Karaoke with Jean

Karaoke Songbook sorted by Artist

Enjoy the show!

Copyright 2016
Paperback Pushers
ISBN-13: 978-1502413925
ISBN-10: 1502413922

ARTIST	SONG TITLE	#	TYPE
? & the Mysterians	96 Tears	3-284	MM
(HED) Planet Earth	Blackout	32-183	THM
10 Years	Beautiful	36-499	CB
10 Years	Wasteland	30-230	PHM
10 Years	Wasteland	30-285	SC
10,000 Maniacs	Because The Night	2-111	SC
10,000 Maniacs	Candy Everybody Wants	12-112	DK
10,000 Maniacs	Like The Weather	46-234	MM
10,000 Maniacs	More Than This	46-235	MM
10,000 Maniacs	These Are Days	13-237	P
10,000 Maniacs	Trouble Me	29-286	SC
100 Proof Aged in S	Somebody's Been Sleeping	15-9	SC
10CC	I'm Not In Love	12-122	DK
10CC	I'm Not In Love	7-495	MM
10CC	Things We Do For Love	15-806	SC
112	Peaches & Cream	23-591	PHM
112	Peaches & Cream	16-394	SGB
1910 Fruitgum Co.	1-2-3 Red Light	22-448	SC
1910 Fruitgum Co.	Simon Says	11-419	DK
1910 Fruitgum Co.	Simon Says	16-668	LC
2 Live Crew	Me So Horny **	5-547	SC
2 Pac	Changes **	25-471	MM
2 Pac	Dear Mama	28-218	DK
2 Pac	How Do U Want It **	25-474	MM
20 Fingers	Short Dick Man **	2-723	SC
3 Doors Down	Away From The Sun	20-530	CB
3 Doors Down	Be Like That	33-373	CB
3 Doors Down	Be Like That	18-402	MM
3 Doors Down	Be Like That	16-309	TT
3 Doors Down	Behind Those Eyes	47-652	CB
3 Doors Down	Citizen Soldier	36-511	CB
3 Doors Down	Citizen Soldier	36-291	PHM
3 Doors Down	Dangerous Game	47-658	CB
3 Doors Down	Duck And Run	34-161	CB
3 Doors Down	Everytime You Go	47-656	CB
3 Doors Down	Going Down In Flames	47-659	SBI
3 Doors Down	Here By Me	47-653	CB
3 Doors Down	Here Without You	20-222	MM
3 Doors Down	Here Without You	32-365	THM
3 Doors Down	It's Not My Time (I Won't Go)	36-439	CB
3 Doors Down	Kryptonite	13-844	PHM
3 Doors Down	Kryptonite	18-565	TT
3 Doors Down	Let Me Be Myself	36-231	PHM
3 Doors Down	Let Me Go	22-364	CB
3 Doors Down	Life Of My Own	47-662	SBI
3 Doors Down	Live For Today	47-654	CB
3 Doors Down	Loser	15-642	THM
3 Doors Down	Loser	18-566	TT
3 Doors Down	Road I'm On the	32-215	THM
3 Doors Down	Smack	47-660	SBI
3 Doors Down	So I Need You	47-657	CB
3 Doors Down	Ticket To Heaven	47-661	SBI
3 Doors Down	Train	47-655	CB
3 Doors Down	When I'm Gone	35-279	CB
3 Doors Down	When I'm Gone	25-425	MM

ARTIST	SONG TITLE	#	TYPE
3 Doors Down	When I'm Gone	18-826	THM
3 Doors Down	When You're Young	37-266	CB
3 Of Hearts	Love Is Enough	15-106	ST
311	Beyond The Gray Sky	23-273	THM
311	Creatures (For A While)	23-175	PHM
311	Down	6-41	SC
38 Special	Caught Up In You	18-155	CB
38 Special	Caught Up In You	7-465	MM
38 Special	Caught Up In You	2-530	SC
38 Special	Hold On Loosely	2-527	SC
38 Special	Hold On Loosely	13-767	SGB
38 Special	If I'd Been The One	7-458	MM
38 Special	Second Chance	16-246	AMS
3LW	No More (Baby I'm A Doo Right)	18-529	TT
3OH!3	Don't Trust Me	36-284	PHM
4 Non Blondes	Spaceman	46-236	KRG
4 Non Blondes	What's Up	28-431	DK
4 Non Blondes	What's Up	6-419	MM
4 PM	Sukiyaki	12-196	DK
4 Runner	Cain's Blood	6-809	MM
4 Runner	Cain's Blood	2-826	SC
4 Runner	Heart With A 4-Wheel Drive	6-854	MM
4 Runner	Ripples	4-124	SC
4 Runner	That Was Him	7-319	MM
4 Runner	That Was Him	4-413	SC
42nd Street	Show - 42nd Street	2-293	SC
42nd Street	Show - We're In The Money	2-291	SC
4Him	Basics Of Life	35-319	CB
4Him	For Future Generations - Gospel	34-428	CB
4HIM	Gospel - Basics Of Life	35-319	CB
4Him	Gospel - For Future Generations	34-428	CB
4PM	Lay Down Your Love	14-876	SC
5 Stairsteps	Ooh Child	25-276	MM
5 Star	Rain Or Shine	30-790	SF
50 Cent	Disco Inferno (Radio Vers)	37-102	SC
50 Cent	In Da Club	32-160	THM
50 Cent	In Da Club **	25-724	MM
50 Cent	P.I.M.P. (Radio Verson) **	21-792	SC
50 Cent	P.I.M.P. (Remix	32-381	THM
50 Cent & Dogg	21 Questions	25-712	MM
50 Cent & Dogg	Duet - 21 Questions	25-712	MM
50 Cent & Nate Dogg	21 Questions	32-276	THM
5th Dimension	Aquarius	11-337	DK
5th Dimension	Go Where You Wanna Go	48-92	LE
5th Dimension	Last Night I Didn't Get To Sleep..	37-71	SC
5th Dimension	Never My Love	48-91	LE
5th Dimension	One Less Bell To Answer	15-544	MM
5th Dimension	Stoned Soul Picnic	11-288	DK

ARTIST	SONG TITLE	#	TYPE
5th Dimension	Stoned Soul Picnic	9-703	SAV
5th Dimension	Up Up and Away	11-526	DK
5th Dimension	Wedding Bell Blues	35-74	CB
5th Dimension	Wedding Bell Blues	11-289	DK
5th Dimension	Wedding Bell Blues	2-865	SC
5th Harmony	Boss	48-329	MRH
5th Harmony & Trainor	Brave Honest Beautiful - duet	48-440	KCD
5th Harmony & Trainor	Duet - Brave Honest Beautiful	48-440	KCD
702	I Still Love You	32-234	THM
702	Steelo	24-371	SC
702	Where My Girls' At	8-378	PHT
98 Degrees	Because Of You	16-222	MM
98 Degrees	Because Of You	15-371	SKG
98 Degrees	Do You Wanna Dance	15-375	SKG
98 Degrees	Fly With Me	15-377	SKG
98 Degrees	Give Me Just One Night	14-4	PHM
98 Degrees	Hardest Thing the	29-174	MH
98 Degrees	Hardest Thing the	7-847	PHM
98 Degrees	Hardest Thing the	13-780	SGB
98 Degrees	Hardest Thing the	15-370	SKG
98 Degrees	Heat It Up	15-378	SKG
98 Degrees	I Do	7-703	PHM
98 Degrees	I Do (Cherish You)	29-179	MH
98 Degrees	I Do (Cherish You)	8-500	PHT
98 Degrees	I Do (Cherish You)	10-204	SC
98 Degrees	I Do (Cherish You)	13-789	SGB
98 Degrees	I Do (Cherish You)	15-369	SKG
98 Degrees	If She Only Knew	15-379	SKG
98 Degrees	Invisible Man	15-372	SKG
98 Degrees	My Everything	17-717	THM
98 Degrees	My Everything	18-570	TT
98 Degrees	Still	15-373	SKG
98 Degrees	Take My Breath Away	15-380	SKG
98 Degrees	To Me You're Everything	15-376	SKG
98 Degrees	Was It Something I Didn't Do	15-374	SKG
98 Degrees	Why Are We Still Friends	18-353	CB
A-Ha	Cry Wolf	46-240	SFM
A-Ha	Living Daylights the	9-66	SC
A-Ha	Livingdaylights the	46-241	SC
A-Ha	Stay On These Roads	46-238	KV
A-Ha	Sun Always Shines On TV	46-237	CK
A-Ha	Take On Me	20-302	CB
A-Ha	Take On Me	28-340	DK
A-Ha	Take On Me	13-249	P
A-Ha	Take On Me	20-82	SC
A-Ha	You Are The One	46-239	KV
A-Teens	Bouncing Off The Ceiling	18-549	TT
A3	Woke Up This Morning	16-238	PHM
Aaliyah	Are You That Somebody	7-783	PHT
Aaliyah	Come Over	20-522	CB
Aaliyah	Duet - Are You That Somebody	7-783	PHT

ARTIST	SONG TITLE	#	TYPE
Aaliyah	If Your Girl Only Knew	24-300	SC
Aaliyah	Journey To The Past	10-120	SC
Aaliyah	Kiss You	20-466	CB
Aaliyah	Miss You	34-142	CB
Aaliyah	Miss You	32-58	THM
Aaliyah	More Than A Woman	18-291	CB
Aaliyah	More Than A Woman	18-147	PHM
Aaliyah	One I Gave My Heart To	9-96	PS
Aaliyah	Try Again	35-224	CB
Aaliyah	Try Again	15-632	THM
Aaliyah	Try Again	18-540	TT
Aaliyah & Tank	Come Over	32-352	THM
Abandoned Pools	Remedy the	32-175	THM
Abba	Andante	46-218	FUN
Abba	Angel Eyes	19-85	MM
Abba	As Good As New	19-76	MM
Abba	Chiquitita	7-497	MM
Abba	Dance (While the Music Still Goes On)	49-303	LRT
Abba	Dancing Queen	11-518	DK
Abba	Dancing Queen	7-496	MM
Abba	Day Before You Came the	46-217	FUN
Abba	Does Your Mother Know	7-498	MM
Abba	Eagle	46-219	FUN
Abba	Fernando	7-506	MM
Abba	Gimme Gimme Gimme	7-499	MM
Abba	Happy New Year	19-81	MM
Abba	Hasta Manana	19-82	MM
Abba	He Is Your Brother	46-220	FUN
Abba	Head Over Heels	19-78	MM
Abba	Honey Honey	19-75	MM
Abba	I Do I Do I Do I Do	7-500	MM
Abba	I Have A Dream	7-501	MM
Abba	Knowing Me Knowing You	7-502	MM
Abba	Knowing Me Knowing You	10-535	SF
Abba	Lay All Your Love On Me	19-74	MM
Abba	Mamma Mia	7-508	MM
Abba	Money Money Money	15-532	CMC
Abba	Money Money Money	19-72	MM
Abba	Name Of The Game the	7-505	MM
Abba	One Of Us	19-79	MM
Abba	Ring Ring	19-77	MM
Abba	Rock Me	19-83	MM
Abba	So Long	19-86	MM
Abba	SOS	7-503	MM
Abba	Summer Night City	19-80	MM
Abba	Super Trouper	7-507	MM
Abba	Take A Chance On Me	7-509	MM
Abba	Take A Chance On Me	4-317	SC
Abba	Thank You For The Music	7-504	MM
Abba	Under Attack	46-221	FUN
Abba	Voulez Vous	19-87	MM
Abba	Waterloo	11-519	DK

ARTIST	SONG TITLE	#	TYPE
Abba	Waterloo	7-510	MM
Abba	Way Old Friends Do the	46-223	KV
Abba	When All Is Said And Done	46-222	KV
Abba	When I Kissed The Teacher	46-224	KV
Abba	Winner Takes All	19-73	MM
Abbott, Gregory	Shake You Down	18-493	SAV
Abbott, Gregory	Shake You Down	29-641	SC
ABC	Be Near Me	18-382	SAV
ABC	Be Near Me	5-604	SC
ABC	Look Of Love the	16-455	MH
ABC	When Smokey Sings	18-388	SAV
Abdul, Paula	Cold Hearted	14-583	SC
Abdul, Paula	Duet - Opposites Attract	18-241	DK
Abdul, Paula	Knocked Out	12-813	P
Abdul, Paula	Opposites Attract	18-241	DK
Abdul, Paula	Vibeology	18-390	SAV
Abrams Brothers	Northern Redemption	41-60	PHN
AC/DC	Back In Black	13-753	SGB
AC/DC	Big Balls **	5-551	SC
AC/DC	Dirty Deeds Done Dirt Cheap	4-556	SC
AC/DC	Hells Bells	13-743	SGB
AC/DC	You Shook Me All Night Long	9-354	AH
Ace	How Long	3-452	SC
Ace	How Long	10-545	SF
Ace Of Base	All That She Wants	12-244	DK
Ace Of Base	All That She Wants	6-408	MM
Ace Of Base	All That She Wants	9-269	SC
Ace Of Base	All That She Wants	8-614	TT
Ace Of Base	Don't Turn Around	6-632	MM
Ace Of Base	Living In Danger	16-622	MM
Ace Of Base	Sign the	12-245	DK
Ace Of Base	Sign the	19-573	MH
Ace Of Base	Sign the	13-604	P
Ace Of Base	Sign the	8-604	TT
Ace Of Base	Whenever You're Near Me	14-284	MM
Acuff & Nitty Gritty Dirt Band	Wreck On The Highway	46-242	CB
Acuff, Roy	Great Speckled Bird	8-417	CB
Acuff, Roy	Great Speckled Bird	11-819	DK
Acuff, Roy	Wabash Cannonball	21-635	CB
Acuff, Roy	Wabash Cannonball	12-302	DK
Acuff, Roy	Wabash Cannonball	3-605	SC
Acuff, Roy	Wreck On The Highway	38-67	CB
Ad Libs	Boy From New York City the	19-607	MH
Ad Libs	Boy From New York City the	3-297	MM
Adam Ant	Goody Two Shoes	21-742	MH
Adamo, Salvadore	Latino - Mauvals Garcon	15-528	CMC
Adamo, Salvadore	Latino - Tombe La Neige	15-572	CMC
Adams & Raitt	Duet - Rock Steady	35-314	CB
Adams & Raitt	Rock Steady - duet	35-314	CB
Adams, Bryan	Back To You	23-448	CB

ARTIST	SONG TITLE	#	TYPE
Adams, Bryan	Back To You	15-405	SC
Adams, Bryan	Can't Stop This Thing We Started	21-465	CB
Adams, Bryan	Can't Stop This Thing We Started	16-408	PR
Adams, Bryan	Do I Have To Say The Words	23-441	CB
Adams, Bryan	Everything I Do I Do It For You	21-454	CB
Adams, Bryan	Everything I Do I Do It For You	11-71	JTG
Adams, Bryan	Everything I Do I Do It For You	6-93	MM
Adams, Bryan	Have You Ever Really Loved a Woman	23-443	CB
Adams, Bryan	Have You Ever Really Loved a Woman	14-877	SC
Adams, Bryan	Heat Of The Night	23-438	CB
Adams, Bryan	Heaven	23-436	CB
Adams, Bryan	Heaven	11-154	DK
Adams, Bryan	Heaven	16-549	P
Adams, Bryan	Here I Am	18-418	MM
Adams, Bryan	I'll Always Be Right There	23-444	CB
Adams, Bryan	Let's Make A Night To Remember	23-445	CB
Adams, Bryan	Let's Make A Night To Remember	24-226	SC
Adams, Bryan	On A Day Like Today	14-289	MM
Adams, Bryan	Only Thing That Looks Good On Me..	23-446	CB
Adams, Bryan	Only Thing That Looks Good...	4-683	SC
Adams, Bryan	Please Forgive Me	23-442	CB
Adams, Bryan	Please Forgive Me	2-116	SC
Adams, Bryan	Please Forgive Me	8-606	TT
Adams, Bryan	Run To You	23-435	CB
Adams, Bryan	Star	23-447	CB
Adams, Bryan	Straight From The Heart	23-434	CB
Adams, Bryan	Summer Of ' 69	23-437	CB
Adams, Bryan	Summer Of ' 69	7-487	MM
Adams, Bryan	Summer Of ' 69	16-527	P
Adams, Bryan	Why Do You Have To Be So Hard To	29-283	PHM
Adams, Faye	Shake A Hand	10-225	SS
Adams, Oleta	At Last	17-432	KC
Adams, Oleta	Circle Of One	46-383	SC
Adams, Oleta	Day I Stop Loving You the	46-382	SC
Adams, Oleta	Embraceable You	23-343	MM
Adams, Oleta	Get Here	17-426	KC
Adams, Oleta	Get Here	19-570	MH
Adams, Oleta	Get Here	12-876	P
Adams, Oleta	Holy Is The Lamb - xmas	46-391	PR
Adams, Oleta	I Just Had To Hear Your Voice	46-390	HKC
Adams, Oleta	I Knew You When	46-384	PS
Adams, Oleta	If This Love Should End	46-386	PS
Adams, Oleta	Life Keeps Moving On	46-387	PS

ARTIST	SONG TITLE	#	TYPE
Adams, Oleta	Never Knew Love	4-172	SC
Adams, Oleta	Rhythm Of Life	46-388	PS
Adams, Oleta	Slow Motion	46-385	PS
Adams, Oleta	Wanna Be	46-389	ESS
Adams, Oleta	We Will Meet Again	23-344	MM
Adams, Oleta	Xmas - Holy Is The Lamb	46-391	PR
Adams, Ryan	New York New York	25-39	MM
Adams, Ryan	New York New York	30-652	THM
Adams, Ryan	Two	30-596	PHM
Adams, Yolanda	Open My Heart	20-619	CB
Adams&Sting&Stewar	Duet - All For Love	8-608	TT
Adams&Sting&Stewart	All For Love	8-608	TT
Addotta, Kip	Wet Dream **	23-19	SC
Adele	All I Ask	46-87	DCK
Adele	Best For Last	44-171	KV
Adele	Black And Gold	44-176	KV
Adele	Can't Let Go	49-6	DCK
Adele	Chasing Pavements	38-180	SC
Adele	Cold Shoulder	38-228	CB
Adele	Crazy For You	44-170	KV
Adele	Daydreamer	38-229	CB
Adele	Don't You Remember	44-167	KV
Adele	First Love	46-2	KV
Adele	Fool That I Am	38-230	CB
Adele	He Won't Go	40-31	KV
Adele	Hello	49-128	SBI
Adele	Hello	45-291	DCK
Adele	Hiding My Heart	44-174	KV
Adele	Hometown Glory	38-231	CB
Adele	I Can't Make You Love Me	38-237	CB
Adele	I Found A Boy	44-173	KV
Adele	I Miss You	45-819	DCK
Adele	I'll Be Waiting	39-19	KV
Adele	If It Hadn't Been For Love	40-33	KV
Adele	Love In The Dark	46-86	DCK
Adele	Lovesong	40-34	ASK
Adele	Make You Feel My Love	38-186	CB
Adele	Many Shades Of Black	44-177	KV
Adele	Melt My Heart To Stone	44-168	KV
Adele	Million Years Ago	45-821	DCK
Adele	My Same	44-169	KV
Adele	One And Only	40-35	ZM
Adele	Promise This	40-36	SF
Adele	Promise This (Live Version)	47-432	KV
Adele	Remedy	49-790	BKD
Adele	Remedy	46-8	DCK
Adele	Right As Rain	36-292	PHM
Adele	River Lea	46-4	DCK
Adele	Rollin' In The Deep	38-181	CB
Adele	Rumour Has it	38-232	PHM
Adele	Send My Love (To Your New Girlfriend)	46-7	DCK

ARTIST	SONG TITLE	#	TYPE
Adele	Set Fire To The Rain	38-182	PHM
Adele	Skyfall	44-178	MRH
Adele	Someone Like You	38-183	PHM
Adele	Sweetest Devotion	46-88	DCK
Adele	Take It All	44-172	KV
Adele	That's It, I Quit, I'm Movin' On	44-175	KV
Adele	Tired	46-1	SBI
Adele	Turning Tables	38-187	CB
Adele	Water Under The Bridge	46-9	DCK
Adele	Water Under The Bridge (Inst)	49-410	BKD
Adele	When We Were Young	46-3	DCK
Adema	Unstable	23-180	PHM
Adema	Way You Like It the	30-654	THM
Adkins, Trace	All I Ask For Anymore	37-57	CB
Adkins, Trace	Arlington	23-287	CB
Adkins, Trace	Arlington	29-605	ST
Adkins, Trace	Big Time	7-765	CHM
Adkins, Trace	Chrome	34-390	CB
Adkins, Trace	Chrome	25-357	MM
Adkins, Trace	Chrome	18-336	ST
Adkins, Trace	Chrome	32-4	THM
Adkins, Trace	Don't Lie	10-229	SC
Adkins, Trace	Don't Lie	22-376	ST
Adkins, Trace	Every Light In The House Is On	4-435	SC
Adkins, Trace	Help Me Understand	25-194	MM
Adkins, Trace	Help Me Understand	16-331	ST
Adkins, Trace	Honky Tonk Badonkadonk	23-470	CB
Adkins, Trace	Honky Tonk Badonkadonk	23-376	SC
Adkins, Trace	Hot Mama	35-448	CB
Adkins, Trace	Hot Mama	19-529	ST
Adkins, Trace	I Got My Game On	30-543	CB
Adkins, Trace	I Left Something Turned On At Home	7-640	CHM
Adkins, Trace	I Left Something Turned On At Home	10-88	SC
Adkins, Trace	I'm Gonna Love You Anyway	14-113	CB
Adkins, Trace	I'm Gonna Love You Anyway	14-12	CHM
Adkins, Trace	I'm Tryin'	33-145	CB
Adkins, Trace	I'm Tryin'	15-608	ST
Adkins, Trace	Just Fishin'	40-7	CB
Adkins, Trace	Ladies Love Country Boys	30-114	CB
Adkins, Trace	Lonely Won't Leave Me Alone	8-32	CB
Adkins, Trace	Lonely Won't Leave Me Alone	7-734	CHM
Adkins, Trace	More	13-813	CHM
Adkins, Trace	More	22-482	ST
Adkins, Trace	More (Radio Version)	23-369	SC
Adkins, Trace	Muddy Water	36-215	PHM
Adkins, Trace	Rest Of Mine the	22-630	ST
Adkins, Trace	Rough & Ready	20-338	ST

ARTIST	SONG TITLE	#	TYPE
Adkins, Trace	Songs About Me	23-1	CB
Adkins, Trace	Swing	29-588	CB
Adkins, Trace	Then They Do	25-572	MM
Adkins, Trace	Then They Do	19-8	ST
Adkins, Trace	Then They Do	32-265	THM
Adkins, Trace	There's A Girl In Texas	7-280	MM
Adkins, Trace	This Ain't No Thinkin' Thing	7-421	MM
Adkins, Trace	You're Gonna Miss This	36-424	CB
Aerosmith	Angel	4-319	SC
Aerosmith	Angel	13-669	SGB
Aerosmith	Back In The Saddle	12-772	P
Aerosmith	Big Ten Inch Record **	2-184	SC
Aerosmith	Cryin'	18-479	NU
Aerosmith	Draw The Line	5-70	SC
Aerosmith	Dream On	33-302	CB
Aerosmith	Dream On	12-709	P
Aerosmith	Dude (Looks Like A Lady)	43-211	SC
Aerosmith	I Don't Want To Miss A Thing	34-130	CB
Aerosmith	I Don't Want To Miss A Thing	21-556	PHM
Aerosmith	Jaded	16-474	MH
Aerosmith	Jaded	16-257	TT
Aerosmith	Janie's Got A Gun	43-212	SC
Aerosmith	Last Child	23-102	SC
Aerosmith	Love In An Elevator	2-730	SC
Aerosmith	Pandora's Box	10-487	DA
Aerosmith	Rag Doll	24-199	SC
Aerosmith	Same Old Song And Dance	12-771	P
Aerosmith	Same Old Song And Dance	5-885	SC
Aerosmith	Sunshine	16-83	ST
Aerosmith	Sunshine (Radio Version)	16-88	SC
Aerosmith	Sweet Emotion	12-773	P
Aerosmith	Sweet Emotion	16-154	SC
Aerosmith	Toys In The Attic	4-561	SC
Aerosmith	Train Kept A Rollin'	13-757	SGB
Aerosmith	Walk This Way	35-137	CB
Aerosmith	Walk This Way	16-601	MM
AFI	Leaving Song the (Pt. 2)	23-177	PHM
Afroman	Because I Got High	16-377	SGB
After 7	Duet - Till You Do Me Right	3-433	SC
After 7	Ready Or Not	11-820	DK
After 7	Till You Do Me Right	3-433	SC
After The Fire	Der Kommissar	29-15	MH
Agostino, Gigi	I'll Fly With You	16-307	PHM
Aguilera & Elliott	Car Wash	20-554	PHM
Aguilera & Hancock	Song For You a	29-280	PHM
Aguilera & Lil Kim	Can't Hold Us Down **	21-796	SC
Aguilera & Lil Kim	Duet - Can't Hold Us Down **	21-796	SC
Aguilera & Shelton	Duet - Just A Fool	43-181	ASK
Aguilera & Shelton	Just A Fool - Duet	43-181	ASK

ARTIST	SONG TITLE	#	TYPE
Aguilera, Christina	Ain't No Other Man	30-724	SF
Aguilera, Christina	Beautiful	25-424	MM
Aguilera, Christina	Beautiful	18-603	PHM
Aguilera, Christina	Blessed	14-491	SC
Aguilera, Christina	Come On Over	15-438	PHM
Aguilera, Christina	Come On Over	20-6	SGB
Aguilera, Christina	Come On Over (Radio Version)	14-501	SC
Aguilera, Christina	Dirty	18-338	PHM
Aguilera, Christina	Fighter	25-578	MM
Aguilera, Christina	Fighter	19-338	STP
Aguilera, Christina	Fighter	32-206	THM
Aguilera, Christina	Genie In A Bottle	13-571	LE
Aguilera, Christina	Genie In A Bottle	8-196	PHT
Aguilera, Christina	Genie In A Bottle	10-187	SC
Aguilera, Christina	Genie In A Bottle	13-778	SGB
Aguilera, Christina	I Turn To You	14-175	CB
Aguilera, Christina	I Turn To You	13-570	LE
Aguilera, Christina	I Turn To You	10-219	SC
Aguilera, Christina	What A Girl Wants	13-569	LE
Aguilera&Mya&Lil Ki	Duet - Lady Marmalade	18-526	TT
Aguilera&Mya&Lil Ki	Lady Marmalade	15-454	PHM
Aguilera&Mya&Lil Ki	Lady Marmalade	16-110	PRT
Aiken, Clay	Bridge Over Troubled Water	19-546	SC
Aiken, Clay	I Will Carry You	20-544	PHM
Aiken, Clay	I Will Carry You	36-321	PS
Aiken, Clay	Invisible	20-532	CB
Aiken, Clay	Invisible	36-320	PS
Aiken, Clay	Solitaire	36-322	PS
Aiken, Clay	This Is The Night	25-651	MM
Aiken, Clay	This Is The Night	19-540	SC
Aiken, Clay	This Is The Night	32-316	THM
Aiken, Clay	Way the	36-323	PS
Ain't Misbehavin'	I Got A Feeling I'm Falling - show	48-790	MM
Ain't Misbehavin'	Show - I Got A Feeling I'm Falling	6-329	MM
Ain't Misbehavin'	Show - I Got A Feeling I'm Falling	48-790	MM
Ain't Misbehavin'	Show - Your Feet's Too Big	7-366	MM
Air	All I Need	30-780	SF
Air Supply	All Out Of Love	18-121	DK
Air Supply	All Out Of Love	9-786	SAV
Air Supply	Always	46-401	SBI
Air Supply	Book Of Love the	46-403	SBI
Air Supply	Chances	46-399	CB
Air Supply	Even The Nights Are Better	46-393	SC
Air Supply	Every Woman In The World	46-392	SC
Air Supply	Goodbye	46-400	SBI
Air Supply	Here I Am (Just When I)	46-394	SC
Air Supply	I Can Wait Forever	46-587	CB
Air Supply	I Want To Give It All	46-589	CB
Air Supply	Just As I Am	46-398	CB
Air Supply	Lost In Love	35-159	CB

ARTIST	SONG TITLE	#	TYPE
Air Supply	Lost In Love	15-523	CMC
Air Supply	Lost In Love	16-795	DK
Air Supply	Making Love Out Of Nothing At All	14-580	SC
Air Supply	Now And Forever	46-588	CB
Air Supply	One That You Love the	11-324	DK
Air Supply	One That You Love the	4-324	SC
Air Supply	Strong Strong Wind	46-402	SBI
Air Supply	Sweet Dreams	46-395	CB
Air Supply	Two Less Lonely People In The World	46-397	CB
Air Supply	Young Love	46-396	CB
Airborne Toxic Event	Sometime Around Midnight	36-380	SC
Akens, Jewel	Birds And The Bees the	17-108	DK
Akens, Jewel	Birds And The Bees the	13-269	P
Akens, Jewel	Birds And The Bees the	3-267	SC
Akins, Rhett	Better Than It Used To Be	8-305	CB
Akins, Rhett	Don't Get Me Started	7-232	MM
Akins, Rhett	Don't Get Me Started	22-885	ST
Akins, Rhett	I Brake For Brunettes	6-713	MM
Akins, Rhett	I Brake For Brunettes	22-856	ST
Akins, Rhett	Kiss My Country Ass	29-35	CB
Akins, Rhett	Love You Back	4-499	SC
Akins, Rhett	More Than Everything	8-132	CB
Akins, Rhett	More Than Everything	22-663	ST
Akins, Rhett	She Said Yes	3-575	SC
Akins, Rhett	That Ain't My Truck	35-407	CB
Akins, Rhett	That Ain't My Truck	3-418	SC
Akins, Rhett	What They're Talkin' About	6-714	MM
Akon	Don't Matter (Radio Vers)	37-123	SC
Akon	Lonely (Radio Vers)	37-106	SC
Akon & Styles P	Locked Up	30-812	PHM
Al B. Sure!	Alone With You	18-488	SAV
Al B. Sure!	Forever My Lady	18-503	SAV
Al B. Sure!	Nite & Day	28-325	DK
Al B. Sure!	Right Now	9-854	SAV
Al B. Sure!	Stay (Faraway So Close)	18-475	NU
Al Dexter & Troopers	Down At The Roadside Inn	46-411	CB
Al Dexter & Troopers	Honey Do You Think It's Wrong	46-408	CB
Al Dexter & Troopers	I Learned About Love	19-624	CB
Al Dexter & Troopers	I'll Wait For You Dear	46-405	CB
Al Dexter & Troopers	I'm Losing My Mind Over You	38-37	CB
Al Dexter & Troopers	I'm Lost Without You	46-407	CB
Al Dexter & Troopers	It's Up To You	46-409	CB
Al Dexter & Troopers	Ko Ko Mo Island	46-410	CB
Al Dexter & Troopers	New Groom Boogie	46-412	CB
Al Dexter & Troopers	Pistol Packin' Mama	8-769	CB
Al Dexter & Troopers	Rosalita	38-38	CB
Al Dexter & Troopers	So Long Pal	46-404	CB
Al Dexter & Troopers	Too Late To Worry, Too Blue to Cry	34-181	CB

ARTIST	SONG TITLE	#	TYPE
Al Dexter & Troopers	Triflin' Gal	46-406	CB
Al Dexter & Troopers	Wine Women And Song	19-626	CB
Alabama	Angels Among Us	1-24	CB
Alabama	Angels Among Us	2-538	SC
Alabama	Are You Sure Hank Done It This Way	46-245	CB
Alabama	Backwoods Boogie	49-674	KCD
Alabama	Between The Two Of Them	4-106	SC
Alabama	Born Country	4-436	BS
Alabama	Born Country	33-103	CB
Alabama	Born Country	12-195	DK
Alabama	Born Country	6-196	MM
Alabama	Born Country	5-417	SC
Alabama	Can't Keep A Good Man Down	1-11	CB
Alabama	Can't Keep A Good Man Down	5-152	SC
Alabama	Cheap Seats	1-23	CB
Alabama	Cheap Seats	6-585	MM
Alabama	Christmas In Dixie	35-321	CB
Alabama	Close Enough To Perfect	1-4	CB
Alabama	Close Enough To Perfect	4-486	SC
Alabama	Closer You Get the	13-429	P
Alabama	Closer You Get the	9-434	SAV
Alabama	Dancin' On The Boulevard	22-601	ST
Alabama	Dancin' Shaggin' On The Boulevard	1-26	CB
Alabama	Dancin' Shaggin' On The Boulevard	7-655	CHM
Alabama	Dixieland Delight	4-438	BS
Alabama	Dixieland Delight	1-5	CB
Alabama	Down Home	4-439	BS
Alabama	Down Home	13-397	P
Alabama	Down Home	9-475	SAV
Alabama	Duet - Face To Face	12-79	DK
Alabama	Duet - Will You Marry Me	15-98	ST
Alabama	Face To Face	12-79	DK
Alabama	Fallin' Again	26-558	DK
Alabama	Feels So Right	34-262	CB
Alabama	Feels So Right	13-377	P
Alabama	Fire In The Night	4-440	BS
Alabama	Fire In The Night	1-8	CB
Alabama	Forever's As Far As I'll Go	4-441	BS
Alabama	Forever's As Far As I'll Go	17-293	NA
Alabama	Forever's As Far As I'll Go	9-461	SAV
Alabama	Forever's As Far As I'll Go	2-401	SC
Alabama	Forty Hour Week	4-442	BS
Alabama	Forty Hour Week	1-10	CB
Alabama	Give Me One More Shot	2-648	SC
Alabama	Give Me One More Shot	22-869	ST
Alabama	God Must Have Spent	8-958	CB

ARTIST	SONG TITLE	#	TYPE	ARTIST	SONG TITLE	#	TYPE
Alabama	God Must Have Spent	7-880	CHT	Alabama	Reckless	2-331	SC
Alabama	Gonna Have A Party	17-314	NA	Alabama	Roll On Eighteen Wheeler	4-447	BS
Alabama	Here We Are	4-443	BS	Alabama	Roll On Eighteen Wheeler	1-6	CB
Alabama	Here We Are	1-16	CB	Alabama	Roll On Eighteen Wheeler	11-720	DK
Alabama	Here We Are	12-475	P	Alabama	Sad Lookin' Moon	7-608	CHM
Alabama	High Cotton	46-243	CB	Alabama	Say I	1-25	CB
Alabama	Hometown Honeymoon	1-21	CB	Alabama	Say I	7-281	MM
Alabama	Hometown Honeymoon	6-395	MM	Alabama	Say I	22-897	ST
Alabama	Hometown Honeymoon	9-629	SAV	Alabama	She Ain't Your Ordinary Girl	6-823	MM
Alabama	Hometown Honeymoon	2-805	SC	Alabama	She Ain't Your Ordinary Girl	3-413	SC
Alabama	How Do You Fall In Love	8-755	CB	Alabama	She And I	1-12	CB
Alabama	I'm In A Hurry And Don't Know Why	6-303	MM	Alabama	She's Got That Look In Her Eyes	8-407	CB
Alabama	I'm In A Hurry And Don't Know Why	13-490	P	Alabama	She's Got That Look In Her Eyes	22-766	ST
Alabama	I'm In A Hurry And Don't Know Why	2-814	SC	Alabama	Small Stuff	5-806	SC
Alabama	I'm In The Mood	17-589	ST	Alabama	Small Stuff	22-378	ST
Alabama	If I Had You	4-444	BS	Alabama	Song Of The South	4-448	BS
Alabama	If I Had You	1-14	CB	Alabama	Song Of The South	1-13	CB
Alabama	If You're Gonna Play In Texas	1-7	CB	Alabama	Southern Star	4-449	BS
Alabama	In Pictures	7-137	MM	Alabama	Take A Little Trip	1-19	CB
Alabama	In Pictures	3-543	SC	Alabama	Take A Little Trip	6-183	MM
Alabama	It Works	4-131	SC	Alabama	Take Me Down	9-509	SAV
Alabama	Jukebox In My Mind	4-445	BS	Alabama	Tennessee River	4-450	BS
Alabama	Jukebox In My Mind	1-17	CB	Alabama	Tennessee River	13-471	P
Alabama	Jukebox In My Mind	6-623	MM	Alabama	Then Again	1-18	CB
Alabama	Jukebox In My Mind	17-292	NA	Alabama	Then Again	9-530	SAV
Alabama	Katy Brought My Guitar Back Today	24-1	SC	Alabama	There's No Way	1-9	CB
Alabama	Keepin' Up	8-867	CB	Alabama	Thistlehair The Christmas Bear	45-755	CB
Alabama	Keepin' Up	22-696	ST	Alabama	TLCASAP	1-22	CB
Alabama	Lady Down On Love	33-75	CB	Alabama	TLCASAP	6-460	MM
Alabama	Lady Down On Love	5-395	SC	Alabama	Touch Me When We're Dancing	4-818	SC
Alabama	Louisiana Moon	49-106	CDG	Alabama	Twentieth Century	23-364	SC
Alabama	Love In The First Degree	13-468	P	Alabama	Twentieth Century	22-539	ST
Alabama	Love In The First Degree	9-479	SAV	Alabama	Wasn't Through Loving You Yet	49-672	KCD
Alabama	Maker Said Take Her the	7-345	MM	Alabama	We Can't Love Like This	2-461	SC
Alabama	Maker Said Take Her the	4-895	SC	Alabama	We Made Love	9-427	CB
Alabama	Mountain Music	35-387	CB	Alabama	We Made Love	22-552	ST
Alabama	Mountain Music	26-342	DK	Alabama	When It All Goes South	22-457	ST
Alabama	Mountain Music	13-368	P	Alabama	When We Make Love	9-439	SAV
Alabama	Mountain Music	2-100	SC	Alabama	Why Lady Why	1-2	CB
Alabama	My Home's In Alabama	4-446	BS	Alabama	Why Lady Why	4-552	SC
Alabama	My Home's In Alabama	1-1	CB	Alabama	Will You Marry Me	15-98	SC
Alabama	Of Course I'm Alright	22-657	ST	Alabama	Will You Marry Me	16-278	TT
Alabama	Of Course I'm Right	1-29	CB	Alabama	Woman He Loves the	16-9	ST
Alabama	Old Flame	8-23	CB	Alabama	Xmas - Christmas In Dixie	4-437	BS
Alabama	Old Flame	17-311	NA	Alabama	Xmas - Christmas In Dixie	8-51	CB
Alabama	On This Side Of The Moon	24-90	SC	Alabama	Xmas - Christmas In Dixie	14-544	SC
Alabama	Once Upon A Lifetime	1-20	CB				
Alabama	Once Upon A Lifetime	12-172	DK				
Alabama	Once Upon A Lifetime	6-126	MM				
Alabama	Pass It On Down	1-15	CB				
Alabama	Pictures And Memories	46-247	SC				
Alabama	Reckless	6-401	MM				

ARTIST	SONG TITLE	#	TYPE
Alabama	Xmas - Thistlehair The Christmas Bear	45-755	CB
Alabama	You've Got The Touch	29-76	CB
Alabama	You've Got The Touch	11-429	DK
Alabama	You've Got The Touch	13-347	P
Aladdin	Show - Whole New World a	20-187	Z
Aladdin	Whole New World a	20-187	Z
Alan Parsons Projec	Time	16-241	AMS
Albert, Herb	This Guy's In Love With You	35-100	CB
Albert, Herb	This Guy's In Love With You	11-594	DK
Albert, Herb	This Guy's In Love With You	19-110	SAV
Albert, Morris	Feelings	26-262	DK
Albert, Morris	Feelings	2-195	SC
Alcazar	Crying At The Discoteque	21-723	TT
Aldean & Clarkson	Don't You Wanna Stay - duet	37-208	AS
Aldean & Clarkson	Duet - Don't You Wanna Stay	37-208	AS
Aldean, Jason	1994	44-203	KV
Aldean, Jason	Amarillo Sky	30-107	CB
Aldean, Jason	Big Green Tractor	37-55	CB
Aldean, Jason	Black Tears	44-291	BKD
Aldean, Jason	Black Tears	45-277	BKD
Aldean, Jason	Burnin' It Down	44-320	SBI
Aldean, Jason	Church Pew Or Barstool	47-712	BKD
Aldean, Jason	Crazy Town	37-327	PHM
Aldean, Jason	Dirt Road Anthem	37-231	CB
Aldean, Jason	Do You Wish It Was Me	44-292	BKD
Aldean, Jason	Feel That Again	44-134	ASK
Aldean, Jason	Gonna Know We Were Here	45-100	BK
Aldean, Jason	Hicktown	23-117	CB
Aldean, Jason	Johnny Cash	30-339	CB
Aldean, Jason	Just Gettin' Started	45-99	BKD
Aldean, Jason	Laughed Until We Cried	30-553	CB
Aldean, Jason	Lights Come On	49-640	DCK
Aldean, Jason	Miss That Girl	48-669	BKD
Aldean, Jason	My Kinda Party	37-343	CB
Aldean, Jason	Night Train	41-70	ASK
Aldean, Jason	Only Way I Know the	45-857	SBI
Aldean, Jason	See You When I See You	48-670	KV
Aldean, Jason	She's Country	45-458	CB
Aldean, Jason	Sweet Little Somethin'	49-21	SSC
Aldean, Jason	Take A Little Ride	39-25	ASK
Aldean, Jason	Tattoo's On This Town	45-429	BKD
Aldean, Jason	Tonight Looks Good On You	45-368	BKD
Aldean, Jason	Water Tower	44-293	BKD
Aldean, Jason	When She Says Baby	43-140	ASK
Aldean, Jason	Why	29-39	CB
Aldean, Jason	Why	29-502	SC
Aldean, Jason	Why	23-454	ST
Aldo Nova	Fantasy	35-209	CB

ARTIST	SONG TITLE	#	TYPE
Aldo Nova	Fantasy	5-492	SC
Alexander, Jessi	Honeysuckle Sweet	20-345	ST
Ali	Show - Change Is Gonna Come a	18-676	PS
Ali	Show - World's Greatest Hero the	18-675	PS
Alice Cooper	Ballad Of Dwight Fry	16-453	SGB
Alice Cooper	Be My Lover	16-450	SGB
Alice Cooper	Billion Dollar Babies	16-447	SGB
Alice Cooper	Dead Babies	16-454	SGB
Alice Cooper	Desperado	16-445	SGB
Alice Cooper	Feed My Frankenstein	16-448	SGB
Alice Cooper	Generation Landslide	16-443	SGB
Alice Cooper	Hello Hooray	16-452	SGB
Alice Cooper	Hey Stoopid	21-779	SC
Alice Cooper	I Love The Dead	16-441	SGB
Alice Cooper	I Never Cry	16-446	SGB
Alice Cooper	I'm Eighteen	19-144	SGB
Alice Cooper	Only Women Bleed	14-566	AH
Alice Cooper	Only Women Bleed	20-361	SC
Alice Cooper	Raped And Freezing	16-444	SGB
Alice Cooper	School's Out	17-355	DK
Alice Cooper	Sick Things	16-451	SGB
Alice Cooper	Some Folks	16-449	SGB
Alice Cooper	Under My Wheels	16-442	SGB
Alice Cooper	Welcome To My Nightmare	19-288	SGB
Alice Cooper	You And Me	15-750	AMS
Alice In Chains	Again	4-334	SC
Alice In Chains	No Excuses	30-766	SF
Alien Ant Farm	Glow	32-441	THM
Alien Ant Farm	Smooth Criminal	35-255	CB
Alien Ant Farm	Smooth Criminal	25-22	MM
Alien Ant Farm	Smooth Criminal	16-395	SGB
Alien Ant Farm	These Days	23-178	PHM
Alien Ant Farm	These Days (Album Version)	32-362	THM
All American Reject	Swing Swing	32-147	THM
All American Rejects	Future Has Arrived the	30-495	CB
All American Rejects	Gives You Hell	36-253	PHM
All American Rejects	Move Along	30-277	SC
All American Rejects	Swing Swing	32-147	THM
All Saints	I Know Where It's At	7-716	PHM
All Saints	Never Ever	16-230	PHM
All Star Tribute	Duet - What's Goin' On	25-45	MM
All Star Tribute	Duet - What's Goin' On	16-81	ST
All Star Tribute	What's Goin' On	25-45	MM
All Star Tribute	What's Goin' On	16-300	PHM
All Star Tribute	What's Goin' On	16-81	ST
All Time Low	Backseat Serenade	39-125	PHM
All Time Low	Damned If I Do (Darned If..)	36-307	PHM
All-4-One	Beautiful As U	18-355	CB
All-4-One	I Can Love You Like That	3-428	SC
All-4-One	I Swear	34-133	CB
All-4-One	I Swear	26-314	DK
All-4-One	I Swear	13-289	P

ARTIST	SONG TITLE	#	TYPE
All-4-One	I Swear	2-226	SC
All-4-One	I Will Be Right There	5-790	SC
All-4-One	Skillz - She's Got	13-307	P
All-4-One	So Much In Love	49-481	MM
All-American Reject	Future Has Arrived the	30-496	CB
All-American Reject	Move Along	30-155	PT
All-American Reject	Move Along	30-277	SC
All-American Reject	Swing Swing	23-165	PHM
Allan, Gary	Best I Ever Had	23-280	CB
Allan, Gary	Bones	43-190	ASK
Allan, Gary	Drinkin' Dark Whiskey	45-872	VH
Allan, Gary	Every Storm (Runs Out Of Rain)	47-711	BKD
Allan, Gary	Feelin' Like That a	30-193	CB
Allan, Gary	From Where I'm Sitting	10-82	SC
Allan, Gary	Get Off On The Pain	37-333	CB
Allan, Gary	Her Man	4-424	SC
Allan, Gary	I'll Take Today	22-706	ST
Allan, Gary	It Ain't The Whiskey	44-156	BKD
Allan, Gary	It Would Be You	8-402	CB
Allan, Gary	It Would Be You	7-768	CHM
Allan, Gary	Kiss Me When I'm Down	38-108	CB
Allan, Gary	Learning How To Bend	36-409	CB
Allan, Gary	Life Ain't Always Beautiful	29-189	CB
Allan, Gary	Living In A House Full Of Love	8-138	CB
Allan, Gary	Living In A House Full Of Love	22-651	ST
Allan, Gary	Lovin' You Against My Will	9-399	CB
Allan, Gary	Man Of Me	15-602	ST
Allan, Gary	Man To Man	34-364	CB
Allan, Gary	Man To Man	25-410	MM
Allan, Gary	Man To Man	18-329	ST
Allan, Gary	Man To Man	32-2	THM
Allan, Gary	No Man In His Wrong Heart	8-760	CB
Allan, Gary	No Man In His Wrong Heart	22-829	ST
Allan, Gary	Nothing On But The Radio	20-473	ST
Allan, Gary	One the	25-127	MM
Allan, Gary	One the	16-326	ST
Allan, Gary	Pieces	43-258	KCDC
Allan, Gary	Right Where I Need To Be	14-715	CB
Allan, Gary	Right Where I Need To Be	10-259	SC
Allan, Gary	Right Where I Need To Be	22-579	ST
Allan, Gary	She's So California	36-243	PHM
Allan, Gary	Smoke Rings In The Dark	5-734	SC
Allan, Gary	Smoke Rings In The Dark	22-504	ST
Allan, Gary	Songs About Rain	20-268	SC
Allan, Gary	Songs About Rain	19-847	ST

ARTIST	SONG TITLE	#	TYPE
Allan, Gary	Today	38-127	CB
Allan, Gary	Today	36-318	PHM
Allan, Gary	Tough Little Boys	25-643	MM
Allan, Gary	Tough Little Boys	19-173	ST
Allan, Gary	Tough Little Boys	32-336	THM
Allan, Gary	Watching Airplanes	30-538	CB
Allen, Chris	No Boundaries	36-294	PHM
Allen, Deborah	Baby I Lied	20-679	SC
Allen, Deborah	Break These Chains	17-253	NA
Allen, Deborah	Wrong Side Of Love	4-138	SC
Allen, Deborah	Xmas - Rockin' Little Christmas	8-57	CB
Allen, Kitty	Little Things Mean A Lot	19-613	MH
Allen, Kitty	Little Things Mean A Lot	9-747	SAV
Allen, Lily	Smile	30-732	SF
Allman Brothers	Ain't Wastin' Time No More	13-771	SGB
Allman Brothers	Everyday I Have The Blues	7-219	MM
Allman Brothers	It's Not My Cross To Bear	15-16	SC
Allman Brothers	Melissa	9-326	AG
Allman Brothers	Melissa	13-760	SGB
Allman Brothers	Midnight Rider	18-157	CB
Allman Brothers	No One To Run With	2-535	SC
Allman Brothers	One Way Out	9-374	AH
Allman Brothers	One Way Out	15-28	SC
Allman Brothers	One Way Out	13-769	SGB
Allman Brothers	Please Call Home	21-811	SC
Allman Brothers	Ramblin' Man	18-154	CB
Allman Brothers	Ramblin' Man	16-787	DK
Allman Brothers	Ramblin' Man	12-777	P
Allman Brothers	Ramblin' Man	2-524	SC
Allman Brothers	Statesboro Blues	15-312	SC
Allman Brothers	Stormy Monday Blues	11-296	DK
Allman Brothers	Stormy Monday Blues	7-222	MM
Allman Brothers	Whipping Post	2-526	SC
Allman Brothers Band	Dreams	45-589	OZP
Allman, Greg	Midnight Rider	12-696	P
Allure & 112	All Cried Out	20-122	PHM
Allure & 112	Duet - All Cried Out	20-122	PHM
Almost Famous	Show - America	18-677	PS
Almost Famous	Show - Something In The Air	18-679	PS
Almost Famous	Show - Tiny Dancer	18-678	PS
Aly & AJ	Rush	30-160	PT
Amazing Rhythm Aces	Dancing The Night Away	45-836	VH
Amazing Rhythm Aces	I Got The Feeling	45-835	VH
Amazing Rhythm Aces	I'm Setting You Free	47-788	SRK
Amazing Rhythm Aces	I'm Setting You Free	45-834	VH
Amazing Rhythm Aces	You Left The Water Running	47-789	SRK
Amber	Above The Clouds	21-719	TT

ARTIST	SONG TITLE	#	TYPE
Amber	This Is Your Night	24-554	SC
Amber	Yes (Hex Hector Mix)	21-736	TT
Amboy Dukes	Journey To The Center Of The Mind	14-457	SC
Ambrosia	Biggest Part Of Me	29-645	SC
Ambrosia	Holdin' On To Yesterday	17-535	SC
Ambrosia	How Much I Feel	17-563	PR
America	Daisy Jane	20-96	SC
America	Don't Cross The River	46-414	CB
America	From A Moving Train	46-421	SC
America	Horse With No Name	16-774	DK
America	Horse With No Name	7-485	MM
America	Horse With No Name a	35-109	CB
America	I Need You	4-79	SC
America	Lonely People	3-529	SC
America	Muskrat Love	46-413	CB
America	Only In Your Heart	46-418	CB
America	Sandman	46-416	CB
America	Sister Golden Hair	11-138	DK
America	Sister Golden Hair	9-788	SAV
America	Tin Man	33-295	CB
America	To Each His Own	46-419	CB
America	Ventura Highway	33-288	CB
America	Ventura Highway	13-305	P
America	Ventura Highway	4-54	SC
America	Woman Tonight	46-417	CB
America	You Can Do Magic	34-74	CB
America	You Can Do Magic	18-265	DK
America	You Can Do Magic	18-500	SAV
American Breed	Bend Me Shape Me	7-65	MM
American Breed	Bend Me Shape Me	14-337	SC
American Breed	Bend Me Shape Me	10-639	SF
American Hi-Fi	Art Of Losing the	32-145	THM
American HiFi	Another Perfect Day	18-400	MM
Amerie	Talkin' To Me	32-14	THM
Amerie feat. Eve	1 Thing	23-308	CB
Amerson, Steve	Gospel - On Eagles Wings	49-716	VH
Amerson, Steve	On Eagles Wings	49-716	VH
Ames Brothers	Hawaiian War Chant	9-749	SAV
Amitri, Del	Driving With the Brakes On	30-793	SF
Amitri, Del	Roll To Me	48-575	DK
Amos, Tori	Caught A Lite Sneeze	4-667	SC
Amos, Tori	Cornflake Girl	5-343	SC
Amos, Tori	Crucify	6-34	SC
Amos, Tori	Precious Things	5-744	SC
Amos, Tori	Silent All These Years	10-691	HH
Amos, Tori	Sorta Fairytale a	25-393	MM
Amos, Tori	Sorta Fairytale a	18-606	PHM
Amos, Tori	Talula	24-745	SC
Anastacia	You'll Never Be Alone	32-59	THM
Anastasia	At The Beginning	17-652	PR
Anastasia	Show - At The Beginning - Duet	17-652	PR
Anastasia	Show - I'm Outta Love	13-842	PHM
Anastasia	Show - Journey To The	17-653	PR

ARTIST	SONG TITLE	#	TYPE
	Past		
Anastasia	Show - Once Upon A December	17-651	PR
Anastasia	Show - One Day In Your Life	25-252	MM
Anastasia	Show - One Day In Your Life	21-731	TT
Anastasia	You'll Never Be Alone	32-59	THM
Anderson & Howard	Dis-Satisfied	20-797	CB
Anderson & Howard	Dis-Satisfied - duet	40-75	CB
Anderson & Howard	Duet - Dis-Satisfied	20-797	CB
Anderson & Howard	Duet - For Loving You	40-65	CB
Anderson & Howard	For Loving You - duet	40-65	CB
Anderson & Turner	Duet - Sometimes	40-69	CB
Anderson & Turner	Sometimes - duet	40-69	CB
Anderson, Bill	8 X 10	20-785	CB
Anderson, Bill	Bright Lights And Country Music	5-420	SC
Anderson, Bill	Corner Of My Life the	20-796	CB
Anderson, Bill	Corner Of My Life the	5-249	SC
Anderson, Bill	Don't She Look Good	20-792	CB
Anderson, Bill	For Loving You	46-213	CB
Anderson, Bill	Happy State Of Mind	20-789	CB
Anderson, Bill	I Can't Wait Any Longer	5-813	SC
Anderson, Bill	I Get The Fever	20-786	CB
Anderson, Bill	I Get The Fever	5-96	SC
Anderson, Bill	If It's All The Same To You	20-795	CB
Anderson, Bill	If You Can Live With it	20-793	CB
Anderson, Bill	Mama Sang A Song	20-784	CB
Anderson, Bill	My Life (I'll Throw It Away If I..)	20-790	CB
Anderson, Bill	My Life Throw It Away If I Want To	5-361	SC
Anderson, Bill	Po' Folk	46-211	CK
Anderson, Bill	Sometimes	46-212	CB
Anderson, Bill	Southern Fried	5-40	SC
Anderson, Bill	Still	20-783	CB
Anderson, Bill	Still	12-308	DK
Anderson, Bill	Wild Week End	20-788	CB
Anderson, Bill	World Of Make Believe	20-794	CB
Anderson, Bill	Xmas - First Noel the	8-79	CB
Anderson, Bill	Xmas - It Came Upon A Midnight Clea	8-71	CB
Anderson, Bill w Howard	If It's All The Same To You	40-73	CB
Anderson, John	Bend It Until It Breaks	22-853	ST
Anderson, John	Bend Until It Breaks	20-113	CB
Anderson, John	Bend Until It Breaks	6-711	MM
Anderson, John	Bend Until It Breaks	17-280	NA
Anderson, John	Bend Until It Breaks	2-572	SC
Anderson, John	Black Sheep	13-515	P
Anderson, John	Black Sheep	5-620	SC
Anderson, John	Chicken Truck	5-43	SC
Anderson, John	Country 'Til I Die	2-460	SC
Anderson, John	Goin' Down Hill	14-252	SC
Anderson, John	Honky Tonk Crowd	6-81	SC
Anderson, John	I Wish I Could Have	20-404	MH

ARTIST	SONG TITLE	#	TYPE	ARTIST	SONG TITLE	#	TYPE
	Been There			Anderson, Lynn	Blue Bayou	47-651	SFI
Anderson, John	I'm Just An Old Chunk Of Coal	44-67	DFK	Anderson, Lynn	Cry	47-641	CB
Anderson, John	I've Got It Made	2-361	SC	Anderson, Lynn	Fool Me	47-645	CB
Anderson, John	If Her Lovin' Don't Kill Me	30-42	CB	Anderson, Lynn	How Can I Unlove You	13-503	P
Anderson, John	Long Hard Lesson Learned	7-204	MM	Anderson, Lynn	If I Kiss You (Will You Go Away)	47-637	CB
Anderson, John	Long Hard Lesson Learned	4-239	SC	Anderson, Lynn	Keep Me In Mind	47-642	CB
Anderson, John	Mississippi Moon	20-114	CB	Anderson, Lynn	Listen To A Country Song	5-157	SC
Anderson, John	Mississippi Moon	2-764	SC	Anderson, Lynn	No Other Time	47-646	CB
Anderson, John	Money In The Band	2-429	SC	Anderson, Lynn	Oh Superman	47-648	SF
Anderson, John	My Kind Of Crazy	4-416	SC	Anderson, Lynn	Promises Promises	47-638	CB
Anderson, John	Nobody's Got It All	14-152	CB	Anderson, Lynn	Rocky Top	47-650	P
Anderson, John	Paradise	22-453	SC	Anderson, Lynn	Rose Garden	8-24	CB
Anderson, John	Seminole Wind	34-302	CB	Anderson, Lynn	Rose Garden	17-4	DK
Anderson, John	Seminole Wind	2-398	SC	Anderson, Lynn	Rose Garden	13-431	P
Anderson, John	Small Town	8-134	CB	Anderson, Lynn	Sing About Love	47-644	CB
Anderson, John	Small Town	22-665	ST	Anderson, Lynn	Stay There Til I Get There	47-643	CB
Anderson, John	Solid Ground	4-147	SC	Anderson, Lynn	Talkin' To The Wall	47-647	CB
Anderson, John	Somebody Slap Me	7-666	CHM	Anderson, Lynn	That's A No No	47-639	CB
Anderson, John	Somebody Slap Me	4-839	SC	Anderson, Lynn	Top Of The World	47-649	KT
Anderson, John	Straight Tequila Night	13-527	P	Anderson, Lynn	What A Man My Man Is	34-222	CB
Anderson, John	Straight Tequila Night	9-539	SAV	Anderson, Lynn	What A Man My Man Is	7-108	MM
Anderson, John	Straight Tequila Night	2-635	SC	Anderson, Lynn	What A Man My Man Is	5-562	SC
Anderson, John	Swingin'	8-16	CB	Anderson, Lynn	You're My Man	47-640	CB
Anderson, John	Swingin'	17-419	DK	Andrea True Conn.	More More More Pt. 1	17-531	SC
Anderson, John	Swingin'	6-758	MM	Andrew Sisters	Alexander's Ragtime Band	2-250	SC
Anderson, John	Swingin'	13-466	P	Andrew Sisters	Back In Your Own Backyard	46-425	KV
Anderson, John	Takin' The Country Back	8-303	CB	Andrew Sisters	Beat Me Daddy 8 To The Bar	46-429	KV
Anderson, John	Takin' The Country Back	22-790	ST	Andrew Sisters	Beer Barrel Polka	2-62	SC
Anderson, John	When It Comes To You	20-115	CB	Andrew Sisters	Bei Mir Bist Du Schon	12-569	P
Anderson, John	When It Comes To You	24-359	SC	Andrew Sisters	Bei Mir Bist Du Schon	9-563	SAV
Anderson, John	Wild And Blue	5-156	SC	Andrew Sisters	Boogie Woogie Bugle Boy	11-581	DK
Anderson, John	Woman Knows a	30-315	CB	Andrew Sisters	Boogie Woogie Bugle Boy	12-532	P
Anderson, John	Would You Catch A Falling Star	5-767	SC	Andrew Sisters	Boogie Woogie Bugle Boy	2-238	SC
Anderson, John	Xmas - Christmas Time	18-755	CB	Andrew Sisters	Chattanooga Choo Choo	46-426	KV
Anderson, John	You Ain't Hurt Nothin' Yet	9-417	CB	Andrew Sisters	Coffee Song the	48-641	KV
Anderson, Jordin	Toxic	41-66	PHN	Andrew Sisters	Hold Tight Hold Tight	46-428	KV
Anderson, Keith	C'Mon!	36-220	PHM	Andrew Sisters	I Wanna Be Loved	46-422	CB
Anderson, Keith	Every Time I Hear Your Name	29-44	CB	Andrew Sisters	I'll Be With You In Apple Blossom Time	46-430	KV
Anderson, Keith	Every Time I Hear Your Name	29-711	ST	Andrew Sisters	In The Mood	46-427	KV
Anderson, Keith	I Still Miss You	36-415	CB	Andrew Sisters	Lullaby Of Broadway	46-423	EK
Anderson, Keith	Patriotic - Sunday Morning In Amer	30-443	CB	Andrew Sisters	Pensylvania 6-5000	46-434	KV
Anderson, Keith	Pickin' Wildflowers	23-4	CB	Andrew Sisters	Roll Out The Barrel	46-436	SC
Anderson, Keith	Podunk	30-105	CB	Andrew Sisters	Rum And Coca Cola	46-424	KV
Anderson, Keith	Sunday Morning In America	30-443	CB	Andrew Sisters	Say Si Si (Para Vigo Me Voy)	46-433	KV
Anderson, Keith	Three Chords Country & American	30-18	CB	Andrew Sisters	Shoo Shoo Baby	46-432	KV
Anderson, Keith	XXL	36-374	SC	Andrew Sisters	Sing Sing Sing	9-564	SAV
Anderson, Keith	XXL - (Double XL)	23-412	CB	Andrew Sisters	Tico Tico	46-431	KV

ARTIST	SONG TITLE	#	TYPE
Andrew Sisters	Tuxedo Junction	46-435	KV
Andrew Sisters	Woodpecker Song the	9-820	SAV
Andrews & Hearts	Teardrops	49-456	MM
Andrews, Chris	Yesterday Man	10-576	SF
Andrews, Jessica	Everything	36-276	PHM
Andrews, Jessica	Good Times	25-706	MM
Andrews, Jessica	Good Times	19-269	ST
Andrews, Jessica	Helplessly Hopelessly	29-352	CB
Andrews, Jessica	Helplessly Hopelessly	15-186	ST
Andrews, Jessica	I Do Now	14-728	CB
Andrews, Jessica	I Will Be There For You	8-930	CB
Andrews, Jessica	Karma	16-334	ST
Andrews, Jessica	Now	36-367	CB
Andrews, Jessica	Summer Girl	23-294	CB
Andrews, Jessica	There's More To Me Than That	25-446	MM
Andrews, Jessica	There's More To Me Than You	34-356	CB
Andrews, Jessica	There's More To Me Than You	18-595	ST
Andrews, Jessica	There's More To Me Than You	32-119	THM
Andrews, Jessica	Unbreakable Heart	8-910	CB
Andrews, Jessica	Unbreakable Heart	22-479	ST
Andrews, Jessica	Who Am I	14-167	CB
Andrews, Jessica	Who I Am	33-147	CB
Andrews, Jessica	Who I Am	22-462	ST
Andrews, Jessica	You Go First (Do You Wanna Kiss)	22-489	ST
Andrews, Julie	I Could Have Danced All Night	19-107	SAV
Andrews, Julie	Show - My Favorite Things	12-534	P
Andrews,L & Hearts	Long Lonely Nights	25-173	MM
Androids	Do It With Madonna	32-250	THM
Angelle, Lisa	I Wear your Love	5-722	SC
Angelle, Lisa	I Will Love You	14-842	ST
Angelle, Lisa	I Will Love You	15-216	THM
Angelle, Lisa	Woman Gets Lonely a	14-97	CB
Angels	Am I Ever Gonna See You Again	46-438	CK
Angels	My Boyfriend's Back	11-115	DK
Angels	My Boyfriend's Back	10-726	JVC
Angels	My Boyfriend's Back	3-367	MH
Angels	My Boyfriend's Back	6-153	MM
Angels	My Boyfriend's Back	13-84	P
Angels	My Boyfriend's Back	9-289	SC
Angels	Take A Long Line	46-437	CDA
Angels	Till	5-79	SC
Angels & Airwaves	Everything's Magic	37-141	SC
Animals	Boom Boom	12-28	DK
Animals	Bring it On Home To Me	43-423	EZH
Animals	Bring It On Home To Me	37-273	ZM
Animals	Don't Bring Me Down	15-467	LE
Animals	Don't Let Me Be Misunderstood	11-553	DK
Animals	Don't Let Me Be Misunderstood	15-49	LE

ARTIST	SONG TITLE	#	TYPE
Animals	Don't Let Me Be Misunderstood	13-232	P
Animals	Don't Let Me Be Misunderstood	19-102	SAV
Animals	Don't Let Me Be Misunderstood	5-180	SC
Animals	House Of The Rising Sun	11-354	DK
Animals	House Of The Rising Sun	15-46	LE
Animals	House Of The Rising Sun	13-168	P
Animals	House Of The Rising Sun	29-834	SC
Animals	I Put A Spell On You	11-367	DK
Animals	I'm Crying	46-439	CB
Animals	It's My Life	11-277	DK
Animals	It's My Life	15-48	LE
Animals	It's My Life	13-231	P
Animals	San Franciscan Nights	15-52	LE
Animals	See See Rider	43-422	DKM
Animals	Sky Pilot	43-424	SC
Animals	We Gotta Get Out Of This Place	11-275	DK
Animals	We Gotta Get Out Of This Place	15-47	LE
Animals	We Gotta Get Out Of This Place	9-704	SAV
Animation	Obsession	11-279	DK
Animotion	Duet - Obsession	11-279	DK
Anka, Paul	But I Do Love You	46-594	DCK
Anka, Paul	Crazy Love	45-584	OZP
Anka, Paul	Dance On Little Girl	4-224	SC
Anka, Paul	Diana	33-235	CB
Anka, Paul	Diana	27-500	DK
Anka, Paul	Diana	13-124	P
Anka, Paul	Diana	9-171	SO
Anka, Paul	Eye Of The Tiger	44-113	KV
Anka, Paul	Having My Baby	9-173	SO
Anka, Paul	Hello	49-246	DFK
Anka, Paul	I Don't Like To Sleep Alone	9-174	SO
Anka, Paul	I Love You Because	5-224	SC
Anka, Paul	It's A Sin	49-244	DFK
Anka, Paul	It's My Life	44-114	KV
Anka, Paul	It's Time To Cry	5-524	SC
Anka, Paul	Jump	49-243	DFK
Anka, Paul	Kissin' On The Phone	9-551	SAV
Anka, Paul	Lonely Boy	3-505	SC
Anka, Paul	Longest Day the	45-598	OZP
Anka, Paul	My Home Town	9-552	SAV
Anka, Paul	My Home Town	14-455	SC
Anka, Paul	Puppy Love	35-42	CB
Anka, Paul	Puppy Love	27-501	DK
Anka, Paul	Puppy Love	9-176	SO
Anka, Paul	Put Your Head On My Shoulder	12-11	DK
Anka, Paul	Put Your Head On My Shoulder	2-206	SC

ARTIST	SONG TITLE	#	TYPE
Anka, Paul	Put Your Head On My Shoulder	9-175	SO
Anka, Paul	Smells Like Teen Spirit	49-245	DFK
Anka, Paul	Way You Make Me Feel the	49-247	DFK
Anka, Paul	You Are My Destiny	9-553	SAV
Anka, Paul	You Are My Destiny	3-511	SC
Anka, Paul	You Are My Destiny	9-172	SO
Anka, Paul	You're Having My Baby	15-595	DK
Anka, Paul & ??	Duet - Having My Baby	28-252	DK
Anka, Paul & ??	Duet - You're Havin' My Baby	15-595	DK
Annie	Show - It's The Hard Knock Life	6-880	MM
Annie	Show - Maybe	5-650	SC
Annie	Show - Thank Heaven for Little Girl	6-898	MM
Annie	Show - Tomorrow	33-220	CB
Annie	Show - Tomorrow	26-507	DK
Annie	Show - Tomorrow	6-328	MM
Annie	Show - Tomorrow	13-196	P
Annie	Tomorrow - Show	33-220	CB
Annie Get Your Gun	Anything You Can Do	19-585	SC
Annie Get Your Gun	Show - Anything You Can Do	19-585	SC
Annie Get Your Gun	Show - Girl That I Marry the	18-197	PS
Annie Get Your Gun	Show - There's No Busines Like Show	2-282	SC
Annie Get Your Gun	Show - There's No Business Like Sho	6-886	MM
Annie Get Your Gun	Show - They Say It's Wonderful	17-800	PS
Anthony & Arena	Duet - I Want To Spend My Life...	20-130	PHM
Anthony & Arena	I Want To Spend My Life With You	20-130	PHM
Anthony & Imperials	Going Out Of My Head	17-35	DK
Anthony & Imperials	Going Out Of My Head	6-678	MM
Anthony & Imperials	Going Out Of My Head	4-254	SC
Anthony & Imperials	I'm On The Outside Lookin' In	10-495	DA
Anthony & Imperials	I'm On The Outside Lookin' In	25-284	MM
Anthony, Derek	Cowboy Way	42-9	PHN
Anthony, Marc	How Could I	17-736	PS
Anthony, Marc	I Need To Know	35-248	CB
Anthony, Marc	I Need To Know	29-176	MH
Anthony, Marc	I Need To Know	8-516	PHT
Anthony, Marc	I Need To Know	5-782	SC
Anthony, Marc	I Need You	25-198	MM
Anthony, Marc	I've Got You	18-223	CB
Anthony, Marc	I've Got You	25-256	MM
Anthony, Marc	Latino - Celos	23-234	AI
Anthony, Marc	Latino - Contra La Lorriente	17-806	PS
Anthony, Marc	Latino - Da La Vuelta	17-734	PS
Anthony, Marc	Latino - Dimalo (I Need To Know)	17-733	PS

ARTIST	SONG TITLE	#	TYPE
Anthony, Marc	Latino - No Sabes Como	17-807	PS
Anthony, Marc	Latino - Suceden	17-808	PS
Anthony, Marc	Love Is All	17-732	PS
Anthony, Marc	My Baby You	33-383	CB
Anthony, Marc	My Baby You	15-434	PHM
Anthony, Marc	Remember Me	17-737	PS
Anthony, Marc	She's Been Good To Me	17-731	PS
Anthony, Marc	That's Okay	17-735	PS
Anthony, Marc	Tragedy	25-27	MM
Anthony, Marc	When I Dream At Night	14-503	SC
Anthony, Marc	You Sang To Me	16-236	PHM
Anthony, Marc	You Sang To Me	17-730	PS
Anthony, Ray	Bunny Hop the - DANCE #	22-387	SC
Anything Goes	Show - You're The One	19-588	SC
Anything Goes	You're The One	29-588	SC
Apple, Fiona	Across The Universe	16-210	MM
Apple, Fiona	Fast As You Can - Radio Version	17-537	SC
Apple, Fiona	Shadow Boxer	33-357	CB
Apple, Fiona	Shadowboxer	24-549	SC
April Wine	Just Between You And Me	24-677	SC
Aqua	Barbie Girl	13-568	LE
Aqua	Duet - Barbie Girl	13-568	LE
Aqua	Turn Back Time	5-276	SC
Aqualung	Brighter Than Sunshine	30-283	SC
Archer & Park	Where There's Smoke	24-133	SC
Archer, Tasmin	Sleeping Satellite	18-387	SAV
Archies	Archies the - TV theme	46-440	SC
Archies	Sugar Sugar	35-67	CB
Archies	Sugar Sugar	27-521	DK
Archies	Sugar Sugar	13-113	P
Archies	Sugar Sugar	9-697	SAV
Archies	TV Theme - Archies the	46-440	SC
Archuleta, David	Crush	36-494	CB
Archuleta, David	Crush	36-233	PHM
Archulets, David	Little Too Not Over You a	36-287	PHM
Arctic Monkeys	I Bet You Look Good On the Dance...	30-287	SC
Arden, Jann	Good Mother	24-550	SC
Arden, Jann	Insensitive	19-581	MH
Arden, Jann	Insensitive	4-672	SC
Arena, Tina	Chains	14-903	SC
Arjona, Ricardo	Latino - Cuando	17-787	SC
Arjona, Ricardo	Latino - El Problema	23-231	AI
Armed Development	Tennessee	18-383	SAV
Arminger, Katie	I Do But Do I	38-90	PHM
Armstrong & Fitzgerald	Duet - Summertime	44-112	KV
Armstrong & Fitzgerald	Summertime - Duet	44-112	KV
Armstrong, Louis	Blueberry Hill	9-560	SAV
Armstrong, Louis	Cabaret	46-445	PS
Armstrong, Louis	Gospel - When The Saints Go Marchin	11-480	DK
Armstrong, Louis	Hello Dolly	12-107	DK

ARTIST	SONG TITLE	#	TYPE
Armstrong, Louis	Hello Dolly	12-510	P
Armstrong, Louis	If	17-378	DK
Armstrong, Louis	Kiss To Build A Dream On	6-450	MM
Armstrong, Louis	La Vie En Rose	46-446	TU
Armstrong, Louis	Mack The Knife	46-443	LE
Armstrong, Louis	Mame	46-444	LE
Armstrong, Louis	Show - Hello Dolly	9-561	SAV
Armstrong, Louis	Show - What A Wonderful World	6-323	MM
Armstrong, Louis	We Have All the Time In the World	46-441	SF
Armstrong, Louis	What A Wonderful World	9-351	AH
Armstrong, Louis	What A Wonderful World	18-242	DK
Armstrong, Louis	What A Wonderful World	6-323	MM
Armstrong, Louis	What A Wonderful World	9-562	SAV
Armstrong, Louis	What A Wonderful World	10-585	SF
Armstrong, Louis	When The Saints Go Marching In	10-708	JVC
Armstrong, Louis	When The Saints Go Marching In	46-442	LE
Armstrong, Louis	When You Wish Upon A Star	21-14	CB
Armstrong, Louis	Xmas - Zat You Santa Claus	45-744	SC
Armstrong, Louis	Zat You Santa Claus	45-744	SC
Arnaz, Desi	Babalu (Spanish)	49-19	KV
Arnold, Eddy	Anytime	19-638	CB
Arnold, Eddy	Anytime	17-626	THM
Arnold, Eddy	Bouquet Of Roses	3-673	CB
Arnold, Eddy	Bouquet Of Roses	15-409	NK
Arnold, Eddy	Bouquet Of Roses	17-625	THM
Arnold, Eddy	Cattle Call	19-30	CB
Arnold, Eddy	Cattle Call	4-259	SC
Arnold, Eddy	Cattle Call	17-628	THM
Arnold, Eddy	Don't Rob Another Man's Castle	19-843	CB
Arnold, Eddy	Each Minute Seems Like A Million..	6-9	SC
Arnold, Eddy	Easy On The Eyes	45-569	CB
Arnold, Eddy	Full Time Job a	45-570	CB
Arnold, Eddy	Heart Full Of Love	19-841	CB
Arnold, Eddy	Here Comes Heaven	19-43	CB
Arnold, Eddy	I Really Don't Want To Know	17-17	DK
Arnold, Eddy	I Really Don't Want To Know	9-525	SAV
Arnold, Eddy	I Really Don't Want To Know	5-692	SC
Arnold, Eddy	I Wanna Play House With You	44-222	CKC
Arnold, Eddy	I Want To Go With You	19-34	CB
Arnold, Eddy	I Want To Go With You	4-797	SC
Arnold, Eddy	I'll Hold You In My Heart	19-629	CB
Arnold, Eddy	I'll Hold You In My Heart	3-599	SC
Arnold, Eddy	I'll Hold You In My Heart	17-627	THM
Arnold, Eddy	I'm Throwing Rice At The Girl That	19-643	CB
Arnold, Eddy	It Comes And Goes	44-223	DCK
Arnold, Eddy	It's A Sin	19-630	CB
Arnold, Eddy	Just A Little Lovin'	19-838	CB
Arnold, Eddy	Just A Little Lovin'	19-398	SC
Arnold, Eddy	Just A Little Lovin'	17-624	THM
Arnold, Eddy	Just Call Me Lonesome	45-571	CB
Arnold, Eddy	Last Word In Lonesome Is Me	19-39	CB
Arnold, Eddy	Lonely Again	19-41	CB
Arnold, Eddy	Make The World Go Away	19-33	CB
Arnold, Eddy	Make The World Go Away	13-480	P
Arnold, Eddy	Make The World Go Away	8-659	SAV
Arnold, Eddy	Make The World Go Away	2-193	SC
Arnold, Eddy	Make The World Go Away	17-622	THM
Arnold, Eddy	Make To World Go Away	11-434	DK
Arnold, Eddy	Misty Blue	44-221	CKC
Arnold, Eddy	One Kiss To Many	19-642	CB
Arnold, Eddy	Out Of The Blue	4-476	SC
Arnold, Eddy	Somebody Like Me	19-40	CB
Arnold, Eddy	Streets Of Laredo	7-355	MM
Arnold, Eddy	Tennessee Stud	19-38	CB
Arnold, Eddy	Texarkana	19-840	CB
Arnold, Eddy	That Do Make It Nice	19-44	CB
Arnold, Eddy	That's How Much I Love You	17-631	THM
Arnold, Eddy	That's What I Get For Loving You	45-573	OZP
Arnold, Eddy	Then You Can Tell Me Goodbye	17-629	THM
Arnold, Eddy	There's Been A Change In Me	45-572	CKC
Arnold, Eddy	Turn The World Around	19-42	CB
Arnold, Eddy	Up On The Housetop - Xmas	44-224	SC
Arnold, Eddy	Wagon Wheels	19-32	CB
Arnold, Eddy	Wayward Wind the	7-359	MM
Arnold, Eddy	Welcome To My World	12-304	DK
Arnold, Eddy	Welcome To My World	8-660	SAV
Arnold, Eddy	What Is Life Without Love	19-635	CB
Arnold, Eddy	What's He Doin' In My World	19-35	CB
Arnold, Eddy	What's He Doin' In My World	5-99	SC
Arnold, Eddy	What's He Doin' In My World	17-623	THM
Arnold, Eddy	Xmas - Up On The Housetop	14-519	SC
Arnold, Eddy	You Don't Know Me	19-31	CB
Arnold, Eddy	You Don't Know Me	13-530	P
Arnold, Eddy	You Don't Know Me	17-630	THM

ARTIST	SONG TITLE	#	TYPE	ARTIST	SONG TITLE	#	TYPE
Arrested Developmen	Duet - Tennessee	28-393	DK	Astley, Rick	Ones You Love the	18-483	NU
Arthur's Theme	Best That You Can Do	6-889	MM	Astley, Rick	Together Forever	11-261	DK
Arthur's Theme	Show - Best That You Can Do	6-889	MM	Ataris	Boys Of Summer	25-664	MM
Arthur's Theme	Show - Best That You Can Do	12-877	P	Ataris	Boys Of Summer the	32-327	THM
Ashanti	Dreams	20-628	NS	Ataris	In This Diary	32-222	THM
Ashanti	Foolish	18-297	CB	Ataris	Saddest Song the	32-443	THM
Ashanti	Foolish	25-215	MM	ATC	Around The World	12-393	PHM
Ashanti	Only U	22-347	CB	Athenaeum	What I Didn't Know	7-776	PHT
Ashanti	Rain On Me	32-386	THM	Atkins & Knopfler	Poor Boy Blues	44-80	KV
Ashanti	Rock Wit U (Awww Baby)	25-723	MM	Atkins, Chet	I Still Can't Say Goodbye	46-448	DFK
Ashanti	Rock Wit U (Awww Baby)	32-308	THM	Atkins, Chet	I Still Write Your Name In The Snow	18-487	SC
Ashley, Leon	Laura What's He Got That I Ain't Go	13-535	P	Atkins, Chet	Poor Boy Blues	46-447	KV
Ashton, Susan	Closer	8-898	CB	Atkins, Rodney	15 Minutes	37-50	CB
Ashton, Susan	Faith Of The Heart	8-916	CB	Atkins, Rodney	Angel's Hands	30-552	CB
Ashton, Susan	Faith Of The Heart	7-856	CHT	Atkins, Rodney	Chasin' Girls	37-325	CB
Ashton, Susan	She Is	19-372	ST	Atkins, Rodney	Cleaning This Gun	30-573	CB
Ashton, Susan	You're Lucky I Love You	8-968	CB	Atkins, Rodney	Farmer's Daughter	37-329	CB
Ashton, Susan	You're Lucky I Love You	22-492	ST	Atkins, Rodney	Honesty (Write Me A List)	30-36	CB
Ashworth, Ernie	Talk Back Trembling Lips	15-84	CB	Atkins, Rodney	Honesty (Write Me A List)	19-273	ST
Ashworth, Ernie	Talk Back Trembling Lips	4-302	SC	Atkins, Rodney	Honesty (Write Me A List)	32-337	THM
Asia	Heat Of The Moment	4-321	SC	Atkins, Rodney	If Her Lovin' Don't Kill Me	30-42	CB
Asia	Only Time Will Tell	5-689	SC	Atkins, Rodney	If You're Goin' Through Hell	30-40	CB
Asleep at the Wheel	Blues For Dixie	24-124	SC	Atkins, Rodney	If You're Going Through Hell	29-714	ST
Asleep At The Wheel	Boogie Back To Texas	45-863	VH	Atkins, Rodney	It's America - Patriotic	36-261	PHM
Asleep at the Wheel	Cherokee Maiden	14-737	CB	Atkins, Rodney	Monkey In The Middle	23-14	CB
Asleep At The Wheel	Don't Ask Me Why I'm Going To Texas	45-862	VH	Atkins, Rodney	My Old Man	30-39	CB
Asleep At The Wheel	Kind Of Love I Can't Forget the	46-215	VH	Atkins, Rodney	My Old Man	18-596	ST
Asleep at the Wheel	Letter That Johnny Walker Read	5-765	SC	Atkins, Rodney	My Old Man	32-84	THM
Asleep At The Wheel	Miles And Miles Of Texas	45-861	VH	Atkins, Rodney	Patriotic - It's America	36-261	PHM
Asleep at the Wheel	Route 66	15-75	CB	Atkins, Rodney	Sing Along	30-37	CB
Asleep at the Wheel	Route 66	43-18	CB	Atkins, Rodney	Sing Along	17-572	ST
Asleep At The Wheel	Silver Dew On the Blue Grass Tonight	46-216	VH	Atkins, Rodney	Someone To Share It With	30-41	CB
Asleep At The Wheel	Texas Fiddle Man	45-864	VH	Atkins, Rodney	Someone To Share It With	20-342	ST
Aspects Of Love	Show - Love Changes Everything	6-255	MM	Atkins, Rodney	Take A Back Road	38-118	CB
Association	Along Comes Mary	21-529	SC	Atkins, Rodney	These Are My People	30-354	CB
Association	Cherish	11-634	DK	Atkins, Rodney	Watching You	30-111	CB
Association	Cherish	9-695	SAV	ATL	Calling All Girls	32-423	THM
Association	Never My Love	12-312	DK	Atlanta	Sweet Country Music	5-419	SC
Association	Never My Love	13-108	P	Atlanta Rhythm Sec	Champagne Jam	7-464	MM
Association	Never My Love	9-474	SAV	Atlanta Rhythm Sec	Doraville	7-93	MM
Association	Windy	35-64	CB	Atlanta Rhythm Sec	So Into You	7-56	MM
Association	Windy	17-117	DK	Atlanta Rhythm Sec	So Into You	3-481	SC
Astaire, Fred	Cheek To Cheek	12-539	P	Atlantic Star	Secret Lovers	2-845	SC
Astley, Rick	Never Gonna Give You Up	11-243	DK	Atlantic Starr	Always	6-344	MM
				Atlantic Starr	Always - duet	35-193	CB
				Atlantic Starr	Duet - Always	35-193	CB
				Atlantic Starr	Duet - Always	28-105	DK
				Atlantic Starr	Duet - Always	6-344	MM

ARTIST	SONG TITLE	#	TYPE
Atlantic Starr	Duet - Secret Lovers	2-845	SC
Atomic Kid	Tide Is High the (Get The Feeling)	32-324	THM
Audio Adrenaline	Gospel - Big House	20-151	KB
Audio Slave	Cochise	20-465	CB
Audio Slave	Cochise	23-145	PHM
Audio Slave	I Am The Highway	20-534	CB
Audio Slave	Like A Stone	25-586	MM
Audio Slave	Like A Stone	32-141	THM
Audio Slave	Show Mw How To Live	32-325	THM
August & Spur of th	I-95 Asshole Song **	30-660	RSX
August & Spur of th	I-95 Asshole Song **	2-180	SC
Aurty, Gene	Be Honest With Me	45-658	OZP
Austin & Ingram	Duet - Baby Come To Me	11-406	DK
Austin, Paul	Mood Indigo	12-566	P
Austin, Sherrie	Driving Into The Sun	20-174	ST
Austin, Sherrie	Innocent Man	8-749	CB
Austin, Sherrie	Lucky In Love	7-663	CHM
Austin, Sherrie	Never Been Kissed	8-959	CB
Austin, Sherrie	Never Been Kissed	14-628	SC
Austin, Sherrie	Put Your Heart In To It	8-307	CB
Austin, Sherrie	Put Your Heart Into It	22-789	ST
Austin, Sherrie	Son Of A Preacher Man	20-481	ST
Austin, Sherrie	Streets Of Heaven	34-421	CB
Austin, Sherrie	Streets Of Heaven	25-648	MM
Austin, Sherrie	Streets Of Heaven	19-178	ST
Austin, Sherrie	Streets Of Heaven	32-342	THM
Authority Zero	One More Minute	32-107	THM
Automatic	Monster	30-730	SF
Autry, Gene	At Mail Call Today	22-174	CB
Autry, Gene	Back In The Saddle Again	12-284	DK
Autry, Gene	Back In The Saddle Again	5-430	SC
Autry, Gene	Don't Fence Me In	22-173	CB
Autry, Gene	Don't Hang Around Me Anymore	22-175	CB
Autry, Gene	Don't Live A Lie	22-176	CB
Autry, Gene	Easter - Peter Cottontail	45-660	DCK
Autry, Gene	Frosty The Snowman	45-659	DKM
Autry, Gene	Gonna Build A Big Fence Around TX	22-172	CB
Autry, Gene	Have I Told You Lately	33-4	CB
Autry, Gene	Here Comes Santa Claus	45-661	KKS
Autry, Gene	I Hang My Head And Cry	22-171	CB
Autry, Gene	I Want To Be Sure	22-177	CB
Autry, Gene	I Wish I Had Never Met Sunshine	22-182	CB
Autry, Gene	I'm Thinking Tonight Of My Blue Eye	22-170	CB
Autry, Gene	My Blue Heaven	46-291	CB
Autry, Gene	My Old Kentucky Home	43-320	CB
Autry, Gene	Peter Cottontail	45-660	DCK
Autry, Gene	Show - Back In The Saddle Again	12-284	DK
Autry, Gene	Silver Haired Daddy Of	45-657	TB

ARTIST	SONG TITLE	#	TYPE
	Mine		
Autry, Gene	Silver Spurs (On Golden Stairs)	22-178	CB
Autry, Gene	Someday You'll Want Me To Want U	22-181	CB
Autry, Gene	Twilight On The Trail	8-818	CB
Autry, Gene	Up On The Housetop	45-662	SY
Autry, Gene	Xmas - Frosty The Snowman	45-659	DKM
Autry, Gene	Xmas - Here Comes Santa Claus	45-661	KKS
Autry, Gene	Xmas - Rudolph the Red-Nosed Rein	14-511	SC
Autry, Gene	Xmas - Up On The Housetop	45-662	SY
Autry, Gene	You Are My Sunshine	8-437	CB
Autry, Gene	You're Not My Darlin' Anymore	22-180	CB
Avalon	Gospel - Testify To Love	20-155	KB
Avalon	Testify To Love	46-450	SC
Avalon, Frankie	Beauty School Drop Out	9-278	SC
Avalon, Frankie	Bobby Sox To Stockings	46-449	LE
Avalon, Frankie	Dede Dinah	5-462	SC
Avalon, Frankie	I Want To Be With You Always	5-225	SC
Avalon, Frankie	Just Ask Your Heart	5-525	SC
Avalon, Frankie	Venus	11-365	DK
Avalon, Frankie	Venus	13-86	P
Avalon, Frankie	Why	4-215	SC
Avalon, Frankie	Why Do Fools Fall In Love	46-451	KBA
Avenged Sevenfold	Almost Easy (Radio Version)	37-139	SC
Avenged Sevenfold	Bat Country	29-257	SC
Average White Band	Work To Do	2-564	SC
Axton, Hoyt	Della And The Dealer	44-62	HM
Axton, Hoyt	Honky Tonk Music	46-452	VH
Axton, Hoyt	Rusty Old Halo	44-64	SRK
Ayala, Ramon y Sus	Latino - Quemame Los Ojos	17-758	SC
AZ Yet	Last Night	24-298	SC
Azar, Steve	Doin' It Right	23-284	CB
Azar, Steve	I Don't Have To Be Me 'Til Monday	16-42	ST
Azar, Steve	I Don't Have To Be Me Till Monday	25-56	MM
Azar, Steve	I Never Stopped Lovin' You	7-340	MM
Azar, Steve	I Never Stopped Lovin' You	4-398	SC
Azar, Steve	My Heart Wants To Run	17-583	ST
Azar, Steve	Nights Like This	4-597	SC
Azar, Steve	Someday	7-210	MM
Azar, Steve	Waitin' On Joe	18-134	ST
Azar, Steve	Waiting On Joe	34-387	CB
Azar, Steve	You Don't Know A Thing	30-93	CB
B Talent	Try Honesty	32-406	THM
B-52-s	Love Shack	16-520	P

ARTIST	SONG TITLE	#	TYPE
B-52-s	Love Shack	2-43	SC
B-52-s	Love Shack	10-525	SF
B-52's	Bedrock Twitch	46-455	SBI
B-52's	Dance This Mess Around	46-454	KV
B-52's	Deadbeat Club	46-453	DK
B-52's	Debbie	46-456	SC
B-52's	Duet - Love Shack	26-232	DK
B-52's	Duet - Love Shack	16-520	P
B-52's	Duet - Love Shack	2-43	SC
B-52's	Duet - Love Shack	10-525	SF
B-52's	Meet The Flintstones	46-458	KV
B-52's	Private Idaho	46-457	SC
B-52's	Roam	12-786	P
B-52's	Rock Lobster	11-714	DK
B-52's	TV Theme - Meet The Flintstones	46-458	KV
B.O.B. & Bruno Mars	Duet - Nothin' On You	38-238	BH
B.O.B. & Bruno Mars	Nothin' On You - duet	38-238	BH
B.T. Express	Do It Till Your Satisfied	11-386	DK
B.T.O.	You Ain't Seen Nothin' Yet	13-171	P
B.T.O.	You Ain't Seen Nothin' Yet	4-760	SC
B*Witched	C'Est La Vie	7-845	PHM
B2K	Girlfriend	32-196	THM
B2K	Gots Ta Be	18-227	CB
B2K	Uh Huh	17-597	PHM
B2K & P Diddy	Bump Bump Bump	32-122	THM
Baby & P Diddy	Do That	32-129	THM
Babyface	Everytime I Close My Eyes	15-473	SC
Babyface	For The Cool In You	13-608	P
Babyface	How Come How Long	21-552	PHM
Babyface	My Kinda Girl	11-730	DK
Babyface	Never Keeping Secrets	2-235	SC
Babyface	Sorry For The Stupid Things	29-318	PHM
Babyface	When Can I See You	34-114	CB
Babyface	When Can I See You	12-184	DK
Babys	Back On My Feet Again	5-143	SC
Babys	Every Time I Think Of You	3-133	SC
Babys	Isn't It Time	15-802	SC
Backstreet & Mia	Duet - Take Me There	16-203	PHT
Backstreet & Mia	Take Me There	7-816	PHM
Backstreet Boys	All I Have To Give	18-712	MM
Backstreet Boys	All I Have To Give	7-802	PHT
Backstreet Boys	Anywhere For You	18-703	MM
Backstreet Boys	Anywhere For You	30-415	THM
Backstreet Boys	As Long As You Love Me	18-714	MM
Backstreet Boys	As Long As You Love Me	7-708	PHM
Backstreet Boys	As Long As You Love Me	10-135	SC
Backstreet Boys	Back To Your Heart	10-206	SC
Backstreet Boys	Boys Will Be Boys	30-409	THM

ARTIST	SONG TITLE	#	TYPE
Backstreet Boys	Call the	12-387	PHM
Backstreet Boys	Darlin'	18-706	MM
Backstreet Boys	Drowning	33-389	CB
Backstreet Boys	Drowning	25-34	MM
Backstreet Boys	Drowning	16-305	PHM
Backstreet Boys	Drowning	16-90	SC
Backstreet Boys	Everybody	18-713	MM
Backstreet Boys	Everybody	10-129	SC
Backstreet Boys	Everytime I Close My Eyes	30-410	THM
Backstreet Boys	Get Down	30-416	THM
Backstreet Boys	Get Down (You're The One...)	18-707	MM
Backstreet Boys	Hey Mr. DJ	30-417	THM
Backstreet Boys	Hey Mr. DJ (Keep Playing...)	18-705	MM
Backstreet Boys	I Wanna Be With You	30-411	THM
Backstreet Boys	I Want It That Way	29-175	MH
Backstreet Boys	I Want It That Way	18-711	MM
Backstreet Boys	I Want It That Way	7-896	PHT
Backstreet Boys	I Want It That Way	13-779	SGB
Backstreet Boys	I'll Never Break Your Heart	11-65	JTG
Backstreet Boys	I'll Never Break Your Heart	18-710	MM
Backstreet Boys	I'll Never Break Your Heart	7-770	PHT
Backstreet Boys	If You Want To Be A Good Girl	30-418	THM
Backstreet Boys	If You Want To Be Good Girl	18-708	MM
Backstreet Boys	It's True	15-446	PHM
Backstreet Boys	Larger Than Life	18-716	MM
Backstreet Boys	Larger Than Life	8-522	PHT
Backstreet Boys	Let's Have A Party	30-412	THM
Backstreet Boys	More Than That	18-567	TT
Backstreet Boys	Nobody But You	30-413	THM
Backstreet Boys	One the	33-385	CB
Backstreet Boys	One the	29-177	MH
Backstreet Boys	One the	13-839	PHM
Backstreet Boys	One the	14-468	SC
Backstreet Boys	Quit Playing Games With My Heart	18-709	MM
Backstreet Boys	Quit Playing Games With My Heart	21-549	PHM
Backstreet Boys	Set Adrift On Memory Bliss	18-704	MM
Backstreet Boys	Shape Of My Heart	35-203	CB
Backstreet Boys	Shape Of My Heart	23-260	HS
Backstreet Boys	Shape Of My Heart	16-478	MH
Backstreet Boys	Shape Of My Heart	14-38	THM
Backstreet Boys	Show Me The Meaning of Being Lonely	18-715	MM
Backstreet Boys	Show Me The Meaning Of Being Lonely	5-886	SC
Backstreet Boys	Show Me The Meaning of Being Lonely	30-405	THM
Backstreet Boys	Show Me The Meaning of...	35-213	CB

ARTIST	SONG TITLE	#	TYPE
Backstreet Boys	We've Got It Goin' On	34-157	CB
Backstreet Boys	We've Got It Goin' On	30-414	THM
Backstreet Boys	We've Got It Going On	18-702	MM
Backstreet Boyz	One the	30-633	THM
Bad Company	Feel Like Makin' Love	2-143	SC
Bad Company	Good Lovin' Gone Bad	4-562	SC
Bad Company	Movin' On	10-489	DA
Bad Company	Seagull	15-753	AMS
Bad Company	Shooting Star	5-588	SC
Bad Company	Young Blood	24-202	SC
Bad English	When I See You Smile	13-215	P
Bad English	When I See You Smile	15-740	SC
Badfinger	Come And Get It	15-747	SC
Badfinger	Day After Day	12-705	P
Badfinger	Day After Day	29-293	SC
Badfinger	Without You	17-524	SC
Badlees	Angeline Is Coming Home	24-54	SC
Badu, Erykah	Bag Lady	23-257	HS
Badu, Erykah	Bag Lady	25-690	MM
Badu, Erykah	Next Lifetime	10-90	SC
Badu, Erykah	On And On	33-363	CB
Badu, Erykah	On And On	25-685	MM
Baez, Joan	All My Trials	46-465	SBI
Baez, Joan	Banks Of The Ohio	46-463	KVD
Baez, Joan	Diamonds And Rust	46-462	SC
Baez, Joan	Donna Donna	46-466	JVC
Baez, Joan	Farewell Angelina	46-461	SBI
Baez, Joan	Help Me Make It Through The Night	46-459	KV
Baez, Joan	Love Is Just A Four Letter Word	49-772	PS
Baez, Joan	Night They Drove Old Dixie Down	7-348	MM
Baez, Joan	Night They Drove Old Dixie Down	5-383	SC
Baez, Joan	We Shall Overcome	46-460	MIK
Baha Men	Who Let The Dogs Out	14-7	PHM
Bailey, Razzy	Anywhere There's A Jukebox	29-390	CB
Bailey, Razzy	Everytime You Cross My Mind	29-387	CB
Bailey, Razzy	Friends	29-377	CB
Bailey, Razzy	I Ain't Got No Business Doin...	29-384	CB
Bailey, Razzy	I Can't Get Enough Of You	29-382	CB
Bailey, Razzy	I Keep Coming Back	29-378	CB
Bailey, Razzy	If Love Had A Face	29-385	CB
Bailey, Razzy	Love's Gonna Fall Here Tonight	29-388	CB
Bailey, Razzy	Loving Up A Storm	29-379	CB
Bailey, Razzy	Midnight Hauler	29-380	CB
Bailey, Razzy	Scratch My Back/Whisper In My Ear	29-386	CB
Bailey, Razzy	She Left Love All Over Me	29-381	CB
Bailey, Razzy	Tonight She's Gonna Love Me	29-383	CB

ARTIST	SONG TITLE	#	TYPE
Bailey, Razzy	Too Old To Play Cowboy	29-391	CB
Bailey, Razzy	What Time Do You Have To Be Back	29-389	CB
Baillie & The Boys	Long Shot	5-568	SC
Bainbridge, Merrill	Mouth	10-680	HE
Bainbridge, Merrill	Mouth	24-365	SC
Bainbridge, Merrill	Mouth	19-167	SGB
Bainbridge, Merrill	Under The Water	10-690	HH
Bainbridge, Merrill	Under The Water	10-89	SC
Baker & Myers	Little Bit Of Honey	24-164	SC
Baker & Myers	Years From Here	4-133	SC
Baker, Anita	Bewitched Bothered & Bewildered	9-792	SAV
Baker, Anita	Body & Soul	27-306	DK
Baker, Anita	Body And Soul	13-611	P
Baker, Anita	Caught Up In The Rapture	12-884	P
Baker, Anita	Caught Up In the Rapture	4-299	SC
Baker, Anita	Giving You The Best That I Got	2-280	SC
Baker, Anita	I Apologize	29-128	ST
Baker, Anita	Just Because	11-538	DK
Baker, Anita	Sweet Love	12-628	P
Baker, Anita	Years From Here	7-237	MM
Baker, Chet	But Not For Me	9-793	SAV
Baker, Laverne	I Cried A Tear	17-318	SS
Ball, David	Circle Of Friends	7-277	MM
Ball, David	Hangin' In & Hangin' On	24-151	SC
Ball, David	Hangin' In & Hangin' On	7-328	MM
Ball, David	Honky Tonk Healin'	7-86	MM
Ball, David	Look What Followed Me Home	22-859	ST
Ball, David	Riding With Private Malone	33-151	CB
Ball, David	Riding With Private Malone	25-6	MM
Ball, David	Riding With Private Malone	15-857	ST
Ball, David	She Always Talked About Mexico	16-694	ST
Ball, David	Thinkin' Problem	34-310	CB
Ball, David	Thinkin' Problem	6-587	MM
Ball, David	Thinkin' Problem	2-319	SC
Ball, David	Watching My Baby Not Comin' Back	14-632	SC
Ball, David	What Do You Want With Him	6-808	MM
Ball, David	What Do You Want With Him	2-769	SC
Ball, David	When The Thought Of You Catches...	17-232	NA
Ball, David	When The Thought Of You Catches...	21-299	NA
Ball, David	When The Thought Of You Catches...	2-447	SC
Ballard & Midnights	Finger Poppin' Time	4-223	SC
Ballard & Midnights	Finger Poppin' Time	10-242	SS

ARTIST	SONG TITLE	#	TYPE
Ballard, Frankie	Buncha Girls a	37-352	CB
Ballard, Frankie	Helluva Life	43-16	KCDC
Ballard, Frankie	Sunshine And Whiskey	49-757	BKD
Ballard, Frankie	Tell Me You Get Lonely	49-758	CB
Ballard, Frankie	Young And Crazy	49-745	KRG
Ballerini, Kelsea	Dibs	45-386	BKD
Ballerini, Kelsea	Love Me Like You Mean It	45-456	SSC
Ballerini, Kelsea	Peter Pan	45-457	BKD
Ballerini, Kelsea	XO	47-396	BKD
Ballerini, Kelsea	Yeah Boy	45-387	BKD
Bamford, Gord	Drinkin' Buddy	44-85	KV
Bananarama	Cruel Summer	17-520	SC
Bananarama	I Heard A Rumour	17-149	DK
Bananarama	I Want You Back	48-782	P
Bananarama	Love In The First Degree	48-566	DK
Band	I Shall Be Released	12-61	DK
Band	I Shall Be Released	46-468	DK
Band	Live Is A Carnival	6-58	SC
Band	Night They Drove Old Dixie Down	17-70	DK
Band	Up On Cripple Creek	46-467	MM
Band	Weight the	6-482	MM
Band	Weight the	13-235	P
Band Aid	Xmas - Do They Know It's Christmas	14-527	SC
Band Of Horses	Is There A Ghost	49-909	SC
Band Perry	All Your Life	40-37	CB
Band Perry	Better Dig Two	40-38	ASK
Band Perry	Don't Let Me Be Lonely	44-336	SSC
Band Perry	Done	40-39	ASK
Band Perry	Done	40-18	PHN
Band Perry	End Of Time	48-108	KV
Band Perry	End Of Time	45-56	BKD
Band Perry	Forever Mine Nevermind	44-389	ASK
Band Perry	Forever Mine Nevermind	41-53	PHN
Band Perry	Hip To My Heart	37-331	CB
Band Perry	I'm A Keeper	44-390	KV
Band Perry	If I Die Young	44-142	BKD
Band Perry	If I Die Young	40-40	PHN
Band Perry	Independence	40-41	ASK
Band Perry	Live Forever	45-545	BKD
Band Perry	Mother Like Mine	41-58	PHN
Band Perry	Mother Like Mine a	43-458	ASK
Band Perry	Pioneer	40-42	ASK
Band Perry	Postcard From Paris	39-46	ASK
Band Perry	Walk Me Down The Middle	44-391	KV
Band Perry	You Lie	37-203	AS
Band Perry	Chainsaw	43-142	KV
Banda La Costena	Latino - Por La Espalda	17-755	SC
Bandy & Hobbs	Duet - Following The Feeling	9-577	SAV
Bandy & Hobbs	Duet - Let's Get Over Them Together	9-575	SAV
Bandy & Hobbs	Following The Feeling	9-577	SAV
Bandy & Hobbs	Let's Get Over Them	9-575	SAV

ARTIST	SONG TITLE	#	TYPE
	Together		
Bandy & Stampley	Duet - Hey Joe Hey Moe	19-509	CB
Bandy & Stampley	Duet - Holding The Bag	19-505	CB
Bandy & Stampley	Duet - Just Good Ol' Boys	19-496	CB
Bandy & Stampley	Hey Joe Hey Moe - duet	34-245	CB
Bandy & Stampley	Holding The Bag	19-505	CB
Bandy & Stampley	Just Good Ol' Boys	19-496	CB
Bandy & Stanpley	Hey Joe Hey Moe	19-509	CB
Bandy, Moe	Americana	19-499	CB
Bandy, Moe	Americana	5-155	SC
Bandy, Moe	Bandy The Rodeo Clown	19-501	CB
Bandy, Moe	Barstool Mountain	19-508	CB
Bandy, Moe	Hank Williams You Wrote My Life	3-688	CB
Bandy, Moe	Here I Am I'm Drunk Again	19-510	CB
Bandy, Moe	I Cheated Me Right Out Of You	19-497	CB
Bandy, Moe	I Cheated Me Right Out Of You	4-645	SC
Bandy, Moe	I'm Sorry For You My Friend	19-504	CB
Bandy, Moe	It Was Always So Easy To Forget	19-507	CB
Bandy, Moe	It Was Always So Easy To Forget	20-284	SC
Bandy, Moe	It's A Cheatin' Situation	19-498	CB
Bandy, Moe	It's A Cheatin' Situation	4-268	SC
Bandy, Moe	She's Not Really Cheatin'	19-500	CB
Bandy, Moe	She's Not Really Cheatin'	5-668	SC
Bandy, Moe	Till I'm Too Old To Die Young	19-503	CB
Bandy, Moe	Till I'm Too Old To Die Young	9-446	SAV
Bandy, Moe	Till I'm Too Old To Die Young	5-811	SC
Bandy, Moe	Two Lonely People	19-506	CB
Bangles	Be With You	46-469	CB
Bangles	Eternal Flame	12-812	P
Bangles	Going Down To Liverpool	46-473	SF
Bangles	Hazy Shade Of Winter	46-471	LE
Bangles	Hero Takes A Fall	46-472	SF
Bangles	If She Knew What She Wanted	15-734	SC
Bangles	In Your Room	24-423	SC
Bangles	Manic Monday	12-845	P
Bangles	Manic Monday	4-535	SC
Bangles	Walk Down Your Street	46-470	JVC
Bangles	Walk Like An Egyptian	7-104	MM
Bangles	Walk Like An Egyptian	4-294	SC
Bangles	Walk Like An Eqyptian	17-412	DK
Banks, Lloyd	I'm So Fly	30-806	PHM
Bardo, Sharie	These Boots Are Made For Walkin'	14-46	THM

ARTIST	SONG TITLE	#	TYPE
Bare & Anderson's	Duet - Game Of Triangles the	3-709	CB
Bare & Anderson's	Game Of Triangles the	3-709	CB
Bare, Bobby	500 Miles Away From Home	18-267	CB
Bare, Bobby	Alimony	45-734	VH
Bare, Bobby	All American Boy	18-278	CB
Bare, Bobby	Chicken Every Sunday	18-277	CB
Bare, Bobby	Come Sundown	18-275	CB
Bare, Bobby	Detroit City	15-78	CB
Bare, Bobby	Detroit City	17-162	DK
Bare, Bobby	Detroit City	8-620	SAV
Bare, Bobby	Dropkick Me Jesus	6-78	SC
Bare, Bobby	Four Strong Winds	18-270	CB
Bare, Bobby	Game Of Triangles the	18-276	CB
Bare, Bobby	How I Got To Memphis	18-273	CB
Bare, Bobby	It's Alright	18-271	CB
Bare, Bobby	Jogger the	23-26	SC
Bare, Bobby	Joggers	47-902	DCK
Bare, Bobby	Lincoln Park Inn	3-704	CB
Bare, Bobby	Lincoln Park Inn	20-285	SC
Bare, Bobby	Margie's At The Lincoln Park Inn	18-272	CB
Bare, Bobby	Marie Laveau	3-700	CB
Bare, Bobby	Marie Laveau	14-311	SC
Bare, Bobby	Mermaid the	46-47	SSK
Bare, Bobby	Miller's Cave	18-269	CB
Bare, Bobby	Numbers	45-713	VH
Bare, Bobby	Please Don't Tell Me How The Story	18-274	CB
Bare, Bobby	Streets Of Baltimore the	3-708	CB
Bare, Bobby	Streets Of Baltimore the	5-367	SC
Bare, Bobby	Tequila Sheila	44-71	SRK
Bare, Bobby	That's How I Got To Memphis	5-817	SC
Bare, Bobby	Winner the	15-146	SC
Bare, Bobby Jr & Sr	Daddy What If	18-268	CB
Bare, Bobby Sr & Jr	Duet - Daddy What If	18-268	CB
Bareillas, Sara	Brave	48-209	KV
Bareillas, Sara	Hold My Heart	48-208	KV
Bareillas, Sara	I Choose You	48-210	KV
Bareillas, Sara	King Of Anything	48-206	CB
Bareillas, Sara	Let The Rain	48-212	KV
Bareillas, Sara	She Used To Be Mine	48-211	KV
Bareillas, Sara	Uncharted	48-207	CB
Bareilles, Sara	Goodbye Yellow Brick Road	49-643	KV
Bareilles, Sara	Goodbye Yellow Brick Road (Live)	49-15	KV
Bareilles, Sara	Islands	49-22	KV
Bareilles, Sara	Love Song	36-454	CB
Bareilles, Sara	Love Song	37-23	PS
Bareilles, Sara	Morningside	37-21	PS
Bareilles, Sara	One Sweet Love	37-22	PS
Barenaked Ladies	Alcohol	30-625	RS
Barenaked Ladies	Another Postcard (Chimps)	32-430	THM
Barenaked Ladies	Be My Yoko Ono	30-626	RS

ARTIST	SONG TITLE	#	TYPE
Barenaked Ladies	Big Bang Theory Theme Song	49-751	KV
Barenaked Ladies	Brian Wilson	5-748	SC
Barenaked Ladies	Brian Wilson - 2000 Vers	30-615	RS
Barenaked Ladies	Brian Wilson - Original Vers	30-627	RS
Barenaked Ladies	Call And Answer	34-131	CB
Barenaked Ladies	Call And Answer	7-890	PHT
Barenaked Ladies	Call And Answer	30-622	RS
Barenaked Ladies	Duet - Get In Line	30-620	RS
Barenaked Ladies	Duet - If I Had $1,000,000	30-613	RS
Barenaked Ladies	Duet - If I Had A $1,000,000	5-332	SC
Barenaked Ladies	Duet - If I Had A Million Dollars	33-362	CB
Barenaked Ladies	Enid	30-623	RS
Barenaked Ladies	Falling For The First Time	18-405	MM
Barenaked Ladies	Falling For The First Time	23-99	SC
Barenaked Ladies	Get In Line	16-181	PHM
Barenaked Ladies	Get In Line - Duet	30-620	RS
Barenaked Ladies	Get In Line (Solo Verses)	30-628	RS
Barenaked Ladies	If I Had $1,000,000	30-613	RS
Barenaked Ladies	If I Had $1,000,000	5-332	SC
Barenaked Ladies	If I Had A Million Dollars - duet	33-362	CB
Barenaked Ladies	It's All Been Done	33-366	CB
Barenaked Ladies	It's All Been Done	16-216	MM
Barenaked Ladies	It's All Been Done	7-778	PHT
Barenaked Ladies	It's All Been Done	30-612	RS
Barenaked Ladies	Jane	30-617	RS
Barenaked Ladies	Never Is Enough	30-624	RS
Barenaked Ladies	Old Apartment the	30-611	RS
Barenaked Ladies	One Week	7-773	PHT
Barenaked Ladies	One Week	30-614	RS
Barenaked Ladies	Shoe Box	30-616	CB
Barenaked Ladies	Shoe Box	30-616	RS
Barenaked Ladies	Straw Hat And Old Dirty Hank	30-618	RS
Barenaked Ladies	Thanks That Was Fun	18-296	CB
Barenaked Ladies	TV Themes - Big Bang Theory	49-751	KV
Barenaked Ladies	What A Good Boy	30-621	RS
Barenaked Ladies	When I Fall	30-619	RS
Barkley, Gnarls	Crazy	30-606	SF
Barkley, Gnarls	Gone Daddy Gone	30-59	PHM
Barkley, Gnarls	Smiley Faces	30-728	SF
Barlow, Gary	So Help Me Girl	7-699	PHM
Barnes & Barnes	Fish Heads	5-636	SC
Barnett, Mandy	I've Got A Right To Cry	14-620	SC
Barnett, Mandy	Maybe	7-274	MM
Barnett, Mandy	Now That's All Right With Me	4-158	SC
Barnett, Mandy	Planet Of Love	7-622	CHM
Barnett, Mandy	Simple I Love You a	4-427	SC
Barnett, Mandy	Whispering Wind Blows On & On	5-728	SC

ARTIST	SONG TITLE	#	TYPE
Barrino, Fantasia	I Believe	23-563	MM
Barrino, Fantasia	Truth Is	22-345	CB
Bartels, Joanie	Xmas - I Want A Hippopatamus For..	14-303	MM
Barton, Eileen	If I Knew You Were Comin'	5-83	SC
Base & DJ Ez Rock	It Takes Two	18-370	AH
Base & DJ Ez Rock	It Takes Two	12-177	DK
Basia	Miles Away	14-865	PS
Basia	New Day For You	14-862	PS
Basia	New Day For You	16-70	SC
Basia	Promises	14-863	PS
Basia	Time And Tide	14-864	PS
Basil, Toni	Mickey	11-328	DK
Basil, Toni	Mickey	16-533	P
Bass, Fontella	Rescue Me	35-77	CB
Bass, Fontella	Rescue Me	19-618	MH
Bass, Fontella	Rescue Me	6-557	MM
Bass, Fontella	Rescue Me	9-230	PT
Bassey, Shirley	And I Love You So	46-478	LGK
Bassey, Shirley	As Long As He Needs Me	46-485	SF
Bassey, Shirley	Big Spender	11-19	PX
Bassey, Shirley	Climb Every Mountain	46-480	P
Bassey, Shirley	Diamonds Are Forever	9-71	SC
Bassey, Shirley	For All We Know	46-481	PS
Bassey, Shirley	Get The Party Started	46-479	MRH
Bassey, Shirley	Goldfinger	12-649	P
Bassey, Shirley	Goldfinger	9-60	SC
Bassey, Shirley	Greatest Performance Of My Life	46-477	KV
Bassey, Shirley	If You Go Away	46-476	KV
Bassey, Shirley	Kiss Me Honey Honey Kiss Me	46-474	EK
Bassey, Shirley	Light My Fire	46-475	KV
Bassey, Shirley	Never Never Never	46-482	PS
Bassey, Shirley	Show - Goldfinger	19-106	SAV
Bassey, Shirley	Show Is Over the	46-483	SBI
Bassey, Shirley	This Is My Life	46-484	SBI
Bassey, Shirley	What Now My Love	46-486	SF
Bates, Greg	Brothers	39-75	PHN
Bates, Jeff	Did It For The Girl	44-149	BKD
Bates, Jeff	Don't Hate Me For Lovin' You	36-588	CB
Bates, Jeff	Good People	23-298	CB
Bates, Jeff	I Wanna Make You Cry	19-775	ST
Bates, Jeff	Long Slow Kisses	22-85	CB
Bates, Jeff	Love Song the	25-520	MM
Bates, Jeff	Love Song the	18-786	ST
Bates, Jeff	Love Song the	32-114	THM
Bates, Jeff	No Shame	29-51	CB
Bates, Jeff	One Second Chance	30-83	CB
Bates, Jeff	Rainbow Man	19-533	ST
Bates, Jeff	Riverbank	36-618	CB
Battaglia, Kaci	Crazy Possessive	36-300	PHM
Baxley, Tori	Half A Man	23-141	CB
Bay Ciry Rollers	Shang A Lang	45-943	KV
Bay City Rollers	I Only Want To Be With	4-390	SC

ARTIST	SONG TITLE	#	TYPE
	You		
Bay City Rollers	Saturday Night	11-267	DK
BB Mak	Back Here	13-841	PHM
BB Mak	Back Here	14-476	SC
BB Mak	Back Here	18-546	TT
BB Mak	Out Of My Heart	25-312	MM
BB Mak	Still On Your Side	14-40	THM
Beach Boys	409	3-557	SC
Beach Boys	All Summer Long	46-494	NT
Beach Boys	Barbara Ann	5-496	BS
Beach Boys	Barbara Ann	33-257	CB
Beach Boys	Barbara Ann	17-46	DK
Beach Boys	Be True To Your School	5-497	BS
Beach Boys	California Girls	5-498	BS
Beach Boys	California Girls	16-758	DK
Beach Boys	Catch A Wave	5-510	BS
Beach Boys	Cottonfields	46-489	KV
Beach Boys	Dance Dance Dance	5-499	BS
Beach Boys	Darlin'	46-174	SC
Beach Boys	Do It Again	46-502	ZM
Beach Boys	Do You Wanna Dance	46-493	LE
Beach Boys	Don't Worry Baby	5-901	BS
Beach Boys	Don't Worry Baby	11-652	DK
Beach Boys	Don't Worry Baby	13-118	P
Beach Boys	Fun Fun Fun	5-500	BS
Beach Boys	Fun Fun Fun	11-632	DK
Beach Boys	Fun Fun Fun	12-669	P
Beach Boys	Fun Fun Fun	4-41	SC
Beach Boys	Getcha Back	46-487	CB
Beach Boys	Girls Don't Tell Me	46-496	NT
Beach Boys	Girls On The Beach	46-497	NT
Beach Boys	God Only Knows	17-544	DK
Beach Boys	Good Timin'	46-488	DK
Beach Boys	Good Vibrations	5-501	BS
Beach Boys	Good Vibrations	33-242	CB
Beach Boys	Good Vibrations	11-812	DK
Beach Boys	Good Vibrations	12-856	P
Beach Boys	Help Me Rhonda	5-502	BS
Beach Boys	Help Me Rhonda	11-233	DK
Beach Boys	Heroes And Villians	46-500	SC
Beach Boys	I Can Hear Music	46-501	SC
Beach Boys	I Get Around	5-503	BS
Beach Boys	I Get Around	33-252	CB
Beach Boys	I Get Around	11-398	DK
Beach Boys	I Get Around	12-867	P
Beach Boys	I'm Waiting For The Day	45-607	OZP
Beach Boys	In My Room	5-902	BS
Beach Boys	Ko Ko Mo	5-504	BS
Beach Boys	Ko Ko Mo	18-63	MM
Beach Boys	Let Him Run Wild	46-490	KV
Beach Boys	Little Deuce Coupe	5-509	BS
Beach Boys	Little Deuce Coupe	35-40	CB
Beach Boys	Little Deuce Coupe	11-651	DK
Beach Boys	Little Deuce Coupe	13-265	P
Beach Boys	Little Deuce Coupe	3-554	SC
Beach Boys	Little Saint Nick - Xmas	33-208	CB
Beach Boys	Rock & Roll Music	5-505	BS

ARTIST	SONG TITLE	#	TYPE
Beach Boys	Rock And Roll Music	34=65	CB
Beach Boys	Sail On Sailor	15-746	SC
Beach Boys	Sloop John B	5-506	BS
Beach Boys	Sloop John B	46-597	LE
Beach Boys	Sloop John B	46-596	CB
Beach Boys	Sloop John B	46-595	SC
Beach Boys	Surfer Girl	12-670	P
Beach Boys	Surfin' Safari	46-492	LE
Beach Boys	Surfin' USA	5-507	BS
Beach Boys	Surfin' USA	16-776	DK
Beach Boys	Surfin' USA	3-324	MH
Beach Boys	Surfin' USA	12-733	P
Beach Boys	Then I Kissed Her	46-503	ZM
Beach Boys	Warmth Of The Sun	46-498	NT
Beach Boys	Wendy	46-495	NT
Beach Boys	When I Grow Up To Be A Man	46-491	LE
Beach Boys	Wipe Out	11-769	DK
Beach Boys	Wouldn't It Be Nice	5-508	BS
Beach Boys	Wouldn't It Be Nice	17-545	DK
Beach Boys	Wouldn't It Be Nice	12-913	P
Beach Boys	Xmas - Little Saint Nick	33-208	CB
Beach Boys	Xmas - Little Saint Nick	3-401	SC
Beach Boys	Xmas - Little Saint Nick	22-840	ST
Beach, Viola	Swings & Waterslides	49-932	MRH
Beaches	Show - Otto Titsling	7-361	MM
Beamer,Keola/Kapona	Honolulu City Lights	6-839	MM
Beamer,Keola/Kapona	Lovely Hula Hands	6-833	MM
Beamer,Keola/Kapono	Hawaii - Honolulu City Lights	6-839	MM
Beamer,Keola/Kapono	Hawaii - Lovely Hula Hands	6-833	MM
Bear, Edward	Last Song	2-781	SC
Beard, Jan	Speakin' Of The Devil	24-355	SC
Beard, Kendall	Drinkin'	42-6	PHN
Beastie Boys	Brass Monkey	14-440	SC
Beastie Boys	No Sleep 'Til Brooklyn	25-482	MM
Beastie Boys	You Gotta Fight For Your Right...	34-87	CB
Beastie Boys	You Gotta Fight for Yr Right/Party	10-499	DA
Beat	Mirror In The Bathroom	49-112	SF
Beat	Twist And Crawl	49-108	CDG
Beatles	Across The Universe	7-522	SAV
Beatles	Act Naturally	16-656	DK
Beatles	All My Loving	11-127	DK
Beatles	All My Loving	12-739	P
Beatles	All My Loving	7-548	SAV
Beatles	All My Loving	29-342	SC
Beatles	All You Need Is Love	16-744	DK
Beatles	And I Love Her	11-128	DK
Beatles	And I Love Her	13-61	P
Beatles	Ask Me Why	9-642	SAV
Beatles	Back In The U.S.S.R.	16-842	DK
Beatles	Back In The U.S.S.R.	12-725	P
Beatles	Besame Mucho	44-121	KV

ARTIST	SONG TITLE	#	TYPE
Beatles	Birthday	17-63	DK
Beatles	Birthday	19-135	KC
Beatles	Birthday	12-870	P
Beatles	Blackbird	13-106	P
Beatles	Can't Buy Me Love	11-87	DK
Beatles	Can't Buy Me Love	13-80	P
Beatles	Can't Buy Me Love	9-643	SAV
Beatles	Chains	11-260	DK
Beatles	Come Together	11-193	DK
Beatles	Come Together	11-72	JTG
Beatles	Come Together	12-914	P
Beatles	Come Together	9-645	SAV
Beatles	Day In The Life a	17-64	DK
Beatles	Day Tripper	16-801	DK
Beatles	Day Tripper	12-912	P
Beatles	Do You Want To Know A Secret	11-250	DK
Beatles	Do You Want To Know A Secret	13-259	P
Beatles	Do You Want To Know A Secret	29-339	SC
Beatles	Don't Bother Me	9-641	SAV
Beatles	Don't Let Me Down	20-195	SC
Beatles	Drive My Car	12-720	P
Beatles	Drive My Car	20-196	SC
Beatles	Eight Days A Week	16-732	DK
Beatles	Eight Days A Week	3-322	MH
Beatles	Eight Days A Week	29-345	SC
Beatles	Eleanor Rigby	11-166	DK
Beatles	Eleanor Rigby	13-234	P
Beatles	Everybody's Got Something To Hide	47-770	SRK
Beatles	Everybody's Trying To Be My Baby	44-118	KV
Beatles	Fool On The Hill the	28-456	DK
Beatles	Fool On The Hill the	12-919	P
Beatles	For No One	7-525	SAV
Beatles	From Me To You	15-478	MM
Beatles	From Me To You	29-333	SC
Beatles	Get Back	11-180	DK
Beatles	Get Back	13-47	P
Beatles	Get Back	7-528	SAV
Beatles	Girl	7-512	SAV
Beatles	Halloween - Helter Skelter	45-120	SC
Beatles	Happiness Is A Warm Gun	10-491	DA
Beatles	Hard Day's Night a	11-176	DK
Beatles	Hard Day's Night a	13-48	P
Beatles	Hard Day's Night a	7-519	SAV
Beatles	Hello Goodbye	16-726	DK
Beatles	Hello Goodbye	13-95	P
Beatles	Hello Goodbye	9-644	SAV
Beatles	Help	16-760	DK
Beatles	Help	15-489	SC
Beatles	Help!	35-53	CB
Beatles	Helter Skelter - Halloween	45-120	SC

ARTIST	SONG TITLE	#	TYPE
Beatles	Here Comes The Sun	33-264	CB
Beatles	Here Comes The Sun	7-520	SAV
Beatles	Here There And Everywhere	11-108	DK
Beatles	Here There And Everywhere	7-514	SAV
Beatles	Hey Jude	16-830	DK
Beatles	I Am The Walrus	21-510	SC
Beatles	I Call Your Name	11-552	DK
Beatles	I Feel Fine	37-272	CB
Beatles	I Feel Fine	11-133	DK
Beatles	I Feel Fine	29-336	SC
Beatles	I Me Mine	44-119	KV
Beatles	I Saw Her Standing There	16-771	DK
Beatles	I Saw Her Standing There	12-737	P
Beatles	I Saw Her Standing There	29-340	SC
Beatles	I Should Have Known Better	11-550	DK
Beatles	I Should Have Known Better	13-62	P
Beatles	I Want To Hold Your Hand	29-346	SC
Beatles	I'm A Loser	20-198	SC
Beatles	I'm Down	20-197	SC
Beatles	I'm Down	46-127	SC
Beatles	In My Life	16-747	DK
Beatles	In My Life	7-515	SAV
Beatles	It's All Too Much	20-200	SC
Beatles	Kansas City (Hey Hey Hey Hey)	44-123	KV
Beatles	Lady Madonna	34-68	CB
Beatles	Lady Madonna	16-780	DK
Beatles	Lady Madonna	7-526	SAV
Beatles	Let It Be	16-762	DK
Beatles	Let It Be	13-141	P
Beatles	Long And Winding Road	16-815	DK
Beatles	Long And Winding Road	13-153	P
Beatles	Love Me Do	11-681	DK
Beatles	Love Me Do	12-723	P
Beatles	Love Me Do	29-335	SC
Beatles	Lucy In The Sky With Diamonds	33-250	CB
Beatles	Lucy In The Sky With Diamonds	15-274	DK
Beatles	Lucy In The Sky With Diamonds	12-872	P
Beatles	Lucy In The Sky With Diamonds	7-521	SAV
Beatles	Lucy In The Sky With Diamonds	2-761	SC
Beatles	Michelle	11-139	DK
Beatles	Michelle	13-46	P
Beatles	Mr. Moonlight	11-452	DK
Beatles	Night Before the	20-207	SC
Beatles	No Reply	11-144	DK
Beatles	Norwegian Wood	17-546	DK

ARTIST	SONG TITLE	#	TYPE
Beatles	Not A Second Time	44-120	KV
Beatles	Nowhere Man	11-217	DK
Beatles	Nowhere Man	12-858	P
Beatles	Nowhere Man	7-518	SAV
Beatles	Ob La Di Ob La Da	11-147	DK
Beatles	Ob La Di Ob La Da	7-517	SAV
Beatles	Ob La Di Ob La Da	46-599	P
Beatles	Ob La Di Ob La Da	46-598	SC
Beatles	Octopus's Garden	20-203	SC
Beatles	Oh Darling	17-547	DK
Beatles	Oh Darling	13-105	P
Beatles	P.S. I Love You	29-334	SC
Beatles	Paperback Writer	18-116	DK
Beatles	Penny Lane	16-799	DK
Beatles	Penny Lane	13-179	P
Beatles	Penny Lane	7-524	SAV
Beatles	Please Please Me	16-872	DK
Beatles	Please Please Me	13-119	P
Beatles	Please Please Me	7-523	SAV
Beatles	Please Please Me	29-338	SC
Beatles	Ps I Love You	11-682	DK
Beatles	Rain	20-205	SC
Beatles	Revolution	16-857	DK
Beatles	Revolution	13-178	P
Beatles	Rock & Roll Music	7-511	SAV
Beatles	Roll Over Beethoven	29-332	SC
Beatles	She Loves You	16-813	DK
Beatles	She Loves You	12-738	P
Beatles	She Loves You	29-344	SC
Beatles	She's A Woman	11-199	DK
Beatles	She's A Woman	29-337	SC
Beatles	She's Leaving Home	17-61	DK
Beatles	Shot Of Rhythm And Blues a	45-610	OZP
Beatles	Something	7-513	SAV
Beatles	Strawberry Fields Forever	11-234	DK
Beatles	Strawberry Fields Forever	12-926	P
Beatles	Strawberry Fields Forever	7-527	SAV
Beatles	Sun King	44-122	KV
Beatles	This Boy	29-343	SC
Beatles	Ticket To Ride	11-91	DK
Beatles	Till There Was You	11-451	DK
Beatles	Twist & Shout	16-835	DK
Beatles	Twist & Shout	3-323	MH
Beatles	Twist & Shout	7-516	SAV
Beatles	Twist & Shout	2-55	SC
Beatles	Twist & Shout	29-341	SC
Beatles	We Can Work it Out	11-210	DK
Beatles	What You're Doing	44-124	KV
Beatles	When I'm 64	17-62	DK
Beatles	When I'm 64	13-68	P
Beatles	With A Little Help From My Friends	13-167	P
Beatles	Words Of Love	11-270	DK

ARTIST	SONG TITLE	#	TYPE
Beatles	Yellow Submarine	11-109	DK
Beatles	Yesterday	11-100	DK
Beatles	You're Gonna Lose That Girl	28-471	DK
Beatles	You've Got To Hide Your Love Away	11-551	DK
Beau Brummels	Laugh Laugh	5-176	SC
Bedingfield, Daniel	If You're Not The One	20-523	CB
Bedingfield, Daniel	If You're Not The One	25-583	MM
Bedingfield, Daniel	If You're Not The One	19-339	STP
Bedingfield, Daniel	If You're Not The One	32-169	THM
Bedingfield, Daniel	James Dean	18-778	PHM
Bedingfield, Natasha	Pocketful Of Sunshine	36-456	CB
Bedingfield, Natasha	Unwritten	30-146	PT
Bedingfield, Natasha	Unwritten	29-255	SC
Bee Gees	Alone	48-689	KB
Bee Gees	And The Sun Will Shine	48-687	FMK
Bee Gees	Don't Throw It All Away	48-681	CB
Bee Gees	Emotion	48-692	ZMP
Bee Gees	ESP	9-777	SAV
Bee Gees	Fanny (Be Tender With My Love)	48-690	P
Bee Gees	Grease	9-779	SAV
Bee Gees	Holiday	12-7	DK
Bee Gees	Holiday	17-503	LE
Bee Gees	How Can You Mend A Broken Heart	11-674	DK
Bee Gees	How Can You Mend A Broken Heart	17-504	LE
Bee Gees	How Can You Mend A Broken Heart	13-162	P
Bee Gees	How Can You Mend A Broken Heart	2-432	SC
Bee Gees	How Deep is Your Love	11-84	DK
Bee Gees	How Deep Is Your Love	11-76	JTG
Bee Gees	How Deep Is Your Love	17-492	LE
Bee Gees	How Deep Is Your Love	9-653	SAV
Bee Gees	How Deep Is Your Love	2-843	SC
Bee Gees	I Can't See Nobody	48-682	DFK
Bee Gees	I Just Want To Be Your Everything	11-441	DK
Bee Gees	I Started A Joke	17-491	LE
Bee Gees	I've Got To Get A Message To You	17-495	LE
Bee Gees	If I Can't Have You	11-249	DK
Bee Gees	If I Can't Have You	9-778	SAV
Bee Gees	If I Can't Have You	10-548	SF
Bee Gees	Immortality	48-684	DCK
Bee Gees	Islands In The Stream	17-499	LE
Bee Gees	Jive Talkin'	11-331	DK
Bee Gees	Jive Talkin'	17-506	LE
Bee Gees	Jive Talkin'	9-780	SAV
Bee Gees	Jive Talkin'	20-369	SC
Bee Gees	Lonely Days	17-490	LE
Bee Gees	Lonely Days	22-932	SC
Bee Gees	Love So Right	17-500	LE
Bee Gees	Love You Inside Out	48-688	JV
Bee Gees	Love You Inside Out	48-680	CB

ARTIST	SONG TITLE	#	TYPE
Bee Gees	Massachusettes (Lights Went Out)	11-827	DK
Bee Gees	More Than A Woman	17-501	LE
Bee Gees	Night Fever	11-663	DK
Bee Gees	Night Fever	9-654	SAV
Bee Gees	Night Fever	2-497	SC
Bee Gees	Nights on Broadway	17-498	LE
Bee Gees	One	48-683	DFK
Bee Gees	Only One Woman	9-781	SAV
Bee Gees	Secret Love	48-693	ZMP
Bee Gees	Spicks And Specks	48-691	ZMP
Bee Gees	Stayin' Alive	18-111	DK
Bee Gees	Stayin' Alive	17-497	LE
Bee Gees	Stayin' Alive	2-499	SC
Bee Gees	This Is Where I Came In	48-686	EG
Bee Gees	To Love Somebody	17-494	LE
Bee Gees	Too Much Heaven	17-496	LE
Bee Gees	Too Much Heaven	21-808	SC
Bee Gees	Tragedy	11-415	DK
Bee Gees	Tragedy	17-493	LE
Bee Gees	Tragedy	9-784	SAV
Bee Gees	Words	17-505	LE
Bee Gees	Words	6-50	SC
Bee Gees	You Should Be Dancing	11-414	DK
Bee Gees	You Should Be Dancing	17-502	LE
Bee Gees	You Should Be Dancing	9-776	SAV
Bee Gees	You Should Be Dancing	2-500	SC
Bee Gees	You Win Again	48-685	P
Beene Man/Ms Thing	Duet - Dude	20-550	PHM
Beene Man&Ms Thing	Dude	20-550	PHM
Bega, Lou	Mambo #5	8-506	PHT
Bega, Lou	Mambo No 5	29-178	MH
Bega, Lou	Tricky Tricky	9-340	PS
Bega, Lou	Tricky Tricky	5-891	SC
Belafonte, Harry	Cocoanut Woman	46-506	LE
Belafonte, Harry	Day O (Banana Boat Song)	12-97	DK
Belafonte, Harry	Day O (Banana Boat Song)	13-60	P
Belafonte, Harry	Island In The Sun	48-773	P
Belafonte, Harry	Island In The Sun	46-507	LE
Belafonte, Harry	Jamaica Farewell	46-504	JVC
Belafonte, Harry	Jump In Line	46-508	LE
Belafonte, Harry	Mama Look At Boo Boo	6-866	MM
Belafonte, Harry	Matilda	46-505	KV
Belafonte, Harry	Show - Banana Boat Song (Day-O)	6-330	MM
Bell & Fontana	Duet - Love Is An Open Door - Frozen	43-189	SBIG
Bell & Fontana	Love Is An Open Door - duet - Frozen	43-189	SBIG
Bell & Fontana	Show - Love Is An Open Door - Frozen	43-189	SBIG
Bell & James	Loving It Up	9-769	SAV
Bell Biv Devoe	Do Me **	28-399	DK
Bell Biv Devoe	Do Me **	5-552	SC
Bell Biv Devoe	Poison	25-478	MM

ARTIST	SONG TITLE	#	TYPE
Bell, Benny	Shaving Cream	5-632	SC
Bell, Benny	Shaving Cream **	30-668	RSX
Bell, Kristen	Do You Want To Build A Snowman - Frozen	43-186	ASK
Bell, Kristen	Show - Do You Want To Build A Snowman	43-186	ASK
Bellamy Brothers	Almost Jamaica	44-76	SRK
Bellamy Brothers	Blame It On The Fire In My Heart	45-301	DCK
Bellamy Brothers	Blue California	47-744	SRK
Bellamy Brothers	Can I Come Home	24-129	SC
Bellamy Brothers	Cowboy Beat	6-755	MM
Bellamy Brothers	Crazy From The Heart	45-299	CDG
Bellamy Brothers	Crossfire	45-297	KV
Bellamy Brothers	Dancin' Cowboys	14-430	SC
Bellamy Brothers	Do You Love As Good As You Look	33-67	CB
Bellamy Brothers	Do You Love As Good As You Look	13-460	P
Bellamy Brothers	Do You Love As Good As You Look	5-616	SC
Bellamy Brothers	Feelin' The Feelin'	44-75	KV
Bellamy Brothers	For All The Wrong Reasons	4-811	SC
Bellamy Brothers	Forget About Me	45-303	KV
Bellamy Brothers	Get Into Reggae Cowboy	44-72	KV
Bellamy Brothers	I Love You More And More	45-292	DCK
Bellamy Brothers	I Need More Of You	5-815	SC
Bellamy Brothers	If I Said You Had A Beautiful Body	8-832	CB
Bellamy Brothers	If I Said You Had A Beautiful Body	12-117	DK
Bellamy Brothers	If I Said You Had A Beautiful Body	13-334	P
Bellamy Brothers	If I Said You Had A Beautiful Body	10-510	SF
Bellamy Brothers	Jalapenos	45-304	KST
Bellamy Brothers	Kids Of The Baby Boom	34-274	CB
Bellamy Brothers	Let Your Love Flow	15-69	CB
Bellamy Brothers	Let Your Love Flow	13-432	P
Bellamy Brothers	Let Your Love Flow	10-513	SF
Bellamy Brothers	Lie To You For Your Love	6-85	SC
Bellamy Brothers	Lord Help Me Be The Kind Of Person	47-760	SRK
Bellamy Brothers	Not	46-50	SSK
Bellamy Brothers	Old Hippie (The Sequel)	7-206	MM
Bellamy Brothers	Old Hippie Christmas - xmas	45-306	CB
Bellamy Brothers	Redneck Girl	13-391	P
Bellamy Brothers	Redneck Girl	5-26	SC
Bellamy Brothers	Rip Off The Knob	6-753	MM
Bellamy Brothers	Rock A Billy	47-807	SRK
Bellamy Brothers	Shine Them Buckles	4-414	SC
Bellamy Brothers	Slippin' Away	45-300	DCK
Bellamy Brothers	Some Broken Hearts	45-298	KVD
Bellamy Brothers	Vertical Expression (of	44-77	KV

ARTIST	SONG TITLE	#	TYPE
	Horizontal)		
Bellamy Brothers	We Dared The Lightning	3-658	SC
Bellamy Brothers	What'll I Do	45-305	CB
Bellamy Brothers	When I'm Away From You	5-159	SC
Bellamy Brothers	Xmas - Old Hippie Christmas	45-306	CB
Bellamy Brothers	You Ain't Just Whistlin' Dixie	4-644	SC
Bellamy Brothers	You'll Never Be Sorry	47-771	SRK
Bellamy Brothers	You'll Never Be Sorry	45-302	KV
Bellamy Brothers	You're The World	45-307	KV
Belle Stars	Iko Iko	3-527	SC
Belle, Regina	If I Could	17-425	KC
Belle, Regina	If I Could	15-509	PS
Belle, Regina	Make It Like It Was	16-552	P
Ben Folds Five	Brick	5-193	SC
Ben Folds Five	Song For The Dumped **	37-86	SC
Benatar, Par	Little Too Late	46-510	MH
Benatar, Pat	All Fired Up	24-432	SC
Benatar, Pat	Fire And Ice	9-12	MH
Benatar, Pat	Fire And Ice	19-156	SGB
Benatar, Pat	Heartbreaker	12-769	P
Benatar, Pat	Heartbreaker	4-528	SC
Benatar, Pat	Hell Is For Children	9-376	AH
Benatar, Pat	Hell Is For Children	9-10	MH
Benatar, Pat	Hell Is For Children	19-548	SC
Benatar, Pat	Hell Is For Children	19-151	SGB
Benatar, Pat	Hit Me With Your Best Shot	16-870	DK
Benatar, Pat	Hit Me With Your Best Shot	13-283	P
Benatar, Pat	Hit Me With Your Best Shot	2-150	SC
Benatar, Pat	Hot Child In The City	35-138	CB
Benatar, Pat	Hot Child In The City	11-417	DK
Benatar, Pat	I'm Gonna Follow You	46-513	MH
Benatar, Pat	Invincible (Legend of Billy Jean)	46-125	SC
Benatar, Pat	Looking For A Stranger	46-511	MH
Benatar, Pat	Love Is A Battlefield	28-282	DK
Benatar, Pat	Love Is A Battlefield	3-613	SC
Benatar, Pat	Promises In The Dark	20-93	SC
Benatar, Pat	Sex As A Weapon	46-126	SC
Benatar, Pat	Shadows Of The Night	19-560	SC
Benatar, Pat	Shadows Of The Night	19-163	SGB
Benatar, Pat	Treat Me Right	18-243	DK
Benatar, Pat	Treat Me Right	5-145	SC
Benatar, Pat	True Love	46-124	SC
Benatar, Pat	We Belong	11-661	DK
Benatar, Pat	We Belong	9-691	SAV
Benatar, Pat	We Live For Love	46-512	MH
Benatar, Pat	You Better Run	24-565	SC
Benet,McDonald,Judd	Duet - Heart Of America	29-50	CB
Bennett & Krall	All Right Okay You Win	25-670	MM
Bennett & Krall	Duet - All Right Okay	25-670	MM

ARTIST	SONG TITLE	#	TYPE
	You Win		
Bennett & Lady Gaga	Duet - Let's Face the Music & Dance	49-720	KV
Bennett & Lady Gaga	Let's Face the Music & Dance	49-720	KV
Bennett & Lang	Duet - Moonglow	29-129	ST
Bennett & Lang	Duet - What A Wonderful World	45-518	SC
Bennett & Lang	What A Wonderful World - duet	45-518	SC
Bennett & Underwood	Duet - It Had To Be You	45-949	KV
Bennett & Underwood	It Had To Be You - duet	45-949	KV
Bennett, Tony	Because Of You	17-364	DK
Bennett, Tony	Blue Moon	34-445	CB
Bennett, Tony	Body And Soul	10-712	JVC
Bennett, Tony	Can You Find It In Your Heart	25-258	MM
Bennett, Tony	Door Is Still Open To My Heart	10-407	LE
Bennett, Tony	Firefly	10-415	LE
Bennett, Tony	Fly Me To The Moon	28-502	DK
Bennett, Tony	Foggy Day a	10-411	LE
Bennett, Tony	Good Life the	10-413	LE
Bennett, Tony	I Left My Heart In San Francisco	16-728	DK
Bennett, Tony	I Left My Heart In San Francisco	10-410	LE
Bennett, Tony	I Left My Heart In San Francisco	12-519	P
Bennett, Tony	I Left My Heart In San Francisco	2-192	SC
Bennett, Tony	I Wanna Be Around	10-414	LE
Bennett, Tony	I Wanna Be Around	18-69	MM
Bennett, Tony	It's A Sin To Tell A Lie	10-711	JVC
Bennett, Tony	It's A Sin To Tell A Lie	19-99	SAV
Bennett, Tony	Jeepers Creepers	34-442	CB
Bennett, Tony	Just In Time	18-45	MM
Bennett, Tony	Naughty Lady Of Shady Lane	10-408	LE
Bennett, Tony	Nice Work If You Can Get It	7-183	MM
Bennett, Tony	Old Devil Moon	10-409	LE
Bennett, Tony	Put On A Happy Face	43-227	CB
Bennett, Tony	Rags To Riches	49-213	MM
Bennett, Tony	Sh-Boom	11-602	DK
Bennett, Tony	Shadow Of Your Smile	16-755	DK
Bennett, Tony	Shadow Of Your Smile	12-515	P
Bennett, Tony	Shadow Of Your Smile	19-782	SGB
Bennett, Tony	Standing On The Corner	10-406	LE
Bennett, Tony	Steppin' Out With My Baby	18-246	DK
Bennett, Tony	Stranger In Paradise	10-412	LE
Bennett, Tony	Stranger In Paradise	10-606	SF
Bennett, Tony	Who Can I Turn To	10-416	LE
Bennett/Vaught/Sina	My Funny Valentine	16-750	DK
Benson, George	Give Me The Night	9-52	MM
Benson, George	Give Me The Night	14-639	SC

ARTIST	SONG TITLE	#	TYPE
Benson, George	Love Ballad	12-820	P
Benson, George	On Broadway	18-61	MM
Benson, George	On Broadway	13-152	P
Benson, George	This Masquerade	16-785	DK
Benson, George	This Masquerade	14-353	MH
Benson, George	This Masquerade	16-536	P
Benson, George	Turn Your Love Around	35-164	CB
Benson, George	Turn Your Love Around	12-791	P
Benson, George	Turn Your Love Around	15-798	SC
Bentley, Dierks	5-1-5-0	39-43	ASK
Bentley, Dierks	Am I The Only One	44-382	BKD
Bentley, Dierks	Am I The Only One	37-354	CB
Bentley, Dierks	Bartenders, Barstools & Barmaids	45-48	TBR
Bentley, Dierks	Breathe You In	45-164	PHN
Bentley, Dierks	Come A Little Closer	23-409	CB
Bentley, Dierks	Come A Little Closer	29-506	SC
Bentley, Dierks	Come A Little Closer	29-604	ST
Bentley, Dierks	Country And Cold Cans	45-49	ASK
Bentley, Dierks	Domestic Light And Cold	23-466	CB
Bentley, Dierks	Draw Me A Map	37-345	PHM
Bentley, Dierks	Drunk On A Plane	46-232	PHN
Bentley, Dierks	Every Mile A Memory	30-22	CB
Bentley, Dierks	Feel That Fire	36-221	PHM
Bentley, Dierks	Free And Easy Down the Road I Go	30-453	CB
Bentley, Dierks	Gonna Die Young	45-166	PHN
Bentley, Dierks	Heart Of A Lonely Girl	45-165	PHN
Bentley, Dierks	Home	38-216	ASK
Bentley, Dierks	How Am I Doin	20-386	ST
Bentley, Dierks	How Am I Doin'	30-796	PHM
Bentley, Dierks	How Am I Doin'	21-663	SC
Bentley, Dierks	I Hold On	41-48	ASK
Bentley, Dierks	I Wanna Make You Close Your Eyes	49-376	CB
Bentley, Dierks	I Wanna Make You Close Your Eyes	45-167	SF
Bentley, Dierks	Long Trip Alone	30-195	CB
Bentley, Dierks	Lot Of Leavin' Left To Do	22-21	CB
Bentley, Dierks	My Last Name	22-5	CB
Bentley, Dierks	My Last Name	20-266	SC
Bentley, Dierks	My Last Name	19-676	ST
Bentley, Dierks	Riser	44-146	BKD
Bentley, Dierks	Say You Do	48-741	BKD
Bentley, Dierks	Say You Do	46-233	SSC
Bentley, Dierks	Settle For A Slowdown	29-188	CB
Bentley, Dierks	Settle For A Slowdown	29-852	SC
Bentley, Dierks	Settle For A Slowdown	29-707	ST
Bentley, Dierks	Sideways	37-26	CB
Bentley, Dierks	Somewhere On A Beach	48-747	BKD
Bentley, Dierks	Somewhere On A Beach	47-700	DCK
Bentley, Dierks	Somewhere On A Beach (Inst)	49-411	BKD
Bentley, Dierks	Sweet & Wild	36-247	PHM
Bentley, Dierks	Tip It On Back	39-23	ASK
Bentley, Dierks	Tip It On Back	45-50	SBI

ARTIST	SONG TITLE	#	TYPE
Bentley, Dierks	Trying To Stop Your Leaving	36-400	CB
Bentley, Dierks	Up On The Ridge	45-163	CB
Bentley, Dierks	What Was I Thinkin'	34-412	CB
Bentley, Dierks	What Was I Thinkin'	25-614	MM
Bentley, Dierks	What Was I Thinkin'	19-57	ST
Bentley, Dierks	What Was I Thinkin'	32-264	THM
Bentley, Lambert & Johnson	Bad Angel - duet	37-351	CB
Bentley, Stephanie	Dead Ringer	4-500	SC
Bentley, Stephanie	Once I Was The Light Of Your Life	7-329	MM
Bentley, Stephanie	Once I Was The Light Of Your Life	4-886	SC
Bentley, Stephanie	Who's That Girl	4-155	SC
Benton, Brook	Endlessly	4-214	SC
Benton, Brook	Endlessly	10-258	SS
Benton, Brook	Fools Rush In	10-234	SS
Benton, Brook	It's Just A Matter Of Time	3-516	SC
Benton, Brook	Kiddio	12-370	DK
Benton, Brook	Rainy Night In Georgia	17-143	DK
Benton, Brook	Rainy Night In Georgia	13-18	P
Benton&Washington	Baby You've Got What It Takes	6-684	MM
Benton&Washington	Duet - Baby You've got What it Take	6-684	MM
Berg, Martraca	Back In The Saddle	8-408	CB
Berg, Martraca	Back In The Saddle	7-735	CHM
Berg, Martraca	Back In The Saddle	22-777	ST
Berg, Martraca	That Train Don't Run	22-650	ST
Berg, Martraca	Won't Let Go	2-314	SC
Berlin	Duet - Sex (I'm A...) **	30-671	RSX
Berlin	No More Words	24-561	SC
Berlin	Sex (I'm A ...) **	30-671	RSX
Berlin	Sex (I'm a...)	19-550	SC
Berlin	Take My Breath Away	12-377	DK
Bernard, Crystal	Have We Forgotten What Love Is	7-425	MM
Bernard, Crystal	Have We Forgotten What Love Is	4-616	SC
Berry, Chuck	Almost Grown	46-229	DCK
Berry, Chuck	Back In The USA	46-231	SRK
Berry, Chuck	Brown Eyed Handsome Man	46-227	SC
Berry, Chuck	C'Est La Vie	11-43	PX
Berry, Chuck	Carol	12-337	DK
Berry, Chuck	Johnny B. Goode	17-413	DK
Berry, Chuck	Johnny B. Goode	9-19	PS
Berry, Chuck	Johnny B. Goode	17-322	SS
Berry, Chuck	Johnny B. Goode	46-601	MM
Berry, Chuck	Johnny B. Goode	46-600	LE
Berry, Chuck	Johnny B. Goode	46-226	SC
Berry, Chuck	Little Queenie	46-225	KV
Berry, Chuck	Maybelline	12-48	DK
Berry, Chuck	Maybelline	2-49	SC
Berry, Chuck	Memphis Tennessee	27-486	DK
Berry, Chuck	My Ding A Ling **	2-186	SC

ARTIST	SONG TITLE	#	TYPE
Berry, Chuck	My Ding-A-Ling **	30-666	RSX
Berry, Chuck	Nadine (Is It You)	43-438	LG
Berry, Chuck	No Particular Place To Go	11-42	PX
Berry, Chuck	No Particular Place To Go	3-12	SC
Berry, Chuck	Promised Land the	46-228	THM
Berry, Chuck	Reeling And A-Rocking	11-48	PX
Berry, Chuck	Rock & Roll Music	27-485	DK
Berry, Chuck	Rock & Roll Music	7-290	MM
Berry, Chuck	Roll Over Beethoven	35-8	CB
Berry, Chuck	Roll Over Beethoven	12-103	DK
Berry, Chuck	Roll Over Beethoven	5-87	SC
Berry, Chuck	Route 66	46-230	SRK
Berry, Chuck	School Days	43-389	CBEP
Berry, Chuck	Sweet Little Sixteen	12-140	DK
Berry, Chuck	Sweet Little Sixteen	4-7	SC
Berry, Chuck	Xmas - Merry Christmas Baby	7-11	MM
Berry, Chuck	Xmas - Run Rudolph Run	5-717	SC
Berry, Chuck	You Never Can Tell	43-437	LG
Berry, John	Change My Mind	7-325	MM
Berry, John	Change My Mind	24-153	SC
Berry, John	Every Time My Heart Calls	4-196	SC
Berry, John	Faithfully	22-620	ST
Berry, John	I Think About It All The Time	7-18	MM
Berry, John	I Think About It All The Time	3-425	SC
Berry, John	I Will If You Will	7-633	CHM
Berry, John	If I Had Any Pride Left At All	3-574	SC
Berry, John	Kiss Me In The Car	2-128	SC
Berry, John	Love Is For Giving	8-981	CB
Berry, John	Love Is For Giving	16-197	THM
Berry, John	Mind Of Her Own a	24-347	SC
Berry, John	Over My Shoulder	8-107	CB
Berry, John	Power Windows	5-805	SC
Berry, John	Power Windows	22-522	ST
Berry, John	She's Taken A Shine	7-577	CHM
Berry, John	She's Taken A Shine	22-913	ST
Berry, John	Standing On The Edge Of Goodbye	2-657	SC
Berry, John	Stone the	8-135	CB
Berry, John	Stone the	22-652	ST
Berry, John	What's In It For Me	17-252	NA
Berry, John	What's In It For Me	2-483	SC
Berry, John	You And Only You	2-579	SC
Berry, John	Your Love Amazes Me	35-403	CB
Berry, John	Your Love Amazes Me	6-502	MM
Berry, John	Your Love Amazes Me	2-491	SC
Best Little Whorehs	Show - Hard Candy Christmas	6-252	MM
Bethel, Hannah	Medicine	42-11	PHN
Better Than Ezra	At The Stars	7-811	PHT

ARTIST	SONG TITLE	#	TYPE
Better Than Ezra	Extra Ordinary	23-94	SC
Better Than Ezra	Good	3-489	SC
Better Than Ezra	King Of New Orleans	4-674	SC
Beverly Hills Cop	Show - Heat Is On the	6-887	MM
Beyonce	07/11/16	48-328	MRH
Beyonce	Check On It	48-387	DKM
Beyonce	Crazy In Love	30-168	CB
Beyonce	Ego	36-293	PHM
Beyonce	Get Me Bodied	30-559	CB
Beyonce	Halo	36-29	PT
Beyonce	If I Were A Boy	36-513	CB
Beyonce	If I Were A Boy	36-249	PHM
Beyonce	Irreplaceable	30-258	CB
Beyonce	Love On Top	48-389	MRH
Beyonce	Me Myself & I	19-661	CB
Beyonce	Naughty Girl	48-385	SC
Beyonce	Pretty Hurts	48-388	KV
Beyonce	Single Ladies	36-489	CB
Beyonce	Work It Out	48-386	SC
Beyonce & Shakira	Beautiful Liar	30-485	CB
Beyonce & Shakira	Duet - Beautiful Liar	30-485	CB
Beyonce feat Jay-Z	Crazy In Love	19-597	CB
Beyonce feat Sean Paul	Baby Boy	35-272	CB
Beyonce w Slim Thug	Check On It	30-158	PT
Beyonce&Slim Thug	Duet - Check On It	30-158	PT
Bieber, Justin	Baby	36-57	ASK
Bieber, Justin	Be Alright	48-628	KVD
Bieber, Justin	Company	48-622	DCK
Bieber, Justin	Fall	48-627	KVD
Bieber, Justin	Life Is Worth Living	49-881	DCK
Bieber, Justin	Life Is Worth Living	48-623	DCK
Bieber, Justin	Love Me	36-58	ASK
Bieber, Justin	Love Yourself	48-629	SF
Bieber, Justin	Love Yourself	48-621	DCK
Bieber, Justin	Mark My Words	48-624	DCK
Bieber, Justin	Mistletoe	48-625	KVD
Bieber, Justin	Nothing Like Us	48-626	KVD
Bieber, Justin	One Less Lonely Girl	36-59	ASK
Bieber, Justin	One Time	36-60	ASK
Bieber, Justin	Purpose	49-721	KV
Bieber, Justin	Somebody To Love	36-61	ASK
Bieber, Justin	U Smile	36-62	ASK
Bieber, Justin	What Do You Mean	48-620	BKD
Bieber, Justin	Xmas - Mistletoe	48-625	KVD
Bif Naked	Moment Of Weakness	10-223	SC
Big & Rich	8th Of November	30-90	CB
Big & Rich	Between Raisin' Hell & Amazing...	30-549	CB
Big & Rich	Big Time	22-24	CB
Big & Rich	Comin' To Your City	23-467	CB
Big & Rich	Duet - Kick My Ass (Radio Version)	21-651	SC
Big & Rich	Duet - Live This Life	23-380	SC
Big & Rich	Duet - Never Mind Me	29-857	SC
Big & Rich	Duet - Rollin' (Ballad of	23-45	SC

ARTIST	SONG TITLE	#	TYPE
	Big&Rich)		
Big & Rich	Duet - Rollin' (Ballad Rap Style)	23-46	SC
Big & Rich	Holy Water	22-103	CB
Big & Rich	Kick My Ass (Radio Version)	21-651	SC
Big & Rich	Live This Life	23-380	SC
Big & Rich	Look At You	49-781	SSC
Big & Rich	Lost In The Moment	30-347	CB
Big & Rich	Lost In This Moment (Radio Vers)	38-208	SC
Big & Rich	Loud	30-539	CB
Big & Rich	Never Mind Me	29-183	CB
Big & Rich	Never Mind Me	29-857	SC
Big & Rich	Rollin' (Ballad - Rap Style)	23-46	SC
Big & Rich	Rollin' (Ballad of Big&Rich)	23-45	SC
Big & Rich	Run Away With You	48-710	BKD
Big & Rich	Save A Horse Ride A Cowboy	20-387	ST
Big & Rich	Wild West Show	22-8	CB
Big & Rich	Wild West Show	19-772	ST
Big & Rich	You Shook Me All Night Long	30-482	CB
Big Bad Voodoo Dadd	Mr. Pinstripe Suit	15-209	AMS
Big Bad Voodoo Dadd	So Long Farewell	15-210	AMS
Big Bad Voodoo Dadd	You & Me & The Bottle Makes Three	15-208	AMS
Big Bad Voodoo Dadd	You & Me & The Bottle Makes Three	13-687	SGB
Big Bopper	Chantilly Lace	3-315	MH
Big Bopper	Chantilly Lace	6-137	MM
Big Bopper	Chantilly Lace	2-48	SC
Big Country	In A Big Country	28-341	DK
Big Country	In A Big Country	18-386	SAV
Big Daddy Weave	Gospel - In Christ	34-430	CB
Big House	Buck These Haggard Blues	14-727	CB
Big House	Cold Outside	7-613	CHM
Big House	Cold Outside	7-423	MM
Big House	Faith	5-289	SC
Big House	You Ain't That Lonely Yet	16-581	SC
Big Mountain	Baby I Love Your Way	34-116	CB
Big Timers/Boo/Gott	Oh Yeah!	32-11	THM
Big Twist	Turn Back The Hands Of Time	19-802	SGB
Big Tymers	Oh Yeah **	32-11	THM
Billie	Girlfriend	17-24	DK
Billie	She Wants You	10-183	SC
Bishop, Elvin	Fooled Around & Fell In Love	35-386	CB
Bishop, Elvin	Fooled Around And Fell In Love	18-151	CB
Bishop, Elvin	Fooled Around And Fell In Love	7-459	MM

ARTIST	SONG TITLE	#	TYPE
Bishop, Elvin	Fooled Around And Fell In Love	16-528	P
Bishop, Elvin	Struttin' My Stuff	46-518	CB
Bishop, Elvin	Travelin' Shoes	46-519	CB
Bishop, Stephen	It Might Be You	46-515	MH
Bishop, Stephen	On And On	9-787	SAV
Bishop, Stephen	Save It For A Rainy Day	9-789	SAV
Bishop, Stephen	Save It For A Rainy Day	21-511	SC
Bishop, Stephen	Save It For A Rainy Day	46-516	SAV
Bishop, Stephen	Separte Lives (Acoustic Version)	46-517	SBI
Bishop, Stephen	Show - It Might Be You	13-187	P
Biz Markie	This Is Something For The Radio	28-224	SF
Black & Hartman	Duet - Easy For Me To Say	15-851	ST
Black & Hartman	Duet - When I Said I Do	30-420	THM
Black & Hartman	Easy For Me To Say	15-851	ST
Black & Hartman	When I Said I Do - Duet	30-420	THM
Black & Hartman-Bla	Duet - When I Said I Do	30-420	THM
Black & McBride	Duet - Still Holdin' On	1-840	CB
Black & McBride	Duet - Still Holdin' On	7-639	CHM
Black & McBride	Still Holding On	1-840	CB
Black & McBride	Still Holding On	7-639	CHM
Black & Wariner	Been There	22-473	ST
Black & Wariner	Been There - duet	30-419	THM
Black & Wariner	Duet - Been There	30-419	THM
Black & Wynonna	Bad Goodbye a	8-115	CB
Black & Wynonna	Bad Goodbye a	30-5	MM
Black & Wynonna	Bad Goodbye a	12-396	P
Black & Wynonna	Bad Goodbye a	30-437	THM
Black & Wynonna	Duet - A Bad Goodbye	30-5	MM
Black & Wynonna	Duet - A Bad Goodbye	30-437	THM
Black & Wynonna	Duet - Bad Goodbye a	8-115	CB
Black & Wynonna	Duet - Bad Goodbye a	12-396	P
Black Crowes	Blackberry	24-545	SC
Black Crowes	Good Friday	24-58	SC
Black Crowes	Hard To Handle	34-104	CB
Black Crowes	Hard To Handle	5-336	SC
Black Crowes	Jealous Again	6-33	SC
Black Crowes	Remedy the	13-279	P
Black Crowes	Remedy the	19-340	STP
Black Crowes	She Talks To Angels	13-280	P
Black Eyed Peas	Don't Phunk With My Heart	23-321	CB
Black Eyed Peas	Duet - Don't Phunk With My Heart	23-321	CB
Black Eyed Peas	Duet - My Humps	30-747	SF
Black Eyed Peas	Let's Get It Started	46-205	SC
Black Eyed Peas	My Humps	30-139	PT
Black Eyed Peas	My Humps	30-747	SF
Black Eyed Peas	Pump It (Radio Vers) **	37-117	SC
Black Eyed Peas	Rock That Body	46-189	BHK
Black Eyed Peas	Shut Up	47-584	MRH
Black Eyed Peas	Where Is The Love	19-594	CB
Black Eyed Peas	Where Is The Love	25-714	MM
Black Eyed Peas	Where Is The Love	32-360	THM
Black Lab	Time Ago	16-228	PHM

ARTIST	SONG TITLE	#	TYPE
Black Label Society	Blessed Hellride the	19-856	PHM
Black Lace	Agadoo	16-369	SF
Black Lace	Do The Conga	49-49	ZVS
Black Lace	Hokey Cokey	49-53	ZVS
Black Lace	I Am The Music Man	49-50	ZVS
Black Lace	Superman	49-52	ZVS
Black Oak Arkansas	Jim Dandy	18-150	CB
Black Sabbath	Black Night	45-113	ZM
Black Sabbath	Halloween - Black Night	45-113	ZM
Black Sabbath	Mob Rules the	21-765	SC
Black Sabbath	Paranoid	20-363	SC
Black Sabbath	Paranoid/War Pigs LIVE	13-656	SGB
Black Sabbath	War Pigs	10-477	DA
Black, Cilla	Anyone Who Had A Heart	48-781	P
Black, Cilla	You're My World	10-581	SF
Black, Clint	Better Man a	1-106	CB
Black, Clint	Better Man a	13-523	P
Black, Clint	Better Man a	8-691	SAV
Black, Clint	Boogie Man the	43-263	CB
Black, Clint	Boogie Man the	20-344	ST
Black, Clint	Burn One Down	30-422	THM
Black, Clint	Burn One Down For Me	1-116	CB
Black, Clint	Burn One Down For Me	6-121	MM
Black, Clint	Desperado	1-828	CB
Black, Clint	Desperado	30-423	THM
Black, Clint	Drinkin' Songs & Other Logic	29-203	CB
Black, Clint	Good Run Of Bad Luck a	1-827	CB
Black, Clint	Good Run Of Bad Luck a	30-6	MM
Black, Clint	Half The Man	1-829	CB
Black, Clint	Half Way Up	1-830	CB
Black, Clint	Hard Way the	30-432	THM
Black, Clint	I Raq And Roll	34-410	CB
Black, Clint	Iraq And Roll	19-50	ST
Black, Clint	Killin' Time	1-107	CB
Black, Clint	Killin' Time	6-208	MM
Black, Clint	Killin' Time	13-398	P
Black, Clint	Killin' Time	30-424	THM
Black, Clint	Life Gets Away	3-573	SC
Black, Clint	Like The Rain	4-453	SC
Black, Clint	Loosen Up My Strings	8-762	CB
Black, Clint	Loosen Up My Strings	22-825	ST
Black, Clint	Love She Can't Live Without	14-74	CB
Black, Clint	Love She Can't Live Without	13-848	CHM
Black, Clint	Love She Can't Live Without	19-255	CSZ
Black, Clint	Loving Blind	1-112	CB
Black, Clint	Loving Blind	12-399	P
Black, Clint	Loving Blind	30-425	THM
Black, Clint	Money Or Love	16-434	ST
Black, Clint	My Imagination	20-497	ST
Black, Clint	No Time To Kill	1-119	CB
Black, Clint	No Time To Kill	30-426	THM

ARTIST	SONG TITLE	#	TYPE
Black, Clint	Nobody's Home	1-108	CB
Black, Clint	Nobody's Home	12-164	DK
Black, Clint	Nobody's Home	13-469	P
Black, Clint	Nobody's Home	30-427	THM
Black, Clint	Nothin' But The Taillights	1-826	CB
Black, Clint	Nothin' But The Taillights	7-723	CHM
Black, Clint	Nothin' But The Taillights	22-613	ST
Black, Clint	Nothing's New	30-428	THM
Black, Clint	Nothing's News	1-110	CB
Black, Clint	One Emotion	1-833	CB
Black, Clint	One Emotion	30-429	THM
Black, Clint	One More Payment	1-113	CB
Black, Clint	Patriotic - I Raq & Roll	34-410	CB
Black, Clint	Put Yourself In My Shoes	1-111	CB
Black, Clint	Put Yourself In My Shoes	12-398	P
Black, Clint	Put Yourself In My Shoes	30-430	THM
Black, Clint	Rainbow In The Rain	23-419	CB
Black, Clint	Rainbow In The Rain	29-612	ST
Black, Clint	Shoes You're Wearing	1-834	CB
Black, Clint	Shoes You're Wearing	7-743	CHM
Black, Clint	Something That We Do	1-835	CB
Black, Clint	Something That We Do	7-682	CHM
Black, Clint	Something That We Do	22-629	ST
Black, Clint	Spend My Time	19-680	ST
Black, Clint	State Of Mind	1-120	CB
Black, Clint	State Of Mind	6-456	MM
Black, Clint	State Of Mind	30-431	THM
Black, Clint	Still Holding On	22-598	ST
Black, Clint	Strong One the	30-479	CB
Black, Clint	Summer's Comin'	1-836	CB
Black, Clint	Summer's Comin'	2-824	SC
Black, Clint	This Nightlife	1-837	CB
Black, Clint	Til Santa's Gone (Milk & Cookies) - xmas	45-242	BS
Black, Clint	Walkin' Away	1-109	CB
Black, Clint	Walkin' Away	12-169	DK
Black, Clint	Walkin' Away	30-433	THM
Black, Clint	We Tell Ourselves	1-115	CB
Black, Clint	We Tell Ourselves	6-116	MM
Black, Clint	We Tell Ourselves	30-434	THM
Black, Clint	When I Said I Do	19-236	SC
Black, Clint	When I Said I Do	22-498	ST
Black, Clint	When My Ship Comes In	1-117	CB
Black, Clint	When My Ship Comes In	6-127	MM
Black, Clint	When My Ship Comes In	12-479	P
Black, Clint	When My Ship Comes In	30-435	THM
Black, Clint	Where Are You Now	1-114	CB
Black, Clint	Where Are You Now	12-397	P
Black, Clint	Where Are You Now	30-436	THM
Black, Clint	Wherever You Go	1-839	CB
Black, Clint	Wherever You Go	16-400	PR
Black, Clint	Xmas - Til Santa's Gone	45-242	BS

ARTIST	SONG TITLE	#	TYPE
	(Milk & Cookies)		
Black, Clint	Xmas - Till Santa's Gone	8-63	CB
Black, Clint	You Don't Need Me Now	8-397	CB
Black, Clint	You Don't Need Me Now	7-855	CHT
Black, Clint	You Don't Need Me Now	22-725	ST
Black, Clint	You Don't Need Me Now	30-421	THM
Blackfoot	Train Train	18-158	CB
Blackfoot	Train Train	2-531	SC
Blackhawk	Almost A Memory Now	4-202	SC
Blackhawk	Big Guitar	4-394	SC
Blackhawk	Big Guitar	22-894	ST
Blackhawk	Days Of America	16-40	ST
Blackhawk	Down In Flames	2-646	SC
Blackhawk	Every Once In Awhile	6-579	MM
Blackhawk	Goodbye Says It All	6-474	MM
Blackhawk	Hole In My Heart	7-674	CHM
Blackhawk	I Need You All The Time	6-67	SC
Blackhawk	I Sure Can Smell The Rain	2-418	SC
Blackhawk	I'm Not Strong Enough To Say No	6-841	MM
Blackhawk	King Of The World	7-403	MM
Blackhawk	King Of The World	4-624	SC
Blackhawk	Like There Ain't No Yesterday	3-629	SC
Blackhawk	One Night In New Orleans	17-575	ST
Blackhawk	Postmarked Birmingham	22-664	ST
Blackhawk	That's Just About Right	2-740	SC
Blackhawk	There You Have It	8-181	CB
Blackhawk	Your Own Little Corner Of My Heart	8-376	CB
Blackhawk	Your Own Little Corner Of My Heart	22-733	ST
Blaine, Marcie	Bobby's Girl	10-327	KC
Blaine, Marcie	Bobby's Girl	9-288	SC
Blair	Have Fun Go Mad	5-272	SC
Blake & Brian	Amnesia	8-105	CB
Blake & Brian	Another Perfect Day	4-827	SC
Blake Shelton w Pistol Annies	Boys Round Here	40-54	ASK
Blanchard&Morgan	Duet - Tennessee Birdwalk	8-716	CB
Blanchard&Morgan	Duet - You've Got Your Troubles	9-590	SAV
Blanchard&Morgan	Tennessee Birdwalk	8-716	CB
Blanchard&Morgan	You've Got Your Troubles	9-590	SAV
Bland, Bobby	Turn On Your Love Light	21-574	SC
Bland, Bobby	Turn On Your Love Light	10-246	SS
Bland, Bobby Blu	Stormy Monday Blues	47-725	KV
Blaque & N'Sync	Bring It All To Me	15-774	BS
Blaque & N'Sync	Bring It All To Me	15-296	CB
Blaque & N'Sync	Bring It All To Me	5-898	SC
Blaque & N'Sync	Duet - Bring It All To Me	15-774	BS
Blaque & N'Sync	Duet - Bring It All To Me	15-296	CB

ARTIST	SONG TITLE	#	TYPE
Blaque & N'Sync	Duet - Bring It All To Me	5-898	SC
Blassie, Freddie	Pencil Necked Geek	37-85	SC
Blazer, Justine	Not Gonna Take You Back	41-67	PHN
Blessed Union of Souls	Let Me Be The One	34-159	CB
Blessed Union/Soul	All Along	24-55	SC
Blessed Union/Soul	All Along	7-574	THM
Blessed Union/Soul	Hey Leonardo	7-893	PHT
Blessed Union/Soul	Mr. Leonardo	7-878	PHM
Blige & Ja Rule	Duet - Rainy Dayz	25-225	MM
Blige & Ja Rule	Rainy Dayz	18-220	CB
Blige & Method Man	Duet - Love At First Sight	32-346	THM
Blige & Method Man	Love At First Sight	32-346	THM
Blige & U2	Duet - One	30-757	SF
Blige & U2	One	30-757	SF
Blige, Mary J.	Be Without You	48-601	DK
Blige, Mary J.	Family Affair	33-399	CB
Blige, Mary J.	Family Affair	25-35	MM
Blige, Mary J.	Just Fine	36-462	CB
Blige, Mary J.	No More Drama	20-612	CB
Blige, Mary J.	No More Drama	25-146	MM
Blige, Mary J.	No More Drama	16-86	ST
Blige, Mary J.	Not Gon' Cry	4-684	SC
Blige, Mary J.	Ooh!	19-650	CB
Blige, Mary J.	Ooh!	32-419	THM
Blige, Mary J.	Real Love	34-111	CB
Blige, Mary J.	Real Love	28-223	SF
Blige, Mary J.	Real Love	32-204	THM
Blind Faith	Can't Find My Way Back Home	10-479	DA
Blind Melon	No Rain	28-401	DK
Blind Melon	No Rain	6-417	MM
Blindside	Sleepwalking	32-184	THM
Blink 182	All The Small Things	16-185	PHM
Blink 182	First Date	35-266	CB
Blink 182	Rock Show	16-385	SGB
Blink 182	Stay Together For the Kids	36-138	SGB
Blink 182	Stay Together For The Kids	16-322	TT
Blink 182	What's My Age Again	8-512	PHT
Blink 182	What's My Age Again	19-828	SGB
Blondie	Atomic	49-130	LG
Blondie	Call Me	15-412	DK
Blondie	Call Me	24-558	SC
Blondie	Denis Denis	49-131	LG
Blondie	Dreaming	15-745	SC
Blondie	Good Boys	49-139	TU
Blondie	Hanging On The Telephone	49-129	CB
Blondie	Heart Of Glass	17-151	DK
Blondie	I'm Always Touched By Your Presence	49-132	LG
Blondie	Island Of Lost Souls	49-133	LG
Blondie	Maria	28-193	SF
Blondie	Maria	13-782	SGB

ARTIST	SONG TITLE	#	TYPE
Blondie	Nothing Is Real But The Girl	49-134	LG
Blondie	One Way Or Another	12-144	DK
Blondie	One Way Or Another	4-533	SC
Blondie	Picture This	49-135	LG
Blondie	Rapture	11-823	DK
Blondie	Rapture	13-34	P
Blondie	Rip Her To Shreds	49-137	SC
Blondie	Sunday Girl	10-549	SF
Blondie	Tide Is High the	33-314	CB
Blondie	Tide Is High the	17-65	DK
Blondie	Tide Is High the	13-15	P
Blondie	Union City Blue	49-136	LG
Blondie	X-Offender	49-138	SF
Blood Sweat & Tears	You've Made Me So Very Happy	48-587	DK
Blood Sweat &Tears	And When I Die	11-256	DK
Blood Sweat &Tears	And When I Die	13-233	P
Blood Sweat &Tears	God Bless The Child	19-129	KC
Blood Sweat &Tears	Hi Dee Ho That Old Sweet Roll	9-728	SAV
Blood Sweat &Tears	Hi Dee Ho That Old Sweet Roll	5-615	SC
Blood Sweat &Tears	Spinning Wheel	16-800	DK
Blood Sweat &Tears	Spinning Wheel	12-859	P
Bloodhound	Ballad Of Chassey Lain	20-4	SGB
Bloodhound Gang	Bad Touch the	16-232	PHM
Bloodhound Gang	Lap Dance Is So Much Better... **	37-79	SC
Bloodhound Gang	You're Pretty When I'm Drunk	47-582	KV
Bloodstone	Natural High	25-275	MM
Bloom, Bobby	Montego Bay	9-716	SAV
Blount, Benton	Patriotic - That's An American	39-67	PHN
Blount, Benton	That's An American - Patriotic	39-67	PHN
Blue Cantrell	Hit 'Em Up Style	33-410	CB
Blue County	Good Little Girls	19-678	ST
Blue County	I Get To	30-203	CB
Blue County	I Get To	30-203	CB
Blue County	Nothin' But Cowboy Boots	43-265	SD
Blue County	Nothin' But Cowboy Boots	23-15	CB
Blue County	That Summer Song	22-335	CB
Blue County	That's Cool	20-388	ST
Blue Mink	Duet - Melting Pot	10-635	SF
Blue Mink	Melting Pot	10-635	SF
Blue Moon Boys	Santabilly Boogie - xmas	46-287	CB
Blue Moon Boys	Xmas - Santabilly Boogie	46-287	CB
Blue Oyster Cult	Don't Fear The Reaper	34-48	CB
Blue Oyster Cult	Don't Fear The Reaper	11-512	DK
Blue Oyster Cult	Don't Fear The Reaper	7-494	MM
Blue Oyster Cult	Don't Fear The Reaper	14-647	SC
Blue, Evans	Cold (But I'm Still Here - Radio)	30-281	SC

ARTIST	SONG TITLE	#	TYPE
Blues Brothers	634-5789 Soulville USA	35-78	CB
Blues Brothers	6345-789	29-153	ZM
Blues Brothers	Blues Brothers Medley No 1	29-164	ZM
Blues Brothers	Blues Brothers Medley No 2	29-165	ZM
Blues Brothers	Can't Turn You Loose	38-30	TT
Blues Brothers	Do You Love Me	29-162	ZM
Blues Brothers	Everybody Needs Somebody	38-31	SF
Blues Brothers	Everybody Needs Somebody	29-156	ZM
Blues Brothers	Funky Nassau	38-33	TT
Blues Brothers	Gimme Some Lovin'	16-162	SC
Blues Brothers	Gimme Some Lovin'	29-163	ZM
Blues Brothers	Going Back To Miami	38-34	SBII
Blues Brothers	Hey Bartender	20-142	KB
Blues Brothers	Hey Bartender	19-804	SGB
Blues Brothers	Hey Bartender	29-161	ZM
Blues Brothers	Minnie The Moocher	29-155	ZM
Blues Brothers	New Orleans	38-35	SBII
Blues Brothers	Rawhide	29-152	ZM
Blues Brothers	Riot In Cell Block No. 9	38-36	LE
Blues Brothers	Rubber Biscuit	38-29	SC
Blues Brothers	Shake Your Tailfeather	29-157	ZM
Blues Brothers	She Caught The Katy	19-805	SGB
Blues Brothers	She Caught The Katy	29-160	ZM
Blues Brothers	Soul Man	29-154	ZM
Blues Brothers	Sweet Home Chicago	9-382	AH
Blues Brothers	Sweet Home Chicago	20-134	KB
Blues Brothers	Sweet Home Chicago	19-791	SGB
Blues Brothers	Sweet Home Chicago	29-159	ZM
Blues Brothers	Who's Making Love	29-158	ZM
Blues Image	Ride Captain Ride	9-360	MG
Blues Image	Ride Captain Ride	3-472	SC
Blues Traveler	But Anyway	33-335	CB
Blues Traveler	But Anyway	24-47	SC
Blues Traveler	Hook	34-119	CB
Blues Traveler	Hook	24-746	SC
Blues Traveler	Run Around	9-322	AG
Blues Traveler	Run Around	3-431	SC
Blunt, James	1973 (Radio Vers)	49-907	SC
Blunt, James	You're Beautiful (Radio Version)	29-258	SC
Blur	Crazy Beat	32-251	THM
Blush	All Stars	39-127	PHM
Bo Bice	Inside Your Heaven	23-317	CB
Bob & Tom	Drinking Song the	44-74	KV
Bob & Tom Band	Blow Me A Kiss **	37-89	SC
Bob & Tom Band	Prisoner Of Love **	37-87	SC
Bobbettes	Mr. Lee	5-236	SC
Bobby Fuller Four	I Fought The Law	11-366	DK
Bobby Fuller Four	I Fought The Law	13-123	P
Bobby Fuller Four	I Fought The Law	9-464	SAV
Bodeans	Feed The Fire	18-480	NU
Bodeans	Hurt By Love	24-636	SC
Bogguss, Suzy	Aces	1-559	CB

ARTIST	SONG TITLE	#	TYPE
Bogguss, Suzy	Aces	6-117	MM
Bogguss, Suzy	Aces	2-705	SC
Bogguss, Suzy	Cross My Broken Heart	1-556	CB
Bogguss, Suzy	Drive South	1-561	CB
Bogguss, Suzy	Drive South	6-224	MM
Bogguss, Suzy	Drive South	12-456	P
Bogguss, Suzy	From Where I Stand	8-869	CB
Bogguss, Suzy	From Where I Stand	10-155	SC
Bogguss, Suzy	Give Me Some Wheels	4-362	SC
Bogguss, Suzy	Give Me Some Wheels	22-903	ST
Bogguss, Suzy	Goodnight	14-707	CB
Bogguss, Suzy	Goodnight	10-231	SC
Bogguss, Suzy	Heartache	1-562	CB
Bogguss, Suzy	Hey Cinderella	1-565	CB
Bogguss, Suzy	Hey Cinderella	6-454	MM
Bogguss, Suzy	Hey Cinderella	2-96	SC
Bogguss, Suzy	Just Like The Weather	1-563	CB
Bogguss, Suzy	Just Like The Weather	6-396	MM
Bogguss, Suzy	Letting Go	1-560	CB
Bogguss, Suzy	Letting Go	6-120	MM
Bogguss, Suzy	Letting Go	12-444	P
Bogguss, Suzy	Lovin' A Hurricane	1-564	CB
Bogguss, Suzy	No Way Out	1-567	CB
Bogguss, Suzy	No Way Out	4-455	SC
Bogguss, Suzy	Nobody Love Nobody Gets Hurt	8-184	CB
Bogguss, Suzy	Ourbound Plane	6-192	MM
Bogguss, Suzy	Outbound Plane	1-558	CB
Bogguss, Suzy	Outbound Plane	13-489	P
Bogguss, Suzy	Outbound Plane	2-329	SC
Bogguss, Suzy	Somebody To Love	8-99	CB
Bogguss, Suzy	Somebody To Love	7-767	CHM
Bogguss, Suzy	Somebody To Love	22-815	ST
Bogguss, Suzy	Someday Soon	1-557	CB
Bogguss, Suzy	Someday Soon	13-507	P
Bogguss, Suzy	Somewhere Between	1-566	CB
Bogguss, Suzy	Souvenirs	6-670	MM
Bogguss, Suzy	Souvenirs	2-427	SC
Bogguss, Suzy	Take It To The Limit	6-470	MM
Bogguss, Suzy	Xmas - I'll Be Home For Christmas	18-752	CB
Bogguss, Suzy	You Wouldn't Say That To A Stranger	6-576	MM
Bolton, Michael	Best Of Love the	10-115	SC
Bolton, Michael	Completely	12-168	DK
Bolton, Michael	Completely	2-110	SC
Bolton, Michael	Completely	8-610	TT
Bolton, Michael	How Am I Supposed To Live w/o You	17-109	DK
Bolton, Michael	How Am I Supposed To Live w/o You	18-502	SAV
Bolton, Michael	How Am I Supposed To Live...	33-338	CB
Bolton, Michael	Lean On Me	46-275	KV
Bolton, Michael	Love Is A Wonderful Thing	35-201	CB
Bolton, Michael	Love Is A Wonderful Thing	9-670	SAV

ARTIST	SONG TITLE	#	TYPE
Bolton, Michael	Love Is Beautiful a	4-167	SC
Bolton, Michael	Love Is The Power	4-607	SC
Bolton, Michael	Only A Woman Like You	25-202	MM
Bolton, Michael	Reach Out I'll Be There	6-95	MM
Bolton, Michael	Safe Place From The Storm	5-278	SC
Bolton, Michael	Said I Loved You But I Lied	2-108	SC
Bolton, Michael	Time Love & Tenderness	34-107	CB
Bolton, Michael	To Love Somebody	24-137	SC
Bolton, Michael	When A Man Loves A Woman	21-467	CB
Bolton, Michael	When I'm Back On My Feet	17-91	DK
Bolton, Michael	You Wouldn't Know Love	14-587	SC
Bomshel	Ain't My Day To Care	30-88	CB
Bomshel	Country Music Love Song	37-286	SC
Bomshel	Fight Like A Girl	37-31	CB
Bomshel	It Was An Absolutely Finger Lickin'	29-208	CB
Bomshel	Power Of One	30-551	CB
Bon Jovi	Always	28-448	DK
Bon Jovi	Always	2-472	SC
Bon Jovi	Bad Medicine	21-713	CB
Bon Jovi	Bad Medicine	26-101	DK
Bon Jovi	Bed Of Roses	12-37	DK
Bon Jovi	Bed Of Roses	18-548	TT
Bon Jovi	Blaze Of Glory	17-110	DK
Bon Jovi	Blaze Of Glory	13-210	P
Bon Jovi	Born To Be My Baby	21-718	CB
Bon Jovi	Born To Be My Baby	11-753	DK
Bon Jovi	Halloween - One Wild Night	16-287	TT
Bon Jovi	I'll Be There For You	21-715	CB
Bon Jovi	It's My Life	10-665	SF
Bon Jovi	It's My Life	19-836	SGB
Bon Jovi	It's My Life	15-641	THM
Bon Jovi	It's My Life	18-563	TT
Bon Jovi	Lay Your Hands On Me	21-759	SC
Bon Jovi	Livin' On A Prayer	21-714	CB
Bon Jovi	Livin' On A Prayer	28-301	DK
Bon Jovi	Living In Sin	21-716	CB
Bon Jovi	Misunderstood	20-463	CB
Bon Jovi	Misunderstood	25-433	MM
Bon Jovi	Never Say Goodbye	14-565	AH
Bon Jovi	Raise Your Hands	21-782	SC
Bon Jovi	Runaway	21-717	CB
Bon Jovi	Runaway	23-50	MH
Bon Jovi	Runaway	5-491	SC
Bon Jovi	Runaway	13-665	SGB
Bon Jovi	Say It Isn't So	20-1	SGB
Bon Jovi	Thank You For Loving Me	30-216	PHM
Bon Jovi	Thank You For Loving Me	18-577	TT

ARTIST	SONG TITLE	#	TYPE
Bon Jovi	This Ain't A Love Song	3-435	SC
Bon Jovi	Wanted Dead Or Alive	11-770	DK
Bon Jovi	Wanted Dead Or Alive	20-308	MH
Bon Jovi	You Give Love A Bad Name	12-59	DK
Bon Jovi & Nettles	Duet - Who Says You Can't Go Home	29-41	CB
Bon Jovi & Nettles	Duet - Who Says You Can't Go Home	30-242	RS
Bon Jovi & Nettles	Who Says You Can't Go Home	30-242	RS
Bon Jovi, Jon	Xmas - Please Come Home For Christmas	41-41	CB
Bonamy, James	All I Do Is Love Her	7-583	CHM
Bonamy, James	All I Do Is Love Her	4-591	SC
Bonamy, James	I Don't Think I Will	7-279	MM
Bonamy, James	I Don't Think I Will	4-367	SC
Bonamy, James	Little Blue Dot	8-31	CB
Bonamy, James	Naked To The Pain	4-828	SC
Bonamy, James	She's Got A Mind Of Her Own	4-105	SC
Bonamy, James	Swing the	7-612	CHM
Bonamy, James	Swing the	10-84	SC
Bonamy, James	Swing the	22-610	ST
Bondi, Renee	Gospel - On Eagles Wings	49-715	VH
Bondi, Renee	On Eagles Wings	49-715	VH
Bonds, Gary U.S.	Quarter To Three	10-742	JVC
Bonds, Gary U.S.	Quarter To Three	12-648	P
Bonds, Gary U.S.	Quarter To Three	10-252	SS
Bonham, Tracy	Mother Mother	4-337	SC
Bonham, Tracy	One the	24-230	SC
Bonoff & Nitty Grit	You Believed In Me	4-373	SC
Bonoff, Karla	Standing Right Next To Me	2-229	SC
Boomcat	What U Do 2 Me	32-319	THM
Boomkat	Wreckoning the **	20-630	NS
Boone, Debbie	Beautiful Sunday	9-370	MG
Boone, Debbie	You Light Up My Life	12-42	DK
Boone, Pat	April Love	11-205	DK
Boone, Pat	April Love	9-557	SAV
Boone, Pat	Don't Forbid Me	12-646	P
Boone, Pat	Exodus Song	9-558	SAV
Boone, Pat	Friendly Persuasion	10-601	SF
Boone, Pat	I'll Be Home	9-559	SAV
Boone, Pat	I'll See You In My Dreams	45-595	OZP
Boone, Pat	I've Heard That Song Before	45-828	VH
Boone, Pat	If Dreams Came True	49-263	DFK
Boone, Pat	Love Letters In The Sand	35-7	CB
Boone, Pat	Love Letters In The Sand	11-454	DK
Boone, Pat	Love Letters In The Sand	13-69	P
Boone, Pat	Moody River	18-248	DK
Boone, Pat	Moody River	4-357	SC
Boone, Pat	Remember You're Mine	48-775	P

ARTIST	SONG TITLE	#	TYPE
Boone, Pat	Speedy Gonzales	13-446	P
Boone, Pat	Sugar Moon	47-792	SRK
Boone, Pat	Xmas - We Wish You A Merry Xmas	14-306	MM
Born Free	Born Free	12-30	DK
Born Free	Show - Born Free	12-30	DK
Borrowed Blue	Porch People	39-64	PHN
Bosson	We Live	14-475	SC
Boston	Amanda	35-183	CB
Boston	Amanda	16-598	MM
Boston	Don't Look Back	5-595	SC
Boston	Long Time	4-882	SC
Boston	More Than Feeling	16-602	MM
Boston	Peace Of Mind	5-73	SC
Boston	Rock & Roll Band	4-564	SC
Boston	Smokin'	5-874	SC
Bow Wow Wow	I Want Candy	24-430	SC
Bowen & Palladio	Duet - If I Didn't Know Better - Nash	45-472	KVD
Bowen & Palladio	Duet - When The Right One Comes Along	45-471	KVD
Bowen & Palladio	I Will Never let You Know - Nashville	45-467	BKD
Bowen & Palladio	If I Didn't Know Better - Nashville	45-472	KVD
Bowen & Palladio	Show - I Will Never Let You Know	45-467	BKD
Bowen & Palladio	Show - If I Didn't Know Better - duet	45-472	KVD
Bowen & Palladio	Show - When the Right One Comes Along	45-471	KVD
Bowen & Palladio	When The Right One Comes Along - duet	45-471	KVD
Bowen, Clare	Black Roses - Nashville	45-461	BKD
Bowen, Clare	Looking For A Place To Shine - Nashville	45-475	KVD
Bowen, Clare	Show - Black Roses - Nashville	45-461	BKD
Bowen, Clare	Show - Looking for A Place To Shine	45-475	KVD
Bowie, David	Let's Dance	21-749	MH
Bowie, David	Modern Love	20-84	SC
Bowie, David	Seven	19-826	SGB
Bowie, David	Space Oddity	14-567	AH
Bowie, David	Space Oddity	30-741	SF
Bowie, David	Young Americans	21-407	SC
Bowie, David	Ziggy Stardust	13-752	SGB
Bowling For Soup	1985	20-551	PHM
Bowling For Soup	Almost	22-360	CB
Bowling For Soup	Girl All The Bad Guys Want	20-461	CB
Bowling For Soup	Girl All The Bad Guys Want	20-624	NS
Bowling For Soup	Ohio (Come Back To Texas)	23-311	CB
Box Car Racer	There Is	32-71	THM
Box Tops	Cry Like A Baby	11-338	DK
Box Tops	Letter the	16-876	DK
Box Tops	Letter the	6-658	MM

ARTIST	SONG TITLE	#	TYPE
Box Tops	Letter the	12-671	P
Box Tops	Letter the	21-572	SF
Boxcar Willie	Xmas - Deck The Halls	8-74	CB
Boxcar Willie	Xmas - Up On The Housetop	8-69	CB
Boxtops	Sweet Dreams Ladies, Forward March	46-520	SC
Boy George	Crying Game the	12-151	DK
Boy George	Crying Game the	24-140	SC
Boy George	Everything I Own	46-522	P
Boy George	Sold	46-521	KV
Boy Howdy	Bigger Fish To Fry	2-741	SC
Boy Howdy	She Can't Love You	3-545	SC
Boy Howdy	She's Give Anything	6-463	MM
Boy Howdy	They Don't Make 'Em Like...	6-593	MM
Boy Howdy	True To His Word	24-123	SC
Boyce Avenue	Because Of You	46-60	KV
Boyce Avenue	Call Me Maybe	46-95	KV
Boyce Avenue	Here Without You	46-59	KV
Boyce Avenue	I'll Be There For You	46-93	KV
Boyce Avenue	Let Her Go	45-5	KV
Boyce Avenue	Love Me Like You Do	48-511	KVD
Boyce Avenue	PayPhone	46-279	KV
Boyce Avenue	We Are Young	45-11	KV
Boyce Avenue	Wherever You Will Go	46-94	KV
Boyce, Tommy	I Wonder What She's Doin' Tonight	49-744	KRG
Boyd, Craig Wayne	I Ain't No Quitter	39-61	PHN
Boys Like Girls	Hero/Heroine	37-143	SC
Boys Like Girls	Thunder	36-531	CB
Boyz II Men	4 Seasons Of Lonliness	7-700	PHM
Boyz II Men	Color Of Love the	18-221	CB
Boyz II Men	Color Of Love the	25-220	MM
Boyz II Men	Duet - I'll Make Love To You	12-182	DK
Boyz II Men	End Of The Road	6-411	MM
Boyz II Men	I Remember	4-178	SC
Boyz II Men	I Will Get There	7-820	PHM
Boyz II Men	I'll Make Love To You	12-182	DK
Boyz II Men	I'll Make Love To You	6-642	MM
Boyz II Men	It's So Hard To Say Goodbye	17-427	KC
Boyz II Men	It's So Hard To Say Goodbye	15-515	PS
Boyz II Men	On Bended Knee	28-400	DK
Boyz II Men	On Bended Knee	16-632	MM
Boyz II Men	On Bended Knee	2-464	SC
Boyz II Men	On Bended Knee	29-122	ST
Boyz II Men	Pass You By	23-261	HS
Boyz II Men	Song For Mama	5-182	SC
Boyz II Men	Water Runs Dry	29-131	ST
Boyz II Men	Xmas - Let It Snow	22-835	ST
Boyz II Men	I'll Make Love To You	33-376	CB
Boyz II Men	In The Still Of The Night	34-112	CB
Boyz II Men	Motownphilly	33-334	CB
Boyz II Men	Water Runs Dry	33-374	CB
Boz Scaggs	JoJo	17-533	SC

ARTIST	SONG TITLE	#	TYPE
Boz Skaggs	Lido Shuffle	15-176	MH
BR5-49	Cherokee Boogie	7-380	MM
BR5-49	Cherokee Boogie	4-506	SC
BR5-49	Too Lazy To Work, Nervous to Steal	17-477	TT
BR5-49	Too Lazy To Work/Nervous to Steal	29-356	CB
Bradbery, Danielle	Heart Of Dixie	43-90	HM
Brady, Johnny	Gambler the	49-860	DCK
Bragg, Billy	Sexuality	30-778	SF
Branch & Santana	Game Of Love the	32-21	THM
Branch, Michelle	All You Wanted	25-84	MM
Branch, Michelle	Are You Happy Now	34-165	CB
Branch, Michelle	Are You Happy Now	25-621	MM
Branch, Michelle	Are You Happy Now	23-338	SC
Branch, Michelle	Are You Happy Now	32-284	THM
Branch, Michelle	Breathe	19-657	CB
Branch, Michelle	Breathe	32-428	THM
Branch, Michelle	Everywhere	15-815	CB
Branch, Michelle	Everywhere	23-589	PHM
Branch, Michelle	Game Of Love the	32-21	THM
Branch, Michelle	Goodbye To You	18-438	CB
Branch, Michelle	Goodbye To You	25-309	MM
Branch, Michelle	Till I Get Over You	20-539	CB
Branch, Michelle	Till I Get Over You	20-358	PHM
Branch, Michelle	Wanting Out	32-390	THM
Brandt, Lindsay	Call Me Red	41-83	PHN
Brandt, Paul	I Do	7-330	MM
Brandt, Paul	I Do	4-454	SC
Brandt, Paul	I Meant To Do That	7-395	MM
Brandt, Paul	I Meant To Do That	4-628	SC
Brandt, Paul	I Meant To Do That	22-907	ST
Brandt, Paul	It's A Beautiful Thing	14-702	CB
Brandt, Paul	It's A Beautiful Thing	5-810	SC
Brandt, Paul	It's A Beautiful Thing	22-540	ST
Brandt, Paul	Little In Love a	22-660	ST
Brandt, Paul	My Heart Has A History	7-199	MM
Brandt, Paul	Take It From Me	10-98	SC
Brandt, Paul	That's The Truth	14-616	SC
Brandt, Paul	What Comes Over You	22-764	ST
Brandt, Paul	What's Come Over You	8-306	CB
Brandy	Almost Doesn't Count	8-218	PHT
Brandy	Brokenhearted - duet	34-123	CB
Brandy	Duet - Brokenhearted	34-123	CB
Brandy	Full Moon	18-224	CB
Brandy	Full Moon	17-600	PHM
Brandy	Have You Ever	28-213	DK
Brandy	I Wanna Be Down	33-348	CB
Brandy	Long Distance	36-269	PHM
Brandy	Right Here (Departed)	36-500	CB
Brandy	Sittin' Up In My Room	4-166	SC
Brandy	U Don't Know Me Like U Used To	5-788	SC
Brandy	What About Us	25-219	MM
Brandy & Monica	Boy Is Mine the	21-560	PHM
Brandy & Monica	Duet - Boy Is Mine the	21-560	PHM
Brandy/Tamia/Knight	Missing You	24-234	SC

ARTIST	SONG TITLE	#	TYPE
Branigan, Laura	Gloria	26-324	DK
Branigan, Laura	Gloria	4-536	SC
Branigan, Laura	Lucky One	16-634	MM
Branigan, Laura	Self Control	16-639	MM
Branigan, Laura	Self Control	24-425	SC
Branigan, Laura	Solitaire	34-63	CB
Branigan, Laura	Solitaire	3-617	SC
Braxton & Loon	Hit The Freeway	32-18	THM
Braxton, Toni	7 Whole Days	13-609	P
Braxton, Toni	Another Sad Love Song	34-118	CB
Braxton, Toni	Another Sad Love Song	6-412	MM
Braxton, Toni	Another Sad Love Song	18-817	PS
Braxton, Toni	Breathe Again	12-131	DK
Braxton, Toni	Breathe Again	16-551	P
Braxton, Toni	Breathe Again	18-816	PS
Braxton, Toni	Find Me A Man	18-820	PS
Braxton, Toni	He Wasn't Man Enough	14-181	CB
Braxton, Toni	He Wasn't Man Enough	14-5	PHM
Braxton, Toni	He Wasn't Man Enough	14-471	SC
Braxton, Toni	He Wasn't Man Enough	18-516	TT
Braxton, Toni	Hit The Freeway	32-18	THM
Braxton, Toni	How Could An Angel Break A Heart	18-822	PS
Braxton, Toni	How Could An Angel Break A Heart	15-496	SC
Braxton, Toni	How Many Ways	2-471	SC
Braxton, Toni	I Belong To You	16-619	MM
Braxton, Toni	I Don't Want To	10-692	HH
Braxton, Toni	Just Be A Man About It	14-509	SC
Braxton, Toni	Just Be A Man About It	20-2	SGB
Braxton, Toni	Just Be A Man About It	30-642	THM
Braxton, Toni	Please	29-314	PHM
Braxton, Toni	Seven Whole Days	18-819	PS
Braxton, Toni	Unbreak My Heart	33-360	CB
Braxton, Toni	Unbreak My Heart	18-815	PS
Braxton, Toni	Unbreak My Heart	24-374	SC
Braxton, Toni	You Mean The World To Me	2-222	SC
Braxton, Toni	You Mean The World To Me	8-615	TT
Braxton, Toni	You're Makin' Me High	18-818	PS
Braxton, Toni	You're Makin' Me High	4-677	SC
Braxton, Toni	You're Makin' Me High	7-568	THM
Braxtons	So Many Ways	24-238	SC
Bread	Audrey	46-528	PR
Bread	Baby I'm A Want You	12-316	DK
Bread	Baby I'm A Want You	9-717	SAV
Bread	Diary	9-720	SAV
Bread	Diary	5-612	SC
Bread	Down On My Knees	46-526	CB
Bread	Everything I Own	34-39	CB
Bread	Everything I Own	11-230	DK
Bread	Everything I Own	16-541	P
Bread	Everything I Own	9-724	SAV
Bread	Guitar Man	4-325	SC
Bread	If	35-212	CB
Bread	If	12-318	DK

ARTIST	SONG TITLE	#	TYPE
Bread	It Don't Matter To Me	26-355	DK
Bread	Last Time	46-523	CB
Bread	Let Your Love Go	46-524	CB
Bread	Lost Without Your Love	39-3	CB
Bread	Make It With You	11-229	DK
Bread	Make It With You	13-128	P
Bread	Mother Freedom	46-525	CB
Bread	Sweet Surrender	46-529	PR
Bread	Too Much Love	46-527	CB
Breakfast at Tiffan	Show - Moon River	6-879	MM
Breaking Benjamin	Rain	30-222	PHM
Breaking Benjamin	So Cold	30-821	PHM
Breaking Benjamin	Sooner Or Later	48-544	DK
Breathe	Hands To Heaven	16-67	SC
Breeders	Cannonball	5-738	SC
Breelan, Angel	It's My Turn	41-81	PHN
Breen, Ann	Irish - Too Ra Loo Ra Loo Ral	21-495	SC
Brennan, Walter	Gospel - Old Rivers	43-105	CB
Brennan&McDonald	Don't Give Up On Us	21-622	SF
Brennan&McDonald	Duet - Don't Give Up On Us	21-622	SF
Brewer & Shipley	One Toke Over The Line	10-362	KC
Brewer, Teresa	Music Music Music	35-4	CB
Brewer, Teresa	Music Music Music	4-194	SC
Brian Setzer Orch	Dirty Boogie the	46-530	KV
Brian Setzer Orch	Everytime I Hear That Mellow Sax	46-533	MM
Brian Setzer Orch	Gettin' In The Mood	46-534	MM
Brian Setzer Orch	Jump Jive & Wail	7-775	PHT
Brian Setzer Orch	Jump Jive & Wail	13-692	SGB
Brian Setzer Orch	Mystery Train	46-531	KV
Brian Setzer Orch	Summertime Blues	46-532	KV
Brian Setzer Orch	This Cat's On A Hot Tin Roof	13-688	SGB
Brian Setzer Orch	This Old House	13-699	SGB
Brian Setzer Orch	This Old House	46-535	SGB
Brice, Lee	Beautiful Every Time	45-549	CB
Brice, Lee	Don't Believe Everything You Think	49-92	PHN
Brice, Lee	Drinking Class	49-202	BKD
Brice, Lee	Girls In Bikinis	48-735	DCK
Brice, Lee	Happy Endings	36-560	CB
Brice, Lee	Happy Endings	49-38	SC
Brice, Lee	Hard To Love	45-547	ASK
Brice, Lee	I Don't Dance	43-145	SBIG
Brice, Lee	I Drive Your Truck	43-191	ASK
Brice, Lee	Love Like Crazy	45-548	CB
Brice, Lee	One More Day	41-74	PHN
Brice, Lee	Parking Lot Party	43-255	ASK
Brice, Lee	See About A Girl	39-54	PHN
Brice, Lee	Seven Days A Thousand Times	39-95	PHN
Brice, Lee	She Ain't Right	45-383	ST
Brice, Lee	Summer Country Friday Night	38-92	PHM
Brice, Lee	That Way Again	39-85	PHN
Brice, Lee	That Way Again	45-381	PHN

ARTIST	SONG TITLE	#	TYPE
Brice, Lee	That's When You Know It's Over	41-51	ASK
Brice, Lee	That's When You Know It's Over	39-74	PHN
Brice, Lee	Upper Middle Class White Trash	36-610	CB
Brice, Lee	Upper Middle Class White Trash	36-202	PHM
Brice, Lee	Woman Like You a	45-382	SBI
Brice, Lee	Woman Like You a	45-61	BKD
Brickman & Ash	Duet - Gift the	7-710	PHM
Brickman & Ash	Gift the	7-710	PHM
Brickman, Jim	Simple Things	23-96	SC
Brickman, Raye, Ashton	Peace (Where the Heart Is)	32-391	THM
Bridges, Alicia	I Love The Nightlife	9-229	PT
Bridges, Alicia	I Love The Nightlife	2-496	SC
Brigadoon	Show - Almost Like Being In Love	12-290	DK
Brigadoon	Show - Almost Like Being In Love	18-813	PS
Britt & Elton John	Duet - Where We Both Say...	36-379	SC
Britt & Elton John	Where We Both Say... - duet	36-379	SC
Britt, C & John, E	Where We Both Say Goodbye	23-135	CB
Britt, C & John, E.	Duet - Where We Both Say Goodbye	23-135	CB
Britt, Catherine	Upside Of Being Down the	23-397	CB
Britt, Catherine	Upside Of Being Down the	20-509	ST
Britt, Catherine	What I Did Last Night	30-308	CB
Britton & Chase	Ball And Chain - Nashville	45-476	KVD
Britton & Chase	Show - Ball And Chain - Nashville	45-476	KVD
Broadman Hymnal	Gospel - Alas And Did My Saviour...	21-82	SX
Broadman Hymnal	Gospel - All Hail The Power	21-84	SX
Broadman Hymnal	Gospel - Amazing Grace	21-60	SX
Broadman Hymnal	Gospel - Are You Washed In The...	21-49	SX
Broadman Hymnal	Gospel - At The Cross	21-50	SX
Broadman Hymnal	Gospel - Banner Of The Cross the	21-30	SX
Broadman Hymnal	Gospel - Blessed Assurance	21-55	SX
Broadman Hymnal	Gospel - Blessed Be The Name	21-92	SX
Broadman Hymnal	Gospel - Brethren We Have Met To...	21-70	SX
Broadman Hymnal	Gospel - Bringing In The Sheaves	21-103	SX
Broadman Hymnal	Gospel - Christ Receiveth Sinful Me	21-51	SX
Broadman Hymnal	Gospel - Christ the Lord Is Risen..	21-116	SX
Broadman Hymnal	Gospel - Close To Thee	21-74	SX

ARTIST	SONG TITLE	#	TYPE	ARTIST	SONG TITLE	#	TYPE
Broadman Hymnal	Gospel - Come Thou Fount	21-66	SX	Broadman Hymnal	Gospel - Keep Walkin'	21-124	SX
Broadman Hymnal	Gospel - Face To Face	21-46	SX	Broadman Hymnal	Gospel - Last Mile of the Day the	21-129	SX
Broadman Hymnal	Gospel - Fairest Lord Jesus	21-73	SX	Broadman Hymnal	Gospel - Lead On O Eternal King	21-78	SX
Broadman Hymnal	Gospel - Footsteps Of Jesus	21-75	SX	Broadman Hymnal	Gospel - Leaning On The Everlasting	21-91	SX
Broadman Hymnal	Gospel - Glory To His Name	21-65	SX	Broadman Hymnal	Gospel - Let The Lord's Light Beam	21-87	SX
Broadman Hymnal	Gospel - Have Faith In God	21-27	SX	Broadman Hymnal	Gospel - Love Lifted Me	21-101	SX
Broadman Hymnal	Gospel - Have Thine Own Way Lord	21-85	SX	Broadman Hymnal	Gospel - Make Me A Channel of Bless	21-31	SX
Broadman Hymnal	Gospel - He Keeps Me Singing	21-106	SX	Broadman Hymnal	Gospel - My Jesus I Love Thee	21-57	SX
Broadman Hymnal	Gospel - Heavenly Sunlight	21-54	SX	Broadman Hymnal	Gospel - Near The Cross	21-97	SX
Broadman Hymnal	Gospel - Here They Come	21-132	SX	Broadman Hymnal	Gospel - Nearer My God To Thee	21-72	SX
Broadman Hymnal	Gospel - Higher Ground	21-89	SX	Broadman Hymnal	Gospel - Nearer My God To Thee	21-90	SX
Broadman Hymnal	Gospel - His Way With Thee	21-56	SX	Broadman Hymnal	Gospel - Nothing But The Blood	21-110	SX
Broadman Hymnal	Gospel - Hold Bible Book Divine	21-79	SX	Broadman Hymnal	Gospel - Nothing Can Compare	21-117	SX
Broadman Hymnal	Gospel - Holy Holy Holy	21-21	SX	Broadman Hymnal	Gospel - Oh Say But I'm Glad	21-128	SX
Broadman Hymnal	Gospel - How About Your Heart	21-118	SX	Broadman Hymnal	Gospel - Old Rugged Cross the	21-36	SX
Broadman Hymnal	Gospel - How Firm A Foundation	21-71	SX	Broadman Hymnal	Gospel - On Jordan's Stormy Banks	21-83	SX
Broadman Hymnal	Gospel - I Am Resolved	21-45	SX	Broadman Hymnal	Gospel - Only Believe	21-98	SX
Broadman Hymnal	Gospel - I Am Thine Oh Lord	21-28	SX	Broadman Hymnal	Gospel - Only Trust Him	21-69	SX
Broadman Hymnal	Gospel - I Love To Tell The Story	21-104	SX	Broadman Hymnal	Gospel - Onward Christain Soldiers	21-26	SX
Broadman Hymnal	Gospel - I Need Thee Every Hour	21-68	SX	Broadman Hymnal	Gospel - Other Side Of Jordan the	21-119	SX
Broadman Hymnal	Gospel - I Was Glad When They...	21-113	SX	Broadman Hymnal	Gospel - Pass Me Not	21-76	SX
Broadman Hymnal	Gospel - I Will Sing the Wondrous..	21-105	SX	Broadman Hymnal	Gospel - Peace Of Prayer	21-131	SX
Broadman Hymnal	Gospel - I've Found A New Way	21-115	SX	Broadman Hymnal	Gospel - Praise Him All Ye Little C	21-111	SX
Broadman Hymnal	Gospel - If Jesus Said It	21-125	SX	Broadman Hymnal	Gospel - Praise Him Praise Him	21-102	SX
Broadman Hymnal	Gospel - In The Shelter Of His Arms	21-121	SX	Broadman Hymnal	Gospel - Redeemed	21-41	SX
Broadman Hymnal	Gospel - In The sweet By & By	21-100	SX	Broadman Hymnal	Gospel - Rescue The Perishing	21-39	SX
Broadman Hymnal	Gospel - It Is Well With My Soul	21-37	SX	Broadman Hymnal	Gospel - Rest Of Heaven the	21-38	SX
Broadman Hymnal	Gospel - Jesus Is Calling	21-29	SX	Broadman Hymnal	Gospel - Revive Us Again	21-58	SX
Broadman Hymnal	Gospel - Jesus Loves Me	21-112	SX	Broadman Hymnal	Gospel - Rock Of Ages	21-63	SX
Broadman Hymnal	Gospel - Jesus Loves the Little Chi	21-114	SX	Broadman Hymnal	Gospel - Saved Saved	21-99	SX
Broadman Hymnal	Gospel - Jesus Paid It All	21-86	SX	Broadman Hymnal	Gospel - Saviour Like a Shepherd ..	21-23	SX
Broadman Hymnal	Gospel - Jesus Saves	21-24	SX	Broadman Hymnal	Gospel - Send The Light	21-53	SX
Broadman Hymnal	Gospel - Jesus the Very Thought of.	21-80	SX	Broadman Hymnal	Gospel - Shall We Gather At The Riv	21-109	SX
Broadman Hymnal	Gospel - Just As I Am	21-61	SX	Broadman Hymnal	Gospel - Since I Have Been Redeemed	21-48	SX
				Broadman Hymnal	Gospel - Softly And Tenderly	21-44	SX
				Broadman Hymnal	Gospel - Solid Rock the	21-42	SX

ARTIST	SONG TITLE	#	TYPE
Broadman Hymnal	Gospel - Stand Up Stand Up for Jesu	21-25	SX
Broadman Hymnal	Gospel - Standing On The Promises	21-52	SX
Broadman Hymnal	Gospel - Sweet Hour Of Prayer	21-88	SX
Broadman Hymnal	Gospel - Take My Life & Let It Be..	21-64	SX
Broadman Hymnal	Gospel - Take the Name of Jesus…	21-108	SX
Broadman Hymnal	Gospel - Take Time To Be Holy	21-96	SX
Broadman Hymnal	Gospel - Tell It To Jesus	21-47	SX
Broadman Hymnal	Gospel - Thanks To Calvary	21-123	SX
Broadman Hymnal	Gospel - There Is a Name I Love To	21-94	SX
Broadman Hymnal	Gospel - There Shall Be Showers Of.	21-43	SX
Broadman Hymnal	Gospel - There's A God Somewhere	21-130	SX
Broadman Hymnal	Gospel - Till The Storm Passes By	21-126	SX
Broadman Hymnal	Gospel - Tis So Sweet To Trust In J	21-95	SX
Broadman Hymnal	Gospel - To The Work	21-33	SX
Broadman Hymnal	Gospel - Trust And Obey	21-107	SX
Broadman Hymnal	Gospel - Uncloudy Day the	21-40	SX
Broadman Hymnal	Gospel - Way That He Loves the	21-120	SX
Broadman Hymnal	Gospel - We're Marching To Zion	21-22	SX
Broadman Hymnal	Gospel - What A Friend We Have In..	21-59	SX
Broadman Hymnal	Gospel - When God Dips His Love…	21-127	SX
Broadman Hymnal	Gospel - When I See Jesus	21-122	SX
Broadman Hymnal	Gospel - When I Survey the Wondrous	21-67	SX
Broadman Hymnal	Gospel - When We All Get To Heaven	21-93	SX
Broadman Hymnal	Gospel - Where He Leads Me	21-62	SX
Broadman Hymnal	Gospel - Who Is On The Lord's Side	21-32	SX
Broadman Hymnal	Gospel - Will Jesus Find Us Watchin	21-34	SX
Broadman Hymnal	Gospel - Wonderful Words Of Life	21-77	SX
Broadman Hymnal	Gospel - Work For The Night Is Comi	21-81	SX
Broadman Hymnal	Gospel - Ye Must Be Born Again	21-35	SX
Broadway Arrangemen	Show - I'll String Along With You	19-777	SGB
Broadway Arrangemen	Show - Put The Blame On Mama	19-783	SGB
Brock, Chad	Country Boy Can	8-909	CB

ARTIST	SONG TITLE	#	TYPE
	Survive - (Y2K)		
Brock, Chad	Country Boy Can Survive Y2K	22-537	ST
Brock, Chad	Lightening Does The Work	8-963	CB
Brock, Chad	Lightning Does The Work	34-322	CB
Brock, Chad	Lightning Does The Work	14-624	SC
Brock, Chad	Man's Gotta Do a	18-139	ST
Brock, Chad	Ordinary Life	8-854	CB
Brock, Chad	Ordinary Life	7-857	CHT
Brock, Chad	Ordinary Life	22-732	ST
Brock, Chad	Tell Me How	16-169	CB
Brock, Chad	Tell Me How	25-12	MM
Brock, Chad	Tell Me How	15-676	ST
Brock, Chad	That Was Us	19-13	ST
Brock, Chad	That Was Us	32-191	THM
Brock, Chad	Visit the	14-909	CB
Brock, Chad	Visit the	13-861	CHM
Brock, Chad	Visit the	19-221	CSZ
Brock, Chad	Visit the	22-555	ST
Brock, Chad	Visit the	14-34	THM
Brock, Chad	Yes!	13-822	CHM
Brock, Chad	Yes!	6-72	SC
Brock, Chad	You Are	19-708	ST
Brody, Dean	Brothers	36-275	PHM
Brokop, Lisa	Before He Kissed Me	7-201	MM
Brokop, Lisa	Before He Kissed Me	4-238	SC
Brokop, Lisa	Big Picture	23-300	CB
Brokop, Lisa	How Do I Let Go	8-487	CB
Brokop, Lisa	She Can't Save Him	4-29	SC
Brokop, Lisa	Take That	17-261	NA
Brokop, Lisa	Take That	2-570	SC
Brokop, Lisa	When You Get To Be You	8-857	CB
Brokop, Lisa	When You Get To Be You	10-159	SC
Brokop, Lisa	Who Needs You	3-534	SC
Brokup, Lisa	One Of Those Nights	2-737	SC
Brooklyn Bridge	Worst That Could Happen	3-583	SC
Brooks & Dunn	Ain't Nothing 'Bout You	14-833	ST
Brooks & Dunn	Are You Ever Gonna Love Me	14-687	CB
Brooks & Dunn	Beer Thirty	5-828	SC
Brooks & Dunn	Beer Thirty	22-514	ST
Brooks & Dunn	Believe	23-482	CB
Brooks & Dunn	Believe	49-898	SC
Brooks & Dunn	Best Of My Love	1-85	CB
Brooks & Dunn	Boot Scootin' Boogie	1-79	CB
Brooks & Dunn	Boot Scootin' Boogie	10-762	JVC
Brooks & Dunn	Boot Scootin' Boogie	13-379	P
Brooks & Dunn	Boot Scootin' Boogie	26-325	DK
Brooks & Dunn	Brand New Man	1-76	CB
Brooks & Dunn	Brand New Man	12-419	P
Brooks & Dunn	Building Bridges	29-593	CB
Brooks & Dunn	Every River	25-358	MM

ARTIST	SONG TITLE	#	TYPE
Brooks & Dunn	Every River	18-205	ST
Brooks & Dunn	God Must Be Busy	36-550	CB
Brooks & Dunn	Good Girls Go To Heaven	17-476	TT
Brooks & Dunn	Hard Workin' Man	1-81	CB
Brooks & Dunn	Hard Workin' Man	6-315	MM
Brooks & Dunn	He's Got You	22-666	ST
Brooks & Dunn	Heartbroke Out Of My Mind	1-83	CB
Brooks & Dunn	Hillbilly Deluxe	30-192	CB
Brooks & Dunn	Honky Tonk Truth	7-676	CHM
Brooks & Dunn	Honky Tonk Truth	22-627	ST
Brooks & Dunn	How Long Gone	8-742	CB
Brooks & Dunn	How Long Gone	22-809	ST
Brooks & Dunn	Husbands & Wives	10-151	SC
Brooks & Dunn	Husbands & Wives	22-668	ST
Brooks & Dunn	I Am That Man	4-365	SC
Brooks & Dunn	I Can't Get Over You	22-710	ST
Brooks & Dunn	I Can't Get Over You	8-350	CB
Brooks & Dunn	I'll Never Forgive My Heart	1-89	CB
Brooks & Dunn	I'll Never Forgive My Heart	17-256	NA
Brooks & Dunn	I'll Never Forgive My Heart	2-448	SC
Brooks & Dunn	Indian Summer	37-51	CB
Brooks & Dunn	It Won't Be Christmas Without You	45-749	CB
Brooks & Dunn	It's Getting Better All The Time	23-2	CB
Brooks & Dunn	It's Getting Better All The Time	23-31	SC
Brooks & Dunn	Johnny Cash Junkie	45-676	DCK
Brooks & Dunn	Little Miss Honky Tonk	2-662	SC
Brooks & Dunn	Little Miss Honky Tonk	22-867	ST
Brooks & Dunn	Little Miss Honky-Tonk	1-90	CB
Brooks & Dunn	Long Goodbye the	25-59	MM
Brooks & Dunn	Long Goodbye the	15-853	ST
Brooks & Dunn	Lost And Found	1-80	CB
Brooks & Dunn	Lost And Found	6-219	MM
Brooks & Dunn	Lost And Found	12-418	P
Brooks & Dunn	Mama Don't Get Dressed Up For Nothi	4-465	SC
Brooks & Dunn	Man This Lonely a	22-906	ST
Brooks & Dunn	Missing You	5-725	SC
Brooks & Dunn	Missing You	22-484	ST
Brooks & Dunn	My Heart Is Lost To You	25-226	MM
Brooks & Dunn	My Heart Is Lost To You	16-699	ST
Brooks & Dunn	My Maria	35-409	CB
Brooks & Dunn	My Maria	7-226	MM
Brooks & Dunn	My Maria	22-879	ST
Brooks & Dunn	My Next Broken Heart	1-77	CB
Brooks & Dunn	My Next Broken Heart	13-511	P
Brooks & Dunn	My Next Broken Heart	2-343	SC
Brooks & Dunn	Neon Moon	1-78	CB
Brooks & Dunn	Neon Moon	13-510	P
Brooks & Dunn	Neon Moon	2-4	SC
Brooks & Dunn	Only In America	33-152	CB

ARTIST	SONG TITLE	#	TYPE
Brooks & Dunn	Only In America	15-184	ST
Brooks & Dunn	Play Something Country	23-143	CB
Brooks & Dunn	Proud Of The House We Built	30-468	CB
Brooks & Dunn	Put A Girl In It	36-406	CB
Brooks & Dunn	Red Dirt Road	34-400	CB
Brooks & Dunn	Red Dirt Road	25-612	MM
Brooks & Dunn	Red Dirt Road	19-47	ST
Brooks & Dunn	Red Dirt Road	32-266	THM
Brooks & Dunn	Rock My World Little Country Girl	1-86	CB
Brooks & Dunn	Rock My World Little Country Girl	6-464	MM
Brooks & Dunn	Rock My World Little Country Girl	2-92	SC
Brooks & Dunn	She Used To Be Mine	1-84	CB
Brooks & Dunn	She Used To Be Mine	26-561	DK
Brooks & Dunn	She Used To Be Mine	10-774	JVC
Brooks & Dunn	She Used To Be Mine	6-379	MM
Brooks & Dunn	She's Not The Cheatin' Kind	1-88	CB
Brooks & Dunn	She's Not The Cheatin' Kind	26-560	DK
Brooks & Dunn	She's Not The Cheatin' Kind	6-667	MM
Brooks & Dunn	She's Not The Cheatin' Kind	2-477	SC
Brooks & Dunn	South Of Santa Fe	7-881	CHT
Brooks & Dunn	South Of Santa Fe	14-631	SC
Brooks & Dunn	South Of Santa Fe	22-747	ST
Brooks & Dunn	Texas Women Don't Stay Lonely Long	4-113	SC
Brooks & Dunn	That Ain't No Way To Go	1-87	CB
Brooks & Dunn	That Ain't No Way To Go	2-212	SC
Brooks & Dunn	That's What It's All About	30-800	PHM
Brooks & Dunn	That's What It's All About	20-486	ST
Brooks & Dunn	That's What She Gets For Loving Me	20-167	ST
Brooks & Dunn	We'll Burn That Bridge When We...	1-82	CB
Brooks & Dunn	We'll Burn That Bridge When We...	2-335	SC
Brooks & Dunn	Whiskey Under The Bridge	7-149	MM
Brooks & Dunn	Whiskey Under The Bridge	3-532	SC
Brooks & Dunn	Who Says There Ain't No Santa	49-367	CB
Brooks & Dunn	Why Would I Say Goodbye	14-658	CB
Brooks & Dunn	Why Would I say Goodbye	7-606	CHM
Brooks & Dunn	Xmas - It Won't Be Christmas Without You	45-749	CB
Brooks & Dunn	Xmas - Who Says There Ain't No Santa	49-367	CB
Brooks & Dunn	You Can't Take The Honky Tonk Out..	19-675	ST

ARTIST	SONG TITLE	#	TYPE
Brooks & Dunn	You'll Always Be Loved By Me	9-387	CB
Brooks & Dunn	You'll Always Be Loved By Me	13-819	CHM
Brooks & Dunn	You'll Always Be Loved By Me	19-247	CSZ
Brooks & Dunn	You're Gonna Miss Me When I'm Gone	3-412	SC
Brooks & Jones	Beer Run	16-4	ST
Brooks & Jones	Beer Run - Duet	33-141	CB
Brooks & Jones	Duet - Beer Run	33-141	CB
Brooks & Yearwood	Call the - duet	48-346	KV
Brooks & Yearwood	Duet - Call the	48-346	KV
Brooks & Yearwood	Duet - In Another's Eyes	7-675	CHM
Brooks & Yearwood	Duet - In Another's Eyes	22-625	ST
Brooks & Yearwood	Duet - Like We Never Had a Broken..	2-304	SC
Brooks & Yearwood	Duet - Love Will Always Win	29-195	CB
Brooks & Yearwood	Duet - Squeeze Me In	18-12	CB
Brooks & Yearwood	Duet - Squeeze Me In	25-121	MM
Brooks & Yearwood	Duet - Where Your Road Leads	22-667	ST
Brooks & Yearwood	Duet - Wild As The Wind	8-871	CB
Brooks & Yearwood	Duet - Wild As The Wind	10-165	SC
Brooks & Yearwood	In Another's Eyes	22-625	ST
Brooks & Yearwood	Like We Never Had A Broken Heart	2-304	SC
Brooks & Yearwood	Love Will Always Win	29-195	CB
Brooks & Yearwood	Squeeze Me In	18-12	CB
Brooks & Yearwood	Squeeze Me In	25-121	MM
Brooks & Yearwood	Squeeze Me In	16-108	ST
Brooks & Yearwood	Where Your Road Leads	22-667	ST
Brooks & Yearwood	Wild As The Wind	8-871	CB
Brooks & Yearwood	Wild As The Wind	10-165	SC
Brooks & Yearwood]	In Another's Eyes	7-675	CHM
Brooks, Elkie	Pearl's A Singer	11-21	PX
Brooks, Garth	Against The Grain	12-109	DK
Brooks, Garth	Against The Grain	6-272	MM
Brooks, Garth	Ain't Goin' Down	1-217	CB
Brooks, Garth	Ain't Goin' Down	6-404	MM
Brooks, Garth	American Honky Tonk Bar Assn.	6-376	MM
Brooks, Garth	American Honky-Tonk Bar Assn.	2-409	SC
Brooks, Garth	Beaches Of Cheyenne	7-166	MM
Brooks, Garth	Beaches Of Cheyenne	4-152	SC
Brooks, Garth	Belleau Woods	8-228	CB
Brooks, Garth	Big Money	18-10	CB
Brooks, Garth	Callin' Baton Rouge	20-410	MH
Brooks, Garth	Callin' Baton Rouge	2-704	SC
Brooks, Garth	Change the	20-103	CB
Brooks, Garth	Change the	7-179	MM
Brooks, Garth	Change the	22-891	ST
Brooks, Garth	Cowboy Cadillac	48-351	MM
Brooks, Garth	Cowboys And Angels	15-465	SC
Brooks, Garth	Dance the	1-213	CB
Brooks, Garth	Dance the	17-349	DK

ARTIST	SONG TITLE	#	TYPE
Brooks, Garth	Dance the	6-275	MM
Brooks, Garth	Dance the	13-325	P
Brooks, Garth	Dance the	2-675	SC
Brooks, Garth	Dixie Chicken	1-220	CB
Brooks, Garth	Do What You Gotta Do	23-363	SC
Brooks, Garth	Do What You Gotta Do	22-471	ST
Brooks, Garth	Don't Cross The River	48-357	SC
Brooks, Garth	Face To Face	48-344	JVC
Brooks, Garth	Fever the	4-20	SC
Brooks, Garth	Friend To Me a	48-354	PC
Brooks, Garth	Friends In Low Places	1-214	CB
Brooks, Garth	Friends In Low Places	11-802	DK
Brooks, Garth	Friends In Low Places	6-273	MM
Brooks, Garth	Friends In Low Places	12-433	P
Brooks, Garth	Friends In Low Places (Live Version	2-672	SC
Brooks, Garth	Good Ride Cowboy	23-449	ST
Brooks, Garth	Hard Luck Woman	48-349	MM
Brooks, Garth	I Ain't Never	4-260	SC
Brooks, Garth	I Don't Have To Wonder	9-407	CB
Brooks, Garth	If Tomorrow Never Comes	1-211	CB
Brooks, Garth	If Tomorrow Never Comes	6-278	MM
Brooks, Garth	If Tomorrow Never Comes	2-673	SC
Brooks, Garth	Ireland 99	7-850	CHT
Brooks, Garth	It Don't Matter To The Sun	19-227	SC
Brooks, Garth	It Don't Matter To The Sun	22-511	ST
Brooks, Garth	It's Midnight Cinderella	4-160	SC
Brooks, Garth	It's Your Song	8-850	CB
Brooks, Garth	It's Your Song	22-683	ST
Brooks, Garth	Kickin' And Screamin'	4-137	SC
Brooks, Garth	Learning To Live Again	6-308	MM
Brooks, Garth	Learning To Live Again	2-685	SC
Brooks, Garth	Lonesome Dove the	48-352	PT
Brooks, Garth	Longneck Bottle	22-411	ST
Brooks, Garth	Longneck Bottle	8-151	CB
Brooks, Garth	Longneck Bottle	15-522	SC
Brooks, Garth	Lost In You	22-497	ST
Brooks, Garth	Mom	48-348	KV
Brooks, Garth	More Than A Memory	30-583	CB
Brooks, Garth	Mr. Blue	48-343	DKM
Brooks, Garth	Mr. Midnight	18-11	CB
Brooks, Garth	Mr. Right	20-102	CB
Brooks, Garth	Much Too Young To Feel This Damn Ol	6-279	MM
Brooks, Garth	Neon Moon	48-358	SC
Brooks, Garth	New Way To Fly	48-360	TU
Brooks, Garth	Night I Called The Old Man Out	6-629	MM
Brooks, Garth	Night Will Only Know the	24-2	SC
Brooks, Garth	Not Counting You	1-212	CB
Brooks, Garth	Not Counting You	6-280	MM
Brooks, Garth	Not Counting You	2-684	SC

ARTIST	SONG TITLE	#	TYPE
Brooks, Garth	Old Stuff the	48-350	MM
Brooks, Garth	One Night A Day	6-575	MM
Brooks, Garth	One Night A Day	12-482	P
Brooks, Garth	Papa Loved Mama	6-281	MM
Brooks, Garth	Papa Loved Mama	2-681	SC
Brooks, Garth	People Loving People	48-347	KV
Brooks, Garth	Pushing Up Daisies	48-356	SC
Brooks, Garth	Red Strokes the	17-260	NA
Brooks, Garth	Right Now	5-792	SC
Brooks, Garth	River the	6-283	MM
Brooks, Garth	River the	2-682	SC
Brooks, Garth	Rodeo	6-282	MM
Brooks, Garth	Rodeo	2-683	SC
Brooks, Garth	Rodeo Or Mexico	18-14	CB
Brooks, Garth	Rollin'	7-171	MM
Brooks, Garth	Same Old Story	48-353	PT
Brooks, Garth	Shameless	1-215	CB
Brooks, Garth	Shameless	6-274	MM
Brooks, Garth	Shameless	2-676	SC
Brooks, Garth	She's Every Woman	7-76	MM
Brooks, Garth	She's Gonna Make It	8-300	CB
Brooks, Garth	Somewhere Other Than The Night	6-271	MM
Brooks, Garth	Somewhere Other Than The Night	2-686	SC
Brooks, Garth	Standing Outside The Fire	6-466	MM
Brooks, Garth	Standing Outside The Fire	3-37	SC
Brooks, Garth	Steam	48-359	THM
Brooks, Garth	Tearin' It Up & Burnin' It Down	8-872	CB
Brooks, Garth	Tearin' It Up & Burnin' It Down	10-153	SC
Brooks, Garth	Tearin' It Up & Burnin' It Down	22-699	ST
Brooks, Garth	That Girl Is A Cowboy	48-355	PHN
Brooks, Garth	That Ol' Wind	1-216	CB
Brooks, Garth	That Ol' Wind	7-384	MM
Brooks, Garth	That Summer	6-388	MM
Brooks, Garth	That Summer	2-677	SC
Brooks, Garth	Thicker Than Blood	25-290	MM
Brooks, Garth	Thicker Than Blood	17-579	ST
Brooks, Garth	Thicker Than Water	18-13	CB
Brooks, Garth	This Ain't Tennessee	8-750	CB
Brooks, Garth	Thunder Rolls the	6-276	MM
Brooks, Garth	Thunder Rolls the	2-678	SC
Brooks, Garth	To Make You Feel My Love	8-484	CB
Brooks, Garth	To Make You Feel My Love	7-759	CHM
Brooks, Garth	Two Of A Kind Working On A Full	13-326	P
Brooks, Garth	Two Of A Kind Working On A Full	2-679	SC
Brooks, Garth	Two Of a Kind Working On A Full..	12-146	DK
Brooks, Garth	Two Of A Kind Working On A Full...	6-284	MM

ARTIST	SONG TITLE	#	TYPE
Brooks, Garth	Two Pina Coladas	1-221	CB
Brooks, Garth	Two Pina Coladas	7-730	CHM
Brooks, Garth	Two Pina Coladas	22-779	ST
Brooks, Garth	Unanswered Prayers	6-277	MM
Brooks, Garth	Unanswered Prayers	2-680	SC
Brooks, Garth	Uptown Down-Home Good Ol' Boy	8-730	CB
Brooks, Garth	Walking After Midnight	48-345	JVC
Brooks, Garth	We Bury The Hatchet	17-217	NA
Brooks, Garth	We Shall Be Free	20-590	CB
Brooks, Garth	What She's Doing Now	6-285	MM
Brooks, Garth	What She's Doing Now	2-674	SC
Brooks, Garth	When You Come Back To Me Again	14-720	CB
Brooks, Garth	When You Come Back To Me Again	19-252	CSZ
Brooks, Garth	When You Come Back To Me Again	22-544	ST
Brooks, Garth	White Christmas	45-794	PS
Brooks, Garth	Why Ain't I Running	32-188	THM
Brooks, Garth	Why Ain't I Running	18-9	CB
Brooks, Garth	Why Ain't I Running	25-524	MM
Brooks, Garth	Why Ain't I Running	18-796	ST
Brooks, Garth	Wild As The Wind	7-822	CHT
Brooks, Garth	Wild Horses	10-268	CB
Brooks, Garth	Wild Horses	22-583	ST
Brooks, Garth	Wolves	17-227	NA
Brooks, Garth	Wrapped Up In You	17-601	CB
Brooks, Garth	Wrapped Up In You	25-48	MM
Brooks, Garth	Wrapped Up In You	16-1	ST
Brooks, Garth	Xmas - Gift the	30-390	SC
Brooks, Garth	Xmas - Old Man's Back In Town the	18-731	CB
Brooks, Garth	Xmas - Old Man's Back In Town the	7-2	MM
Brooks, Garth	Xmas - Old Man's Back In Town the	15-657	THM
Brooks, Garth	Xmas - Santa Looked a Lot Like Dadd	7-13	MM
Brooks, Garth	Xmas - Santa Looked A Lot Like Dadd	22-843	ST
Brooks, Garth	Xmas - White Christmas	45-794	PS
Brooks, Garth	You Move Me	8-176	CB
Brooks, Meredith	Bitch **	10-93	SC
Brooks, Meredith	Sin City	13-682	SGB
Brooks, Meredith	Stop	16-227	PHM
Brooks, Meredith	What Would Happen	7-704	PHM
Brooks, Meredith	What Would Happen	10-113	SC
Brother Cane	I Lie In The Bed I Make	10-143	SC
Brother Phelps	Eagle Over Angel	4-115	SC
Brother Phelps	Ever Changing Woman	2-422	SC
Brother Phelps	Let Go	2-368	SC
Brother Phelps	Were You Really Livin'	24-127	SC
Brotherhood Of Man	Duet - United We Stand	33-271	CB
Brotherhood Of Man	Save All Your Kisses For Me	47-588	ZM
Brotherhood Of Man	Save All Your Kisses For Me	47-587	P

ARTIST	SONG TITLE	#	TYPE
Brotherhood Of Man	United We Stand - duet	33-271	CB
Brothers Four	Green Green	15-484	CMC
Brothers Four	Green Leaves Of Summer	18-168	DK
Brothers Four	Greenfields	18-166	DK
Brothers Four	Michael Row The Boat Ashore	9-821	SAV
Brothers Four	Try To Remember	27-530	DK
Brothers Johnson	Stomp	15-45	SS
Brothers Osborne	Stay A Little Longer	49-785	SS
Brown & Cornelius	Duet - I Don't Wanna Have To Marry	13-485	P
Brown & Cornelius	Duet - I Don't Wanna Have To Marry.	9-603	SAV
Brown & Cornelius	I Don't Wanna Have To Marry You	13-485	P
Brown & Cornelius	I Don't Wanna Have To Marry You	9-603	SAV
Brown & Schmidt	Duet - Let It Be Me	14-881	SC
Brown & Schmidt	Let It Be Me	14-881	SC
Brown & T-Pain	Duet - Kiss Kiss	49-895	SC
Brown & T-Pain	Kiss Kiss - duet	49-895	SC
Brown T. Graham	Darlene	34-279	CB
Brown, Bobby	Don't Be Cruel	11-315	DK
Brown, Bobby	Don't Be Cruel	13-198	P
Brown, Bobby	Every Little Step	12-844	P
Brown, Bobby	Girlfriend	16-563	P
Brown, Bobby	My Perogative	34-92	CB
Brown, Bobby	Roni	29-287	SC
Brown, Chris	Forever	36-469	CB
Brown, Chris	Run It!	30-153	PT
Brown, Chris	Take You Down	36-479	CB
Brown, Chris	With You	36-442	CB
Brown, Cooter	Pure Bred Redneck	4-93	SC
Brown, Horace	Things We Do For Love	24-233	SC
Brown, James	Bewildered	29-146	LE
Brown, James	Cold Sweat	29-145	LE
Brown, James	Get Up Offa That Thing	29-140	LE
Brown, James	Hot Pants	29-142	LE
Brown, James	I Got The Feeling	29-139	LE
Brown, James	I Got You I Feel Good	14-564	AH
Brown, James	I Got You I Feel Good	26-327	DK
Brown, James	I Got You I Feel Good	29-151	LE
Brown, James	I Got You I Feel Good	13-92	P
Brown, James	I Got You I Feel Good	2-38	SC
Brown, James	I'll Go Crazy	14-598	SC
Brown, James	It's A Man's Man's Man's World	15-308	SC
Brown, James	Licking Stick	29-148	LE
Brown, James	Livin' In America	29-149	LE
Brown, James	Living In America	20-163	BCI
Brown, James	Living In America	33-315	CB
Brown, James	Living In America	9-681	SAV
Brown, James	Mother Popcorn	29-147	LE
Brown, James	Papa's Got A Brand New Bag	29-143	LE
Brown, James	Papa's Got A Brand New Bag	10-254	SS

ARTIST	SONG TITLE	#	TYPE
Brown, James	Please Please Please	29-150	LE
Brown, James	Please Please Please	14-589	SC
Brown, James	Prisoner Of Love	29-141	LE
Brown, James	Say It Loud (I'm Black & Proud)	29-144	LE
Brown, James	Sex Machine	27-278	DK
Brown, James	Sex Machine	29-137	LE
Brown, James	Super Bad	29-138	LE
Brown, Jim Ed	Ain't You Even Gonna Cry	47-772	SRK
Brown, Jim Ed	Bottle Bottle	45-691	BAT
Brown, Jim Ed	Just For Old Time's Sake	9-850	SAV
Brown, Jim Ed	Morning	5-769	SC
Brown, Jim Ed	Pop A Top	8-805	CB
Brown, Jim Ed	Pop A Top	5-432	SC
Brown, Jim Ed	Southern Lovin'	46-536	SSK
Brown, Jim Ed	You're The Part Of Me	45-714	VH
Brown, Joe	Picture Of You	11-52	PX
Brown, Joe	Picture Of You	10-558	SF
Brown, Julie	Cause I'm A Blonde	15-138	SC
Brown, Julie	Homecoming Queen's Got A Gun	5-639	SC
Brown, Junior	Better Call Saul	47-545	SF
Brown, Junior	Highway Patrol	40-76	CB
Brown, Junior	Holding Pattern	40-79	CB
Brown, Junior	I Hung It Up	40-81	CB
Brown, Junior	My Wife Thinks You're Dead	40-77	CB
Brown, Junior	My Wife Thinks You're Dead	4-134	SC
Brown, Junior	Party Lights	40-78	CB
Brown, Junior	Venom Wearin' Denim	7-320	MM
Brown, Junior	Venom Wearing Denim	40-80	CB
Brown, Kane	I Love That I Hate You	49-626	BKD
Brown, Kane	I Love That I Hate You - Inst	49-629	BKD
Brown, Kane	Last Minute Late Night	49-628	DCK
Brown, Kane	Used To Love You Sober	49-627	DCK
Brown, Marty	You Can't Wrap Your Arms/Memory	24-653	SC
Brown, Shannon	Baby I Lied	25-58	MM
Brown, Shannon	Baby I Lied	16-107	ST
Brown, Shannon	Corn Fed	23-484	CB
Brown, Shannon	Corn Fed	23-459	ST
Brown, Shannon	I Won't Lie	8-853	CB
Brown, Shannon	Pearls	29-369	CB
Brown, T. Graham	Darlene	5-777	SC
Brown, T. Graham	Don't Go To Strangers	47-550	SC
Brown, T. Graham	Happy Ever After	47-551	SC
Brown, T. Graham	Hell and High Water	20-286	SC
Brown, T. Graham	I Tell It Like It Used To Be	9-526	SAV
Brown, T. Graham	I Wish That I Could Hurt That Way Again	47-549	SAV
Brown, T. Graham	If You Could See Me Now	47-548	CB
Brown, T. Graham	Memphis Women &	5-833	SC

ARTIST	SONG TITLE	#	TYPE	ARTIST	SONG TITLE	#	TYPE
	Chicken				For Me		
Brown, T. Graham	Moonshadow Road	47-546	CB	Bryan, Luke	Country Man	36-582	CB
Brown, T. Graham	Never In A Million Tears	8-975	CB	Bryan, Luke	Country Man	36-214	PHM
Brown, T. Graham	Never In A Million Tears	10-191	SC	Bryan, Luke	Crash My Party	40-60	ASL
Brown, T. Graham	Wine Into Water	10-146	SC	Bryan, Luke	Dirt Road Diary	46-376	ASK
Brown, T. Graham	Wine Into Water	22-707	ST	Bryan, Luke	Do I	45-479	AC
Brown, T. Graham	With This Ring	47-547	CB	Bryan, Luke	Drinkin' Beer & Wasting Bullets	43-13	BKD
Browne, Jackson	Cocaine	23-612	BS	Bryan, Luke	Drunk On A Plane	44-183	SBIG
Browne, Jackson	Doctor My Eyes	17-180	SC	Bryan, Luke	Drunk On You	44-1	ASK
Browne, Jackson	Here Come Those Tears Again	7-94	MM	Bryan, Luke	Drunk On You	46-294	BKD
Browne, Jackson	Here Come Those Tears Again	23-616	BS	Bryan, Luke	Games	45-29	BKD
Browne, Jackson	I'm The Cat	24-229	SC	Bryan, Luke	Huntin' Fishin' & Lovin' Everyday	48-110	DCK
Browne, Jackson	In The Shape Of A Heart	23-618	BS	Bryan, Luke	I Don't Want This Night To End	38-117	CB
Browne, Jackson	Love Needs A Heart	23-614	BS	Bryan, Luke	I Knew You That Way	45-430	CK
Browne, Jackson	Nothing But Time	23-615	BS	Bryan, Luke	I See You	45-403	BKD
Browne, Jackson	Road the	23-609	BS	Bryan, Luke	If You Ain't Here To Party	43-279	BKD
Browne, Jackson	Rosie	23-610	BS	Bryan, Luke	If You Ain't Here To Party	45-98	KV
Browne, Jackson	Running On Empty	23-608	BS	Bryan, Luke	In Love With The Girl	48-109	BKD
Browne, Jackson	Running On Empty	17-181	SC	Bryan, Luke	Just A Sip	40-52	ASK
Browne, Jackson	Shaky Town	23-613	BS	Bryan, Luke	Just A Sip	45-97	ASK
Browne, Jackson	Somebody's Baby	5-306	SC	Bryan, Luke	Kick The Dust Up	45-41	SSC
Browne, Jackson	Stay	23-617	BS	Bryan, Luke	Kiss Tomorrow Goodbye	44-163	BKD
Browne, Jackson	You Love The Thunder	23-611	BS	Bryan, Luke	Kiss Tomorrow Goodbye	45-428	BKD
Browns	Duet - Looking Back To See	8-717	CB	Bryan, Luke	Play It Again	43-147	ASK
Browns	Foolish Pride	47-544	DFK	Bryan, Luke	Rain Is A Good Thing	45-96	CB
Browns	Looking Back To See	8-717	CB	Bryan, Luke	Roller Coaster	44-111	KV
Browns	Old Lamplighter the	6-54	SC	Bryan, Luke	She Get Me High	44-270	SSC
Browns	Scarlet Ribbons	9-605	SAV	Bryan, Luke	Someone Else Calling You Baby	45-32	CB
Browns	Scarlet Ribbons For Her Hair	47-543	SAV	Bryan, Luke	Strip It Down	45-30	BKD
Browns	Three Bells the	22-450	SC	Bryan, Luke	Suntan City	45-856	KCD
Bruce, Ed	After All	29-692	SC	Bryan, Luke	Take My Drunk Ass Home	43-262	BFK
Bruce, Ed	Diane	14-260	SC	Bryan, Luke	Take My Drunk Ass Home	43-270	KV
Bruce, Ed	Ever Never Loving You	19-449	SC	Bryan, Luke	That's My Kind Of Night	45-31	SBI
Bruce, Ed	Girls Women And Ladies	46-538	SC	Bryan, Luke	We Rode In Trucks	36-556	CB
Bruce, Ed	Hundred Dollar Lady	48-410	DFK	Bryan, Luke	You Don't Know Jack	38-101	PHM
Bruce, Ed	Last Cowboy Song the	46-537	KV	Bryant, Chase	Little Bit Of You	49-736	SBI
Bruce, Ed	My First Taste Of Texas	5-824	SC	Bryant, Chase	Take It On Back	45-398	BKD
Bruce, Ed	Nights	5-154	SC	Bryson & Flack	Duet - Tonight I Celebrate My Love.	6-228	MM
Bruce, Ed	You Turn Me On Like A Radio	4-490	SC	Bryson & Flack	Duet - Tonight I Celebrate My Love.	9-211	SO
Bruce, Ed	You're The Best Break This Heart..	12-449	P	Bryson & Flack	Duet - Tonight I Celebrate..	35-311	CB
Bruce, Tommy	Ain't Misbehavin'	10-613	SF	Bryson & Flack	Tonight I Celebrate My Love - duet	35-311	CB
Bryan & Fairchild	Duet - Home Alone Tonight	45-822	DCK	Bryson & Flack	Tonight I Celebrate My Love For U	6-228	MM
Bryan & Fairchild	Home Alone Tonight - duet	45-822	DCK	Bryson & Flack	Tonight I Celebrate My Love For U	9-208	SC
Bryan, Luke	All My Friends Say	30-256	CB				
Bryan, Luke	Been There Done That	45-322	SSC				
Bryan, Luke	Beer In The Headlights	45-480	ASK				
Bryan, Luke	Blood Brothers	45-427	YBK				
Bryan, Luke	Buzzkill	44-328	SSC				
Bryan, Luke	Country Girl Shake It	37-202	AS				

ARTIST	SONG TITLE	#	TYPE
Bryson & LaBelle	Duet - Whole New World a	17-424	KC
Bryson & LaBelle	Duet - Whole New World a	9-208	SO
Bryson & LaBelle	Whole New World a	17-424	KC
Bryson & LaBelle	Whole New World a	9-208	SC
Bryson w/Kenny G..	By The Time This Night Is Over	2-268	SC
Bryson, Peabo	By The Time This Night Is Over	6-369	MM
Bryson, Peabo	By The time This Night Is Over	9-214	SO
Bryson, Peabo	Closer Than Close	24-265	SC
Bryson, Peabo	If Ever You're In My Arms Again	49-480	MM
BTO	Four Wheel Drive	46-550	CB
BTO	Gimme Your Money Please	46-546	CB
BTO	Give It Time	46-547	CB
BTO	Hey You	46-540	CB
BTO	Hold Back The Water	46-543	CB
BTO	Let It Ride	35-121	CB
BTO	Let It Ride	20-91	SC
BTO	Letter the	46-539	CB
BTO	Lookin' Out For #1	46-548	CB
BTO	Not Fragile	46-545	CB
BTO	Rock Is My Life & This Is My Song	46-549	CB
BTO	Roll On Down The Highway	5-600	SC
BTO	Take It Like A Man	46-544	CB
BTO	Takin' Care Of Business	11-332	DK
BTO	Takin' Care Of Business	13-170	P
BTO	Thank You For The Feelin'	46-541	CB
BTO	You Ain't Seen Nothing Yet	46-542	CB
Buble & Twain	White Christmas - duet	45-792	KV
Buble & Twain	Xmas - White Christmas - duet	45-792	KV
Buble, Michael	All I Do Is Dream Of You	40-88	PS
Buble, Michael	All Of Me	40-84	PS
Buble, Michael	At This Moment	40-87	PS
Buble, Michael	Crazy Little Thing Called Love	30-177	LE
Buble, Michael	Crazy Love	40-86	PS
Buble, Michael	Cry Me A River	40-83	PS
Buble, Michael	Everything	30-489	CB
Buble, Michael	Everything	37-119	SC
Buble, Michael	Feeling Good	38-175	CB
Buble, Michael	Fever	30-178	LE
Buble, Michael	Foggy Day In London Town	38-178	PS
Buble, Michael	Georgia On My Mind	40-85	PS
Buble, Michael	Haven't Met You Yet	38-176	CB
Buble, Michael	Hold On	38-174	CB
Buble, Michael	Hold On	40-89	PS
Buble, Michael	Hollywood	38-173	CB
Buble, Michael	Home	30-179	LE

ARTIST	SONG TITLE	#	TYPE
Buble, Michael	How Can You Mend A Broken Heart	30-180	LE
Buble, Michael	I'm Your Man	38-179	BIP
Buble, Michael	Kissing A Fool	30-181	LE
Buble, Michael	Let It Snow	45-739	ZP
Buble, Michael	Lost	38-172	SC
Buble, Michael	Moondance	30-182	LE
Buble, Michael	Save the Last Dance For Me	38-171	SC
Buble, Michael	Song For You a	38-177	ZM
Buble, Michael	Summer Wind	30-183	LE
Buble, Michael	Sway	30-184	LE
Buble, Michael	Xmas - Let It Snow	45-739	Zp
Buble, Michael	You'll Never Find Another Love Like	30-185	LE
Buble, Michael	You're Nobody Till Somebody...	40-90	PS
Buckcherry	All Night Long	48-474	CB
Buckcherry	Crazy Bitch **	30-656	RSX
Buckcherry	Don't Go Away Mad	48-472	CB
Buckcherry	For The Movies	8-531	PHT
Buckcherry	For The Movies	5-787	SC
Buckcherry	For The Movies	48-475	SC
Buckcherry	Lit Up	48-476	SC
Buckcherry	Rescue Me	48-473	CB
Buckcherry	Ridin'	15-299	THM
Buckcherry	Ridin'	48-477	SC
Buckcherry	Sorry	36-461	CB
Buckingham, Lindsey	Soul Drifter	24-258	SC
Buckinghams	Hey Baby They're Playing Our Song	20-34	SC
Buckinghams	Kind Of A Drag	7-63	MM
Buckinghams	Kind Of A Drag	3-16	SC
Buckner & Garcia	Pac-Man Fever	37-84	SC
Buffalo Club	Heart Hold On	8-146	CB
Buffalo Club	Heart Hold On	22-662	ST
Buffalo Club	If She Don't Love You	14-660	CB
Buffalo Club	If She Don't Love You	22-409	CHM
Buffalo Club	If She Don't Love You	7-433	MM
Buffalo Club	Nothin' Less Than Love	22-634	ST
Buffalo Springfield	For What It's Worth	17-122	DK
Buffalo Springfield	For What It's Worth	12-909	P
Buffalo Springfield	For What It's Worth	9-666	SAV
Buffett & Keith	Duet - Piece Of Work	38-168	SC
Buffett & Keith	Piece Of Work - duet	38-168	SC
Buffett & McBride	Duet - Trip Around The Sun	22-65	CB
Buffett & McBride	Duet - Trip Around The Sun	30-7	SC
Buffett & McBride	Duet - Trip Around The Sun	20-506	ST
Buffett & McBride	Trip Around The Sun	21-168	CB
Buffett & McBride	Trip Around The Sun	30-7	SC
Buffett & McBride	Trip Around The Sun	20-506	ST
Buffett & Strait	Sea Of Heartbreak	20-498	ST
Buffett, Jimmy	Another Saturday Night	46-137	SC
Buffett, Jimmy	Bama Breeze	46-136	ST
Buffett, Jimmy	Beautiful Swimmers	46-152	PS

ARTIST	SONG TITLE	#	TYPE
Buffett, Jimmy	Boat Drinks	42-17	SC
Buffett, Jimmy	California Promises	47-793	SRK
Buffett, Jimmy	Changes In Latitude Changes In..	6-426	MM
Buffett, Jimmy	Changes In Latitude...	33-287	CB
Buffett, Jimmy	Cheeseburger In Paradise	6-424	MM
Buffett, Jimmy	Cheeseburger In Paradise	2-137	SC
Buffett, Jimmy	Christmas Island - xmas	45-251	SC
Buffett, Jimmy	Come Monday	6-421	MM
Buffett, Jimmy	Come Monday	12-694	P
Buffett, Jimmy	Fins	42-18	SC
Buffett, Jimmy	Fruit Cakes	46-130	SC
Buffett, Jimmy	God's Own Drunk	7-417	MM
Buffett, Jimmy	God's Own Drunk	46-151	MM
Buffett, Jimmy	Grapefruit Juicy Fruit	46-139	SC
Buffett, Jimmy	Growing Older But Not Up	46-150	ZM
Buffett, Jimmy	He Went To Paris	46-142	SC
Buffett, Jimmy	Hey Good Lookin'	46-293	CB
Buffett, Jimmy	Ho Ho Ho And A Bottle Of Rum	46-144	SC
Buffett, Jimmy	Honey Do	46-147	TU
Buffett, Jimmy	Last Mango In Paris	46-146	CKC
Buffett, Jimmy	Livingston Saturday Night	46-143	SC
Buffett, Jimmy	Margaritaville	12-55	DK
Buffett, Jimmy	Margaritaville	20-312	MH
Buffett, Jimmy	Margaritaville	6-429	MM
Buffett, Jimmy	Margaritaville	2-36	SC
Buffett, Jimmy	Margaritaville (With lost verse)	49-296	HM
Buffett, Jimmy	Merry Christmas Alabama	46-145	TU
Buffett, Jimmy	Off To See The Lizard	45-846	VH
Buffett, Jimmy	Pencil Thin Mustache	46-141	SC
Buffett, Jimmy	Pirate Looks At 40 a	46-138	SC
Buffett, Jimmy	Son Of A Son Of A Sailor	42-16	SC
Buffett, Jimmy	Souvenirs	46-131	SC
Buffett, Jimmy	Summerzcool	46-149	PS
Buffett, Jimmy	Take Another Road	45-847	VH
Buffett, Jimmy	Tin Cup Chalace	46-148	SBI
Buffett, Jimmy	Trip Around The Sun	46-135	ASK
Buffett, Jimmy	Volcano	6-432	MM
Buffett, Jimmy	We Are the People Our Parents Warned..	44-69	KV
Buffett, Jimmy	Weather Is Here With You	46-140	SC
Buffett, Jimmy	Why Don't We Get Drunk & Screw **	9-353	AH
Buffett, Jimmy	Why Don't We Get Drunk & Screw **	7-411	MM
Buffett, Jimmy	Why Don't We Get Drunk & Screw **	2-177	SC
Buffett, Jimmy	Xmas - Christmas Island	45-251	SC
Buffett, Jimmy	Xmas - Mele Kalikimaka	5-716	SC
Buffett, Jimmy	Xmas - Merry Christmas	46-145	TU

ARTIST	SONG TITLE	#	TYPE
	Alabama		
Buffett/Black/Chesn	Hey Good Lookin'	20-395	ST
Buggles	Video Killed The Radio Star	11-672	DK
Bullens, Cindy	Freddy My Love	10-14	SC
Bullens, Cindy	It's Raining On Prom Night	10-15	SC
Bulletboys	Smooth Up In Ya	21-763	SC
Bundy, Laura Bell	Two-Step	47-507	KV
Burdon, Eric & War	Spill The Wine	15-51	LE
Burdon, Eric & War	Spill The Wine	7-57	MM
Burdon, Eric & War	Spill The Wine	3-132	SC
Burnette, Billy	What a Woman Feels	10-270	CB
Burnin' Daylight	Like To Love Again	4-830	SC
Burnin' Daylight	Say Yes	10-100	SC
Burns, George	I Wish I Was Eighteen Again	44-58	KV
Burns, George	Simon Smith & His Amazing Dancing	21-603	SF
Bus Boys	Boys Are Back In Town the	13-660	SGB
Bush	Chemicals Between Us the	5-794	SC
Bush	Comedown	24-749	SC
Bush	Everything Zen	5-745	SC
Bush	Headful Of Ghosts	30-649	THM
Bush	Little Things	6-36	SC
Bush	People That We Love	16-323	TT
Bush	Warm Machine	14-484	SC
Bush, Kate	Babooshka	48-753	P
Bush, Kate	Wuthering Heights	48-760	P
Busta Rhymes	Gimme Some More	28-221	DK
Busta Rhymes	Put Your Hands Where My Eyes Can	14-449	SC
Busta Rhymes, Carey, Flipmo	Duet- I Know What You Want	32-311	THM
Busta Rhymes, Carey, Flipmo	I Know What You Want	32-311	THM
Busted	What I Go To School For	20-556	PHM
Butch Cassidy/Sunda	Show - Raindrops Keep Falling On...	6-892	MM
Butler & Impression	Make It Easy On Yourself	7-471	MM
Butler, Carl	Don't Let Me Cross Over	8-719	CB
Butler, Carl	Don't Let Me Cross Over	4-257	SC
Butler, Carl & Pearl	Don't Let Me Cross Over - duet	35-332	CB
Butler, Carl & Pearl	Duet - Don't Let Me Cross Over	35-332	CB
Butler, Jerry	Only The Strong Survive	4-706	SC
Buxton, Sarah	Innocence	30-52	CB
Buxton, Sarah	Innocence	30-100	PHM
Buxton, Sarah	Outside My Window	36-314	PHM
Buxton, Sarah	That Kind Of Day	30-343	CB
Bye Bye Birdie	Put On A Happy Face - show	48-786	MM
Bye Bye Birdie	Show - Begin The Beguine	27-423	DK
Bye Bye Birdie	Show - Kids	12-291	DK

ARTIST	SONG TITLE	#	TYPE	ARTIST	SONG TITLE	#	TYPE
Bye Bye Birdie	Show - Kids	7-363	MM		Again		
Bye Bye Birdie	Show - Lots Of Living Left To Do	6-872	MM	Byrd, Tracy	I Wanna Feel That Way Again	22-814	ST
Bye Bye Birdie	Show - Put On A Happy Face	48-786	MM	Byrd, Tracy	I'm From The Country	8-401	CB
				Byrd, Tracy	I'm From The Country	22-770	ST
Byrd & Chesnutt	Good Way To Get On My Bad Side	9-868	ST	Byrd, Tracy	Just Let Me Be In Love	25-15	MM
Byrd, Griggs, Shelton, Mont	Truth About Men the	34-406	CB	Byrd, Tracy	Just Let Me Be In Love	15-677	ST
				Byrd, Tracy	Keeper Of The Stars	1-545	CB
Byrd, Griggs, Shelton, Mont	Truth About Men the	32-226	THM	Byrd, Tracy	Keeper Of The Stars	2-568	SC
				Byrd, Tracy	Keeper Of The Stars the	22-872	ST
Byrd, Tracy	4 To 1 In Atlanta	22-902	ST	Byrd, Tracy	Lately (Been Dreamin' 'Bout Babies)	18-465	ST
Byrd, Tracy	Better Place Than This	30-439	CB				
Byrd, Tracy	Big Love	1-549	CB	Byrd, Tracy	Lately (Been Dreamin' 'Bout Babies)	32-78	THM
Byrd, Tracy	Big Love	4-462	SC				
Byrd, Tracy	Christmas Like Mama Used To Make It	45-768	CB	Byrd, Tracy	Lifestyles Of The Not So Rich&Famou	20-106	CB
Byrd, Tracy	Don't Love Make A Diamond Shine	1-551	CB	Byrd, Tracy	Lifestyles Of The Not So Rich&Famou	6-583	MM
Byrd, Tracy	Don't Love Make A Diamond Shine	7-644	CHM	Byrd, Tracy	Love Lessons	20-108	CB
				Byrd, Tracy	Love Lessons	7-87	MM
Byrd, Tracy	Don't Love Make A Diamond Shine	10-104	SC	Byrd, Tracy	Love Lessons	3-536	SC
Byrd, Tracy	Love You Ain't Seen The Last of Me	9-410	CB
Byrd, Tracy	Don't Take Her She's All I Got	14-649	CB	Byrd, Tracy	Love You Ain't Seen The Last Of Me	13-831	CHM
Byrd, Tracy	Don't Take Her She's All I Got	7-589	CHM	Byrd, Tracy	No Ordinary Man	20-111	CB
				Byrd, Tracy	On Again Off Again	8-222	CB
Byrd, Tracy	Don't Take Her She's All I Got	7-435	MM	Byrd, Tracy	Pink Flamingos	20-110	CB
				Byrd, Tracy	Put Your Hand In Mind	14-704	CB
Byrd, Tracy	Drinkin' Bone	25-700	MM	Byrd, Tracy	Put Your Hand In Mine	19-233	SC
Byrd, Tracy	Drinkin' Bone	19-363	ST	Byrd, Tracy	Put Your Hand In Mine	22-379	ST
Byrd, Tracy	Drinkin' Bone	32-378	THM	Byrd, Tracy	Revenge Of A Middle Aged Woman	22-78	CB
Byrd, Tracy	Drinking Bone	35-421	CB				
Byrd, Tracy	Duet - Good Way To Get On My…	16-263	TT	Byrd, Tracy	Take Me With You When You Go	14-116	CB
Byrd, Tracy	First Steo the	20-112	CB	Byrd, Tracy	Ten Rounds With Jose Quervo	33-182	CB
Byrd, Tracy	First Step the	17-266	NA				
Byrd, Tracy	First Step the	2-548	SC	Byrd, Tracy	Ten Rounds With Jose Quervo	25-189	MM
Byrd, Tracy	First Step the	22-852	ST				
Byrd, Tracy	Four To One In Atlanta	20-104	CB	Byrd, Tracy	Ten Rounds With Jose Quervo	16-433	ST
Byrd, Tracy	Good Ol' Fashioned Love	8-129	CB				
				Byrd, Tracy	Tiny Town	22-322	CB
Byrd, Tracy	Good Ol' Fashioned Love	22-633	ST	Byrd, Tracy	Truth About Men the	25-563	MM
				Byrd, Tracy	Truth About Men the	19-4	ST
Byrd, Tracy	Good Way To Get On My Bad Side	16-263	TT	Byrd, Tracy	Walking To Jerusalem	20-107	CB
				Byrd, Tracy	Walking To Jerusalem	6-803	MM
Byrd, Tracy	Heaven In My Woman's Eyes	20-109	CB	Byrd, Tracy	Watermelon Crawl	1-543	CB
				Byrd, Tracy	Watermelon Crawl	2-576	SC
Byrd, Tracy	Heaven In My Woman's Eyes	4-91	SC	Byrd, Tracy	Whan Mama Ain't Happy	1-555	CB
				Byrd, Tracy	When Mama Ain't Happy	7-827	CHT
Byrd, Tracy	Holdin' Heaven	1-541	CB	Byrd, Tracy	When Mama Ain't Happy	22-718	ST
Byrd, Tracy	Holdin' Heaven	2-354	SC	Byrd, Tracy	Why Don't That Telephone Ring	20-105	CB
Byrd, Tracy	Holdin' Heaven	8-602	TT				
Byrd, Tracy	How'd I Wind Up In Jamaica	20-256	PHM	Byrd, Tracy	Xmas - Christmas Like Mama Used To…	45-768	CB
Byrd, Tracy	How'd I Wind Up In Jamaica	20-336	ST	Byrds	All I Really Want To Do	47-555	LC
				Byrds	Ballad Of Easy Rider	47-553	KV
Byrd, Tracy	I Wanna Feel That Way Again	8-734	CB	Byrds	Eight Miles High	2-759	SC
Byrd, Tracy	I Wanna Feel That Way	5-293	SC	Byrds	Mr. Spaceman	47-554	KV

ARTIST	SONG TITLE	#	TYPE
Byrds	Mr. Tambourine Man	17-44	DK
Byrds	Mr. Tambourine Man	12-860	P
Byrds	My Back Pages	14-459	SC
Byrds	So You Want To Be A Rock N Roll...	20-57	SC
Byrds	Teach Your Children	47-556	SC
Byrds	Turn Turn Turn	35-95	CB
Byrds	Turn Turn Turn	26-323	DK
Byrds	Turn Turn Turn	15-574	MM
Byrds	You Ain't Going Nowhere	47-552	KV
C, Al	Don't Like This Bar (Parody)	38-281	ALC
C&C Music Factory	Gonna Make You Sweat	33-341	CB
C&C Music Factory	Gonna Make You Sweat	21-458	CB
C&C Music Factory	Just A Touch Of Love (Everyday)	49-917	KVD
C&C Music Factory	Things That Make You Go Hmmm	27-331	DK
Cab the	Bounce	36-289	PHM
Cabaret	Show - Cabaret	16-45	MM
Cabaret	Show - Don't Tell Mama	16-46	MM
Cabaret	Show - Maybe This Time	10-381	KC
Cabaret	Show - Mein Herr	15-720	MM
Cabaret	Show - Money Makes the World Go..	10-369	KC
Cabrera, Ryan	On The Way Down	20-548	PHM
Cabrera, Ryan	On The Way Down	48-711	SC
Cabrera, Ryan	True	22-362	CB
Cabrera, Ryan	True	21-163	PHM
Cactus Choir	Step Right Up	8-309	CB
Cadillac 3, FGL, etc	South, The	44-290	KC
Cadillac Three	South the	48-457	ASK
Cadillac Three	Tennessee Mojo	44-312	SBI
Cadillacs	Gloria	35-163	CB
Cadillacs	Gloria	25-558	MM
Cadillacs	Speedo	25-554	MM
Cadillad Three	White Lightning	48-444	KCD
Cafferty, John	Betty Lou's Got A New Pair Of Shoes	45-162	KV
Cafferty, John	Hearts On Fire	30-768	SF
Cafferty, John	Hearts On Fire	45-161	SFM
Cafferty, John	On The Dark Side	19-127	KC
Cafferty, John	On The Dark Side	17-489	LC
Cafferty, John	Pride And Passion	45-158	SB
Cafferty, John	Runnin' Through The Fire	45-160	KV
Cafferty, John	Some Like It Hot	45-159	KV
Cagle, Chris	Chicks Dig It	34-416	CB
Cagle, Chris	Chicks Dig It	25-642	MM
Cagle, Chris	Chicks Dig It	19-267	ST
Cagle, Chris	Chicks Dig It	32-338	THM
Cagle, Chris	Country By The Grace Of God	16-703	ST
Cagle, Chris	I Breathe In I Breathe Out	33-143	CB
Cagle, Chris	I Breathe In I Breathe Out	25-51	MM

ARTIST	SONG TITLE	#	TYPE
Cagle, Chris	I Breathe In I Breathe Out	15-859	ST
Cagle, Chris	I'd Be Lyin'	19-768	ST
Cagle, Chris	Laredo	14-844	ST
Cagle, Chris	Miss Me Baby	23-295	CB
Cagle, Chris	Miss Me Baby	29-512	SC
Cagle, Chris	Miss Me Baby	29-611	ST
Cagle, Chris	My Love Goes On And On	14-104	CB
Cagle, Chris	My Love Goes On And On	14-17	CHM
Cagle, Chris	My Love Goes On And On	19-226	CSZ
Cagle, Chris	Southern Girl	41-63	PHN
Cagle, Chris	Wal-Mart Parking Lot	29-206	CB
Cagle, Chris	What A Beautiful Day	34-355	CB
Cagle, Chris	What A Beautiful Day	25-444	MM
Cagle, Chris	What A Beautiful Day	18-467	ST
Cagle, Chris	What A Beautiful Day	32-82	THM
Cagle, Chris	What Kinda Gone	30-536	CB
Caillat, Colbie	Bubbly	30-591	PHM
Caillat, Colbie	Bubbly	37-16	PS
Caillat, Colbie	Fallin' For You	36-302	PHM
Caillat, Colbie	Feelings Show	37-20	PS
Caillat, Colbie	I Do	37-262	CB
Caillat, Colbie	Little Things the	36-532	CB
Caillat, Colbie	Little Things the	37-17	PS
Caillat, Colbie	Oxygen	37-19	PS
Caillat, Colbie	Realize	36-459	CB
Caillat, Colbie	Realize	37-18	PS
Caillat, Colbie	Shadow	38-209	PHM
Cailliat, Colbie	Brighter Than The Sun	48-222	PHM
Cailliat, Colbie	Fearless	48-221	KV
Cailliat, Colbie	Hold On	48-219	KV
Cailliat, Colbie	I Never Told You	48-216	CB
Cailliat, Colbie	Midnight Bottle	48-220	KV
Cailliat, Colbie	One Fine Wire	48-217	KV
Cailliat, Colbie	Try	45-10	BKD
Cailliat, Colbie	You Got Me	48-218	KV
Caitlin & Will	Address In The Stars	37-47	CB
Cajun	Cajun - Mona Lisa	49-405	SCK
Cajun	Cajun - Tee Na Na	49-293	GS
Cajun	Mona Lisa - Cajun Style	49-405	SCK
Cajun	Tee Na Na - Cajun	49-293	GS
Cajun Classic	Diggy Liggy Lo	45-725	VH
Cake	Short Skirt Long Jacket	16-393	SGB
Calabrese, Kayla	Kiss Me	41-88	PHN
Calamity Jane	Deadwood Stage the - show	49-852	SGB
Calamity Jane	Show - Deadwood Stage the	49-852	SGB
Caldwell, Bobby	Love Lite	24-20	SC
Caldwell, Bobby	Stuck On You	9-384	AH
Caldwell, Bobby	What You Won't Do For Love	17-409	DK
Caldwell, Bobby	What You Won't Do For Love	25-286	MM
Calling	Could It Be Any Harder	18-427	CB

ARTIST	SONG TITLE	#	TYPE
Calling	Wherever You Will Go	33-424	CB
Calling	Wherever You Will Go	20-375	HP
Calling	Wherever You Will Go	25-25	MM
Calloway, Cab	Minnie The Moocher	12-538	P
Cam	Burning House	45-409	BKD
Cam	Country Ain't Never Been Pretty	49-753	KV
Cam	Half Broken Heart	48-750	BKD
Cam	Half Broken Heart (Inst)	49-412	BKD
Cam	Mayday	49-8	KV
Cam	My Mistake	49-537	KVD
Cam	My Mistake	49-9	FMK
Cam	Runaway Train	49-535	KVD
Cam	Village	49-755	KVD
Cam'ron & Juelz	Duet - Hey Ma	25-460	MM
Cam'ron & Juelz	Hey Ma	25-460	MM
Camelot	Show - If Ever I Would Leave You	12-294	DK
Camelot	Show - If Ever I Would Leave You	18-187	PS
Cameo	Word Up	11-516	DK
Cameo	Word Up	16-543	P
Cameo	Word Up	16-69	SC
Camp, Shawn	Fallin' Never Felt So Good	9-625	SAV
Campbell, Craig	Family Man	37-346	CB
Campbell, Craig	Fish	40-6	CB
Campbell, Craig	Keep Them Kisses Comin'	44-186	KCDC
Campbell, Craig	Outta My Head	44-195	ASK
Campbell, Craig	Outta My Head	45-390	ASK
Campbell, Craig	Wake Up Lovin' You	45-399	BKD
Campbell, Glen	Burning Bridges	47-525	VH
Campbell, Glen	By The Time I Get To Phoenix	16-869	DK
Campbell, Glen	By The Time I Get To Phoenix	13-447	P
Campbell, Glen	Country Boy You Got /Feet In LA	15-68	CB
Campbell, Glen	Country Boy You Got /Feet In LA	5-412	SC
Campbell, Glen	Country Boy You Got Your...	33-34	CB
Campbell, Glen	Dream Baby	8-453	CB
Campbell, Glen	Dreams Of The Everyday Housewife	9-616	SAV
Campbell, Glen	Dreams Of The Everyday Housewife	5-434	SC
Campbell, Glen	Faithless Love	19-433	SC
Campbell, Glen	Galveston	35-66	CB
Campbell, Glen	Galveston	12-300	DK
Campbell, Glen	Gentle On My Mind	17-14	DK
Campbell, Glen	Gentle On My Mind	13-418	P
Campbell, Glen	Gentle On My Mind	8-657	SAV
Campbell, Glen	Grow Old With Me	49-266	DFK
Campbell, Glen	Hey Little One	47-803	SRK
Campbell, Glen	Honey Come Back	5-36	SC
Campbell, Glen	I Love How You Love Me	34-255	CB
Campbell, Glen	I Wanna Love	48-490	CKC

ARTIST	SONG TITLE	#	TYPE
Campbell, Glen	I'm So Lonesome I Could Cry	48-489	CKC
Campbell, Glen	It's Only Make Believe	11-106	DK
Campbell, Glen	Lady Like You a	5-161	SC
Campbell, Glen	Let It Be Me	48-494	CKC
Campbell, Glen	My Elusive Butterfly	48-492	CKC
Campbell, Glen	Old Hometown	9-631	SAV
Campbell, Glen	Rhinestone Cowboy	8-358	CB
Campbell, Glen	Rhinestone Cowboy	15-275	DK
Campbell, Glen	Rhinestone Cowboy	9-635	SAV
Campbell, Glen	She's Gone Gone Gone	48-493	CKC
Campbell, Glen	Southern Nights	11-618	DK
Campbell, Glen	Southern Nights	13-426	P
Campbell, Glen	Southern Nights	8-658	SAV
Campbell, Glen	Southern Nights	5-126	SC
Campbell, Glen	Then You Can Tell Me Goodbye	9-523	SAV
Campbell, Glen	Try A Little Kindness	33-24	CB
Campbell, Glen	Try A Little Kindness	9-619	SAV
Campbell, Glen	Try A Little Kindness	14-328	SC
Campbell, Glen	Turn Around Look At Me	48-491	CKC
Campbell, Glen	Wichita Lineman	8-286	CB
Campbell, Glen	Wichita Lineman	12-298	DK
Campbell, Glen	Wichita Lineman	10-744	JVC
Campbell, Glen	Wichita Lineman	13-454	P
Campbell, Glen	Wichita Lineman	5-216	SC
Campbell, Stacy D.	Honey I Do	6-853	MM
Campbell, Stacy D.	Honey I Do	3-563	SC
Campbell, Stacy D.	Rosalee	20-116	CB
Campbell, Tevin	Can We Talk	28-116	DK
Campbell, Tevin	Confused	9-843	SAV
Campbell, Tevin	Don't Say Goodbye Girl	29-135	ST
Campbell, Tevin	I Got It Bad	24-297	SC
Campbell, Tevin	I'm Ready	28-443	DK
Campbell, Tevin	I'm Ready	2-234	SC
Campbell, Tevin	Xmas - Oh Holy Night	22-836	ST
Candyman	Knockin' Boots	49-16	KV
Canned Heat	Christmas Blues	45-762	CB
Canned Heat	Xmas - Christmas Blues	45-762	CB
Cannel, Bruce	Hey Baby	6-154	MM
Cannon, Freddie	Palisades Park	17-50	DK
Cannon, Freddie	Tallahassee Lassie	6-677	MM
Cannon, Freddie	Way Down Yonder In New Orleans	4-248	SC
Cannon, Freddie	Way Down Yonder In New Orleans	10-622	SF
Cannon, Melanie	And The Wheels Turn	36-278	PHM
Cantor, Eddie	Ida! Sweet As Apple Cider	43-217	CB
Cantor, Eddie	If You Knew Susie (Like I Know Susie)	43-215	CB
Cantor, Eddie	Yes Sir! That's My Baby	43-216	CB
Cantrell & Paul	Breathe	25-718	MM
Cantrell & Paul	Duet - Breathe	25-718	MM
Cantrell, Blu	Breathe	34-144	CB
Cantrell, Blu	Hit 'Em Up Style	15-807	CB
Cantrell, Blu	Hit 'Em Up Style	23-584	PHM
Cantrell, Blu	Hit 'Em Up Style	16-389	SGB

ARTIST	SONG TITLE	#	TYPE
Cantrell, Blu	Hit 'Em Up Style	18-518	TT
Cantrell, Jerry	Leave Me Alone	24-119	SC
Canyon, George	I'll Never Do Better Than You	22-73	CB
Canyon, George	My Name	22-334	CB
Capitols	Cool Jerk	35-83	CB
Capitols	Cool Jerk	3-580	SC
Capris	There's A Moon Out Tonight	6-264	MM
Capris	There's A Moon Out Tonight	13-271	P
Capris	There's A Moon Out Tonight	5-240	SC
Captain & Tennille	Can't Stop Dancin'	46-554	CB
Captain & Tennille	Come In From The Rain	46-590	CB
Captain & Tennille	Do That To Me One More Time	11-522	DK
Captain & Tennille	Do That To Me One More Time	2-866	SC
Captain & Tennille	I'm On My Way	46-559	CB
Captain & Tennille	Keeping Our Love Warm	46-556	CB
Captain & Tennille	Lonely Night (Angel Face)	46-552	CB
Captain & Tennille	Love Will Keep Us Together	26-102	DK
Captain & Tennille	Love Will Keep Us Together	9-9	MH
Captain & Tennille	Love Will Keep Us Together	12-831	P
Captain & Tennille	Muskrat Love	34-30	CB
Captain & Tennille	Shop Around	46-553	CB
Captain & Tennille	Song Of Joy	46-558	CB
Captain & Tennille	Way That I Want To Touch You the	46-551	CB
Captain & Tennille	We Never Really Say Goodbye	46-557	CB
Captain & Tennille	Wedding Song the	49-324	CB
Captain & Tennille	Wedding Song the	46-561	CB
Captain & Tennille	You Need A Woman Tonight	46-560	CB
Captain & Tennille	You Never Done It Like That	46-555	CB
Cara, Irene	Fame	11-343	DK
Cara, Irene	Fame	9-4	MH
Cara, Irene	Fame	18-57	MM
Cara, Irene	Flashdance (What A Feeling)	11-265	DK
Cara, Irene	Out Here On My Own	17-428	KC
Cara, Irene	Out Here On My Own	12-759	P
Caravelles	You Don't Have To Be A Baby To Cry	3-591	SC
Cardigans	Lovefool	24-640	SC
Carey & Boyz II	One Sweet Day	15-547	THM
Carey & Houston	When You Believe	7-787	PHT
Carey & Lorenz	Duet - I'll Be There	11-712	DK
Carey & Lorenz	Duet - I'll Be There	6-94	MM
Carey & Lorenz	I'll Be There	11-713	DK
Carey & Lorenz	I'll Be There	6-94	MM
Carey & Snoop Dogg	Duet - Say Something	23-310	CB

ARTIST	SONG TITLE	#	TYPE
Carey & Snoop&JD	Duet - It's Like That	22-365	CB
Carey, Mariah	Against All Odds	19-831	SGB
Carey, Mariah	Always Be My Baby	34-90	CB
Carey, Mariah	Always Be My Baby	19-577	MH
Carey, Mariah	Always Be My Baby	21-139	SC
Carey, Mariah	Anytime You Need A Friend	2-236	SC
Carey, Mariah	Boy (I Need You)	20-464	CB
Carey, Mariah	Butterfly	7-695	PHM
Carey, Mariah	Bye Bye	36-483	CB
Carey, Mariah	Can't Let Go	9-662	SAV
Carey, Mariah	Crybaby	15-634	THM
Carey, Mariah	Dreamlover	6-420	MM
Carey, Mariah	Dreamlover	17-172	SC
Carey, Mariah	Duet - I'll Be There	33-345	CB
Carey, Mariah	Hero	19-571	MH
Carey, Mariah	Hero	6-406	MM
Carey, Mariah	Hero	9-268	SC
Carey, Mariah	I Don't Wanna Cry	21-463	CB
Carey, Mariah	I Still Believe	16-200	PHT
Carey, Mariah	I'll Be There - duet	30-345	CB
Carey, Mariah	Love Takes Time	34-86	CB
Carey, Mariah	Make It Happen	6-173	MM
Carey, Mariah	Miss You Most At Christmas Time	45-799	SBI
Carey, Mariah	Never Too Far	23-583	PHM
Carey, Mariah	Say Somethin'	30-717	SF
Carey, Mariah	Someday	21-461	CB
Carey, Mariah	Through The Rain	25-426	MM
Carey, Mariah	Through The Rain	18-584	NS
Carey, Mariah	Through The Rain	32-100	THM
Carey, Mariah	Touch My Body	36-440	CB
Carey, Mariah	Underneath The Stars	24-632	SC
Carey, Mariah	Vision Of Love	21-237	SC
Carey, Mariah	We Belong Together	30-136	PT
Carey, Mariah	When You Believe	35-218	CB
Carey, Mariah	When You Believe	16-397	PR
Carey, Mariah	Without You	2-119	SC
Carey, Mariah	Xmas - All I Want For Christmas	7-8	MM
Carey, Mariah	Xmas - All I Want For Christmas	3-383	SC
Carey, Mariah	Xmas - Miss You Most At Christmas Time	45-799	SBI
Carey, Mariah w Snoop Dogg	Say Somethin'	30-717	SF
Carey/Joe/98 Degree	Duet - Thank God I Found You	16-183	PHM
Carey/Joe/98 Degree	Duet - Thank God I Found You	17-542	SC
Carey&Joe&98 Degree	Thank God I Found You	16-183	PHM
Carey&Joe&98 Degree	Thank God I Found You	17-542	SC
Carey&Scoop&JD	It's Like That	22-365	CB
Carey&Snoop Dogg	Say Something	23-310	CB
Cargill, Henson	Skip A Rope	10-745	JVC
Cargill, Henson	Skip A Rope	4-868	SC

ARTIST	SONG TITLE	#	TYPE
Carlisle, Belinda	Circle In The Sand	5-603	SC
Carlisle, Belinda	Heaven Is A Place On Earth	18-239	DK
Carlisle, Belinda	Heaven Is A Place On Earth	16-547	P
Carlisle, Belinda	I Get Weak	11-283	DK
Carlisle, Belinda	I Get Weak	5-146	SC
Carlisle, Belinda	Mad About You	28-273	DK
Carlisle, Belinda	Mad About You	4-538	SC
Carlisle, Belinda	Summer Rain	21-599	SF
Carlisle, Bob	Butterfly Kisses	10-20	SC
Carlisle, Bob	Butterfly Kisses (Country Version)	7-636	CHM
Carlisles	No Help Wanted	39-15	CB
Carlson, Paulette	Not With My Heart You Don't	4-466	SC
Carlton, Carl	She's A Bad Mama Jama	18-367	AH
Carlton, Carl	Willin'	17-357	DK
Carlton, Vanessa	Ordinary Day	25-341	MM
Carlton, Vanessa	Pretty Baby	25-430	MM
Carlton, Vanessa	Pretty Baby	32-97	THM
Carlton, Vanessa	Thousand Miles a	33-429	CB
Carlton, Vanessa	Thousand Miles a	25-204	MM
Carlton, Vanessa	White Houses	20-555	PHM
Carmen, Eric	All By Myself	11-333	DK
Carmen, Eric	Change Of Heart	9-774	SAV
Carmen, Eric	Hungry Eyes	46-563	MM
Carmen, Eric	I'd Really Love To See You Tonight	11-334	DK
Carmen, Eric	Love Is All That Matters	46-562	KV
Carmen, Eric	Make Me Lose Control	11-319	DK
Carmen, Eric	Never Gonna Fall In Love Again	11-416	DK
Carnes, Kim	Bette Davis Eyes	2-148	SC
Carnes, Kim	Crazy In The Night	5-473	SC
Carolina Liar	Show Me What I Am Looking For	36-290	PHM
Carolina Rain	American Radio	36-195	PHM
Carolina Rain	Get Outta My Way	30-94	CB
Carolina Rain	I Ain't Scared	22-87	CB
Carolina Rain	Isn't She	30-255	CB
Caroline's Spine	Nothing To Prove (Radio Version)	14-472	SC
Caron, Leslie	Hi LiLi Hi Lo	9-827	SAV
Carousel	Show - Highest Judge Of All	14-386	PS
Carousel	Show - June Is Busting Out All Over	6-874	MM
Carousel	Show - You'll Never Walk Alone	2-284	SC
Carpenter & Diffie	Duet - Not Too Much To Ask	1-425	CB
Carpenter & Diffie	Duet - Not Too Much To Ask	15-155	THM
Carpenter & Diffie	Not Too Much To Ask	1-425	CB
Carpenter & Diffie	Not Too Much To Ask	15-155	THM
Carpenter, M C	Almost Home	22-431	ST
Carpenter, M C	Better To Dream Of You	47-665	CB
Carpenter, M C	Bug the	6-389	MM

ARTIST	SONG TITLE	#	TYPE
Carpenter, M C	Bug the	15-164	THM
Carpenter, M C	Come On Come On	8-883	CB
Carpenter, M C	Come On Come On	12-469	P
Carpenter, M C	Down At The Twist & Shout	1-421	CB
Carpenter, M C	Down At The Twist & Shout	12-19	DK
Carpenter, M C	Down At The Twist & Shout	13-508	P
Carpenter, M C	Down At The Twist & Shout	2-9	SC
Carpenter, M C	Down At The Twist & Shout	15-163	THM
Carpenter, M C	Going Out Tonight	15-159	THM
Carpenter, M C	Going Out Tonight	6-630	MM
Carpenter, M C	Going Out Tonight	2-797	SC
Carpenter, M C	Grow Old With Me	1-434	CB
Carpenter, M C	Hard Way the	6-306	MM
Carpenter, M C	Hard Way the	2-810	SC
Carpenter, M C	Hard Way the	15-156	THM
Carpenter, M C	He Thinks He'll Keep Her	1-424	CB
Carpenter, M C	He Thinks He'll Keep Her	6-452	MM
Carpenter, M C	He Thinks He'll Keep Her	2-816	SC
Carpenter, M C	He Thinks He'll Keep Her	15-152	THM
Carpenter, M C	House Of Cards	8-885	CB
Carpenter, M C	House Of Cards	4-70	SC
Carpenter, M C	House Of Cards	15-158	THM
Carpenter, M C	How Do	47-666	CB
Carpenter, M C	I Feel Lucky	1-422	CB
Carpenter, M C	I Feel Lucky	6-113	MM
Carpenter, M C	I Feel Lucky	15-150	THM
Carpenter, M C	I Take My Chances	8-884	CB
Carpenter, M C	I Take My Chances	6-572	MM
Carpenter, M C	I Take My Chances	15-153	THM
Carpenter, M C	I Want To Be Your Girlfriend	7-434	MM
Carpenter, M C	It's Only Love	8-873	CB
Carpenter, M C	John Doe No. 24	2-578	SC
Carpenter, M C	Let Me In To Your Heart	1-429	CB
Carpenter, M C	My Dear Old Friend	47-670	SC
Carpenter, M C	Never Had It So Good	14-685	CB
Carpenter, M C	Not Too Much To Ask	6-134	MM
Carpenter, M C	Only A Dream	47-668	SC
Carpenter, M C	Passionate Kisses	1-423	CB
Carpenter, M C	Passionate Kisses	6-132	MM
Carpenter, M C	Passionate Kisses	12-435	P
Carpenter, M C	Passionate Kisses	9-633	SAV
Carpenter, M C	Passionate Kisses	15-154	THM
Carpenter, M C	Passionate Kisses	8-594	TT
Carpenter, M C	Passionate Kisses	34-303	CB
Carpenter, M C	Quittin' Time	1-432	CB
Carpenter, M C	Quittin' Time	15-157	THM
Carpenter, M C	Right Now	1-433	CB
Carpenter, M C	Right Now	15-162	THM

ARTIST	SONG TITLE	#	TYPE
Carpenter, M C	Shut Up And Kiss Me	1-427	CB
Carpenter, M C	Shut Up and Kiss Me	17-245	NA
Carpenter, M C	Shut Up And Kiss Me	2-456	SC
Carpenter, M C	Shut Up And Kiss Me	15-151	THM
Carpenter, M C	Simple Life	47-663	CB
Carpenter, M C	Something Of A Dreamer	1-430	CB
Carpenter, M C	Something Of A Dreamer	15-161	THM
Carpenter, M C	Stones In The Road	47-669	SC
Carpenter, M C	Tender When I Wanna Be	8-888	CB
Carpenter, M C	Tender When I Wanna Be	17-273	NA
Carpenter, M C	Tender When I Wanna Be	2-580	SC
Carpenter, M C	Tender When I Wanna Be	15-165	THM
Carpenter, M C	This Is Me Leaving You	29-359	CB
Carpenter, M C	This Shirt	8-887	CB
Carpenter, M C	What Would You Say To Me	49-332	CB
Carpenter, M C	What Would You Say To Me	47-664	CB
Carpenter, M C	Wherever You Are	47-667	MM
Carpenter, M C	Why Walk When You Can Fly	8-886	CB
Carpenter, M C	Why Walk When You Can Fly	3-635	SC
Carpenter, M C	You Win Again	1-431	CB
Carpenter, M C	You Win Again	15-160	THM
Carpenters	All Of My Life	45-803	KV
Carpenters	All You Get From Love is a Love Song	44-357	ZMPA
Carpenters	Calling Occupants Of Interplanetary...	45-804	LE
Carpenters	Can't Smile Without You	44-350	KV
Carpenters	Close To You	16-740	DK
Carpenters	Close To You	12-829	P
Carpenters	Close To You	10-538	SF
Carpenters	End Of The World	45-801	DKM
Carpenters	For All We Know	35-68	CB
Carpenters	For All We Know	11-683	DK
Carpenters	Goodbye To Love	44-349	JVC
Carpenters	Have Yourself a Merry Little Xmas	44-338	CB
Carpenters	Hurting Each Other	33-265	CB
Carpenters	Hurting Each Other	11-684	DK
Carpenters	Hurting Each Other	2-434	SC
Carpenters	Hurting Each Other	45-802	DKM
Carpenters	I Kept On Loving You	44-342	OZP
Carpenters	I Won't Last A Day Without You	33-286	CB
Carpenters	I Won't Last A Day Without You	4-848	SC
Carpenters	It's Going To Take Some Time	9-718	SAV
Carpenters	It's Going To Take Some Time	20-56	SC

ARTIST	SONG TITLE	#	TYPE
Carpenters	Jambalaya	44-348	DK
Carpenters	Let Me Be The One	44-343	OZP
Carpenters	Make It With You	44-344	OZP
Carpenters	Now the	45-800	SBI
Carpenters	Only Yesterday	44-352	MFK
Carpenters	Our Day Will Come	44-355	SKG
Carpenters	Please Mr. Postman	44-346	CBE
Carpenters	Rainy Days & Mondays	16-856	DK
Carpenters	Rainy Days & Mondays	12-687	P
Carpenters	Rainy Days & Mondays	2-437	SC
Carpenters	Sing	13-140	P
Carpenters	Sleigh Ride	45-805	SF
Carpenters	Solitaire	44-351	LG
Carpenters	Superstar	11-733	DK
Carpenters	Sweet Sweet Smile	44-356	TB
Carpenters	There's A Kind Of Hush	44-347	DK
Carpenters	This Masquerade	44-354	SFG
Carpenters	Ticket To Ride	44-353	MFK
Carpenters	Top Of The World	12-688	P
Carpenters	Touch Me When We're Dancing	44-345	CBE
Carpenters	Two Of Us	44-339	OZP
Carpenters	We've Only Just Begun	18-112	DK
Carpenters	We've Only Just Begun	12-689	P
Carpenters	Xmas - Have Yourself A Merry...	44-338	CB
Carpenters	Xmas - Merry Christmas Darling	3-406	SC
Carpenters	Xmas - Merry Christmas Darling	22-841	ST
Carpenters	Xmas - Sleigh Ride	45-805	SF
Carpenters	Yesterday Once More	34-23	CB
Carpenters	Yesterday Once More	11-235	DK
Carpenters	You	44-340	OZP
Carpenters	You're The One	44-341	OZP
Carr, Vicki	For Once In My Life	6-443	MM
Carr, Vicki	I'll Wait For You	46-564	MM
Carr, Vicki	It Must Be Him	11-637	DK
Carr, Vicki	It Must Be Him	14-339	SC
Carrack, Paul	Don't Shed A Tear	12-376	DK
Carrington, Rodney	Dancing With A Man	15-147	SC
Carrington, Rodney	Don't Look Now **	44-98	SC
Carrington, Rodney	Fred	44-102	SC
Carrington, Rodney	Great To Be A Man	44-101	SC
Carrington, Rodney	Letter To My P#N#S **	44-100	SC
Carrington, Rodney	Man Song the	44-103	SRK
Carrington, Rodney	More Of A Man	14-161	CB
Carrington, Rodney	More Of A Man	44-99	SC
Carrington, Rodney	Morning Wood **	44-97	SC
Carrington, Rodney	Show Them To Me	30-358	CB
Carrington, Rodney	Who Put The D### On The Snowman **	44-95	SC
Carroll, Jason M.	Alyssa Lies	30-169	CB
Carroll, Jason M.	Alyssa Lies	30-169	CB
Carroll, Jason M.	Hurry Home	36-317	PHM
Carroll, Jason M.	I Can Sleep When I'm Dead	36-418	CB
Carroll, Jason M.	Livin' Our Love Song	30-442	CB

ARTIST	SONG TITLE	#	TYPE
Carroll, Jason M.	Livin' Our Love Song	30-442	CB
Carroll. Jason M.	Where I'm From	36-265	PHM
Cars	Drive	11-659	DK
Cars	Drive	13-192	P
Cars	Drive	14-643	SC
Cars	My Best Friend's Girl	13-646	SGB
Cars	Shake It Up	17-75	DK
Cars	You Might Think	20-51	SC
Carson, Jeff	Butterfly Kisses	22-599	ST
Carson, Jeff	Car the	3-564	SC
Carson, Jeff	Cheatin' On Her Heart	8-235	CB
Carson, Jeff	Holdin' On To Something	4-209	SC
Carson, Jeff	I Can Only Imagine	19-179	ST
Carson, Jeff	Not On Your Love	6-825	MM
Carson, Jeff	Not On Your Love	3-414	SC
Carson, Jeff	Real Life (I Never Was The Same..)	29-354	CB
Carson, Jeff	Real Life (I Never Was The Same)	15-607	ST
Carson, Jeff	Shine On	8-740	CB
Carson, Jeff	That Last Mile	24-155	SC
Carson, Jeff	Until We Fall Back In Love Again	25-193	MM
Carson, Jeff	Until We Fall Back In Love Again	16-691	ST
Carson, Jeff	When You Said You Loved Me	30-319	CB
Carson, Jeff	Xmas - Santa Got Lost In Texas	8-81	CB
Carson, Jeff	Yeah Buddy	2-735	SC
Carter Family	Wildwood Frower	34-198	CB
Carter-Cash, June	Keep On The Sunny Side	49-394	SC
Carter, Aaron	Aaron's Party Come And Get It	16-249	TT
Carter, Aaron	Bounce	16-250	TT
Carter, Aaron	How I Beat Shaq	16-253	TT
Carter, Aaron	I Want Candy	16-255	TT
Carter, Carlene	Come On Back	2-616	SC
Carter, Carlene	Heart Is Right	49-759	KRG
Carter, Carlene	Hurricane	2-660	SC
Carter, Carlene	I Fell In Love	6-529	MM
Carter, Carlene	I Love You 'Cause I Want To	6-743	MM
Carter, Carlene	Unbreakable Heart	24-131	SC
Carter, Carlene	We Danced Anyway	7-578	CHM
Carter, Clarence	Kiss You All Over **	2-185	SC
Carter, Clarence	Patches	17-144	DK
Carter, Clarence	Slip Away **	5-521	SC
Carter, Clarence	Strokin' **	30-665	RSX
Carter, Clarence	Strokin' **	2-188	SC
Carter, Deana	Absence Of The Heart	10-145	SC
Carter, Deana	Absence Of The Heart	22-669	ST
Carter, Deana	Angels Working Overtime	7-864	CHT
Carter, Deana	Angels Working Overtime	14-603	SC
Carter, Deana	Angels Working	22-744	ST

ARTIST	SONG TITLE	#	TYPE
	Overtime		
Carter, Deana	Count Me In	14-655	CB
Carter, Deana	Count Me In	7-617	CHM
Carter, Deana	Did I Shave My Legs For This	33-133	CB
Carter, Deana	Did I Shave My Legs For This	22-412	ST
Carter, Deana	Every Little Thing	19-301	MH
Carter, Deana	Girl You Left Me For the	23-123	CB
Carter, Deana	How Do I Get There	7-667	CHM
Carter, Deana	How Do I Get There	4-831	SC
Carter, Deana	How Do I Get There	22-612	ST
Carter, Deana	I'm Just A Girl	20-216	CB
Carter, Deana	I'm Just A Girl	25-610	MM
Carter, Deana	I'm Just A Girl	19-65	ST
Carter, Deana	I'm Just A Girl	32-303	THM
Carter, Deana	Once Upon A December	22-762	ST
Carter, Deana	One Day At A Time	22-320	CB
Carter, Deana	Ruby Brown	22-518	ST
Carter, Deana	Strawberry Wine	4-422	SC
Carter, Deana	That's How You Know It's Love	24-652	SC
Carter, Deana	There's No Limit	34-349	CB
Carter, Deana	There's No Limit	25-422	MM
Carter, Deana	There's No Limit	18-468	ST
Carter, Deana	There's No Limit	32-41	THM
Carter, Deana	You Still Shake Me	8-330	CB
Carter, Deana	You Still Shake Me	7-826	CHT
Carter, Deana	You Still Shake Me	22-716	ST
Carter, June	Jukebox Blues	49-297	HM
Carter, Mel	Hold Me Thrill Me Kiss Me	6-257	MM
Carter, Mel	Hold Me Thrill Me Kiss Me	2-60	SC
Carter, Nick	Do I Have To Cry For You	18-607	PHM
Carter's Chord	Different Breed	36-196	PHM
Carter's Chord	Young Love	36-567	CB
Cartman, Eric	Come Sail Away	13-716	SGB
Cartman, Eric	Kyle's Mom's A Bitch **	13-726	SGB
Cartwright, Lionel	Give Me His Last Chance	9-626	SAV
Cartwright, Lionel	I Watched It All On My Radio	9-456	SAV
Cartwright, Lionel	Leap Of Faith	13-525	P
Cartwright, Lionel	Miles And Years	8-972	CB
Cascada	Faded	36-234	PHM
Cascada	What Hurts The Most (Radio Vers)	49-904	SC
Cascades	Rhythm Of The Rain	12-659	P
Cash & Carter	Daddy Sang Bass	11-836	DK
Cash & Carter	Duet - Far Side Banks Of Jordan	47-785	SRK
Cash & Carter	Duet - If I Were A Carpenter	29-558	CB
Cash & Carter	Duet - Jackson	29-754	CB
Cash & Carter	Duet - Jackson	4-267	SC
Cash & Carter	Duet - Long Legged Guitar Pickin'..	29-719	CB

ARTIST	SONG TITLE	#	TYPE
Cash & Carter	Duet - Time's A Wastin'	49-294	HKC
Cash & Carter	Far Side Banks Of Jordan - duet	47-785	SRK
Cash & Carter	If I Were A Carpenter	29-558	CB
Cash & Carter	Jackson	29-754	CB
Cash & Carter	Jackson	4-267	SC
Cash & Carter	Long Legged Guitar Pickin' Man	29-719	CB
Cash & Carter	Time's A Wastin' - duet	49-294	HKC
Cash & Fiona Apple	Duet - Father & Son	43-403	SC
Cash & Fiona Apple	Father & Son - Duet	43-403	SC
Cash & Jennings	Duet - There Ain't No Good Chain..	29-562	CB
Cash & Jennings	Duet - There Ain't No Good Chain...	20-663	SC
Cash & Jennings	There Ain't No Good Chain Gang	29-562	CB
Cash & Jennings	There Ain't No Good Chain Gang	20-663	SC
Cash & Matthews	Duet - For You	37-243	CB
Cash & Matthews	For You - duet	37-243	CB
Cash, J. & Cash, R.	Duet - September When It Comes	37-252	CB
Cash, J. & Cash, R.	September When It Comes - duet	37-252	CB
Cash, Johnny	25 Minutes To Go	21-608	SF
Cash, Johnny	Ain;t No Grave	45-663	BBH
Cash, Johnny	All Over Again	29-765	CB
Cash, Johnny	All Over Again	43-418	SRK
Cash, Johnny	Any Old Wind That Blows	29-560	CB
Cash, Johnny	Any Old Wind That Blows	6-82	SC
Cash, Johnny	Away In A Manger - xmas	45-37	SC
Cash, Johnny	Ballad Of A Teenage Queen	14-240	CB
Cash, Johnny	Ballad Of A Teenage Queen	21-579	SC
Cash, Johnny	Ballad Of Ira Hayes the	29-726	CB
Cash, Johnny	Ballad Of Ira Hayes the	21-588	SC
Cash, Johnny	Big Battle	45-688	BAT
Cash, Johnny	Big River	29-741	CB
Cash, Johnny	Big River	5-844	SC
Cash, Johnny	Blistered	29-752	CB
Cash, Johnny	Boy Named Sue a	14-238	CB
Cash, Johnny	Boy Named Sue a	6-516	MM
Cash, Johnny	Boy Named Sue a	21-583	SC
Cash, Johnny	Cat's In The Cradle	45-89	SBI
Cash, Johnny	Cats In The Cradle	43-406	DCK
Cash, Johnny	Cocaine Blues	37-218	SF
Cash, Johnny	Come In Stranger	29-564	CB
Cash, Johnny	Cry Cry Cry	29-567	CB
Cash, Johnny	Daddy Sang Bass	21-581	SC
Cash, Johnny	Desperado	43-409	KCA
Cash, Johnny	Devil To Pay the	49-283	BAT
Cash, Johnny	Doin' My Time	43-412	SRK
Cash, Johnny	Don't Take Your Guns To Town	14-243	CB

ARTIST	SONG TITLE	#	TYPE
Cash, Johnny	Don't Take Your Guns To Town	21-586	SC
Cash, Johnny	Drive On	24-349	SC
Cash, Johnny	Drive On	49-743	SC
Cash, Johnny	Five Feet High And Rising	14-245	CB
Cash, Johnny	Flesh And Blood	14-248	CB
Cash, Johnny	Folsum Prison Blues	14-234	CB
Cash, Johnny	Folsum Prison Blues	17-161	DK
Cash, Johnny	Folsum Prison Blues	13-424	P
Cash, Johnny	Folsum Prison Blues	21-580	SC
Cash, Johnny	Folsum Prison Blues (Faster Vers)	29-735	CB
Cash, Johnny	For The Good Times	43-407	KCA
Cash, Johnny	For The Good Times	49-295	HKC
Cash, Johnny	For You	43-382	CKC
Cash, Johnny	Forever Young	43-420	SBI
Cash, Johnny	Forever Young	45-90	SB
Cash, Johnny	Frankie & Johnny	43-401	KV
Cash, Johnny	Further On Up The Road	49-282	BAT
Cash, Johnny	Get Rhythm	29-568	CB
Cash, Johnny	Get Rhythm	4-858	SC
Cash, Johnny	Ghost Riders In The Sky	29-563	CB
Cash, Johnny	Ghost Riders In The Sky	13-509	P
Cash, Johnny	Ghost Riders In The Sky	5-210	SC
Cash, Johnny	Give My Love To Rose	29-565	CB
Cash, Johnny	Give My Love To Rose	21-584	SC
Cash, Johnny	God's Gonna Cut You Down	45-36	SC
Cash, Johnny	God's Gonna Cut You Down - Gospel	37-244	CB
Cash, Johnny	God's Hands	47-806	SRK
Cash, Johnny	Goodbye Little Darlin'	43-416	SRK
Cash, Johnny	Gospel - God's Gonna Cut You Down	37-244	CB
Cash, Johnny	Gospel - I Talk To Jesus Every Day	49-714	VH
Cash, Johnny	Greystone Chapel	43-32	HM
Cash, Johnny	Guess Things Happen That Way	14-241	CB
Cash, Johnny	Guess Things Happen That Way	21-593	SC
Cash, Johnny	Hey Porter	29-731	CB
Cash, Johnny	Home Of The Blues	29-722	CB
Cash, Johnny	Home Of The Blues	47-720	CB
Cash, Johnny	Honky Tonk Girl	45-665	HSK
Cash, Johnny	Hurt	29-733	CB
Cash, Johnny	Hurt	21-590	SC
Cash, Johnny	Hurt	19-14	ST
Cash, Johnny	Hurt	32-219	THM
Cash, Johnny	I Got Stripes	29-766	CB
Cash, Johnny	I Got Stripes	6-5	SC
Cash, Johnny	I Heard That Lonesome Whistle Blow	29-742	CB
Cash, Johnny	I Talk To Jesus Every Day	49-714	VH
Cash, Johnny	I Walk The Line	14-236	CB
Cash, Johnny	I Walk The Line	11-763	DK

ARTIST	SONG TITLE	#	TYPE
Cash, Johnny	I Walk The Line	13-365	P
Cash, Johnny	I Walk The Line	9-481	SAV
Cash, Johnny	I Walk The Line	21-589	SC
Cash, Johnny	I'd Rather Die Young	43-415	SRK
Cash, Johnny	I've Been Everywhere	43-380	ASK
Cash, Johnny	In The Jailhouse Now	43-402	LG
Cash, Johnny	It Ain't Me Babe	29-730	CB
Cash, Johnny	It's Just About Time	29-764	CB
Cash, Johnny	Kate	29-559	CB
Cash, Johnny	Kneeling Drunkard's Plea	49-289	CWK
Cash, Johnny	Legend Of John Henry's Hammer	43-404	VH
Cash, Johnny	Lost On The Desert	46-21	SSK
Cash, Johnny	Luther Played The Boogie	22-243	SC
Cash, Johnny	Man Comes Around the	43-400	KV
Cash, Johnny	Man In Black	14-235	CB
Cash, Johnny	Man In Black	4-573	SC
Cash, Johnny	Man In White	45-671	DCK
Cash, Johnny	Night Hank Williams Came To Town	43-419	KV
Cash, Johnny	On The Evening Train	45-715	VH
Cash, Johnny	One On The Right Is On The Left	14-247	CB
Cash, Johnny	One On The Right Is On The Left..	5-203	SC
Cash, Johnny	One Piece At A Time	14-242	CB
Cash, Johnny	One Piece At A Time	2-513	SC
Cash, Johnny	Oney	29-571	CB
Cash, Johnny	Oney	5-207	SC
Cash, Johnny	Orange Blossom Special	14-246	CB
Cash, Johnny	Orange Blossom Special	21-585	SC
Cash, Johnny	Personal Jesus	43-398	KV
Cash, Johnny	Ragged Old Flag	29-566	CB
Cash, Johnny	Rebel, Johnny Yuma the	46-34	SSK
Cash, Johnny	Ring Of Fire	3-159	CB
Cash, Johnny	Ring Of Fire	11-435	DK
Cash, Johnny	Ring Of Fire	8-662	SAV
Cash, Johnny	Ring Of Fire	21-591	SC
Cash, Johnny	Ring Of Fire (Faster Version)	29-753	CB
Cash, Johnny	Rock Island Line	45-35	CBE
Cash, Johnny	Rockabilly Blues	43-414	SRK
Cash, Johnny	Rosanna's Going Wild	29-740	CB
Cash, Johnny	Rose Of My Heart	45-664	DCK
Cash, Johnny	Rusty Cage	43-410	KCA
Cash, Johnny	Sam Hall	47-811	SRK
Cash, Johnny	San Quentin	21-614	SF
Cash, Johnny	Sea Of Heartbreak	45-92	KV
Cash, Johnny	Seasons Of My Heart	29-725	CB
Cash, Johnny	See Ruby Fall	45-88	DFK
Cash, Johnny	Smiling Bill McCall	29-572	CB
Cash, Johnny	So Doggone Lonesome	29-760	CB
Cash, Johnny	So Doggone Lonesome	5-572	SC
Cash, Johnny	Solitary Man	43-408	KCA
Cash, Johnny	Sunday Mornin' Comin' Down	8-423	CB
Cash, Johnny	Sunday Mornin' Comin' Down	9-601	SAV
Cash, Johnny	Sunday Mornin' Comin' Down	5-196	SC
Cash, Johnny	Thanks A Lot	29-569	CB
Cash, Johnny	There You Go	29-746	CB
Cash, Johnny	There You Go	5-214	SC
Cash, Johnny	These Hands	48-432	VH
Cash, Johnny	Thing Called Love a	29-561	CB
Cash, Johnny	Thing Called Love a	20-650	SC
Cash, Johnny	Trouble In Mind	46-35	SSK
Cash, Johnny	Understand Your Man	14-244	CB
Cash, Johnny	Understand Your Man	21-592	SC
Cash, Johnny	Wanted Man	43-411	KCA
Cash, Johnny	Wanted Man	44-4	VH
Cash, Johnny	Ways Of A Woman In Love the	29-763	CB
Cash, Johnny	Ways Of A Woman In Love the	5-427	SC
Cash, Johnny	What Do I Care	29-762	CB
Cash, Johnny	What Is Truth	29-734	CB
Cash, Johnny	What Is Truth	29-698	SC
Cash, Johnny	When The Man Comes Around	43-417	SRK
Cash, Johnny	Why Me Lord	43-421	SF
Cash, Johnny	Wind Changes the	45-689	BAT
Cash, Johnny	Without Love	43-405	KC
Cash, Johnny	Wreck Of The Old ' 97 the	29-570	CB
Cash, Johnny	Xmas - Away In A Manger	30-389	SC
Cash, Johnny	Xmas - Away In A Manger	45-37	SC
Cash, Johnny	You're The Nearest Thing To Heaven	29-743	CB
Cash, Johnny & Roseann	Duet - September When It Comes	43-460	CB
Cash, Johnny & Roseann	September When It Comes	43-460	CB
Cash, Roseanne	Blue Moon With Heartache	14-255	SC
Cash, Roseanne	I Don't Know Why You Don't Want Me	5-818	SC
Cash, Roseanne	I Don't Want To Spoil The Party	7-115	MM
Cash, Roseanne	I'm Moving On	45-396	DCK
Cash, Roseanne	If You Change Your Mind	12-77	DK
Cash, Roseanne	If You Change Your Mind	5-24	SC
Cash, Roseanne	My Baby Thinks He's A Train	49-631	CB
Cash, Roseanne	Never Be You	5-761	SC
Cash, Roseanne	Runaway Train	11-788	DK
Cash, Roseanne	Runaway Train	13-332	P
Cash, Roseanne	Seven Year Ache	8-266	CB
Cash, Roseanne	Seven Year Ache	13-366	P
Cash, Roseanne	Tennessee Flat Top Box	9-638	SAV

ARTIST	SONG TITLE	#	TYPE
Cash, Roseanne	Tennessee Flat Top Box	12-426	P
Cash, Tommy	One Song Away	47-756	SRK
Cashman & West	American City Suite	15-754	AMS
Casinos	Then You Can Tell Me Goodbye	6-267	MM
Casinos	Then You Can Tell Me Goodbye	2-844	SC
Cassidy & Gray	Duet - You Don't Know Me	25-673	MM
Cassidy & Gray	You Don't Know Me	25-673	MM
Cassidy, Eva	Blue Skies	25-675	MM
Cassie	Long Way 2 Go	30-60	PHM
Castaways	Liar Liar	20-38	SC
Cathedrals	Gospel - Champion Of Love	16-16	SX
Cathedrals	Gospel - Dry Bones	16-17	SX
Catherine Wheel Th	Sparks Are Gonna Fly	15-791	THM
Cats	Show - Memory	6-319	MM
Cave In	Anchor	32-294	THM
Caviar	Tangerine Speedo (Radio Version)	23-30	SC
Cavo	Champagne	36-304	PHM
CCR	Bad Moon Risin'	11-363	DK
CCR	Bad Moon Risin'	7-44	MM
CCR	Bad Moon Risin'	5-351	SC
CCR	Born On The Bayou	48-366	SC
CCR	Commotion	48-363	CB
CCR	Cotton Fields	19-103	SAV
CCR	Cross-Tie Walker	48-372	KV
CCR	Don't Look Now (It Ain't You Or Me)	48-369	KV
CCR	Down On The Corner	33-262	CB
CCR	Down On The Corner	11-339	DK
CCR	Down On The Corner	15-172	MH
CCR	Down On The Corner	5-347	SC
CCR	Fortunate	17-29	DK
CCR	Fortunate Son	5-358	SC
CCR	Good Golly Miss Molly	48-362	ASK
CCR	Green River	34-21	CB
CCR	Green River	17-28	DK
CCR	Green River	13-230	P
CCR	Green River	5-350	SC
CCR	Halloween - I Put A Spell On You	16-282	TT
CCR	Have You Ever Seen The Rain	35-104	CB
CCR	Have You Ever Seen The Rain	11-465	DK
CCR	Have You Ever Seen The Rain	6-793	MM
CCR	Have You Ever Seen The Rain	12-865	P
CCR	Have You Ever Seen The Rain	5-353	SC
CCR	Heard It Through The Grapevine	48-361	THM
CCR	Hey Tonight	5-357	SC
CCR	I Put A Spell On You	5-606	SC
CCR	I Put A Spell On You	16-282	TT

ARTIST	SONG TITLE	#	TYPE
CCR	It Came Out Of The Sky	48-368	KV
CCR	Keep On Chooglin'	48-365	KV
CCR	Lodi	5-356	SC
CCR	Long As I Can See The Light	5-360	SC
CCR	Lookin' Out My Back Door	11-340	DK
CCR	Lookin' Out My Back Door	13-8	P
CCR	Lookin' Out My Back Door	5-346	SC
CCR	Lookin' Out My Back Door	34-69	CB
CCR	Midnight Special	33-258	CB
CCR	Midnight Special	13-169	P
CCR	Pagan Baby	48-371	KV
CCR	Proud Mary	11-353	DK
CCR	Proud Mary	12-924	P
CCR	Proud Mary	5-348	SC
CCR	Run Through The Jungle	5-359	SC
CCR	Someday Never Comes	48-367	SC
CCR	Susie Q	5-349	SC
CCR	Suzie-Q	33-255	CB
CCR	Sweet Hitch-Hiker	48-364	CB
CCR	Travelin' Band	11-420	DK
CCR	Travelin' Band	5-355	SC
CCR	Up Around The Bend	5-354	SC
CCR	Who'll Stop The Rain	35-93	CB
CCR	Who'll Stop The Rain	5-352	SC
CCR	Wrote A Song For Everyone	48-370	KV
Cetera & Cher	After All	6-338	MM
Cetera & Cher	After All	14-52	RS
Cetera & Grant	Duet - Next Time I Fall In Love	13-158	P
Cetera & Grant	Duet - Next Time I Fall In Love	9-203	SO
Cetera & Grant	Next Time I Fall In Love	13-158	P
Cetera & Grant	Next Time I Fall In Love	9-203	SO
Cetera & Kahn	Duet - Feels Like Heaven	6-103	MM
Cetera & Kahn	Feels Like Heaven	6-103	MM
Cetera, Peter	Glory Of Love	11-78	JTG
Cetera, Peter	One Clear Voice	24-178	SC
Chainsmokers	#Selfie	43-288	ASK
Chainsmokers	#Selfie	43-187	SBI
Chairman of Board	Give Me Just A Little More Time	12-139	DK
Chairman of Board	Give Me Just A Little More Time	4-705	SC
Chamandy, Chantal	Feels Like Love	36-180	PHM
Chambers Brothers	Time Has Come Today	14-451	SC
Champs, T.	Tequila	12-120	DK
Chandler, Gene	Duke Of Earl	11-467	DK
Chandler, Gene	Duke Of Earl	13-260	P
Chandler, Gene	Duke Of Earl	2-56	SC
Chandler, Gene	Groovy Situation	5-119	SC
Change	Lover's Holiday	30-743	SF

ARTIST	SONG TITLE	#	TYPE
Change	Lover's Holiday a	30-743	SF
Channel, Bruce	Hey Baby	14-348	SC
Channing, Stockard	Show - There Are Worse Things I...	10-9	SC
Channing, Stockard	Show -Look At Me I'm Sandra Dee	9-279	SC
Chantels	Look In My Eyes	25-178	MM
Chantels	Maybe	25-276	MM
Chapin, Harry	50,000 Pounds Of Bananas	21-519	SC
Chapin, Harry	Cat's In The Cradle	6-445	MM
Chapin, Harry	Cat's In The Cradle	13-172	P
Chapin, Harry	I Wonder What Would Happen	46-565	KV
Chapin, Harry	Sequel	21-509	SC
Chapin, Harry	Sunday Morning Sunshine	46-566	KV
Chapin, Harry	Taxi	9-350	AH
Chapin, Harry	Taxi	29-294	SC
Chapin, Harry	WOLD	21-515	SC
Chapman, Beth Niels	All I Have	29-325	PS
Chapman, Donovan	House Like That	30-311	CB
Chapman, Donovan	There Is No War	19-690	ST
Chapman, Steven C	Gospel - Lord Of The Dance	20-148	KB
Chapman, Tracy	Baby Can I Hold You	44-190	MRE
Chapman, Tracy	Crossroads	44-192	SBI
Chapman, Tracy	Fast Car	9-320	AG
Chapman, Tracy	Fast Car	9-5	MH
Chapman, Tracy	Fast Car	21-620	SF
Chapman, Tracy	Fast Car	19-158	SGB
Chapman, Tracy	Give Me One Reason	14-906	SC
Chapman, Tracy	Mountains Of Things	44-193	SBI
Chapman, Tracy	New Beginning	24-239	SC
Chapman, Tracy	Promise, the	44-185	KV
Chapman, Tracy	Smoke & Ashes	24-639	SC
Chapman, Tracy	Talkin' 'Bout A Revolution	24-570	SC
Chapman, Tracy	Talkin' 'Bout A Revolution	44-194	SCB
Chapman, Tracy	Telling Stories	44-187	SC
Chapman, Tracy	Wedding Song	44-191	MM
Chapmen, Stacy	How Do I Love Her	32-398	THM
Charlene	I've Never Been To Me	12-3	DK
Charles & Eddie	Would I Lie To You	24-144	SC
Charles, Ray	America The Beautiful	20-162	BCI
Charles, Ray	Blue Bayou	46-579	KV
Charles, Ray	Born To Lose	12-188	DK
Charles, Ray	Busted	46-576	JVC
Charles, Ray	Bye Bye Love	46-573	CB
Charles, Ray	Cryin' Time	12-173	DK
Charles, Ray	Don't Set Me Free	46-582	LE
Charles, Ray	Drown In My Own Tears	46-570	CB
Charles, Ray	Drown In My Own Tears	46-210	SC
Charles, Ray	Duet - Night Time Is The Right Time	35-69	CB
Charles, Ray	Georgia On My Mind	12-145	DK
Charles, Ray	Georgia On My Mind	19-779	SGB

ARTIST	SONG TITLE	#	TYPE
Charles, Ray	Halleujah I Love Her So	9-534	SAV
Charles, Ray	Hard Times (No One Knows)	46-572	CB
Charles, Ray	Here We Go Again	4-246	SC
Charles, Ray	Hit The Road Jack	10-671	HE
Charles, Ray	Hit The Road Jack	2-52	SC
Charles, Ray	I Believe To My Soul	46-581	LE
Charles, Ray	I Can't Stop Loving You	35-48	CB
Charles, Ray	I Can't Stop Loving You	16-805	DK
Charles, Ray	I Can't Stop Loving You	13-349	P
Charles, Ray	I Can't Stop Loving You	2-269	SC
Charles, Ray	I Got A Woman	27-230	DK
Charles, Ray	I Got A Woman	46-575	DKM
Charles, Ray	In The Heat Of The Night	12-555	P
Charles, Ray	It Had To Be You	46-583	LE
Charles, Ray	Let The Good Times Roll	46-574	CB
Charles, Ray	Let's Go Get Stoned	46-306	SC
Charles, Ray	Mary Ann	46-571	CB
Charles, Ray	Mess Around	46-569	CB
Charles, Ray	Night Time Is The Right Time - duet	35-69	CB
Charles, Ray	Precious Thing	46-577	KV
Charles, Ray	Ruby	46-585	PS
Charles, Ray	Shake A Tail Feather	46-568	AH
Charles, Ray	Take These Chains From My Heart	46-580	LE
Charles, Ray	Unchain My Heart	12-148	DK
Charles, Ray	What'd I Say	16-798	DK
Charles, Ray	What'd I Say	12-664	P
Charles, Ray	What'd I Say	4-5	SC
Charles, Ray	Yesterday	46-578	KV
Charles, Ray	You Are My Sunshine	46-584	LE
Charles, Ray	You Don't Know Me	17-305	NA
Charles, Tina	I Love To Love	11-29	PX
Charlie Daniels & Tritt	Duet - Southern Boy	34-557	CB
Charlie Daniels & Tritt	Southern Boy - duet	34-357	CB
Charlie Daniels Band	Boogie Woogie Fiddle Country Blues	5-406	SC
Charlie Daniels Band	Boogie Woogie Fiddle Country Blues	37-287	SC
Charlie Daniels Band	Devil Went Down To Georgia	7-451	MM
Charlie Daniels Band	Devil Went Down To Georgia	13-540	P
Charlie Daniels Band	Devil Went Down To Georgia	2-15	SC
Charlie Daniels Band	Devil Went Down To Georgia	8-596	TT
Charlie Daniels Band	Drinkin' My Baby Goodbye	7-410	MM
Charlie Daniels Band	Drinkin' My Baby Goodbye	5-242	SC
Charlie Daniels Band	Drinkin' My Baby Goodbye	43-19	CB
Charlie Daniels Band	Few More Rednecks (What the World..)	46-608	CB

ARTIST	SONG TITLE	#	TYPE
Charlie Daniels Band	Funky Junky the	43-272	CB
Charlie Daniels Band	In America	46-607	CB
Charlie Daniels Band	In America - patriotic	34-240	CB
Charlie Daniels Band	Last Fallen Hero	46-606	CB
Charlie Daniels Band	Legend Of Wooley Swamp	20-648	SC
Charlie Daniels Band	Little Folks	46-609	CB
Charlie Daniels Band	Long Haired Country Boy	4-546	SC
Charlie Daniels Band	Long Haired Country Boy	13-762	SGB
Charlie Daniels Band	Patriotic - In America	34-240	CB
Charlie Daniels Band	Road Dogs	14-729	CB
Charlie Daniels Band	Road Dogs	43-274	CB
Charlie Daniels Band	Simple Man	20-281	SC
Charlie Daniels Band	Simple Man	35-394	CB
Charlie Daniels Band	South's Gonna Do It Again	2-17	SC
Charlie Daniels Band	Texas	45-690	BAT
Charlie Daniels Band	This Ain't No Rag It's A Flag	16-31	ST
Charlie Daniels Band	This Ain't No Rag It's A Flag	20-579	CB
Charlie Daniels Band	Trudy	49-372	CB
Charlie Daniels Band	Uneasy Rider	2-533	SC
Charlie Daniels Band	Uneasy Rider	43-276	CB
Charlie Daniels Band	Wichita Jail	43-273	CB
Charlie Daniels/Tri	Southern Boy	18-802	ST
Chas & Dave	Gertcha	30-745	SF
Chasez, JC	Blowin' Me Up (With Her Love)	32-132	THM
Chasez, JC	Country Girl	18-772	PHM
Chayanne	Latino - Yo Te Amo	18-5	PS
Cheap Trick	Can't Stop Fallin' Into Love	17-82	DK
Cheap Trick	Can't Stop Fallin' Into Love	9-678	SAV
Cheap Trick	Don't Be Cruel	48-543	DK
Cheap Trick	Dream Police	9-725	SAV
Cheap Trick	Flame the	4-883	SC
Cheap Trick	I Want You To Want Me	13-19	P
Cheap Trick	Surrender	17-81	DK
Cheap Trick	Surrender	4-566	SC
Checker, Chubby	Hucklebuck the	4-708	SC
Checker, Chubby	Let's Twist Again	17-344	DK
Checker, Chubby	Let's Twist Again	13-318	P
Checker, Chubby	Let's Twist Again	5-86	SC
Checker, Chubby	Limbo Rock - DANCE #	22-440	SC
Checker, Chubby	Maybelline	48-558	DK
Checker, Chubby	Memphis	48-557	DK
Checker, Chubby	Pony Time	11-564	DK
Checker, Chubby	Rock And Roll Music	46-611	DKM
Checker, Chubby	Slow Twistin'	46-610	CB
Checker, Chubby	Sweet Little Sixteen	48-559	DK
Checker, Chubby	Twist the	26-498	DK
Checker, Chubby	Twist the	3-316	MH
Checker, Chubby	Twist the	2-41	SC
Cheech & Chong	Earache My Eye	37-88	SC

ARTIST	SONG TITLE	#	TYPE
Cheetam, Oliver	Get Down Saturday Night	15-702	LE
Chef	Chocolate Salty Balls **	5-541	SC
Chef	Chocolate Salty Balls **	13-721	SGB
Chef	Love Gravy **	13-717	SGB
Chef	No Substitute/Oh Cathy Lee **	13-718	SGB
Chef	Simultaneous **	13-715	SGB
Chef & Meatloaf	Duet - Tonight is Right for Lovin**	13-720	SGB
Chef & Meatloaf	Tonight Is Right For Loving **	13-720	SGB
Cher	All I Really Want To Do	47-674	LE
Cher	All Or Nothing	14-68	RS
Cher	Baby Don't Go	15-125	SGB
Cher	Bang Bang	14-61	RS
Cher	Bang Bang	15-126	SGB
Cher	Believe	28-4	DK
Cher	Believe	7-841	PHM
Cher	Believe	14-47	RS
Cher	Body To Body	21-720	TT
Cher	Cowboy's Work Is Never Done - duet	47-678	RSZ
Cher	Dark Lady	11-654	DK
Cher	Dark Lady	14-56	RS
Cher	Dark Lady	15-132	SGB
Cher	Different Kind Of Love Song	47-671	CB
Cher	Dov L' Amor	47-677	PS
Cher	Duet - Cowboy's Work Is Never Done	47-678	RSZ
Cher	Gypsies Tramps & Thieves	17-115	DK
Cher	Gypsies Tramps & Thieves	14-60	RS
Cher	Gypsies Tramps & Thieves	2-445	SC
Cher	Gypsies Tramps & Thieves	15-131	SGB
Cher	Half Breed	34-20	CB
Cher	Half Breed	11-687	DK
Cher	Half Breed	14-58	RS
Cher	Half Breed	15-134	SGB
Cher	Heart Of Stone	15-130	SGB
Cher	I Found Someone	11-323	DK
Cher	I Found Someone	14-62	RS
Cher	I Found Someone	15-120	SGB
Cher	I Hope You Find It	47-680	KV
Cher	I Walk Alone	47-686	SBI
Cher	If I Could Turn Back Time	11-750	DK
Cher	If I Could Turn Back Time	6-342	MM
Cher	If I Could Turn Back Time	14-49	RS
Cher	Just Like Jesse James	14-63	RS
Cher	Just Like Jesse James	15-129	SGB
Cher	Little Man	47-685	RSZ
Cher	Love And	15-128	SGB

ARTIST	SONG TITLE	#	TYPE
	Understanding		
Cher	Love Hurts	15-122	SGB
Cher	Music's No Good Without You	21-730	TT
Cher	One By One	24-48	SC
Cher	Power the	47-676	PS
Cher	Runaway	47-673	CB
Cher	Save Up All Your Tears	15-123	SGB
Cher	Shoop Shoop Song	11-643	DK
Cher	Shoop Shoop Song	19-128	KC
Cher	Shoop Shoop Song	14-64	RS
Cher	Shoop Shoop Song	15-124	SGB
Cher	Sirens	47-681	KV
Cher	Song For The Lonely	25-141	MM
Cher	Song For The Lonely	21-733	TT
Cher	Strong Enough	33-375	CB
Cher	Strong Enough	8-34	PHT
Cher	Strong Enough	14-53	RS
Cher	Strong Enough	10-182	SC
Cher	Strong Enough	13-701	SGB
Cher	Take Me Home	14-66	RS
Cher	Walking In Memphis	47-684	MRE
Cher	Way Of Love the	14-51	RS
Cher	We All Sleep Alone	14-50	RS
Cher	Welcome To Burlesque	47-683	KV
Cher	Woman's Word	47-682	KV
Cher	Working Girl	47-679	SC
Cher	You Better Sit Down Kids	14-54	RS
Cher	You Haven't Seen The Last Of Me	47-672	CB
Cher & Cetera	Duet - After All	6-338	MM
Cher & Cetera	Duet - After All	14-52	RS
Cherie	Older Than My Years	20-546	PHM
Cherrelle	Duet - Saturday Love	12-372	DK
Cherrelle	Saturday Love	12-372	DK
Cherry Poppin Daddy	Ding Dong Daddy Of The D Car Line	13-693	SGB
Cherry Poppin Daddy	Zoot Suit Riot	21-562	PHM
Cherry Poppin Daddy	Zoot Suit Riot	5-283	SC
Cherry Poppin Daddy	Zoot Suit Riot	13-690	SGB
Cherry Poppin' Daddys	Ding Dong Daddy Of The D Car Line	49-797	SGB
Cherry, Don	Band Of Gold	22-449	SC
Chesney & McGraw	Duet - Feel Like A Rock Star	45-126	BKD
Chesney & McGraw	Duet - Feels Like A Rock Star	39-37	ASK
Chesney & McGraw	Feel Like A Rock Star - duet	45-126	BKD
Chesney & McGraw	Feels Like A Rock Star - duet	39-37	ASK
Chesney & Nelson	Duet - That Lucky Old Sun	36-241	PHM
Chesney & Nelson	That Lucky Old Sun - duet	36-241	PHM

ARTIST	SONG TITLE	#	TYPE
Chesney & Potter	Duet - Wild Child	45-46	BKD
Chesney & Potter	Wild Child - duet	45-46	BKD
Chesney & Strait	Duet - Shift Work	30-585	CB
Chesney & Strait	Shift Work - Duet	30-585	CB
Chesney & Uncle Kracker	Duet - When The Sun Goes Down	35-445	CB
Chesney & Uncle Kracker	When the Sun Goes Down - duet	35-445	CB
Chesney, Kenny	Ain't Back Yet	37-312	CB
Chesney, Kenny	All I Need To Know	1-317	CB
Chesney, Kenny	All I Need To Know	7-24	MM
Chesney, Kenny	American Kids	44-272	SBI
Chesney, Kenny	American Kids	44-337	SSC
Chesney, Kenny	Anything But Mine	23-5	CB
Chesney, Kenny	Back In My Arms Again	1-321	CB
Chesney, Kenny	Back Where I Come From	48-81	CB
Chesney, Kenny	Because Of Your Love	48-90	CB
Chesney, Kenny	Beer In Mexico	29-589	CB
Chesney, Kenny	Beer In Mexico	29-501	SC
Chesney, Kenny	Being Drunk's A Lot Like Loving You	47-580	CB
Chesney, Kenny	Better As A Memory	36-427	CB
Chesney, Kenny	Big Star	29-423	CB
Chesney, Kenny	Big Star	25-440	MM
Chesney, Kenny	Big Star	18-779	ST
Chesney, Kenny	Big Star	32-116	THM
Chesney, Kenny	Boys Of Fall the	37-341	CB
Chesney, Kenny	Chance a	8-124	CB
Chesney, Kenny	Chance a	22-656	ST
Chesney, Kenny	Coastal	48-74	BKD
Chesney, Kenny	Come Over	39-27	ASK
Chesney, Kenny	Don't Blink	30-576	CB
Chesney, Kenny	Don't Happen Twice	29-432	CB
Chesney, Kenny	Down The Road	45-384	BKD
Chesney, Kenny	Dreams	48-85	CB
Chesney, Kenny	El Cerrito Place	39-65	PHN
Chesney, Kenny	Everybody Wants To Go To Heaven	36-212	PHM
Chesney, Kenny	Fall In Love	1-316	CB
Chesney, Kenny	Fall In Love	2-689	SC
Chesney, Kenny	Flip Flop Summer	30-529	CB
Chesney, Kenny	Flora-Bama	45-129	BKD
Chesney, Kenny	For The First Time	30-34	CB
Chesney, Kenny	From Hillbilly Heaven to Honky-Tonk	8-137	CB
Chesney, Kenny	Good Stuff the	29-425	CB
Chesney, Kenny	Good Stuff the	25-230	MM
Chesney, Kenny	Good Stuff the	17-567	ST
Chesney, Kenny	Got A Little Crazy	48-88	CB
Chesney, Kenny	Grandpa Told Me So	1-320	CB
Chesney, Kenny	Grandpa Told Me So	3-653	SC
Chesney, Kenny	Guitars And Tiki Bars	22-16	CB
Chesney, Kenny	High And Dry	48-80	CB
Chesney, Kenny	How Forever Feels	8-875	CB
Chesney, Kenny	How Forever Feels	22-714	ST
Chesney, Kenny	I Go Back	29-430	CB
Chesney, Kenny	I Go Back	20-382	ST

ARTIST	SONG TITLE	#	TYPE
Chesney, Kenny	I Lost It	29-434	CB
Chesney, Kenny	I Lost It	19-218	CSZ
Chesney, Kenny	I Remember	48-77	CB
Chesney, Kenny	I Will Stand	8-764	CB
Chesney, Kenny	I Will Stand	22-827	ST
Chesney, Kenny	I'm Alive	48-73	BKD
Chesney, Kenny	It Don't Happen Twice	22-589	ST
Chesney, Kenny	Keg In The Closet	23-131	CB
Chesney, Kenny	Live A Little	37-237	CB
Chesney, Kenny	Live Those Songs	48-84	CB
Chesney, Kenny	Live Those Songs	45-131	SC
Chesney, Kenny	Living In Fast Forward	29-32	CB
Chesney, Kenny	Living In Fast Forward	29-500	SC
Chesney, Kenny	Living In Fast Forward	29-704	ST
Chesney, Kenny	Lot Of Things Different a	29-424	CB
Chesney, Kenny	Lot Of Things Different a	25-360	MM
Chesney, Kenny	Lot Of Things Different a	18-327	ST
Chesney, Kenny	Me And You	1-322	CB
Chesney, Kenny	Me And You	7-338	MM
Chesney, Kenny	Me And You	4-402	SC
Chesney, Kenny	Never Gonna Feel That Way Again	48-78	CB
Chesney, Kenny	Never Wanted Nothing More	30-469	CB
Chesney, Kenny	No Shoes No Shirt No Problem	29-426	CB
Chesney, Kenny	No Shoes No Shirt No Problem	25-620	MM
Chesney, Kenny	No Shoes No Shirt No Problem	19-58	ST
Chesney, Kenny	No Shoes No Shirt No Problem	32-297	THM
Chesney, Kenny	Noise	49-390	DCK
Chesney, Kenny	On the Coast of Somewhere Beautiful	49-786	TU
Chesney, Kenny	Out Last Night	37-38	CB
Chesney, Kenny	Outta Here	48-83	CB
Chesney, Kenny	Pirate Flag	44-327	SSC
Chesney, Kenny	Reality	44-380	BKD
Chesney, Kenny	Save It For A Rainy Day	45-135	KRG
Chesney, Kenny	She Gets That Way	1-328	CB
Chesney, Kenny	She Gets That Way	48-86	CB
Chesney, Kenny	She Thinks My Tractor's Sexy	19-195	CB
Chesney, Kenny	She Thinks My Tractor's Sexy	5-803	SC
Chesney, Kenny	She Thinks My Tractor's Sexy	22-374	ST
Chesney, Kenny	She's Got It All	1-324	CB
Chesney, Kenny	She's Got It All	7-662	CHM
Chesney, Kenny	She's Got It All	22-616	ST
Chesney, Kenny	Some People Change	48-87	CB
Chesney, Kenny	Somebody's Callin'	1-319	CB
Chesney, Kenny	Somewhere In The Sun	48-82	CB
Chesney, Kenny	Somewhere With You	37-233	CB
Chesney, Kenny	Summertime	29-573	CB
Chesney, Kenny	Summertime	37-311	SC
Chesney, Kenny	Ten With A Two	48-89	CB

ARTIST	SONG TITLE	#	TYPE
Chesney, Kenny	That's Why I'm Here	8-234	CB
Chesney, Kenny	That's Why I'm Here	7-746	CHM
Chesney, Kenny	That's Why I'm Here	22-773	ST
Chesney, Kenny	There Goes My Life	22-2	CB
Chesney, Kenny	There Goes My Life	19-674	ST
Chesney, Kenny	This Is Our Moment	37-330	CB
Chesney, Kenny	Til It's Gone	45-128	BKD
Chesney, Kenny	Tin Man the	1-318	CB
Chesney, Kenny	Tin Man the	15-603	ST
Chesney, Kenny	Welcome To The Fishbowl	48-76	BKD
Chesney, Kenny	What I Need To Do	29-428	CB
Chesney, Kenny	What I Need To Do	13-812	CHM
Chesney, Kenny	What I Need To Do	22-529	ST
Chesney, Kenny	What I Need To Do (Radio Version)	23-375	SC
Chesney, Kenny	Whatever It Takes	45-130	CB
Chesney, Kenny	When I Close My Eyes	1-323	CB
Chesney, Kenny	When I Close My Eyes	15-583	RIS
Chesney, Kenny	When I See This Bar	44-333	SSC
Chesney, Kenny	When I See This Bar	45-127	BKD
Chesney, Kenny	When I Think About Leaving	29-436	CB
Chesney, Kenny	When The Sun Goes Down	20-165	ST
Chesney, Kenny	Who You'd Be Today	23-479	CB
Chesney, Kenny	Woman With You the	22-66	CB
Chesney, Kenny	Woman With You the	20-499	ST
Chesney, Kenny	You And Tequila	37-217	CB
Chesney, Kenny	You Had Me From Hello	19-207	CB
Chesney, Kenny	You Had Me From Hello	7-885	CHT
Chesney, Kenny	You Had Me From Hello	14-623	SC
Chesney, Kenny	You Had Me From Hello	22-750	ST
Chesney, Kenny	You Save Me	30-56	CB
Chesney, Kenny	Young	29-427	CB
Chesney, Kenny	Young	25-122	MM
Chesney, Kenny	Young	16-325	ST
Chesney, Kenny	Down The Road	36-259	PHM
Chesnutt, Mark	Almost Goodbye	1-354	CB
Chesnutt, Mark	Almost Goodbye	2-819	SC
Chesnutt, Mark	As The Honky Tonk Turns	3-576	SC
Chesnutt, Mark	Blame It On Texas	8-845	CB
Chesnutt, Mark	Broken Promised Land	1-350	CB
Chesnutt, Mark	Brother Jukebox	8-848	CB
Chesnutt, Mark	Brother Jukebox	20-398	MH
Chesnutt, Mark	Brother Jukebox	17-212	NA
Chesnutt, Mark	Bubba Shot The Jukebox	8-846	CB
Chesnutt, Mark	Bubba Shot The Jukebox	10-761	JVC
Chesnutt, Mark	Bubba Shot The Jukebox	6-112	MM
Chesnutt, Mark	Down In Tennessee	6-846	MM
Chesnutt, Mark	Down In Tennessee	3-420	SC
Chesnutt, Mark	Fallin' Never Felt So Good	9-413	CB
Chesnutt, Mark	Goin' Through The Big	8-847	CB

ARTIST	SONG TITLE	#	TYPE
	"D"		
Chesnutt, Mark	Goin' Through The Big "D"	3-369	SC
Chesnutt, Mark	Goin' Through The Big "D"	33-116	CB
Chesnutt, Mark	Gonna Get A Life	1-357	CB
Chesnutt, Mark	Gonna Get A Life	2-659	SC
Chesnutt, Mark	Hard Secret To Keep a	23-120	CB
Chesnutt, Mark	I Am A Saint	22-98	CB
Chesnutt, Mark	I Don't Want To Miss A Thing	8-865	CB
Chesnutt, Mark	I Don't Want To Miss A Thing	10-166	SC
Chesnutt, Mark	I Don't Want To Miss A Thing	22-702	ST
Chesnutt, Mark	I Just Wanted You To Know	1-355	CB
Chesnutt, Mark	I Just Wanted You To Know	2-93	SC
Chesnutt, Mark	I Might Even Quit Lovin' You	8-471	CB
Chesnutt, Mark	I Might Even Quit Lovin' You	22-786	ST
Chesnutt, Mark	I Want My Baby Back	18-331	ST
Chesnutt, Mark	I'll Think Of Something	2-333	SC
Chesnutt, Mark	I'm In Love With A Married Woman	25-564	MM
Chesnutt, Mark	I'm In Love With A Married Woman	18-800	ST
Chesnutt, Mark	I'm In Love With A Married Woman	32-157	THM
Chesnutt, Mark	It Sure Is Monday	8-844	CB
Chesnutt, Mark	It Sure Is Monday	6-761	MM
Chesnutt, Mark	It Sure Is Monday	17-246	NA
Chesnutt, Mark	It Wouldn't Hurt To Have Wings	22-455	SC
Chesnutt, Mark	It Wouldn't Hurt To Have Wings	8-849	CB
Chesnutt, Mark	It's A Little Too Late	1-358	CB
Chesnutt, Mark	It's A Little Too Late	4-502	SC
Chesnutt, Mark	It's Not Over	8-232	CB
Chesnutt, Mark	It's Not Over	7-727	CHM
Chesnutt, Mark	It's Not Over	22-755	ST
Chesnutt, Mark	Let It Rain	7-627	CHM
Chesnutt, Mark	Lord Loves The Drinking Man	20-451	ST
Chesnutt, Mark	Lost In The Feeling	14-122	CB
Chesnutt, Mark	Lovin' Her Was Easier (Than Any...	49-739	CB
Chesnutt, Mark	Old Country	6-124	MM
Chesnutt, Mark	Old Country	2-712	SC
Chesnutt, Mark	Old Flames Have New Names	1-351	CB
Chesnutt, Mark	Old Flames Have New Names	6-534	MM
Chesnutt, Mark	Old Flames Have New Names	2-365	SC
Chesnutt, Mark	Rollin' With The Flow	30-542	CB
Chesnutt, Mark	She Dreams	6-610	MM
Chesnutt, Mark	She Dreams	2-569	SC

ARTIST	SONG TITLE	#	TYPE
Chesnutt, Mark	She Never Got Me Over You	37-48	CB
Chesnutt, Mark	She Was	34-374	CB
Chesnutt, Mark	She Was	25-131	MM
Chesnutt, Mark	She Was	16-333	ST
Chesnutt, Mark	Thank God For Believers	4-826	SC
Chesnutt, Mark	Thank God For Believers	22-618	ST
Chesnutt, Mark	Things To Do In Wichita	48-706	BKD
Chesnutt, Mark	This Heartache Never Sleeps	7-886	CHT
Chesnutt, Mark	This Heartache Never Sleeps	14-610	SC
Chesnutt, Mark	This Heartache Never Sleeps	22-742	ST
Chesnutt, Mark	Too Cold At Home	1-346	CB
Chesnutt, Mark	Trouble	7-147	MM
Chesnutt, Mark	Trouble	3-542	SC
Chesnutt, Mark	Wherever You Are	10-150	SC
Chesnutt, Mark	Wherever You Are	22-675	ST
Chesnutt, Mark	Woman Sensuous Woman	6-504	MM
Chesnutt, Mark	Woman Sensuous Woman	2-220	SC
Chesnutt, Mark	Wrong Place Wrong Time	1-359	CB
Chesnutt, Mark	Wrong Place Wrong Time	22-905	ST
Chesnutt, Mark	Your Love Is A Miracle	1-349	CB
Chess	Show - Anthem	15-239	PR
Chess	Show - Anthem	17-697	PS
Chess	Show - Heaven Help My Heart	17-698	PS
Chess	Show - I Know Him So Well	17-701	PS
Chess	Show - Lullaby	17-703	PS
Chess	Show - No Contest	17-699	PS
Chess	Show - Nobody's Side	17-696	PS
Chess	Show - One Night In Bangkok	17-694	PS
Chess	Show - Pity The Child	17-702	PS
Chess	Show - Someone Else's Story	17-798	PS
Chess	Show - Story Of Chess	17-691	PS
Chess	Show - Terrace Dust	17-695	PS
Chess	Show - Where I Want To Be	17-692	PS
Chess	Show - You And I	15-238	PR
Chess	Show - You And I	17-700	PS
Chess	Show - You And I (Reprise)	17-704	PS
Chevelle	Closure	19-851	PHM
Chevelle	Red the	23-161	PHM
Chevelle	Send The Pain Below	32-180	THM
Chi-Lites	Have You Seen Her	16-565	P
Chi-Lites	Oh Girl	27-317	DK
Chi-Lites	Oh Girl	12-883	P
Chic	Dance Dance Dance	9-754	SAV

ARTIST	SONG TITLE	#	TYPE
Chic	Good Times	27-300	DK
Chic	Good Times	9-759	SAV
Chic	Le Freak	11-626	DK
Chic	Le Freak	16-567	P
Chic	Le Freak	20-370	SC
Chicago	25 Or 6 To 4	13-219	P
Chicago	Along Comes A Woman	24-197	SC
Chicago	Baby What A Big Surprise	35-135	CB
Chicago	Baby What A Big Surprise	17-508	SC
Chicago	Colour My World	13-220	P
Chicago	Colour My World	2-841	SC
Chicago	Does Anybody Really Know..	4-878	SC
Chicago	Does Anybody Really Know...	34-37	CB
Chicago	Hard Habit To Break	12-816	P
Chicago	I Don't Wanna Live Without Your..	17-77	DK
Chicago	Jolly Old Saint Nicholas - xmas	45-255	SC
Chicago	Saturday In The Park	34-25	CB
Chicago	Saturday in The Park	17-78	DK
Chicago	Saturday In The Park	13-218	P
Chicago	Saturday In The Park	4-286	SC
Chicago	Xmas - Jolly Old Saint Nicholas	45-255	SC
Chicago	You're The Inspiration	2-857	SC
Chicago - Show	Show - All I Care About	19-515	STS
Chicago - Show	Show - All That Jazz	25-590	MM
Chicago - Show	Show - All That Jazz	18-809	PS
Chicago - Show	Show - All That Jazz	19-511	STS
Chicago - Show	Show - Cell Block Tango	19-513	STS
Chicago - Show	Show - Class	19-523	STS
Chicago - Show	Show - Funny Honey	16-48	MM
Chicago - Show	Show - Funny Honey	19-512	STS
Chicago - Show	Show - Little Bit Of Good a	19-516	STS
Chicago - Show	Show - Me And My Baby	19-520	STS
Chicago - Show	Show - Mr. Cellophane	16-50	MM
Chicago - Show	Show - My Own Best Friend	19-519	STS
Chicago - Show	Show - Nowadays	19-524	STS
Chicago - Show	Show - Razzle Dazzle	16-47	MM
Chicago - Show	Show - Razzle Dazzle	19-522	STS
Chicago - Show	Show - Roxie	19-518	STS
Chicago - Show	Show - We Both Reached For The...	19-517	STS
Chicago - Show	Show - When You're Good To Mama	16-49	MM
Chicago - Show	Show - When You're Good To Mama	19-514	STS
Chicago - Show	Show – Mr. Cellophane	19-521	STS
Chico	Chico Time	30-701	CB
Chico	Chico Time	30-701	SF
Chiffons	He's So Fine	10-333	KC
Chiffons	One Fine Day	27-531	DK
Chiffons	One Fine Day	6-161	MM

ARTIST	SONG TITLE	#	TYPE
Chiffons	One Fine Day	13-63	P
Chiffons	Sweet Talkin' Guy	10-330	KC
Chiffons	Sweet Talkin' Guy	6-561	MM
Chiffons	Sweet Talkin' Guy	4-33	SC
Childs, Andy	Broken	24-79	SC
Chilites	I Found Sunshine	35-116	CB
Chimes	Once In A While	7-67	MM
Chingy	Right Thurr **	25-713	MM
Chingy	Right Thurr ** (Radio Version)	21-789	SC
Chipmunk Christmas	Xmas - Chipmunk Christmas Song	18-733	CB
Chitty Chitty Bang	Chitty Chitty Bang Bang	9-809	SAV
Chitty Chitty Bang	Show - Chitty Chitty Bang Bang	9-809	SAV
Chitty Chitty Bang	Show - Truly Scrumptious	9-810	SAV
Chordettes	Lollipop	19-609	MH
Chordettes	Lollipop	9-287	SC
Chordettes	Mr. Sandman	33-230	CB
Chordettes	Mr. Sandman	11-833	DK
Chordettes	Mr. Sandman	13-67	P
Chords	Sh-Boom	27-507	DK
Chords	Sh-Boom Life Could Be A Dream	12-658	P
Chorus Line	Show - Dance Ten Looks Three	7-371	MM
Chorus Line	Show - Nothing	5-649	SC
Chorus Line	Show - One	6-243	MM
Chorus Line	Show - One	15-237	PR
Chorus Line	Show - What I Did For Love	12-282	DK
Chorus Line	Show - What I Did For Love	6-324	MM
Chris Weaver Band	Everything I Used To Be	41-69	PHN
Chris Weaver Band	So Damn Beautiful	41-64	PHN
Chris Weaver Band	Standing In Line	39-62	PHN
Chris Weaver Band	Travelin' On	42-1	PHN
Christain Christmas	Xmas - Angels We Have Heard On High	10-448	BF
Christain Christmas	Xmas - Deck The Halls	10-436	BF
Christain Christmas	Xmas - It Came Upon a Midnight Clea	10-437	BF
Christain Christmas	Xmas - Joy To The World	10-435	BF
Christain Christmas	Xmas - Silent Night	10-438	BF
Christian Christmas	Xmas - Away In A Manger	10-443	BF
Christian Christmas	Xmas - First Noel the	10-442	BF
Christian Christmas	Xmas - God Rest Ye Merry Gentlemen	10-449	BF
Christian Christmas	Xmas - Hark The Herald Angels Sing	10-447	BF
Christian Christmas	Xmas - Oh Come All Ye Faithful	10-439	BF
Christian Christmas	Xmas - Oh Come Oh Come Emmanuel	10-444	BF
Christian Christmas	Xmas - Oh Holy Night	10-434	BF
Christian Christmas	Xmas - Oh Little Town of	10-440	BF

ARTIST	SONG TITLE	#	TYPE
	Bethlehem		
Christian Christmas	Xmas - We Three Kings	10-445	BF
Christian Christmas	Xmas - We Wish You A Merry Xmas	10-441	BF
Christian Christmas	Xmas - What Child Is This	10-446	BF
Christie, Lou	Gypsy Cried the	6-649	MM
Christie, Lou	Lightnin' Strikes	34-24	CB
Christie, Lou	Lightnin' Strikes	11-357	DK
Christie, Lou	Lightnin' Strikes	10-666	SF
Christie, Lou	Two Faces Have I	43-213	MM
Christmas	Carol Of The Bells	45-747	CB
Christmas	Ding Dong Merrily On High - xmas	45-14	KV
Christmas	Friendly Beast the - xmas	45-12	KV
Christmas	I Saw Three Ships - xmas	45-13	KV
Christmas	Xmas - All I Want For Xmas Is My Tw	14-517	SC
Christmas	Xmas - Angels From The Realms/Glory	10-257	SC
Christmas	Xmas - Angels We Have Heard on High	14-419	SC
Christmas	Xmas - Ave Maria (in Latin)	22-289	TT
Christmas	Xmas - Away In A Manger	25-365	MM
Christmas	Xmas - Away In A Manger	14-409	SC
Christmas	Xmas - Blue Christmas	12-583	P
Christmas	Xmas - Carol Of The Bells	45-747	CB
Christmas	Xmas - Christ Was Born On Xmas Day	25-368	MM
Christmas	Xmas - Christmas Song the	6-292	MM
Christmas	Xmas - Christmas Song the	12-591	P
Christmas	Xmas - Christmas Time Is Here	25-372	MM
Christmas	Xmas - Deck The Halls	17-206	CMC
Christmas	Xmas - Deck The Halls	11-728	DK
Christmas	Xmas - Deck The Halls	21-273	NCG
Christmas	Xmas - Deck The Halls	14-407	SC
Christmas	Xmas - Ding Dong Merrily On High	45-14	KV
Christmas	Xmas - Do You Hear What I Hear	25-366	MM
Christmas	Xmas - Do You Hear What I Hear	10-253	SC
Christmas	Xmas - Feliz Navidad	6-297	MM
Christmas	Xmas - First Noel the	17-202	CMC
Christmas	Xmas - First Noel the	6-288	MM
Christmas	Xmas - First Noel the	21-269	NCG
Christmas	Xmas - First Noel the	12-585	P
Christmas	Xmas - First Noel the	10-251	SC
Christmas	Xmas - Friendly Beast the	45-12	KV
Christmas	Xmas - Frosty The	17-210	CMC
Christmas	Xmas - Frosty The Snowman	11-239	DK
Christmas	Xmas - Frosty The Snowman	21-277	NCG
Christmas	Xmas - Frosty The Snowman	12-577	P
Christmas	Xmas - Frosty The Snowman	14-513	SC
Christmas	Xmas - God Rest Ye Merry Gentlemen	17-204	CMC
Christmas	Xmas - God Rest Ye Merry Gentlemen	21-271	NCG
Christmas	Xmas - God Rest Ye Merry Gentlemen	14-418	SC
Christmas	Xmas - Good Christain Friends Rejoi	10-243	SC
Christmas	Xmas - Hark The Herald Angels Sing	25-363	MM
Christmas	Xmas - Hark The Herald Angels Sing	14-443	SC
Christmas	Xmas - Have Yourself A Merry Little	12-500	P
Christmas	Xmas - Here Comes Santa Claus	14-524	SC
Christmas	Xmas - Holly Jolly Christmas	6-298	MM
Christmas	Xmas - I Heard The Bells On Xmas..	25-373	MM
Christmas	Xmas - I Saw Mommy Kissing Santa	17-53	DK
Christmas	Xmas - I Saw Mommy Kissing Santa	12-593	P
Christmas	Xmas - I Saw Mommy Kissing Santa..	6-295	MM
Christmas	Xmas - I Saw Mommy Kissing Santa..	14-516	SC
Christmas	Xmas - I Saw Three Ships	45-13	KV
Christmas	Xmas - I Wonder As I Wander	14-414	SC
Christmas	Xmas - I'll Be Home For Christmas	12-579	P
Christmas	Xmas - I'll Be Home For Christmas	14-541	SC
Christmas	Xmas - It Came Upon A Midnight Clea	25-364	MM
Christmas	Xmas - It Came Upon a Midnight Clea	14-413	SC
Christmas	Xmas - It's Beginning To Look A Lot	10-456	BF
Christmas	Xmas - It's Beginning To Look A Lot	6-299	MM
Christmas	Xmas - It's Beginning To Look A Lot	12-582	P
Christmas	Xmas - It's Beginning To Look A Lot	14-510	SC
Christmas	Xmas - Jingle Bell Rock	27-469	DK
Christmas	Xmas - Jingle Bell Rock	12-589	P
Christmas	Xmas - Jingle Bells	10-450	BF
Christmas	Xmas - Jingle Bells	17-209	CMC

ARTIST	SONG TITLE	#	TYPE
Christmas	Xmas - Jingle Bells	11-238	DK
Christmas	Xmas - Jingle Bells	6-286	MM
Christmas	Xmas - Jingle Bells	21-276	NCG
Christmas	Xmas - Jingle Bells	12-642	P
Christmas	Xmas - Jingle Bells	14-514	SC
Christmas	Xmas - Jolly Old St. Nicholas	14-512	SC
Christmas	Xmas - Joy To The World	17-199	CMC
Christmas	Xmas - Joy To The World	27-474	DK
Christmas	Xmas - Joy To The World	25-369	MM
Christmas	Xmas - Joy To The World	21-266	NCG
Christmas	Xmas - Joy To The World	10-249	SC
Christmas	Xmas - Let It Snow	6-290	MM
Christmas	Xmas - Let It Snow	12-588	P
Christmas	Xmas - Let There Be Peace On Earth	10-245	SC
Christmas	Xmas - Little Drummer Boy	26-358	DK
Christmas	Xmas - Little Drummer Boy	6-294	MM
Christmas	Xmas - Little Drummer Boy	12-578	P
Christmas	Xmas - Mistletoe And Holly	6-296	MM
Christmas	Xmas - Oh Christmas Tree	14-406	SC
Christmas	Xmas - Oh Come All Ye Faithful	25-376	MM
Christmas	Xmas - Oh Come All Ye Faithful	14-410	SC
Christmas	Xmas - Oh Come Oh Come Emmanuel	14-412	SC
Christmas	Xmas - Oh Holy Night	17-208	CMC
Christmas	Xmas - Oh Holy Night	25-370	MM
Christmas	Xmas - Oh Holy Night	21-275	NCG
Christmas	Xmas - Oh Holy Night	14-415	SC
Christmas	Xmas - Oh Holy Night	22-290	TT
Christmas	Xmas - Oh Little Town of Bethlehem	17-205	CMC
Christmas	Xmas - Oh Little Town Of Bethlehem	25-367	MM
Christmas	Xmas - Oh Little Town of Bethlehem	21-272	NCG
Christmas	Xmas - Oh Little Town of Bethlehem	12-594	P
Christmas	Xmas - Oh Little Town Of Bethlehem	10-255	SC
Christmas	Xmas - Oh Tannenbaum	12-592	P
Christmas	Xmas - Rockin' Around the Xmas Tree	12-590	P
Christmas	Xmas - Rudolph the Red-Nosed Rein	10-453	BF
Christmas	Xmas - Rudolph The Red-Nosed Rein	11-727	DK
Christmas	Xmas - Santa Claus is	10-457	BF
Christmas	Coming/Town		
Christmas	Xmas - Santa Claus is Coming/Town	12-266	DK
Christmas	Xmas - Santa Claus Is Coming/Town	12-580	P
Christmas	Xmas - Santa Claus Is Coming/Town	14-515	SC
Christmas	Xmas - Silent Night	17-200	CMC
Christmas	Xmas - Silent Night	25-362	MM
Christmas	Xmas - Silent Night	21-267	NCG
Christmas	Xmas - Silent Night	12-586	P
Christmas	Xmas - Silent Night	14-408	SC
Christmas	Xmas - Silver Bells	14-522	SC
Christmas	Xmas - Sleigh Bells	10-454	BF
Christmas	Xmas - Sleigh Ride	27-471	DK
Christmas	Xmas - Sleigh Ride	12-581	P
Christmas	Xmas - Twelve Days Of Christmas	10-455	BF
Christmas	Xmas - Twelve Days Of Christmas	17-207	CMC
Christmas	Xmas - Twelve Days Of Christmas	17-54	DK
Christmas	Xmas - Twelve Days Of Christmas	6-287	MM
Christmas	Xmas - Twelve Days Of Christmas	21-274	NCG
Christmas	Xmas - Twelve Days Of Christmas	12-587	P
Christmas	Xmas - Twelve Days Of Christmas	14-405	SC
Christmas	Xmas - We Three Kings	25-374	MM
Christmas	Xmas - We Three Kings	14-417	SC
Christmas	Xmas - We Wish You A Merry Xmas	17-203	CMC
Christmas	Xmas - We Wish You A Merry Xmas	17-52	DK
Christmas	Xmas - We Wish You A Merry Xmas	21-270	NCG
Christmas	Xmas - We Wish You A Merry Xmas	12-584	P
Christmas	Xmas - We Wish You a Merry Xmas	14-525	SC
Christmas	Xmas - What Child Is This	17-201	CMC
Christmas	Xmas - What Child Is This	25-371	MM
Christmas	Xmas - What Child Is This	21-268	NCG
Christmas	Xmas - What Child Is This	14-416	SC
Christmas	Xmas - White Christmas	12-576	P
Christmas	Xmas - Winter Wonderland	10-452	BF
Christmas	Xmas - Winter Wonderland	14-523	SC
Christy Minstrels	This Land Is Your Land	7-349	MM
Christy, Lauren	Color Of The Night	16-628	MM
Christy, Lauren	Magazine	7-718	PHM
Chuck Wagon Gang	Gospel - Someone To Talk To	16-27	SX

ARTIST	SONG TITLE	#	TYPE
Chuck Wagon&Wheels	Beauty's In The Eye Of The Beerhold	14-725	CB
Chuck Wagon&Wheels	Play That Country Music	14-163	CB
Chumbawamba	Amnesia	10-140	SC
Chumbawamba	Duet - Tubthumping	7-692	PHM
Chumbawamba	Tubthumping	30-214	CB
Chumbawamba	Tubthumping	7-692	PHM
Chumbawamba	Tubthumping	10-116	SC
Church, Claudia	Home In My Heart	8-480	CB
Church, Claudia	It's All Your Fault	19-241	SC
Church, Claudia	What's The Matter With You Baby	8-331	CB
Church, Claudia	What's The Matter With You Baby	22-735	ST
Church, Eric	Cold One	46-621	SBI
Church, Eric	Creepin'	46-616	ASK
Church, Eric	Drink In My Hand	44-211	CB
Church, Eric	Give Me Back My Home Town	43-125	ASK
Church, Eric	Guys Like Me	30-314	CB
Church, Eric	Hell On The Heart	46-619	CB
Church, Eric	His Kinda Money (My Kinda Love)	46-618	CB
Church, Eric	Homeboy	46-620	CB
Church, Eric	How 'Bout You	29-194	CB
Church, Eric	Hungover And Hard Up	48-7	KCD
Church, Eric	Jack Daniels	49-525	BKD
Church, Eric	Lightning	46-623	ST
Church, Eric	Love Your Love The Most	44-217	CB
Church, Eric	Mr. Misunderstood	46-10	BKD
Church, Eric	Outsiders	46-617	ASK
Church, Eric	Over When It's Over	46-615	ASK
Church, Eric	Sinners Like Me	30-21	CB
Church, Eric	Smoke A Little Smoke	37-61	CB
Church, Eric	Springsteen	43-11	ASK
Church, Eric	Talladega	46-622	SBI
Church, Eric	Two Pink Lines	30-246	CB
Ciara	Like A Boy	30-495	CB
Ciara	Promise	30-270	CB
Ciara & Missy Elliott	1, 2 Step	37-98	SC
Ciara & Petey Pablo	Goodies	37-105	SC
Cinderella	Don't Know What You Got (Till It's.	23-54	MH
Cinderella	Don't Know What You Got (Till It's)	24-676	SC
Cinderella	I'm Coming Home	10-501	DA
Cinderella	I'm Coming Home	10-625	SF
Cinderella	Nobody's Fool	17-87	DK
Cinderella	Nobody's Fool	5-486	SC
Cinderella	Shake Me	21-772	SC
Citizen King	Better Days	7-894	PHT
City High	Caramel	20-613	CB
City High	What Would You Do	18-541	TT
Civilles & Cole	Deeper Love a	9-841	SAV
Clanton & Rockets	Just A Dream	3-513	SC
Clanton, Jimmy	Another Sleepless Night	47-564	DCK

ARTIST	SONG TITLE	#	TYPE
Clanton, Jimmy	Just A Dream	7-36	MM
Clanton, Jimmy	Venus In Blue Jeans	5-14	SC
Clapton & Cream	White Room	15-60	LE
Clapton, Eric	After Midnight	33-267	CB
Clapton, Eric	After Midnight	17-69	DK
Clapton, Eric	After Midnight	15-54	LE
Clapton, Eric	After Midnight	12-708	P
Clapton, Eric	Anything For Your Love	13-797	SGB
Clapton, Eric	Badge	13-805	SGB
Clapton, Eric	Before You Accuse Me	20-133	KB
Clapton, Eric	Before You Accuse Me	14-601	SC
Clapton, Eric	Believe In Life	15-819	CB
Clapton, Eric	Believe In Life	18-404	MM
Clapton, Eric	Blue Eyes Blue	5-783	SC
Clapton, Eric	Change The World	33-388	CB
Clapton, Eric	Change The World	28-202	DK
Clapton, Eric	Change The World	13-803	SGB
Clapton, Eric	Cocaine	9-343	AH
Clapton, Eric	Cocaine	28-204	DK
Clapton, Eric	Cocaine	15-53	LE
Clapton, Eric	Cocaine	20-310	MH
Clapton, Eric	Cocaine	2-139	SC
Clapton, Eric	Crossroads	20-147	KB
Clapton, Eric	Don't Think Twice It's Alright	19-795	SGB
Clapton, Eric	Have You Ever Loved A Woman	13-799	SGB
Clapton, Eric	I Shot The Sheriff	16-847	DK
Clapton, Eric	I Shot The Sheriff	15-55	LE
Clapton, Eric	I Shot The Sheriff	13-166	P
Clapton, Eric	It's In The Way That You Use It	46-203	SC
Clapton, Eric	Lay Down Sally	11-670	DK
Clapton, Eric	Lay Down Sally	15-56	LE
Clapton, Eric	Layla - Electric Version	13-804	SGB
Clapton, Eric	Layla (Slow Version)	15-58	LE
Clapton, Eric	Let It Grow	13-801	SGB
Clapton, Eric	Let It Rain	5-589	SC
Clapton, Eric	Lonely Stranger	13-793	SGB
Clapton, Eric	Miss You	13-795	SGB
Clapton, Eric	Motherless Child	46-204	SC
Clapton, Eric	My Father's Eyes	10-131	SC
Clapton, Eric	No Alibis	13-796	SGB
Clapton, Eric	Old Love	10-485	DA
Clapton, Eric	Only You Know And I Know	13-802	SGB
Clapton, Eric	Outside Woman Blues	13-792	SGB
Clapton, Eric	Promises	5-477	SC
Clapton, Eric	Running On Faith	4-272	SC
Clapton, Eric	Running On Faith	13-798	SGB
Clapton, Eric	San Franciscan Nights	15-555	LE
Clapton, Eric	She's Gone	5-282	SC
Clapton, Eric	Superman Inside	15-302	THM
Clapton, Eric	Swalbr	13-794	SGB
Clapton, Eric	Tales Of Great Ulysses	13-791	SGB
Clapton, Eric	Tears In Heaven	11-79	JTG
Clapton, Eric	Tears In Heaven	15-59	LE

ARTIST	SONG TITLE	#	TYPE
Clapton, Eric	Tulsa Time	15-61	LE
Clapton, Eric	Why Does Love Got To Be So Sad	13-800	SGB
Clapton, Eric	Willie & The Hand Jive	26-360	DK
Clapton, Eric	Willie & The Hand Jive	15-62	LE
Clapton, Eric	Wonderful Tonight	15-57	LE
Clapton, Eric	Wonderful Tonight	6-436	MM
Clapton, Eric	Wonderful Tonight	28-203	SF
Clara	Like A Boy	30-495	CB
Clara	Promise	30-270	CB
Clark Family Exp.	Going Away	17-571	ST
Clark Family Exp.	Meanwhile Back At The Ranch	19-219	CSZ
Clark Family Exp.	Standing Still	15-332	CB
Clark Family Exp.	Standing Still	15-194	ST
Clark Family Exp.	To Quote Shakespeare	17-605	CB
Clark Family Exp.	To Quote Shakespeare	16-14	ST
Clark, Brandi	Girl Next Door (Inst)	49-791	BKD
Clark, Claudine	Party Lights	6-648	MM
Clark, D	Raindrops	35-35	CB
Clark, Dee	Hey Little Girl	9-734	SAV
Clark, Dee	Nobody But You	14-342	SC
Clark, Dee	Raindrops	6-679	MM
Clark, J	You Da Man	32-8	THM
Clark, Jameson	Still Smokin'	16-695	ST
Clark, Jameson	You Da Man	18-335	ST
Clark, Jameson	You Da Man	32-6	THM
Clark, Petula	Don't Sleep In The Subway	9-87	PS
Clark, Petula	Don't Sleep In The Subway	20-63	SC
Clark, Petula	Downtown	6-350	MM
Clark, Petula	Downtown	9-84	PS
Clark, Petula	Downtown	10-661	SF
Clark, Petula	I Couldn't Live Without Your Love	6-53	SC
Clark, Petula	I Know A Place	9-88	PS
Clark, Petula	My Love	19-619	MH
Clark, Petula	My Love	9-85	PS
Clark, Petula	My Love	5-12	SC
Clark, Petula	Sign Of The Times the	9-86	PS
Clark, Petula	This Is My Song	10-589	SF
Clark, Roy	Come Live With Me & Be My Love	9-578	SAV
Clark, Roy	Honeymoon Feelin'	5-160	SC
Clark, Roy	I Never Picked Cotton	5-820	SC
Clark, Roy	I Never Picked Cotton	46-624	SC
Clark, Roy	If I Had To Do It All Over Again	29-647	SC
Clark, Roy	Shotgun Wedding	10-620	SF
Clark, Roy	Thank God And Greyhound	4-580	SC
Clark, Roy	Tips Of My Fingers	19-393	SC
Clark, Roy	Yesterday (Guitar Version)	45-656	TBR
Clark, Roy	Yesterday When I Was Young	8-290	CB
Clark, Roy	Yesterday When I Was Young	10-752	JVC

ARTIST	SONG TITLE	#	TYPE
Clark, Roy	Yesterday When I Was Young	4-264	SC
Clark, Sanford	Fool the	5-846	SC
Clark, Terri	Better Things To Do	19-302	MH
Clark, Terri	Better Things To Do	6-822	MM
Clark, Terri	Damn Right	29-184	CB
Clark, Terri	Dirty Girl	30-353	CB
Clark, Terri	Emotional Girl	7-588	CHM
Clark, Terri	Everytime I Cry	34-330	CB
Clark, Terri	Everytime I Cry	7-852	CHT
Clark, Terri	Everytime I Cry	22-713	ST
Clark, Terri	Getting There	29-349	CB
Clark, Terri	Getting There	15-612	ST
Clark, Terri	Girls Lie Too	35-434	CB
Clark, Terri	Girls Lie Too	20-339	ST
Clark, Terri	I Just Wanna Be Mad	33-193	CB
Clark, Terri	I Just Wanna Be Mad	25-352	MM
Clark, Terri	I Just Wanna Be Mad	18-209	ST
Clark, Terri	I Think The World Needs A Drink	22-76	CB
Clark, Terri	I Wanna Do It All	35-423	CB
Clark, Terri	I Wanna Do It All	25-709	MM
Clark, Terri	I Wanna Do It All	19-370	ST
Clark, Terri	I Wanna Do It All	32-412	THM
Clark, Terri	If I Were You	34-327	CB
Clark, Terri	If I Were You	7-196	MM
Clark, Terri	If I Were You	4-207	SC
Clark, Terri	In My Next Life	36-551	CB
Clark, Terri	Just The Same	7-631	CHM
Clark, Terri	Just The Same	10-99	SC
Clark, Terri	Just The Same	22-605	ST
Clark, Terri	Little Gasoline a	14-110	CB
Clark, Terri	No Fear	14-148	CB
Clark, Terri	No Fear	14-786	ST
Clark, Terri	Northern Girl	38-1	CB
Clark, Terri	Now That I Found You	8-463	CB
Clark, Terri	Now That I Found You	7-744	CHM
Clark, Terri	One Of The Guys	23-393	CB
Clark, Terri	Poor Poor Pitiful Me	7-387	MM
Clark, Terri	Poor Poor Pitiful Me	4-595	SC
Clark, Terri	She Didn't Have Time	23-303	CB
Clark, Terri	She Didn't Have Time	29-610	ST
Clark, Terri	Something You Should've Said	7-327	MM
Clark, Terri	Suddenly Single	4-403	SC
Clark, Terri	Three Mississippi	20-217	CB
Clark, Terri	Three Mississippi	25-571	MM
Clark, Terri	Three Mississippi	19-2	ST
Clark, Terri	Three Mississippi	32-267	THM
Clark, Terri	Unsung Hero	10-193	SC
Clark, Terri	When Boy Meets Girl	7-169	MM
Clark, Terri	When Boy Meets Girl	3-665	SC
Clark, Terri	You're Easy On The Eyes	8-158	CB
Clarkson & Guari	Duet - Timeless	25-633	MM
Clarkson & Guari	Timeless	25-633	MM

ARTIST	SONG TITLE	#	TYPE
Clarkson, Kelly	Addicted	47-687	CB
Clarkson, Kelly	All I Ever Wanted	47-692	CB
Clarkson, Kelly	Already Gone	47-690	CB
Clarkson, Kelly	Because Of You	29-254	SC
Clarkson, Kelly	Before Your Love	25-332	MM
Clarkson, Kelly	Before Your Love	36-363	SC
Clarkson, Kelly	Before Your Love	32-102	THM
Clarkson, Kelly	Behind These Hazel Eyes	30-134	PT
Clarkson, Kelly	Breakaway	20-543	PHM
Clarkson, Kelly	Breakaway	30-712	SF
Clarkson, Kelly	Breaking Your Own Heart	47-695	KV
Clarkson, Kelly	Don't Waste Your Time	47-688	CB
Clarkson, Kelly	I Do Not Hook Up	47-691	CB
Clarkson, Kelly	I Hate Myself For Losing You	47-693	KV
Clarkson, Kelly	If I Can't Have You	47-697	KV
Clarkson, Kelly	Let Your Tears Fall	48-436	KCD
Clarkson, Kelly	Low	19-648	CB
Clarkson, Kelly	Low	20-223	MM
Clarkson, Kelly	Low	32-394	THM
Clarkson, Kelly	Miss Independent	25-623	MM
Clarkson, Kelly	Miss Independent	36-324	PS
Clarkson, Kelly	Miss Independent	23-337	SC
Clarkson, Kelly	Miss Independent	32-279	THM
Clarkson, Kelly	Moment Like This a	33-425	CB
Clarkson, Kelly	Moment Like This a	25-333	MM
Clarkson, Kelly	Moment Like This a	18-581	NS
Clarkson, Kelly	Moment Like This a	18-341	PHM
Clarkson, Kelly	Moment Like This a	36-357	SC
Clarkson, Kelly	My Life Would Suck Without You	47-689	CB
Clarkson, Kelly	Never Again	30-483	CB
Clarkson, Kelly	Piece By Piece	48-653	DCK
Clarkson, Kelly	Since You've Been Gone	22-349	CB
Clarkson, Kelly	Sober	30-571	CB
Clarkson, Kelly	Some Kind Of Miracle	47-698	SC
Clarkson, Kelly	Someone	48-438	KCD
Clarkson, Kelly	Stranger (What Doesn't Kill You)	39-49	ASK
Clarkson, Kelly	Take You High	48-437	KCD
Clarkson, Kelly	Tie It Up	43-151	BKD
Clarkson, Kelly	Trouble With Love Is the	35-288	CB
Clarkson, Kelly	Underneath The Tree	45-773	KV
Clarkson, Kelly	Walk Away	30-152	PT
Clarkson, Kelly	Walk Away	30-703	SF
Clarkson, Kelly	War Paint	47-696	KV
Clarkson, Kelly	White Christmas	45-793	KV
Clarkson, Kelly	Xmas - Underneath The Tree	45-773	KV
Clarkson, Kelly	Xmas - White Christmas	45-793	KV
Clarkson, Kelly	You Can't Win	48-505	KVD
Clarkson, Kelly	You Love Me	47-694	KV
Clash	Rock The Casbah	11-752	DK
Clash	Rock The Casbah	5-137	SC
Clash	Should I Stay Or Should I Go	27-196	DK
Clash	Should I Stay Or Should I Go	12-800	P
Clash	Should I Stay Or Should I Go	10-530	SF
Class Of 99	Another Brick In The Wall	16-206	PHT
Classics	Till Then	7-312	MM
Classics IV	Halloween - Spooky	16-289	TT
Classics IV	Spooky	34-47	CB
Classics IV	Spooky	26-343	DK
Classics IV	Spooky	6-688	MM
Classics IV	Spooky	16-289	TT
Classics IV	Stormy	6-789	MM
Classics IV	Traces	12-319	DK
Claypool, Philip	Circus Leaving Town	46-625	SC
Claypool, Philip	Feel Like Makin' Love	7-81	MM
Claypool, Philip	Perfect World	46-626	CB
Claypool, Philip	Strength Of A Woman the	4-127	SC
Clean Living	In Heaven There Is No Beer	2-416	SC
Cleftones	Heart And Soul	48-390	KRG
Cleftones	Little Girl Of Mine	25-179	MM
Cleveland, Mel	Fifteen Beers Ago	47-499	HM
Cliff, Jimmy	Games People Play	46-630	HSW
Cliff, Jimmy	Harder They Come the	12-702	P
Cliff, Jimmy	Harder They Come the	46-633	HSW
Cliff, Jimmy	I Can See Clearly Now	16-575	SC
Cliff, Jimmy	I Can See Clearly Now	8-607	TT
Cliff, Jimmy	Many Rivers To Cross	46-628	SC
Cliff, Jimmy	Raggae Nights	46-631	XPK
Cliff, Jimmy	We Are All One	46-629	SC
Cliff, Jimmy	Wild World	46-632	HSG
Cliff, Jimmy	Wonderful World Beautiful People	46-627	MFK
Cliff, Richard	Bachelor Boy	48-759	P
Cliff, Richard	I Just Don't Have A Heart	48-767	P
Cliff, Richard	Living Doll	48-765	P
Cliff, Richard	Miss You Nights	48-776	P
Cliff, Richard	Summer Holiday	48-752	P
Cliff, Richard	Travellin' Light	48-768	P
Cliff, Richard	We Don't Talk Anymore	48-758	P
Climax	Precious & Few	27-597	DK
Climax	Precious & Few	2-839	SC
Climax Blues Band	Couldn't Get it Right	4-876	SC
Cline, Patsy	Always	22-184	CB
Cline, Patsy	Always	6-732	MM
Cline, Patsy	Always	5-162	SC
Cline, Patsy	Anytime	16-359	CB
Cline, Patsy	Back In Baby's Arms	6-721	MM
Cline, Patsy	Back In Baby's Arms	22-256	SC
Cline, Patsy	Bill Bailey Won't You Please Come..	22-185	CB
Cline, Patsy	Blue Moon Of Kentucky	2-628	SC
Cline, Patsy	Church, A Courtroom And Then Goodbye a	45-485	CB
Cline, Patsy	Crazy	16-864	DK

ARTIST	SONG TITLE	#	TYPE
Cline, Patsy	Crazy	6-725	MM
Cline, Patsy	Crazy	8-667	SAV
Cline, Patsy	Crazy	10-506	SF
Cline, Patsy	Crazy Arms	6-749	MM
Cline, Patsy	Crazy Arms	13-448	P
Cline, Patsy	Dear God	45-487	CB
Cline, Patsy	Eyes Of A Child the	6-731	MM
Cline, Patsy	Faded Love	6-730	MM
Cline, Patsy	Faded Love	2-636	SC
Cline, Patsy	Fingerprints	45-484	CB
Cline, Patsy	Foolin' Around	43-176	CB
Cline, Patsy	Gospel - Dear God	43-107	CB
Cline, Patsy	Gospel - Just A Closer Walk With Thee	45-493	CB
Cline, Patsy	Half As Much	45-496	RCA
Cline, Patsy	Have You Ever Been Lonely	22-186	CB
Cline, Patsy	Have You Ever Been Lonely	13-319	P
Cline, Patsy	He Called Me Baby	22-187	CB
Cline, Patsy	He Called Me Baby	6-729	MM
Cline, Patsy	Heart You Break May Be Your Own the	45-488	CB
Cline, Patsy	Heartaches	3-183	CB
Cline, Patsy	Honky Tonk Merry Go Round	45-489	CB
Cline, Patsy	How Can I Face Tomorrow	45-495	CB
Cline, Patsy	I Can See An Angel	45-492	CB
Cline, Patsy	I Can't Forget You	45-491	CB
Cline, Patsy	I Cried All The Way To The Altar	45-486	CB
Cline, Patsy	I Don't Wanta	45-482	CB
Cline, Patsy	I Fall To Pieces	16-763	DK
Cline, Patsy	I Fall To Pieces	6-733	MM
Cline, Patsy	I Fall To Pieces	13-344	P
Cline, Patsy	I Fall To Pieces	2-11	SC
Cline, Patsy	I Love You Honey	47-511	VH
Cline, Patsy	I Love You So Much It Hurts	22-188	CB
Cline, Patsy	I'm Blue Again	45-514	MM
Cline, Patsy	I've Loved And Lost Again	45-515	MM
Cline, Patsy	If I Could See The World Thru/Eyes.	22-189	CB
Cline, Patsy	Imagine That	19-395	SC
Cline, Patsy	In Care Of The Blues	8-819	CB
Cline, Patsy	In Care Of The Blues	45-510	CB
Cline, Patsy	Just A Closer Walk With Thee	45-493	CB
Cline, Patsy	Just Out Of Reach	45-498	MM
Cline, Patsy	Leavin' On Your Mind	26-509	DK
Cline, Patsy	Leavin' On Your Mind	6-724	MM
Cline, Patsy	Leavin' On Your Mind	2-23	SC
Cline, Patsy	Let The Teardrops Fall	45-483	CB
Cline, Patsy	Life's Railway To Heaven	45-494	CB
Cline, Patsy	Love Letters In The Sand	45-517	JTG

ARTIST	SONG TITLE	#	TYPE
Cline, Patsy	Lovesick Blues	45-502	KV
Cline, Patsy	Pick Me Up On Your Way Down	22-197	CB
Cline, Patsy	Poor Man's Roses a	22-183	CB
Cline, Patsy	Poor Man's Roses a	6-726	MM
Cline, Patsy	Rose Of San Antone	45-503	KV
Cline, Patsy	San Antonio Rose	22-190	CB
Cline, Patsy	Seven Lonely Days	45-501	LE
Cline, Patsy	Shake Rattle And Roll	45-511	DIG
Cline, Patsy	She's Got You	17-9	DK
Cline, Patsy	She's Got You	13-373	P
Cline, Patsy	So Wrong	22-196	CB
Cline, Patsy	So Wrong	16-588	MM
Cline, Patsy	Someday	6-722	MM
Cline, Patsy	South Of The Border	22-191	CB
Cline, Patsy	Stop Look And Listen	45-490	CB
Cline, Patsy	Stop The World	45-509	CB
Cline, Patsy	Strange	6-723	MM
Cline, Patsy	Stranger In My Arms	45-505	LE
Cline, Patsy	Stupid Cupid	45-516	MM
Cline, Patsy	Sweet Dreams	11-203	DK
Cline, Patsy	Sweet Dreams	12-415	P
Cline, Patsy	There He Goes	22-192	CB
Cline, Patsy	Three Cigarettes In An Ashtray	22-193	CB
Cline, Patsy	Tra Le La Le La Triangle	5-697	SC
Cline, Patsy	Turn The Cards Slowly	45-513	MM
Cline, Patsy	Walkin' After Midnight	16-823	DK
Cline, Patsy	Walkin' After Midnight	13-415	P
Cline, Patsy	Walkin' After Midnight	9-484	SAV
Cline, Patsy	Wayward Wind the	22-194	CB
Cline, Patsy	When I Get Through With You	45-504	CB
Cline, Patsy	When My Dreamboat Comes Home	45-512	MM
Cline, Patsy	When You Need A Laugh	45-506	OZP
Cline, Patsy	Who Can I Count On	45-500	ABA
Cline, Patsy	Why Can't He Be You	6-727	MM
Cline, Patsy	You Made Me Love You	45-507	KVD
Cline, Patsy	You Made Me Love You	45-481	ABA
Cline, Patsy	You Took Him Off My Hands	22-195	CB
Cline, Patsy	You Took Him Off My Hands	6-734	MM
Cline, Patsy	You Were Only Fooling	45-499	ABA
Cline, Patsy	You're Stronger Than Me	6-728	MM
Cline, Patsy	Your Cheatin' Heart	45-497	PS
Clingy	Right Thurr	32-313	THM
Clinton, George	Atomic Dog	14-354	MH
Clipse	When The Last Time **	32-130	THM
Clooney, Rosemary	Anniversary Song	15-400	MM
Clooney, Rosemary	Come On-A-My Place	4-187	SC
Clooney, Rosemary	Don't Worry 'Bout Me	11-456	DK
Clooney, Rosemary	This Ole House	2-241	SC
Clooney, Rosemary & Betty	Duet - Sisters	49-768	MM

ARTIST	SONG TITLE	#	TYPE
Clooney, Rosemary & Betty	Sisters - duet	49-768	MM
Clovers	Chains Of Love	10-274	SS
Clovers	Devil Or Angel	25-559	MM
Club 7	Never Had A Dream Come True	18-528	TT
Clydesiders	My Love Is Like A Red Red Rose	48-766	P
Coasters	Along Came Jones	6-687	MM
Coasters	Along Came Jones **	23-23	SC
Coasters	Charlie Brown	17-107	DK
Coasters	Charlie Brown	13-270	P
Coasters	Charlie Brown	29-829	SC
Coasters	Down In Mexico	43-83	VH
Coasters	Framed	6-681	MM
Coasters	Little Egypt	10-698	JVC
Coasters	Poison Ivy	11-509	DK
Coasters	Poison Ivy	10-697	JVC
Coasters	Poison Ivy	6-160	MM
Coasters	Searchin'	11-412	DK
Coasters	Searchin'	10-694	JVC
Coasters	Yakety Yak	35-12	CB
Coasters	Yakety Yak	26-144	DK
Coasters	Yakety Yak	10-696	JVC
Coasters	Young Blood	11-413	DK
Coasters	Young Blood	10-695	JVC
Coasters	Young Blood	12-905	P
Cobra Starship & Gym...	Duet - Snakes On A Plane	30-65	PHM
Cobra Starship & Gym...	Snakes On A Plane - duet	30-65	PHM
Cochran & Wariner	Duet - What If I Said	8-143	CB
Cochran & Wariner	Duet - What If I Said	22-761	ST
Cochran & Wariner	What If I Said	8-143	CB
Cochran & Wariner	What If I Said	22-761	ST
Cochran, Anita	Good Times	9-426	CB
Cochran, Anita	I Cry	16-35	ST
Cochran, Anita	Will You Be Here	8-96	CB
Cochran, Anita	You With Me	14-103	CB
Cochran, Eddie	C'Mon Everybody	27-494	DK
Cochran, Eddie	Sitting In The Balcony	16-863	DK
Cochran, Eddie	Summertime Blues	11-188	DK
Cochran, Eddie	Three Steps To Heaven	10-550	SF
Cochran, Tammy	Angels In Waiting	33-144	CB
Cochran, Tammy	Angels In Waiting	9-869	ST
Cochran, Tammy	I Cry	25-74	MM
Cochran, Tammy	If You Can	9-415	CB
Cochran, Tammy	If You Can	22-566	ST
Cochran, Tammy	Life Happened	33-195	CB
Cochran, Tammy	Life Happened	25-300	MM
Cochran, Tammy	Life Happened	17-585	ST
Cochran, Tammy	Love Won't Let Me	18-592	ST
Cochran, Tammy	Love Won't Let Me	32-155	THM
Cochran, Tammy	So What	14-115	CB
Cochran, Tammy	What Kind Of A Woman Would I Be	19-55	ST
Cochran, Tammy	What Kind Of Woman Would I Be	25-616	MM

ARTIST	SONG TITLE	#	TYPE
Cocker & Warnes	Duet - Up Where We Belong	26-138	DK
Cocker & Warnes	Duet - Up Where We Belong	6-227	MM
Cocker & Warnes	Duet - Up Where We Belong	13-190	P
Cocker & Warnes	Up Where We Belong	6-227	MM
Cocker & Warnes	Up Where We Belong	13-190	P
Cocker, Joe	Ain't No Sunshine	49-536	KVD
Cocker, Joe	Cry Me A River	21-442	LE
Cocker, Joe	Feelin' Alright	12-918	P
Cocker, Joe	Feeling Alright	21-440	LE
Cocker, Joe	High Time We Went	48-540	DK
Cocker, Joe	Letter the	18-254	DK
Cocker, Joe	Letter the	21-439	LE
Cocker, Joe	Letter the	15-803	SC
Cocker, Joe	Night Calls	45-621	DCK
Cocker, Joe	She Came In Through The Bathroom	5-683	SC
Cocker, Joe	Unchain My Heart	34-53	CB
Cocker, Joe	Unchain My Heart	21-436	LE
Cocker, Joe	When The Night Comes	5-339	SC
Cocker, Joe	With A Little Help From My Friends	33-320	CB
Cocker, Joe	With A Little Help From My Friends	17-60	DK
Cocker, Joe	With A Little Help From My Friends	21-441	LE
Cocker, Joe	You Are So Beautiful	26-277	DK
Cocker, Joe	You Are So Beautiful	21-443	LE
Cocker, Joe	You Are So Beautiful	13-131	P
Cocker, Joe	You Can Leave Your Hat On	21-438	LE
Coe & Anderson	Duet - Get A Little Dirt On You	18-319	CB
Coe & Anderson	Get A Little Dirt On You	18-319	CB
Coe & Jones	Duet - This Bottle In My Hand	18-322	CB
Coe & Jones	Duet - This Bottle In My Hand	48-425	CB
Coe & Jones	This Bottle In My Hand	18-322	CB
Coe & Jones	This Bottle In My Hand - duet	48-425	CB
Coe, David Allan	Divers Do It Deeper	18-323	CB
Coe, David Allan	Hank Williams Junior Junior	18-321	CB
Coe, David Allan	If That Ain't Country	18-317	CB
Coe, David Allan	Jack Daniels If You Please	18-313	CB
Coe, David Allan	Jimmy Buffett Don't Live In Key West	48-426	HC
Coe, David Allan	Just To Prove My Love To You	18-316	CB
Coe, David Allan	Long Haired Redneck	18-311	CB
Coe, David Allan	Longhaired Redneck	5-857	SC
Coe, David Allan	Mona Lisa Lost Her Smile	18-312	CB
Coe, David Allan	Mona Lisa Lost Her Smile	14-315	SC
Coe, David Allan	Now I Lay Me Down To	18-320	CB

ARTIST	SONG TITLE	#	TYPE
	Cheat		
Coe, David Allan	Ride the	18-310	CB
Coe, David Allan	She Used To Love Me A Lot	14-250	SC
Coe, David Allan	Tennessee Whiskey	18-315	CB
Coe, David Allan	What Made You Change Your Mind	18-318	CB
Coe, David Allan	Willie Waylon And Me	18-314	CB
Coe, David Allan	You Never Even Called Me By My..	18-309	CB
Coe, David Allan	You Never Even Called Me By My..	13-414	P
Coe, David Allan	You Never Even Called Me By My…	17-243	NA
Coffey, Kelly	At The End Of The Day	34-366	CB
Coffey, Kelly	At The End Of The Day	25-354	MM
Coffey, Kelly	At The End Of The Day	18-132	ST
Coffey, Kelly	Dance With My Father	20-475	ST
Coffey, Kelly	Texas Plates	19-538	ST
Coffey, Kelly	Whatever It Takes	25-522	MM
Coffey, Kelly	Whatever It Takes	18-795	ST
Coffey, Kelly	Whatever It Takes	32-192	THM
Coffey, Kelly	When You Lie Next To Me	33-150	CB
Coffey, Kelly	When You Lie Next To Me	25-73	MM
Coffey, Kelly	When You Lie Next To Me	16-329	ST
Cogan, Alma	Dreamboat	10-608	SF
Cohn, Marc	Silver Thunderbird	47-702	DCK
Cohn, Marc	True Companion	29-323	PS
Cohn, Mark	Paper Walls	24-19	SC
Cohn, Mark	Walking In Memphis	17-460	SC
Cold	Different Kind Of Pain a	29-277	PHM
Cold	Stupid Girl	19-602	CB
Cold	Stupid Girl	32-221	THM
Cold	Suffocate **	23-181	PHM
Coldplay	Clocks	35-283	CB
Coldplay	Clocks	25-542	MM
Coldplay	Clocks	23-162	PHM
Coldplay	Clocks	23-335	SC
Coldplay	Every Teardrop Is A Waterfall	48-257	MRH
Coldplay	Fix You	48-256	SC
Coldplay	God Put A Smile Upon Your Face	32-442	THM
Coldplay	Green Eyes	48-259	SBI
Coldplay	Hardest Part the	30-275	SC
Coldplay	Hardest Part the	30-694	SF
Coldplay	Head Full Of Dreams	48-415	BKD
Coldplay	Hurts Like Heaven	39-103	PHM
Coldplay	In My Place	25-307	MM
Coldplay	In My Place	18-588	NS
Coldplay	Life In Technicolor II	48-255	SC
Coldplay	Lost!	36-236	PHM
Coldplay	Lovers In Japan	36-271	PHM
Coldplay	Magic	46-187	BHK
Coldplay	Paradise	48-258	MRH

ARTIST	SONG TITLE	#	TYPE
Coldplay	Scientist the	20-233	MM
Coldplay	Scientist the	32-295	THM
Coldplay	Speed Of Sound	23-316	CB
Coldplay	Speed Of Sound	30-140	PT
Coldplay	Talk	29-248	SC
Coldplay	Trouble	48-254	SC
Coldplay	Violet Hill	36-533	CB
Coldplay	Viva La Vida	36-490	CB
Coldplay	Yellow	21-640	TT
Cole, Keyshia	Heaven Sent	36-534	CB
Cole, Keyshia	I Remember	36-465	CB
Cole, Nat "King"	Answer Me My Love	28-511	DK
Cole, Nat "King"	Around The World	46-374	ZM
Cole, Nat "King"	Ballerina	29-458	LE
Cole, Nat "King"	Blossom Fell a	29-454	LE
Cole, Nat "King"	Darling Je Vous Aime Beaucoup	46-347	CB
Cole, Nat "King"	Dinner For One Please James	46-372	SBI
Cole, Nat "King"	Don't Get Around Much Anymore	46-354	SC
Cole, Nat "King"	Embraceable You	9-799	SAV
Cole, Nat "King"	Fascination	46-373	TU
Cole, Nat "King"	For All We Know	46-358	LE
Cole, Nat "King"	For Sentimental Reasons	28-515	DK
Cole, Nat "King"	For Sentimental Reasons	12-880	P
Cole, Nat "King"	For Sentimental Reasons	4-360	SC
Cole, Nat "King"	Gee Baby Ain't I Good To You	46-364	PS
Cole, Nat "King"	I Found A Million Dollar Baby	46-366	PS
Cole, Nat "King"	I Love You For Sentimental Reasons	11-572	DK
Cole, Nat "King"	I Should Care	45-603	OZP
Cole, Nat "King"	I'm In The Mood For Love	28-514	DK
Cole, Nat "King"	I'm Through With Love	46-359	MM
Cole, Nat "King"	If I May	46-349	CB
Cole, Nat "King"	It's Only A Paper Moon	11-222	DK
Cole, Nat "King"	It's Only A Paper Moon	15-838	MM
Cole, Nat "King"	L-O-V-E	12-501	P
Cole, Nat "King"	L-O-V-E	19-781	SGB
Cole, Nat "King"	Let There Be Love	29-457	LE
Cole, Nat "King"	Looking Back	46-350	CB
Cole, Nat "King"	Love Is A Many Splendored Thing	16-773	DK
Cole, Nat "King"	Love Letters	46-375	ZM
Cole, Nat "King"	Lover Come Back To Me	46-352	SAV
Cole, Nat "King"	Makin' Whoopie	46-363	PS
Cole, Nat "King"	Mona Lisa	11-297	DK
Cole, Nat "King"	Mona Lisa	12-525	P
Cole, Nat "King"	My Baby Just Cares For Me	46-360	MM
Cole, Nat "King"	My Foolish Heart	46-371	SAV
Cole, Nat "King"	Nature Boy	46-353	SAV
Cole, Nat "King"	Perfidia	46-357	KV

ARTIST	SONG TITLE	#	TYPE
Cole, Nat "King"	Pretend	29-459	LE
Cole, Nat "King"	Pretend	5-229	SC
Cole, Nat "King"	Quizas, Quizas, Quizas	46-369	SAV
Cole, Nat "King"	Ramblin' Rose	11-97	DK
Cole, Nat "King"	Ramblin' Rose	29-452	LE
Cole, Nat "King"	Ramblin' Rose	2-197	SC
Cole, Nat "King"	Ramblin' Rose	17-327	SS
Cole, Nat "King"	Route 66	46-355	DK
Cole, Nat "King"	Send For Me	46-351	CB
Cole, Nat "King"	Smile	29-453	LE
Cole, Nat "King"	Somewhere Along The Way	46-348	CB
Cole, Nat "King"	Stardust	43-226	CB
Cole, Nat "King"	Straighten Up And Fly Right	12-574	P
Cole, Nat "King"	Sweet Lorraine	46-356	KV
Cole, Nat "King"	Tenderly	46-370	SAV
Cole, Nat "King"	That Sunday That Summer	45-875	DCK
Cole, Nat "King"	There Is No Greater Love	46-368	PS
Cole, Nat "King"	This Is All I Ask Of You	46-367	PS
Cole, Nat "King"	Those Lazy Hazy Crazy Days Of Summer	29-456	LE
Cole, Nat "King"	Those Lazy Hazy Crazy Days Of Summer	11-304	DK
Cole, Nat "King"	Those Lazy Hazy Crazy Days Of Summer	35-19	CB
Cole, Nat "King"	Too Young	12-526	P
Cole, Nat "King"	Unforgettable	7-187	MM
Cole, Nat "King"	Very Thought Of You the	16-413	PR
Cole, Nat "King"	Very Thought Of You the	46-365	PS
Cole, Nat "King"	Walkin' My Baby Back Home	15-576	MM
Cole, Nat "King"	When I Fall In Love	29-455	LE
Cole, Nat "King"	Xmas - Christmas Song the	14-539	SC
Cole, Nat "King"	Xmas - Deck The Halls	14-298	MM
Cole, Nat "King"	You Stepped Out Of A Dream	46-361	MM
Cole, Nat "King"	Answer Me My Love	34-12	CB
Cole, Nat "King"	Rambling Rose	33-212	CB
Cole, Nat & Natalie	Duet - Unforgettable	12-127	DK
Cole, Nat & Natalie	Duet - When I Fall In Love	24-548	SC
Cole, Nat & Natalie	Unforgettable	12-127	DK
Cole, Nat & Natalie	When I Fall In Love	24-548	SC
Cole, Natalie	Dindi	48-643	KV
Cole, Natalie	Fascination	18-245	DK
Cole, Natalie	I'm In The Mood For Love	12-156	DK
Cole, Natalie	Inseparable	17-429	KC
Cole, Natalie	Inseparable	7-475	MM
Cole, Natalie	Inseparable	29-329	PS
Cole, Natalie	It Might As Well Be Spring	11-797	DK
Cole, Natalie	LOVE	36-361	SC
Cole, Natalie	Miss You Like Crazy	33-328	CB
Cole, Natalie	Miss You Like Crazy	6-352	MM
Cole, Natalie	Miss You Like Crazy	2-271	SC
Cole, Natalie	Orange Colored Sky	15-549	MM
Cole, Natalie	Our Love	24-342	SC
Cole, Natalie	Pink Cadillac	9-220	PT
Cole, Natalie	Pink Cadillac	3-552	SC
Cole, Natalie	Smile Like Yours a	10-105	SC
Cole, Natalie	Take A Look	24-267	SC
Cole, Natalie	This Will Be	34-71	CB
Cole, Natalie	Very Thought Of You the	15-575	MM
Cole, Paula	I Don't Want To Wait	15-501	SC
Cole, Paula	I Don't Want To Wait	49-509	PHG
Cole, Paula	Me	5-192	SC
Cole, Paula	Me	49-512	PHM
Cole, Paula	Where Have All The Cowboys Gone	10-689	HH
Cole, Paula	Where Have All The Cowboys Gone	24-638	SC
Collective Soul	Counting The Days	30-819	CB
Collective Soul	Counting The Days	30-819	PHM
Collective Soul	December	3-496	SC
Collective Soul	Precious Declaration	34-55	CB
Collective Soul	Run	7-810	PHT
Collie, Mark	Born To Love You	2-350	SC
Collie, Mark	Even The Man In The Moon Is Cryin	17-163	JVC
Collie, Mark	Even The Man In The Moon Is Cryin'	2-334	SC
Collie, Mark	Lipstick Don't Lie	7-236	MM
Collie, Mark	Love To Burn	16-644	MM
Collie, Mark	Steady As She Goes	3-631	SC
Collie, Mark	Three Words Two Hearts One Night	6-848	MM
Collins & Baskey	Duet - Easy Lover	49-310	BC
Collins & Baskey	Easy Lover - duet	49-310	BC
Collins & Martin	Duet - Separate Lives	20-306	CB
Collins & Martin	Duet - Separate Lives	6-235	MM
Collins & Martin	Separate Lives	20-306	CB
Collins & Martin	Separate Lives	6-235	MM
Collins, Jim	My First Last One And Only	8-413	CB
Collins, Jim	Next Step the	8-145	CB
Collins, Judy	Both Sides Now	11-630	DK
Collins, Judy	Send In The Clowns	12-517	P
Collins, Judy	Someday Soon	11-439	DK
Collins, Phil	Against All Odds	44-7	CBEP
Collins, Phil	All Of My Life	44-16	SBI
Collins, Phil	Another Day In Paradise	44-6	CBEP
Collins, Phil	Both Sides Of The Story	44-21	SC
Collins, Phil	Can't Stop Loving You	25-398	MM
Collins, Phil	Can't Stop Loving You	23-339	SC
Collins, Phil	Can't Turn Back The Years	44-20	SC
Collins, Phil	Dance Into The Light	24-367	SC

ARTIST	SONG TITLE	#	TYPE	ARTIST	SONG TITLE	#	TYPE
Collins, Phil	Do You Remember	44-9	LG	Combo Oldies	Wonder Who's Kissing Her Now	16-415	PR
Collins, Phil	Don't Let Him Steal Your Heart	44-23	SD	Comeaux, Amie	Moving Out	24-85	SC
Collins, Phil	Don't Lose My Number	21-600	SF	Commander Cody	Hot Rod Lincoln	3-553	SC
Collins, Phil	Easy Lover	44-25	TOS	Commodores	Brick House	14-363	MH
Collins, Phil	Everyday	2-117	SC	Commodores	Easy	11-699	DK
Collins, Phil	Father To Son	44-17	SBI	Commodores	Easy	10-364	KC
Collins, Phil	Find A Way To My Heart	44-12	PSJT	Commodores	Lady (You Bring Me Up)	16-832	DK
Collins, Phil	Groovy Kind Of Love a	11-225	DK	Commodores	Lady (You Bring Me Up)	14-358	MH
Collins, Phil	Groovy Kind Of Love a	21-743	MH	Commodores	Lady (You Bring Me Up)	15-44	SS
Collins, Phil	Heatwave (Love Is Like A)	44-32	SB	Commodores	Still	26-472	DK
Collins, Phil	I Can't Dance	44-26	AH	Commodores	Still	14-355	MH
Collins, Phil	I Don't Care Anymore	44-10	LG	Commodores	Three Times A Lady	35-145	CB
Collins, Phil	I Missed Again	44-22	SC	Commodores	Three Times A Lady	7-470	MM
Collins, Phil	I Wish It Would Rain	44-14	PSJT	Commodores	Three Times A Lady	21-617	SF
Collins, Phil	In The Air Tonight	44-11	MH	Common & Blige	Come Close To Me	32-88	THM
Collins, Phil	Invisible Touch	44-28	BS	Common & Blige	Duet - Come Close To Me	32-88	THM
Collins, Phil	It's In Your Eyes	44-19	SC	Common Feat&Blige	Come Close To Me	20-515	CB
Collins, Phil	Land Of Confusion	44-30	BS	Common Feat&Blige	Duet - Come Close To Me	20-515	CB
Collins, Phil	Long Long Way To Go	44-15	SBI	Como, Perry	And I Love You So	26-474	DK
Collins, Phil	Look Through My Eyes	44-31	KV	Como, Perry	And I Love You So	13-547	LE
Collins, Phil	Never A Time	44-27	BS	Como, Perry	And I Love You So	12-507	P
Collins, Phil	One More Night	20-296	CB	Como, Perry	As Time Goes By	16-789	DK
Collins, Phil	One More Night	24-70	SC	Como, Perry	As Time Goes By	13-542	LE
Collins, Phil	Something Happened on/to Heaven	24-256	SC	Como, Perry	Catch A Falling Star	13-543	LE
Collins, Phil	Sussuidio	20-299	CB	Como, Perry	Catch A Falling Star	20-776	PS
Collins, Phil	Take Me Home	44-13	PSJT	Como, Perry	Catch A Falling Star	2-198	SC
Collins, Phil	Thru' These Walls	44-33	SBI	Como, Perry	Delaware	49-40	ZVS
Collins, Phil	Tonight, Tonight, Tonight	44-29	BS	Como, Perry	Don't Let The Stars Get In Your Eye	25-267	MM
Collins, Phil	True Colors	16-221	MM	Como, Perry	Don't Let The Stars Get In Your Eye	20-779	PS
Collins, Phil	Two Hearts	44-8	LG	Como, Perry	Don't Let The Stars Get In Your Eye	10-607	SF
Collins, Phil	Why Can't it Wait 'Till Morning	44-34	SBI	Como, Perry	Hot Diggity	13-541	LE
Collins, Phil	You Can't Hurry Love	44-24	SF	Como, Perry	Hot Diggity	20-778	PS
Collins, Phil	You'll Be In My Heart	11-68	JTG	Como, Perry	Hot Diggity	3-509	SC
Collins, Phil	You'll Be In My Heart	13-783	SGB	Como, Perry	If	13-545	LE
Collins, Simon	Unconditional	36-232	PHM	Como, Perry	If	20-781	PS
Color Me Badd	Bells the	15-760	NU	Como, Perry	It's Impossible	33-217	CB
Color Me Badd	Earth The Sun The Rain the	4-338	SC	Como, Perry	It's Impossible	11-299	DK
Color Me Badd	I Wanna Sex You Up	34-105	CB	Como, Perry	It's Impossible	20-774	PS
Color Me Badd	I Wanna Sex You Up **	2-718	SC	Como, Perry	It's Impossible	4-352	SC
Colter & Jennings	Duet - Storms Never Last	44-66	KV	Como, Perry	It's Impossible	13-546	LE
Colter & Jennings	Storms Never Last - Duet	44-66	KV	Como, Perry	Love Makes The World Go Round	49-41	ZVS
Colter, Ben	Big Sweet John - parody	45-287	BS	Como, Perry	Magic Moments	16-411	PR
Colter, Ben	Parody - Big Sweet John	45-287	BS	Como, Perry	Make Someone Happy	25-260	MM
Colter, Jessi	I'm Not Lisa	8-204	CB	Como, Perry	Me And You And A Dog Named Boo	48-561	DK
Colter, Jessi	What's Happened To Blue Eyes	5-397	SC	Como, Perry	No Other Love	20-780	PS
Colvin, Shawn	Get Out Of This House	4-608	SC	Como, Perry	Papa Loves Mambo	20-782	PS
Colvin, Shawn	Sunny Came Home	16-398	PR	Como, Perry	Round and Round	13-548	LE
Colvin, Shawn	Sunny Came Home	15-564	SC	Como, Perry	Round And Round	20-773	PS
Colvin, Shawn	You And The Mona Lisa	7-696	PHM	Como, Perry	Some Enchanted Evening	11-303	DK

72

ARTIST	SONG TITLE	#	TYPE
Como, Perry	Some Enchanted Evening	13-544	LE
Como, Perry	Some Enchanted Evening	20-777	PS
Como, Perry	There Is No Xmas Like A Home Xmas	45-748	CB
Como, Perry	Till The End Of Time	11-575	DK
Como, Perry	Till The End Of Time	20-775	PS
Como, Perry	When You Were Sweet Sixteen	12-68	DK
Como, Perry	Xmas - Have Yourself A Merry Little	14-534	SC
Como, Perry	Xmas - There Is No Xmas Like A Home...	45-748	CB
Como, Perry	Xmas - There's No Place Like Home..	14-294	MM
Company B	Fascinated	18-376	AH
Con Air	Show - How Do I Live	18-180	DK
Concrete Blond	Joey	24-566	SC
Confederate RR	Bill's Laundromat Bar & Grill	7-79	MM
Confederate RR	Cowboy Cadillac	8-946	CB
Confederate RR	Cowboy Cadillac	14-607	SC
Confederate RR	Daddy Never Was The Cadillac Kind	2-221	SC
Confederate RR	Elvis & Andy	6-615	MM
Confederate RR	Elvis & Andy	2-360	SC
Confederate RR	Jesus And Mama	2-339	SC
Confederate RR	Keep On Rockin'	8-192	CB
Confederate RR	One You Love The Most	4-587	SC
Confederate RR	Queen Of Memphis	34-304	CB
Confederate RR	Queen Of Memphis	10-754	JVC
Confederate RR	Queen Of Memphis	6-307	MM
Confederate RR	Queen Of Memphis	12-458	P
Confederate RR	Queen Of Memphis	2-707	SC
Confederate RR	Summer In Dixie	17-262	NA
Confederate RR	That's What Brothers Do	25-14	MM
Confederate RR	That's What Brothers Do	16-10	ST
Confederate RR	Toss A Little Bone	14-105	CB
Confederate RR	Trashy Women	6-403	MM
Confederate RR	When And Where	6-804	MM
Confederate RR	When You Leave That Way	2-567	SC
Conlee, John	As Long As I'm Rockin' With You	47-617	CB
Conlee, John	Baby You're Something	5-570	SC
Conlee, John	Back Side Of Thirty	9-502	SAV
Conlee, John	Backside Of Thirty	8-829	CB
Conlee, John	Before My Time	47-620	CB
Conlee, John	Busted	17-400	DK
Conlee, John	Busted	17-303	NA
Conlee, John	Busted	5-124	SC
Conlee, John	Common Man	33-77	CB
Conlee, John	Friday Night Blues	17-296	NA
Conlee, John	Friday Night Blues	5-163	SC
Conlee, John	Got My Heart Set On You	29-690	SC
Conlee, John	I Don't Remember Loving You	20-283	SC

ARTIST	SONG TITLE	#	TYPE
Conlee, John	I'm Only In It For The Love	47-618	CB
Conlee, John	I'm Only In It For The Love	46-110	SC
Conlee, John	In My Eyes	47-615	CB
Conlee, John	Lady Lay Down	34-238	CB
Conlee, John	Lady Lay Down	4-813	SC
Conlee, John	Miss Emily's Picture	5-250	SC
Conlee, John	Old School	47-623	SRK
Conlee, John	Old School	47-622	PCD
Conlee, John	Rose Colored Glasses	33-44	CB
Conlee, John	Rose Colored Glasses	9-529	SAV
Conlee, John	She Can't Say That Anymore	47-619	CB
Conlee, John	Working Man	47-621	CB
Conlee, John	Years After You	47-616	CB
Conley, E.T.	Angel In Disguise	47-605	CB
Conley, E.T.	Bring Back Your Lovin' To Me	47-601	CB
Conley, E.T.	Hard Days & Honky Tonk Nights	47-776	SRK
Conley, E.T.	I Have Loved You Girl (But Not Like This	47-606	SC
Conley, E.T.	Love's The Only Voice	47-603	CB
Conley, E.T.	Shadow Of A Doubt	47-600	CB
Conley, E.T.	What She Is (Is A Woman In Love)	47-604	CB
Conley, E.T.	Your Love's On The Line	47-602	CB
Conley, Earl Thomas	Chance Of Lovin' You	5-823	SC
Conley, Earl Thomas	Don't Make It Easy For Me	12-473	P
Conley, Earl Thomas	Don't Make It Easy For Me	5-772	SC
Conley, Earl Thomas	Fire & Smoke	4-815	SC
Conley, Earl Thomas	Fire And Smoke	33-68	CB
Conley, Earl Thomas	Heavenly Bodies	29-701	SC
Conley, Earl Thomas	Holding Her And Loving You	16-582	SC
Conley, Earl Thomas	Holding Her And Loving You	33-72	CB
Conley, Earl Thomas	Honor Bound	5-529	SC
Conley, Earl Thomas	I Can't Win For Losing You	4-493	SC
Conley, Earl Thomas	Love Don't Care Who's Heart It Brea	12-405	P
Conley, Earl Thomas	Love Out Loud	34-288	CB
Conley, Earl Thomas	Nobody Falls Like A Fool	29-783	CB
Conley, Earl Thomas	Once In A Blue Moon	9-565	SAV
Conley, Earl Thomas	Once In A Blue Moon	5-153	SC
Conley, Earl Thomas	Right From The Start	29-64	CB
Conley, Earl Thomas	Right From The Start	5-134	SC
Conley, Earl Thomas	Somewhere Between Right & Wrong	13-538	P
Conley, Earl Thomas	Somewhere Between Right & Wrong	14-420	SC
Conley, Earl Thomas	What I'd Say	5-394	SC
Connick, Harry Jr.	But Not For Me	3-124	KB
Connick, Harry Jr.	But Not For Me	19-715	PS

73

ARTIST	SONG TITLE	#	TYPE
Connick, Harry Jr.	Don't Get Around Much Anymore	19-716	PS
Connick, Harry Jr.	For Once In My Life	48-504	KVD
Connick, Harry Jr.	Forever For Now	19-719	PS
Connick, Harry Jr.	Goodnight My Love	30-186	LE
Connick, Harry Jr.	Hear Me In The Harmony	24-369	SC
Connick, Harry Jr.	I Could Write A Book	19-722	PS
Connick, Harry Jr.	It Had To Be You	20-764	KB
Connick, Harry Jr.	It Had To Be You	30-188	LE
Connick, Harry Jr.	It Had To Be You	19-713	PS
Connick, Harry Jr.	It's All Right With Me	19-721	PS
Connick, Harry Jr.	Let's Call The Whole Thing Off	19-717	PS
Connick, Harry Jr.	Our Love Is Here To Stay	3-126	KB
Connick, Harry Jr.	Our Love Is Here To Stay	19-714	PS
Connick, Harry Jr.	Recipe For Love	19-720	PS
Connick, Harry Jr.	Show - Where Or When	12-293	DK
Connick, Harry Jr.	We Are In Love	30-189	LE
Connick, Harry Jr.	We Are In Love	19-718	PS
Connick, Harry Jr.	Whisper Your Name (If I Could)	30-187	LE
Contours	Do You Love Me	16-791	DK
Conway, Liana	Free	39-80	PHN
Cook, David	Light On	36-250	PHM
Cook, David	Time Of My Life the	36-492	CB
Cook, Elizabeth	Stupid Things	18-601	ST
Cook, Kristy Lee	15 Minutes Of Shame	36-213	PHM
Cooke, Sam	Another Saturday Night	46-639	PS
Cooke, Sam	Bring It On Home To Me	46-640	RB
Cooke, Sam	Chain Gang	46-634	SC
Cooke, Sam	Everybody Loves To Cha Cha Cha	46-641	RB
Cooke, Sam	Having A Party	46-636	LE
Cooke, Sam	Only Sixteen	46-637	LE
Cooke, Sam	Send Me Some Lovin'	12-897	P
Cooke, Sam	Shake the	46-638	LE
Cooke, Sam	Summertime	46-635	KV
Cooke, Sam	Twistin' The Night Away	10-244	SS
Cooke, Sam	Wonderful World	21-240	SC
Cooke, Sam	You Send Me	43-21	LEG
Cooke, Sam	You Send Me	21-236	SC
Cooke, Sam	You Send Me	10-188	SS
Cookies	Chains	9-707	SAV
Cookies	Don't Say Nothin' About My Baby	20-64	SC
Cooley, Spade	Shame On You	38-39	CB
Coolidge, Rita	All Time High	9-69	SC
Coolidge, Rita	Higher And Higher	15-493	DK
Coolidge, Rita	I'd Rather Leave While I'm In Love	10-517	SF
Coolio	Gansta's Paradise	34-120	CB
Cooper, Alice	Billion Dollar Babies	37-65	SC
Corbett, John	Good To Go	29-211	CB
Corbin, Easton	All Over The Road	44-269	KCDC
Corbin, Easton	Are You With Me	45-392	BKD

ARTIST	SONG TITLE	#	TYPE
Corbin, Easton	Baby Be My Love Song	46-642	SSC
Corbin, Easton	Baby Be My Love Song	45-410	BKD
Corbin, Easton	Clockwork	44-280	KCDC
Corbin, Easton	I Can't Love You Back	43-150	CB
Corbin, Easton	I Can't Love You Back	38-105	CB
Corbin, Easton	I Think Of You	41-54	PHN
Corbin, Easton	Little More Country Than That	37-230	CB
Corbin, Easton	Lovin' You Is Fun	44-392	KV
Corbin, Easton	Roll With It	44-209	CB
Corbin, Easton	Roll With It	45-391	CB
Corbin, Easton	This Feels a Lot Like Love	40-20	PHN
Corbin, Easton	Yup	48-452	KCD
Cornelius & Rose	Too Late To Turn Back Now	16-566	P
Cornelius & Rose	Too Late To Turn Back Now	5-376	SC
Cornelius & Rose	Treat Her Like A Lady	9-722	SAV
Cornelius & Rose	Treat Her Like A Lady	2-858	SC
Cornelius Brothers	It's Too Late To Turn Back Now	27-322	DK
Cornell, Kristina	Little Red Balloon	30-346	CB
Corrs	All The Love In The World	49-191	SBI
Corrs	Angel	49-189	MRH
Corrs	Breathless	20-621	CB
Corrs	Breathless	14-41	THM
Corrs	Breathless	18-510	TT
Corrs	Dreams	49-196	SF
Corrs	Give Me A Reason	49-199	SF
Corrs	I Never Loved You Anyway	49-195	SF
Corrs	Irresistible	49-198	SF
Corrs	Long Night	49-201	SF
Corrs	On My Father's Wings	49-194	SC
Corrs	One Night	49-200	SF
Corrs	Radio	49-197	SF
Corrs	Right Time the	49-193	SC
Corrs	Runaway	49-190	MM
Corrs	So Young	49-188	LG
Corrs	Summer Sunshine	23-565	MM
Corrs	What Can I Do	49-187	LG
Corrs	Would You Be Happier	49-192	SBI
Corrs & Bond	Duet - When The Stars Go Blue	18-413	MM
Corrs & Bond	When The Stars Go Blue	18-413	MM
Corrs & White	Duet - Looking Through Your Eyes	17-667	PR
Corrs & White	Looking Through Your Eyes	17-667	PR
Corrs & White	Show - Looking Thru Your Eyes (Duet	17-667	PR
Cosgrove, Amanda	About You Now	36-288	PHM
Cosgrove, Miranda	Kissin' U	44-143	BKD
Costa, Paul	Never On Sunday	12-498	P
Costello, Elvis	Alison (My Aim Is True)	9-327	AG
Costello, Elvis	Everyday I Write The	16-59	SC

ARTIST	SONG TITLE	#	TYPE
	Book		
Costello&Bacharach	She	13-784	SGB
Cotter, Brad	Can't Tell Me Nothin'	22-70	CB
Cotter, Brad	I Meant To	20-384	ST
Cotter, Brad	I Miss Me	22-88	CB
Cotton, Graham	Best Days	48-595	DK
Coty, Neal	Legacy	14-129	CB
Coty, Neal	Legacy	22-595	ST
Coty, Neal	Right Down Through The Middle Of Us	29-351	CB
Couch, Danny	Ah My Hawaii	6-830	MM
Counting Crows	Accidentally In Love	23-557	MM
Counting Crows	American Girls	18-425	CB
Counting Crows	Angels Of The Silences	24-555	SC
Counting Crows	Big Yellow Taxi	20-470	CB
Counting Crows	Big Yellow Taxi	32-137	THM
Counting Crows	Hanginaround	18-701	CB
Counting Crows	Hanginaround	8-527	PHT
Counting Crows	Hanginaround	17-541	SC
Counting Crows	Have You Seen Me Lately	18-698	CB
Counting Crows	Long December a	18-700	CB
Counting Crows	Mr. Jones	18-696	CB
Counting Crows	Raining In Baltimore	18-699	CB
Counting Crows	Round Here	18-697	CB
Counting Crows	Round Here	2-466	SC
Country Christmas	Xmas - Carol Of The Bells	18-738	CB
Country Christmas	Xmas - Christ Was Born on Xmas Day	18-734	CB
Country Christmas	Xmas - Do You Hear What I Hear	18-744	CB
Country Christmas	Xmas - Little Drummer Boy	18-739	CB
Country Christmas	Xmas - Marvelous Little Boy	18-740	CB
Country Christmas	Xmas - Mary's Little Boy Child	18-741	CB
Country Christmas	Xmas - My Favorite Things	18-732	CB
Country Christmas	Xmas - Nuttin' For Christmas	18-742	CB
Country Christmas	Xmas - Twas the Night Before Xmas	18-737	CB
Country Christmas	Xmas - Twas The Night Before Xmas	15-665	THM
Country Christmas	Xmas - We Need A Little Christmas	18-736	CB
Country Christmas	Xmas - We Three Kings	18-743	CB
Country Gentlemen	Fox On The Run	8-256	CB
Country Gentlemen	Nine Pound Hammer	8-254	CB
Coven	One Tin Soldier	9-356	MG
Coven	One Tin Soldier	9-11	MH
Cover Girls	Wishing On A Star	24-141	SC
Covington, Bucky	Different World a	30-310	CB
Covington, Bucky	Hold A Woman	39-63	PHN
Covington, Bucky	I Want My Life Back	39-52	CB
Covington, Bucky	It's Good To Be Us	30-556	CB
Covington, Bucky	Mexicoma	38-78	PHN

ARTIST	SONG TITLE	#	TYPE
Cowboy Copas	Alabam	8-711	CB
Cowboy Crush	Hillbilly Nation	29-205	CB
Cowboy Crush	Miss Difficult	30-554	CB
Cowboy Crush	Nobody Ever Died Of A Broken Heart	23-128	CB
Cowsills	Hair	11-794	DK
Cowsills	Indian Lake	14-462	SC
Cowsills	Rain The Park And Other Things	12-46	DK
Cox, Deborah	Absolutely Not	25-216	MM
Cox, Deborah	Nobody's Supposed To Be Here	7-840	PHM
Cox, Deborah	Play Your Part	32-277	THM
Cox, Deborah	Up & Down (In & Out)	32-17	THM
Cox, Deborah	Where Do We Go From Here	24-60	SC
Cox, Deborah	Who Do U Love	4-171	SC
Cox, Don	I Never Met A Woman I Didn't Like	4-164	SC
Cox, Michael	Angela Jones	29-816	SF
Cracker	Nothing To Believe In	24-59	SC
Craddock, Billy C	Ain't Nothin' Shakin'	46-648	CB
Craddock, Billy C	Broken Down In Tiny Pieces	4-825	SC
Craddock, Billy C	Dream Lover	46-647	CB
Craddock, Billy C	Easy As Pie	5-34	SC
Craddock, Billy C	I Cheated On A Good Woman	5-764	SC
Craddock, Billy C	I Love The Blues & the Boogie Woogie	46-645	CB
Craddock, Billy C	I'm Gonna Knock On Your Door	46-644	CB
Craddock, Billy C	One Last Kiss	45-830	VH
Craddock, Billy C	Rub It In	2-133	SC
Craddock, Billy C	Ruby Baby	35-374	CB
Craddock, Billy C	Still Thinkin' 'Bout You	5-663	SC
Craddock, Billy C	Sweet Magnolia Blossom	5-399	SC
Craddock, Billy C	Tear Fell a	46-646	CB
Craddock, Billy C	You Rubbed It In All Wrong	34-224	CB
Craddock, Billy C	You Rubbed It In All Wrong	20-278	SC
Craft, Paul "Earl"	Hey Girls This Is Earl I Didn't Die	14-159	CB
Craig, David	Don't Love you No More	30-774	SF
Craig, David	Hidden Agenda	34-169	CB
Craig, David	Hidden Agenda	32-173	THM
Cramer, Floyd	Bonaparte's Retreat	45-579	OZP
Cramer, Floyd	Piano Roll Blues	47-523	VH
Cranberries	Analyse	25-23	MM
Cranberries	Free To Decide	24-108	SC
Cranberries	Linger	33-351	CB
Cranberries	Linger	13-239	P
Cranberries	Salvation	7-570	THM
Cranberries	Salvation Song	13-602	P
Cranberries	Tomorrow	38-250	PHM
Cranberries	Zombie	16-633	MM
Crash Test Dummies	Afternoons & Coffee	30-773	SF

ARTIST	SONG TITLE	#	TYPE
	Spoons		
Crash Test Dummies	Mmm Mmm Mmm Mmm	12-163	DK
Crash Test Dummies	Mmm Mmm Mmm Mmm	8-605	TT
Crawford, Randy	Mad Over You	24-266	SC
Crawford, Randy	One Day I'll Fly Away	11-24	PX
Crawford, Randy	Street Life	11-18	PX
Cray, Robert	Foul Play	7-218	MM
Cray, Robert	Nothin' But A Woman	7-217	MM
Cray, Robert	Smoking Gun	15-311	SC
Cray, Robert	Smoking Gun	19-803	SGB
Crazy Elephant	Gimme Gimme Good Lovin'	9-363	MG
Crazy Elephant	Gimme Gimme Good Lovin'	4-212	SC
Crazy Town	Butterfly	34-121	CB
Crazy Town	Butterfly	16-475	MH
Crazy Town	Butterfly	12-392	PHM
Crazy Town	Butterfly	16-111	PRT
Crazy Town	Butterfly	18-550	TT
Crazy Town	Drowning	32-72	THM
Crazy World of Arthur Brown	Fire - Halloween	45-114	SC
Crazy World of Arthur Brown	Halloween - Fire	45-114	SC
Cream	Crossroads	15-19	SC
Cream	I Feel Free	5-882	SC
Cream	Outside Woman Blues	19-801	SGB
Cream	Strange Brew	12-327	DK
Cream	Sunshine Of Your Love	3-128	SC
Cream	Tales Of Brave Ulysses	19-279	SGB
Cream	White Room	11-650	DK
Cream	White Room	12-855	P
Creed	Bullets	18-295	CB
Creed	Don't Stop Dancing	25-432	MM
Creed	Don't Stop Dancing	32-64	THM
Creed	Higher	14-174	CB
Creed	Higher	5-793	SC
Creed	Higher	15-786	THM
Creed	I'm Eighteen	16-207	PHT
Creed	My Sacrifice	33-404	CB
Creed	My Sacrifice	25-38	MM
Creed	My Sacrifice	16-74	ST
Creed	One Last Breath	18-419	MM
Creed	Weathered	32-108	THM
Creed	What If	5-889	SC
Creed	What's This Life For	7-777	PHT
Creed	With Arms Wide Open	30-208	PHM
Creed	With Arms Wide Open	16-120	PRT
Creed	With Arms Wide Open	14-474	SC
Crests	Angels Listened In	6-680	MM
Crests	Angels Listened In	4-247	SC
Crests	Sixteen Candles	11-149	DK
Crests	Sixteen Candles	10-323	KC
Crests	Sixteen Candles	25-171	MM
Crests	Sixteen Candles	13-56	P
Crests	Sixteen Candles	9-20	PS
Crests	Sixteen Candles	4-696	SC

ARTIST	SONG TITLE	#	TYPE
Crests	Step By Step	7-266	MM
Crittenden, Melodie	Broken Road	8-406	CB
Crittenden, Melodie	Broken Road	7-733	CHM
Crittenden, Melodie	I Should've Known	5-291	SC
Croce, Jim	Bad Bad Leroy Brown	17-374	DK
Croce, Jim	Bad Bad Leroy Brown	13-135	P
Croce, Jim	Changes In Latitude, Changes In Attitude	48-465	LE
Croce, Jim	I Got A Name	7-48	MM
Croce, Jim	I Got A Name	9-535	SAV
Croce, Jim	I'll Have To Say I Love You...	3-479	SC
Croce, Jim	I'll Have To Say I Love You...	33-292	CB
Croce, Jim	I've Got A Name	34-64	CB
Croce, Jim	Junk Food Junkie	5-640	SC
Croce, Jim	Lover's Cross	19-351	PS
Croce, Jim	Lover's Cross	29-644	SC
Croce, Jim	New York's Not My Home	48-463	CB
Croce, Jim	One Less Set Of Footsteps	19-352	PS
Croce, Jim	Operator	33-285	CB
Croce, Jim	Operator	2-555	SC
Croce, Jim	Photographs & Memories	5-601	SC
Croce, Jim	Rapid Roy (That Stock Car Boy)	48-461	CB
Croce, Jim	Roller Derby Queen	48-462	CB
Croce, Jim	Speedball Tucker	48-464	CB
Croce, Jim	Time In a Bottle	13-133	P
Croce, Jim	Workin' At The Car Wash Blues	19-353	PS
Croce, Jim	You Don't Mess Around With Jim	19-354	PS
Crosby & Andrew S	Duet - Don't Fence Me In	29-421	CB
Crosby & David Bowie	Xmas - Peace On Earth/Little Drummer - duet	41-42	CB
Crosby & Kelly	Duet - True Love	29-417	CB
Crosby Stills & Nash	Carry On - WN	48-61	SC
Crosby Stills & Nash	Duet - Wooden Ships - WN	48-56	SC
Crosby Stills & Nash	Find The Cost Of Freedom - WN	48-58	SC
Crosby Stills & Nash	Helplessly Hopelessly - WN	48-59	SC
Crosby Stills & Nash	Judy Blue Eyes	7-481	MM
Crosby Stills & Nash	Just A Song Before I Go	24-74	SC
Crosby Stills & Nash	Long Time Gone	12-866	P
Crosby Stills & Nash	Marakesh Express - WN	48-55	SC
Crosby Stills & Nash	Ohio	4-80	SC
Crosby Stills & Nash	Only Waiting For You - WN	48-71	SC
Crosby Stills & Nash	Our House	2-779	SC
Crosby Stills & Nash	Suite Judy Blue Eyes	3-447	SC
Crosby Stills & Nash	Teach Your Children	3-480	SC
Crosby Stills & Nash	Wasted On The Way	3-517	SC
Crosby Stills & Nash	Wooden Ships - duet -	48-56	SC

ARTIST	SONG TITLE	#	TYPE
	WN		
Crosby Stills & Nash	Woodstock	12-910	P
Crosby, Bing	Ac-Cent-Tchu-Ate The Positive	21-8	CB
Crosby, Bing	April Showers	29-474	LE
Crosby, Bing	Around The World	29-481	LE
Crosby, Bing	Count Your Blessings Instead Of Sheep	21-15	CB
Crosby, Bing	Dear Hearts And Gentle People	9-546	SAV
Crosby, Bing	Deep In The Heart Of Texas	29-409	CB
Crosby, Bing	Deep In The Heart Of Texas	29-477	LE
Crosby, Bing	Deep In The Heart Of Texas	4-354	SC
Crosby, Bing	Did You Ever See A Dream Walking	29-420	CB
Crosby, Bing	Far Away Places	4-186	SC
Crosby, Bing	Goodnight Sweetheart	29-410	CB
Crosby, Bing	I Kiss Your Hand Madame	9-547	SAV
Crosby, Bing	In My Merry Oldsmobile	29-411	CB
Crosby, Bing	In The Good Old Summertime	29-412	CB
Crosby, Bing	Irish - When Irish Eyes Are Smiling	29-415	CB
Crosby, Bing	Let Me Call You Sweetheart	29-413	CB
Crosby, Bing	Pennies From Heaven	29-478	LE
Crosby, Bing	Pennies From Heaven	12-546	P
Crosby, Bing	Singing In The Rain	29-479	LE
Crosby, Bing	Some Enchanted Evening	9-548	SAV
Crosby, Bing	Stardust	29-419	CB
Crosby, Bing	Swanee	9-549	SAV
Crosby, Bing	Swinging On A Star	29-414	CB
Crosby, Bing	Swinging On A Star	17-379	DK
Crosby, Bing	Swinging On A Star	29-475	LE
Crosby, Bing	Swinging On A Star	15-844	MM
Crosby, Bing	Till We Meet Again	29-418	CB
Crosby, Bing	True Love	29-480	LE
Crosby, Bing	Xmas - Silver Bells	11-242	DK
Crosby, Bing	Xmas - Silver Bells	29-482	LE
Crosby, Bing	Xmas - White Christmas	11-726	DK
Crosby, Bing	Xmas - White Christmas	29-483	LE
Crosby, Bing	Xmas - White Christmas	14-536	SC
Crosby, Bing	Xmas - White Christmas	22-848	ST
Crosby, Bing	You Are My Sunshine	29-476	LE
Crosby, Bing	You Are My Sunshine	9-550	SAV
Crosby, Bing	You Must've Been A Beautiful Baby	21-5	CB
Crosby, Bing	You Must've Been A Beautiful Baby	12-545	P
Crosby, Stills, Nash & Young	4 + 20	46-175	SC
Crosby, Stills, Nash & Young	Teach Your Children	34-35	CB
Cross Can Ragweed	17	18-597	ST

ARTIST	SONG TITLE	#	TYPE
Cross Can Ragweed	Alabama	23-12	CB
Cross Can Ragweed	Constantly	19-694	ST
Cross Can Ragweed	Fightin' For	23-476	CB
Cross Can Ragweed	Sick And Tired	20-175	ST
Cross Can Ragweed	This Time Around	29-582	CB
Cross Section	Hi Heel Sneakers	30-784	SF
Cross, Christopher	Arthur's Theme	16-812	DK
Cross, Christopher	Ride Like The Wind	11-330	DK
Cross, Christopher	Ride Like The Wind	14-646	SC
Cross, Christopher	Sailing	17-118	DK
Cross, Christopher	Save Your Sadness	14-871	SC
Cross, Christopher	Show - Arthur's Theme	16-812	DK
Crossfade	Cold	30-614	PHM
Crossin' Dixon	Guitar Singer	30-540	CB
Crossin' Dixon	Make You Mine	36-574	CB
Crouch, Andre	Soon And Very Soon	13-83	P
Crow, Sheryl	All I Wanna Do	19-569	MH
Crow, Sheryl	All I Wanna Do	6-641	MM
Crow, Sheryl	All I Wanna Do	29-664	RS
Crow, Sheryl	Anything But Down	28-192	DK
Crow, Sheryl	Anything But Down	29-667	RS
Crow, Sheryl	Anything But Down	10-51	SC
Crow, Sheryl	C'Mon C'Mon	25-436	MM
Crow, Sheryl	C'mon C'mon	18-609	PHM
Crow, Sheryl	C'Mon C'Mon	29-677	RS
Crow, Sheryl	Can't Cry Anymore	29-668	RS
Crow, Sheryl	Change Would Do You Good	10-52	SC
Crow, Sheryl	Change Would Do You Good a	29-671	RS
Crow, Sheryl	Difficult Kind the	8-521	PHT
Crow, Sheryl	Difficult Thing the	29-673	RS
Crow, Sheryl	Everyday Is A Winding Road	29-670	RS
Crow, Sheryl	Everyday Is A Winding Road	10-49	SC
Crow, Sheryl	Everyday Is A Winding Road	19-160	SGB
Crow, Sheryl	First Cut Is The Deepest the	21-633	CB
Crow, Sheryl	First Cut Is The Deepest the	29-663	RS
Crow, Sheryl	If It Makes You Happy	29-672	RS
Crow, Sheryl	If It Makes You Happy	10-56	SC
Crow, Sheryl	Leaving Las Vegas	29-669	RS
Crow, Sheryl	Leaving Las Vegas	17-465	SC
Crow, Sheryl	Light In Your Eyes	29-662	RS
Crow, Sheryl	My Favorite Mistake	29-675	RS
Crow, Sheryl	My Favorite Mistake	10-50	SC
Crow, Sheryl	Soak Up The Sun	18-350	CB
Crow, Sheryl	Soak Up The Sun	25-201	MM
Crow, Sheryl	Soak Up The Sun	29-665	RS
Crow, Sheryl	Steve McQueen	18-428	CB
Crow, Sheryl	Steve McQueen	25-343	MM
Crow, Sheryl	Steve McQueen	29-676	RS
Crow, Sheryl	Strong Enough	29-674	RS
Crow, Sheryl	Strong Enough	10-53	SC
Crow, Sheryl	Sweet Child O' Mine	8-247	PHT

ARTIST	SONG TITLE	#	TYPE
Crow, Sheryl	Sweet Child O' Mine	29-679	RS
Crow, Sheryl	Sweet Child O' Mine	10-55	SC
Crow, Sheryl	There Goes The Neighborhood	7-800	PHT
Crow, Sheryl	There Goes The Neighborhood	29-678	RS
Crow, Sheryl	Tomorrow Never Dies	9-65	SC
Crow, Sheryl	Woman In The White House	46-298	BKD
Crow, Sheryl & Kid Rock	Duet - Picture	32-10	THM
Crow, Sheryl & Kid Rock	Picture	32-10	THM
Crowded House	Don't Dream It's Over	4-880	SC
Crowded House	Something So Strong	7-492	MM
Crowded House	Something So Strong	12-808	P
Crowded House	Something So Strong	15-797	SC
Crowell & Cash, J.	Duet - I Walk The Line	10-154	SC
Crowell & Cash, J.	I Walk The Line	10-154	SC
Crowell & Cash, R.	Duet - It's Such A Small World	5-437	SC
Crowell & Cash, R.	It's Such A Small World	5-437	SC
Crowell, Rodney	Big Heart	17-247	NA
Crowell, Rodney	Earthbound	19-710	ST
Crowell, Rodney	I Couldn't Leave You If I Tried	12-40	DK
Crowell, Rodney	I Couldn't Leave You If I Tried	5-255	SC
Crowell, Rodney	I Don't Fall In Love So Easy	24-14	SC
Crowell, Rodney	If Looks Could Kill	2-348	SC
Crowell, Rodney	Lovin' All Night	2-330	SC
Crowell, Rodney	Many A Long & Lonesome Highway	14-434	SC
Crowell, Rodney	Please Remember Me	2-745	SC
Crowell, Rodney	Say You Love Me	29-60	CB
Crush	Jellyhead	24-237	SC
Cryner, Bobbie	You'd Think He'd Know Me	4-165	SC
Crystal Waters	100% Pure Love	13-293	P
Crystal Waters	100% Pure Love	2-467	SC
Crystal Waters	Say If You Feel Alright	10-686	HH
Crystals	Da Doo Ron Ron	3-359	MH
Crystals	Da Doo Ron Ron	25-174	MM
Crystals	Da Doo Ron Ron	9-283	SC
Crystals	He's A Rebel	11-200	DK
Crystals	He's A Rebel	19-620	MH
Crystals	He's A Rebel	7-42	MM
Crystals	He's A Rebel	9-803	SAV
Crystals	He's A Rebel	4-11	SC
Crystals	He's Sure The Boy I Love	45-593	OZP
Crystals	Then He Kissed Me	3-291	MM
Crystals	Then He Kissed Me	10-652	SF
Crystals	Uptown	9-701	SAV
Cult	Painted On My Heart	15-436	PHM
Cult	She Sells Sanctuary	21-767	SC
Culture Club	Church Of The Poison Mind	46-652	SF

ARTIST	SONG TITLE	#	TYPE
Culture Club	Do You Really Want To Hurt Me	18-492	SAV
Culture Club	Do You Really Want To Hurt Me	5-120	SC
Culture Club	I Just Wanna Be Loved	47-1	SF
Culture Club	I'll Tumble 4 Ya	46-650	SC
Culture Club	It's A Miracle	47-4	ZM
Culture Club	Karma Chameleon	35-175	CB
Culture Club	Karma Chameleon	29-6	MH
Culture Club	Karma Chameleon	3-523	SC
Culture Club	Miss Me Blind	46-651	ST
Culture Club	Mr. Vain	47-3	SF
Culture Club	Time (Clock Of The Heart)	46-649	SBI
Culture Club	Victims	47-2	SF
Cupids Inspiration	Yesterday Has Gone	10-634	SF
Cure	Just Like Heaven	16-569	SC
Curfman, Shannon	Playing With Fire	14-485	SC
Curfman, Shannon	True Friends	5-900	SC
Currington, Billy	All Day Long	46-297	BKD
Currington, Billy	Don't	36-606	CB
Currington, Billy	Don't It	45-44	BKD
Currington, Billy	Drinkin' Town With A Football Problem	45-273	KCD
Currington, Billy	Enjoy Yourself	48-214	KV
Currington, Billy	Give It To Me Straight	45-274	DCK
Currington, Billy	Good Directions	30-162	CB
Currington, Billy	Hey Girl	40-57	ASK
Currington, Billy	I Got A Feelin'	19-766	ST
Currington, Billy	I Got A Feelin'	43-316	CB
Currington, Billy	Let Me Down Easy	37-348	CB
Currington, Billy	Like My Dog	38-205	SRK
Currington, Billy	Love Done Gone	43-313	CB
Currington, Billy	Must Be Doin' Somethin' Right	23-142	CB
Currington, Billy	Off My Rocker	43-315	CB
Currington, Billy	People Are Crazy	37-30	CB
Currington, Billy	People Are Crazy	47-558	SC
Currington, Billy	Pretty Good At Drinkin' Beer	37-205	AS
Currington, Billy	Tangled Up	30-478	CB
Currington, Billy	That's How Country Boys Roll	36-44	PT
Currington, Billy	Walk A Little Straighter	25-618	MM
Currington, Billy	Walk A Little Straighter	19-175	ST
Currington, Billy	Walk A Little Straighter	32-373	THM
Currington, Billy	Why Why Why	29-209	CB
Currington, Billy	Wingman	43-314	CB
Cutting Crew	I Just Died In Your Arms	33-350	CB
Cutting Crew	I Just Dies in Your Arms	5-389	SC
Cymbal, Johnny	Mr. Bass Man	6-660	MM
Cypress Hill	Insane In The Brain **	25-479	MM
Cypress Hill	Insane In The Brain **	14-436	SC
Cyrkle	Red Rubber Ball	7-62	MM
Cyrkle	Red Rubber Ball	3-21	SC
Cyrus, Billy Ray	Achy Breaky Heart	11-784	DK
Cyrus, Billy Ray	Achy Breaky Heart	6-106	MM
Cyrus, Billy Ray	Achy Breaky Heart	12-432	P

ARTIST	SONG TITLE	#	TYPE
Cyrus, Billy Ray	Ain't Your Dog No More	4-112	SC
Cyrus, Billy Ray	Always Sixteen	22-15	CB
Cyrus, Billy Ray	Burn Down The Trailer Park	14-788	ST
Cyrus, Billy Ray	Busy Man	8-859	CB
Cyrus, Billy Ray	Busy Man	22-700	ST
Cyrus, Billy Ray	Could've Been Me	10-756	JVC
Cyrus, Billy Ray	Could've Been Me	3-641	SC
Cyrus, Billy Ray	Crazy 'Bout You Baby	9-870	ST
Cyrus, Billy Ray	Give My Heart To You	14-612	SC
Cyrus, Billy Ray	Give My Heart To You	22-746	ST
Cyrus, Billy Ray	I'm So Miserable	39-79	PHN
Cyrus, Billy Ray	In The Heart Of A Woman	9-628	SAV
Cyrus, Billy Ray	In The Heart Of A Woman	2-356	SC
Cyrus, Billy Ray	It's All The Same To Me	7-673	CHM
Cyrus, Billy Ray	It's All The Same To Me	22-624	ST
Cyrus, Billy Ray	One Last Thrill	2-743	SC
Cyrus, Billy Ray	Runway Lights	38-91	PHM
Cyrus, Billy Ray	She's Not Cryin' Anymore	26-543	DK
Cyrus, Billy Ray	She's Not Cryin' Anymore	6-304	MM
Cyrus, Billy Ray	Somebody New	12-167	DK
Cyrus, Billy Ray	Somebody New	17-167	JVC
Cyrus, Billy Ray	Somebody New	17-231	NA
Cyrus, Billy Ray	Somebody New	2-802	SC
Cyrus, Billy Ray	Somebody Said A Prayer	36-217	PGM
Cyrus, Billy Ray	Storm In The Heartland	17-269	NA
Cyrus, Billy Ray	Storm In The Heartland	2-542	SC
Cyrus, Billy Ray	Trail Of Tears	4-431	SC
Cyrus, Billy Ray	We The People	20-583	CB
Cyrus, Billy Ray	When I'm Gone	24-4	SC
Cyrus, Billy Ray	Where'm I Gonna Live	33-114	CB
Cyrus, Billy Ray	Where'm I Gonna Live	6-220	MM
Cyrus, Billy Ray	Where'm I Gonna Live	3-381	SC
Cyrus, Billy Ray	Words By Heart	6-475	MM
Cyrus, Billy Ray	Words By Heart	3-41	SC
Cyrus, Billy Ray	You Won't Be Lonely Now	14-98	CB
Cyrus, Billy Ray	You Won't Be Lonely Now	19-222	CSZ
Cyrus, Billy Ray	You Won't Be Lonely Now	22-564	ST
Cyrus, Billy Ray	You Won't Be Lonely Now	14-29	THM
Cyrus, Miley	Adore You	42-20	ASK
Cyrus, Miley	Adore You	43-163	PHM
Cyrus, Miley	As I Am	36-77	WD
Cyrus, Miley	E.N.H.	36-75	WD
Cyrus, Miley	G.N.O. Girls Night Out	36-73	WD
Cyrus, Miley	I Miss You	36-78	WD
Cyrus, Miley	Let's Dance	36-74	WD
Cyrus, Miley	Right Here	36-76	WD
Cyrus, Miley	See You Again	36-71	WD
Cyrus, Miley	Start All Over	36-72	WD

ARTIST	SONG TITLE	#	TYPE
Cyrus, Miley	Wrecking Ball	42-19	ZM
D J Casper	Cha Cha Slide	45-75	CK
D-Train	You're The One For Me - Pt. 1	15-34	SS
D-Train	You're The One For Me - Pt. 2	15-35	SS
D.H.T.	Listen To Your Heart	30-145	PT
D'Angelo	Cruisin'	4-680	SC
D'Arby, Terrance T.	Sign Your Name	18-490	SAV
D'Arby, Terrence T.	Sign Your Name	5-614	SC
D4L	Duet - Becha Can't Do It Like Me **	29-252	SC
Da Vinci's Notebook	Enormous P#n#s	37-92	SC
Daddy Yankee	Duet - Rompe (Radio Version)	29-251	SC
Dahl, Ian Van	Castles In The Sky	21-722	TT
Dakota Moon	Another Day Goes By	14-281	MM
Dakota Moon	Looking For A Place To Land	24-85	MM
Dale & Gale	Duet - I'm Leavin' It Up To You	8-714	CB
Dale & Gale	I'm Leavin' It Up To You	8-714	CB
Dale & Gale	I'm Leavin' It Up To You	6-268	MM
Dale & Grace	Duet - I'm Leaving It Up To You	35-336	CB
Dale & Grace	I'm Leaving It Up To You - duet	35-336	CB
Dalley, Amy	Everybody's Got A Vice	30-251	CB
Dalley, Amy	Good Kind Of Crazy	30-355	CB
Dalley, Amy	I Think You're Beautiful	19-537	ST
Dalley, Amy	I Would Cry	23-3	CB
Dalley, Amy	Let's Try Goodbye	30-466	CB
Dalley, Amy	Living Together	22-82	CB
Dalley, Amy	Love's Got An Attitude	34-393	CB
Dalley, Amy	Love's Got An Attitude	24-570	MM
Dalley, Amy	Love's Got An Attitude	18-801	ST
Dalley, Amy	Love's Got An Attitude	32-300	THM
Dalley, Amy	Men Don't Change	35-428	CB
Dalley, Amy	Men Don't Change	20-172	ST
Dalton, Lacy J.	16th Avenue	14-319	SC
Dalton, Lacy J.	Black Coffee	4-73	SC
Dalton, Lacy J.	Crazy Blue Eyes	45-827	OZP
Dalton, Lacy J.	Deal the	45-825	VH
Dalton, Lacy J.	Dream Baby	45-823	KC
Dalton, Lacy J.	Everybody Makes Mistakes	5-630	SC
Dalton, Lacy J.	Hard Times	5-627	SC
Dalton, Lacy J.	Hillbilly Girl With The Blues	29-689	SC
Dalton, Lacy J.	Life's Railway To Heaven	45-826	VH
Dalton, Lacy J.	Losin' Kind Of Love	3-87	SC
Dalton, Lacy J.	Takin' It Easy	9-566	SAV
Dalton, Lacy J.	Takin' It Easy	5-245	SC
Dalton, Lacy J.	Where Did We Go Right	45-820	DCK
Dalton, Lacy J.	Whisper	45-824	SC
Daltry, Roger	Without Your Love	16-242	AMS
Dames At Sea	Broadway Baby - show	48-784	MM

ARTIST	SONG TITLE	#	TYPE
Dames At Sea	Show - Broadway Baby	48-784	MM
Dames At Sea	Show – Broadway Baby	7-374	MM
Damn Yankees	High Enough	34-57	CB
Damn Yankees	Show - Coming Of Age	5-66	SC
Damn Yankees	Show - Heart	7-375	MM
Damn Yankees	Show - High Enough	9-668	SAV
Damn Yankees	Show - Lola	10-370	KC
Damn Yankees	Show - Two Lost Souls	19-589	SC
Damn Yankees	Show - You Gotta Have Heart	6-896	MM
Damned	New Rose	21-610	SF
Damone, Vic	On The Street Where You Live	11-574	DK
Dan + Shay	19 You And Me	43-188	SBI
Dan + Shay	Nothin' Like You	47-397	BKD
Dan + Shay	Show You Off	44-284	KCD
Dan + Shay	What You Do To Me	44-379	BKD
Dana	It's Goinna Be A Cold Cold Christmas	45-591	OZP
Dana	Xmas - It's Gonna Be a Cold Cold Xmas	45-591	OZP
Danger, Harvey	Flagpole Sitta	7-769	PHT
Dangerman	Let's Make A Deal	7-875	PHM
Daniel, Dale	You Gave Her Your Name	24-254	SC
Daniel, Davis	I Miss Her Missing Me	4-118	SC
Daniel, Davis	I'm Not Listening Anymore	4-887	SC
Daniel, Davis	Tyler	4-477	SC
Daniels, Clint	Letter the	34-405	CB
Daniels, Clint	Letter the (Almost Home)	19-71	ST
Daniels, Clint	When I Grow Up	8-224	CB
Danleers	One Summer Night	6-263	MM
Danleers	Rock & Roll Is Here To Stay	6-653	MM
Danny & Juniors	At The Hop	17-51	DK
Danny & Juniors	At The Hop	13-255	P
Darin, Bobby	18 Yellow Roses	4-216	SC
Darin, Bobby	18 Yellow Roses	30-762	SF
Darin, Bobby	Artificial Flowers	23-356	PS
Darin, Bobby	Artificial Flowers	47-11	PS
Darin, Bobby	Baby Face	47-10	MM
Darin, Bobby	Beyond The Sea	7-185	MM
Darin, Bobby	Beyond The Sea	12-506	P
Darin, Bobby	Bill Bailey Won't You Please Come	12-653	P
Darin, Bobby	Clementine	23-357	PS
Darin, Bobby	Dream Lover	11-629	DK
Darin, Bobby	Feeling Good	48-646	KV
Darin, Bobby	I Got Rhythm	47-5	KV
Darin, Bobby	If I Were A Carpenter	7-31	MM
Darin, Bobby	If I Were A Carpenter	10-626	SF
Darin, Bobby	Lazy River	4-711	SC
Darin, Bobby	Lonesome Whistle (I Heard That)	47-751	SRK
Darin, Bobby	Mack The Knife	11-110	DK
Darin, Bobby	Mack The Knife	7-189	MM

ARTIST	SONG TITLE	#	TYPE
Darin, Bobby	More	47-8	MM
Darin, Bobby	Multiplication	47-7	MFK
Darin, Bobby	Queen Of Hop	5-511	SC
Darin, Bobby	Queen Of The Hop	47-12	SC
Darin, Bobby	Song Sung Blue	49-722	KV
Darin, Bobby	Splish Splash	11-628	DK
Darin, Bobby	Splish Splash	10-326	KC
Darin, Bobby	Sunday In New York	47-9	MM
Darin, Bobby	That's All	23-358	PS
Darin, Bobby	There's A Rainbow 'Round My Shoulder	47-6	KV
Darin, Bobby	Things	21-531	SC
Darin, Bobby	You Must've Been A Beautiful Baby	18-43	MM
Darin, Bobby	You Must've Been A Beautiful Baby	4-15	SC
Darin, Bobby	You Must've Been A Beautiful Baby	9-312	STR
Darin, Bobby	You're The Reason I'm Living	47-13	SC
Darkness	Friday Night	29-227	ZM
Darkness	Get Your Hands Off My Woman **	29-231	ZM
Darkness	Girlfriend	30-755	SF
Darkness	Givin' Up **	29-232	ZM
Darkness	Holding My Own	29-230	ZM
Darkness	I Believe In A Thing Called Love	29-228	ZM
Darkness	Love Is Only A Feeling	29-229	ZM
Darkness	One Way Ticket (Radio Version)	29-245	SC
Darling, Helen	Full Deck Of Cards	4-588	SC
Darling, Helen	I Haven't Found It Yet	4-122	SC
Darling, Helen	Jenny Come Back	7-19	MM
Darren, James	Goodbye Cruel World	7-37	MM
Darren, James	Goodbye Cruel World	5-457	SC
Darren, James	Her Royal Majesty	14-458	SC
Dashboard Confessional	Hands Down	32-404	THM
Dashboard Confessional	Hands Down	23-188	PHM
Daughtry	Feels Like Tonight	36-448	CB
Daughtry	Home	30-484	CB
Daughtry	It's Not Over	30-266	CB
Daughtry	Over You	38-138	CB
Daughtry	Renegade	38-263	PHM
Daughtry	Waiting For Superman	43-160	PHM
Daughtry	What About Now	36-26	PT
Daughtry	What I Want	30-558	CB
Dave Clark Five	Any Way You Want It	45-82	OZP
Dave Clark Five	Because	12-654	P
Dave Clark Five	Bits & Pieces	10-648	SF
Dave Clark Five	Can't You See That She's Mine	43-214	SC
Dave Clark Five	Can't You See That She's Mine	45-81	LE
Dave Clark Five	Catch Us If You Can	45-80	LC
Dave Clark Five	Do You Love Me	49-776	SC
Dave Clark Five	Do You Love Me	45-78	CB

ARTIST	SONG TITLE	#	TYPE
Dave Clark Five	Everybody Knows	45-83	ZMP
Dave Clark Five	Glad All Over	45-76	LE
Dave Clark Five	Here Comes That Rainy Day Feeling	3-858	SC
Dave Clark Five	I Like It Like That	45-79	LC
Dave Clark Five	Over And Over	45-77	CB
Dave Mattherw Band	Too Much	34-125	CB
Dave Matthews Band	Crash Into Me	49-451	MM
Dave Matthews Band	Crush	14-287	MM
Dave Matthews Band	Everyday	36-135	SGB
Dave Matthews Band	Everyday	16-85	ST
Dave Matthews Band	I Did It	35-246	CB
Dave Matthews Band	I Did It	16-481	MH
Dave Matthews Band	So Much To Say	24-107	SC
Dave Matthews Band	Space Between	33-418	CB
Dave Matthews Band	Space Between	16-390	SGB
Dave Matthews Band	Space Between	16-324	TT
Dave Matthews Band	What Would You Say	3-441	SC
Dave Matthews Band	Where Are You Going	33-411	CB
David Rose Band	Stripper the	2-76	SC
David, Craig	7 Days	25-89	MM
David, Craig	Don't Love You No More (I'm Sorry)	30-774	SF
David, Craig	Fill Me In	15-816	CB
David, Craig	Hidden Agenda	18-775	PHM
David, Craig	Hidden Angels	20-459	CB
David, Craig	Walking Away	18-347	CB
David, Craig	Walking Away	25-221	MM
David, Craig	Walking Away	17-598	PHM
David, Craig	What's Your Flava?	32-54	THM
Davidson, Clay	I Can't Lie To Me	14-111	CB
Davidson, Clay	I Can't Lie To Me	19-225	CSZ
Davidson, Clay	I Can't Lie To Me	22-556	ST
Davidson, Clay	Sometimes	14-790	ST
Davidson, Clay	Unconditional	14-184	CB
Davidson, Clay	Unconditional	19-244	CSZ
Davidson, Clay	Unconditional	23-370	SC
Davis Sisters	I Forgot More Than You'll Ever Know	13-389	P
Davis, Alana	32 Flavors	5-186	SC
Davis, Linda	Company Time	6-509	MM
Davis, Linda	Company Time	2-132	SC
Davis, Linda	From The Inside Out	8-950	CB
Davis, Linda	How Can I Make You Love Me	4-467	SC
Davis, Linda	I Wanna Remember This	8-493	CB
Davis, Linda	I Wanna Remember This	22-817	ST
Davis, Linda	I'm Yours	8-246	CB
Davis, Linda	I'm Yours	22-704	ST
Davis, Linda	Love Didn't Do It	6-609	MM
Davis, Linda	Love Didn't Do It	17-238	NA
Davis, Linda	Love Didn't Do It	2-316	SC
Davis, Linda	Love Story In The Making	7-233	MM
Davis, Linda	Love Story In The Making	4-226	SC
Davis, Linda	Love Story In The Making a	22-886	ST

ARTIST	SONG TITLE	#	TYPE
Davis, Linda	Some Things Are Meant To Be	3-666	SC
Davis, Linda	Walk Away	24-161	SC
Davis, Linda	Walk Away	22-918	ST
Davis, Mac	Baby Don't Get Hooked On Me	23-509	CB
Davis, Mac	Baby Don't Get Hooked On Me	17-16	DK
Davis, Mac	Forever Lovers	23-520	CB
Davis, Mac	Friend Lover Woman Wife	23-518	CB
Davis, Mac	Hard To Be Humble	10-480	DA
Davis, Mac	Hooked On Music	23-511	CB
Davis, Mac	Hooked On Music	19-426	SC
Davis, Mac	I Believe In Music	23-519	CB
Davis, Mac	I Believe In Music	11-781	DK
Davis, Mac	I Believe In Music	12-830	P
Davis, Mac	It's Hard To Be Humble	23-508	CB
Davis, Mac	It's Hard To Be Humble	5-629	SC
Davis, Mac	Kiss It And Make It Better	23-522	CB
Davis, Mac	Let's Keep It That Way	23-521	CB
Davis, Mac	One Hell Of A Woman	23-510	CB
Davis, Mac	One Hell Of A Woman	47-595	CB
Davis, Mac	Rock 'N Roll (I Gave You The Best..	23-515	CB
Davis, Mac	Stop And Smell The Roses	23-514	CB
Davis, Mac	Stop And Smell The Roses	4-330	SC
Davis, Mac	Texas In My Rear View Mirror	23-516	CB
Davis, Mac	Texas in My Rear View Mirror	4-542	SC
Davis, Mac	Watching Scotty Grow	23-517	CB
Davis, Mac	You're My Bestest Friend	23-512	CB
Davis, Mac	You're My Bestest Friend	4-487	SC
Davis, Paul	65 Love Affair	16-158	SC
Davis, Paul	Cool Night	15-743	SC
Davis, Paul	Do Right	48-613	SC
Davis, Paul	I Go Crazy	18-52	MM
Davis, Paul	I Go Crazy	13-154	P
Davis, Sammy Jr.	Birth Of The Blues the	15-849	MM
Davis, Sammy Jr.	Candy Man	34-5	CB
Davis, Sammy Jr.	Candy Man the	11-311	DK
Davis, Sammy Jr.	Candy Man the	20-760	KB
Davis, Sammy Jr.	Hello Detroit	45-608	OZP
Davis, Sammy Jr.	Hey There	7-193	MM
Davis, Sammy Jr.	Hey There	10-603	SF
Davis, Sammy Jr.	I've Gotta Be Me	15-508	MM
Davis, Sammy Jr.	I've Gotta Be Me	19-780	SGB
Davis, Sammy Jr.	I've Gotta Be Me	47-14	MM
Davis, Sammy Jr.	Mr. Bojangles	47-16	SC
Davis, Sammy Jr.	Something's Gotta Give	7-195	MM
Davis, Sammy Jr.	That Old Black Magic	47-15	PS
Davis, Sammy Jr.	Too Close For Comfort	47-17	PS
Davis, Skeeter	Am I That Easy To	34-201	CB

ARTIST	SONG TITLE	#	TYPE
	Forget		
Davis, Skeeter	End Of The World	43-323	CB
Davis, Skeeter	End Of The World the	17-1	DK
Davis, Skeeter	End Of The World the	6-164	MM
Davis, Skeeter	End Of The World the	13-428	P
Davis, Skeeter	Fuel To The Flame	43-332	CB
Davis, Skeeter	Gonna Get Along Without You Now	43-329	CB
Davis, Skeeter	He Says The Same Things To Me	43-335	CB
Davis, Skeeter	Homebreaker	43-333	CB
Davis, Skeeter	I Can't Help You, I'm Falling Too	15-92	CB
Davis, Skeeter	I Can't Stay Mad At You	43-336	CB
Davis, Skeeter	I'm A Lover (Not A Fighter)	43-331	CB
Davis, Skeeter	My Last Date (With You)	43-326	CB
Davis, Skeeter	Optimistic	43-327	CB
Davis, Skeeter	Set Him Free	43-325	CB
Davis, Skeeter	What Does It Take	43-330	CB
Davis, Skeeter	What Does It Take	5-848	SC
Davis, Skeeter	Where I Ought Not To Be	43-328	CB
Davis, Spencer	Gimme Some Lovin'	49-460	MM
Davis, Tyrone	Turn Back The Hands Of Time	10-670	HE
Davis, Tyrone	Turn Back The Hands Of Time	5-390	SC
Davy Dee Dozy Bee	Zabadak	10-612	SF
Dawn, P.M.	I'd Die Without You	13-247	P
Day, Dennis	Christmas In Killarney	45-771	THX
Day, Dennis	Xmas - Christmas In Killarney	45-771	THX
Day, Doris	Again	45-581	OZP
Day, Doris	Bewitched Bothered & Bewildered	48-138	ZMP
Day, Doris	Black Hills Of Dakota the	48-136	ZMP
Day, Doris	By The Light Of The Silvery Moon	48-144	SFD
Day, Doris	Deadwood Stage the	48-137	ZMP
Day, Doris	Dream	9-798	SAV
Day, Doris	Everybody Loves A Lover	34-10	CB
Day, Doris	Everybody Loves A Lover	9-93	PS
Day, Doris	Everybody Loves A Lover	5-1	SC
Day, Doris	Fly Me To The Moon	46-276	KV
Day, Doris	Guy Is Just A Guy a	48-132	SC
Day, Doris	I'll Remember April	45-594	OZP
Day, Doris	If I Give My Heart To You	9-750	SAV
Day, Doris	If I Give My Heart To You	20-70	SC
Day, Doris	It's Magic	34-13	CB
Day, Doris	It's Magic	9-89	PS
Day, Doris	Just Blew In From the Windy City - show	48-143	SBI

ARTIST	SONG TITLE	#	TYPE
Day, Doris	Little Girl Blue	48-142	LE
Day, Doris	Lullaby Of Broadway	48-141	LE
Day, Doris	Move Over Darling	48-135	ZMP
Day, Doris	On Moonlight Bay	48-145	SFM
Day, Doris	On The Sunny Side Of The Street	12-527	P
Day, Doris	Perhaps Perhaps Perhaps	48-133	SFM
Day, Doris	Pillow Talk	48-134	ZMP
Day, Doris	Que Sera Sera	11-578	DK
Day, Doris	Que Sera Sera	3-354	MH
Day, Doris	Que Sera Sera	12-513	P
Day, Doris	Que Sera Sera	9-90	PS
Day, Doris	Que Sera Sera	2-240	SC
Day, Doris	Ready Willing and Able	48-139	ZMP
Day, Doris	Secret Love	11-577	DK
Day, Doris	Sentimental Journey	35-27	CB
Day, Doris	Sentimental Journey	16-827	DK
Day, Doris	Sentimental Journey	12-496	P
Day, Doris	Sentimental Journey	2-239	SC
Day, Doris	Sugarbush	48-140	ZMP
Day, Doris	Tea For Two	11-798	DK
Day, Doris	Tea For Two	12-537	P
Day, Doris	Teacher's Pet	9-92	PS
Day, Doris	When I Fall In Love	33-218	CB
Day, Doris	When I Fall In Love	9-91	PS
Day, Doris	You Took Advantage Of Me	48-131	KV
Day, Doris (Calamity Jane)	Show - Just Blew In From the Windy City	48-143	SBI
Day, Jennifer	Completely	36-358	SC
Day, Jennifer	Fun Of Your Love the	13-816	CHM
Day, Jennifer	Fun Of Your Love the	22-481	ST
Day, Jennifer	What If It's Me	9-386	CB
Day, Otis & Knights	Shout	2-35	SC
Daya	Hide Away	48-619	BKD
Daya	Sit Still Look Pretty	49-861	DCK
Dayne, Taylor	Can't Get Enough Of Your Love	24-150	SC
Dayne, Taylor	I'll Always Love You	13-160	P
Dayne, Taylor	I'll Always Love You	29-292	SC
Dayne, Taylor	I'll Be Your Shelter	12-798	P
Dayne, Taylor	It Only Takes A Minute	11-408	DK
Dayne, Taylor	Love Will Lead You Back	17-92	DK
Dayne, Taylor	Love Will Lead You Back	6-100	MM
Dayne, Taylor	Naked Without You	13-709	SGB
Dayne, Taylor	Prove Your Love	28-291	DK
Dayne, Taylor	Tell It To My Heart	11-497	DK
Dayne, Taylor	Tell It To My Heart	12-815	P
Dayne, Taylor	Whatever You Want	21-734	TT
Dayne, Taylor	With Every Beat Of My Heart	11-713	DK
Dayne, Taylor	With Every Beat Of My Heart	12-757	P
Days Of The New	Enemy	5-785	SC
Days Of The New	Shelf In The Room	5-279	SC

ARTIST	SONG TITLE	#	TYPE
Daz Sampson	Teenage Life	30-695	SF
DC Talk	Consume Me	34-424	CB
De Azlan, Star	She's Pretty	36-565	CB
De La Soul	Me Myself & I	14-441	SC
Dead Milkmen	Punk Rock Girl	21-408	SC
Deadeye Dick	New Age Girl	2-719	SC
Dean, Billy	Billy The Kid	2-614	SC
Dean, Billy	Cowboy Band	6-595	MM
Dean, Billy	Cowboy Band	17-251	NA
Dean, Billy	I Wouldn't Be A Man	7-398	MM
Dean, Billy	I Wouldn't Be A Man	4-618	SC
Dean, Billy	I Wouldn't Be A Man	22-911	ST
Dean, Billy	I'm In Love With You	19-684	ST
Dean, Billy	I'm Not Built That Way	4-111	SC
Dean, Billy	If There Hadn't Been You	17-224	NA
Dean, Billy	If There Hadn't Been You	3-49	SC
Dean, Billy	Innocent Bystander	8-935	CB
Dean, Billy	It's What I Do	4-161	SC
Dean, Billy	Let Them Be Little	22-105	CB
Dean, Billy	Let Them Be Little	20-512	ST
Dean, Billy	Only The Wind	13-491	P
Dean, Billy	Race You To The Bottom	23-304	CB
Dean, Billy	Real Man	8-752	CB
Dean, Billy	Shine On	29-53	CB
Dean, Billy	Somewhere In My Broken Heart	35-401	CB
Dean, Billy	Somewhere In My Broken Heart	17-351	DK
Dean, Billy	Swinging For The Fence	29-600	CB
Dean, Billy	Thank God I'm A Country Boy	20-350	ST
Dean, Billy	This Is The Life	23-129	CB
Dean, Billy	Tryin' To Hide A Fire In The Dark	6-530	MM
Dean, Billy	We Just Disagree	6-458	MM
Dean, Billy	We Just Disagree	2-25	SC
Dean, Jimmy	Big Bad John	8-787	CB
Dean, Jimmy	Big Bad John	9-471	SAV
Dean, Jimmy	I Won't Go Hunting With You Jake	47-19	BFK
Dean, Jimmy	Little Black Book	47-18	SRK
Dean, Roxie	Everyday Girl	19-535	ST
Dean, Roxie	Soldier's Wife a	23-403	CB
Dean, Roxie	Soldier's Wife a	20-483	ST
Dean, Tyler	Built For Blue Jeans	30-118	CB
Dean, Tyler	Somebody Who Would Die For You	29-54	CB
Dean, Tyler	That Smile	38-247	PHN
Death Cab for Cutie	Crooked Teeth	29-219	PHM
DeBarge	All This Love	24-334	SC
DeBarge	Rhythm Of The Night	28-348	DK
DeBarge	Rhythm Of The Night	4-884	SC
DeBurgh, Chris	Lady In Red	34-88	CB
DeBurgh, Chris	Lady In Red	6-346	MM
DeBurgh, Chris	Lady In Red	13-186	P

ARTIST	SONG TITLE	#	TYPE
Dee & Starlighters	Peppermint Twist	11-508	DK
Dee & Starlighters	Peppermint Twist - DANCE #	22-394	SC
Dee-Lite	Groove Is In The Heart	10-493	DA
Dee-Lite	Groove Is In The Heart	5-340	SC
Dee, Kiki	I've Got The Music In Me	49-482	MM
DeeJay, Alice	Better Off Alone	30-630	THM
Deep Blue Something	Truly Madly Deeply	13-683	SGB
Deep Purple	Highway Star	4-568	SC
Deep Purple	Hush	11-444	DK
Deep Purple	Hush	6-792	MM
Deep Purple	Knocking At Your Back Door	21-753	SC
Deep Purple	Smoke On The Water	34-56	CB
Deep Purple	Smoke On The Water	11-772	DK
Deep Purple	Smoke On The Water	15-167	MH
Deep Purple	Space Truckin'	13-756	SGB
Deep Purple	Woman From Tokyo	5-871	SC
Dees & Idiots	Disco Duck - Part 1	23-28	SC
Dees & Idiots	Duet - Disco Duck - Part 1	23-28	SC
Def Leppard	Armageddon It	3-518	SC
Def Leppard	Bringin' On The Heartbreak	23-47	MH
Def Leppard	Foolin'	5-484	SC
Def Leppard	Let's Get Rocked	49-318	CB
Def Leppard	Let's Get Rocked	46-172	SC
Def Leppard	Love Bites	35-189	CB
Def Leppard	Love Bites	4-81	SC
Def Leppard	Photograph	46-166	SC
Def Leppard	Pour Some Sugar On Me	13-744	SGB
Def Leppard	Promises	46-170	SC
Def Leppard	Rock Of Ages	46-167	SC
Def Leppard	Rocket	46-171	SC
Def Leppard	Too Late For Love	46-169	SC
Def Leppard	Two Steps Behind	6-373	MM
Def Leppard	When Love And Hate Collide	46-168	SC
Default	Live A Lie	32-73	THM
Default	Wasting My Time	25-147	MM
Deftones	Minerva	32-289	THM
DeGarmo, Diana	Dreams	20-553	PHM
Deggs, Cole & Lonesome	Girl Next Door	30-555	CB
Deggs, Cole & Lonesome	I Got More	30-313	CB
DeGraw, Gavin	Cheated On Me	36-535	CB
DeGraw, Gavin	I Don't Want To Be	20-193	PHM
DeGraw, Gavin	In Love With a Girl	36-466	CB
DeGraw, Gavin	In Love With A Girl	49-853	SC
Dekker & the Aces	Israelites	25-385	MM
Dekker & the Aces	You Can Get It If You Really Want	25-378	MM
Del Amitri	Driving With The Brakes On	30-793	SF
Del Amitri	Roll To Me	28-420	DK
Del Ray, Lana	Diet Mountain Dew	44-108	KV

ARTIST	SONG TITLE	#	TYPE
Del Rey, Lana	Born To Die	49-72	ZPC
Del Rey, Lana	Lucky Ones	49-24	KV
Del Rey, Lana	Shades Of Cool	45-283	BKD
Del Rey, Lana	Summertime Sadness	43-81	MRH
Del Rey, Lana	This Is What Makes Us Girls	48-506	KVD
Del Rey, Lana	Young And Beautiful	46-188	BHK
Del Shannon	Hats Off To Larry	6-647	MM
Del Shannon	Runaway	35-36	CB
Del Shannon	Runaway	26-356	DK
Del Shannon	Runaway	3-290	MM
Del Shannon	Runaway	2-58	SC
Del Shannon	Two Kinds Of Teardrops	29-813	SF
Del Vikings	Come Go With Me	33-233	CB
Del Vikings	Come Go With Me	25-553	MM
Del Vikings	Come Go With Me	15-463	P
Delaney, Bonnie	Never Ending Song Of Love	9-369	MG
Delaney, Bonnie	Never Ending Song Of Love	9-721	SAV
Delfonics	Didn't I Blow Your Mind	9-797	SAV
Delfonics	La La Means I Love You	7-314	MM
Delfonics	La La Means I Love You	12-923	P
Dells	Oh What A Night	3-299	MM
Dells	Oh What A Night	10-207	SS
Dells	Stay In My Corner	25-169	MM
Dem Franchize Boyz	White Tees	30-811	PHM
Denney, K	It'll Go Away	32-44	THM
Denney, Kevin	Cadillac Tears	25-295	MM
Denney, Kevin	Cadillac Tears	17-582	ST
Denney, Kevin	It'll Go Away	18-457	ST
Denney, Kevin	It'll Go Away	32-44	THM
Denney, Kevin	That's Just Jessie	33-186	CB
Denney, Kevin	That's Just Jessie	25-71	MM
Denney, Kevin	That's Just Jessie	16-105	ST
Denney, Kevin	Year At A Time a	19-681	ST
Dennis, Cathy	Just Another Dream	9-679	SAV
Dennis, Cathy	Too Many Walls	9-684	SAV
Dennis, Wesley	Borrowed Angel	2-771	SC
Dennis, Wesley	I Don't Know	2-701	SC
Denver, John	Annie's Song	11-614	DK
Denver, John	Annie's Song	36-142	LE
Denver, John	Annie's Song	10-507	SF
Denver, John	Back Home Again	36-150	LE
Denver, John	Back Home Again	4-820	SC
Denver, John	Calypso	36-146	LE
Denver, John	Eagles And Horses	48-404	DCK
Denver, John	Fly Away	36-149	LE
Denver, John	Follow Me	15-620	THM
Denver, John	Grandma's Feather Bed	49-235	DFK
Denver, John	Heart To Heart	15-618	THM
Denver, John	I'm Sorry	36-147	LE
Denver, John	I'm Sorry	4-635	SC
Denver, John	I'm Sorry	48-487	CKC
Denver, John	If Ever	48-408	DFK
Denver, John	My Sweet Lady	29-694	SC
Denver, John	My Sweet Lady	15-613	THM
Denver, John	Perhaps Love	15-615	THM
Denver, John	Poems Prayers And Promises	48-411	DFK
Denver, John	Relatively Speaking	15-617	THM
Denver, John	Rocky Mountain High	16-358	CB
Denver, John	Rocky Mountain High	36-144	LE
Denver, John	Rocky Mountain High	9-38	MM
Denver, John	Rocky Mountain High	13-369	P
Denver, John	Shanghai Breezes	15-614	THM
Denver, John	Somedays Are Diamonds	4-488	SC
Denver, John	Somedays Are Diamonds	15-619	THM
Denver, John	Starry Starry Nights (Vincent)	48-488	CKC
Denver, John	Starwood In Aspen	49-250	DFK
Denver, John	Sunshine On My Shoulder	36-143	LE
Denver, John	Sunshine On My Shoulder	11-613	DK
Denver, John	Sweet Surrender	5-528	SC
Denver, John	Take Me Home Country Roads	17-30	DK
Denver, John	Take Me Home Country Roads	36-145	LE
Denver, John	Take Me Home Country Roads	12-827	P
Denver, John	Thank God I'm A Country Boy	8-19	CB
Denver, John	Thank God I'm A Country Boy	11-615	DK
Denver, John	Thank God I'm A Country Boy	36-147	LE
Denver, John	Thank God I'm A Country Boy	13-450	P
Denver, John	This Ol' Guitar	15-621	THM
Denver, John	Today	15-616	THM
Denver, John	What One Man Can Do	15-622	THM
Denver, Mike	Let's Go Waltzing Together	45-806	KV
Denver, Mike	Party's Over the (Turn Out The Lights)	45-807	KV
Depeche Mode	Dream On	33-377	CB
Depeche Mode	I Feel Loved	16-318	TT
Depeche Mode	People Are People	5-385	SC
Depeche Mode	Personal Jesus	21-410	SC
Depeche Mode	Policy of Truth	16-524	P
Derailers	More Of Your Love	17-483	CB
Derek & Dominos	Bell Bottom Blues	28-206	DK
Derek & Dominos	Bell Bottom Blues	20-72	SC
Derek & Dominos	Layla	9-371	AH
Derek & Dominos	Layla	15-178	MH
Derek & Dominos	Nobody Knows You When You're…	15-315	SC
Dern, Daisy	Getting Back To You	25-68	MM
Derringer, Rick	Rock & Roll Hoochie Koo	17-120	DK
Desario & KC	Duet - Yes I'm Ready	35-79	CB
Desario & KC	Duet - Yes I'm Ready	12-384	DK

ARTIST	SONG TITLE	#	TYPE
Desario & KC	Yes I'm Ready	12-384	DK
Desario & KC	Yes I'm Ready - duet	35-79	CB
Desert Rose Band	Ashes Of Love	8-621	SAV
Desert Rose Band	He's Back And I'm Blue	5-759	SC
Desert Rose Band	Hello Trouble	9-497	SAV
Desert Rose Band	I Still Believe In You	5-531	SC
Desert Rose Band	One Step Forward	5-770	SC
DeShannon, Jackie	Put A Little Love In Your Heart	11-402	DK
DeShannon, Jackie	What The World Needs Now	11-528	DK
Destiny's Child	Bills Bills Bills	13-564	LE
Destiny's Child	Bills Bills Bills	8-505	PHT
Destiny's Child	Bills Bills Bills	10-201	SC
Destiny's Child	Bills Bills Bills	13-775	SGB
Destiny's Child	Bootylicious	18-394	MM
Destiny's Child	Bootylicious	18-508	TT
Destiny's Child	Emotion	25-18	MM
Destiny's Child	Independent Woman	16-109	PRT
Destiny's Child	Independent Women	35-226	CB
Destiny's Child	Independent Women Part 1	14-21	THM
Destiny's Child	Jumpin' Jumpin'	34-180	CB
Destiny's Child	Jumpin' Jumpin'	13-566	LE
Destiny's Child	Jumpin' Jumpin'	30-635	THM
Destiny's Child	Say My Name	14-171	CB
Destiny's Child	Say My Name	13-565	LE
Destiny's Child	Say My Name	15-329	PHM
Destiny's Child	So Good	19-823	SGB
Destiny's Child	Soldier	20-24	PHM
Destiny's Child	Survivor	15-453	PHM
Destiny's Child	Survivor	18-534	TT
Destiny's Child&Lil	Duet - Soldier	22-343	CB
Destiny's Child&Lil	Soldier	22-343	CB
Detroit Spinners	Could It Be I'm Falling In Love	9-753	SAV
Deuce	America	39-100	PHM
Devo	Whip It	26-357	DK
Devo	Whip It	29-12	MH
Devo	Whip It	13-217	P
Devo	Working In A Coal Mine	12-896	P
Dewdrop, Daddy	Chick A Boom	4-83	SC
DF Dub	Country Girl	32-159	THM
Diamond & Jennings	Duet - One Good Love	7-235	MM
Diamond & Jennings	Duet - One Good Love	45-172	SC
Diamond & Jennings	One Good Love	7-235	MM
Diamond & Jennings	One Good Love	4-199	SC
Diamond & Jennings	One Good Love - duet	45-172	SC
Diamond Rio	Beautiful Mess	25-191	MM
Diamond Rio	Beautiful Mess	16-701	ST
Diamond Rio	Bubba Hyde	1-173	CB
Diamond Rio	Bubba Hyde	6-707	MM
Diamond Rio	Bubba Hyde	4-65	SC
Diamond Rio	Can't You Tell	23-399	CB
Diamond Rio	Can't You Tell	30-11	SC
Diamond Rio	Completely	19-704	ST
Diamond Rio	Finish What We Started	6-816	MM

ARTIST	SONG TITLE	#	TYPE
Diamond Rio	Finish What We Started	3-546	SC
Diamond Rio	God Only Cries	29-576	CB
Diamond Rio	Gone Out Of My Mind	4-141	SC
Diamond Rio	Holdin'	1-176	CB
Diamond Rio	Holdin'	7-585	CHM
Diamond Rio	Holdin'	22-912	ST
Diamond Rio	How Your Love Makes Me Feel	7-664	CHM
Diamond Rio	How Your Love Makes Me Feel	22-619	ST
Diamond Rio	I Believe	34-367	CB
Diamond Rio	I Believe	25-442	MM
Diamond Rio	I Believe	18-461	ST
Diamond Rio	I Believe	32-45	THM
Diamond Rio	I Know How The River Feels	8-957	CB
Diamond Rio	Imagine That	8-141	CB
Diamond Rio	Imagine That	22-646	ST
Diamond Rio	In A Week Or Two	1-170	CB
Diamond Rio	In A Week Or Two	2-337	SC
Diamond Rio	In God We Still Trust	29-19	CB
Diamond Rio	It's All In Your Head	1-175	CB
Diamond Rio	It's All In Your Head	4-498	SC
Diamond Rio	Love A Little Stronger	6-602	MM
Diamond Rio	Love A Little Stronger	2-806	SC
Diamond Rio	Mama Don't Forget To Pray	1-168	CB
Diamond Rio	Meet In The Middle	1-166	CB
Diamond Rio	Meet In The Middle	26-565	DK
Diamond Rio	Meet In The Middle	13-335	P
Diamond Rio	Meet In The Middle	2-512	SC
Diamond Rio	Mirror Mirror	1-167	CB
Diamond Rio	Mirror Mirror	2-392	SC
Diamond Rio	Night Is Fallin' In My Heart	2-543	SC
Diamond Rio	Norma Jean Riley	1-169	CB
Diamond Rio	Nowhere Bound	1-180	CB
Diamond Rio	Nowhere Bound	2-624	SC
Diamond Rio	Oh Me Oh My Sweet Baby	1-171	CB
Diamond Rio	Oh Me Oh My Sweet Baby	2-370	SC
Diamond Rio	One Believer	22-316	CB
Diamond Rio	One More Day	33-134	CB
Diamond Rio	One More Day	22-461	ST
Diamond Rio	Stuff	14-713	CB
Diamond Rio	Sweet Summer	15-97	ST
Diamond Rio	That's Just That	17-602	CB
Diamond Rio	That's Just That	25-54	MM
Diamond Rio	That's Just That	16-5	ST
Diamond Rio	That's What I Get For Loving You	1-174	CB
Diamond Rio	This Romeo Ain't Got Julie Yet	1-172	CB
Diamond Rio	This Romeo Ain't Got Julie Yet	6-532	MM
Diamond Rio	This Romeo Ain't Got Julie Yet	2-821	SC

ARTIST	SONG TITLE	#	TYPE
Diamond Rio	Unbelievable	1-179	CB
Diamond Rio	Unbelievable	22-686	ST
Diamond Rio	Walkin' Away	4-101	SC
Diamond Rio	We All Fall Down	19-764	ST
Diamond Rio	Wild Blue Yonder	4-470	SC
Diamond Rio	Workin' Man's Blues	2-643	SC
Diamond Rio	Workin' Man's Blues	22-862	ST
Diamond Rio	Wrinkles	25-702	MM
Diamond Rio	Wrinkles	19-261	ST
Diamond Rio	Wrinkles	32-410	THM
Diamond Rio	You're Gone	1-178	CB
Diamond Rio	You're Gone	5-290	SC
Diamond Rio	You're Gone	22-811	ST
Diamond Rio,Warner	Duet - Workin' Mans Blues	2-643	SC
Diamond, Neil	America	20-161	BCI
Diamond, Neil	America	30-679	LE
Diamond, Neil	America	13-296	P
Diamond, Neil	And The Grass Won't Pay No Mind	30-498	THM
Diamond, Neil	Beautiful Noise	30-683	LE
Diamond, Neil	Brother Love's Travelin' Salvation Show	7-530	AH
Diamond, Neil	Brother Love's Travelin' Salvation Show	18-689	PS
Diamond, Neil	Brother Love's Travelin' Salvation Show	24-698	SC
Diamond, Neil	Brother Love's Travelin' Salvation Show	30-499	THM
Diamond, Neil	Can Anybody Hear Me	47-416	PS
Diamond, Neil	Cherry Cherry	7-531	AH
Diamond, Neil	Cherry Cherry	18-686	PS
Diamond, Neil	Cherry Cherry	24-700	SC
Diamond, Neil	Cracklin' Rosie	7-532	AH
Diamond, Neil	Cracklin' Rosie	30-677	LE
Diamond, Neil	Cracklin' Rosie	24-692	SC
Diamond, Neil	Cracklin' Rosie	30-500	THM
Diamond, Neil	Crunchy Granola Suite (Hot August Night)	47-411	BHK
Diamond, Neil	Desiree	47-420	PS
Diamond, Neil	Don't Make Me Over	47-424	PS
Diamond, Neil	Done Too Soon	48-413	DFK
Diamond, Neil	Forever In Blue Jeans	7-533	AH
Diamond, Neil	Forever In Blue Jeans	30-678	LE
Diamond, Neil	Girl You'll Be A Woman Soon	7-534	AH
Diamond, Neil	Girl You'll Be A Woman Soon	30-680	LE
Diamond, Neil	Girl You'll Be A Woman Soon	13-299	P
Diamond, Neil	Girl You'll Be A Woman Soon	24-705	SC
Diamond, Neil	Glory Road	47-410	BHK
Diamond, Neil	Groovy Kind Of Love	47-421	PS
Diamond, Neil	He Ain't Heavy He's My Brother	30-676	LE
Diamond, Neil	He Ain't Heavy He's My Brother	24-203	SC
Diamond, Neil	Headed For The Future	30-501	THM
Diamond, Neil	Heartlight	30-690	LE
Diamond, Neil	Heartlight	24-696	SC
Diamond, Neil	Hello Again	7-535	AH
Diamond, Neil	Hello Again	24-702	SC
Diamond, Neil	Hello Again	30-502	THM
Diamond, Neil	Holly Holy	7-536	AH
Diamond, Neil	Holly Holy	30-682	LE
Diamond, Neil	Holly Holy	13-297	P
Diamond, Neil	Holly Holy	18-695	PS
Diamond, Neil	Holly Holy	24-693	SC
Diamond, Neil	I Am I Said	7-537	AH
Diamond, Neil	I Am I Said	30-674	LE
Diamond, Neil	I Am I Said	30-503	THM
Diamond, Neil	I Believe In Happy Endings	47-423	THM
Diamond, Neil	I Got The Feelin' (Oh No No)	47-418	MM
Diamond, Neil	I Haven't Played This Song In Years	30-504	THM
Diamond, Neil	I Thank The Lord For The Nighttime	30-684	LE
Diamond, Neil	I'm A Believer	18-688	PS
Diamond, Neil	I'm Alive	30-505	THM
Diamond, Neil	I'm Glad You're Here With Me Tonite	24-691	SC
Diamond, Neil	I've Been This Way Before	47-412	DFK
Diamond, Neil	If You Know What I Mean	30-687	LE
Diamond, Neil	If You Know What I Mean	18-690	PS
Diamond, Neil	Kentucky Woman	7-538	AH
Diamond, Neil	Kentucky Woman	24-699	SC
Diamond, Neil	Lady Oh	47-414	DCK
Diamond, Neil	Last Thing On My Mind	11-350	DK
Diamond, Neil	Leave A Little Room For God	30-506	THM
Diamond, Neil	Longfellow Serenade	7-539	AH
Diamond, Neil	Longfellow Serenade	30-675	LE
Diamond, Neil	Longfellow Serenade	15-748	SC
Diamond, Neil	Love On The Rocks	7-540	AH
Diamond, Neil	Love On The Rocks	30-681	LE
Diamond, Neil	Love On The Rocks	30-507	THM
Diamond, Neil	Marry Me	4-395	SC
Diamond, Neil	Midnight Train To Georgia	47-415	DCK
Diamond, Neil	One Hand One Heart	10-24	SC
Diamond, Neil	Play Me	7-541	AH
Diamond, Neil	Play Me	18-694	PS
Diamond, Neil	Play Me	24-694	SC
Diamond, Neil	Play Me	30-508	THM
Diamond, Neil	Red Red Wine	7-542	AH
Diamond, Neil	Red Red Wine	13-295	P
Diamond, Neil	Red Red Wine (Slower Version)	30-688	LE
Diamond, Neil	Red Red Wine (Slower Version)	24-701	SC
Diamond, Neil	Save The Last Dance For Me	47-422	PS

ARTIST	SONG TITLE	#	TYPE
Diamond, Neil	September Morn	7-543	AH
Diamond, Neil	September Morn	30-689	LE
Diamond, Neil	September Morn	4-298	SC
Diamond, Neil	Shilo	18-687	PS
Diamond, Neil	Shilo	24-695	SC
Diamond, Neil	Shilo	30-509	THM
Diamond, Neil	Solitary Man	7-544	AH
Diamond, Neil	Solitary Man	18-691	PS
Diamond, Neil	Solitary Man	24-703	SC
Diamond, Neil	Something Blue	46-593	DCK
Diamond, Neil	Song Sung Blue	7-545	AH
Diamond, Neil	Song Sung Blue	13-298	P
Diamond, Neil	Song Sung Blue	16-409	PR
Diamond, Neil	Song Sung Blue	24-697	SC
Diamond, Neil	Songs Of Life	18-692	PS
Diamond, Neil	Soolaimon	18-693	PS
Diamond, Neil	Soolaimon	30-510	THM
Diamond, Neil	Stones	47-419	MM
Diamond, Neil	Story Of My Life	47-413	DKM
Diamond, Neil	Sweet Caroline	7-546	AH
Diamond, Neil	Sweet Caroline	30-686	LE
Diamond, Neil	Sweet Caroline	30-511	THM
Diamond, Neil	Tennessee Moon	7-197	MM
Diamond, Neil	Until It's Time For You To Go	47-417	PS
Diamond, Neil	Xmas - Sleigh Ride	14-295	MM
Diamond, Neil	Yesterday's Song	30-685	LE
Diamond&Streisand	Duet - You Don't Bring Me Flowers	30-512	THM
Diamond&Streisand	You Don't Bring Me Flowers	30-512	THM
Diamonds	Little Darlin'	12-114	DK
Diamonds	Little Darlin'	6-141	MM
Diamonds	Little Darlin'	13-50	P
Diamonds	Little Darlin'	19-100	SAV
Diamonds	Stroll the	27-490	DK
Diamonds	Stroll the - DANCE #	22-396	SC
Diaz, Dian	No More Tears	36-181	PHM
Dickens, Little Jimmy	Country Boy	14-914	SC
Dickens, Little Jimmy	Country Boy	45-336	SC
Dickens, Little Jimmy	Hillbilly Fever	8-770	CB
Dickens, Little Jimmy	Hillbilly Fever	45-335	CBE P
Dickens, Little Jimmy	May The Bird Of Paradise Fly Up…	8-712	CB
Dickens, Little Jimmy	May The Bird Of Paradise Fly Up…	19-391	SC
Dickens, Little Jimmy	Out Behind The Barn	45-334	CK
Dickens, Little Jimmy	Tomorrow Never Comes	45-576	SSK
Dickens, Little Jimmy	You Only Want Me For My Body	45-681	VH
Dickens, Little Jimmy	You Only Want Me For My Body	45-330	BSP
Dickies	Banana Splits	48-769	P

ARTIST	SONG TITLE	#	TYPE
Diddley, Bo	Bo Diddley	6-690	MM
Diddley, Bo	Road Runner	11-46	PX
Diddley, Bo	Road Runner	10-248	SS
Diddy/P Feat/Usher	Duet - I Need A Girl	17-596	PHM
Dido	Don't Leave Home	29-237	ZM
Dido	Here With Me	18-517	TT
Dido	Hunter	15-818	CB
Dido	Hunter	18-408	MM
Dido	Hunter	18-519	TT
Dido	Mary's In India	29-235	ZM
Dido	See You When You're 40	29-236	ZM
Dido	Stoned	29-234	ZM
Dido	Thank You	35-240	CB
Dido	Thank You	16-121	PRT
Dido	Thank You	18-535	TT
Dido	White Flag	19-652	CB
Dido	White Flag	20-225	MM
Dido	White Flag	32-356	THM
Dido	White Flag	29-233	ZM
Dido	Who Makes You Feel	29-238	ZM
Diffie, Joe	Behind Closed Doors	10-163	SC
Diffie, Joe	Bigger Than The Beatles	1-284	CB
Diffie, Joe	Bigger Than The Beatles	7-178	MM
Diffie, Joe	Bigger Than The Beatles	3-660	SC
Diffie, Joe	Country	4-237	SC
Diffie, Joe	Honky Tonk Attitude	1-277	CB
Diffie, Joe	Honky Tonk Attitude	6-313	MM
Diffie, Joe	I'm In Love With A Capital U	1-283	CB
Diffie, Joe	I'm In Love With A Capital U	2-836	SC
Diffie, Joe	If The Devil Danced In Empty Pocket	1-272	CB
Diffie, Joe	If The Devil Danced In Empty Pocket	17-370	DK
Diffie, Joe	If The Devil Danced In Empty Pocket	13-403	P
Diffie, Joe	If You Want Me To Go	1-271	CB
Diffie, Joe	In Another World	15-674	ST
Diffie, Joe	In My Own Backyard	2-216	SC
Diffie, Joe	Is It Cold In Here Or Is It Me	1-274	CB
Diffie, Joe	Is It Cold In Here Or Is It Me	13-409	P
Diffie, Joe	It's Always Something	22-477	ST
Diffie, Joe	It's Always Something	33-133	CB
Diffie, Joe	It's Always Something	6-66	SC
Diffie, Joe	John Deere Green	1-279	CB
Diffie, Joe	John Deere Green	26-539	DK
Diffie, Joe	John Deere Green	6-455	MM
Diffie, Joe	New Way To Light Up An Old Flame	1-273	CB
Diffie, Joe	New Way To Light Up An Old Flame	20-403	MH
Diffie, Joe	Next Thing Smokin'	1-276	CB
Diffie, Joe	Next Thing Smokin'	15-538	MM
Diffie, Joe	Night To Remember	8-943	CB
Diffie, Joe	Night To Remember	7-868	CHT

ARTIST	SONG TITLE	#	TYPE
Diffie, Joe	Night To Remember a	22-745	ST
Diffie, Joe	Pickup Man	1-281	CB
Diffie, Joe	Pickup Man	2-458	SC
Diffie, Joe	Poor Me	1-285	CB
Diffie, Joe	Poor Me	22-679	ST
Diffie, Joe	Prop Me Up Beside The Jukebox	1-278	CB
Diffie, Joe	Prop Me Up Beside The Jukebox	12-138	DK
Diffie, Joe	Prop Me Up Beside The Jukebox	6-380	MM
Diffie, Joe	Quittin' Kind the	14-699	CB
Diffie, Joe	Quittin' Kind the	19-231	SC
Diffie, Joe	Quittin' Kind the	22-506	ST
Diffie, Joe	Ships that Don't Come In	1-275	CB
Diffie, Joe	So Help Me Girl	1-282	CB
Diffie, Joe	So Help Me Girl	4-69	SC
Diffie, Joe	So Help Me Girl	22-871	ST
Diffie, Joe	Somethin' Like This	22-623	ST
Diffie, Joe	Startin' Over Blues	24-356	SC
Diffie, Joe	Texas Size Heartache	8-468	CB
diffie, Joe	That Road Not Taken	6-852	MM
Diffie, Joe	Third Rock From The Sun	1-280	CB
Diffie, Joe	Third Rock From The Sun	6-614	MM
Diffie, Joe	Third Rock From The Sun	2-478	SC
Diffie, Joe	This Is Your Brain	7-626	CHM
Diffie, Joe	This Is Your Brain	10-74	SC
Diffie, Joe	This Pretender	25-195	MM
Diffie, Joe	This Pretender	16-686	ST
Diffie, Joe	Tougher Than Nails	30-8	SC
Diffie, Joe	Tougher Than Nails	20-177	ST
Diffie, Joe	White Light'nin'	4-146	SC
Diffie, Joe	Whole Lotta Gone	4-412	SC
Diffie, Joe	Xmas - Leroy the Redneck Reindeer	18-720	CB
Digital Underground	Humpty Dance	25-475	MM
Digital Underground	Humpty Dance	5-344	SC
Dillards	Dooley	46-192	SC
Dillards	Somebody Touched Me	36-356	CB
Dillon, Dean	Hot Country And Single	4-473	SC
Dinning, Mark	Teen Angel	35-39	CB
Dinning, Mark	Teen Angel	11-507	DK
Dinning, Mark	Teen Angel	10-743	JVC
Dinning, Mark	Teen Angel	4-695	SC
DIO	Last In Line the	21-755	SC
Dio, Ronnie James	Holy Diver	5-483	SC
Dion	Abraham Martin & John	33-254	CB
Dion	Abraham Martin & John	3-13	SC
Dion	Donna The Prima Donna	20-28	SC
Dion	Drip Drop	5-230	SC
Dion	Runaround Sue	7-288	MM
Dion	Runaround Sue	12-908	P
Dion	Runaround Sue	9-17	PS
Dion	Teenager In Love	11-96	DK

ARTIST	SONG TITLE	#	TYPE
Dion	Teenager In Love	7-296	MM
Dion	Teenager In Love	12-906	P
Dion	Teenager In Love	9-895	SAV
Dion	Wanderer the	11-656	DK
Dion	Wanderer the	10-334	KC
Dion	Wanderer the	6-159	MM
Dion	Wanderer the	12-892	P
Dion	Wanderer the	9-26	PS
Dion & Belmonts	I Wonder Why	47-20	LE
Dion & Belmonts	Lonely Teenager	47-23	SC
Dion & Belmonts	Ruby Baby	47-21	SC
Dion & Belmonts	Runaround Sue	29-840	SC
Dion & Belmonts	Sea Cruise	47-22	BC
Dion & Belmonts	That's My Desire	25-549	MM
Dion & Belmonts	Where Or When	25-556	MM
Dion & Bryson	Beauty And The Beast	9-213	SC
Dion & Bryson	Duet - Beauty & The Beast	9-213	SO
Dion & Griffin	Duet - When I Fall In Love	12-239	DK
Dion & Griffin	Duet - When I Fall In Love	6-331	MM
Dion & Griffin	When I Fall In Love	12-239	DK
Dion & Griffin	When I Fall In Love	6-331	MM
Dion & Kelly, R.	Duet - I'm Your Angel	14-195	CB
Dion & Kelly, R.	Duet - I'm Your Angel	20-124	PHM
Dion & Kelly, R.	I'm Your Angel	14-195	CB
Dion & Kelly, R.	I'm Your Angel	20-124	PHM
Dion & Pavaratti	Duet - I Hate You Then I Love You	17-655	PR
Dion & Pavaratti	I Hate You Then I Love You	17-655	PR
Dion & Pavaratti	Show - I Hate You Then I Love You	17-655	PR
Dion, Celine	All By Myself	15-112	BS
Dion, Celine	At Last	25-679	MM
Dion, Celine	At Last	19-19	PS
Dion, Celine	Aun Existe Amor	19-25	PS
Dion, Celine	Beauty And The Beast	15-108	BS
Dion, Celine	Because You Love Me	15-111	BS
Dion, Celine	Because You Love Me	19-568	MH
Dion, Celine	Because You Loved Me	14-197	CB
Dion, Celine	Call The Man	15-116	BS
Dion, Celine	Colour Of My Love	15-117	BS
Dion, Celine	Dance With My Father	29-212	PHM
Dion, Celine	Falling Into You	24-232	SC
Dion, Celine	God Bless America	16-299	PHM
Dion, Celine	Goodbye's The Saddes Word	19-26	PS
Dion, Celine	Greatest Love the	19-28	PS
Dion, Celine	Have You Ever Been In Love	34-158	CB
Dion, Celine	Have You Ever Been In Love	25-624	MM
Dion, Celine	Have You Ever Been In Love	19-15	PS
Dion, Celine	Here There and Everywhere	14-193	CB

ARTIST	SONG TITLE	#	TYPE
Dion, Celine	Here There And Everywhere	16-218	MM
Dion, Celine	I Drove All Night	20-460	CB
Dion, Celine	I Drove All Night	25-531	MM
Dion, Celine	I Drove All Night	20-626	NS
Dion, Celine	I Drove All Night	18-774	PHM
Dion, Celine	I Surrender	19-20	PS
Dion, Celine	I Want You To Need Me	13-838	PHM
Dion, Celine	I'm Alive	18-228	CB
Dion, Celine	I'm Alive	19-21	PS
Dion, Celine	I'm Your Angel	16-208	MM
Dion, Celine	If You Asked Me To	33-339	CB
Dion, Celine	If You Asked Me To	6-99	MM
Dion, Celine	It's All Coming Back To Me Now	15-118	BS
Dion, Celine	It's All Coming Back To Me Now	4-690	SC
Dion, Celine	Misled	34-138	CB
Dion, Celine	Misled	2-233	SC
Dion, Celine	My Heart Will Go On	15-107	BS
Dion, Celine	My Heart Will Go On	14-194	CB
Dion, Celine	My Heart Will Go On	7-711	PHM
Dion, Celine	Nature Boy	19-17	PS
Dion, Celine	New Day Has Come	18-300	CB
Dion, Celine	New Day Has Come	19-16	PS
Dion, Celine	New Day Has Come a	25-196	MM
Dion, Celine	Nothing Broken But My Heart	34-160	CB
Dion, Celine	Only One Road	15-109	BS
Dion, Celine	Power Of Love	15=113	BS
Dion, Celine	Power Of Love	14-196	CB
Dion, Celine	Power Of Love	26-340	DK
Dion, Celine	Power Of Love	9-266	SC
Dion, Celine	Power Of The Dream the	4-661	SC
Dion, Celine	Prayer	19-22	PS
Dion, Celine	Prayer the	15-119	BS
Dion, Celine	Rain Tax (It's Inevitable)	19-29	PS
Dion, Celine	Reason the	14-192	CB
Dion, Celine	Right In Front Of You	19-18	PS
Dion, Celine	Send Me A Lover	4-610	SC
Dion, Celine	Sorry For Love	19-27	PS
Dion, Celine	Taking Chances	49-914	SC
Dion, Celine	Tell Him	15-115	BS
Dion, Celine	Ten Days	19-24	PS
Dion, Celine	That's The Way It Is	15-293	CB
Dion, Celine	That's The Way It Is	8-525	PHT
Dion, Celine	That's The Way It Is	17-539	SC
Dion, Celine	Think Twice	6-645	MM
Dion, Celine	To Love You More	15-114	BS
Dion, Celine	To Love You More	21-554	PHM
Dion, Celine	When The Wrong One Loves U Right	19-23	PS
Dion, Celine	Where Does My Heart Beat	15-110	BS
Dion, Celine	Where Does My Heart Beat	33-336	CB
Dion, Celine	Where Does My Heart Beat	28-407	DK

ARTIST	SONG TITLE	#	TYPE
Dion, Celine & ?	Duet - I'm Your Angel	16-208	MM
Dire Straits	Money For Nothing	2-149	SC
Dire Straits	Sultans Of Swing	11-645	DK
Dire Straits	Walk Of Life	6-487	MM
Dire Straits	Walk Of Life	12-803	P
Dire Straits	Walk Of Life	4-845	SC
Dirty Polka Band	Dirty Polka **	30-667	RSX
Dirty Polka Band	Duet - Dirty Polka **	30-667	RSX
Dirty Vegas	Days Go By	18-149	PHM
Dishwalla	Charlie Brown's Parents	24-541	SC
Dishwalla	Counting Blue Cars	7-573	THM
Disturbed	Down With The Sickness **	16-315	TT
Disturbed	Night the	36-383	SC
Disturbed	Remember	23-146	PHM
Disturbed	Sound Of Silence	49-1	DCK
Disturbed	Stricken	29-249	SC
Divine	Lately	7-793	PHT
Divinyls	I Touch Myself	30-662	RSX
Divinyls	I Touch Myself **	18-255	DK
Divinyls	I Touch Myself **	2-190	SC
Dixie Chicks	Am I The Only One	16-653	RS
Dixie Chicks	Cold Day in July	8-903	CB
Dixie Chicks	Cold Day In July	30-597	RS
Dixie Chicks	Cold Day In July	22-542	ST
Dixie Chicks	Cowboy Take Me Away	20-210	CB
Dixie Chicks	Cowboy Take Me Away	30-598	RS
Dixie Chicks	Cowboy Take Me Away	22-513	ST
Dixie Chicks	Don't Waste Your Heart	8-905	CB
Dixie Chicks	Don't Waste Your Heart	30-599	RS
Dixie Chicks	Everybody Knows	29-596	CB
Dixie Chicks	Give It Up Or Let Me Go	16-652	RS
Dixie Chicks	Godspeed (Sweet Dreams)	34-351	CB
Dixie Chicks	Godspeed (Sweet Dreams)	25-644	MM
Dixie Chicks	Godspeed (Sweet Dreams)	19-172	ST
Dixie Chicks	Godspeed (Sweet Dreams)	32-306	THM
Dixie Chicks	Goodbye Earl	14-177	CB
Dixie Chicks	Goodbye Earl	13-811	CHM
Dixie Chicks	Goodbye Earl	30-600	RS
Dixie Chicks	Goodbye Earl	5-801	SC
Dixie Chicks	Goodbye Earl	16-264	TT
Dixie Chicks	Heartbreak Town	8-906	CB
Dixie Chicks	Heartbreak Town	30-601	RS
Dixie Chicks	Heartbreak Town	15-599	ST
Dixie Chicks	Hello Mr. Heartache	20-213	CB
Dixie Chicks	Hello Mr. Heartache	30-602	RS
Dixie Chicks	Hole In My Head	14-730	CB
Dixie Chicks	Hole In My Head	30-603	RS
Dixie Chicks	I Can Love You Better	35-414	CB
Dixie Chicks	I Can Love You Better	10-63	SC
Dixie Chicks	I Can Love You Better	22-760	ST
Dixie Chicks	I Hope	29-29	CB
Dixie Chicks	I Hope	23-461	ST

ARTIST	SONG TITLE	#	TYPE
Dixie Chicks	I'll Take Care Of You	16-651	RS
Dixie Chicks	If I Fall You're Goin' Down With Me	8-901	CB
Dixie Chicks	If I Fall You're Goin' Down With Me	30-604	RS
Dixie Chicks	If I Fall You're Goin' Down With Me	14-832	ST
Dixie Chicks	Landslide	25-348	MM
Dixie Chicks	Landslide	18-325	ST
Dixie Chicks	Let 'Er Rip	8-756	CB
Dixie Chicks	Let 'Er Rip	10-60	SC
Dixie Chicks	Let Him Fly	20-214	CB
Dixie Chicks	Let Him Fly	30-605	RS
Dixie Chicks	Long Time Gone	25-287	MM
Dixie Chicks	Long Time Gone	17-578	ST
Dixie Chicks	Long Way Around the	30-338	CB
Dixie Chicks	Loving Arms	8-478	CB
Dixie Chicks	Lubbock Or Leave It	30-360	CB
Dixie Chicks	Neighbor the	49-916	SC
Dixie Chicks	Never Say Die	16-650	RS
Dixie Chicks	Not Ready To Make Nice	29-376	CB
Dixie Chicks	Once You've Loved Somebody	15-543	SGB
Dixie Chicks	Ready To Run	8-974	CB
Dixie Chicks	Ready To Run	30-606	RS
Dixie Chicks	Ready To Run	10-61	SC
Dixie Chicks	Ready To Run	22-426	ST
Dixie Chicks	Roly Poly	16-654	RS
Dixie Chicks	Sin Wagon	14-703	CB
Dixie Chicks	Sin Wagon	30-607	RS
Dixie Chicks	Sin Wagon	22-460	ST
Dixie Chicks	Sin Wagon	14-37	THM
Dixie Chicks	Some Days You Gotta Dance	8-904	CB
Dixie Chicks	Some Days You Gotta Dance	25-60	MM
Dixie Chicks	Some Days You Gotta Dance	30-608	RS
Dixie Chicks	Some Days You Gotta Dance	15-855	ST
Dixie Chicks	There's Your Trouble	8-466	CB
Dixie Chicks	There's Your Trouble	7-742	CHM
Dixie Chicks	There's Your Trouble	10-57	SC
Dixie Chicks	Tonight The Heartache's On Me	8-862	CB
Dixie Chicks	Tonight The Heartache's On Me	7-862	CHT
Dixie Chicks	Tonight The Heartache's On Me	22-737	ST
Dixie Chicks	Tonight The Heartaches On Me	10-64	SC
Dixie Chicks	Travelin' Soldier	25-186	MM
Dixie Chicks	Travelin' Soldier	16-439	ST
Dixie Chicks	Travelin' Soldier	32-115	THM
Dixie Chicks	Travelin' Soldier	34-333	CB
Dixie Chicks	Truth No. 2	36-368	CB
Dixie Chicks	Truth No. 2	19-59	ST
Dixie Chicks	Voice Inside My Head	36-176	PHM
Dixie Chicks	White Trash Wedding	20-215	CB

ARTIST	SONG TITLE	#	TYPE
Dixie Chicks	Wide Open Spaces	8-155	CB
Dixie Chicks	Wide Open Spaces	10-58	SC
Dixie Chicks	Wide Open Spaces	22-828	ST
Dixie Chicks	Without You	20-212	CB
Dixie Chicks	Without You	13-856	CHM
Dixie Chicks	Without You	30-609	RS
Dixie Chicks	Without You	30-609	RS
Dixie Chicks	You Can't Hurry Love	30-610	RS
Dixie Chicks	You Were Mine	8-876	CB
Dixie Chicks	You Were Mine	10-59	SC
Dixie Chicks	You Were Mine	22-697	ST
Dixie Chicks&Skaggs	Duet - Walk Softly	14-158	CB
Dixie Chicks&Skaggs	Walk Softly	14-158	CB
Dixie Cups	Chapel Of Love (Going To The...)	10-336	KC
Dixie Cups	Iko Iko	47-24	SBI
Dixie Cups	People Say	47-25	SC
Dixon, Willie	I'm Your Hoochie Coochie Man	15-322	SC
Dixon, Willie	Little Red Rooster	15-316	SC
Dixon, Willie	You Shook Me	14-592	SC
DJ Jazzy Jeff & Fresh Prince	Parents Just Don't Understand	34-137	CB
DJ Sammy&Yanou	Heaven (Disco Version)	21-724	TT
DNCE	Cake By The Ocean	49-658	BKD
Dodd, Deryl	Bitter End a	8-939	CB
Dodd, Deryl	Bitter End a	22-721	ST
Dodd, Deryl	Friends Don't Drive Friends To Dr..	7-386	MM
Dodd, Deryl	Friends Don't Drive Friends To Drink	4-586	SC
Dodd, Deryl	Good Idea Tomorrow	8-934	CB
Dodd, Deryl	Good Idea Tomorrow	14-608	SC
Dodd, Deryl	That's How I Got To Memphis	7-397	MM
Dodd, Deryl	That's How I Got To Memphis	24-654	SC
Dodd, Deryl	Time On My Hands	8-103	CB
Doe, Ernie K.	I Cried My Last Tear	45-577	OZP
Doe, Ernie K.	Mother In Law	26-454	DK
Dog's Eye View	Small Wonders	24-547	SC
Dogg, Nate & Eve	Duet - Get Up	32-126	THM
Dogg, Nate & Eve	Get Up - duet	32-126	THM
Dokken	In My Dreams	23-49	MH
Dokken	In My Dreams	6-25	SC
Dokken	Into The Fire	21-780	SC
Dolan, Joe	Aching Breaking Heart	49-140	SRK
Dolan, Joe	It's You It's You It's You	49-141	SRK
Dolan, Joe	Sweet Little Rock N' Roller	49-142	SRK
Dolby, Thomas	She Blinded Me With Science	18-364	AH
Dolby, Thomas	She Blinded Me With Science	29-9	MH
Dolby, Thomas	She Blinded Me With Science	30-781	SF
Dolce, Joe	Shaddap A You Face	6-522	MM

ARTIST	SONG TITLE	#	TYPE
Dolce, Joe	Shaddap A You Face	16-375	SF
Domino, Fats	Ain't That A Shame	11-254	DK
Domino, Fats	Ain't That A Shame	12-731	P
Domino, Fats	Be My Guest	45-732	VH
Domino, Fats	Blue Monday	9-741	SAV
Domino, Fats	Blueberry Hill	11-313	DK
Domino, Fats	Blueberry Hill	14-554	SC
Domino, Fats	Hello Josephine	44-110	KV
Domino, Fats	I Want To Walk You Home	9-742	SAV
Domino, Fats	I Want To Walk You Home	22-452	SC
Domino, Fats	I'm Gonna Be A Wheel Someday	9-743	SAV
Domino, Fats	I'm In Love Again	9-733	SAV
Domino, Fats	I'm In Love Again	5-239	SC
Domino, Fats	I'm Ready	4-709	SC
Domino, Fats	I'm Walkin'	17-136	DK
Domino, Fats	I'm Walkin'	12-665	P
Domino, Fats	I'm Walkin'	4-4	SC
Domino, Fats	Lady Lady	47-804	SRK
Domino, Fats	Lazy Lady	45-853	VH
Domino, Fats	Let The Four Winds Blow	10-216	SS
Domino, Fats	My Girl Josephine	45-845	VH
Domino, Fats	One Night	47-805	SRK
Domino, Fats	Walking To New Orleans	10-250	SS
Domino, Fats	Whole Lotta Loving	4-707	SC
Don & Juan	What's Your Name	7-301	MM
Don Juan De Marco	Show - Have You Ever Really Loved..	6-899	MM
Donaldson, Bo	Billy Don't Be A Hero	16-157	SC
Donegan, Lonnie	Does Your Chewing Gum Lose It's Flavor...	6-514	MM
Donegan, Lonnie	Gamblin' Man	10-596	SF
Donnas	Take It Off	25-543	MM
Donnas	Take It Off	23-171	PHM
Donnas	Take It Off	23-336	SC
Donnas	Who Invited You	32-256	THM
Donovan	Hurdy Gurdy Man	27-110	DK
Donovan	Hurdy Gurdy Man	5-234	SC
Donovan	Mellow Yellow	12-161	DK
Donovan	Sunshine Superman	27-108	DK
Donovan	Sunshine Superman	3-463	SC
Donovan	Sunshine Superman	30-763	SF
Donovan	Wear Your Love Like Heaven	27-111	DK
Doobie Brothers	Biggest Part Of Me	47-29	TT
Doobie Brothers	Black Water	29-82	CB
Doobie Brothers	Black Water	11-662	DK
Doobie Brothers	Black Water	13-6	P
Doobie Brothers	Black Water	9-772	SAV
Doobie Brothers	China Grove	29-78	CB
Doobie Brothers	China Grove	15-170	MH
Doobie Brothers	China Grove	13-30	P
Doobie Brothers	Doctor the	29-77	CB
Doobie Brothers	It Keeps You Runnin'	29-86	CB
Doobie Brothers	Jesus Is Just Alright	29-85	CB

ARTIST	SONG TITLE	#	TYPE
Doobie Brothers	Jesus Is Just Alright	20-50	SC
Doobie Brothers	Listen To The Music	29-79	CB
Doobie Brothers	Listen To The Music	12-349	DK
Doobie Brothers	Listen To The Music	13-28	P
Doobie Brothers	Little Darlin' (I Need You(	47-27	PS
Doobie Brothers	Long Train Runnin'	11-824	DK
Doobie Brothers	Long Train Runnin'	13-29	P
Doobie Brothers	Long Train Runnin'	29-80	CB
Doobie Brothers	Minute By Minute	29-90	CB
Doobie Brothers	Natural Thing	47-26	KV
Doobie Brothers	Need A Little Taste Of Love	18-392	SAV
Doobie Brothers	Real Love	29-91	CB
Doobie Brothers	Rockin' Down The Highway	29-84	CB
Doobie Brothers	South City Midnight Lady	29-87	CB
Doobie Brothers	Take Me In Your Arms (Rock Me)	29-88	CB
Doobie Brothers	Takin' It To The Streets	29-81	CB
Doobie Brothers	What A Fool Believes	29-83	CB
Doobie Brothers	What A Fool Believes	11-247	DK
Doobie Brothers	What A Fool Believes	13-129	P
Doobie Brothers	Without You	29-89	CB
Doobie Brothers	You Belong To Me	47-28	PS
Doors	Alabama Song	18-653	SO
Doors	Back Door Man **	15-5	SC
Doors	Back Door Man **	18-641	SO
Doors	Been Down So Long	13-647	SGB
Doors	Break On Through	34-50	CB
Doors	Break On Through	18-642	SO
Doors	End the	18-655	SO
Doors	Hello I Love You	35-65	CB
Doors	Hello I Love You	3-14	SC
Doors	Hello I Love You	18-643	SO
Doors	L.A. Woman	18-644	SO
Doors	Light My Fire	2-749	SC
Doors	Light My Fire	18-645	SO
Doors	Love Her Madly	33-277	CB
Doors	Love Her Madly	18-646	SO
Doors	Love Me Two Times	18-647	SO
Doors	People Are Strange	4-699	SC
Doors	People Are Strange	18-648	SO
Doors	Riders On The Storm	33-280	CB
Doors	Riders On The Storm	18-649	SO
Doors	Roadhouse Blues	18-652	SO
Doors	Strange Days	18-654	SO
Doors	Touch Me **	2-727	SC
Doors	Touch Me **	18-650	SO
Doors	When The Music's Over	18-651	SO
Dorsey, Jimmy	All Or Nothing At All	47-32	PS
Dorsey, Jimmy	Brazil	47-33	PS
Dorsey, Jimmy	I Remember You	15-504	DK
Dorsey, Jimmy	I Understand	47-31	PS
Dorsey, Jimmy	Maria Elena	47-34	PS
Dorsey, Jimmy	Tangerine	47-30	PS

ARTIST	SONG TITLE	#	TYPE
Dorsey, Jimmy	Yours	47-35	PS
Dorsey, Lee	Holy Cow	47-36	SF
Dorsey, Lee	Working In A Coal Mine	5-174	SC
Dorsey, Lee	Ya Ya	6-864	MM
Dotson, Amber	I Ain't Your Mama	23-477	CB
Dotson, Amber	I'll Try Anything	22-314	CB
DoubleDrive	Imprint	32-296	THM
Douglas, Carl	Kung Fu Fighting	16-734	DK
Douglas, Carl	Kung Fu Fighting	4-881	SC
Downday	Back In The Day	41-89	PHN
Dr Dre/Snoop Doggy	Nuttin' But A "G" Thang	14-435	SC
Dr. Hook	Better Love Next Time	21-506	SC
Dr. Hook	Cover Of The Rolling Stone	15-174	MH
Dr. Hook	Cover Of The Rolling Stone	7-453	MM
Dr. Hook	Cover Of The Rolling Stone	2-138	SC
Dr. Hook	Everybody's Makin' It But Me	47-48	SFM
Dr. Hook	Freakin' At The Freakers Ball	47-40	SC
Dr. Hook	Happy Ever After Love	47-52	ZM
Dr. Hook	I Don't Want To Be Alone Tonight	47-46	SFM
Dr. Hook	If Not You	47-43	PSH
Dr. Hook	In Over My Head	47-49	SFM
Dr. Hook	Knowing She's There	47-51	ZM
Dr. Hook	Little Bit More	48-771	P
Dr. Hook	Little Bit More	47-39	SC
Dr. Hook	Living Next Door To Alice	47-37	BMG
Dr. Hook	Millionaire the	47-44	SC
Dr. Hook	More Like The Movies	47-45	SFM
Dr. Hook	Only Sixteen	47-41	SFG
Dr. Hook	Sexy Eyes	9-690	SAV
Dr. Hook	Sharing The Night Together	47-38	SC
Dr. Hook	Storms Never Last	47-50	ZM
Dr. Hook	Sweetest Of All	47-42	SFG
Dr. Hook	Sylvia's Mother	5-598	SC
Dr. Hook	When You're In Love With A Beautiful Woman	13-130	P
Dr. Hook	When You're In Love With A Beautiful Woman	15-741	SC
Dr. Hook	Years From Now	47-47	SFM
Dr. John	Right Place Wrong Time	4-89	SC
Drake, Dusty	And Then	49-857	SC
Drake, Dusty	I Am The Working Man	22-72	CB
Drake, Dusty	One Last Time	25-565	MM
Drake, Dusty	One Last Time	19-52	ST
Drake, Dusty	Say Yes	30-342	CB
Drake, Dusty	Smaller Pieces	19-369	ST
Dramatics	Whatcha See Is Whatcha Get	25-280	MM
Dream	He Loves U Not	16-122	PRT
Dream	He Loves U Not	14-43	THM
Dream	He Loves U Not	33-447	CB

ARTIST	SONG TITLE	#	TYPE
Dream	This Is Me	18-539	TT
Dream Academy	Life In A Northern Town	16-245	AMS
Dreamgirls	Show - Dreamgirls	2-294	SC
Dreamgirls	Show - I Am Changing	10-375	KC
Dreamlovers	When We Get Married	2-853	SC
Drifters	At The Club	45-898	SF
Drifters	Come On Over To My Place	45-900	SF
Drifters	Dance With Me	45-896	RB
Drifters	Down On The Beach Tonight	45-894	MFK
Drifters	Fools Fall In Love	45-884	VH
Drifters	Hello Happiness	45-901	SF
Drifters	Honey Love	17-323	SS
Drifters	I Count The Tears	45-895	MM
Drifters	I'll Take You Where The Music Is Playing	45-886	VH
Drifters	I've Got Sand In My Shoes	45-883	VH
Drifters	Kissin' In The Dark	45-889	EZC
Drifters	Like Sister And Brother	45-902	SF
Drifters	Little Red Book	46-199	SC
Drifters	My Girl	45-891	LE
Drifters	On Broadway	33-239	CB
Drifters	On Broadway	12-360	DK
Drifters	Saturday Night At The Movies	45-892	MFK
Drifters	Save The Last Dance For Me	16-770	DK
Drifters	Save The Last Dance For Me	13-256	P
Drifters	Save The Last Dance For Me	2-852	SC
Drifters	Some Kind Of Wonderful	12-359	DK
Drifters	Spanish Harlem	45-890	LE
Drifters	There Goes My Baby	12-357	DK
Drifters	There Goes My Baby	5-452	SC
Drifters	There Goes My First Love	45-893	MFK
Drifters	This Magic Moment	35-43	CB
Drifters	This Magic Moment	11-219	DK
Drifters	This Magic Moment	12-656	P
Drifters	This Magic Moment	9-838	SAV
Drifters	This Magic Moment	17-328	SS
Drifters	Under The Boardwalk	17-103	DK
Drifters	Under The Boardwalk	3-328	MH
Drifters	Under The Boardwalk	2-90	SC
Drifters	Up On The Roof	16-834	DK
Drifters	Up On The Roof	12-672	P
Drifters	When My Little Girl Is Smiling	45-885	VH
Drifters	White Christmas	45-897	SBI
Drifters	Xmas - White Christmas	45-898	SBI
Drifters	You're More Than A Number	45-899	SF
Driskoll&Womak,Jo	Duet - I'd Give My Right Nut To....	14-10	CHM
Driskoll&Womak,Jo	I'd Give My Right Nut To	14-10	CHM

ARTIST	SONG TITLE	#	TYPE
	Save…		
Dropline	Fly Away From Here	21-646	MM
Drowning Pool	Bodies	16-311	TT
Drusky & Mitchell	Duet - Yes Mr. Peters	20-742	CB
Drusky & Mitchell	Duet - Yes Mr. Peters	9-611	SAV
Drusky & Mitchell	Yes Mr. Peters	20-742	CB
Drusky & Mitchell	Yes Mr. Peters	9-611	SAV
Drusky, Roy	All My Hard Times	20-755	CB
Drusky, Roy	Another	20-743	CB
Drusky, Roy	Anymore	20-744	CB
Drusky, Roy	From Now On All My Friends Are…	20-751	CB
Drusky, Roy	I Went Out Of My Way To Make…	20-750	CB
Drusky, Roy	Long Long Texas Road	20-747	CB
Drusky, Roy	Peel Me A Nanner	20-748	CB
Drusky, Roy	Pick Of The Week	20-756	CB
Drusky, Roy	Second Hand Rose	20-746	CB
Drusky, Roy	Such A Fool	20-754	CB
Drusky, Roy	Three Hearts In A Tangle	20-745	CB
Drusky, Roy	Tips Of My Fingers	20-749	CB
Drusky, Roy	Where The Blue And Lonely Go	20-753	CB
Drusky, Roy	World Is Round the	20-752	CB
Duarte, Ryan	You	20-536	CB
Dub, DF	Blowin' Me Up	18-773	PHM
Dubliners	Irish - Black Velvet Band	21-493	SC
Dubliners	Irish - Seven Drunken Nights	21-494	SC
Ducas, George	Every Time She Passes By	4-368	SC
Ducas, George	Hello Cruel World	2-768	SC
Ducas, George	Lipstick Promises	6-706	MM
Ducas, George	Lipstick Promises	17-283	NA
Ducas, George	Lipstick Promises	2-647	SC
Ducas, George	Lipstick Promises	22-857	ST
Dudley, Dave	Comin' Down	43-298	CB
Dudley, Dave	Cowboy Boots	43-291	CB
Dudley, Dave	Fly Away Again	47-53	CB
Dudley, Dave	George (And The North Woods)	43-297	CB
Dudley, Dave	If It Feels Good Do It	47-55	CB
Dudley, Dave	Last Day In The Mines	43-292	CB
Dudley, Dave	Mad	43-293	CB
Dudley, Dave	Me And Ole CB	43-296	CB
Dudley, Dave	Pool Shark the	43-289	CB
Dudley, Dave	Six Days On The Road	8-271	CB
Dudley, Dave	Six Days On The Road	12-17	DK
Dudley, Dave	Six Days On The Road	8-626	SAV
Dudley, Dave	There Ain't no Easy Run	43-295	CB
Dudley, Dave	Truck Drivin' Man	8-390	CB
Dudley, Dave	Truck Drivin' Son Of A Gun	43-294	CB
Dudley, Dave	Two Six Packs Away	47-54	CB
Dudley, Dave	What We're Fighting For	43-290	CB
Dudley, Dave	White Line Fever	46-27	SSK
Due West	Taste Of Your Love	39-82	PHN

ARTIST	SONG TITLE	#	TYPE
Duff, Hilary	So Yesterday	32-357	THM
Duff, Hilary	Wake Up	35-302	CB
Duff, Hillary	Come Clean	20-566	CB
Duff, Hillary	Fly	20-552	PHM
Duff, Hillary	So Yesterday	21-632	CB
Duffy	Mercy	36-452	CB
Dugan, Jeff	Don't Tell Her	8-941	CB
Dugger, Tim	Way Past My Beer Time	38-261	PHN
Dukes, Amboy	Halloween - Journey to the Center..	16-284	TT
Dukes, Amboy	Journey To The Center Of The Earth	16-284	TT
Duncan, Johnny	It Couldn't Have Been Any Better	19-428	SC
Duncan, Johnny	Last Train To San Fernando	10-602	SF
Duncan, Johnny	She Can Put Her Shoes Under My…	29-774	CB
Duncan, Johnny	She Can Put Her Shoes Under My…	5-758	SC
Duncan, Johnny	Thinkin' Of A Rendezvous	5-533	SC
Duncan, Whitney	Bed That You Made the	48-707	BKD
Duncan, Whitney	Skinny Dippin'	37-52	CB
Dunn, Holly	Are You Ever Gonna Love Me	2-358	SC
Dunn, Holly	As Long As You Belong To Me	6-190	MM
Dunn, Holly	Daddy's Hands	26-359	DK
Dunn, Holly	Daddy's Hands	13-383	P
Dunn, Holly	Daddy's Hands	8-696	SAV
Dunn, Holly	Golden Years	6-225	MM
Dunn, Holly	I Am Who I Am	2-691	SC
Dunn, Holly	It's Not About Blame	3-630	SC
Dunn, Holly	Love Someone Like Me	6-744	MM
Dunn, Holly	Maybe I Mean Yes	6-199	MM
Dunn, Holly	No Love Have I	24-357	SC
Dunn, Holly	Only When I Love	34-269	CB
Dunn, Holly	Only When I Love	5-617	SC
Dunn, Holly	You Really Had Me Going	17-221	NA
Dunn, Holly	You Really Had Me Going	12-443	P
Dunn, Holly	You Really Had Me Going	3-374	SC
Dunn, Ronnie	Cost Of Livin'	38-223	FTX
Dunn, Ronnie	How Far To Waco	45-236	SRK
Dunn, Ronnie	Kiss You There	45-235	KCDC
Dunn, Ronnie	Let The Cowboy Ride	45-233	DFK
Dunn, Ronnie	She's Acting Single	42-26	PHN
Dunn, Ronnie	They Still Play Country Music In Texas	45-234	VH
Dunn, Ronnie	Your Kind Of Love	42-28	PHN
Dupree, Robbie	Steal Away	14-568	AH
Dupree, Robbie	Steal Away	28-323	DK
Duprees	Have You Heard	6-258	MM
Duprees	My Own True Love	49-453	MM
Duprees	You Belong To Me	15-589	MM

ARTIST	SONG TITLE	#	TYPE
Duran Duran	Hungry Like The Wolf	35-169	CB
Duran Duran	Hungry Like The Wolf	11-539	DK
Duran Duran	Is There Something I Should Know	17-98	DK
Duran Duran	Notorious	28-307	DK
Duran Duran	Notorious	18-381	SAV
Duran Duran	Reflex the	17-97	DK
Duran Duran	Reflex the	21-739	MH
Duran Duran	Rio	34-80	CB
Duran Duran	Rio	17-462	SC
Duran Duran	Show - View To A Kill	18-234	DK
Duran Duran	View To A Kill	4-387	SC
Durante, Jimmy	As Time Goes By	3-121	KB
Durante, Jimmy	Make Someone Happy	20-769	KB
Durbin, James	Love Me Bad	38-264	PHM
Durrance, Eric	Angels Fly Away	36-229	PHM
Dusty, Slim	Pub With No Beer	47-490	ARC
Dwight Twilly Band	I'm On Fire	7-452	MM
Dylan, Bob	Blowin' In The Wind	29-98	CB
Dylan, Bob	Don't Think Twice It's All Right	29-99	CB
Dylan, Bob	Forever Young	29-103	CB
Dylan, Bob	Gotta Serve Somebody	40-30	SC
Dylan, Bob	Hurricane	29-104	CB
Dylan, Bob	It Ain't Me Babe	29-101	CB
Dylan, Bob	Just Like A Woman	29-94	CB
Dylan, Bob	Just Like A Woman	12-43	DK
Dylan, Bob	Knockin' On Heaven's Door	29-95	CB
Dylan, Bob	Knockin' On Heaven's Door	12-64	DK
Dylan, Bob	Knockin' On Heaven's Door	13-175	P
Dylan, Bob	Lay Lady Lay	29-92	CB
Dylan, Bob	Lay Lady Lay	12-44	DK
Dylan, Bob	Lay Lady Lay	13-228	P
Dylan, Bob	Lay Lady Lay	2-855	SC
Dylan, Bob	Like A Rolling Stone	29-93	CB
Dylan, Bob	Like A Rolling Stone	11-469	DK
Dylan, Bob	Maggie's Farm	29-102	CB
Dylan, Bob	Man Gave Names To All The Animals	47-796	SRK
Dylan, Bob	Positively 4th Street	29-96	CB
Dylan, Bob	Quinn The Eskimo	13-177	P
Dylan, Bob	Rainy Day Woman #12 & 35	29-97	CB
Dylan, Bob	Rainy Day Woman #12 & 35	12-190	DK
Dylan, Bob	Rainy Day Women #12 & 35	2-747	SC
Dylan, Bob	Subterranean Homesick Blues	29-106	CB
Dylan, Bob	Subterranean Homesick Blues	18-175	DK
Dylan, Bob	Take Me As I Am	45-840	VH
Dylan, Bob	Tangled Up In Blue	29-105	CB
Dylan, Bob	Times They Are A-Changin'	29-100	CB
Dylan, Bob	Times They Are A-	18-174	DK

ARTIST	SONG TITLE	#	TYPE
	Changin'		
Dyllon, Marshall	Live It Up	14-133	CB
Dyllon, Marshall	Live It Up	22-580	ST
Dyllon, Marshall	You	15-214	THM
Dynamite Hack	Boyz In The Hood	19-837	SGB
E.U.	Da Butt **	2-189	SC
Eagle Eye Cherry	Feels So Right	18-299	CB
Eagle Eye Cherry	Feels So Right	25-90	MM
Eagle Eye Cherry	Long Way Around	19-833	SGB
Eagle Eye Cherry	Save Tonight	15-629	PHM
Eagles	After The Thrill Is Gone	15-704	LE
Eagles	Already Gone	2-257	SC
Eagles	Best Of My Love	7-549	BS
Eagles	Best Of My Love	6-422	MM
Eagles	Best Of My Love	2-263	SC
Eagles	Busy Being Fabulous	49-708	ST
Eagles	Certain Kind Of Fool	49-83	ZPA
Eagles	Chug All Night	44-92	LG
Eagles	Desperado	7-560	BS
Eagles	Desperado	2-255	SC
Eagles	Doolin-Dalton	49-82	ZPA
Eagles	Get Over It	7-550	BS
Eagles	Get Over It	43-113	LG
Eagles	Good Day In Hell	44-105	ZMP
Eagles	Greeks Don't Want No Freaks	49-85	ZPA
Eagles	Heartache Tonight	7-551	BS
Eagles	Heartache Tonight	6-430	MM
Eagles	Heartache Tonight	2-259	SC
Eagles	Hole In The World	32-353	THM
Eagles	Hotel California	7-552	BS
Eagles	Hotel California	6-428	MM
Eagles	Hotel California	2-264	SC
Eagles	I Can't Tell You Why	7-562	BS
Eagles	I Can't Tell You Why	2-266	SC
Eagles	In The City	5-880	SC
Eagles	James Dean	36-130	SGB
Eagles	Last Resort	15-705	LE
Eagles	Life In The Fast Lane	7-559	BS
Eagles	Life In The Fast Lane	2-260	SC
Eagles	Long Run the	7-553	BS
Eagles	Long Run the	2-254	SC
Eagles	Love Will Keep Us Alive	17-168	SC
Eagles	Love Will Keep Us Alive	30-752	SF
Eagles	Lyin' Eyes	7-554	BS
Eagles	Lyin' Eyes	6-433	MM
Eagles	Lyin' Eyes	2-256	SC
Eagles	New Kid In Town	7-555	BS
Eagles	New Kid In Town	2-261	SC
Eagles	Nightingale	49-86	ZPA
Eagles	Ol' 55	15-706	LE
Eagles	On The Border	44-94	ZMP
Eagles	One Of These Nights	7-556	BS
Eagles	One Of These Nights	2-253	SC
Eagles	Out Of Control	44-93	LG
Eagles	Peaceful Easy Feeling	7-563	BS
Eagles	Peaceful Easy Feeling	2-252	SC

ARTIST	SONG TITLE	#	TYPE
Eagles	Sad Cafe the	44-106	ZMP
Eagles	Saturday Night	49-84	ZPA
Eagles	Seven Bridges Road	7-565	BS
Eagles	Take It Easy	7-557	BS
Eagles	Take It To The Limit	7-558	BS
Eagles	Take It To The Limit	6-425	MM
Eagles	Take It To The Limit	2-265	SC
Eagles	Tequila Sunrise	2-258	SC
Eagles	Victim Of Love	7-561	BS
Eagles	Wasted Time	44-91	ZMP
Eagles	Witchy Woman	7-564	BS
Eagles	Witchy Woman	2-262	SC
Eagles	Xmas - Please Come Home For Xmas	7-4	MM
Eagles	Xmas - Please Come Home For Xmas	14-533	SC
Eagles	You Never Cry Like A Lover	44-104	ZMP
Earl & Stacy	Duet - Romeo & Juliet	9-855	SAV
Earl & Stacy	Romeo & Juliet	9-855	SAV
Earle, Steve	Continental Trailways Blues	46-176	CB
Earle, Steve	Copperhead Road	45-951	KV
Earle, Steve	Devil's Right Hand the	45-954	KV
Earle, Steve	Feel Alright	46-185	SC
Earle, Steve	Galway Girl	46-181	KV
Earle, Steve	Goodbye's All We Got Left	46-178	CB
Earle, Steve	Guitar Town	11-779	DK
Earle, Steve	Hillbilly Highway	46-177	CB
Earle, Steve	Jerusalem	46-182	TU
Earle, Steve	Johnny Come Lately	45-953	KV
Earle, Steve	Mystery Train Pt. 2	46-183	DCK
Earle, Steve	Six Days On The Road	46-179	CB
Earle, Steve	Sugarland	46-180	KV
Earle, Steve	Transcendental Blues	46-184	SC
Earls	Remember Then	7-68	MM
Earth Wind & Fire	After The Love Has Gone	4-381	SC
Earth Wind & Fire	Boogie Wonderland	11-378	DK
Earth Wind & Fire	Duet - Boogie Wonderland	11-378	DK
Earth Wind & Fire	Getaway	11-264	DK
Earth Wind & Fire	Got To Get You Into My Life	11-284	DK
Earth Wind & Fire	Let's Groove	18-372	AH
Earth Wind & Fire	September	27-319	DK
Earth Wind & Fire	September	15-698	LE
Earth Wind & Fire	Shining Star	27-321	DK
Earth Wind & Fire	Shining Star	16-554	P
Earth Wind & Fire	Sing A Song	34-419	CB
Earth Wind & Fire	Spend The Night	4-284	SC
Earth Wind & Fire	That's The Way Of The World	16-555	P
Easter, Jeff&Sheri	My Country	22-11	CB
Easton, Sheena	Almost Over You	20-47	SC
Easton, Sheena	For Your Eyes Only	33-324	CB
Easton, Sheena	For Your Eyes Only	28-295	DK

ARTIST	SONG TITLE	#	TYPE
Easton, Sheena	For Your Eyes Only	9-70	SC
Easton, Sheena	Lover In Me the	16-529	P
Easton, Sheena	Machinery	15-526	CMC
Easton, Sheena	Morning Train (9 to 5)	11-131	DK
Easton, Sheena	Morning Train (9 to 5)	9-782	SAV
Easton, Sheena	Nearness Of You the	18-266	DK
Easton, Sheena	Strut	17-510	SC
Easton, Sheena	Sugar Walls **	15-4	SC
Easton, Sheena	Telefone	5-690	SC
Easybeats	Friday On My Mind	14-463	SC
Echelons	Christmas Long Ago	45-766	CB
Echelons	Xmas - Christmas Long Ago	45-766	CB
Eckstine, Billy	Green Dolphin Street	15-483	SGB
Eckstine, Billy	I'm In The Mood For Love	12-491	P
Eden Xo	Too Cool To Dance	48-400	DCK
Eder, Linda	Anything Can Happen	17-441	PS
Eder, Linda	Big Time	16-715	PS
Eder, Linda	Don Quixote	16-714	PS
Eder, Linda	Don't Ask Me Why	17-442	PS
Eder, Linda	Havana	17-436	PS
Eder, Linda	Hero	17-766	PS
Eder, Linda	I Want More	17-443	PS
Eder, Linda	I'll Forget You	17-444	PS
Eder, Linda	I'm Afraid This Must Be Love	17-445	PS
Eder, Linda	Is This Anyway To Fall	17-446	PS
Eder, Linda	It's No Secret Anymore	17-437	PS
Eder, Linda	It's Time	16-712	PS
Eder, Linda	Man That Got Away the	17-447	PS
Eder, Linda	New Life a	16-720	PS
Eder, Linda	Next Time I Love	16-716	PS
Eder, Linda	No One Knows Who I Am	16-719	PS
Eder, Linda	Someone Like You	16-718	PS
Eder, Linda	Something To Believe In	16-713	PS
Eder, Linda	This Time Around	17-440	PS
Eder, Linda	Till You Come Back To Me	17-448	PS
Eder, Linda	Unusual Way	17-449	PS
Eder, Linda	Vienna	17-435	PS
Eder, Linda	When Autumn Comes	17-450	PS
Eder, Linda	Why Do People Fall In Love	17-439	PS
Eder, Linda	You Never Remind Me	17-438	PS
Edgar Winter Group	Free Ride	34-46	CB
Edgar Winter Group	Free Ride	16-594	MM
Edgar Winter Group	Free Ride	29-295	SC
Edison Lighthouse	Love Grows	4-323	SC
Editors	Bullets	30-748	SF
Edmunds, Kevin	24/7	5-896	SC
Edmunds, Kevin	No Love	19-829	SGB
Edsels	Rama Lama Ding Dong	6-861	MM
Edwards, Jonathan	Sunshine	7-58	MM
Edwards, Jonathan	Sunshine	2-780	SC
Edwards, Kathleen	Instate	29-321	PHM
Edwards, Meredith	Bird Song a	15-333	CB

ARTIST	SONG TITLE	#	TYPE
Edwards, Meredith	Rose Is A Rose a	14-793	ST
Edwards, Meredith	Rose Is A Rose a	15-197	THM
Edwards, Tommy	It's All In The Game	11-737	DK
Edwards, Tommy	It's All In The Game	6-439	MM
Eels	Novocaine For The Soul	24-361	SC
Eiffel 65	Blue (Da Da Dee)	5-887	SC
Eiffel 85	Blue (Da Da Dee)	34-145	CB
El Coyote	Latino - No Puedo Olvidar Tu Voz	17-752	SC
El DeBarge	Where You Are	14-872	SC
El Dorados	At My Front Door	14-456	SC
Elam, Katrina	Flat On The Floor	30-349	CB
Elam, Katrina	I Want A Cowboy	22-29	CB
Elam, Katrina	I Won't Say Goodbye	20-478	ST
Elam, Katrina	Love Is	30-204	CB
Elam, Katrina	No End In Sight	23-405	CB
Elam, Katrina	No End In Sight	23-43	SC
Elam, Katrina	No End In Sight	20-493	ST
Eldridge & Rhett	You Can't Stop Me	45-349	BKD
Eldridge, Brett	Beat Of The Music	43-136	PHN
Eldridge, Brett	Don't Ya	47-433	SSC
Eldridge, Brett	Drunk On Your Love	49-661	BKD
Eldridge, Brett	Drunk On Your Love	48-450	KCD
Eldridge, Brett	Drunk On Your Love	47-707	DCK
Eldridge, Brett	Lose My Mind	45-134	SC
Eldridge, Brett	Mean To Me	45-290	BKD
Eldridge, Brett	One Mississippi	45-278	BKD
Eldridge, Brett	Raymond	46-591	FTX
Eldridge, Jimmy	Funny How Time Slips Away	10-747	JVC
Elegants	Little Star	25-560	MM
Elegants	Little Star	14-349	SC
Eli Young Band	10,000 Towns	44-381	BKD
Eli Young Band	Always The Love Song	44-202	CB
Eli Young Band	Always The Love Song	36-225	PHM
Eli Young Band	Crazy Girl	37-220	CB
Eli Young Band	Drunk Last Night	43-88	HM
Eli Young Band	Dust	44-205	DCK
Eli Young Band	Dust	44-325	SSC
Eli Young Band	Even If It Breaks Your Heart	44-298	PHN
Eli Young Band	Guinevere	47-59	CB
Eli Young Band	Just Add Moonlight	45-279	BKD
Eli Young Band	Life At Best	47-60	PHN
Eli Young Band	Radio Waves	47-58	CB
Eli Young Band	Say Goodnight	47-56	ASK
Eli Young Band	When It Rains	47-57	CB
Elliman, Yvonne	If I Can't Have You	2-505	SC
Ellington, Dale	Satin Doll	10-704	JVC
Ellington, Dale	Take The A-Train	10-707	JVC
Ellington, Duke	Do Nothin' 'Til You Hear From Me	12-567	P
Elliot, Cass	Dream A Little Dream Of Me	49-513	MM
Elliot, Cass	It's Getting Better	49-514	ZM
Elliot, Cass	Make Your Own Kind Of Music	49-515	SAV
Elliot, Cass	Words Of Love	49-473	MM

ARTIST	SONG TITLE	#	TYPE
Elliot, M. & Ludacris	Duet - Gossip Folks	32-127	THM
Elliot, M. & Ludacris	Gossip Folks - duet	32-127	THM
Elliot, Missy	Get Your Freak On	18-514	TT
Elliot, Missy	Lose Control	37-104	SC
Elliot, Missy	Pussycat **	21-793	SC
Elliot, Missy	Work It	32-91	THM
Elliot, Missy	Work It **	25-456	MM
Elliott, Alecia	I'm Diggin' It	5-798	SC
Elliott, Alecia	You Wanna What	9-389	CB
Elliott/Tweet/Ginuw	Duet - Take Away	20-614	CB
Elliott&Tweet&Ginuw	Take Away	20-614	CB
Ellis-Bextor,Sophie	Murder On The Dance Floor	25-346	MM
Ellis, Shirley	Clapping Song	47-91	P
Ellis, Shirley	Name Game the	16-860	DK
Ellis, Shirley	Name Game the	21-573	SC
Elmo & Patsy	Xmas - Grandma Got Run Over By..	8-55	CB
Elmo & Patsy	Xmas - Grandma Got Run Over By..	3-390	SC
Elmo & Patsy	Xmas - Grandma Got Run Over By...	6-291	MM
Elmo & Patsy	Xmas - Senor Santa Claus	3-388	SC
ELO	Can't Get It Out Of My Head	17-514	SC
ELO	Don't Bring Me Down	16-597	MM
ELO	Evil Woman	16-596	MM
ELO	Hold On Tight	5-685	SC
ELO	Strange Magic	3-130	SC
ELO	Sweet Talkin' Woman	5-593	SC
ELO	Turn To Stone	20-85	SC
Embrace	Nature's Law	30-691	SF
Emerald, Caro	I'm Yours	48-213	KV
Emerick, Scotty	Coast Is Clear the	20-334	ST
Emerick, Scotty	I Can't Take You Anywhere	25-707	MM
Emerick, Scotty	I Can't Take You Anywhere	19-271	ST
Emerick, Scotty	Watch the	43-264	CB
Emerick, Scotty	Watch the	20-394	ST
Emerick, Scotty	What's Up With That	29-597	CB
Emerick, Scotty	Where's My Beer	47-497	CB
Emerson Drive	Fall Into Me	25-301	MM
Emerson Drive	Fall Into Me	18-131	ST
Emerson Drive	Good Man a	29-583	CB
Emerson Drive	I Should Be Sleeping	34-348	CB
Emerson Drive	I Should Be Sleeping	25-67	MM
Emerson Drive	I Should Be Sleeping	16-102	ST
Emerson Drive	Last One Standing	19-770	ST
Emerson Drive	Moments	30-247	CB
Emerson Drive	November	23-401	CB
Emerson Drive	Only God (Could Stop Me Lovin...)	25-574	MM
Emerson Drive	Only God Could Stop Me Loving You	19-6	ST
Emerson Drive	You Still Own Me	30-535	CB

ARTIST	SONG TITLE	#	TYPE
Emerson Lake Palmer	From The Beginning	4-84	SC
Emerson Lake Palmer	Lucky Man	3-519	SC
EMF	Unbelievable	21-453	CB
EMF	Unbelievable	5-341	SC
Emilia	Big Big World	7-797	PHT
Emilio	Even If I Tried	4-102	SC
Emilio	I Think We're On To Something	4-375	SC
Emilio	I Think We're On To Something	7-285	MM
Emilio	It's Not The End Of The World	7-168	MM
Emilio	It's Not The End Of The World	4-30	SC
Emilio	Secret Love	4-350	SC
Eminem	Cleaning Out My Closet **	25-458	MM
Eminem	Lose Yourself **	25-455	MM
Eminem	Lose Yourself **	32-13	THM
Eminem	My Name Is **	25-463	MM
Eminem	Real Slim Shady **	25-469	MM
Eminem	Real Slim Shady (Radio Version) **	14-480	SC
Eminem	Real Slim Shady **	19-827	SGB
Eminem	Stan **	21-643	TT
Eminem	Superman	32-198	THM
Eminem	Without Me **	25-466	MM
Eminem	Without Me **	18-143	PHM
Eminem & Dido	Stan **	25-465	MM
Emotions	Best Of My Love	11-290	DK
Emotions	Best Of My Love	12-706	P
Emotions	Best Of My Love	5-107	SC
EMS	Unbelievable	34-106	CB
En Vogue	Don't Let Go (Love)	4-602	SC
En Vogue	Free Your Mind	16-571	SC
En Vogue	Giving Him Something He Can Feel	12-749	P
En Vogue	My Lovin' (You're Never Gonna Get I	6-104	MM
En Vogue	My Loving (You're Never...)	34-108	CB
En Vogue	Riddle	33-282	CB
En Vogue	Riddle (Radio Version)	14-467	SC
En Vogue	Too Gone Too Long	7-690	PHM
England Dan&Coley	I'd Really Love To See You Tonight	28-230	DK
England Dan&Coley	Love Is The Answer	15-739	SC
England, Ty	Irresistible You	24-156	SC
England, Ty	Redneck Son	4-206	SC
England, Ty	Should've Asked Her Faster	20-396	MH
England, Ty	Should've Asked Her Faster	6-821	MM
England, Ty	Should've Asked Her Faster	3-419	SC
England, Ty	Smoke In Her Eyes	3-626	SC
England, Tyler	I Drove Her To Dallas	10-271	CB

ARTIST	SONG TITLE	#	TYPE
England, Tyler	Irresistible You	7-318	MM
England, Tyler	Too Many Highways	5-834	SC
English, Robin	Girl In Love	25-52	MM
Engvall & Friends	Now That's Awesome!	14-162	CB
Engvall & Montgomer	Warning Signs	12-932	CB
Engvall & Tritt	Here's Your Sign	14-648	CB
Engvall, Bill	Fruitcake Makes Me Puke	47-61	CB
Engvall, Bill	I'm A Cowboy	8-213	CB
Engvall, Bill	I'm A Cowboy	49-176	CB
Engvall, Foxworthy & Stuart	Blue Collar Dollar	47-62	CB
Engvall,Bill,Byrd,M	Now That's Awesome!	10-264	SC
Enrique, Luis	Latino - Que So Yo	17-792	SC
Enriquez, Jocelyn	Do You Miss Me	24-553	SC
Enya	Only If	18-530	TT
Enya	Only Time	33-405	CB
Enya	Only Time	16-302	PHM
Enya	Only Time	23-93	SC
Enya	Only Time (Radio Version)	21-520	SGB
Equals	Baby Come Back	12-652	P
Erasure	Chains Of Love	16-526	P
Erika Jo	I Break Things	23-137	CB
Ernie K Doe	Mother In Law	6-521	MM
Ernie K Doe	Mother In Law	2-74	SC
Error 404 & C J Watson	If Trucks Drank Beer	45-132	DFK
Escape Club	Wild Wild West	35-217	CB
Escape Club	Wild Wild West	11-640	DK
Escape Club	Wild Wild West	5-378	SC
Esquires	Get On Up	6-57	SC
Essex	Easier Said Than Done	6-149	MM
Essex	Easier Said Than Done	4-32	SC
Essex, David	Rock On	34-61	CB
Essex, David	Rock On	4-762	SC
Estefan & Miami Sound	Conga	34-79	CB
Estefan & Miami Sound	Rhythm Is Gonna Get You	34-82	CB
Estefan & N'Sync	Duet - Music Of My Heart	35-315	CB
Estefan & N'Sync	Music Of My Heart - duet	35-315	CB
Estefan, Gloria	Always Tomorrow	17-749	PT
Estefan, Gloria	Anything For You	17-746	PT
Estefan, Gloria	Can't Stay Away From You	30-1	PT
Estefan, Gloria	Coming Out Of The Dark	17-743	PT
Estefan, Gloria	Conga	17-741	PT
Estefan, Gloria	Cut Both Ways	17-742	PT
Estefan, Gloria	Don't Want To Lose You Now	49-461	MM
Estefan, Gloria	Everlasting Love	26-338	DK
Estefan, Gloria	Everlasting Love	16-635	MM
Estefan, Gloria	Everlasting Love	29-127	ST
Estefan, Gloria	Get On Your Feet	30-756	SF
Estefan, Gloria	Get On Your Feet	23-574	MM

ARTIST	SONG TITLE	#	TYPE
Estefan, Gloria	Get On Your Feet	17-740	PT
Estefan, Gloria	Get On Your Feet	30-758	SF
Estefan, Gloria	Heaven's What I Feel	23-572	MM
Estefan, Gloria	Here We Are	17-744	PT
Estefan, Gloria	I Can See You Smile	23-575	MM
Estefan, Gloria	I See Your Smile	17-750	PT
Estefan, Gloria	It's Too Late	23-573	MM
Estefan, Gloria	It's Too Late	3-492	SC
Estefan, Gloria	Latino - Oye Mi Canto	17-745	PT
Estefan, Gloria	Live For Loving You	17-751	PT
Estefan, Gloria	Rhythm Is Gonna Get You the	17-739	PT
Estefan, Gloria	Talk To Me	6-371	MM
Estefan, Gloria	Words Get In The Way	17-748	PT
Estefan, Gloria	You'll Be Mine (Party Time)	24-180	SC
Estelle & Kanye West	American Boy - duet	48-591	DK
Estelle & Kanye West	Duet - American Boy	48-591	DK
Esten, Charles	Show - This Town - Nashville	45-478	KVD
Esten, Charles	Show - Undermine - Nashville	45-474	KVD
Esten, Charles	This Town - Nashville	45-478	KVD
Esten, Charles	Undermine - Nashville	45-474	KVD
Eternal	Stay	15-759	NU
Etherdige, Melissa	I Want To Come Over	19-164	SGB
Etheridge, Melissa	An Unusual Kiss	47-71	SC
Etheridge, Melissa	Angels Would Fall	8-515	PHT
Etheridge, Melissa	Breathe	20-359	PHM
Etheridge, Melissa	Bring Me Some Water	4-540	SC
Etheridge, Melissa	Chrome Plated Heart	5-678	SC
Etheridge, Melissa	Come To My Window	19-574	MH
Etheridge, Melissa	Come To My Window	6-637	MM
Etheridge, Melissa	Come To My Window	13-292	P
Etheridge, Melissa	Come To My Window	10-238	PS
Etheridge, Melissa	Come To My Window	9-271	SC
Etheridge, Melissa	Enough Of Me	49-423	SC
Etheridge, Melissa	Enough Of Me	47-64	MM
Etheridge, Melissa	Falling Up	39-105	PHM
Etheridge, Melissa	Fearless Love	47-66	PHM
Etheridge, Melissa	I Need To Wake Up	47-65	NSP
Etheridge, Melissa	I Want To Be In Love	23-98	SC
Etheridge, Melissa	I Want To Come Over	10-235	PS
Etheridge, Melissa	I Want To Come Over	4-180	SC
Etheridge, Melissa	I'm The Only One	16-625	MM
Etheridge, Melissa	I'm The Only One	13-291	P
Etheridge, Melissa	I'm The Only One	10-236	PS
Etheridge, Melissa	I'm The Only One	2-468	SC
Etheridge, Melissa	If I Wanted To	10-237	PS
Etheridge, Melissa	Like The Way I Do	9-378	AH
Etheridge, Melissa	Like The Way I Do	7-486	MM
Etheridge, Melissa	Like The Way I Do	19-154	SGB
Etheridge, Melissa	Lover Please	47-63	ASK
Etheridge, Melissa	Lucky	47-67	PHR
Etheridge, Melissa	No Souveniers	15-738	SC
Etheridge, Melissa	Nowhere To Go	24-51	SC

ARTIST	SONG TITLE	#	TYPE
Etheridge, Melissa	Piece Of My Heart	47-69	RSZ
Etheridge, Melissa	Similar Features	24-564	SC
Etheridge, Melissa	This Moment	23-558	MM
Etheridge, Melissa	Yes I Am	47-68	RSZ
Etheridge, Melissa	You Can Sleep While I Drive	19-547	SC
Etheridge, Melissa	Your Little Secret	47-70	SC
Europe	Carrie	29-302	SC
Eurythmics	Don't Ask Me Why	47-77	SBI
Eurythmics	Here Comes The Rain Again	13-294	P
Eurythmics	I Saved The World Today	47-80	SF
Eurythmics	I've Got A Life	47-73	EZ
Eurythmics	It's Alright Baby's Coming Back	47-82	SFM
Eurythmics	Love Is A Stranger	47-76	LE
Eurythmics	Miracle Of Love	47-75	KV
Eurythmics	Missionary Man	9-886	DK
Eurythmics	Missionary Man	29-296	SC
Eurythmics	Money Can't Buy It	47-78	SFG
Eurythmics	Stay By Me	47-113	SFG
Eurythmics	Sweet Dreams Are Made Of This	11-207	DK
Eurythmics	Sweet Dreams Are Made Of This	13-242	P
Eurythmics	There Must Be An Angel	47-74	EZ
Eurythmics	Thorn In My Side	47-72	DMG
Eurythmics	Walking On Broken Glass	47-79	SFG
Eurythmics	Who's That Girl	34-83	CB
Eurythmics	Who's That Girl	47-81	SFM
Eurythmics	Would I Lie To You	11-94	DK
Eurythmics	Would I Lie To You	13-245	P
Eurythmics	Would I Lie To You	4-534	SC
Eurythmics&Franklin	Sisters Are Doing It For Themselves	16-637	MM
Evan & Jaron	Crazy For This Girl	16-485	MH
Evan & Jaron	Distance the	33-406	CB
Evanescence	Bring Me To Life	20-514	CB
Evanescence	Bring Me To Life	25-584	MM
Evanescence	Bring Me To Life	32-178	THM
Evanescence	Everybody's Fool	20-562	CB
Evanescence	Going Under	19-593	CB
Evanescence	Going Under	32-363	THM
Evanescence	Lithium	30-272	CB
Evanescence	Lithium	30-272	CB
Evanescence	My Immortal	19-663	CB
Evanescence	Sweet Sacrifice	30-492	CB
Evanescence	Sweet Sacrifice	30-492	CB
Evanescense	Call Me When You're Sober	48-602	DK
Evanescense	Call Me When You're Sober	47-873	CB
Evans Blue	Cold (But I'm Still Here)	30-281	SC
Evans, Faith	Can't Believe	18-511	TT
Evans, Faith	Duet - Can't Believe	18-511	TT
Evans, Faith	I Love You	20-617	CB

ARTIST	SONG TITLE	#	TYPE
Evans, Faith	I Love You	25-217	MM
Evans, Faith	Love Like This	15-524	SGB
Evans, Sara	As If	30-470	CB
Evans, Sara	Backseat Of A Greyhound Bus	29-549	CB
Evans, Sara	Backseat Of A Greyhound Bus	25-562	MM
Evans, Sara	Backseat Of A Greyhound Bus	18-793	ST
Evans, Sara	Backseat Of A Greyhound Bus	32-189	THM
Evans, Sara	Bible Song	29-509	SC
Evans, Sara	Born To Fly	14-91	CB
Evans, Sara	Born To Fly	22-561	ST
Evans, Sara	Cheatin'	29-18	CB
Evans, Sara	Cheatin'	23-453	ST
Evans, Sara	Coalmine	29-575	CB
Evans, Sara	Cryin' Game	8-733	CB
Evans, Sara	Cryin' Game	5-296	SC
Evans, Sara	Cryin' Game	22-832	ST
Evans, Sara	Fool I'm A Woman	29-548	CB
Evans, Sara	Fool I'm A Woman	7-867	CHT
Evans, Sara	Fool I'm A Woman	22-741	ST
Evans, Sara	I Could Not Ask For More	29-545	CB
Evans, Sara	I Could Not Ask For More	14-835	ST
Evans, Sara	I Keep Looking	29-550	CB
Evans, Sara	I Keep Looking	25-181	MM
Evans, Sara	I Keep Looking	16-430	ST
Evans, Sara	Let's Dance	29-556	CB
Evans, Sara	Love You With All My Heart	36-595	CB
Evans, Sara	Missing Missouri	30-248	CB
Evans, Sara	My Heart Can't Tell You No	38-135	PHM
Evans, Sara	No Place That Far	29-553	CB
Evans, Sara	No Place That Far	22-705	ST
Evans, Sara	Perfect	29-547	CB
Evans, Sara	Perfect	19-530	ST
Evans, Sara	Real Fine Place To Start a	23-121	CB
Evans, Sara	Real Fine Place To Start a	23-377	SC
Evans, Sara	Saints And Angels	25-10	MM
Evans, Sara	Saints And Angels	29-552	CB
Evans, Sara	Saints And Angels	15-671	ST
Evans, Sara	Shame About That	8-310	CB
Evans, Sara	Shame About That	10-123	SC
Evans, Sara	Slow Me Down	43-154	ASK
Evans, Sara	Some Things Never Change	36-414	CB
Evans, Sara	Suds In The Bucket	29-543	CB
Evans, Sara	Suds In The Bucket	20-383	ST
Evans, Sara	Three Chords and The Truth	4-833	SC
Evans, Sara	Three Chords And The Truth	22-636	ST
Evans, Sara	Tonight	22-99	CB

ARTIST	SONG TITLE	#	TYPE
Evans, Sara	Tonight (Radio Version)	21-665	SC
Evans, Sara	Xmas - Oh Come All Ye Faithful	30-395	SC
Evans, Sara	You'll Always Be My Baby	30-55	CB
Evans, Sara	You'll Always Be My Baby	30-102	PHM
Eve & Keys	Duet - Gansta Lovin'	18-436	CB
Eve & Keys	Gansta Lovin'	18-436	CB
Eve 6	Here's To The Night	18-559	TT
Eve 6	Inside Out	7-786	PHT
Eve 6	Think Twice	32-333	THM
Everclear	Father Of Mine	7-792	PHT
Everclear	Heartspark Dollar Sign	4-331	SC
Everclear	I Will Buy You A New Life	7-774	PHT
Everclear	I Will Buy You A New Life	10-137	SC
Everclear	Santa Monica	4-673	SC
Everclear	Wonderful	35-235	CB
Everclear	Wonderful	15-441	PHM
Everclear	Wonderful	20-8	SGB
Everclear	Wonderful (Radio Version)	14-499	SC
Everett, Betty	It's In His Kiss	15-514	MM
Everett, Jace	Bad Things	29-24	CB
Everett, Jace	Bad Things	23-460	ST
Everett, Jace	Nowhere In The Neighborhood	29-375	CB
Everett, Jace	That's The Kind Of Love I'm In	23-296	CB
Everlast	What It's Like	7-803	PHT
Everly Brothers	All I Have To Do Is Dream	11-400	DK
Everly Brothers	All I have To Do Is Dream	3-321	MH
Everly Brothers	All I Have To Do Is Dream	7-315	MM
Everly Brothers	All I Have To Do Is Dream	13-49	P
Everly Brothers	All I Have To Do Is Dream	3-338	PS
Everly Brothers	All I Have To Do Is Dream	9-458	SAV
Everly Brothers	All I Have To Do Is Dream	14-551	SC
Everly Brothers	Arms Of Mary	45-550	OZP
Everly Brothers	Be Bop A Lula	45-865	VH
Everly Brothers	Bird Dog	11-546	DK
Everly Brothers	Bye Bye Love	17-343	DK
Everly Brothers	Bye Bye Love	7-295	MM
Everly Brothers	Bye Bye Love	13-77	P
Everly Brothers	Bye Bye Love	3-334	PS
Everly Brothers	Bye Bye Love	19-104	SAV
Everly Brothers	Cathy's Clown	11-506	DK
Everly Brothers	Cathy's Clown	13-76	P
Everly Brothers	Cathy's Clown	3-337	PS
Everly Brothers	Claudette	38-21	ZM
Everly Brothers	Crying In The Rain	38-17	CB

ARTIST	SONG TITLE	#	TYPE
Everly Brothers	Devoted To You	38-18	CB
Everly Brothers	Ebony Eyes	38-22	CB
Everly Brothers	How Can I Meet Her	45-551	DCK
Everly Brothers	Let It Be Me	11-665	DK
Everly Brothers	Like Strangers	45-293	DCK
Everly Brothers	Lucille	45-866	VH
Everly Brothers	On the Wings of a Nightingale	38-19	SF
Everly Brothers	Price Of Love the	10-575	SF
Everly Brothers	Problems	38-23	CB
Everly Brothers	So Sad (To Watch Good Love...)	38-24	CB
Everly Brothers	Take A Message To Mary	38-20	CB
Everly Brothers	Temptation	38-25	ZM
Everly Brothers	That's Old Fashioned	38-26	CB
Everly Brothers	Till I Kissed Ya	35-14	CB
Everly Brothers	Till I Kissed Ya	7-286	MM
Everly Brothers	Till I Kissed Ya	3-335	PS
Everly Brothers	Wake Up Little Susie	11-448	DK
Everly Brothers	Wake Up Little Susie	13-78	P
Everly Brothers	Wake Up Little Susie	3-336	PS
Everly Brothers	Wake Up Little Susie	29-828	SC
Everly Brothers	Walk Right Back	43-22	CB
Everly Brothers	Walk Right Back	9-640	SAV
Everly Brothers	When Will I Be Loved	38-27	CB
Everly Brothers	When Will I Be Loved	45-294	ZMP
Everly, Phil	Words In Your Eyes the	47-810	SRK
Every Mother's Son	Come On Down To My Boat	4-255	SC
Every Which Way But	Show - Every Which Way But Loose	6-890	MM
Everything B T Girl	Lullaby Of Clubland	17-718	THM
Everything B T Girl	Single	4-611	SC
Everything B T Girl	Wrong	4-335	SC
Evita	Show - Another Suitcase In Another	15-243	PS
Evita	Show - Buenos Aires	15-240	PS
Evita	Show - Don't Cry For Me Argentina	15-246	PS
Evita	Show - Don't Cry For Me Argentina	2-288	SC
Evita	Show - Goodnight And Thank You	15-241	PS
Evita	Show - High Flying Adored	15-247	PS
Evita	Show - I'd Be Surprisingly Good	15-242	PS
Evita	Show - Lament	15-250	PS
Evita	Show - New Argentina a	15-245	PS
Evita	Show - Peron's Last Flame	15-244	PS
Evita	Show - Rainbow Tour	15-248	PS
Evita	Show - Waltz For Eva & Che	15-249	PS
Evita	Show - You Must Love Me	18-179	DK
Ewing, Skip	Gospel According To Luke	3-74	SC

ARTIST	SONG TITLE	#	TYPE
Ewing, Skip	It's You Again	5-775	SC
Ewing, Skip	Xmas - Christmas Carol	22-291	CB
Exciters	Tell Him	18-250	DK
Exciters	Tell Him	6-659	MM
Exciters	Tell Him	13-72	P
Exciters	Tell Him	3-587	SC
Exies	Kickout	32-291	THM
Exies	My Goddess	32-111	THM
Exile	Crazy For Your Love	11-428	DK
Exile	Give Me One More Chance	33-80	CB
Exile	Give Me One More Chance	11-721	DK
Exile	Give Me One More Chance	20-279	SC
Exile	Hang On To Your Heart	17-15	DK
Exile	I Can't Get Close Enough	29-659	SC
Exile	I Could Get Used To You	17-365	DK
Exile	I Don't Want To Be A Memory	17-12	DK
Exile	I Don't Want To Be A Memory	16-585	SC
Exile	It'll Be Me	20-659	SC
Exile	It's You Again	12-35	DK
Exile	Kiss You All Over	11-395	DK
Exile	Kiss You All Over	2-838	SC
Exile	She's A Miracle	11-741	DK
Exile	She's A Miracle	9-516	SAV
Exile	She's A Miracle	5-628	SC
Exile	Super Love	17-347	DK
Exile	Woke Up In Love	33-86	CB
Exile	Woke Up In Love	11-433	DK
Expose	Come Go With Me	24-208	SC
Expose	I'll Never Get Over You Getting…	28-409	DK
Expose	I'll Never Get Over You Getting…	6-362	MM
Expose	In Walked Love	2-224	SC
Expose	Let Me Be The One	20-43	SC
Expose	Season's Change	12-374	DK
Expose	Tell Me Why	13-194	P
Expose	Tell Me Why	18-501	SAV
Expose	When I Looked At Him	12-758	P
Expose	When I Looked At Him	18-491	SAV
Extreme	Get The Funk Out	5-74	SC
Extreme	Hole Hearted	17-352	DK
Extreme	More Than Words	21-464	CB
Extreme	More Than Words	12-767	P
EZ-Rock & Rob Base	Joy & Pain	14-446	SC
Fabares, Shelly	Johnny Angel	17-125	DK
Fabares, Shelly	Johnny Angel	3-358	MH
Fabares, Shelly	Johnny Angel	13-125	P
Fabian	Turn Me Loose	3-469	SC
Fabian, Lara	I Will Love Again	15-639	THM
Fabian, Lara	Love By Grace	17-720	THM
Fabolous	Breathe	37-99	SC
Fabolous & Tamia	Duet - Into You	32-418	THM

ARTIST	SONG TITLE	#	TYPE
Fabolous & Tamia	Into You	32-418	THM
Fabolous&Ashanti	Duet - Into You (Radio Version) **	21-784	SC
Fabolous&Ashanti	Into You (Radio Version)	21-784	SC
Fabulous T-Birds	Amnesia	48-610	MM
Fabulous T-Birds	My Babe	48-611	NT
Fabulous T-Birds	Powerful Stuff	48-612	PCD
Fabulous T-Birds	Tuff Enuff	35-186	CB
Fabulous T-Birds	Tuff Enuff	7-215	MM
Fabulous T-Birds	Wrap It Up	7-216	MM
Fagen, Donald	Tomorrow's Girls	16-631	MM
Fairchild, Barbara	Gospel - He's a Mighty Good Friend	47-84	VHG
Fairchild, Barbara	He's A Mighty Good Friend - gospel	47-84	VHG
Fairchild, Barbara	Hidden Heroes	47-83	DWG
Fairchild, Barbara	Kid Stuff	29-693	SC
Fairchild, Barbara	Teddy Bear Song	8-17	CB
Fairchild, Barbara	Teddy Bear Song	8-623	SAV
Fairchild, Barbara	Teddy Bear Song	4-784	SC
Fairchild, Shelly	Kiss Me	23-291	CB
Fairchild, Shelly	Tiny Town	22-23	CB
Fairchild, Shelly	You Don't Lie Here Anymore	22-80	CB
Fairchild, Shelly	You Don't Lie Here Anymore	23-39	SC
Fairground Attracti	Perfect	10-527	SF
Faith No More	We Care A Lot	30-783	SF
Faith, A.	How About That	29-817	SF
Faith, Adam	What Do You Want	48-755	P
Faithfull, Marianne	Come & Stay With Me	10-659	SF
Fall Out Boy	Dance Dance	30-147	PT
Fall Out Boy	I'm Like A Lawyer	30-595	PHM
Fall Out Boy	Irresistible	48-435	KCD
Fall Out Boy	Little Less 16 Candles, Little More	30-280	SC
Fall Out Boy	My Songs Know What You Did...	45-446	SS
Fall Out Boy	Sugar We're Goin' Down	30-137	PT
Fall Out Boy	Sugar We're Goin' Out	45-447	EZH
Fall Out Boy	Thanks For The Memories	48-606	DK
Fall Out Boy	This Ain't A Scene it's An Arms Race **	48-607	DK
Fall Out Boy	Uma Thurman	45-655	SBI
Fall Out Boy	Young Volcanoes	45-444	SFK
Family Force 5	Can You Feel It	38-251	PHM
Fantasia	Baby Mama	22-369	CB
Fantasia	When I See U	30-572	CB
Fargo, Donna	Another Goodbye	48-666	SC
Fargo, Donna	Do I Love You (Yes In Every Way)	48-665	CB
Fargo, Donna	Don't Be Angry	48-661	CB
Fargo, Donna	Funny Face	12-410	P
Fargo, Donna	Funny Face	8-629	SAV
Fargo, Donna	Happiest Girl In The Whole USA	15-833	CB
Fargo, Donna	Happiest Girl In The Whole USA	13-388	P

ARTIST	SONG TITLE	#	TYPE
Fargo, Donna	Heartbreak Hotel	8-807	CB
Fargo, Donna	I'll Try A Little Bit Harder	48-660	CB
Fargo, Donna	It Do Feel Good	5-755	SC
Fargo, Donna	Little Girl Gone	48-659	CB
Fargo, Donna	Manhattan Kansas	48-667	VH
Fargo, Donna	Mockingbird Hill	48-662	CB
Fargo, Donna	Shame On Me	29-699	SC
Fargo, Donna	Somebody Special	48-664	SC
Fargo, Donna	Superman	8-837	CB
Fargo, Donna	That Was Yesterday	48-663	CB
Fargo, Donna	U S of A	8-365	CB
Fargo, Donna	You Can't Be A Beacon	13-495	P
Fargo, Donna	You Can't Be a Beacon...	35-365	CB
Fargo, Donna	You Were Always There	39-9	CB
Fargo, Donna	You Were Always There	4-787	SC
Farley, Rachel	Ain't Easy	41-52	PHN
Farr, Tyler	Better In Boots	47-928	BKD
Farr, Tyler	Cowgirl	44-388	BKD
Farr, Tyler	Guy Walks Into A Bar a	45-672	BKD
Farr, Tyler	Redneck Crazy	44-332	SSC
Farr, Tyler	Redneck Crazy	49-704	KV
Farr, Tyler	Whiskey In My Water	43-179	ASK
Farr, Tyler	Withdrawals	45-673	SBI
Farrell & Jay-Z	Duet - Frontin'	32-347	THM
Farrell & Jay-Z	Frontin' - duet	32-347	THM
Farris, Dionne	Hopeless	9-97	PS
Farris, Dionne	I Know	28-408	DK
Farris, Dionne	I Know	14-874	SC
Farris, Dionne	I Know	29-125	ST
Farris, Matt	Redneck Radio	41-75	PHN
Farris, R.	I'm Not The Girl	32-210	THM
Fastball	Better Than It Was	47-86	CB
Fastball	Fire Escape	47-85	MM
Fastball	Out Of My Head	7-805	PHT
Fastball	Sooner Or Later	47-87	CB
Fastball	Way the	33-394	CB
Fastball	Way the	5-281	SC
Fastball	You're An Ocean	15-449	PHM
Fat Boys/Beach Boys	Wipe Out	28-395	DK
Fatboy Slim	Duet - That Old Pair Of Jeans	30-707	SF
Fatboy Slim	That Old Pair Of Jeans	30-707	SF
Feat & Blige	911	14-45	THM
Feat & Blige	Duet - 911	14-45	THM
Feeling	Fill My Little World	30-713	SF
Feliciano, Jose	Listen To The Falling Rain	47-808	SRK
Feliciano, Jose	Xmas - Feliz Navidad	14-538	SC
Female Country	Xmas - Blue Christmas	15-660	THM
Female Country	Xmas - May The Good Lord Bless &...	15-654	THM
Fender, Freddie	Before The Next Teardrop Falls	29-784	CB
Fender, Freddie	I'm Leaving It All Up To You	48-501	CKC
Fender, Freddie	I'm Not A Fool Anymore	49-292	GS
Fender, Freddie	Secret Love	37-360	CK

ARTIST	SONG TITLE	#	TYPE
Fender, Freddie	Since I Met You Baby	37-358	CK
Fender, Freddie	Talk To Me	48-499	CKC
Fender, Freddie	Vaya Con Dios	48-500	CKC
Fender, Freddie	Wasted Days & Wasted Nights	8-49	CB
Fender, Freddie	Wasted Days & Wasted Nights	18-240	DK
Fender, Freddie	Wasted Days & Wasted Nights	13-45	P
Fender, Freddie	Wasted Days & Wasted Nights	9-599	SAV
Fender, Freddie	You'll Lose A Good Thing	37-359	CK
Fender, Freddie	You'll Lose A Good Thing	20-290	SC
Fergie	Big Girls Don't Cry	30-568	CB
Fergie	Clumsy	46-321	SC
Fergie	Fergalicious **	48-235	DKM
Fergie	Finally	36-491	CB
Fergie	Finally	46-323	SC
Fergie	Glamorous	48-234	CB
Fergie	Labels Or Love	48-233	CB
Fergie	London Bridge (Radio Version)	48-232	SC
Fergie	Won't Let You Fall	48-236	KV
Fernando, Vincente	Latino - Gorracho Te Recuerdo	18-8	PS
Ferrell, Rick	Different Point Of View	17-481	CB
Fiddler On The Roof	Do You Love Me	19-585	SC
Fiddler On The Roof	Matchmaker - show	48-785	MM
Fiddler On The Roof	Show - Do You Love Me - duet	19-586	SC
Fiddler On The Roof	Show - If I Were A Rich Man	6-246	MM
Fiddler On The Roof	Show - If I Were A Rich Man	18-192	PS
Fiddler On The Roof	Show - If I Were A Rich Man	5-654	SC
Fiddler On The Roof	Show - Matchmaker	48-785	MM
Fiddler On The Roof	Show - Miracle Of Miracles	14-381	PS
Fiddler On The Roof	Show - Sunrise Sunset	6-321	MM
Fiddler On The Roof	Sunrise Sunset	6-321	MM
Fifth Dimension	Last Night I Didn't Get To Sleep At All	49-470	MM
Fifth Dimension	One Less Bell To Answer	33-249	CB
Filter	Hey Man Nice Shot	5-742	SC
Filter	Hey Man Nice Shot (Album Version)	21-762	SC
Filter	Take A Picture	34-143	CB
Filter	Take A Picture	16-184	PHM
Filter	Take A Picture	5-888	SC
Finch	What Is It To Burn	32-181	THM
Fine Young Cannibal	Good Thing	14-562	AH
Fine Young Cannibal	She Drives Me Crazy	18-253	DK
Fine Young Cannibal	She Drives Me Crazy	6-169	MM
Fine Young Cannibal	She Drives Me Crazy	5-136	SC
Fine Young Cannibal	She Drives Me Crazy	33-333	CB

ARTIST	SONG TITLE	#	TYPE
Finger Eleven	One Thing	19-852	PHM
Finger Eleven	Paralyzer	48-603	DK
Fireballs	Bottle Of Wine	2-403	SC
Firefall	Just Remember I Love You	3-450	SC
Firefall	Strange Way	16-406	PR
Firefall	You Are The Woman	2-842	SC
Firehouse	Hold The Dream	24-21	SC
Firehouse	Love Of A Lifetime	16-570	SC
Firehouse	When I Look Into Your Eyes	23-107	SC
Firm	Radioactive	5-476	SC
First Edition	2001 Space Odessey	10-354	KC
First Edition	Just Dropped In...	2-754	SC
First Edition	Rueben James	9-732	SAV
First Edition	Something's Burning	9-731	SAV
Fisher, Eddie	Dungaree Doll	7-294	MM
Fisher, Eddie	I'm Walking Behind You	49-46	ZVS
Fisher, Eddie	Oh My Pa Pa	33-229	CB
Fisher, Eddie	Oh My Papa	7-298	MM
Fisher, Eddie	Outside Of Heaven	49-47	ZVS
Fitzgerald & Armstrong	Duet - Nearness Of You	49-723	KV
Fitzgerald & Armstrong	Nearness Of You - duet	49-723	KV
Fitzgerald, Ella	A Tisket A Tasket	9-819	SAV
Fitzgerald, Ella	Ain't Got Nothin' But The Blues	47-517	VH
Fitzgerald, Ella	And The Angels Sing	45-583	OZP
Fitzgerald, Ella	Begin The Beguine	12-554	P
Fitzgerald, Ella	Don't Get Around Much Anymore	12-549	P
Fitzgerald, Ella	Embraceable You	12-502	P
Fitzgerald, Ella	How High The Moon	12-550	P
Fitzgerald, Ella	I Let A Song Go Out Of My Heart	12-563	P
Fitzgerald, Ella	I Only Have Eyes For You	23-350	MM
Fitzgeralds, Ella	It's Alright With Me	23-351	MM
Fitzgerald, Ella	Night And Day	44-117	KV
Fitzgerald, Ella	Sweet Georgia Brown	15-837	MM
Fitzgerald, Ella	Tisket A Tasket a	16-414	PR
Fitzgerald, Ella	You'll Have To Swing It	46-274	KV
Fitzgerald&Armstron	Duet - Let's Call The Whole Thing..	12-489	P
Fitzgerald&Armstron	Let's Call The Whole Thing Off	12-489	P
Five Americans	Western Union	16-667	LC
Five Bells	Moody Manitoba Morning	49-253	DFK
Five Blobs	Blob the - Halloween	45-121	SC
Five Blobs	Halloween - Blob the	45-121	SC
Five For Fighting	100 Years	20-572	CB
Five For Fighting	Chances	42-29	PHM
Five For Fighting	Slice	42-30	PHM
Five For Fighting	Superman	15-812	CB
Five For Fighting	Superman	20-378	HP
Five For Fighting	Superman	18-401	MM

102

ARTIST	SONG TITLE	#	TYPE
Five For Fighting	World	43-6	PHM
Five Man Elec Band	Signs	12-778	P
Five Man Elec Band	Signs	5-311	SC
Five Satins	In The Still Of The Night	35-5	CB
Five Satins	In The Still Of The Night	16-738	DK
Five Satins	In The Still Of The Night	7-308	MM
Five Satins	In The Still Of The Night	12-734	P
Five Satins	In The Still Of The Night	9-21	PS
Five Satins	To The Aisle	2-862	SC
Fixx	One Thing Leads To Another	29-8	MH
Fixx	One Thing Leads To Another	3-135	SC
Fixx	Red Skies	21-409	SC
Fixx	Stand Or Fall	16-68	SC
Flack & Hathaway	Back Together Again	12-850	P
Flack & Hathaway	Duet - Back Together Again	12-850	P
Flack & Priest	Duet - Set The Night To Music	6-226	MM
Flack & Priest	Set The Night To Music	6-226	MM
Flack, Roberta	Closer I Get To You	47-90	MM
Flack, Roberta	Feel Like Making Love	11-627	DK
Flack, Roberta	First Time Ever I Saw Your Face	11-124	DK
Flack, Roberta	First Time Ever I Saw Your Face	5-114	SC
Flack, Roberta	Killing Me Softly	11-521	DK
Flack, Roberta	Where Is The Love	47-89	LE
Flack, Roberta	You Make Me Feel Brand New	24-269	SC
Flack, Roberta	You've Got A Friend	47-88	KV
Flaming Lips	She Don't Use Jelly	5-750	SC
Flamingos	I Only Have Eyes For You	12-662	P
Flamingos	I Only Have Eyes For You	9-806	SAV
Flamingos	I'll Be Home	10-256	SS
Flashdance	Show - Maniac	11-696	DK
Flatt & Scruggs	Ballad Of Jed Clampett - TV	33-222	CB
Flatt & Scruggs	I'll Go Steppin' Too	8-259	CB
Flatt & Scruggs	Mountain Dew	12-159	DK
Flatt & Scruggs	Preachin' Prayin' Singin'	49-329	CB
Flatt & Scruggs	Roll In My Sweet Baby's Arms	8-255	CB
Flatt & Scruggs	Salty Dog	8-248	CB
Flatt & Scruggs	TV - Ballad Of Jed Clampett	33-222	CB
Fleetwood Mac	As Lone As You Follow	47-912	LE
Fleetwood Mac	Big Love	47-911	LE
Fleetwood Mac	Chain the	29-272	SC
Fleetwood Mac	Don't Stop	17-390	DK
Fleetwood Mac	Don't Stop	10-31	SC
Fleetwood Mac	Dreams	7-47	MM
Fleetwood Mac	Dreams	12-699	P
Fleetwood Mac	Dreams	10-28	SC
Fleetwood Mac	Everywhere	47-913	SBI
Fleetwood Mac	Go Your Own Way	33-290	CB

ARTIST	SONG TITLE	#	TYPE
Fleetwood Mac	Go Your Own Way	10-32	SC
Fleetwood Mac	Go Your Own Way	10-542	SF
Fleetwood Mac	Gold Dust Woman	5-467	SC
Fleetwood Mac	Gypsy	10-29	SC
Fleetwood Mac	Hold Me	4-85	SC
Fleetwood Mac	Hold Me	10-571	SF
Fleetwood Mac	Hypnotized	13-648	SGB
Fleetwood Mac	Jungle Love	4-873	SC
Fleetwood Mac	Landslide	10-27	SC
Fleetwood Mac	Little Lies	4-320	SC
Fleetwood Mac	Never Going Back Again	17-522	SC
Fleetwood Mac	No Questions Asked	47-910	LE
Fleetwood Mac	Oh Daddy	47-907	DCK
Fleetwood Mac	Oh Daddy	46-116	SC
Fleetwood Mac	Oh Diane	47-914	SBI
Fleetwood Mac	Over My Head	47-909	LE
Fleetwood Mac	Peacekeeper	25-577	MM
Fleetwood Mac	Peacekeeper	32-207	THM
Fleetwood Mac	Prove Your Love	11-680	DK
Fleetwood Mac	Rhiannon	10-30	SC
Fleetwood Mac	Sara	3-528	SC
Fleetwood Mac	Save Me	47-915	SBI
Fleetwood Mac	Say You Love Me	17-392	DK
Fleetwood Mac	Say You Love Me	4-527	SC
Fleetwood Mac	Say You Will	25-658	MM
Fleetwood Mac	Say You Will	32-354	THM
Fleetwood Mac	Second Hand News	47-916	SC
Fleetwood Mac	Seven Wonders	48-908	LE
Fleetwood Mac	Silver Springs	7-685	PHM
Fleetwood Mac	You Make Loving Fun	12-352	DK
Fleetwood Mac	You Make Loving Fun	10-25	SC
Fleetwoods	Come Softly To Me	27-505	DK
Fleetwoods	Come Softly To Me	12-898	P
Fleetwoods	Duet - Come Softly To Me	27-505	DK
Fleetwoods	Mr. Blue	11-547	DK
Fleetwoods	Mr. Blue	12-899	P
Fleming & John	Ugly Girl	10-220	SC
Flirts	Jukebox (Don't Put Another Dime...)	24-421	SC
Flo Rida	Club Can't Handle Me	45-654	KV
Flo Rida	Duet - Right Round	45-649	B
Flo Rida	Good Feeling	45-653	MRH
Flo Rida	How I Feel	45-648	SBI
Flo Rida	I Cry	45-650	MRH
Flo Rida	Let It Roll	45-652	MRH
Flo Rida	Low	45-647	DKM
Flo Rida	Right Round - duet	45-649	B
Flo Rida	Whistle	45-651	MRH
Floaters	Float On	16-557	P
Flock Of Seagulls	I Ran (So Far Away)	29-7	MH
Floetry	Floetic	32-12	THM
Floetry	Say Yes	25-684	MM
Floetry	Say Yes	32-270	THM
Flogging Molly	Drunken Lullabies	48-614	SC
Flogging Molly	If I Ever Leave This World Alive	48-618	KV

ARTIST	SONG TITLE	#	TYPE
Flogging Molly	Salty Dog	48-616	KV
Flogging Molly	Seven Deadly Sins	48-615	KV
Flogging Molly	What's Left Of The Flag	48-617	KV
Florence & Machine	Breath Of Life	39-113	PHM
Florence & Machine	No Light No Light	38-242	PHM
Florida Georgia Line	Anything Goes	45-136	BKD
Florida Georgia Line	Bumpin' The Night	46-99	SBI
Florida Georgia Line	Confession	48-733	BKD
Florida Georgia Line	Confession (Inst)	49-413	BKD
Florida Georgia Line	Cruise	44-131	ASK
Florida Georgia Line	Dayum Baby	47-92	ASK
Florida Georgia Line	Dirt	44-319	SBI
Florida Georgia Line	Get Your Shine On	44-273	ASK
Florida Georgia Line	H.O.L.Y.	49-858	DCK
Florida Georgia Line	Hands On You	43-238	ASK
Florida Georgia Line	Hell Raisin' Heat Of The Summer	47-94	ASK
Florida Georgia Line	Here's To The Good Times	45-154	ASK
Florida Georgia Line	It's Just What We Do	43-126	ASK
Florida Georgia Line	Party People	43-459	ASK
Florida Georgia Line	Party People	40-23	PHN
Florida Georgia Line	People Back Home	43-130	ASK
Florida Georgia Line	Round Here	47-93	ASK
Florida Georgia Line	Sippin' On Fire	45-156	DCK
Florida Georgia Line	Stay	43-95	HM
Florida Georgia Line	Sun Daze	45-155	BKD
Florida Georgia Line	Take It Out On Me	44-313	SBI
Florida Georgia Line	Tell Me How You Like It	45-153	ASK
Florida Georgia Line	This Is How We Roll	43-123	ASK
Flower Drum Song	Show - I Enjoy Being A Girl	17-801	PS
Floyd, Eddie	Knock On Wood	11-501	DK
Floyd, Eddie	Knock On Wood	12-721	P
Flying Burrito Bros	Dark End Of The Street	11-440	DK
Flying Machine	Smile a Little Smile For Me	4-713	SC
Flyleaf	All Around Me	36-510	CB
Flynnville Train	Last Good Time	30-441	CB
Flynnville Train	Tequila Sheila	30-577	CB
Fogelberg, Dan	Longer Than	10-359	KC
Fogelberg, Dan	Longer Than	9-209	SO
Fogelberg, Dan	Xmas - Same Old Lang Syne	14-532	SC
Fogerty, John	Big Train From Memphis	49-104	CDG
Fogerty, John	Blue Moon Nights	48-650	DCK
Fogerty, John	Centerfield	21-575	SC
Fogerty, John	Green River	48-652	DCK
Fogerty, John	Gunslinger	48-655	KV
Fogerty, John	Rockin' All Over The World	48-651	DCK
Fogerty, John	Southern Streamline	47-734	SRK
Foghat	Fool For The City	5-599	SC
Foghat	I Just Want To Make Love	18-259	DK
Foghat	I Just Want To Make Love	4-570	SC
Foghat	Slow Ride	3-610	SC

ARTIST	SONG TITLE	#	TYPE
Foley, Red	Alabama Jubilee	34-186	CB
Foley, Red	Birmingham Bounce	43-366	CB
Foley, Red	Chattanoogie Shoe Shine	8-718	CB
Foley, Red	Chattanoogie Shoe Shine	4-796	SC
Foley, Red	Midnight	43-355	CB
Foley, Red	Mississippi	43-357	CB
Foley, Red	Never Trust A Woman	43-364	CB
Foley, Red	New Jolie Blond	19-631	CB
Foley, Red	Peace In The Valley	8-669	SAV
Foley, Red	Satisfied Mind	43-365	CB
Foley, Red	Shame On You	43-354	CB
Foley, Red	Smoke On The Water	34-185	CB
Foley, Red	Sugarfoot Rag	5-213	SC
Foley, Red	Tennessee Border No. 2	43-358	CB
Foley, Red	Tennessee Saturday Night	19-641	CB
Foley, Red	Tennessee Saturday Night	6-10	SC
Foley, Red & Kitty Wells	As Long As I Live - Duet	43-362	CB
Foley, Red & Kitty Wells	Duet - As Long As I Live	43-362	CB
Foley, Red & Kitty Wells	Duet - One By One	43-356	CB
Foley, Red & Kitty Wells	One By One - duet	43-356	CB
Foley, Red & Kitty Wells	You And Me - duet	43-363	CB
Folk Implosion	Natural One	4-682	SC
Folk Standard	Sloop John B.	18-169	DK
Folk Standard	When Johnny Comes Marching Home	18-170	DK
Fonsi, Luis	Latino - Imaginame Sin To	17-788	SC
Fontana, Wayne	Game Of Love the	11-356	DK
Fontana, Wayne	Game Of Love the	13-89	P
Fontana, Wayne	Name Game the	21-199	DK
Fontana, Wayne	Um Um Um Um Um Um	10-572	SF
Fontane Sisters	Hearts Of Stone	33-234	CB
Fontane Sisters	Hearts Of Stone	5-78	SC
Foo Fighers	Times Like These (Acoustic Version)	25-625	MM
Foo Fighters	All My Life	23-153	PHM
Foo Fighters	Best Of You	23-307	CB
Foo Fighters	Big Me	34-124	CB
Foo Fighters	Big Me	4-664	SC
Foo Fighters	Breakout	48-228	SC
Foo Fighters	DOA	48-225	SC
Foo Fighters	Everlong	6-40	SC
Foo Fighters	I'll Stick Around	48-226	SC
Foo Fighters	Learn To Fly	33-371	CB
Foo Fighters	Learn To Fly	8-528	PHT
Foo Fighters	Let It Die	36-495	CB
Foo Fighters	Long Road To Run	49-894	SC
Foo Fighters	Long Road To Run	48-224	SC
Foo Fighters	Low	23-172	PHM
Foo Fighters	My Hero	48-229	SC

ARTIST	SONG TITLE	#	TYPE
Foo Fighters	Next Year	48-227	SC
Foo Fighters	No Way Back	30-278	SC
Foo Fighters	One the	18-298	CB
Foo Fighters	Pretender the	37-118	SC
Foo Fighters	Saint Cecelia	48-416	BKD
Foo Fighters	This Is A Call	48-230	SC
Foo Fighters	Times Like These	32-140	THM
Foo Fighters	Walking After You	21-557	PHM
Fools	Life Sucks & Then You Die **	30-657	RSX
For Your Eyes Only	Show - For Your Eyes Only	6-881	MM
Forbert, Steve	Romeo's Tune	16-243	AMS
Force M.D.'s	Tender Love	11-281	DK
Ford & Johnson	Cold Beer - duet	47-493	CB
Ford & Johnson	Duet - Cold Beer	47-493	CB
Ford & Osbourne	Duet - Close My Eyes Forever	29-304	SC
Ford & Otto	Chicken & Biscuits - duet	47-506	CB
Ford & Otto	Duet - Chicken & Biscuits	47-506	CB
Ford & Starr	Ain't Nobody's Business	22-211	CB
Ford & Starr	Ain't Nobody's Business But My Own	49-375	CB
Ford & Starr	Duet - Ain't Nobody's Business But.	22-211	CB
Ford & Starr	Duet - Ain't Nobody's Business But...	49-375	CB
Ford & Starr	Duet - I'll Never Be Free	22-205	CB
Ford & Starr	Duet - I'll Never Be Free	46-193	SC
Ford & Starr	I'll Never Be Free	22-205	CB
Ford & Starr	I'll Never Be Free - Duet	46-193	SC
Ford, Colt	Driving Around Song	47-505	ASK
Ford, Colt	Titty's Beer	47-508	KST
Ford, Colt w Davidson	Country Thang	38-119	CB
Ford, Emile	Lazy Sunday	48-754	P
Ford, Frankie	Sea Cruise	35-34	CB
Ford, Frankie	Sea Cruise	6-145	MM
Ford, Frankie	Sea Cruise	12-904	P
Ford, Frankie	Sea Cruise	2-50	SC
Ford, Lita	Back To The Cave	21-778	SC
Ford, Lita	Kiss Me Deadly	28-290	DK
Ford, Lita	Kiss Me Deadly	4-537	SC
Ford, Lita	Shot Of Poison	19-556	SC
Ford, Robin	Ain't Got Nothin' But The Blues	19-794	SGB
Ford, Tenn Ernie	Anticipation Blues	22-207	CB
Ford, Tenn Ernie	Ballad Of Davy Crockett	22-209	CB
Ford, Tenn Ernie	Country Junction	5-410	SC
Ford, Tenn Ernie	Cry Of The Wild Goose	5-219	SC
Ford, Tenn Ernie	Cry Of The Wild Goose the	22-206	CB
Ford, Tenn Ernie	Hey Mr. Cottonpicker	8-432	CB
Ford, Tenn Ernie	Hey Mr. Cottonpicker	18-618	PS
Ford, Tenn Ernie	Hicktown	22-210	CB
Ford, Tenn Ernie	Kissin' Bug Boogie	8-418	CB

ARTIST	SONG TITLE	#	TYPE
Ford, Tenn Ernie	Kissin' Bug Boogie	18-619	PS
Ford, Tenn Ernie	Mr. And Mississippi	22-203	CB
Ford, Tenn Ernie	Mule Train	19-846	CB
Ford, Tenn Ernie	Mule Train	3-881	PS
Ford, Tenn Ernie	Patriotic - This Is My Country	34-438	CB
Ford, Tenn Ernie	Shot Gun Boogie	4-865	SC
Ford, Tenn Ernie	Shot Gun Boogie	22-204	CB
Ford, Tenn Ernie	Sixteen Tons	15-827	CB
Ford, Tenn Ernie	Sixteen Tons	16-862	DK
Ford, Tenn Ernie	Sixteen Tons	7-117	MM
Ford, Tenn Ernie	Sixteen Tons	13-320	P
Ford, Tenn Ernie	Sixteen Tons	18-616	PS
Ford, Tenn Ernie	Sixteen Tons	9-495	SAV
Ford, Tenn Ernie	Smokey Mountain Boogie	22-208	CB
Ford, Tenn Ernie	Tailor Made Woman	22-212	CB
Ford, Tenn Ernie	Tennessee Local	8-817	CB
Ford, Tenn Ernie	Tennessee Local	18-620	PS
Ford, Tenn Ernie	This Is My Country	34-438	CB
Ford, Tenn Ernie	This Is My Country	21-11	SC
Ford, Willa	I Wanna Be Bad	18-406	MM
Foreigner	Blue Morning Blue Day	16-599	MM
Foreigner	Cold As Ice	13-13	P
Foreigner	Dirty White Boy	13-748	SGB
Foreigner	Double Vision	17-79	DK
Foreigner	Hot Blooded	35-136	CB
Foreigner	Hot Blooded	13-284	P
Foreigner	I Don't Want To Live Without You	17-80	DK
Foreigner	I Want To Know What Love Is	20-293	CB
Foreigner	I Want To Know What Love Is	11-82	DK
Foreigner	I Want To Know What Love Is	13-286	P
Foreigner	I Want To Know What Love Is	9-202	SO
Foreigner	Say You Will	5-140	SC
Foreigner	Waiting For A Girl Like You	11-121	DK
Foreigner	Waiting For A Girl Like You	4-764	SC
Foreigner	With Heaven On Our Side	24-16	SC
Forrester Sisters	I Fell In Love Again Last Night	12-406	P
Forrester Sisters	Just In Case	33-45	CB
Forrester Sisters	Just In Case	11-425	DK
Forrester Sisters	Just In Case	8-687	SAV
Forrester Sisters	Just In Case	5-28	SC
Forrester Sisters	Leave It Alone	16-590	MM
Forrester Sisters	Lonely Alone	19-432	SC
Forrester Sisters	Lyin' In His Arms Again	26-570	DK
Forrester Sisters	Mama's Never Seen Those Eyes	34-259	CB
Forrester Sisters	Mama's Never Seen Those Eyes	12-472	P
Forrester Sisters	Men	18-264	DK

ARTIST	SONG TITLE	#	TYPE
Forrester Sisters	Men	6-109	MM
Forrester Sisters	Men	13-390	P
Forrester Sisters	Men	2-126	SC
Forrester Sisters	That's What You Do When You're In	20-682	SC
Forrester Sisters	When You're In Love (That's What..)	19-443	SC
Fortunes	This Golden Ring	45-600	OZP
Fortunes	You've Got Your Troubles	48-751	P
Foster & Lloyd	Crazy Over You	5-621	SC
Foster & Lloyd	Fair Shake	20-280	SC
Foster & Lloyd	Sure Thing	5-867	SC
Foster & Lloyd	What Do You Want From Me	5-766	SC
Foster, Radney	Close Up The Honky Tonks	47-99	SSK
Foster, Radney	Closing Time	47-96	SC
Foster, Radney	Easier Said Than Done	2-328	SC
Foster, Radney	Everyday Angel	18-211	ST
Foster, Radney	Everyday Angel	49-28	KCD
Foster, Radney	Half Of My Mistakes	47-98	ST
Foster, Radney	Just Call Me Lonesome	12-457	P
Foster, Radney	Labor Of Love	2-320	SC
Foster, Radney	Nobody Wins	2-622	SC
Foster, Radney	Running Kind	47-97	SC
Foster, Radney	Scary Old World	19-12	ST
Foster, Radney	Willin' To Walk	2-668	SC
Foster, Stephen	Beautiful Dreamer	46-290	CB
Foundations	Baby Now That I've Found You	7-473	MM
Foundations	Baby Now That I've Found You	3-134	SC
Foundations	Baby Now That I've Found You	10-594	SF
Foundations	Build Me Up Buttercup	12-47	DK
Fountains of Wayne	Rock Me Tonight	48-570	DK
Fountains of Wayne	Stacy's Mom	35-292	CB
Fountains of Wayne	Stacy's Mom	20-226	MM
Fountains of Wayne	Stacy's Mom	23-183	PHM
Four Aces	Gang That Sang Heart Of My Heart	9-746	SAV
Four Aces	Heart And Soul	4-358	SC
Four Aces	Love Is A Many Splendored Thing	48-762	P
Four Lads	Gilly Gilly Ossenfeffer	21-597	SF
Four Lads	Moments To Remember	45-69	JVC
Four Lads	Standing On The Corner	21-536	SC
Four Pennies	Juliet	10-569	SF
Four Preps	26 Miles	9-735	SAV
Four Preps	Organ Grinder's Swing	9-824	SAV
Four Seasons	Ain't That A Shame	45-798	SBI
Four Seasons	Big Girls Don't Cry	35-41	CB
Four Seasons	Big Girls Don't Cry	16-840	DK
Four Seasons	Big Girls Don't Cry	13-120	P
Four Seasons	Big Girls Don't Cry	4-10	SC
Four Seasons	Big Man In Town	43-436	LG
Four Seasons	Bye Bye Baby (Baby	43-434	LG

ARTIST	SONG TITLE	#	TYPE
	Goodbye)		
Four Seasons	Candy Girl	22-441	SC
Four Seasons	Dawn	4-716	SC
Four Seasons	Dawn (Go Away)	33-247	CB
Four Seasons	December 1963	10-539	SF
Four Seasons	December 1963 (Oh What A Night)	11-789	DK
Four Seasons	Don't Think Twice	43-435	LG
Four Seasons	Let's Hang On	20-36	SC
Four Seasons	Oh What A Night	35-90	CB
Four Seasons	Oh What A Night	10-539	SF
Four Seasons	Rag Doll	34-16	CB
Four Seasons	Rag Doll	11-701	DK
Four Seasons	Ronnie	43-385	LG
Four Seasons	Save It For Me	43-433	LG
Four Seasons	Sherry	35-49	CB
Four Seasons	Sherry	11-214	DK
Four Seasons	Sherry	13-85	P
Four Seasons	Sherry	19-113	SAV
Four Seasons	Tell It To The Rain	43-432	CBE P
Four Seasons	Walk Like A Man	27-142	DK
Four Seasons	Who Loves You	43-384	CB
Four Seasons	Working My Way Back To You	35-160	CB
Four Seasons	Working My Way Back To You	22-445	SC
Four Tops	7 Rooms Of Gloom	34-32	CB
Four Tops	Ain't No Woman (Like The One...)	26-436	DK
Four Tops	Ain't No Woman Like The One I Got	35-113	CB
Four Tops	Baby I Need Your Lovin'	16-797	DK
Four Tops	Baby I Need Your Lovin'	12-634	P
Four Tops	Bernadette	26-520	DK
Four Tops	I Can't Help Myself	11-102	DK
Four Tops	I Can't Help Myself	2-86	SC
Four Tops	If I Were A Carpenter	43-428	EZC
Four Tops	Indestructible	43-383	CB
Four Tops	It's The Same Old Song	11-146	DK
Four Tops	It's The Same Old Song	2-78	SC
Four Tops	Loco In Acapulco	43-429	EZC
Four Tops	Reach Out I'll Be There	11-142	DK
Four Tops	Shake Me Wake Me (When It's Over	43-427	CB
Four Tops	Something About You	43-426	CB
Four Tops	Standing In The Shadows	16-764	DK
Four Tops	Still Water	43-425	CB
Four Tops	Walk Away Renee	2-80	SC
Four Tops	When She Was My Girl	43-387	CB
Four Tops	When She Was My Girl	43-431	SF
Fowler, Kevin	Cheaper To Keep Her	48-708	BKD
Fowler, Kevin	Don't Touch My Willie	29-613	ST
Fowler, Kevin	Hard Man To Love	49-91	YBK
Fowler, Kevin	Hell Yeah I Like Beer	47-500	JRM
Fox, Samantha	I Only Wanna Be With You	35-190	CB

ARTIST	SONG TITLE	#	TYPE
Fox, Samantha	I Only Wanna Be With You	11-697	DK
Fox, Samantha	I Only Wanna Be With You	6-484	MM
Fox, Samantha	I Wanna Have Some Fun	15-10	SC
Fox, Samantha	Naughty Girls Need Love Too	11-534	DK
Fox, Samantha	Touch Me **	5-554	SC
Foxworthy, Jeff	Xmas - Redneck 12 Days Of Xmas	18-719	CB
Foxworthy&Engvall	Blue Collar Dollar	9-422	CB
Foxx, Inez	Mockingbird	3-579	SC
Frampton, Peter	Baby I Love Your Way	24-209	SC
Frampton, Peter	Show Me The Way	12-698	P
Frampton, Peter	Show Me The Way	5-872	SC
Frances, Connie	Three Good Reasons	45-871	VH
Francis, Cleve	Love Or The Lack Thereof	2-395	SC
Francis, Cleve	Walkin'	24-252	SC
Francis, Connie	Among My Souvenirs	8-825	CB
Francis, Connie	Among My Souvenirs	3-510	SC
Francis, Connie	Don't Break The Heart That Loves U	8-816	CB
Francis, Connie	Don't Break The Heart That Loves U	4-218	SC
Francis, Connie	Everybody's Somebody's Fool	11-271	DK
Francis, Connie	Lipstick On Your Collar	10-729	JVC
Francis, Connie	My Happiness	20-40	SC
Francis, Connie	My Heart Has A Mind Of It's Own	5-90	SC
Francis, Connie	Robot Man	29-814	SF
Francis, Connie	Stupid Cupid	10-332	KC
Francis, Connie	Stupid Cupid	4-694	SC
Francis, Connie	Tennessee Waltz	8-810	CB
Francis, Connie	Vacation	16-364	CB
Francis, Connie	Where The Boys Are	11-251	DK
Francis, Connie	Where The Boys Are	9-24	PS
Francis, Connie	Who's Sorry Now	19-608	MH
Francis, Connie	Who's Sorry Now	7-292	MM
Francis, Connie	Who's Sorry Now	4-693	SC
Francis, Connie	Who's Sorry Now	10-514	SF
Frankie Goes Hollyw	Relax	29-13	MH
Frankie Goes Hollyw	Relax	5-117	SC
Frankie J	Don't Wanna Try	21-636	CB
Frankie J	How To Deal	23-313	CB
Frankie J w Baby Bash	Obsession (No Es Amor)	37-96	SC
Frankie, J	Don't Wanna Try	32-237	THM
Franklin & Michael	Duet - I knew You Were Waiting	35-310	CB
Franklin & Michael	Duet - I Knew You Were Waiting For	17-350	DK
Franklin & Michael	I Knew You Were Waiting	35-310	CB
Franklin & Michael	I Knew You Were Waiting	17-350	DK
Franklin, Aretha	Ain't No Way	9-660	SAV
Franklin, Aretha	Chain Of Fools	26-477	DK
Franklin, Aretha	Chain Of Fools	36-160	JT
Franklin, Aretha	Chain Of Fools	19-612	MH
Franklin, Aretha	Chain Of Fools	12-722	P
Franklin, Aretha	Chain Of Fools	9-664	SAV
Franklin, Aretha	Deeper Love a	36-161	JT
Franklin, Aretha	Do Right Woman Do Right Man	11-293	DK
Franklin, Aretha	Don't Play That Song	17-102	DK
Franklin, Aretha	Freeway Of Love	34-33	CB
Franklin, Aretha	Freeway Of Love	36-162	JT
Franklin, Aretha	Freeway Of Love	4-877	SC
Franklin, Aretha	Here We Go Again	36-163	JT
Franklin, Aretha	Higher Ground	13-87	P
Franklin, Aretha	How Many Times	36-164	JT
Franklin, Aretha	I Knew You Were Waiting	48-551	DK
Franklin, Aretha	I Never Loved a Man....	36-165	JT
Franklin, Aretha	I Say a Little Prayer	10-627	SF
Franklin, Aretha	In the Morning	36-166	JT
Franklin, Aretha	It Hurts Like Hell	36-167	JT
Franklin, Aretha	Love Pang	36-168	JT
Franklin, Aretha	Natural Woman	12-710	P
Franklin, Aretha	Natural Woman	2-267	SC
Franklin, Aretha	Natural Woman (You Make Me...)	25-170	MM
Franklin, Aretha	Natural Woman a (You Make Me...)	26-108	DK
Franklin, Aretha	Respect	17-48	DK
Franklin, Aretha	Respect	36-169	JT
Franklin, Aretha	Respect	10-735	JVC
Franklin, Aretha	Respect	13-74	P
Franklin, Aretha	Respect	9-225	PT
Franklin, Aretha	Respect	9-286	SC
Franklin, Aretha	Rock Steady	36-170	JT
Franklin, Aretha	Rock Steady	19-559	SC
Franklin, Aretha	Rose Is Still A Rose a	36-159	JT
Franklin, Aretha	Rose Is Still A Rose a	9-95	PS
Franklin, Aretha	Say A Little Prayer	10-593	SF
Franklin, Aretha	Think	33-245	CB
Franklin, Aretha	Think	11-810	DK
Franklin, Aretha	Think	3-357	MH
Franklin, Aretha	Think	12-718	P
Franklin, Aretha	Till You Come Back To Me	10-478	DA
Franklin, Aretha	Until You Come Back To Me	34-44	CB
Franklin, Aretha	Until You Come Back To Me	36-173	JT
Franklin, Aretha	Who's Zoomin' Who	36-174	JT
Franklin, Aretha	Willing To Forgive	6-635	MM
Franklin, Aretha	Willing To Forgive	15-762	NU
Franklin, Aretha	Woman the	36-171	JT
Franklin, Aretha	You Make Me Feel Like a Natural...	36-175	JT
Fray	Cable Car (Over My Head)	30-282	SC
Fray	How To Save A Life	36-191	PHM
Fray	Over My Head (Cable	30-149	PT

ARTIST	SONG TITLE	#	TYPE
	(Car)		
Fray	You Found Me	36-266	PHM
Frazier River	Last Request	4-619	SC
Frazier River	She got What She Deserved	7-203	MM
Frazier River	Tangled Up In Texas	7-322	MM
Frazier River	Tangled Up In Texas	4-396	SC
Frazier, Morgan	Yellow Brick Road	39-96	PHN
Freberg, Stan	Xmas - Nuttin' For Christmas	14-297	MM
Freberg, Stan	Xmas - Nuttin' For Christmas	5-708	SC
Freddie & Dreamers	I'm Telling You Now	11-558	DK
Freddie & Dreamers	If You Gotta Make A Fool Of Some-	10-561	SF
Freddie & Dreamers	You Were Made For Me	10-566	SF
Free	All Right Now	17-88	DK
Free	All Right Now	20-309	MH
Free	All Right Now	12-774	P
Free Movement	I've Found Someone Of My Own	25-281	MM
Freeman, Adrianna	Just A Girl	42-3	PHN
Freeman, Bobby	C'mon And Swim - DANCE #	22-397	SC
Freeman, Bobby	Do You Wanna Dance	7-287	MM
Freeman, Bobby	Do You Wanna Dance	13-51	P
Frehley, Ace	New York Groove	17-468	SC
French, Nicki	Total Eclipse Of The Heart	3-434	SC
Frey, Glenn	Heat Is On the	26-142	DK
Frey, Glenn	Heat Is On the	5-111	SC
Frey, Glenn	I've Got Mine	4-275	SC
Frey, Glenn	One You Love the	15-712	LE
Frey, Glenn	You Belong To The City	15-713	LE
Fricke, Janie	Always Have Always Will	29-652	SC
Fricke, Janie	Do Me With Love	34-247	CB
Fricke, Janie	Down To My Last Broken Heart	19-420	SC
Fricke, Janie	He's A Heartache	9-627	SAV
Fricke, Janie	He's A Heartache Lookin' For A	13-519	P
Fricke, Janie	He's A Heartache Lookin' For A...	5-21	SC
Fricke, Janie	I'll Need Someone To Hold Me When	7-165	MM
Fricke, Janie	Place To Fall Apart a	12-411	P
Fricke, Janie	She's Single Again	13-537	P
Fricke, Janie	Tell Me A Lie	8-210	CB
Fricke, Janie	Tell Me A Lie	7-152	MM
Fricke, Janie	You Don't Know Love	14-429	SC
Fricke, Janie	Your Heart's Not In It	4-782	SC
Frickie, Janie	It Ain't Easy Being Easy	49-633	CB
Frickie, Janie	Let's Stop Talking About It	49-635	CB
Frickie, Janie	Somebody Else's Fire	49-810	CB
Frida	I Know There's Something Goin' On	18-494	SAV
Frida	I Know There's	5-608	SC

ARTIST	SONG TITLE	#	TYPE
	Something Goin' On		
Friend & Lover	Duet - Reach Out In The Darkness	6-781	MM
Friend & Lover	Reach Out In The Darkness	6-781	MM
Frizzell & West	Duet - I Just Came Here To Dance	45-411	CB
Frizzell & West	Duet - You're The Reason God Made	2-311	SC
Frizzell & West	Duet - You're The Reason God Made..	8-120	CB
Frizzell & West	Duet - You're The Reason God Made..	13-522	P
Frizzell & West	I Just Came Here To Dance - duet	45-411	CB
Frizzell & West	You're The Reason God Made OK	8-120	CB
Frizzell & West	You're The Reason God Made OK	13-523	P
Frizzell & West	You're The Reason God Made OK	2-311	SC
Frizzell, David	I'm Gonna Hire A Wino	16-355	CB
Frizzell, David	I'm Gonna Hire A Wino	7-419	MM
Frizzell, David	I'm Gonna Hire A Wino	13-392	P
Frizzell, Lefty	Always Late With Your Kisses	19-483	CB
Frizzell, Lefty	Always Late With Your Kisses	7-151	MM
Frizzell, Lefty	Always Late With Your Kisses	4-810	SC
Frizzell, Lefty	Cigarettes And Coffee Blues	46-16	SSK
Frizzell, Lefty	Don't Stay Away Till Love Grows…	19-493	CB
Frizzell, Lefty	Forever And Always	19-495	CB
Frizzell, Lefty	Give Me More More More	19-491	CB
Frizzell, Lefty	Give Me More More More	5-421	SC
Frizzell, Lefty	I Love You A Thousand Ways	19-486	CB
Frizzell, Lefty	I Love You A Thousand Ways	5-374	SC
Frizzell, Lefty	I Overlooked An Orchid	19-484	CB
Frizzell, Lefty	I Want To Be With You Always	3-735	CB
Frizzell, Lefty	I'm An Old Old Man	19-494	CB
Frizzell, Lefty	If You've Got The Money I've Got…	19-481	CB
Frizzell, Lefty	If You've Got The Money I've Got…	7-106	MM
Frizzell, Lefty	If You've Got The Money I've Got…	3-592	SC
Frizzell, Lefty	Long Black Veil	19-492	CB
Frizzell, Lefty	Long Black Veil	12-311	DK
Frizzell, Lefty	Look What Thoughts Will Do	19-487	CB
Frizzell, Lefty	Mama - xmas	46-51	SSK
Frizzell, Lefty	Mom And Dad's Waltz	19-485	CB
Frizzell, Lefty	Mom And Dad's Waltz	7-162	MM

ARTIST	SONG TITLE	#	TYPE
Frizzell, Lefty	Saginaw Michigan	19-482	CB
Frizzell, Lefty	Saginaw Michigan	7-111	MM
Frizzell, Lefty	She's Gone Gone Gone	20-642	SC
Frizzell, Lefty	Shine Shave Shower It's Sat Nite	3-734	CB
Frizzell, Lefty	Travelin' Blues	19-490	CB
Frizzell, Lefty	Watermelon Time In Georgia	47-812	SRK
Frizzell, Lefty	Xmas - Mama	46-51	SSK
Frozen	Let It Go - Frozen	46-378	DIS
Frozen	Fixer Upper - Frozen	46-381	DIS
Frozen	For The First Time In Forever	46-377	DIS
Frozen	In Summer - Frozen	46-380	DIS
Frozen	Reindeers Are Better Than People	46-379	DIS
Frozen	Show - Fixer Upper - Frozen	46-381	DIS
Frozen	Show - For The First Time In Forever	46-377	DIS
Frozen	Show - In Summer - Frozen	46-380	DIS
Frozen	Show - Let It Go - Frozen	46-378	DIS
Frozen	Show - Reindeers Are Better Than People	46-379	DIS
Fudd, Ozzy	Kill The Wabbit	47-777	SRK
Fuel	Bad Day	33-418	CB
Fuel	Bad Day	18-397	MM
Fuel	Falls On Me	20-565	CB
Fuel	Falls On Me	23-174	PHM
Fuel	Hemmorage In My Hands	35-245	CB
Fuel	Hemmorage In My Hands	15-428	PHM
Fuel	Hemmorage In My Hands	18-558	TT
Fuel	Last Time	18-293	CB
Fuel	Last Time	30-653	THM
Fuel	Wasted Time	36-485	CB
Fuel	Won't Back Down	32-144	THM
Fugees	Killing Me Softly	14-905	SC
Full Monty	Big Black Man (With Vocals)	36-132	SGB
Fun.	We Are Young	39-116	SF
Funny Girl	Don't Rain On My Parade	49-440	MM
Funny Girl	My Man	49-441	MM
Funny Girl	My Man - show	48-789	MM
Funny Girl	Show - Don't Rain On My Parade	49-440	MM
Funny Girl	Show - My Man	49-441	MM
Funny Girl	Show - My Man	48-789	MM
Funny Girl	Show - Sadie Sadie	7-365	MM
Funny Girl	Show - Second Hand Rose	10-375	KC
Funny Girl - Streisand	Show - Who Are You Now	49-581	PS
Funny Lady - Streisand	Show - Am I Blue	49-585	PS

ARTIST	SONG TITLE	#	TYPE
Funny Lady - Streisand	Show - I Found a Million Dollar Baby	49-583	PS
Funny Lady - Streisand	Show - If I Love Again	49-586	PS
Funny Lady - Streisand	Show - Isn't This Better	49-584	PS
Funny Lady - Streisand	Show - Me An My Shadow	49-587	PS
Funny Lady - Streisand	Show - More Than You Know	49-582	PS
Fureys	Red Rose Cafe the	44-109	KV
Furtado & Timbaland	Duet - Promiscuous	48-605	DK
Furtado & Timbaland	Promiscuous	30-146	PT
Furtado & Timbaland	Promiscuous - duet	48-605	DK
Furtado, Nelly	All Good Things (Come to an End)	30-497	CB
Furtado, Nelly	I'm Like A Bird	35-236	CB
Furtado, Nelly	I'm Like A Bird	16-114	PRT
Furtado, Nelly	I'm Like A Bird	18-522	TT
Furtado, Nelly	On The Radio	21-649	CB
Furtado, Nelly	On The Radio	25-144	MM
Furtado, Nelly	Powerless (Say What You Want)	19-665	CB
Furtado, Nelly	Say It Right	30-265	CB
Furtado, Nelly	Try	20-564	CB
Furtado, Nelly	Turn Off The Lights	23-587	PHM
Furtado, Nelly	Turn Off The Lights	15-820	CB
Furtado, Nelly	Turn Off The Lights	18-403	MM
Furtado&Timbaland	Duet - Promiscuous	30-146	PT
Furtado&Timbaland	Promiscuous	30-146	PT
Fury, Billy	Halfway To Paradise	10-554	SF
Fury, Billy	I'd Never Find Another You	10-557	SF
Fury, Billy	Once Upon A Dream	10-660	SF
Fury, Billy	When Will You Say I Love You	10-619	SF
Future Leaders of the World	Let Me Out	30-815	PHM
G.Q.	Disco Nights	18-366	AH
Gabe Dixon Band	Five More Hours	36-256	PHM
Gabriel, Peter	In Your Eyes	16-247	AMS
Gabriel, Peter	Shock The Monkey	21-403	SC
Gabriel, Peter	Sledge Hammer	2-556	SC
Gallery	I Believe In Music	47-568	MKP
Gallery	Nice To Be With You	9-365	MG
Gallery	Nice To Be With You	3-20	SC
Game & 50 Cent	How We Do (Radio Vers)	37-100	SC
Gap Band	Big Fun	48-278	SFM
Gap Band	Early In The Morning	14-366	MH
Gap Band	Oops Upside Your Head	16-372	SF
Gap Band	Party Train	18-361	AH
Gap Band	You Dropped A Bomb On Me	16-643	MM
Garbage	I Think I'm Paranoid	19-553	SC
Garbage	Milk	24-642	SC
Garbage	Only Happy When It Rains	4-668	SC
Garbage	Push It	5-275	SC
Garbage	Special	13-786	SGB

ARTIST	SONG TITLE	#	TYPE
Garbage	Stupid Girl	24-115	SC
Garfunkel, Art	I Only Have Eyes For You	12-287	DK
Garfunkel, Art	Show - I Only Have Eyes For You	12-287	DK
Garland, Judy	But The World Goes 'Round	48-274	LE
Garland, Judy	Come Rain Or Come Shine	28-103	DK
Garland, Judy	Come Rain Or Come Shine	12-541	P
Garland, Judy	Get Happy	43-379	PS
Garland, Judy	I Can't Give You Anything But Love	48-276	MM
Garland, Judy	I Got Rhythm	48-272	KV
Garland, Judy	Man I Love the	48-273	LE
Garland, Judy	Man That Got Away the	7-181	MM
Garland, Judy	Meet Me In St. Louis Louis	16-412	PR
Garland, Judy	Meet Me In St. Louis Louis	9-823	SAV
Garland, Judy	On the Atchison Topeka & the Santa Fe	48-271	KV
Garland, Judy	Over The Rainbow	11-170	DK
Garland, Judy	Over The Rainbow	12-511	P
Garland, Judy	Rock A Bye Your Baby	2-237	SC
Garland, Judy	Swanee	7-194	MM
Garland, Judy	That's Entertainment	48-275	PS
Garland, Judy	Trolley Song the	12-540	P
Garland, Judy	Trolley Song the	9-822	SAV
Garland, Judy	When You're Smiling	17-420	DK
Garland, Judy	When You're Smiling	12-543	P
Garland, Judy	When You're Smiling	4-359	SC
Garland, Judy	Xmas - Have Yourself A Merry Little	11-241	DK
Garland, Judy	You Made Me Love You	33-215	CB
Garland, Judy	You Made Me Love You	15-846	MM
Garland, Judy	You're Nearer	48-277	PS
Garland, Judy	Zing! Went the Strings of My Heart	43-378	PSJT
Garnett, Gale	We'll Sing In The Sunshine	11-449	DK
Garnett, Gale	We'll Sing In The Sunshine	3-253	SC
Gary Lee & Showdowns	Rodeo Song the **	30-659	RSX
Gates, David	Love Is Always Seventeen	24-242	SC
Gates, David	Save The Last Dance For Me	2-738	SC
Gatlin, Larry	All The Gold In California	33-43	CB
Gatlin, Larry	Broken Lady	34-221	CB
Gatlin, Larry	I Don't Wanna Cry	47-103	CB
Gatlin, Larry	I Heard The Bells On Christmas Day	47-100	CB
Gatlin, Larry	I Heard The Bells On Xmas Day - xmas	45-253	CB
Gatlin, Larry	I've Done Enough Dying Today	33-51	CB

ARTIST	SONG TITLE	#	TYPE
Gatlin, Larry	Love Is Just A Game	47-104	CB
Gatlin, Larry	Love Of A Lifetime	47-110	CB
Gatlin, Larry	Night Time Magic	47-101	CB
Gatlin, Larry	She Used To Be Somebody's Baby	47-102	CB
Gatlin, Larry	Statues Without Hearts	34-226	CB
Gatlin, Larry	Sure Feels Like Love	47-108	CB
Gatlin, Larry	Take Me To Your Loving Place	47-106	CB
Gatlin, Larry	Talkin' To The Moon	47-109	CB
Gatlin, Larry	What Are We Doin' Lonesome	47-107	CB
Gatlin, Larry	Xmas - I Heard the Bells On Xmas Day	47-100	CB
Gatlin, Larry	Xmas - I Heard The Bells On Xmas Day	45-253	CB
Gatlins	All The Gold In California	6-768	MM
Gatlins	All The Gold In California	13-327	P
Gatlins	Broken Lady	13-516	P
Gatlins	Broken Lady	8-688	SAV
Gatlins	Houston (Means I'm One Day Closer	13-484	P
Gatlins	I Just Wish You Were Someone I Loved	47-105	CB
Gatlins	I've Done Enough Dying Today	8-803	CB
Gatlins	Take Me To Your Lovin' Place	4-489	SC
Gatlins	Xmas - Oh Holy Night	8-75	CB
Gattis, Keith	Little Drops Of My Heart	7-239	MM
Gattis, Keith	Little Drops Of My Heart	4-234	SC
Gattis, Keith	Real Deal	4-417	SC
Gaye & Terrell	Ain't No Mountain High Enough	11-112	DK
Gaye & Terrell	Ain't Nothin' Like The Real Thing	6-240	MM
Gaye & Terrell	Ain't Nothin' Like The Real Thing	4-38	SC
Gaye & Terrell	Duet - Ain't No Mountain High Enoug	11-112	DK
Gaye & Terrell	Duet - Ain't Nothin' Like the Real	6-240	MM
Gaye & Terrell	Duet - Ain't Nothin' Like the Real	4-38	SC
Gaye & Terrell	Duet - You're All I Need To Get By	11-829	DK
Gaye & Terrell	You're All I Need To Get By	11-829	DK
Gaye & Weston	Duet - It Takes Two	35-308	CB
Gaye & Weston	It Takes Two - duet	36-308	CB
Gaye, Marvin	Ain't That Peculiar	17-156	DK
Gaye, Marvin	Got To Give It Uo	22-933	SC
Gaye, Marvin	Got To Give It Up	36-113	JTG
Gaye, Marvin	Got To Give It Up	15-703	LE
Gaye, Marvin	How Sweet It Is	36-114	JTG
Gaye, Marvin	How Sweet It Is To Be Loved By You	4-40	SC
Gaye, Marvin	I Heard It Through The	16-778	DK

ARTIST	SONG TITLE	#	TYPE
	Grapevine		
Gaye, Marvin	I Heard It Through the Grapevine	36-118	JTG
Gaye, Marvin	I Heard It Through The Grapevine	12-627	P
Gaye, Marvin	I Heard It Through The Grapevine	2-77	SC
Gaye, Marvin	I'll Be Doggone	12-62	DK
Gaye, Marvin	Inner City Blues	47-723	DK
Gaye, Marvin	Let's Get It On	36-115	JTG
Gaye, Marvin	Mercy Mercy Me	11-757	DK
Gaye, Marvin	Mercy Mercy Me - the Ecology	14-352	MH
Gaye, Marvin	Sexual Healing	11-370	DK
Gaye, Marvin	Sexual Healing	36-117	JTG
Gaye, Marvin	Sexual Healing	12-888	P
Gaye, Marvin	Too Busy Thinking About My Baby	12-10	DK
Gaye, Marvin	Too Busy Thnking About My Baby	2-84	SC
Gaye, Marvin	What's Goin' On	11-371	DK
Gaye, Marvin	What's Goin' On	13-144	P
Gaye, Marvin	What's Goin' On	4-290	SC
Gaye, Marvin	What's Going On?	36-116	JTG
Gayle & Morris	Duet - Making Up For Lost Time	34-265	CB
Gayle & Morris	Making Up for Lost Time - Duet	34-265	CB
Gayle & Rabbitt	Duet - I Made A Promise	2-835	SC
Gayle & Rabbitt	I Made A Promise	2-835	SC
Gayle, Crystal	Baby What About You	49-634	CB
Gayle, Crystal	Blue Side the	48-498	CKC
Gayle, Crystal	Cry	34-261	CB
Gayle, Crystal	Cry	13-498	P
Gayle, Crystal	Don't It Make My Brown Eyes Blue	8-20	CB
Gayle, Crystal	Don't It Make My Brown Eyes Blue	16-746	DK
Gayle, Crystal	Don't It Make My Brown Eyes Blue	13-358	P
Gayle, Crystal	Don't It Make My Brown Eyes Blue	9-597	SAV
Gayle, Crystal	Don't It Make My Brown Eyes Blue	10-512	SF
Gayle, Crystal	Half The Way	48-496	CKC
Gayle, Crystal	Half The Way	46-111	SC
Gayle, Crystal	Hallelujah - xmas	45-254	CB
Gayle, Crystal	I'll Do It All Over Again	29-619	CB
Gayle, Crystal	I'll Get Over You	15-73	CB
Gayle, Crystal	I'll Get Over You	5-48	SC
Gayle, Crystal	I've Cried	5-60	SC
Gayle, Crystal	If You Ever Change Your Mind	5-391	SC
Gayle, Crystal	It's Like We Never Said Goodbye	5-54	SC
Gayle, Crystal	Our Love Is On The Fault Line	9-519	SAV
Gayle, Crystal	Ready For The Times To Get Better	29-782	CB

ARTIST	SONG TITLE	#	TYPE
Gayle, Crystal	River Road	47-755	SRK
Gayle, Crystal	Somebody Loves You	8-454	CB
Gayle, Crystal	Somebody Loves You	5-51	SC
Gayle, Crystal	Sound Of Goodbye	45-832	VH
Gayle, Crystal	Talkin' In Your Sleep	15-830	CB
Gayle, Crystal	Talkin' In Your Sleep	13-375	P
Gayle, Crystal	Talkin' In Your Sleep	10-515	SF
Gayle, Crystal	Three Good Reasons	24-250	SC
Gayle, Crystal	Too Many Lovers	48-497	CKC
Gayle, Crystal	Turning Away	38-42	CB
Gayle, Crystal	When I Dream	4-791	SC
Gayle, Crystal	Why Have You Left The One You Left Me For	13-341	P
Gayle, Crystal	Why Have You Left The One You Left Me For	33-36	CB
Gayle, Crystal	Xmas - Hallelujah	45-254	CB
Gayle, Crystal	Xmas - Have Yourself A Merry Little	18-756	CB
Gayle, Crystal	Xmas - What Child Is This	8-72	CB
Gayle, Crystal	You Never Gave Up On Me	9-490	SAV
Gayle, Crystal	You Never Miss A Real Good Thing	8-834	CB
Gayle, Crystal	You'll Never Miss A Real Good Thing	5-53	SC
Gaylor, Ruth	My Funny Valentine	12-542	P
Gaynor, Gloria	I Will Survive	11-89	DK
Gaynor, Gloria	I Will Survive	12-834	P
Gaynor, Gloria	I Will Survive	9-224	PT
Gaynor, Gloria	I Will Survive	19-165	SGB
Gaynor, Gloria	Never Can Say Goodbye	11-754	DK
Gearing, Ashley	Can You Hear Me When I Talk To U	25-650	MM
Gearing, Ashley	Can You Hear Me When I Talk To U	19-177	ST
Gearing, Ashley	Can You Hear Me When I Talk To You	32-341	THM
Gearing, Ashley	Me My Heart And I	38-246	PHN
Geiger, Teddy	These Walls	36-186	PHM
General Public	I'll Take You There	15-765	NU
General Public	Tenderness	29-262	SC
Genesis	Follow You Follow Me	21-798	SC
Genesis	Invisible Touch	35-166	CB
Genesis	Man On The Corner	37-76	SC
Genesis	That's All	15-737	SC
Genies	Who's That Knocking	49-454	MM
Gentry, Bobbie	I'll Never Fall In Love Again	48-223	SF
Gentry, Bobbie	Ode To Billy Joe	8-291	CB
Gentry, Bobbie	Ode To Billy Joe	11-401	DK
Gentry, Bobbie	Ode To Billy Joe	13-126	P
Gentrys	Keep On Dancin'	11-360	DK
George, Barbara	I Know	6-150	MM
Georgia Satellites	Hippy Hippy Shake	34-117	CB
Georgia Sattelites	Keep Your Hands To Yourself	18-159	CB
Georgia Sattelites	Keep Your Hands To Yourself	11-822	DK

ARTIST	SONG TITLE	#	TYPE
Georgia Sattelites	Keep Your Hands To Yourself	20-307	MH
Georgia Sattelites	Keep Your Hands To Yourself	12-793	P
Gerblansky, Ned	Feel Like Makin' Love	13-722	SGB
Gerry & Pacemakers	Don't Let The Sun Catch You Cryin'	12-325	DK
Gerry & Pacemakers	Ferry Cross The Mersey	11-287	DK
Gerry & Pacemakers	How Do You Do It	48-778	P
Gerry & Pacemakers	I Like It	10-562	SF
Getz & Gilberto	Girl From Ipanema the	12-518	P
Gibb, Andy	I Just Want To Be Your Everything	27-574	DK
Gibb, Andy	I Just Want To Be Your Everything	2-851	SC
Gibb, Andy	Love Is Thicker Than Water	11-442	DK
Gibb, Andy	Love Is Thicker Than Water	20-360	SC
Gibb, Andy	Shadow Dancing	11-105	DK
Gibb, Andy	Shadow Dancing	5-474	SC
Gibb, Robin	Boys Do Fall In Love	49-27	SBI
Gibb, Robin	Juliet	49-25	KV
Gibb, Robin	Saved By The Bell	10-630	SF
Gibb, Robin	Saved By The Bell	49-26	SF
Gibb, Terri	Somebody's Knockin'	13-529	P
Gibbs, Georgia	Dance With Me Henry (The Wall)	33-236	CB
Gibbs, Grant	Kiss Of Fire	11-458	DK
Gibson Miller Band	Johnny Get Your Gun	24-352	SC
Gibson Miller Band	Red White & Blue Collar	17-228	NA
Gibson Miller Band	Stone Cold Country	47-872	NT
Gibson Miller Band	Texas Tattoo	6-398	MM
Gibson Miller Band	Texas Tattoo	12-459	P
Gibson, Debbie	Lost In Your Eyes	7-96	MM
Gibson, Debbie	Only In My Dreams	12-754	P
Gibson, Don	Blue Blue Day	3-595	SC
Gibson, Don	Give Myself A Party	43-287	CB
Gibson, Don	I Can Mend Your Broken Heart	43-285	CB
Gibson, Don	Just One Time	5-423	SC
Gibson, Don	Lonesome #1	43-284	CB
Gibson, Don	Lonesome Number One	5-696	SC
Gibson, Don	Oh Lonesome Me	8-808	CB
Gibson, Don	Oh Lonesome Me	13-444	P
Gibson, Don	Oh Lonesome Me	8-654	SAV
Gibson, Don	Rings Of Gold	43-286	CB
Gibson, Don	Sea Of Heartbreak	34-200	CB
Gibson, Don	Sea Of Heartbreak	2-629	SC
Gibson, Don	Too Soon To Know	8-821	CB
Gibson, Don	Touch The Morning	5-130	SC
Gibson, Don	Who Cares	5-853	SC
Gibson, Don	Woman Sensuous Woman	35-362	CB
Gibson, Don	Woman Sensuous Woman	5-392	SC
Gilbert, Brantley	17 Again	44-196	KCD
Gilbert, Brantley	Bottoms Up	43-129	ASK

ARTIST	SONG TITLE	#	TYPE
Gilbert, Brantley	Bottoms Up	46-605	KVD
Gilbert, Brantley	Bottoms Up	46-604	BKD
Gilbert, Brantley	Bottoms Up	46-603	PHN
Gilbert, Brantley	Country Must Be Country Wide	38-87	CB
Gilbert, Brantley	Country Must Be Country Wide	46-157	CB
Gilbert, Brantley	Friday Night	44-158	BKD
Gilbert, Brantley	G.R.I.T.S.	44-300	BKD
Gilbert, Brantley	Kick It In The Sticks	38-100	CB
Gilbert, Brantley	Kick It In The Sticks	46-158	CB
Gilbert, Brantley	More Than Miles	44-299	SBI
Gilbert, Brantley	More Than Miles	42-24	ASK
Gilbert, Brantley	My Baby's Guns & Roses	44-281	KCD
Gilbert, Brantley	My Kind Of Crazy	44-302	DCK
Gilbert, Brantley	One Hell Of An Amen	45-448	SSC
Gilbert, Brantley	Read Me My Rights	46-159	BKD
Gilbert, Brantley	Stone Cold Sober	49-371	BKD
Gilbert, Brantley	Take It Outside	44-159	BKD
Gilbert, Brantley	You Don't Know Her Like I Do	42-25	ASK
Gilbert, Moore & Rhett	Small Town Throwdown	44-274	KCD
Gilder, Nick	Hot Child In The City	28-267	DK
Gilder, Nick	Hot Child In The City	4-761	SC
Gill & Grant	Duet - When I Look Into Your Heart	9-871	ST
Gill & Grant	When I Look Into Your Heart	9-871	ST
Gill & Loveless	Duet - My Kind Of Woman/Man	8-970	CB
Gill & Loveless	Duet - My Kind Of Woman/Man	14-625	SC
Gill & Loveless	My Kind of Woman/My Kind of Man	8-970	CB
Gill & Loveless	My Kind of Woman/My Kind of Man	14-625	SC
Gill & McEntire	Duet - Oklahoma Swing	1-795	CB
Gill & McEntire	Oklahoma Swing	1-795	CB
Gill, Johnny	Let's Get The Mood Right	24-294	SC
Gill, Johnny	My My My	34-94	CB
Gill, Johnny	Rub You The Right Way	28-426	DK
Gill, Johnny	Rub You The Right Way	16-556	P
Gill, Vince	Cinderella	4-551	SC
Gill, Vince	Don't Come Cryin' To Me	8-355	CB
Gill, Vince	Don't Come Cryin' To Me	7-823	CHT
Gill, Vince	Don't Come Cryin' To Me	22-715	ST
Gill, Vince	Don't Let Our Love Start Slippin'	6-216	MM
Gill, Vince	Don't Let Our Love Start Slippin'..	1-592	CB
Gill, Vince	Don't Let Our Love Start Slippin'..	8-603	TT
Gill, Vince	Feels Like Love	14-722	CB
Gill, Vince	Feels Like Love	13-850	CHM

ARTIST	SONG TITLE	#	TYPE
Gill, Vince	Feels Like Love	19-213	CSZ
Gill, Vince	Go Rest High On That Mountain	1-595	CB
Gill, Vince	Go Rest High On That Mountain	7-150	MM
Gill, Vince	High Lonesome Sound	7-241	MM
Gill, Vince	High Lonesome Sound	22-882	ST
Gill, Vince	I Never Knew Lonely	3-38	SC
Gill, Vince	I Still Believe In you	1-591	CB
Gill, Vince	I Still Believe In You	12-476	P
Gill, Vince	I Still Believe In You	3-642	SC
Gill, Vince	If You Ever Have Forever In Mind	8-724	CB
Gill, Vince	If You Ever Have Forever In Mind	7-763	CHM
Gill, Vince	If You Ever Have Forever In Mind	5-286	SC
Gill, Vince	If You Ever Have Forever In Mind	22-794	ST
Gill, Vince	In These Last Few Days	20-335	ST
Gill, Vince	Kindly Keep It Country	8-215	CB
Gill, Vince	Kindly Keep It Country	22-685	ST
Gill, Vince	Let's Make Sure We Kiss Goodbye	23-361	SC
Gill, Vince	Let's Make Sure We Kiss Goodbye	22-483	ST
Gill, Vince	Little More Love a	7-607	CHM
Gill, Vince	Little More Love a	10-78	SC
Gill, Vince	Liza Jane	1-589	CB
Gill, Vince	Liza Jane	13-488	P
Gill, Vince	Look At Us	1-590	CB
Gill, Vince	Look At Us	9-536	SAV
Gill, Vince	Loving You Makes Me A Better Man	5-804	SC
Gill, Vince	Never Knew Lonely	1-587	CB
Gill, Vince	Next Big Thing	34-398	CB
Gill, Vince	Next Big Thing	25-452	MM
Gill, Vince	Next Big Thing	18-464	ST
Gill, Vince	Next Big Thing	32-76	THM
Gill, Vince	No Future In The Past	1-598	CB
Gill, Vince	No Future In The Past	26-527	DK
Gill, Vince	Nobody's Fool But Yours	49-710	VH
Gill, Vince	Oklahoma Borderline	3-108	SC
Gill, Vince	One More Last Chance	26-313	DK
Gill, Vince	One More Last Chance	6-392	MM
Gill, Vince	Pocket Full Of Gold	1-588	CB
Gill, Vince	Pocket Full Of Gold	6-207	MM
Gill, Vince	Pretty Little Adriana	1-596	CB
Gill, Vince	Pretty Little Adriana	7-391	MM
Gill, Vince	Pretty Little Adriana	24-651	SC
Gill, Vince	Reason Why the	30-117	CB
Gill, Vince	Shoot Straight From Your Heart	14-785	ST
Gill, Vince	Shoot Straight From Your Heart	15-196	THM
Gill, Vince	Someday	25-575	MM
Gill, Vince	Someday	19-7	ST
Gill, Vince	Someday	32-261	THM

ARTIST	SONG TITLE	#	TYPE
Gill, Vince	Take Your Memory With You	17-391	DK
Gill, Vince	Tryin' To Get Over You	1-600	CB
Gill, Vince	Tryin' To Get Over You	6-468	MM
Gill, Vince	Tryin' To Get Over You	2-97	SC
Gill, Vince	What The Cowgirl's Do	2-479	SC
Gill, Vince	What The Cowgirls Do	1-594	CB
Gill, Vince	What The Cowgirls Do	20-411	MH
Gill, Vince	What The Cowgirls Do	6-607	MM
Gill, Vince	What You Give Away	30-365	CB
Gill, Vince	When I Call Your Name	1-586	CB
Gill, Vince	When I Call Your Name	9-444	SAV
Gill, Vince	When Love Finds You	1-599	CB
Gill, Vince	When Love Finds You	2-457	SC
Gill, Vince	Whenever You Come Around	1-593	CB
Gill, Vince	Whenever You Come Around	6-571	MM
Gill, Vince	Whenever You Come Around	2-213	SC
Gill, Vince	Which Bridge To Cross	4-75	SC
Gill, Vince	Which Bridge To Cross	22-850	ST
Gill, Vince	World's Apart	7-343	MM
Gill, Vince	World's Apart	4-897	SC
Gill, Vince	Xmas - Let There Be Peace On Earth -duet	41-35	CB
Gill, Vince	Xmas - One Bright Star	18-729	CB
Gill, Vince	Xmas - One Bright Star	22-846	ST
Gill, Vince	Xmas - What Child Is This	30-397	SC
Gill, Vince	You And You Alone	7-668	CHM
Gill, Vince	You Better Think Twice	6-799	MM
Gill, Vince	You Better Think Twice	2-830	SC
Gill, Vince	Young Man's Town	19-683	ST
Gilley, Mickey	Bring It On Home To Me	16-175	THM
Gilley, Mickey	Chains Of Love	16-178	THM
Gilley, Mickey	City Lights	22-226	CB
Gilley, Mickey	Don't The Girls All Get Prettier At Closing Time	8-48	CB
Gilley, Mickey	Don't The Girls All Get Prettier At Closing Time	7-416	MM
Gilley, Mickey	Doo Wah Days	47-778	SRK
Gilley, Mickey	Fool For Your Love	22-217	CB
Gilley, Mickey	Headache Tomorrow, Heartache Tonight	16-173	THM
Gilley, Mickey	Headache Tomorrow, Heartache Tonight	22-216	CB
Gilley, Mickey	Here Comes The Hurt Again	5-870	SC
Gilley, Mickey	Honky Tonk Wine	5-44	SC
Gilley, Mickey	I Overlooked An Orchid	22-222	CB
Gilley, Mickey	I Overlooked An Orchid	4-576	SC
Gilley, Mickey	Lawdy Miss Clawdy	16-176	THM
Gilley, Mickey	Lonely Nights	22-227	CB
Gilley, Mickey	Power Of Positive Drinking	16-179	THM
Gilley, Mickey	Put Your Dreams Away	22-213	CB
Gilley, Mickey	Rockin' Around The Christmas Tree	45-757	CB

ARTIST	SONG TITLE	#	TYPE
Gilley, Mickey	Room Full Of Roses	12-428	P
Gilley, Mickey	Room Full Of Roses	22-215	CB
Gilley, Mickey	She's Pulling Me Back Again	16-177	THM
Gilley, Mickey	Stand By Me	8-36	CB
Gilley, Mickey	Stand By Me	16-170	THM
Gilley, Mickey	Talk To Me	22-219	CB
Gilley, Mickey	Tears Of The Lonely	22-224	CB
Gilley, Mickey	That's All That Matters	22-221	CB
Gilley, Mickey	That's All That Matters	5-246	SC
Gilley, Mickey	That's All That Matters	16-172	THM
Gilley, Mickey	True Love Ways	22-223	CB
Gilley, Mickey	True Love Ways	5-132	SC
Gilley, Mickey	True Love Ways	16-171	THM
Gilley, Mickey	Xmas - Blue Christmas	33-205	CB
Gilley, Mickey	Xmas - Joy To The World	8-65	CB
Gilley, Mickey	Xmas - Oh Little Town of Bethlehem	8-68	CB
Gilley, Mickey	Xmas - Rockin' Around The Christmas Tree	45-757	CB
Gilley, Mickey	You Don't Know Me	22-225	CB
Gilley, Mickey	You Don't Know Me	16-174	THM
Gilley, Mickey	You've Really Got A Hold On Me	22-218	CB
Gilman, Billy	Elisabeth	16-13	ST
Gilman, Billy	Oklahoma	14-141	CB
Gilman, Billy	Oklahoma	22-581	ST
Gilman, Billy	Oklahoma	14-33	THM
Gilman, Billy	One Voice	14-726	CB
Gilman, Billy	One Voice	19-250	CSZ
Gilman, Billy	Patriotic - There's A Hero	33-146	CB
Gilman, Billy	She's My Girl	15-189	ST
Gilman, Billy	There's A Hero - Patriotic	36-339	CB
Gilmer, Jimmy	Sugar Shack	12-115	DK
Gin Blossoms	As Long As It Matters	4-670	SC
Gin Blossoms	Baby I Love Your Way	12-241	DK
Gin Blossoms	Day Job	24-744	SC
Gin Blossoms	Follow You Down	33-361	CB
Gin Blossoms	Found Out About You	35-208	CB
Gin Blossoms	Found Out About You	12-240	DK
Gin Blossoms	Found Out About You	18-476	NU
Gin Blossoms	Hey Jealousy	34-58	CB
Gin Blossoms	Hey Jealousy	13-236	P
Gin Blossoms	Until I Fall Away	6-644	MM
Gina G.	Gimme Some Love	21-553	PHM
Gina G.	Gimme Some Love	10-106	SC
Ginuwine	Differences	35-264	CB
Ginuwine	Differences	16-82	ST
Ginuwine	In Those Jeans	32-383	THM
Ginuwine	In Those Jeans (Radio Version)	21-783	SC
Ginuwine w Baby	Hell Yeah	32-162	THM
Gisselle	Latino - Marchate	23-243	AI
Glaser, Tompall	Put Another Log On The Fire	8-446	CB

ARTIST	SONG TITLE	#	TYPE
Glaser, Tompall	Show - It's A Mad Mad Mad World	9-811	SAV
Glass Tiger	Don't Forget Me When I'm Gone	21-752	MH
Glass Tiger	Someday	24-200	SC
Gleaming Spires	Are You Ready For The Sex **	15-7	SC
Glen Miller Orchestra	Chatanooga Choo Choo	34-435	CB
Glitter, Gary	Another Rock & Roll Christmas	45-780	SF
Glitter, Gary	Hello Hello I'm Back Again	49-147	SF
Glitter, Gary	I Love You Love Me Love	49-144	SF
Glitter, Gary	Leader Of The Gang	49-145	SF
Glitter, Gary	Rock And Roll Part 2	49-143	SC
Glitter, Gary	So You Want To Touch Me	49-146	SF
Glitter, Gary	Xmas - Another Rock & Roll Christmas	45-780	SF
Gloriana	Best Night Ever - duet	43-237	ASK
Gloriana	Duet - Best Night Ever	43-237	ASK
Gloriana	Wanna Take You Home	49-862	DCK
Gloriana	Wild At Heart	37-29	CB
Glover, Dana	Rain	20-516	CB
Glover, Dana	Thinking Over	32-26	THM
Go West	King Of Wishful Thinking	16-72	SC
Go-Go's	Head Over Heels	20-86	SC
Go-Go's	Our Lips Are Sealed	13-213	P
Go-Go's	Our Lips Are Sealed	4-539	SC
Go-Go's	Vacation	28-278	DK
Go-Go's	Vacation	5-109	SC
Go-Go's	We Got The Beat	11-228	DK
Go-Go's	We Got The Beat	16-548	P
Go-Go's	We Got The Beat	9-773	SAV
Go, Gary	Wonderful	36-308	PHM
Godfather Theme	Show - Speak Softly Love	12-121	DK
Godsmack	Greed	16-382	SGB
Godspell	Show - Day By Day	18-201	PS
Gold, Andrew	Lonely Boy	24-206	SC
Golden Earring	Halloween - Twilight Zone Music	16-295	TT
Golden Earring	Radar Love	2-146	SC
Golden Earring	Twilight Zone Music	15-794	SC
Goldsboro, Bobby	Autumn Of My Life	4-219	SC
Goldsboro, Bobby	Hello Summertime	45-879	VH
Goldsboro, Bobby	Honey	35-98	CB
Goldsboro, Bobby	Honey	11-95	DK
Goldsboro, Bobby	Honey	10-750	JVC
Goldsboro, Bobby	Honey	12-645	P
Goldsboro, Bobby	Honey	4-702	SC
Goldsboro, Bobby	I Know You Better Than That	49-648	DFK
Goldsboro, Bobby	It's Too Late	45-604	OZP
Goldsboro, Bobby	Little Things	14-454	SC
Goldsboro, Bobby	Me And The Elephant	44-65	SAV

ARTIST	SONG TITLE	#	TYPE
			P
Goldsboro, Bobby	Straight Life the	45-877	TB
Goldsboro, Bobby	Summer (The First Time)	45-876	SF
Goldsboro, Bobby	Watching Scotty Grow	4-639	SC
Goldsboro, Bobby	With Pen In Hand	45-878	TB
Gomez, Selena	Nobody Does It Like You	48-399	DCK
Gonzales, Babs	Be Bop Santa Claus - xmas	45-245	CB
Gonzales, Babs	Xmas - Be Bop Santa Claus	45-245	CB
Goo Goo Dolls	Big Machine	18-431	CB
Goo Goo Dolls	Big Machine	25-316	MM
Goo Goo Dolls	Black Balloon	33-368	CB
Goo Goo Dolls	Black Balloon	16-190	THM
Goo Goo Dolls	Broadway	35-223	CB
Goo Goo Dolls	Dizzy	34-59	CB
Goo Goo Dolls	Give A Little Bit	22-352	CB
Goo Goo Dolls	Here Is Gone	34-149	CB
Goo Goo Dolls	Here Is Gone	25-199	MM
Goo Goo Dolls	Iris	16-224	PHM
Goo Goo Dolls	Iris	5-274	SC
Goo Goo Dolls	Iris	21-595	SF
Goo Goo Dolls	Learn To Fly	30-218	PHM
Goo Goo Dolls	Let Love In	30-269	CB
Goo Goo Dolls	Long Way Down	4-671	SC
Goo Goo Dolls	Naked	13-610	P
Goo Goo Dolls	Naked	4-177	SC
Goo Goo Dolls	Not Broken	37-265	PHM
Goo Goo Dolls	Real	36-238	PHM
Goo Goo Dolls	Slide	14-282	MM
Goo Goo Dolls	Slide	7-782	PHT
Goo Goo Dolls	Slide	13-676	SGB
Goo Goo Dolls	Sympathy	25-587	MM
Goo Goo Dolls	Sympathy	19-341	STP
Goo Goo Dolls	Sympathy	32-217	THM
Good Charlotte	Anthem the	35-281	CB
Good Charlotte	Anthem the	32-143	THM
Good Charlotte	Girls And Boys	25-655	MM
Good Charlotte	Girls And Boys	32-396	THM
Good Charlotte	I Just Wanna Live	22-356	CB
Good Charlotte	Lifestyles Of The Rich & Famous	20-457	CB
Good Charlotte	Lifestyles Of The Rich & Famous	25-434	MM
Good Charlotte	Lifestyles Of The Rich & Famous	18-825	THM
Good Charlotte	Show - Hold On	19-660	CB
Good Charlotte	Young And The Hopeless	34-175	CB
Good Charlotte	Young And The Hopeless	32-328	THM
Goodman, Benny	Moonglow	45-606	OZP
Goodrem, Delta	In This Life	36-493	CB
Gore, Lesley	California Nights	4-715	SC
Gore, Lesley	It's My Party	11-114	DK
Gore, Lesley	It's My Party	3-364	MH

ARTIST	SONG TITLE	#	TYPE
Gore, Lesley	It's My Party	12-901	P
Gore, Lesley	It's My Party	9-25	PS
Gore, Lesley	It's My Party	9-284	SC
Gore, Lesley	Judy's Turn To Cry	5-7	SC
Gore, Lesley	Maybe I Know	4-718	SC
Gore, Lesley	No More Tears (Left To Cry)	47-112	DFK
Gore, Lesley	She's A Fool	5-168	SC
Gore, Lesley	Sunshine Lollipops And Rainbows	47-111	SBI
Gore, Lesley	That's The Way Boys Are	5-88	SC
Gore, Lesley	You Don't Own Me	19-621	MH
Gore, Lesley	You Don't Own Me	5-80	SC
Gore, Lesley	You Don't Own Me	11-527	DK
Gorillaz	Clint Eastwood	16-313	TT
Gorillaz	Clint Eastwood (Radio Version)	16-87	SC
Gorillaz	Duet - Clint Eastwood - Radio Vers	16-87	SC
Gorillaz	Feel Good Inc (Radio Vers)	37-108	SC
Gorillaz	Kids With Guns	30-767	SF
Gorme, Eydie	Blame It On The Bossanova	11-257	DK
Gorme, Eydie	I'll Take Romance	25-271	MM
Gorme, Steve&Eydie	Bei Mir Bist Du Schon	15-842	MM
Gorme, Steve&Eydie	Duet - Bei Mir Mist Du Shoen	15-842	MM
Gorme, Steve&Eydie	It Never Rains In Southern CA	16-749	DK
Gosdin, Vern	Baby That's Cold	48-431	VH
Gosdin, Vern	Chiseled In Stone	8-690	SAV
Gosdin, Vern	Do You Believe Me Now	19-444	SC
Gosdin, Vern	Dream Of Me	47-120	CB
Gosdin, Vern	Garden the	47-114	CB
Gosdin, Vern	I Can Tell By The Way You Dance	4-555	SC
Gosdin, Vern	I Can Tell By The Way You Dance	33-83	CB
Gosdin, Vern	I'm Still Crazy	21-630	SC
Gosdin, Vern	If You're Gonna o Me Wrong Do It Right	29-696	SC
Gosdin, Vern	If You're Gonna o Me Wrong Do It Right	34-258	CB
Gosdin, Vern	Is It Raining At Your House	47-115	CB
Gosdin, Vern	Right In The Wrong Direction	47-118	CB
Gosdin, Vern	Set 'Em Up Joe	15-822	CB
Gosdin, Vern	Slow Burning Memory	47-117	CB
Gosdin, Vern	That Just About Does It	16-354	CB
Gosdin, Vern	This Ain't My First Rodeo	29-648	SC
Gosdin, Vern	Til The End	47-121	SC
Gosdin, Vern	Way Down Deep	47-116	CB
Gosdin, Vern	What Would Your Memories Do	47-119	CB
Gosdin, Vern	Who You Gonna Blame It On	5-398	SC

ARTIST	SONG TITLE	#	TYPE
Gospel	Gospel - Abide With Me	12-203	DK
Gospel	Gospel - Amazing Grace	11-477	DK
Gospel	Gospel - Battle Hymn Of/Republic	12-219	DK
Gospel	Gospel - Beautiful Isle Of Somewher	12-218	DK
Gospel	Gospel - Bible Tells Me So	12-221	DK
Gospel	Gospel - Blessed Assurance	12-228	DK
Gospel	Gospel - Brighten The Corner	12-237	DK
Gospel	Gospel - Bringing In The Sheaves	12-223	DK
Gospel	Gospel - Flow Gently Sweet Afton	12-213	DK
Gospel	Gospel - Give Me That Old Time Reli	12-224	DK
Gospel	Gospel - Go Down Moses	12-233	DK
Gospel	Gospel - Go Tell It On The Mountain	12-204	DK
Gospel	Gospel - Go Tell It On The Mountain	12-647	P
Gospel	Gospel - He's Got The Whole World	12-225	DK
Gospel	Gospel - How Great Thou Art	12-205	DK
Gospel	Gospel - I Love To Tell The Story	12-229	DK
Gospel	Gospel - I Need Thee Every Hour	12-209	DK
Gospel	Gospel - I'll Fly Away	33-202	CB
Gospel	Gospel - I'll Fly Away	12-217	DK
Gospel	Gospel - In The Garden	12-207	DK
Gospel	Gospel - In The Sweet By & By	12-227	DK
Gospel	Gospel - It Is No Secret What God..	12-234	DK
Gospel	Gospel - Jesus Is Coming Soon	12-208	DK
Gospel	Gospel - Jesus Loves Me	12-201	DK
Gospel	Gospel - Just A Closer Walk W/Thee	12-222	DK
Gospel	Gospel - Lily Of The Valley	12-230	DK
Gospel	Gospel - Little Brown Church In The	12-210	DK
Gospel	Gospel - Lord's Prayer the	12-220	DK
Gospel	Gospel - Nearer My God To Thee	12-206	DK
Gospel	Gospel - Old Rugged Cross the	12-236	DK
Gospel	Gospel - One Day At A Time	33-203	CB
Gospel	Gospel - Onward Christain Soldiers	12-200	DK
Gospel	Gospel - Peace In The Valley	12-235	DK

ARTIST	SONG TITLE	#	TYPE
Gospel	Gospel - Precious Memories	12-215	DK
Gospel	Gospel - Rock Of Ages	12-199	DK
Gospel	Gospel - Standing On The Promises	12-232	DK
Gospel	Gospel - Sweet Hour Of Prayer	12-212	DK
Gospel	Gospel - Take My Hand Precious Lord	12-214	DK
Gospel	Gospel - Wait For the Light To Shine	49-713	VH
Gospel	Gospel - What A Friend We Have In..	12-226	DK
Gospel	Gospel - When The Roll Is Called Up	12-211	DK
Gospel	Gospel - When They Ring Those...	12-231	DK
Gospel	Gospel - Whispering Hope	12-216	DK
Gospel	Gospel - Wings Of A Dove	12-202	DK
Gospel	I'll Fly Away - Gospel	33-202	CB
Gospel	One Day At A Time - Gospel	33-203	CB
Gospel	Wait For The Light To Shine	49-713	VH
Goulding, Ellie	Burn	43-183	ASK
Goulet, Robert	If Ever I Would Leave You	28-102	DK
Goulet, Robert	If Ever I Would Leave You	12-568	P
Goulet, Robert	Impossible Dream the	3-116	KB
Grace, Stephanie	Hey There	39-56	PHN
Grace, Stephanie	Would U Be Mine	39-93	PHN
Gracin , Josh	Favorite State Of Mind	29-366	CB
Gracin, Josh	I Keep Coming Back	30-171	CB
Gracin, Josh	I Want To Live	35-450	CB
Gracin, Josh	I Want To Live	20-261	PHM
Gracin, Josh	I Want To Live	20-333	ST
Gracin, Josh	Nothin' To Lose	22-69	CB
Gracin, Josh	Nothin' To Lose	23-36	SC
Gracin, Josh	Nothin' To Lose	20-505	ST
Gracin, Josh	Stay With Me (Brass Bed)	23-122	CB
Gracin, Josh	We Weren't Crazy	36-434	CB
Graham, Larry	One in A Million You	6-556	MM
Graham, Larry	One In A Million You	13-306	P
Graham, Larry	One In A Million You	2-278	SC
Graham, Lukas	7 Years	48-792	DCK
Graham, Lukas	Drunk In The Morning	48-791	KV
Graham, Terry	Dozen Red Roses A	7-623	CHM
Gramm, Lou	Just Between You And Me	18-380	SAV
Grams, Shannon	You Got It All	17-73	DK
Grand Funk RR	Bad Time	3-520	SC
Grand Funk RR	Footstompin' Music	20-89	SC
Grand Funk RR	Loco-Motion the	2-40	SC
Grand Funk RR	Mean Mistreater	5-594	SC
Grand Funk RR	Some Kind Of	4-77	SC

ARTIST	SONG TITLE	#	TYPE
	Wonderful		
Grand Funk RR	We're An American Band	17-89	DK
Grand Funk RR	We're An American Band	4-753	SC
Grand Masters Flash	Message the	14-439	SC
Grand, Gil	Let's Start Living	8-937	CB
Grandpa Jones	Christmas Guest	45-789	DW
Grandpa Jones	Mountain Dew	35-329	CB
Grandpa Jones	Xmas - Christmas Guest	45-789	DW
Grant & Cetera	Duet - Next Time I Fall In Love	35-312	CB
Grant & Cetera	Next Time I Fall In Love - duet	35-312	CB
Grant, Amy	Baby Baby	21-462	CB
Grant, Amy	Baby Baby	18-764	PS
Grant, Amy	Big Yellow Taxi	3-430	SC
Grant, Amy	Big Yellow Taxi	19-346	STP
Grant, Amy	Every Heartbeat	6-102	MM
Grant, Amy	Giggle	49-34	SHER
Grant, Amy	Good For Me	16-623	MM
Grant, Amy	House Of Love	18-769	PS
Grant, Amy	I Will Remember You	18-765	PS
Grant, Amy	Like I Love You	18-766	PS
Grant, Amy	Lucky One	6-639	MM
Grant, Amy	Next Time I Fall In Love	18-768	PS
Grant, Amy	Say You'll Be Mine	29-134	ST
Grant, Amy	Takes A Little Time	7-684	PHM
Grant, Amy	Takes A Little Time	18-763	PS
Grant, Amy	That's What Love Is For	18-762	PS
Grant, Amy	Whatever It Takes	18-767	PS
Grant, Amy	Xmas - I'll Be Home For Christmas	7-3	MM
Grant, Amy	Xmas - Tennessee Christmas	8-50	CB
Grant, Amy	Xmas - Winter Wonderland	14-299	MM
Grant, Gogi	Wayward Wind the	3-514	SC
Grant, Natalie	Real Me the	36-177	PHM
Grant, Natalie	What Are You Waiting For	29-55	CB
Grass Roots	Heaven Knows	45-157	SC
Grass Roots	Let's Live For Today	16-769	DK
Grass Roots	Let's Live For Today	12-650	P
Grass Roots	Midnight Confession	7-260	MM
Grass Roots	Sooner Or Later	11-545	DK
Grass Roots	Sooner Or Later	9-719	SAV
Grass Roots	Temptation Eyes	4-55	SC
Grass Roots	Two Divided By Love	17-523	SC
Grass Roots	Want A Million Years	20-95	SC
Grateful Dead	Casey Jones	2-750	SC
Grateful Dead	Friend of The Devil	9-321	AG
Grateful Dead	Ripple	29-263	SC
Grateful Dead	Touch Of Grey	3-522	SC
Gray, David	Babylon	16-482	MH
Gray, David	One I Love the	29-319	PHM
Gray, David	Tell Me Something	29-220	PHM

ARTIST	SONG TITLE	#	TYPE
Gray, Dobie	Drift Away	2-440	SC
Gray, Dobie	In Crowd the	12-668	P
Gray, Joel	Money Makes The World Go Round	6-524	MM
Gray, Macy	I Try	14-173	CB
Gray, Macy	I Try	13-567	LE
Gray, Macy	I Try	15-327	PHM
Gray, Macy	She Ain't Right For You	19-601	CB
Gray, Macy	Still	23-263	HS
Gray, Macy	When I See You	25-544	MM
Gray, Macy	Why Didn't You Call Me	14-497	SC
Gray, Macy	Why Didn't You Call Me	19-830	SGB
Gray, Macy	Why Didn't You Call Me	30-639	THM
Greapo, Elvis	Latino - Pintame	17-812	PS
Greapo, Elvis	Latino - Si Tu Te A Lejas	17-813	PS
Grease	Born To Hand Jive - Grease	49-425	SDK
Grease	Greased Lightnin'	49-430	SDK
Grease	Hopelessly Devoted To You	49-427	SDK
Grease	Rock And Roll Is Here To Stay	49-429	SDK
Grease	Show - Born To Hand Jive	49-425	SDK
Grease	Show - Grease	16-761	DK
Grease	Show - Greased Lightnin'	49-430	SDK
Grease	Show - Hopelessly Devoted To You	49-427	SDK
Grease	Show - Look At Me I'm Sandra Dee	6-878	MM
Grease	Show - Rock And Roll Is Here To Stay	49-429	SDK
Grease	Show - Summer Nights - duet	49-426	SDK
Grease	Show - There Are Worse Things I …	6-891	MM
Grease	Show - We Go Together	49-431	SDK
Grease	Show - You're The One That I Want	49-428	SDK
Grease	Summer Nights - duet	49-426	SDK
Grease	We Go Together	49-431	SDK
Grease	You're The One That I Want	49-428	SDK
Great Big World & Aguilera	Say Something	43-252	BKD
Great Big World & Aguilera	Say Something	43-253	SBI
Great Divide	Break In The Storm	8-868	CB
Great Divide	Pour Me A Vacation	8-194	CB
Great Divide	San Isabella	8-952	CB
Great Divide	San Isabella	14-614	SC
Great Plains	Healing Hands	4-432	SC
Great White	Once Bitten Twice Shy	23-48	MH
Great White	Once Bitten Twice Shy	13-281	P
Great White	Once Bitten Twice Shy	5-602	SC
Great White	Rock Me	6-19	SC
Great White	Rollin' Stoned	21-781	SC
Greaves, R. B.	Take A Letter Maria	27-548	DK

ARTIST	SONG TITLE	#	TYPE
Green & Lovett	Duet - Funny How Time Slips Away	26-566	DK
Green & Lovett	Funny How Time Slips Away	26-566	DK
Green Day	American Idiot	20-558	PHM
Green Day	Basket Case	19-285	SGB
Green Day	Brain Stew	4-175	SC
Green Day	Longview	19-287	SGB
Green Day	Walking Contradiction	4-675	SC
Green, Al	For The Good Times	46-160	SC
Green, Al	Let's Stay Together	11-369	DK
Green, Al	Let's Stay Together	7-467	MM
Green, Al	Let's Stay Together	13-145	P
Green, Al	Tired Of Being Alone	12-717	P
Green, Al	What Locks The Door	48-5	KCD
Green, Al	Your Heart's In Good Hands	4-173	SC
Green, Pat	All Just To Get To You	47-125	PHN
Green, Pat	Baby Doll	22-319	CB
Green, Pat	Break It Back Down	45-622	DCK
Green, Pat	Carry On	25-11	MM
Green, Pat	Carry On	16-12	ST
Green, Pat	Country Star	47-122	CB
Green, Pat	Dixie Lullaby	47-124	NSC
Green, Pat	Don't Break My Heart Again	22-100	CB
Green, Pat	Don't Break My Heart Again	20-504	ST
Green, Pat	Feels Just Like It Should	30-91	CB
Green, Pat	Guy Like Me	19-702	ST
Green, Pat	Let Me	36-616	CB
Green, Pat	Let Me	36-200	PHM
Green, Pat	Somewhere Between TX & Mexico	23-140	CB
Green, Pat	Three Days	16-437	ST
Green, Pat	Wave On Wave	25-646	MM
Green, Pat	Wave On Wave	19-68	ST
Green, Pat	Way Back Texas	30-475	CB
Green, Pat	What I'm For	47-123	CB
Green, V.	Emotional Rollercoaster	32-164	THM
Green, V.	Fanatic	32-309	THM
Greenbaum, Norman	Spirit In The Sky	35-102	CB
Greenbaum, Norman	Spirit In The Sky	12-132	DK
Greenbaum, Norman	Spirit In The Sky	5-149	SC
Greene & Seely	Duet - Wish I Didn't Have To Miss U	5-444	SC
Greene & Seely	Wish I Didn't Have To Miss You	5-444	SC
Greene, Jack	All The Time	43-338	CB
Greene, Jack	All The Time	4-312	SC
Greene, Jack	Back In The Arms Of Love	43-343	CB
Greene, Jack	I Need Somebody Bad	43-350	CB
Greene, Jack	If This Is Love	43-347	CB
Greene, Jack	It's Time To Cross That Bridge	43-351	CB
Greene, Jack	Lord Is That Me	43-349	CB
Greene, Jack	Love Takes Care Of Me	43-345	CB

ARTIST	SONG TITLE	#	TYPE
Greene, Jack	Statue Of A Fool	43-342	CB
Greene, Jack	There Goes My Everything	8-774	CB
Greene, Jack	There Goes My Everything	8-671	SAV
Greene, Jack	There's A Whole Lot About A Woman	43-348	CB
Greene, Jack	Until My Dreams Come True	43-341	CB
Greene, Jack	What Locks The Door	43-339	CB
Greene, Jack	Whole World Comes To Me the	43-346	CB
Greene, Jack	Wish I Didn't Have To Miss You	43-344	CB
Greene, Jack	You Are My Treasure	43-340	CB
Greene, Lorne	Ringo	5-845	SC
Greenwood, Lee	Another Year Of Love	47-130	MM
Greenwood, Lee	Before I'm Ever Over You	47-131	SC
Greenwood, Lee	Between A Rock And A Heartache	47-128	CB
Greenwood, Lee	Dixie Road	11-744	DK
Greenwood, Lee	Fool's Gold	5-626	SC
Greenwood, Lee	God Bless The USA	20-156	BCI
Greenwood, Lee	God Bless The USA	13-410	P
Greenwood, Lee	God Bless The USA	2-22	SC
Greenwood, Lee	Going Going Gone	4-492	SC
Greenwood, Lee	Great Defenders the	47-132	SC
Greenwood, Lee	Hearts Aren't Made To Break	20-19	SC
Greenwood, Lee	Holdin' A Good Hand	6-619	MM
Greenwood, Lee	I'll Be Loving You	47-127	CB
Greenwood, Lee	IOU	2-637	SC
Greenwood, Lee	It Turns Me Inside Out	8-686	SAV
Greenwood, Lee	It Turns Me Inside Out	5-29	SC
Greenwood, Lee	Mornin' Ride	4-550	SC
Greenwood, Lee	Ring On Her Finger Time On Her Hand	17-294	NA
Greenwood, Lee	Rocks That You Can't Move	32-47	THM
Greenwood, Lee	Somebody's Gonna Love You	9-477	SAV
Greenwood, Lee	Touch And Go Crazy	46-113	SC
Greenwood, Lee	We've Got It Made	47-129	CB
Greenwood, Lee	You've Got A Good Love Comin'	47-126	CB
Greenwood&Boggus s	Duet - Hopelessly Yours	2-308	SC
Greenwood&Boggus s	Hopelessly Yours	2-308	SC
Greenwood&Mandrel l	Duet - To Me	2-307	SC
Greenwood&Mandrel l	To Me	2-307	SC
Greg Khin Band	Jeopardy	5-139	SC
Greg Khin Band	Breakup Song	9-342	AH
Greg Khin Band	Breakup Song	21-398	SC
Gregg, Ricky Lynn	If I Had A Cheatin' Heart	24-7	SC
Gregg, Ricky Lynn	To Find Where I Belong	2-733	SC

ARTIST	SONG TITLE	#	TYPE
Gregory, Adam	Crazy Days	36-612	CB
Gregory, Clinton	Rocking The Country	8-979	CB
Gregory, Clinton	Standing On The Edge Of Love	24-255	SC
Gregory, Clinton	You Didn't Miss A Thing	2-665	SC
Gregory, Clinton	You Smile	41-82	PHN
Griffin, Merv	I've Got A Lovely Bunch Of Coconuts	27-432	DK
Griffiths, Marcia	Electric Slide (Electric Boogie)	22-392	SC
Griggs w/McBride	Practice Life	18-328	ST
Griggs, Andy	How Cool Is That	15-335	CB
Griggs, Andy	How Cool Is That	15-191	ST
Griggs, Andy	I Never Had A Chance	29-56	CB
Griggs, Andy	I'll Go Crazy	19-203	CB
Griggs, Andy	I'll Go Crazy	10-213	SC
Griggs, Andy	I'll Go Crazy	22-488	ST
Griggs, Andy	If Heaven	22-104	CB
Griggs, Andy	If Heaven	23-42	SC
Griggs, Andy	Practice Life	25-355	MM
Griggs, Andy	Practice Life	32-5	THM
Griggs, Andy	She Thinks She Needs Me	35-447	CB
Griggs, Andy	She Thinks She Needs Me	20-173	ST
Griggs, Andy	She's More	22-531	ST
Griggs, Andy	Tattoo Rose	30-474	CB
Griggs, Andy	This I Gotta See	23-290	CB
Griggs, Andy	Tonight I Wanna Be Your Man	33-153	CB
Griggs, Andy	Tonight I Wanna Be Your Man	25-132	MM
Griggs, Andy	Tonight I Wanna Be Your Man	16-328	ST
Griggs, Andy	Waitin' On Sundown	14-102	CB
Griggs, Andy	Waitin' On Sundown	13-854	CHM
Griggs, Andy	You Made Me That Way	14-140	CB
Griggs, Andy	You Made Me That Way	14-11	CHM
Griggs, Andy	You Made Me That Way	10-265	SC
Griggs, Andy	You Made Me That Way	22-576	ST
Griggs, Andy	You Won't Ever Be Lonely	7-859	CHT
Groban, Josh	Awake	36-447	CB
Groban, Josh	Believe	48-47	CB
Groban, Josh	Broken Vow	43-305	CB
Groban, Josh	Falling Slowly	48-645	KV
Groban, Josh	February Song	43-304	CB
Groban, Josh	Hidden Away	48-48	CB
Groban, Josh	Higher Window	48-50	KVD
Groban, Josh	Home To Stay	48-43	CB
Groban, Josh	Let Me Fall	48-45	CB
Groban, Josh	My Confession	48-42	CB
Groban, Josh	Never Let Go	48-46	CB
Groban, Josh	Remember When It Rained	20-547	PHM
Groban, Josh	She's Out Of My Life	48-49	KVD
Groban, Josh	Sometimes I Dream	48-52	PSJT
Groban, Josh	To Where You Are	35-307	CB

ARTIST	SONG TITLE	#	TYPE
Groban, Josh	To Where You Are	18-415	MM
Groban, Josh	To Where You Are	17-592	PHM
Groban, Josh	Vincent (Starry Starry Night)	43-303	CB
Groban, Josh	What I Did For Love	48-51	KVD
Groban, Josh	When You Say You Love Me	43-306	CB
Groban, Josh	You Are Loved (Don't Give Up)	48-44	CB
Groban, Josh	You Raise Me Up	20-354	PHM
Groban, Josh	You're Still You	18-776	PHM
Groove Generation	You Make Me Feel Like Dancing	17-38	DK
Groove Theory	Baby Luv	24-176	SC
Groove Theory	Tell Me	4-686	SC
Grover, Dana	Rain	25-588	MM
Guess Who	American Woman	11-132	DK
Guess Who	American Woman	7-45	MM
Guess Who	American Woman	12-862	P
Guess Who	Hand Me Down World	5-591	SC
Guess Who	Laughing	12-324	DK
Guess Who	Laughing	5-454	SC
Guess Who	No Sugar Tonight/Mother Nature	20-94	SC
Guess Who	No Time	26-363	DK
Guess Who	These Eyes	9-355	MG
Guess Who	These Eyes	7-269	MM
Guess Who	Undun	26-508	DK
Guns 'N Roses	Knickin' On Heaven's Door	46-165	SC
Guns 'N Roses	Knockin' On Heaven's Door	48-53	SC
Guns 'N Roses	Live And Let Die - WN	48-60	SC
Guns 'N Roses	My Michelle - WN	48-57	SC
Guns 'N Roses	Nightrain - WN	48-67	KV
Guns 'N Roses	Since I Don't Have You	48-54	SC
Guns 'N Roses	Sympathy For The Devil - WN	48-66	KV
Guns & Roses	Back Off Bitch **	23-113	SC
Guns & Roses	Don't Cry (Original)	6-29	SC
Guns & Roses	Mr. Brownstone	5-482	SC
Guns & Roses	November Rain	6-172	MM
Guns & Roses	November Rain	12-764	P
Guns & Roses	November Rain	23-108	SC
Guns & Roses	Paradise City	10-504	DA
Guns & Roses	Paradise City	17-22	DK
Guns & Roses	Paradise City	13-278	P
Guns & Roses	Patience	12-766	P
Guns & Roses	Sweet Child O' Mine	11-320	DK
Guns & Roses	Sweet Child O' Mine	12-765	P
Guns & Roses	Used To Love Her	21-766	SC
Guns & Roses	Welcome To The Jungle	17-21	DK
Guns & Roses	Welcome To The Jungle	13-277	P
Guns & Roses	You Could Be Mine	21-769	SC
Guthrie, Arlo	Alice's Restaurant	7-353	MM
Guthrie, Arlo	City Of New Orleans	9-361	MG
Guthrie, Gwen	Ain't Nothing Going On But The Rent	48-777	P

ARTIST	SONG TITLE	#	TYPE	ARTIST	SONG TITLE	#	TYPE
Guthrie, Woody	This Land Is Your Land	35-33	CB	Haggard, Merle	Are The Good Times Really Over	12-90	DK
Guthrie, Woody	This Land Is Your Land	26-322	DK	Haggard, Merle	Back To The Barrooms Again	29-447	DK
Guy	Dancin'	9-332	PS	Haggard, Merle	Better Love Next Time a	8-326	CB
Guy	Dancin'	5-899	SC	Haggard, Merle	Big City	1-364	CB
Guy, Buddy	Damn Right I Got The Blues	20-139	KB	Haggard, Merle	Big City	11-432	DK
Guys & Dolls	I've Never Been In Love Before	19-584	SC	Haggard, Merle	Bottle Let Me Down the	8-313	CB
Guys & Dolls	Show - Adelaide's Lament	7-364	MM	Haggard, Merle	Branded Man	1-367	CB
Guys & Dolls	Show - I've Never Been In Love Befo	18-194	PS	Haggard, Merle	Branded Man	4-724	SC
Guys & Dolls	Show - I've Never Been In Love Befo	19-584	SC	Haggard, Merle	Carolyn	22-237	CB
Guys & Dolls	Show - Luck Be A Lady	27-397	DK	Haggard, Merle	Carolyn	12-15	DK
Guys & Dolls	Show - Luck Be A Lady	10-377	KC	Haggard, Merle	CC Water Back	43-52	CB
Guys & Dolls	Show - Luck Be A Lady	5-655	SC	Haggard, Merle	Cherokee Maiden	15-71	CB
Guys And Dolls	Bushel And A Peck	49-773	PS	Haggard, Merle	Chill Factor	29-449	DK
Guys And Dolls	Show - Bushel And A Peck	49-773	PS	Haggard, Merle	Daddy Frank The Guitar Man	7-120	MM
Guys And Dolls - Streisand	Show - Luck Be A Lady	49-563	PS	Haggard, Merle	Daddy Frank The Guitar Man	8-316	CB
Gypsy	Show - Everything's Coming Up Roses	5-646	SC	Haggard, Merle	Duet - Pick Me Up On Your Way Down	49-168	KV
Gypsy	Show - Let Me Entertain You	6-241	MM	Haggard, Merle	Emptiest Arms In The World	17-382	DK
H-Town	Knockin' Da Boots	16-568	P	Haggard, Merle	Emptiest Arms In The World the	37-171	CB
Hagar, Sammy	I Can't Drive 55	3-555	SC	Haggard, Merle	Every Fool Has A Rainbow	49-805	CB
Hagar, Sammy	There's Only One Way To Rock	21-768	SC	Haggard, Merle	Everybody's Had The Blues	8-322	CB
Haggard & Eastwood	Bar Room Buddies	22-234	CB	Haggard, Merle	Everybody's Had The Blues	49-804	CB
Haggard & Eastwood	Duet - Bar Room Buddies	22-234	CB	Haggard, Merle	Farmer's Daughter	8-314	CB
Haggard & Jewel	Duet - That's the Way Love Goes	49-809	CB	Haggard, Merle	Fightin' Side Of Me the	8-312	CB
Haggard & Jewel	That's the Way Love Goes - duet	49-809	CB	Haggard, Merle	Fightin' Side Of Me the	4-633	SC
Haggard & Jones	CC Water Back	22-232	CB	Haggard, Merle	From Graceland to the Promised...	37-175	CB
Haggard & Jones	Duet - CC Water Back	22-232	CB	Haggard, Merle	Fugitive the	8-315	CB
Haggard & Jones	Duet - Yesterday's Wine	22-242	CB	Haggard, Merle	Fugitive the	4-732	SC
Haggard & Jones	Yesterday's Wine	22-242	CB	Haggard, Merle	Going Where The Lonely Go	22-241	CB
Haggard & Nelson	Duet - Pancho & Lefty	33-78	CB	Haggard, Merle	Going Where The Lonely Go	19-412	SC
Haggard & Nelson	Duet - Pick Me Up On Your Way Down	49-816	KV	Haggard, Merle	Good Hearted Woman a	49-822	SRK
Haggard & Nelson	Pancho & Lefty - duet	33-78	CB	Haggard, Merle	Goodbye Comes Hard For Me	49-818	SSK
Haggard & Nelson	Pick Me Up On Your Way Down	49-816	KV	Haggard, Merle	Grandma Harp	8-842	CB
Haggard & Williams	Bull And The Beaver the	5-445	SC	Haggard, Merle	Harold's Super Service	46-17	SSK
Haggard & Williams	Duet - Bull & The Beaver the	5-445	SC	Haggard, Merle	Here Comes The Freedom Train	8-456	CB
Haggard & Wilson	Duet - Politically Uncorrect	49-424	ST	Haggard, Merle	Here In Frisco	49-880	DCK
Haggard & Wilson	Politically Uncorrect - duet	49-424	ST	Haggard, Merle	Holding Things Together	44-55	KV
Haggard, Marty	Hello God	4-627	SC	Haggard, Merle	Hungry Eyes	1-374	CB
Haggard, Marty	In The Afterlife	4-423	SC	Haggard, Merle	Hungry Eyes	5-33	SC
Haggard, Merle	Always Wanting You	22-238	CB	Haggard, Merle	I Am An Island	49-821	SC
Haggard, Merle	America First	49-170	SC	Haggard, Merle	I Am An Island	49-169	SC
Haggard, Merle	Are The Good Times Really Over	37-178	CB	Haggard, Merle	I Can't Be Myself	37-173	CB
				Haggard, Merle	I Forget You Every Day	49-820	SSK
				Haggard, Merle	I Had A Beautiful Time	44-73	KV

ARTIST	SONG TITLE	#	TYPE
Haggard, Merle	I Take A Lot Of Pride	22-229	CB
Haggard, Merle	I Take A Lot Of Pride In What I Am	43-49	CB
Haggard, Merle	I Take A Lot Of Pride In What I Am	4-727	SC
Haggard, Merle	I Think I'll Just Stay Here & Drink	8-317	CB
Haggard, Merle	I Think I'll Just Stay Here & Drink	17-10	DK
Haggard, Merle	I Think I'll Just Stay Here & Drink	13-386	P
Haggard, Merle	I Threw Away The Rose	8-370	CB
Haggard, Merle	I Wonder If They Ever Think Of Me	37-170	CB
Haggard, Merle	I'm Always On a Mountain When...	37-180	CB
Haggard, Merle	I've Had A Beautiful Time	46-23	SSK
Haggard, Merle	If I Left It Up To You	45-575	SSK
Haggard, Merle	If We Make It Through December	17-6	DK
Haggard, Merle	If We Make It Through December	13-459	P
Haggard, Merle	If We're Not Back In Love By Monday	34-233	CB
Haggard, Merle	If We're Not Back In Love By Monday	4-579	SC
Haggard, Merle	If We're Not Back In Love By Monday	8-325	CB
Haggard, Merle	In My Next Life	46-46	SSK
Haggard, Merle	It Makes No Difference Now	46-28	SSK
Haggard, Merle	It's All Going To Pot	45-947	KV
Haggard, Merle	It's All In The Movies	8-319	CB
Haggard, Merle	It's Been A Great Afternoon	37-181	CB
Haggard, Merle	It's Been A Great Afternoon	11-837	DK
Haggard, Merle	It's Been A Great Afternoon	10-777	JVC
Haggard, Merle	It's Not Love But It's Not Bad	8-321	CB
Haggard, Merle	It's Not Love But It's Not Bad	5-129	SC
Haggard, Merle	Jesus Takes A Hand	37-172	CB
Haggard, Merle	Kentucky Gambler	16-663	CB
Haggard, Merle	Legend Of Bonnie & Clyde	5-92	SC
Haggard, Merle	Legend Of Bonnie & Clyde	37-174	CB
Haggard, Merle	Let's Chase Each Other 'Round..	7-153	MM
Haggard, Merle	Let's Chase Each Other 'Round...	8-320	CB
Haggard, Merle	Let's Chase Each Other 'Round...	4-660	SC
Haggard, Merle	Life's Just Not The Way It Used To Be	46-43	SSK
Haggard, Merle	Long Black Limousine	49-819	SSK
Haggard, Merle	Makeup And Faded Blue Jeans	46-45	SSK

ARTIST	SONG TITLE	#	TYPE
Haggard, Merle	Mama Tried	8-277	CB
Haggard, Merle	Mama Tried	16-788	DK
Haggard, Merle	Mama Tried	17-306	NA
Haggard, Merle	Mama Tried	13-501	P
Haggard, Merle	Mamma's Hungry Eyes	49-171	CB
Haggard, Merle	Misery & Gin	22-233	CB
Haggard, Merle	Misery And Gin	49-811	CB
Haggard, Merle	Motorcycle Cowboy	9-428	CB
Haggard, Merle	Movin' On	22-239	CB
Haggard, Merle	Movin' On	13-340	P
Haggard, Merle	My Favorite Memory	22-235	CB
Haggard, Merle	My Favorite Memory	12-53	DK
Haggard, Merle	My Friends Are All Gonna...	3-908	CB
Haggard, Merle	My Own Kind Of Hat	37-179	CB
Haggard, Merle	Natural High	22-228	CB
Haggard, Merle	Nobody's Darlin' But Mine	48-485	CKC
Haggard, Merle	Okie From Muskogee	1-362	CB
Haggard, Merle	Okie From Muskogee	11-765	DK
Haggard, Merle	Okie From Muskogee	13-374	P
Haggard, Merle	Old Man From The Mountain	22-230	CB
Haggard, Merle	Pancho & Lefty	43-56	CB
Haggard, Merle	Pick Me Up On Your Way Down - duet	49-168	KV
Haggard, Merle	Place To Fall Apart a	49-817	PS
Haggard, Merle	Rainbow Stew	37-176	CB
Haggard, Merle	Rainbow Stew	5-41	SC
Haggard, Merle	Ramblin' Fever	8-281	CB
Haggard, Merle	Ramblin' Fever	17-401	DK
Haggard, Merle	Ramblin' Fever	8-644	SAV
Haggard, Merle	Reasons To Quit	29-437	DK
Haggard, Merle	Red Bandana	37-182	CB
Haggard, Merle	Roots Of My Raising the	37-169	CB
Haggard, Merle	Running Kind	49-815	KV
Haggard, Merle	Santa Claus And Popcorn - xmas	45-247	CB
Haggard, Merle	Shelly's Winter Love	45-722	VH
Haggard, Merle	Silver Wings	8-39	CB
Haggard, Merle	Sing A Sad Song	49-814	VH
Haggard, Merle	Sing Me Back Home	8-323	CB
Haggard, Merle	Sing Me Back Home	4-734	SC
Haggard, Merle	Soldier's Last Letter	37-183	CB
Haggard, Merle	Someday We'll Look Back	49-339	CB
Haggard, Merle	Someday When Things Are Good	16-664	CB
Haggard, Merle	Somewhere Between	44-59	KV
Haggard, Merle	Somewhere Between	46-22	SSK
Haggard, Merle	Swinging Doors	8-318	CB
Haggard, Merle	Swinging Doors	6-772	MM
Haggard, Merle	Swinging Doors	8-645	SAV
Haggard, Merle	Swinging Doors	4-723	SC
Haggard, Merle	Teach Me To Forget	45-712	VH
Haggard, Merle	That's The Way Love Goes	1-366	CB
Haggard, Merle	That's The Way Love	9-466	SAV

ARTIST	SONG TITLE	#	TYPE
	Goes		
Haggard, Merle	That's The Way Love Goes	22-382	ST
Haggard, Merle	Things Aren't Funny Anymore	8-324	CB
Haggard, Merle	Things Have Gone To Pieces	49-813	DCK
Haggard, Merle	Think About A Lullaby	49-807	CB
Haggard, Merle	Think About A Lullaby	49-343	CB
Haggard, Merle	Today I Started Loving You Again	8-425	CB
Haggard, Merle	Today I Started Loving You Again	11-125	DK
Haggard, Merle	Truck Driver's Blues	4-374	SC
Haggard, Merle	Turnin' Off A Memory	37-177	CB
Haggard, Merle	Twinkle Twinkle Lucky Star	1-369	CB
Haggard, Merle	Twinkle Twinkle Lucky Star	11-747	DK
Haggard, Merle	Waiting For A Train	46-24	SSK
Haggard, Merle	Wake Up	49-812	DFK
Haggard, Merle	Way I Am the	46-25	SSK
Haggard, Merle	Way I Am the	45-719	VH
Haggard, Merle	Way It Was In '51 the	46-44	SSK
Haggard, Merle	We Never Touch At All	49-806	CB
Haggard, Merle	We Never Touch At All	49-342	CB
Haggard, Merle	What Am I Gonna Do (With The Rest...)	46-32	SSK
Haggard, Merle	When It Rains It Pours	49-808	CB
Haggard, Merle	When It Rains It Pours	49-344	CB
Haggard, Merle	When My Blue Moon Turns To Gold	44-61	KV
Haggard, Merle	Workin' Man Can't Get Nowhere Today	8-823	CB
Haggard, Merle	Workin' Man's Blues	6-776	MM
Haggard, Merle	Xmas - If We Make It Thru December	8-67	CB
Haggard, Merle	Xmas - If We Make It Thru December	14-548	SC
Haggard, Merle	Xmas - Santa Claus And Popcorn	45-247	CB
Haggard, Merle	You Take Me For Granted	22-240	CB
Haggard, Nelson & Price	Duet - Pick Me Up On Your Way Down	44-87	KV
Haggard, Nelson & Price	Pick Me Up On Your Way Down	44-87	KV
Haircut One Hundred	Love Plus One	21-402	SC
Hale, Lucy	You Sound Good To Me	43-239	ASK
Haley & Comets	Choo Choo Ch' Boogie	49-533	KRG
Haley & Comets	Rock Around The Clock	12-119	DK
Haley & Comets	Rock Around The Clock	12-728	P
Haley & Comets	Rock Around The Clock	49-534	SC
Haley & Comets	Saints' Rock & Roll the	12-551	P
Haley & Comets	See Ya Later Alligator	33-228	CB
Haley & Comets	See You Later Alligator	11-44	PX
Haley & Comets	See You Later Alligator	3-465	SC
Haley & Comets	Shake Rattle & Roll	11-668	DK
Haley & Comets	Shake Rattle & Roll	11-49	PX

ARTIST	SONG TITLE	#	TYPE
Haley & Comets	Shake Rattle & Roll	2-47	SC
Haley & Comets	Skinny Minnie	49-532	DCK
Halfway To Hazard	Daisy	30-445	CB
Halfway To Hazard	Devil And The Cross	36-575	CB
Hall & Oates	Did It In A Minute - WN	48-62	CB
Hall & Oates	Do It For Love	18-416	MM
Hall & Oates	Everything Your Heart Desires - WN	48-63	CB
Hall & Oates	Family Man	9-199	SO
Hall & Oates	I Can't Go For That	3-524	SC
Hall & Oates	I Can't Go For That (No Can Do)	33-309	CB
Hall & Oates	Kiss On My List - WN	48-64	CB
Hall & Oates	ManEater	4-327	SC
Hall & Oates	ManEater	9-201	SO
Hall & Oates	One On One - WN	48-68	LC
Hall & Oates	Out Of Touch - WN	48-65	CB
Hall & Oates	Private Eyes	35-152	CB
Hall & Oates	Private Eyes	4-87	SC
Hall & Oates	Promise Ain't Enough - WN	48-69	MM
Hall & Oates	Rich Girl	11-83	DK
Hall & Oates	Rich Girl	4-851	SC
Hall & Oates	Sara Smile	13-667	SGB
Hall & Oates	Say It Isn't So - WN	48-72	SC
Hall & Oates	She's Gone	20-76	SC
Hall & Oates	So Close	9-198	SO
Hall & Oates	Throw The Roses Away - WN	48-70	SC
Hall & Oates	You Make My Dreams	21-737	MH
Hall, Aaron	I Miss You	15-767	NU
Hall, Daryl	Gloryland	9-200	SO
Hall, Tom T.	Ballad Of Forty Dollars	18-283	CB
Hall, Tom T.	Chattanooga Dog	45-341	BSP
Hall, Tom T.	Country Is	15-65	CB
Hall, Tom T.	Country Is	5-416	SC
Hall, Tom T.	Deal	18-285	CB
Hall, Tom T.	Everything From Jesus To Jack Daniels	45-838	VH
Hall, Tom T.	Faster Horses	8-439	CB
Hall, Tom T.	Fox On The Run	18-279	CB
Hall, Tom T.	Gospel - Me And Jesus - VR	49-711	VH
Hall, Tom T.	Homecoming	45-928	SSK
Hall, Tom T.	I Care	18-282	CB
Hall, Tom T.	I Care	29-700	SC
Hall, Tom T.	I Like Beer	7-409	MM
Hall, Tom T.	I Like Beer	3-603	SC
Hall, Tom T.	I Like Beer	8-447	CB
Hall, Tom T.	I Love	8-43	CB
Hall, Tom T.	I Love	5-402	SC
Hall, Tom T.	In The Summertime	45-929	ESS
Hall, Tom T.	Me And Jesus - VR - Gospel	49-711	VH
Hall, Tom T.	Negatory Romance	18-280	CB
Hall, Tom T.	Old Dogs Children & Watermelon Wine	3-748	CB
Hall, Tom T.	Old Dogs Children &	13-482	P

ARTIST	SONG TITLE	#	TYPE
	Watermelon Wine		
Hall, Tom T.	Old Farts Jackasses Steel Guitars &	45-927	DCK
Hall, Tom T.	Pamala Brown	45-669	DCK
Hall, Tom T.	Ravishing Ruby	3-752	CB
Hall, Tom T.	Ravishing Ruby	5-821	SC
Hall, Tom T.	Second Hand Flowers	45-716	VH
Hall, Tom T.	Sneaky Snake	45-837	VH
Hall, Tom T.	That Song Is Driving Me Crazy	3-753	CB
Hall, Tom T.	That Song Is Driving Me Crazy	6-2	SC
Hall, Tom T.	Tulsa Telephone Book	45-926	VH
Hall, Tom T.	Week In A Country Jail a	18-281	CB
Hall, Tom T.	Xmas - Jolly Old St. Nicholas	8-77	CB
Hall, Tom T.	Xmas - Oh Christmas Tree	8-70	CB
Hall, Tom T.	Year That Clayton Delany Died	8-283	CB
Hall, Tom T.	Year That Clayton Delany Died	4-308	SC
Hall, Tom T.	Your Man Loves You Honey	18-284	CB
Halloween Songs	Halloween - Jack O Lantern Jump	45-102	KV
Halloween Songs	Halloween - Skeleton Dance	45-101	KV
Halloween Songs	Jack O Lantern Jump - Halloween	45-102	KV
Halloween Songs	Skeleton Dance - Halloween	45-101	KV
Hamilton, Anthony	Charlene	30-813	PHM
Hamilton, Anthony	Comin' From Where I'm From	32-425	THM
Hamilton, George IV	Abilene	8-782	CB
Hamilton, George IV	Abilene	8-663	SAV
Hamilton, George IV	Abilene	2-630	SC
Hamilton, Roy	Ebb Tide	9-738	SAV
Hamilton/Frank/Reyn	Don't Pull Your Love	17-113	DK
Hamilton/Frank/Reyn	Don't Pull Your Love	13-70	P
Hamilton/Frank/Reyn	Don't Pull Your Love	4-841	SC
Hamilton/Frank/Reyn	Fallin' In Love	2-849	SC
Hammer, MC	Too Legit To Quit	12-126	DK
Hammer, MC	Too Legit To Quit	25-484	MM
Hammer, MC	U Can't Touch This	33-439	CB
Hammer, MC	U Can't Touch This	25-472	MM
Hammer, MC	U Can't Touch This	24-138	SC
Hammond, Albert	It Never Rains In Southern CA	5-113	SC
Hanna-McEuen	Something Like A Broken Heart	22-324	CB
Hanson	I Will Come To You	7-697	PHM
Hanson	If Only (Radio Version)	14-486	SC
Hanson	Mmm Bop	33-358	CB
Hanson	Mmm Bop	15-531	SC
Hanson	This Time Around	29-172	MH
Hanson	This Time Around	16-240	PHM
Hanson	Where's The Love	15-585	SC

ARTIST	SONG TITLE	#	TYPE
Hanson, Jennifer	Beautiful Goodbye	34-354	CB
Hanson, Jennifer	Beautiful Goodbye	25-415	MM
Hanson, Jennifer	Beautiful Goodbye	18-210	ST
Hanson, Jennifer	Half A Heart Tattoo	25-698	MM
Hanson, Jennifer	Half A Heart Tattoo	19-366	ST
Hanson, Jennifer	Half A Heart Tattoo	32-379	THM
Hanson, Jennifer	Joyride	30-537	CB
Hanson, Jennifer	This Far Gone	20-220	CB
Hanson, Jennifer	This Far Gone	19-49	ST
Hanson, Jennifer	This Far Gone	32-262	THM
Happenings	I Got Rhythm	16-855	DK
Happenings	See You In September	10-365	KC
Happenings	See You In September	7-39	MM
Harbey Danger	Flagpole Sitta	10-139	SC
Hardiman, Gloria	Meet Me With Your Black Drawers On	14-595	SC
Harling, Keith	Coming Back For You	8-758	CB
Harling, Keith	Easy Makin' Love	9-424	CB
Harling, Keith	Papa Bear	8-95	CB
Harling, Keith	Papa Bear	22-805	ST
Harling, Keith	Santa's Got A Semi - xmas	45-243	CB
Harling, Keith	There Goes The Neighborhood	8-915	CB
Harling, Keith	Write It In Stone	8-870	CB
Harling, Keith	Write It In Stone	10-156	SC
Harling, Keith	Xmas - Santa's Got A Semi	45-243	CB
Harper, Ben	Get It Like You Like It	36-188	PHM
Harper, Ben	Steal My Kisses	13-840	PHM
Harper& Innocent Cr	Steal My Kisses (Radio Version)	14-465	SC
Harpo, Slim	I'm A King Bee	14-599	SC
Harptones	Life Is But A Dream	25-557	MM
Harptones	Sunday Kind Of Love a	25-180	MM
Harris, EmmyLou	Beneath Still Waters	1-226	CB
Harris, EmmyLou	Beneath Still Waters	4-794	SC
Harris, EmmyLou	Blue Kentucky Girl	8-275	CB
Harris, EmmyLou	Blue Kentucky Girl	11-708	DK
Harris, EmmyLou	Blue Kentucky Girl	13-421	P
Harris, EmmyLou	Blue Moon Of Kentucky	6-735	MM
Harris, EmmyLou	Born To Run	19-447	SC
Harris, EmmyLou	Goodbye	46-278	KV
Harris, Emmylou	Gospel - Wayfaring Stranger	43-102	CB
Harris, EmmyLou	Heartbreak Hill	1-228	CB
Harris, EmmyLou	Heaven Only Knows	8-827	CB
Harris, EmmyLou	Heaven Only Knows	6-748	MM
Harris, EmmyLou	High Powered Love	1-230	CB
Harris, EmmyLou	High Powered Love	4-472	SC
Harris, EmmyLou	If I Could Only Win Your Love	8-282	CB
Harris, EmmyLou	If I Could Only Win Your Love	5-158	SC
Harris, EmmyLou	Lost His Love On Our First Date	8-207	CB
Harris, EmmyLou	Making Believe	8-460	CB
Harris, EmmyLou	Mr. Sandman	1-234	CB

ARTIST	SONG TITLE	#	TYPE
Harris, EmmyLou	Mr. Sandman	7-110	MM
Harris, EmmyLou	Once More	1-235	CB
Harris, EmmyLou	One Of These Days	15-76	CB
Harris, EmmyLou	Rollin' & Ramblin'	16-356	CB
Harris, EmmyLou	Save The Last Dance For Me	1-238	CB
Harris, EmmyLou	Thanks To You	16-591	MM
Harris, EmmyLou	Till I Gain Control Again	45-717	VH
Harris, EmmyLou	To Daddy	13-342	P
Harris, EmmyLou	Together Again	46-195	SC
Harris, EmmyLou	Two More Bottles Of Wine	1-239	CB
Harris, EmmyLou	Two More Bottles Of Wine	6-741	MM
Harris, EmmyLou	Two More Bottles Of Wine	13-477	P
Harris, EmmyLou	Two More Bottles Of Wine	5-127	SC
Harris, EmmyLou	Wayfaring Stranger	1-240	CB
Harris, EmmyLou	Xmas - Oh Little Town of Bethlehem	30-400	SC
Harris, EmmyLou	You Never Can Tell (C' Est La Vie)	14-249	SC
Harris, Major	Love Won't Let Me Wait	28-108	DK
Harris, Richard	McArthur Park	19-131	KC
Harris, Rolf	Tie Me Kangaroo Down Sport	26-339	DK
Harris, Rolf	Tie Me Kangaroo Down Sport	9-826	SAV
Harris, Rolf	Tie Me Kangaroo Down Sport	37-80	SC
Harris, Sam	Over The Rainbow	7-478	MM
Harris, Thurston	Little Bitty Pretty One	3-458	SC
Harrison, George	All Those Years Ago	24-67	SC
Harrison, George	Gospel - My Sweet Lord	33-270	CB
Harrison, George	Got My Mind Set On You	14-563	AH
Harrison, George	What Is Life	5-686	SC
Harrison, Wilbert	Kansas City	35-16	CB
Harrison, Wilbert	Kansas City	11-355	DK
Harrison, Wilbert	Kansas City	6-155	MM
Harry James Orchestra	You Made Me Love You	43-218	CB
Hart, Beth	LA Song	16-188	PHM
Hart, Corey	Sunglasses At Night	14-569	AH
Hart, Corey	Sunglasses At Night	5-382	SC
Hart, Freddie	Easy Lovin'	12-89	DK
Hart, Freddie	Easy Lovin'	8-633	SAV
Hart, Freddie	Easy Lovin'	5-27	SC
Hart, Freddie	Easy Loving	35-360	CB
Hart, Freddie	First Time the	45-842	VH
Hart, Freddie	My Hang-Up Is You	12-51	DK
Hart, Freddie	My Hang-Up Is You	19-441	SC
Hart, Freddie	Super Kind Of Woman	29-649	SC
Hart, Tara Lyn	That's When You Came Along	14-714	CB
Harter, J. Michael	Hard Call To Make	18-136	ST
Hartford, John	Big Rock Candy Mountain	49-327	CB
Hartman, Dan	I Can Dream About You	35-172	CB

ARTIST	SONG TITLE	#	TYPE
Hartman, Dan	I Can Dream About You	17-559	PR
Hartman, Dan	I Can Dream About You	9-687	SAV
Harvey, Adam	Beauty Is In the Eye of the Beerholder	47-491	CKA
Harvey, P.J.	Down By The Water	19-549	SC
Harvick, Kerry	Cowgirls	22-86	CB
Harvick, Kerry	That's What Your Love Does	23-288	CB
Hatchett, Molly	Dreams	9-375	AH
Hatchett, Molly	Dreams	13-772	SGB
Hatchett, Molly	Flirtin' With Disaster	7-461	MM
Hatchett, Molly	Flirtin' With Disaster	16-149	SC
Hathaway, Donny	Xmas - This Christmas	41-38	CB
Haun, Lindsey	Broken	30-176	CB
Havens, Richie	Here Comes The Sun	3-620	SC
Hawkins, Edwin	Oh Happy Day	11-385	DK
Hawkins, Hankshaw	Lonesome 7-7203	8-713	CB
Hawkins, Ronnie	Mary Lou	5-522	SC
Hayes, Amber	I Built This Wall	39-77	PHM
Hayes, Hunter	21	45-94	KV
Hayes, Hunter	All You Ever	39-69	PHN
Hayes, Hunter	Cry With You	39-73	PHN
Hayes, Hunter	Everybody's Got Somebody But Me	43-91	HM
Hayes, Hunter	Faith To Fall Back On	39-84	PHN
Hayes, Hunter	I Want Crazy	40-51	ASK
Hayes, Hunter	Invisible	43-132	PHN
Hayes, Hunter	Somebody's Heartbreak	38-254	PHN
Hayes, Hunter	Storm Warning	39-53	ASK
Hayes, Hunter	Storm Warning	38-249	PHN
Hayes, Hunter	Storyline	45-460	BKD
Hayes, Hunter	Tattoo	45-95	ASK
Hayes, Hunter	Thing About You	44-315	SBI
Hayes, Hunter	Wanted	39-50	ASK
Hayes, Wade	Day She Left Tulsa the	8-142	CB
Hayes, Wade	Day She Left Tulsa the	7-736	CHM
Hayes, Wade	Day She Left Tulsa the	22-423	ST
Hayes, Wade	Don't Stop	6-814	MM
Hayes, Wade	Don't Stop	3-422	SC
Hayes, Wade	Goodbye Is The Wrong Way	9-425	CB
Hayes, Wade	How Do You Sleep At Night	8-754	CB
Hayes, Wade	How Do You Sleep At Night	22-678	ST
Hayes, Wade	I'm Still Dancing With You	2-700	SC
Hayes, Wade	It's Over My Head	22-914	ST
Hayes, Wade	Old Enough To Know Better	6-715	MM
Hayes, Wade	Old Enough To Know Better	17-275	NA
Hayes, Wade	Old Enough To Know Better	2-544	SC
Hayes, Wade	On A Good Night	7-272	MM
Hayes, Wade	On A Good Night	4-370	SC
Hayes, Wade	On A Good Night	22-896	ST
Hayes, Wade	Tore Up From The Floor	8-351	CB

ARTIST	SONG TITLE	#	TYPE
	Up		
Hayes, Wade	Tore Up From The Floor Up	22-722	ST
Hayes, Wade	Up North	6-61	SC
Hayes, Wade	What I Meant To Say	3-624	SC
Hayes, Wade	When The Wrong One Loves U Right	8-100	CB
Hayes, Wade	Where Do I Go To Start All Over	4-459	SC
Hayes, Wade	Wichita Lineman	22-637	ST
Haymes, Dick	It Might As Well Be Spring	4-181	SC
Haynes, Susan	Drinkin' In My Sunday Dress	29-52	CB
Haynes, Susan	Drinkin' In My Sunday Dress	29-710	ST
Head East	Never Been Any Reason	21-812	SC
Head, Murray	One Night In Bangkok	17-467	SC
Head, Roy	Treat Her Right	7-33	MM
Head, Roy &Traits	Just A Little Bit	10-267	SS
Headley, H.	I Wish I Wasn't	32-275	THM
Healy, Jeff	While My Guitar Gently Weeps	36-126	SGB
Heard	From The Underworld	10-645	SF
Heart	All I Wanna Do Is Make Love To You	14-633	SC
Heart	Alone	11-388	DK
Heart	Alone	13-157	P
Heart	Barracuda	17-511	SC
Heart	Crazy On You	48-160	LE
Heart	Dog & Butterfly	24-680	SC
Heart	Dreamboat Annie	24-568	SC
Heart	Even It Up	4-530	SC
Heart	Fanatic	39-129	PHM
Heart	If Looks Could Kill	19-552	SC
Heart	Kick It Out	48-161	KV
Heart	Magic Man	6-489	MM
Heart	Magic Man	12-697	P
Heart	Magic Man	2-147	SC
Heart	Never	20-53	SC
Heart	Nothin' At All	24-63	SC
Heart	Straight On	24-424	SC
Heart	Tell It Like It Is	46-117	SC
Heart	These Dreams	35-192	CB
Heart	Walkin' Good	48-162	PHM
Heart	What About Love	11-280	DK
Heart	Will You Be There In The Mornin'	2-114	SC
Heart	Woman In Me the	2-231	SC
Heartland	I Loved Her First	30-29	CB
Heartland	Sound A Dream Makes the	39-55	PHN
Heat Miser/Snow Miser	Xmas - Year Without A Santa Claus	45-249	SC
Heat Miser/Snow Miser	Year Without A Santa Claus - xmas	45-249	SC
Heatherly, Eric	Flowers On The Wall	6-70	SC
Heatherly, Eric	Last Man Committed	25-299	MM
Heatherly, Eric	Last Man Committed	17-588	ST

ARTIST	SONG TITLE	#	TYPE
Heatherly, Eric	Sometimes It's Just Your Time	18-471	ST
Heatherly, Eric	Swimming In Champagne	14-120	CB
Heatherly, Eric	Swimming In Champagne	10-260	SC
Heatherly, Eric	Wrong Five O'Clock	22-466	ST
Heatwave	Always And Forever	2-272	SC
Heatwave	Boogie Nights	14-362	MH
Heatwave	Boogie Nights	15-33	SS
Hebb, Bobby	Sunny	35-60	CB
Hebb, Bobby	Sunny	17-133	DK
Hebb, Bobby	Sunny	6-266	MM
Hebb, Bobby	Sunny	13-52	P
Heep, Uriah	Easy Livin'	29-636	SC
Heinz	Just Like Eddie	10-650	SF
Hello Dolly	Show - Hello Dolly	6-247	MM
Hello Dolly	Show - It Only Takes A Moment	18-199	PS
Helms, Bobby	Fraulein	34-2	CB
Helms, Bobby	Fraulein	5-582	SC
Helms, Bobby	My Special Angel	33-441	CB
Helms, Bobby	My Special Angel	6-270	MM
Helms, Bobby	Xmas - Jingle Bell Rock	35-323	CB
Helms, Bobby	Xmas - Jingle Bell Rock	3-408	SC
Henderson, Ella	Yours	48-327	MRH
Hendricks, Bobby	Itchy Twitchy Feeling	45-831	VH
Hendrix, A.	Joy And Pain	32-350	THM
Hendrix, Jimi	All Along The Watchtower	19-277	SGB
Hendrix, Jimi	Are You Experienced	28-198	DK
Hendrix, Jimi	Crosstown Traffic	10-475	DA
Hendrix, Jimi	Foxy Lady	28-194	DK
Hendrix, Jimi	Hey Joe	11-667	DK
Hendrix, Jimi	Little Miss Lover	10-490	DA
Hendrix, Jimi	Purple Haze	2-758	SC
Hendrix, Jimi	Purple Haze	28-196	SF
Hendrix, Jimi	Red House	9-380	AH
Hendrix, Jimi	Red House	15-318	SC
Hendrix, Jimi	Wind Cries Mary the	28-197	SF
Henley, Don	All She Wants To Do Is Dance	15-707	LE
Henley, Don	Boys Of Summer the	48-151	LE
Henley, Don	Dirty Laundry	48-148	AH
Henley, Don	End Of The Innocence	48-156	ZMP
Henley, Don	Everybody Knows	48-153	SBI
Henley, Don	For My Wedding	14-154	CB
Henley, Don	Heart Of The Matter	48-150	LE
Henley, Don	I Will Not Go Quietly	48-158	ZMP
Henley, Don	Last Worthless Evening the	48-157	ZMP
Henley, Don	New York Minute	15-708	LE
Henley, Don	Not Enough Love In The World	48-149	AH
Henley, Don	Sit Down You're Rockin' The Boat	48-152	MM
Henley, Don	Sunset Grill	48-155	ZMP
Henley, Don	Taking You Home	30-643	THM

ARTIST	SONG TITLE	#	TYPE
Henley, Don	Through Your Hands	48-154	SC
Henley, Don	You Don't Know Me At All	48-159	ZMP
Henry, C. Frogman	Ain't Got No Home	5-644	SC
Henry, C. Frogman	But I Do	7-303	MM
Henry, C. Frogman	But I Do	11-47	PX
Henry, C. Frogman	But I Do	4-252	SC
Henry, C. Frogman	I Don't Know Why But I Do	3-300	MM
Herman's Hermits	Can't You Hear My Heartbeat	12-194	DK
Herman's Hermits	Can't You Hear My Heartbeat	30-776	SF
Herman's Hermits	Dandy	4-222	SC
Herman's Hermits	End Of The World	47-136	LE
Herman's Hermits	I'm Henry The VIII I Am	11-557	DK
Herman's Hermits	I'm Henry The VIII I Am	6-862	MM
Herman's Hermits	I'm Henry The VIII I Am	9-310	STR
Herman's Hermits	I'm Into Something Good	18-258	DK
Herman's Hermits	I'm Into Something Good	13-82	P
Herman's Hermits	Just A Little Bit Better	49-777	SC
Herman's Hermits	Just A Little Bit Better	47-137	SC
Herman's Hermits	Listen People	14-453	SC
Herman's Hermits	Mother In Law	47-134	DKM
Herman's Hermits	Mrs. Brown You've Got A Lovely..	16-790	DK
Herman's Hermits	Mrs. Brown You've Got A Lovely...	35-55	CB
Herman's Hermits	Mrs. Brown You've Got A Lovely...	9-783	SAV
Herman's Hermits	Mrs. Brown You've Got A Lovely...	5-173	SC
Herman's Hermits	Must To Avoid a	47-140	ZM
Herman's Hermits	My Sentimental Friend	10-629	SF
Herman's Hermits	No Milk Today	47-138	SF
Herman's Hermits	Silhouettes	4-515	SC
Herman's Hermits	Sleepy Joe	47-142	ZM
Herman's Hermits	Something's Happening	47-139	SF
Herman's Hermits	Sunshine Girl	47-141	ZM
Herman's Hermits	There's A Kind Of Hush	16-880	DK
Herman's Hermits	There's A Kind Of Hush	12-921	P
Herman's Hermits	There's A Kind Of Hush	5-465	SC
Herman's Hermits	This Door Swings Both Ways	45-599	OZP
Herman's Hermits	What A Wonderful World	47-135	LE
Herman's Hermits	Years May Come Years May Go	47-143	ZM
Hernandez, Patrick	Born To Be Alive	18-368	AH
Hernandez, Patrick	Born To Be Alive	15-697	LE
Herndon & Bentley	Duet - Heart Half Empty	7-146	MM
Herndon & Bentley	Duet - Heart Half Empty	4-100	SC
Herndon & Bentley	Heart Half Empty	4-100	SC
Herndon & Bentley	Heart Half Empty	7-146	MM
Herndon & Tucker	Don't Go Breakin' My Heart	19-711	ST
Herndon & Tucker	Duet - Don't Go Breakin'	19-711	ST

ARTIST	SONG TITLE	#	TYPE
	My Heart		
Herndon, Ty	Few Short Years a	17-591	ST
Herndon, Ty	Hands Of A Working Man	8-878	CB
Herndon, Ty	Hands Of A Working Man	7-830	CHT
Herndon, Ty	Hands Of A Working Man	22-703	ST
Herndon, Ty	Heather's Wail	16-106	ST
Herndon, Ty	I Have To Surrender	8-131	CB
Herndon, Ty	I Have To Surrender	22-642	ST
Herndon, Ty	I Want My Goodbye Back	7-16	MM
Herndon, Ty	In Your Face	7-207	MM
Herndon, Ty	In Your Face	4-231	SC
Herndon, Ty	It Must Be Love	8-159	CB
Herndon, Ty	It Must Be Love	22-830	ST
Herndon, Ty	Love Like That a	14-73	CB
Herndon, Ty	Love Like That a	22-562	ST
Herndon, Ty	Loved Too Much	7-628	CHM
Herndon, Ty	Lying In A Moment	7-337	MM
Herndon, Ty	Man Holdin' On A	7-749	CHM
Herndon, Ty	No Mercy	13-836	CHM
Herndon, Ty	No Mercy	23-371	SC
Herndon, Ty	No Mercy	22-532	ST
Herndon, Ty	She Wants To Be Wanted Again	7-402	MM
Herndon, Ty	She Wants To Be Wanted Again	24-660	SC
Herndon, Ty	Steam	14-694	CB
Herndon, Ty	Steam	5-732	SC
Herndon, Ty	Steam	22-507	ST
Herndon, Ty	What Mattered Most	2-658	SC
Hero/Heroine	Boys Like Girls	37-143	SC
Herrara, Eddy	Latino - Tu Eres Ajena	23-240	AI
Hewitt, Jennifer Lo	Barenaked	25-308	MM
Hewitt, Jennifer Lo	Barenaked	18-346	PHM
Hewitt, Jennifer Lo	How Do I Deal	7-798	PHT
Hey Romeo	Maybe You Remember Me Now	39-71	PHN
Hi-Five	Never Should've Let You Go	4-271	SC
Hicks, Taylor	Do I Make You Proud	30-151	PT
Hicks, Tim	Here Comes The Thunder	47-509	DCK
Hicks, Tim	Stronger Beer	47-498	DFK
Higgins, Bertie	Just Another Day In Paradise	7-50	MM
Higgins, Bertie	Key Largo	8-828	CB
Higgins, Bertie	Key Largo	18-50	MM
Highway 101	Bed You Made For Me the	9-514	SAV
Highway 101	Bed You Made For Me the	5-17	SC
Highway 101	Cry Cry Cry	34-280	CB
Highway 101	Do You Love Me Just Say Yes	5-752	SC
Highway 101	Honky Tonk Baby	6-193	MM
Highway 101	Honky Tonk Heart	14-318	SC

ARTIST	SONG TITLE	#	TYPE
Highway 101	Somewhere Tonight	13-497	P
Highway 101	Walkin' Talkin' Cryin' Barely...	2-514	SC
Highway 101	Walkin' Talkin' Cryin' Barely......	17-332	DK
Highway 101	Where'd You Get Your Cheatin' From	7-209	MM
Highway 101	Whiskey If You Were A Woman	29-65	CB
Highway 101	Whiskey If You Were A Woman	19-297	MH
Highway 101	Whiskey If You Were A Woman	13-395	P
Highway 101	Whiskey If You Were A Woman	8-695	SAV
Highway 101	Who's Gonna Love You	24-360	SC
Highway 101	Who's Lonely Now	14-689	CB
Highwaymen	Cotton Fields	16-357	CB
Highwaymen	Desperados Waiting For A Train	48-407	DFK
Highwaymen	Gospel - Michael Row The Boat Ashor	16-756	DK
Highwaymen	Highwayman	11-711	DK
Highwaymen	It Is What It Is	2-742	SC
Highwaymen	It Is What It Is	47-736	SRK
Hill & McGraw	Duet - Let's Make Love	35-335	CB
Hill & McGraw	Duet - Let's Make Love	22-530	ST
Hill & McGraw	Duet - Like We Never Loved At All	36-377	SC
Hill & McGraw	Let's Make Love	22-530	ST
Hill & McGraw	Let's Make Love - Duet	35-335	CB
Hill & McGraw	Like We Never Loved At All - duet	36-377	SC
Hill, D	I Should Be	32-56	THM
Hill, Dan	Sometimes When We Touch	16-66	SC
Hill, Dru	Tell Me	24-544	SC
Hill, Dru	These Are The Times	13-674	SGB
Hill, Dru	You Are Everything	28-225	SF
Hill, Faith	Breathe	22-371	ST
Hill, Faith	Bring Out The Elvis	14-724	CB
Hill, Faith	But I Will	15-681	CB
Hill, Faith	But I Will	6-594	MM
Hill, Faith	But I Will	17-223	NA
Hill, Faith	But I Will	2-315	SC
Hill, Faith	Cry	33-187	CB
Hill, Faith	Cry	25-336	MM
Hill, Faith	Cry	18-203	ST
Hill, Faith	Hard Way the	15-682	CB
Hill, Faith	I Can't Do That Anymore	15-683	CB
Hill, Faith	I Can't Do That Anymore	7-382	MM
Hill, Faith	I Can't Do That Anymore	4-600	SC
Hill, Faith	If My Heart Had Wings	14-784	ST
Hill, Faith	It Matters To Me	15-684	CB
Hill, Faith	It Matters To Me	7-145	MM
Hill, Faith	It Matters To Me	3-632	SC
Hill, Faith	Just About Now	24-351	SC
Hill, Faith	Just To Hear You Say That You Love Me	8-486	CB
Hill, Faith	Just To Hear You Say That You Love Me	7-762	CHM
Hill, Faith	Just To Hear You Say That You Love Me	22-793	ST
Hill, Faith	Let Me Let Go	15-685	CB
Hill, Faith	Let's Go To Vegas	15-686	CB
Hill, Faith	Let's Go To Vegas	7-30	MM
Hill, Faith	Life's Too Short To Love Like That	17-268	NA
Hill, Faith	Like We Never Loved At All	23-411	CB
Hill, Faith	Lost	30-460	CB
Hill, Faith	Love Ain't Like That	8-328	CB
Hill, Faith	Love Ain't Like That	7-824	CHT
Hill, Faith	Love Ain't Like That	22-709	ST
Hill, Faith	Love Is A Sweet Thing	9-392	CB
Hill, Faith	Lucky One the	29-192	CB
Hill, Faith	Mississippi Girl	23-279	CB
Hill, Faith	One	32-243	THM
Hill, Faith	Piece Of My Heart	15-688	CB
Hill, Faith	Piece Of My Heart	6-467	MM
Hill, Faith	Piece Of My Heart	2-317	SC
Hill, Faith	Red Umbrella	30-575	CB
Hill, Faith	Secret Of Life the	14-622	SC
Hill, Faith	Somebody Stand By Me	15-689	CB
Hill, Faith	Someone Else's Dream	15-690	CB
Hill, Faith	Someone Else's Dream	4-198	SC
Hill, Faith	Stealing Kisses	29-591	CB
Hill, Faith	Sunshine And Summertime	30-85	CB
Hill, Faith	Take Me As I Am	15-695	CB
Hill, Faith	Take Me As I Am	2-399	SC
Hill, Faith	That's How Love Moves	6-74	SC
Hill, Faith	There Will Come A Day	20-587	CB
Hill, Faith	There Will Come A Day	16-303	PHM
Hill, Faith	There Will Come A Day	22-569	ST
Hill, Faith	There You'll Be	33-445	CB
Hill, Faith	There You'll Be	15-182	ST
Hill, Faith	There You'll Be	18-537	TT
Hill, Faith	This Kiss	15-691	CB
Hill, Faith	This Kiss	7-731	CHM
Hill, Faith	This Kiss	22-767	ST
Hill, Faith	This Kiss (Pop Version)	15-624	PHM
Hill, Faith	Way You Love Me the	23-366	SC
Hill, Faith	Way You Love Me the	22-470	ST
Hill, Faith	What's In It For Me	14-151	CB
Hill, Faith	When The Lights Go Down	25-441	MM
Hill, Faith	When The Lights Go Down	18-466	ST
Hill, Faith	When The Lights Go Down	32-77	THM
Hill, Faith	When You Cry	8-983	CB
Hill, Faith	Wild One	15-692	CB
Hill, Faith	Wild One	2-20	SC
Hill, Faith	You Can't Lose Me	15-693	CB
Hill, Faith	You Can't Lose Me	19-291	MH
Hill, Faith	You Can't Lose Me	7-344	MM

ARTIST	SONG TITLE	#	TYPE
Hill, Faith	You Can't Lose Me	4-407	SC
Hill, Faith	You Give Me Love	15-694	CB
Hill, Faith	You're Still Here	34-352	CB
Hill, Faith	You're Still Here	25-608	MM
Hill, Faith	You're Still Here	19-63	ST
Hill, Faith	You're Still Here	32-269	THM
Hill, Goldie	I Let The Stars Get In My Eyes	8-775	CB
Hill, Ingram	Those Three Words	39-58	PHN
Hill, Jordan	For The Love Of You	7-575	THM
Hill, Jordan	Ooh Poo Pah Doo	11-468	DK
Hill, Jordan	Remember Me This Way	3-429	SC
Hill, Kim	Janie's Gone Fishing	6-584	MM
Hill, Lauryn	Can't Take My Eyes Off Of You	19-723	CB
Hill, Lauryn	Can't Take My Eyes Off Of You	13-672	SGB
Hill, Lauryn	Doo Wap (That Thing)	16-201	PHT
Hill, Lauryn	Doo Wop (That Thing)	19-725	CB
Hill, Lauryn	Doo Wop (That Thing)	28-219	DK
Hill, Lauryn	Doo Wop (That Thing)	25-682	MM
Hill, Lauryn	Doo Wop (That Thing)	21-611	SF
Hill, Lauryn	Doo Wop (That Thing)	13-679	SGB
Hill, Lauryn	Duet - Nothing Ever Matters	13-708	SGB
Hill, Lauryn	Everything Is Everything	25-695	MM
Hill, Lauryn	Ex Factor	25-688	MM
Hill, Lauryn	Ex-Factor	19-724	CB
Hill, Lauryn	Ex-Factor	28-220	DK
Hill, Lauryn	Ex-Factor	7-821	PHM
Hill, Lauryn	Ex-Factor	13-675	SGB
Hill, Lauryn	Lost Ones	19-726	CB
Hill, Lauryn	Nothing Ever Matters	13-708	SGB
Hill, Lauryn	To Zion	19-727	CB
Hill, Lauryn/Fugees	Killing Me Softly	19-728	CB
Hilltoppers	Marianne	9-852	SAV
Hilson, Keri	Energy	36-527	CB
Hilton, Ronnie	Around The World	10-600	SF
him	Wings Of A Butterfly	30-274	SC
Hinder	All American Nightmare	48-633	CB
Hinder	Best Is Yet To Come	48-630	CB
Hinder	Better Than Me	30-494	CB
Hinder	Get Stoned (Radio Version)	30-279	SC
Hinder	Lips Of An Angel	30-264	CB
Hinder	Loaded And Alone	48-631	BKD
Hinder	Use Me	36-514	CB
Hinder	What Ya Gonna Do	48-632	CB
Hinder	Without You	36-254	PHM
Hives	Hate To Say I Told You So	18-437	CB
Ho, Don	E Lei Ka Lei Lei	6-831	MM
Ho, Don	Hawaii - E Lei Ka Lei Lei	6-831	MM
Ho, Don	Hawaii - Hawaiian Wedding Song	6-834	MM
Ho, Don	Hawaii - I'll Remember	6-836	MM
Ho, Don	Hawaii - Ku'Uipo/Bora Bora	6-838	MM

ARTIST	SONG TITLE	#	TYPE
Ho, Don	Hawaii - Lover's Prayer	6-828	MM
Ho, Don	Hawaii - Molokai	6-827	MM
Ho, Don	Hawaii - Pua Carnation	6-837	MM
Ho, Don	Hawaii - Sweet Someone	6-835	MM
Ho, Don	Hawaii - Tiny Bubbles	6-826	MM
Ho, Don	Hawaiian Wedding Song	6-834	MM
Ho, Don	I'll Remember	6-836	MM
Ho, Don	Ku' Uipo/Bora Bora	6-838	MM
Ho, Don	Lover's Prayer	6-828	MM
Ho, Don	Molokai	6-827	MM
Ho, Don	Pua Carnation	6-837	MM
Ho, Don	Sweet Someone	6-835	MM
Ho, Don	Tiny Bubbles	6-826	MM
Hobbs, Becky	Country Girls	8-759	CB
Hobbs, Becky	I Can't Fight this Feeling	4-114	SC
Hobbs, Becky	Jones On The Jukebox	6-533	MM
Hobbs, Becky	Talk Back Trembling Lips	9-492	SAV
Hoffs, Susanna	All I Want	24-551	SC
Hogan, Brooks,Stacks	Falling	36-309	PHM
Hoku	Another Dumb Blonde	15-297	CB
Hole	Gold Dust Woman	24-227	SC
Holiday, Billie	Ain't Nobody's Business If I Do	49-474	MM
Holiday, Billie	All Of Me	49-459	MM
Holiday, Billie	God Bless The Child	6-569	MM
Holiday, Billie	Good Morning Heartache	49-467	MM
Holiday, Billie	He's Funny That Way	15-486	MM
Holiday, Billie	Nite & Day	11-588	DK
Holiday, J.	Suffocate	36-460	CB
Holland, Greg	When I Come Back	2-581	SC
Hollies	Air That I Breathe	44-358	LG
Hollies	Bus Stop	17-359	DK
Hollies	Bus Stop	44-364	LG
Hollies	Bus Stop	19-101	SAV
Hollies	Carrie Anne	3-131	SC
Hollies	Gasoline Alley Bred	44-376	ZM
Hollies	He Ain't Heavy, He's My Brother	12-321	DK
Hollies	Here I Go Again	17-86	DK
Hollies	Here I Go Again	10-646	SF
Hollies	I Can't Let Go	44-368	ZM
Hollies	I Can't Tell the Bottom From the Top	44-374	ZPK
Hollies	I'm Alive	10-570	SF
Hollies	I'm Down	44-373	DCK
Hollies	If I Needed Someone	44-375	ZM
Hollies	Jennifer Eccles	44-372	ZM
Hollies	Just One Look	44-363	LG
Hollies	King Midas In Reverse	48-423	DCK
Hollies	Let Love Pass	44-377	ZM
Hollies	Listen To Me	44-370	ZM
Hollies	Long Cool Woman In A Black Dress	9-346	AH
Hollies	Long Cool Woman in a Black Dress	44-365	LG

ARTIST	SONG TITLE	#	TYPE
Hollies	Long Cool Woman In A Black Dress	20-314	MH
Hollies	Look Through Any Window	44-360	EK
Hollies	On A Carousel	44-362	LG
Hollies	Sorry Suzanne	44-367	ZM
Hollies	Stay	44-371	ZM
Hollies	Stop Stop Stop	44-359	LG
Hollies	Suspended Animation	44-378	ZM
Hollies	We're Through	44-369	ZM
Hollies	Yes I Will	44-361	EK
Hollister, Dave	Tell Me Why	20-527	CB
Holly, Buddy	Baby Don't Care	3-210	LG
Holly, Buddy	Baby I Don't Care	11-39	PX
Holly, Buddy	Be Bop A Lula	47-879	PS
Holly, Buddy	Bo Diddley	3-212	LG
Holly, Buddy	Bo Diddley	11-38	PX
Holly, Buddy	Brown Eyed Handsome Man	3-217	LG
Holly, Buddy	Brown Eyed Handsome Man	11-35	PX
Holly, Buddy	Brown Eyed Handsome Man	10-641	SF
Holly, Buddy	Crying, Waiting, Hoping	47-889	ZM
Holly, Buddy	Early In The Morning	3-222	LG
Holly, Buddy	Everyday	12-175	DK
Holly, Buddy	Everyday	3-220	LG
Holly, Buddy	Fool's Paradise	47-888	ZM
Holly, Buddy	Heartbeat	3-224	LG
Holly, Buddy	I'm Gonna Love You Too	47-882	ZM
Holly, Buddy	It Doesn't Matter Anymore	17-362	DK
Holly, Buddy	It Doesn't Matter Anymore	3-208	LG
Holly, Buddy	It's So Easy	9-884	DK
Holly, Buddy	It's So Easy	12-683	P
Holly, Buddy	It's So Easy	11-32	PX
Holly, Buddy	Learning The Game	47-886	ZM
Holly, Buddy	Listen To Me	3-223	LG
Holly, Buddy	Listen To Me	11-36	PX
Holly, Buddy	Look At Me	47-891	ZM
Holly, Buddy	Love Is Strange	47-883	ZM
Holly, Buddy	Love's Made A Fool Of You	49-81	ZPA
Holly, Buddy	Mailman Bring Me No More Blues	45-718	VH
Holly, Buddy	Maybe Baby	35-10	CB
Holly, Buddy	Maybe Baby	3-215	LG
Holly, Buddy	Maybe Baby	7-291	MM
Holly, Buddy	Maybe Baby	4-513	SC
Holly, Buddy	Midnight Shift	47-885	ZM
Holly, Buddy	Not Fade Away	11-37	PX
Holly, Buddy	Oh Boy	12-99	DK
Holly, Buddy	Oh Boy	3-213	LG
Holly, Buddy	Oh Boy	6-689	MM
Holly, Buddy	Oh Boy	13-41	P
Holly, Buddy	Oh Boy	3-264	SC
Holly, Buddy	Peggy Sue	11-218	DK

ARTIST	SONG TITLE	#	TYPE
Holly, Buddy	Peggy Sue	3-216	LG
Holly, Buddy	Peggy Sue	12-735	P
Holly, Buddy	Peggy Sue	11-40	PX
Holly, Buddy	Peggy Sue Got Married	3-214	LG
Holly, Buddy	Raining In My Heart	3-219	LG
Holly, Buddy	Raining In My Heart	11-30	PX
Holly, Buddy	Rave On	3-218	LG
Holly, Buddy	Rave On	11-34	PX
Holly, Buddy	Reminiscing	48-673	DCK
Holly, Buddy	Reminiscing	47-884	ZM
Holly, Buddy	Rock Around With Ollie Vee	47-881	ZM
Holly, Buddy	Rock Me My Baby	48-674	DCK
Holly, Buddy	Send Me Some Loving	45-585	OZP
Holly, Buddy	Take Your Time	47-892	ZM
Holly, Buddy	That'll Be The Day	15-281	DK
Holly, Buddy	That'll Be The Day	11-33	PX
Holly, Buddy	That'll Be The Day	29-841	SC
Holly, Buddy	That's What They Say	48-675	DCK
Holly, Buddy	Think It Over	3-209	LG
Holly, Buddy	Think It Over	11-41	PX
Holly, Buddy	Ting A Ling	48-676	DCK
Holly, Buddy	True Love Ways	11-31	PX
Holly, Buddy	Valley Of Tears	47-890	ZM
Holly, Buddy	Well Alright	47-880	CB
Holly, Buddy	What To Do	47-887	ZM
Holly, Buddy	Wishing	3-221	LG
Holly, Buddy	Words Of Love	3-211	LG
Holly, Doyle	Queen Of The Silver Dollar	8-630	SAV
Hollywood Argyles	Alley Oop	29-832	SC
Hollywood Beyond	What's The Colour Of Money	9-800	SAV
Holman, Eddie	Hey There Lonely Girl	35-73	CB
Holman, Eddie	Hey There Lonely Girl	26-104	DK
Holmes, Monty	Leave My Mama Out Of This	8-874	CB
Holmes, Monty	Leave My Mama Out Of This	10-160	SC
Holmes, Rupert	Escape (the Pina Colada Song)	11-211	DK
Holmes, Rupert	Escape (the Pina Colada Song)	4-765	SC
Holmes, Rupert	Escape (the Pina Coloda Song)	35-155	CB
Holmes, Rupert	Try To Remember	11-212	DK
Holt, John	Killing Me Softly with Her Song	49-769	MRE
Holy, Steve	Blue Moon	14-712	CB
Holy, Steve	Blue Moon	19-254	CSZ
Holy, Steve	Brand New Girlfriend	29-198	CB
Holy, Steve	Come On Rain	30-250	CB
Holy, Steve	Don't Make Me Beg	5-809	SC
Holy, Steve	Don't Make Me Beg	22-520	ST
Holy, Steve	Go Home	22-339	CB
Holy, Steve	Good Morning Beautiful	16-167	CB
Holy, Steve	Good Morning Beautiful	15-678	ST
Holy, Steve	Hauled Off And Kissed	39-66	PHN

ARTIST	SONG TITLE	#	TYPE
	Me		
Holy, Steve	Hunger the	22-586	ST
Holy, Steve	I'm Not Breakin'	25-353	MM
Holy, Steve	I'm Not Breakin'	18-207	ST
Holy, Steve	I'm Not Breakin'	19-349	THM
Holy, Steve	It's My Time (Waste It If I Want To	23-416	CB
Holy, Steve	Love Don't Run	38-106	CB
Holy, Steve	Men Buy The Drinks, Girls Call The Shots	30-459	CB
Holy, Steve	Might Have Been	36-613	CB
Holy, Steve	Might Have Been	36-280	PHM
Holy, Steve	Put Your Best Dress On	43-266	CB
Holy, Steve	Put Your Best Dress On	20-390	ST
Holy, Steve	Rock A Bye Heart	25-527	MM
Holy, Steve	Rock A Bye Heart	18-797	ST
Holy, Steve	Rock A Bye Heart	32-154	THM
Hombres	Let It Out	3-26	SC
Homer & Jethro	Battle Of Kokamonga	15-348	MM
Hometown News	Minivan	16-706	ST
Hometown News	Wheels	18-334	ST
Hondells	Little Honda	3-549	SC
Honey Cone	Want Ads	35-108	CB
Honey Cone	Want Ads	17-375	DK
Honeydrippers	Sea Of Love	12-192	DK
Honeydrippers	Sea Of Love	6-163	MM
Honeymoon Suite	New Girl Now	5-468	SC
Hoobastank	Crawling In The Dark	49-315	CB
Hoobastank	Disappear	20-26	PHM
Hoobastank	If I Were You	30-286	SC
Hoobastank	Out Of Control	23-271	THM
Hoobastank	Reason the	20-352	PHM
Hoobastank	Remember Me	18-829	THM
Hoobastank	Running Away	35-270	CB
Hoobastank	This Is Gonna Hurt	39-121	PHM
Hooker, John Lee	Boom Boom Boom	20-137	KB
Hooker, John Lee	Boom Boom Boom	7-46	MM
Hooker, John Lee	Boom Boom Boom	15-319	SC
Hooker, John Lee	I'm In The Mood	49-477	MM
Hooker, John Lee	Keep It To Yourself	46-26	SSK
Hooker, John Lee	One Bourbon One Scotch One Beer	20-143	KB
Hooray For Hollywoo	Show - Hooray For Hollywood	6-871	MM
Hootie & Blowfish	Hannah Jane	13-597	P
Hootie & Blowfish	Hannah Jane	4-689	SC
Hootie & Blowfish	Hold My Hand	21-134	CB
Hootie & Blowfish	Hold My Hand	28-422	DK
Hootie & Blowfish	Hold My Hand	2-475	SC
Hootie & Blowfish	Hold My Hand	29-126	ST
Hootie & Blowfish	I Go Blind	4-170	SC
Hootie & Blowfish	I Only Wanna Be With You	21-135	CB
Hootie & Blowfish	Let Her Cry	21-137	CB
Hootie & Blowfish	Let Her Cry	28-49	DK
Hootie & Blowfish	Old Man And Me	21-136	CB
Hootie & Blowfish	Only Lonely	7-791	PHT

ARTIST	SONG TITLE	#	TYPE
Hootie & Blowfish	Only Wanna Be With You	18-251	DK
Hootie & Blowfish	Only Wanna Be With You	3-427	SC
Hootie & Blowfish	Sad Caper	24-373	SC
Hootie & Blowfish	Time	21-138	CB
Hootie & Blowfish	Time	24-747	SC
Hootie & Blowfish	Tucker's Town	21-133	CB
Hope, Bob	Duet - Thanks For The Memory	11-457	DK
Hope, Bob	Thanks For The Memory	21-13	SC
Hope, Bob & ?	Thanks For The Memory	11-457	DK
Hopkins, Mary	Those Were The Days	12-193	DK
Hopkins, Mary	Those Were The Days	7-34	MM
Hopkins, Mary	Those Were The Days	10-587	SF
Horn, S.	Hit The Road Jack	23-349	MM
Horne, Lena	Stormy Weather	2-242	SC
Horne, Lena	Xmas - Let It Snow	14-518	SC
Hornsby & Range	Way It Is the	5-478	SC
Hornsby, Bruce	Great Divide	14-290	MM
Hornsby, Bruce	Valley Road the	12-176	DK
Hornsby, Bruce	Walk In The Sun	3-495	SC
Horton, Johnny	All For The Love Of A Girl	18-628	PS
Horton, Johnny	Battle Of New Orleans the	6-523	MM
Horton, Johnny	Battle Of New Orleans the	13-127	P
Horton, Johnny	Battle Of New Orleans the	18-625	PS
Horton, Johnny	Honky Tonk Man	17-11	DK
Horton, Johnny	Honky Tonk Man	14-325	SC
Horton, Johnny	Johnny Reb	14-327	SC
Horton, Johnny	Mansion You Stole the	4-307	SC
Horton, Johnny	North To Alaska	8-380	CB
Horton, Johnny	North To Alaska	11-835	DK
Horton, Johnny	North To Alaska	18-627	PS
Horton, Johnny	Sink The Bismarck	18-626	PS
Horton, Johnny	Sink The Bismarck	4-145	SC
Horton, Johnny	When It's Springtime In Alaska	5-435	SC
Horton, Johnny	Whispering Pines	3-894	PS
Horton, Johnny	Words	45-574	SSK
Hot 'N Juicy	I'm Horny **	13-723	SGB
Hot Apple Pie	Easy Does It	29-373	CB
Hot Apple Pie	Hillbillies	22-330	CB
Hot Apple Pie	We're Makin' Up	29-20	CB
Hot Chocolate	Every 1's A Winner	17-71	DK
Hot Chocolate	You Sexy Thing	11-381	DK
Hot Chocolate	You Sexy Thing	5-380	SC
Hot Chocolate	You Sexy Thing	10-543	SF
Hot Hot Heat	Bandages	32-293	THM
Hot Hot Heat	Middle Of Nowhere	30-225	PHM
Hough, Julianne	My Hallelujah Song	36-224	PHM
Hough, Julianne	That Song In My Head	36-429	CB
House Of Pain	Jump Around	25-480	MM
House Of Pain	Jump Around	20-90	SC
House, James	Little By Little	2-651	SC

ARTIST	SONG TITLE	#	TYPE
House, James	This Is Me Missing You	6-817	MM
House, James	This Is Me Missing You	2-770	SC
Houser, Randy	Absolutely Nothing	39-90	PHN
Houser, Randy	Anything Goes	36-599	CB
Houser, Randy	Anything Goes	36-198	PHM
Houser, Randy	Boots On	45-552	AC
Houser, Randy	Goodnight Kiss	43-144	ASK
Houser, Randy	How Country Feels	45-321	SBI
Houser, Randy	I'm All About It	45-555	CB
Houser, Randy	Like A Cowboy	45-553	ASK
Houser, Randy	Man Like Me a	38-103	CB
Houser, Randy	Man Like Me a	45-556	CB
Houser, Randy	Runnin' Outta Moonlight	45-404	BKD
Houser, Randy	We Went	49-369	BKD
Houser, Randy	Whistlin' Dixie	45-554	CB
Houston & Iglesias	Could I Have This Kiss Forever	14-478	SC
Houston & Iglesias	Could I Have This Kiss Forever	15-636	THM
Houston & Iglesias	Duet - Could I Have This Kiss Forev	14-478	SC
Houston & Iglesias	Duet - Could I Have This Kiss Forev	15-636	THM
Houston & Iglesias	Latino - Could I Have This Kiss For	14-478	SC
Houston & Mandrell	After Closing Time	9-588	SAV
Houston & Winans	Count On Me	14-902	SC
Houston & Winans	Duet - Count On Me	14-902	SC
Houston, David	Almost Persuaded	8-427	CB
Houston, David	Almost Persuaded	13-514	P
Houston, David	Almost Persuaded	9-617	SAV
Houston, David	Already It's Heaven	48-188	CB
Houston, David	Baby Baby I Know You're A Lady	13-533	P
Houston, David	Baby Baby I Know You're A Lady	6-7	SC
Houston, David	Good Things	48-192	CB
Houston, David	Have A Little Faith	5-431	SC
Houston, David	I Do My Swinging At Home	14-433	SC
Houston, David	I'm Down To My Last "I Love You"	48-191	CB
Houston, David	Living In A House Full Of Love	34-209	CB
Houston, David	My Woman's Good To Me	48-193	CB
Houston, David	She's All Woman	48-190	CB
Houston, David	Where Love Used To Live	48-189	CB
Houston, David	With One Exception	22-249	SC
Houston, David	Woman Always Knows	5-254	SC
Houston, David	You Mean The World To Me	9-606	SAV
Houston, David	You Mean The World To Me	5-105	SC
Houston, M.	That Girl	32-163	THM
Houston, Marques	All Because Of You	23-309	CB
Houston, Thelma	Don't Leave Me This Way	35-133	CB
Houston, Thelma	Don't Leave Me This Way	16-833	DK
Houston, Walter	September Song	15-558	CMC
Houston, Whitney	All At Once	48-636	SAV
Houston, Whitney	All The Man That I Need	21-459	CB
Houston, Whitney	All The Man That I Need	12-248	DK
Houston, Whitney	All The Man That I Need	13-204	P
Houston, Whitney	Didn't We Almost Have It All	43-373	CB
Houston, Whitney	Exhale (Shoop Shoop)	19-583	MH
Houston, Whitney	Greatest Love Of All	11-263	DK
Houston, Whitney	Greatest Love Of All	17-431	KC
Houston, Whitney	Greatest Love Of All	9-1	MH
Houston, Whitney	Greatest Love Of All	6-349	MM
Houston, Whitney	Greatest Love Of All	12-676	P
Houston, Whitney	Heartbreak Hotel	7-806	PHT
Houston, Whitney	Heartbreak Hotel	13-673	SGB
Houston, Whitney	How Will I Know	16-745	DK
Houston, Whitney	How Will I Know	12-825	P
Houston, Whitney	I Believe In You And Me	49-312	BC
Houston, Whitney	I Learned From The Best	16-180	PHM
Houston, Whitney	I Wanna Dance With Somebody	11-135	DK
Houston, Whitney	I Wanna Dance With Somebody	13-188	P
Houston, Whitney	I Will Always Love You	17-385	DK
Houston, Whitney	I Will Always Love You	6-91	MM
Houston, Whitney	I Will Always Love You	12-873	P
Houston, Whitney	I Will Always Love You	29-326	PS
Houston, Whitney	I'm Every Woman	11-27	PX
Houston, Whitney	I'm Every Woman	19-551	SC
Houston, Whitney	I'm Your Baby Tonight	34-89	CB
Houston, Whitney	I'm Your Baby Tonight	11-785	DK
Houston, Whitney	I'm Your Baby Tonight	12-841	P
Houston, Whitney	If I Told You That	19-832	SGB
Houston, Whitney	It's Not Right But It's Okay	8-327	PHT
Houston, Whitney	It's Not Right But It's Okay	13-677	SGB
Houston, Whitney	Love Will Save The Day	43-372	CB
Houston, Whitney	Lover For Life	48-638	PS
Houston, Whitney	Million Dollar Bill	48-634	BKD
Houston, Whitney	Miracle	48-635	MM
Houston, Whitney	My Heart Is Calling	48-637	PI
Houston, Whitney	My Love Is Your Love	34-134	CB
Houston, Whitney	My Love Is Your Love	8-526	PHT
Houston, Whitney	One Moment In Time	33-331	CB
Houston, Whitney	One Moment In Time	6-357	MM
Houston, Whitney	One Moment In Time	12-874	P
Houston, Whitney	One Of Those Days	32-52	THM
Houston, Whitney	Run To You	6-416	MM
Houston, Whitney	Saving All My Love For You	20-303	CB
Houston, Whitney	Saving All My Love For You	15-556	CMC
Houston, Whitney	So Emotional	11-318	DK
Houston, Whitney	Star Spangled Banner	20-158	BCI
Houston, Whitney	Step By Step	49-311	BC

131

ARTIST	SONG TITLE	#	TYPE
Houston, Whitney	Try It On My Own	34-178	CB
Houston, Whitney	Try It On My Own	25-537	MM
Houston, Whitney	Try It On My Own	32-240	THM
Houston, Whitney	Whatchalookinat	32-202	THM
Houston, Whitney	Whatchalookinat	18-426	CB
Houston, Whitney	Where Do Broken Hearts Go	27-314	DK
Houston, Whitney	Where Do Broken Hearts Go	8-613	TT
Houston, Whitney	Xmas - Do You Hear What I Hear	7-14	MM
Houston, Whitney	You Give Good Love	11-461	DK
Houston, Whitney	You Give Good Love	13-189	P
Houston,Feat,Evan	Heartbreak Hotel	7-817	PHM
Houston/Evans/Price	Heartbreak Hotel	28-191	DK
How Grinch Stole...	Xmas - You're a Mean One Mr Grinch	5-719	SC
Howard, Jan	Evil On Your Mind	8-789	CB
Howard, Rebecca L	Forgive	25-237	MM
Howard, Rebecca L	Forgive	17-574	ST
Howard, Rebecca L	Forgive	33-189	CB
Howard, Rebecca L	I Don't Paint Myself Into Corners	14-87	CB
Howard, Rebecca L	I Don't Paint Myself Into Corners	25-296	MM
Howard, Rebecca L	I Need A Vacation	19-693	ST
Howard, Rebecca L	No One'll Ever Love Me	22-338	CB
Howard, Rebecca L	Out Here In The Water	6-62	SC
Howard, Rebecca L	Sing Cause I Love To	36-216	PHM
Howard, Rebecca L	What A Shame	25-704	MM
Howard, Rebecca L	What A Shame	19-272	ST
Howard, Rebecca L	When My Dreams Come True	8-987	CB
Howlin' Wolf	Killing Floor	20-144	KB
Howlin' Wolf	Smokestack Lightning	14-588	SC
Hudson, Jennifer	Spotlight	36-498	CB
Hudson, Jennifer	Spotlight	38-203	PHM
Hudson, Jennifer	Where You At	37-267	CB
Hues Corporation	Rock The Boat	16-824	DK
Hues Corporation	Rock The Boat	13-132	P
Hues Corporation	So Emotional	27-313	DK
Hughes, Judd	High Lonesome	20-453	ST
Human Beings	Nobody But Me	9-359	MG
Human League	Duet - Fascination (Keep Feeling)	24-210	SC
Human League	Fascination (Keep Feeling)	24-210	SC
Human League	Human	33-313	CB
Human League	Human	16-866	DK
Humble Pie	30 Days In The Hole	5-590	SC
Hummon, Marcus	God's Country USA	7-202	MM
Hummon, Marcus	Honky Tonk Mona Lisa	4-397	SC
Humperdinck, E.	After The Lovin'	26-484	DK
Humperdinck, E.	After The Lovin'	6-438	MM
Humperdinck, E.	After The Lovin'	2-201	SC
Humperdinck, E.	After The Lovin'	37-156	CB
Humperdinck, E.	Am I That Easy To Forget	37-158	CB

ARTIST	SONG TITLE	#	TYPE
Humperdinck, E.	Am I That Easy To Forget	48-393	ZMV
Humperdinck, E.	Another Time Another Place	37-160	CB
Humperdinck, E.	Can't You See	49-260	DFK
Humperdinck, E.	Chance To Be A Hero a	49-261	DFK
Humperdinck, E.	Eternally	49-262	DFK
Humperdinck, E.	Funny Familiar Forgotten Feelings	48-515	LE
Humperdinck, E.	Green Green Grass Of Home	11-471	DK
Humperdinck, E.	How I Love You	49-258	DFK
Humperdinck, E.	I Never Said Goodbye	37-161	CB
Humperdinck, E.	I'm A Better Man	37-167	CB
Humperdinck, E.	I'm Leavin' You	37-162	CB
Humperdinck, E.	In Time	49-259	DFK
Humperdinck, E.	Last Waltz the	10-468	MG
Humperdinck, E.	Last Waltz the	19-115	SAV
Humperdinck, E.	Last Waltz the	10-583	SF
Humperdinck, E.	Last Waltz the	37-168	CB
Humperdinck, E.	Love Me With All Your Heart	37-163	CB
Humperdinck, E.	Love Will Set You Free	49-254	DFK
Humperdinck, E.	Man Without Love a	37-154	CB
Humperdinck, E.	Quando Quando Quando	15-850	MM
Humperdinck, E.	Quando Quando, Quando	34-6	CB
Humperdinck, E.	Red Roses For My Lady	49-248	DFK
Humperdinck, E.	Release Me	16-859	DK
Humperdinck, E.	Release Me	12-497	P
Humperdinck, E.	Release Me	2-196	SC
Humperdinck, E.	Release Me	37-157	CB
Humperdinck, E.	Spanish Eyes	9-315	STR
Humperdinck, E.	Spanish Eyes	37-155	CB
Humperdinck, E.	Sweetheart	37-164	CB
Humperdinck, E.	Ten Guitars	48-392	LE
Humperdinck, E.	There Goes My Everything	49-45	ZVS
Humperdinck, E.	This Is My Song	48-391	KV
Humperdinck, E.	Way It Used To Be the	37-165	CB
Humperdinck, E.	Winter World Of Love	35-105	CB
Hunt, Sam	House Party	45-23	BKD
Hunt, Sam	Leave The Night On	44-321	SBI
Hunt, Sam	Make You Miss Me (Inst)	49-793	K2G
Hunt, Sam	Take Your Time	45-22	KVD
Hunter Sisters	Your Love Has Lifted Me Higher	17-114	DK
Hunter Sisters	Your Love Keeps Lifting Me Higher	35-87	CB
Hunter, Ian	Cleveland Rocks	37-73	SC
Hunter, Ivory Joe	Empty Arms	17-329	SS
Hunter, Ivory Joe	Since I Met You Baby	3-508	SC
Hunter, Jesse	By The Way She's Lookin'	24-346	SC
Hunter, Jesse	Long Legged Hannah...	2-574	SC
Hurricane Chris	Bay Bay A (Radio Vers)	49-887	SC
Hush	Limelight	5-65	SC

ARTIST	SONG TITLE	#	TYPE
Husky, Ferlin	Country Music Is Here To Stay	22-260	CB
Husky, Ferlin	Country Music Is Here To Stay	5-375	SC
Husky, Ferlin	Cuzz You're So Sweet	22-266	CB
Husky, Ferlin	Fallen Star a	22-267	CB
Husky, Ferlin	Gone	8-773	CB
Husky, Ferlin	Gone	4-867	SC
Husky, Ferlin	Heavenly Sunshine	22-271	CB
Husky, Ferlin	I Can't Stop Loving You	22-269	CB
Husky, Ferlin	I Feel Better All Over	5-428	SC
Husky, Ferlin	I Feel Better All Over	22-264	CB
Husky, Ferlin	I Hear Little Rock Calling	45-565	SSK
Husky, Ferlin	I Really Don't Want To Know	22-272	CB
Husky, Ferlin	Just For You	22-262	CB
Husky, Ferlin	Little Tom	22-265	CB
Husky, Ferlin	Money Greases The Wheels	22-270	CB
Husky, Ferlin	My Reason For Living	22-268	CB
Husky, Ferlin	Once	22-261	CB
Husky, Ferlin	Timber I'm Falling	22-263	CB
Husky, Ferlin	Waltz You Saved For Me the	45-344	BSP
Husky, Ferlin	Wings Of A Dove	8-366	CB
Husky, Ferlin	Wings Of A Dove	3-604	SC
Hutchinson, Eric	Ok It's Alright With Me	36-305	PHM
Hyland, Bryan	Duet - Itsy Bitsy Teenie Weenie...	10-329	KC
Hyland, Bryan	Gypsy Woman	7-257	MM
Hyland, Bryan	Itsy Bitsy Teenie Weenie	6-867	MM
Hyland, Bryan	Itsy Bitsy Teenie Weenie	12-644	P
Hyland, Bryan	Itsy Bitsy Teenie Weenie	16-376	SF
Hyland, Bryan	Itsy Bitsy Teenie Weenie...	10-329	KC
Hyland, Bryan	Itsy Bitsy Teenie Weenie...	4-1	SC
Hyland, Bryan	Sealed With A Kiss	35-51	CB
Hyland, Bryan	Sealed With A Kiss	11-692	DK
Hyland, Bryan	Sealed With A Kiss	7-265	MM
I Am Sam	Show - Blackbird	18-672	PS
I Am Sam	Show - I'm Looking Through You	18-674	PS
I Am Sam	Show - Nowhere Man	18-673	PS
I Am Sam	Show - Two Of Us	18-671	PS
Ian, Janis	At 17	19-162	SGB
Ian, Janis	Days Like These	24-28	SC
Ian, Janis	From Me To You	29-266	SC
Ice Castles	Show - Through The Eyes Of Love	6-320	MM
Ice Castles	Show - Through The Eyes Of Love	13-147	P
Icehouse	Electric Blue	11-321	DK
Ides Of March	Vehicle	19-132	KC
Ides Of March	Vehicle	3-550	SC
Idol, Billy	Cradle Of Love	12-165	DK
Idol, Billy	Cradle Of Love	12-779	P
Idol, Billy	Dancing With Myself	12-124	DK

ARTIST	SONG TITLE	#	TYPE
Idol, Billy	Dancing With Myself	13-212	P
Idol, Billy	Eyes Without a Face	4-879	SC
Idol, Billy	I Forgot To Be Your Love	13-211	P
Idol, Billy	Mony Mony	26-290	DK
Idol, Billy	White Wedding	2-854	SC
Iglesias & Houston	Could I Have This Kiss Forever	20-119	PHM
Iglesias & Houston	Duet - Could I Have This Kiss Forev	20-119	PHM
Iglesias & Kelis	Not In Love	20-351	PHM
Iglesias & Nelson	Duet - To All the Girls I've Loved...	35-333	CB
Iglesias & Nelson	To All the Girls I've Loved... - duet	35-333	CB
Iglesias & Parton	Duet - When You Tell Me That You...	49-771	PS
Iglesias & Parton	When You Tell Me That You Love Me	29-327	PS
Iglesias & Parton	When You Tell Me That You Love Me	49-771	PS
Iglesias & Pitbull	I'm A Freak	43-269	SF
Iglesias w Pitbull	I Like It	40-9	BH
Iglesias, Enrique	Addicted	19-664	CB
Iglesias, Enrique	Bailamos	35-215	CB
Iglesias, Enrique	Bailamos	29-168	MH
Iglesias, Enrique	Bailamos	8-503	PHT
Iglesias, Enrique	Be With You	14-176	CB
Iglesias, Enrique	Be With You	29-167	MH
Iglesias, Enrique	Be With You	16-237	PHM
Iglesias, Enrique	Do You Know (Ping-Pong Song)	30-560	CB
Iglesias, Enrique	Do You Know (Ping-Pong Song)	46-317	SC
Iglesias, Enrique	Don't Turn Off The Light	18-414	MM
Iglesias, Enrique	Escape	25-136	MM
Iglesias, Enrique	Hero	33-398	CB
Iglesias, Enrique	Hero	16-301	PHM
Iglesias, Enrique	Hero (Fast Version)	25-21	MM
Iglesias, Enrique	Latino - Costas Del Amor	17-809	PS
Iglesias, Enrique	Latino - Esperanza	17-810	PS
Iglesias, Enrique	Latino - Heroe	23-233	AI
Iglesias, Enrique	Latino - Mentiroso	23-232	AI
Iglesias, Enrique	Latino - Ruelta Rusa	17-811	PS
Iglesias, Enrique	Maybe	20-469	CB
Iglesias, Enrique	Rhythm Divine	17-540	SC
Iglesias, Enrique	Sad Eyes	14-23	THM
Iglesias, Enrique	Tonight (I'm Loving You)	49-70	ZPC
Iglesias, Julio	Crazy	47-560	LE
Iglesias, Julio	Hey	47-561	MM
Iglesias, Julio	Latino - Gozar La Vida	17-789	SC
Iglesias, Julio	Moonlight Lady	47-563	CAK
Iglesias, Julio Jr.	One More Chance	47-562	PS
III Nino	How Can I Live	23-186	PHM
Imbruglia, Natalie	Wrong Impression	33-450	CB
Imbruglio, Natalie	Torn	8-513	PHT
Imbruglio, Natalie	Torn	13-713	SGB

ARTIST	SONG TITLE	#	TYPE
Imbruglio, Natalie	Wishing I Was There	15-623	PHM
Imbruglio, Natalie	Wrong Impression	18-288	CB
Imbruglio, Natalie	Wrong Impression	25-137	MM
Immature	Lover's Groove	24-288	SC
Immature	Please Don't Go	4-340	SC
Impalas	Soorry I Ran All The Way Home	6-683	MM
Imperials	Gospel - Oh Buddah	16-29	SX
Impressions	Duet - People Get Ready	27-234	DK
Impressions	It's All Right	12-716	P
Impressions	People Get Ready	27-234	DK
Impressions	People Get Ready	13-100	P
Incubus	Anna Molly	37-111	SC
Incubus	Drive	35-239	CB
Incubus	Drive	16-387	SGB
Incubus	I Wish You Were Here	33-400	CB
Incubus	I Wish You Were Here	16-319	TT
Incubus	Love Hurts	36-272	PHM
Incubus	Make A Move	30-224	PHM
Incubus	Stellar	15-643	THM
Incubus	Warning	18-225	CB
India.Arie	Brown Skin	25-687	MM
India.Arie	Little Things the	34-154	CB
India.Arie	Ready For Love	25-689	MM
India.Arie	Truth the	32-200	THM
India.Arie	Video	18-354	CB
India.Arie	Video	25-149	MM
Indigo Girls	Closer To Fine	14-638	SC
Indigo Girls	Least Complicated	4-285	SC
Indigo Girls	Power Of Two the	14-873	SC
Indigo Swing	Indigo Swing the	13-696	SGB
Inferno	From Paris To Berlin	30-706	SF
Information Society	What's On Your Mind	21-405	SC
Ingram & Austin	Baby Come To Me	11-406	DK
Ingram & Austin	Baby Come To Me	6-238	MM
Ingram & Austin	Baby Come To Me	21-604	SF
Ingram & Austin	Baby Come To Me	9-207	SO
Ingram & Austin	Duet - Baby Come To Me	6-238	MM
Ingram & Austin	Duet - Baby Come To Me	21-604	SF
Ingram & Austin	Duet - Baby Come To Me	9-207	SO
Ingram & Austin	Duet - How Do You Keep the Music...	49-463	MM
Ingram & Austin	How Do You Keep the Music Playing	49-463	MM
Ingram, Jack	Barefoot And Crazy	37-42	CB
Ingram, Jack	How Many Days	5-830	SC
Ingram, Jack	I Don't Have The Heart	33-340	CB
Ingram, Jack	Lips Of An Angel	30-249	CB
Ingram, Jack	Love You	30-87	CB
Ingram, Jack	Maybe She'll Get Lonely	36-552	CB
Ingram, Jack	Measure Of A Man	30-447	CB
Ingram, Jack	Mustang Burn	14-723	CB
Ingram, Jack	Wherever You Are	29-30	CB
Ingram, Jack	Work This Out	9-419	CB
Ingram, James	I Don't Have The Heart	2-273	SC

ARTIST	SONG TITLE	#	TYPE
Ingram, James	If Loving You Is Wrong	48-589	DK
Ingram, James	Just Once	26-365	DK
Ingram, James	Just Once	17-434	KC
Ingram, James	Just Once	6-558	MM
Ingram, James	Just Once	9-210	SO
Ingram, James	One Hundred Ways	9-55	MM
Ingram, James	Someone Like You	4-277	SC
Ingram, James	Whatever We Imagine	9-212	SO
Ingram, James	Where Did My Heart Go	24-252	SC
Ingram, Luther	I Don't Want To Be Right	7-476	MM
Ingram, Luther	If Lovin' You Is Wrong I Don't...	16-562	P
Ini Kamoze	Here Comes The Hotstepper	2-724	SC
Inner Circle	Ob La Di Ob La Da	25-383	MM
Inner Circle	Sweat (A la la la la lon...)	6-365	MM
INOJ	Time After Time	14-292	MM
INOJ	Time After Time	15-627	PHM
Inspiral Carpets	I Want You	30-770	SF
Intruders	Cowboys To Girls	6-55	SC
INXS	Beautiful Girl	4-276	SC
Inxs	Devil Inside	34-95	CB
Inxs	Need You Tonight	33-325	CB
INXS	Need You Tonight	11-786	DK
INXS	New Sensation	27-200	DK
INXS	Tears Are Falling	11-790	DK
Inxs	What You Need	33-317	CB
Iris, Donnie	Ah Leah	6-27	SC
Irish Rovers	Irish - Whiskey In The Jar	21-490	SC
Irish Rovers	Irish - Whiskey On A Sunday	48-723	KV
Irish Songs	Irish - Aye Aye Aye (The Limerick Song)	48-730	SDK
Irish Songs	Irish - Danny Boy	9-142	AH
Irish Songs	Irish - Danny Boy	12-492	P
Irish Songs	Irish - Danny Boy	21-499	SC
Irish Songs	Irish - Danny Boy	23-218	SM
Irish Songs	Irish - Daughter Of Rosie O'Grady	48-726	PS
Irish Songs	Irish - Does Your Mother Come From...	48-727	PS
Irish Songs	Irish - Drunken Sailor	48-721	KV
Irish Songs	Irish - Fields Of Atheny	48-715	DCK
Irish Songs	Irish - Foggy Dew	48-729	PR
Irish Songs	Irish - Green Fields Of Ireland	48-724	KWD
Irish Songs	Irish - Harrigan	9-143	AH
Irish Songs	Irish - Harrigan	23-216	SM
Irish Songs	Irish - I'll Take You Home Again...	9-144	AH
Irish Songs	Irish - I'll Take You Home Again...	21-488	SC
Irish Songs	Irish - Irish Washerwoman the	9-145	AH
Irish Songs	Irish - It's A Long Way To Tipperary	48-716	EZC
Irish Songs	Irish - Kerrigan	9-162	AH

ARTIST	SONG TITLE	#	TYPE
Irish Songs	Irish - Kerry Dance the	9-146	AH
Irish Songs	Irish - Lanigan's Ball	48-731	SF
Irish Songs	Irish - Little Bit Of Heaven a	48-728	PS
Irish Songs	Irish - Loch Lamond	27-438	DK
Irish Songs	Irish - Londonderry Air (Old Irish Air)	48-725	MM
Irish Songs	Irish - MacNamara's Band	9-147	AH
Irish Songs	Irish - Molly Malone	9-148	AH
Irish Songs	Irish - Molly Malone (Cockles...)	21-496	SC
Irish Songs	Irish - Mountains Of Mourne	48-719	KCD
Irish Songs	Irish - My Bonnie	11-482	DK
Irish Songs	Irish - My Wild Irish Rose	9-149	AH
Irish Songs	Irish - My Wild Irish Rose	2-70	SC
Irish Songs	Irish - My Wild Irish Rose	23-217	SM
Irish Songs	Irish - Orange And The Green the	21-502	SC
Irish Songs	Irish - Paddy McGinty's Goat	48-732	SF
Irish Songs	Irish - Peg O' My Heart	9-150	AH
Irish Songs	Irish - Rose Of Tralee the	9-151	AH
Irish Songs	Irish - Rothesay-O	48-718	LRT
Irish Songs	Irish - St. Patrick's Day	9-152	AH
Irish Songs	Irish - Sweet Rosie O'Grady	9-153	AH
Irish Songs	Irish - There Is A Tavern In The Town	48-714	DK
Irish Songs	Irish - Too Ra Loo Ra Loo Ral	9-154	AH
Irish Songs	Irish - Too-Ra-Loo Ra-Loo-Ra	27-436	DK
Irish Songs	Irish - Trotting To The Fair	48-717	LRT
Irish Songs	Irish - Unicorn the	9-155	AH
Irish Songs	Irish - Unicorn the	2-64	SC
Irish Songs	Irish - Unicorn the	21-500	SC
Irish Songs	Irish - Wearin' O' The Green	9-156	AH
Irish Songs	Irish - When Irish Eyes Are Smiling	9-157	AH
Irish Songs	Irish - When Irish Eyes Are Smiling	12-108	DK
Irish Songs	Irish - When Irish Eyes Are Smiling	2-68	SC
Irish Songs	Irish - When Irish Eyes Are Smiling	23-215	SM
Irish Songs	Irish - Whiskey In The Jar	9-158	AH
Irish Songs	Irish - Whistling Gypsy Rover	9-159	AH
Irish Songs	Irish - Who Threw the Overalls in..	9-160	AH
Irish Songs	Irish - Wild Rover the	9-161	AH
Irish Songs	Irish - Wild Rover the	21-498	SC
Irish Songs	It's The Same Old Shillelagh - Irish	49-35	SHER
Iron Butterfly	In A Gadda Da Vida	9-669	SAV
Iron Butterfly	In A Gadda Da Vida	5-609	SC
Irwin, B.	Swinging On A Star	29-825	SF
Isaacs, Sonya	Barefoot In The Grass	14-118	CB
Isaacs, Sonya	How Can I Forget	14-166	CB
Isaacs, Sonya	I've Forgotten How You Feel	13-815	CHM
Isaacs, Sonya	No Regrets...Yet	22-9	CB
Isaacs, Sonya	No Regrets...Yet	19-697	ST
Isaacs, Sonya	Since I Gave My Heart Away	14-721	CB
Isaacs, Sonya	That's What Love Demands	14-910	CB
Isaak, Chris	Baby Did A Bad Bad Thing	22-496	ST
Isaak, Chris	Baby Did A Bad Bad Thing	8-511	PHT
Isaak, Chris	Dark Moon	24-244	SC
Isaak, Chris	Let Me Down Easy	18-351	CB
Isaak, Chris	Let Me Down Easy	25-208	MM
Isaak, Chris	Please	14-283	MM
Isaak, Chris	Please	7-784	PHT
Isaak, Chris	Solitary Man	24-26	SC
Isaak, Chris	Somebody's Crying	3-493	SC
Isaak, Chris	Think Of Tomorrow	4-614	SC
Isaak, Chris	Wicked Game	12-147	DK
Isaak, Chris	Wicked Game	12-807	P
Isley Brothers	Between The Sheets	18-489	SAV
Isley Brothers	Don't Say Goodnight Pt. 1	17-320	SS
Isley Brothers	Don't Say Goodnight Pt. 2	17-321	SS
Isley Brothers	Fight The Power	2-503	SC
Isley Brothers	It's Your Thing	17-393	DK
Isley Brothers	It's Your Thing	7-49	MM
Isley Brothers	It's Your Thing	12-724	P
Isley Brothers	It's Your Thing	5-453	SC
Isley Brothers	Say You Will	11-679	DK
Isley Brothers	Shout	11-791	DK
Isley Brothers	Shout	12-891	P
Isley Brothers	Shout	11-23	PX
Isley Brothers	That Lady	16-877	DK
Isley Brothers	This Old Heart Of Mine	27-334	DK
Isley Brothers & Mr. Biggs	What Would You Do	32-235	THM
Isyss	Single For The Rest Of My Life	32-55	THM
Ives, Burl	Big Rock Candy Mountain	44-5	SF
Ives, Burl	Down In The Valley	43-440	CB
Ives, Burl	Funny Way Of Laughing	10-748	JVC
Ives, Burl	Little Bitty Tear a	4-258	SC
Ives, Burl	Lonesome 77203	45-924	OZP
Ives, Burl	My Gal Sal	43-391	CBEP
Ives, Burl	Pearly Shells (Popo O	43-441	CB

ARTIST	SONG TITLE	#	TYPE
	Ewa)		
Ives, Burl	Xmas - Holly Jolly Christmas	35-322	CB
Ives, Burl	Xmas - Holly Jolly Christmas	14-540	SC
Ivy League	Funny How Love Can Be	10-616	SF
J-Kwon	Tipsy **	23-252	THM
J. Geils Band	Ain't Nothing But A House Party	46-325	SC
J. Geils Band	Centerfold	27-201	DK
J. Geils Band	Centerfold	13-12	P
J. Geils Band	Detroit Breakdown	17-472	SC
J. Geils Band	First I Look At The Purse	46-326	SC
J. Geils Band	Flame Thrower	37-74	SC
J. Geils Band	Freeze Frame	3-521	SC
J. Geils Band	Give It To Me	10-486	DA
J. Geils Band	I Do	46-329	SC
J. Geils Band	Looking For A Love	46-324	SC
J. Geils Band	Love Stinks	46-586	SC
J. Geils Band	Musta Got Lost	4-78	SC
J. Geils Band	One Last Kiss	46-328	LE
J. Geils Band	Take It Back	46-327	LE
J'Son	I'll Never Stop Loving You	24-53	SC
Ja Rule & Ashanti	Duet - Mesmerize	32-123	THM
Ja Rule & Ashanti	Mesmerize - duet	32-123	THM
Jacks, Terry	Seasons In The Sun	29-633	SC
Jacks, Terry	Seasons In The Sun	10-547	SF
Jackson & Buffett	Duet - It's Five O'Clock Somewhere	25-636	MM
Jackson & Buffett	Duet - It's Five O'Clock Somewhere	35-427	CB
Jackson & Buffett	Duet - It's Five O'Clock Somewhere	32-334	THM
Jackson & Buffett	It's 5 O'Clock Somewhere - duet	35-427	CB
Jackson & Buffett	It's Five O'Clock Somewhere	25-636	MM
Jackson & Buffett	It's Five O'Clock Somewhere	19-168	ST
Jackson & Buffett	It's Five O'Clock Somewhere - Duet	32-334	THM
Jackson & Elliot	Son Of A Gun	16-75	ST
Jackson & Houston	Duet - If You Say My Eyes/Beautiful	22-927	SC
Jackson & Houston	If You Say My Eyes R Beautiful	22-927	SC
Jackson & Krauss	Angels Cried the - duet	49-175	CB
Jackson & Krauss	Duet - Angels Cried the	49-175	CB
Jackson & Strait	Designated Drinker	40-100	CB
Jackson & Strait	Designated Drinker	16-327	ST
Jackson & Strait	Duet - Designated Drinker	40-100	CB
Jackson & Strait	Duet - Murder On Music Row	43-68	CB
Jackson & Strait	Murder On Music Row	43-68	CB
Jackson & Strait	Murder On Music Row	13-829	CHM
Jackson Five	ABC	11-411	DK

ARTIST	SONG TITLE	#	TYPE
Jackson Five	Dancing Machine	49-316	CB
Jackson Five	I Want You Back	11-377	DK
Jackson Five	I'll Be There	49-317	CB
Jackson Five	Never Can Say Goodbye	24-331	SC
Jackson w Buffett	Barefootin'	40-15	SD
Jackson, Alan	1976	49-182	KV
Jackson, Alan	Amarillo	47-774	SRK
Jackson, Alan	Angels And Alcohol	45-338	KRG
Jackson, Alan	Another Good Reason Not To Drink	40-99	CB
Jackson, Alan	Between The Devil And Me	22-653	ST
Jackson, Alan	Between The Devil And Me	1-57	CB
Jackson, Alan	Blue Ridge Mountain Song	49-14	KV
Jackson, Alan	Blue Ridge Mountain Song	45-104	KV
Jackson, Alan	Blues Man the	13-806	CHM
Jackson, Alan	Blues Man the	19-256	CSZ
Jackson, Alan	Blues Man the	6-63	SC
Jackson, Alan	Buicks To The Moon	44-81	PS
Jackson, Alan	Chasin' That Neon Rainbow	1-33	CB
Jackson, Alan	Chasin' That Neon Rainbow	12-421	P
Jackson, Alan	Chattahoochee	26-494	DK
Jackson, Alan	Chattahoochie	1-42	CB
Jackson, Alan	Chattahoochie	6-302	MM
Jackson, Alan	Chattahoochie	12-461	P
Jackson, Alan	Country Boy	36-222	PHM
Jackson, Alan	Dallas	1-37	CB
Jackson, Alan	Dallas	6-206	MM
Jackson, Alan	Dallas	2-706	SC
Jackson, Alan	Dixie Highway	45-106	KV
Jackson, Alan	Dog River Blues	45-103	DFK
Jackson, Alan	Don't Rock The Jukebox	1-35	CB
Jackson, Alan	Don't Rock The Jukebox	12-21	DK
Jackson, Alan	Don't Rock The Jukebox	6-118	MM
Jackson, Alan	Don't Rock The Jukebox	13-329	P
Jackson, Alan	Drive (For Daddy Gene)	33-167	CB
Jackson, Alan	Drive (For Daddy Gene)	25-133	MM
Jackson, Alan	Drive (For Daddy Gene)	16-426	ST
Jackson, Alan	Every Now And Then	45-107	KV
Jackson, Alan	Everything I Love	1-54	CB
Jackson, Alan	Everything I Love	7-587	CHM
Jackson, Alan	Everything I Love	24-656	SC
Jackson, Alan	Gone Country	2-577	SC
Jackson, Alan	Gone Crazy	8-394	CB
Jackson, Alan	Gone Crazy	7-851	CHT
Jackson, Alan	Gone Crazy	22-723	ST
Jackson, Alan	Gonna Come Back As A Country Song	39-60	PHN
Jackson, Alan	Good Time	36-389	CB
Jackson, Alan	Gospel - I Love To Tell The Story	43-109	CB
Jackson, Alan	Gospel - It's So Sweet To Trust...	43-98	CB

ARTIST	SONG TITLE	#	TYPE
Jackson, Alan	Gospel - Leaning on the Everlasting..	43-104	CB
Jackson, Alan	Hard Hat & A Hammer	49-178	CB
Jackson, Alan	Here In The Real World	14-678	CB
Jackson, Alan	Hole In The Wall	47-746	SRK
Jackson, Alan	Hole In The Wall	46-300	BKD
Jackson, Alan	Home	1-52	CB
Jackson, Alan	Home	7-242	MM
Jackson, Alan	House With No Curtains	8-238	CB
Jackson, Alan	House With No Curtains	7-724	CHM
Jackson, Alan	I Could Get Used To This Lovin' Thing	45-105	KV
Jackson, Alan	I Don't Even Know Your Name	1-50	CB
Jackson, Alan	I Don't Even Know Your Name	2-829	SC
Jackson, Alan	I Love To Tell The Story	49-174	ASK
Jackson, Alan	I Still Like Bologna	36-313	PHM
Jackson, Alan	I'd Love You All Over Again	1-34	CB
Jackson, Alan	I'd Love You All Over Again	2-387	SC
Jackson, Alan	I'll Go On Loving You	8-767	CB
Jackson, Alan	I'll Go On Loving You	22-821	ST
Jackson, Alan	I'll Try	1-51	CB
Jackson, Alan	I'll Try	7-249	MM
Jackson, Alan	I'll Try	4-125	SC
Jackson, Alan	If Love Was A River	49-234	DFK
Jackson, Alan	It Must Be Love	9-430	CB
Jackson, Alan	It Must Be Love	19-245	CSZ
Jackson, Alan	It Must Be Love	22-546	ST
Jackson, Alan	It's All About Him (Moby Edit)	30-547	CB
Jackson, Alan	It's Alright To Be A Redneck	15-860	ST
Jackson, Alan	It's Just That Way	44-144	BKD
Jackson, Alan	Jim And Jack And Hank	45-53	BKD
Jackson, Alan	Job Description	4-109	SC
Jackson, Alan	Laid Back 'N Low Key	44-126	KV
Jackson, Alan	Life Keeps Bringing Me Down	49-183	PHN
Jackson, Alan	Like Red On A Rose	30-47	CB
Jackson, Alan	Little Bitty	1-53	CB
Jackson, Alan	Little Bitty	4-620	SC
Jackson, Alan	Little Man	34-331	CB
Jackson, Alan	Little Man	10-194	SC
Jackson, Alan	Little Man	22-743	ST
Jackson, Alan	Livin' On Love	1-47	CB
Jackson, Alan	Livin' On Love	20-408	MH
Jackson, Alan	Livin' On Love	6-661	MM
Jackson, Alan	Long Long Way	49-238	DFK
Jackson, Alan	Long Way To Go	49-237	DFK
Jackson, Alan	Long Way To Go	49-180	CB
Jackson, Alan	Love's Got A Hold On You	1-39	CB
Jackson, Alan	Margaritaville	8-899	CB
Jackson, Alan	Meat And Potato Man	29-347	CB
Jackson, Alan	Mercury Blues	1-44	CB
Jackson, Alan	Mercury Blues	6-382	MM
Jackson, Alan	Merry Christmas To Me	49-177	CB
Jackson, Alan	Mexico Tequila And Me	45-21	KVD
Jackson, Alan	Midnight In Montgomery	1-38	CB
Jackson, Alan	Midnight In Montgomery	2-393	SC
Jackson, Alan	Monday Morning Church	22-81	CB
Jackson, Alan	Monday Morning Church	21-652	SC
Jackson, Alan	Must've Had A Ball	45-109	SC
Jackson, Alan	My Own Kind Of Hat	8-912	CB
Jackson, Alan	Pop A Top	19-204	CB
Jackson, Alan	Pop A Top	5-807	SC
Jackson, Alan	Pop A Top	22-372	ST
Jackson, Alan	Rainy Day In June	47-745	SRK
Jackson, Alan	Rainy Day In June	45-339	LM
Jackson, Alan	Remember When	19-673	ST
Jackson, Alan	Right On The Money	8-219	CB
Jackson, Alan	Right On The Money	22-681	ST
Jackson, Alan	Ring Of Fire	49-179	CB
Jackson, Alan	She Just Started Liking Cheatin Songs	40-97	CB
Jackson, Alan	She's Got The Rhythm	1-40	CB
Jackson, Alan	She's Got The Rhythm	6-114	MM
Jackson, Alan	She's Got The Rhythm	12-436	P
Jackson, Alan	She's Got The Rhythm	2-424	SC
Jackson, Alan	Short Sweet Ride	47-747	SRK
Jackson, Alan	Sissy's Song	37-27	CB
Jackson, Alan	Small Town Saturday Night	43-64	CB
Jackson, Alan	Small Town Southern Man	36-435	CB
Jackson, Alan	So You Don't Have to Love Me...	38-256	PHN
Jackson, Alan	Someday	3-40	SC
Jackson, Alan	Someday When Things Are Good	1-36	CB
Jackson, Alan	Song For The Life	1-49	CB
Jackson, Alan	Song For The Life	2-653	SC
Jackson, Alan	Strong Enough	49-181	KV
Jackson, Alan	Summertime Blues	1-46	CB
Jackson, Alan	Summertime Blues	20-401	MH
Jackson, Alan	Summertime Blues	6-601	MM
Jackson, Alan	Summertime Blues	17-218	NA
Jackson, Alan	Summertime Blues	2-312	SC
Jackson, Alan	Talk Is Cheap	45-108	KV
Jackson, Alan	Talkin' Song Repair Blues	22-326	CB
Jackson, Alan	Talkin' Song Repair Blues the	23-383	SC
Jackson, Alan	Tall Tall Trees	3-634	SC
Jackson, Alan	Tequila Sunrise	1-45	CB
Jackson, Alan	Thank GOD For The Radio	44-125	KV
Jackson, Alan	That'd Be Alright	32-113	THM
Jackson, Alan	That'd Be Alright	25-449	MM
Jackson, Alan	That'd Be Alright	18-781	ST
Jackson, Alan	There Goes	1-56	CB

ARTIST	SONG TITLE	#	TYPE
Jackson, Alan	There Goes	7-657	CHM
Jackson, Alan	Three Minute Up Tempo Love Song	49-173	ASK
Jackson, Alan	To Do What I Do	46-309	SC
Jackson, Alan	Tonight I Climbed The Wall	12-462	P
Jackson, Alan	Tonight I Climbed The Wall	2-417	SC
Jackson, Alan	Too Much Of A Good Thing	20-442	ST
Jackson, Alan	Tropical Depression	40-98	CB
Jackson, Alan	USA Today	23-406	CB
Jackson, Alan	Walk On The Rocks	49-185	SC
Jackson, Alan	Walkin' The Floor Over You	47-748	SRK
Jackson, Alan	Wanted	1-32	CB
Jackson, Alan	When Somebody Loves You	40-101	CB
Jackson, Alan	When Somebody Loves You	14-834	ST
Jackson, Alan	When Somebody Loves You	15-218	THM
Jackson, Alan	Where I Come From	33-155	CB
Jackson, Alan	Where I Come From	15-604	ST
Jackson, Alan	Where Were You	20-578	CB
Jackson, Alan	Where Were You	25-62	MM
Jackson, Alan	Where Were You	16-38	ST
Jackson, Alan	Who Says You Can't Have It All	1-43	CB
Jackson, Alan	Who Says You Can't Have It All	6-477	MM
Jackson, Alan	Who Says You Can't Have It All	2-106	SC
Jackson, Alan	Who's Cheatin' Who	1-55	CB
Jackson, Alan	Who's Cheatin' Who	7-604	CHM
Jackson, Alan	Woman's Love a	30-243	CB
Jackson, Alan	Work In Progress	40-103	CB
Jackson, Alan	Work In Progress	25-291	MM
Jackson, Alan	Work In Progress	17-580	ST
Jackson, Alan	Www.Memory	14-123	CB
Jackson, Alan	Www.Memory	19-215	CSZ
Jackson, Alan	Www.Memory	22-570	ST
Jackson, Alan	Www.Memory	14-30	THM
Jackson, Alan	Xmas - I Only Want You For Xmas	8-52	CB
Jackson, Alan	Xmas - Let It Be Christmas	30-396	SC
Jackson, Alan	Xmas - Merry Christmas To Me	49-177	CB
Jackson, Alan	Xmas - Santa's Gonna Come/Pickup	18-717	CB
Jackson, Alan	Xmas - Santa's Gonna Come/Pickup	22-842	ST
Jackson, Alan	You Can Always Come Home	45-340	KV
Jackson, Alan	You Can't Give Up On Lovin'	2-431	SC
Jackson, Alan	You Never Know	48-512	KVD
Jackson, Freddie	Baby You Are My Lady	17-509	SC
Jackson, Freddie	I Don't Want To Lose	17-131	DK
	You		
Jackson, Freddie	Make Love Easy	18-486	NU
Jackson, Freddie	Rock Me Tonight	17-132	DK
Jackson, Freddie	You Are My Lady	15-721	LE
Jackson, Janet	Again	2-118	SC
Jackson, Janet	All For You	35-230	CB
Jackson, Janet	All For You	15-452	PHM
Jackson, Janet	All For You	16-112	PRT
Jackson, Janet	All For You	18-505	TT
Jackson, Janet	Any Time Any Place	15-445	CB
Jackson, Janet	Because Of Love	2-112	SC
Jackson, Janet	Control	11-227	DK
Jackson, Janet	Control	12-752	P
Jackson, Janet	Doesn't Really Matter	33-379	CB
Jackson, Janet	Doesn't Really Matter	14-6	PHM
Jackson, Janet	Doesn't Really Matter	15-413	PS
Jackson, Janet	Doesn't Really Matter	20-10	SGB
Jackson, Janet	Escapade	15-415	PS
Jackson, Janet	Every Time	15-414	PS
Jackson, Janet	Everything	6-413	MM
Jackson, Janet	Go Deep	15-444	CB
Jackson, Janet	Go Deep	15-626	PHM
Jackson, Janet	Go Deep	15-416	PS
Jackson, Janet	I Get Lonely	15-443	CB
Jackson, Janet	I Get Lonely	15-417	PS
Jackson, Janet	Just A Little While	20-529	CB
Jackson, Janet	Just A Little While	20-356	PHM
Jackson, Janet	Let's Wait Awhile	2-281	SC
Jackson, Janet	Love Will Never Do	21-457	CB
Jackson, Janet	Love Will Never Do	15-418	PS
Jackson, Janet	Miss You Much	11-387	DK
Jackson, Janet	Miss You Much	16-544	P
Jackson, Janet	Nasty	27-304	DK
Jackson, Janet	Nasty	15-419	PS
Jackson, Janet	Rhythm Dancer	15-420	PS
Jackson, Janet	Runaway	15-421	PS
Jackson, Janet	Someone To Call My Lover	18-398	MM
Jackson, Janet	Someone To Call My Lover	18-532	TT
Jackson, Janet	Tell Me I'm Not Dreaming	11-590	DK
Jackson, Janet	Together Again	7-709	PHM
Jackson, Janet	Together Again	9-100	PS
Jackson, Janet	Twenty Foreplay	4-174	SC
Jackson, Janet	What Have You Done For Me Lately	27-305	DK
Jackson, Janet	What Have You Done For Me Lately	12-824	P
Jackson, Janet	When I Think Of You	27-303	DK
Jackson, Janet	When I Think Of You	4-854	SC
Jackson, Joe	Is She Really Going Out With Him	11-657	DK
Jackson, Joe	Is She Really Going Out With Him	5-308	SC
Jackson, Joe	Steppin' Out	28-369	DK
Jackson, M &	Duet - I Just Can't Stop Loving You	27-276	DK

ARTIST	SONG TITLE	#	TYPE
Jackson, M &	I Just Can't Stop Loving You	27-276	DK
Jackson, M & Ross	Ease On Down The Road	9-834	SAV
Jackson, Mahalia	Gospel - We Shall Overcome	33-211	CB
Jackson, Mahalia	We Shall Overcome	33-211	CB
Jackson, Michael	Bad	35-191	CB
Jackson, Michael	Bad	11-190	DK
Jackson, Michael	Beat It	33-306	CB
Jackson, Michael	Beat It	17-19	DK
Jackson, Michael	Beat It	12-755	P
Jackson, Michael	Billie Jean	17-20	DK
Jackson, Michael	Billie Jean	14-356	MH
Jackson, Michael	Black Or White	21-456	CB
Jackson, Michael	Black Or White	28-111	DK
Jackson, Michael	Black Or White	6-180	MM
Jackson, Michael	Black Or White	12-804	P
Jackson, Michael	Butterflies	25-76	MM
Jackson, Michael	Butterflies	16-76	ST
Jackson, Michael	Childhood	3-488	SC
Jackson, Michael	Don't Stop Till You Get Enough	28-112	DK
Jackson, Michael	Don't Stop Till You Get Enough	36-120	JTG
Jackson, Michael	Don't Stop Till You Get Enough	7-92	MM
Jackson, Michael	Duet - I Just Can't Stop Loving You	16-564	P
Jackson, Michael	Halloween - Thriller	16-292	TT
Jackson, Michael	Heal The World	6-105	MM
Jackson, Michael	Human Nature	12-375	DK
Jackson, Michael	I Just Can't Stop Loving You	15-503	CMC
Jackson, Michael	I Just Can't Stop Loving You	16-564	P
Jackson, Michael	Little Christmas Tree	47-478	DCK
Jackson, Michael	Man In The Mirror	34-102	CB
Jackson, Michael	Man In The Mirror	14-582	SC
Jackson, Michael	Off The Wall	36-121	JTG
Jackson, Michael	Pretty Young Thing	11-462	DK
Jackson, Michael	Remember The Time	33-355	CB
Jackson, Michael	Rock With You	36-122	JTG
Jackson, Michael	Rock With You	12-700	P
Jackson, Michael	Rockin' Robin	12-60	DK
Jackson, Michael	Rockin' Robin	13-136	P
Jackson, Michael	She's Out Of My Life	25-278	MM
Jackson, Michael	Thriller	16-865	DK
Jackson, Michael	Thriller	16-292	TT
Jackson, Michael	Way You Make Me Feel the	11-768	DK
Jackson, Michael	Way You Make Me Feel the	13-214	P
Jackson, Michael	Will You Be There	6-374	MM
Jackson, Michael	Xmas - Little Christmas Tree	47-478	DCK
Jackson, Michael	You Are Not Alone	36-124	JTG
Jackson, Michael	You Rock My World	25-16	MM
Jackson, Michael	You Rock My World	16-306	PHM

ARTIST	SONG TITLE	#	TYPE
Jackson, Slan	Like Red On A Rose	30-47	CB
Jackson, Stonewall	BJ The DJ	8-715	CB
Jackson, Stonewall	BJ The DJ	5-103	SC
Jackson, Stonewall	Blues Plus Booze (Mean I Lose)	46-38	SSK
Jackson, Stonewall	Don't Be Angry	8-788	CB
Jackson, Stonewall	Don't Be Angry	5-221	SC
Jackson, Stonewall	Help Stamp Out Lonliness	49-284	BFK
Jackson, Stonewall	Leona	46-40	SSK
Jackson, Stonewall	Life To Go	5-372	SC
Jackson, Stonewall	Waterloo	8-779	CB
Jackson, Stonewall	Waterloo	4-859	SC
Jackson, Stonewall	Why I'm Walkin'	5-433	SC
Jackson, Stonewall	Wound Time Can't Erase a	5-693	SC
Jackson, Wanda	Breathless	46-55	SSK
Jackson, Wanda	Girl I Used To Know a	20-646	SC
Jackson, Wanda	In The Middle Of A Heartache	19-404	SC
Jackson, Wanda	Let Me Go Lover	47-798	SRK
Jackson, Wanda	Oh Boy!	46-56	SSK
Jackson, Wanda	Please Love Me Forever	47-797	SRK
Jackson, Wanda	Right Or Wrong	8-781	CB
Jackson, Wanda	Right Or Wrong	12-409	P
Jackson, Wanda	Window Up Above the	8-792	CB
Jackson, Wanda	Woman Lives For Love a	45-592	OZP
Jackson&Chipmunks	Xmas - Santa's Gonna Come/Pickup...	8-80	CB
Jackson&McCartney	Duet - Girl Is Mine the	17-150	DK
Jackson&McCartney	Duet - Girl Is Mine the	24-205	SC
Jackson&McCartney	Girl Is Mine the	17-150	DK
Jackson&McCartney	Girl Is Mine the	24-205	SC
Jacksons	Blame It On The Boogie	30-789	SF
Jadakiss & Carey	U Make Me Wanna	20-192	PHM
Jade	Looking For Mr. Right	18-485	NU
Jagged Edge	Promise	15-435	PHM
Jagger, Mick	God Gave Me Everything	16-89	SC
Jaheim	Never	36-504	CB
Jaheim	Put That Woman First	20-525	CB
Jaheim	Put That Woman First	32-274	THM
Jain	Come	48-644	KV
James	Say Something	30-772	SF
James & Barnes	Duet - Wrong Song - Nashville	45-470	KVD
James & Barnes	Show - Wrong Song - duet - Nashville	45-470	KVD
James & Barnes	Wrong Song - duet - Nashville	45-470	KVD
James & Claybourne	Duet - No One Will Ever Love You	45-473	KVD
James & Claybourne	No One Will Ever Love You - Nashville	45-473	KVD
James & Claybourne	Show - No One Will Ever Love You	45-473	KVD
James & Orchestra	You Made Me Love You	21-7	CB
James & Shondells	Crimson And Clover	11-418	DK

ARTIST	SONG TITLE	#	TYPE
James & Shondells	Crimson And Clover	12-868	P
James & Shondells	Crimson And Clover	4-704	SC
James & Shondells	Crystal Blue Persuasion	33-260	CB
James & Shondells	Crystal Blue Persuasion	12-134	DK
James & Shondells	Draggin' The Line	9-344	AH
James & Shondells	Draggin' The Line	20-321	MH
James & Shondells	Hanky Panky	11-813	DK
James & Shondells	Hanky Panky	6-140	MM
James & Shondells	I Think We're Alone Now	20-65	SC
James & Shondells	Mony Mony	10-331	KC
James & Shondells	Mony Mony	13-207	P
James & Shondells	Sweet Cherry Wine	3-466	SC
James Bond Movies	Show - All Time High	18-85	SC
James Bond Movies	Show - Diamonds Are Forever	18-87	SC
James Bond Movies	Show - For Your Eyes Only	18-86	SC
James Bond Movies	Show - From Russia With Love	18-79	SC
James Bond Movies	Show - Goldeneyes	18-84	SC
James Bond Movies	Show - Goldfinger	18-76	SC
James Bond Movies	Show - License To Kill	18-83	SC
James Bond Movies	Show - Live And Let Die	18-77	SC
James Bond Movies	Show - Living Daylights the	18-82	SC
James Bond Movies	Show - Man With The Golden Gun	18-80	SC
James Bond Movies	Show - Nobody Does It Better	18-73	SC
James Bond Movies	Show - Thunderball	18-75	SC
James Bond Movies	Show - Tomorrow Never Dies	18-81	SC
James Bond Movies	Show - View To A Kill	18-74	SC
James Bond Movies	Show - You Only Live Twice	18-78	SC
James Gang	Walk Away	3-609	SC
James-Decker, Jessie	Clint Eastwood	48-460	BKD
James-Decker, Jessie	Coming Home	48-459	BKD
James-Decker, Jessie	Lights Down Low	48-448	KCD
James-Decker, Jessie	Rain On The Roof Of This Car	48-458	BKD
James, Brett	After All	32-193	THM
James, Brett	After All	18-803	ST
James, Brett	Chasing Amy	25-188	MM
James, Brett	Chasing Amy	16-696	ST
James, Brett	Female Bonding	6-812	MM
James, Brett	Worth The Fall	4-130	SC
James, Duncan	Sooner Or Later	30-720	SF
James, Elmore	Shake Your Money Maker	20-141	KB
James, Etta	At Last	23-359	CR
James, Etta	At Last	15-402	JTG
James, Etta	At Last	19-610	MH
James, Etta	At Last	21-693	PS
James, Etta	At Last	36-359	SC
James, Etta	Don't Cry Baby	21-695	PS

ARTIST	SONG TITLE	#	TYPE
James, Etta	I Just Want To Make Love To You	19-561	SC
James, Etta	My Dearest Darling	21-696	PS
James, Etta	Sunday Kind Of Love a	25-667	MM
James, Etta	Tell Mama	21-697	PS
James, Etta	Trust In Me	21-694	PS
James, Joni	Why Don't You Believe Me	5-85	SC
James, Mickie	Somebody's Gonna Pay	40-22	PHN
James, Rick	Give It To Me Baby **	15-3	SC
James, Rick	Superfreak	15-700	LE
James, Sonny	Because Of You	48-469	DKM
James, Sonny	Behind The Tear	19-468	CB
James, Sonny	Behind The Tear	5-583	SC
James, Sonny	Born To Be With You	19-473	CB
James, Sonny	Bright Lights Big City	19-477	CB
James, Sonny	Bright Lights Big City	29-651	SC
James, Sonny	Don't Keep Me Hangin' On	19-474	CB
James, Sonny	Empty Arms	19-476	CB
James, Sonny	Endlessly	19-475	CB
James, Sonny	Heaven Says Hello	19-472	CB
James, Sonny	Heaven Says Hello	5-694	SC
James, Sonny	I'll Never Find Another You	19-469	CB
James, Sonny	I'll Never Find Another You	5-705	SC
James, Sonny	Is It Wrong For Loving You	48-468	GS
James, Sonny	It's The Little Things	19-471	CB
James, Sonny	It's The Little Things	14-335	SC
James, Sonny	My Love	3-770	CB
James, Sonny	Running Bear	15-91	CB
James, Sonny	Running Bear	10-738	JVC
James, Sonny	Running Bear (Faster Version)	19-466	CB
James, Sonny	Since I Met You Baby	4-856	SC
James, Sonny	Take Good Care Of Her	19-470	CB
James, Sonny	World Of Our Own a	19-467	CB
James, Sonny	You're The Only World I Know	19-478	CB
James, Sonny	You're The Only World I Know	4-262	SC
James, Sonny	Young Love	19-480	CB
James, Sonny	Young Love	27-233	DK
James, Sonny	Young Love	7-114	MM
James, Sonny	Young Love	3-506	SC
James, Tommy	Draggin' The Line	29-285	SC
Jan & Dean	Dead Man's Curve	34-17	CB
Jan & Dean	Dead Man's Curve	4-250	SC
Jan & Dean	Drag City	3-556	SC
Jan & Dean	Honolulu Lulu	45-602	OZP
Jan & Dean	Little Old Lady From Pasadena	11-633	DK
Jan & Dean	Little Old Lady From Pasadena	13-66	P
Jan & Dean	Little Old Lady From Pasadena	3-561	SC
Jan & Dean	Summer Means Fun	49-36	SHE

ARTIST	SONG TITLE	#	TYPE
			R
Jan & Dean	Surf City	33-246	CB
Jan & Dean	Surf City	15-565	DK
Jana	Ooh Baby Baby	10-186	SC
Jana	Ooh It's Kinda Crazy	12-389	PHM
Jane's Addiction	Irresistible Force	38-241	PHM
Jane's Addiction	Just Because	32-326	THM
Jane's Addiction	True Nature	19-853	PHM
Janet	Doesn't Really Matter	30-641	THM
Janet, Joanna	Since I've Seen You Last	16-693	ST
Janson, Chris	Better I Don't	45-379	ASK
Janson, Chris	Buy Me A Boat	45-28	BKD
Janson, Chris	Buy Me A Boat (Inst)	49-738	BKD
Janson, Chris	Cut Me Some Slack	41-98	PHN
Janson, Chris	Cut Me Some Slack	45-380	PHN
Janson, Chris	Power Of Positive Drinkin'	49-654	KV
Janson, Chris	Till A Woman Comes Along	45-370	BKD
Jareau, Al	Mornin'	48-780	P
Jarreau, Al	We're In This Love Together	18-48	MM
Jarreau, Al	We're In This Love Together	18-504	SAV
Jars Of Clay	Flood	7-571	THM
Jars Of Clay	Gospel - Flood	20-150	KB
Jason & the Long Road	It's A Good Thing	38-225	CB
Javier	Crazy	32-314	THM
Jay & Americans	Cara Mia	7-32	MM
Jay & Americans	Cara Mia	14-375	PS
Jay & Americans	Cara Mia	4-245	SC
Jay & Americans	Come A Little Bit Closer	11-638	DK
Jay & Americans	Come A Little Bit Closer	6-162	MM
Jay & Americans	Come A Little Bit Closer	13-88	P
Jay & Americans	Come A Little Bit Closer	14-374	PS
Jay & Americans	Come Dance With Me	14-371	PS
Jay & Americans	Crying	14-373	PS
Jay & Americans	Let's Lock The Door & Throw Away..	14-372	PS
Jay & Americans	Only In America	14-378	PS
Jay & Americans	She Cried	14-376	PS
Jay & Americans	Some Enchanted Evening	14-379	PS
Jay & Americans	Sunday And Me	14-369	PS
Jay & Americans	Think Of The Good Times	14-368	PS
Jay & Americans	Think Of The Good Times	45-168	PS
Jay & Americans	This Magic Moment	26-387	DK
Jay & Americans	This Magic Moment	14-377	PS
Jay & Americans	Walkin' In The Rain	14-370	PS
Jay & Techniques	Apples Peaches Pumpkin Pie	35-86	CB
Jay & Techniques	Keep The Ball Rollin'	9-698	SAV
Jay-Z	Dirt Off Your Shoulder **	23-249	THM
Jay-Z & Beyonce	03 Bonnie & Clyde	25-459	MM
Jay-Z & Beyonce	Crazy In Love	25-653	MM

ARTIST	SONG TITLE	#	TYPE
Jay-Z & Knowles	03 Bonnie & Clyde	32-48	THM
Jay-Z & Knowles	Duet - 03 Bonnie & Clyde	32-48	THM
Jay-Z&Amil&Ja-Rule	Can I Get A...	14-445	SC
Jay-Z&Amil&Ja-Rule	Duet - Can I Get A...	14-445	SC
Jazz Standard	Ain't Misbehavin'	47-717	VH
Jazz Standard	Alright Ok You Win	47-718	VH
Jazz Standard	Basin Street Blues	47-520	VH
Jazz Standard	Birth Of The Blues	47-519	VH
Jazz Standard	St. Louis Blues	47-522	VH
Jazz Standard	Tangerine	47-715	KV
Jean, Norma	Let's Go All The Way	46-19	SSK
Jeff Beck Group	I Ain't Superstitious	15-24	SC
Jeff Healy Band	Angel Eyes	9-341	AH
Jeff Healy Band	Angel Eyes	34-98	CB
Jeff Healy Band	Confidence Man	9-373	AH
Jeff Healy Band	Confidence Man	19-797	SGB
Jeff Healy Band	I Think I Love You Too Much	17-96	DK
Jeff Healy Band	Lost In Your Eyes	4-280	SC
Jeff Healy Band	Roadhouse Blues	47-724	KV
Jefferson Airplane	Somebody To Love	11-185	DK
Jefferson Airplane	Somebody To Love	3-265	SC
Jefferson Airplane	White Rabbit	17-121	DK
Jefferson Airplane	White Rabbit	12-917	P
Jefferson Airplane	White Rabbit	2-753	SC
Jefferson Starship	Count On Me	24-201	SC
Jefferson Starship	Miracles	12-353	DK
Jefferson Starship	Runaway	20-75	SC
Jefferson Starship	Sara	12-354	DK
Jefferson, Paul	Fear Of A Broken Heart	7-326	MM
Jefferson, Paul	Fear Of A Broken Heart	24-158	SC
Jefferson, Paul	I Might Just Make It	7-388	MM
Jekyll & Hyde	Show - Love Has Come Of Age	16-51	PS
Jekyll & Hyde	Show - New Life a	16-56	PS
Jekyll & Hyde	Show - No One Knows Who I Am	16-55	PS
Jekyll & Hyde	Show - Once Upon A Dream	17-656	PS
Jekyll & Hyde	Show - Once Upon A Dream (Reprise)	17-663	PS
Jekyll & Hyde	Show - Someone Like You	16-53	PS
Jekyll & Hyde	Show - This Is The Moment	10-382	KC
Jekyll & Hyde	Show - This Is The Moment	15-236	PR
Jekyll & Hyde	Show - This Is The Moment	18-189	PS
Jekyll & Hyde	Show - Till You Came Into My Life	17-660	PS
Jelly Beans	I Wanna Love Him So Bad	6-47	SC
Jenai	Cool Me Down	18-791	ST
Jenkins	Blame It On Mama	20-260	PHM
Jenkins	Blame It On Mama	20-347	ST
Jenkins	Getaway Car	23-400	CB
Jenkins	Getaway Car	20-508	ST

ARTIST	SONG TITLE	#	TYPE
Jenkins, Matt	King Of The Castle	23-301	CB
Jennings & Carter	Duet - I Got You	45-170	RCA
Jennings & Carter	I Got You - duet	45-170	RCA
Jennings & Colter	Duet - I Got You	22-151	CK
Jennings & Colter	Duet - I Got You	9-621	SAV
Jennings & Colter	Duet - Out Of The Rain	45-183	DCK
Jennings & Colter	Duet - Storms Never Last	45-185	DCK
Jennings & Colter	Duet - Wild Side Of Life	45-195	SSK
Jennings & Colter	I Got You	22-151	CK
Jennings & Colter	I Got You	9-621	SAV
Jennings & Colter	Out Of The Rain - duet	45-183	DCK
Jennings & Colter	Storms Never Last - duet	45-185	DCK
Jennings & Colter	Wild Side Of Life - duet	45-195	SSK
Jennings & Nelson	Duet - Just To Satisfy You	45-176	CB
Jennings & Nelson	Good Hearted Woman	11-151	DK
Jennings & Nelson	Just To Satisfy You - duet	45-176	CB
Jennings, Shooter	4th Of July	22-340	CB
Jennings, Shooter	Gone To Carolina	30-54	CB
Jennings, Shooter	Real Me the	49-637	PHN
Jennings, Shooter	Steady At The Wheel	29-47	CB
Jennings, Shooter	Walk Of Life	49-638	ST
Jennings, Shooter	Wild And Lonesome	41-56	PHN
Jennings, Waylon	Amanda	22-152	CK
Jennings, Waylon	Amanda	12-448	P
Jennings, Waylon	America	22-145	CK
Jennings, Waylon	America	20-666	SC
Jennings, Waylon	Anita You're Dreaming	45-191	SRK
Jennings, Waylon	Are You Ready For The Country	22-144	CK
Jennings, Waylon	Are You Sure Hank Done It This Way	1-617	CB
Jennings, Waylon	Are You Sure Hank Done It This Way	22-143	CK
Jennings, Waylon	Are You Sure Hank Done It This Way	4-309	SC
Jennings, Waylon	Bob Wills Is Still The King	22-142	CK
Jennings, Waylon	Can't You See	22-146	CK
Jennings, Waylon	Clyde	45-171	SC
Jennings, Waylon	Come With Me	29-781	CB
Jennings, Waylon	Cowboy Movies	24-132	SC
Jennings, Waylon	Delia's Gone	46-52	SSK
Jennings, Waylon	Don't You Think This Outlaw Thing Has...	45-178	TU
Jennings, Waylon	Door Is Always Open the	47-753	SRK
Jennings, Waylon	Down Came The World	45-187	SRK
Jennings, Waylon	Drinkin' And Dreamin'	22-141	CK
Jennings, Waylon	Drinkin' And Dreamin'	20-653	SC
Jennings, Waylon	Dukes Of Hazzard Theme	22-147	CK
Jennings, Waylon	Eagle the	20-582	CB
Jennings, Waylon	Eagle the	45-1`73	CB
Jennings, Waylon	Eagle the - Americana	36-340	CB
Jennings, Waylon	Good Hearted Woman	8-18	CB

ARTIST	SONG TITLE	#	TYPE
Jennings, Waylon	Good Hearted Woman	12-425	P
Jennings, Waylon	Good Hearted Woman a	22-136	CK
Jennings, Waylon	Good Ol' Boys	1-618	CB
Jennings, Waylon	Good Ol' Boys	4-721	SC
Jennings, Waylon	Honky Tonk Heroes	45-174	CB
Jennings, Waylon	I Ain't Living Long Like This	6-84	SC
Jennings, Waylon	I'm A Ramblin' Man	1-619	CB
Jennings, Waylon	I'm A Ramblin' Man	22-150	CK
Jennings, Waylon	I've Always Been Crazy	8-208	CB
Jennings, Waylon	I've Always Been Crazy	22-138	CK
Jennings, Waylon	I've Always Been Crazy	4-640	SC
Jennings, Waylon	Kissing You Goodbye	45-181	DCK
Jennings, Waylon	Ladies Love Outlaws	44-60	KV
Jennings, Waylon	Let's Turn Back The Years	46-18	SSK
Jennings, Waylon	Listen They're Playing Our Song	45-190	KV
Jennings, Waylon	Lonely Weekends	45-194	SSK
Jennings, Waylon	Lonesome Orn'ry & Mean	26-194	DK
Jennings, Waylon	Lonesome Orn'ry & Mean	45-175	DK
Jennings, Waylon	Lot Of Good	47-809	SRK
Jennings, Waylon	Lovin' Her Was Easier	1-621	CB
Jennings, Waylon	Lucille	22-148	CK
Jennings, Waylon	Lucille (You Won't Do Your Daddy..)	4-735	SC
Jennings, Waylon	Luckenbach Texas	1-622	CB
Jennings, Waylon	Luckenbach Texas	22-137	CK
Jennings, Waylon	Luckenbach Texas	17-3	DK
Jennings, Waylon	Luckenbach Texas	13-463	P
Jennings, Waylon	Luckenbach Texas	8-685	SAV
Jennings, Waylon	Mama Don't Let Your Babies Grow...	22-149	CK
Jennings, Waylon	Mamas Don't Let Your Babies Grow...	1-623	CB
Jennings, Waylon	Mason Dixon Lines	47-514	VH
Jennings, Waylon	Never Could Toe The Mark	45-192	TU
Jennings, Waylon	Only Daddy That'll Walk The Line	22-140	CK
Jennings, Waylon	Only Daddy That'll Walk The Line	5-91	SC
Jennings, Waylon	Rainy Day Woman	22-139	CK
Jennings, Waylon	Rainy Day Woman	4-733	SC
Jennings, Waylon	Rose In Paradise	5-393	SC
Jennings, Waylon	Sally Was A Good Old Girl	45-182	DCK
Jennings, Waylon	Six White Horses	45-184	DCK
Jennings, Waylon	This Time	45-193	VH
Jennings, Waylon	Waymore's Blues	45-189	SRK
Jennings, Waylon	Whatever Happened To The Blues	45-188	SRK
Jennings, Waylon	Wrong	16-586	MM
Jennings, Waylon	Wurlitzer Prize	35-377	CB
Jennings, Waylon	Wurlitzer Prize the	8-267	CB
Jennings, Waylon	Wurlitzer Prize the	4-728	SC
Jennings, Waylon	Xmas - Away In A	8-66	CB

ARTIST	SONG TITLE	#	TYPE
	Manger		
Jennings, Waylon	Xmas - Oh Come All Ye Faithful	8-78	CB
Jennings, Waylon	You Asked Me To	45-179	ASK
Jennings, Waylon	You Can Have Her	14-258	SC
Jensen, Gordon	Gospel - Inside Out	16-24	SX
Jensen, Gordon	Gospel - Warm Kind of Family Feelin	16-614	CB
Jepsen, Carly Rae	Curiosity	49-111	SBI
Jepsen, Carly Rae	Everywhere You Look	49-792	BKD
Jepsen, Carly Rae	I Really Love You	45-275	BKD
Jepsen, Carly Rae	Take A Picture	49-127	BKD
Jepsen, Carly Rae	This Kiss	49-109	BKD
Jepsen, Carly Rae	Tonight I'm Getting Over You	49-110	KCD
Jepson, Carly Rae	Call Me Maybe	39-44	ASK
Jesus Christ Supers	Show - Damned For All Time	15-256	PS
Jesus Christ Supers	Show - Everything's Allright	15-253	PS
Jesus Christ Supers	Show - Heaven On Their Minds	15-252	PS
Jesus Christ Supers	Show - Hosanna	15-254	PS
Jesus Christ Supers	Show - I Don't Know How To Love Him	6-327	MM
Jesus Christ Supers	Show - I Don't Know How to Love Him	15-255	PS
Jesus Christ Supers	Show - I Only Want To Say	15-258	PS
Jesus Christ Supers	Show - Jesus Christ Superstar	15-260	PS
Jesus Christ Supers	Show - John 19:41	15-261	PS
Jesus Christ Supers	Show - King Herod's Song	15-259	PS
Jesus Christ Supers	Show - Last Supper the	15-257	PS
Jesus Christ Supers	Show - Superstar Overture	15-251	PS
Jet	Are You Gonna Be My Girl	20-540	CB
Jet	Are You Gonna Be My Girl	19-855	PHM
Jet	Rollover DJ	20-549	PHM
Jets	Make It Real	11-390	DK
Jets	Rocket 2 You	11-282	DK
Jett, Joan	Bad Reputation	35-202	CB
Jett, Joan	Crimson And Clover	16-640	MM
Jett, Joan	Dirty Deeds, Done Dirt Cheap	43-388	PS
Jett, Joan	Do You Wanna Touch Me...	15-8	SC
Jett, Joan	I Hate Myself For Loving You	18-385	SAV
Jett, Joan	I Hate Myself For Loving You	5-315	SC
Jett, Joan	I Love Rock & Roll	11-325	DK
Jett, Joan	I Love Rock & Roll	13-3	P
Jett, Joan	I Love Rock & Roll	10-522	SF
Jewel	Absence Of Fear	19-355	PS
Jewel	Angel Standing By	36-335	SC
Jewel	Break Me	18-218	CB

ARTIST	SONG TITLE	#	TYPE
Jewel	Break Me	25-197	MM
Jewel	Don't	36-332	SC
Jewel	Down So Long	19-356	PS
Jewel	Foolish Games	19-357	PS
Jewel	Foolish Games	36-334	SC
Jewel	Good Day	36-192	PHM
Jewel	Hands	28-189	DK
Jewel	Hands	19-358	PS
Jewel	Hands	13-678	SGB
Jewel	I'm Sensitive	36-333	SC
Jewel	Intuition	25-627	MM
Jewel	Intution	32-280	THM
Jewel	Morning Song	36-331	SC
Jewel	Near You Always	36-330	SC
Jewel	Stand	20-235	MM
Jewel	Stand	32-433	THM
Jewel	Standing Still	25-42	MM
Jewel	Standing Still	16-78	ST
Jewel	This Way	18-432	CB
Jewel	What's Simple Is True - (Radio Ver)	17-543	SC
Jewel	Who Will Save Your Soul	4-345	SC
Jewel	You Were Meant For Me	19-576	MH
Jewel	You Were Meant For Me	4-601	SC
Jewell, Buddy	Help Pour Out The Rain	34-402	CB
Jewell, Buddy	Help Pour Out The Rain	25-638	MM
Jewell, Buddy	Help Pour Out The Rain	32-296	THM
Jewell, Buddy	Help Pour Out The Rain	19-70	ST
Jewell, Buddy	If She Were Any Other Woman	22-318	CB
Jewell, Buddy	One Step At A Time	20-476	ST
Jewell, Buddy	So Gone	23-490	CB
Jewell, Buddy	Sweet Southern Comfort	22-13	CB
Jewell, Buddy	Sweet Southern Comfort	19-677	ST
Jim & Jesse	Knoxville Girl	33-225	CB
Jim & Jesse	Old Slew Foot	8-261	CB
Jimmy Eat World	Big Casino	49-889	SC
Jimmy Eat World	Middle the	18-349	CB
Jimmy Eat World	Middle the	25-203	MM
Jimmy Eat World	Middle the	30-651	THM
Jimmy Eat World	Pain	30-822	PHM
Jimmy Eat World	Praise Chorus a	23-148	PHM
Jimmy Eat World	Sweetness	18-417	MM
Jimmy's Chickens	Do Right	8-530	PHT
Jive Five	My True Story	7-270	MM
Jo Jo	Leave (Get Out)	23-560	MM
Jodeci	Come And Talk To Me	9-686	SAV
Jodeci	Get On Up	4-685	SC
Jodeci	I'm Still Waiting	9-849	SAV
Joe	I Wanna Know	35-231	CB
Joe	I Wanna Know	16-123	PRT
Joe	I Wanna Know	15-633	THM
Joe & Mystikal	Stutter	15-457	PHM
Joe & Mystikal	Stutter	18-576	TT
Joe And Jake	You're Not Alone	49-882	SF
Joe Public	Live & Learn	28-441	DK

ARTIST	SONG TITLE	#	TYPE
Joel, Billy	All About Soul	2-228	SC
Joel, Billy	Allentown	17-463	SC
Joel, Billy	Always A Woman	16-139	LE
Joel, Billy	And So It Goes	12-271	DK
Joel, Billy	Ballad Of Billy The Kid	46-173	SC
Joel, Billy	Big Shot	6-553	MM
Joel, Billy	Big Shot	17-518	SC
Joel, Billy	Captain Jack	15-751	AMS
Joel, Billy	Captain Jack	21-517	SC
Joel, Billy	Close To The Borderline	45-580	OZP
Joel, Billy	Entertainer the	12-275	DK
Joel, Billy	Entertainer the	16-141	LE
Joel, Billy	Flesh For Fantasy	47-147	LE
Joel, Billy	For The Longest Time	33-312	CB
Joel, Billy	Honesty	12-277	DK
Joel, Billy	Honesty	16-517	P
Joel, Billy	Hot In The City	47-148	LE
Joel, Billy	Hot In The City	47-144	BSP
Joel, Billy	I Go To Extremes	12-268	DK
Joel, Billy	I Go To Extremes	16-144	LE
Joel, Billy	I Go To Extremes	16-518	P
Joel, Billy	It's Still Rock & Roll To Me	12-274	DK
Joel, Billy	It's Still Rock & Roll To Me	16-147	LE
Joel, Billy	It's Still Rock & Roll To Me	12-801	P
Joel, Billy	Just The Way You Are	12-278	DK
Joel, Billy	Just The Way You Are	11-74	JTG
Joel, Billy	Just The Way You Are	16-132	LE
Joel, Billy	Just The Way You Are	6-440	MM
Joel, Billy	Keeping The Faith	48-9	SC
Joel, Billy	Leave A Tender Moment Alone	12-273	DK
Joel, Billy	Leave A Tender Moment Alone	6-555	MM
Joel, Billy	Longest Time the	16-140	LE
Joel, Billy	Longest Time the	6-543	MM
Joel, Billy	Lullabye Goodnight My Angel	12-269	DK
Joel, Billy	Lullabye Goodnight My Angel	2-120	SC
Joel, Billy	Movin' Out (Anthony's Song)	12-279	DK
Joel, Billy	Movin' Out (Anthony's Song)	16-136	LE
Joel, Billy	My Life	16-138	LE
Joel, Billy	My Life	5-116	SC
Joel, Billy	New York State Of Mind	33-298	CB
Joel, Billy	New York State Of Mind	16-133	LE
Joel, Billy	Only The Good Die Young	12-280	DK
Joel, Billy	Only The Good Die Young	16-143	LE
Joel, Billy	Only The Good Die Young	6-550	MM
Joel, Billy	Piano Man	34-62	CB
Joel, Billy	Piano Man	12-276	DK
Joel, Billy	Piano Man	16-148	LE

ARTIST	SONG TITLE	#	TYPE
Joel, Billy	Piano Man	6-541	MM
Joel, Billy	Pressure	5-379	SC
Joel, Billy	Rebel Yell	47-150	SC
Joel, Billy	Rebel Yell	47-145	DM
Joel, Billy	River Of Dreams	12-270	DK
Joel, Billy	River Of Dreams	16-137	LE
Joel, Billy	River Of Dreams	6-361	MM
Joel, Billy	River Of Dreams	2-230	SC
Joel, Billy	Say Goodbye To Hollywood	12-802	P
Joel, Billy	Scenes From An Italian Restaurant	16-135	LE
Joel, Billy	Scenes From An Italian Restaurant	20-367	SC
Joel, Billy	Scream	47-146	LE
Joel, Billy	Shameless	48-10	SC
Joel, Billy	She's Always A Woman	12-281	DK
Joel, Billy	She's Always A Woman	6-549	MM
Joel, Billy	Shock To The System	47-149	NT
Joel, Billy	Stiletto	5-687	SC
Joel, Billy	Stranger the	48-11	SC
Joel, Billy	Sweet Sixteen	47-151	ZM
Joel, Billy	Tell Her About It	35-170	CB
Joel, Billy	Tell Her About It	16-145	LE
Joel, Billy	Tell Her About It	16-516	P
Joel, Billy	Tell Her About It	21-615	SF
Joel, Billy	Uptown Girl	34-75	CB
Joel, Billy	Uptown Girl	12-272	DK
Joel, Billy	Uptown Girl	21-750	MH
Joel, Billy	Vienna	9-385	AH
Joel, Billy	We Didn't Start The Fire	34-97	CB
Joel, Billy	We Didn't Start The Fire	12-267	DK
Joel, Billy	We Didn't Start The Fire	16-142	LE
Joel, Billy	We Didn't Start The Fire	14-579	SC
Joel, Billy	You May Be Right	16-146	LE
Joel, Billy	You May Be Right	6-546	MM
Joey & Rory	Cheater Cheater	45-812	CB
Joey & Rory	Duet - Play The Song	45-813	BKD
Joey & Rory	Duet - This Song's For You	45-815	CB
Joey & Rory	Duet - When I'm Gone	45-817	BKD
Joey & Rory	Love Your Man	45-816	BKD
Joey & Rory	Play The Song - duet	45-813	BKD
Joey & Rory	That's Important To Me	45-818	BKD
Joey & Rory	This Song's For You - duet	45-815	CB
Joey & Rory	To Say Goodbye	45-814	BKD
Joey & Rory	When I'm Gone - duet	45-817	BKD
John Fred & Playboy Band	Judy In Disguise	48-582	DK
John, E & Clapton	Duet - Runaway Train	24-25	SC
John, E & Clapton	Runaway Train	24-25	SC
John, E & Dee, Kiki	Don't Go Breakin' My Heart	6-334	MM
John, E & Dee, Kiki	Don't Go Breakin' My Heart	13-253	P
John, E & Dee, Kiki	Don't Go Breakin' My Heart	4-757	SC

ARTIST	SONG TITLE	#	TYPE
John, E & Dee, Kiki	Duet - Don't Go Breakin' My Heart	6-334	MM
John, E & Dee, Kiki	Duet - Don't Go Breakin' My Heart	13-252	P
John, E & Dee, Kiki	Duet - Don't Go Breakin' My Heart	4-757	SC
John, E & Dee, Kiki	Duet - True Love	24-148	SC
John, E & Dee, Kiki	True Love	24-148	SC
John, E & Rimes	Duet - Written In The Stars	16-204	PHT
John, E & Rimes	Duet - Written In The Stars	13-712	SGB
John, E & Rimes	Written In The Stars	16-204	PHT
John, E & Rimes	Written In The Stars	13-713	SGB
John, E & Rupaul	Don't Go Breakin' My Heart	4-278	SC
John, E & Rupaul	Duet - Don't Go Breakin' My Heart	4-278	SC
John, Elton	Believe	12-75	DK
John, Elton	Bennie & The Jets	11-92	DK
John, Elton	Bennie & The Jets	12-680	P
John, Elton	Bitch Is Back the **	6-490	MM
John, Elton	Bitch Is Back the **	2-380	SC
John, Elton	Blessed	13-596	P
John, Elton	Blessed	4-679	SC
John, Elton	Can You Feel The Love Tonight	11-67	JTG
John, Elton	Candle In The Wind	33-327	CB
John, Elton	Candle In The Wind	11-295	DK
John, Elton	Candle In The Wind	16-521	P
John, Elton	Candle In The Wind	2-378	SC
John, Elton	Club At The End Of The Street	2-373	SC
John, Elton	Come Down In Time	48-396	DCK
John, Elton	Crocodile Rock	11-123	DK
John, Elton	Crocodile Rock	12-823	P
John, Elton	Daniel	16-849	DK
John, Elton	Daniel	3-241	LG
John, Elton	Daniel	12-679	P
John, Elton	Daniel	9-655	SAV
John, Elton	Daniel	2-376	SC
John, Elton	Don't Let The Sun Go Down On Me	6-98	MM
John, Elton	Don't Let The Sun Go Down On Me	13-310	P
John, Elton	Don't Let The Sun So Down On Me	17-552	DK
John, Elton	Friends	2-382	SC
John, Elton	Friends Never Say Goodbye	14-25	THM
John, Elton	Funeral For A Friend/Lover	9-381	AH
John, Elton	Goodbye England's Rose (Diana)	12-933	CB
John, Elton	Goodbye Yellow Brick Road	11-208	DK
John, Elton	Goodbye Yellow Brick Road	12-822	P
John, Elton	Goodbye Yellow Brick Road	9-656	SAV

ARTIST	SONG TITLE	#	TYPE
John, Elton	Goodbye Yellow Brick Road	5-377	SC
John, Elton	Goodbye Yellow Brock Road	34-29	CB
John, Elton	Healing Hands	2-381	SC
John, Elton	Honky Cat	15-179	MH
John, Elton	I Don't Wanna Go On With You Like	6-545	MM
John, Elton	I Don't Wanna Go On With You Like..	2-372	SC
John, Elton	I Don't Want To Go On Without You	17-553	DK
John, Elton	I Guess That's Why They Call It The Blues	17-554	DK
John, Elton	I Guess That's Why They Call It The Blues	13-312	P
John, Elton	I Guess That's Why They Call It The Blues	2-379	SC
John, Elton	I Want Love	25-19	MM
John, Elton	I Want Love	16-84	ST
John, Elton	I'm Still Standing	13-309	P
John, Elton	Island Girl	15-511	CMC
John, Elton	Island Girl	20-364	SC
John, Elton	Kiss The Bride	2-861	SC
John, Elton	Last Song the	9-40	MM
John, Elton	Levon	6-548	MM
John, Elton	Levon	2-375	SC
John, Elton	Little Jeannie	35-151	CB
John, Elton	Little Jeannie	2-384	SC
John, Elton	Looking Up	47-699	DCK
John, Elton	Love Lies Bleeding	13-670	SGB
John, Elton	Made In England	3-437	SC
John, Elton	Madman Across The Water	46-132	SC
John, Elton	Mama Can't Buy You Love	9-894	SAV
John, Elton	One the	12-243	DK
John, Elton	One the	13-308	P
John, Elton	One the	9-837	SAV
John, Elton	Philadelphia Freedom	17-555	DK
John, Elton	Philadelphia Freedom	6-554	MM
John, Elton	Philadelphia Freedom	17-459	SC
John, Elton	Rocket Man	34-41	CB
John, Elton	Rocket Man	17-404	DK
John, Elton	Rocket Man	16-399	PR
John, Elton	Sacrifice	13-313	P
John, Elton	Sacrifice	2-377	SC
John, Elton	Sad Songs (Say So Much)	30-3	DK
John, Elton	Sad Songs Say So Much	13-311	P
John, Elton	Sad Songs Say So Much	2-385	SC
John, Elton	Saturday Night's Alright For Fighting	11-525	DK
John, Elton	Saturday Night's Alright For Fighting	13-137	P
John, Elton	Simple Life	6-92	MM
John, Elton	Simple Life	9-673	SAV
John, Elton	Something About The Way	7-686	PHM

ARTIST	SONG TITLE	#	TYPE
John, Elton	Sorry Seems To Be The Hardest...	34-45	CB
John, Elton	Sorry Seems To Be The Hardest...	2-386	SC
John, Elton	This Train Don't Stop	25-138	MM
John, Elton	Tiny Dancer	6-542	MM
John, Elton	Tiny Dancer	2-374	SC
John, Elton	Wake Up Wendy	13-719	SGB
John, Elton	Xmas - Step Into Christmas	13-314	P
John, Elton	Xmas - Step Into Christmas	14-531	SC
John, Elton	Xmas - Who'd Be a Turkey at Xmas	5-720	SC
John, Elton	You Can Make History Young Again	24-368	SC
John, Elton	Your Song	11-103	DK
John, Elton	Your Song	3-240	LG
John, Elton	Your Song	12-691	P
John, Elton	Your Song	2-383	SC
John, Fred	Judy In Disguise With Glasses	35-99	CB
John, Fred	Judy In Disguise With Glasses	11-561	DK
John, Robert	Sad Eyes	35-157	CB
John, Robert	Sad Eyes	11-410	DK
Johnnie & Joe	Over The Mountain, Across the Sea	7-263	MM
Johnny Hates Jazz	Shattered Dreams	3-444	SC
Johns, Sammy	Chevy Van	14-561	AH
Johns, Sammy	Chevy Van	20-46	SC
Johns, Sarah	One In The Middle the	30-480	CB
Johnson, Carolyn D.	Complicated	14-843	ST
Johnson, Carolyn D.	Complicated	33-157	CB
Johnson, Carolyn D.	Georgia	14-136	CB
Johnson, Carolyn D.	Georgia	22-577	ST
Johnson, Carolyn D.	Georgia	14-35	THM
Johnson, Carolyn D.	Got A Good Day	30-363	CB
Johnson, Carolyn D.	I Don't Want You To Go	25-70	MM
Johnson, Carolyn D.	I Don't Want You To Go	16-96	ST
Johnson, Carolyn D.	I Don't Want You To Go	34-339	CB
Johnson, Carolyn D.	Love And Negotiation	30-48	CB
Johnson, Carolyn D.	One Day Closer To You	18-128	ST
Johnson, Carolyn D.	Simple Life	20-264	SC
Johnson, Carolyn D.	Simple Life	19-689	ST
Johnson, Carolyn D.	Taking Back My Brave	30-116	CB
Johnson, J	Bubbletoes	32-63	THM
Johnson, J.	Horizon Has Been Defeated the	32-257	THM
Johnson, Jack	Banana Pancakes	48-704	BKD
Johnson, Jack	Breakdown	29-281	PHM
Johnson, Jack	Flake	25-310	MM
Johnson, Jack	Upside Down	29-214	PHM
Johnson, Jack	Upside Down	30-769	SF
Johnson, Jamey	Dollar the	23-473	CB
Johnson, Jamey	Dollar the	29-854	SC
Johnson, Jamey	Living For A Song	39-87	PHN
Johnson, Jamey	Ray Ray's Juke Joint	48-508	KVD

ARTIST	SONG TITLE	#	TYPE
Johnson, Jamey	Rebelicious	29-577	CB
Johnson, Lonnie	Sucu Sucu	29-821	SF
Johnson, Lonnie	Tomorrow Night	10-399	SS
Johnson, Mary	You Got What It Takes	6-568	MM
Johnson, Michael	Bluer Than Blue	20-44	SC
Johnson, Michael	Give Me Wings	34-275	CB
Johnson, Michael	Give Me Wings	11-706	DK
Johnson, Michael	Give Me Wings	20-14	SC
Johnson, Michael	Moon Is Still Over Her Shoulder the	29-653	SC
Johnson, Puff	Forever More	4-678	SC
Johnson, Puff	Over And Over	4-603	SC
Johnson, Robert	Sweet Home Chicago	7-225	MM
Johnson, S	Guess What	32-124	THM
JoJo	Anything	30-488	CB
JoJo	How To Touch A Girl	30-262	CB
JoJo	Not That Kinda Girl	22-361	CB
JoJo	Say Love	48-397	DCK
Jolie & The Wanted	I Would	14-155	CB
Jolie & The Wanted	I'm Beautiful (When I Look In ..Eye	15-337	CB
Jolson, Al	After You've Gone	29-473	LE
Jolson, Al	After You've Gone	12-942	PS
Jolson, Al	Anniversary Song	11-300	DK
Jolson, Al	Anniversary Song	12-509	P
Jolson, Al	Back In Your Own Backyard	12-934	PS
Jolson, Al	California Here I Come	29-469	LE
Jolson, Al	California Here I Come	12-935	PS
Jolson, Al	I'm Sitting On Top Of The World	29-470	LE
Jolson, Al	I'm Sitting On Top Of The World	12-936	PS
Jolson, Al	Let Me Sing And I'm Happy	12-937	PS
Jolson, Al	Liza (All The Clouds Float Away)	12-938	PS
Jolson, Al	My Mammy	29-472	LE
Jolson, Al	My Mammy	12-939	PS
Jolson, Al	Rock-A-Bye Your Baby	29-467	LE
Jolson, Al	Rock-A-Bye Your Baby With A Dixie	15-836	MM
Jolson, Al	Rock-A-Bye Your Baby With A Dixie	12-940	PS
Jolson, Al	Swanee	29-468	LE
Jolson, Al	Swanee	12-941	PS
Jolson, Al	Toot Toot Tootsie	29-471	LE
Jolson, Al	Toot Toot Tootsie Goodbye	12-943	PS
Jolson, Al	Toot Toot Tootsie Goodbye	21-1	SC
Jon B with Babyface	Duet - Someone To Love	3-436	SC
Jon B with Babyface	Someone To Love	3-436	SC
Jonas Brothers	Burnin' Up	36-488	CB
Jonas Brothers	Goodnight And Goodbye	36-538	WD
Jonas Brothers	Hello Beautiful	36-539	WD
Jonas Brothers	Hold On	36-455	CB
Jonas Brothers	Just Friends	36-541	WD

ARTIST	SONG TITLE	#	TYPE
Jonas Brothers	Kids Of The Future	36-545	WD
Jonas Brothers	Lovebug	36-518	CB
Jonas Brothers	Pushing Me Away	36-508	CB
Jonas Brothers	SOS	30-592	PHM
Jonas Brothers	Still In Love With You	36-543	WD
Jonas Brothers	Tonight	36-523	CB
Jonas Brothers	When You Look Me In The Eyes	36-451	CB
Jones & Jackson	Duet - Good Year For The Roses	49-184	SC
Jones & Jackson	Good Year For The Roses a - duet	49-184	SC
Jones & McClinton	Duet - You're the Reason Our Kids..	14-160	CB
Jones & McClinton	You're The Reason Our Kids R Ugly	14-160	CB
Jones & Paycheck	Duet - You Can Have Her	9-584	SAV
Jones & Paycheck	You Can Have Her	9-584	SAV
Jones & Wynette	Duet - Golden Ring	5-441	SC
Jones & Wynette	Duet - Near You	5-447	SC
Jones & Wynette	Duet - We Loved It Away	49-374	CB
Jones & Wynette	Duet - We're Gonna Hold On	8-122	CB
Jones & Wynette	Near You	5-447	SC
Jones & Wynette	We Loved It Away	49-374	CB
Jones & Wynette	We're Gonna Hold On	8-122	CB
Jones, Donell	You Know What's Up	9-339	PS
Jones, George	50,000 Names	20-585	CB
Jones, George	50,000 Names	16-697	ST
Jones, George	Bartender's Blues	15-821	CB
Jones, George	Bartender's Blues	6-771	MM
Jones, George	Choices	14-630	SC
Jones, George	Choices	22-436	ST
Jones, George	Cold Hard Truth the	14-701	CB
Jones, George	Cold Hard Truth the	5-832	SC
Jones, George	Door the	8-341	CB
Jones, George	Door the	4-822	SC
Jones, George	Girl I Used To Know a	19-403	SC
Jones, George	Good Year For The Roses a	4-637	SC
Jones, George	Grand Tour the	8-280	CB
Jones, George	Grand Tour the	7-116	MM
Jones, George	Grand Tour the	9-574	SAV
Jones, George	Grand Tour the	5-666	SC
Jones, George	He Stopped Loving Her Today	12-33	DK
Jones, George	He Stopped Loving Her Today	13-363	P
Jones, George	He Stopped Loving Her Today	9-515	SAV
Jones, George	Her Name Is ...	14-253	SC
Jones, George	High Tech Redneck	8-337	CB
Jones, George	High Tech Redneck	6-757	MM
Jones, George	Honky Tonk Myself To Death	8-342	CB
Jones, George	Honky Tonk Myself To Death	4-136	SC
Jones, George	Honky Tonk Song	4-456	SC

ARTIST	SONG TITLE	#	TYPE
Jones, George	I Always Get Lucky With You	5-396	SC
Jones, George	I Don't Need Your Rockin' Chair	33-115	CB
Jones, George	I Don't Need Your Rockin' Chair	2-641	SC
Jones, George	I'll Share My World With You	6-14	SC
Jones, George	I'm Ragged But I'm Right	49-644	VH
Jones, George	Just One More	4-800	SC
Jones, George	Love Bug	8-336	CB
Jones, George	Man He Was the	16-164	CB
Jones, George	Once You've Had The Best	8-347	CB
Jones, George	One I Loved Back Then the	4-653	SC
Jones, George	Our Bed Of Roses	49-350	CB
Jones, George	Pass Me By	47-741	SRK
Jones, George	Picture Of Me Without You	12-191	DK
Jones, George	Race Is On the	8-265	CB
Jones, George	Race Is On the	17-290	NA
Jones, George	Race Is On the	13-472	P
Jones, George	Race Is On the	9-506	SAV
Jones, George	Right Left Hand the	8-338	CB
Jones, George	She Loved A Lot In Her Time	8-346	CB
Jones, George	She Thinks I Still Care	8-339	CB
Jones, George	She Thinks I Still Care	11-818	DK
Jones, George	She Thinks I Still Care	8-631	SAV
Jones, George	She's My Rock	8-343	CB
Jones, George	Sinners And Saints	14-706	CB
Jones, George	Six Foot Deep, Six Foot Down	47-752	SRK
Jones, George	Somebody Wants Me Out Of The Way	47-731	SRK
Jones, George	Still Doin' Time	8-205	CB
Jones, George	Still Doin' Time	4-731	SC
Jones, George	Take Me	8-345	CB
Jones, George	Tell Me My Lying Eyes Are Wrong	6-90	SC
Jones, George	Tender Years	4-725	SC
Jones, George	Tennessee Whiskey	34-260	CB
Jones, George	Tennessee Whiskey	14-321	SC
Jones, George	Walk Through This World With Me	8-340	CB
Jones, George	Walk Through This World With Me	4-256	SC
Jones, George	Walls Can Fall	24-11	SC
Jones, George	What My Woman Can't Do	46-282	KV
Jones, George	When Did You Stop Loving Me	45-711	VH
Jones, George	When The Grass Grows Over Me	8-348	CB
Jones, George	When The Last Curtain Falls	49-349	CB
Jones, George	White Light'nin'	3-602	SC
Jones, George	Who's Gonna Fill Their	33-69	CB

ARTIST	SONG TITLE	#	TYPE
	Shoes		
Jones, George	Who's Gonna Fill Their Shoes	4-729	SC
Jones, George	Why Baby Why	4-726	SC
Jones, George	Window Up Above the	4-730	SC
Jones, George	Wine Colored Roses	8-335	CB
Jones, George	Writing On The Wall	8-344	CB
Jones, George	Wrong's What I Do Best	24-83	SC
Jones, George	You Comb Her Hair	20-643	SC
Jones, George	You Never Know Just How Good You've..	49-348	CB
Jones, George	You're Still On My Mind	49-90	YBK
Jones, Grandpa	Mountain Dew	8-257	CB
Jones, Howard	Everlasting Love	21-738	MH
Jones, Howard	Lift Me Up	4-282	SC
Jones, Howard	Things Can Only Get Better	16-641	MM
Jones, Jack	Day In The Life Of A Fool a	29-485	LE
Jones, Jack	Good Times	17-336	DK
Jones, Jack	Impossible Dream the	29-484	LE
Jones, Jack	Lady	29-486	LE
Jones, Jack	Love Boat Theme	29-488	LE
Jones, Jack	Somewhere My Love	19-785	SGB
Jones, Jack	Windmills Of Your Mind	12-487	P
Jones, Jack	Wives And Lovers	29-487	LE
Jones, Jesus	Right Here Right Now	12-38	DK
Jones, Jesus	Right Here Right Now	5-345	SC
Jones, Jiggley	Baby Blue	41-102	PHN
Jones, Jimmy	Good Timin'	11-364	DK
Jones, Jimmy	Good Timin'	29-815	SF
Jones, Jimmy	Handy Man	5-170	SC
Jones, Joe	You Talk Too Much	3-285	MM
Jones, Joe	You Talk Too Much	3-578	SC
Jones, Kacey	Show Up Naked Bring Beer	47-501	KAC
Jones, Norah	Cold Cold Heart	19-184	Z
Jones, Norah	Come Away With Me	35-249	CB
Jones, Norah	Come Away With Me	25-406	MM
Jones, Norah	Come Away With Me	36-362	SC
Jones, Norah	Come Away With Me	19-337	STP
Jones, Norah	Come Away With Me	32-133	THM
Jones, Norah	Come Away With Me	19-186	Z
Jones, Norah	Don't Know Why	33-436	CB
Jones, Norah	Don't Know Why	18-421	MM
Jones, Norah	Don't Know Why	32-50	THM
Jones, Norah	Don't Know Why	19-182	Z
Jones, Norah	Feelin' The Same Way	25-672	MM
Jones, Norah	Feelin' The Same Way	32-241	THM
Jones, Norah	Feelin' The Same Way	19-185	Z
Jones, Norah	I've Got To See You Again	25-676	MM
Jones, Norah	I've Got To See You Again	19-190	Z
Jones, Norah	Lonestar	19-189	Z
Jones, Norah	Long Day Is Over the	19-193	Z
Jones, Norah	Nightingale	19-192	Z
Jones, Norah	One Flight Down	19-191	Z

ARTIST	SONG TITLE	#	TYPE
Jones, Norah	Seven Years	19-183	Z
Jones, Norah	Shoot The Moon	19-187	Z
Jones, Norah	Sunrise	20-537	CB
Jones, Norah	Those Sweet Words	22-351	CB
Jones, Norah	Turn Me On	19-669	CB
Jones, Norah	Turn Me On	25-666	MM
Jones, Norah	Turn Me On	19-188	Z
Jones, Quincy	You Put A Move On My Heart	21-145	SC
Jones, Sarah	One In The Middle the	30-480	CB
Jones, Spike	Xmas - All I Want For Xmas Is My Tw	5-713	SC
Jones, Spike	Yes We Have No Bananas	17-417	DK
Jones, Tom	Black Betty	49-269	DFK
Jones, Tom	Delilah	12-9	DK
Jones, Tom	Detroit City	15-466	JTG
Jones, Tom	Give A Little Love	49-270	DFK
Jones, Tom	Green Green Grass Of Home	12-494	P
Jones, Tom	Green Green Grass Of Home	10-582	SF
Jones, Tom	Help Yourself	15-488	MM
Jones, Tom	I Who Have Nothing	18-44	MM
Jones, Tom	I'll Never Fall In Love	35-94	CB
Jones, Tom	I'll Never Fall In Love Again	27-552	DK
Jones, Tom	I'll Never Fall In Love Again	4-346	SC
Jones, Tom	I'll Never Fall In Love Again	10-628	SF
Jones, Tom	I'm Not Feelin' It No More	47-780	SRK
Jones, Tom	If I Only Knew	15-510	JTG
Jones, Tom	It's Not Unusual	13-300	P
Jones, Tom	Linda Lu	49-257	DFK
Jones, Tom	Love Me Tonight	12-655	P
Jones, Tom	Most Beautiful Girl the	25-270	MM
Jones, Tom	She's A Lady	33-281	CB
Jones, Tom	She's A Lady	12-149	DK
Jones, Tom	Thunderball	9-59	SC
Jones, Tom	What's New Pussycat	12-488	P
Jones, Tom	What's New Pussycat	4-44	SC
Jones, Tom	With These Hands	18-262	DK
Jones, Tom	With These Hands	15-586	PS
Joplin, Janis	Ball And Chain	15-221	LE
Joplin, Janis	Cry Baby	28-199	DK
Joplin, Janis	Cry Baby	7-482	MM
Joplin, Janis	Down On Me	15-220	LE
Joplin, Janis	Get It While You Can	15-223	LE
Joplin, Janis	Kizmic Blues	15-222	LE
Joplin, Janis	Little Girl Blue	49-752	KV
Joplin, Janis	Me & Bobby McGee	11-140	DK
Joplin, Janis	Me & Bobby McGee	9-309	STR
Joplin, Janis	Mercedes Benz	34-40	CB
Joplin, Janis	Mercedes Benz	10-673	HE
Joplin, Janis	Mercedes Benz	19-155	SGB
Joplin, Janis	Move Over	46-311	SC

ARTIST	SONG TITLE	#	TYPE
Joplin, Janis	One Good Man	46-307	SC
Joplin, Janis	Piece Of My Heart	14-641	SC
Joplin, Janis	Piece Of My Heart	28-201	SF
Joplin, Janis	Summertime	15-224	LE
Joplin, Janis	Try Just a Little Bit Harder	5-676	SC
Joplin, Janis	Turtle Blues	49-748	KV
Jordan, Montell	Falling	24-552	SC
Jordan, Montell	Get It On Tonight	15-328	PHM
Jordan, Montell	Get It On Tonight	5-897	SC
Jordan, Montell	This Is How We Do It	49-446	MM
Jordan, Sass	You Don't Have To Remind Me	24-556	SC
Joseph & Amazing	Show - Any Dream Will Do	10-374	KC
Joseph & Amazing	Show - Any Dream Will Do	5-659	SC
Joseph & Amazing	Show - Any Dream Will Do	18-631	STS
Joseph & Amazing	Show - Benjamin Calypso	18-640	STS
Joseph & Amazing	Show - Close Every Door To Me	18-636	STS
Joseph & Amazing	Show - Go Go Joseph	18-637	STS
Joseph & Amazing	Show - Jacob & Sons	18-632	STS
Joseph & Amazing	Show - Joseph's Coat	18-633	STS
Joseph & Amazing	Show - One More Angel In Heaven	18-634	STS
Joseph & Amazing	Show - Potiphar	18-635	STS
Joseph & Amazing	Show - Prologue	18-630	STS
Joseph & Amazing	Show - Song Of The King	18-638	STS
Joseph & Amazing	Show - Those Canaan Days	18-639	STS
Joseph & Amazing..	Show - Close Every Door To Me	18-195	PS
Josh Abbot Band	I'll Sing About Mine	40-26	PHM
Josh Abbott & Musgraves	Duet - Oh Tonight	45-436	CB
Josh Abbott & Musgraves	Oh Tonight - duet	45-436	CB
Journey	Any Way You Want It	4-871	SC
Journey	Don't Stop Believin'	4-82	SC
Journey	I'll Be Alright Without You	17-536	SC
Journey	Lights	14-576	SC
Journey	Lovin' Touchin' Squeezin'	15-166	MH
Journey	Lovin' Touchin' Squeezin'	3-531	SC
Journey	Message of Love	4-613	SC
Journey	Open Arms	10-360	KC
Journey	Open Arms	3-484	SC
Journey	Remember Me	13-707	SGB
Journey	Separate Ways (Worlds)	4-885	SC
Journey	When You Love A Woman	24-375	SC
Journey	Who's Crying Now	4-51	SC
Juanes & Furtado	Latino - Fotografia	23-238	AI

ARTIST	SONG TITLE	#	TYPE
Judas Priest	Breaking The Law	5-489	SC
Judas Priest	Green Manalishi (W/2-Pronged Crown)	21-760	SC
Judas Priest	You've Got Another Thing Comin'	23-55	MH
Judd & Keith	Duet - I Love Nascar	38-169	SC
Judd & Keith	I Love Nascar - duet	38-169	SC
Judd, Cledus T.	Cledus The Karaoke King	16-515	CB
Judd, Cledus T.	Coronary Life	16-506	CB
Judd, Cledus T.	Did I Shave My Back For This	16-513	CB
Judd, Cledus T.	Double D Cups - parody	47-874	HM
Judd, Cledus T.	Duet - Jackson (Alan That Is)	16-511	CB
Judd, Cledus T.	Every Bulb In The House Is Blown	16-512	CB
Judd, Cledus T.	Goodbye Squirrel (Parody)	16-265	TT
Judd, Cledus T.	Goodbye Squirrell	44-308	SBI
Judd, Cledus T.	Grandpa Got Runned Over/John Deere	16-514	CB
Judd, Cledus T.	Hip Hop To Honky Tonk	16-510	CB
Judd, Cledus T.	How Do You Milk A Cow	16-505	CB
Judd, Cledus T.	If George Strait Starts Dancing	45-735	VH
Judd, Cledus T.	If Shania Was Mine	16-502	CB
Judd, Cledus T.	Indian In-Laws (Parody)	16-270	TT
Judd, Cledus T.	It's A Great Day To Be A Guy	44-307	SBI
Judd, Cledus T.	Jackson (Alan That Is)	16-511	CB
Judd, Cledus T.	More Beaver (Parody)	16-273	TT
Judd, Cledus T.	My Cellmate Thinks I'm Sexy	35-419	CB
Judd, Cledus T.	My Cellmate Thinks I'm Sexy	14-164	CB
Judd, Cledus T.	My Cellmate Thinks I'm Sexy	15-136	SC
Judd, Cledus T.	Paycheck Woman	23-388	SC
Judd, Cledus T.	Shania I'm Broke	16-509	CB
Judd, Cledus T.	She's Got A Butt Bigger Than The..	16-507	CB
Judd, Cledus T.	She's Inflatable	16-504	CB
Judd, Cledus T.	Where The Grass Don't Grow	16-508	CB
Judd, Cledus T.	Wives Do It All The Time	16-503	CB
Judd, W & English	Duet - Healing	24-80	SC
Judd, W & English	Healing	24-80	SC
Judd, W & English, M	Duet - Healing	48-322	SC
Judd, W & English, M	Healing - duet	48-322	SC
Judd, W & Wynette, T	Duet - Girl Thang	48-319	MH
Judd, W & Wynette, T	Girl Thang - duet	48-319	MH
Judd, Wynonna	Always Will	8-104	CB
Judd, Wynonna	Attitude	29-21	CB
Judd, Wynonna	Burning Love	48-318	KV
Judd, Wynonna	Can't No Body Love You	22-523	ST

ARTIST	SONG TITLE	#	TYPE
	Like I Do		
Judd, Wynonna	Come Some Rainy Day	8-227	CB
Judd, Wynonna	Come Some Rainy Day	10-122	SC
Judd, Wynonna	Come Some Rainy Day	22-752	ST
Judd, Wynonna	Flies On The Butter	19-767	ST
Judd, Wynonna	Freedom	8-863	CB
Judd, Wynonna	Girls With Guitars	1-654	CB
Judd, Wynonna	Girls With Guitars	6-586	MM
Judd, Wynonna	Girls With Guitars	2-324	SC
Judd, Wynonna	Going Nowhere	22-565	ST
Judd, Wynonna	Heaven Help Me	19-532	ST
Judd, Wynonna	Heaven Help My Heart	1-656	CB
Judd, Wynonna	Heaven Help My Heart	7-243	MM
Judd, Wynonna	I Hear You Knocking	48-317	CB
Judd, Wynonna	I Saw The Light	1-647	CB
Judd, Wynonna	I Saw The Light	7-747	CHM
Judd, Wynonna	I Saw The Light	13-506	P
Judd, Wynonna	I Saw The Light	2-511	SC
Judd, Wynonna	Is It Over Yet	1-652	CB
Judd, Wynonna	It's Never Easy To Say Goodbye	48-321	SC
Judd, Wynonna	Let's Make A Baby King	6-478	MM
Judd, Wynonna	Little Bit Of Love	6-194	MM
Judd, Wynonna	My Angel Is Here	1-657	CB
Judd, Wynonna	My Angel Is Here	4-363	SC
Judd, Wynonna	My Strongest Weakness	1-649	CB
Judd, Wynonna	My Strongest Weakness	6-223	MM
Judd, Wynonna	No One Else On Earth	1-648	CB
Judd, Wynonna	No One Else On Earth	19-294	MH
Judd, Wynonna	No One Else On Earth	6-107	MM
Judd, Wynonna	No One Else On Earth	13-505	P
Judd, Wynonna	No One Else On Earth	2-715	SC
Judd, Wynonna	Only Love	1-651	CB
Judd, Wynonna	Only Love	6-405	MM
Judd, Wynonna	Rock Bottom	6-497	MM
Judd, Wynonna	Rock Bottom	12-413	P
Judd, Wynonna	She Is His Only Need	1-646	CB
Judd, Wynonna	She Is His Only Need	6-198	MM
Judd, Wynonna	She Is His Only Need	13-336	P
Judd, Wynonna	She Is His Only Need	2-801	SC
Judd, Wynonna	Sing	49-419	BKD
Judd, Wynonna	Sing	48-316	CB
Judd, Wynonna	Somebody To Love You	22-916	ST
Judd, Wynonna	Tell Me Why	1-650	CB
Judd, Wynonna	Tell Me Why	18-249	DK
Judd, Wynonna	Tell Me Why	6-314	MM
Judd, Wynonna	Tell Me Why	12-412	P
Judd, Wynonna	Tell Me Why	2-818	SC
Judd, Wynonna	Testify To Love	48-320	SC
Judd, Wynonna	To Be Loved By You	1-655	CB
Judd, Wynonna	To Be Loved By You	4-126	SC
Judd, Wynonna	What The World Needs	25-606	MM
Judd, Wynonna	What The World Needs	19-69	ST
Judd, Wynonna	When Love Starts Talkin'	8-130	CB
Judd, Wynonna	When Love Starts Talkin'	22-654	ST

ARTIST	SONG TITLE	#	TYPE
Judd, Wynonna	Why Not Me	13-396	P
Judd, Wynonna	Without Your Love I'm Going Nowhere	14-80	CB
Judd, Wynonna	Woman To Woman	8-186	CB
Judd, Wynonna	Woman To Woman	22-680	ST
Judd, Wynonna	Xmas - Let's Make A Baby King	15-662	THM
Judds	Born To Be Blue	6-537	MM
Judds	Cathy's Clown	9-447	SAV
Judds	Change Of Heart	1-142	CB
Judds	Change Of Heart	2-618	SC
Judds	Don't Be Cruel	5-401	SC
Judds	Girl's Night Out	1-143	CB
Judds	Girls Night Out	13-330	P
Judds	Girls Night Out	2-101	SC
Judds	Give a Little Love	1-144	CB
Judds	Give A Little Love	12-58	DK
Judds	Give A Little Love	9-503	SAV
Judds	Grandpa (Tell Me 'Bout The...)	1-136	CB
Judds	Grandpa (Tell Me 'Bout The...)	11-202	DK
Judds	Grandpa (Tell Me 'Bout The...)	13-360	P
Judds	Had A Dream (For The Heart)	19-437	SC
Judds	Have Mercy	1-137	CB
Judds	Have Mercy	11-707	DK
Judds	Have Mercy	12-470	P
Judds	Have Mercy	9-507	SAV
Judds	I Know Where I'm Going	1-138	CB
Judds	I Know Where I'm Going	4-789	SC
Judds	John Deere Tractor	17-242	NA
Judds	Let Me Tell You About Love	1-145	CB
Judds	Let Me Tell You About Love	9-441	SAV
Judds	Love Can Build A Bridge	1-139	CB
Judds	Love Can Build A Bridge	12-39	DK
Judds	Love Can Build A Bridge	6-203	MM
Judds	Love Is Alive	1-146	CB
Judds	Love Is Alive	9-528	SAV
Judds	Mama He's Crazy	1-140	CB
Judds	Mama He's Crazy	13-362	P
Judds	Mama He's Crazy	8-704	SAV
Judds	Maybe Your Baby's Got the Blues	1-147	CB
Judds	Maybe Your Baby's Got The Blues	9-496	SAV
Judds	One Hundred And Two	12-2	DK
Judds	One Hundred And Two	19-295	MH
Judds	One Hundred And Two	9-537	SAV
Judds	One Man Woman	2-369	SC
Judds	Only Love	12-484	P
Judds	Rockin' With The Rhythm of the Rain	1-148	CB
Judds	Rockin' With the Rhythm of the Rain	6-628	MM
Judds	Rockin' With the	5-16	SC

ARTIST	SONG TITLE	#	TYPE
	Rhythm of the Rain		
Judds	Stuck In Love	13-820	CHM
Judds	Turn It Loose	1-149	CB
Judds	Why Not Me	1-141	CB
Judds	Why Not Me	9-467	SAV
Judds	Xmas - Beautiful Star Of Bethlehem	15-652	THM
Judds	Xmas - What Child Is This	30-391	SC
Judds	Young Love	1-150	CB
Judds	Young Love	6-775	MM
Judds	Young Love	9-450	SAV
Jump 5	I've Got The Music In Me	48-584	DK
Jungle Book	Show - Bare Necessities	20-179	Z
Jungle Book	Show - I Wanna Be Like You	20-180	Z
Junior	Mama Used To Say - Pt. 1	15-31	SS
Junior	Mama Used To Say - Pt. 2	15-32	SS
Junior Senior	Move Your Feet	25-661	MM
Justice, Jimmy	When My Little Girl Is Smiling	10-623	SF
Juvenile&Little Way	Back That Thang Up	14-448	SC
Jypsi	I Don't Love You Like That	36-573	CB
Jypsi	Love Is A Drug	36-554	CB
K-Ci & JoJo	All My Life	10-22	SC
K-Ci & JoJo	Crazy	18-551	TT
K-Ci & JoJo	It's Me	32-53	THM
K-Ci & JoJo	This Very Moment	32-87	THM
K-Ci & JoJo	This Very Moment	20-467	CB
Kadison, Joshua	Beautiful In My Eyes	29-324	PS
Kadison, Joshua	Beautiful In My Eyes	2-223	SC
Kadison, Joshua	Picture Postcards From LA	2-469	SC
Kajagoogoo	Too Shy	21-401	SC
Kalapana	Hawaii - Naturally	6-840	MM
Kalapana	Naturally	6-840	MM
Kandi	Don't Think I'm Not	15-448	PHM
Kane, Christian	House Rules the	43-84	PHN
Kane, Christian	Let Me Go	43-85	CB
Kane, Eden	Boy's Cry	10-614	SF
Kane, Eden	Forget Me Not	29-823	SF
Kane, Helen	I Wanna Be Loved By You	12-544	P
Kansas	Carry On Wayward Son	4-47	SC
Kansas	Dust In The Wind	11-327	DK
Kansas	Fight Fire With Fire	37-70	SC
Kansas	Play The Game Tonight	17-528	SC
Kaoma	Lambada - Spanish	49-458	MM
Kaperton, Kaley	White Red & Beautiful	41-59	PHN
Kasino F	Nite And Day	48-569	DK
Kate & Leopold	Show - Until	18-680	PS
Katrina & Waves	That's The Way	9-857	SAV
Katrina & Waves	Walking On Sunshine	3-607	SC
Kaufman, Irving	Hail Hail The Gang's All Here	34-443	CB

ARTIST	SONG TITLE	#	TYPE
Kaye, Danny	Five Pennies Saints the	48-467	TDS
Kaye, Danny	Kids - Ugly Duckling	48-466	SBI
Kaye, Danny	Thumbelina	48-429	VH
Kaye, Danny	Ugly Duckling - kids	48-466	SBI
KC & Sunshine Band	Get Down Tonight	13-251	P
KC & Sunshine Band	Get Down Tonight	2-501	SC
KC & Sunshine Band	I'm Your Boogie Man	35-146	CB
KC & Sunshine Band	I'm Your Boogie Man	2-493	SC
KC & Sunshine Band	I'm Your Boogie Man	49-314	CB
KC & Sunshine Band	Please Don't Go	24-333	SC
KC & Sunshine Band	Shake Shake Shake	4-60	SC
KC & Sunshine Band	That's The Way I Like It	15-568	CMC
KC & Sunshine Band	That's The Way I Like It	17-129	DK
Keane	Bedshaped	21-690	Z
Keane	Can't Stop Now	21-688	Z
Keane	Somewhere Only We Know	21-687	Z
Keane	Sunshine	21-691	Z
Keane	This Is The Last Time	21-692	Z
Keane	Your Eyes Open	21-689	Z
Kearney, Mat	Breathe In Breathe Out	49-886	SC
Kearney, Mat	Closer To Love	36-297	PHM
Kearney, Mat	One Black Sheep	48-401	DCK
Keating, Ronan	Lovin' Each Day	23-95	SC
Keith	98.6	9-705	SAV
Keith	98.6	5-514	SC
Keith & Buffett	Duet - Piece Of Work	30-17	SC
Keith & Buffett	Duet - Too Drunk To Karaoke	41-44	ASK
Keith & Buffett	Piece Of Work - duet	40-17	SC
Keith & Buffett	Too Drunk To Karaoke - duet	41-44	ASK
Keith & Haggard	Duet - She Ain't Hooked On Me...	49-778	SC
Keith & Haggard	She Ain't Hooked On Me No More	49-778	SC
Keith & Nelson	Beer For My Horses - duet	34-391	CB
Keith & Nelson	Duet - Beer For My Horses	23-391	CB
Keith, Toby	35 MPH Town	46-301	BKD
Keith, Toby	Ain't It Just Like You	47-157	CB
Keith, Toby	American Ride	38-157	CB
Keith, Toby	American Soldier	20-271	SC
Keith, Toby	American Soldier	19-700	ST
Keith, Toby	Angry American (Courtesy of...)	33-164	CB
Keith, Toby	As Good As I Once Was	23-133	CB
Keith, Toby	Baddest Boots	47-161	CB
Keith, Toby	Beautiful Stranger	49-675	KCD
Keith, Toby	Beer For My Horses	19-48	ST
Keith, Toby	Beer For My Horses	32-227	THM
Keith, Toby	Beers Ago	38-218	PHN
Keith, Toby	Big Blue Note	23-463	CB
Keith, Toby	Big Dog Daddy	40-28	SC
Keith, Toby	Big Ol' Truck	1-691	CB
Keith, Toby	Big Ol' Truck	6-820	MM
Keith, Toby	Big Ol' Truck	3-423	SC

ARTIST	SONG TITLE	#	TYPE	ARTIST	SONG TITLE	#	TYPE
Keith, Toby	Blame It On The Mistletoe	48-486	CKC	Keith, Toby	I Like Girls That Drink Beer	39-18	SB
Keith, Toby	Bullets In The Gun	38-162	PHM	Keith, Toby	I Love This Bar	35-422	CB
Keith, Toby	Cabo San Lucas	45-67	DFK	Keith, Toby	I Love This Bar	25-710	MM
Keith, Toby	Christmas Rock	45-752	CB	Keith, Toby	I Love This Bar	19-525	ST
Keith, Toby	Country Comes To Town	14-716	CB	Keith, Toby	I Love This Bar	32-414	THM
Keith, Toby	Country Comes To Town	13-833	CHM	Keith, Toby	I Wanna Talk About Me	33-137	CB
Keith, Toby	Country Comes To Town	19-246	CSZ	Keith, Toby	I Wanna Talk About Me	25-1	MM
Keith, Toby	Country Comes To Town	38-159	SC	Keith, Toby	I Wanna Talk About Me	15-669	ST
Keith, Toby	Courtest Of The Red White & Blue	33-164	CB	Keith, Toby	I'm Just Talkin' 'Bout Tonight	15-183	ST
Keith, Toby	Courtesy Of The Red White & Blue	17-564	ST	Keith, Toby	I'm So Happy I Can't Stop Cryin'	1-705	CB
Keith, Toby	Courtesy Of The Red, White & Blue	25-236	MM	Keith, Toby	If a Man Answers	8-913	CB
Keith, Toby	Crash Here Tonight	30-46	CB	Keith, Toby	If A Man Answers	22-730	ST
Keith, Toby	Cryin' For Me	38-156	AC	Keith, Toby	It's All Good	47-155	CB
Keith, Toby	Does That Blue Moon Ever Shine On You	1-692	CB	Keith, Toby	Just The Guy To Do It	47-153	AMM
Keith, Toby	Does That Blue Moon Ever Shine On You	7-208	MM	Keith, Toby	Knock Yourself Out	47-154	AMM
Keith, Toby	Does That Blue Moon Ever Shine On You	4-210	SC	Keith, Toby	Last Living Cowboy	45-65	KV
Keith, Toby	Don't Leave, I Think I Love You	47-160	CB	Keith, Toby	Little Less Talk Lot More Action	1-703	CB
Keith, Toby	Double Wide Paradise	1-693	CB	Keith, Toby	Little Less Talk Lot More Action	17-405	DK
Keith, Toby	Double Wide Paradise	5-292	SC	Keith, Toby	Little Less Talk Lot More Action	6-461	MM
Keith, Toby	Dream Walkin'	8-296	CB	Keith, Toby	Little Too Late a	29-590	CB
Keith, Toby	Drinks After Work	44-303	ASK	Keith, Toby	Little Too Late the	38-164	SC
Keith, Toby	Drunk Americans	45-66	BKD	Keith, Toby	Losing My Touch	47-156	CB
Keith, Toby	Get Drunk And Be Somebody	29-182	CB	Keith, Toby	Lost You Anyway	44-137	BKD
Keith, Toby	Get Drunk And Be Somebody	29-851	SC	Keith, Toby	Love Me If You Can	30-472	CB
Keith, Toby	Get Drunk And Be Somebody	29-706	ST	Keith, Toby	Made In America - Patriotic	38-165	PHM
Keith, Toby	Get My Drink On	36-422	CB	Keith, Toby	Me Too	1-697	CB
Keith, Toby	Get Out Of My Car	44-145	BKD	Keith, Toby	Me Too	7-581	CHM
Keith, Toby	Getcha Some	8-190	CB	Keith, Toby	Me Too	7-400	MM
Keith, Toby	Getcha Some	10-147	SC	Keith, Toby	Me Too	22-910	ST
Keith, Toby	Getcha Some	22-672	ST	Keith, Toby	My List	25-135	MM
Keith, Toby	Go With Her	23-33	SC	Keith, Toby	My List	16-97	ST
Keith, Toby	God Love Her	36-239	PHM	Keith, Toby	Nights I Can't Remember, Friends I'll...	47-162	CB
Keith, Toby	Good To Go To Mexico	47-158	CB	Keith, Toby	Note To Self	38-166	SC
Keith, Toby	Grain Of Salt	48-430	VH	Keith, Toby	Patriotic - Courtesy of the...	33-164	CB
Keith, Toby	He Ain't Worth Missing	6-384	MM	Keith, Toby	Patriotic - Made In America	38-165	PHM
Keith, Toby	Hell No	38-163	SC	Keith, Toby	RED SOLO CUP	38-155	AT
Keith, Toby	High Maintenance Woman	30-336	CB	Keith, Toby	Rock You Baby	34-389	CB
Keith, Toby	Honky Tonk U	22-17	CB	Keith, Toby	Rock You Baby	25-517	MM
Keith, Toby	Hope On The Rocks	40-46	ASK	Keith, Toby	Rock You Baby	38-167	SC
Keith, Toby	Hope On The Rocks	40-19	PHN	Keith, Toby	Rock You Baby	18-782	ST
Keith, Toby	How Do You Like Me Now	8-907	CB	Keith, Toby	Rock You Baby	32-118	THM
Keith, Toby	How Do You Like Me Now	22-534	ST	Keith, Toby	Rum Is The Reason	45-388	BKD
				Keith, Toby	She Ain't Hooked On Me No More	47-152	AMM
				Keith, Toby	She Never Cried In Front Of Me	47-163	CB
				Keith, Toby	She Never Cries In Front Of Me	36-609	CB
				Keith, Toby	She Never Cries In Front	36-204	PHM

ARTIST	SONG TITLE	#	TYPE
	of Me		
Keith, Toby	She's A Hottie	36-388	CB
Keith, Toby	Should've Been A Cowboy	1-698	CB
Keith, Toby	Should've Been A Cowboy	26-554	DK
Keith, Toby	Should've Been A Cowboy	6-397	MM
Keith, Toby	Should've Been A Cowboy	12-452	P
Keith, Toby	Should've Been A Cowboy	2-29	SC
Keith, Toby	Shut Up And Hold On	43-94	HM
Keith, Toby	Size I Wear the	47-165	KV
Keith, Toby	Stays In Mexico	23-394	CB
Keith, Toby	Stays In Mexico	30-12	SC
Keith, Toby	Stays In Mexico	20-487	ST
Keith, Toby	Sweet	47-159	CB
Keith, Toby	Taliban Song the	20-267	SC
Keith, Toby	That Don't Make Me A Bad Guy	47-164	CB
Keith, Toby	Time For Me To Ride	38-161	SC
Keith, Toby	Trailerhood	38-158	PHM
Keith, Toby	Upstairs Downtown	1-699	CB
Keith, Toby	Upstairs Downtown	6-719	MM
Keith, Toby	Upstairs Downtown	17-271	NA
Keith, Toby	Upstairs Downtown	2-575	SC
Keith, Toby	We Were In Love	1-700	CB
Keith, Toby	We Were In Love	7-661	CHM
Keith, Toby	We Were In Love	22-603	ST
Keith, Toby	Weed With Willie	20-274	SC
Keith, Toby	When Love Fades	5-796	SC
Keith, Toby	When Love Fades	22-380	ST
Keith, Toby	Whiskey Girl	20-253	PHM
Keith, Toby	Whiskey Girl	20-326	ST
Keith, Toby	Who's That Man	1-704	CB
Keith, Toby	Who's That Man	17-241	NA
Keith, Toby	Who's That Man	2-482	SC
Keith, Toby	Who's Your Daddy	33-184	CB
Keith, Toby	Who's Your Daddy	25-350	MM
Keith, Toby	Who's Your Daddy	18-204	ST
Keith, Toby	Wish I Didn't Know Now	1-701	CB
Keith, Toby	Wish I Didn't Know Now	12-454	P
Keith, Toby	Wish I Didn't Know Now...	2-359	SC
Keith, Toby	Woman's Touch a	7-333	MM
Keith, Toby	Woman's Touch a	4-418	SC
Keith, Toby	Xmas - Blame It On The Mistletoe	48-486	CKC
Keith, Toby	Xmas - Christmas Rock	45-752	CB
Keith, Toby	Xmas - Night Before Christmas the	30-388	SC
Keith, Toby	Xmas - Santa I'm Right Here	8-89	CB
Keith, Toby	You Ain't Much Fun	1-702	CB
Keith, Toby	You Ain't Much Fun	3-370	SC
Keith, Toby	You Can't Read My Mind	47-166	KV
Keith, Toby	You Caught Me At A	36-378	SC

ARTIST	SONG TITLE	#	TYPE
	Bad Time		
Keith, Toby	You Shouldn't Kiss Me Like This	14-157	CB
Keith, Toby	You Shouldn't Kiss Me Like This	14-18	CHM
Keith, Toby	You Shouldn't Kiss Me Like This	22-458	ST
Keith, Toby	You Shouldn't Kiss Me Like This	16-279	TT
Keith, Toby w/Nelso	Beer For My Horses	25-451	MM
Keith, Toby w/Sting	I'm So Happy I Can't Stop Cryin'	22-658	ST
Keith, Toby&Krystal	Duet - Mockingbird	21-661	SC
Keith, Toby&Krystal	Mockingbird	21-661	SC
Keller, Joanie	Three Little Teardrops	9-398	CB
Kelley, Josh	Amazing	32-247	THM
Kelley, Josh	Amazing	25-652	MM
Kelley, Josh	To Remember	36-255	PHM
Kelly Family	An Angel	49-717	KV
Kelly, Gene	Moses Supposes (Tongue Twister)	9-818	SAV
Kelly, Gene	Singin' In The Rain	11-816	DK
Kelly, Gene	Singin' In The Rain	25-266	MM
Kelly, Gene	Singin' In The Rain	12-508	P
Kelly, Kristen	Ex Old Man	39-36	ASK
Kelly, R	I Wish	35-252	CB
Kelly, R	Ignition	32-49	THM
Kelly, R.	Bad Man	20-7	SGB
Kelly, R.	Bump 'N Grind	2-473	SC
Kelly, R.	Down Low (Nobody Has To Know)	49-517	CB
Kelly, R.	Fiesta	18-555	TT
Kelly, R.	Gotham City	34-128	CB
Kelly, R.	Gotham City	10-109	SC
Kelly, R.	Happy People (Radio Vers)	49-531	SC
Kelly, R.	I Believe I Can Fly	11-77	JTG
Kelly, R.	I Believe I Can Fly	24-637	SC
Kelly, R.	I Can't Sleep Baby	49-521	SC
Kelly, R.	If I Could Turn Back The Hands..	49-516	CB
Kelly, R.	Ignition	25-721	MM
Kelly, R.	Ignition	19-344	STP
Kelly, R.	Ignition	32-49	THM
Kelly, R.	Step In The Name Of Love	49-520	SC
Kelly, R.	Storm Is Over the	16-260	TT
Kelly, R.	Summer Buddies	49-705	KV
Kelly, R.	When A Woman's Fed Up	49-519	PS
Kelly, R.	World's Greatest	33-413	CB
Kelly, R.	World's Greatest the	49-510	PHM
Kelly, R.	You Remind Me Of Something	49-518	CB
Kelly, Tori	Dear No One	48-649	DCK
Kelly, Tori	Funny	48-677	DCK
Kelly, Tori	Hollow	48-640	KV
Kelly, Tori	Nobody Love	48-648	BKD
Kelly, Tori	Should've Been Us	48-647	BKD

ARTIST	SONG TITLE	#	TYPE
Kelly&P Diddy&Les	Shake Ya Tailfeather (Radio Version	21-790	SC
Kem	Love Calls	32-421	THM
Kemp, Johnny	Just Got Paid	18-369	AH
Kendall, Jeannie	That's What Your Love Does To Me	20-218	CB
Kendalls	Heaven's Just A Sin Away	3-593	SC
Kendalls	It Don't Feel Like Sinning To Me	5-540	SC
Kendalls	Put It Off Until Tomorrow	9-604	SAV
Kendalls	Sweet Desire	5-403	SC
Kendalls	Thank God For The Radio	29-654	SC
Kendalls	You'd Make An Angel Want To Cheat	20-675	SC
Kendrick, Anna	Cups (When I'm Gone)	42-13	PHM
Kendricks, Eddie	Boogie Down	14-899	DK
Kendricks, Eddie	Keep On Truckin'	14-898	DK
Kenner, Chris	I Like It Like That	3-585	SC
Kenny G	Don't Make Me Wait For Love	49-746	KRG
Kentucky HH	Dumas Walker	2-27	SC
Kentucky HH	Oh Lonesome Me	8-598	TT
Kentucky HH	Spirit In The Sky	49-706	KV
Kentucky HH	Too Much To Lose	14-147	CB
Kentucky HH	Walk Softly On This Heart Of Mine	6-765	MM
Kentucky HH	Walk Softly On This Heart Of Mine	17-310	NA
Kentucky HH	Walk Softly On This Heart Of Mine	2-619	SC
Kernaghan, Lee	Ute Me	39-98	PHN
Kersh, David	Another You	14-653	CB
Kersh, David	Another You	22-408	CHM
Kersh, David	Day In Day Out	22-608	ST
Kersh, David	Goodnight Sweetheart	4-421	SC
Kersh, David	If I Never Stop Lovin' You	22-772	ST
Kersh, David	If I Never Stop Loving You	8-237	CB
Kersh, David	If I Never Stop Loving You	7-732	CHM
Kersh, David	If I Never Stop Loving You	10-128	SC
Kersh, David	Wonderful Tonight	8-482	CB
Kershaw & Morgan	Duet - He Drinks Tequila	30-31	CB
Kershaw & Morgan	Duet - He Drinks Tequila	14-838	ST
Kershaw & Morgan	Duet - He Drinks Tequila	16-267	TT
Kershaw & Morgan	Duet - I Finally Found Someone	17-482	CB
Kershaw & Morgan	Duet - Maybe Not Tonight	8-924	CB
Kershaw & Morgan	He Drinks Tequila	30-31	CB
Kershaw & Morgan	He Drinks Tequila	14-838	ST
Kershaw & Morgan	He Drinks Tequila	16-267	TT
Kershaw & Morgan	He Drinks Tequila - duet	30-31	CB
Kershaw & Morgan	I Finally Found Someone	17-483	CB

ARTIST	SONG TITLE	#	TYPE
Kershaw & Morgan	Maybe Not Tonight	8-924	CB
Kershaw, Doug	Diggy Liggy Lo	44-53	KV
Kershaw, Sammy	Anywhere But Here	2-355	SC
Kershaw, Sammy	Beer Bait And Ammo	22-1	CB
Kershaw, Sammy	Cadillac Style	1-466	CB
Kershaw, Sammy	Cadillac Style	13-512	P
Kershaw, Sammy	Double Wide Paradise	22-797	ST
Kershaw, Sammy	Haunted Heart	20-406	MH
Kershaw, Sammy	Honky Tonk America	1-479	CB
Kershaw, Sammy	Honky Tonk America	22-813	ST
Kershaw, Sammy	I Can't Reach Her Anymore	1-470	CB
Kershaw, Sammy	I Can't Reach Her Anymore	6-479	MM
Kershaw, Sammy	I Know A Little	24-6	SC
Kershaw, Sammy	I Want My Money Back	25-526	MM
Kershaw, Sammy	I Want My Money Back	18-789	ST
Kershaw, Sammy	I Want My Money Back	32-151	THM
Kershaw, Sammy	If You're Gonna Walk I'm Gonna..	2-694	SC
Kershaw, Sammy	If You're Gonna Walk I'm Gonna...	1-474	CB
Kershaw, Sammy	Louisiana Hot Sauce	14-117	CB
Kershaw, Sammy	Love Of My Life	8-139	CB
Kershaw, Sammy	Love Of My Life	22-414	ST
Kershaw, Sammy	Matches	22-788	ST
Kershaw, Sammy	Matches	8-462	CB
Kershaw, Sammy	Matches	7-737	CHM
Kershaw, Sammy	Me And Maxine	22-478	ST
Kershaw, Sammy	Meant To Be	1-475	CB
Kershaw, Sammy	Meant To Be	7-229	MM
Kershaw, Sammy	National Working Woman's Holiday	6-589	MM
Kershaw, Sammy	National Working Woman's Holiday...	1-471	CB
Kershaw, Sammy	One Day Left To Live	1-480	CB
Kershaw, Sammy	One Day Left To Live	22-691	ST
Kershaw, Sammy	Politics Religion And Her	24-647	SC
Kershaw, Sammy	Politics Religion And Her	22-919	ST
Kershaw, Sammy	Queen Of My Double-Wide Trailer	1-469	CB
Kershaw, Sammy	Queen Of My Double-Wide Trailer	3-637	SC
Kershaw, Sammy	She Don't Know She's Beautiful	1-468	CB
Kershaw, Sammy	She Don't Know She's Beautiful	6-305	MM
Kershaw, Sammy	Southbound	1-473	CB
Kershaw, Sammy	Southbound	6-716	MM
Kershaw, Sammy	Southbound	17-272	NA
Kershaw, Sammy	Southbound	2-539	SC
Kershaw, Sammy	Still Lovin' You	4-25	SC
Kershaw, Sammy	Tennessee Girl	30-92	CB
Kershaw, Sammy	Third Rate Romance	1-472	CB
Kershaw, Sammy	Third Rate Romance	17-230	NA
Kershaw, Sammy	Third Rate Romance	2-798	SC
Kershaw, Sammy	Vidalia	1-476	CB

ARTIST	SONG TITLE	#	TYPE
Kershaw, Sammy	Vidalia	7-273	MM
Kershaw, Sammy	Vidalia	4-425	SC
Kershaw, Sammy	When You Love Someone	22-487	ST
Kershaw, Sammy	Xmas - Daddy Stuff	8-88	CB
Kershaw, Sammy	Yard Sale	1-467	CB
Kershaw, Sammy	Yard Sale	3-372	SC
Kershaw, Sammy	Your Tattoo	7-83	MM
Ketchum, Hal	Girl Like You a	8-178	CB
Ketchum, Hal	Hang In There Superman	4-399	SC
Ketchum, Hal	Hearts Are Gonna Roll	12-466	P
Ketchum, Hal	Hearts Are Gonna Roll	2-341	SC
Ketchum, Hal	I Know Where Love Lives	12-424	P
Ketchum, Hal	I Miss My Mary	4-461	SC
Ketchum, Hal	I Saw The Light	8-464	CB
Ketchum, Hal	Just This Side Of Heaven - Hal-lelu	29-200	CB
Ketchum, Hal	Mama Knows The Highway	10-776	JVC
Ketchum, Hal	My Love Will Not Change	20-450	ST
Ketchum, Hal	Past The Point Of Rescue	4-150	SC
Ketchum, Hal	She Is	15-104	ST
Ketchum, Hal	Small Town Saturday Night	13-470	P
Ketchum, Hal	Someplace Far Away	24-354	SC
Ketchum, Hal	Stay Forever	2-652	SC
Ketchum, Hal	That's What I Get	2-799	SC
Ketchum, Hal	Tonight We Just Might Fall In Love	6-590	MM
Ketchum, Hal	Tonight We Just Might Fall In Love	17-222	NA
Ketchum, Hal	Veil Of Tears	3-633	SC
Keys, Alicia	Diary	35-253	CB
Keys, Alicia	Fallin'	35-228	CB
Keys, Alicia	Fallin'	23-585	PHM
Keys, Alicia	Fallin'	16-379	SGB
Keys, Alicia	Fallin'	18-513	TT
Keys, Alicia	How Come You Don't Call Me	18-352	CB
Keys, Alicia	How Come You Don't Call Me	25-211	MM
Keys, Alicia	How Come You Don't Call Me	17-594	PHM
Keys, Alicia	If I Ain't Got You	20-531	CB
Keys, Alicia	If I Ain't Got You	23-250	THM
Keys, Alicia	Like You'll Never See Me Again	36-449	CB
Keys, Alicia	Like You'll Never See Me Again	49-893	SC
Keys, Alicia	No One	36-480	CB
Keys, Alicia	Teenage Love Affair	36-507	CB
Keys, Alicia	Woman's Worth a	33-390	CB
Keys, Alicia	Woman's Worth a	25-31	MM
Keys, Alicia & Eve	Gansta' Lovin'	25-467	MM
Keys, Alicia & Usher	My Boo	37-97	SC

ARTIST	SONG TITLE	#	TYPE
Khan, Chaka	Ain't Nobody	15-43	SS
Khan, Chaka	I Feel For You	16-875	DK
Khan, Chaka	Sweet Thing	27-296	DK
Kid & Pirates	I'll Never Get Over You	29-818	SF
Kid & Pirates	Shakin' All Over	10-551	SF
Kid Rock	All Summer Long	36-467	CB
Kid Rock	Amen	36-475	CB
Kid Rock	American Bad Ass (Radio Version) **	14-487	SC
Kid Rock	Bawitdaba	36-345	SC
Kid Rock	Born Free	37-269	CB
Kid Rock	Cocky **	36-346	SC
Kid Rock	Cold And Empty	49-511	PHM
Kid Rock	Cowboy	10-221	SC
Kid Rock	First Kiss	45-17	KVD
Kid Rock	Forever (Radio Version)	16-91	SC
Kid Rock	Let's Ride	46-61	BKD
Kid Rock	Lonely Road Of Faith	18-292	CB
Kid Rock	Lonely Road Of Faith	36-349	SC
Kid Rock	Only God Knows Why	14-180	CB
Kid Rock	Only God Knows Why	15-326	PHM
Kid Rock	Only God Knows Why	5-894	SC
Kid Rock	Roll On	49-319	CB
Kid Rock	Single Father	20-484	ST
Kid Rock	Wasting Time	15-429	PHM
Kid Rock	Where U At Rock **	36-348	SC
Kid Rock & Crow	Collide - duet	38-204	FTX
Kid Rock & Crow	Duet - Collide	38-204	FTX
Kid Rock & Crow	Duet - Picture	18-433	CB
Kid Rock & Crow	Duet - Picture	25-400	MM
Kid Rock & Crow	Duet - Picture	29-666	RS
Kid Rock & Crow	Duet - Picture	32-10	THM
Kid Rock & Crow	Picture	18-433	CB
Kid Rock & Crow	Picture	29-666	RS
Kid Rock & Crow	Picture	32-10	THM
Kids	Clementine	10-297	SC
Kids	Do The Holey Pokey	33-197	CB
Kids	Gospel - Jesus Loves the Little...	33-198	CB
Kids	He's Got The Whole World	33-450	CB
Kids	Head Shoulders Knees & Toes	49-351	CB
Kids	Home On The Range	10-303	SC
Kids	How Much Is That Doggy In The...	12-263	DK
Kids	I'm Popeye The Sailor Man - kids	49-32	SHER
Kids	I've Been Workin' On The RR	34-447	CB
Kids	If You're Happy & U Know It	34-449	CB
Kids	Kids - All Around The Mulberry Bush	23-200	SM
Kids	Kids - Alouette	12-623	P
Kids	Kids - Alphabet Song	12-605	P
Kids	Kids - Alphabet Song	17-193	SC
Kids	Kids - Alphabet Song	23-206	SM

ARTIST	SONG TITLE	#	TYPE
Kids	Kids - Ants Go Marching In	17-185	SC
Kids	Kids - B-I-N-G-O	17-190	SC
Kids	Kids - Baa Baa Black Sheep	12-613	P
Kids	Kids - Baa Baa Black Sheep	17-186	SC
Kids	Kids - Baa Baa Black Sheep	23-202	SM
Kids	Kids - Battle Hymn of the Republic	10-305	SC
Kids	Kids - Be Kind to Your Web-Footed..	10-306	SC
Kids	Kids - Billy Boy	10-298	SC
Kids	Kids - Billy Boy	23-212	SM
Kids	Kids - Bolweevil	10-301	SC
Kids	Kids - Boom Boom Ain't It Great	10-307	SC
Kids	Kids - Camptown Races	10-312	SC
Kids	Kids - Candy Man the	12-602	P
Kids	Kids - Chitty Chitty Bang Bang	12-595	P
Kids	Kids - Clapping Song the	12-624	P
Kids	Kids - Clementine	10-297	SC
Kids	Kids - Do The Hokey Pokey	33-197	CB
Kids	Kids - Do Your Ears Hang Low	16-402	PR
Kids	Kids - Do Your Ears Hang Low	17-184	SC
Kids	Kids - Do-Re-Mi	12-618	P
Kids	Kids - Eensy Weensy Spider	33-448	CB
Kids	Kids - Farmer In The Dell	12-615	P
Kids	Kids - Farmer In The Dell	23-207	SM
Kids	Kids - Found A Peanut	10-294	SC
Kids	Kids - Frere Jacques	12-621	P
Kids	Kids - Froggie Went A Courtin'	10-275	SC
Kids	Kids - Georgie Porgie	10-318	SC
Kids	Kids - Happy Talk	12-603	P
Kids	Kids - He's Got The Whole World	33-450	CB
Kids	Kids - He's Got The Whole World	12-619	P
Kids	Kids - Head Shoulders Knees & Toes	49-351	CB
Kids	Kids - Here We Go Loopty Loo	10-293	SC
Kids	Kids - Hey Diddle Diddle	10-280	SC
Kids	Kids - Hey Diddle Diddle	23-205	SM
Kids	Kids - Hickory Dickory Dock	10-277	SC
Kids	Kids - Hickory Dickory Dock	23-201	SM
Kids	Kids - Hokey Pokey	12-610	P
Kids	Kids - Hokey Pokey	2-71	SC

ARTIST	SONG TITLE	#	TYPE
Kids	Kids - Hokey Pokey	16-371	SF
Kids	Kids - Home On The Range	10-303	SC
Kids	Kids - How Much Is That Doggy In Th	12-263	DK
Kids	Kids - Humpty Dumpty	10-284	SC
Kids	Kids - I'm A Little Teapot	17-187	SC
Kids	Kids - I've Been Workin' On the RR	33-447	CB
Kids	Kids - I've Been Working on the RR	12-265	DK
Kids	Kids - I've Been Working on the RR	17-183	SC
Kids	Kids - If You're Happy & U Know It	34-449	CB
Kids	Kids - If Your Happy & You Know It	17-198	SC
Kids	Kids - It's Raining It's Pouring	12-598	P
Kids	Kids - Jack & Jill	17-191	SC
Kids	Kids - Jeepers Creepers	12-262	DK
Kids	Kids - Jesus Loves The Little Children	33-198	CB
Kids	Kids - Jimmy Crack Corn	10-311	SC
Kids	Kids - John Jacob Jingleheimer Schm	10-292	SC
Kids	Kids - Kum Ba Yah	10-300	SC
Kids	Kids - Little Bo Peep	17-189	SC
Kids	Kids - Little Boy Blue	10-283	SC
Kids	Kids - Little Bunny Foo Foo	17-195	SC
Kids	Kids - Little Jack Horner	10-278	SC
Kids	Kids - Little Miss Muffet	10-285	SC
Kids	Kids - Little White Duck	35-326	CB
Kids	Kids - London Bridge	12-255	DK
Kids	Kids - London Bridge	12-601	P
Kids	Kids - London Bridge	17-188	SC
Kids	Kids - London Bridge	23-199	SM
Kids	Kids - Mary Had A Little Lamb	35-327	CB
Kids	Kids - Mary Had A Little Lamb	12-252	DK
Kids	Kids - Mary Had A Little Lamb	12-600	P
Kids	Kids - Mary Had A Little Lamb	17-196	SC
Kids	Kids - Mary Had A Little Lamb	23-211	SM
Kids	Kids - Mary Mary Quite Contrary	10-308	SC
Kids	Kids - Michael Row the Boat Ashore	12-596	P
Kids	Kids - My Bonnie	10-321	SC
Kids	Kids - Nobody Likes Me	10-313	SC
Kids	Kids - Oh Susanna	12-611	P
Kids	Kids - Oh Susanna	17-192	SC
Kids	Kids - Old Grey Mare	49-352	CB
Kids	Kids - Old King Cole	10-281	SC
Kids	Kids - Old King Cole	23-208	SM

ARTIST	SONG TITLE	#	TYPE
Kids	Kids - Old MacDonald Had a Farm	12-599	P
Kids	Kids - Old MacDonald Had A Farm	17-194	SC
Kids	Kids - On Top Of Old Smokey	10-310	SC
Kids	Kids - On Top Of Old Smoky	33-199	CB
Kids	Kids - On Top Of Spaghetti	12-606	P
Kids	Kids - Paper Of Pins a	10-317	SC
Kids	Kids - Pat A Cake	10-282	SC
Kids	Kids - Pease Porrige Hot	10-288	SC
Kids	Kids - Pick A Bale Of Cotton	10-304	SC
Kids	Kids - Polly Wolly Doodle	12-256	DK
Kids	Kids - Pop Goes The Weasel	23-204	SM
Kids	Kids - Puff The Magic Dragon	12-264	DK
Kids	Kids - Put On A Happy Face	12-259	DK
Kids	Kids - Rain Rain Go Away	10-286	SC
Kids	Kids - Ring Around The Rosy	23-210	SM
Kids	Kids - Row Row Row Your Boat	12-620	P
Kids	Kids - Row Row Row Your Boat	10-290	SC
Kids	Kids - Rub A Dub Dub	10-316	SC
Kids	Kids - Sally The Camel	16-403	PR
Kids	Kids - She'll Be Comin' 'Round the	12-257	DK
Kids	Kids - She'll Be Comin' 'Round the.	10-291	SC
Kids	Kids - Simple Simon	10-315	SC
Kids	Kids - Sing A Song of Sixpence	10-289	SC
Kids	Kids - Skip To My Lou	12-258	DK
Kids	Kids - Skip To My Lou	10-296	SC
Kids	Kids - Skip To My Lou	23-213	SM
Kids	Kids - Swanee River	10-302	SC
Kids	Kids - Taps	10-299	SC
Kids	Kids - There Was a Crooked Man	10-309	SC
Kids	Kids - There Was An Old Woman	10-320	SC
Kids	Kids - There's a Hole in the Middle	10-322	SC
Kids	Kids - This Old Man	12-261	DK
Kids	Kids - This Old Man	12-612	P
Kids	Kids - This Old Man	23-203	SM
Kids	Kids - Three Blind Mice	12-253	DK
Kids	Kids - Three Blind Mice	12-617	P
Kids	Kids - Three Blind Mice	23-214	SM
Kids	Kids - Three Little Kittens	10-287	SC
Kids	Kids - Tisket A Tasket a	10-279	SC

ARTIST	SONG TITLE	#	TYPE
Kids	Kids - Tra La La Boom De Ay	12-260	DK
Kids	Kids - Twinkle Twinkle Little Star	12-254	DK
Kids	Kids - Twinkle Twinkle Little Star	12-622	P
Kids	Kids - Twinkle Twinkle Little Star	17-197	SC
Kids	Kids - Twinkle Twinkle Little Star	23-209	SM
Kids	Kids - Wheels On The Bus the	33-200	CB
Kids	Kids - Where Has My Little Dog Gone	10-276	SC
Kids	Kids - Where Is Thumbkin?	10-319	SC
Kids	Kids - Yankee Doodle	12-604	P
Kids	Kids - Yankee Doodle	10-295	SC
Kids	Kids - Yankee Doodle Dandy	16-401	PR
Kids	Old Grey Mare - kids	49-352	CB
Kids	Puff The Magic Dragon	12-264	DK
Kihn, Greg	Breakup Song	18-578	TT
Kiki Dee Band	I've Got The Music In Me	18-236	DK
Kiki Dee Band	I've Got The Music In Me	9-727	SAV
Kiki Dee Band	I've Got The Music In Me	4-855	SC
Kilgore, Jerry	Cactus In A Coffee Can	14-79	CB
Kilgore, Jerry	Love Trip	14-696	CB
Kilgore, Jerry	Love Trip	5-724	SC
Kilgore, Jerry	Love Trip	22-384	ST
Killer Mike & Big Boi	A.D.I.D.A.S.	32-165	THM
Killers	All These Things That I've Done	30-226	PHM
Killers	Dustland Fairytale a	36-310	PHM
Killers	Human	36-273	PHM
Killers	Mr. Brightside	30-133	PT
Killers	Spaceman	36-385	SC
Kim, Andy	Baby I Love You	47-407	DFK
Kim, Andy	Rock Me Gently	27-576	DK
Kim, Andy	Rock Me Gently	3-608	SC
Kimes, Royal Wade	Night Birds	19-11	ST
Kinder, Ryan	Mine	42-8	PHN
Kinder, Ryan	Tonight	41-99	PHN
King And I, the	Show - Getting To Know You	6-249	MM
King And I, the	Show - Getting To Know You	2-286	SC
King And I, the	Show - I Have Dreamed	18-193	PS
King Harvest	Dancing In The Moonlight	27-578	DK
King Harvest	Dancing In The Moonlight	9-368	MG
King Harvest	Dancing In The Moonlight	9-714	SAV
King, Albert	Born Under A Bad Sign	20-135	KB
King, Albert	Born Under A Bad Sign	15-309	SC
King, Albert	Call My Job	19-800	SGB
King, Albert	Good Time Charlie	19-793	SGB
King, B.B.	Big Boss Man	20-136	KB

ARTIST	SONG TITLE	#	TYPE
King, B.B.	Caldonia	14-591	SC
King, B.B.	Choo Choo Ch'Boogie	45-367	DFK
King, B.B.	Every Day I Have The Blues	46-308	SC
King, B.B.	Paying The Cost to Be The Boss	14-602	SC
King, B.B.	Rock Me Baby	15-20	SC
King, B.B.	Thrill Is Gone the	12-94	DK
King, B.B.	Thrill Is Gone the	20-140	KB
King, B.B.	Thrill Is Gone the	12-666	P
King, B.B.	Thrill Is Gone the	14-590	SC
King, B.B.	Why I Sing The Blues	15-320	SC
King, Ben E.	Don't Play That Song	4-217	SC
King, Ben E.	I Who Have Nothing	10-737	JVC
King, Ben E.	Love Come Down	11-463	DK
King, Ben E.	Spanish Harlem	22-443	SC
King, Ben E.	Stand By Me	11-372	DK
King, Ben E.	Stand By Me	10-736	JVC
King, Ben E.	Stand By Me	12-626	P
King, Ben E.	Stand By Me	2-81	SC
King, Carole	Anyone At All	43-451	MM
King, Carole	Beautiful	16-882	DK
King, Carole	Been To Canaan	43-444	CB
King, Carole	Carry Your Load	43-445	CB
King, Carole	City Streets	43-2	KV
King, Carole	Crying In The Rain	43-453	UB
King, Carole	Home Again	43-452	MM
King, Carole	I Feel The Earth Move	26-337	DK
King, Carole	I Feel The Earth Move	13-303	P
King, Carole	I Feel The Earth Move	19-166	SGB
King, Carole	It Might As Well Rain Until September	43-446	LG
King, Carole	It's Too late	11-215	DK
King, Carole	It's Too Late	12-682	P
King, Carole	It's Too Late	19-116	SAV
King, Carole	Jazzman	3-618	SC
King, Carole	Jazzman	47-716	LE
King, Carole	Nightingale	43-450	LG
King, Carole	Now And Forever	24-22	SC
King, Carole	One Fine Day	24-73	SC
King, Carole	Only Love Is Real	43-447	CB
King, Carole	Smackwater Jack	5-681	SC
King, Carole	So Far Away	33-256	CB
King, Carole	So Far Away	12-878	P
King, Carole	So Far Away	9-715	SAV
King, Carole	So Far Away	4-843	SC
King, Carole	Sweet Seasons	33-261	CB
King, Carole	Sweet Seasons	43-122	SC
King, Carole	Tapestry	43-449	KV
King, Carole	That's How Things Go Down	43-442	CB
King, Carole	Way Over Yonder	43-448	CBE
King, Carole	Where You Lead	43-4	CB
King, Carole	Will You Still Love Me Tomorrow	42-36	SC
King, Carole	You've Got A Friend	43-443	CB
King, Claude	All For The Love Of A Girl	47-921	SSK
King, Claude	Catch A Little Raindrop	47-917	SSK
King, Claude	He Ain't Country	47-923	SSK
King, Claude	I've Got The World By The Tail	47-920	SSK
King, Claude	Laura (What's He Got That I Ain't Got)	47-924	SSK
King, Claude	Mary's Vineyard	47-918	SSK
King, Claude	She Knows Why	47-922	SSK
King, Claude	Tiger Woman	47-919	SSK
King, Claude	Wolverton Mountain	8-709	CB
King, Claude	Wolverton Mountain	22-447	SC
King, Elle	America's Sweetheart	46-123	BKD
King, Elle	Ex's & Oh's	46-121	BKD
King, Elle	Playing For Keeps	46-122	ASK
King, Elle	Under The Influence	49-927	KVD
King, Evelyn C.	Love Come Down	27-354	DK
King, Evelyn C.	Love Come Down - Pt. 1	15-40	SS
King, Evelyn C.	Love Come Down - Pt. 2	15-41	SS
King, Evelyn C.	Shame	17-135	DK
King, Evelyn C.	Shame	5-110	SC
King, Freddy	Down Home Blues	7-224	MM
King, Matt	From Your Knees	8-961	CB
King, Matt	Rub It In	5-731	SC
King, Pee Wee	Slow Poke	8-721	CB
King, Pee Wee	Tennessee Waltz	15-825	CB
King, Solomon	She Wears My Ring	10-631	SF
Kings	Switch Into Glide	13-661	SGB
Kings Of Leon	Notion	36-306	PHM
Kings Of Leon	Sex On Fire	36-270	PHM
Kings Of Leon	Use Somebody	36-18	PT
Kingsmen	Louie Louie	11-688	DK
Kingsmen	Louie Louie	13-110	P
Kingsmen	Louie Louie	2-59	SC
Kingsmen	Money Honey	17-326	SS
Kingsmen	Money! That's What I Want	11-179	DK
Kingsmen	Money! That's What I Want	12-637	P
Kingston Trio	Scotch & Soda	2-415	SC
Kingston Trio	Sloop John B	7-360	MM
Kingston Trio	They Call The Wind Maria	7-350	MM
Kingston Trio	Tom Dooley	35-11	CB
Kingston Trio	Tom Dooley	27-370	DK
Kingston Trio	Tom Dooley	7-346	MM
Kingston Trio	When The Saints Go Marching In	7-354	MM
Kingston Trio	Where Have All The Flowers Gone	18-163	DK
Kingston Trio	Where Have All The Flowers Gone	7-356	MM
Kingston Trip	Greenback Dollar	47-754	SRK
Kinison, Sam	Wild Thing (Rock Version)	21-770	SC
Kinks	All Day & All Of The Night	13-165	P
Kinks	All Day & All Of The Night	5-226	SC

ARTIST	SONG TITLE	#	TYPE
Kinks	Ape Man	48-175	LE
Kinks	Autumn Almanac	48-174	LE
Kinks	Celluloid Heroes	48-183	SC
Kinks	Come Dancing	3-619	SC
Kinks	Days	48-181	LE
Kinks	Dead End Street	48-178	LE
Kinks	Dedicated Follower Of Fashion	48-180	LE
Kinks	Don't Forget To Dance	48-176	LE
Kinks	Everybody's Gonna Be Happy	48-184	ZMJ
Kinks	Father Christmas - xmas	45-250	SC
Kinks	Lola	48-182	MM
Kinks	Lola	48-169	LE
Kinks	See My Friend	48-170	LE
Kinks	Set Me Free	48-172	LE
Kinks	Stop Your Sobbing	48-185	ZMJ
Kinks	Sunny Afternoon	3-726	SC
Kinks	Sunny Afternoon	10-668	SF
Kinks	Sunny Afternoon	48-179	LE
Kinks	Supersonic Rocket Ship	48-177	LE
Kinks	Tired Of Waiting For You	10-663	SF
Kinks	Waterloo Sunset	48-173	LE
Kinks	Well Respected Man	48-171	LE
Kinks	Xmas - Father Christmas	45-250	SC
Kinks	You Really Got Me	13-223	P
Kinks	You Really Got Me	3-266	SC
Kinleys	Crazy Kind Of Love Thing	19-566	CB
Kinleys	Dance In The Boat	19-567	CB
Kinleys	I'm In	14-125	CB
Kinleys	I'm In	22-469	ST
Kinleys	Just Between You & Me	19-563	CB
Kinleys	Just Between You & Me	10-121	SC
Kinleys	Just Between You & Me	22-758	ST
Kinleys	My Heart Is Still Beating	5-721	SC
Kinleys	My Heart Is Still Beating	22-493	ST
Kinleys	Please	12-931	CB
Kinleys	Please	7-683	CHM
Kinleys	Please	22-661	ST
Kinleys	She Ain't The Girl For You	9-395	CB
Kinleys	She Ain't The Girl For You	13-826	CHM
Kinleys	Somebody's Out There Watching	19-564	CB
Kinleys	Somebody's Out There Watching	22-689	ST
Kinleys	You Make It Seem So Easy	8-751	CB
Kismet	Show - Stranger In Paradise	18-188	PS
Kiss	Beth	14-558	AH
Kiss	Beth	10-36	SC
Kiss	Detroit Rock City	10-39	SC
Kiss	Deuce	10-37	SC

ARTIST	SONG TITLE	#	TYPE
Kiss	Forever	23-103	SC
Kiss	God Gave Rock & Roll To You	13-653	SGB
Kiss	Hard Luck Woman	10-33	SC
Kiss	Lick It Up	6-26	SC
Kiss	Nothing Can Keep Me From You	8-509	PHT
Kiss	Psycho Circus	10-38	SC
Kiss	Rock & Roll All Night	9-349	AH
Kiss	Rock & Roll All Night	10-40	SC
Kiss	Shout It Out Loud	10-34	SC
Kiss	Strutter	10-35	SC
Kiss	Tears Are Falling	21-774	SC
Kix	Don't Close Your Eyes	6-30	SC
Klymaxx	I Miss You	15-796	SC
Knack	My Sharona	33-301	CB
Knack	My Sharona	6-486	MM
Knack	My Sharona	12-796	P
Knight & Pips	Best Thing That Ever Happened To Me	13-315	P
Knight & Pips	Best Thing That Ever Happened To Me	2-446	SC
Knight & Pips	Every Beat Of My Heart	7-66	MM
Knight & Pips	I've Got To Use My Imagination	11-504	Dk
Knight & Pips	If I Were Your Woman	17-356	DK
Knight & Pips	License To Kill	9-67	SC
Knight & Pips	Midnight Train To Georgia	16-808	DK
Knight & Pips	Midnight Train To Georgia	13-146	P
Knight & Pips	Midnight Train To Georgia	9-228	PT
Knight & Pips	Midnight Train To Georgia	9-791	SAV
Knight & Pips	Midnight Train To Georgia	2-438	SC
Knight & Pips	Neither One Of Us	10-677	HE
Knight & Pips	Neither One Of Us..	17-104	DK
Knight, Beverly	Come As You Are	30-775	SF
Knight, Beverly	Piece of My Heart	30-756	SF
Knight, Chris	It Ain't Easy Being Me	8-223	CB
Knight, Jean	Mr. Big Stuff	35-85	CB
Knight, Jean	Mr. Big Stuff	10-674	HE
Knight, Jordan	I Could Never Take The Place Of...	8-520	PHT
Knight, Jordan	I Could Never Take The Place Of...	10-199	SC
Knowles & Jay-Z	03 Bonnie & Clyde - Duet	32-48	THM
Knowles & Jay-Z	Crazy In Love - Duet	32-307	THM
Knowles & Jay-Z	Duet - 03 Bonnie & Clyde	32-48	THM
Knowles & Jay-Z	Duet - Crazy In Love	32-307	THM
Knowles & Paul	Baby Boy	25-715	MM
Knowles & Paul	Baby Boy	21-787	SC
Knowles & Paul	Baby Boy - Duet	32-382	THM
Knowles & Paul	Duet - Baby Boy	25-715	MM
Knowles & Paul	Duet - Baby Boy	21-787	SC

ARTIST	SONG TITLE	#	TYPE
Knowles & Paul	Duet - Baby Boy	32-382	THM
Knowles&Vandross	Closer I Get To You the	21-791	SC
Knowles&Vandross	Duet - Closer I Get To You	21-791	SC
Knox, Buddy	Party Doll	33-237	CB
Knox, Buddy	Party Doll	3-294	MM
Knox, Buddy	Party Doll	3-468	SC
Kooks	Naive	30-753	SF
Kooks	She Moves In Her Own Way	30-733	SF
Kool & The Gang	Celebration	16-874	DK
Kool & The Gang	Celebration	16-530	P
Kool & The Gang	Celebration	9-663	SAV
Kool & the Gang	Fresh	39-5	CB
Kool & The Gang	Get Down On It	14-357	MH
Kool & The Gang	Get Down On It	15-36	SS
Kool & The Gang	JoAnna	16-558	P
Kool & the Gang	Jungle Boogie	39-4	CB
Kool & The Gang	Ladies Night	27-571	DK
Kool & The Gang	Ladies Night	12-701	P
Kool & The Gang	Ladies Night	9-761	SAV
Kool & The Gang	Too Hot	49-475	MM
Korn	Alone I Break	32-74	THM
Korn	Coming Undone	49-890	SC
Korn	Twisted Transistor	29-253	SC
Krall, Diana	Let's Face The Music & Dance	23-342	MM
Krall, Diana	Peel Me A Grape	23-341	MM
Krall, Diana	You're Getting To Be A Habit w/Me	23-346	MM
Kramer & Dacotas	Bad To Me	10-560	SF
Kramer & Dacotas	Little Children	10-567	SF
Kramer & Dacotas	Trains & Boats & Planes	10-653	SF
Kramer, Billy J.	Bad To Me	20-37	SC
Kramer, Jana	Circles	48-197	BKD
Kramer, Jana	Good As You Were Bad	44-165	BKD
Kramer, Jana	I Got The Boy	48-198	BKD
Kramer, Jana	I Hope It Rains	48-194	KCD
Kramer, Jana	I Won't Give Up	48-195	PHN
Kramer, Jana	Love	48-199	BKD
Kramer, Jana	When You're Lonely	48-196	PHN
Kramer, Jana	Whiskey	47-578	ASK
Kramer, Jana	Why Ya Wanna?	43-280	BKD
Krauss & Plant	Duet - Gone Gone Gone (Done ...	37-116	SC
Krauss & Plant	Gone Gone Gone (Done... - duet	37-116	SC
Krauss & Union Station	Baby Now That I've Found You	34-322	CB
Krauss & Union Station	If I Didn't Know Any Better	36-185	PHM
Krauss, Alison	Baby Now That I've Found You	8-893	CB
Krauss, Alison	Baby Now That I've Found You	6-824	MM
Krauss, Alison	Everybody Wants To Go To Heaven	49-712	VH
Krauss, Alison	Find My Way Back To My Heart	7-620	CHM

ARTIST	SONG TITLE	#	TYPE
Krauss, Alison	Goodbye Is All We Have	23-487	CB
Krauss, Alison	Goodbye Is All We Have	29-616	ST
Krauss, Alison	How's The World Treating You	19-774	ST
Krauss, Alison	I Give You To His Heart	10-158	SC
Krauss, Alison	I've Got That Old Feelin'	8-892	CB
Krauss, Alison	Let Me Touch You For Awhile	25-134	MM
Krauss, Alison	Let Me Touch You For Awhile	16-436	ST
Krauss, Alison	Lucky One the	25-55	MM
Krauss, Alison	Lucky One the	16-41	ST
Krauss, Alison	My Poor Old Heart	29-49	CB
Krauss, Alison	New Favorite	25-417	MM
Krauss, Alison	New Favorite	18-472	ST
Krauss, Alison	New Fool	24-86	sC
Krauss, Alison	Oh Atlanta	4-27	SC
Krauss, Alison	Restless	23-13	CB
Krauss, Alison	Restless	23-384	SC
Krauss, Alison	Simple Love	30-477	CB
Krauss, Alison	When You Say Nothing At All	2-656	SC
Kravitz, Lenny	Again	23-258	HS
Kravitz, Lenny	Again	16-473	MH
Kravitz, Lenny	American Woman	8-529	PHT
Kravitz, Lenny	American Woman	16-192	THM
Kravitz, Lenny	Dig In	25-33	MM
Kravitz, Lenny	Fly Away	11-69	JTG
Kravitz, Lenny	Fly Away	7-801	PHT
Kravitz, Lenny	Fly Away	13-710	SGB
Kravitz, Lenny	I Belong To You	16-239	PHM
Kravitz, Lenny	I'll Be Waiting	49-902	SC
Kravitz, Lenny	If I Could Fall In Love	18-435	CB
Kravitz, Lenny	It Ain't Over	17-331	DK
Kravitz, Lenny	Stillness Of Heart	18-289	CB
Kravitz, Lenny	That Lady	48-555	DK
Kreviazuk, Chantel	In This Life	25-539	MM
Kristofferson, Kris	Come Sundown	47-750	SRK
Kristofferson, Kris	Come Sundown	45-199	DCK
Kristofferson, Kris	For The Good Times	45-200	DCK
Kristofferson, Kris	Help Me Make It Through The Night	45-208	PT
Kristofferson, Kris	Jesus Was A Capricorn	45-201	DCK
Kristofferson, Kris	Loving Her Was Easier	45-203	DCK
Kristofferson, Kris	Me & Bobby McGee	13-173	P
Kristofferson, Kris	Pilgrim Chapter 33	45-205	DCK
Kristofferson, Kris	Silver Tounged Devil And I	45-198	ASK
Kristofferson, Kris	Stranger	45-206	OZP
Kristofferson, Kris	Sunday Mornin' Comin' Down	45-204	DCK
Kristofferson, Kris	Who's To Bless And Who's To Blame	45-202	DCK
Kristofferson, Kris	Why Me Lord	8-682	SAV
Kristofferson, Kris	You Show Me Yours & I'll Show You Mine	45-197	JBK
Kroeger & Scott	Hero	18-217	CB
Kroeger & Scott	Hero	18-409	MM

ARTIST	SONG TITLE	#	TYPE
Krokus	Eat The Rich	23-105	SC
Krush	Hawaii - My Hawaii	6-832	MM
Krush	My Hawaii	6-832	MM
Kyper	Tic Tac Toe	2-187	SC
Kyser, Kay	Jingle Jangle Jingle	4-189	SC
La Bouche	Sweet Dreams	4-336	SC
La Cage Au Folle	Show - Best Of Times	6-245	MM
La Cage Au Folle	Show - I Am What I Am	10-371	KC
Laballo, Kevin	Latino - Mi Primer Amor (Salsa	18-7	PS
Labelle & Blige	Ain't No Way	29-316	PHM
Labelle & McDonald	Duet - On My Own	16-725	DK
LaBelle & McDonald	Duet - On My Own	12-832	P
LaBelle & McDonald	On My Own	16-725	DK
LaBelle & McDonald	On My Own	12-832	P
LaBelle, Patti	Lady Marmalade	11-194	DK
LaBelle, Patti	Lady Marmalade	34-27	CB
LaBelle, Patti	My Love Sweet Love	4-332	SC
LaBelle, Patti	New Attitude	28-364	DK
LaBelle, Patti	New Attitude	5-141	SC
LaBelle, Patti	Shoe Was On The Other Foot	9-101	PS
LaBelle, Patti	Stir It Up	49-240	DFK
LaBelle, Patti	When You've Been Blessed	24-270	SC
Lace	I Want A Man	14-705	CB
Lace	I Want A Man	5-733	SC
Lace	I Want A Man	22-494	ST
Lace	Kiss 'Em All	14-717	CB
Lace	You Could've Had Me	9-406	CB
Lachey, Nick	What's Left Of Me	30-159	PT
Lady Antebellum	American Honey	36-55	PT
Lady Antebellum	And The Radio Played	44-160	BKD
Lady Antebellum	As You Turn Away	47-925	KV
Lady Antebellum	Baby It's Cold Outside	45-775	KV
Lady Antebellum	Bartender	44-201	SBIG
Lady Antebellum	Bottle Up Lightining	38-111	KV
Lady Antebellum	Can't Take My Eyes Off You	46-85	BKD
Lady Antebellum	Cold As Stone - duet	47-870	KV
Lady Antebellum	Compass	43-93	HM
Lady Antebellum	Dancing Away With My Heart	46-295	BKD
Lady Antebellum	Dancing Away With My Heart - duet	46-80	BKD
Lady Antebellum	Downtown	46-83	BKD
Lady Antebellum	Duet - Dancing Away With My Heart	46-80	BKD
Lady Antebellum	Duet - Just A Kiss	38-88	AT
Lady Antebellum	Duet - Need You Now	36-49	PT
Lady Antebellum	Duet - One Great Mystery	48-445	KCD
Lady Antebellum	Duet - Our Kind Of Love	37-336	CB
Lady Antebellum	Duet - Wanted You More	46-81	BKD
Lady Antebellum	Friday Night	38-253	PHN
Lady Antebellum	Get To Me	46-82	BKD
Lady Antebellum	Goodbye Town	43-143	BK3D

ARTIST	SONG TITLE	#	TYPE
Lady Antebellum	Hello World	37-232	CB
Lady Antebellum	I Run To You	40-2	CB
Lady Antebellum	I Was Here	37-56	CB
Lady Antebellum	It Ain't Pretty	46-84	BKD
Lady Antebellum	Just A Kiss - duet	38-88	AT
Lady Antebellum	Let It Snow	45-741	KVD
Lady Antebellum	Long Stretch Of Love - duet	48-442	KCD
Lady Antebellum	Lookin' For A Good Time	36-601	CB
Lady Antebellum	Lookin' For A Good Time	36-197	PHM
Lady Antebellum	Love Don't Live Here	36-559	CB
Lady Antebellum	Need You Now - duet	36-49	PT
Lady Antebellum	One Day You Will	40-48	DFK
Lady Antebellum	One Great Mystery - duet	48-445	KCD
Lady Antebellum	Our Kind Of Love - duet	37-336	CB
Lady Antebellum	Ready To Love Again	44-127	KV
Lady Antebellum	Silver Bells	45-776	KV
Lady Antebellum	Wanted You More - duet	46-81	BKD
Lady Antebellum	We Owned The Night	38-114	CB
Lady Antebellum	When You Got A Good Thing	44-128	KV
Lady Antebellum	Xmas - Baby it's Cold Outside	45-775	KV
Lady antebellum	Xmas - Let It Snow	45-741	KVD
Lady Antebellum	Xmas - Silver Bells	45-776	KV
Lady Gaga	Alejandro	38-184	CB
Lady Gaga	Bad Romance	38-188	CB
Lady Gaga	Boys Boys Boys	38-189	PS
Lady Gaga	Edge Of Glory	38-185	CB
Lady Gaga	Love Game	38-191	SC
Lady Gaga	Paparazzi	38-192	CB
Lady Gaga	Poker Face	38-193	CB
Lady Gaga	You And I	38-202	SF
Lady Gaga & Beyonce	Duet - Telephone	38-194	CB
Lady Gaga & Beyonce	Telephone - duet	38-194	CB
Lady Gaga & O'Donis	Duet - Just Dance	38-190	SC
Lady Gaga & O'Donis	Just Dance - duet	36-1	PT
Lady Is A Tramp	Show - Bella Notte	20-181	Z
Lady Is A Tramp	Show - He's A Tramp	20-182	Z
Laine, Frankie	Cry Of The Wild Goose	18-613	PS
Laine, Frankie	Moonlight Gambler	3-878	PS
Laine, Frankie	My Friend	45-601	OZP
Laine, Frankie	On The Sunny Side Of The Street	3-879	PS
Laine, Frankie	Rain Rain Rain	10-597	SF
Laine, Frankie	Rawhide	12-893	P
Laine, Frankie	Rawhide	19-112	SAV
Laine, Frankie	That Lucky Old Sun	3-875	PS
Laine, Frankie	That's My Desire	21-639	PS
Lamar, Holly	There Are The Days	18-453	ST
Lambert & Underwood	Duet - Something Bad	44-278	PHN

161

ARTIST	SONG TITLE	#	TYPE
Lambert & Underwood	Something Bad - Duet	44-278	PHN
Lambert & Urban	Duet - We Were Us	46-249	ASK
Lambert & Urban	We Were Us - duet	46-249	ASK
Lambert, Miranda	Airstream Song	46-258	KV
Lambert, Miranda	All Kinds Of Kinds	41-46	ASK
Lambert, Miranda	All That's Left For You To Do Is Leave	45-308	KV
Lambert, Miranda	Another Sunday In The South	45-282	BKD
Lambert, Miranda	Automatic	43-124	ASK
Lambert, Miranda	Babies Makin' Babies	49-923	KVD
Lambert, Miranda	Baggage Claim	44-130	ASK
Lambert, Miranda	Better In The Long Run	46-267	KV
Lambert, Miranda	Boots And Wings	46-273	KCD
Lambert, Miranda	Bring Me Down	23-118	CB
Lambert, Miranda	Bring Me Down	23-381	SC
Lambert, Miranda	Crazy Ex-Girlfriend	30-194	CB
Lambert, Miranda	Dead Flowers	46-252	CB
Lambert, Miranda	Dear Diamond	44-396	KV
Lambert, Miranda	Desperation	46-265	KV
Lambert, Miranda	Down	46-270	QH
Lambert, Miranda	Dry Town	45-431	KV
Lambert, Miranda	Easy Living	45-956	KV
Lambert, Miranda	Famous In A Small Town	30-359	CB
Lambert, Miranda	Fastest Girl In Town	39-31	ASK
Lambert, Miranda	Fine Tune	46-254	KV
Lambert, Miranda	Girl Like Me	46-253	KV
Lambert, Miranda	Girls	45-632	BKD
Lambert, Miranda	Gravity Is A Bitch	45-946	KV
Lambert, Miranda	Greyhound Bound For Nowhere	46-251	CB
Lambert, Miranda	Guilty In Here	46-261	KV
Lambert, Miranda	Gunpowder & Lead	36-571	CB
Lambert, Miranda	Hard Staying Sober	46-263	KV
Lambert, Miranda	Heart Like Mine	37-223	CB
Lambert, Miranda	Holding On To You	46-272	BKD
Lambert, Miranda	House That Built Me the	36-54	PT
Lambert, Miranda	Hurts To Think	45-674	DCK
Lambert, Miranda	I Can't Be Bothered	46-266	KV
Lambert, Miranda	I Wanna Die	46-260	KV
Lambert, Miranda	Jack Daniels	44-83	BKD
Lambert, Miranda	Kerosene	22-336	CB
Lambert, Miranda	Kerosene	23-387	SC
Lambert, Miranda	Little Red Wagon	46-268	KV
Lambert, Miranda	Look At Miss Ohio	46-256	KV
Lambert, Miranda	Love Is Looking For You	44-395	KV
Lambert, Miranda	Love Letters	46-259	KV
Lambert, Miranda	Love Song	46-248	AC
Lambert, Miranda	Makin' Plans	44-394	KV
Lambert, Miranda	Mama's Broken Heart	39-92	PHN
Lambert, Miranda	Me And Charlie Talking	22-97	CB
Lambert, Miranda	Me And Charlie Talking	23-44	SC
Lambert, Miranda	More Like Her	43-377	CB
Lambert, Miranda	New Strings	29-581	CB
Lambert, Miranda	New Strings	45-33	ASK

ARTIST	SONG TITLE	#	TYPE
Lambert, Miranda	Nobody's Fool	38-259	PHN
Lambert, Miranda	Oklahoma Sky	46-255	KV
Lambert, Miranda	Old Shit	45-945	KV
Lambert, Miranda	Only Prettier	37-224	KS
Lambert, Miranda	Over You	45-64	BKD
Lambert, Miranda	Platinum	46-271	SSC
Lambert, Miranda	Priceilla	44-305	BKD
Lambert, Miranda	Run Daddy Run	39-47	ASK
Lambert, Miranda	Same Old You	45-952	KV
Lambert, Miranda	Sin For A Sin	46-257	KV
Lambert, Miranda	Smokin' And Drinkin'	45-19	KV
Lambert, Miranda	Sweet By And By	48-749	BKD
Lambert, Miranda	Sweet By And By (Inst)	49-414	BKD
Lambert, Miranda	That's the Way the World Goes...	38-222	CB
Lambert, Miranda	Time To Get A Gun	45-34	ASK
Lambert, Miranda	Two Of A Crime	45-408	BKD
Lambert, Miranda	Two Rings Shy	46-269	KV
Lambert, Miranda	Virginia Bluebell	46-264	KV
Lambert, Miranda	What About Georgia	46-250	CB
Lambert, Miranda	White Liar	36-39	PT
Lampa, Rachael	Blessed	34-423	CB
Lane, Chris	Fix	49-789	BKD
Lane, Christy	One Day At A Time	12-69	DK
Lane, Christy	Simple Little Words	20-657	SC
Lang, Johnny	Lie To Me	5-747	SC
Lang, k.d.	Air That I Breathe the	47-167	KV
lang, k.d.	Big Big Love	8-891	CB
lang, k.d.	Constant Craving	8-889	CB
lang, k.d.	Constant Craving	6-367	MM
lang, k.d.	Constant Craving	13-238	P
lang, k.d.	Constant Craving	9-265	SC
lang, k.d.	Down To My Last Cigarette	6-740	MM
lang, k.d.	Hallelujah	41-43	PS
Lang, k.d.	Helpless	47-169	PHR
lang, k.d.	I'm Down To My Last Cigarette	34-321	CB
lang, k.d.	I'm Down To My Last Cigarette	26-571	DK
Lang, k.d.	If I Were You	47-171	SC
Lang, k.d.	Joker the	47-170	SC
lang, k.d.	Lock Stock & Teardrops	18-34	CB
Lang, k.d.	Miss Chatelaine	4-273	SC
Lang, k.d.	Sexuality	47-172	SC
Lang, k.d.	Summerfling	47-168	MM
lang, k.d.	Three Days	18-31	CB
lang, k.d.	Trail Of Broken Hearts	8-890	CB
Lanza, Mario	Be My Love	9-748	SAV
Larsen, Blaine	Best Man the	23-139	CB
Larsen, Blaine	Chillin'	37-338	CB
Larsen, Blaine	How Do You Get That Lonely	23-6	CB
Larsen, Blaine	How Do You Get That Lonely	21-658	SC
Larsen, Blaine	I Don't Know What She Said...	29-715	ST
Larsen, Blaine	In My High School	20-392	ST

ARTIST	SONG TITLE	#	TYPE
Larsen, Blaine	Spoken Like A Man	30-252	CB
Las Ketchup	Ketchup Song the	25-396	MM
Las Ketchup	Ketchup Song the	18-585	NS
Las Ketchup	Ketchup Song the	32-23	THM
Las Ketchup	Latino - Ketchup Song the	25-407	MM
Lasgo	Something	18-610	PHM
Lasgo	Something	32-101	THM
Last Goodnight	Pictures Of You	49-912	SC
Lauper, Cyndi	All Through The Night	33-319	CB
Lauper, Cyndi	All Through The Night	16-163	SC
Lauper, Cyndi	Girls Just Want To Have Fun	11-389	DK
Lauper, Cyndi	Girls Just Want To Have Fun	9-8	MH
Lauper, Cyndi	Girls Just Want To Have Fun	16-534	P
Lauper, Cyndi	I Drove All Night	5-688	SC
Lauper, Cyndi	She Bop	3-476	SC
Lauper, Cyndi	Time After Time	17-37	DK
Lauper, Cyndi	Time After Time	4-754	SC
Lauper, Cyndi	True Colors	11-244	DK
Lauper, Cyndi	True Colors	12-684	P
Lauper, Cyndi	Who Let In The Rain	24-24	SC
Laurel & Hardy	Trail Of The Lonesome Pines	47-592	P
Lavigne, Avril	Complicated	33-432	CB
Lavigne, Avril	Complicated	25-302	MM
Lavigne, Avril	Complicated	18-145	PHM
Lavigne, Avril	Don't Tell Me	20-568	CB
Lavigne, Avril	Girlfriend	30-487	CB
Lavigne, Avril	Hot	37-120	SC
Lavigne, Avril	I'm With You	35-261	CB
Lavigne, Avril	I'm With You	25-427	MM
Lavigne, Avril	I'm With You	18-604	PHM
Lavigne, Avril	Losing Grip	20-518	CB
Lavigne, Avril	Losing Grip	25-576	MM
Lavigne, Avril	Losing Grip	19-335	STP
Lavigne, Avril	Losing Grip	32-209	THM
Lavigne, Avril	My Happy Ending	23-555	MM
Lavigne, Avril	Nobody's Home	20-191	PHM
Lavigne, Avril	Sk8er Boi	33-448	CB
Lavigne, Avril	Sk8er Boi	25-334	MM
Lavigne, Avril	Sk8er Boy	18-339	PHM
Lawrence & Gorme	Duet - Green Eyes	25-268	MM
Lawrence & Gorme	Duet - I Want To Stay Here	29-491	LE
Lawrence & Gorme	Duet - Together (Wherever We Go)	25-257	MM
Lawrence & Gorme	Green Eyes	25-268	MM
Lawrence & Gorme	Together (Wherever We Go)	25-257	MM
Lawrence, Steve	Go Away Little Girl	16-807	DK
Lawrence, Steve	Go Away Little Girl	29-492	LE
Lawrence, Steve	I've Gotta Be Me	29-489	LE
Lawrence, Steve	Poor Little Rich Girl	29-490	LE
Lawrence, Steve	Portrait Of My Love	15-552	MM
Lawrence, Steve	Pretty Blue Eyes	5-517	SC

ARTIST	SONG TITLE	#	TYPE
Lawrence, Tracy	Alibis	1-574	CB
Lawrence, Tracy	Alibis	12-76	DK
Lawrence, Tracy	Alibis	10-757	JVC
Lawrence, Tracy	Alibis	6-310	MM
Lawrence, Tracy	Alibis	12-463	P
Lawrence, Tracy	All Wrapped Up In Christmas	48-382	CB
Lawrence, Tracy	As Any Fool Can See	1-579	CB
Lawrence, Tracy	As Any Fool Can See	6-710	MM
Lawrence, Tracy	As Any Fool Can See	17-279	NA
Lawrence, Tracy	Better Man Better Off	14-654	CB
Lawrence, Tracy	Better Man Better Off	22-406	CHM
Lawrence, Tracy	Can't Break It To My Heart	6-400	MM
Lawrence, Tracy	Can't Break It To My Heart	1-575	CB
Lawrence, Tracy	Coast Is Clear the	22-640	ST
Lawrence, Tracy	Find Out Who Your Friends Are	30-43	CB
Lawrence, Tracy	How A CowgirL Says Goodbye	1-585	CB
Lawrence, Tracy	How A Cowgirl Says Goodbye	7-642	CHM
Lawrence, Tracy	I Hope Heaven Has A Honky Tonk	48-379	CB
Lawrence, Tracy	I See It Now	1-578	CB
Lawrence, Tracy	I See It Now	17-235	NA
Lawrence, Tracy	I See It Now	2-488	SC
Lawrence, Tracy	I'll Never Pass This Way Again	8-220	CB
Lawrence, Tracy	If I Don't Make It Back	29-853	SC
Lawrence, Tracy	If I Don't Make It Back	23-458	ST
Lawrence, Tracy	If I Don't Make It Back	29-45	CB
Lawrence, Tracy	If The Good Die Young	1-576	CB
Lawrence, Tracy	If The Good Die Young	20-402	MH
Lawrence, Tracy	If The Good Die Young	17-214	NA
Lawrence, Tracy	If The World Had A Front Porch	1-581	CB
Lawrence, Tracy	If The World Had A Front Porch	7-20	MM
Lawrence, Tracy	If You Loved Me	4-96	SC
Lawrence, Tracy	Is That A Tear	7-393	MM
Lawrence, Tracy	Is That A Tear	4-890	SC
Lawrence, Tracy	It's All How You Look At It	30-801	PHM
Lawrence, Tracy	It's All How You Look At It	20-474	ST
Lawrence, Tracy	Lessons Learned	5-835	SC
Lawrence, Tracy	Lessons Learned	22-536	ST
Lawrence, Tracy	Life Don't Have To Be So Hard	16-8	ST
Lawrence, Tracy	Lonely	14-718	CB
Lawrence, Tracy	Lonely	13-851	CHM
Lawrence, Tracy	Lonely	19-249	CSZ
Lawrence, Tracy	My Second Home	2-7	SC
Lawrence, Tracy	One Step Ahead Of The Storm	48-383	MM
Lawrence, Tracy	Paint Me A Birmingham	19-679	ST
Lawrence, Tracy	Renegades Rebels &	6-596	MM

ARTIST	SONG TITLE	#	TYPE
	Rogues		
Lawrence, Tracy	Renegades Rebels & Rogues	2-318	SC
Lawrence, Tracy	Runnin' Behind	1-573	CB
Lawrence, Tracy	Runnin' Behind	2-796	SC
Lawrence, Tracy	Sawdust On Her Halo	22-83	CB
Lawrence, Tracy	Somebody Paints The Wall	2-815	SC
Lawrence, Tracy	Stars Over Texas	1-583	CB
Lawrence, Tracy	Stars Over Texas	7-339	MM
Lawrence, Tracy	Sticks And Stones	1-571	CB
Lawrence, Tracy	Sticks And Stones	10-786	JVC
Lawrence, Tracy	Stop Drop And Roll	44-182	ASK
Lawrence, Tracy	Texas Tornado	1-580	CB
Lawrence, Tracy	Texas Tornado	2-765	SC
Lawrence, Tracy	Til I Was A Daddy Too	36-408	CB
Lawrence, Tracy	Time Marches On	1-582	CB
Lawrence, Tracy	Time Marches On	7-205	MM
Lawrence, Tracy	Time Marches On	22-881	ST
Lawrence, Tracy	Today's Lonely Fool	1-572	CB
Lawrence, Tracy	Unforgiven	14-796	ST
Lawrence, Tracy	Unforgiven	48-384	MM
Lawrence, Tracy	Up To Him	48-381	CB
Lawrence, Tracy	Used To The Pain	23-305	CB
Lawrence, Tracy	Used To The Pain	29-608	ST
Lawrence, Tracy	We Don't Love Here Anymore	48-378	CB
Lawrence, Tracy	What A Memory	16-438	ST
Lawrence, Tracy	While You Sleep	22-831	ST
Lawrence, Tracy	Xmas - All Wrapped Up In Christmas	48-382	CB
Lawrence, Tracy	You Can't Hide Redneck	48-380	CB
Lawrence, Vicki	Night The Lights Went Out In GA	13-14	P
Lawson, Jamie	Wasn't Expecting That	48-447	KCD
Lawson, Jamie	Wasn't Expecting That	47-704	BKD
Lawson, Melissa	What If It All Goes Right	36-246	PHM
Lawson, Shannon	Everybody Wants	20-257	PHM
Lawson, Shannon	Goodbye On A Bad Day	30-386	CB
Lawson, Shannon	Goodbye On A Bad Day	25-227	MM
Lawson, Shannon	Goodbye On A Bad Day	16-432	ST
Lawson, Shannon	Just Like A Redneck	20-482	ST
Lawson, Shannon	Smokin' Grass	20-348	ST
Leace, Donal	Sad Lisa	21-612	SF
Leary, Denis	Asshole **	30-658	RSX
Led Zeppelin	All My Love	5-876	SC
Led Zeppelin	Black Dog	4-558	SC
Led Zeppelin	Dazed And Confused	19-274	SGB
Led Zeppelin	I Can't Quit You Baby	15-22	SC
Led Zeppelin	Immigrant Song	12-770	P
Led Zeppelin	Kashmir	19-286	SGB
Led Zeppelin	Ramble On	5-71	SC
Led Zeppelin	Rock & Roll	11-499	DK
Led Zeppelin	Rock & Roll	13-224	P
Led Zeppelin	Stairway To Heaven	11-771	DK
Led Zeppelin	Stairway To Heaven	13-225	P
Led Zeppelin	Whole Lotta Love	17-85	DK

ARTIST	SONG TITLE	#	TYPE
Led Zeppelin	Whole Lotta Love	12-768	P
Ledoux & Brooks	Whatcha Goona Do With A Cowboy	6-181	MM
LeDoux, Chris	Airborne Cowboy	23-491	CB
LeDoux, Chris	Cadillac Ranch	17-165	JVC
LeDoux, Chris	County Fair	14-731	CB
LeDoux, Chris	Dallas Days And Fort Worth Nights	3-636	SC
LeDoux, Chris	Everytime I Roll The Dice	2-104	SC
LeDoux, Chris	Five Dollar Fine	4-625	SC
LeDoux, Chris	Get Back On That Pony	10-780	JVC
LeDoux, Chris	Gravitational Pull	7-250	MM
LeDoux, Chris	Horsepower	20-178	ST
LeDoux, Chris	I Believe In America	20-586	CB
LeDoux, Chris	Life Is A Highway	8-964	CB
LeDoux, Chris	Patriotic - I Believe In America	34-360	CB
LeDoux, Chris	Riding For A Fall	24-89	SC
LeDoux, Chris	Silence On The Line	14-107	CB
LeDoux, Chris	Slow Down	2-772	SC
LeDoux, Chris	Stampede	5-840	SC
LeDoux, Chris	Under This Old Hat	4-108	SC
LeDoux, Chris	Wild And Wooly	24-13	SC
Lee & Brody	Duet - Yellow Rose Of Texas	49-645	VH
Lee & Brody	Yellow Rose Of Texas - duet	49-645	VH
Lee & Showdown	Rodeo Song the **	30-659	RSX
Lee, Amos	Keep It Loose Keep It Tight	29-317	PHM
Lee, Brenda	All Alone Am I	30-326	CB
Lee, Brenda	All Alone Am I	22-442	SC
Lee, Brenda	As Usual	45-454	ZM
Lee, Brenda	Big Four Poster Bed	30-330	CB
Lee, Brenda	Break It To Me Gently	30-328	CB
Lee, Brenda	Broken Trust	30-335	CB
Lee, Brenda	Coming On Strong	49-7	DCK
Lee, Brenda	Coming On Strong	45-733	VH
Lee, Brenda	Cowgirl And The Dandy	30-334	CB
Lee, Brenda	Dum Dum	4-710	SC
Lee, Brenda	Emotions	11-603	DK
Lee, Brenda	End Of The World	45-453	SAV
Lee, Brenda	Everybody Loves Me But You	45-905	CB
Lee, Brenda	Fly Me To The Moon	15-475	CMC
Lee, Brenda	Fool #1	16-367	CB
Lee, Brenda	Fool #1	4-304	SC
Lee, Brenda	Grass Is Greener the	45-888	VH
Lee, Brenda	He's My Rock	30-332	CB
Lee, Brenda	Here Comes That Feeling	45-908	EZ
Lee, Brenda	Hold Me	45-364	OZP
Lee, Brenda	I Want To Be Wanted	5-81	SC
Lee, Brenda	I Want To Be Wanted	30-795	SF
Lee, Brenda	I Wish That I Could Hurt That Way..	9-435	SAV
Lee, Brenda	I'm In The Mood For	45-907	DKM

ARTIST	SONG TITLE	#	TYPE
	Love		
Lee, Brenda	I'm Sorry	30-323	CB
Lee, Brenda	I'm Sorry	11-505	DK
Lee, Brenda	I'm Sorry	10-725	JVC
Lee, Brenda	I'm Sorry	3-363	MH
Lee, Brenda	I'm Sorry	12-741	P
Lee, Brenda	If You Love Me Really Love Me	47-894	SF
Lee, Brenda	If You Love Me Really Love Me	47-893	SAV
Lee, Brenda	Is It True	45-911	ZM
Lee, Brenda	It's Only A Paper Moon	48-579	DK
Lee, Brenda	Jingle Bell Rock	45-904	DMG
Lee, Brenda	Johnny One Time	30-325	CB
Lee, Brenda	Let's Jump The Broomstick	29-827	SF
Lee, Brenda	Losing You	47-727	DCK
Lee, Brenda	Lover Come Back To Me	45-910	TO
Lee, Brenda	Nobody Wins	30-327	CB
Lee, Brenda	Nobody Wins	45-450	CB
Lee, Brenda	Only You	45-881	VH
Lee, Brenda	Papa Noel	45-903	CB
Lee, Brenda	Pennies From Heaven	48-577	DK
Lee, Brenda	Pennies From Heaven	45-906	DKM
Lee, Brenda	Rock On Baby	30-331	CB
Lee, Brenda	Rocking Around the Christmas Tree	35-324	CB
Lee, Brenda	Rose Garden	45-909	IDM
Lee, Brenda	Speak To Me Pretty	45-452	EZC
Lee, Brenda	Sunday Sunrise	9-615	SAV
Lee, Brenda	Sweet Nothins'	30-322	CB
Lee, Brenda	Sweet Nothins'	11-26	PX
Lee, Brenda	Sweet Nothins'	3-293	MM
Lee, Brenda	Sweet Nothins'	4-6	SC
Lee, Brenda	Tell Me What It's Like	30-333	CB
Lee, Brenda	That's All You Gotta Do	47-726	SRK
Lee, Brenda	Too Many Rivers	30-324	CB
Lee, Brenda	Too Many Rivers	45-449	CB
Lee, Brenda	Weep No More My Baby	49-241	DFK
Lee, Brenda	Wrong Ideas	30-329	CB
Lee, Brenda	Xmas - Jingle Bell Rock	45-904	DMG
Lee, Brenda	Xmas - Papa Noel	45-903	CB
Lee, Brenda	Xmas - Rockin' Around The Xmas Tree	8-53	CB
Lee, Brenda	Xmas - Rockin' Around the Xmas Tree	11-729	DK
Lee, Brenda	Xmas - Rockin' Around the Xmas Tree	6-300	MM
Lee, Brenda	Xmas - Rockin' Around The Xmas Tree	3-398	SC
Lee, Brenda	You Can Depend On Me	45-451	CBE
Lee, Brice	Drinking Class	45-47	BKD
Lee, Curtis	Pretty Little Angel Eyes	6-685	MM
Lee, Curtis	Pretty Little Angel Eyes	10-383	SS
Lee, Gary & Sundown	Rodeo Song **	2-181	SC
Lee, Jesse	Like My Mother Does	38-226	CB
Lee, Johnny	Be There For My Baby	5-771	SC

ARTIST	SONG TITLE	#	TYPE
Lee, Johnny	Bet Your Heart On Me	47-174	SC
Lee, Johnny	Cherokee Fiddle	47-173	SC
Lee, Johnny	Hey Bartender	2-408	SC
Lee, Johnny	Lookin' For Love	29-629	CB
Lee, Johnny	Lookin' For Love	17-414	DK
Lee, Johnny	Lookin' For Love	12-431	P
Lee, Johnny	Lookin' For Love	8-678	SAV
Lee, Johnny	One In A Million	4-544	SC
Lee, Johnny	Pickin' Up Strangers	47-175	SC
Lee, Johnny	Prisoner Of Hope	5-538	SC
Lee, Johnny	She Even Woke Me Up To Say Goodbye	9-491	SAV
Lee, Johnny	Sometimes	47-787	SRK
Lee, Johnny	Sometimes	45-841	VH
Lee, Johnny	Sounds Like Love	5-861	SC
Lee, Peggy	Big Spender	47-179	KV
Lee, Peggy	Black Coffee	47-178	KV
Lee, Peggy	Come Rain Or Come Shine	49-935	SC
Lee, Peggy	Fever	26-331	DK
Lee, Peggy	Fever	10-324	KC
Lee, Peggy	Fever	23-352	MM
Lee, Peggy	Fever	4-192	SC
Lee, Peggy	Golden Earrings	47-180	KV
Lee, Peggy	How Long Has This Been Going On	47-177	KV
Lee, Peggy	I Can't Give You Anything But Love	49-926	KVD
Lee, Peggy	I Wanna Be Seduced	45-850	VH
Lee, Peggy	I'm A Woman	25-668	MM
Lee, Peggy	I've Got You Under My Skin	9-807	SAV
Lee, Peggy	Is That All There Is	47-182	PS
Lee, Peggy	It's A Good Day	47-181	KV
Lee, Peggy	Johnny Guitar	47-176	JVC
Lee, Peggy	Manana	47-183	PS
Lee, Peggy	Moments Like This	49-934	PS
Lee, Peggy	My Heart Belongs To Daddy	25-261	MM
Lee, Peggy	Sing A Rainbow	49-933	KV
Lee, Peggy	Why Don't You Do Right	25-677	MM
Lee, Robin	Black Velvet	6-620	MM
Lee, Robin	Black Velvet	17-304	NA
Lee, Robin	Black Velvet	4-63	SC
Lee, Scooter	Roll Back The Rug And Dance	45-855	VH
Left Banke	Walk Away Renee	18-237	DK
Legend, John	All Of Me	45-2	KV
Legend, John	Another Again	45-295	CB
Legend, John	Each Day Gets Better	36-464	CB
Legend, John	Ordinary People	30-135	PT
Legend, John	Save Room	37-114	SC
Legend, John	Save Room	46-322	SC
Legend, John	You And I (Nobody In The World)	45-808	KV
Legend, John w Andre 3000	Green Light	36-512	CB
Legend, John w	Hey Girl	38-265	PHM

ARTIST	SONG TITLE	#	TYPE
Estelle			
Lehrer, Tom	Masochism Tango the **	23-21	SC
Lehrer, Tom	Poisoning Pigeons In The Park	23-29	SC
Lehrer, Tom	Xmas - Christmas Carol a	5-710	SC
Leigh, Danni	29 Nights	8-936	CB
Leigh, Danni	I Don't Feel This Way Anymore	14-736	CB
Leigh, Danni	If The Jukebox Took Teardrops	8-187	CB
Leigh, Danni	Longnecks Cigarettes	14-170	CB
Leigh, Danni	Sometimes	16-692	ST
Lekakis, Paul	Boom Boom (Let's Go Back..) **	15-1	SC
Lemon Pipers	Green Tambourine	11-113	DK
Lemonheads	If I Could Talk I'd Tell You	24-645	SC
Lemonheads	Into Your Arms	6-43	SC
Len	Duet - Steal My Sunshine	33-407	CB
Len	Duet - Steal My Sunshine	8-497	PHT
Len	Duet - Steal My Sunshine	10-205	SC
Len	Steal My Sunshine	8-497	PHT
Len	Steal My Sunshine	10-205	SC
Len	Steal My Sunshine - duet	33-407	CB
Lennon, John	#9 Dream	30-291	RS
Lennon, John	Cold Turkey	30-298	RS
Lennon, John	Give Peace A Chance	30-293	RS
Lennon, John	Happy Xmas - The War Is Over	30-305	RS
Lennon, John	Happy Xmas (The War Is Over)	3-389	SC
Lennon, John	Imagine	6-157	MM
Lennon, John	Imagine	30-292	RS
Lennon, John	Imagine	9-649	SAV
Lennon, John	Instant Karma	30-294	RS
Lennon, John	Instant Karma	16-65	SC
Lennon, John	Jealous Guy	30-303	RS
Lennon, John	Just Like Starting Over	30-295	RS
Lennon, John	Love	30-302	RS
Lennon, John	Mind Games	30-290	RS
Lennon, John	Mother	30-304	RS
Lennon, John	No. 9 Dreams	30-291	RS
Lennon, John	Nobody Told Me	7-488	MM
Lennon, John	Nobody Told Me	30-296	RS
Lennon, John	Power To The People	30-289	RS
Lennon, John	Stand By Me	30-300	RS
Lennon, John	Strarting Over	9-650	SAV
Lennon, John	Watchin' The Wheels	30-299	RS
Lennon, John	Watching The Wheels	29-261	SC
Lennon, John	Whatever Gets You Thru the Night	30-288	RS
Lennon, John	Woman	17-372	DK
Lennon, John	Woman	30-297	RS
Lennon, John	Working Class Hero	30-301	RS

ARTIST	SONG TITLE	#	TYPE
Lennon, John	Xmas - And So This Is Christmas	7-15	MM
Lennon, John	Xmas - Happy Christmas (War/Over)	3-389	SC
Lennon, John	Xmas - Happy Xmas The War Is Over	30-305	RS
Lennon, Julian	Too Late For Goodbyes	5-682	SC
Lennox & Green	Duet - Put A Little Love In Your...	18-379	SAV
Lennox & Green	Duet - Put A Little Love in/Heart	6-336	MM
Lennox & Green	Put A Little Love In Your Heart	6-336	MM
Lennox & Green	Put A Little Love In Your Heart	18-379	SAV
Lennox, Annie	Here Comes The Rain Again	17-724	PS
Lennox, Annie	Little Bird	13-246	P
Lennox, Annie	Little Bird	17-728	PS
Lennox, Annie	No More I Love Yous	16-618	MM
Lennox, Annie	No More I Love Yous	17-722	PS
Lennox, Annie	Put A Little Love In Your Heart	49-462	MM
Lennox, Annie	Sweet Dreams Are Made Of This	17-726	PS
Lennox, Annie	Thin Line Between Love & Hate	19-554	SC
Lennox, Annie	Train In Vain	17-725	PS
Lennox, Annie	Walkin' On Broken Glass	17-729	PS
Lennox, Annie	Walking On Broken Glass	12-246	DK
Lennox, Annie	Walking On Broken Glass	13-243	P
Lennox, Annie	Walking On Broken Glass	5-338	SC
Lennox, Annie	Whiter Shade Of Pale	17-727	PS
Lennox, Annie	Why	12-247	DK
Lennox, Annie	Why	13-244	P
Lennox, Annie	Why	17-723	PS
Les Miserables	Show - Bring Him Home	17-643	PR
Les Miserables	Show - Bring Him Home	18-186	PS
Les Miserables	Show - Castle On A Cloud	17-644	PR
Les Miserables	Show - Castle On A Cloud	18-89	PS
Les Miserables	Show - Empty Chairs at Empty Tables	17-649	PR
Les Miserables	Show - I Dreamed A Dream	6-318	MM
Les Miserables	Show - I Dreamed A Dream	17-645	PR
Les Miserables	Show - I Dreamed A Dream	18-88	PS
Les Miserables	Show - In My Life	6-242	MM
Les Miserables	Show - Little Fall Of Rain a	17-648	PR
Les Miserables	Show - Master Of The House	7-368	MM
Les Miserables	Show - On My Own	17-646	PR

ARTIST	SONG TITLE	#	TYPE
Les Miserables	Show - On My Own	9-94	PS
Les Miserables	Show - Stars	17-647	PR
Les Miserables	Show - Stars	18-90	PS
Les Paul/Mary Ford	Duet - How High The Moon	4-190	SC
Les Paul/Mary Ford	How High The Moon	4-190	SC
Less Th	Silence Of Selling Yourself Short the	32-367	THM
Lettermen	Almost There	48-531	L1
Lettermen	Be My Girl	48-534	L1
Lettermen	Dear Heart	48-519	L1
Lettermen	Dearly Beloved	48-533	L1
Lettermen	Goin' Out Of My Head	48-526	L1
Lettermen	Here There And Everywhere	48-539	PIX
Lettermen	Hurt So Bad	48-523	L1
Lettermen	I Only Have Eyes For You	48-518	L1
Lettermen	Love Letters In The Sand	48-537	L1
Lettermen	My Cup Runneth Over	48-517	L1
Lettermen	Polka Dots And Moonbeams	48-522	L1
Lettermen	Portrait Of My Love	48-521	L1
Lettermen	Put Your Head On My Shoulder	48-525	L1
Lettermen	She Cried	48-532	L1
Lettermen	Sincerely	48-536	L1
Lettermen	Smile	48-520	L1
Lettermen	Summer Place a	48-527	L1
Lettermen	Things We Did Last Summer	48-528	L1
Lettermen	Till Then	48-538	L1
Lettermen	To Know Her Is To Love Her	48-530	L1
Lettermen	Traces/Memories	48-524	L1
Lettermen	Venus	48-529	L1
Lettermen	Way You Look Tonight the	48-516	THM
Lettermen	What Now My Love	19-108	SAV
Lettermen	Young Love	48-535	L1
Letters To Cleo	Dangerous Type	4-339	SC
Letters To Cleo	Here And Now	24-750	SC
Level 42	Running In The Family	44-184	ZMH
Level 42	Something About You	15-793	SC
Levert, Gerald	Taking Everything	7-819	PHM
Lewis & Durtz	Duet - Outside	16-480	MH
Lewis & Durtz	Outside	16-480	MH
Lewis & Durtz	Outside	15-459	PHM
Lewis & Marx	At The Beginning	10-114	SC
Lewis & Marx	Duet - At The Beginning	10-114	SC
Lewis & Paltrow	Cruisin'	14-22	THM
Lewis & Paltrow	Duet - Cruisin'	14-22	THM
Lewis & Playboys	Birds And The Bees the	48-560	DK
Lewis & Playboys	Count Me In	43-31	CB
Lewis & Playboys	Count Me In	7-41	MM
Lewis & Playboys	Everybody Loves A Clown	3-18	SC

ARTIST	SONG TITLE	#	TYPE
Lewis & Playboys	Save Your Heart For Me	6-59	SC
Lewis & Playboys	She's Just My Style	3-459	SC
Lewis & Playboys	Sure Gonna Miss Her	14-464	SC
Lewis & Playboys	This Diamond Ring	35-56	CB
Lewis & Playboys	This Diamond Ring	11-90	DK
Lewis & Playboys	This Diamond Ring	10-328	KC
Lewis & The News	100 Years From Now	47-190	SC
Lewis & The News	Back In Time	47-189	KV
Lewis & The News	Bad Is Bad	47-193	SC
Lewis & The News	Bring It All For My Baby	9-790	SAV
Lewis & The News	But It's Alright	6-640	MM
Lewis & The News	Couple Days Off	47-185	CB
Lewis & The News	Do You Believe In Love	47-184	CB
Lewis & The News	Doin' It All For My Baby	11-329	DK
Lewis & The News	Doing It All For My Baby	33-321	CB
Lewis & The News	Feeling Alright	47-192	SC
Lewis & The News	Heart And Soul	11-101	DK
Lewis & The News	Heart Of Rock & Roll	16-811	DK
Lewis & The News	Heart Of Rock N Roll	35-171	CB
Lewis & The News	Hip To Be Square	16-793	DK
Lewis & The News	I Want A New Drug	34-77	CB
Lewis & The News	I Want A New Drug	2-748	SC
Lewis & The News	If This Is It	11-245	DK
Lewis & The News	It Hit Me Like A Hammer	47-186	CB
Lewis & The News	Jacob's Ladder	24-69	SC
Lewis & The News	Jacob's Ladder	47-187	CB
Lewis & The News	Let Her Go & Start Over	25-26	MM
Lewis & The News	Perfect World	11-393	DK
Lewis & The News	Power Of Love	20-301	CB
Lewis & The News	Power Of Love	11-136	DK
Lewis & The News	Power Of Love	12-836	P
Lewis & The News	Some Kind Of Wonderful	24-143	SC
Lewis & The News	Stuck With You	15-563	CMC
Lewis & The News	Stuck With You	17-112	DK
Lewis & The News	Stuck With You	21-741	MH
Lewis & The News	Walking On A Thin Line	47-191	SC
Lewis & The News	Working For A Living	47-188	JVC
Lewis, Aaron	Country Boy	48-770	BKD
Lewis, Barbara	Baby I'm Yours	26-100	DK
Lewis, Barbara	Baby I'm Yours	3-362	MH
Lewis, Barbara	Baby I'm Yours	3-288	MM
Lewis, Barbara	Baby I'm Yours	12-907	P
Lewis, Barbara	Hello Stranger	25-168	MM
Lewis, Barbara	Make Me Your Baby	20-69	SC
Lewis, Bobby	Tossin' And Turnin'	11-565	DK
Lewis, Bobby	Tossin' And Turnin'	10-741	JVC
Lewis, Bobby	Tossin' And Turnin'	6-147	MM
Lewis, Bobby	Tossin' And Turnin'	13-122	P
Lewis, Bobby	Tossin' And Turnin'	3-254	SC
Lewis, Donna	I Love You Always Forever	24-46	SC
Lewis, Donna	Without Love	24-643	SC
Lewis, Glenn	Don't You Forget It	25-214	MM
Lewis, Huey	Heart And Soul	48-572	DK
Lewis, Huey	Hip To Be Square	48-571	DK
Lewis, Huey	Power Of Love the	48-573	DK

ARTIST	SONG TITLE	#	TYPE
Lewis, Jerry Lee	Another Place Another Time	47-195	CB
Lewis, Jerry Lee	Boogie Woogie Country Man	47-813	SRK
Lewis, Jerry Lee	Breathless	5-455	SC
Lewis, Jerry Lee	Chantilly Lace	47-202	EK
Lewis, Jerry Lee	Country Memories	47-799	SRK
Lewis, Jerry Lee	Drinkin' Wine	7-408	MM
Lewis, Jerry Lee	Drinking Wine (Spo Dee O Dee)	33-27	CB
Lewis, Jerry Lee	Great Balls Of Fire	11-164	DK
Lewis, Jerry Lee	Great Balls Of Fire	12-894	P
Lewis, Jerry Lee	Great Balls Of Fire	9-501	SAV
Lewis, Jerry Lee	Halloween - Haunted House	45-140	OZP
Lewis, Jerry Lee	Haunted House - Halloween	45-140	OZP
Lewis, Jerry Lee	High School Confidential	47-204	SC
Lewis, Jerry Lee	Honky Tonk Woman	47-814	SRK
Lewis, Jerry Lee	I Believe In You	47-802	SRK
Lewis, Jerry Lee	I Saw Her Standing There	47-203	KV
Lewis, Jerry Lee	I Saw Her Standing There	45-874	VH
Lewis, Jerry Lee	Lonely Weekends	47-800	SRK
Lewis, Jerry Lee	Middle Age Crazy	34-236	CB
Lewis, Jerry Lee	No More Than I Got	47-801	SRK
Lewis, Jerry Lee	Once More With Feeling	47-197	CB
Lewis, Jerry Lee	One Minute Past Eternity	47-196	CB
Lewis, Jerry Lee	Rockin' My Life Away	47-201	CB
Lewis, Jerry Lee	She Even Woke Me Up To Say Goodbye	47-198	CB
Lewis, Jerry Lee	There Must Be More To Love Than This	47-199	CB
Lewis, Jerry Lee	Thirty Nine & Holding	13-496	P
Lewis, Jerry Lee	Thirty Nine & Holding	33-69	CB
Lewis, Jerry Lee	Trouble In Mind	45-731	VH
Lewis, Jerry Lee	Walkin' The Floor Over You	46-41	SSK
Lewis, Jerry Lee	What Made Milwaukee Famous..	3-375	SC
Lewis, Jerry Lee	Whole Lotta Shakin' Goin' On	3-320	MH
Lewis, Jerry Lee	Whole Lotta Shakin' Goin' On	13-55	P
Lewis, Jerry Lee	Would You Take Another Chance On Me	47-200	CB
Lewis, Jerry Lee	You Win Again	34-196	CB
Lewis, Jerry Lee	You Win Again	47-194	CB
Lewis, Jerry Lee.	What'd I Say	29-820	SF
Lewis, Leona	Better In Time	36-529	CB
Lewis, Leona	Bleeding Love	36-446	CB
Lewis, Smiley	I Hear You Knockin'	13-266	P
Lewis, Smiley	I Hear You Knockin'	5-459	SC
Lewis, Ted	Baby Face	21-6	SC
Leyton, John	Johnny Remember Me	10-564	SF
LFO	Back In Love Again	14-359	MH

ARTIST	SONG TITLE	#	TYPE
LFO	Girl On TV	16-182	PHM
LFO	I Don't Wanna Kiss You Goodnight	16-235	PHM
LFO	I Don't Wanna Kiss You Goodnight	14-479	SC
LFO	I Don't Wanna Kiss You Goodnight	14-172	CB
LFO	Life Is Good	18-287	CB
LFO	Life Is Good	16-77	ST
LFO	Summer Girls	10-203	SC
Liberacion	Latino - En La Misma Cama	23-239	AI
Liberty X	Just A Little	25-337	MM
Liberty X	X	30-719	SF
Lifehouse	Breathing	35-237	CB
Lifehouse	Breathing	25-78	MM
Lifehouse	Broken	36-503	CB
Lifehouse	First Time	30-562	CB
Lifehouse	First Time	37-113	SC
Lifehouse	Hanging By A Moment	15-808	CB
Lifehouse	Hanging By A Moment	16-470	MH
Lifehouse	Hanging By A Moment	16-113	PRT
Lifehouse	Hanging By A Moment	18-557	TT
Lifehouse	Sick Cycle Carousel	18-574	TT
Lifehouse	Spin	25-344	MM
Lifehouse	Take Me Away (Remix Edit)	32-211	THM
Lifehouse	Whatever It Takes	36-477	CB
Lifehouse	You And Me	30-142	PT
Light, Jan	Mr. Big Stuff	6-650	MM
Lightfoot, Gordon	Baby Step Back	43-492	SK
Lightfoot, Gordon	Beautiful	43-494	SK
Lightfoot, Gordon	Bitter Green	43-491	SK
Lightfoot, Gordon	Canadian RR Trilogy	43-496	SK
Lightfoot, Gordon	Carefree Highway	2-791	SC
Lightfoot, Gordon	Carefree Highway	43-487	SK
Lightfoot, Gordon	Circle Is Small (I Can See It In,,,)	21-805	SC
Lightfoot, Gordon	Circle Too Small	43-478	SK
Lightfoot, Gordon	Cotton Jenny	43-115	SK
Lightfoot, Gordon	Daylight Katy	43-490	SK
Lightfoot, Gordon	Don Quixote	43-493	SK
Lightfoot, Gordon	Early Morning Rain	43-486	SK
Lightfoot, Gordon	For Lovin Me/Did She Mention My Name	43-477	SK
Lightfoot, Gordon	Go-Go 'Round	43-482	SK
Lightfoot, Gordon	I'm Not Sayin'/Ribbon Of Darkness	43-489	SK
Lightfoot, Gordon	If You Could Read My Mind	43-25	CBE
Lightfoot, Gordon	If You Could Read My Mind	9-358	MG
Lightfoot, Gordon	If You Could Read My Mind	43-476	SK
Lightfoot, Gordon	Inspiration Lady	43-475	SK
Lightfoot, Gordon	Pussywillows Cat Tails	43-495	SK
Lightfoot, Gordon	Race Among The Ruins	43-483	SK
Lightfoot, Gordon	Rainy Day People	43-484	SK

ARTIST	SONG TITLE	#	TYPE
Lightfoot, Gordon	Song For A Winter's Night	43-485	SK
Lightfoot, Gordon	Summer Side of Life	43-481	SK
Lightfoot, Gordon	Sundown	9-319	AG
Lightfoot, Gordon	Sundown	43-26	CB
Lightfoot, Gordon	Sundown	4-379	SC
Lightfoot, Gordon	Sundown	43-488	SK
Lightfoot, Gordon	Wreck Of The Edmond Fitzgerald	5-301	SC
Lightfoot, Gordon	You Are What I Am	43-480	SK
Lightman, Toby	Real Love	20-559	PHM
Lil Jon&Eastside&YY	Duet - Get Low **	21-794	SC
Lil Jon&Eastside&YY	Get Low **	21-794	SC
Lil Kim & 50 Cent	Duet - Magic Stick	32-387	THM
Lil Kim & 50 Cent	Magic Stick - Duet	32-387	THM
Lil Kim w Mr. Cheeks	Jump Off the	32-351	THM
Lil Mo	Shoulda Known	32-385	THM
Lil Romeo	My Baby	18-569	TT
Lil' Shop of Horror	Show - Da-Doo	17-680	PS
Lil' Shop of Horror	Show - Dentist	7-362	MM
Lil' Shop of Horror	Show - Dentist	17-684	PS
Lil' Shop of Horror	Show - Don't Feed The Plants	17-690	PS
Lil' Shop of Horror	Show - Feed Me (Get It)	17-685	PS
Lil' Shop of Horror	Show - Grow For Me	17-681	PS
Lil' Shop of Horror	Show - Grow For Me	5-658	SC
Lil' Shop of Horror	Show - Mean Green Mother From...	17-689	PS
Lil' Shop of Horror	Show - Meek Shall Inherit the	17-688	PS
Lil' Shop of Horror	Show - Prologue	17-678	PS
Lil' Shop of Horror	Show - Skid Row - Downtown	17-679	PS
Lil' Shop of Horror	Show - Some Fun Now	17-683	PS
Lil' Shop of Horror	Show - Somewhere That's Green	17-682	PS
Lil' Shop of Horror	Show - Suddenly Seymour	17-686	PS
Lil' Shop of Horror	Show - Suddenly Seymour - (best)	19-590	SC
Lil' Shop of Horror	Show - Suppertime	17-687	PS
Lillix	It's About Time	25-582	MM
Lillix	It's About Time	19-544	SC
Lillix	It's About Time	32-248	THM
Limi-T 21	Latino - Como Tu Mi Quiere A Mi	17-794	SC
Limi-T 21	Latino - Y Dale.....	18-4	PS
Limite	Latino - Acariciame	17-756	SC
Limite	Latino - Por Encima Te Todo	18-6	PS
Limp Bizkit	My Way	15-301	THM
Limp Bizkit	Re-Arranged	5-781	SC
Limp Bizkit	Show - Take A Look Around (M-2)	14-494	SC
Lind, Bob	Elusive Butterfly	11-362	DK
Lind, Bob	Elusive Butterfly	9-845	SAV
Lindell, Eric	Give It Time	36-183	PHM

ARTIST	SONG TITLE	#	TYPE
Lines, Aaron	It Takes A Man	23-302	CB
Lines, Aaron	Love Changes Everything	25-619	MM
Lines, Aaron	Love Changes Everything	19-53	ST
Lines, Aaron	Waitin' On The Wonderful	23-9	CB
Lines, Aaron	You Can't Hide Beautiful	25-415	MM
Lines, Aaron	You Can't Hide Beautiful	18-214	ST
Linkin Park	Crawlin'	16-381	SGB
Linkin Park	In the End	36-136	SGB
Linkin Park	In The End	16-320	TT
Linkin Park	Pushin' Me Away	16-321	TT
Linkin Park	Somewhere I Belong	32-214	THM
Lion King	Can You Feel The Love Tonight	20-185	Z
Lion King	Show - Can You Feel the Love Tonite	20-185	Z
Lion King	Show - Circle Of Life	20-186	Z
Lipps Inc.	Funkytown	18-365	AH
Lipps Inc.	Funkytown	18-244	DK
Lipps Inc.	Funkytown	9-14	MH
Lipps Inc.	Funkytown	20-372	SC
Lisa Lisa & Cult J	All Cried Out	11-592	DK
Lisa Lisa & Cult J	Duet - All Cried Out	11-592	DK
Lisa Lisa & Cult J	Head To Toe	11-317	DK
Lisa Lisa & Cult J	Lost In Emotion	11-593	DK
Lit	My Own Worst Enemy	7-895	PHT
Lit	Over My Head	15-644	THM
Little Anthony	Goin' Out Of My Head	30-514	LE
Little Anthony	Hurt So Bad	30-515	LE
Little Anthony	Hurt So Bad	35-54	CB
Little Anthony	I Miss You So	30-520	LE
Little Anthony	I'm On The Outside (Lookin' In)	30-517	LE
Little Anthony	Shimmy Shimmy Ko Ko Bop	30-516	LE
Little Anthony	Shimmy Shimmy Ko Ko Bop	5-637	SC
Little Anthony	Take Me Back	30-518	LE
Little Anthony	Tears On My Pillow	30-513	LE
Little Anthony	Tears On My Pillow	12-12	DK
Little Anthony	Tears On My Pillow	6-269	MM
Little Anthony	Wishful Thinking	30-519	LE
Little Big Town	Bones	30-201	CB
Little Big Town	Boondocks	23-283	CB
Little Big Town	Boondocks	29-503	SC
Little Big Town	Bring It On Home	29-193	CB
Little Big Town	Day Drinking	44-324	SSC
Little Big Town	Don't Waste My Time	25-190	MM
Little Big Town	Don't Waste My Time	16-690	ST
Little Big Town	Duet - Boondocks	23-283	CB
Little Big Town	Duet - Don't Waste My Time	25-190	MM
Little Big Town	Duet - Reason Why the	38-220	CB
Little Big Town	Everything Changes	18-135	ST
Little Big Town	Fine Line	36-592	CB
Little Big Town	Fine Line	36-207	PHM

ARTIST	SONG TITLE	#	TYPE
Little Big Town	Front Porch Thing	40-25	PHM
Little Big Town	Girl Crush	45-6	KV
Little Big Town	Girl Crush (Inst)	49-737	BKD
Little Big Town	Good As Gone	30-108	CB
Little Big Town	Good Lord Willing	47-206	CB
Little Big Town	I'm With The Band	30-579	CB
Little Big Town	Kiss Goodbye	37-349	CB
Little Big Town	Little More You a	30-345	CB
Little Big Town	Little White Church	37-328	CB
Little Big Town	Looking For A Reason	29-595	CB
Little Big Town	Pain Killer	45-362	BKD
Little Big Town	PONTOON	39-39	ASK
Little Big Town	Pontoon	47-404	SRK
Little Big Town	Pontoon	47-403	BKD
Little Big Town	Pontoon	47-402	MRH
Little Big Town	Reason Why the - duet	38-220	CB
Little Big Town	Shut Up Train	47-205	KV
Little Big Town	Sober	40-3	ASK
Little Big Town	Tornado	40-4	ASK
Little Big Town	We Go Together	40-5	PHM
Little Big Town	Your Side Of The Bed	41-45	ASK
Little Caesar&Roman	Those Oldies But Goodies	3-584	SC
Little Eva	Keep Your Hands Off My Baby	5-76	SC
Little Eva	Loco-Motion the	35-187	CB
Little Eva	Loco-Motion the	23-360	CR
Little Eva	Loco-Motion the	10-733	JVC
Little Eva	Loco-Motion the	3-356	MH
Little Eva	Loco-Motion the	12-636	P
Little Feat	Dixie Chicken	12-25	DK
Little Feat	Fat Man In The Bathtub	47-207	SC
Little Feat	Oh Atlanta	17-461	SC
Little Feat	Willin'	37-75	SC
Little Milton	Grits Ain't Groceries	21-576	SC
Little People the	O White Christmas	45-795	SC
Little People the	Xmas - O White Christmas	45-795	SC
Little Richard	Good Golly Miss Molly	3-313	MH
Little Richard	Good Golly Miss Molly	6-165	MM
Little Richard	Good Golly Miss Molly	3-470	SC
Little Richard	Jenny Jenny	11-88	DK
Little Richard	Long Tall Sally	15-276	DK
Little Richard	Long Tall Sally	13-57	P
Little Richard	Long Tall Sally	11-51	PX
Little Richard	Long Tall Sally	14-557	SC
Little Richard	Lucille	16-858	DK
Little Richard	Lucille	14-340	SC
Little Richard	Slippin' And Slidin'	10-198	SS
Little Richard	Tutti Frutti	11-220	DK
Little Richard	Tutti Frutti	13-42	P
Little Richard	Tutti Frutti	3-257	SC
Little River Band	Cool Change	18-303	SC
Little River Band	Happy Anniversary	18-308	SC
Little River Band	Help Is On The Way	18-307	SC
Little River Band	Lady	18-304	SC
Little River Band	Lonesome Loser	18-302	SC

ARTIST	SONG TITLE	#	TYPE
Little River Band	Night Owls the	4-326	SC
Little River Band	Other Guy the	18-306	SC
Little River Band	Reminiscing	19-130	KC
Little River Band	Reminiscing	18-305	SC
Little River Band	Take It Easy On Me	18-301	SC
Little Texas	Amy's Back In Austin	6-708	MM
Little Texas	Amy's Back In Austin	17-282	NA
Little Texas	Amy's Back In Austin	3-533	SC
Little Texas	Bad For Us	48-100	MM
Little Texas	Country Crazy	4-103	SC
Little Texas	First Time For Everything	12-400	P
Little Texas	God Blessed Texas	12-460	P
Little Texas	God Blessed Texas	2-28	SC
Little Texas	I'd Rather Miss You	2-620	SC
Little Texas	Kick A Little	20-407	MH
Little Texas	Kick A Little	6-665	MM
Little Texas	Kick A Little	2-481	SC
Little Texas	Life Goes On	7-140	MM
Little Texas	Missing Years	30-450	CB
Little Texas	My Love	10-785	JVC
Little Texas	My Love	6-472	MM
Little Texas	Some Guys Have All The Luck	12-401	P
Little Texas	Southern Grace	6-802	MM
Little Texas	Southern Grace	2-767	SC
Little Texas	What Might Have Been	2-115	SC
Little Willies	For The Good Times	38-262	PHN
Littrell, Brian	Welcome Home	36-187	PHM
Live	All Over You	17-354	DK
Live	Heaven	19-649	CB
Live	Heaven	25-628	MM
Live	Heaven	32-397	THM
Live	I Alone	3-498	SC
Live	Lightning Crashes	13-664	SGB
Livewire	Whiskey Sunday	41-79	PHN
Living Colour	Cult Of Personality	27-206	DK
Living Colour	Love Rears It's Ugly Head	6-45	SC
LL Cool J	Hey Lover	4-681	SC
LL Cool J	Hush (Pop Mix)	20-276	PHM
LL Cool J & Amerie	Duet - Paradise	32-86	THM
LL Cool J & Amerie	Paradise - Duet	32-86	THM
Lo Cash Cowboys	Best Seat In The House	44-279	KCDC
Lobo	Carribean Disco Show - Day-O	46-333	FMG
Lobo	Don't Expect Me To Be Your Friend	46-330	SC
Lobo	Don't Tell Me Goodnight	21-806	SC
Lobo	How Can I Tell Her About You	46-332	AH
Lobo	I'd Love You To Want Me	11-396	DK
Lobo	I'd Love You To Want Me	2-433	SC
Lobo	Me & You & A Dog Named Boo	17-36	DK

ARTIST	SONG TITLE	#	TYPE		ARTIST	SONG TITLE	#	TYPE
Lobo	Me & You & A Dog Named Boo	7-99	MM		Loggins, Dave	Please Come To Boston	9-325	AG
Lobo	My First Time	46-336	SBI		Loggins, Kenny	Danger Zone	28-319	DK
Lobo	Simple Man a	46-335	ZP		Loggins, Kenny	Danny's Song	9-329	AG
Lobo	Stoney	46-334	MDG		Loggins, Kenny	Footloose	26-139	DK
Lobo	Where Were You When I Was Falling...	46-331	SC		Loggins, Kenny	Footloose	12-828	P
LoCash	Duet - I Love This Life	49-529	ZP		Loggins, Kenny	For The First Time	10-23	SC
LoCash	I Love This Life	49-526	BKD		Loggins, Kenny	I'm Alright	34-72	CB
LoCash	I Love This Life - duet	49-529	ZP		Loggins, Kenny	I'm Alright	14-635	SC
LoCash Cowboys	C.O.U.N.T.R.Y.	49-530	ZP		Loggins, Kenny	Nobody's Fool	4-318	SC
LoCash Cowboys	Chase A Little Love	49-527	KCD		Loggins, Kenny	This Is It	34-67	CB
LoCash Cowboys	Here Comes Summer	49-528	CB		Loggins, Kenny	This Is It	14-577	SC
Locke, Kimberly	8th World Wonder	20-357	PHM		Lohan, Lindsay	Over	22-363	CB
Locke, Kimberly	8th World Wonder	36-325	PS		London, Julie	Cry Me A River	11-579	DK
Locke, Kimberly	Band Of Gold	49-903	SC		London, Julie	Cry Me A River	12-564	P
Locke, Kimberly	I Could	29-315	PHM		London, Julie	Cry Me A River	4-355	SC
Locke, Kimberly	Wrong	20-560	PHM		Londonbeat	I've Been Thinking About You	21-460	CB
Locklin, Hank	Country Hall Of Fame	37-283	CB		Lonesome River Road	Sittin' On Top Of The World	49-326	CB
Locklin, Hank	Geisha Girl	5-695	SC		Lonestar	Amazed	19-196	CB
Locklin, Hank	Happy Birthday To Me	44-213	CB		Lonestar	Amazed	7-882	CHT
Locklin, Hank	It's A Little More Like Heaven	5-691	SC		Lonestar	Amazed	14-606	SC
Locklin, Hank	Jealous Heart	47-512	VH		Lonestar	Class Reunion (That Used To Be Us)	22-26	CB
Locklin, Hank	Let Me Be The One	37-290	CB		Lonestar	Come Cryin' To Me	7-643	CHM
Locklin, Hank	Let Me Be The One	5-363	SC		Lonestar	Come Cryin' To Me	10-102	SC
Locklin, Hank	Please Help Me I'm Falling	8-650	SAV		Lonestar	Come Cryin' To Me	22-602	ST
Locklin, Hank	Please Help Me I'm Falling	2-634	SC		Lonestar	County Fair	22-77	CB
Locklin, Hank	Send Me The Pillow	8-777	CB		Lonestar	Every Little Thing She Does	48-478	CKC
Locklin, Hank	Send Me The Pillow	8-651	SAV		Lonestar	Everything's Changed	22-812	ST
Locklin, Hank	Send Me The Pillow	19-392	SC		Lonestar	Heartbroke Every Day	22-402	CHM
Locklin, Hank	We're Goinna Go Fishin'	40-8	CB		Lonestar	Heartbroke Every Day	7-396	MM
Locklin, Hank	Why Baby Why	44-215	CB		Lonestar	I'll Die Tryin'	29-57	CB
Locklin, Hank	You're The Reason	44-214	CB		Lonestar	I'm Already There	33-138	CB
Loeb & Nine Stories	Stay (I Missed You)	4-666	SC		Lonestar	I'm Already There	15-93	ST
Loeb, Lisa	Do You Sleep	14-202	CB		Lonestar	I'm Already There	16-268	TT
Loeb, Lisa	Do You Sleep	24-743	SC		Lonestar	Let's Be Us Again	35-435	CB
Loeb, Lisa	Firecracker	14-203	CB		Lonestar	Let's Be Us Again	20-166	ST
Loeb, Lisa	I Do	14-199	CB		Lonestar	Maybe Someday	41-78	PHN
Loeb, Lisa	I Do	10-117	SC		Lonestar	Mountains	30-19	CB
Loeb, Lisa	Let's Forget About It	14-201	CB		Lonestar	Mr. Mom	23-398	CB
Loeb, Lisa	Stay (I Missed You)	14-198	CB		Lonestar	Mr. Mom	21-662	SC
Loeb, Lisa	Stay (I Missed You)	6-631	MM		Lonestar	Mr. Mom	20-489	ST
Loeb, Lisa	Truthfully	14-200	CB		Lonestar	My Front Porch Looking In	32-225	THM
Loeb, Lisa	Underdog	25-435	MM		Lonestar	My Front Porch Looking In	25-566	MM
Loggins & Messina	Danger Zone	48-567	DK		Lonestar	My Front Porch Looking In	19-1	ST
Loggins & Messina	Your Mama Don't Dance	13-139	P		Lonestar	No News	22-454	SC
Loggins & Messina	Your Mama Don't Dance	11-137	DK		Lonestar	Not A Day Goes By	25-130	MM
Loggins & Nicks	Duet - Whenever I Call You Friend	11-292	DK		Lonestar	Not A Day Goes By	16-100	ST
Loggins & Nicks	Duet - Whenever I Call You Friend	13-159	P		Lonestar	Nothing To Prove	30-317	CB
Loggins & Nicks	Whenever I Call You Friend	11-292	DK		Lonestar	Runnin' Away With My Heart	22-899	ST
Loggins & Nicks	Whenever I Call You Friend	13-159	P		Lonestar	Saturday Night	8-917	CB
					Lonestar	Saturday Night	22-727	ST

ARTIST	SONG TITLE	#	TYPE
Lonestar	Say When	8-308	CB
Lonestar	Say When	7-766	CHM
Lonestar	Say When	22-769	ST
Lonestar	Smile	10-230	SC
Lonestar	Smile	22-501	ST
Lonestar	Tell Her	14-139	CB
Lonestar	Tell Her	13-855	CHM
Lonestar	Tell Her	19-216	CSZ
Lonestar	Tell Her	10-262	SC
Lonestar	Tequila Talkin'	7-88	MM
Lonestar	Tequila Talkin'	3-656	SC
Lonestar	Unusually Unusual	34-377	CB
Lonestar	Unusually Unusual	25-351	MM
Lonestar	Unusually Unusual	15-606	ST
Lonestar	Walking In Memphis	25-699	MM
Lonestar	Walking In Memphis	19-364	ST
Lonestar	Walking In Memphis	32-409	THM
Lonestar	What About Now	9-416	CB
Lonestar	What About Now	13-807	CHM
Lonestar	What About Now	22-543	ST
Lonestar	When Cowboys Didn't Dance	4-503	SC
Lonestar	With Me	25-2	MM
Lonestar	With Me	15-667	ST
Lonestar	Xmas - Winter Wonderland	30-399	SC
Lonestar	You Walked In	22-631	ST
Lonestar	You're Like Coming Home	23-281	CB
Long, Brice	Anywhere But Here	23-483	CB
Long, Brice	It's Only Monday	23-299	CB
Long, Brice	Meat And Potato Man	29-598	CB
Long, Janna	Gospel - Greater Is He	34-429	CB
Look	I Am The Beat	30-782	SF
Looking Glass	Brandy (You're A Fine Girl)	11-702	DK
Looking Glass	Brandy (You're A Fine Girl)	12-704	P
Lopez & Anthony	Latino - No Me Ames	23-237	AI
Lopez & Fabolous	Duet - Get Right	22-359	CB
Lopez & Fabolous	Get Right	22-359	CB
Lopez & Fat Joe	Duet - Hold You Down	33-395	CB
Lopez & Fat Joe	Hold You Down - duet	33-395	CB
Lopez & Ja Rule	Duet - I'm Real	23-586	PHM
Lopez & LL Cool J	All I Have	20-458	CB
Lopez & LL Cool J	All I Have	32-96	THM
Lopez & LL Cool J	Duet - All I Have	20-458	CB
Lopez & LL Cool J	Duet - All I Have	32-96	THM
Lopez & Pitbull	Dance Again - duet	40-10	BH
Lopez & Pitbull	Duet - Dance Again	40-10	BH
Lopez & Pitbull	Duet - On The Floor	40-11	CB
Lopez & Pitbull	On The Floor - duet	40-11	CB
Lopez w LL Cool J	All I Have	32-96	THM
Lopez, Jennifer	Ain't It Funny	33-393	CB
Lopez, Jennifer	Ain't It Funny	25-81	MM
Lopez, Jennifer	Alive	18-356	CB
Lopez, Jennifer	Alive	18-410	MM

ARTIST	SONG TITLE	#	TYPE
Lopez, Jennifer	Alive	18-142	PHM
Lopez, Jennifer	Baby I Love You	19-647	CB
Lopez, Jennifer	Baby I Love You	21-795	SC
Lopez, Jennifer	Could This Be Love	23-327	CB
Lopez, Jennifer	Could This Be Love	23-576	MM
Lopez, Jennifer	Feelin' So Good	15-295	CB
Lopez, Jennifer	Feelin' So Good	5-895	SC
Lopez, Jennifer	Feeling So Good	23-582	MM
Lopez, Jennifer	I'm Glad	20-520	CB
Lopez, Jennifer	I'm Glad	32-236	THM
Lopez, Jennifer	I'm Gonna Be Alright	17-595	PHM
Lopez, Jennifer	I'm Real	16-391	SGB
Lopez, Jennifer	If You Had My Love	23-322	CB
Lopez, Jennifer	If You Had My Love	13-563	LE
Lopez, Jennifer	If You Had My Love	23-580	MM
Lopez, Jennifer	If You Had My Love	8-189	PHT
Lopez, Jennifer	If You Had My Love	10-181	SC
Lopez, Jennifer	If You Had My Love	13-776	SGB
Lopez, Jennifer	Jenny From The Block	18-586	NS
Lopez, Jennifer	Jenny From The Block	32-16	THM
Lopez, Jennifer	Love Don't Cost A Thing	16-116	PRT
Lopez, Jennifer	Love Don't Cost A Thing	17-714	THM
Lopez, Jennifer	Play	16-124	PRT
Lopez, Jennifer	Promise Me You'll Try	23-326	CB
Lopez, Jennifer	Promise Me You'll Try	23-577	MM
Lopez, Jennifer	Should've Been	23-325	CB
Lopez, Jennifer	Should've Never	23-578	MM
Lopez, Jennifer	Too Late	23-323	CB
Lopez, Jennifer	Too Late	23-579	MM
Lopez, Jennifer	Waiting For Tonight	23-324	CB
Lopez, Jennifer	Waiting For Tonight	23-581	MM
Lopez, Jennifer	Waiting For Tonight	8-518	PHT
Lopez, Trini	Lemon Tree	11-734	DK
Lord!	Hard Rock Hallelujah	30-711	SF
Loring & Anderson	Friends & Lovers	15-477	CMC
Los Bravos	Black Is Black	11-596	DK
Los Bravos	Black Is Black	5-178	SC
Los Del Rios	Duet - Macarena the	7-567	THM
Los Del Rios	Macarena	10-684	HE
Los Del Rios	Macarena	7-567	THM
Los Del Rios	Macarena (Bayside Boyz Mix)	13-612	P
Los Del Rios	Macarena (Female only) - DANCE #	22-388	SC
Los Lobos	Come On Let's Go	47-208	SBI
Los Lobos	Kiko And The Lavender Moon	7-51	MM
Los Lobos	La Bamba	34-85	CB
Los Lobos	La Bamba	22-395	SC
Los Lobos	We Belong Together	13-102	P
Los Lonely Boys	Heaven	22-67	CB
Los Lonely Boys	More Than Love	20-557	PHM
Los Tigres Del Nort	Latino - De Paisano A Paisano	18-1	SC
Los Tigres Del Nort	Latino - Prision De Amor	17-757	SC
Lost Trailers	Call Me Crazy	29-579	CB
Lost Trailers	Country Folks Livin'	37-285	PHM

ARTIST	SONG TITLE	#	TYPE
	Loud		
Lost Trailers	Holler Back	36-590	CB
Lost Trailers	How 'Bout You Don't	36-244	PHM
Lost Trailers	Why Me	30-113	CB
Lost Trailors	All This Love	47-209	CB
Lostprophets	Rooftops (A Liberation Broadcast)	30-725	SF
Lostprophets	Wake Up Make A Move	30-818	PHM
Lou, Louchie	10 Out Of 10	12-395	PHM
Louvin Brothers	Duet - I Don't Believe You Met My..	3-207	SC
Louvin Brothers	I Don't Believe You've Met My…	3-207	SC
Lovato, Demi	Here We Go Again	36-23	PT
Lovato, Demi	Let It Go	43-166	ASK
Lovato, Demi	Without The Love	48-654	DCK
Love Affair	Everlasting Love	10-584	SF
Love And Theft	Angel Eyes	38-252	PHN
Love And Theft	Night That You'll Never Forget	49-666	SBI
Love And Theft	Runaway	37-46	CB
Love And Theft	Runnin' Out Of Air	39-81	PHN
Loveless & Tritt	Duet - Out of Control Raging Fire	16-43	ST
Loveless & Tritt	Out Of Control Raging Fire	16-43	ST
Loveless, Patty	Blame It On Your Heart	1-721	CB
Loveless, Patty	Blame it On Your Heart	6-301	MM
Loveless, Patty	Blame It On Your Heart	12-467	P
Loveless, Patty	Blame It On Your Heart	2-520	SC
Loveless, Patty	Blue Memories	1-716	CB
Loveless, Patty	Blue Side Of Town the	1-708	CB
Loveless, Patty	Boys Are Back In Town the	17-488	CB
Loveless, Patty	Can't Get Enough	1-729	CB
Loveless, Patty	Can't Get Enough	22-726	ST
Loveless, Patty	Can't Stop Myself From Loving You	1-719	CB
Loveless, Patty	Can't Stop Myself From Loving You	2-709	SC
Loveless, Patty	Chains	1-712	CB
Loveless, Patty	Chains	9-505	SAV
Loveless, Patty	Chains	2-811	SC
Loveless, Patty	Don't Toss Us Away	1-709	CB
Loveless, Patty	Don't Toss Us Away	2-612	SC
Loveless, Patty	Halfway Down	1-726	CB
Loveless, Patty	Halfway Down	6-842	MM
Loveless, Patty	Halfway Down	3-421	SC
Loveless, Patty	Here I Am	1-724	CB
Loveless, Patty	Here I Am	17-270	NA
Loveless, Patty	Here I Am	2-547	SC
Loveless, Patty	High On Love	8-729	CB
Loveless, Patty	High On Love	5-298	SC
Loveless, Patty	High On Love	22-796	ST
Loveless, Patty	How Can I Help You Say Goodbye	1-722	CB
Loveless, Patty	How Can I Help You Say Goodbye	19-296	MH

ARTIST	SONG TITLE	#	TYPE
Loveless, Patty	How Can I Help You Say Goodbye	6-503	MM
Loveless, Patty	How Can I Help You Say Goodbye	2-207	SC
Loveless, Patty	Hurt Me Bad In A Real Good Way	1-717	CB
Loveless, Patty	Hurt Me Bad In A Real Good Way	13-331	P
Loveless, Patty	I Try To Think About Elvis	1-723	CB
Loveless, Patty	I Try To Think About Elvis	6-662	MM
Loveless, Patty	I Try To Think About Elvis	2-453	SC
Loveless, Patty	I Wanna Believe	20-393	ST
Loveless, Patty	I'm That Kind Of Girl	1-715	CB
Loveless, Patty	I'm That Kind Of Girl	9-473	SAV
Loveless, Patty	I'm That Kind Of Girl	2-21	SC
Loveless, Patty	If My Heart Had Windows	1-706	CB
Loveless, Patty	If My Heart Had Windows	8-698	SAV
Loveless, Patty	Jealous Bone	1-718	CB
Loveless, Patty	Jealous Bone	13-528	P
Loveless, Patty	Keep Your Distance	23-420	CB
Loveless, Patty	Last Thing On My Mind the	22-596	ST
Loveless, Patty	Like Water Into Wine	22-673	ST
Loveless, Patty	Like Water Into Wine	1-731	CB
Loveless, Patty	Little Bit In Love a	1-707	CB
Loveless, Patty	Lonely Side Of Love	14-681	CB
Loveless, Patty	Lonely Side Of Love	17-234	NA
Loveless, Patty	Lonely Too Long	1-732	CB
Loveless, Patty	Lonely Too Long	4-434	SC
Loveless, Patty	Lovin' All Night	25-641	MM
Loveless, Patty	Lovin' All Night	19-180	ST
Loveless, Patty	Lovin' All Night	32-304	THM
Loveless, Patty	Lovin' All Night	35-430	CB
Loveless, Patty	Nights' Too Long the	1-714	CB
Loveless, Patty	Nothing But The Wheel	1-720	CB
Loveless, Patty	Nothing But The Wheel	6-386	MM
Loveless, Patty	On Down The Line	1-713	CB
Loveless, Patty	On Down the Line	6-626	MM
Loveless, Patty	On Your Way Home	36-369	CB
Loveless, Patty	On Your Way Home	19-691	ST
Loveless, Patty	She Drew A Broken Heart	1-733	CB
Loveless, Patty	She Drew A Broken Heart	7-582	CHM
Loveless, Patty	Tear Stained Letter	7-427	MM
Loveless, Patty	That's The Kind Of Mood I'm In	14-77	CB
Loveless, Patty	That's The Kind Of Mood I'm In	13-846	CHM
Loveless, Patty	Thousand Times A Day	1-728	CB
Loveless, Patty	Thousand Times A Day	7-253	MM
Loveless, Patty	Thousand Times A Day a	22-884	ST
Loveless, Patty	Timber I'm Falling In	1-710	CB

ARTIST	SONG TITLE	#	TYPE
	Love		
Loveless, Patty	Timber I'm Falling In Love	2-342	SC
Loveless, Patty	To Have You Back Again	8-301	CB
Loveless, Patty	Trouble With The Truth	1-734	CB
Loveless, Patty	Trouble With The Truth	7-618	CHM
Loveless, Patty	When The Fallen Angels Fall	20-13	SC
Loveless, Patty	You Can Feel Bad	1-727	CB
Loveless, Patty	You Can Feel Bad	4-104	SC
Loveless, Patty	You Don't Even Know Who I Am	1-725	CB
Loveless, Patty	You Don't Even Know Who I Am	2-687	SC
Loveless, Patty	You Don't Seem To Miss Me	1-735	CB
Loveless, Patty	You Don't Seem To Miss Me	22-641	ST
Loveless, Patty	You Will	6-465	MM
Loveless, Patty	You Will	2-95	SC
Loverboy	Hot Girls In Love	18-498	SAV
Loverboy	Hot Girls In Love	5-144	SC
Loverboy	Queen Of The Broken Hearts	37-77	SC
Loverboy	Working For The Weekend	28-351	DK
Loverboy	Working For The Weekend	4-389	SC
Lovett, Lyle	She's No Lady	12-136	DK
Lovett, Ruby	Little Bitty Crack In His Heart	8-491	CB
Lovin' Spoonful	Darling Be Home Soon	47-212	LE
Lovin' Spoonful	Daydream	47-210	CB
Lovin' Spoonful	Did You Ever Have To Make Up Your Mind	3-19	SC
Lovin' Spoonful	Do You Believe In Magic	11-666	DK
Lovin' Spoonful	Nashville Cats	47-213	PRI
Lovin' Spoonful	Summer In The City	35-61	CB
Lovin' Spoonful	Summer In The City	11-647	DK
Lovin' Spoonful	Welcome Back	47-211	LE
Lovin' Spoonful	You Didn't Have To Be So Nice	6-46	SC
Lovin' Spoonful	Younger Girl	47-214	PS
Low Millions	Statue	29-322	PHM
Lowe, Jim	Green Door the	3-504	SC
Lowe, Nick	I Knew The Bride	19-139	SGB
Lucas, Lauren	Carolina Kind the	23-297	CB
Lucas, Lauren	What You Ain't Gonna Get	23-125	CB
Ludacris	Act A Fool	32-310	THM
Ludacris	Act A Fool (Radio Version) **	21-797	SC
Ludacris	Area Codes **	18-545	TT
Ludacris	Pimpin' All Over The World	30-144	PT
Luhrmann, Baz	Everybody's Free	7-849	PHM
Lulu	Boom Bang-A-Bang	49-54	ZVS
Lulu	Man With The Golden	9-64	SC

ARTIST	SONG TITLE	#	TYPE
	Gun the		
Lulu	To Sir With Love	11-359	DK
Lulu	To Sir With Love	10-724	JVC
Lulu	To Sir With Love	12-885	P
Luman, Bob	Let's Think About Living	29-826	SF
Luman, Bob	Lonely Women Make Beautiful Lovers	5-565	SC
Luman, Bob	Still Loving You	5-778	SC
Luman, Bob	When You Say Love	5-865	SC
Lumidee	Never Leave You - Uh Ooh Uh Oooh	32-312	THM
Lumineers	Flowers In Your Hair	48-422	ASK
Lumineers	Gale Song	48-421	SBI
Lumineers	Ho Hey	48-418	BKD
Lumineers	Ophelia	48-403	DCK
Lumineers	Slow It Down	48-420	SBI
Lumineers	Stubborn Love	48-419	SBI
Lund, Corb	Bible On The Dash	39-89	PHN
Lymon & Teenagers	Goody Goody	6-146	MM
Lymon & Teenagers	Goody Goody	4-221	SC
Lymon & Teenagers	Why Do Fools Fall In Love	33-232	CB
Lymon & Teenagers	Why Do Fools Fall In Love	12-150	DK
Lymon & Teenagers	Why Do Fools Fall In Love	12-660	P
Lymon, Frankie	ABC's Of Love the	30-526	LE
Lymon, Frankie	Goody Goody	30-522	LE
Lymon, Frankie	I Want You To Be My Girl	30-523	LE
Lymon, Frankie	Little Bitty Pretty One	30-521	LE
Lymon, Frankie	Promise To Remember	30-524	LE
Lymon, Frankie	Who Can Explain	30-525	LE
Lymon, Frankie	Why Do Fools Fall In Love	30-527	LE
Lynch, Dustin	Cowboys And Angels	44-129	ASK
Lynch, Dustin	Hell Of A Night	47-930	BKD
Lynch, Dustin	She Cranks My Tractor	44-153	BKD
Lynch, Dustin	Where It's At (Yep, Yep)	44-204	KCDC
Lynch, Dustin	Wild In Your Smile	47-929	ASK
Lynch, Dustin	Your Plan	47-931	PHN
Lynch, L.	United States Of Whatever	32-259	THM
Lynn & Jack White	Duet - Portland Oregon	48-251	SC
Lynn & Jack White	Portland Oregon - duet	48-251	SC
Lynn, Barbara	You'll Lose A Good Thing	7-307	MM
Lynn, Loretta	Another Man Loved Me Last Night	48-253	VH
Lynn, Loretta	Before I'm Over You	48-249	CB
Lynn, Loretta	Blue Kentucky Girl	8-385	CB
Lynn, Loretta	Coal Miner's Daughter	11-426	DK
Lynn, Loretta	Coal Miner's Daughter	13-357	P
Lynn, Loretta	Coal Miner's Daughter	8-706	SAV
Lynn, Loretta	Country In My Genes	14-95	CB
Lynn, Loretta	Dear Uncle Sam	5-849	SC
Lynn, Loretta	Don't Come Home A-Drinkin'	8-46	CB

ARTIST	SONG TITLE	#	TYPE	ARTIST	SONG TITLE	#	TYPE
Lynn, Loretta	Don't Come Home A-Drinkin'	6-739	MM		You Think I Am		
Lynn, Loretta	Don't Come Home A-Drinkin'	13-406	P	Lynn, Loretta	When The Tingle Becomes A Chill	4-750	SC
Lynn, Loretta	Fist City	11-430	DK	Lynn, Loretta	Will The Circle Be Unbroken	47-636	CB
Lynn, Loretta	Fist City	5-574	SC	Lynn, Loretta	Wine, Women & Song	43-232	CB
Lynn, Loretta	Gospel - How Great Thou Art	47-635	CB	Lynn, Loretta	Wings Of A Dove	43-230	CB
Lynn, Loretta	Gospel - In The Garden	47-633	CB	Lynn, Loretta	Woman Of The World	43-231	CB
Lynn, Loretta	Gospel - In The Sweet Bye and Bye	47-634	CB	Lynn, Loretta	Xmas - To Heck With Ole Santa Claus	46-49	SSK
Lynn, Loretta	Gospel - Just A Closer Walk With Thee	47-631	CB	Lynn, Loretta	You Ain't Woman Enough	15-835	CB
Lynn, Loretta	Gospel - Precious Memories	43-97	CB	Lynn, Loretta	You Ain't Woman Enough	13-474	P
Lynn, Loretta	Gospel - the Old Rugged Cross	43-101	CB	Lynn, Loretta	You Just Stepped In (From Stepping Out)	47-628	CB
Lynn, Loretta	Gospel - What a Friend We Have In Jesus	43-106	CB	Lynn, Loretta	You're Lookin' At Country	8-294	CB
Lynn, Loretta	Gospel - Will the Circle Be Unbroken	47-636	CB	Lynn, Loretta	You're Lookin' At Country	5-413	SC
Lynn, Loretta	Happy Birthday	47-629	CB	Lynn, Loretta	Your Squaw Is On The Warpath	4-736	SC
Lynn, Loretta	Here I Am Again	48-250	CB	Lynn, Loretta	Wings Upon Your Horns	45-683	VH
Lynn, Loretta	Hey Loretta	5-566	SC	Lynn, Lorretta	Tippy Toeing	45-709	VH
Lynn, Loretta	Honky Tonk Girl	47-624	CB	Lynne, Rockie	Do We Still	30-86	CB
Lynn, Loretta	How Great Thou Art	47-635	CB	Lynne, Rockie	I Can't Believe It's Me	36-572	CB
Lynn, Loretta	I Can't Feel You Anymore	43-233	CB	Lynne, Rockie	Lipstick	29-26	CB
Lynn, Loretta	I Can't Hear The Music	47-627	CB	Lynne, Rockie	Lipstick	23-456	ST
Lynn, Loretta	I've Got A Picture Of Us On My Mind	43-236	CB	Lynne, Rockie	More	30-206	CB
Lynn, Loretta	If You're Not Gone Too Long	45-723	VH	Lynne, Shelby	How Can I Be Sure	49-915	SC
Lynn, Loretta	In The Garden - gospel	47-633	CB	Lynne, Shelby	I Won't Die Alone	23-417	CB
Lynn, Loretta	In The Sweet Bye And Bye	47-634	CB	Lynne, Shelby	Slow Me Down	6-815	MM
Lynn, Loretta	Just A Closer Walk With Thee	47-631	CB	Lynne, Shelby	Things Are Tough All Over	7-161	MM
Lynn, Loretta	Lonesome 7-7203	10-516	SF	Lynne, Shelby	Wall In Your Heart	25-43	MM
Lynn, Loretta	Love Is The Foundation	47-626	CB	Lynns	Nights Like These	10-126	SC
Lynn, Loretta	Miss Being Mrs.	20-449	ST	Lynns	What Am I Doin' Loving You	8-747	CB
Lynn, Loretta	Morning After Baby Let Me Down	47-773	SRK	Lynns	Woman To Woman	8-415	CB
Lynn, Loretta	One's On The Way	4-741	SC	Lynns	Woman To Woman	22-791	ST
Lynn, Loretta	Out Of My Head & Back In My Bed	47-625	CB	Lynryd Skynyrd	Swamp Music	5-266	SC
Lynn, Loretta	Out Of My Head & Back In My Bed	46-194	SC	Lynyrd Skynyrd	Ballad Of Curtis Lowe	19-816	SGB
Lynn, Loretta	Pill the	47-630	CB	Lynyrd Skynyrd	Ballad Of Curtis Lowe	5-256	SC
Lynn, Loretta	Rated X	4-740	SC	Lynyrd Skynyrd	Call Me The Breeze	5-257	SC
Lynn, Loretta	Red White And Blue	48-252	THM	Lynyrd Skynyrd	Call Me The Breeze	19-807	SGB
Lynn, Loretta	Somebody Somewhere	4-743	SC	Lynyrd Skynyrd	Don't Ask Me No Questions	5-263	SC
Lynn, Loretta	Success	47-632	CB	Lynyrd Skynyrd	Don't Ask Me No Questions	19-814	SGB
Lynn, Loretta	Table For Two	43-235	CB	Lynyrd Skynyrd	Free Bird	18-152	CB
Lynn, Loretta	They Don't Make 'Em Like My Daddy Anymore	8-368	CB	Lynyrd Skynyrd	Free Bird	12-692	P
Lynn, Loretta	To Heck With Ole Santa Claus - xmas	46-49	SSK	Lynyrd Skynyrd	Free Bird	5-267	SC
Lynn, Loretta	Trouble In Paradise	8-813	CB	Lynyrd Skynyrd	Free Bird	13-774	SGB
Lynn, Loretta	What Kind Of Girl Do	43-234	CB	Lynyrd Skynyrd	Gimme Back My Bullets	19-810	SGB
				Lynyrd Skynyrd	Gimme Three Steps	18-160	CB
				Lynyrd Skynyrd	Gimme Three Steps	7-456	MM
				Lynyrd Skynyrd	Gimme Three Steps	5-269	SC
				Lynyrd Skynyrd	Gimme Three Steps	19-806	SGB
				Lynyrd Skynyrd	I Ain't The One	19-809	SGB

ARTIST	SONG TITLE	#	TYPE
Lynyrd Skynyrd	I Know A Little	19-820	SGB
Lynyrd Skynyrd	Needle & The Spoon the	5-270	SC
Lynyrd Skynyrd	Needle & The Spoon the	19-817	SGB
Lynyrd Skynyrd	Poison Whiskey	5-260	SC
Lynyrd Skynyrd	Poison Whiskey	19-812	SGB
Lynyrd Skynyrd	Saturday Night Special	5-264	SC
Lynyrd Skynyrd	Searchin'	19-811	SGB
Lynyrd Skynyrd	Swamp Music	19-819	SGB
Lynyrd Skynyrd	Sweet Home Alabama	12-355	DK
Lynyrd Skynyrd	Sweet Home Alabama	12-693	P
Lynyrd Skynyrd	Sweet Home Alabama	5-265	SC
Lynyrd Skynyrd	Sweet Home Alabama	13-773	SGB
Lynyrd Skynyrd	T Is For Texas	19-808	SGB
Lynyrd Skynyrd	That Smell	5-259	SC
Lynyrd Skynyrd	Tuesday's Gone	19-821	SGB
Lynyrd Skynyrd	What's Your Name	12-356	DK
Lynyrd Skynyrd	What's Your Name	5-268	SC
Lynyrd Skynyrd	Whiskey Rock A Roller	19-813	SGB
Lynyrd Skynyrd	Workin' For MCA	5-258	SC
Lynyrd Skynyrd	Workin' For MCA	19-818	SGB
Lynyrd Skynyrd	You Got That Right	5-261	SC
Lyons, Elizabeth	Everything Tonite	41-80	PHN
Lyric	Hot And Tipsy	32-278	THM
M	Muzic	14-1	PHM
M	Muzic	16-119	PRT
M	Pop Muzik	6-519	MM
M	Pop Muzik	22-931	SC
M-People	Moving On Up	2-227	SC
M2M	Don't Say You Love Me	16-186	PHM
M2M	Mirror Mirror	14-493	SC
M2M	Mirror Mirror	30-634	THM
MacColl, Kirsty	England 2 Columbia 0	30-787	SF
MacGregor, Mary	Torn Between Two Lovers	22-928	SC
Mack & Mabel	Show - I Won't Send Roses	17-796	PS
Mack & Mabel	Show - Time Heals Everything	17-797	PS
Mack, Warner	Bridge Washed Out the	15-85	CB
Mack, Warner	Bridge Washed Out the	4-805	SC
Mackelmore & Lewis	Cowboy Boots	43-456	ASK
Maddie & Tae	After The Storm Blows Through	46-5	DCK
Maddie & Tae	Downside Of Growing Up	49-754	KVD
Maddie & Tae	Fly	45-42	BKD
Maddie & Tae	Girl In A Country Song	45-111	BKD
Maddie & Tae	Shut Up And Fish	49-642	KV
Maddie & Tae	Shut Up And Fish	47-927	BKD
Maddie & Tae	Shut Up And Fish - instrumental	48-745	BKD
Maddie & Tae	Sierra	48-502	KVD
Maddie & Tae	Your Side Of Town	45-112	KVD
Made In London	Shut Your Mouth	21-634	SGB
Maderios, Glenn	She Ain't Worth It	33-330	CB
Madness	Our House	28-367	DK
Madness	Our House	29-5	MH
Madonna	4 Minutes	48-592	DK

ARTIST	SONG TITLE	#	TYPE
Madonna	American Life	20-524	CB
Madonna	American Life	25-589	MM
Madonna	American Life	32-242	THM
Madonna	American Pie	15-298	CB
Madonna	American Pie	15-324	PHM
Madonna	Angel	24-65	SC
Madonna	Beautiful Stranger	8-101	PHT
Madonna	Borderline	11-807	DK
Madonna	Borderline	21-154	LE
Madonna	Borderline	14-637	SC
Madonna	Cherish	12-851	P
Madonna	Crazy For You	20-295	CB
Madonna	Crazy For You	21-153	LE
Madonna	Crazy For You	9-2	MH
Madonna	Crazy For You	13-216	P
Madonna	Crazy For You	4-853	SC
Madonna	Deeper And Deeper	6-101	MM
Madonna	Die Another Day	25-394	MM
Madonna	Die Another Day	18-582	NS
Madonna	Die Another Day	32-20	THM
Madonna	Don't Cry For Me Argentina	21-161	LE
Madonna	Don't Tell Me	17-715	THM
Madonna	Dress You Up	28-345	DK
Madonna	Dress You Up	21-156	LE
Madonna	Express Yourself	21-158	LE
Madonna	Express Yourself	9-665	SAV
Madonna	Frozen	21-148	LE
Madonna	Hanky Panky	6-179	MM
Madonna	Hanky Panky	15-11	SC
Madonna	Holiday	13-25	P
Madonna	Hollywood	19-605	CB
Madonna	Hollywood	25-634	MM
Madonna	Hollywood	32-318	THM
Madonna	I'll Remember	21-160	LE
Madonna	I'll Remember	2-225	SC
Madonna	Into The Groove	2-37	SC
Madonna	Justify My Love	21-455	CB
Madonna	La Isla Bonita	13-26	P
Madonna	Like A Prayer	6-347	MM
Madonna	Like A Prayer	12-852	P
Madonna	Like A Virgin	11-81	DK
Madonna	Like A Virgin	21-146	LE
Madonna	Like A Virgin	12-675	P
Madonna	Like A Virgin	10-524	SF
Madonna	Live To Tell	12-853	P
Madonna	Love Don't Live Here Anymore	14-900	SC
Madonna	Lucky Star	12-847	P
Madonna	Material Girl	11-274	DK
Madonna	Material Girl	21-147	LE
Madonna	Open My Heart	14-44	THM
Madonna	Open Your Heart	15-548	CMC
Madonna	Open Your Heart	19-555	SC
Madonna	Papa Don't Preach	11-586	DK
Madonna	Papa Don't Preach	21-157	LE
Madonna	Papa Don't Preach	12-817	P

ARTIST	SONG TITLE	#	TYPE
Madonna	Physical Attraction	18-375	AH
Madonna	Power Of Goodbye	21-152	LE
Madonna	Rain	21-159	LE
Madonna	Rain	6-372	MM
Madonna	Rain	13-24	P
Madonna	Ray Of Light	21-149	LE
Madonna	Secret	2-465	SC
Madonna	Show - Musiq	20-3	SGB
Madonna	Take A Bow	21-150	LE
Madonna	Take A Bow	9-267	SC
Madonna	Take A Bow	29-123	ST
Madonna	This Used To Be My Playground	9-675	SAV
Madonna	True Blue	15-573	CMC
Madonna	Vogue	19-579	MH
Madonna	Vogue	6-175	MM
Madonna	Vogue	12-854	P
Madonna	Xmas - Santa Baby	6-289	MM
Madonna	Xmas - Santa Baby	14-530	SC
Madonna	You Must Love Me	4-609	SC
Madonna	You'll See	21-151	LE
Madonna	You'll See	15-594	THM
Maestro, J.	Worst That Could Happen	9-357	MG
Magnapop	Open The Door	24-118	SC
Main Ingredient	Everybody Plays The Fool	35-200	CB
Main Ingredient	Everybody Plays The Fool	22-934	SC
Maisonettes	Heartache Avenue	30-746	SF
Major, Charlie	Tell Me Something I Don't Know	4-630	SC
Male Country	Xmas - Friendly Beasts the	15-661	THM
Male Country	Xmas - Home For The Holidays	15-666	THM
Malibu Storm	Photograph	20-452	ST
Mallan, Peter	Irish - Annie Laurie	11-489	DK
Malo & McBride	Duet - Feels Like Home	30-257	CB
Malo & McBride	Feels Like Home - duet	30-257	CB
Malone & Rapparees	Irish - Wearin' O' The Green	21-489	SC
Mamas & Papas	California Dreamin'	11-351	DK
Mamas & Papas	California Dreamin'	6-156	MM
Mamas & Papas	California Dreamin'	13-54	P
Mamas & Papas	California Dreamin'	9-115	PS
Mamas & Papas	Creeque Alley	14-452	SC
Mamas & Papas	Dancing In The Street	47-215	KV
Mamas & Papas	Dedicated To The One I Love	9-116	PS
Mamas & Papas	Dream A Little Dream Of Me	9-117	PS
Mamas & Papas	Dream A Little Dream Of Me	19-152	SGB
Mamas & Papas	Duet - Creeque Alley	14-452	SC
Mamas & Papas	Duet - I Call Your Name	49-724	KV
Mamas & Papas	I Call Your Name - duet	49-724	KV
Mamas & Papas	I Dig Rock And Roll Music	47-218	ST

ARTIST	SONG TITLE	#	TYPE
Mamas & Papas	I Saw Her Again	47-217	LE
Mamas & Papas	Make Your Own Kind Of Music	9-706	SAV
Mamas & Papas	Monday Monday	35-96	CB
Mamas & Papas	Monday Monday	11-358	DK
Mamas & Papas	Monday Monday	12-864	P
Mamas & Papas	Monday Monday	9-118	PS
Mamas & Papas	Spanish Harlem	47-216	KV
Mamas & Papas	Words Of Love	9-119	PS
Mamas & Papas	Words Of Love	5-228	SC
Mame	Show - If He Walked Into My Life	6-253	MM
Mame	Show - If He Walked Into My Life	17-799	PS
Mame	Show - We Need a Little Christmas	12-283	DK
Man of La Mancha	Show - Don Quixote	18-808	PS
Man of La Mancha	Show - Dulcenia	5-656	SC
Man of La Mancha	Show - Impossible Dream the	12-87	DK
Man of La Mancha	Show - Impossible Dream the	6-326	MM
Man of La Mancha	Show - Impossible Dream the	15-235	PR
Man of La Mancha	Show - Impossible Dream the	2-285	SC
Man of La Mancha	Show - Man Of La Mancha	5-660	SC
Manchester,Melissa	Come In From The Rain	14-586	SC
Manchester,Melissa	Don't Cry Out Loud	15-468	MM
Manchester,Melissa	I Want To Be In Love	18-396	MM
Manchester,Melissa	Midnight Blue	4-46	SC
Manchester,Melissa	Through The Eyes Of Love	26-366	DK
Mandrell & Greenwood	Duet - It Should Have Been Love By Now	48-696	CB
Mandrell & Greenwood	It Should Have Been Love By Now - duet	48-696	CB
Mandrell & Houston	Duet - After Closing Time	9-588	SAV
Mandrell, Barbara	Crackers	33-33	CB
Mandrell, Barbara	Crackers	5-49	SC
Mandrell, Barbara	Fast Lanes & Country Roads	5-407	SC
Mandrell, Barbara	Happy Birthday Dear Heartache	5-46	SC
Mandrell, Barbara	I Was Country When Country Wasn't	13-457	P
Mandrell, Barbara	I Was Country When Country Wasn't C	11-745	DK
Mandrell, Barbara	If Lovin' You Is Wrong I Don't	4-781	SC
Mandrell, Barbara	In Times Like These	5-50	SC
Mandrell, Barbara	Keys In The Mailbox	47-775	SRK
Mandrell, Barbara	Married But Not To Each Other	8-288	CB
Mandrell, Barbara	No One Mends A Broken Heart	5-567	SC
Mandrell, Barbara	One Of a Kind Pair Of Fools	9-632	SAV

ARTIST	SONG TITLE	#	TYPE	ARTIST	SONG TITLE	#	TYPE
Mandrell, Barbara	Only A Lonely Heart Now	5-247	SC	Manilow, Barry	Looks Like We Made It	9-43	MM
Mandrell, Barbara	Sleeping Single In A Double Bed	8-27	CB	Manilow, Barry	Looks Like We Made it	9-81	PS
Mandrell, Barbara	Sleeping Single In A Double Bed	26-465	DK	Manilow, Barry	Mandy	29-108	CB
Mandrell, Barbara	Sleeping Single In A Double Bed	13-442	P	Manilow, Barry	Mandy	13-161	P
Mandrell, Barbara	Standing Room Only	48-694	CB	Manilow, Barry	Mandy	9-74	PS
Mandrell, Barbara	Ten Pound Hammer	24-130	SC	Manilow, Barry	Old Songs the	29-121	CB
Mandrell, Barbara	There's No Love In Tennessee	5-59	SC	Manilow, Barry	One Voice	46-305	SC
Mandrell, Barbara	Till You're Gone	5-57	SC	Manilow, Barry	Ready To Take A Chance Again	12-123	DK
Mandrell, Barbara	Tonight My Baby's Comin' Home	20-689	SC	Manilow, Barry	Ready To Take A Chance Again	15-840	MM
Mandrell, Barbara	Wish You Were Here	48-695	CB	Manilow, Barry	Ships	29-118	CB
Mandrell, Barbara	Xmas - Christmas At Our House	15-650	THM	Manilow, Barry	Ships	6-552	MM
Mandrell, Barbara	Years	15-587	DK	Manilow, Barry	Somewhere In The Night	6-544	MM
Mandrell, Louise	All I Want For Christmas Is You - xmas	45-256	CB	Manilow, Barry	This One's For You	29-117	CB
Mandrell, Louise	I Wanna Say Yes	20-678	SC	Manilow, Barry	Tryin' To Get The Feeling Again	29-114	CB
Mandrell, Louise	Xmas - All I Want For Christmas Is You	45-256	CB	Manilow, Barry	Weekend In New England	9-82	PS
Manhattan Transfer	Boy From New York City the	26-330	DK	Manilow, Barry	Weekend In New England	16-64	SC
Manhattan Transfer	Operator	7-472	MM	Manilow, Barry	When October Goes	9-80	PS
Manhattans	Kiss And Say Goodbye	16-837	DK	Mann, Barry	Who Put The Bomp	6-652	MM
Manhattans	Kiss And Say Goodbye	7-468	MM	Mann, Barry	Who Put The Bomp	12-903	P
Manhattans	Shining Star	35-131	CB	Mann, Manfred	5-4-3-2-1	10-644	SF
Manhattans	Shining Star	17-101	DK	Mann, Manfred	Blinded By The Light	3-455	SC
Manilow, Barry	Bandstand Boogie	29-111	CB	Mann, Manfred	Do Wah Diddy Diddy	26-329	DK
Manilow, Barry	Can't Smile Without You	29-115	CB	Mann, Manfred	Do Wah Diddy Diddy	3-289	MM
Manilow, Barry	Can't Smile Without you	11-689	DK	Mann, Manfred	Do Wah Diddy Diddy	13-75	P
Manilow, Barry	Can't Smile Without You	6-547	MM	Mann, Manfred	Mighty Qunin the	5-466	SC
Manilow, Barry	Can't Smile Without You	13-151	P	Mann, Manfred	Pretty Flamingo	10-579	SF
Manilow, Barry	Can't Smile Without You	9-78	PS	Marano, Laura	Boombox	49-863	DCK
Manilow, Barry	Copacabana	29-107	CB	Marathons	Peanut Butter	6-517	MM
Manilow, Barry	Copacabana	17-56	DK	Marcel	Country Rock Star	25-233	MM
Manilow, Barry	Copacabana	9-76	PS	Marcel	Country Rock Star	17-570	ST
Manilow, Barry	Copacabana	9-771	SAV	Marcels	Blue Moon	16-828	DK
Manilow, Barry	Copacabana	10-541	SF	Marcels	Blue Moon	6-152	MM
Manilow, Barry	Could It Be Magic	29-112	CB	Marcels	Blue Moon	13-79	P
Manilow, Barry	Could It Be Magic	18-49	MM	March, Peggy	I Will Follow Him	7-73	MM
Manilow, Barry	Daybreak	29-113	CB	March, Peggy	I Will Follow Him	4-36	SC
Manilow, Barry	Even Now	29-116	CB	Marcy Playground	Sex & Candy	5-191	SC
Manilow, Barry	Even Now	6-551	MM	Marcy Playground	Sherry Frazier	16-213	MM
Manilow, Barry	Even Now	9-79	PS	Maresca, Ernie	Shout Shout	3-577	SC
Manilow, Barry	I Made It Through The Rain	29-119	CB	Mariah	Loverboy	35-269	CB
Manilow, Barry	I Made It Through The Rain	9-75	PS	Marie Sisters	Real Bad Mood	16-702	ST
Manilow, Barry	I Write The Songs	29-109	CB	Marie, Teena	Lovergirl	18-374	AH
Manilow, Barry	I Write The Songs	16-759	DK	Marie, Teena	Lovergirl	24-567	SC
Manilow, Barry	I Write The Songs	9-77	PS	Marilyn Manson	Personal Jesus	30-820	PHM
Manilow, Barry	It's A Miracle	29-120	CB	Marino, Frank	King Bee/Back Door Man Medley	19-798	SGB
Manilow, Barry	It's A Miracle	17-532	SC	Mario	C'Mon	18-771	PHM
Manilow, Barry	Looks Like We Made It	29-110	CB	Mario	Crying Out For Me	36-487	CB
Manilow, Barry	Looks Like We Made It	11-635	DK	Mario	How Do I Breathe	30-486	CB
				Mario	Let Me Love You	22-358	CB
				Mario	Music For Love	36-478	CB
				Mark, Marky	Good Vibrations	6-176	MM
				Marley, Bob	Could You Be Loved	25-391	MM
				Marley, Bob	Is This Love	12-6	DK

ARTIST	SONG TITLE	#	TYPE
Marley, Bob	Is This Love	25-377	MM
Marley, Bob	Kaya	25-389	MM
Marley, Bob	Lively Up Yourself	25-382	MM
Marley, Bob	Put It On	25-380	MM
Marley, Bob	Stir It Up	12-797	P
Marley, Ziggy	Beautiful Day	25-388	MM
Marley, Ziggy	Love is My Religion	36-190	PHM
Maroon 5	Harder To Breathe	35-294	CB
Maroon 5	Harder To Breathe	25-585	MM
Maroon 5	Harder To Breathe	32-323	THM
Maroon 5	Harder To Breathe	21-682	Z
Maroon 5	Ladykiller	39-104	PHM
Maroon 5	Love Somebody	44-147	BKD
Maroon 5	Lucky Strike	39-111	PHM
Maroon 5	Makes Me Wonder	30-567	CB
Maroon 5	Moves Like Jagger	49-71	ZPC
Maroon 5	Must Get Out	21-684	Z
Maroon 5	Never Gonna Leave This Bed	37-268	PHM
Maroon 5	One More Night	39-108	PHM
Maroon 5	Sad	39-118	PHM
Maroon 5	She Will Be Loved	46-206	SC
Maroon 5	Sugar	48-434	KCD
Maroon 5	Sun the	21-686	Z
Maroon 5	Sunday Morning	22-344	CB
Maroon 5	Sunday Morning	21-683	Z
Maroon 5	Sweetest Goodbye	21-685	Z
Maroon 5	This Love	20-561	CB
Maroon 5	This Love	21-681	Z
Maroon 5	This Summer's Gonna Hurt Like A...	48-443	KCD
Maroon 5	Tickets	39-132	PHM
Maroon 5	Won't Go Home Without You	36-444	CB
Maroon 5 & Lady Antebellum	Duet - Out Of Goodbyes	38-239	CB
Maroon 5 & Lady Antebellum	Out Of Goodbyes - duet	38-239	CB
Maroon 5 feat Rihanna	If I Never See Your Face Again	36-472	CB
Marquees	Santa Done Got Hip - xmas	45-244	CB
Marquees	Xmas - Santa Done Got Hip	45-244	CB
Mars, Bruno	Gorilla	47-219	KV
Mars, Bruno	It Will Rain	39-117	SB
Mars, Bruno	Just The Way You Are	37-264	CB
Mars, Bruno	Lazy Song the	37-263	CB
Mars, Bruno	Locked Out Of Heaven	47-222	ZP
Mars, Bruno	Marry You	38-201	PHM
Mars, Bruno	Natalie	47-221	KV
Mars, Bruno	Treasure	47-220	KV
Mars, Bruno	Uptown Funk	45-15	KV
Mars, Bruno	Young Girls	43-161	PHM
Mars, Charlie	Let The Meter Run	39-107	PHM
Marshall Tucker Ban	24 Hours At A Time	9-383	AH
Marshall Tucker Ban	24 Hours At A Time	13-770	SGB
Marshall Tucker Ban	Can't You See	9-323	AG

ARTIST	SONG TITLE	#	TYPE
Marshall Tucker Ban	Can't You See	18-153	CB
Marshall Tucker Ban	Can't You See	3-611	SC
Marshall Tucker Ban	Can't You See	13-761	SGB
Marshall Tucker Ban	Can't You See	20-311	MH
Marshall Tucker Ban	Fire On The Mountain	18-161	CB
Marshall Tucker Ban	Heard It In A Love Song	2-528	SC
Marshall Tucker Band	Can't You See	47-559	SC
Marshall Tucker Band	Down We Go	47-225	DCK
Marshall Tucker Band	Last Of The Singing Cowboys	47-224	SC
Marshall Tucker Band	Searchin' For A Rainbow	47-223	CB
Marshall, Amanda	Birmingham	24-363	SC
Marshall, Amanda	This Could Take All Night	19-157	SGB
Martha & Vandellas	Dancing In The Street	11-126	DK
Martha & Vandellas	Dancing In The Street	3-355	MH
Martha & Vandellas	Dancing In The Street	12-632	P
Martha & Vandellas	Heat Wave	16-743	DK
Martha & Vandellas	Heat Wave	12-633	P
Martha & Vandellas	Jimmy Mack	16-853	DK
Martika	I Fell The Earth Move	18-497	SAV
Martika	Toy Soldier	7-102	MM
Martika	Toy Soldier	21-601	SF
Martin & ?	Duet - Nobody Wants to be Lonely	20-123	PHM
Martin & 7	Nobody Wants To Be Lonely	20-123	PHM
Martin & Madonna	Be Careful	9-128	PS
Martin & Madonna	Be Careful	13-730	SGB
Martin & Madonna	Duet - Be Careful	9-128	PS
Martin & Madonna	Duet - Be Careful	13-730	SGB
Martin & Modugno	Volare	26-344	DK
Martin & Renaud	Duet - Two Sleepy People	23-76	MM
Martin & Renaud	Two Sleepy People	23-76	MM
Martin, B	Rub Me The Right Way	32-3	THM
Martin, Billie Ray	Your Loving Arms	24-171	SC
Martin, Brad	Before i Knew Better	33-159	CB
Martin, Brad	Before I Knew Better	25-240	MM
Martin, Brad	Before I Knew Better	16-431	ST
Martin, Brad	Just Like Love	18-333	ST
Martin, Brad	One Of Those Days	19-66	ST
Martin, Brad	Rub Me In The Right Way	18-459	ST
Martin, Brad	Rub Me The Right Way	32-3	THM
Martin, Dean	Ain't That A Kick In The Head	23-71	MM
Martin, Dean	Baby It's Cold Outside	23-72	MM
Martin, Dean	Carolina In The Morning	21-2	CB
Martin, Dean	Dream	23-79	MM
Martin, Dean	Everybody Loves Somebody	11-309	DK
Martin, Dean	Everybody Loves Somebody	20-758	KB
Martin, Dean	Everybody Loves Somebody	10-405	LE

ARTIST	SONG TITLE	#	TYPE
Martin, Dean	Everybody Loves Somebody	23-65	MM
Martin, Dean	Everybody Loves Somebody	12-505	P
Martin, Dean	Everybody Loves Somebody	2-205	SC
Martin, Dean	Gentle On My Mind	10-588	SF
Martin, Dean	Houston	23-84	MM
Martin, Dean	I Wish You Love	23-92	MM
Martin, Dean	I'll Always Love You	23-75	MM
Martin, Dean	I've Got My Love To Keep Me Warm	23-78	MM
Martin, Dean	Imagination	23-73	MM
Martin, Dean	Imagination	19-778	SGB
Martin, Dean	In The Chapel In The Moonlight	23-86	MM
Martin, Dean	Innamorata	10-403	LE
Martin, Dean	Innamorata	23-66	MM
Martin, Dean	Kiss Me	10-404	LE
Martin, Dean	Let Me Go Lover	23-80	MM
Martin, Dean	Little Old Wine Drinker Me	10-400	LE
Martin, Dean	Little Old Wine Drinker Me	23-77	MM
Martin, Dean	Mambo Italiano	23-90	MM
Martin, Dean	Marshmallow World a - xmas	46-277	KV
Martin, Dean	Memories Are Made Of This	11-573	DK
Martin, Dean	Memories Are Made Of This	10-401	LE
Martin, Dean	Memories Are Made Of This	7-188	MM
Martin, Dean	Money Burns a Hole In My Pocket	49-647	DFK
Martin, Dean	Object Of My Affection	23-74	MM
Martin, Dean	Old Bones	49-646	DFK
Martin, Dean	Please Don't Talk About Me When…	23-88	MM
Martin, Dean	Powder Your Face With Sunshine	23-83	MM
Martin, Dean	Return To Me	10-402	LE
Martin, Dean	Return To Me	7-192	MM
Martin, Dean	Send Me The Pillow That You Dream..	23-85	MM
Martin, Dean	Someday You'll Want Me To Want U	23-91	MM
Martin, Dean	Somewhere There's A Someone	23-87	MM
Martin, Dean	Standing On The Corner	23-81	MM
Martin, Dean	Sway	7-182	MM
Martin, Dean	That's Amore	28-517	DK
Martin, Dean	That's Amore	23-64	MM
Martin, Dean	That's Amore	4-351	SC
Martin, Dean	Under The Bridges Of Paris	49-48	ZVS
Martin, Dean	Volare	35-13	CB
Martin, Dean	Volare	23-63	MM
Martin, Dean	Xmas - Baby It's Cold Outside	14-301	MM

ARTIST	SONG TITLE	#	TYPE
Martin, Dean	Xmas - Marshmallow World a	46-277	KV
Martin, Dean	You Belong To Me	23-82	MM
Martin, Dean	You're Nobody 'Til Somebody Loves U	15-596	MM
Martin, Dean	You're Nobody Til Somebody Loves	34-9	CB
Martin, Dean & ?	Duet - Sam's Song	23-89	MM
Martin, Dean & ?	Sam's Song	23-89	MM
Martin, Dusty	Wrong Mr. Right Again the	4-480	SC
Martin, Jimmy	Gospel - Will the Circle be unbroken	33-204	CB
Martin, Jimmy	Honey You Don't Know My Mind	8-252	CB
Martin, Jimmy	Long Journey Home	8-263	CB
Martin, Jimmy	Will the Circle be Unbroken - Gospel	33-204	CB
Martin, Marilyn	Through His Eyes	2-654	SC
Martin, Ricky	Cup Of Life	33-365	CB
Martin, Ricky	Cup Of Life, the	9-130	PS
Martin, Ricky	I Am Made Of You	9-140	PS
Martin, Ricky	I Am Made Of You	13-732	SGB
Martin, Ricky	I Count The Minutes	9-139	PS
Martin, Ricky	I Count The Minutes	13-733	SGB
Martin, Ricky	Latino - Bella She's All I Ever Had	9-135	PS
Martin, Ricky	Latino - Bella She's All I Ever Had	13-731	SGB
Martin, Ricky	Latino - La Copa De La Vida	13-734	SGB
Martin, Ricky	Latino - Livin' La Vida Loca	9-134	PS
Martin, Ricky	Latino - Livin' La Vida Loca	13-736	SGB
Martin, Ricky	Latino - Maria	9-131	PS
Martin, Ricky	Latino - Tal Vez	23-236	AI
Martin, Ricky	Livin' La Vida Loca	11-80	JTG
Martin, Ricky	Livin' La Vida Loca	7-870	PHM
Martin, Ricky	Livin' La Vida Loca	9-126	PS
Martin, Ricky	Livin' La Vida Loca	13-735	SGB
Martin, Ricky	Love You For A Day	9-132	PS
Martin, Ricky	Love You For A Day	13-737	SGB
Martin, Ricky	Private Emotion	15-325	PHM
Martin, Ricky	Private Emotion	9-137	PS
Martin, Ricky	Private Emotion	13-738	SGB
Martin, Ricky	Shake Your Bon Bon	29-181	MH
Martin, Ricky	Shake Your Bon Bon	9-136	PS
Martin, Ricky	Shake Your Bon Bon	13-739	SGB
Martin, Ricky	She Bangs	34-151	CB
Martin, Ricky	She Bangs	23-256	HS
Martin, Ricky	She Bangs	14-42	THM
Martin, Ricky	She's All I Ever Had	35-221	CB
Martin, Ricky	She's All I Ever Had	29-180	MH
Martin, Ricky	She's All I Ever Had	8-501	PHT
Martin, Ricky	She's All I Ever Had	9-127	PS
Martin, Ricky	She's All I Ever Had	13-740	SGB
Martin, Ricky	Spanish Eyes	9-138	PS
Martin, Ricky	Spanish Eyes	13-741	SGB

ARTIST	SONG TITLE	#	TYPE
Martin, Ricky	You Stay With Me	9-129	PS
Martin, Ricky	You Stay With Me	13-742	SGB
Martin, Steve	King Tut	6-511	MM
Martin, Steve	King Tut	5-634	SC
Martin, Tony	I Get Ideas	4-183	SC
Martinez & Kelis	Take You Home	32-125	THM
Martinez, Angie	If I Could Go	18-345	PHM
Martinez, Rosco	Neon Moonlight	15-766	NU
Martino, Al	Daddy's Little Girl	29-493	LE
Martino, Al	Daddy's Little Girl	2-63	SC
Martino, Al	Here In My Heart	4-191	SC
Martino, Al	I Have But One Heart	46-209	SC
Martino, Al	Mary In The Morning	29-496	LE
Martino, Al	More Than The Eyes Can See	29-495	LE
Martino, Al	My Foolish Heart	29-494	LE
Martino, Al	Spanish Eyes	18-238	DK
Martino, Al	Spanish Eyes	29-497	LE
Martino, Al	Spanish Eyes	4-356	SC
Martino, Al	Spanish Eyes	19-786	SGB
Martino, Al	Wanted	29-498	LE
Martins	I Can't Help Myself	22-12	CB
Marvalettes	Don't Mess With Bill	11-774	DK
Marvalettes	Don't Mess With Bill	25-172	MM
Marvalettes	Please Mr. Postman	7-72	MM
Marvalettes	Please Mr. Postman	12-640	P
Marx, Groucho	I'm Against It (Whatever It Is)	48-8	KV
Marx, Groucho	Lydia The Tattooed Lady	47-926	KV
Marx, Richard	Angelia	14-584	SC
Marx, Richard	Endless Summer Nights	34-96	CB
Marx, Richard	Endless Summer Nights	15-792	SC
Marx, Richard	Hold On To The Nights	35-195	CB
Marx, Richard	Hold On To The Nights	21-746	MH
Marx, Richard	Now And Forever	18-477	NU
Marx, Richard	Now And Forever	16-574	SC
Marx, Richard	Right Here Waiting	33-332	CB
Marx, Richard	Right Here Waiting	6-348	MM
Marx, Richard	Satisfied	13-663	SGB
Marx, Richard	Way She Loves Me the	6-633	MM
Marx, Richard	Way She Loves Me the	2-462	SC
Mary Poppins	Show - Feed The Birds	20-183	Z
Mary Poppins	Show - Supercalifragilisticexpe alido...	49-851	SGB
Mary Poppins	Supercalifragilisticexpe alidocious	49-851	SGB
Mase & P Diddy	Breathe Stretch Shake	30-809	PHM
Mason, Dave	We Just Disagree	9-331	AG
Mason, Dave	We Just Disagree	26-341	DK
Mason, Mila	Closer To Heaven	8-298	CB
Mason, Mila	Closer To Heaven	22-774	ST
Mason, Mila	Dark Horse	22-403	CHM
Mason, Mila	Strong One the	8-483	CB
Mason, Mila	That's Enough Of That	7-405	MM
Mason, Mila	That's Enough Of That	4-428	SC
Mason, Mila	That's The Kind Of Love	16-579	SC

ARTIST	SONG TITLE	#	TYPE
	I'm In		
Mason, Mila	This Heart	8-763	CB
Massive Attack	Unfinished Sympathy	30-749	SF
Master P	Kenny's Dead **	13-725	SGB
Matchbox 20	3 A.M.	7-706	PHM
Matchbox 20	Back 2 Good	33-359	CB
Matchbox 20	Back To Good	16-217	MM
Matchbox 20	Bent	33-408	CB
Matchbox 20	Bent	13-837	PHM
Matchbox 20	Bent	14-469	SC
Matchbox 20	Bright Lights	19-651	CB
Matchbox 20	Bright Lights	20-224	MM
Matchbox 20	Bright Lights	32-393	THM
Matchbox 20	Disease	25-395	MM
Matchbox 20	Disease	18-583	NS
Matchbox 20	Disease	32-22	THM
Matchbox 20	Downfall	20-542	CB
Matchbox 20	Feel	19-600	CB
Matchbox 20	Feel	32-369	THM
Matchbox 20	How Far We've Gone	49-892	SC
Matchbox 20	If You're Gone	16-476	MH
Matchbox 20	If You're Gone	15-426	PHM
Matchbox 20	Last Beautiful Girl	25-17	MM
Matchbox 20	Long Day	34-127	CB
Matchbox 20	Long Day	24-635	SC
Matchbox 20	Mad Season	35-229	CB
Matchbox 20	Mad Season	15-458	PHM
Matchbox 20	Push	10-108	SC
Matchbox 20	Real World	21-555	PHM
Matchbox 20	These Hard Times	36-481	CB
Matchbox 20	Unwell	35-295	CB
Matchbox 20	Unwell	25-536	MM
Matchbox 20	Unwell	20-632	NS
Matchbox 20	Unwell	32-172	THM
Mathis & Streisand	Duet - I Have A Love (One Hand...)	6-345	MM
Mathis & Streisand	I Have A Love (One Hand One Heart)	6-345	MM
Mathis & Williams	Duet - Too Much Too Little Too Late	11-460	DK
Mathis & Williams	Duet - Too Much Too Little Too Late	6-341	MM
Mathis & Williams	Duet - Too Much Too Little Too Late	13-156	P
Mathis & Williams	Duet - Too Much Too Little Too...	35-309	CB
Mathis & Williams	Too Much Too Little Too Late	35-309	CB
Mathis & Williams	Too Much Too Little Too Late	11-460	DK
Mathis & Williams	Too Much Too Little Too Late	6-341	MM
Mathis & Williams	Too Much Too Little Too Late	13-156	P
Mathis, Johnny	Certain Smile	9-736	SAV
Mathis, Johnny	Certain Smile a	29-460	LE
Mathis, Johnny	Chances Are	29-465	LE
Mathis, Johnny	Chances Are	10-458	MG

181

ARTIST	SONG TITLE	#	TYPE
Mathis, Johnny	Chances Are	2-848	SC
Mathis, Johnny	Gina	49-322	CB
Mathis, Johnny	Hold Me Thrill Me Kiss Me	9-740	SAV
Mathis, Johnny	It's Not For Me To Say	10-467	MG
Mathis, Johnny	Misty	29-466	LE
Mathis, Johnny	Someone	29-462	LE
Mathis, Johnny	Too Much Too Little Too Late	29-464	LE
Mathis, Johnny	Twelfth Of Never	10-462	MG
Mathis, Johnny	Twelfth Of Never	18-47	MM
Mathis, Johnny	Twelfth Of Never	2-860	SC
Mathis, Johnny	Twelfth Of Never	19-787	SGB
Mathis, Johnny	Twelfth Of Never the	29-463	LE
Mathis, Johnny	What Child Is This	45-782	SBI
Mathis, Johnny	What Will Mary Say	29-461	LE
Mathis, Johnny	When A Child Is Born	45-781	ZM
Mathis, Johnny	When Sunny Gets Blue	15-584	MM
Mathis, Johnny	Wonderful Wonderful	18-55	MM
Mathis, Johnny	Xmas - Sleigh Ride	14-521	SC
Mathis, Johnny	Xmas - What Child Is This	45-782	SBI
Mathis, Johnny	Xmas - When A Child Is Born	45-781	ZM
Mathis, Johnny`	Twelfth Of Never	35-9	CB
Mattea & O'Brien	Battle Hymn Of Love the	1-198	CB
Mattea & O'Brien	Battle Hymn Of Love the	2-305	SC
Mattea & O'Brien	Duet - Battle Hymn Of Love the	1-190	CB
Mattea & O'Brien	Duet - Battle Hymn Of Love the	2-305	SC
Mattea, Kathy	455 Rocket	14-659	CB
Mattea, Kathy	455 Rocket	22-407	CHM
Mattea, Kathy	455 Rocket	7-431	MM
Mattea, Kathy	Asking Us To Dance	17-229	NA
Mattea, Kathy	Asking Us To Dance	49-29	KCD
Mattea, Kathy	BFD	14-908	CB
Mattea, Kathy	BFD	22-568	ST
Mattea, Kathy	Burning Old Memories	4-74	SC
Mattea, Kathy	Clown In Your Rodeo	2-666	SC
Mattea, Kathy	Come From The Heart	1-187	CB
Mattea, Kathy	Come From The Heart	3-645	SC
Mattea, Kathy	Eighteen Wheels & A Dozen Roses	1-184	CB
Mattea, Kathy	Eighteen Wheels & A Dozen Roses	13-413	P
Mattea, Kathy	Eighteen Wheels & A Dozen Roses	9-432	SAV
Mattea, Kathy	Eighteen Wheels & A Dozen Roses	2-16	SC
Mattea, Kathy	Few Good Things Remain a	6-737	MM
Mattea, Kathy	Few Good Things Remain, a	1-191	CB
Mattea, Kathy	Goin' Gone	1-183	CB
Mattea, Kathy	Goin' Gone	6-747	MM
Mattea, Kathy	Goin' Gone	5-19	SC
Mattea, Kathy	Life As We Knew it	1-186	CB
Mattea, Kathy	Life As We Knew It	7-158	MM

ARTIST	SONG TITLE	#	TYPE
Mattea, Kathy	Listen To The Radio	17-265	NA
Mattea, Kathy	Lonesome Standard Time	6-133	MM
Mattea, Kathy	Love At The Five And Dime	1-181	CB
Mattea, Kathy	Love Travels	8-136	CB
Mattea, Kathy	Love Travels	22-635	ST
Mattea, Kathy	Maybe She's Human	2-549	SC
Mattea, Kathy	Nobody's Gonna Rain On Our Parade	6-603	MM
Mattea, Kathy	She Came From Fort Worth	1-189	CB
Mattea, Kathy	She Came From Fort Worth	19-304	MH
Mattea, Kathy	Standing Knee Deep In A ...	2-716	SC
Mattea, Kathy	Time Passes By	1-192	CB
Mattea, Kathy	Train Of Memories	5-530	SC
Mattea, Kathy	Trouble With Angels	9-409	CB
Mattea, Kathy	Untold Stories	1-185	CB
Mattea, Kathy	Walk The Way The Wind Blows	1-182	CB
Mattea, Kathy	Walk The Way The Wind Blows	5-135	SC
Mattea, Kathy	Walking Away A Winner	1-193	CB
Mattea, Kathy	Walking Away A Winner	10-784	JVC
Mattea, Kathy	Walking Away A Winner	12-455	P
Mattea, Kathy	Walking Away A Winner	2-215	SC
Mattea, Kathy	Where've You Been	14-679	CB
Mattea, Kathy	Where've You Been	9-452	SAV
Mattea, Kathy	Xmas - Star the	18-758	CB
Mattea, Kathy	You're The Power	6-79	SC
Matthews, Lee	Irish - There's Irish In Our Eyes	48-720	KV
Mavericks	All That Heaven Will Allow	2-776	SC
Mavericks	All You ever Do Is Bring/Down	3-652	SC
Mavericks	Amazing Grace	6-591	MM
Mavericks	Here Comes My Baby	5-831	SC
Mavericks	Here Comes The Rain	7-144	MM
Mavericks	I Should Have Been True	22-858	ST
Mavericks	Missing You	4-410	SC
Mavericks	Oh What A Thrill	6-604	MM
Mavericks	There Goes My Heart	2-490	SC
Mavericks	To Be With You	7-725	CHM
Mavericks	To Be With You	22-775	ST
Mavericks	Tonight The Bottle Let Me Down	44-115	KV
Mavericks	What A Cryin' Shame	12-451	P
Mavericks	What A Cryin' Shame	2-516	SC
Maxi Priest	Close To You	11-678	DK
Maxi Priest	Close To You	5-342	SC
Maxwell	Ascension (Don't Ever Wonder)	24-240	SC
Maxwell	Fortunate	7-848	PHM
Mayer, John	Bigger Than My Body	19-646	CB
Mayer, John	Bigger Than My Body	20-221	MM

ARTIST	SONG TITLE	#	TYPE
Mayer, John	Bigger Than My Body	32-395	THM
Mayer, John	Call Me The Breeze	42-15	PHM
Mayer, John	Clarity	20-563	CB
Mayer, John	No Such Thing	18-219	CB
Mayer, John	No Such Thing	20-377	HP
Mayer, John	No Such Thing	18-412	MM
Mayer, John	Waiting On The World To Change	36-184	PHM
Mayer, John	Why Georgia	25-535	MM
Mayer, John	Why Georgia	19-343	STP
Mayer, John	Why Georgia	32-246	THM
Mayer, John	Your Body Is A Wonderland	25-338	MM
Mayer, John	Your Body Is A Wonderland	18-342	PHM
Mayfield, Curtis	Superfly	28-110	DK
McAlyster	I Know How The River Feels	10-272	CB
McAnally, Shane	Are Your Eyes Still Blue	8-982	CB
McAnally, Shane	Are Your Eyes Still Blue	22-381	ST
McAnally, Shane	Run Away	14-88	CB
McAnally, Shane	Say Anything	8-377	CB
McBride & The Ride	Can I Count On You	2-613	SC
McBride & The Ride	Hurry Sundown	2-711	SC
McBride & The Ride	Just One Night	2-347	SC
McBride & The Ride	Love On The Loose Heart	2-357	SC
McBride, Martina	Anything's Better Than Feelin'/Blue	8-896	CB
McBride, Martina	Anyway	30-200	CB
McBride, Martina	Be That Way	8-864	CB
McBride, Martina	Blessed	29-533	CB
McBride, Martina	Blessed	25-63	MM
McBride, Martina	Blessed	16-30	ST
McBride, Martina	Broken Wing a	1-387	CB
McBride, Martina	Broken Wing a	22-645	ST
McBride, Martina	Cheap Whiskey	6-108	MM
McBride, Martina	Cheap Whiskey	2-404	SC
McBride, Martina	City Of Love	29-541	CB
McBride, Martina	City Of Love	20-263	SC
McBride, Martina	Concrete Angel	29-530	CB
McBride, Martina	Concrete Angel	25-420	MM
McBride, Martina	Concrete Angel	18-462	ST
McBride, Martina	Concrete Angel	32-79	THM
McBride, Martina	Cry On The Shoulder Of The Road	1-382	CB
McBride, Martina	Cry On The Shoulder Of The Road	7-592	CHM
McBride, Martina	Cry On The Shoulder Of The Road	7-429	MM
McBride, Martina	Cry On The Shoulder Of The Road	3-568	SC
McBride, Martina	For These Times	30-578	CB
McBride, Martina	God's Will	23-10	CB
McBride, Martina	God's Will	20-265	SC
McBride, Martina	Great Disguise a	4-393	SC
McBride, Martina	Happy Girl	8-102	CB
McBride, Martina	Happy Girl	7-764	CHM

ARTIST	SONG TITLE	#	TYPE
McBride, Martina	Heart Trouble	1-379	CB
McBride, Martina	Heart Trouble	2-541	SC
McBride, Martina	Help Me Make It Through The Night	29-37	CB
McBride, Martina	How Far	29-537	CB
McBride, Martina	How Far	20-337	ST
McBride, Martina	How I Feel	30-455	CB
McBride, Martina	I Just Call You Mine	37-39	CB
McBride, Martina	I Love You	29-534	CB
McBride, Martina	I Love You	22-485	ST
McBride, Martina	I Still Miss Someone	29-190	CB
McBride, Martina	I Still Miss Someone	29-844	SC
McBride, Martina	I'm Gonna Love You Through It	38-219	CB
McBride, Martina	In My Daughter's Eyes	29-535	CB
McBride, Martina	In My Daughter's Eyes	19-688	ST
McBride, Martina	Independence Day	1-378	CB
McBride, Martina	Independence Day	6-574	MM
McBride, Martina	Independence Day	12-464	P
McBride, Martina	It's My Time	33-154	CB
McBride, Martina	It's My Time	22-588	ST
McBride, Martina	Life # 9	1-377	CB
McBride, Martina	Life # 9	19-292	MH
McBride, Martina	Life # 9	6-459	MM
McBride, Martina	Love's The Only House	29-531	CB
McBride, Martina	Love's The Only House	22-524	ST
McBride, Martina	My Baby Loves Me	1-376	CB
McBride, Martina	My Baby Loves Me	26-582	DK
McBride, Martina	My Baby Loves Me	6-402	MM
McBride, Martina	Over The Rainbow	29-542	CB
McBride, Martina	Over The Rainbow (Live Version)	23-38	SC
McBride, Martina	Phones Are Ringing All Over Town	7-228	MM
McBride, Martina	Ride	36-258	PHM
McBride, Martina	Rose Garden	36-371	SC
McBride, Martina	Rose Garden (I Never Promised...)	23-414	CB
McBride, Martina	Safe In The Arms Of Love	1-380	CB
McBride, Martina	Safe In The Arms Of Love	7-22	MM
McBride, Martina	Swingin' Doors	1-385	CB
McBride, Martina	Swingin' Doors	4-433	SC
McBride, Martina	Teenage Daughters	37-222	CB
McBride, Martina	That's Me	1-383	CB
McBride, Martina	That's Me	6-182	MM
McBride, Martina	There You Are	9-423	CB
McBride, Martina	There You Are	13-823	CHM
McBride, Martina	There You Are	22-545	ST
McBride, Martina	This One's For The Girls	29-528	CB
McBride, Martina	This One's For The Girls	25-637	MM
McBride, Martina	This One's For The Girls	19-169	ST
McBride, Martina	This One's For The Girls	32-335	THM
McBride, Martina	Til I Can Make It On My Own	30-28	CB
McBride, Martina	Time Has Come the	6-189	MM
McBride, Martina	Valentine	8-133	CB

ARTIST	SONG TITLE	#	TYPE	ARTIST	SONG TITLE	#	TYPE
McBride, Martina	Valentine	22-768	ST	McCann, Lila	Yippy Ky Yay	22-819	ST
McBride, Martina	Whatever You Say	8-947	CB	McCarter Sisters	Up And Gone	14-691	CB
McBride, Martina	Whatever You Say	7-828	CHT	McCartney & Wings	Band On The Run	17-406	DK
McBride, Martina	When God Fearin' Women Get The	15-601	ST	McCartney & Wings	Band On The Run	14-578	SC
McBride, Martina	When God Fearing Women Get The..	29-529	CB	McCartney & Wings	Coming Up	28-327	DK
McBride, Martina	When You Love Me	29-540	CB	McCartney & Wings	From A Lover To A Friend	25-36	MM
McBride, Martina	Where I Used To Have A Heart	1-384	CB	McCartney & Wings	Hi Hi Hi	12-81	DK
McBride, Martina	Where I Used To Have a Heart	2-671	SC	McCartney & Wings	Jet	17-557	DK
McBride, Martina	Where I Used To Have A Heart	22-874	ST	McCartney & Wings	Junior's Farm	17-558	DK
McBride, Martina	Where Would You Be	29-532	CB	McCartney & Wings	Let 'Em In	15-756	AMS
McBride, Martina	Where Would You Be	25-234	MM	McCartney & Wings	Live And Let Die	13-32	P
McBride, Martina	Where Would You Be	16-698	ST	McCartney & Wings	My Love	11-248	DK
McBride, Martina	Wild Angels	1-381	CB	McCartney & Wings	With A Little Luck	12-82	DK
McBride, Martina	Wild Angels	7-176	MM	McCartney, Jesse	Beautiful Soul	22-370	CB
McBride, Martina	Wild Angels	3-663	SC	McCartney, Jesse	Beautiful Soul	30-742	SF
McBride, Martina	Wrong Again	8-183	CB	McCartney, Jesse	How Do You Sleep	36-286	PHM
McBride, Martina	Wrong Again	10-149	SC	McCartney, Jesse	It's Over	36-497	CB
McBride, Martina	Wrong Again	22-671	ST	McCartney, Jesse	Leavin'	36-445	CB
McBride, Martina	Wrong Baby Wrong Baby Wrong	37-326	CB	McCartney, Jesse	Right Where You Want Me	30-62	PHM
McBride, Martina	Xmas - Have Yourself A Merry Little	30-387	SC	McCartney, Paul	Band On The Run	48-562	DK
McBride, Martina	You Ain't Woman Enough	29-599	CB	McCartney, Paul	Freedom	33-391	CB
McBusted	Air Guitar	48-330	MRH	McCartney, Paul	Freedom (NYC Version)	16-94	SC
McCabe, Coley	Grow Young With You	6-73	SC	McCartney, Paul	From A Lover To A Friend	16-92	SC
McCain, Edwin	Hearts Fall	18-407	MM	McCartney, Paul	Hi Hi Hi	48-565	DK
McCain, Edwin	I Could Not Ask For More	49-508	PHC	McCartney, Paul	Jet	21-516	SC
McCain, Edwin	I'll Be	10-21	SC	McCartney, Paul	Let Me Roll It	15-755	AMS
McCall, C.W.	Convoy	8-21	CB	McCartney, Paul	Live And Let Die	9-61	SC
McCall, C.W.	Convoy	6-870	MM	McCartney, Paul	Maybe I'm Amazed	6-493	MM
McCall, C.W.	Wolf Creek Pass **	23-24	SC	McCartney, Paul	Maybe I'm Amazed	29-290	SC
McCann, Lila	Almost Over You	8-411	CB	McCartney, Paul	My Love	48-563	DK
McCann, Lila	Almost Over You	7-739	CHM	McCartney, Paul	Say Say Say	15-557	CMC
McCann, Lila	Almost Over You	22-784	ST	McCartney, Paul	Silly Love Songs	16-782	DK
McCann, Lila	Come A Little Closer	15-101	ST	McCartney, Paul	Silly Love Songs	14-645	SC
McCann, Lila	Crush	10-212	SC	McCartney, Paul	Uncle Albert/Admiral Halsey	20-49	SC
McCann, Lila	Crush	22-435	ST	McCartney, Paul	With A Little Love	48-564	DK
McCann, Lila	Down Came A Blackbird	7-656	CHM	McCartney, Paul	Xmas - Wonderful Christmastime	34-431	CB
McCann, Lila	Go Easy On Me	22-323	CB	McCartney&Wonder	Duet - Ebony & Ivory	11-117	DK
McCann, Lila	I Can Do This	23-306	CB	McCartney&Wonder	Ebony And Ivory	11-117	DK
McCann, Lila	I Wanna Fall In Love	35-415	CB	McClain, Charley	Dancing Your Memory Away	38-41	SC
McCann, Lila	I Wanna Fall In Love	22-649	ST	McClain, Charley	Radio Heart	5-244	SC
McCann, Lila	I Will Be	8-908	CB	McClain, Charley	Sentimental Ol' You	5-862	SC
McCann, Lila	I'm Amazed	23-486	CB	McClain, Charley	Sleepin' With The Radio On	8-201	CB
McCann, Lila	I'm Amazed	23-457	ST	McClain, Charley	Who's Cheatin' Who	2-131	SC
McCann, Lila	Kiss Me Now	6-71	SC	McClinton, Delbert	Givin' It Up For Your Love	2-565	SC
McCann, Lila	To Get Me To You	8-193	CB	McClinton, Delbert	Sending Me Angels	8-302	CB
McCann, Lila	With You	8-332	CB	McClinton, Delbert	When Rita Leaves	17-478	TT
McCann, Lila	With You	7-854	CHT	McCloud, Nicole	One Good Reason	21-732	TT
McCann, Lila	With You	22-734	ST	McComas, Brian	99.9% Sure	25-567	MM
McCann, Lila	Yippy Ky Yay	8-731	CB	McComas, Brian	99.9% Sure	19-10	ST
				McComas, Brian	99.9% Sure	32-195	THM

ARTIST	SONG TITLE	#	TYPE
McComas, Brian	99.9% Sure (I've Never Been...)	34-395	CB
McComas, Brian	All Comes Floodin' Down	30-199	CB
McComas, Brian	Good Good Lovin'	29-585	CB
McComas, Brian	I Could Never Love You Enough	16-689	ST
McComas, Brian	Middle Of Nowhere the	22-315	CB
McComas, Brian	Middle Of Nowhere the	23-389	SC
McComas, Brian	Night Disappear With You	16-168	CB
McComas, Brian	Night Disappear With You	25-9	MM
McComas, Brian	Night Disappear With You	15-862	ST
McComas, Brian	You're In My Head	19-534	ST
McComb, Jeremy	Cold	36-281	PHM
McCoo & Davis Jr.	Duet - You Don't Have To Be A Star	17-140	DK
McCoo & Davis Jr.	You Don't Have To Be A Star	17-140	DK
McCoy, Neal	A-Ok	38-245	PHN
McCoy, Neal	Beatin' It In	14-794	ST
McCoy, Neal	Billy's Got His Beer Goggles On	23-286	CB
McCoy, Neal	City Put The Country Back In Me	1-855	CB
McCoy, Neal	City Put The Country Back In Me	6-675	MM
McCoy, Neal	City Put The Country Back In Me	17-220	NA
McCoy, Neal	City Put The Country Back In Me	2-394	SC
McCoy, Neal	Every Man For Himself	14-108	CB
McCoy, Neal	Every Man For Himself	22-574	ST
McCoy, Neal	For A Change	1-842	CB
McCoy, Neal	For A Change	6-720	MM
McCoy, Neal	For A Change	17-278	NA
McCoy, Neal	For A Change	2-645	SC
McCoy, Neal	Forever Works For Me	9-388	CB
McCoy, Neal	Forever Works For Me	13-832	CHM
McCoy, Neal	Forever Works For Me	19-259	CSZ
McCoy, Neal	Girls Of Summer the	1-844	CB
McCoy, Neal	Girls Of Summer the	10-196	SC
McCoy, Neal	Girls Of Summer the	22-434	ST
McCoy, Neal	Girls Of Summer the	16-194	THM
McCoy, Neal	Going Going Gone	1-845	CB
McCoy, Neal	Going Going Gone	4-400	SC
McCoy, Neal	Hillbilly Rap	7-341	MM
McCoy, Neal	Hillbilly Rap	24-154	SC
McCoy, Neal	I Was	8-920	CB
McCoy, Neal	I Was	22-731	ST
McCoy, Neal	If I Was A Drinkin' Man	1-847	CB
McCoy, Neal	If I Was A Drinkin' Man	6-851	MM
McCoy, Neal	If You Can't Be Good, Be Good At It	22-419	ST
McCoy, Neal	If You Can't Be Good, Be Good At It	1-848	CB
McCoy, Neal	If You Can't Be Good, Be Good At It	7-729	CHM
McCoy, Neal	Last Of A Dying Breed the	29-586	CB
McCoy, Neal	Last Of A Dying Breed the	29-716	ST
McCoy, Neal	Love Happens Like That	8-732	CB
McCoy, Neal	Love Happens Like That	22-818	ST
McCoy, Neal	Luckiest Man In The World	18-469	ST
McCoy, Neal	Luckiest Man In The World the	32-7	THM
McCoy, Neal	No Doubt About It	1-850	CB
McCoy, Neal	No Doubt About It	26-534	DK
McCoy, Neal	No Doubt About It	10-775	JVC
McCoy, Neal	No Doubt About It	6-469	MM
McCoy, Neal	No Doubt About It	2-426	SC
McCoy, Neal	Party On	8-470	CB
McCoy, Neal	Shake the	1-841	CB
McCoy, Neal	Shake the	7-654	CHM
McCoy, Neal	Shake the	22-609	ST
McCoy, Neal	Tailgate	30-27	CB
McCoy, Neal	That Woman Of Mine	1-852	CB
McCoy, Neal	That Woman Of Mine	22-915	ST
McCoy, Neal	Then You Can Tell Me Goodbye	7-276	MM
McCoy, Neal	They're Playing Our Song	1-853	CB
McCoy, Neal	They're Playing Our Song	6-798	MM
McCoy, Neal	They're Playing Our Song	2-823	SC
McCoy, Neal	Wink	1-843	CB
McCoy, Neal	Wink	6-581	MM
McCoy, Neal	Wink	12-450	P
McCoy, Neal	You Gotta Love That	1-854	CB
McCoy, Neal	You Gotta Love That	4-129	SC
McCoy, T. & Bruno Mars	Billionaire - duet	38-235	CB
McCoy, T. & Bruno Mars	Duet - Billionaire	38-235	CB
McCoy's	Hang On Sloopy	17-155	DK
McCoy's	Hang On Sloopy	6-138	MM
McCoys	Hang On Sloopy	35-52	CB
McCrae, George	Rock Your Baby	33-251	CB
McCrae, George	Rock Your Baby	11-409	DK
McCready, Mindy	All I Want Is Everything	14-700	CB
McCready, Mindy	All I Want Is Everything	19-234	SC
McCready, Mindy	Girl's Gotta Do a	7-614	CHM
McCready, Mindy	Guys Do It All The Time	4-391	SC
McCready, Mindy	Let's Talk About Love	8-243	CB
McCready, Mindy	Maybe He'll Notice Her Now	34-323	CB
McCready, Mindy	Maybe He'll Notice Her Now	7-390	MM
McCready, Mindy	Maybe He'll Notice Her Now	4-510	SC
McCready, Mindy	Maybe He'll Notice Her Now	22-908	ST
McCready, Mindy	Maybe Maybe Not	16-335	ST

ARTIST	SONG TITLE	#	TYPE
McCready, Mindy	One In A Million	10-192	SC
McCready, Mindy	Other Side	34-329	CB
McCready, Mindy	Other Side Of This Kiss the	8-727	CB
McCready, Mindy	Other Side Of This Kiss the	5-295	SC
McCready, Mindy	Other Side Of This Kiss the	22-802	ST
McCready, Mindy	Scream	14-169	CB
McCready, Mindy	Scream	22-594	ST
McCready, Mindy	Ten Thousand Angels	4-232	SC
McCready, Mindy	What If I Do	8-127	CB
McCready, Mindy	What If I Do	22-643	ST
McCready, Mindy	You'll Never Know	8-239	CB
McCready, Rich	Hangin' On	4-154	SC
McCready, Rich	Thinkin' Strait	7-255	MM
McCready, Rich	When Hell Freezes Over	4-891	SC
McCreary, Scotty	I Love You This Big	38-110	CB
McCreary, Scotty	Water Tower Town	39-40	ASK
McCreery, Scotty	Christmas In Heaven	45-638	KV
McCreery, Scotty	Feelin' It	44-136	ASK
McCreery, Scotty	Feelin' It	45-45	BKD
McCreery, Scotty	See You Tonight	44-2	BKD
McCreery, Scotty	See You Tonight	43-139	KCD
McCreery, Scotty	Trouble With Girls the	45-636	ASK
McCreery, Scotty	Water Tower Town	45-637	ASK
McCreery, Scotty	Xmas - Christmas In Heaven	45-638	KV
McDaniel, Mel	Baby's Got Her Blue Jeans On	35-390	CB
McDaniel, Mel	Baby's Got Her Blue Jeans On	17-402	DK
McDaniel, Mel	Baby's Got Her Blue Jeans On	7-113	MM
McDaniel, Mel	Baby's Got Her Blue Jeans On	12-447	P
McDaniel, Mel	Baby's Got Her Blue Jeans On	3-597	SC
McDaniel, Mel	Big Ole Blew	4-821	SC
McDaniel, Mel	Let It Roll	5-670	SC
McDaniel, Mel	Louisiana Saturday Night	2-366	SC
McDaniel, Mel	Mama's Bible	49-39	DFK
McDaniel, Mel	Ride This Train	49-121	SHER
McDaniel, Mel	Stand On It	49-123	DFK
McDaniel, Mel	Stand Up	2-125	SC
McDaniel, Mel	Take Me To The Country	49-124	DFK
McDaniels, Gene	Another Tear Falls	49-122	DFK
McDaniels, Gene	Hundred Pounds Of Clay	10-325	KC
McDaniels, Gene	Hundred Pounds Of Clay	5-89	SC
McDawn, Karen	Cajun - Cajun Hoedown	49-386	VH
McDawn, Karen	Cajun Hoedown	45-870	VH
McDonald, Michael	I Keep Forgettin'	4-383	SC
McDonald, Michael	Matters Of The Heart	13-600	P
McDonald, Richie	How Do I Just Stop	36-279	PHM
McDonald&Mattea	Among The Missing	8-914	CB

ARTIST	SONG TITLE	#	TYPE
McDonald&Mattea	Duet - Among The Missing	8-914	CB
McDowell, Ronnie	All Tied Up	5-535	SC
McDowell, Ronnie	Don't Let Go	47-233	CB
McDowell, Ronnie	I Dream Of Women Like You	47-228	CB
McDowell, Ronnie	I Got A Million Of 'Em	47-229	CB
McDowell, Ronnie	In A New York Minute	34-272	CB
McDowell, Ronnie	In A New York Minute	5-763	SC
McDowell, Ronnie	It's Only Make Believe	47-231	CB
McDowell, Ronnie	King Is Gone the	8-458	CB
McDowell, Ronnie	Life Has It's Little Ups & Downs	47-234	SAV
McDowell, Ronnie	Love Talks	47-230	CB
McDowell, Ronnie	Older Women	8-211	CB
McDowell, Ronnie	Older Women	13-499	P
McDowell, Ronnie	Personally	47-226	CB
McDowell, Ronnie	Wandering Eyes	4-823	SC
McDowell, Ronnie	Watching Girls Go By	34-253	CB
McDowell, Ronnie	When You Hurt I Hurt	47-232	CB
McDowell, Ronnie	You Made A Wanted Man Out Of Me	47-227	CB
McDowell, Ronnie	You're Gonna Ruin My Bad Reputation	11-742	DK
McDowell, Ronny	Bedroom Eyes	45-675	DCK
McEntire & B&D	Duet - If You See Him/Her	8-97	CB
McEntire & B&D	Duet - If You See Him/Her	7-760	CHM
McEntire & B&D	If You See Him If You See Her	8-97	CB
McEntire & B&D	If You See Him If You See Her	7-760	CHM
McEntire & Chesney	Duet - Every Other Weekend	49-707	ST
McEntire & Chesney	Every Other Weekend - duet	49-707	ST
McEntire & Clarkson	Because Of You - duet	30-464	CB
McEntire & Clarkson	Duet - Because Of You	30-464	CB
McEntire & Davis	Does He Love You	1-808	CB
McEntire & Davis	Does He Love You	6-399	MM
McEntire & Davis	Duet - Does He Love You	1-808	CB
McEntire & Davis	Duet - Does He Love You	6-399	MM
McEntire & Ewing	Every Other Weekend	36-581	CB
McEntire & Gill	Duet - Heart Won't Lie the	1-806	CB
McEntire & Gill	Duet - Heart Won't Lie the	12-402	P
McEntire & Gill	Duet - Heart Won't Lie the	2-301	SC
McEntire & Gill	Duet - Oklahoma Swing	1-795	CB
McEntire & Gill	Duet - Oklahoma Swing	6-751	MM
McEntire & Gill	Duet - Oklahoma Swing - DANCE	22-390	SC
McEntire & Gill	Heart Won't Lie the	1-806	CB
McEntire & Gill	Heart Won't Lie the	12-402	P
McEntire & Gill	Heart Won't Lie the	2-301	SC

ARTIST	SONG TITLE	#	TYPE
McEntire & Gill	Oklahoma Swing	6-751	MM
McEntire & Gill	Oklahoma Swing	22-390	SC
McEntire & Hill	Sleeping With The Telephone	36-548	CB
McEntire, Joey	I Love You Came Too Late	7-897	PHT
McEntire, Joey	I Love You Came Too Late	10-188	SC\
McEntire, Joey	Stay The Same	7-844	PHM
McEntire, Reba	And Still	1-819	CB
McEntire, Reba	And Still	6-813	MM
McEntire, Reba	And Still	2-833	SC
McEntire, Reba	Baby's Gone Blues	4-468	SC
McEntire, Reba	Before I Met You	1-818	CB
McEntire, Reba	Can't Even Get The Blues	1-783	CB
McEntire, Reba	Can't Even Get The Blues	13-412	P
McEntire, Reba	Can't Even Get The Blues	5-30	SC
McEntire, Reba	Cathy's Clown	17-302	NA
McEntire, Reba	Christmas Guest	45-767	CB
McEntire, Reba	Climb That Mountain High	6-819	MM
McEntire, Reba	Consider Me Gone	36-37	PT
McEntire, Reba	Don't Touch Me There	6-202	MM
McEntire, Reba	Enough	45-406	BKD
McEntire, Reba	Falling Out Of Love	1-799	CB
McEntire, Reba	Falling Out Of Love	10-779	JVC
McEntire, Reba	Fancy	1-796	CB
McEntire, Reba	Fancy	13-478	P
McEntire, Reba	Fancy	2-390	SC
McEntire, Reba	Fear Of Being Alone the	1-821	CB
McEntire, Reba	Fear Of Being Alone the	4-505	SC
McEntire, Reba	For Herself	1-804	CB
McEntire, Reba	For Herself	7-142	MM
McEntire, Reba	For My Broken Heart	1-800	CB
McEntire, Reba	For My Broken Heart	19-298	MH
McEntire, Reba	For My Broken Heart	2-793	SC
McEntire, Reba	Forever Love	8-743	CB
McEntire, Reba	Forever Love	22-808	ST
McEntire, Reba	Going Out Like That	45-405	BKD
McEntire, Reba	Greatest Man I Never Knew	33-110	Cb
McEntire, Reba	Greatest Man I Never Knew	6-209	MM
McEntire, Reba	Greatest Man I Never Knew	2-807	SC
McEntire, Reba	Have I Got A Deal For You	1-811	CB
McEntire, Reba	Have I Got A Deal For You	17-299	NA
McEntire, Reba	He Gets That From Me	22-64	CB
McEntire, Reba	He Gets That From Me	20-503	ST
McEntire, Reba	Heart Is A Lonely Hunter	6-717	MM
McEntire, Reba	Heart Is A Lonely Hunter	2-642	SC
McEntire, Reba	Heart Is A Lonely Hunter	22-864	ST
McEntire, Reba	Heart Won't Lie the	6-129	MM
McEntire, Reba	How Was I To Know	1-813	CB

ARTIST	SONG TITLE	#	TYPE
McEntire, Reba	How Was I To Know	7-586	CHM
McEntire, Reba	I Don't Think Love Ought To Be That	5-863	SC
McEntire, Reba	I Know How He Feels	1-794	CB
McEntire, Reba	I Wouldn't Know	9-336	PS
McEntire, Reba	I'd Rather Ride Around With You	1-815	CB
McEntire, Reba	I'd Rather Ride Around With You	7-625	CHM
McEntire, Reba	I'd Rather Ride Around With You	10-81	SC
McEntire, Reba	I'll Be	13-808	CHM
McEntire, Reba	I'll Be	6-64	SC
McEntire, Reba	I'm A Survivor	15-668	ST
McEntire, Reba	I'm Gonna Take That Mountain	19-526	ST
McEntire, Reba	I'm Gonna Take That Mountain	32-408	THM
McEntire, Reba	I'm In Love All Over	1-817	CB
McEntire, Reba	I'm Not That Lonely Yet	1-791	CB
McEntire, Reba	If I Had Only Known	6-212	MM
McEntire, Reba	Is There Life Out There	1-801	CB
McEntire, Reba	Is There Life Out There	12-403	P
McEntire, Reba	It's Not Over	1-798	CB
McEntire, Reba	It's Your Call	1-807	CB
McEntire, Reba	It's Your Call	6-128	MM
McEntire, Reba	Last One To Know the	29-67	CB
McEntire, Reba	Let The Music Lift you Under..	1-803	CB
McEntire, Reba	Little Girl	1-781	CB
McEntire, Reba	Little Girl	24-125	SC
McEntire, Reba	Little Rock	6-539	MM
McEntire, Reba	Little Rock	3-378	SC
McEntire, Reba	Love Needs A Holiday	29-187	CB
McEntire, Reba	Love Will Find It's Way	1-792	CB
McEntire, Reba	My Sister	22-331	CB
McEntire, Reba	My Sister	23-379	SC
McEntire, Reba	New Fool At An Old Game	1-793	CB
McEntire, Reba	Night The Lights Went Out in GA	1-802	CB
McEntire, Reba	Night The Lights Went Out In GA	6-191	MM
McEntire, Reba	On My Own	1-784	CB
McEntire, Reba	On My Own	7-80	MM
McEntire, Reba	On My Own	3-535	SC
McEntire, Reba	One Honest Heart	8-945	CB
McEntire, Reba	One Honest Heart	7-865	CHT
McEntire, Reba	One Last Good Hand	24-246	SC
McEntire, Reba	One Promise Too Late	34-273	CB
McEntire, Reba	Only In My Mind	5-131	SC
McEntire, Reba	Please Come To Boston	15-550	SC
McEntire, Reba	Read My Mind	1-797	CB
McEntire, Reba	Read My Mind	17-226	NA
McEntire, Reba	Red Roses	1-785	CB
McEntire, Reba	Ring On Her Finger	1-782	CB
McEntire, Reba	Ring On Her Finger	7-172	MM
McEntire, Reba	Ring On Her Finger	3-622	SC

ARTIST	SONG TITLE	#	TYPE
McEntire, Reba	Rumor Has It	6-624	MM
McEntire, Reba	She Thinks His Name Was John	1-820	CB
McEntire, Reba	She Thinks His Name Was John	6-599	MM
McEntire, Reba	She Thinks His Name Was John	2-455	SC
McEntire, Reba	Silly Me	1-786	CB
McEntire, Reba	Silly Me	24-12	SC
McEntire, Reba	So So Long	1-812	CB
McEntire, Reba	Somebody	19-765	ST
McEntire, Reba	Somebody Should Leave	13-402	P
McEntire, Reba	Somebody Should Leave	3-376	SC
McEntire, Reba	Starting Over Again	1-790	CB
McEntire, Reba	Starting Over Again	4-204	SC
McEntire, Reba	Strange	49-421	KV
McEntire, Reba	Sunday Kind Of Love	1-816	CB
McEntire, Reba	Sweet Music Man	25-123	MM
McEntire, Reba	Sweet Music Man	16-98	ST
McEntire, Reba	Take It Back	1-805	CB
McEntire, Reba	Take It Back	6-215	MM
McEntire, Reba	Take It Back	2-5	SC
McEntire, Reba	Take It Back	8-593	TT
McEntire, Reba	There Ain't No Future In This	14-426	SC
McEntire, Reba	They Asked About You	1-809	CB
McEntire, Reba	They Asked About You	6-457	MM
McEntire, Reba	They Asked About You	2-425	SC
McEntire, Reba	Till Love Comes Again	14-683	CB
McEntire, Reba	Till Love Comes Again	9-522	SAV
McEntire, Reba	Till You Love Me	2-486	SC
McEntire, Reba	Today All Over Again	1-787	CB
McEntire, Reba	Walk On	11-704	DK
McEntire, Reba	Walk On	17-249	NA
McEntire, Reba	Walk On	2-517	SC
McEntire, Reba	We're So Good Together	14-734	CB
McEntire, Reba	We're So Good Together	13-860	CHM
McEntire, Reba	What Am I Gonna Do About You	11-740	DK
McEntire, Reba	What Am I Gonna Do About You	12-438	P
McEntire, Reba	What Do You Say	19-240	SC
McEntire, Reba	What Do You Say	22-373	ST
McEntire, Reba	What If	8-150	CB
McEntire, Reba	What If	22-754	ST
McEntire, Reba	What If It's You	1-823	CB
McEntire, Reba	What If It's You	7-681	CHM
McEntire, Reba	What If It's You	22-628	ST
McEntire, Reba	Whoever's In New England	13-339	P
McEntire, Reba	Whoever's In New England	8-693	SAV
McEntire, Reba	Whoever's In New England	22-780	ST
McEntire, Reba	Why Haven't I Heard From You	1-810	CB
McEntire, Reba	Why Haven't I Heard	2-214	SC

ARTIST	SONG TITLE	#	TYPE
	From You		
McEntire, Reba	Will He Ever Go Away	24-84	SC
McEntire, Reba	Wrong Night	8-851	CB
McEntire, Reba	Wrong Night	22-684	ST
McEntire, Reba	Xmas - Christmas Guest	45-767	CB
McEntire, Reba	Xmas - Christmas Letter a	8-59	CB
McEntire, Reba	Xmas - On This Day	18-723	CB
McEntire, Reba	Xmas - On This Day	15-658	THM
McEntire, Reba	You Lie	16-587	MM
McEntire, Reba	You're Gonna Be	23-471	CB
McEntire, Reba	You're The First Time I Thought...	1-788	CB
McEntire, Reba	You're The First Time I Thought...	4-788	SC
McEntire&Clarkson	Because Of You	30-464	CB
McEntire&Clarkson	Duet - Because Of You	30-464	CB
McFadden&Whitehead	Ain't No Stoppin' Us Now	7-491	MM
McFatter, Clyde	Long Lonely Nights	10-337	SS
McFerrin, Bobby	Don't Worry Be Happy	26-309	DK
McGovern, Maureen	Can You Read My Mind	7-184	MM
McGovern, Maureen	Morning After the	17-32	DK
McGraw & Dunn, C	Diamond Rings & Old Barstools - duet	45-43	BKD
McGraw & Dunn, C	Duet - Diamond Rings & Old Barstools	45-43	BKD
McGraw & Hill	Angry All The Time	15-600	ST
McGraw & Hill	Duet - Angry All The Time	15-600	ST
McGraw & Hill	Duet - I Need You	40-29	SC
McGraw & Hill	Duet - I Need You	46-316	SC
McGraw & Hill	Duet - It's Your Love	7-634	CHM
McGraw & Hill	I Need You - duet	40-29	SC
McGraw & Hill	I Need You - duet	46-316	SC
McGraw & Hill	It's Your Love	7-634	CHM
McGraw & Swift	Duet - Highway Don't Care	40-45	ASK
McGraw & Swift	Highway Don't Care - duet	40-45	ASK
McGraw, Tim	All I Want Is A Life	1-533	CB
McGraw, Tim	All We Ever Find	49-75	ZPA
McGraw, Tim	Angel Boy	25-72	MM
McGraw, Tim	Angel Boy	16-330	ST
McGraw, Tim	Angry All The Time	29-348	CB
McGraw, Tim	Back When	22-62	CB
McGraw, Tim	Back When	20-502	ST
McGraw, Tim	Better Than I Used To Be	47-763	SRK
McGraw, Tim	Can't Be Really Gone	1-532	CB
McGraw, Tim	Can't Be Really Gone	7-173	MM
McGraw, Tim	Can't Be Really Gone	3-627	SC
McGraw, Tim	City Lights	44-285	KCDC
McGraw, Tim	City Lights	45-285	BKD
McGraw, Tim	Cowboy In Me	16-95	ST
McGraw, Tim	Cowboy In Me the	25-61	MM
McGraw, Tim	Dear Santa	47-238	CB

ARTIST	SONG TITLE	#	TYPE
McGraw, Tim	Do You Want Fries With That	23-277	CB
McGraw, Tim	Don't Take The Girl	1-527	CB
McGraw, Tim	Don't Take The Girl	6-573	MM
McGraw, Tim	Don't Take The Girl	2-218	SC
McGraw, Tim	Down On The Farm	1-528	CB
McGraw, Tim	Down On The Farm	6-613	MM
McGraw, Tim	Down On The Farm	2-480	SC
McGraw, Tim	Drugs Or Jesus	22-19	CB
McGraw, Tim	Everywhere	12-927	CB
McGraw, Tim	Everywhere	7-680	CHM
McGraw, Tim	Everywhere	4-837	SC
McGraw, Tim	Everywhere	22-611	ST
McGraw, Tim	Felt Good On My Lips	37-347	SC
McGraw, Tim	For A Little While	1-540	CB
McGraw, Tim	For A Little While	22-682	ST
McGraw, Tim	Forget About Us	47-240	CB
McGraw, Tim	Grown Men Don't Cry	9-860	ST
McGraw, Tim	Grown Men Don't Cry	16-266	TT
McGraw, Tim	Home	47-244	CB
McGraw, Tim	How Bad Do You Want It	23-40	SC
McGraw, Tim	Humble And Kind	48-678	BKD
McGraw, Tim	I Know How To Love You Well	49-77	ZPA
McGraw, Tim	I Like It I Love It	1-531	CB
McGraw, Tim	I Like It I Love It	6-844	MM
McGraw, Tim	I've Got Friends That Do	29-574	CB
McGraw, Tim	I've Got Friends That Do	49-313	BC
McGraw, Tim	If You're Reading This	30-456	CB
McGraw, Tim	Illegal	47-245	CB
McGraw, Tim	Indian Outlaw	1-526	CB
McGraw, Tim	Indian Outlaw	6-508	MM
McGraw, Tim	Indian Outlaw	2-94	SC
McGraw, Tim	Indian Outlaw	16-269	TT
McGraw, Tim	It's A Business Doing Pleasure With You	47-236	CB
McGraw, Tim	It's Your Love (Solo)	1-535	CB
McGraw, Tim	It's Your Love (Solo)	7-624	CHM
McGraw, Tim	It's Your Love (Solo)	10-101	SC
McGraw, Tim	Just To See You Smile	1-536	CB
McGraw, Tim	Just To See You Smile	22-751	ST
McGraw, Tim	Kill Myself	23-35	SC
McGraw, Tim	Kristofferson	36-410	CB
McGraw, Tim	Last Dollar (Fly Away)	30-306	CB
McGraw, Tim	Let It Go	47-235	CB
McGraw, Tim	Let Me Love You	47-241	CB
McGraw, Tim	Live Like You Were Dying	29-516	CB
McGraw, Tim	Live Like You Were Dying	20-471	ST
McGraw, Tim	Lookin' For That Girl	43-134	PHN
McGraw, Tim	Maybe We Should Just Sleep On It	7-376	MM
McGraw, Tim	Maybe We Should Just Sleep On It	4-458	SC
McGraw, Tim	Meanwhile Back At Mama's	44-197	KCD
McGraw, Tim	My Best Friend	5-808	SC
McGraw, Tim	My Best Friend	22-512	ST
McGraw, Tim	My Little Girl	30-45	CB
McGraw, Tim	My Little Girl	30-99	PHM
McGraw, Tim	My Next Thirty Years	14-708	CB
McGraw, Tim	My Next Thirty Years	19-210	CSZ
McGraw, Tim	My Next Thirty Years	14-28	THM
McGraw, Tim	My Old Friend	23-478	CB
McGraw, Tim	Nashville Without You	44-157	BKD
McGraw, Tim	Not A Moment Too Soon	1-529	CB
McGraw, Tim	Not A Moment Too Soon	17-264	NA
McGraw, Tim	Not A Moment Too Soon	2-545	SC
McGraw, Tim	Nothin' To Die For	36-387	SC
McGraw, Tim	Old Town New	23-386	SC
McGraw, Tim	One Of These Days	8-474	CB
McGraw, Tim	One Of These Days	7-741	CHM
McGraw, Tim	One Of Those Nights	43-257	ASK
McGraw, Tim	One Part Two Part	38-258	PHN
McGraw, Tim	Place In The Sun a	14-150	CB
McGraw, Tim	Please Remember Me	8-955	CB
McGraw, Tim	Please Remember Me	7-860	CHT
McGraw, Tim	Real Good Man	29-513	CB
McGraw, Tim	Real Good Man	25-640	MM
McGraw, Tim	Real Good Man	19-170	ST
McGraw, Tim	Real Good Man	32-299	THM
McGraw, Tim	Red Rag Top	29-515	CB
McGraw, Tim	Red Rag Top	32-1	THM
McGraw, Tim	Red Ragtop	25-347	MM
McGraw, Tim	Red Ragtop	18-326	ST
McGraw, Tim	Refried Dreams	1-530	CB
McGraw, Tim	Refried Dreams	4-71	SC
McGraw, Tim	Refried Dreams	22-870	ST
McGraw, Tim	Right Back Atcha Babe	39-51	ASK
McGraw, Tim	Set This Circus Down	29-520	CB
McGraw, Tim	Seventeen	8-971	CB
McGraw, Tim	She Never Lets It Go To Her Heart	1-534	CB
McGraw, Tim	She's My Kind Of Rain	29-514	CB
McGraw, Tim	She's My Kind Of Rain	25-516	MM
McGraw, Tim	She's My Kind Of Rain	18-783	ST
McGraw, Tim	She's My Kind Of Rain	32-149	THM
McGraw, Tim	Shotgun Rider	47-246	KVD
McGraw, Tim	Sing Me Home	47-243	CB
McGraw, Tim	Sleep Tonight	49-787	TU
McGraw, Tim	Smilin'	29-524	CB
McGraw, Tim	Some Things Never Change	9-411	CB
McGraw, Tim	Some Things Never Change	13-817	CHM
McGraw, Tim	Some Things Never Change	22-541	ST
McGraw, Tim	Somebody Must Be Praying	8-967	CB
McGraw, Tim	Something Like That	19-194	CB
McGraw, Tim	Something Like That	22-486	ST
McGraw, Tim	Southern Girl	45-402	BKD
McGraw, Tim	Southern Voice	47-237	CB
McGraw, Tim	Still	47-239	CB

ARTIST	SONG TITLE	#	TYPE
McGraw, Tim	Suspicions	30-440	CB
McGraw, Tim	Take Me Away From Here	47-242	CB
McGraw, Tim	Telluride	29-521	CB
McGraw, Tim	Telluride	15-195	ST
McGraw, Tim	That's Why God Made Mexico	49-76	ZPA
McGraw, Tim	Things Change	10-269	CB
McGraw, Tim	Things Change	22-465	ST
McGraw, Tim	Tiny Dancer	18-602	ST
McGraw, Tim	Tiny Dancer	32-80	THM
McGraw, Tim	Top Of The World	45-38	BKD
McGraw, Tim	Trouble With Never the	8-960	CB
McGraw, Tim	Truck Yeah	39-26	ASK
McGraw, Tim	Unbroken	29-518	CB
McGraw, Tim	Unbroken	25-288	MM
McGraw, Tim	Unbroken	17-566	ST
McGraw, Tim	Watch The Wind Blow By	22-4	CB
McGraw, Tim	Watch The Wind Blow By	19-687	ST
McGraw, Tim	When The Stars Go Blue	29-365	CB
McGraw, Tim	Where The Green Grass Grows	8-753	CB
McGraw, Tim	Where The Green Grass Grows	22-823	ST
McGraw, Tim	Who Are They	49-78	ZPA
McGraw, Tim	Why We Said Goodbye	29-526	CB
McGraw, Tim	You Get Used To Somebody	29-527	CB
McGraw, Tim	You Had To Be There	44-164	BKD
McGuinn, Mark	More Beautiful Day	18-140	ST
McGuinn, Mark	Mrs. Steven Rudy	14-839	ST
McGuinn, Mark	She Doesn't Dance	25-69	MM
McGuinn, Mark	She Doesn't Dance	16-34	ST
McGuinn, Mark	That's A Plan	15-609	ST
McGuinn, Rudy	Mrs. Steven Rudy	33-148	CB
McGuire Sisters	Little Things Mean A Lot	46-197	KV
McGuire Sisters	Sincerely	46-198	SC
McGuire Sisters	Sugartime	2-247	SC
McGuire, Barry	Eve Of Destruction	21-201	DK
McGuire, Barry	Eve Of Destruction	10-355	KC
McHayes	It Don't Mean I Don't Love You	19-9	ST
McHayes	Tulsa Time	20-455	ST
McKenna, Lori	Unglamorous	36-558	CB
McKennitt, Loreena	Mummer's Dance the	7-715	PHM
McKennitt, Loreena	Mummer's Dance the	5-195	SC
McKenzie, Scott	San Francisco (Be Sure To Wear..)	12-922	P
McKnight & Williams	Duet - Love Is	34-113	CB
McKnight & Williams	Love Is - duet	34-113	CB
McKnight, Brian	6-8-12	19-834	SGB
McKnight, Brian	After The Love	18-484	NU
McKnight, Brian	Back At One	5-786	SC
McKnight, Brian	Crazy Love	14-879	SC
McKnight, Brian	Everytime You Go Away	22-368	CB
McKnight, Brian	Love Of My Life	33-402	CB

ARTIST	SONG TITLE	#	TYPE
McKnight, Brian	Shoulda Woulda Coulda	20-517	CB
McKnight, Brian	Shoulda Woulda Coulda	25-581	MM
McKnight, Brian	Shoulda Woulda Coulda	32-197	THM
McKnight, Brian	Still	25-83	MM
McKnight, Brian	Try Our Love Again	19-672	CB
McKnight, Brian	What's It Gonna Be	18-357	CB
McKnight, Brian	Win	25-29	MM
McLachlan, Sarah	Adia	14-187	CB
McLachlan, Sarah	Adia	10-133	SC
McLachlan, Sarah	Adia	29-239	ZM
McLachlan, Sarah	Angel	14-186	CB
McLachlan, Sarah	Angel	28-188	DK
McLachlan, Sarah	Angel	7-781	PHT
McLachlan, Sarah	Angel	13-702	SGB
McLachlan, Sarah	Angel	29-241	ZM
McLachlan, Sarah	Angel Of Mine	48-186	SC
McLachlan, Sarah	Building A Mystery	14-189	CB
McLachlan, Sarah	Building A Mystery	15-461	SC
McLachlan, Sarah	Dirty Little Secret	29-240	ZM
McLachlan, Sarah	Do What You Have To Do	43-3	SC
McLachlan, Sarah	Fallen	35-274	CB
McLachlan, Sarah	Fallen	32-431	THM
McLachlan, Sarah	Fallen	29-244	ZM
McLachlan, Sarah	Good Enough	14-191	CB
McLachlan, Sarah	Good Enough	16-627	MM
McLachlan, Sarah	Hold On	29-132	ST
McLachlan, Sarah	I Will Remember You	8-182	PHT
McLachlan, Sarah	I Will Remember You	4-662	SC
McLachlan, Sarah	I Will Remember You	13-790	SGB
McLachlan, Sarah	Ice Cream (Live)	10-222	SC
McLachlan, Sarah	Ice Cream (Live)	48-164	SC
McLachlan, Sarah	In Your Shoes	48-163	BKD
McLachlan, Sarah	Ordinary Miracle	43-5	PHM
McLachlan, Sarah	Possession	14-190	CB
McLachlan, Sarah	Push	29-242	ZM
McLachlan, Sarah	River the	43-1	ST
McLachlan, Sarah	Stupid	20-574	CB
McLachlan, Sarah	Sweet Surrender	14-188	CB
McLachlan, Sarah	Train Wreck	29-243	ZM
McLachlan, Sarah	World On Fire	48-187	MM
McLaughlin & Bareilles	Duet - Summer Is Over	48-734	PHM
McLaughlin & Bareilles	Summer Is Over - duet	48-734	PHM
McLean, Don	American Pie	11-716	DK
McLean, Don	And I Love You So	21-507	SC
McLean, Don	Castles In The Air	37-66	SC
McLean, Don	Crying	47-247	CB
McLean, Don	Every Day	47-248	SBI
McLean, Don	On The Amazon	47-250	SFM
McLean, Don	Vincent (Starry Starry Night)	16-152	SC
McLean, Don	Winterwood	47-249	SFM
McNeal, Lutricia	Ain't That Just The Way	7-716	PHM
McPhatter, Clyde	Lover Please	5-520	SC
McPhee, Katharine	Over The Rainbow	30-156	PT

ARTIST	SONG TITLE	#	TYPE
McPhee, Katherine	Over It	30-490	CB
McPhee, Katherine	Over The Rainbow	30-156	PT
McPotts	Put Me Out Of My Misery	4-405	SC
MDO	Groove With Me Tonight	10-224	SC
Meat Loaf	All Revved Up With No Place To Go	37-78	SC
Meat Loaf	Bat Out Of Hell - Halloween	45-141	LE
Meat Loaf	Couldn't Have Said It Better	46-304	SC
Meat Loaf	Couldn't Have Said It Better - duet	45-524	SC
Meat Loaf	Duet - Couldn't Have Said It Better	45-524	SC
Meat Loaf	Duet - Paradise by the Dashboard..	26-328	DK
Meat Loaf	Duet - Paradise by the Dashboard..	20-315	MH
Meat Loaf	Duet - Paradise by the Dashboard...	9-348	AH
Meat Loaf	Duet - Paradise by the Dashboard...	2-31	SC
Meat Loaf	Halloween - Bat Out Of Hell	45-141	LE
Meat Loaf	Heaven Can Wait	6-488	MM
Meat Loaf	Heaven Can Wait	30-765	SF
Meat Loaf	I Would Do Anything For Love	28-428	DK
Meat Loaf	I'd Do Anything For Love	6-407	MM
Meat Loaf	I'd Lie For You	15-507	THM
Meat Loaf	Paradise By The Dashboard Lights	9-348	AH
Meat Loaf	Paradise By The Dashboard Lights	26-328	DK
Meat Loaf	Paradise By The Dashboard Lights	20-315	MH
Meat Loaf	Paradise By The Dashboard Lights	2-31	SC
Meat Loaf	Rock & Roll Dreams Come...	2-107	SC
Meat Loaf	Two Out Of Three Ain't Bad	6-481	MM
Meat Loaf	Two Out Of Three Ain't Bad	22-920	SC
Meat Loaf	You Took The Words Right Out..	6-494	MM
Meat Loaf & Russo	Duet - I'd Lie For You	33-352	CB
Meat Loaf & Russo	I'd Lie For You - duet	33-352	CB
Meat Puppets	Backwater	15-768	NU
Medley & Warnes	Duet - Time Of My Life the	6-333	MM
Medley & Warnes	Time Of My Life the	6-333	MM
Melako	Pure Pleasere Seeker	20-9	SGB
Melancholy Ramblers	Take An Old Cold Tater And Wait	45-682	VH
Melanie	Bitter Bad	45-609	OZP
Melanie	Brand New Key	11-597	DK
Melanie	Brand New Key	4-755	SC

ARTIST	SONG TITLE	#	TYPE
Melanie	Look What They Done To My Song Ma	28-261	DK
Melanie C	I Turn To You	23-262	HS
Mellencamp & ?	Duet - Up Where We Belong	21-437	LE
Mellencamp & ?	Up Where We Belong	21-437	LE
Mellencamp, John	Again Tonight	19-97	PS
Mellencamp, John	Ain't Even Done With The Night	5-307	SC
Mellencamp, John	Americans the	30-451	CB
Mellencamp, John	Americans the	45-426	CB
Mellencamp, John	Americans the - Patriotic	30-451	CB
Mellencamp, John	Authority Song	21-434	LE
Mellencamp, John	Authority Song	21-427	SC
Mellencamp, John	Authority Song	45-413	LE
Mellencamp, John	Check It Out	45-420	CB
Mellencamp, John	Cherry Bomb	19-91	PS
Mellencamp, John	Cherry Bomb	21-415	SC
Mellencamp, John	Crumblin' Down	21-433	LE
Mellencamp, John	Crumblin' Down	19-96	PS
Mellencamp, John	Crumblin' Down	20-78	SC
Mellencamp, John	Dance Naked	19-94	PS
Mellencamp, John	Emotional Love	45-422	SC
Mellencamp, John	Get A Leg Up	5-741	SC
Mellencamp, John	Hard To Hold On To	45-421	OZP
Mellencamp, John	Human Wheels	4-283	SC
Mellencamp, John	Hurts So Good	21-430	LE
Mellencamp, John	Hurts So Good	19-93	PS
Mellencamp, John	Hurts So Good	4-328	SC
Mellencamp, John	Hurts So Good	34-66	CB
Mellencamp, John	I Need A Lover	46-207	SC
Mellencamp, John	I'm Not Running Anymore	21-414	SC
Mellencamp, John	Jack & Diane	21-432	LE
Mellencamp, John	Jack & Diane	6-485	MM
Mellencamp, John	Jack & Diane	19-92	PS
Mellencamp, John	Jack & Diane	21-424	SC
Mellencamp, John	Jackie Brown	45-424	SC
Mellencamp, John	Junior	45-414	SC
Mellencamp, John	Just Another Day	45-415	MM
Mellencamp, John	Just Like You	45-425	TU
Mellencamp, John	Key West Intermezzo	21-421	SC
Mellencamp, John	Lonely Ol' Night	45-419	CB
Mellencamp, John	Our Country	30-205	CB
Mellencamp, John	Our Country	30-205	CB
Mellencamp, John	Our Country	45-418	CB
Mellencamp, John	Paper In Fire	21-422	SC
Mellencamp, John	Patriotic - Americans the	30-451	CB
Mellencamp, John	Peaceful World	16-80	ST
Mellencamp, John	Pink Houses	21-429	LE
Mellencamp, John	Pink Houses	5-471	SC
Mellencamp, John	Pink Houses	35-167	CB
Mellencamp, John	R.O.C.K. In The USA	21-431	LE
Mellencamp, John	R.O.C.K. In The USA	19-88	PS
Mellencamp, John	R.O.C.K. In The USA	21-420	SC
Mellencamp, John	Rain On The Scarecrow	21-428	LE

ARTIST	SONG TITLE	#	TYPE
Mellencamp, John	Rain On The Scarecrow	45-416	SC
Mellencamp, John	ROCK In The USA	33-293	CB
Mellencamp, John	Show - Yours Forever - Perfect Storm	45-417	SC
Mellencamp, John	Show - Yours Forever (Perfect Storm	14-502	SC
Mellencamp, John	Small Town	21-435	LE
Mellencamp, John	Small Town	19-90	PS
Mellencamp, John	Small Town	21-417	SC
Mellencamp, John	Teardrops Will Fall	19-696	ST
Mellencamp, John	Under The Boardwalk	45-423	KV
Mellencamp, John	What If I Came Knocking	24-261	SC
Mellencamp, John	Whatever We Wanted	19-95	PS
Mellencamp, John	Wild Night	19-89	PS
Mellencamp, John	Your Life Is Now	14-285	MM
Mellencamp, John	Yours Forever	45-417	SC
Mellencamp&India.Ar	Duet - Peaceful World	25-24	MM
Mellencamp&India.Ar	Duet - Peaceful World	23-97	SC
Mellencamp&India.Ar	Peaceful World	25-24	MM
Mellencamp&India.Ar	Peaceful World	23-97	SC
Mellencamp&Ndege'o	Wild Night	21-423	SC
Mellencamp&Ndege'oc	Duet - Wild Night	21-423	SC
Mellokings	Tonight Tonight	6-265	MM
Mellons, Ken	Bundle Of Nerves	8-852	CB
Mellons, Ken	I Can Bring Her Back	2-650	SC
Mellons, Ken	Jukebox Junkie	34-313	CB
Mellons, Ken	Jukebox Junkie	6-671	MM
Mellons, Ken	Jukebox Junkie	2-451	SC
Mellons, Ken	Rub A Dubbin'	3-664	SC
Mellons, Ken	Stanger In Your Eyes	7-283	MM
Mellons, Ken	Workin' For The Weekend	2-695	SC
Melvin & Bluenotes	Bad Luck	10-498	DA
Melvin & Bluenotes	Love I Lost the	27-237	DK
Melvin & Bluenotes	Love I Lost the	12-916	P
Men At Work	Be Good Johnny	47-251	KV
Men At Work	Down under	34-76	CB
Men At Work	Down Under	16-739	DK
Men At Work	Down Under	12-763	P
Men At Work	Down Under	5-386	SC
Men At Work	It's A Mistake	9-689	SAV
Men At Work	Overkill	18-499	SAV
Men At Work	Who Can It Be Now	33-310	CB
Men At Work	Who Can It Be Now	16-878	DK
Men At Work	Who Can It Be Now	16-550	P
Men At Work	Who Can It Be Now	4-846	SC
Men In Black	Show - Men In Black	18-181	DK
Mena, Maria	You're The Only One	23-562	MM
Mendel, Idina	Let It Go - Frozen	45-459	ASK
Mendel, Idina	Show - Let It Go - Frozen	45-459	ASK
Mendes & Brazil 66	Look Of Love the	16-733	DK

ARTIST	SONG TITLE	#	TYPE
Mendes, Shawn	Stitches	48-439	KCD
Mendez & Brazil 66	Look Of Love the	13-53	P
Mercedes	It's Your Thing	48-554	DK
Mercer, Johnny	Ac-Cent-Tchu-Ate The Positive	4-188	SC
Merchant, Natalie	Carnival	34-129	CB
Merchant, Natalie	Carnival	10-681	HE
Merchant, Natalie	Carnival	19-578	MH
Merchant, Natalie	Carnival	18-35	PS
Merchant, Natalie	Carnival	3-491	SC
Merchant, Natalie	In The Ghetto	8-400	PHT
Merchant, Natalie	Jealousy	18-39	PS
Merchant, Natalie	Kind And Generous	16-226	PHM
Merchant, Natalie	River	18-37	PS
Merchant, Natalie	Seven Years	18-38	PS
Merchant, Natalie	Wonder	19-572	MH
Merchant, Natalie	Wonder	18-36	PS
Merchant, Natalie	Wonder	4-663	SC
Mercy Me	I Can Only Imagine	35-305	CB
Mercy Me	I Can Only Imagine	32-286	THM
MercyMe	I Can Only Imagine	20-380	HP
Merman, Ethel	Everything's Coming Up Roses	7-191	MM
Merman, Ethel	There's No Business Like Show...	12-571	P
Merman, Ethel	There's No Business Like Show...	2-244	SC
Merritt,Tift	Good Hearted Woman	22-325	CB
Messina, Jo Dee	Because You Love Me	8-858	CB
Messina, Jo Dee	Because You Love Me	22-375	ST
Messina, Jo Dee	Biker Chick	30-530	CB
Messina, Jo Dee	Biker Chick	30-530	CB
Messina, Jo Dee	Bring On The Rain	33-132	CB
Messina, Jo Dee	Bring On The Rain	15-852	ST
Messina, Jo Dee	Burn	14-146	CB
Messina, Jo Dee	Burn	22-456	ST
Messina, Jo Dee	Burn	14-32	THM
Messina, Jo Dee	Bye Bye	8-236	CB
Messina, Jo Dee	Bye Bye	22-759	ST
Messina, Jo Dee	Closer	14-142	CB
Messina, Jo Dee	Dare To Dream	25-232	MM
Messina, Jo Dee	Dare To Dream	16-700	ST
Messina, Jo Dee	Delicious Surprise (I Believe It)	23-285	CB
Messina, Jo Dee	Delicious Surprise (I Believe)	29-603	ST
Messina, Jo Dee	Do You Wanna Make Something Of It	24-646	SC
Messina, Jo Dee	Do You Wanna Make Something...	7-394	MM
Messina, Jo Dee	Downtime	15-94	ST
Messina, Jo Dee	Even God Must Get The Blues	23-362	SC
Messina, Jo Dee	He'd Never Seen Julie Cry	10-87	SC
Messina, Jo Dee	Heads Carolina Tails California	4-135	SC
Messina, Jo Dee	I Wish	25-701	MM

ARTIST	SONG TITLE	#	TYPE
Messina, Jo Dee	I Wish	19-263	ST
Messina, Jo Dee	I Wish	32-380	THM
Messina, Jo Dee	I'm Alright	8-489	CB
Messina, Jo Dee	I'm Done	36-433	CB
Messina, Jo Dee	It's Too Late To Worry	30-17	CB
Messina, Jo Dee	Lesson In Leavin'	8-476	CB
Messina, Jo Dee	Lesson In Leavin'	14-621	SC
Messina, Jo Dee	My Give A Damn's Busted	23-7	CB
Messina, Jo Dee	No Time For Tears	9-401	CB
Messina, Jo Dee	No Time For Tears	13-818	CHM
Messina, Jo Dee	Not Going Down	29-43	CB
Messina, Jo Dee	Shine	37-37	CB
Messina, Jo Dee	Silver Thunderbird	8-977	CB
Messina, Jo Dee	Stand Beside Me	8-214	CB
Messina, Jo Dee	Stand Beside Me	22-688	ST
Messina, Jo Dee	That's The Way	9-420	CB
Messina, Jo Dee	That's The Way	13-849	CHM
Messina, Jo Dee	Walk To The Light	7-247	MM
Messina, Jo Dee	Was That My Life	34-358	CB
Messina, Jo Dee	Was That My Life	25-519	MM
Messina, Jo Dee	Was That My Life	18-780	ST
Messina, Jo Dee	Was That My Life	32-120	THM
Messina, Jo Dee	You're Not In Kansas Anymore	7-332	MM
Messina, Jo Dee	You're Not In Kansas Anymore	4-900	SC
Metallica	Battery	47-257	SBI
Metallica	Day That Never Comes the	47-256	SBI
Metallica	Die Die My Darling	47-258	SC
Metallica	Enter Sandman	13-626	LE
Metallica	Fade To Black	21-764	SC
Metallica	Fuel	47-259	SC
Metallica	Hero Of The Day	47-252	AH
Metallica	I Disappear	14-492	SC
Metallica	Mama Said	47-255	SBI
Metallica	Master Of Puppets	13-624	LE
Metallica	Memory Remains the	47-253	MH
Metallica	Nothing Else Matters	13-622	LE
Metallica	Nothing Else Matters	5-736	SC
Metallica	One	13-625	LE
Metallica	Sad But True	47-260	SC
Metallica	Seek And Destroy	47-284	SC
Metallica	Turn The Page	7-796	PHT
Metallica	Unforgiven the	13-621	LE
Metallica	Unnamed Feeling	47-254	PHR
Metallica	Until It Sleeps	7-569	THM
Metallica	Wherever I May Roam	13-623	LE
Metallica	Whiskey in The Jar	7-812	PHT
Metro Station	Seventeen Forever	36-248	PHM
Metro Station	Shake It	36-30	PT
MGMT	Kids	36-301	PHM
MIA	Paper Planes	36-230	PHM
Miami Sound Mach	1-2-3	11-111	DK
Miami Sound Mach	1-2-3	17-738	PT
Miami Sound Mach	1-2-3	17-178	SC

ARTIST	SONG TITLE	#	TYPE
Miami Sound Mach	Bad Boys	17-171	SC
Michael, G & Queen	Somebody To Love	4-279	SC
Michael, George	An Easier Affair	30-735	CB
Michael, George	An Easier Affair	30-735	SF
Michael, George	Faith	28-311	DK
Michael, George	Faith	12-750	P
Michael, George	Faith	29-288	SC
Michael, George	Fast Love	4-342	SC
Michael, George	Father Figure	11-660	DK
Michael, George	Father Figure	12-751	P
Michael, George	Freedom 90	11-804	DK
Michael, George	I Want Your Sex **	17-94	DK
Michael, George	I Want Your Sex **	21-748	MH
Michael, George	I Want Your Sex **	5-550	SC
Michael, George	Jesus To A Child	11-73	JTG
Michael, George	Jesus To A Child	4-179	SC
Michael, George	Kissing A Fool	11-624	DK
Michael, George	Monkey	11-677	DK
Michael, George	One More Try	33-380	CB
Michael, George	One More Try	11-676	DK
Michael, George	Praying For Time	17-93	DK
Michael, George	Too Funky	12-837	P
Michael, George	Too Funky	5-746	SC
Michaels, Lee	Do You Know What I Mean	29-274	SC
Michaelson, Ingrid	Girls Chase Boys	45-4	KV
Michaelson, Ingrid	Keep Breathing	49-910	SC
Michaelson, Ingrid	Way I Am the	36-519	CB
Michel'le	No More Lies	12-846	P
Mickey & Sylvia	Duet - Love Is Strange	4-243	SC
Mickey & Sylvia	Love Is Strange	4-243	SC
Middle of the Road	Chirpy Chirpy Cheep Cheep	16-373	SF
Middleman, Georgia	Kick Down The Door	14-165	CB
Middleman, Georgia	No Place Like Home	14-89	CB
Middleman, Georgia	No Place Like Home	22-578	ST
Midler & Love	Duet - He's Sure The Boy I Love	45-359	KV
Midler & Love	He's Sure The Boy I Love - duet	45-359	KV
Midler & Ronstadt	Duet - Sisters	45-914	HSW
Midler & Ronstadt	Sisters - duet	45-914	HSW
Midler, Bette	Baby Mine	45-916	KV
Midler, Bette	Boogie Woogie Bugle Boy	45-922	LE
Midler, Bette	Boogie Woogie Bugle Boy	45-912	CB
Midler, Bette	Friends	45-913	CB
Midler, Bette	From A Distance	26-233	DK
Midler, Bette	From A Distance	12-875	P
Midler, Bette	Gift Of Love the	45-941	PC
Midler, Bette	Glory Of Love	16-757	DK
Midler, Bette	I Put A Spell On You	45-920	KV
Midler, Bette	I've Still Got My Health	45-915	KV
Midler, Bette	In The Mood	45-921	KV
Midler, Bette	Lullaby In Blue	13-705	SGB
Midler, Bette	My One True Friend	14-279	MM
Midler, Bette	My One True Friend	45-939	MM

ARTIST	SONG TITLE	#	TYPE
Midler, Bette	One Fine Day	45-918	KV
Midler, Bette	One For My Baby (Live)	45-360	KV
Midler, Bette	Perfect Kiss the	45-942	PS
Midler, Bette	Rose the	11-85	DK
Midler, Bette	Rose the	10-529	SF
Midler, Bette	Rose the (Faster Version)	13-2	P
Midler, Bette	Rose the (Slow Version)	13-1	P
Midler, Bette	Rose the (With Harmonies)	9-636	SAV
Midler, Bette	Show - Every Road Leads Back To U	12-285	DK
Midler, Bette	Stuff Like That There	45-935	KV
Midler, Bette	Tell Him	45-917	KV
Midler, Bette	That's The Way Love Moves	45-940	MM
Midler, Bette	Too Many Fish In The Sea	45-938	KV
Midler, Bette	Waterfalls	45-936	KV
Midler, Bette	White Christmas	45-779	PS
Midler, Bette	Wind Beneath My Wings	26-367	DK
Midler, Bette	Wind Beneath My Wings	6-356	MM
Midler, Bette	Wind Beneath My Wings	2-61	SC
Midler, Bette	Xmas - White Christmas	45-779	PS
Midler, Bette	You Can't Hurry Love	45-937	KV
Midler, Bette	You Don't Own Me	45-919	KV
Midnight Oil	Beds Are Burning	17-74	DK
Midnight Runners	Come On Eileen	29-11	MH
Midnight Star	Duet - Freak-A-Zoid	17-526	SC
Midnight Star	Freak-A-Zoid	17-526	SC
Mighty Bosstones	So Sad To Say	14-489	SC
Miguel, Luis	Latino - La Bikina	17-791	SC
Mika	Relax Take It Easy	37-115	SC
Mikaila	So In Love With Two	34-167	CB
Mikalia	So In Love With Two	15-432	PHM
Mike & Mechanics	All I Need Is A Miracle	24-62	SC
Mike & Mechanics	Living Years the	34-103	CB
Mike & Mechanics	Over My Shoulder	14-883	SC
Miles, Alannah	Still Got This Thing	48-507	KVD
Milian, Christina	Us Against The World	36-285	PHM
Milian, Christina	When You Look At Me	21-735	TT
Miller & Orchestra	Chattanooga Choo Choo	21-3	CB
Miller & Orchestra	Don't Fence Me In	21-18	SC
Miller & Orchestra	Yellow Rose Of Texas the	11-762	DK
Miller & Orchestra	Yellow Rose Of Texas the	3-515	SC
Miller, Dean	Nowhere USA	4-829	SC
Miller, Dean	Wake up And Smell The Whiskey	8-414	CB
Miller, Frankie	Darlin'	44-57	SF
Miller, Glen	Chattanooga Choo Choo	12-530	P
Miller, Glen	I've Got A Gal In Kalamazoo	12-557	P
Miller, Glen	Little Brown Jug	10-706	JVC
Miller, Jodi	Queen Of The House	20-638	SC

ARTIST	SONG TITLE	#	TYPE
Miller, Lance	She Really Loves Me	30-350	CB
Miller, Marie	You're Not Alone	40-21	PHN
Miller, Mitch	Ain't We Got Fun	23-538	CB
Miller, Mitch	By The Light Of The Silvery Moon	23-540	CB
Miller, Mitch	Bye Bye Blackbird	23-541	CB
Miller, Mitch	Clementine	45-923	CB
Miller, Mitch	Don't Fence Me In	43-225	CB
Miller, Mitch	Down By The Old Mill Stream	23-543	CB
Miller, Mitch	Five Foot Two Eyes Of Blue	23-542	CB
Miller, Mitch	I Love My Baby (My Baby Loves Me)	23-548	CB
Miller, Mitch	I'm Looking Over A 4-Leaf Clover	23-544	CB
Miller, Mitch	Moonlight Bay	49-331	CB
Miller, Mitch	Oh Susanna	43-395	CB
Miller, Mitch	She Wore A Yellow Ribbon	43-396	SAV
Miller, Mitch	Shine On Harvest Moon	23-547	CB
Miller, Mitch	Side By Side	23-539	CB
Miller, Mitch	Sweet Adeline	23-550	CB
Miller, Mitch	Sweet Violets	23-551	CB
Miller, Mitch	That Old Gang Of Mine	23-549	CB
Miller, Mitch	Till We Meet Again	23-552	CB
Miller, Mitch	Tip Toe Through The Tulips	34-444	CB
Miller, Mitch	When The Red Red Robin Comes…	23-545	CB
Miller, Mitch	While Strolling Thru The Park 1 Day	23-546	CB
Miller, Mitch	Yellow Rose Of Texas	43-224	CB
Miller, Mitch	You Are My Sunshine	43-223	CB
Miller, Ned	Do What You Do Do Well	49-227	DFK
Miller, Ned	From A Jack To A King	2-129	SC
Miller, Roger	Chug A Lug	22-274	CB
Miller, Roger	Chug A Lug	2-405	SC
Miller, Roger	Dang Me	8-293	CB
Miller, Roger	Dang Me	11-764	DK
Miller, Roger	Dang Me	6-774	MM
Miller, Roger	Dang Me	17-287	NA
Miller, Roger	Dang Me	13-483	P
Miller, Roger	Dang Me	9-521	SAV
Miller, Roger	Do Wacka Do	22-285	CB
Miller, Roger	Engine Engine # 9	8-421	CB
Miller, Roger	Engine Engine # 9	4-305	SC
Miller, Roger	England Swings	22-280	CB
Miller, Roger	England Swings	22-451	SC
Miller, Roger	Husbands & Wives	6-11	SC
Miller, Roger	Husbands & Wives	22-281	CB
Miller, Roger	I'm A Nut	15-350	MM
Miller, Roger	Kansas City Star	22-279	CB
Miller, Roger	Kansas City Star	3-195	SC
Miller, Roger	King Of The Road	3-896	CB
Miller, Roger	King Of The Road	17-33	DK
Miller, Roger	King Of The Road	6-769	MM

ARTIST	SONG TITLE	#	TYPE
Miller, Roger	King Of The Road	17-286	NA
Miller, Roger	King Of The Road	12-789	P
Miller, Roger	King Of The Road	14-552	SC
Miller, Roger	Little Green Apples	22-283	CB
Miller, Roger	Little Green Apples	5-39	SC
Miller, Roger	Lock Stock And Teardrops	45-342	BSP
Miller, Roger	Lovin' Her Was Easier (Than...)	22-286	CB
Miller, Roger	Me And Bobby McGee	45-930	VH
Miller, Roger	My Uncle Used to Love....She Died	22-287	CB
Miller, Roger	Old Toy Trains	45-365	OZP
Miller, Roger	One Dyin' And A Buryin'	22-278	CB
Miller, Roger	Walkin' In The Sunshine	22-282	CB
Miller, Roger	Walking In The Sunshine	16-646	JVC
Miller, Roger	When Two Worlds Collide	22-284	CB
Miller, Roger	You Can't Rollerskate In A Buffalo	8-811	CB
Miller, Steve	Abracadabra	23-631	BS
Miller, Steve	Dance Dance Dance	23-629	BS
Miller, Steve	Fly Like An Eagle	23-627	BS
Miller, Steve	Jet Airliner	23-628	BS
Miller, Steve	Joker the	23-626	BS
Miller, Steve	Jungle Love	23-620	BS
Miller, Steve	Rockin' Me	23-622	BS
Miller, Steve	Serenade	23-623	BS
Miller, Steve	Stake the	23-625	BS
Miller, Steve	Swingtown	23-619	BS
Miller, Steve	Take The Money And Run	23-621	BS
Miller, Steve	True Fine Love	23-624	BS
Miller, Steve	Wild Mountain Honey	23-632	BS
Miller, Steve	Winter Time	23-630	BS
Milli Vanilli	Girl I'm Gonna Miss You	33-329	CB
Milli Vanilli	Girl I'm Gonna Miss You	11-495	DK
Milli Vanilli	Girl You Know It's True	11-587	DK
Mills & Friend	Lovesick Blues	10-559	SF
Mills Brothers	Cab Driver	47-261	AH
Mills Brothers	In The Shade Of The Old Apple Tree	43-219	CB
Mills Brothers	Let Me Call You Sweetheart	47-263	P
Mills Brothers	Me And My Shadow	43-220	CB
Mills Brothers	Old Folks At Home	43-221	CB
Mills Brothers	Rockin' Chair	47-264	LRT
Mills Brothers	Til Then	47-262	AH
Mills, Frank	Hair - show	49-264	SC
Mills, Frank	Love Me Love Me Love	49-251	DFK
Mills, Frank	Show - Hair	49-264	SC
Mills, Stephanie	Never Knew Love Like This Before	9-42	MM
Milsap, Ronnie	All Is Fair In Love And War	24-8	SC
Milsap, Ronnie	Almost Like A Song	17-295	NA
Milsap, Ronnie	Am I Losing You	47-271	CB

ARTIST	SONG TITLE	#	TYPE
Milsap, Ronnie	Any Day Now	11-743	DK
Milsap, Ronnie	Any Day Now	13-425	P
Milsap, Ronnie	Are You Lovin' Me Like I'm...	38-124	CB
Milsap, Ronnie	Back On My Mind Again	8-209	CB
Milsap, Ronnie	Back On My Mind Again	5-400	SC
Milsap, Ronnie	Cowboys And Clowns	47-270	CB
Milsap, Ronnie	Daydreams About Night Things	15-63	CB
Milsap, Ronnie	Daydreams About Night Things	8-683	SAV
Milsap, Ronnie	Don't You Ever Get Tired Of...	1-447	CB
Milsap, Ronnie	Happy Happy Birthday Darling	47-272	CB
Milsap, Ronnie	He Got You	47-273	CB
Milsap, Ronnie	Houston Solution	1-448	CB
Milsap, Ronnie	How Do I Turn You On	5-563	SC
Milsap, Ronnie	I Wouldn't Have Missed It For The..	17-411	DK
Milsap, Ronnie	I Wouldn't Have Missed It For The..	12-446	P
Milsap, Ronnie	I'd Be A Legend In My Time	1-437	CB
Milsap, Ronnie	I'd Be A Legend In My Time	4-269	SC
Milsap, Ronnie	I'm A Stand By My Woman Man	1-439	CB
Milsap, Ronnie	I'm Playing For You	24-78	SC
Milsap, Ronnie	In Love	47-265	CB
Milsap, Ronnie	In No Time At All	47-277	CB
Milsap, Ronnie	Inside	5-536	SC
Milsap, Ronnie	It Was Almost Like A Song	1-440	CB
Milsap, Ronnie	It Was Almost Like A Song	11-620	DK
Milsap, Ronnie	It's Christmas	45-756	CB
Milsap, Ronnie	Just In Case	47-276	CB
Milsap, Ronnie	Let Me Be Your Love Pillow	47-268	CB
Milsap, Ronnie	Let's Take The Long Way Around the World	35-383	CB
Milsap, Ronnie	Livin' On Love	47-266	CB
Milsap, Ronnie	Local Girls	29-368	CB
Milsap, Ronnie	Lost In The Fifties Tonight	1-445	CB
Milsap, Ronnie	Lost In The Fifties Tonight	9-482	SAV
Milsap, Ronnie	Lost In The Fifties Tonight	2-10	SC
Milsap, Ronnie	My Heart	11-621	DK
Milsap, Ronnie	No Getting' Over You	9-569	SAV
Milsap, Ronnie	Nobody Likes Sad Songs	29-775	CB
Milsap, Ronnie	Only One Love In My Life	19-438	SC
Milsap, Ronnie	Play Born To Lose Again	47-280	VH
Milsap, Ronnie	Please Don't Tell Me How The Story.	4-638	SC

ARTIST	SONG TITLE	#	TYPE
Milsap, Ronnie	Pure Love	1-436	CB
Milsap, Ronnie	Pure Love	5-251	SC
Milsap, Ronnie	She Keeps The Home Fires Burnin'	4-482	SC
Milsap, Ronnie	She Keeps the Home Fires Burning	34-264	CB
Milsap, Ronnie	Since I Don't Have You	1-449	CB
Milsap, Ronnie	Smoky Mountain Rain	1-443	CB
Milsap, Ronnie	Snap Your Fingers	1-446	CB
Milsap, Ronnie	Stand By My Woman Man	4-572	SC
Milsap, Ronnie	Stranger In My House	8-684	SAV
Milsap, Ronnie	Stranger In My House	14-425	SC
Milsap, Ronnie	Stranger Things Have Happened	2-521	SC
Milsap, Ronnie	There's No Getting Over Me	1-444	CB
Milsap, Ronnie	There's No Getting Over Me	11-619	DK
Milsap, Ronnie	There's No Getting' Over Me	13-423	P
Milsap, Ronnie	Time Love And Money	14-72	CB
Milsap, Ronnie	Too Late To Worry Too Blue To Cry	47-275	CB
Milsap, Ronnie	True Believer	47-278	SC
Milsap, Ronnie	Turn That Radio On	16-363	CB
Milsap, Ronnie	What A Difference You've Made..	11-710	DK
Milsap, Ronnie	What A Difference You've Made...	1-441	CB
Milsap, Ronnie	What A Difference You've Made…	13-475	P
Milsap, Ronnie	When The Sun Goes Down	47-267	CB
Milsap, Ronnie	Why Don't You Spend The Night	47-269	CB
Milsap, Ronnie	Woman In Love a	47-279	SC
Milsap, Ronnie	Xmas - It's Christmas	45-756	CB
Mimms & Enchanters	Cry Baby	5-515	SC
Mims	This Is Why I'm Hot **	48-604	DK
Mindbenders	Groovy Kind Of Love a	10-610	SF
Minelli, Liza	Blue Skies	49-221	ASK
Minelli, Liza	Cabaret	49-224	MM
Minelli, Liza	City Lights	49-218	LG
Minelli, Liza	Duet - Money Makes the World Go Round	49-223	LG
Minelli, Liza	Get Happy	49-220	MFK
Minelli, Liza	I Dreamed A Dream	49-216	KH
Minelli, Liza	It Was A Good Time	49-222	ASK
Minelli, Liza	Lost In You	8-504	PHT
Minelli, Liza	Maybe This Time	49-447	MM
Minelli, Liza	Maybe This Time	49-214	MM
Minelli, Liza	Money Makes The World Go Round - duet	49-223	LG
Minelli, Liza	New York New York	49-217	LG
Minelli, Liza	Ring Them Bells	49-219	LG
Minelli, Liza	Show - Cabaret	18-233	DK
Minogue, Kylie	Can't Get You Out Of My	33-430	CB

ARTIST	SONG TITLE	#	TYPE
	Head		
Minogue, Kylie	Can't Get You Out Of My Head	25-142	MM
Minogue, Kylie	Can't Get You Out Of My Head	21-721	TT
Minogue, Kylie	Come Into My World	25-402	MM
Minogue, Kylie	Come Into My World	32-95	THM
Minogue, Kylie	In Your Eyes	21-725	TT
Minogue, Kylie	Love At First Sight	18-226	CB
Minogue, Kylie	Love At First Sight	25-311	MM
Minogue, Kylie	Love At First Sight	21-729	TT
Minogue, Kylie	Slow	20-571	CB
Minor, Shane	I Think You're Beautiful	23-367	SC
Minor, Shane	I Think You're Beautiful	22-476	ST
Minor, Shane	Ordinary Love	10-210	SC
Minor, Shane	Ordinary Love	22-491	ST
Minor, Shane	Slave To The Heart	8-944	CB
Mint Condition	What Kind Of Man Would I Be	24-293	SC
Miracles	Love Machine Part 1	17-153	DK
Miracles	Mickey's Monkey	17-360	DK
Miracles	Shop Around	11-141	DK
Miracles	Shop Around	3-292	MM
Miracles	You've Really Got A Hold On Me	49-478	MM
Miss Saigon	Show - Last Night Of The World	10-378	KC
Miss Saigon	Show - Last Night of the World	17-650	PR
Miss Saigon	Show - Why God Why	18-191	PS
Missing Persons	Waking In L.A.	24-433	SC
Missing Persons	Words	24-559	SC
Mitchell, Guy	Singing The Blues	33-231	CB
Mitchell, Guy	Singing The Blues	45-68	CB
Mitchell, Joni	Big Yellow Taxi	12-101	DK
Mitchell, Joni	Big Yellow Taxi	29-273	SC
Mitchell, Joni	Free Man In Paris	16-63	SC
Mitchell, Joni	Help Me	9-330	AG
Mitchell, Joni	Help Me	2-787	SC
Mitchell, Ross	See The Day	21-618	SF
Mizzy, Vic	Addams Family TV Theme	16-280	TT
Moby	Natural Blue (Grammy Version)	16-258	TT
Moby	Porcelain	15-649	THM
Moby	South Side	16-259	TT
Moby	We Are All Made Of Stars	35-277	CB
Moby	We Are All Made Of Stars	25-205	MM
Moby	Why Does My Heart Feel So Bad	16-262	TT
Modern English	I Melt With You	9-345	AH
Modest Mouse	Float On	23-564	MM
Moffats	Xmas - When God Made You	18-727	CB
Mojo	Lady	34-166	CB
Mojo Nixon	Don Henley Must Die	15-142	SC
Moke	Down	32-109	THM

ARTIST	SONG TITLE	#	TYPE
Moman, Chips	This Time	16-649	JTG
Moments	Love On A Two Way Street	27-325	DK
Moments	Love On a Two Way Street	25-279	MM
Mona Lisa	You Said	24-50	SC
Monahan, Pat	Her Eyes	49-891	SC
Monet, J	Work It Out	32-199	THM
Money, Eddie	Baby Hold On	15-180	MH
Money, Eddie	Fall In Love Again	47-285	SC
Money, Eddie	I Wanna Go Back	47-286	SC
Money, Eddie	I'll Get By	4-274	SC
Money, Eddie	I've Been In Love Before	47-283	LC
Money, Eddie	Shakin'	14-644	SC
Money, Eddie	Shakin'	13-662	SGB
Money, Eddie	Think I'm In Love	47-282	LC
Money, Eddie	Two Tickets To Paradise	4-382	SC
Money, Eddie	Walk On Water	47-281	KV
Monheit, Jane	I'm Through With Love	25-678	MM
Monheit, Jane	If	25-674	MM
Monheit, Jane	My Foolish Heart	25-671	MM
Monica	All Eyez On Me	18-430	CB
Monica	Angel Of Mine	16-212	MM
Monica	Angel Of Mine	7-795	PHT
Monica	Angel Of Mine	16-396	PR
Monica	First Night	33-372	CB
Monica	Jupiter	8-334	PHT
Monica	Knock Knock	19-671	CB
Monica	Knock Knock	32-424	THM
Monica	So Gone	34-174	CB
Monica	So Gone	32-273	THM
Monica	So Gone (Radio Version)	21-788	SC
Monica	Street Symphony	8-356	PHT
Monica	U Should've Known Better	20-541	CB
Monica	Why I Love You So Much	7-572	THM
Monica & Brandy	Boy Is Mine the	13-685	SGB
Monifah	Touch It	7-799	PHT
Monkees	Daydream Believer	16-748	DK
Monkees	Daydream Believer	9-648	SAV
Monkees	Daydream Believer	14-556	SC
Monkees	Gonna Buy Me A Dog	47-779	SRK
Monkees	Hey Hey We're The Monkees	35-59	CB
Monkees	Hey Hey We're The Monkees	27-403	DK
Monkees	Hey Hey We're The Monkees	15-491	MM
Monkees	I Wanna Be Free	47-293	ABS
Monkees	I'm A Believer	9-646	SAV
Monkees	I'm Not Your Stepping Stone	11-693	DK
Monkees	I'm Not Your Stepping Stone	9-712	SAV
Monkees	Last Train To Clarksville	16-768	DK
Monkees	Last Train To Clarksville	12-863	P

ARTIST	SONG TITLE	#	TYPE
Monkees	Last Train To Clarksville	9-647	SAV
Monkees	Last Train To Clarksville	3-471	SC
Monkees	Little Bit Me Little Bit You a	20-27	SC
Monkees	Mary Mary	47-292	SC
Monkees	Pleasant Valley Sunday	9-711	SAV
Monkees	Randy Scouse Git	47-287	EZ
Monkees	She	47-291	SC
Monkees	Take A Giant Step	47-289	EZ
Monkees	Theme From The Monkees	6-858	MM
Monkees	Valleri	11-231	DK
Monkees	What Am I Doing Hangin' Around	47-290	EZ
Monkees	Words	47-288	EZ
Monotones	Book Of Love	35-6	CB
Monotones	Book Of Love	3-467	SC
Monro, Matt	Always On My Mind	11-57	PT
Monro, Matt	And I Love You So	11-63	PT
Monro, Matt	Around The World	18-100	PS
Monro, Matt	Around The World	9-215	SO
Monro, Matt	Born Again	11-55	PT
Monro, Matt	Come Back To Me	18-107	PS
Monro, Matt	Come In From The Rain	11-59	PT
Monro, Matt	From Russia With Love	9-63	SC
Monro, Matt	I'll Take Romance	20-765	KB
Monro, Matt	I'll Take Romance	18-104	PS
Monro, Matt	I've Never Been To Me	11-56	PT
Monro, Matt	If	11-61	PT
Monro, Matt	If She Walked Into My Life	18-103	PS
Monro, Matt	MacArthur Park	11-60	PT
Monro, Matt	My Kind Of Girl	9-181	PS
Monro, Matt	On A Clear Day	9-231	PS
Monro, Matt	Portrait Of My Love	9-247	PS
Monro, Matt	Real Live Girl	18-105	PS
Monro, Matt	Softly As I Leave You	18-99	PS
Monro, Matt	Softly As I Leave You	11-54	PT
Monro, Matt	Wednesday's Child	18-108	PS
Monro, Matt	Yesterday/Something	11-58	PT
Monro, Matt	You Needed Me	11-62	PT
Monro, Matt	You've Got Possibilities	18-106	PS
Monroe, Ashley	Can't Let Go	48-737	VH
Monroe, Ashley	I Don't Want To	30-109	CB
Monroe, Ashley	Satisfied	29-210	CB
Monroe, Bill	Blue Moon Of Kentucky	8-249	CB
Monroe, Bill	Dark Hollow	8-251	CB
Monroe, Bill	Drifting Too Far From The Shore	47-296	CB
Monroe, Bill	In The Pines	8-250	CB
Monroe, Bill	Kentucky Waltz	47-295	CB
Monroe, Bill	KentuckyWaltz	49-325	CB
Monroe, Bill	Little Georgia Rose	8-262	CB
Monroe, Bill	New Mule Skinner Blues	47-294	CB
Monroe, Bill	Nine Pound Hammer	47-297	SC
Monroe, Bill	Walking In Jerusalem Just Like John	47-298	CB
Monroe, Marilyn	Diamonds Are A Girl's	2-251	SC

ARTIST	SONG TITLE	#	TYPE
	Best Friend		
Monroe, Marilyn	Diamonds Are A Girl's Best Friend	19-776	SGB
Monroe, Marilyn	My Heart Belongs To Daddy	49-330	CB
Monroe, Rick	Just The Same	41-65	PHN
Monroe, Vaughn	Ghost Riders In The Sky (Fast)	48-542	DK
Monroe, Vaughn	There I've Said It Again	4-195	SC
Montana, Billy	Didn't Have You	2-736	SC
Montana, Billy	No Yesterday	4-26	SC
Montana, Billy	Rain Through The Roof	7-29	MM
Montana, Hannah	Best Of Both Worlds the	36-66	WD
Montana, Hannah	I Got Nerve	36-65	WD
Montana, Hannah	If We Were A Movie	36-67	WD
Montana, Hannah	Just Like You	36-70	WD
Montana, Hannah	Other Side of Me the	36-68	WD
Montana, Hannah	Pumpin' Up The Party	36-63	WD
Montana, Hannah	This Is The Life	36-69	WD
Montana, Hannah	Who Said	36-64	WD
Montana, Joey	Picky	49-924	KVD
Montana, Randy	Ain't Much Left Of Loving You	49-30	KVD
Montaner, Ricardo	Latino - Resumiendo	23-244	AI
Monte, Lou	Darktown Strutters Ball	9-744	SAV
Monte, Lou	Lazy Mazy	7-289	MM
Montero, Pablo	Latino - Vuelve Junto A Mi	23-246	AI
Montez, Chris	Let's Dance	13-262	P
Montez, Chris	Let's Dance	5-171	SC
Montez, Chris	More I See You the	10-667	SF
Montgomery Gentry	All Night Long	14-138	CB
Montgomery Gentry	All Night Long	14-15	CHM
Montgomery Gentry	All Night Long	10-263	SC
Montgomery Gentry	All Night Long	22-573	ST
Montgomery Gentry	All Night Long	14-36	THM
Montgomery Gentry	Back When I Knew It All	36-412	CB
Montgomery Gentry	Cold One Comin' On	25-4	MM
Montgomery Gentry	Cold One Comin' On	15-670	ST
Montgomery Gentry	Daddy Won't Sell The Farm	8-911	CB
Montgomery Gentry	Daddy Won't Sell The Farm	22-516	ST
Montgomery Gentry	Didn't I	16-684	ST
Montgomery Gentry	Fine Line a	17-475	TT
Montgomery Gentry	Folks Like Us	48-702	BKD
Montgomery Gentry	Gone	22-95	CB
Montgomery Gentry	Gone	23-34	SC
Montgomery Gentry	Hell Yeah	34-415	CB
Montgomery Gentry	Hell Yeah	25-696	MM
Montgomery Gentry	Hell Yeah	19-265	ST
Montgomery Gentry	Hell Yeah	32-375	THM
Montgomery Gentry	Hillbilly Shoes	8-938	CB
Montgomery Gentry	I Got Drunk	46-201	SC
Montgomery Gentry	If You Ever Stop Loving Me	20-170	ST
Montgomery Gentry	Lonely And Gone	19-205	CB
Montgomery Gentry	Lonely And Gone	22-433	ST

ARTIST	SONG TITLE	#	TYPE
Montgomery Gentry	Long Line Of Losers	37-63	CB
Montgomery Gentry	Lucky Man	30-337	CB
Montgomery Gentry	Merry Christmas From The Family	45-750	CB
Montgomery Gentry	My Town	33-177	CN
Montgomery Gentry	My Town	25-293	MM
Montgomery Gentry	My Town	17-584	ST
Montgomery Gentry	Self Made Man	9-414	CB
Montgomery Gentry	Self Made Man	13-853	CHM
Montgomery Gentry	Self Made Man	22-548	ST
Montgomery Gentry	She Couldn't Change Me	30-30	CB
Montgomery Gentry	She Couldn't Change Me	14-792	ST
Montgomery Gentry	She Don't Tell Me To	29-17	CB
Montgomery Gentry	She Don't Tell Me To	29-507	SC
Montgomery Gentry	She Don't Tell Me To	23-451	ST
Montgomery Gentry	Something To Be Proud Of	23-130	CB
Montgomery Gentry	Speed	34-380	CB
Montgomery Gentry	Speed	25-453	MM
Montgomery Gentry	Speed	18-591	ST
Montgomery Gentry	Speed	32-117	THM
Montgomery Gentry	Till Nothing Comes Between Us	25-447	MM
Montgomery Gentry	What Do Ya Think About That	30-532	CB
Montgomery Gentry	Xmas - Merry Christmas From The Family	45-750	CB
Montgomery Gentry	You Do Your Thing	30-802	PHM
Montgomery Gentry	You Do Your Thing	20-488	ST
Montgomery, J M	Ain't Got Nothin' On Us	24-280	SC
Montgomery, J M	Ain't Got Nothing On Us	14-218	CB
Montgomery, J M	Angel In My Eyes	14-215	CB
Montgomery, J M	Angel In My Eyes	22-655	ST
Montgomery, J M	Be My Baby Tonight	14-207	CB
Montgomery, J M	Be My Baby Tonight	12-483	P
Montgomery, J M	Be My Baby Tonight	2-219	SC
Montgomery, J M	Beer & Bones	2-412	SC
Montgomery, J M	Beer & Bones	6-526	MM
Montgomery, J M	Country Thang	18-787	ST
Montgomery, J M	Country Thang	32-152	THM
Montgomery, J M	Cover You In Kisses	14-217	CB
Montgomery, J M	Cover You In Kisses	5-300	SC
Montgomery, J M	Cowboy Love	7-174	MM
Montgomery, J M	Cowboy Love	3-661	SC
Montgomery, J M	Dream On Texas Ladies	4-142	SC
Montgomery, J M	Even Then	15-336	CB
Montgomery, J M	Four Wheel Drive	19-181	ST
Montgomery, J M	Friends	14-212	CB
Montgomery, J M	Friends	7-381	MM
Montgomery, J M	Friends	4-590	SC
Montgomery, J M	Goes Good With Beer	23-391	CB
Montgomery, J M	Goes Good With Beer	20-495	ST
Montgomery, J M	Goes Good With Beer	30-798	PHM
Montgomery, J M	Heaven Sent Me You	4-415	SC
Montgomery, J M	Hello L-O-V-E	7-863	CHT
Montgomery, J M	Hello L-O-V-E	22-740	ST
Montgomery, J M	Hold On To Me	8-212	CB

ARTIST	SONG TITLE	#	TYPE
Montgomery, J M	Hold On To Me	22-670	ST
Montgomery, J M	Home To You	22-430	ST
Montgomery, J M	How Was I To Know	14-214	CB
Montgomery, J M	How Was I To Know	7-658	CHM
Montgomery, J M	I Can Love You Like That	2-688	SC
Montgomery, J M	I Can Love You Like That	14-208	CB
Montgomery, J M	I Love The Way You Love Me	14-205	CB
Montgomery, J M	I Love The Way You Love Me	6-385	MM
Montgomery, J M	I Love The Way You Love Me	12-414	P
Montgomery, J M	I Love The Way You Love Me	2-2	SC
Montgomery, J M	I Miss You A Little	14-213	CB
Montgomery, J M	I Miss You A Little	22-404	CHM
Montgomery, J M	I Swear	14-206	CB
Montgomery, J M	I Swear	6-451	MM
Montgomery, J M	If You Ever Went Away	36-282	PHM
Montgomery, J M	If You've Got Love	14-210	CB
Montgomery, J M	If You've Got Love	17-250	NA
Montgomery, J M	If You've Got Love	2-459	SC
Montgomery, J M	It's What I Am	7-252	MM
Montgomery, J M	Kick It Up	17-237	NA
Montgomery, J M	Letters From Home	20-168	ST
Montgomery, J M	Life's A Dance	14-204	CB
Montgomery, J M	Little Girl the	14-119	CB
Montgomery, J M	Little Girl the	13-859	CHM
Montgomery, J M	Little Girl the	19-242	CSZ
Montgomery, J M	Long As I Live	14-211	CB
Montgomery, J M	Long As I Live	4-229	SC
Montgomery, J M	Love Working On You	14-216	CB
Montgomery, J M	Love Working On You	22-781	ST
Montgomery, J M	My Christmas Wish	45-753	CB
Montgomery, J M	Nickels & Dimes & Love	49-422	SC
Montgomery, J M	No Man's Land	7-138	MM
Montgomery, J M	Nothing Catches Jesus by Surprise	23-368	SC
Montgomery, J M	Nothing Catches Jesus By Surprise	22-474	ST
Montgomery, J M	Pictures	34-371	CB
Montgomery, J M	Rope The Moon	2-210	SC
Montgomery, J M	Sold	6-796	MM
Montgomery, J M	Sold	2-739	SC
Montgomery, J M	Sold	14-209	CB
Montgomery, J M	That's What I Like About You	14-783	ST
Montgomery, J M	Till Nothing Comes Between Us	18-138	ST
Montgomery, J M	Till Nothing Comes Between Us	19-350	THM
Montgomery, J M	Till Nothing Comes Between Us	33-188	CB
Montgomery, J M	Xmas - My Christmas Wish	45-753	CB
Monty Python	Always Look On The Bright Side	15-141	SC
Monty Python	Galaxy Song	15-144	SC
Moody Blues	Black & White	17-519	SC
Moody Blues	Breaking Point	45-586	OZP
Moody Blues	Deep the	45-587	OZP
Moody Blues	Go Now	20-97	SC
Moody Blues	Go Now	10-573	SF
Moody Blues	I Know You're Out There	20-87	SC
Moody Blues	I'm Just A Singer In A Rock & Roll	17-507	SC
Moody Blues	Legend Of A Mind	28-139	DK
Moody Blues	Lovely To See You	28-140	DK
Moody Blues	Never Comes The Day	28-141	DK
Moody Blues	Nights In White Satin	33-284	CB
Moody Blues	Nights in White Satin	12-331	DK
Moody Blues	Nights In White Satin	13-176	P
Moody Blues	Tuesday Afternoon	28-138	DK
Moody Blues	Tuesday Afternoon	10-358	KC
Moonglows	Sincerely	7-311	MM
Moore & Lambert	Duet - Old Habits	44-283	KCDC
Moore & Lambert	Old Habits - Duet	44-283	KCDC
Moore, Chanti	Love's Taken Over	9-851	SAV
Moore, Dorothy	Misty Blue	24-335	SC
Moore, Gary	King Of The Blues	36-134	SGB
Moore, Gary	Sky Is Crying the	19-792	SGB
Moore, Gary	Still Got The Blues	14-594	SC
Moore, Jeff	Wrangler Butts	49-205	CB
Moore, Justin	Back That Thing Up	38-120	CB
Moore, Justin	Backwoods	43-310	CB
Moore, Justin	Bait A Hook	38-115	CB
Moore, Justin	Home Sweet Home	49-304	KRG
Moore, Justin	How I Got To Be This Way	38-112	CB
Moore, Justin	I Could Kick Your Ass	44-383	BKD
Moore, Justin	I'd Want It To Be Yours	45-646	BKD
Moore, Justin	If Heaven Wasn't So Far Away	37-236	CB
Moore, Justin	Lettin' The Night Roll	43-141	KCDC
Moore, Justin	Old Habits	43-178	ASK
Moore, Justin	Point At You	43-308	ASK
Moore, Justin	Small Town USA	43-309	CB
Moore, Justin	This Kind Of Town	45-645	BKD
Moore, Justin	Til My Last Day	43-307	ASK
Moore, Justin	You Look Like I Need A Drink	45-619	DCK
Moore, Kip	Beer Money	45-633	SBI
Moore, Kip	Crazy One More Time	45-634	PHN
Moore, Kip	Everything But You	45-635	PHN
Moore, Kip	Hey Pretty Girl	44-330	SSC
Moore, Kip	I'm To Blame	46-6	DCK
Moore, Kip	Somethin' 'Bout A Truck	45-352	KST
Moore, Kip	Young Love	49-204	BKD
Moore, Kip	Young Love	49-37	SBI
Moore, Lathan	Burn These Memories Down	41-87	PHN
Moore, Lathan	Forever Man	39-94	PHN

ARTIST	SONG TITLE	#	TYPE
Moore, Mandy	Crush	15-809	CB
Moore, Mandy	Crush	23-590	PHM
Moore, Mandy	Cry	25-88	MM
Moore, Mandy	Have A Little Faith In Me	32-434	THM
Moore, Mandy	I Wanna Be With You	35-222	CB
Moore, Mandy	I Wanna Be With You	30-636	THM
Moore, Mandy	I Wanna Be With You	18-521	TT
Moore, Mandy	In My Pocket	21-644	TT
Moore, Mandy	Nothing That You Are	37-25	PS
Moore, Mandy	Slummin' In Paradise	37-24	PS
Moore, Seamus	Viagra Song	49-203	KWD
Moorer, Allison	Alabama Song	8-244	CB
Moorer, Allison	Dancing Barefoot	49-206	CB
Moorer, Allison	Pardon Me	8-919	CB
Moorer, Allison	Send Down An Angel	14-83	CB
Moorer, Allison	Set You Free	8-188	CB
Moorer, Allison	Soft Place To Fall a	8-735	CB
Moorer, Allison	Think It Over	49-346	SC
Moorer, Allison	Think It Over	49-226	SC
Moorer, Allison	Up This High	49-207	CB
Morgan & Randall	By My Side	8-123	CB
Morgan & Randall	By My Side	7-251	MM
Morgan & Randall	Duet - By My Side	8-123	CB
Morgan & Randall	Duet - By My Side	7-251	MM
Morgan, Craig	Almost Home	34-362	CB
Morgan, Craig	Almost Home	18-474	ST
Morgan, Craig	Almost Home	32-224	THM
Morgan, Craig	Bein' Alive And Livin'	48-282	PHN
Morgan, Craig	Bonfire	37-53	CB
Morgan, Craig	Corn Star	30-28	ASK
Morgan, Craig	Every Friday Afternoon	25-705	MM
Morgan, Craig	Every Friday Afternoon	19-268	ST
Morgan, Craig	Every Friday Afternoon	32-411	THM
Morgan, Craig	God Family And Country	17-474	THM
Morgan, Craig	God Must Really Love Me	48-279	CB
Morgan, Craig	I Got You	29-38	CB
Morgan, Craig	I Want Us Back	30-33	CB
Morgan, Craig	International Harvester	30-574	CB
Morgan, Craig	Little Bit Of Life	30-51	CB
Morgan, Craig	Look At Us	19-771	ST
Morgan, Craig	Love Loves A Long Night	48-281	PHN
Morgan, Craig	Love Remembers	36-594	CB
Morgan, Craig	More Trucks Than Cars	48-283	SBI
Morgan, Craig	Paradise	14-81	CB
Morgan, Craig	Redneck Yacht Club	23-136	CB
Morgan, Craig	Something To Write Home About	6-75	SC
Morgan, Craig	Something To Write Home About	22-553	ST
Morgan, Craig	Still A Lot Of Chicken Left On That Bone	48-280	CB
Morgan, Craig	That's What I Love About Sunday	22-101	CB
Morgan, Craig	This Ain't Nothin'	37-227	CB
Morgan, Craig	This Ole Boy	48-284	CB

ARTIST	SONG TITLE	#	TYPE
Morgan, Craig	Tough	30-309	CB
Morgan, Craig	Wake Up Lovin' You	44-155	BKD
Morgan, Debelah	Dance With Me	14-505	SC
Morgan, Debelah	Dance With Me	18-512	TT
Morgan, George	Alright I'll Sign The Papers	46-20	SSK
Morgan, George	Candy Kisses	19-842	CB
Morgan, George	Candy Kisses	8-664	SAV
Morgan, George	Red Rose From the Blue Side/Town	29-630	CB
Morgan, George	Room Full Of Roses	5-577	SC
Morgan, Lorrie	Ain't Got Time To Rock No Baby	47-781	SRK
Morgan, Lorrie	Back In Your Arms Again	1-342	CB
Morgan, Lorrie	Back In Your Arms Again	7-90	MM
Morgan, Lorrie	Behind His Last Goodbye	49-119	SC
Morgan, Lorrie	By My Side	22-888	ST
Morgan, Lorrie	Color Of Roses the	49-120	SC
Morgan, Lorrie	Cryin' Time	3-47	SC
Morgan, Lorrie	Dear Me	1-331	CB
Morgan, Lorrie	Dear Me	2-623	SC
Morgan, Lorrie	Do You Still Want To Buy Me That…	19-709	ST
Morgan, Lorrie	Don't Stop In My World	4-419	SC
Morgan, Lorrie	Except For Monday	1-338	CB
Morgan, Lorrie	Except For Monday	13-400	P
Morgan, Lorrie	Five Minutes	1-334	CB
Morgan, Lorrie	Five Minutes	26-584	DK
Morgan, Lorrie	Five Minutes	2-389	SC
Morgan, Lorrie	Go Away	1-345	CB
Morgan, Lorrie	Go Away	7-665	CHM
Morgan, Lorrie	Good As I Was To You	14-651	CB
Morgan, Lorrie	Good As I Was To You	7-590	CHM
Morgan, Lorrie	Good As I Was To You	7-432	MM
Morgan, Lorrie	Good As I Was To You	4-617	SC
Morgan, Lorrie	Half Enough	6-383	MM
Morgan, Lorrie	He Talks To Me	1-335	CB
Morgan, Lorrie	He Talks To Me	19-293	MH
Morgan, Lorrie	He Talks To Me	6-622	MM
Morgan, Lorrie	He Talks To Me	9-476	SAV
Morgan, Lorrie	Heart Over Mind	6-674	MM
Morgan, Lorrie	Heart Over Mind	3-46	SC
Morgan, Lorrie	Here I Go Again	14-695	CB
Morgan, Lorrie	Here I Go Again	5-723	SC
Morgan, Lorrie	I Can Buy My Own Roses	4-599	SC
Morgan, Lorrie	I Didn't Know My Own Strength	6-807	MM
Morgan, Lorrie	I Didn't Know My Own Strength	2-762	SC
Morgan, Lorrie	I Guess You Had To Be There	6-309	MM
Morgan, Lorrie	I Just Might Be	7-323	MM
Morgan, Lorrie	I Just Might Be	24-163	SC
Morgan, Lorrie	I'll Take The Memories	49-116	CB

ARTIST	SONG TITLE	#	TYPE
Morgan, Lorrie	I'm Not That Easy To Forget	8-469	CB
Morgan, Lorrie	If You Came Back From Heaven	1-341	CB
Morgan, Lorrie	If You Came Back From Heaven	6-578	MM
Morgan, Lorrie	If You Came Back From Heaven	45-412	CB
Morgan, Lorrie	My Night To Howl	6-500	MM
Morgan, Lorrie	My Night To Howl	2-127	SC
Morgan, Lorrie	One Of Those Nights Tonight	22-418	ST
Morgan, Lorrie	Out Of Your Shoes	1-332	CB
Morgan, Lorrie	Out Of Your Shoes	6-745	MM
Morgan, Lorrie	Picture Of Me Without You	1-337	CB
Morgan, Lorrie	Picture Of Me Without You	26-583	DK
Morgan, Lorrie	Picture Of Me Without You	13-531	P
Morgan, Lorrie	Picture Of Me Without You	9-609	SAV
Morgan, Lorrie	Reading My Heart	47-782	SRK
Morgan, Lorrie	She's Taking Him Back Again	49-115	CB
Morgan, Lorrie	Someone To Call Me Darlin'	49-117	CB
Morgan, Lorrie	Something In Red	1-343	CB
Morgan, Lorrie	Something In Red	6-115	MM
Morgan, Lorrie	Something In Red	2-13	SC
Morgan, Lorrie	Standing Tall	4-123	SC
Morgan, Lorrie	Things We Do the	49-113	CB
Morgan, Lorrie	To Get To You	49-114	CB
Morgan, Lorrie	Trainwreck Of Emotion	1-333	CB
Morgan, Lorrie	War Paint	49-118	SC
Morgan, Lorrie	Watch Me	1-339	CB
Morgan, Lorrie	Watch Me	6-750	MM
Morgan, Lorrie	Watch Me	13-401	P
Morgan, Lorrie	We Both Walk	1-336	CB
Morgan, Lorrie	What Part Of No	1-340	CB
Morgan, Lorrie	What Part Of No	6-130	MM
Morgan, Lorrie	You'd Think He'd Know Me Better	8-741	CB
Morris & Gayle	Duet - Making Up For Lost Time	49-636	CB
Morris & Gayle	Making Up For Lost Time - duet	49-636	CB
Morris, Gary	100 Percent Chance Of Rain	34-266	CB
Morris, Gary	100% Chance Of Rain	5-534	SC
Morris, Gary	Don't Look Back	9-624	SAV
Morris, Gary	I'll Never Stop Loving You	20-20	SC
Morris, Gary	Lasso The Moon	45-620	DCK
Morris, Gary	Second Hand Heart	20-25	SC
Morris, Gary	Wind Beneath My Wings	9-440	SAV
Morris, Maren	My Church	48-639	KV
Morris, Maren	My Church (Inst)	49-415	BKD
Morris, Nathan	Wishes	24-177	SC

ARTIST	SONG TITLE	#	TYPE
Morrisette, Alanis	Crazy (James Michael Mix)	29-246	SC
Morrisette, Alanis	Empathy	39-120	PHM
Morrisette, Alanis	Guardian	39-114	PHM
Morrisette, Alanis	Hand in My Pocket	18-41	PS
Morrisette, Alanis	Hands Clean	25-139	MM
Morrisette, Alanis	Head Over Feet	24-174	SC
Morrisette, Alanis	Ironic	18-42	PS
Morrisette, Alanis	So Pure	8-311	PHT
Morrisette, Alanis	Thank U	7-780	PHT
Morrisette, Alanis	Uninvited	13-684	SGB
Morrisette, Alanis	Unsent	16-202	PHT
Morrisette, Alanis	Unsent	13-680	SGB
Morrisette, Alanis	Woman Down	39-130	PHM
Morrisette, Alanis	You Learn	39-128	SC
Morrisette, Alanis	You Learn	10-682	HE
Morrisette, Alanis	You Learn	19-159	SGB
Morrisette, Alanis	You Oughta Know	18-40	PS
Morrisette, Alanis	You Oughta Know	3-487	SC
Morrisette, Alanis	You Oughta Know	19-153	SGB
Morrison, James	Better Man	38-268	ZM
Morrison, James	Broken Strings - duet	38-274	EK
Morrison, James	Duet - Broken Strings	38-274	EX
Morrison, James	Get To You	38-273	MH
Morrison, James	How Come	38-269	ZM
Morrison, james	I Won't Let You Go	38-267	ZM
Morrison, James	If The Rain Must Fall	38-270	ZM
Morrison, James	One Last Chance	38-271	ZM
Morrison, James	Undiscovered	38-276	SF
Morrison, James	Wonderful World	38-275	EK
Morrison, James	You Give Me Something	38-272	SF
Morrison, Van	And It Stoned Me	23-601	BS
Morrison, Van	And It Stoned Me	15-728	SI
Morrison, Van	Baby Please Don't Go	23-595	BS
Morrison, Van	Blue Money	23-607	BS
Morrison, Van	Blue Money	15-733	SI
Morrison, Van	Bright Side Of The Road	23-592	BS
Morrison, Van	Bright Side Of The Road	15-722	SI
Morrison, Van	Brown Eyed Girl	23-597	BS
Morrison, Van	Brown Eyed Girl	17-339	DK
Morrison, Van	Brown Eyed Girl	13-254	P
Morrison, Van	Caravan	17-534	SC
Morrison, Van	Crazy Love	5-873	SC
Morrison, Van	Domino	23-603	BS
Morrison, Van	Domino	4-844	SC
Morrison, Van	Full Force Gale	23-600	BS
Morrison, Van	Full Force Gale	15-727	SI
Morrison, Van	Gloria	23-593	BS
Morrison, Van	Gloria	21-198	DK
Morrison, Van	Gloria	12-925	P
Morrison, Van	Have I Told You Lately	23-596	BS
Morrison, Van	Have I Told You Lately	15-724	SI
Morrison, Van	Here Comes The Night	23-602	BS
Morrison, Van	Here Comes The Night	15-729	SI
Morrison, Van	Irish - One Irish Rover	21-503	SC
Morrison, Van	Moondance	23-594	BS
Morrison, Van	Moondance	13-10	P

ARTIST	SONG TITLE	#	TYPE
Morrison, Van	Please Baby Please Don't Go	15-723	SI
Morrison, Van	Queen Of The Slip Stream	15-732	SI
Morrison, Van	Queen Of The Slip Stream	23-606	BS
Morrison, Van	Sweet Thing	23-598	BS
Morrison, Van	Sweet Thing	15-725	SI
Morrison, Van	Tupelo Honey	17-464	SC
Morrison, Van	Warm Love	23-599	BS
Morrison, Van	Warm Love	15-726	SI
Morrison, Van	Whenever God Shines His Light	23-605	BS
Morrison, Van	Whenever God Shines His Light On..	15-731	SI
Morrison, Van	Wild Night	23-604	BS
Morrison, Van	Wild Night	15-730	SI
Morrissey	More You Ignore Me the	6-38	SC
Morrissey	You Have Killed Me	30-698	SF
Motels	Only The Lonely	19-361	DK
Motels	Only The Lonely	5-148	SC
Motels	Suddenly Last Summer	19-360	DK
Motels	Suddenly Last Summer	24-569	SC
Mother's Finest	Baby Love	24-431	SC
Mother's Finest	Truth'll Set You Free	24-557	SC
Motley Crue	Dr. Feelgood	23-52	MH
Motley Crue	Girls Girls Girls	7-484	MM
Motley Crue	Girls Girls Girls	5-75	SC
Motley Crue	Home Sweet Home	24-685	SC
Motley Crue	Live Wire	23-104	SC
Motley Crue	Primal Scream **	21-773	SC
Motley Crue	Shout At The Devil	5-481	SC
Motley Crue	Smokin' In The Boy's Room	2-558	SC
Motley Crue	Smokin' In The Boys Room	35-182	CB
Motley Crue	Too Young To Fall In Love	6-23	SC
Motley Crue	Without You	12-775	P
Motograter	Down	23-189	PHM
Motorhead	Ace Of Spades	21-757	SC
Moulin Rouge	Come What May	19-121	PR
Moulin Rouge	Come What May	18-664	PS
Moulin Rouge	Elephant Love Medley	19-120	PR
Moulin Rouge	Lady Marmalade	18-665	PS
Moulin Rouge	Show - Come What May	19-121	PR
Moulin Rouge	Show - Come What May	18-664	PS
Moulin Rouge	Show - Elephant Love Medley	19-120	PR
Moulin Rouge	Show - Lady Marmalade	18-665	PS
Moulin Rouge	Show - Nature Boy	18-666	PS
Moulin Rouge	Show - One Day I'll Fly Away	19-119	PR
Moulin Rouge	Show - Sparkling Diamonds	19-117	PR
Moulin Rouge	Show - Sparkling Diamonds	18-668	PS
Moulin Rouge	Show - Your Song	19-118	PR
Moulin Rouge	Show - Your Song	18-667	PS

ARTIST	SONG TITLE	#	TYPE
Mountain	Mississippi Queen	17-90	DK
Move	Flowers In The Rain	10-642	SF
Moving Pictures	What About Me	21-801	SC
Moyet, Allison	All Cried Out	11-28	PX
Moyet, Allison	Love Letters	43-86	SF
Moyet, Allison	Love Letters	11-25	PX
Moyet, Allison	That Old Devil Called Love	11-22	PX
Mr. Big	To Be With You	6-170	MM
Mr. Big	Wild World	23-112	SC
Mr. Magic	I Smoke I Drink	30-808	PHM
Mr. Mister	Broken Wings	11-658	DK
Mr. Mister	Broken Wings	12-819	P
Mr. Mister	Kyrie	21-740	MH
Mraz, Jason	3 Things	47-304	KV
Mraz, Jason	93 Million Miles	47-303	KV
Mraz, Jason	Beautiful Mess a	47-305	KV
Mraz, Jason	Bella Luna	47-300	KV
Mraz, Jason	Curbside Prophet	23-556	MM
Mraz, Jason	Geek In The Pink	47-306	PHM
Mraz, Jason	I Won't Give Up	44-384	BKD
Mraz, Jason	I'm Yours	36-515	CB
Mraz, Jason	I'm Yours	48-593	DK
Mraz, Jason	It's So Hard To Say Goodbye	44-318	SBI
Mraz, Jason	Live High	47-301	KV
Mraz, Jason	Long Drive	45-284	BKD
Mraz, Jason	Love Someone	47-302	KV
Mraz, Jason	Make It Mine	44-386	CB
Mraz, Jason	Remedy	25-545	MM
Mraz, Jason	Remedy the (I Won't Worry)	34-177	CB
Mraz, Jason	Rough Water	43-167	ASK
Mraz, Jason	Summer Breeze	47-299	KV
Mraz, Jason	Wordplay	44-385	CB
Mraz, Jason	You And I Both	44-387	SC
Muddy Waters	Got My Mojo Workin'	15-313	SC
Muddy Waters	Hoochie Coochie Man	27-238	DK
Muddy Waters	Hoochie Coochie Man	7-221	MM
Muddy Waters	Mannish Boy	20-145	KB
Muddy Waters	Mannish Boy	15-27	SC
Muddy Waters	Rollin' & Tumblin'	14-593	SC
Mudhog	I Don't Know If I'm Coming Home	30-557	CB
Mudvayne	Not Falling	23-156	PHM
Mullen, Nicole C	Gospel - Redeemer	35-318	CB
Mullen, Nicole C	Redeemer	35-318	CB
Mullican, Moon	I'll Sail My Ship Alone	5-579	SC
Mullins, Megan	Ain't What It Used To Be	29-584	CB
Mullins, Megan	Cryin' Days	30-446	CB
Mullins, Megan	Cryin' Days	30-446	CB
Mullins, Rich	Awesome GOD	35-320	CB
Mullins, Rich	Gospel - Awesome GOD	35-320	CB
Mullins, Shawn	Beautiful Wreck	29-218	PHM
Mullins, Shawn	Everywhere I Go	14-24	THM
Mullins, Shawn	Lullabye	14-288	MM
Mullins, Shawn	Lullabye	7-779	PHT

ARTIST	SONG TITLE	#	TYPE
Mullins, Shawn	Lullabye	13-711	SGB
Multi-Voice	Duet - Voices That Care	18-682	PR
Multi-Voice	Ease On Down The Road	18-685	PR
Multi-Voice	I'd Like To Teach The World To Sing	11-544	DK
Multi-Voice	I'd Like To Teach The World To Sing	18-684	PR
Multi-Voice	That's What Friends Are For	18-683	PR
Multi-Voice	Voices That Care	18-682	PR
Mumba, Samantha	Always Come Back To Your ...	18-506	TT
Mumba, Samantha	Baby Come Over	18-507	TT
Mumba, Samantha	Gotta Tell You	14-39	THM
Mumba, Samantha	Gotta Tell You	18-515	TT
Mumba, Samantha	I Don't Need To Tell You I'm Pretty	15-813	CB
Mumford & Sons	Babel	39-126	PHM
Mumford & Sons	Ditmas	48-433	BKD
Mumford & Sons	Feel The Tide	39-115	PHM
Mumford & Sons	I Will Wait	39-123	PHM
Mumford & Sons	Lover Of The Light	39-119	PHM
Mumford & Sons	Snake Eyes	48-427	MRH
Mungo, Jerry	In The Summertime	13-321	P
Munster's Theme	Halloween - Theme from Musters	16-290	TT
Muppet Movie	Show - Rainbow Connection the	6-325	MM
Murdock, Shirley	As We Lay	5-470	SC
Muriel's Wedding	Fernando	6-900	MM
Muriel's Wedding	Show - Fernando	6-900	MM
Murmaids	Popsicles and Icicles	3-586	SC
Murmurs	You Suck **	5-739	SC
Murphy, David Lee	All Lit Up In Love	4-838	SC
Murphy, David Lee	Breakfast In Birmingham	48-99	MM
Murphy, David Lee	Dust On The Bottle	6-850	MM
Murphy, David Lee	Every Time I Get Around	7-230	MM
Murphy, David Lee	Every Time I Get Around You	22-883	ST
Murphy, David Lee	Fish Ain't Bitin'	3-544	SC
Murphy, David Lee	Genuine Rednecks	7-430	MM
Murphy, David Lee	Inspiration	22-90	CB
Murphy, David Lee	Just Don't Wait Around	8-152	CB
Murphy, David Lee	Just Don't Wait Around	7-726	CHM
Murphy, David Lee	Just Don't Wait Around Til She's...	22-416	ST
Murphy, David Lee	Just Once	24-251	SC
Murphy, David Lee	Loco	35-440	CB
Murphy, David Lee	Loco	19-773	ST
Murphy, David Lee	Out With A Bang	7-170	MM
Murphy, David Lee	Out With A Bang	3-657	SC
Murphy, David Lee	Party Crowd	35-406	CB
Murphy, David Lee	Party Crowd	2-667	SC
Murphy, David Lee	Road You Leave Behind the	7-321	MM
Murphy, David Lee	Road You Leave Behind the	4-894	SC

ARTIST	SONG TITLE	#	TYPE
Murphy, David Lee	She's Really Something To See	22-917	ST
Murphy, Eddie	Party All The Time	6-518	MM
Murphy, George	Oh You Beautiful Doll	21-4	SC
Murphy, Michael M	Carolina In The Pines	3-621	SC
Murphy, Michael M	Still Taking Chances	5-539	SC
Murphy, Michael M	What's Forever For	13-486	P
Murphy, Michael M	Wildfire	17-562	PR
Murphy, Michael M	Wildfire	2-788	SC
Murphy, Michael M.	What's Forever For	34-251	CB
Murphy, Michael M.	Wildfire	34-319	CB
Murray & Loggins	Duet - Nobody Loves Me Like U Do	12-118	DK
Murray & Loggins	Duet - Nobody Loves Me Like U Do	11-4	PL
Murray & Loggins	Duet - Nobody Loves Me Like You Do	38-3	CB
Murray & Loggins	Nobody Loves Me Like You Do	12-118	DK
Murray & Loggins	Nobody Loves Me Like You Do	11-4	PL
Murray & Loggins	Nobody Loves Me Like You Do - duet	38-3	CB
Murray Head	One Night In Bangkok	29-16	MH
Murray, Anne	Another Sleepless Night	13-408	P
Murray, Anne	As Time Goes By	49-928	KVD
Murray, Anne	Blessed Are The Believers	11-11	PL
Murray, Anne	Blessed Are The Believers	6-77	SC
Murray, Anne	Bluebird the	38-4	SC
Murray, Anne	Bridge Over Troubled Water	46-13	CKC
Murray, Anne	Broken Hearted Me	29-788	CB
Murray, Anne	Broken Hearted Me	11-12	PL
Murray, Anne	Broken Hearted Me	9-831	SAV
Murray, Anne	Broken Hearted Me	5-25	SC
Murray, Anne	Cotton Jenny	11-7	PL
Murray, Anne	Could I Have This Dance	17-123	DK
Murray, Anne	Could I Have This Dance	6-762	MM
Murray, Anne	Could I Have This Dance	13-355	P
Murray, Anne	Could I Have This Dance	11-3	PL
Murray, Anne	Could I Have This Dance	9-517	SAV
Murray, Anne	Danny's Song	8-448	CB
Murray, Anne	Daydream Believer	38-5	SC
Murray, Anne	Feed The Fire	38-2	CB
Murray, Anne	He Thinks I Still Care	11-13	PL
Murray, Anne	He Thinks I Still Care	4-790	SC
Murray, Anne	I Can See Arkansas	11-15	PL
Murray, Anne	I Just Fall In Love Again	11-598	DK
Murray, Anne	I Just Fall In Love Again	11-16	PL
Murray, Anne	I'll Be Your Baby Tonight	11-9	PL
Murray, Anne	Just Another Woman In Love	33-39	CB
Murray, Anne	Just Another Woman In Love	12-430	P
Murray, Anne	Little Good News a	11-10	PL
Murray, Anne	Love Song	15-67	CB

ARTIST	SONG TITLE	#	TYPE
Murray, Anne	Love Song	11-2	PL
Murray, Anne	Love Song	2-638	SC
Murray, Anne	Nobody Loves Me Like You Do	46-15	THM
Murray, Anne	Now And Forever (You And Me)	14-263	SC
Murray, Anne	Put Your Hand In The Hand	11-8	PL
Murray, Anne	Shadows In The Moonlight	33-311	CB
Murray, Anne	Shadows In The Moonlight	29-660	SC
Murray, Anne	Snowbird	17-124	DK
Murray, Anne	Snowbird	13-354	P
Murray, Anne	Snowbird	8-622	SAV
Murray, Anne	Somebody's Always Saying Goodbye	46-14	SC
Murray, Anne	Son Of A Rotten Gambler	38-7	PHM
Murray, Anne	Son Of A Rotten Gambler	11-14	PL
Murray, Anne	Stranger In My Place a	11-17	PL
Murray, Anne	There Goes My Everything	11-6	PL
Murray, Anne	Walk Right Back	46-89	OZP
Murray, Anne	Xmas - Little Drummer Boy	30-392	SC
Murray, Anne	Xmas - Sweet Little Jesus Boy	11-5	PL
Murray, Anne	You Are My Sunshine/Open Up Your Heart	45-950	KV
Murray, Anne	You Needed Me	16-838	DK
Murray, Anne	You Needed Me	13-81	P
Murray, Anne	You Needed Me	11-1	PL
Murray, Anne	You Needed Me	9-451	SAV
Murray, Anne	You Won't See Me	38-6	PS
Murray, Ruby	Softly Softly	10-604	SF
Muse	Supermassive Black Hole	30-721	SF
Musgraves & Nelson	Are You Sure - duet	49-93	FMK
Musgraves, Kacey	Biscuits	45-314	KV
Musgraves, Kacey	Blowin' Smoke	41-47	ASK
Musgraves, Kacey	Blowin' Smoke	45-315	ASK
Musgraves, Kacey	Dime Store Cowgirl	45-316	KRG
Musgraves, Kacey	Family Is Family	45-318	KV
Musgraves, Kacey	Follow Your Arrow	49-94	BKD
Musgraves, Kacey	Follow Your Arrow	45-309	KV
Musgraves, Kacey	High Time	45-435	ZM
Musgraves, Kacey	It Is What It Is	45-310	KV
Musgraves, Kacey	Keep It To Yourself	45-319	BKD
Musgraves, Kacey	Late To The Party	45-366	KV
Musgraves, Kacey	Merry Go 'Round	43-260	KCD
Musgraves, Kacey	My House	45-312	KV
Musgraves, Kacey	Pageant Material	45-320	KV
Musgraves, Kacey	Silver Lining	45-311	KV
Musgraves, Kacey	Somebody To Love	45-317	KRG
Musgraves, Kacey	Step Off	45-313	KV
Musgraves, Kacey	Stupid	45-434	KVD

ARTIST	SONG TITLE	#	TYPE
Musgraves, Kacey	This Town	45-375	KV
Musgraves, Kacey	Trailer Song the	45-276	BKD
Musgraves, Kacey	Walkashame	45-955	KV
Music Explosion	Little Bit O' Soul	3-590	SC
Music Man	Show - Sadder But Wiser Girl the	18-198	PS
Music Man	Show - Seventy-Six Trombones	27-388	DK
Music Man	Show - Seventy-Six Trombones	6-895	MM
Music Man	Show - Seventy-Six Trombones	2-295	SC
Music Man	Show - Shipoopi	14-388	PS
Music Man	Show - Till There Was You	6-884	MM
Musiq	Halfcrazy	35-262	CB
Musiq	Halfcrazy	18-148	PHM
MXPX	Chick Magnet	45-590	OZP
My Fair Lady	Show - Get Me to the Church on Time	6-882	MM
My Fair Lady	Show - Get Me To the Church on Time	18-200	PS
My Fair Lady	Show - Get Me To The Church on Time	2-289	SC
My Fair Lady	Show - I Could've Danced All Night	17-804	PS
My Fair Lady	Show - I Could've Danced All Night	2-296	SC
My Fair Lady	Show - On The Street Where U Live	27-390	DK
My Fair Lady	Show - On the Street Where U Live	18-185	PS
My Fair Lady	Show - Show Me	5-651	SC
My Fair Lady	Show - With A Little Bit Of Luck	5-653	SC
My Fair Lady	Show - Wouldn't It Be Loverly	6-893	MM
Mya	Case Of The Ex	15-431	PHM
Mya	Fallen	19-667	CB
Mya	Free	12-394	PHM
Mya	My First Night With You	13-787	SGB
Mya	My Love Is Like - Wooh	32-426	THM
Mya	My Love Is Like... WO!	25-725	MM
Mya	My Love Is Like....WO!	21-785	SC
Mya	My Love Is Like...Wooh	35-284	CB
Myers, Billie	Kiss The Rain	7-714	PHM
Myers, Billie	Kiss The Rain	5-183	SC
Myles, Alannah	Black Velvet	26-299	DK
Myles, Alannah	Black Velvet	6-171	MM
Myles, Heather	Love Me A Little Bit Longer	14-609	SC
Myles, Heather	True Love	8-195	CB
N'Sync	Bye Bye Bye	20-427	CB
N'Sync	Bye Bye Bye	29-170	MH
N'Sync	Crazy For You	15-781	BS
N'Sync	Crazy For You	20-438	CB
N'Sync	Drive Myself Crazy	15-777	BS
N'Sync	Everything I Own	15-773	BS
N'Sync	For The Girl Who Has	15-770	BS

ARTIST	SONG TITLE	#	TYPE
	Everything		
N'Sync	For The Girl Who Has Everything	20-441	CB
N'Sync	Giddy Up	15-779	BS
N'Sync	Girlfriend	20-436	CB
N'Sync	Girlfriend	25-150	MM
N'Sync	God Must Have Spent	15-776	BS
N'Sync	God Must Have Spent	20-430	CB
N'Sync	God Must Have Spent	11-64	JTG
N'Sync	God Must Have Spent	7-789	PHT
N'Sync	God Must Have Spent	13-788	SGB
N'Sync	Gone	20-432	CB
N'Sync	Gone	25-30	MM
N'Sync	Here We Go	15-782	BS
N'Sync	I Drive Myself Crazy	20-435	CB
N'Sync	I Drive Myself Crazy	29-173	MH
N'Sync	I Just Want To Be With You	15-769	BS
N'Sync	I Need Love	15-772	BS
N'Sync	I Need Love	20-437	CB
N'Sync	I Want You Back	15-778	BS
N'Sync	I Want You Back	20-433	CB
N'Sync	It's Gonna Be Me	20-428	CB
N'Sync	It's Gonna Be Me	14-470	SC
N'Sync	It's Gonna Be Me	30-632	THM
N'Sync	It's Gonna Be Me	18-562	TT
N'Sync	Pop	20-431	CB
N'Sync	Pop	18-572	TT
N'Sync	Sailing	15-780	BS
N'Sync	Sailing	20-440	CB
N'Sync	Tearin' Up My Heart	15-775	BS
N'Sync	Tearin' Up My Heart	20-429	CB
N'Sync	Tearin' Up My Heart	29-166	MH
N'Sync	This I Promise You	20-434	CB
N'Sync	This I Promise You	16-484	MH
N'Sync	This I Promise You	16-115	PRT
N'Sync	This I Promise You	14-507	SC
N'Sync	This I Promise You	14-19	THM
N'Sync	You Got It	15-771	BS
N'Sync & Estefan	Duet - Music Of My Heart	20-439	CB
N'Sync & Estefan	Duet - Music Of My Heart	8-498	PHT
N'Sync & Estefan	Music Of My Heart	20-439	CB
N'Sync & Estefan	Music Of My Heart	8-498	PHT
N2 Deep	Back To The Hotel	28-394	DK
Naess, Leona	Charm Attack	13-845	PHM
Nail, David	Clouds	45-561	KV
Nail, David	I'm About To Come Alive	36-619	CB
Nail, David	Kiss You Tonight	45-289	BKD
Nail, David	Let It Rain	45-557	ASK
Nail, David	Memphis	17-573	ST
Nail, David	Night's On Fire	45-57	BKD
Nail, David	Red Light	45-559	AC
Nail, David	Sound Of A Million Dreams	45-558	ZP
Nail, David	Turning Home	45-560	CB

ARTIST	SONG TITLE	#	TYPE
Nail, David	Whatever She's Got	43-146	ASK
Nail, David	Whatever She's Got	44-335	SSC
Nail, David	Whatever She's Got	45-400	BKD
Nail, Jason	Kiss You Tonight	44-294	BKD
Nail, Jimmy	Calling Out Your Name	47-706	DCK
Nails	88 Lines About 44 Women **	30-672	RSX
Nails	88 Lines About 44 Women **	23-16	SC
Naked Eyes	Always Something There To Remind	18-362	AH
Naked Eyes	Always Something There To Remind	29-291	SC
Naked Eyes	Promises Promises	21-406	SC
Nalick, Anna	Breathe (2am)	30-154	PT
Nalick, Anna	Wreck Of The Day	36-193	PHM
Napoleon XIV	They're Coming To Take Me Away	6-860	MM
Napoleon XIV	They're Coming To Take Me Away	5-631	SC
Napoleon XIV	They're Coming To Take Me Away	16-291	TT
Nappy Roots	Roun' The Globe	32-348	THM
Nas	I Can	25-720	MM
Nas	I Can	32-239	THM
Nas	If I Ruled The World (Imagine That)	25-477	MM
Nas	Made You Look	32-51	THM
Nas	One Mic	25-464	MM
Nash, Johnny	I Can See Clearly Now	35-111	CB
Nash, Johnny	I Can See Clearly Now	17-410	DK
Nash, Kate	Foundations (Radio Vers)	37-147	SC
Nash, Leigh	Need To Be Next To You	17-719	THM
Nashville Cast	Show - When the Right One Comes Along	45-465	AHN
Nashville Cast	When The Right One Comes Along - show	45-465	AHN
Nashville Cast	When the Right One Comes...	39-91	PHN
Nashville Teens	Tobacco Road	10-655	SF
Natalie&Baby Bash	Duet - Energy	23-319	CB
Natalie&Baby Bash	Energy	23-319	CB
Nate Dogg & Eve	Duet - Get Up **	32-126	THM
Nate Dogg & Eve	Get Up **	32-126	THM
Nathanson, Marr	Come On Get Higher	49-856	SC
Nathanson, Matthew	All We Are	36-274	PHM
Nathanson, Matthew	Come On Get Higher	36-237	PHM
Naughty By Nature	Hip Hop Hooray	16-572	SC
Naughty By Nature	O.P.P.	25-483	MM
Naughty By Nature	O.P.P.	14-438	SC
Nazareth	Bad Bad Boy	30-740	SF
Nazareth	Hair Of The Dog	10-483	DA
Nazareth	Love Hurts	7-490	MM
Nazareth	Love Hurts	3-474	SC
Nazario, Ednita	Latino - Dime	23-242	AI
Ne-Yo	Closer	36-458	CB
Ne-Yo	Miss Independence	36-509	CB
Ne-Yo	Miss Independent	49-854	SC

ARTIST	SONG TITLE	#	TYPE
Neil, Vince	You're Invited (...Friend Can't Come)	21-775	SC
Nelly	Air Force One	32-85	THM
Nelly	Air Force Ones	25-461	MM
Nelly	Country Grammar (Hot....)	14-495	SC
Nelly	Grillz	30-699	SF
Nelly	Hot In Here	25-306	MM
Nelly	Hot In Here	18-146	PHM
Nelly	Ride With Me	18-573	TT
Nelly & McGraw	Duet - Over & Over	22-350	CB
Nelly & McGraw	Over & Over	22-350	CB
Nelly & P Diddy	Shake Ya Tail Feathers **	25-711	MM
Nelly & Rowland	Dilemma - duet	33-433	CB
Nelly & Rowland	Duet - Dilemma	33-433	CB
Nelly & Rowland, K.	Dilemma	25-457	MM
Nelly w/McGraw	Over And Over	20-190	PHM
Nelly w/Timberlake	Work It (Remix)	20-353	PHM
Nelly, P. Diddy, Lee	Duet - Shake Ya Tail Feather	32-344	THM
Nelly, P. Diddy, Lee	Shake Ya Tail Feather - Duet	32-344	THM
Nelly/Kyjuan/Ali/Le	Air Force Ones	32-85	THM
Nelson	Love & Affection	24-683	SC
Nelson & Collie	Duet - Willingly	38-96	CB
Nelson & Collie	Willingly - duet	38-96	CB
Nelson & Haggard	Pancho & Lefty	22-236	CB
Nelson & Haggard	Pancho & Lefty	13-411	P
Nelson & Haggard	Reasons To Quit	11-436	DK
Nelson & Iglesias	Duet - To All The Girls I've Loved	9-204	SO
Nelson & Iglesias	Duet - To All The Girls I've Loved.	16-848	DK
Nelson & Iglesias	Duet - To All The Girls I've Loved.	13-183	P
Nelson & Iglesias	To All The Girls I've Loved Before	16-848	DK
Nelson & Iglesias	To All The Girls I've Loved Before	13-183	P
Nelson & Iglesias	To All The Girls I've Loved Before	9-204	SO
Nelson & Jennings	Duet - Just To Satisfy You	38-97	CB
Nelson & Jennings	Just To Satisfy You - duet	38-97	CB
Nelson & Jennings	Mamas Don't Let Your Babies Grow	16-786	DK
Nelson & Jennings	Mamas Don't Let Your Babies Grow	13-359	P
Nelson & Jennings	Mamas Don't Let Your Babies Grow..	9-433	SAV
Nelson & Jennings	Mamas Don't Let Your Babies Grow...	8-22	CB
Nelson & Keith	Midnight Rider	22-75	CB
Nelson & Womack	Duet - Mendocino County Line	25-129	MM
Nelson & Womack	Duet - Mendocino County Line	16-332	ST
Nelson & Womack	Mendocino County Line	25-129	MM

ARTIST	SONG TITLE	#	TYPE
Nelson & Womack	Mendocino County Line	16-332	ST
Nelson w Keith	Midnight Rider	38-70	CB
Nelson, Ricky	Be Bop Baby	21-708	CB
Nelson, Ricky	Believe What You Say	21-709	CB
Nelson, Ricky	Fools Rush In	38-99	ZM
Nelson, Ricky	Garden Party	21-699	CB
Nelson, Ricky	Garden Party	26-510	DK
Nelson, Ricky	Hello Mary Lou	21-698	CB
Nelson, Ricky	Hello Mary Lou	12-135	DK
Nelson, Ricky	Hello Mary Lou	9-480	SAV
Nelson, Ricky	Hello Mary Lou	10-509	SF
Nelson, Ricky	I'm Walking	38-98	LE
Nelson, Ricky	It's Late	21-700	CB
Nelson, Ricky	It's Late	20-30	SC
Nelson, Ricky	It's Up To You	21-711	CB
Nelson, Ricky	It's Up To You	15-764	NU
Nelson, Ricky	It's Up To You	5-513	SC
Nelson, Ricky	Just A Little Too Much	21-701	CB
Nelson, Ricky	Lonesome Town	21-702	CB
Nelson, Ricky	My Babe	46-37	SSK
Nelson, Ricky	Never Be Anyone Else But You	21-703	CB
Nelson, Ricky	Never Be Anyone Else But You	6-60	SC
Nelson, Ricky	Poor Little Fool	21-704	CB
Nelson, Ricky	Poor Little Fool	2-51	SC
Nelson, Ricky	Stood Up	21-705	CB
Nelson, Ricky	Stood Up	20-39	SC
Nelson, Ricky	Teenage Idol	21-706	CB
Nelson, Ricky	Teenager's Romance a	21-707	CB
Nelson, Ricky	That's All She Wrote	47-842	DCK
Nelson, Ricky	Travelin' Man	21-701	CB
Nelson, Ricky	Travelin' Man	11-134	DK
Nelson, Ricky	Travelin' Man	13-261	P
Nelson, Ricky	Travelin' Man	9-499	SAV
Nelson, Ricky	Travelin' Man	29-839	SC
Nelson, Ricky	You Just Can't Quit	47-843	DCK
Nelson, Ricky	Young World	21-712	CB
Nelson, Ricky	Young World	5-238	SC
Nelson, Willie	Ain't Goin Down on Brokeback Mrn	49-291	FMK
Nelson, Willie	Ain't It Funny How Time Slips Away	9-457	SAV
Nelson, Willie	All Of Me	16-589	MM
Nelson, Willie	Always On My Mind	8-14	CB
Nelson, Willie	Always On My Mind	11-143	DK
Nelson, Willie	Always On My Mind	13-433	P
Nelson, Willie	Angel Flying Too Close/Ground	8-199	CB
Nelson, Willie	Angel Flying Too Close/Ground	4-541	SC
Nelson, Willie	Bigbooty	47-733	SRK
Nelson, Willie	Bloody Mary Morning	5-757	SC
Nelson, Willie	Blue Eyes Crying In The Rain	15-66	CB
Nelson, Willie	Blue Eyes Crying In The Rain	17-2	DK
Nelson, Willie	Blue Eyes Crying In The	8-707	SAV

ARTIST	SONG TITLE	#	TYPE
	Rain		
Nelson, Willie	Blue Eyes Crying In The Rain	3-638	SC
Nelson, Willie	Blue Skies	35-380	CB
Nelson, Willie	Blue Skies	13-451	P
Nelson, Willie	Bring Me Sunshine	47-515	VH
Nelson, Willie	City Of New Orleans	1-630	CB
Nelson, Willie	City Of New Orleans	8-708	SAV
Nelson, Willie	City Of New Orleans	14-317	SC
Nelson, Willie	Corina Corina	46-90	SSK
Nelson, Willie	Cry Cry Darling	38-75	PS
Nelson, Willie	Devil In A Sleeping Bag	46-36	SSK
Nelson, Willie	Don't Mess With My Toot Toot	47-759	SRK
Nelson, Willie	Drinking Champagne	38-76	PS
Nelson, Willie	Forgiving You Was Easy	4-655	SC
Nelson, Willie	Freight Train Boogie	38-77	PS
Nelson, Willie	Gravedigger	49-709	ST
Nelson, Willie	Half A Mind	47-758	SRK
Nelson, Willie	Hard To Be A Hippie	45-328	KV
Nelson, Willie	He Was A Friend Of Mine	47-743	SRK
Nelson, Willie	I Gotta Get Drunk	45-849	VH
Nelson, Willie	If I Were The Man You Wanted	45-326	DCK
Nelson, Willie	If You Can Touch Her At All	38-68	CB
Nelson, Willie	If You've Got The Money	4-584	SC
Nelson, Willie	Last Thing I Needed First Thing This Morning	43-28	CB
Nelson, Willie	Last Thing I Needed First Thing This Morning	4-495	SC
Nelson, Willie	Let It Be Me	38-69	SC
Nelson, Willie	Man With The Blues	38-78	PS
Nelson, Willie	Maria (Shut Up And Kiss Me)	25-297	MM
Nelson, Willie	Maria (Shut Up and Kiss Me)	18-137	ST
Nelson, Willie	Me And Paul	5-860	SC
Nelson, Willie	Midnight Rider	38-71	CB
Nelson, Willie	Mountain Dew	17-313	NA
Nelson, Willie	My Heroes Have Always Been...	34-241	CB
Nelson, Willie	My Heros Have Always Been Cowboys	13-464	P
Nelson, Willie	Nothing I Can Do About It Now	38-72	CB
Nelson, Willie	Ocean Of Diamonds	38-79	PS
Nelson, Willie	On The Road Again	1-627	CB
Nelson, Willie	On The Road Again	16-843	DK
Nelson, Willie	On The Road Again	13-350	P
Nelson, Willie	Party's Over the	5-703	SC
Nelson, Willie	Remember Me	38-73	CB
Nelson, Willie	Roll Me Up And Smoke Me When I Die	45-18	KV
Nelson, Willie	Seven Spanish Angels	9-469	SAV
Nelson, Willie	Stardust	38-80	CB
Nelson, Willie	There'll Be No Teardrops Tonight	47-524	VH

ARTIST	SONG TITLE	#	TYPE
Nelson, Willie	Uncloudy Day	38-74	CB
Nelson, Willie	Undo The Right	46-48	SSK
Nelson, Willie	Whiskey River	1-628	CB
Nelson, Willie	Whiskey River	7-406	MM
Nelson, Willie	Whiskey River	2-639	SC
Nelson, Willie	Who Put All My Ex's In Texas	46-91	SSK
Nelson, Willie	Won't You Ride In My Little Red Wagon	46-92	SSK
Nelson, Willie	Xmas - Pretty Paper	8-61	CB
Nelson, Willie	Xmas - Pretty Paper	14-546	SC
Nelson, Willie	You Done Me Wrong	38-81	PS
Nelson, Willie	You Remain	45-327	DCK
Nena	99 Luftbaloons	11-685	DK
Nena	99 Red Balloons	4-532	SC
Neon Trees	Everybody Talks	39-30	PHM
Neon Trees	Sleeping With A Friend	43-165	ASK
Nerney, Declan	Stop The World And Let Me Off	45-852	VH
Nesbitt, Jim	Running Bare	15-143	SC
Nesler, Mark	Baby Ain't Rockin' Me Right	8-926	CB
Nesler, Mark	Slow Down	8-217	CB
Nesler, Mark	Used To The Pain	5-299	SC
Nesmith, Michael	Rio	30-761	SF
Nettles & Bon Jovi	Duet - Who Says You Can't Go Home	30-242	RS
Nettles & Bon Jovi	Who Says You Can't Go Home - duet	30-242	RS
Nettles, Jennifer	Falling	44-277	PHN
Nettles, Jennifer	Me Without You	43-267	BKD
Nettles, Jennifer	Me Without You	44-282	KCD
Nettles, Jennifer	Sugar	49-784	SS
Nettles, Jennifer	That Girl	43-92	HM
Nettles, Jennifer	Unlove You	49-660	BKD
Neville, Aaron	Can't Stop My Heart From Loving You	14-870	SC
Neville, Aaron	Crazy Love	24-366	SC
Neville, Aaron	Don't Take Away My Heaven	12-125	DK
Neville, Aaron	Grand Tour the	2-617	SC
Neville, Aaron	Tell It Like It Is	12-100	DK
Neville, Aaron	Tell It Like It Is	6-563	MM
Neville, Aaron	Tell It Like It Is	3-263	SC
New Edition	Hit Me Off	24-291	SC
New Edition	If It Isn't Love	28-336	DK
New Found Glory	Head On Collision	32-106	THM
New Found Glory	I Don't Wanna Know	22-355	CB
New Kids On Block	Cover Girl	11-514	DK
New Kids On Block	Hangin' Tough	11-515	DK
New Kids On Block	Hanging Tough	31-110	CB
New Kids On Block	I'll Be Loving You Forever	9-688	SAV
New Kids On Block	Step By Step	33-347	CB
New Kids On Block	Step By Step	11-531	DK
New Kids on Block	Summertime	36-441	CB
New Kids On Block	This One's For The Children	9-859	SAV

ARTIST	SONG TITLE	#	TYPE
New Kids On Block	Tonight	9-682	SAV
New Kids On Block	You Got It (The Right Stuff)	16-867	DK
New Kids On Block	You Got It (The Right Stuff)	9-694	SAV
New Kids On Block w Ne-Yo	Single	36-501	CB
New Kids On Block w Ne-Yo	Single	36-235	PHM
New Order	Bizarre Love Triangle	6-31	SC
New Order	True Faith	21-596	SF
New Radicals	You Get What You Give	7-788	PHT
New Seekers	I'd Like To Teach the World to Sing	28-237	DK
New Seekers	Look What They've Done To My Song	49-471	MM
New Vaudeville Band	Winchester Cathedral	27-112	DK
New Vaudeville Band	Winchester Cathedral	3-582	SC
New Years Eve	Auld Lang Syne	21-472	DK
New Years Eve	Auld Lang Syne	14-520	SC
Newbeats	Bread & Butter	6-865	MM
Newbeats	Bread & Butter	4-700	SC
Newfield, Heidi	Johnny & June	36-208	PHM
Newfield, Heidi	Stay Up Late	38-221	CB
Newley, Anthony	Show - Talk To The Animals	9-817	SAV
Newley, Anthony	Strawberry Fair	29-819	SF
Newley, Anthony	What Kind Of Fool Am I	27-382	DK
Newman, Jimmy	Fallen Star a	4-807	SC
Newman, John	Love Me Again	43-162	PHM
Newman, Randy	I Love L.A.	29-270	SC
Newman, Randy	Short People	35-144	CB
Newman, Randy	Short People	26-263	DK
Newman, Randy	Short People	5-475	SC
Newsboys	Gospel - Shine	20-154	KB
Newsong	Xmas - Christmas Shoes	34-434	CB
Newton-John & Travolta	Duet - Summer Nights	33-253	CB
Newton-John & Travolta	Summer Nights - duet	33-253	CB
Newton-John, Olivia	Can't We Talk It Over In Bed	18-391	SAV
Newton-John, Olivia	Have You Never Been Mellow	33-283	CB
Newton-John, Olivia	Have You Never Been Mellow	11-122	DK
Newton-John, Olivia	Have You Never Been Mellow	4-751	SC
Newton-John, Olivia	Heart Attack	5-680	SC
Newton-John, Olivia	Hopelessly Devoted To You	15-273	DK
Newton-John, Olivia	Hopelessly Devoted To You	9-273	SC
Newton-John, Olivia	Hopelessly Devoted To You	10-521	SF
Newton-John, Olivia	I Honestly Love You	11-183	DK
Newton-John, Olivia	I Honestly Love You	12-685	P
Newton-John, Olivia	I Honestly Love You	2-442	SC
Newton-John, Olivia	If You Love Me Let Me	9-582	SAV

ARTIST	SONG TITLE	#	TYPE
	Know		
Newton-John, Olivia	Let Me Be There	17-49	DK
Newton-John, Olivia	Let Me Be There	13-346	P
Newton-John, Olivia	Let Me Be There	9-587	SAV
Newton-John, Olivia	Long Live Love	49-55	ZVS
Newton-John, Olivia	Look At Me I'm Sandra Dee	10-16	SC
Newton-John, Olivia	Love Is A Gift	45-588	OZP
Newton-John, Olivia	Magic	33-275	CB
Newton-John, Olivia	Magic	11-498	DK
Newton-John, Olivia	Physical	17-57	DK
Newton-John, Olivia	Physical	5-147	SC
Newton-John, Olivia	Please Mister Please	4-380	SC
Newton-John, Olivia	Sweetest Thing the	8-198	CB
Newton-John, Olivia	Sweetest Thing the	45-9	MM
Newton, Juice	Angel Of The Morning	16-724	DK
Newton, Juice	Angel Of The Morning	9-571	SAV
Newton, Juice	Break It To Me Gently	5-22	SC
Newton, Juice	Break It To Me Gently	8-600	TT
Newton, Juice	Cheap Love	6-746	MM
Newton, Juice	Emotions	17-291	NA
Newton, Juice	Love's Been A Little Bit Hard On Me	33-42	CB
Newton, Juice	Love's Been A Little Bit Hard On Me	2-136	SC
Newton, Juice	Queen Of Hearts	35-161	CB
Newton, Juice	Queen Of Hearts	11-107	DK
Newton, Juice	Queen Of Hearts	13-440	P
Newton, Juice	Sweetest Thing the	6-738	MM
Newton, Juice	Sweetest Thing the	2-837	SC
Newton, Juice	They Never Made It To Me	14-732	CB
Newton, Juice	You Make Me Want To Make You...	34-257	CB
Newton, Juice	You Make Me Want To Make You...	38-133	SC
Newton, Wayne	Baby I'm A Want You	16-722	DK
Newton, Wayne	Baby I'm A Want You	47-319	MM
Newton, Wayne	But Not For Me	47-316	LE
Newton, Wayne	Bye Bye Blackbird	47-311	LE
Newton, Wayne	Can't Take That Away From Me	47-313	LE
Newton, Wayne	Daddy Don't You Walk So Fast	47-307	LE
Newton, Wayne	Danke Schoen	12-529	P
Newton, Wayne	Danke Schoen	9-314	STR
Newton, Wayne	Has Anybody Seen My Gypsy Rose	47-318	LE
Newton, Wayne	I Know So	47-794	SRK
Newton, Wayne	L-O-V-E	47-308	LE
Newton, Wayne	More	47-310	LE
Newton, Wayne	Old Man Moses	47-314	LE
Newton, Wayne	Playground In My Mind	47-309	LE
Newton, Wayne	Red Roses For A Blue Lady	21-19	CB
Newton, Wayne	Remember When	47-315	LE
Newton, Wayne	Toot Toot Tootsie Goodbye	47-317	LE

ARTIST	SONG TITLE	#	TYPE
Newton, Wayne	Wives And Lovers	47-312	LE
Next	Duet - Too Close	21-561	PHM
Next	Imagine That	32-89	THM
Next	Too Close	21-561	PHM
Nichols, Gary	I Can't Love You Anymore	30-198	CB
Nichols, Gary	Unbroken Ground	30-89	CB
Nichols, Joe	Ain't Nobody Gonna Take That From Me	47-571	PS
Nichols, Joe	All I Need Is A Heart	47-573	PS
Nichols, Joe	Another Side Of You	30-454	CB
Nichols, Joe	Believers	37-40	CB
Nichols, Joe	Brokenheartsville	34-370	CB
Nichols, Joe	Brokenheartsville	25-413	MM
Nichols, Joe	Brokenheartsville	18-450	ST
Nichols, Joe	Brokenheartsville	32-42	THM
Nichols, Joe	Cool To Be A Fool	35-439	CB
Nichols, Joe	Cool To Be A Fool	19-531	ST
Nichols, Joe	Freaks Like Me	48-6	KCD
Nichols, Joe	Gimme That Girl	38-125	CB
Nichols, Joe	I'll Wait For You	30-50	CB
Nichols, Joe	If I Could Only Fly	47-574	PS
Nichols, Joe	If Nobody Believed In You	35-441	CB
Nichols, Joe	If Nobody Believed In You	20-325	ST
Nichols, Joe	Impossible the	33-174	CB
Nichols, Joe	Impossible the	25-192	MM
Nichols, Joe	Impossible the	16-705	ST
Nichols, Joe	It Ain't No Crime	36-395	CB
Nichols, Joe	It Ain't No Crime	47-324	THC
Nichols, Joe	It's All Good	47-321	KV
Nichols, Joe	Let It Snow	45-740	CB
Nichols, Joe	Let's Get Drunk And Fight	47-570	PS
Nichols, Joe	Shape I'm In the	47-320	CB
Nichols, Joe	She Only Smokes When She Drinks	25-607	MM
Nichols, Joe	She Only Smokes When She Drinks	19-60	ST
Nichols, Joe	She Only Smokes When She Drinks	32-268	THM
Nichols, Joe	She's All Lady	47-572	PS
Nichols, Joe	Size Matters (Someday)	29-186	CB
Nichols, Joe	Size Matters (Someday)	29-849	SC
Nichols, Joe	Size Matters (Someday)	29-709	ST
Nichols, Joe	Sunny And 75	42-34	ASK
Nichols, Joe	Sunny And 75	44-329	SSC
Nichols, Joe	Take It Off	37-356	CB
Nichols, Joe	Tequila Makes Her Clothes Fall Off	23-410	CB
Nichols, Joe	This Ole Boy	47-322	KV
Nichols, Joe	To Tell You The Truth I Lied	47-323	SC
Nichols, Joe	What's A Guy Gotta Do	22-91	CB
Nichols, Joe	What's a Guy Gotta Do	23-41	SC
Nichols, Joe	Who Are You When I'm Not Looking	47-569	PS

ARTIST	SONG TITLE	#	TYPE
Nichols, Joe	Xmas - Let It Snow	45-740	CB
Nichols, Joe	Yeah!	44-133	ASK
Nichols, Joe	Yeah!	43-256	BKD
Nichols, Turner	She Loves To Hear Me Rock	17-248	NA
Nick Cave & Badseeds	Into My Arms	44-311	SBI
Nick Cave & the Badseeds	Jubilee Street	43-80	SF
Nick Cave & the Badseeds	Mercy Seat the	43-78	SF
Nick Cave & the Badseeds	Red Right Hand	43-79	SF
Nickel Creek	Jealous Of The Moon	29-215	PHM
Nickel Creek	Lighthouses' Tale the	16-336	ST
Nickel Creek	Reasons Why	14-709	CB
Nickel Creek	Speak	19-56	ST
Nickel Creek	This Side	18-337	ST
Nickel Creek	When You Come Back Down	17-479	TT
Nickelback	Because Of You	22-348	CB
Nickelback	Far Away	46-315	SC
Nickelback	Feeling Way Too Damn Good	23-554	MM
Nickelback	Feeling Way Too Damn Good	45-811	SC
Nickelback	Figured You Out	19-668	CB
Nickelback	Figured You Out	23-272	THM
Nickelback	Gotta Be Somebody	45-810	SC
Nickelback	How You Remind Me	35-243	CB
Nickelback	If Everyone Cared	30-259	CB
Nickelback	If Everyone Cared	45-809	SC
Nickelback	If Today Was Your Last Day	36-20	PT
Nickelback	Leader Of Men	46-314	SC
Nickelback	Learn The Hard Way	19-347	STP
Nickelback	Never Again	46-313	SC
Nickelback	Photograph	30-131	PT
Nickelback	Rockstar	30-64	PHM
Nickelback	Savin' Me	30-161	PT
Nickelback	Savin' Me	30-276	SC
Nickelback	Side Of A Bullet	30-569	CB
Nickelback	Someday	19-653	CB
Nickelback	Someday	20-227	MM
Nickelback	Someday	23-173	PHM
Nickelback	Too Bad	30-648	THM
Nicks & Henley	Duet - Leather & Lace	12-378	DK
Nicks & Henley	Duet - Leather & Lace	4-763	SC
Nicks & Henley	Leather And Lace	12-378	DK
Nicks & Henley	Leather And Lace	4-763	SC
Nicks & Perry	Duet - Needles And Pins	47-899	SAV
Nicks & Petty	Duet - Stop Draggin' my Heart Aroun	13-199	P
Nicks & Petty	Needles And Pins - duet	47-899	SAV
Nicks & Petty	Stop Draggin' My Heart Around	13-199	P
Nicks with Dixie Chicks	Too Far From Texas	47-901	TU
Nicks, Stevie	After The Glitter Fades	16-126	SC

ARTIST	SONG TITLE	#	TYPE
Nicks, Stevie	Bella Donna	47-896	LE
Nicks, Stevie	Blue Denim	47-900	SC
Nicks, Stevie	Edge Of Seventeen	16-125	SC
Nicks, Stevie	Gypsy	47-898	PS
Nicks, Stevie	I Can't Wait	16-128	SC
Nicks, Stevie	If Anyone Falls	16-127	SC
Nicks, Stevie	If You Ever Did Believe	16-220	MM
Nicks, Stevie	If You Ever Did Believe	16-132	SC
Nicks, Stevie	Planets Of The Universe	47-897	MM
Nicks, Stevie	Rooms On Fire	47-895	LE
Nicks, Stevie	Stand Back	16-638	MM
Nicks, Stevie	Stand Back	16-130	SC
Nicks, Stevie	Talk To Me	16-636	MM
Nicks, Stevie	Talk To Me	16-129	SC
Nicole, Erica	Better Beer	41-55	PHN
Nicole, Erica	Better Beer	47-503	PHN
Niemann, Jerrod	Blue Bandana	47-326	BKD
Niemann, Jerrod	Drink To That All Night	43-138	ASK
Niemann, Jerrod	Lover Lover	47-325	CB
Niemann, Jerrod	One More Drinking Song	37-221	CB
Niemann, Jerrod	Only GOD Could Love You More	39-72	PHN
Niemann, Jerrod	Shinin' On Me	44-150	BKD
Niemann, Jerrod	What Do You Want From Me	37-209	AS
Night Ranger	Don't Tell Me You Love Me	12-780	P
Night Ranger	Don't Tell Me You Love Me	5-488	SC
Night Ranger	Sister Christain	16-244	AMS
Night Ranger	You Can Still Rock In America	37-64	SC
Nightingale, Maxine	Lead Me On	2-563	SC
Nightingale, Maxine	Right Back Where We Started	2-502	SC
Nightmare B4 Christmas	Halloween - This Is Halloween	45-196	HM
Nightmare B4 Christmas	Show - This Is Halloween	45-196	HM
Nillson	Everybody's Talkin'	11-541	DK
Nillson	Everybody's Talkin'	12-915	P
Nillson	Without You	13-221	P
Nilsson, Harry	Coconut	6-868	MM
Nilsson, Harry	Coconut	12-861	P
Nilsson, Harry	Coconut	5-642	SC
Nine Days	Absolutely (Story of a Girl)	35-219	CB
Nine Days	Absolutely (Story of a Girl)	14-466	SC
Nine Days	Absolutely (Story of a Girl)	15-784	THM
Nine Days	If I Am	15-433	PHM
Nine Inch Nails	Closer **	5-545	SC
Nine Inch Nails	Closer **	13-729	SGB
Nirvana	Heart Shaped Box	24-145	SC
Nirvana	In Bloom	6-42	SC
Nirvana	You Know You're Right	25-405	MM
Nirvana	You Know You're Right	18-823	THM

ARTIST	SONG TITLE	#	TYPE
Nitty Gritty Dirt Band	Bang Bang Bang	49-379	CB
Nitty Gritty Dirt Band	Catfish John	49-290	FMK
Nitty Gritty Dirt Band	Dance Little Jean	5-858	SC
Nitty Gritty Dirt Band	Fishin' In The Dark	8-13	CB
Nitty Gritty Dirt Band	Fishin' In The Dark	10-683	HE
Nitty Gritty Dirt Band	Fishin' In The Dark	5-253	SC
Nitty Gritty Dirt Band	Fishing In The Dark	35-391	CB
Nitty Gritty Dirt Band	I've Been Lookin'	5-618	SC
Nitty Gritty Dirt Band	Long Hard Road	19-413	SC
Nitty Gritty Dirt Band	Modern Day Romance	4-650	SC
Nitty Gritty Dirt Band	Mr. Bojangles	7-455	MM
Nitty Gritty Dirt Band	Mr. Bojangles	9-545	SAV
Nixons	Sister	4-665	SC
Nixons	Wire	24-109	SC
Nizlopi	Girls	30-692	SF
No Authority	Can I Get your Number	15-451	PHM
No Doubt	Don't Speak	15-411	SC
No Doubt	Hella Good	18-348	CB
No Doubt	Hella Good	18-411	MM
No Doubt	Hey Baby	33-401	CB
No Doubt	It's My Life	19-659	CB
No Doubt	Just A Girl	33-354	CB
No Doubt	Just A Girl	4-169	SC
No Doubt	Running	20-462	CB
No Doubt	Running	32-168	THM
No Doubt	Simple Kind Of Life	14-483	SC
No Doubt	Simple Kind Of Life	15-785	THM
No Doubt	Spiderwebs	24-110	SC
No Doubt	Underneath It All	18-434	CB
No Doubt&Lady Saw	Underneath It All	25-403	MM
No Mercy	When I Die	21-551	PHM
No Mercy	Where Do You Go	24-299	SC
Nobb, D.	Come On And Get My Love	9-680	SAV
Noble, Nick	Fallen Star a	10-751	JVC
Nolan, Kenny	I Like Dreamin'	22-925	SC
Nolans	I'm In The Mood For Dancing	49-51	ZVS
Nolen, Gabbie	Almost There	16-707	ST
Noonan, Paddy & Gr.	Irish - McNamara's Band	21-492	SC
NORE, Nina Sky & Daddy Yankee	Oye Mi Canto (Radio Vers)	37-107	SC
Norteno, Oro	Latino - El Coyote	18-3	SC
Norwood, Daron	Bad Dog No Biscuit	22-876	ST
Norwood, Daron	Cowboys Don't Cry	3-42	SC
Norwood, Daron	If I Ever Love Again	24-245	SC
Norwood, Daron	My Girl Friday	2-832	SC
Notorious B.I.G.	Big Poppa **	25-470	MM
Notorious B.I.G.	Hypnotize **	25-476	MM
Notorious BIG/Puff/	Mo Money Mo Problems	25-481	MM
Notorious Cherry Bo	Duet - It's Hard To Kiss The Lips..	23-404	CB
Notorious Cherry Bo	It's Hard To Kiss The Lips At...	23-404	CB
Notorious Cherry Bo	It's Hard To Kiss The Lips At...	30-14	SC
Notorious Cherry Bombs	Duet - It's Hard To Kiss The Lips...	30-14	SC

ARTIST	SONG TITLE	#	TYPE
Nouveau	Lean On Me	20-371	SC
Nu Flavor	Sweet Sexy Thing	10-96	SC
Nugent, Ted	Cat Scratch Fever	14-560	AH
Nugent, Ted	Cat Scratch Fever	35-128	CB
Nugent, Ted	Cat Scratch Fever	20-316	MH
Nugent, Ted	Free For All	4-560	SC
Nugent, Ted	Hey Baby	10-482	DA
Nugent, Ted	Hey Baby	10-740	JVC
Nugent, Ted	Just What The Dr. Ordered	19-278	SGB
Nugent, Ted	Motor City Madhouse	17-473	SC
Nugent, Ted	Stranglehold	36-129	SGB
Nutini, Paolo	Last Request	30-786	SF
Nutmegs	Story Untold	25-550	MM
O Brother Where	Show - Big Rock Candy Mountain	18-661	KB
O Brother Where	Show - Cindy	18-659	KB
O Brother Where	Show - I Am A Man Of Constant Sorro	18-656	KB
O Brother Where	Show - I'll Fly Away	18-658	KB
O Brother Where	Show - In The Jailhouse Now	18-660	KB
O Brother Where	Show - Salty Dog	18-662	KB
O Brother Where	Show - Say Darlin' Say	18-663	KB
O Brother Where	Show - You Are My Sunshine	18-657	KB
O-Town	All Or Nothing	15-460	PHM
O-Town	All Or Nothing	18-543	TT
O-Town	I Showed Her	20-627	NS
O-Town	Liquid Dreams	35-254	CB
O-Town	Liquid Dreams	12-390	PHM
O-Town	These Are The Days	25-404	MM
O-Town	These Are The Days	32-61	THM
O-Town	We Fit Together	25-44	MM
O"Ryan	Take It Slow	30-810	PHM
O'Connor & Scott	Fade Into You - Nashville	45-469	KVD
O'Connor & Scott	Show - Fade Into You - Nashville	45-469	KVD
O'Connor, Sinead	Nothing Compares 2 U	28-438	DK
O'Connor, Sinead	Nothing Compares 2 U	6-174	MM
O'Connor, Sinead	Nothing Compares 2 U	12-842	P
O'Day, Allan	Undercover Angel	4-385	SC
O'Hara, Jamie	50,000 Names	2-428	SC
O'Jays	Back Stabbers	16-765	DK
O'Jays	Back Stabbers	16-561	P
O'Jays	Back Stabbers	9-752	SAV
O'Jays	Backstabbers	9-223	PT
O'Jays	Duet - Love Train	13-180	P
O'Jays	Emotionally Yours	10-679	HE
O'Jays	For The Love Of Money	9-758	SAV
O'Jays	I Love Music	9-762	SAV
O'Jays	Love Train	35-115	CB
O'Jays	Love Train	26-398	DK
O'Jays	Love Train	13-180	P
O'Jays	Love Train	9-227	PT
O'Jays	Love Train	9-770	SAV
O'Jays	Use Ta Be My Girl	17-139	DK

ARTIST	SONG TITLE	#	TYPE
O'Jays	Use Ta Be My Girl	24-340	SC
O'Kaysions	Girl Watcher	35-72	CB
O'Kaysions	Girl Watcher	27-328	DK
O'Kaysions	Girl Watcher	3-255	SC
O'Kaysions	I'm A Girl Watcher	12-667	P
O'Keefe, Danny	Good Time Charlie's Got The Blues	9-500	SAV
O'Neal, Jamie	Every Little Thing	34-399	CB
O'Neal, Jamie	Every Little Thing	19-61	ST
O'Neal, Jamie	Frantic	25-285	MM
O'Neal, Jamie	God Don't Make Mistakes	30-357	CB
O'Neal, Jamie	I Love My Life	29-46	CB
O'Neal, Jamie	Like A Woman	36-262	PHM
O'Neal, Jamie	Shiver	25-7	MM
O'Neal, Jamie	Shiver	15-679	ST
O'Neal, Jamie	Soldier Comin' Home	36-319	PHM
O'Neal, Jamie	Somebody's Hero	22-333	CB
O'Neal, Jamie	There Is No Arizona	14-100	CB
O'Neal, Jamie	Trying To Find Atlantis	22-78	CB
O'Neal, Jamie	Trying To Find Atlantis	21-659	SC
O'Neal, Jamie	When I Think About Angels	33-169	CB
O'Neal, Jamie	When I Think About Angels	9-867	ST
O'Neal. Jamie	Frantic	16-427	ST
O'Neil, Todd	Cajun - Cajun Queen	49-389	CB
O'Neil, Todd	Cajun Queen	49-389	CB
O'Ryan	Take It Slow	30-810	PHM
O'Sullivan, Gilbert	Alone Again	4-384	SC
O'Sullivan, Gilbert	Ooh Baby	24-198	SC
Oak Ridge Boys	American Made	23-493	CB
Oak Ridge Boys	American Made	26-598	DK
Oak Ridge Boys	American Made	13-404	P
Oak Ridge Boys	American Made	29-657	SC
Oak Ridge Boys	Bobbie Sue	23-494	CB
Oak Ridge Boys	Bobbie Sue	9-508	SAV
Oak Ridge Boys	Bobbie Sue	5-665	SC
Oak Ridge Boys	Come On In	9-573	SAV
Oak Ridge Boys	Elvira	8-264	CB
Oak Ridge Boys	Elvira	11-221	DK
Oak Ridge Boys	Elvira	6-764	MM
Oak Ridge Boys	Elvira	13-352	P
Oak Ridge Boys	Elvira	9-438	SAV
Oak Ridge Boys	Everyday	23-506	CB
Oak Ridge Boys	Fancy Free	23-505	CB
Oak Ridge Boys	I'll Be True To You	23-504	CB
Oak Ridge Boys	I'll Be True To You	4-636	SC
Oak Ridge Boys	It Takes A Little Rain (To Make...)	23-496	CB
Oak Ridge Boys	Leavin' Louisiana In The Broad Day-	23-507	CB
Oak Ridge Boys	Love Song	47-330	VH
Oak Ridge Boys	Lucky Moon	23-497	CB
Oak Ridge Boys	No Matter How High	23-498	CB
Oak Ridge Boys	Sail Away	47-327	ASK
Oak Ridge Boys	Thank God For Kids	23-499	CB
Oak Ridge Boys	This Crazy Love	47-329	SC

ARTIST	SONG TITLE	#	TYPE
Oak Ridge Boys	Trying To Love Two Women	33-61	CB
Oak Ridge Boys	Trying To Love Two Women	13-476	P
Oak Ridge Boys	Way Down	47-328	NS
Oak Ridge Boys	Xmas - Thank God For Kids	14-547	SC
Oak Ridge Boys	Y'All Come Back Saloon	23-502	CB
Oak Ridge Boys	Ya'll Come Back Saloon	2-402	SC
Oak Ridge Boys	You're My Soul & Inspiration	23-501	CB
Oak Ridge Boys	You're The One	23-503	CB
Oasis	Acquiesce	16-215	MM
Oasis	Champagne Supernova	43-112	SC
Oasis	Don't Go Away	7-688	PHM
Oasis	Masterplan	21-616	SF
Oasis	Wonderwall	30-219	PHM
Ocean	Duet - Put Your Hand In The Hand	17-27	DK
Ocean	Duet - Put Your Hand In The Hand	24-61	SC
Ocean	Put Your Hand In The Hand	17-27	DK
Ocean	Put Your Hand In The Hand	24-61	SC
Ocean, Billy	Caribbean Queen	11-591	DK
Ocean, Billy	Colour Of Love the	22-921	SC
Ocean, Billy	Get Outta My Dreams Get Into My..	3-547	SC
Ocean, Billy	Suddenly	6-570	MM
Ocean, Billy	Suddenly	2-277	SC
Ocean, Billy	There'll Be Sad Songs (To Make U Cr	25-285	MM
Ocean, Billy	There'll Be Sad Songs To...	35-205	CB
Ocean, Billy	When The Going Gets Tough	48-574	DK
Ofarim, Esther & Ab	Cinderella Rockafella	10-637	SF
Ofarim, Esther & Ab	Duet - Cinderella Rockafella	10-637	SF
Offspring	Come Out And Play	5-749	SC
Offspring	Defy You	30-647	THM
Offspring	Gotta Get Away	6-39	SC
Offspring	Hit That	20-567	CB
Offspring	Pretty Fly (For A White Guy)	7-790	PHT
Ohio Express	Chewy Chewy	16-665	LC
Ohio Express	Yummy Yummy Yummy	22-439	SC
Ohio Players	Fire	35-126	CB
Ohio Players	Fire	12-707	P
Ohio Players	Love Rollercoaster	2-504	SC
Oingo Boingo	Dead Man's Party - Halloween	45-118	SC
Oingo Boingo	Halloween - Dead Man's Party	45-118	SC
Oklahoma	Show - I Cain't Say No	7-370	MM
Oklahoma	Show - Oh What a Beautiful AM	14-382	PS
Oklahoma	Show - Oh What A Beautiful AM	2-283	SC

ARTIST	SONG TITLE	#	TYPE
Oklahoma	Show - Oh What A Beautiful Morning	27-383	DK
Oklahoma	Show - Oklahoma	27-384	DK
Oklahoma	Show - Oklahoma	2-292	SC
Oklahoma	Show - Surrey With the Fringe/Top	12-292	DK
Oklahoma	Surrey With The Fringe On	12-292	DK
Old Dominion	Break Up With Him	45-455	BKD
Old Dominion	Break Up With Him (Inst)	49-794	BKD
Old Dominion	Nowhere Fast	47-398	BKD
Old Dominion	Snapback	48-4	KCD
Oliver	As Long As He Needs Me	15-401	MM
Oliver	As Long As He Needs Me - show	48-788	MM
Oliver	Consider Yourself	12-179	DK
Oliver	Jean	12-572	P
Oliver	Show - As Long As He Needs Me	27-385	DK
Oliver	Show - As Long As He Needs Me	18-811	PS
Oliver	Show - As Long As He Needs Me	48-788	MM
Oliver	Show - Good Morning Starshine	11-346	DK
Oliver	Show - I'd Do Anything	6-250	MM
Oliver	Show - Where Is Love	17-805	PS
Oliver	Who Will Buy	12-197	DK
Olympics	Hully Gully (Baby) - DANCE #	22-398	SC
Olympics	Western Movies	6-682	MM
Olympics	Western Movies	5-463	SC
OMC	How Bizarre	15-495	SC
On A Clear Day	Show - On A Clear Day	6-883	MM
On The Town	Show - N.Y. N.Y. What a Wonderful	10-379	KC
Once Blue	Save Me	24-236	SC
One Direction	Diana	43-180	ASK
One Direction	Drag Me Down	48-446	KCD
One Direction	Night Changes	48-326	MRH
One Direction	One Thing	39-41	ASK
One Direction	Perfect	48-260	SBI
One Direction	Stole My Heart	39-112	PHM
One Direction	Tell Me A Lie	39-109	PHM
One Direction	What Makes You Beautiful	39-42	ASK
One Voice	When U Think About Me	9-335	PS
One Way	Cutie Pie	14-364	MH
OneRepublic	All The Right Moves	44-139	BKD
OneRepublic	Burning Bridges	47-334	KV
OneRepublic	Counting Stars	44-90	ASK
OneRepublic	Counting Stars	45-3	KV
OneRepublic	Good Life the	47-332	CB
OneRepublic	Say (All I Need)	36-517	CB
OneRepublic	Say (All I Need)	47-331	CB
OneRepublic	Secrets	44-140	BKD
OneRepublic	Something I Need	47-333	KV
OneRepublic	Stop & Stare	49-855	SC

ARTIST	SONG TITLE	#	TYPE
OneRepublic	Stop And Stare	36-457	CB
OneRepublic	Stop And Stare	44-107	SC
Oquai, James	Cosmic Girl	21-598	SF
Orbison, Roy	Beautiful Dreamer	47-343	DFK
Orbison, Roy	Blue Angel	35-37	CB
Orbison, Roy	Blue Angel	9-191	SO
Orbison, Roy	Blue Bayou	33-243	CB
Orbison, Roy	Blue Bayou	9-192	SO
Orbison, Roy	Born On The Wind	38-51	ZM
Orbison, Roy	Candy Man	9-193	SO
Orbison, Roy	Claudette	38-52	ZM
Orbison, Roy	Comedians the	45-596	OZP
Orbison, Roy	Crawling Back	47-339	PG
Orbison, Roy	Crowd the	38-53	ZM
Orbison, Roy	Crying	17-26	DK
Orbison, Roy	Crying	14-553	SC
Orbison, Roy	Crying	10-508	SF
Orbison, Roy	Crying	9-182	SO
Orbison, Roy	Crying Time	47-732	SRK
Orbison, Roy	Dream Baby	9-595	SAV
Orbison, Roy	Dream Baby	9-185	SO
Orbison, Roy	Dream You (All I Can Do)	47-346	PS
Orbison, Roy	Falling	38-54	ZM
Orbison, Roy	Gigolette	47-338	HM
Orbison, Roy	Go Go Go	47-347	PS
Orbison, Roy	Goodnight	38-55	CB
Orbison, Roy	Heartache	47-342	DCK
Orbison, Roy	Heartbreak Radio	47-348	RDK
Orbison, Roy	Here Comes That Song Again	38-62	AT
Orbison, Roy	House Without Windows	38-63	PS
Orbison, Roy	I Drove All Night	38-56	SF
Orbison, Roy	I'm Hurtin'	38-57	ZM
Orbison, Roy	In Dreams	20-29	SC
Orbison, Roy	In Dreams	9-189	SO
Orbison, Roy	It Takes One To Know One	47-340	BFK
Orbison, Roy	It's Over	9-190	SO
Orbison, Roy	Lana	38-58	SF
Orbison, Roy	Let's Make A Memory	47-335	BAT
Orbison, Roy	Lonely Wine	47-344	FMK
Orbison, Roy	Look In My Eyes Pretty Woman	47-350	LE
Orbison, Roy	Love Hurts	38-64	PS
Orbison, Roy	Mean Woman Blues	38-59	LE
Orbison, Roy	Oh Pretty Woman	11-181	DK
Orbison, Roy	Oh Pretty Woman	3-326	MH
Orbison, Roy	Oh Pretty Woman	9-465	SAV
Orbison, Roy	Only The Lonely	16-772	DK
Orbison, Roy	Only The Lonely	3-319	MH
Orbison, Roy	Only The Lonely	12-730	P
Orbison, Roy	Only The Lonely	9-493	SAV
Orbison, Roy	Only The Lonely	29-837	SC
Orbison, Roy	Only The Lonely	10-555	SF
Orbison, Roy	Only The Lonely	9-183	SO
Orbison, Roy	Ooby Dooby	9-195	SO

ARTIST	SONG TITLE	#	TYPE
Orbison, Roy	Paper Boy	47-336	BAT
Orbison, Roy	Penny Arcade	38-60	SF
Orbison, Roy	Pretty Paper	9-187	SO
Orbison, Roy	Pretty Woman	9-184	SO
Orbison, Roy	Ride Away	9-196	SO
Orbison, Roy	Running Scared	5-235	SC
Orbison, Roy	Running Scared	9-188	SO
Orbison, Roy	Sentimental	47-341	DCK
Orbison, Roy	Spanish Nights	47-337	BAT
Orbison, Roy	Summer Song	38-65	PS
Orbison, Roy	Sunset	38-66	PS
Orbison, Roy	Sweet Dream Baby	9-194	SO
Orbison, Roy	They Call You Gigolette	38-61	AT
Orbison, Roy	Today's Teardrops	47-735	SRK
Orbison, Roy	Uptown	38-50	PS
Orbison, Roy	Walk On	38-49	PS
Orbison, Roy	When We All Sang Along	47-349	KV
Orbison, Roy	Working For The Man	47-345	KVD
Orbison, Roy	You Got It	9-524	SAV
Orbison, Roy	You Got It	4-289	SC
Orbison, Roy	You Got It	9-186	SO
Ordinary Boys&Lady	Duet - Nine2Five	30-710	SF
Ordinary Boys&Lady	Nine2Five	30-710	SF
Orgy	Opticon	15-305	THM
Orlando & Dawn	Candida	3-245	LG
Orlando & Dawn	Candida	21-809	SC
Orlando & Dawn	Has Anybody Seen My Sweet Gypsy Ros	3-243	LG
Orlando & Dawn	He Don't Love You Like I Love You	35-132	CB
Orlando & Dawn	He Don't Love You Like I Love You	11-523	DK
Orlando & Dawn	Knock Three Times	3-244	LG
Orlando & Dawn	Knock Three Times	13-250	P
Orlando & Dawn	Knock Three Times	8-619	SAV
Orlando & Dawn	Knock Three Times	5-115	SC
Orlando & Dawn	Steppin' Out (Gonna Boogie Tonight)	49-323	CB
Orlando & Dawn	Sweet Gypsy Rose	7-103	MM
Orlando & Dawn	Tie A Yellow Ribbon	12-128	DK
Orlando & Dawn	Tie A Yellow Ribbon	3-246	LG
Orlando & Dawn	Tie A Yellow Ribbon	6-353	MM
Orlando & Dawn	When We All Sang Along	49-33	SHER
Orlando & Dawn	Who's In The Strawberry Patch	3-242	LG
Orleans	Dance With Me	2-863	SC
Orleans	Still The One	16-405	PR
Orleans	Still The One	22-923	SC
Orrico, Stacie	Genuine	35-304	CB
Orrico, Stacie	More To Life	21-613	SF
Orrico, Stacie	More To Life (There's Gotta Be)	32-358	THM
Orrico, Stacie	Stuck	34-176	CB
Orrico, Stacie	Stuck	20-379	HP
Orrico, Stacie	Stuck	25-631	MM
Orrico, Stacie	Stuck	20-625	NS

213

ARTIST	SONG TITLE	#	TYPE
Orrico, Stacie	Stuck	32-208	THM
Orrico, Stacie	There's Got To Be More To Life	19-645	CB
Orson	No Tomorrow	30-700	SF
Orton, Beth	Conceived	29-275	PHM
Osborne, Jeffrey	On The Wings Of Love	27-239	DK
Osborne, Jeffrey	On The Wings Of Love	13-148	P
Osborne, Jeffrey	On The Wings Of Love	2-279	SC
Osborne, Jeffrey	One The Wings Of Love	6-562	MM
Osborne, Jeffrey	Stay With Me Tonight	25-283	MM
Osborne, Joan	One Of Us	19-580	MH
Osborne, Joan	One Of Us	10-240	PS
Osborne, Joan	One Of Us	15-546	THM
Osborne, Joan	Right Hand Man	10-241	PS
Osborne, Joan	St. Theresa	10-239	PS
Osborne, Joan	Who Divided	30-254	CB
Osbourne & Ford	Close My Eyes Forever	23-427	SC
Osbourne & Ford	Duet - Close My Eyes Forever	23-427	SC
Osbourne Brothers	Rocky Top	8-47	CB
Osbourne Brothers	Rocky Top	12-96	DK
Osbourne, Ozzy	Crazy Train	23-424	SC
Osbourne, Ozzy	Crazy Train	13-745	SGB
Osbourne, Ozzy	Flying High Again	23-426	SC
Osbourne, Ozzy	Gets Me Through	16-317	TT
Osbourne, Ozzy	Goodbye To Romance	13-754	SGB
Osbourne, Ozzy	Mama I'm Coming Home	23-421	SC
Osbourne, Ozzy	No More Tears	23-423	SC
Osbourne, Ozzy	Over The Mountain	21-754	SC
Osbourne, Ozzy	Shot In The Dark	5-487	SC
Oslin, K.T.	80's Ladies	6-742	MM
Oslin, K.T.	80's Ladies	2-615	SC
Oslin, K.T.	Come Next Monday	6-618	MM
Oslin, K.T.	Come Next Monday	12-420	P
Oslin, K.T.	Come Next Monday	9-443	SAV
Oslin, K.T.	Come Next Monday	2-809	SC
Oslin, K.T.	Do Ya	29-69	CB
Oslin, K.T.	Hold Me	4-785	SC
Oslin, K.T.	I'll Always Come Back	33-49	CB
Oslin, K.T.	New Way Home	4-148	SC
Oslin, K.T.	Silver Tongue And Gold Plated Lies	4-451	SC
Osmond, Donny	Could She Be Mine	47-868	ZP
Osmond, Donny	Go Away Little Girl	33-274	CB
Osmond, Donny	I Can See Clearly Now	47-865	ZP
Osmond, Donny	Keep Her In Mind	47-863	ZP
Osmond, Donny	Puppy Love	13-316	P
Osmond, Donny	Soldier Of Love	47-853	SFM
Osmond, Donny	Sweet And Innocent	47-851	SBI
Osmond, Donny	What I Meant To Say	47-862	ZP
Osmond, Donny	When Children Rule The World	47-848	BSP
Osmond, Donny	Why	47-857	ZM
Osmond, Donny	Young Love	47-855	ZM
Osmond, Donny & Marie	Duet - Good Life the	47-850	PHN
Osmond, Donny & Marie	Duet - I'm Leaving It All Up To You	47-858	ZM

ARTIST	SONG TITLE	#	TYPE
Osmond, Donny & Marie	Duet - Little Bit Country Little Bit...	47-861	VH
Osmond, Donny & Marie	Duet - Morning Side Of The Mountain	47-845	FMG
Osmond, Donny & Marie	Good Life the - duet	47-850	PHN
Osmond, Donny & Marie	I'm Leaving It All Up To You - duet	47-858	ZM
Osmond, Donny & Marie	Little Bit Country Little Bit Rock&Roll	47-861	VH
Osmond, Donny & Marie	Morning Side Of The Mountain - duet	47-845	FMG
Osmond, Marie	Least Of All You	47-867	ZP
Osmond, Marie	Paper Roses	11-826	DK
Osmond, Marie	Paper Roses	13-427	P
Osmond, Marie	Paper Roses	5-125	SC
Osmond, Marie	Read My Lips	47-852	SC
Osmond, Marie	There's No Stoppin Your Heart	4-795	SC
Osmonds	Crazy Horses	47-849	MFK
Osmonds	Down By The Lasy River	47-864	ZP
Osmonds	Goin' Home	47-859	ZM
Osmonds	I Can't Stop	47-854	SFM
Osmonds	Let Me In	47-860	ZM
Osmonds	Love Me For A Reason	47-856	ZM
Osmonds	One Bad Apple	33-276	CB
Osmonds	One Bad Apple	17-66	DK
Osmonds	Proud One the	47-866	ZP
Osmonds	Remember Me	47-869	ZP
Ottawan	Hands Up	49-457	MM
Otto, James	Days Of Our Lives	20-275	SC
Otto, James	Days Of Our Lives	19-686	ST
Otto, James	For You	36-603	CB
Otto, James	For You	36-211	PHM
Otto, James	Just Got Started Lovin' You	36-392	CB
Otto, James	These Are The Good Old Days	36-263	PHM
Our Lady Peace	Clumsy	5-273	SC
Our Lady Peace	Somewhere Out There	25-401	MM
Our Lady Peace	Superman's Dead	6-37	SC
Outfield	Closer To Me	45-371	OZP
Outfield	For You	45-372	KV
Outfield	Since You've Been Gone	45-373	KV
Outfield	Your Love	45-374	PHM
Outkast	Hey Ya!	20-528	CB
Outkast	Hey Ya!	20-231	MM
Outkast	Ms. Jackson	25-462	MM
Outkast	Ms. Jackson	18-568	TT
Outlaws	Ghost Riders In The Sky	48-656	SC
Outlaws	Green Grass And High Tides	48-657	CB
Outlaws	Hurry Sundown	48-658	CB
Outlaws	There Goes Another Love	7-463	MM
Outlaws	There Goes Another Love	2-522	SC
Outshyne	Country Boy In Me	38-255	PHN
Outsiders	Time Won't Let Me	6-48	SC

ARTIST	SONG TITLE	#	TYPE
Outspoken	Farther	32-148	THM
Overstreet, Paul	All The Fun	14-686	CB
Overstreet, Paul	Ann Don't Go Runnin'	5-564	SC
Overstreet, Paul	Ball And Chain	29-769	CB
Overstreet, Paul	Ball And Chain	12-57	DK
Overstreet, Paul	Ball And Chain	10-781	JVC
Overstreet, Paul	Ball And Chain	9-531	SAV
Overstreet, Paul	Daddy's Come Around	29-768	CB
Overstreet, Paul	Daddy's Come Around	12-41	DK
Overstreet, Paul	Heroes	29-770	CB
Overstreet, Paul	If I Could Bottle This Up	29-773	CB
Overstreet, Paul	Sowin' Love	29-771	CB
Overstreet, Paul	We've Got To Keep On Meeting	4-128	SC
Owen, Jake	After The Music Stopped	44-393	ASK
Owen, Jake	Alone With You	38-210	PHN
Owen, Jake	American Country Love Song	49-4	DCK
Owen, Jake	Anywhere With You	45-397	BKD
Owen, Jake	Barefoot Blue Jean Night	37-215	AS
Owen, Jake	Beachin'	44-18	KCDC
Owen, Jake	Days Of Gold	45-641	ASK
Owen, Jake	Don't Think I Can't Love You	45-643	ASK
Owen, Jake	Eight Second Ride	37-59	CB
Owen, Jake	Eight Second Ride (Inst)	49-391	DCK
Owen, Jake	Ghost Town	45-639	ASK
Owen, Jake	Heaven	49-186	SBI
Owen, Jake	I Like You A Lot	43-131	ASK
Owen, Jake	One That Got Away the	39-21	ASK
Owen, Jake	Something About A Woman	36-420	CB
Owen, Jake	Something About A Woman	49-899	SC
Owen, Jake	Startin' With Me	30-175	CB
Owen, Jake	Tell Me	45-666	CB
Owen, Jake	What We Ain't Got	45-640	SSC
Owen, Jake	Yee-Haw	29-374	CB
Owens & Yoakum	Duet - I Was There	46-104	CB
Owens & Yoakum	I Was There - duet	46-104	CB
Owens, Buck	Above And Beyond	46-101	KWD
Owens, Buck	Act Naturally	8-35	CB
Owens, Buck	Act Naturally	17-297	NA
Owens, Buck	Act Naturally	13-456	P
Owens, Buck	Before You Go	3-909	CB
Owens, Buck	Big In Vegas	5-843	SC
Owens, Buck	Close Up The Honky Tonks	46-108	KVD
Owens, Buck	Crying Time	46-102	VH
Owens, Buck	Excuse Me I Think I've Got A Hearta	14-330	SC
Owens, Buck	Hello Trouble Come On In	46-107	CB
Owens, Buck	I Don't Care	3-200	SC
Owens, Buck	I Don't Care (Just As Long As...)	34-206	CB

ARTIST	SONG TITLE	#	TYPE
Owens, Buck	I've Got A Tiger By The Tail	8-784	CB
Owens, Buck	I've Got A Tiger By The Tail	12-54	DK
Owens, Buck	I've Got A Tiger By The Tail	6-777	MM
Owens, Buck	It Takes People Like You	46-106	CB
Owens, Buck	Kansas City Song	46-109	SC
Owens, Buck	Keys In The Mailbox	44-52	KV
Owens, Buck	Keys In The Mailbox	45-848	VH
Owens, Buck	Love's Gonna Live Here Again	15-81	CB
Owens, Buck	Love's Gonna Live Here Again	12-36	DK
Owens, Buck	Made In Japan	46-105	CB
Owens, Buck	My Heart Skips A Beat	22-244	SC
Owens, Buck	Open Up Your Heart	4-808	SC
Owens, Buck	Pfft You Were Gone	40-49	SRK
Owens, Buck	Rollin' In My Sweet Baby's Arms	8-617	SAV
Owens, Buck	Ruby (Are You Mad at Your Man)	39-8	CB
Owens, Buck	Sam's Place	5-702	SC
Owens, Buck	Together Again	15-829	CB
Owens, Buck	Together Again	17-18	DK
Owens, Buck	Together Again	8-616	SAV
Owens, Buck	Truck Driving Man	46-100	KWD
Owens, Buck	Under Your Spell Again	8-386	CB
Owens, Buck	Under Your Spell Again	8-618	SAV
Owens, Buck	Under Your Spell Again	4-261	SC
Owens, Buck	Waitin' In Your Welfare Line	15-88	CB
Owens, Buck	Waitin' In Your Welfare Line	4-870	SC
Owens, Buck	Who's Gonna Mow Your Grass	46-103	VH
Owens, Buck	Xmas - Santa Looked A Lot Like Dadd	8-64	CB
Owens, Buck	Xmas - Santa Looked a Lot Like Dadd	14-543	SC
Ozark Mtn Daredevil	If You Wanna Get To Heaven	7-454	MM
Ozark Mtn Daredevil	If You Wanna Get To Heaven	2-536	SC
Ozark Mtn Daredevil	Jackie Blue	7-460	MM
Ozark Mtn Daredevil	Jackie Blue	2-532	SC
P Diddy&Feat&Usher	I Need A Girl	17-596	PHM
P. Diddy	Bump Bump Bump	32-122	THM
P. O. D.	Alive	16-308	TT
P.M. Dawn	I'd Die Without You	47-351	SC
Pablo Cruise	Love Will Find A Way	5-607	SC
Pablo Cruise	Whatcha Gonna Do	15-735	SC
Pacifier	Bullitproof	32-110	THM
Page, Martin	In The House Of Stone & Light	28-425	DK
Page, Martin	Keeper Of The Flame	3-494	SC
Page, Patti	Alleghany Moon	2-245	SC
Page, Patti	Allegheny Moon	3-365	MH
Page, Patti	Boogie Woogie Santa	45-248	CB

ARTIST	SONG TITLE	#	TYPE
	Claus - xmas		
Page, Patti	Changing Partners	11-455	DK
Page, Patti	Doggie In The Window	33-213	CB
Page, Patti	I Went To Your Wedding	12-16	DK
Page, Patti	Let Me Go Lover	3-507	SC
Page, Patti	Mockingbird Hill	2-246	SC
Page, Patti	Old Cape Cod	10-463	MG
Page, Patti	Old Cape Cod	3-512	SC
Page, Patti	Tennessee Waltz	11-150	DK
Page, Patti	Tennessee Waltz	13-353	P
Page, Patti	Xmas - Boogie Woogie Santa Claus	45-248	CB
Paige, Allison	End Of The World the	9-429	CB
Paige, Allison	Send A Message	20-219	CB
Paige, Jennifer	Always You	5-784	SC
Paige, Jennifer	Crush	28-187	DK
Paisley & Alabama	Old Alabama	46-246	FTX
Paisley & Jackson	Duet - Out In The Parking Lot	48-495	CKC
Paisley & Jackson	Out On The Parking Lot - duet	48-495	CKC
Paisley & Krauss	Duet - Whiskey Lullaby	20-323	ST
Paisley & Krauss	Whiskey Lullaby	20-323	ST
Paisley & Underwood	Duet - Remind Me	37-355	CB
Paisley & Underwood	Remind Me - duet	37-355	CB
Paisley & Wright	Duet - Hard To Be A Husband/Wife	14-156	CB
Paisley & Wright	Duet - Hard To Be A Husband/Wife	14-789	ST
Paisley & Wright	Hard To Be A Husband/Wife	14-156	CB
Paisley & Wright	Hard To Be A Husband/Wife	14-789	ST
Paisley, Brad	Accidental Racist	43-455	ASK
Paisley, Brad	Alcohol	23-134	CB
Paisley, Brad	Anything Like Me	37-339	CB
Paisley, Brad	Camouflage	44-314	SBI
Paisley, Brad	Camouflage	45-58	KST
Paisley, Brad	Celebrity	34-394	CB
Paisley, Brad	Celebrity	25-568	MM
Paisley, Brad	Celebrity	19-5	ST
Paisley, Brad	Celebrity	32-260	THM
Paisley, Brad	Country Nation	49-879	DCK
Paisley, Brad	Crushin' It	45-39	BKD
Paisley, Brad	Flowers	36-375	SC
Paisley, Brad	He Didn't Have To Be	19-202	CB
Paisley, Brad	He Didn't Have to Be	19-228	SC
Paisley, Brad	He Didn't Have To Be	22-377	ST
Paisley, Brad	I Can't Change The World	43-15	KCDC
Paisley, Brad	I Can't Change The World	47-710	BKD
Paisley, Brad	I Wish You'd Stay	25-414	MM
Paisley, Brad	I Wish You'd Stay	18-202	ST
Paisley, Brad	I'm Gonna Miss Her	33-173	CB
Paisley, Brad	I'm Gonna Miss Her	25-182	MM

ARTIST	SONG TITLE	#	TYPE
Paisley, Brad	I'm Gonna Miss Her	16-429	ST
Paisley, Brad	I'm Still A Guy	36-401	CB
Paisley, Brad	In Times Like These	30-165	CB
Paisley, Brad	Letter To Me	36-430	CB
Paisley, Brad	Little Moments	35-431	CB
Paisley, Brad	Little Moments	19-527	ST
Paisley, Brad	Little Moments	32-415	THM
Paisley, Brad	Make A Mistake With Me	49-507	PCD
Paisley, Brad	Me Neither	13-835	CHM
Paisley, Brad	Me Neither	23-372	SC
Paisley, Brad	Me Neither	16-272	TT
Paisley, Brad	Mona Lisa the	43-152	ASK
Paisley, Brad	Moonshine In The Trunk	47-709	BKD
Paisley, Brad	Mr. Policeman	44-88	KV
Paisley, Brad	Mud On The Tires	21-653	SC
Paisley, Brad	Mud On The Tires	20-501	ST
Paisley, Brad	Online	30-528	CB
Paisley, Brad	Outstanding In Our Field	40-53	ASK
Paisley, Brad	River Bank	44-132	ASK
Paisley, Brad	Shattered Glass	45-347	KV
Paisley, Brad	She's Everything	29-201	CB
Paisley, Brad	She's Everything	30-101	PHM
Paisley, Brad	Then	37-36	CB
Paisley, Brad	Ticks	30-351	CB
Paisley, Brad	Two Feet Of Topsoil	45-578	OZP
Paisley, Brad	Two People Fell In Love	33-156	CB
Paisley, Brad	Two People Fell In Love	9-864	ST
Paisley, Brad	Two People Fell In Love	16-276	TT
Paisley, Brad	Waitin' On A Woman	36-602	CB
Paisley, Brad	Waitin' On A Woman	36-194	PHM
Paisley, Brad	Water	38-132	CB
Paisley, Brad	We Danced	14-913	CB
Paisley, Brad	We Danced	19-211	CSZ
Paisley, Brad	We Danced	22-558	ST
Paisley, Brad	Welcome To The Future	36-312	PHM
Paisley, Brad	When I Get Where I'm Going	23-485	CB
Paisley, Brad	Who Needs Pictures	8-927	CB
Paisley, Brad	Who Needs Pictures	22-748	ST
Paisley, Brad	Working On A Tan	49-231	DFK
Paisley, Brad	World the	29-362	CB
Paisley, Brad	Wrapped Around	33-161	CB
Paisley, Brad	Wrapped Around	25-3	MM
Paisley, Brad	Wrapped Around	15-672	ST
Paisley, Brad	You Need A Man Around Here	44-89	SRK
Paisley, Brad	You Need A Man Around Here	45-59	TBR
Pal Joey	Show - I Could Write A Book	6-875	MM
Palladio, Sam	It Ain't Yours To Throw Away	44-286	KCD
Pallot, Nerina	Everybody's Gone To War	30-708	SF
Palmer, H.	Just So You Know	32-435	THM
Palmer, Rissi	No Air	36-620	CB
Palmer, Robert	Addicted To Love	12-821	P
Palmer, Robert	Addicted To Love	5-118	SC

ARTIST	SONG TITLE	#	TYPE
Palmer, Robert	Addicted To Love	10-534	SF
Palmer, Robert	Bad Case Of Loving You	11-517	DK
Palmer, Robert	Bad Case Of Loving You	17-521	SC
Palmer, Robert	I Didn't Mean To Turn You On	11-226	DK
Palmer, Robert	I Didn't Mean To Turn You On	21-745	MH
Palmer, Robert	Let's Get It On	35-114	CB
Palmer, Robert	Let's Get It On	9-333	PS
Palmer, Robert	Simply Irresistible	11-391	DK
Palmer, Robert	Simply Irresistible	16-537	P
Palmer, Robert	Simply Irresistible	14-634	SC
Paltrow & Babyface	Duet - Just My Imagination	49-770	PR
Paltrow & Babyface	Just My Imagination - duet	49-770	PR
Panettiere, Hayden	Disappear - Nashville	45-466	BKD
Panettiere, Hayden	Love Like Mine - Nashville	45-464	BKD
Panettiere, Hayden	Show - Disappear - Nashville	45-466	BKD
Panettiere, Hayden	Show - Love Like Mine - Nashville	45-464	BKD
Panettiere, Hayden	Show - We Are Water - Nashville	45-468	BKD
Panettiere, Hayden	We Are Water - Nashville	45-468	BKD
Panic at the Disco	But It's Better If You Do	30-58	PHM
Panic at the Disco	Nine In The Afternoon	36-463	CB
Papa Roach	She Loves Me Not	18-429	CB
Papa Roach	Time And Time Again	18-830	THM
Paper Lace	Billy Don't Be A Hero	47-541	ZM
Paper Lace	My Way	47-542	TU
Paper Lace	Night Chicago Died the	9-347	AH
Paragons & Jesters	Please Let Me Love You	25-552	MM
Paramore	Misery Business	49-897	SC
Paramore	That's What You Get	36-526	CB
Pardi, John	Up All Night	41-57	PHN
Pardi, Jon	Head Over Boots	47-399	BKD
Pardi, Jon	Head Over Boots (Inst)	49-417	BKD
Pardi, Jon	Missing You Crazy	47-408	ASK
Pardi, Jon	What I Can't Put Down	47-409	ASK
Paris Sisters	I Love How You Love Me	12-562	P
Paris, Mica	Whisper A Prayer	24-268	SC
Paris, Sarina	Look At Us	34-148	CB
Park, Kyle	Night Is Young the	39-57	PHN
Parker, Caryl Mack	It's Good To Be Me	4-834	SC
Parker, Ray Jr.	Ghostbusters	2-73	SC
Parker, Ray Jr.	Ghostbusters	16-281	TT
Parker, Ray Jr.	Halloween - Ghostbusters	11-262	DK
Parker, Ray Jr.	Halloween - Ghostbusters	2-73	SC
Parker, Ray Jr.	Halloween - Ghostbusters	16-281	TT
Parker, Ray Jr.	Jamie	24-341	SC
Parker, Ray Jr.	Other Woman the	25-273	MM
Parliament	Flash Light	14-365	MH
Parmalee	Already Callin' You Mine	49-657	BKD

ARTIST	SONG TITLE	#	TYPE
Parmalee	Carolina	44-216	KCDC
Parmalee	Close Your Eyes	44-198	KCDC
Parmalee	Musta Had A Good Time	44-210	BKD
Parnell w/Brooks&D	Take These Chains From My Heart	2-326	SC
Parnell, Lee Roy	All That Matters Anymore	8-409	CB
Parnell, Lee Roy	All That Matters Anymore	22-778	ST
Parnell, Lee Roy	Country Down To My Soul	49-255	DFK
Parnell, Lee Roy	Crocodile Tears	49-273	CB
Parnell, Lee Roy	Family Tree	49-278	CB
Parnell, Lee Roy	Givin' Water To A Drowning Man	7-282	MM
Parnell, Lee Roy	Givin' Water To A Drowning Man	22-898	ST
Parnell, Lee Roy	Hearts Desire	49-281	SC
Parnell, Lee Roy	I'm Holding My Own	6-471	MM
Parnell, Lee Roy	If The House Is Rockin'	49-275	SC
Parnell, Lee Roy	Just Lucky That Way	49-279	DFK
Parnell, Lee Roy	Little Bit Of You a	7-27	MM
Parnell, Lee Roy	Little Bit Of You a	2-774	SC
Parnell, Lee Roy	Long Way To Fall	49-280	DFK
Parnell, Lee Roy	Love Without Mercy	49-274	SC
Parnell, Lee Roy	Lucky Me Lucky You	7-630	CHM
Parnell, Lee Roy	On The Radio	2-344	SC
Parnell, Lee Roy	Oughta Be A Law	49-272	CB
Parnell, Lee Roy	Power Of Love the	49-305	SC
Parnell, Lee Roy	She Won't Be Lonely Long	49-271	CB
Parnell, Lee Roy	Tender Moment	6-394	MM
Parnell, Lee Roy	Tender Moment	49-277	CB
Parnell, Lee Roy	We All Get Lucky Sometime	4-497	SC
Parnell, Lee Roy	What Kind Of Fool Do You Think I Am	48-332	CB
Parnell, Lee Roy	When A Woman Loves A Man	7-84	MM
Parnell, Lee Roy	When A Woman Loves A Man	3-570	SC
Parnell, Lee Roy	You Can't Get There From Here	22-622	ST
Parody	50 Ways To Get Bin Laden	49-307	RD
Parody	Bimbo # 5 (Mambo #5 Parody)	15-339	MM
Parody	Cats In The Kettle - parody	46-567	RDK
Parody	Girls In Leather Have Fun	49-309	WMP
Parody	Hair Keeps Falling Off My Head - parody	47-614	WMP
Parody	I Like Queers	47-875	ZP
Parody	I Shot Tequila	47-877	KRZ
Parody	My Favorite S & M Things	47-876	ZP
Parody	Oops I Farted Again	15-338	MM

ARTIST	SONG TITLE	#	TYPE
	(Parody)		
Parody	Parody - 50 Ways To Get Bin Laden	49-307	RD
Parody	Parody - Cats In The Kettle	46-567	RDK
Parody	Parody - Girls In Leather Have Fun	49-309	WMP
Parody	Parody - Hair Keeps Falling Off My Head	47-614	WMP
Parody	Parody - When A Man Loves A Chicken	49-308	RD
Parody	Parody - You Don't Smell Like Flowers	45-288	BS
Parody	Real Slim Shady (Parody)	15-345	MM
Parody	Stranglers In The Night	47-878	ADU
Parody	When A Man Loves A Chicken	49-308	RD
Parody	You Don't Smell Like Flowers - parody	45-288	BS
Parr, John	Naughty Naughty	6-22	SC
Parr, John	St. Elmo's Fire	20-374	SC
Parr, John	St. Elmo's Fire	10-520	SF
Parsons Project	Eye In The Sky	11-118	DK
Parsons Project	Eye In The Sky	9-785	SAV
Partners In Kryme	T-U-R-T-L-E Power	18-389	SAV
Parton & Gill	Duet - I Will Always Love You	7-78	MM
Parton & Gill	Duet - I Will Always Love You	3-566	SC
Parton & Gill	I Will Always Love You	7-78	MM
Parton & Gill	I Will Always Love You	3-566	SC
Parton & Jones, N.	Creepin' In	20-479	ST
Parton & Raye	Duet - Whenever Forever Comes	2-310	SC
Parton & Raye	Whenever Forever Comes	2-310	SC
Parton & Rogers	Christmas Without You	8-85	CB
Parton & Rogers	I Believe In Santa Claus	8-73	CB
Parton & Rogers	Lost Forever In Your Kisses	4-315	SC
Parton & Rogers	Once Upon A Christmas	46-98	DCK
Parton & Rogers	Xmas - Christmas Without You	8-85	CB
Parton & Rogers	Xmas - I Believe In Santa Claus	8-73	CB
Parton & Rogers	Xmas - Once Upon A Christmas	46-98	DCK
Parton & Van Shelton	Duet - Rockin' Years	49-338	CB
Parton & Van Shelton	Rockin' Years - duet	49-338	CB
Parton & Wagoner	Duet - Lost Forever In Your Kisses	4-315	SC
Parton, Dolly	9 To 5	8-544	CB
Parton, Dolly	9 To 5	26-307	DK
Parton, Dolly	9 To 5	12-690	P
Parton, Dolly	Applejack	34-318	CB
Parton, Dolly	Applejack	2-518	SC
Parton, Dolly	Bargain Store the	4-786	SC

ARTIST	SONG TITLE	#	TYPE
Parton, Dolly	Better Get To Livin'	30-581	CB
Parton, Dolly	But You Know I Love You	38-40	SC
Parton, Dolly	Coat Of Many Colors	8-533	CB
Parton, Dolly	Cross My Heart	4-139	SC
Parton, Dolly	Don't Call It Love	49-336	CB
Parton, Dolly	Duet - Real Love	13-394	P
Parton, Dolly	Duet - Romeo	8-545	CB
Parton, Dolly	Eagle When She Flies	3-639	SC
Parton, Dolly	Full Circle	8-822	CB
Parton, Dolly	Gospel - Shine	43-110	CB
Parton, Dolly	Gospel - the Seeker	43-96	CB
Parton, Dolly	Hard Candy Christmas	35-330	CB
Parton, Dolly	He's Alive	24-5	SC
Parton, Dolly	Heartbreaker	8-540	CB
Parton, Dolly	Heartbreaker	13-493	P
Parton, Dolly	Hello God	32-46	THM
Parton, Dolly	Here You Come Again	8-537	CB
Parton, Dolly	Here You Come Again	11-291	DK
Parton, Dolly	Here You Come Again	12-681	P
Parton, Dolly	Here You Come Again	9-600	SAV
Parton, Dolly	Honky Tonk Songs	8-768	CB
Parton, Dolly	I Really Got The Feeling	29-776	CB
Parton, Dolly	I Will Always Love You	17-300	NA
Parton, Dolly	I Will Always Love You	2-14	SC
Parton, Dolly	It's All Wrong But It's Alright	8-538	CB
Parton, Dolly	It's All Wrong But It's Alright	5-532	SC
Parton, Dolly	Jesus & Gravity	36-421	CB
Parton, Dolly	Jolene	8-535	CB
Parton, Dolly	Jolene	12-80	DK
Parton, Dolly	Jolene	13-443	P
Parton, Dolly	Just Someone I Used To Know	8-534	CB
Parton, Dolly	Just When I Needed You Most	7-379	MM
Parton, Dolly	Just When I Needed You Most	4-509	SC
Parton, Dolly	Light Of The Clear Blue Morning the	8-457	CB
Parton, Dolly	Love Is Like A Butterfly	4-313	SC
Parton, Dolly	Me And Little Andy	8-536	CB
Parton, Dolly	More Where That Came From	24-135	SC
Parton, Dolly	My Tennessee Mountain Home	49-333	CB
Parton, Dolly	Old Flames Can't Hold A Candle To U	29-628	CB
Parton, Dolly	Old Flames Can't Hold A Candle To U	8-543	CB
Parton, Dolly	Old Flames Can't Hold A Candle To U	5-662	SC
Parton, Dolly	Old Flames Can't Hold A Candle To U	9-544	SAV
Parton, Dolly	PMS Blues	3-648	SC
Parton, Dolly	Real Love	13-394	P
Parton, Dolly	Romeo	8-545	CB
Parton, Dolly	Romeo	17-388	DK

ARTIST	SONG TITLE	#	TYPE
Parton, Dolly	Romeo	12-404	P
Parton, Dolly	Salt In My Tears the	8-855	CB
Parton, Dolly	Save The Last Dance For Me	45-346	KV
Parton, Dolly	Seeker the	49-334	CB
Parton, Dolly	Silver And Gold	34-291	CB
Parton, Dolly	Silver And Gold	17-215	NA
Parton, Dolly	Single Women	45-667	DCK
Parton, Dolly	Slow Dancing With The Moon	24-249	SC
Parton, Dolly	Starting Over Again	8-542	CB
Parton, Dolly	Straight Talk	8-546	CB
Parton, Dolly	Straight Talk	4-478	SC
Parton, Dolly	Tennessee Homesick Blues	49-335	CB
Parton, Dolly	Tie Our Love In A Double Knot	9-470	SAV
Parton, Dolly	Time For Me To Fly	24-358	SC
Parton, Dolly	To Daddy	8-547	CB
Parton, Dolly	Together You And I	49-740	CB
Parton, Dolly	Two Doors Down	8-539	CB
Parton, Dolly	Two Doors Down	13-372	P
Parton, Dolly	Welcome Home	46-202	SC
Parton, Dolly	White Limozeen	49-337	CB
Parton, Dolly	Why'd You Come In Here Lookin'...	33-58	CB
Parton, Dolly	Why'd You Come In Here Lookin'...	10-778	JVC
Parton, Dolly	Why'd You Come In Here Lookin'...	2-98	SC
Parton, Dolly	Xmas - Hard Candy Christmas	8-54	CB
Parton, Dolly	Xmas - Hard Candy Christmas	3-396	SC
Parton, Dolly	Yellow Roses	17-315	NA
Parton, Dolly	Yellow Roses	4-66	SC
Parton, Dolly	You're The Only One	8-541	CB
Parton, Harris & Ronstadt	To Know Him Is To Love Him	49-353	CB
Parton&VanShelton	Duet - Rockin' Years	8-116	CB
Parton&VanShelton	Duet - Rockin' Years	2-300	SC
Parton&VanShelton	Rockin' Years	8-116	CB
Parton&VanShelton	Rockin' Years	2-300	SC
Partridge Family	Come On Get Happy	34-418	CB
Partridge Family	I Think I Love You	33-269	CB
Partridge Family	I Think I Love You	11-336	DK
Partridge Family	I Think I Love You	13-9	P
Paslay, Eric	Friday Night	43-278	ASK
Paslay, Eric	She Don't Love You	45-16	BKD
Paslay, Eric	Song About A Girl	44-275	PHN
Paslay, Eriic	Never Really Wanted	43-277	PHN
Passions	Just To Be With You	25-548	MM
Pat And Mick	I Haven't Stopped Dancing Yet	49-925	KVD
Patin, Rick	Americana Gold	41-101	PHN
Patriotic	America The Beautiful	44-43	PT
Patriotic	Anchors Away	44-39	PT
Patriotic	Battle Hymn Of The Republic	44-48	PT

ARTIST	SONG TITLE	#	TYPE
Patriotic	Caisson's Song	44-41	PT
Patriotic	God Bless America	44-36	PT
Patriotic	In The Halls Of Montezuma	44-42	PT
Patriotic	My Country 'Tis Of Thee	44-38	PT
Patriotic	Star Spangled Banner	44-35	PT
Patriotic	This Is My Country	44-44	PT
Patriotic	This Land Is Your Land	44-45	PT
Patriotic	When Johnny Comes Marching Home	44-49	PT
Patriotic	Wild Blue Yonder	44-40	PT
Patriotic	Yankee Doodle Boy	44-47	PT
Patriotic	Yankee Doodle Dandy	44-46	PT
Patriotic	You're A Grand Old Flag	44-50	PT
Paul & Ford	Vaya Con Dios	5-516	SC
Paul & Paula	Duet - Hey Paula	11-529	DK
Paul & Paula	Duet - Hey Paula	2-840	SC
Paul & Paula	Hey Paula	11-529	DK
Paul & Paula	Hey Paula	2-840	SC
Paul S	Gimme The Light	32-90	THM
Paul, Billy	Me And Mrs. Jones	11-379	DK
Paul, Billy	Me And Mrs. Jones	17-422	KC
Paul, Les & Ford, Mary	Vaya Con Dios	34-3	CB
Paul, Sean	Get Busy	32-238	THM
Paul, Sean	Get Busy	25-722	MM
Paul, Sean	Gimme The Light	32-90	THM
Paul, Sean	I'm Still In Love With You	23-247	THM
Paul, Sean	Like Glue	32-389	THM
Paul, Sean	Like Glue	25-716	MM
Paul, Sean	Like Glue	21-786	SC
Paula Cole Band	I Believe In Love	5-795	SC
Paxton & Clancy Bro	Wasn't That A Party	18-172	DK
Pay The Girl	Freeze	32-138	THM
Paycheck & Jones	Duet - You Can Have Her	45-214	SAV
Paycheck & Jones	You Can Have Her - duet	45-214	SAV
Paycheck & Miller	Duet - Let's All Go Down To/River	22-33	CB
Paycheck & Miller	Let's All Go Down To The River	22-33	CB
Paycheck & Miller, J	Duet - Let's All Go Down To The River	45-213	CB
Paycheck & Miller, J	Let's All Go Down To The River - duet	45-213	CB
Paycheck, Johnny	A-11	22-40	CB
Paycheck, Johnny	A-11	5-102	SC
Paycheck, Johnny	Apartment #9	45-212	SSK
Paycheck, Johnny	Don't Take Her She's All I Got	45-211	SBI
Paycheck, Johnny	For A Minute There	22-41	CB
Paycheck, Johnny	For A Minute There	45-210	CB
Paycheck, Johnny	Friend Lover Wife	22-35	CB
Paycheck, Johnny	Friend Lover Wife	19-445	SC
Paycheck, Johnny	I'm The Only Hell My Mama Ever Raised	22-37	CB
Paycheck, Johnny	I'm The Only Hell My Mama Ever Raised	3-606	SC

ARTIST	SONG TITLE	#	TYPE	ARTIST	SONG TITLE	#	TYPE
Paycheck, Johnny	Love Is A Good Thing	22-43	CB	Pearl Jam	I Got ID	9-308	RS
Paycheck, Johnny	Mr. Lovemaker	22-39	CB	Pearl Jam	Jeremy	33-353	CB
Paycheck, Johnny	My Part Of Forever	22-44	CB	Pearl Jam	Jeremy	9-298	RS
Paycheck, Johnny	Old Violin	22-45	CB	Pearl Jam	Last Kiss	30-217	PHM
Paycheck, Johnny	Outlaw's Prayer the	22-32	CB	Pearl Jam	Last Kiss	7-889	PHT
Paycheck, Johnny	Slide Off Of Your Satin Sheets	22-38	CB	Pearl Jam	Last Kiss	9-305	RS
Paycheck, Johnny	Slide Off Of Your Satin Sheets	14-309	SC	Pearl Jam	Last Kiss	13-777	SGB
Paycheck, Johnny	Someone To Give My Love To	22-34	CB	Pearl Jam	Light Years	15-646	THM
Paycheck, Johnny	Someone To Give My Love To	5-165	SC	Pearl Jam	Not For You	9-307	RS
Paycheck, Johnny	Something About You I Love	22-42	CB	Pearl Jam	Save You **	23-164	PHM
Paycheck, Johnny	Something About You I Love	5-819	SC	Pearl Jam	Who You Are	24-231	SC
Paycheck, Johnny	Song And Dance Man	22-36	CB	Pearl Jam	Wishlist	33-367	CB
Paycheck, Johnny	Song And Dance Man	5-625	SC	Pearl Jam	Yellow Ledbetter	9-294	RS
Paycheck, Johnny	Take This Job And Shove It	26-200	DK	Pebbles	Girlfriend	12-848	P
Paycheck, Johnny	Take This Job And Shove It	22-31	CB	Pebbles	Mercedes Boy	17-25	DK
Paycheck, Johnny	Take This Job And Shove It	15-341	MM	Pebbles	Mercedes Boy	16-545	P
Paycheck, Johnny	Take This Job And Shove It	12-429	P	Pebbles	Mercedes Boy	15-736	SC
Paycheck, Johnny	Take This Job And Shove It	8-681	SAV	Peck, Danielle	Bad For Me	30-534	CB
Payne, Freda	Band Of Gold	26-230	DK	Peck, Danielle	I Don't	29-31	CB
Payne, Freda	Band Of Gold	13-191	P	Peck, Danielle	Isn't That Everything	30-167	CB
Payne, Leon	I Love You Because	8-666	SAV	Peeples, Audrey	Makes No Sense At All - Nashville	45-462	BKD
Peach Union	On My Own	7-691	PHM	Peeples, Audrey	Show - Makes No Sense At All - Nashville	45-462	BKD
Peaches & Herb	Duet - Reunited	35-158	CB	Peevey, Gayla	Xmas - I Want A Hippopatamus For..	5-712	SC
Peaches & Herb	Duet - Reunited	13-150	P	Pendergrass, Teddy	Close The Door	15-719	LE
Peaches & Herb	Reunited	13-150	P	Pendergrass, Teddy	Love T.K.O.	15-718	LE
Peaches & Herb	Reunited - duet	35-158	CB	Penguins	Earth Angel	35-3	CB
Peaches & Herb	Shake Your Groove Thing	2-498	SC	Penguins	Earth Angel	7-313	MM
Peaches & Herb	Shake Your Groove Thing	15-37	SS	Penguins	Earth Angel	13-112	P
Pearl Jam	Alive	9-292	RS	Penguins	Earth Angel	9-18	PS
Pearl Jam	Animal	9-306	RS	Peniston, CeCe	Finally	17-367	DK
Pearl Jam	Better Man	9-300	RS	Peniston, CeCe	Im In The Mood	16-626	MM
Pearl Jam	Better Man	3-499	SC	Peniston, CeCe	Movin' On	24-290	SC
Pearl Jam	Black	9-303	RS	Peppermint Harris	I Got Loaded	2-406	SC
Pearl Jam	Black	24-139	SC	Perez, Amanda	Angel	34-156	CB
Pearl Jam	Breath	9-299	RS	Perez, Amanda	Angel	20-629	NS
Pearl Jam	Daughter	9-295	RS	Perez, Amanda	Angel	18-770	PHM
Pearl Jam	Dissident	9-297	RS	Perez, Chris	Best I Can the	8-532	PHT
Pearl Jam	Duet - Hunger Strike	9-296	RS	Perfect Circle	Weak And Powerless	23-184	PHM
Pearl Jam	Elderly Woman Behind The Counter	9-304	RS	Perfect Stranger	Coming Up Short Again	9-390	CB
Pearl Jam	Even Flow	9-291	RS	Perfect Stranger	Cut Me Off	4-889	SC
Pearl Jam	Glorified G	9-302	RS	Perfect Stranger	I'm A Stranger Here Myself	4-16	SC
Pearl Jam	Go	9-293	RS	Perfect Stranger	Remember The Ride	4-205	SC
Pearl Jam	Hail Hail	9-301	RS	Perfect Stranger	Ridin' The Rodeo	45-209	CZC
Pearl Jam	Hunger Strike	9-296	RS	Perfect Stranger	You Have The Right to Remain Silent	7-89	MM
Pearl Jam	I Am Mine	18-824	THM	Perfect Stranger	You Have The Right To Remain Silent	3-426	SC
				Perils Of Pauline	Show - I Wish I Didn't Love You So	12-288	DK
				Perkins, Carl	Blue Suede Shoes	33-227	CB
				Perkins, Carl	Blue Suede Shoes	8-648	SAV
				Perkins, Carl	Dixie Fried	5-42	SC
				Perkins, Carl	Honey Don't	11-611	DK
				Perkins, Carl	Matchbox	11-612	DK

ARTIST	SONG TITLE	#	TYPE
Perry, Christina	Human	43-184	ASK
Perry, Katy	Hot 'N Cold	38-195	SC
Perry, Katy	Hot N' Cold	36-536	CB
Perry, Katy	I Kissed A Girl	36-496	CB
Perry, Katy	Last Friday Night	38-196	MH
Perry, Katy	Not Like The Movies	38-197	CB
Perry, Katy	Roar	44-309	SBI
Perry, Katy	Thinking Of You	38-198	CBE
Perry, Katy	This Is How We Do It	46-186	MRH
Perry, Katy	Unconditionally	43-156	PHM
Perry, Katy	Ur So Gay	46-190	KV
Perry, Katy	Waking Up In Vegas	38-199	CB
Perry, Keith	All I Give A Darn About Is You	4-623	SC
Perry, S	Foolish Heart	35-179	CB
Perry, Steve	You Better Wait	6-638	MM
Pet Shop Boys	Duet - What Have I Done To Deserve	17-529	SC
Pet Shop Boys	West End Girls	5-388	SC
Pet Shop Boys	What Have I Done To Deserve This	17-529	SC
Peter & Gordon	Lady Godiva	3-842	SC
Peter & Gordon	World Without Love	11-195	DK
Peter & Gordon	World Without Love	10-357	KC
Peter & Gordon	World Without Love	19-114	SAV
Peter & Gordon	World Without Love	5-172	SC
Peter & Gordon	World Without Love	33-248	CB
Peter, Paul & Mary	500 Miles	12-573	P
Peter, Paul & Mary	Blowin' In The Wind	11-470	DK
Peter, Paul & Mary	Blowin' In The Wind	7-357	MM
Peter, Paul & Mary	Blowin' In The Wind	9-120	PS
Peter, Paul & Mary	Blowin' In The Wind	29-836	SC
Peter, Paul & Mary	I Dig Rock & Roll Music	5-167	SC
Peter, Paul & Mary	If I Had A Hammer	34-446	CB
Peter, Paul & Mary	If I Had A Hammer	18-162	DK
Peter, Paul & Mary	If I Had A Hammer	7-358	MM
Peter, Paul & Mary	If I Had A Hammer	9-121	PS
Peter, Paul & Mary	If I Had A Hammer	4-697	SC
Peter, Paul & Mary	If I Had A Hammer	10-624	SF
Peter, Paul & Mary	Kids - Puff The Magic Dragon	33-442	CB
Peter, Paul & Mary	Leaving On A Jet Plane	35-101	CB
Peter, Paul & Mary	Leaving On A Jet Plane	11-349	DK
Peter, Paul & Mary	Leaving On A Jet Plane	7-351	MM
Peter, Paul & Mary	Leaving On A Jet Plane	13-149	P
Peter, Paul & Mary	Leaving On A Jet Plane	9-122	PS
Peter, Paul & Mary	Puff The Magic Dragon	33-442	CB
Peter, Paul & Mary	Puff The Magic Dragon	11-174	DK
Peter, Paul & Mary	Puff The Magic Dragon	9-123	PS
Peter, Paul & Mary	Stewball	5-237	SC
Peter, Paul & Mary	What Have They Done To The Rain	9-124	PS
Peter, Paul & Mary	Where Have All The Flowers Gone	12-495	P
Peters, Gretchen	I Ain't Ever Satisfied	4-404	SC
Peters, Red	Ballad of a Dog Named Stains **	37-93	SC
Peters, Red	Blow Me **	30-661	RSX

ARTIST	SONG TITLE	#	TYPE
Peters, Red	Blow Me **	5-548	SC
Peters, Red	How's Your Whole....Family **	5-549	SC
Peters, Red	How's Your Whole...Family **	30-663	RSX
Peterson, Michael	By The Book	22-692	ST
Peterson, Michael	Drink Swear Steal & Lie	7-632	CHM
Peterson, Michael	Drink Swear Steal & Lie	22-604	ST
Peterson, Michael	From Here To Eternity	22-647	ST
Peterson, Michael	Modern Man	18-213	ST
Peterson, Michael	Somethin' 'Bout A Sunday	8-949	cB
Peterson, Michael	Sure Feels Real Good	8-973	CB
Peterson, Michael	Sure Feels Real Good	22-509	ST
Peterson, Michael	Sure Feels Real Good	16-198	THM
Peterson, Michael	That's What They Said About the Buffalo	49-107	CDG
Peterson, Michael	Too Good To Be True	8-240	CB
Peterson, Michael	Too Good To Be True	7-738	CHM
Peterson, Michael	When The Bartender Cries	8-490	CB
Peterson, Michael	When The Bartender Cries	22-801	ST
Peterson, Michael	When The Bartender Cries	5-287	SC
Peterson, Ray	Corrina Corrina	9-702	SAV
Peterson, Ray	Tell Laura I Love Her	2-53	SC
Petrone, Shawna	Heaven Bound	8-737	CB
Petrone, Shawna	Something Real	5-802	SC
Petrone, Shawna	This Time	16-195	THM
Petty & Heartbreake	American Girl	2-474	SC
Petty & Heartbreake	Climb That Hill	4-606	SC
Petty & Heartbreake	Don't Do Me Like That	12-792	P
Petty & Heartbreake	Here Comes My Girl	13-17	P
Petty & Heartbreake	Into The Great Wide Open	33-343	CB
Petty & Heartbreake	It's Good To Be King	13-601	P
Petty & Heartbreake	Mary Jane's Last Dance	18-478	NU
Petty & Heartbreake	Mary Jane's Last Dance	5-331	SC
Petty & Heartbreake	Refugee	16-62	SC
Petty & Heartbreake	Runnin' Down A Dream	24-204	SC
Petty & Heartbreake	Waiting the	5-469	SC
Petty & Heartbreake	Walls	24-56	SC
Petty & Heartbreake	You Got Lucky	20-74	SC
Petty & Nicks	Duet - Needles & Pins	9-853	SAV
Petty & Nicks	Needles And Pins	9-853	SAV
Phair, Liz	Extraordinary	20-573	CB
Phair, Liz	Why Can't I	19-654	CB
Phair, Liz	Why Can't I	25-626	MM
Phair, Liz	Why Can't I	32-287	THM
Phantom Of Opera	All I Ask Of You	6-316	MM
Phantom Of Opera	Duet - All I Ask Of You	6-316	MM
Phantom Of Opera	Show - All I Ask Of You	6-316	MM
Phantom Of Opera	Show - All I Ask Of You	9-141	PS
Phantom Of Opera	Show - Music Of The Night	6-322	MM
Phantom Of Opera	Show - Music Of The Night	9-133	PS

ARTIST	SONG TITLE	#	TYPE
Phantom Of Opera	Show - Phantom Of The Opera	18-94	PS
Phantom Of Opera	Show - Think Of Me	6-248	MM
Phantom Of Opera	Show - Think Of Me	18-93	PS
Phantom Of Opera	Show - Wishing You Were Here Again	9-163	PS
Pharrell & Jay Z	Frontin'	25-717	MM
Phillips & Twilight	Sea Of Love	10-335	KC
Phillips, Phillip	Gone Gone Gone	39-102	ASK
Phillips, Phillip	Home	39-99	ASK
Phillips, Phillip	Man On The Moon	39-101	ASK
Phillips, Phillip	Where We Come From	39-100	ASK
Phish	Free	24-634	SC
Phish	Heavy Things	15-787	THM
Phoenix & Witherspoon	Duet - Jackson	29-855	SC
Phoenix & Witherspoon	Duet - Jackson	29-717	ST
Phoenix & Witherspoon	Jackson	29-855	SC
Phoenix & Witherspoon	Jackson	29-717	ST
Pickett, Bobby	Halloween - Monster Mash	11-566	DK
Pickett, Bobby	Halloween - Monster Mash	2-72	SC
Pickett, Bobby	Halloween - Monster Mash	16-286	TT
Pickett, Bobby	Monster Mash	11-566	DK
Pickett, Bobby	Monster Mash	2-72	SC
Pickett, Bobby	Monster Mash	16-286	TT
Pickler, Kellie	Don't You Know You're Beautiful	36-598	CB
Pickler, Kellie	Feeling Tonight	48-701	BKD
Pickler, Kellie	I Wonder	30-341	CB
Pickler, Kellie	Little Bit Gypsy	41-94	PHN
Pickler, Kellie	Mother's Day	38-257	PHN
Pickler, Kellie	Red High Heels	30-173	CB
Pickler, Kellie	Someone Somewhere Tonight	41-71	PHN
Pickler, Kellie	Things That Never Cross a Man's Min	30-586	CB
Pickler, Kellie	Tough	38-227	FTX
Pied Pipers	Mairzy Doats	4-193	SC
Pierce, John	I'd Still Have You	29-207	CB
Pierce, John	I'd Still Have You	29-713	ST
Pierce, Webb	Back Street Affair	8-794	CB
Pierce, Webb	Even Though	29-399	CB
Pierce, Webb	Honky Tonk Song	29-398	CB
Pierce, Webb	I Ain't Never	29-394	CB
Pierce, Webb	I Ain't Never	4-861	SC
Pierce, Webb	I Don't Care	29-393	CB
Pierce, Webb	I Don't Care	6-773	MM
Pierce, Webb	I Just Can't Be True	29-404	CB
Pierce, Webb	I'm Tired	29-406	CB
Pierce, Webb	I'm Walking The Dog	29-396	CB
Pierce, Webb	I'm Walking The Dog	49-31	KCD
Pierce, Webb	In The Jailhouse Now	15-826	CB
Pierce, Webb	In The Jailhouse Now	4-809	SC

ARTIST	SONG TITLE	#	TYPE
Pierce, Webb	It's Been So Long	29-400	CB
Pierce, Webb	Love Love Love	4-857	SC
Pierce, Webb	More And More	29-401	CB
Pierce, Webb	More And More	6-780	MM
Pierce, Webb	Slowly	29-403	CB
Pierce, Webb	There Stands The Glass	8-392	CB
Pierce, Webb	Why Baby Why	29-402	CB
Pierce, Webb	Wondering	8-772	CB
Pillar	Fireproof	32-255	THM
Pilot	Magic	15-744	SC
Pink	Catch Me While I'm Sleeping	20-533	CB
Pink	Don't Let Me Get Me	25-213	MM
Pink	Family Portrait	35-244	CB
Pink	Family Portrait	32-24	THM
Pink	Family Portrait **	25-428	MM
Pink	Feel Good Time	25-656	MM
Pink	Get The Party Started	25-87	MM
Pink	Get The Party Started	16-73	ST
Pink	Just Like A Pill	21-647	CB
Pink	Just Like A Pill	25-315	MM
Pink	Just Like A Pill	18-141	PHM
Pink	Just Like Fire	49-864	DCK
Pink	Most Girls	34-170	CB
Pink	Most Girls	15-450	PHM
Pink	Most Girls	20-11	SGB
Pink	So What	36-505	CB
Pink	There You Go	14-179	CB
Pink	Trouble	19-644	CB
Pink	U & Ur Hand **	48-598	DK
Pink	Who Knew	30-714	SF
Pink	Who Knew	49-884	SC
Pink	Who Knew	48-597	DK
Pink	You Make Me Sick	21-642	TT
Pink & Orbit	Feel Good Time	34-164	CB
Pink & Orbit	Feel Good Time	32-320	THM
Pink Floyd	Another Brick In The Wall	3-449	SC
Pink Floyd	Comfortably Numb	16-248	AMS
Pink Floyd	Comfortably Numb	2-755	SC
Pink Floyd	Have A Cigar	20-98	SC
Pink Floyd	Hey You	5-881	SC
Pink Floyd	Money	5-312	SC
Pink Floyd	Shine On You Crazy Diamond	36-125	SGB
Pink Floyd	Take It Back	24-260	SC
Pink Floyd	Time	19-275	SGB
Pink Floyd	Us And Them	19-280	SGB
Pink Floyd	Wish You Were Here	10-476	DA
Pink Floyd	Wish You Were Here	36-141	SGB
Pink/Feat/Orbit	Feel Good Time	19-595	CB
Pinkard & Bowden	Guns Made America Great	15-148	SC
Pinkard & Bowden	Help Me Make It Thru The Yard	21-543	SC
PinMonkey	Barbed Wire & Roses	25-238	MM
PinMonkey	Barbed Wire & Roses	16-708	ST

ARTIST	SONG TITLE	#	TYPE
PinMonkey	Fly	18-456	ST
Pinmonkey	I Drove All Night	25-421	MM
PinMonkey	I Drove All Night	18-330	ST
PinMonkey	Let's Kill Saturday Night	20-255	PHM
PinMonkey	Let's Kill Saturday Night	20-349	ST
Pinocchio	Show - When You Wish Upon a Star	20-184	Z
Pinson, Bobby	Don't Ask Me How I Know	22-312	CB
Pinson, Bobby	Way Down	29-28	CB
Piper, Jerry	Irish - Galway Bay	21-491	SC
Pirates of Mississi	Feed Jake	13-381	P
Pirates Of Mississippi	Honky Tonk Blues	47-567	NT
Pirates Of Mississippi	Speak Of The Devil	47-565	CB
Pirates Of Mississippi	Wild Side Of Life	47-566	KV
Pires, Alexandre	Latino - Amame	23-235	AI
Pistol Annie's	Hell On Heels	38-207	AS
Pistol Annies	Boys From The South	44-152	BKD
Pitbull	Hotel Room Service	40-12	BH
Pitbull	I Know You Want Me (Calle Ocho)	40-13	PHM
Pitbull & KeSha	Timber	43-192	PHM
Pitbull w T-Pain	Hey Baby (Drop It To the Floor)	40-14	PHM
Pitch Perfect	Cups (You're Gonna Miss Me...)	44-116	KV
Pitney, Gene	Backstage	47-526	ZM
Pitney, Gene	Every Breath I Take	9-846	SAV
Pitney, Gene	Every Breath I Take	9-178	SO
Pitney, Gene	Half Heaven Half Heartache	4-225	SC
Pitney, Gene	I Must Be Seeing Things	47-527	ZM
Pitney, Gene	I'm Gonna Be Strong	9-699	SAV
Pitney, Gene	If I Didn't Have A Dime	47-534	SFM
Pitney, Gene	It Hurts To Be In Love	7-268	MM
Pitney, Gene	It Hurts To Be In Love	5-227	SC
Pitney, Gene	Just One Smile	47-531	ZM
Pitney, Gene	Looking Through The Eyes Of Love	47-529	ZM
Pitney, Gene	Louisiana Mama	47-537	SAV
Pitney, Gene	Man Who Shot Liberty Valance	20-41	SC
Pitney, Gene	Man Who Shot Liberty Valance	9-179	SO
Pitney, Gene	Maria Elena	47-532	ZM
Pitney, Gene	Mecca	17-470	SC
Pitney, Gene	Nobody Needs Your Love	47-533	ZM
Pitney, Gene	Only Love Can Break A Heart	7-262	MM
Pitney, Gene	Only Love Can Break A Heart	22-444	SC
Pitney, Gene	Only Love Can Break A Heart	9-180	SO
Pitney, Gene	Princess In Rags	47-528	ZM
Pitney, Gene	Puppy Love	47-536	SO

ARTIST	SONG TITLE	#	TYPE
Pitney, Gene	Something's Got A Hold Of My Heart	47-530	ZM
Pitney, Gene	Town Without Pity	6-442	MM
Pitney, Gene	Town Without Pity	9-177	SO
Pitney, Gene	Twenty Four Hours From Tulsa	46-118	SC
Pitney, Gene	Twenty Four Sycamore	47-535	SFM
Pitney, Mo	Country	48-757	KCD
Placebo	Because I Want You	30-702	SF
Placebo	Never Ending Why	48-739	KV
Plain White T's	1 2 3 4	36-386	SC
Plain White T's	Hey There Delilah	48-599	DK
Plant & Krauss	Duet - Please Read The Letter	49-905	SC
Plant & Krauss	Please Read The Letter - duet	49-905	SC
Plant, Robert	If I Were A Carpenter	24-257	SC
Plastic Ono Band	Give Peace A Chance	34-26	CB
Platten, Rachel	Fight Song	48-146	BKD
Platten, Rachel	Stand By You (Instrumental Version)	48-147	BKD
Platters	Great Pretender the	12-366	DK
Platters	Great Pretender the	7-310	MM
Platters	Great Pretender the	2-79	SC
Platters	Harbor Lights	16-803	DK
Platters	Harbor Lights	9-554	SAV
Platters	If I Didn't Care	45-72	CB
Platters	Magic Touch the	27-219	DK
Platters	My Prayer	11-759	DK
Platters	My Prayer	6-259	MM
Platters	My Prayer	14-347	SC
Platters	On My Word Of Honor	45-74	DCK
Platters	Only You	11-20	PX
Platters	Only You (And You Alone)	25-175	MM
Platters	Only You And You Alone	13-43	P
Platters	Red Sails In The Sunset	11-302	DK
Platters	Red Sails In The Sunset	9-555	SAV
Platters	Remember When	49-664	DCK
Platters	Sixteen Tons	9-556	SAV
Platters	Smoke Gets In Your Eyes	35-17	CB
Platters	Smoke Gets In Your Eyes	11-310	DK
Platters	Smoke Gets In Your Eyes	13-59	P
Platters	To Each His Own	45-73	DCK
Platters	Twilight Time	12-364	DK
Platters	Twilight Time	2-88	SC
Platters	With This Ring	2-856	SC
Platters	You'll Never Never Know	12-362	DK
Platters	You've Got The Magic Touch	12-365	DK
Platters	You've Got The Magic Touch	22-438	SC
Player	Baby Come Back	12-153	DK
Player	Baby Come Back	4-48	SC

223

ARTIST	SONG TITLE	#	TYPE
Playmates	Beep Beep	5-635	SC
Plimsouls	Million Miles Away	16-60	SC
PM Dawn	I Had No Right	7-785	PHT
Poco	Crazy Love	5-387	SC
Poco	Heart Of The Night	49-267	SC
Poco	Kind Woman	49-268	SC
Poco	Rose Of Cimarron	49-236	DFK
Poco	You Better Think Twice	49-265	DFK
Pocohontas	Show - Colours of the Wind	20-189	Z
Pocohontas	Show - Just Around the River Bend	20-188	Z
POD	Youth Of The Nation	30-650	THM
Poe	Angry Johnny	24-296	SC
Poe, Michelle	Just One Of The Boys	20-391	ST
Poindexter, Buster	Hot Hot Hot	33-437	CB
Poindexter, Buster	Hot Hot Hot	12-113	DK
Point Of Grace	Gospel - Steady On	20-153	KB
Point of Grace	How You Live (Turn Up The Music)	36-589	CB
Pointer Sisters	Automatic	17-43	DK
Pointer Sisters	Fire	3-445	SC
Pointer Sisters	I'm So Excited	11-374	DK
Pointer Sisters	I'm So Excited	9-221	PT
Pointer Sisters	I'm So Excited	10-523	SF
Pointer Sisters	Jump For My Love	3-478	SC
Pointer Sisters	Neutron Dance	11-375	DK
Pointer Sisters	Slow Hand	27-293	DK
Pointer Sisters	Slow Hand	9-222	PT
Pointer Sisters	Slow Hand	19-557	SC
Pointer Sisters	Yes We Can Can	9-729	SAV
Poison	Do Me	17-368	DK
Poison	Every Rose Has It's Thorn	9-372	AH
Poison	Every Rose Has It's Thorn	20-322	MH
Poison	Every Rose Has It's Thorn	24-196	SC
Poison	Every Rose Has It's Thorn	13-746	SGB
Poison	I Won't Forget You	6-16	SC
Poison	Look What The Cat Dragged In	21-776	SC
Poison	Nothin' But A Good Time	5-68	SC
Poison	Something To Believe In	24-682	SC
Poison	Something To Believe In	13-758	SGB
Poison	Talk Dirty To Me	23-53	MH
Poison	Unskinny Bop	5-493	SC
Police	Don't Stand So Close To Me	46-114	SC
Police	Don't Stand Too Close To Me	20-42	SC
Police	Every Breath You Take	35-153	CB
Police	Every Little Thing She Does	4-376	SC
Police	Every Little Thing She Does is Magic	34-51	CB
Police	King Of Pain	17-517	SC

ARTIST	SONG TITLE	#	TYPE
Police	Roxanne	2-140	SC
Police	Wrapped Around Your Finger	46-115	SC
Polka Favorites	Blue Skirt Waltz - w/Words	29-864	SSR
Polka Favorites	Chicken Dance - music only	29-867	SSR
Polka Favorites	E I E I O Polka - w/Words	29-858	SSR
Polka Favorites	E I E I O Polka (Let's Have a Party	29-804	SSR
Polka Favorites	Grab Your Balls We're Going Bowling	29-812	SSR
Polka Favorites	Grab Your Balls We're... - w/Words	29-866	SSR
Polka Favorites	In Heaven There Is No Beer - w/Word	29-860	SSR
Polka Favorites	In Heaven There Is No Beer Polka	29-806	SSR
Polka Favorites	Just Because Polka	29-805	SSR
Polka Favorites	Just Because Polka - w/Words	29-859	SSR
Polka Favorites	Pennsylvania Polka	29-811	SSR
Polka Favorites	Pennsylvania Polka - w/Words	29-865	SSR
Polka Favorites	Polka - E I E I O Polka	29-804	SSR
Polka Favorites	Polka - In Heaven There Is No Beer	29-806	SSR
Polka Favorites	Polka - Just Because Polka	29-805	SSR
Polka Favorites	Polka - Pennsylvania Polka	29-811	SSR
Polka Favorites	Polka - Roll Out The Barrel	29-809	SSR
Polka Favorites	Polka - Too Fat Polka	29-808	SSR
Polka Favorites	Polka - Who Stole The Keishka	29-807	SSR
Polka Favorites	Polka - Grab Your Balls We're Going	29-812	SSR
Polka Favorites	Roll Out The Barrel	29-809	SSR
Polka Favorites	Roll Out The Barrel - w/Words	29-863	SSR
Polka Favorites	Too Fat Polka	29-808	SSR
Polka Favorites	Too Fat Polka - w/Words	29-862	SSR
Polka Favorites	Who Stole The Keishka	29-807	SSR
Polka Favorites	Who Stole The Keishka - w/Words	29-861	SSR
Ponytails	Born Too Late	7-293	MM
Poole & Tremeloes	Candy Man	10-657	SF
Poole & Tremeloes	Do You Love Me	10-563	SF
Pope, Cassadee	11	44-135	ASK
Pope, Cassadee	Good Times	49-669	BKD
Pope, Cassadee	I Am Invincible	49-668	BKD
Pope, Cassadee	I Wish I Could Break Your Heart	44-304	SBI
Pope, Cassadee	Over You	49-671	SBI
Pope, Cassadee	Wasting All These Years	49-670	SSC
Pope, Cassadee	You Hear A Song	49-667	SBI
Porgy & Bess	Show - It Ain't Necessarily So	14-383	PS

ARTIST	SONG TITLE	#	TYPE
Porgy & Bess	Show - There's a Boat Dat's Leavin'	14-387	PS
Portrait	How Deep Is Your Love	3-501	SC
Posner, Mike	Cooler Than Me	40-47	CB
Posner, Mike	I Took A Pill In Ibiza	49-930	MRH
Potentials	You Ought To Be With Me	17-394	DK
Potter, Grace	Empty Heart	48-703	BKD
Potts, MC	Back When	4-162	SC
Powderfinger	My Happiness	15-304	THM
Powell, Jesse	You	7-833	PHM
Power Station	Bang A Gong (Get It On)	5-106	SC
Power Station	Some Like It Hot	34-52	CB
Power Station	Some Like It Hot	21-747	MH
Powerman 5000	Free	32-253	THM
Powers, Summerlyn	Alabama Kinda Girl	41-90	PHN
Pozo Seco Singers	I Can Make It With You	20-35	SC
Prata, Lucas	And She Said (2006 Mets Anthem)	30-63	PHM
Prata, Lucas	Let's Get It On	21-728	TT
Prather, Colt	I Won't Go On And On	20-331	ST
Preacher's Wife	Show - I Believe In You And Me	18-183	DK
Preciado, Julio	Latino - Me Causte Del Cielo	17-753	SC
Presidents of USA	Kitty	5-335	SC
Presidents of USA	Lump	24-748	SC
Presidents of USA	Mach 5	24-641	SC
Presidents of USA	Peaches	13-595	P
Presley & Oakenfold	Rubberneckin'	32-427	THM
Presley & Philharmonics	Steamroller Blues	49-653	KV
Presley, Elvis	Adam & Evil	25-494	MM
Presley, Elvis	Ain't That Lovin' You Baby	7-126	MM
Presley, Elvis	Ain't That Lovin' You Baby	14-816	THM
Presley, Elvis	All I Needed Was Rain	25-495	MM
Presley, Elvis	All Shook Up	11-158	DK
Presley, Elvis	All Shook Up	13-97	P
Presley, Elvis	All Shook Up	9-804	SAV
Presley, Elvis	All Shook Up	2-594	SC
Presley, Elvis	All Shook Up	14-738	THM
Presley, Elvis	Almost	25-757	MM
Presley, Elvis	Almost Always True	25-107	MM
Presley, Elvis	Always On My Mind	18-439	KC
Presley, Elvis	Amazing Grace	30-376	SC
Presley, Elvis	American Trilogy	2-582	SC
Presley, Elvis	An American Trilogy	20-157	BCI
Presley, Elvis	Any Place Is Paradise	14-817	THM
Presley, Elvis	Any Way You Want Me	14-739	THM
Presley, Elvis	Anyone Could Fall In Love W/You	25-485	MM
Presley, Elvis	Anything That's Part Of You	7-131	MM
Presley, Elvis	Anyway You Want Me	7-134	MM
Presley, Elvis	Are You Lonesome Tonight	12-65	DK
Presley, Elvis	Are You Lonesome Tonight	25-758	MM
Presley, Elvis	Are You Lonesome Tonight	13-111	P
Presley, Elvis	Are You Lonesome Tonight	2-603	SC
Presley, Elvis	Are You Lonesome Tonight	14-740	THM
Presley, Elvis	Baby I Don't Care	2-604	SC
Presley, Elvis	Baby Let's Play House	43-240	MM
Presley, Elvis	Baby What You Want Me To Do	45-612	HM
Presley, Elvis	Big Hunk Of Love	14-768	THM
Presley, Elvis	Big Love Big Heartache	25-99	MM
Presley, Elvis	Blue Eyes Crying In The Rain	25-92	MM
Presley, Elvis	Blue Hawaii	12-111	DK
Presley, Elvis	Blue Moon Of Kentucky	12-189	DK
Presley, Elvis	Blue Suede Shoes	15-272	DK
Presley, Elvis	Blue Suede Shoes	12-657	P
Presley, Elvis	Blue Suede Shoes	4-703	SC
Presley, Elvis	Blue Suede Shoes	14-741	THM
Presley, Elvis	Blueberry Hill	43-241	MM
Presley, Elvis	Bossa Nova Baby	8-583	CB
Presley, Elvis	Bossa Nova Baby	4-712	SC
Presley, Elvis	Boy Like Me, A Girl Like You a	25-98	MM
Presley, Elvis	Breathless	43-242	PSJT
Presley, Elvis	Bringin' It Back	25-741	MM
Presley, Elvis	Britches	45-613	HM
Presley, Elvis	Burning Love	11-148	DK
Presley, Elvis	Burning Love	12-677	P
Presley, Elvis	Burning Love	2-584	SC
Presley, Elvis	Burning Love	14-769	THM
Presley, Elvis	C C Rider	14-770	THM
Presley, Elvis	Can't Help Falling In Love	12-86	DK
Presley, Elvis	Can't Help Falling In Love	2-605	SC
Presley, Elvis	Can't Help Falling In Love	14-742	THM
Presley, Elvis	Charro	25-491	MM
Presley, Elvis	Clean Up Your Own Back Yard	8-591	CB
Presley, Elvis	Crawfish	25-761	MM
Presley, Elvis	Crying In The Chapel	11-609	DK
Presley, Elvis	Crying In The Chapel	13-99	P
Presley, Elvis	Crying In The Chapel	9-796	SAV
Presley, Elvis	Crying In The Chapel	30-378	SC
Presley, Elvis	Crying In The Chapel	14-798	THM
Presley, Elvis	Devil In Disguise	17-549	DK
Presley, Elvis	Devil In Disguise	2-583	SC
Presley, Elvis	Do Not Disturb	25-113	MM
Presley, Elvis	Do You Know Who I Am	25-319	MM
Presley, Elvis	Don't	14-743	THM
Presley, Elvis	Don't Ask Me Why	8-579	CB
Presley, Elvis	Don't Be Cruel	11-99	DK
Presley, Elvis	Don't Be Cruel	19-98	SAV

ARTIST	SONG TITLE	#	TYPE
Presley, Elvis	Don't Be Cruel	2-587	SC
Presley, Elvis	Don't Be Cruel	14-744	THM
Presley, Elvis	Don't Cry Daddy	17-548	DK
Presley, Elvis	Don't Cry Daddy	2-599	SC
Presley, Elvis	Don't Leave Me Now	7-123	MM
Presley, Elvis	Don't Think Twice	25-743	MM
Presley, Elvis	Fame And Fortune	7-132	MM
Presley, Elvis	Farther Along	25-509	MM
Presley, Elvis	Fever	18-443	KC
Presley, Elvis	Find Out What's Happenin'	25-744	MM
Presley, Elvis	First Time Ever I Saw Your Face	25-325	MM
Presley, Elvis	Flaming Star	8-580	CB
Presley, Elvis	Follow That Dream	8-581	CB
Presley, Elvis	Fool Such As I a	11-606	DK
Presley, Elvis	Fool Such As I a	14-753	THM
Presley, Elvis	Fool the	25-742	MM
Presley, Elvis	Fools Fall In Love	25-106	MM
Presley, Elvis	Forget Me Never	25-328	MM
Presley, Elvis	Fountain Of Love	25-115	MM
Presley, Elvis	Frankie & Johnny	46-42	SSK
Presley, Elvis	Gentle On My Mind	25-100	MM
Presley, Elvis	Girl I Never Loved the	25-488	MM
Presley, Elvis	Girl Of Mine	25-753	MM
Presley, Elvis	Golden Coins	25-489	MM
Presley, Elvis	Good Luck Charm	3-314	MH
Presley, Elvis	Good Luck Charm	13-98	P
Presley, Elvis	Good Luck Charm	2-598	SC
Presley, Elvis	Gospel - Amazing Grace	30-376	SC
Presley, Elvis	Gospel - By And By	25-510	MM
Presley, Elvis	Gospel - Crying In The Chapel	43-99	CB
Presley, Elvis	Gospel - Crying In The Chapel	6-694	MM
Presley, Elvis	Gospel - Crying In The Chapel	30-378	SC
Presley, Elvis	Gospel - He Touched Me	33-201	CB
Presley, Elvis	Gospel - His Hand In Mine	30-384	SC
Presley, Elvis	Gospel - How Great Thou Art	6-693	MM
Presley, Elvis	Gospel - How Great Thou Art	30-373	SC
Presley, Elvis	Gospel - How Great Thou Art	14-800	THM
Presley, Elvis	Gospel - I Believe	6-692	MM
Presley, Elvis	Gospel - I Believe	30-375	SC
Presley, Elvis	Gospel - If We Never Meet Again	43-111	CB
Presley, Elvis	Gospel - In My Father's House	6-695	MM
Presley, Elvis	Gospel - In My Father's House	14-804	THM
Presley, Elvis	Gospel - Joshua Fit The Battle	30-381	SC
Presley, Elvis	Gospel - Known Only To Him	30-382	SC
Presley, Elvis	Gospel - Lead Me Guide	6-696	MM

ARTIST	SONG TITLE	#	TYPE
	Me		
Presley, Elvis	Gospel - Lead Me Guide Me	30-377	SC
Presley, Elvis	Gospel - Lead Me Guide Me	14-822	THM
Presley, Elvis	Gospel - Let Us Pray	14-805	THM
Presley, Elvis	Gospel - Mansion Over the Hilltop	6-699	MM
Presley, Elvis	Gospel - Mansion Over The Hilltop	14-806	THM
Presley, Elvis	Gospel - Medley ('68 Comeback Sp)	25-500	MM
Presley, Elvis	Gospel - Peace In The Valley	30-374	SC
Presley, Elvis	Gospel - Precious Lord	6-701	MM
Presley, Elvis	Gospel - Promised Land the	6-698	MM
Presley, Elvis	Gospel - Promised Land the	14-810	THM
Presley, Elvis	Gospel - Shake A Hand	6-700	MM
Presley, Elvis	Gospel - Somebody Bigger Than You..	14-809	THM
Presley, Elvis	Gospel - Somebody Bigger Than...	6-702	MM
Presley, Elvis	Gospel - Swing Down Sweet Chariot	30-380	SC
Presley, Elvis	Gospel - Take My Hand Precious Lord	30-386	SC
Presley, Elvis	Gospel - We Call On Him	25-512	MM
Presley, Elvis	Gospel - Where Could I Go	43-108	CB
Presley, Elvis	Gospel - Where Could I Go But To...	30-379	SC
Presley, Elvis	Gospel - Where No One Stands Alone	6-704	MM
Presley, Elvis	Gospel - Where No One Stands Alone	14-811	THM
Presley, Elvis	Gospel - Where Would I Go	6-697	MM
Presley, Elvis	Gospel - Who Am I	6-703	MM
Presley, Elvis	Gospel - Who Am I	30-383	SC
Presley, Elvis	Gospel - Who Am I	14-812	THM
Presley, Elvis	Gospel - Without Him	14-813	THM
Presley, Elvis	Gospel - Working On The Building	30-385	SC
Presley, Elvis	Gospel - You Gave Me A Mountain	6-705	MM
Presley, Elvis	Gospel - You Gave Me A Mountain	14-814	THM
Presley, Elvis	Gospel - You'll Never Walk Alone	6-691	MM
Presley, Elvis	Gospel - You'll Never Walk Alone	30-372	SC
Presley, Elvis	Gospel - You'll Never Walk Alone	14-815	THM
Presley, Elvis	Handy Man	43-243	PSJT
Presley, Elvis	Happy Ending	25-769	MM
Presley, Elvis	Hard Headed Woman	14-745	THM
Presley, Elvis	Hard Knocks	25-498	MM
Presley, Elvis	Hawaii - Blue Hawaii	12-111	DK

ARTIST	SONG TITLE	#	TYPE
Presley, Elvis	Hawaiian Sunset	25-496	MM
Presley, Elvis	Hawaiian Wedding Song	14-771	THM
Presley, Elvis	He'll Have To Go	25-329	MM
Presley, Elvis	Heart Of Rome	25-745	MM
Presley, Elvis	Heartbreak Hotel	11-604	DK
Presley, Elvis	Heartbreak Hotel	2-610	SC
Presley, Elvis	Heartbreak Woman	14-746	THM
Presley, Elvis	Hey Jude	25-760	MM
Presley, Elvis	Hey Little Girl	43-244	PSJT
Presley, Elvis	His Hand In Mine	30-384	SC
Presley, Elvis	His Latest Flame (Marie's the Name)	2-611	SC
Presley, Elvis	Holly Leaves And Christmas Trees	45-777	CB
Presley, Elvis	Hound Dog	11-189	DK
Presley, Elvis	Hound Dog	3-317	MH
Presley, Elvis	Hound Dog	12-729	P
Presley, Elvis	Hound Dog	2-600	SC
Presley, Elvis	Hound Dog	14-747	THM
Presley, Elvis	How Great Thou Art	30-373	SC
Presley, Elvis	How's The World Treating You	25-327	MM
Presley, Elvis	Hurt	18-445	KC
Presley, Elvis	Hurt	14-772	THM
Presley, Elvis	I Beg Of You	14-754	THM
Presley, Elvis	I Believe	18-832	KC
Presley, Elvis	I Believe	30-375	SC
Presley, Elvis	I Believe	14-801	THM
Presley, Elvis	I Can Help	25-752	MM
Presley, Elvis	I Don't Want To Be Tied	25-486	MM
Presley, Elvis	I Forgot To Remember	14-755	THM
Presley, Elvis	I Got A Feeling In My Body	25-746	MM
Presley, Elvis	I Got A Woman	7-133	MM
Presley, Elvis	I Got Stung	14-756	THM
Presley, Elvis	I Gotta Know	7-127	MM
Presley, Elvis	I John	25-511	MM
Presley, Elvis	I Miss You	25-323	MM
Presley, Elvis	I Need Somebody	25-762	MM
Presley, Elvis	I Shall Not Be Moved	25-513	MM
Presley, Elvis	I Want You I Need You I Love You	11-608	DK
Presley, Elvis	I Want You I Need You I Love You	2-597	SC
Presley, Elvis	I Want You I Need You I Love You	14-748	THM
Presley, Elvis	I Was The One	14-749	THM
Presley, Elvis	I'll Be There	25-116	MM
Presley, Elvis	I'll Never Know	25-324	MM
Presley, Elvis	I'll Never Stand In Your Way	45-616	HM
Presley, Elvis	I'm Leavin'	25-755	MM
Presley, Elvis	I'm Left You're Right She's Gone	14-757	THM
Presley, Elvis	I'm Not The Marrying Kind	25-766	MM
Presley, Elvis	I'm So Lonesome I Could Cry	49-445	MM

ARTIST	SONG TITLE	#	TYPE
Presley, Elvis	I've Got A Thing About You	14-818	THM
Presley, Elvis	I've Got A Woman	43-245	PSJT
Presley, Elvis	If I Can Dream	2-602	SC
Presley, Elvis	If I Can Dream	14-773	THM
Presley, Elvis	If I Get Home On Christmas Day	45-761	CB
Presley, Elvis	If I'm A Fool For Loving You	25-759	MM
Presley, Elvis	If We Never Meet Again	25-506	MM
Presley, Elvis	If You Don't Come Back	25-763	MM
Presley, Elvis	If You Talk In Your Sleep	14-819	THM
Presley, Elvis	In The Ghetto	11-342	DK
Presley, Elvis	In The Ghetto	9-709	SAV
Presley, Elvis	In The Ghetto	2-586	SC
Presley, Elvis	Island Of Love	25-112	MM
Presley, Elvis	It Ain't No Big Thing	25-754	MM
Presley, Elvis	It Keeps Right On A-Hurtin'	7-122	MM
Presley, Elvis	It's A Long Lonely Highway	25-117	MM
Presley, Elvis	It's A Matter Of Time	25-751	MM
Presley, Elvis	It's Easy For You	25-326	MM
Presley, Elvis	It's Now Or Never	11-607	DK
Presley, Elvis	It's Now Or Never	13-65	P
Presley, Elvis	It's Now Or Never	2-590	SC
Presley, Elvis	It's Now Or Never	14-758	THM
Presley, Elvis	It's Over	7-121	MM
Presley, Elvis	Jailhouse Rock	16-829	DK
Presley, Elvis	Jailhouse Rock	2-606	SC
Presley, Elvis	Jailhouse Rock	14-750	THM
Presley, Elvis	Johnny B Goode	43-246	MM
Presley, Elvis	Joshua Fit The Battle	30-381	SC
Presley, Elvis	Just Ask Me	14-820	THM
Presley, Elvis	Just Because	43-247	MM
Presley, Elvis	Just Call Me Lonesome	25-111	MM
Presley, Elvis	Just Tell Her Jim Said Hi	14-821	THM
Presley, Elvis	Kentucky Rain	17-550	DK
Presley, Elvis	Kentucky Rain	7-125	MM
Presley, Elvis	Kentucky Rain	2-609	SC
Presley, Elvis	Kissin' Cousins	8-585	CB
Presley, Elvis	Known Only To Him	30-382	SC
Presley, Elvis	Lawdy Miss Clawdy	14-774	THM
Presley, Elvis	Lead Me Guide Me	30-377	SC
Presley, Elvis	Let Me Be Your Teddy Bear	35-2	CB
Presley, Elvis	Let Me Be Your Teddy Bear	18-118	DK
Presley, Elvis	Let's Talk About Us	43-248	PS
Presley, Elvis	Little Less Conversation	25-303	MM
Presley, Elvis	Little Sister	11-177	DK
Presley, Elvis	Little Sister	2-607	SC
Presley, Elvis	Little Sister	14-775	THM
Presley, Elvis	Long Tall Sally	18-542	KC
Presley, Elvis	Long Tall Sally	14-759	THM
Presley, Elvis	Love Coming Down	25-105	MM
Presley, Elvis	Love Letters	13-91	P
Presley, Elvis	Love Me	2-592	SC

227

ARTIST	SONG TITLE	#	TYPE
Presley, Elvis	Love Me Tender	16-723	DK
Presley, Elvis	Love Me Tender	6-260	MM
Presley, Elvis	Love Me Tender	14-760	THM
Presley, Elvis	Love Me Tender	2-591	SC
Presley, Elvis	Love Me Tonight	25-317	MM
Presley, Elvis	Loving You	15-525	MM
Presley, Elvis	Marguerita	25-487	MM
Presley, Elvis	Memories	18-560	KC
Presley, Elvis	Memphis	14-823	THM
Presley, Elvis	Mess Of The Blues	47-719	CB
Presley, Elvis	Milkcow Blues Boogie	7-129	MM
Presley, Elvis	Milky White Way	25-503	MM
Presley, Elvis	Mine	25-101	MM
Presley, Elvis	Moody Blue	17-126	DK
Presley, Elvis	Moody Blue	2-608	SC
Presley, Elvis	Moody Blue	14-824	THM
Presley, Elvis	My Boy	14-825	THM
Presley, Elvis	My Happiness	25-102	MM
Presley, Elvis	My Little Friend	25-118	MM
Presley, Elvis	My Way	18-442	KC
Presley, Elvis	Mystery Train	7-128	MM
Presley, Elvis	Mystery Train - Tiger Man	49-444	MM
Presley, Elvis	Never Again	25-321	MM
Presley, Elvis	Never Ending	25-119	MM
Presley, Elvis	Oh Happy Day	25-514	MM
Presley, Elvis	On A Snowy Christmas Night	45-758	CB
Presley, Elvis	One Boy Two Little Girls	25-497	MM
Presley, Elvis	One Broken Heart For Sale	8-584	CB
Presley, Elvis	One Broken Heart For Sale	7-130	MM
Presley, Elvis	One Night	15-545	MM
Presley, Elvis	One Night	14-751	THM
Presley, Elvis	One Track Heart	25-499	MM
Presley, Elvis	Only Believe	25-504	MM
Presley, Elvis	Only Make Believe	18-441	KC
Presley, Elvis	Paralized	14-776	THM
Presley, Elvis	Party	25-109	MM
Presley, Elvis	Patch It Up (Live)	49-919	KVD
Presley, Elvis	Peace In The Valley	30-374	SC
Presley, Elvis	Plantation Rock the	45-617	HM
Presley, Elvis	Polk Salad Annie	18-440	KC
Presley, Elvis	Poor Boy	8-578	CB
Presley, Elvis	Poor Boy	14-777	THM
Presley, Elvis	Puppet On A String	8-588	CB
Presley, Elvis	Puppet On A String	7-124	MM
Presley, Elvis	Raised On Rock	9-723	SAV
Presley, Elvis	Raised On Rock	14-826	THM
Presley, Elvis	Return To Sender	8-582	CB
Presley, Elvis	Return To Sender	11-152	DK
Presley, Elvis	Return To Sender	12-895	P
Presley, Elvis	Return To Sender	2-595	SC
Presley, Elvis	Return To Sender	14-761	THM
Presley, Elvis	Rip It Up	14-778	THM
Presley, Elvis	Rubber Neckin'	8-592	CB
Presley, Elvis	Run On	25-501	MM
Presley, Elvis	Runaway (Live)	25-748	MM
Presley, Elvis	Scratch My Back	47-768	SRK
Presley, Elvis	Seeing Is Believing	25-502	MM
Presley, Elvis	Sentimental Me	25-93	MM
Presley, Elvis	Separate Ways	9-730	SAV
Presley, Elvis	Shake, Rattle & Roll	43-249	MM
Presley, Elvis	She Thinks I Still Care	25-103	MM
Presley, Elvis	She Thinks I Still Care	14-827	THM
Presley, Elvis	She Wears My Ring	25-764	MM
Presley, Elvis	Singing Tree	25-767	MM
Presley, Elvis	Slowly But Surely	25-492	MM
Presley, Elvis	Snowbird	25-750	MM
Presley, Elvis	So Glad You're Mine	14-828	THM
Presley, Elvis	So High	25-508	MM
Presley, Elvis	Spanish Eyes	25-91	MM
Presley, Elvis	Spinout	8-590	CB
Presley, Elvis	Starting Today	25-95	MM
Presley, Elvis	Stay Away Joe	25-108	MM
Presley, Elvis	Steamroller Blues	18-446	KC
Presley, Elvis	Stop Look & Listen	25-114	MM
Presley, Elvis	Stranger In My Hometown	25-120	MM
Presley, Elvis	Stranger In The Crowd	25-749	MM
Presley, Elvis	Stuck On You	11-605	DK
Presley, Elvis	Stuck On You	13-264	P
Presley, Elvis	Stuck On You	2-601	SC
Presley, Elvis	Stuck On You	14-762	THM
Presley, Elvis	Such An Easy Question	8-589	CB
Presley, Elvis	Suppose	25-96	MM
Presley, Elvis	Suspicion	18-523	KC
Presley, Elvis	Suspicion	14-779	THM
Presley, Elvis	Suspicious Minds	16-851	DK
Presley, Elvis	Suspicious Minds	13-40	P
Presley, Elvis	Suspicious Minds	2-588	SC
Presley, Elvis	Suspicious Minds	14-780	THM
Presley, Elvis	Swing Down Sweet Chariot	30-380	SC
Presley, Elvis	Take My Hand Precious Lord	30-386	SC
Presley, Elvis	Talkin' In Your Sleep	43-250	PSJT
Presley, Elvis	Teddy Bear	9-885	DK
Presley, Elvis	Teddy Bear	3-325	MH
Presley, Elvis	Teddy Bear	12-732	P
Presley, Elvis	Teddy Bear	2-593	SC
Presley, Elvis	Teddy Bear	14-752	THM
Presley, Elvis	Tell Me Why	25-765	MM
Presley, Elvis	Tender Feeling	25-318	MM
Presley, Elvis	That's All Right	11-610	DK
Presley, Elvis	That's All Right	21-569	SAV
Presley, Elvis	That's All Right Mama	14-782	THM
Presley, Elvis	That's Someone You Never Forget	25-320	MM
Presley, Elvis	Thing Called Love a	25-505	MM
Presley, Elvis	Thinking About You	25-104	MM
Presley, Elvis	Three Corn Patches	45-614	HM
Presley, Elvis	Today Tomorrow &	25-756	MM

ARTIST	SONG TITLE	#	TYPE
	Forever		
Presley, Elvis	Tomorrow Never Comes	25-747	MM
Presley, Elvis	Too Much	2-585	SC
Presley, Elvis	Too Much	14-764	THM
Presley, Elvis	Treat Me Nice	14-765	THM
Presley, Elvis	Trouble	14-781	THM
Presley, Elvis	Twelfth Of Never the	25-330	MM
Presley, Elvis	Unchained Melody	18-423	KC
Presley, Elvis	Until It's Time For You To Go	18-579	KC
Presley, Elvis	Vino Dinero Y Amor	25-493	MM
Presley, Elvis	Viva Las Vegas	8-586	CB
Presley, Elvis	Walk A Mile In My Shoes	6-795	MM
Presley, Elvis	Walk A Mile In My Shoes	14-829	THM
Presley, Elvis	Walls Have Ears the	47-769	SRK
Presley, Elvis	Way Down	14-830	THM
Presley, Elvis	Wear My Ring Around Your Neck	2-589	SC
Presley, Elvis	Wear My Ring Around Your Neck	14-766	THM
Presley, Elvis	What A Wonderful Life	25-490	MM
Presley, Elvis	What'd I Say	8-587	CB
Presley, Elvis	Where Could I Go	14-831	THM
Presley, Elvis	Where Could I Go But To The Lord	30-379	SC
Presley, Elvis	White Christmas	45-760	CB
Presley, Elvis	Who Am I	30-383	SC
Presley, Elvis	Wild In The Country	25-94	MM
Presley, Elvis	Without Love (There Is Nothing)	7-135	MM
Presley, Elvis	Wolf Call	25-110	MM
Presley, Elvis	Wonder Of You the	11-450	DK
Presley, Elvis	Wonder Of You the	2-596	SC
Presley, Elvis	Wonder Of You the	14-763	THM
Presley, Elvis	Wonderful World	45-615	HM
Presley, Elvis	Wonderful World Of Christmas	45-759	CB
Presley, Elvis	Wooden Heart	10-553	SF
Presley, Elvis	Wooden Heart	14-767	THM
Presley, Elvis	Working On The Building	25-507	MM
Presley, Elvis	Working On The Building	30-385	SC
Presley, Elvis	World Of Our Own a	25-322	MM
Presley, Elvis	Xmas - Blue Christmas	7-1	MM
Presley, Elvis	Xmas - Blue Christmas	41-17	PR
Presley, Elvis	Xmas - Blue Christmas	14-537	SC
Presley, Elvis	Xmas - Blue Christmas	22-849	ST
Presley, Elvis	Xmas - Blue Christmas	14-797	THM
Presley, Elvis	Xmas - First Noel the	49-876	MM
Presley, Elvis	Xmas - Here Comes Santa Claus	33-206	CB
Presley, Elvis	Xmas - Here Comes Santa Claus	7-5	MM
Presley, Elvis	Xmas - Here Comes Santa Claus	14-799	THM
Presley, Elvis	Xmas - Here Comes Santa Claus	49-870	MM
Presley, Elvis	Xmas - Holly Leaves &	49-867	MM

ARTIST	SONG TITLE	#	TYPE
	Xmas Trees		
Presley, Elvis	Xmas - Holly Leaves And Christmas Trees	45-777	CB
Presley, Elvis	Xmas - I'll Be Home For Christmas	25-770	MM
Presley, Elvis	Xmas - I'll Be Home For Christmas	14-802	THM
Presley, Elvis	Xmas - If Every Day Was Like Xmas	7-9	MM
Presley, Elvis	Xmas - If Every Day Was Like Xmas	3-399	SC
Presley, Elvis	Xmas - If Every Day Was Like Xmas	14-803	THM
Presley, Elvis	Xmas - If Every Day Was Like Xmas	49-877	MM
Presley, Elvis	Xmas - If I Get Home On Christmas Day	45-761	CB
Presley, Elvis	Xmas - If I Get Home On Xmas Day	49-872	MM
Presley, Elvis	Xmas - It Won's Seem Like Christmas..	49-871	MM
Presley, Elvis	Xmas - It Won't Seem Like Christmas	18-735	CB
Presley, Elvis	Xmas - Merry Christmas Baby	14-807	THM
Presley, Elvis	Xmas - O Come All Ye Faithful	49-873	MM
Presley, Elvis	Xmas - O Little Town Of Bethlehem	49-868	MM
Presley, Elvis	Xmas - On A Snowy Christmas Night	45-758	CB
Presley, Elvis	Xmas - On A Snowy Xmas Night	49-874	MM
Presley, Elvis	Xmas - Santa Bring My Baby Back..	14-808	THM
Presley, Elvis	Xmas - Santa Bring My Baby Back...	7-12	MM
Presley, Elvis	Xmas - Santa Claus Is Back In Town	49-875	MM
Presley, Elvis	Xmas - Silver Bells	49-866	MM
Presley, Elvis	Xmas - White Christmas	49-865	MM
Presley, Elvis	Xmas - White Christmas	45-760	CB
Presley, Elvis	Xmas - Winter Wonderland	49-869	MM
Presley, Elvis	Xmas - Wonderful World Of Christmas	45-759	CB
Presley, Elvis	Xmas - Wonderful World of Xmas the	49-878	MM
Presley, Elvis	You Don't Have To Say You Love Me	18-444	KC
Presley, Elvis	You Don't Have To SayYou Love Me	25-768	MM
Presley, Elvis	You'll Never Walk Alone	30-372	SC
Presley, Elvis	You'll Think Of Me	25-97	MM
Presley, Elvis	You're The Devil In Disguise	43-251	PSJT
Presley, Lisa Marie	Lights Out	25-534	MM
Presley, Lisa Marie	Lights Out	23-334	SC
Presley, Lisa Marie	Lights Out	32-176	THM
Presley, Lisa Marie	Sinking In	25-660	MM
Presley, Lisa Marie	Sinking In	19-541	SC

ARTIST	SONG TITLE	#	TYPE
Preston & Syretta	Duet - With You I'm Born Again	12-23	DK
Preston & Syretta	Duet - With You I'm Born Again	10-675	HE
Preston & Syretta	With You I'm Born Again	12-23	DK
Preston & Syretta	With You I'm Born Again	10-675	HE
Preston, Billy	Nothing From Nothing	2-439	SC
Preston, Billy	Will It Go Round In Circles	11-443	DK
Preston, Johnny	Running Bear	12-310	DK
Preston, Robert	Seventy Six Trombones	12-137	DK
Pretenders	Back On The Chain Gang	13-209	P
Pretenders	Back On The Chain Gang	24-451	SC
Pretenders	Brass In Pocket **	5-112	SC
Pretenders	Don't Get Me Wrong	24-563	SC
Pretenders	Everyday Is Like Sunday	14-884	SC
Pretenders	I'll Stand By You	6-643	MM
Pretenders	I'll Stand By You	2-470	SC
Pretenders	Middle Of The Road	24-434	SC
Pretenders	Thin Line Between Love & Hate	13-285	P
Pretenders	Xmas - Have Yourself A Merry Little	14-296	MM
Pretty Poison	Catch Me (I'm Falling)	17-23	DK
Price & Nelson	Duet - Faded Love	45-631	ASK
Price & Nelson	Faded Love - duet	45-631	ASK
Price, Kelly	You Should've Told Me	20-622	CB
Price, Lloyd	I'm Gonna Get Married	11-814	DK
Price, Lloyd	I'm Gonna Get Married	10-703	JVC
Price, Lloyd	I'm Gonna Get Married	14-343	SC
Price, Lloyd	Just Because	10-699	JVC
Price, Lloyd	Lawdy Miss Clawdy	12-371	DK
Price, Lloyd	Personality	17-361	DK
Price, Lloyd	Personality	10-702	JVC
Price, Lloyd	Personality	12-536	P
Price, Lloyd	Personality	10-609	SF
Price, Lloyd	Stagger Lee	35-1	CB
Price, Lloyd	Stagger Lee	11-384	DK
Price, Lloyd	Stagger Lee	10-700	JVC
Price, Lloyd	Stagger Lee	4-701	SC
Price, Lloyd	Where Were You On Our Wedding..	10-701	JVC
Price, Ray	Burning Memories	44-218	DFK
Price, Ray	City Lights	8-382	CB
Price, Ray	Crazy Arms	15-828	CB
Price, Ray	Crazy Arms	12-88	DK
Price, Ray	Crazy Arms	10-749	JVC
Price, Ray	Crazy Arms	5-222	SC
Price, Ray	Different Kind Of Flower a	45-736	VH
Price, Ray	For The Good Times	8-357	CB
Price, Ray	For The Good Times	26-256	DK
Price, Ray	For The Good Times	7-159	MM
Price, Ray	For The Good Times	8-676	SAV
Price, Ray	Heartaches By The Number	8-274	CB
Price, Ray	Heartaches By The Number	12-301	DK
Price, Ray	Heartaches By The Number	17-301	NA
Price, Ray	Heartaches By The Number	8-677	SAV
Price, Ray	Here Comes My Baby Back Again	47-790	SRK
Price, Ray	I Wish I Was 18 Again	45-343	BSP
Price, Ray	I Won't Mention It Again	8-284	CB
Price, Ray	I'll Be There	3-786	CB
Price, Ray	I'll Be There (When You Get Lonely)	45-629	PSJ
Price, Ray	I've Got A New Heartache	3-779	CB
Price, Ray	I've Got A New Heartache	14-331	SC
Price, Ray	Invitation To The Blues	8-420	CB
Price, Ray	Invitation To The Blues	5-104	SC
Price, Ray	Itsy Bitsy Teenie Weenie	45-627	JV
Price, Ray	My Shoes Keep Walking Back To..	4-863	SC
Price, Ray	My Shoes Keep Walking Back To...	3-774	CB
Price, Ray	Night Life	3-785	CB
Price, Ray	One More Time	3-783	CB
Price, Ray	One More Time	22-255	SC
Price, Ray	Other Woman the	45-882	VH
Price, Ray	Pride	22-246	SC
Price, Ray	Release Me	45-630	SV
Price, Ray	Same Old Me the	3-781	CB
Price, Ray	Same Old Me the	4-798	SC
Price, Ray	San Antonio Rose	45-628	P
Price, Ray	Sh's Got To Be A Saint	5-869	SC
Price, Ray	Sittin' And Thinkin'	46-30	SSK
Price, Ray	Soft Rain	3-780	CB
Price, Ray	Take Me As I Am	48-409	DFK
Price, Ray	Touch My Heart	3-778	CB
Price, Ray	Way To Survive a	45-880	VH
Price, Ray	You're The Best Thing That Ever...	8-800	CB
Pride & Ketchum	For Today	4-110	SC
Pride, Charley	All His Children	47-437	CB
Pride, Charley	All I Have To Offer You Is Me	8-360	CB
Pride, Charley	All I Have To Offer You Is Me	14-336	SC
Pride, Charley	Amazing Love	43-203	CB
Pride, Charley	Amazing Love	6-80	SC
Pride, Charley	Burgers And Fries	3-790	CB
Pride, Charley	Burgers And Fries	5-32	SC
Pride, Charley	Crystal Chandeliers	8-802	CB
Pride, Charley	Does My Ring Hurt Your Finger	8-422	CB
Pride, Charley	Don't Fight The Feelings Of Love	47-439	CB
Pride, Charley	Easy Part's Over the	47-436	CB
Pride, Charley	Every Heart Should Have One	43-208	CB

ARTIST	SONG TITLE	#	TYPE
Pride, Charley	Happiness Of Having You the	40-119	CB
Pride, Charley	Honky Tonk Blues	38-122	CB
Pride, Charley	Hope You're Feelin' Me Like I'm...	4-585	SC
Pride, Charley	I Can't Believe That You've Stopped...	47-434	CB
Pride, Charley	I Don't Know Why I Love You But I Do	47-440	FMK
Pride, Charley	I Don't Think She's In Love Anymore	40-107	CB
Pride, Charley	I Know One	6-12	SC
Pride, Charley	I Wonder Could I Love There Anymore	3-793	CB
Pride, Charley	I'd Rather Love You	43-205	CB
Pride, Charley	I'll Be Leaving Alone	3-789	CB
Pride, Charley	I'm Just Me	38-134	CB
Pride, Charley	I'm So Afraid Of Losing You	5-698	SC
Pride, Charley	Is Anybody Goin' To San Antone	8-273	CB
Pride, Charley	Is Anybody Goin' To San Antone	9-485	SAV
Pride, Charley	Is Anybody Going To San Antone	17-308	NA
Pride, Charley	Is Anybody Going To San Antone	20-12	SC
Pride, Charley	It's Gonna Take A Little Bit Longer	47-438	CB
Pride, Charley	Just Between You And Me	22-257	SC
Pride, Charley	Just For The Love Of It	24-247	SC
Pride, Charley	Kiss An Angel Good Morning	3-796	CB
Pride, Charley	Kiss An Angel Good Morning	12-52	DK
Pride, Charley	Kiss An Angel Good Morning	13-393	P
Pride, Charley	Let Me Live In The Light Of His Love	47-435	CB
Pride, Charley	Let The Chips Fall	40-116	CB
Pride, Charley	Me And Bobby McGee	47-441	KV
Pride, Charley	Miracles Music & My Wife	47-443	SRK
Pride, Charley	Missin' You	40-109	CB
Pride, Charley	Mississippi Cotton Pickin'...	38-121	CB
Pride, Charley	More To Me	40-113	CB
Pride, Charley	Mountain Of Love	3-791	CB
Pride, Charley	My Eyes Can Only See As Far As You	43-206	CB
Pride, Charley	Never Been So Loved	3-800	CB
Pride, Charley	Never Been So Loved	4-646	SC
Pride, Charley	Night Games	3-798	CB
Pride, Charley	Roll On Mississippi	38-123	CB
Pride, Charley	She's Just an Old Love Turned Memor	3-797	CB
Pride, Charley	She's Just An Old Love Turned Memor	5-751	SC
Pride, Charley	She's Too Good To Be	6-89	SC

ARTIST	SONG TITLE	#	TYPE
	True		
Pride, Charley	Shoulder To Cry On a	14-251	SC
Pride, Charley	Shutters And Boards	38-137	DFK
Pride, Charley	Snakes Crawl At Night the	8-440	CB
Pride, Charley	Someone Loves You Honey	40-112	CB
Pride, Charley	Someone Loves You Honey	9-856	SAV
Pride, Charley	Someone Loves You Honey	5-624	SC
Pride, Charley	Streets Of Baltimore	47-442	KV
Pride, Charley	Then Who Am I	43-207	CB
Pride, Charley	We Could	40-117	CB
Pride, Charley	When I Stop Leaving I'll Be Gone	40-114	CB
Pride, Charley	Where Do I Put Her Memory	40-108	CB
Pride, Charley	Whole Lot Of Things To Sing About	40-120	CB
Pride, Charley	Why Baby Why	3-799	CB
Pride, Charley	Xmas - Christmas In My Hometown	3-404	SC
Pride, Charley	You Almost Slipped My Mind	40-111	CB
Pride, Charley	You Win Again	43-209	CB
Pride, Charley	You're My Jamaica	40-110	CB
Pride, Charley	You're So Good When You're Bad	3-801	CB
Pride, Charley	You're So Good When You're Bad	34-249	CB
Priest, Maxi&Shaggy	That Girl	25-379	MM
Prima, Louis	That Old Black Magic	12-178	DK
Prima, Louis	That Old Black Magic	12-531	P
Primitive Radio God	Standing Outside a Broken Phone Boo	24-113	SC
Primus	Wynona's Big Brown Beaver **	5-542	SC
Prince	1999	12-809	P
Prince	7	12-761	P
Prince	Adore	49-828	KV
Prince	Alphabet Street	23-328	CB
Prince	Bat Dance	49-835	SAV
Prince	Call My Name	49-823	CB
Prince	Cream **	21-466	CB
Prince	Cream **	15-12	SC
Prince	Darling Nikki **	5-543	SC
Prince	Delirious	12-794	P
Prince	Delirious	5-611	SC
Prince	Diamonds And Pearls	23-329	CB
Prince	Dinner With Delores	49-833	KV
Prince	Do Me Baby	49-831	SC
Prince	Get Off	49-834	LG
Prince	Gold	49-827	KV
Prince	I Could Never Take the Place of Your Man	49-826	KV
Prince	I Hate U	4-687	SC
Prince	I Wanna Be Your Lover	7-95	MM
Prince	I Would Die For U	12-810	P

231

ARTIST	SONG TITLE	#	TYPE
Prince	If I Was Your Girlfriend	49-825	KV
Prince	Kiss	11-622	DK
Prince	Kiss	12-785	P
Prince	Let It Go	49-830	MM
Prince	Let's Go Crazy	11-731	DK
Prince	Let's Go Crazy	13-27	P
Prince	Let's Go Crazy	5-472	SC
Prince	Little Red Corvette	11-286	DK
Prince	Little Red Corvette	12-839	P
Prince	Little Red Corvette	3-560	SC
Prince	Little Red Corvette	21-602	SF
Prince	Morning Papers the	12-840	P
Prince	Morning Papers the	49-832	KV
Prince	Most Beautiful Girl In The World	2-121	SC
Prince	Peach	49-824	KV
Prince	Pop Life	23-330	CB
Prince	Purple Rain	11-642	DK
Prince	Purple Rain	12-756	P
Prince	Purple Rain	8-609	TT
Prince	Raspberry Beret	13-287	P
Prince	Round And Round	12-762	P
Prince	Sign O' The Times	23-331	CB
Prince	Thieves In The Temple	23-333	CB
Prince	U Got The Look	49-829	LG
Prince	When Doves Cry	16-775	DK
Prince	When Doves Cry	12-843	P
Prince & Easton	Duet - U Got The Look	23-332	CB
Prince & Easton	U Got The Look	23-332	CB
Prine, John	Ain't Hurtin' Nobody	23-524	CB
Prine, John	Angel From Montgomery	23-534	CB
Prine, John	Christmas In Prison	46-284	CB
Prine, John	City Of New Orleans	47-596	KV
Prine, John	Dear Abby	23-525	CB
Prine, John	Grandpa Was A Carpenter	23-528	CB
Prine, John	Great Compromise the	23-537	CB
Prine, John	Hello In There	23-529	CB
Prine, John	Illegal Smile	23-523	CB
Prine, John	Illegal Smile	2-756	SC
Prine, John	In A Town This Size	47-597	VH
Prine, John	Let's Talk Dirty In Hawaiian	46-285	RDK
Prine, John	Paradise	23-531	CB
Prine, John	Please Don't Bury Me	23-526	CB
Prine, John	Sam Stone	23-532	CB
Prine, John	Same Thing Happened To Me	45-873	VH
Prine, John	Souvenirs	23-527	CB
Prine, John	Spanish Pipedream	23-533	CB
Prine, John	Take A Look At My Heart	23-536	CB
Prine, John	Xmas - Christmas In Prison	46-284	CB
Prine, John	Yes I Guess They Oughta Name A Drin	23-535	CB
Prine, John	You Got Gold	23-530	CB

ARTIST	SONG TITLE	#	TYPE
Pritchett, Aaron	Hold My Beer	45-678	DCK
Proclaimers	I'm Gonna Be 500 Miles	12-242	DK
Proclaimers	I'm Gonna Be 500 Miles	6-414	MM
Proclaimers	I'm Gonna Be 500 Miles	24-149	SC
Procol Harem	Whiter Shade Of Pale	49-450	MM
Proctor, Rachel	Days Like This	36-366	CB
Proctor, Rachel	Days Like This	25-617	MM
Proctor, Rachel	Days Like This	19-67	ST
Proctor, Rachel	Days Like This	32-371	THM
Proctor, Rachel	Didn't I	19-705	ST
Proctor, Rachel	Me And Emily	20-328	ST
Proctor, Rachel	Where I Belong	22-71	CB
Proctor, Rachel	Where I Belong	30-8	SC
Professor Longhair	Hey Little Girl	17-319	SS
Profyle	Liar	14-26	THM
Prosser, James	Life Goes On	8-396	CB
Provine, D.	Don't Bring Lulu	29-822	SF
Pruett, Jeannie	Satin Sheets	13-371	P
Pruett, Jeannie	Satin Sheets	8-680	SAV
Pseudo Echo	Funky Town	33-323	CB
PSY	Gentleman	43-457	ASK
Psychedelic Furs	Pretty In Pink	13-33	P
Psychedelic Furs	Pretty In Pink	21-619	SF
Public, Joe	Live And Learn	48-576	DK
Puckett & Union Gap	Don't Give It To Him	4-213	SC
Puckett & Union Gap	Lady Willpower	34-22	CB
Puckett & Union Gap	Lady Willpower	3-24	SC
Puckett & Union Gap	Over You	3-15	SC
Puckett & Union Gap	This Girl Is A Woman Now	34-18	CB
Puckett & Union Gap	Woman Woman	20-68	SC
Puckett & Union Gap	Young Girl	33-259	CB
Puckett & Union Gap	Young Girl	11-556	DK
Puckett & Union Gap	Young Girl	13-267	P
Puckett & Union Gap	Young Girl	10-586	SF
Puddle Of Mud	Away From Me	23-269	THM
Puddle Of Mud	Blurry	25-145	MM
Puddle Of Mud	Blurry	16-310	TT
Puddle Of Mud	Blurry	33-426	CB
Puddle Of Mud	Control	16-314	TT
Puddle Of Mud	Psycho	36-438	CB
Puddle Of Mud	She Hates Me	25-340	MM
Puerto Rican Power	Latino - Pena De Amor	23-241	AI
Puff Daddy & Evans	Duet - I'll Be Missing You	20-125	PHM
Puff Daddy & Family	Duet - It's All About The Benjamins	14-442	SC
Puff Daddy& Evans	I'll Be Missing You	20-125	PHM
Puff Daddy& Family	It's All About The Benjamins	14-442	SC
Pullins, Larry	I'm A Nut	5-851	SC
Pure 13	Growing On Me	21-623	SF
Pure Prairie League	Amie	9-328	AG
Pure Prairie League	Amie	26-368	DK
Pure Prairie League	Let Me Love You Tonight	7-457	MM
Purify, James & Bob	I'm Your Puppet	35-80	CB

ARTIST	SONG TITLE	#	TYPE
Purify,James&Bobby	I'm Your Puppet	4-220	SC
Purify,James&Bobby	Shake A Tail Feather	22-399	SC
Pussycat Dolle w Will I Am	Beep **	48-600	DK
Pussycat Dolls	Don't Cha	23-315	CB
Pussycat Dolls	Don't Cha	30-132	PT
Pussycat Dolls	How Many Times How Many Lies	30-263	CB
Pussycat Dolls	Hush Hush	36-295	PHM
Pussycat Dolls	Jai Ho (You Are My Destiny)	44-138	BKD
Pussycat Dolls	When I Grow Up	36-502	CB
Pussycat Dolls w Rhymes	Don't Cha (Radio Vers)	37-103	SC
Pussycat Dolls w Snoop Dogg	Buttons	30-734	SF
Pussycat Dolls&Snoo	Duet - Buttons	30-734	SF
Puth & Trainor	Duet - Marvin Gaye	45-143	BH
Puth & Trainor	Marvin Gaye - duet	45-143	BH
Puth, Charlie	I Won't Tell A Soul	47-576	KV
Puth, Charlie	One Call Away	47-577	BKD
Puth, Charlie	See You Again (Piano Version)	47-575	KV
Puth, Charlie	Some Type Of Love	49-656	KV
Python, Monty	Lumberjack Song	23-27	SC
Q, Stacey	Two Of Hearts	24-550	SC
Quayle, Stephanie	Stand Back	41-91	PHN
Queen	Another One Bites The Dust	12-334	DK
Queen	Bicycle Race	20-77	SC
Queen	Bohemian Rhapsody	26-347	DK
Queen	Bohemian Rhapsody	9-677	SAV
Queen	Crazy Little Thing Called Love	11-625	DK
Queen	Crazy Little Thing Called Love	12-835	P
Queen	Fat Bottomed Girls **	2-725	SC
Queen	Good Old Fashioned Lover Boy	49-80	ZPA
Queen	Killer Queen	12-333	DK
Queen	Now I'm Here	49-79	ZPA
Queen	Somebody To Love	18-261	DK
Queen	Tie Your Mother Down	4-569	SC
Queen	We Are The Champions	35-140	CB
Queen	We Are The Champions	12-185	DK
Queen	We Are The Champions	15-181	MH
Queen	We Will Rock You	17-84	DK
Queen	We Will Rock You	12-776	P
Queen	You're My Best Friend	12-336	DK
Queen	You're My Best Friend	13-7	P
Queens/Stone Age	In My Head	30-229	PHM
Queens/Stone Age	No One Knows	18-827	THM
Queensryche	Silent Lucidity	13-599	P
Queensyrche	Jet City Woman	18-377	SAV
Queensyrche	Jet City Woman	5-605	SC
Queensyrche	Queen Of The Reich	21-758	SC
Queensyrche	Silent Lucidity	18-378	SAV

ARTIST	SONG TITLE	#	TYPE
Quest for Camelot	Show - I Stand All Alone	17-668	PR
Quest for Camelot	Show - In My Father's Wings	17-666	PR
Quest for Camelot	Show - Looking Thru Your Eyes	17-664	PR
Quest for Camelot	Show - Prayer the	17-665	PR
Quiet Riot	Cum On Feel The Noize	12-93	DK
Quiet Riot	Metal Health	23-58	MH
Quiet Riot	Metal Health	5-490	SC
Quinn The Eskimo	Show - Mighty Quinn the	6-897	MM
Ra	Do You Call My Name	23-167	PHM
Rabbitt & Gayle	Duet - Endless Love	11-459	DK
Rabbitt & Gayle	Duet - You And I	8-109	CB
Rabbitt & Gayle	Duet - You And I	26-369	DK
Rabbitt & Gayle	Duet - You And I	6-231	MM
Rabbitt & Gayle	Duet - You And I	13-197	P
Rabbitt & Gayle	Duet - You And I	2-306	SC
Rabbitt & Gayle	Endless Love	11-459	DK
Rabbitt & Gayle	You And I	8-109	CB
Rabbitt & Gayle	You And I	26-369	DK
Rabbitt & Gayle	You And I	6-231	MM
Rabbitt & Gayle	You And I	13-197	P
Rabbitt & Gayle	You And I	2-306	SC
Rabbitt & Newton-John	Both To Each Other (Friends & Lovers)	48-39	CB
Rabbitt & Newton-John	Duet - Both To Each Other	48-39	CB
Rabbitt, Eddie	B-B-Burnin' Up With Love	5-329	SC
Rabbitt, Eddie	Best Year Of My Life the	5-325	SC
Rabbitt, Eddie	Drinkin' My Baby Off My Mind	15-74	CB
Rabbitt, Eddie	Drinkin' My Baby Off My Mind	3-382	SC
Rabbitt, Eddie	Drivin' My Life Away	11-723	DK
Rabbitt, Eddie	Drivin' My Life Away	13-438	P
Rabbitt, Eddie	Hearts On Fire	14-320	SC
Rabbitt, Eddie	I Can't Help Myself	48-34	CB
Rabbitt, Eddie	I Don't Know Where To Start	48-40	CB
Rabbitt, Eddie	I Just Want To Love You	48-36	CB
Rabbitt, Eddie	I Love A Rainy Night	17-7	DK
Rabbitt, Eddie	I Love A Rainy Night	13-439	P
Rabbitt, Eddie	I Wanna Dance With You	11-423	DK
Rabbitt, Eddie	On Second Thought	33-100	CB
Rabbitt, Eddie	On Second Thought	11-703	DK
Rabbitt, Eddie	On Second Thought	2-388	SC
Rabbitt, Eddie	Pour Me Another Tequila	14-310	SC
Rabbitt, Eddie	Repetitive Regret	48-38	CB
Rabbitt, Eddie	Rocky Mountain Music	8-449	CB
Rabbitt, Eddie	Running With The Wind	48-37	CB
Rabbitt, Eddie	She's Comin' Back To Stay	5-324	SC
Rabbitt, Eddie	Someone Could Lose A Heart Tonite	8-203	CB
Rabbitt, Eddie	Someone Could Lose A Heart Tonite	5-669	SC
Rabbitt, Eddie	Step By Step	13-455	P

ARTIST	SONG TITLE	#	TYPE
Rabbitt, Eddie	Suspicions	33-56	CB
Rabbitt, Eddie	Suspicions	9-572	SAV
Rabbitt, Eddie	Suspicions	4-641	SC
Rabbitt, Eddie	That's Why I Fell In Love	12-72	DK
Rabbitt, Eddie	Wanderer the	48-33	CB
Rabbitt, Eddie	Warning Sign	5-327	SC
Rabbitt, Eddie	We Can't Go On Living Like This	48-35	CB
Rabbitt, Eddie	Xmas - We Wish You A Merry Xmas	18-761	CB
Rabbitt, Eddie	You Can't Run From Love	5-322	SC
Rabbitt, Eddie	You Don't Love Me Anymore	48-41	CB
Racey	Some Girls	48-756	P
Radiohead	Creep	13-241	P
Radiohead	Go To Sleep	32-440	THM
Radiohead	There There	32-292	THM
Rae, Corinne Bailey	Put Your Records On	36-182	PHM
Rae, Corinne Bailey	Trouble Sleeping	30-716	SF
RaeLynn	Boyfriend	48-471	BKD
RaeLynn	Careless	48-398	DCK
RaeLynn	For A Boy	48-470	BKD
RaeLynn	God Made Girls	48-417	KV
Rafferty, Gerry	Baker Street	29-265	SC
Rafferty, Gerry	Get It Right Next Time	21-803	SC
Rafferty, Gerry	Right Down The Line	15-742	SC
Rainman	Show - Iko Iko	6-885	MM
Rainwater, Marvin	Gonna Find Me A Bluebird	5-584	SC
Rainwater, Marvin	Whole Lotta Woman	10-605	SF
Raitt, Bonnie	Come To Me	10-767	JVC
Raitt, Bonnie	Dimming Of The Day	45-858	VH
Raitt, Bonnie	Guilty	46-129	SC
Raitt, Bonnie	Have A Heart	11-641	DK
Raitt, Bonnie	Have A Heart	10-772	JVC
Raitt, Bonnie	I Can't Help You Now	25-210	MM
Raitt, Bonnie	I Can't Make You Love Me	6-97	MM
Raitt, Bonnie	I Can't Make You Love Me	10-765	JVC
Raitt, Bonnie	I Don't Want Anything To Change	29-217	PHM
Raitt, Bonnie	Love Letter	43-114	SC
Raitt, Bonnie	Love Me Like A Man	15-21	SC
Raitt, Bonnie	Love Sneakin' Up On You	2-113	SC
Raitt, Bonnie	Marriage Made In Hollywood	39-110	PHM
Raitt, Bonnie	Nick Of Time	17-403	DK
Raitt, Bonnie	Nick Of Time	10-773	JVC
Raitt, Bonnie	Nick Of Time	6-359	MM
Raitt, Bonnie	Nick Of Time	12-882	P
Raitt, Bonnie	No Business	10-768	JVC
Raitt, Bonnie	One Belief Away	5-277	SC
Raitt, Bonnie	Runaway	33-305	CB
Raitt, Bonnie	Runaway	10-769	JVC
Raitt, Bonnie	Silver Lining	25-313	MM

ARTIST	SONG TITLE	#	TYPE
Raitt, Bonnie	Something To Talk About	11-803	DK
Raitt, Bonnie	Something To Talk About	10-764	JVC
Raitt, Bonnie	Something To Talk About	9-264	SC
Raitt, Bonnie	Tangled And Dark	10-766	JVC
Raitt, Bonnie	Thing Called Love	33-334	CB
Raitt, Bonnie	Thing Called Love	10-771	JVC
Raitt, Bonnie	Too Soon To Tell	10-770	JVC
Raitt, Bonnie	You	6-634	MM
Ram Jam Band	Black Betty	4-565	SC
Rambler	Dreamin'	9-408	CB
Rammstein	Du Hast (English Version)	21-761	SC
Ramones	Beat On The Brat	45-85	SC
Ramones	Blitzkrieg Bop	45-84	SC
Ramones	I Wanna Be Sedated	16-456	MH
Ramones	I Wanna Be Sedated	21-411	SC
Ramones	Poison Heart	45-86	DCK
Ramones	Sheena Is A Punk Rocker	45-87	SC
Rancid	Fall Back Down	32-403	THM
Randall, Jon	Cold Coffee Morning	8-951	CB
Randall, Jon	I Came Straight To You	2-827	SC
Randall, Jon	She Don't Believe In Fairy Tales	10-168	SC
Randy & Rainbows	Denise	5-169	SC
Randy & the Rockets	Cajun - Cajun Twist	49-403	SCK
Randy & the Rockets	Cajun Twist	49-403	SCK
Randy Rogers Band	Down And Out	29-48	CB
Randy Rogers Band	Interstate	38-224	CB
Randy Rogers Band	Kiss Me In The Dark	30-49	CB
Randy Rogers Band	One More Goodbye	30-340	CB
Randy Rogers Band	Tonight's Not The Night	22-321	CB
Rare Earth	Get Ready	11-646	DK
Rare Earth	I Just Want To Celebrate	16-407	PR
Rascal Flatts	Banjo	48-503	KVD
Rascal Flatts	Bless The Broken Road	22-93	CB
Rascal Flatts	Bless The Broken Road	21-657	SC
Rascal Flatts	DJ Tonight	44-288	KCDC
Rascal Flatts	Every Day	36-577	CB
Rascal Flatts	Fast Cars And Freedom	22-329	CB
Rascal Flatts	Feels Like Today	20-445	ST
Rascal Flatts	Here Comes Goodbye	48-709	BKD
Rascal Flatts	Here's To You	23-278	CB
Rascal Flatts	I Like The Sound Of That	44-289	KCDC
Rascal Flatts	I Melt	35-426	CB
Rascal Flatts	I Melt	25-647	MM
Rascal Flatts	I Melt	19-260	ST
Rascal Flatts	I Melt	32-339	THM
Rascal Flatts	I'm Movin' On	15-858	ST
Rascal Flatts	I'm Moving On	33-149	CB
Rascal Flatts	I'm Moving On	25-49	MM
Rascal Flatts	Life Is A Highway	30-16	CB
Rascal Flatts	Love You Out Loud	25-515	MM

ARTIST	SONG TITLE	#	TYPE
Rascal Flatts	Love You Out Loud	18-784	ST
Rascal Flatts	Love You Out Loud	32-150	THM
Rascal Flatts	Mayberry	19-701	ST
Rascal Flatts	Me And My Gang	29-592	CB
Rascal Flatts	My Wish	30-110	CB
Rascal Flatts	My Wish	30-97	PHM
Rascal Flatts	My Worst Fear	23-395	CB
Rascal Flatts	One Good Love	22-7	CB
Rascal Flatts	Payback	45-280	BKD
Rascal Flatts	Prayin' For Daylight	13-828	CHM
Rascal Flatts	Revolution	30-546	CB
Rascal Flatts	Rewind	43-133	PHN
Rascal Flatts	She's Leaving	39-48	ASK
Rascal Flatts	Skin	22-313	CB
Rascal Flatts	Stand	30-307	CB
Rascal Flatts	Summer Nights	37-49	CB
Rascal Flatts	Take Me There	30-531	CB
Rascal Flatts	These Days	34-384	CB
Rascal Flatts	These Days	25-294	MM
Rascal Flatts	These Days	17-581	ST
Rascal Flatts	These Days	32-75	THM
Rascal Flatts	This Everyday Love	14-126	CB
Rascal Flatts	This Everyday Love	14-14	CHM
Rascal Flatts	This Everyday Love	19-224	CSZ
Rascal Flatts	Walk The Llama Llama	14-791	ST
Rascal Flatts	What Hurts The Most	29-185	CB
Rascal Flatts	What Hurts The Most	29-705	ST
Rascal Flatts	While You Loved Me	9-866	ST
Rascal Flatts	While You Loved Me	16-277	TT
Rascal Flatts	Winner At A Losing Game	36-549	CB
Rascals	Beautiful Morning a	3-17	SC
Rascals	Good Lovin'	48-588	DK
Rascals	Groovin'	3-256	SC
Rascals	I've Been Lonely Too Long	14-344	SC
Rascals	It's A Beautiful Morning	18-252	DK
Rascals	People Got To Be Free	26-370	DK
Rascals	People Got To Be Free	12-871	P
Rascals	You Better Run	10-494	DA
Raspberries	Go All The Way	2-722	SC
Ratt	Lack Of Communication	21-777	SC
Ratt	Lay It Down	27-402	DK
Ratt	Round & Round	12-5	DK
Ratt	Round & Round	3-616	SC
Ratt	Round And Round	23-57	MH
Raven, Eddy	I Got Mexico	4-649	SC
Raven, Eddy	Joe Knows How To Live	29-656	SC
Raven, Eddy	Shine Shine Shine	20-289	SC
Rawls, Lou	Lady Love	28-106	DK
Rawls, Lou	Lady Love	9-768	SAV
Rawls, Lou	Natural Man	25-272	MM
Rawls, Lou	This Song Will Last Forever	10-500	DA
Rawls, Lou	You'll Never Find Another Love Like	17-141	DK
Rawls, Lou	You'll Never Find	17-433	KC

ARTIST	SONG TITLE	#	TYPE
	Another Love Like		
Rawls, Lou	You'll Never Find Another Love Like	4-293	SC
Ray, Jimmy	Are You Jimmy Ray	5-190	SC
Ray, Johnnie	Cry	12-309	DK
Ray, Johnnie	Cry	7-297	MM
Ray, Johnnie	Cry	18-621	PS
Ray, Johnnie	Cry	4-185	SC
Ray, Johnnie	Just Walkin' In The Rain	13-90	P
Ray, Johnnie	Just Walkin' In The Rain	18-622	PS
Ray, Johnnie	Little White Cloud That Cried	3-887	PS
Ray, Johnnie	Please Mr. Sun	18-624	PS
Ray, Johnnie	Walkin' My Baby Back Home	18-623	PS
Ray, Michael	Kiss You In The Morning	48-699	BKD
Ray, Michael	Real Men Love Jesus	48-700	KCA
Ray/Goodman/Brown	Special Lady	2-561	SC
Raybon Brothers	Butterfly Kisses	16-577	SC
Raybon Brothers	Way She's Looking the	12-929	CB
Raybon, Marty	Cracker Jack Diamond	6-69	SC
Raybon, Marty	Searching For The Missing Peace	14-75	CB
Raye & Eakes	Duet - Tired Of Lovin' This Way	14-82	CB
Raye & Eakes	Tired Of Loving This Way	14-82	CB
Raye, Collin	Ain't Nobody Gonna Take That From	16-165	CB
Raye, Collin	Ain't Nobody Gonna Take That From	15-680	ST
Raye, Collin	Ain't Nobody Gonna Take That From..	25-8	MM
Raye, Collin	All I Can Be Is A Sweet Memory	1-121	CB
Raye, Collin	Anyone Else	19-199	CB
Raye, Collin	Anyone Else	7-853	CHT
Raye, Collin	Anyone Else	22-712	ST
Raye, Collin	Couldn't Last A Moment	13-809	CHM
Raye, Collin	Couldn't Last A Moment	23-374	SC
Raye, Collin	Cover You In Kisses	22-795	ST
Raye, Collin	Every Second	1-123	CB
Raye, Collin	Every Second	26-529	DK
Raye, Collin	Every Second	6-122	MM
Raye, Collin	Every Second	2-509	SC
Raye, Collin	Gift the	10-783	JVC
Raye, Collin	Gift the	22-417	ST
Raye, Collin	Holes In The Floor Of Heaven	22-783	ST
Raye, Collin	I Can Still Feel You	8-98	CB
Raye, Collin	I can Still Feel You	5-294	SC
Raye, Collin	I Know That's Right	29-59	CB
Raye, Collin	I Think About You	1-134	CB
Raye, Collin	I Think About You	4-200	SC
Raye, Collin	I Want You Bad & That Ain't Good	1-125	CB
Raye, Collin	I Want You Bad & That Ain't Good	6-221	MM

ARTIST	SONG TITLE	#	TYPE
Raye, Collin	If I Were You	4-72	SC
Raye, Collin	In This Life	1-124	CB
Raye, Collin	In This Life	10-760	JVC
Raye, Collin	Let It Be Me	1-126	CB
Raye, Collin	Let It Be Me	4-116	SC
Raye, Collin	Little Red Rodeo	8-229	CB
Raye, Collin	Little Red Rodeo	10-124	SC
Raye, Collin	Little Red Rodeo	22-756	ST
Raye, Collin	Little Rock	1-130	CB
Raye, Collin	Little Rock	12-453	P
Raye, Collin	Little Rock	2-421	SC
Raye, Collin	Love Me	1-122	CB
Raye, Collin	Love Me	6-205	MM
Raye, Collin	Love Me	9-540	SAV
Raye, Collin	Love Me	2-19	SC
Raye, Collin	Love Remains	1-135	CB
Raye, Collin	Love Remains	7-336	MM
Raye, Collin	Love Remains	4-236	SC
Raye, Collin	Man Of My Word	6-673	MM
Raye, Collin	Man Of My Word	3-540	SC
Raye, Collin	My Kind Of Girl	1-131	CB
Raye, Collin	My Kind Of Girl	34-309	CB
Raye, Collin	My Kind Of Girl	17-263	NA
Raye, Collin	My Kind Of Girl	2-571	SC
Raye, Collin	Not That Different	1-133	CB
Raye, Collin	Not That Different	7-175	MM
Raye, Collin	Not That Different	3-654	SC
Raye, Collin	On The Verge	14-652	CB
Raye, Collin	On The Verge	22-405	CHM
Raye, Collin	One Boy One Girl	1-132	CB
Raye, Collin	One Boy One Girl	26-530	DK
Raye, Collin	One Boy One Girl	6-843	MM
Raye, Collin	One Boy One Girl	3-434	SC
Raye, Collin	Open Arms	22-648	ST
Raye, Collin	She's All That	22-459	ST
Raye, Collin	Soldier's Prayer a	30-463	CB
Raye, Collin	Somebody Else's Moon	1-127	CB
Raye, Collin	Someone You Used To Know	8-157	CB
Raye, Collin	Start Over Georgia	10-208	SC
Raye, Collin	Start Over Georgia	22-428	ST
Raye, Collin	That Was A River	1-128	CB
Raye, Collin	That's My Story	1-129	CB
Raye, Collin	That's My Story	26-354	DK
Raye, Collin	That's My Story	6-453	MM
Raye, Collin	That's My Story	2-6	SC
Raye, Collin	What I Need	16-435	ST
Raye, Collin	What If Jesus Comes Back Like That	7-177	MM
Raye, Collin	What If Jesus Comes Back Like That	4-23	SC
Raye, Collin	What The Heart Wants	7-672	CHM
Raye, Collin	Xmas - What If Jesus Comes Back	18-747	CB
Raye, Collin	You Still Take Me There	14-840	ST
Raye, Collin	You Still Take Me There	15-219	THM
Raye, Susan	Whatcha Gonna Do With	45-687	VH

ARTIST	SONG TITLE	#	TYPE
	A Dog Like That		
Rays	Silhouettes	11-510	DK
Rays	Silhouettes	25-177	MM
Razorlight	America	46-420	SF
Razorlight	Golden Touch	30-738	SF
Razorlight	In The Morning	30-463	CB
Razorlight	In The Morning	30-731	SF
Rea, Chris	Driving Home For Christmas	45-778	ZM
Rea, Chris	Fool	3-448	SC
Rea, Chris	Xmas - Driving Home For Christmas	45-778	ZM
Ready For The World	Oh Sheila	35-198	CB
Ready for the World	Oh Sheila	12-380	DK
Real Thing	Can't Get By Without You	10-544	SF
Red Hot Chili Peppe	Aeroplane	4-604	SC
Red Hot Chili Peppe	By The Way	25-342	MM
Red Hot Chili Peppe	Californication	15-430	PHM
Red Hot Chili Peppe	Californication	19-606	SGB
Red Hot Chili Peppe	Can't Stop	20-456	CB
Red Hot Chili Peppe	Can't Stop	23-170	PHM
Red Hot Chili Peppe	Dosed	32-331	THM
Red Hot Chili Peppe	Fortune Faded	23-268	THM
Red Hot Chili Peppe	My Friends	15-535	THM
Red Hot Chili Peppe	Otherside	13-843	PHM
Red Hot Chili Peppe	Scar Tissue	8-510	PHT
Red Hot Chili Peppe	Tell Me Baby	30-722	SF
Red Hot Chili Peppe	Under The Bridge	6-167	MM
Red Hot Chili Peppe	Zephyr Song the	25-397	MM
Red Jumpsuit Apparatus	Your Guardian Angel	30-594	PHM
Redbone	Come And Get Your Love	11-294	DK
Redding, Otis	Can't Turn You Loose (Live)	46-163	SC
Redding, Otis	Dock Of The Bay	17-39	DK
Redding, Otis	Dock Of The Bay	12-641	P
Redding, Otis	Dock Of The Bay	19-105	SAV
Redding, Otis	Dock Of The Bay	2-85	SC
Redding, Otis	Dreams To Remember	47-361	MM
Redding, Otis	Fa Fa Fa Fa Fa (Sad Song)	46-162	SC
Redding, Otis	Fa Fa Fa Fa Fa Fa	47-357	LE
Redding, Otis	Happy Song the	47-359	LE
Redding, Otis	Hard To Handle	47-356	LE
Redding, Otis	I Can't Turn You Loose	47-362	PS
Redding, Otis	I've Been Loving You So Long	6-143	MM
Redding, Otis	Mr. Pitiful	47-354	KV
Redding, Otis	Papa's Got A Brand New Bag	47-360	LE
Redding, Otis	Respect	47-355	KV
Redding, Otis	Shake	47-363	SC
Redding, Otis	Sittin' On The Dock Of The Bay	14-550	SC
Redding, Otis	Stand By Me	47-353	KV
Redding, Otis	These Arms Of Mine	33-244	CB

ARTIST	SONG TITLE	#	TYPE
Redding, Otis	Tramp	47-358	LE
Redding, Otis	Try A Little Tenderness	35-75	CB
Redding, Otis	Try A Little Tenderness	12-713	P
Reddmann	Xmas - Chasin' That Neon Reindeer	18-724	CB
Reddmann & Vale	If I Had A Nickle (One Thin Dime)	14-618	SC
Reddy, Helen	Ain't No Way To Treat A Lady	16-156	SC
Reddy, Helen	Angie Baby	16-822	DK
Reddy, Helen	Delta Dawn	11-191	DK
Reddy, Helen	Delta Dawn	13-441	P
Reddy, Helen	Delta Dawn	9-844	SAV
Reddy, Helen	I Am Woman	16-751	DK
Reddy, Helen	I Am Woman	2-436	SC
Reddy, Helen	Leave Me Alone (Ruby Red Dress)	28-269	DK
Reddy, Helen	You And Me Against The World	12-45	DK
Rednex	Cotton Eye Joe	24-437	SC
Rednex	Cotton Eye Joe - DANCE #	22-386	SC
Rednex	Old Pop And An Oak	49-20	KV
Reed, Jerry	Amos Moses	20-723	SC
Reed, Jerry	Bird the	21-471	SC
Reed, Jerry	East Bound And Down	8-25	CB
Reed, Jerry	East Bound And Down	20-724	SC
Reed, Jerry	Good Woman's Love a	20-721	SC
Reed, Jerry	How Do You Do It	3-810	SC
Reed, Jerry	I Love You What Can I Say	20-725	SC
Reed, Jerry	Lord Mr. Ford	20-722	SC
Reed, Jerry	She Got Gold Mine I Got The Shaft	13-461	P
Reed, Jerry	She Got Gold Mine I Got The Shaft	9-463	SAV
Reed, Jerry	She Got Gold Mine I Got The Shaft	20-726	SC
Reed, Jerry	She Got The Goldmine I Got..	33-76	CB
Reed, Jerry	When You're Hot You're Hot	13-504	P
Reed, Jerry	When You're Hot You're Hot	20-720	SC
Reed, Jerry	Xmas - Christmas Time Is Coming	8-56	CB
Reed, Jimmy	Big Boss Man	7-220	MM
Reed, Jimmy	You Got Me Runnin'	7-223	MM
Reed, Lou	Sweet Jane	21-810	SC
Reed, Lou	Sweet Jane	19-283	SGB
Reed, Lou	Walk On The Wild Side	2-717	SC
Reese, Della	S'Wonderful	15-839	MM
Reeves & Cline	Duet - Have You Ever Been Lonely	3-161	CB
Reeves & Cline	Duet - Have You Ever Been Lonely	2-297	SC
Reeves & Cline	Have You Ever Been Lonely	3-161	CB
Reeves & Cline	Have You Ever Been Lonely	2-297	SC

ARTIST	SONG TITLE	#	TYPE
Reeves & West, D	Duet - Love Is No Excuse	45-263	SSK
Reeves & West, D	Love Is No Excuse - duet	45-263	SSK
Reeves, Del	Girl On The Billboard	3-899	CB
Reeves, Del	Girl On The Billboard	12-34	DK
Reeves, Jim	Adios Amigo	8-564	CB
Reeves, Jim	Adios Amigo	3-832	LG
Reeves, Jim	Adios Amigo	5-371	SC
Reeves, Jim	Am I Losing You	8-785	CB
Reeves, Jim	Am I Losing You	3-841	LG
Reeves, Jim	Am I That Easy To Forget	45-266	VH
Reeves, Jim	Angels Don't Lie	44-245	SRK
Reeves, Jim	Anna Marie	40-123	CB
Reeves, Jim	Anna Marie	49-747	KRG
Reeves, Jim	Billy Bayou	40-124	CK
Reeves, Jim	Billy Bayou	4-866	SC
Reeves, Jim	Bimbo	8-574	CB
Reeves, Jim	Blizzard the	45-259	OZP
Reeves, Jim	Blue Boy	8-820	CB
Reeves, Jim	Blue Boy	40-125	CK
Reeves, Jim	Blue Boy	5-575	SC
Reeves, Jim	Blue Side Of Lonesome	8-573	CB
Reeves, Jim	Bottle Takes Effect	45-262	VH
Reeves, Jim	But You Love Me Daddy	44-240	DCK
Reeves, Jim	But You Love Me Daddy	49-741	DCK
Reeves, Jim	Cryin' In My Sleep	44-256	DFK
Reeves, Jim	Dear Hearts And Gentle People	44-265	OZP
Reeves, Jim	Deep Dark Water	44-258	DFK
Reeves, Jim	Distant Drums	8-575	CB
Reeves, Jim	Distant Drums	3-826	LG
Reeves, Jim	Distant Drums	13-520	P
Reeves, Jim	Distant Drums	9-620	SAV
Reeves, Jim	Don't Let Me Cross Over	45-270	DCK
Reeves, Jim	Fallen Star a	49-803	VH
Reeves, Jim	Fool's Paradise	44-239	DCK
Reeves, Jim	Four Walls	8-572	CB
Reeves, Jim	Four Walls	40-122	CK
Reeves, Jim	Four Walls	3-834	LG
Reeves, Jim	Four Walls	3-596	SC
Reeves, Jim	Good Moring Self	45-724	VH
Reeves, Jim	Have I Told You Lately	44-227	EZC
Reeves, Jim	He'll Have To Go	15-831	CB
Reeves, Jim	He'll Have To Go	40-128	CK
Reeves, Jim	He'll Have To Go	3-839	LG
Reeves, Jim	He'll Have To Go	13-370	P
Reeves, Jim	He'll Have To Go	9-610	SAV
Reeves, Jim	Home	40-126	CK
Reeves, Jim	Home	5-94	SC
Reeves, Jim	How's The World Treating You	44-251	SRK
Reeves, Jim	I Don't See Me In Your Eyes Anymore	44-246	SRK
Reeves, Jim	I Guess I'm Crazy	15-82	CB
Reeves, Jim	I Guess I'm Crazy	12-71	DK
Reeves, Jim	I Guess I'm Crazy	14-334	SC

ARTIST	SONG TITLE	#	TYPE
Reeves, Jim	I Heard A Heart Break Last Night	44-257	DFK
Reeves, Jim	I Love You Because	3-827	LG
Reeves, Jim	I Love You Because	10-580	SF
Reeves, Jim	I Missed Me	44-250	SRK
Reeves, Jim	I Won't Come In While He's There	3-829	LG
Reeves, Jim	I Won't Forget You	3-837	LG
Reeves, Jim	I'll Fly Away	44-266	OZP
Reeves, Jim	I'm Beginning To Forget You	44-259	DFK
Reeves, Jim	I'm Getting Better	22-252	SC
Reeves, Jim	I'm Gonna Change Everything	22-250	SC
Reeves, Jim	I've Enjoyed As Much of This as I Can Stand	44-234	DCK
Reeves, Jim	Is It Really Over	8-576	CB
Reeves, Jim	Is It Really Over	40-127	CK
Reeves, Jim	Is It Really Over	3-835	LG
Reeves, Jim	Is It Really Over	5-855	SC
Reeves, Jim	It Hurts So Much	3-836	LG
Reeves, Jim	It's Only A Paper Moon	45-260	DKM
Reeves, Jim	Just Walking In The Rain	45-267	VH
Reeves, Jim	Letter Edged In Black	45-269	STTW
Reeves, Jim	Letter To My Heart a	49-649	DFK
Reeves, Jim	Linda	44-241	DCK
Reeves, Jim	Little Ole Dime	44-230	SRK
Reeves, Jim	Lonesome Waltz	49-796	VH
Reeves, Jim	Losing Your Love	49-800	VH
Reeves, Jim	Memories Are Made Of This	44-228	SRK
Reeves, Jim	Merry Christmas Polka	49-288	CON
Reeves, Jim	Mexicali Rose	44-232	SRK
Reeves, Jim	Mexican Joe	8-577	CB
Reeves, Jim	Missing Angel	46-214	SF
Reeves, Jim	Missing You	8-563	CB
Reeves, Jim	Moonlight And Roses	3-150	LG
Reeves, Jim	Nobody's Fool	45-261	VH
Reeves, Jim	Not Until The Next Time	3-151	LG
Reeves, Jim	Oh How I Miss You Tonight	44-253	DFK
Reeves, Jim	Oklahoma Hills	44-263	SSK
Reeves, Jim	Old Tige	44-229	SRK
Reeves, Jim	One Has My Name, One Has My..	44-264	TU
Reeves, Jim	Read This Letter	49-798	VH
Reeves, Jim	Red Rose From The Blue Side Of Town	8-568	CB
Reeves, Jim	Rosa Rio	44-231	SRK
Reeves, Jim	Roses	44-254	DFK
Reeves, Jim	Senor Santa Claus - xmas	45-268	DFK
Reeves, Jim	Silver Bells - Xmas	44-252	STTW
Reeves, Jim	Snowflake	45-258	CKC
Reeves, Jim	Somewhere Along The Line	44-235	DCK
Reeves, Jim	Stranger Just A Friend, A	44-261	OZP
Reeves, Jim	Sweet Sue Just You	44-242	DCK
Reeves, Jim	Sweet Sue Just You	47-841	DCK
Reeves, Jim	Take Me In Your Arms And Hold Me	45-264	BSP
Reeves, Jim	Talking Walls	47-728	SRK
Reeves, Jim	Talking Walls, The	44-236	DCK
Reeves, Jim	Talking Walls, The	44-233	SRK
Reeves, Jim	That's When I See The Blues	44-249	SRK
Reeves, Jim	There's A Heartache Following Me	3-840	LG
Reeves, Jim	There's Always Me	45-265	BSP
Reeves, Jim	There's Been A Change In Me	44-267	CKC
Reeves, Jim	This Is It	8-809	CB
Reeves, Jim	This Is It	4-799	SC
Reeves, Jim	This World Is Not My Home	44-244	DCK
Reeves, Jim	Trouble In Amen Corner	49-300	LDK
Reeves, Jim	Trouble Is A Woman	44-262	SC
Reeves, Jim	Two Shadows On Your Window	44-260	DFK
Reeves, Jim	We Thank Thee (VR)	44-243	DCK
Reeves, Jim	Welcome To My World	8-571	CB
Reeves, Jim	Welcome To My World	40-121	CK
Reeves, Jim	Welcome To My World	3-828	LG
Reeves, Jim	Welcome To My World	6-788	MM
Reeves, Jim	Welcome To My World	5-212	SC
Reeves, Jim	What Would You Do	49-801	VH
Reeves, Jim	When Two Worlds Collide	3-831	LG
Reeves, Jim	When You Are Gone	44-237	DCK
Reeves, Jim	When You Are Gone	44-247	SRK
Reeves, Jim	Wild Rose	44-248	SRK
Reeves, Jim	Wild Rose	47-739	SRK
Reeves, Jim	World You Left Behind, The	44-255	DFK
Reeves, Jim	Xmas - Merry Christmas Polka	49-288	CON
Reeves, Jim	Xmas - Old Christmas Card	8-58	CB
Reeves, Jim	Xmas - Senor Santa Claus	45-268	DFK
Reeves, Jim	Xmas - Silver Bells	44-252	STTW
Reeves, Jim	You Are My Love	49-799	VH
Reeves, Jim	You're Free To Go	44-238	DCK
Reeves, Jim	You're The Only Good Thing..	3-838	LG
Reeves, Jim	Your Old Love Letters	49-802	VH
Reeves, Julie	He Keeps Me In One Piece	8-965	CB
Reeves, Julie	It's About Time	8-922	CB
Reeves, Julie	Trouble Is A Woman	8-479	CB
Reeves, Ronna	He's My Weakness	3-39	SC
Reeves, Ronna	Rodeo Man	4-409	SC
Reflections	Just Like Romeo &	6-52	SC

ARTIST	SONG TITLE	#	TYPE
	Juliet		
Refreshments	Banditos	24-289	SC
Refugee Camp	Sweetest Thing the	10-111	SC
Rehab & Hank Jr.	Bartender Song (aka Sittin' At a Bar	43-376	CB
Rehab & Hank Jr.	Duet - Bartender Song (aka Sittin at..	43-376	CB
Reid, Mike	I'll Still Be Loving You	9-448	SAV
Reid, Mike	I'll Stop Loving You	9-541	SAV
Reid, Mike	Walk On Faith	13-487	P
Reid, Mike	Walk On Faith	9-532	SAV
Reid, Mike	Walk On Faith	2-391	SC
Reilly, Dee	Nothin's Right And Nothin's Left	45-860	VH
REM	Bang And Blame	16-620	MM
REM	Bang And Blame	13-607	P
REM	Daysleeper	16-214	MM
REM	E-Bow The Letter	24-295	SC
REM	It's The End Of The World	34-60	CB
REM	It's The End Of The World	13-598	P
REM	Leaving New York	30-816	PHM
REM	Losing My Religion	28-436	DK
REM	Losing My Religion	12-783	P
REM	Man On The Moon	12-784	P
REM	Man On The Moon	9-671	SAV
REM	Radio Free Europe	21-404	SC
REM	Shiny Happy People	28-437	DK
REM	Shiny Happy People	33-346	CB
REM	Shiny Happy People	12-806	P
REM	Shiny Happy People	5-337	SC
REM	Stand	12-799	P
Rembrandts	I'll Be There For You	12-238	DK
Rembrandts	I'll Be There For You	3-440	SC
Reminiscing Series	For Me And My Gal	3-32	SC
Reminiscing Series	In the Shade Of the Old Apple Tree	3-28	SC
Reminiscing Series	Margie	3-30	SC
Reminiscing Series	Meet Me In St. Louis Louis	3-29	SC
Reminiscing Series	Peg O' My Heart	3-31	SC
Reminiscing Series	Wait Till The Sun Shines	3-33	SC
Reminiscing Series	When The Red Red Robin Goes...	3-27	SC
Reminiscing Series	When You Wore A Tulip	3-34	SC
Renay, Diane	Navy Blue	4-717	SC
Reno & Wilson	Almost Paradise	17-333	DK
Reno & Wilson	Duet - Almost Paradise	17-333	DK
Rent	Halloween - Rent	45-122	PS
Rent	Show - Another Day	17-635	SSR
Rent	Show - Halloween	17-640	SSR
Rent	Show - Halloween - Rent	45-122	PS
Rent	Show - I'll Cover You	17-636	SSR
Rent	Show - I'll Cover You - Duet	15-263	MM
Rent	Show - Light My Candle	15-149	MM
Rent	Show - Maybe This Time	15-267	MM

ARTIST	SONG TITLE	#	TYPE
Rent	Show - One Song Glory	17-633	SSR
Rent	Show - Out Tonight	15-265	MM
Rent	Show - Out Tonight	17-634	SSR
Rent	Show - Rent	17-632	SSR
Rent	Show - Rent - Duet	15-264	MM
Rent	Show - Seasons Of Love	15-30	MM
Rent	Show - Seasons Of Love	12-486	P
Rent	Show - Seasons Of Love	18-814	PS
Rent	Show - Seasons Of Love	17-637	SSR
Rent	Show - Seasons Of Love - Movie Vers	29-247	SC
Rent	Show - Take Me Or Leave Me	15-266	MM
Rent	Show - Take Me Or Leave Me	17-638	SSR
Rent	Show - What You Own	17-641	SSR
Rent	Show - Without You	17-639	SSR
Rent	Show - Your Eyes	17-642	SSR
REO Soeedwagon	Can't Fight This Feeling	29-297	SC
REO Speedwagon	Can't Fight This Feeling	20-294	CB
REO Speedwagon	Keep On Loving You	11-649	DK
REO Speedwagon	Keep On Loving You	4-756	SC
REO Speedwagon	Take It On The Run	7-98	MM
REO Speedwagon	Take It On The Run	13-288	P
REO Speedwagon	Take It On The Run	3-612	SC
Republica	Ready To Go	24-235	SC
RES	They Say Vision	17-599	PHM
Restless Heart	Big Dreams In A Small Town	1-412	CB
Restless Heart	Big Dreams In A Small Town	5-674	SC
Restless Heart	Big Iron Horses	24-3	SC
Restless Heart	Bluest Eyes In Texas	1-406	CB
Restless Heart	Bluest Eyes In Texas	12-427	P
Restless Heart	Dancy's Dream	4-67	SC
Restless Heart	Danny's Dream	1-407	CB
Restless Heart	Familiar Pain	1-413	CB
Restless Heart	Fast Movin' Train	14-690	CB
Restless Heart	Fast Movin' Train	3-647	SC
Restless Heart	Feel My Way To You	20-496	ST
Restless Heart	For Lack Of Better Words	10-152	SC
Restless Heart	I'll Still Be Loving You	1-416	CB
Restless Heart	I've Never Been So Sure	1-415	CB
Restless Heart	In This Little Town	24-82	SC
Restless Heart	Mending Fences	9-630	SAV
Restless Heart	New York Hold Her Tight	1-417	CB
Restless Heart	No End To This Road	8-488	CB
Restless Heart	No End To This Road	5-288	SC
Restless Heart	No End To This Road	22-820	ST
Restless Heart	Tender Lie a	1-411	CB
Restless Heart	That Rock Won't Roll	13-539	P
Restless Heart	That Rock Won't Roll	5-404	SC
Restless Heart	We Got The Love	1-418	CB
Restless Heart	Wheels	34-283	CB
Restless Heart	Wheels	5-252	SC
Restless Heart	When She Cries	1-409	CB
Restless Heart	When She Cries	6-217	MM

ARTIST	SONG TITLE	#	TYPE
Restless Heart	When Somebody Loves You	1-410	CB
Restless Heart	Why Does It Have To Be ...	1-419	CB
Restless Heart	Why Does It Have to Be Wrong or...	34-277	CB
Restless Heart	You Can Depend On Me	1-420	CB
Revere & Raiders	Good Thing	11-559	DK
Revere & Raiders	Indian Reservation	35-107	CB
Revere & Raiders	Indian Reservation	11-700	DK
Revere & Raiders	Indian Reservation (the Lament of..	14-640	SC
Revere & Raiders	Just Like Me	16-753	DK
Revere & Raiders	Kicks	11-273	DK
Revis	Caught In The Rain	32-252	THM
Reynolds, Debbie	All I Do Is Dream Of You	45-71	OZP
Reynolds, Debbie	Dominique	45-70	CB
Reynolds, Debbie	Show - Dominique - The Singing Nun	45-70	CB
Reynolds, Debbie	Tammy	5-11	SC
Reynolds, Judy	Endless Sleep	9-751	SAV
Reznik, John	I'm Still Here	23-151	PHM
Rhett, Thomas	Beer With Jesus	45-440	SBI
Rhett, Thomas	Crash And Burn	45-296	SBI
Rhett, Thomas	Die A Happy Man	45-442	BKD
Rhett, Thomas	Get Me Some Of That	43-137	ASK
Rhett, Thomas	It Goes Like This	44-331	SSC
Rhett, Thomas	It Goes Like This	45-401	BKD
Rhett, Thomas	Learned It From The Radio	49-5	DCK
Rhett, Thomas	Make Me Wanna	45-180	SSC
Rhett, Thomas	Something To Do With My Hands	43-12	ASK
Rhett, Thomas	Something To Do With My Hands	45-407	BKD
Rhett, Thomas	T-Shirt	49-368	BKD
Rhett, Thomas	Take You Home	43-182	ASK
Rhett, Thomas	Vacation	45-441	BKD
Rhyder, Brandon	Haggard	42-2	PHN
Rice & Malloy	Duet - Ride	48-3	BKD
Rice & Malloy	Ride - duet	48-3	BKD
Rice, Chase	Buzz Back	45-623	PHN
Rice, Chase	Do It Like This	49-663	BKD
Rice, Chase	Gonna Wanna Tonight	45-63	DCK
Rice, Chase	Ready Set Roll	44-199	ASK
Rice, Chase	Ready Set Roll	49-662	KCD
Rice, Chase	Whisper	48-394	DCK
Rice, Damien	Cannonball (Remix)	20-355	PHM
Rich & Fricke	Duet - On My Knees	13-479	P
Rich & Fricke	Duet - On My Knees	5-439	SC
Rich & Fricke	On My Knees	13-479	P
Rich & Fricke	On My Knees	5-439	SC
Rich, Charlie	All Over Me	5-199	SC
Rich, Charlie	Baby Baby	8-424	CB
Rich, Charlie	Beauitful Woman	19-430	SC
Rich, Charlie	Behind Closed Doors	15-823	CB
Rich, Charlie	Behind Closed Doors	17-5	DK
Rich, Charlie	Behind Closed Doors	8-624	SAV

ARTIST	SONG TITLE	#	TYPE
Rich, Charlie	Big Boss Man	8-441	CB
Rich, Charlie	Everytime You Touch Me	4-577	SC
Rich, Charlie	Everytime You Touch Me...	34-228	CB
Rich, Charlie	I Love My Friend	9-576	SAV
Rich, Charlie	I Love My Friend	5-200	SC
Rich, Charlie	Most Beautiful Girl the	17-8	DK
Rich, Charlie	Most Beautiful Girl the	13-422	P
Rich, Charlie	Most Beautiful Girl the	9-580	SAV
Rich, Charlie	My Elusive Dreams	8-361	CB
Rich, Charlie	Road Song	8-452	CB
Rich, Charlie	Rollin' With The Flow	8-459	CB
Rich, Charlie	Rollin' With The Flow	5-209	SC
Rich, Charlie	She Called Me Baby	8-292	CB
Rich, Charlie	She Called Me Baby	9-586	SAV
Rich, Charlie	Since I Fell For You	9-513	SAV
Rich, Charlie	Take It On Home	5-206	SC
Rich, Charlie	There Won't Be Anymore	13-481	P
Rich, Charlie	There Won't Be Anymore	5-204	SC
Rich, Charlie	Very Special Love Song a	8-833	CB
Rich, Charlie	Very Special Love Song a	13-517	P
Rich, Charlie	You're Gonna Love Yourself	9-581	SAV
Rich, Don	Cajun - Loving Cajun Style	49-404	SCK
Rich, Don	Loving Cajun Style	49-404	SCK
Rich, John	Another You	48-705	BKD
Rich, John	Forever Loving You	15-102	ST
Rich, John	I Pray For You	14-86	CB
Richard, Steve	Keep On Rollin'	41-85	PHN
Richards, Cliff	Devil Woman	9-775	SAV
Richards, Cliff	We Don't Talk Anymore	21-804	SC
Richey, Kim	From Where I Stand	7-238	MM
Richey, Kim	Just My Luck	3-562	SC
Richey, Kim	Those Were The Words We Said	3-567	SC
Richie & Dosterhuis	Duet - Face In The Crowd	47-454	KV
Richie & Dosterhuis	Face In The Crowd - duet	47-454	KV
Richie & Ross	Duet - Endless Love	35-207	CB
Richie & Ross	Duet - Endless Love	26-187	DK
Richie & Ross	Duet - Endless Love	6-230	MM
Richie & Ross	Endless Love	26-187	DK
Richie & Ross	Endless Love	15-354	LE
Richie & Ross	Endless Love	13-203	P
Richie & Ross	Endless Love - duet	35-207	CB
Richie & Twain	Duet - Endless Love	47-452	KV
Richie & Twain	Endless Love - duet	47-452	KV
Richie, Lionel	All Night Long	10-398	LE
Richie, Lionel	All Night Long - All Night	13-200	P
Richie, Lionel	All Night Long (All Night)	43-367	CB

ARTIST	SONG TITLE	#	TYPE
Richie, Lionel	Angel	47-450	CB
Richie, Lionel	Angel	45-525	BSK
Richie, Lionel	Ballerina Girl	47-456	LE
Richie, Lionel	Brick House	10-387	LE
Richie, Lionel	Dancing On The Ceiling	34-84	CB
Richie, Lionel	Dancing On The Ceiling	11-537	DK
Richie, Lionel	Dancing On The Ceiling	10-391	LE
Richie, Lionel	Dancing On The Ceiling	14-573	SC
Richie, Lionel	Deep River Woman	33-316	CB
Richie, Lionel	Destiny	47-455	LE
Richie, Lionel	Do It To Me	43-369	CB
Richie, Lionel	Don't Wanna Lose You	47-458	LE
Richie, Lionel	Easy	10-392	LE
Richie, Lionel	Endless Love	10-397	LE
Richie, Lionel	Hello	11-536	DK
Richie, Lionel	Hello	10-384	LE
Richie, Lionel	Hello	13-201	P
Richie, Lionel	I Call It Love	30-271	CB
Richie, Lionel	I Call It Love	36-189	PHM
Richie, Lionel	I Hear Your Voice	16-209	MM
Richie, Lionel	I Still Believe	47-451	PHN
Richie, Lionel	Just Go	47-453	KV
Richie, Lionel	Love Oh Love	47-784	SRK
Richie, Lionel	Love Will Conquer All	47-457	LE
Richie, Lionel	My Love	43-371	CB
Richie, Lionel	My Tender Heart	47-462	SBI
Richie, Lionel	Night Shift	16-873	DK
Richie, Lionel	Night Shift	10-395	LE
Richie, Lionel	Oh No	10-386	LE
Richie, Lionel	Ordinary Girl	24-175	SC
Richie, Lionel	Penny Lover	35-178	CB
Richie, Lionel	Penny Lover	10-389	LE
Richie, Lionel	Sail On	10-394	LE
Richie, Lionel	Say You Say Me	11-535	DK
Richie, Lionel	Say You Say Me	10-390	LE
Richie, Lionel	Say You Say Me	13-202	P
Richie, Lionel	Say You Say Me	4-288	SC
Richie, Lionel	Serves You Right	47-460	LE
Richie, Lionel	Still	10-396	LE
Richie, Lionel	Stuck On You	10-388	LE
Richie, Lionel	Stuck On You	16-161	SC
Richie, Lionel	Three Times A Lady	16-821	DK
Richie, Lionel	Three Times A Lady	17-423	KC
Richie, Lionel	Three Times A Lady	10-393	LE
Richie, Lionel	Time	47-461	MM
Richie, Lionel	To Love A Woman	47-464	SF
Richie, Lionel	Truly	10-385	LE
Richie, Lionel	Truly	12-889	P
Richie, Lionel	Why	47-463	SBI
Richie, Lionel	You Are	34-81	CB
Richie, Lionel	You Mean More To Me	47-459	LE
Richie,, Lionel	Running With The Night	47-465	SFM
Ricochet	Blink Of An Eye	8-126	CB
Ricochet	Blink Of An Eye	22-644	ST
Ricochet	Can't Stop Thinkin' 'Bout You	10-167	SC
Ricochet	Can't Stop Thinking	22-708	ST

ARTIST	SONG TITLE	#	TYPE
	'Bout That		
Ricochet	Connected At The Heart	8-412	CB
Ricochet	Daddy's Money	7-240	MM
Ricochet	Daddy's Money	22-887	ST
Ricochet	Do I Love You Enough	9-400	CB
Ricochet	Ease My Troubled Mind	7-593	CHM
Ricochet	Feel Like Fallin'	20-454	ST
Ricochet	Freedom Isn't Free	20-584	CB
Ricochet	Freedom Isn't Free - Patriotic	36-342	CB
Ricochet	He Left A Lot To Be Desired	7-660	CHM
Ricochet	He Left A Lot To Be Desired	10-103	SC
Ricochet	Honky Tonk Baby	8-757	CB
Ricochet	Honky Tonk Baby	22-834	ST
Ricochet	Love Is Stronger Than Pride	16-660	CHM
Ricochet	Love Is Stronger Than Pride	24-165	SC
Ricochet	Patriotic - Freedom Isn't Free	36-342	CB
Ricochet	She's Gone	14-114	CB
Ricochet	What Do I Know	4-153	SC
Riggs, Levi	There's Still A Place For That	39-68	PHN
Right Said Fred	I'm Too Sexy	6-168	MM
Right Said Fred	I'm Too Sexy	29-637	SC
Righteous Brothers	Ebb Tide	11-232	DK
Righteous Brothers	Ebb Tide	3-332	PS
Righteous Brothers	Ebb Tide	9-316	STR
Righteous Brothers	Just Once In My Life	15-518	JTG
Righteous Brothers	Just Once In My Life	3-333	PS
Righteous Brothers	Rock & Roll Heaven	2-444	SC
Righteous Brothers	Soul & Inspiration	11-237	DK
Righteous Brothers	Soul & Inspiration	3-331	PS
Righteous Brothers	Soul & Inspiration	2-46	SC
Righteous Brothers	Unchained Melody	11-549	DK
Righteous Brothers	Unchained Melody	6-148	MM
Righteous Brothers	Unchained Melody	13-38	P
Righteous Brothers	Unchained Melody	3-329	PS
Righteous Brothers	Unchained Melody	14-555	SC
Righteous Brothers	You're My Soul & Inspiration	35-97	CB
Righteous Brothers	You've Lost That Lovin' Feelin'	16-850	DK
Righteous Brothers	You've Lost That Lovin' Feelin'	6-448	MM
Righteous Brothers	You've Lost That Lovin' Feelin'	3-330	PS
Rihanna	Break It Off	30-260	CB
Rihanna	Breakin' Dishes	36-105	CB
Rihanna	Disturbia	36-104	CB
Rihanna	Don't Stop The Music	36-468	CB
Rihanna	If It's Lovin' That You Want	36-95	CB
Rihanna	If It's Lovin' That You Want (Radio	29-259	SC
Rihanna	It Just Don't Feel Like	36-107	CB

241

ARTIST	SONG TITLE	#	TYPE	ARTIST	SONG TITLE	#	TYPE
	Xmas w/o You			Rimes, LeAnn	I Need You	9-412	CB
Rihanna	Never Ending	48-405	DCK	Rimes, LeAnn	I Need You	22-549	ST
Rihanna	Only Girl In The World	37-270	PHM	Rimes, LeAnn	I'll Get Even With You	4-592	SC
Rihanna	Pon De Replay	36-93	CB	Rimes, LeAnn	Life Goes On	34-369	CB
Rihanna	Pon De Replay (Radio Vers)	37-101	SC	Rimes, LeAnn	Life Goes On	25-339	MM
				Rimes, LeAnn	Life Goes On	18-340	PHM
Rihanna	Shut Up And Drive	30-570	CB	Rimes, LeAnn	Life Goes On (Pop Version)	20-381	HP
Rihanna	SOS	30-150	PT				
Rihanna	SOS (Rescue Me)	36-96	CB	Rimes, LeAnn	Light In Your Eyes the	1-288	CB
Rihanna	Stay	45-8	ASK	Rimes, LeAnn	Light In Your Eyes the	7-615	CHM
Rihanna	Take A Bow	36-102	CB	Rimes, LeAnn	Light In Your Eyes the	7-445	MM
Rihanna	Umbrella	30-493	CB	Rimes, LeAnn	Light In Your Eyes the	24-648	SC
Rihanna	Unfaithful	36-98	CB	Rimes, LeAnn	Looking Through Your Eyes	8-725	CB
Rihanna	Unfaithful	30-729	SF				
Rihanna	We Ride	36-106	CB	Rimes, LeAnn	My Baby	7-447	MM
Rihanna	We Ride	30-57	PHM	Rimes, LeAnn	Nothin' 'Bout Love Makes Sense	22-68	CB
Rihanna	Xmas - It Just Don't Feel Like...	36-95	CB	Rimes, LeAnn	Nothin' 'Bout Love Makes Sense	20-507	ST
Rihanna feat Maroon 5	If I Never See Your Face Again	36-103	CB	Rimes, LeAnn	Nothin' Better To Do	30-462	CB
				Rimes, LeAnn	Nothin' New Under The Moon	8-766	CB
Rihanna feat Ne-Yo	Hate That I Love You	36-100	CB				
Rihanna feat Sean Paul	Break It Off	36-97	CB	Rimes, LeAnn	Nothin' New Under The Moon	22-822	ST
Rihanna w Ne-Yo	Hate That I Love You	36-100	CB	Rimes, LeAnn	On The Side Of Angels	1-290	CB
Riley, Jeannie C	Girl Most Likely the	49-230	DFK	Rimes, LeAnn	On The Side Of Angels	22-659	ST
Riley, Jeannie C.	Harper Valley PTA	16-846	DK	Rimes, LeAnn	One Way Ticket	1-287	CB
Riley, Jeannie C.	Harper Valley PTA	3-361	MH	Rimes, LeAnn	One Way Ticket	7-449	MM
Riley, Jeannie C.	Harper Valley PTA	9-462	SAV	Rimes, Leann	One Way Ticket	4-496	SC
Riley, Jeannie C.	Harper Valley PTA	2-130	SC	Rimes, LeAnn	Please Remember Me	14-134	CB
Rimes, LeAnn	Big Deal	5-800	SC	Rimes, LeAnn	Probably Wouldn't Be This Way	22-328	CB
Rimes, LeAnn	Big Deal	22-503	ST				
Rimes, LeAnn	Blue	1-286	CB	Rimes, LeAnn	Purple Rain	8-861	CB
Rimes, LeAnn	Blue	7-442	MM	Rimes, LeAnn	Right Kind Of Wrong the	14-137	CB
Rimes, LeAnn	Blue	4-372	SC	Rimes, LeAnn	Some People	30-25	CB
Rimes, LeAnn	Blue	22-892	ST	Rimes, LeAnn	Something's Gotta Give	29-34	CB
Rimes, LeAnn	Borrowed	39-83	PHN	Rimes, LeAnn	Soon	25-20	MM
Rimes, LeAnn	Bridge Over Troubled Water	1-298	CB	Rimes, LeAnn	Soon	15-673	ST
				Rimes, LeAnn	Suddenly	25-569	MM
Rimes, LeAnn	But I Do Love You	30-444	CB	Rimes, LeAnn	Suddenly	18-806	ST
Rimes, LeAnn	But I Do Love You	14-837	ST	Rimes, LeAnn	These Arms Of Mine	8-485	CB
Rimes, LeAnn	Can't Fight The Moonlight	14-131	CB	Rimes, LeAnn	These Arms Of Mine	22-701	ST
				Rimes, LeAnn	This Love	20-273	SC
Rimes, LeAnn	Commitment	1-292	CB	Rimes, LeAnn	This Love	19-698	ST
Rimes, LeAnn	Commitment	22-782	ST	Rimes, LeAnn	Tic Toc	36-365	CB
Rimes, LeAnn	Cowboy's Sweetheart	12-928	CB	Rimes, LeAnn	Unchained Melody	1-293	CB
Rimes, LeAnn	Crazy Women	38-109	CB	Rimes, LeAnn	Unchained Melody	7-576	CHM
Rimes, LeAnn	Feels Like Home	14-291	MM	Rimes, LeAnn	We Can	19-599	CB
Rimes, LeAnn	God Bless America	1-299	CB	Rimes, LeAnn	We Can	25-665	MM
Rimes, LeAnn	Good Friend And A Glass Of Wine	36-396	CB	Rimes, LeAnn	We Can	19-542	SC
				Rimes, LeAnn	What I Cannot Change	36-617	CB
Rimes, LeAnn	Honestly	7-440	MM	Rimes, LeAnn	What I Cannot Change	36-218	PHM
Rimes, LeAnn	How Do I Live	22-600	ST	Rimes, LeAnn	Where I Stood	41-93	PHN
Rimes, LeAnn	How Do I Live (Pop Mix)	21-548	PHM	Rimes, LeAnn	You Light Up My Life	8-894	CB
Rimes, LeAnn	Hurt Me	7-437	MM	Rimes, LeAnn	You Light Up My Life	7-678	CHM
Rimes, LeAnn	Hurt Me	4-896	SC	Rimes, Lee Ann	Put A Little Holiday In Your Heart	45-787	SC
Rimes, LeAnn	I Believe	25-80	MM				
Rimes, LeAnn	I Know Who Holds Tomorrow	1-300	CB	Rimes, Lee Ann	Xmas - Put A Little	45-787	SC

ARTIST	SONG TITLE	#	TYPE
	Holiday In Your...		
Rimes, Rob Thomas, Jeff Beck	Duet - Gasoline & Matches	41-86	PHN
Rimes, Rob Thomas, Jeff Beck	Gasoline & Matches - duet	41-86	PHN
Ringside	Tired Of Being Sorry	30-227	PHM
Rio Grand	Kill Me Now	30-84	CB
Rip Chords	Hey Little Cobra	3-548	SC
Riperton, Minnie	Loving You	33-279	CB
Ripperton, Minnie	Lovin' You	7-469	MM
Ripperton, Minnie	Lovin' You	22-930	SC
Rise Against	Good Left Undone the	37-140	SC
Rise Against	Good Left Undone the	49-900	SC
Rise Against	Swing Life Away	30-228	PHM
Ritter, Tex	Daddy's Last Letter the	20-716	CB
Ritter, Tex	Deck Of Cards	20-714	CB
Ritter, Tex	Have I Told You Lately That I Love	20-712	CB
Ritter, Tex	High Noon	45-567	TOS
Ritter, Tex	I Dreamed Of A Hillbilly Heaven	20-717	CB
Ritter, Tex	I Dreamed Of A Hillbilly Heaven	4-301	SC
Ritter, Tex	I Got Spurs That Jingle Jangle Jingle	45-568	DCK
Ritter, Tex	I'm Wastin' My Tears On You	20-705	CB
Ritter, Tex	I'm Wastin' My Tears On You	5-422	SC
Ritter, Tex	Jealous Heart	20-707	CB
Ritter, Tex	Jealous Heart	5-701	SC
Ritter, Tex	Just Beyond The Moon	20-718	CB
Ritter, Tex	Long Time Gone	20-710	CB
Ritter, Tex	Rock & Rye	20-715	CB
Ritter, Tex	Rye Whiskey	20-713	CB
Ritter, Tex	There's A New Moon Over My Shoulder	20-706	CB
Ritter, Tex	When You Leave Don't Slam The Door	20-711	CB
Ritter, Tex	Xmas - Christmas by the old Corral	20-719	CB
Ritter, Tex	You 2-Timed Me 1 Time Too Often	20-708	CB
Ritter, Tex	You Two-Timed Me One Time Too...	5-368	SC
Ritter, Tex	You Will Have To Pay	20-709	CB
River City Gang	This Old Town	38-213	PHN
River Road	Breathless	9-397	CB
River Road	I Broke It I'll Fix It	16-580	SC
River Road	Nickajack	12-930	CB
River Road	Somebody Will	10-125	SC
Rivers & Twisted Radio	Parody - What If God Smoked Cannibus	45-934	SC
Rivers & Twisted Radio	Parody - Wreck The Malls - duet	45-932	SC
Rivers & Twisted Radio	What If God Smoked Cannibus	45-934	SC
Rivers & Twisted Radio	Wreck The Malls - duet	45-932	SC

ARTIST	SONG TITLE	#	TYPE
Rivers, Bob	Dirty Deeds Done With Sheep	45-933	ZP
Rivers, Bob	I Am Santa Claus	45-745	SC
Rivers, Bob	Parody - Dirty Deeds Done With Sheep	45-933	ZP
Rivers, Bob	Parody - What If Eminem Did Jingle...	45-931	SC
Rivers, Bob	Twelve Pains Of Christmas - xmas	45-252	SC
Rivers, Bob	What If Eminem Did Jingle Bells**	45-931	SC
Rivers, Bob	Xmas - I Am Santa Claus	45-745	SC
Rivers, Bob	Xmas - Twelve Pains Of Christmas	45-252	SC
Rivers, Bob	Xmas - Walkin' Round in Women's...	5-706	SC
Rivers, Johnny	Baby I Need Your Loving	47-366	LE
Rivers, Johnny	Do You Wanna Dance	47-368	KBR
Rivers, Johnny	Memphis	3-23	SC
Rivers, Johnny	Midnight Special	47-365	JVC
Rivers, Johnny	Mountain Of Love	17-45	DK
Rivers, Johnny	Mountain Of Love	13-103	P
Rivers, Johnny	Poor Side Of Town	11-130	DK
Rivers, Johnny	Poor Side Of Town	4-39	SC
Rivers, Johnny	Rockin' Pneumonia & Boogie Woogie	26-445	DK
Rivers, Johnny	Rockin' Pneumonia & Boogie Woogie	2-54	SC
Rivers, Johnny	Secret Agent Man	11-447	DK
Rivers, Johnny	Seventh Son	10-496	DA
Rivers, Johnny	Slow Dancin' Swayin' To The Music	35-149	CB
Rivers, Johnny	Summer Rain	47-367	RSX
Rivers, Johnny	Swayin To The Music	21-512	SC
Rivers, Johnny	Too Good To Last	47-369	DFK
Rivers, Johnny	Tracks Of My Tears	47-364	CB
Riviera's	California Sun	12-663	P
Rivingtons	Papa Oo Mau Mau	6-651	MM
Road Hammers	Girl On The Billboard	36-205	PHM
Roar of the Greasep	Who Can I Turn To	27-389	DK
Robbie Seay Band	Rise	49-913	SC
Robbins, Marty	18 Yellow Roses	44-70	KV
Robbins, Marty	All Around Cowboy	45-680	SRK
Robbins, Marty	Among My Souvenirs	4-812	SC
Robbins, Marty	Ballad Of The Alamo	44-54	KV
Robbins, Marty	Begging To You	3-238	CB
Robbins, Marty	Begging To You	22-245	SC
Robbins, Marty	Big Iron	3-227	CB
Robbins, Marty	Big Iron	7-107	MM
Robbins, Marty	Big Iron	4-311	SC
Robbins, Marty	Cowboy In The Continental Suit	48-16	CB
Robbins, Marty	Devil Woman	3-225	CB
Robbins, Marty	Devil Woman	17-383	DK
Robbins, Marty	Devil Woman	7-155	MM
Robbins, Marty	Devil Woman	8-672	SAV
Robbins, Marty	Devil Woman	5-95	SC
Robbins, Marty	Don't Worry	8-287	CB

243

ARTIST	SONG TITLE	#	TYPE	ARTIST	SONG TITLE	#	TYPE
Robbins, Marty	Don't Worry	2-631	SC	Robbins, Marty	Story Of My Life the	4-862	SC
Robbins, Marty	El Paso	7-160	MM	Robbins, Marty	Story Of My Life the	10-599	SF
Robbins, Marty	El Paso	13-449	P	Robbins, Marty	Streets Of Laredo	8-436	CB
Robbins, Marty	El Paso	8-673	SAV	Robbins, Marty	Tonight Carmen	3-239	CB
Robbins, Marty	El Paso	4-582	SC	Robbins, Marty	Tonight Carmen	5-847	SC
Robbins, Marty	El Paso (Long Version)	3-232	CB	Robbins, Marty	Walking Piece Of Heaven	20-649	SC
Robbins, Marty	El Paso City	3-236	CB				
Robbins, Marty	Five Brothers	48-28	VH	Robbins, Marty	Waltz Of The Wind	48-24	DFK
Robbins, Marty	Girl With Gardenias In Her Hair the	48-15	CB	Robbins, Marty	White Sport Coat a	8-40	CB
Robbins, Marty	Hanging Tree the	45-679	VHM	Robbins, Marty	White Sport Coat a	13-364	P
Robbins, Marty	Hark The Herald Angels Sing	48-23	CB	Robbins, Marty	White Sport Coat a	10-595	SF
				Robbins, Marty	Won't You Forgive	48-26	DCK
Robbins, Marty	I Can't Quit (I've Gone Too Far)	48-29	VH	Robbins, Marty	Xmas - Hark The Herald Angels Sing	48-23	CB
Robbins, Marty	I Couldn't Keep From Cryin'	48-19	CB	Robert & Johnny	We Belong Together	25-555	MM
Robbins, Marty	I Don't Know Why (I Just Do)	48-27	VH	Roberts, Emily Ann	She's Got You	47-401	BKD
				Roberts, Julie	Break Down Here	35-432	CB
Robbins, Marty	I Heard The Bluebirds Sing	48-25	DCK	Roberts, Julie	Break Down Here	30-13	SC
				Roberts, Julie	Break Down Here	20-330	ST
Robbins, Marty	I Heard The Bluebirds Sing	47-786	SRK	Roberts, Julie	Chance the	22-89	CB
				Roberts, Julie	Chance the	21-655	SC
Robbins, Marty	I Walk Alone	3-233	CB	Roberts, Julie	First To Never Know	29-58	CB
Robbins, Marty	I Walk Alone	20-636	SC	Roberts, Julie	Girl Next Door	30-20	CB
Robbins, Marty	I'd Trade All Of My Tomorrows	45-868	VH	Roberts, Julie	Men & Mascara	29-578	CB
				Roberts, Julie	Wake Up Older	22-25	CB
Robbins, Marty	I'll Go On Alone	5-365	SC	Roberts, Mica & Keith	Things A Mama Don't Know	36-585	CB
Robbins, Marty	It's A Sin	48-18	CB				
Robbins, Marty	It's Your World	48-22	CB	Robertson & Bryan	Duet - Hairy Christmas	43-82	ASK
Robbins, Marty	Joli Girl	48-20	CB	Robertson & Bryan	Hairy Christmas	43-82	ASK
Robbins, Marty	Judy	48-31	VH	Robertson & Bryan	Xmas - Hairy Christmas - duet	43-82	ASK
Robbins, Marty	Just Married	22-254	SC				
Robbins, Marty	Knee Deep In The Blues	49-172	CB	Robins	Smokey Joe's Café	6-676	MM
Robbins, Marty	Knee Deep In The Blues	48-14	CB	Robinson & Miracles	Baby Baby Don't Cry	27-269	DK
Robbins, Marty	Mr. Shorty	45-272	SSK	Robinson, Smokey	Being With You	16-796	DK
Robbins, Marty	My Woman My Woman My Wife	3-235	CB	Robinson, Smokey	Being With You	36-108	JTG
				Robinson, Smokey	Cruisin'	27-268	DK
Robbins, Marty	My Woman My Woman My Wife	8-674	SAV	Robinson, Smokey	Crusin'	3-558	SC
				Robinson, Smokey	Going To A Go-Go	11-201	DK
Robbins, Marty	Padre	48-21	CB	Robinson, Smokey	I Second That Emotion	16-841	DK
Robbins, Marty	Red River Valley	48-32	KV	Robinson, Smokey	I Second That Emotion	36-111	JTG
Robbins, Marty	Red River Valley	47-765	SRK	Robinson, Smokey	Love Machine	46-133	SC
Robbins, Marty	Return To Me	48-17	CB	Robinson, Smokey	Love Machine (Part 1)	48-550	DK
Robbins, Marty	Ribbon Of Darkness	8-369	CB	Robinson, Smokey	Ooh Baby Baby	16-861	DK
Robbins, Marty	Ribbon Of Darkness	4-801	SC	Robinson, Smokey	Shop Around	36-109	JTG
Robbins, Marty	Ruby Ann	15-79	CB	Robinson, Smokey	Tears Of A Clown	35-103	CB
Robbins, Marty	Running Gun	48-30	VH	Robinson, Smokey	Tears Of A Clown	4-849	SC
Robbins, Marty	San Angelo	47-749	SRK	Robinson, Smokey	Tears Of A Clown	9-313	STR
Robbins, Marty	Shackles & Chains	47-729	SRK	Robinson, Smokey	Tracks Of My Tears	16-806	DK
Robbins, Marty	She Was Only 17 (He Was 1 Yr More)	48-13	CB	Robinson, Smokey	Tracks Of My Tears	12-638	P
				Robinson, Smokey	Tracks Of My Tears	2-91	SC
Robbins, Marty	Singin' The Blues	3-234	CB	Robinson, Smokey	You Really Got A Hold On Me	15-282	DK
Robbins, Marty	Singin' The Blues	13-376	P				
Robbins, Marty	Singin' The Blues	3-601	SC	Robinson, Smokey	You Really Got A Hold On Me	6-564	MM
Robbins, Marty	Some Memories Just Won't Die	5-825	SC	Robinson, Smokey	You Really Got A Hold On Me	36-110	JTG
Robbins, Marty	Stairway Of Love	48-12	CB	Robinson, Vicki Sue	Turn The Beat Around	35-127	CB
Robbins, Marty	Story Of My Life the	3-237	CB	Robinson, Vicki Sue	Turn The Beat Around	9-15	MH

ARTIST	SONG TITLE	#	TYPE
Robison, Bruce	Good Life the	19-230	SC
Robison, Bruce	What Would Willie Do	17-603	CB
Robison, Charlie	Barlight	8-921	CB
Robison, Charlie	I Want You Bad	15-103	ST
Robison, Charlie	My Hometown	5-838	SC
Robison, Charlie	Poor Man's Son	9-404	CB
Robison, Charlie	Right Man For The Job	25-13	MM
Robison, Charlie	Right Man For The Job	16-337	ST
Robison, Charlie	You're Not the Best	8-986	CB
Robyn	Do You Know	21-550	PHM
Robyn	Do You Really Want Me	10-136	SC
Robyn	Show Me Love	7-698	PHM
Robyn	Show Me Love	5-333	SC
Rochelle & Candles	Once Upon A Time	25-551	MM
Rockin' Berries	He's In Town	10-617	SF
Rockwell	Dance the	18-536	TT
Rockwell	Somebody's Watching Me	12-143	DK
Rocky	Show - Eye Of The Tiger	6-876	MM
Rocky Horror Pictur	Show - Hot Patootie	15-352	MM
Rocky Horror Pictur	Show - Sweet Transvestite	7-367	MM
Rocky Horror Pictur	Show - Time Warp	2-141	SC
Rocky Horror Pictur	Show - Time Warp	16-293	TT
Rocky Horror Pictur	Time Warp	2-141	SC
Rocky Horror Pictur	Time Warp	16-293	TT
Rodgers, Jimmie	Honeycomb	11-206	DK
Rodgers, Jimmie	Kisses Sweeter Than Wine	7-299	MM
Rodgers, Jimmie	Kisses Sweeter Than Wine	3-502	SC
Rodgers, Jimmie	Oh Oh I'm Falling In Love Again	4-518	SC
Rodman, Judy	Until I Met You	29-658	SC
Rodriguez, Johnny	Dance With Me Just One More Time	8-841	CB
Rodriguez, Johnny	Down On The Rio Grande	22-59	CB
Rodriguez, Johnny	Foolin'	22-60	CB
Rodriguez, Johnny	Hillbilly Heart	22-56	CB
Rodriguez, Johnny	I Couldn't Be Me Without You	22-54	CB
Rodriguez, Johnny	I Just Can't Get Her Out Of My Mind	22-50	CB
Rodriguez, Johnny	I Just Can't Get Her Out Of My Mind	5-667	SC
Rodriguez, Johnny	I Wonder If I Ever Said Goodbye	22-55	CB
Rodriguez, Johnny	If Practice Makes Perfect	22-57	CB
Rodriguez, Johnny	Just Get Up And Close The Door	22-51	CB
Rodriguez, Johnny	Just Get Up And Close The Door	21-629	SC
Rodriguez, Johnny	Love Put A Song In My Heart	22-52	CB
Rodriguez, Johnny	Love Put A Song In My Heart	37-280	SC
Rodriguez, Johnny	Pass Me By If You're	14-256	SC

ARTIST	SONG TITLE	#	TYPE
	Only Passing T		
Rodriguez, Johnny	Ridin' My Thumb To Mexico	22-48	CB
Rodriguez, Johnny	That's The Way Love Goes	22-49	CB
Rodriguez, Johnny	That's The Way Love Goes	20-282	SC
Rodriguez, Johnny	We Believe In Happy Endings	22-58	CB
Rodriguez, Johnny	We're Over	22-53	CB
Rodriguez, Johnny	You Always Come Back To Hurtin' Me	22-47	CB
Rodriguez, Johnny	You Always Come Back To Hurting Me	5-405	SC
Rodriguez, Johnny	You Can Say That Again	24-157	SC
Roe, Tommy	Dizzy	11-601	DK
Roe, Tommy	Dizzy	6-783	MM
Roe, Tommy	Dollar's Worth Of Pennies a	48-114	CB
Roe, Tommy	Everybody	4-251	SC
Roe, Tommy	Folk Singer the	48-113	CB
Roe, Tommy	Heather Honey	48-111	CB
Roe, Tommy	Hooray For Hazel (Where Were You...)	48-119	DCK
Roe, Tommy	Kiss And Run	48-115	CB
Roe, Tommy	Raining In My Heart	48-112	CB
Roe, Tommy	Sheila	6-794	MM
Roe, Tommy	Some Such Foolishness	48-116	CB
Roe, Tommy	Stop Complainint	48-117	CB
Roe, Tommy	Susie Darling	48-118	CB
Roe, Tommy	Sweet Pea	35-88	CB
Roe, Tommy	Sweet Pea	6-790	MM
Roe, Tommy	Sweet Pea	21-540	SC
Roe, Weller	Jam Up & Jelly Tight	16-647	JTG
Roger	I Want To Be Your Man	48-590	DK
Roger Springer Band	Ain't Nothin' But a Cloud	8-980	CB
Rogers & Carnes	Don't Fall In Love With A Dreamer	17-152	DK
Rogers & Carnes	Don't Fall In Love With A Dreamer	2-303	SC
Rogers & Carnes	Duet - Don't Fall In Love W/Dreamer	17-152	DK
Rogers & Carnes	Duet - Don't Fall in Love W/Dreamer	2-303	SC
Rogers & Duncan	Duet - My World Is Over	20-480	ST
Rogers & Duncan	My World Is Over	20-480	ST
Rogers & Dunn	Duet - Maybe	48-120	CB
Rogers & Dunn	Maybe - duet	48-120	CB
Rogers & Easton	Duet - We've Got Tonight	15-578	MM
Rogers & Easton	We've Got Tonight	15-578	MM
Rogers & Henley	Calling Me - duet	30-348	CB
Rogers & Henley	Duet - Calling Me	30-348	CB
Rogers & Milsap	Duet - Make No Mistake She's Mine	29-74	CB
Rogers & Parton	Christmas To Remember a	18-721	CB
Rogers & Parton	Duet - Greatest Gift Of	48-121	CB

ARTIST	SONG TITLE	#	TYPE
	All		
Rogers & Parton	Duet - Islands In The Stream	8-111	CB
Rogers & Parton	Duet - Islands In The Stream	16-784	DK
Rogers & Parton	Duet - Islands In The Stream	13-419	P
Rogers & Parton	Duet - Islands In The Stream	2-299	SC
Rogers & Parton	Duet - Islands In The Stream	10-511	SF
Rogers & Parton	Duet - Love Is Strange	6-237	MM
Rogers & Parton	Greatest Gift Of All - duet	48-121	CB
Rogers & Parton	I Believe In Santa Claus - duet	48-122	CB
Rogers & Parton	Islands In The Stream	8-111	CB
Rogers & Parton	Islands In The Stream	16-784	DK
Rogers & Parton	Islands In The Stream	13-419	P
Rogers & Parton	Islands In The Stream	2-299	SC
Rogers & Parton	Islands In The Stream	10-511	SF
Rogers & Parton	Love Is Strange	6-237	MM
Rogers & Parton	With Bells On	18-759	CB
Rogers & Parton	With Bells On	3-394	SC
Rogers & Parton	Xmas - Christmas To Remember a	18-721	CB
Rogers & Parton	Xmas - Greatest Gift Of All	22-847	ST
Rogers & Parton	Xmas - I Believe In Santa Claus - duet	48-122	CB
Rogers & Parton	Xmas - With Bells On	18-759	CB
Rogers & Parton	Xmas - With Bells On	3-394	SC
Rogers & Parton	You Can't Make Old Friends	49-23	KV
Rogers & West	All I Ever Need Is You	13-532	P
Rogers & West	All I Ever Need Is You	9-568	SAV
Rogers & West	All I Ever Need Is You	5-438	SC
Rogers & West	Anyone Who Isn't Me Tonight	15-233	CB
Rogers & West	Duet - All I Ever Need Is You	13-532	P
Rogers & West	Duet - All I Ever Need Is You	9-568	SAV
Rogers & West	Duet - All I Ever Need Is You	5-438	SC
Rogers & West	Duet - Anyone Who Isn't Me Tonight	15-233	CB
Rogers & West	Duet - Till I Can Make It On My Own	15-234	CB
Rogers & West	Duet - What Are We Doin' In Love	5-436	SC
Rogers & West	Every Time Two Fools Collide	8-117	CB
Rogers & West	Every Time Two Fools Collide	2-298	SC
Rogers & West	Till I Can Make It On My Own	15-234	CB
Rogers & West	What Are We Doin' In Love	5-436	SC
Rogers, Kenny	All My Life	5-672	SC

ARTIST	SONG TITLE	#	TYPE
Rogers, Kenny	Beautiful - All That You Are	16-166	CB
Rogers, Kenny	Beautiful (All That You Can Be)	15-675	ST
Rogers, Kenny	Buried Treasure	3-175	CB
Rogers, Kenny	Buy Me A Rose	5-836	SC
Rogers, Kenny	Buy Me A Rose	22-521	ST
Rogers, Kenny	Coward Of The County	3-168	CB
Rogers, Kenny	Coward Of The County	11-746	DK
Rogers, Kenny	Coward Of The County	48-129	SC
Rogers, Kenny	Crazy	3-176	CB
Rogers, Kenny	Crazy Me	48-412	DFK
Rogers, Kenny	Daytime Friends	4-643	SC
Rogers, Kenny	Daytime Friends & Nighttime Lovers	3-169	CB
Rogers, Kenny	Duet - If I Knew Then What I Know..	6-234	MM
Rogers, Kenny	Gambler the	3-164	CB
Rogers, Kenny	Gambler the	11-617	DK
Rogers, Kenny	Gambler the	19-134	KC
Rogers, Kenny	Gambler the	7-157	MM
Rogers, Kenny	Gambler the	8-655	SAV
Rogers, Kenny	Greatest the	3-167	CB
Rogers, Kenny	Greatest the	7-883	CHT
Rogers, Kenny	Greatest the	14-615	SC
Rogers, Kenny	Hand Prints On The Wall	19-685	ST
Rogers, Kenny	Harder Cards	16-704	ST
Rogers, Kenny	He Will She Knows	14-911	CB
Rogers, Kenny	He Will She Knows	22-563	ST
Rogers, Kenny	Homeland	20-581	CB
Rogers, Kenny	Homeland	16-37	ST
Rogers, Kenny	Homeland - patriotic	36-337	CB
Rogers, Kenny	I Can't Unlove You	29-42	CB
Rogers, Kenny	I Can't Unlove You	29-712	ST
Rogers, Kenny	I Don't Need You	4-778	SC
Rogers, Kenny	I Prefer The Moonlight	4-816	SC
Rogers, Kenny	I'll Be There For You	48-125	SC
Rogers, Kenny	I'm Missing You	19-54	ST
Rogers, Kenny	I'm Missing You	32-306	THM
Rogers, Kenny	If I Knew Then What I Know Now	6-234	MM
Rogers, Kenny	If You Want To Find Love	16-365	CB
Rogers, Kenny	Just Dropped In	48-124	SC
Rogers, Kenny	Lady	8-270	CB
Rogers, Kenny	Lady	17-55	DK
Rogers, Kenny	Lady	13-387	P
Rogers, Kenny	Last Ten Years the (Superman)	48-128	ST
Rogers, Kenny	Love Or Something Like It	5-768	SC
Rogers, Kenny	Love The World Away	4-772	SC
Rogers, Kenny	Love Will Turn You Around	4-483	SC
Rogers, Kenny	Lucille	8-26	CB
Rogers, Kenny	Lucille	16-871	DK
Rogers, Kenny	Lucille	8-656	SAV
Rogers, Kenny	Lucille	48-130	SC

ARTIST	SONG TITLE	#	TYPE
Rogers, Kenny	Missing You	48-126	SC
Rogers, Kenny	Morning Desire	4-771	SC
Rogers, Kenny	Ol' Red	48-127	SC
Rogers, Kenny	Patriotic - Homeland	36-337	CB
Rogers, Kenny	Ruby Don't Take Your Love To Town	8-38	CB
Rogers, Kenny	Ruby Don't Take Your Love To Town	11-616	DK
Rogers, Kenny	Ruby Don't Take Your Love To Town	10-518	SF
Rogers, Kenny	Rueben James	5-35	SC
Rogers, Kenny	Scarlet Fever	4-777	SC
Rogers, Kenny	She Believes In Me	3-166	CB
Rogers, Kenny	She Believes In Me	26-467	DK
Rogers, Kenny	She Believes In Me	13-445	P
Rogers, Kenny	She Believes In Me	9-794	SAV
Rogers, Kenny	Slow Dance More	19-235	SC
Rogers, Kenny	Someone Must Feel Like A Fool Tonit	24-15	SC
Rogers, Kenny	Stuck On You	45-611	OZP
Rogers, Kenny	Sunshine	9-364	MG
Rogers, Kenny	Sweet Music Man	4-768	SC
Rogers, Kenny	Tell It To Me Brother	48-123	SC
Rogers, Kenny	There You Go Again	14-787	ST
Rogers, Kenny	There You Go Again	15-215	THM
Rogers, Kenny	There You Go Again	16-275	TT
Rogers, Kenny	Through The Years	3-172	CB
Rogers, Kenny	Through The Years	6-444	MM
Rogers, Kenny	Through The Years	12-471	P
Rogers, Kenny	Through The Years	2-3	SC
Rogers, Kenny	Tomb Of Unknown Love	5-243	SC
Rogers, Kenny	Twenty Years Ago	9-639	SAV
Rogers, Kenny	Twenty Years Ago	5-122	SC
Rogers, Kenny	Vows Go Unbroken the	1-765	CB
Rogers, Kenny	While The Feeling's Good	15-77	CB
Rogers, Kenny	You Decorated My Life	3-174	CB
Rogers, Kenny	You Decorated My Life	9-567	SAV
Rogers, Roy	Happy Trails	8-435	CB
Rogers, Roy	Happy Trails	2-166	SC
Rogers, Roy&Dale	Duet - Happy Trails	12-116	DK
Rogers, Roy&Dale	Happy Trails	12-116	DK
Rogue Traders	Voodoo Child	30-788	SF
Rolling Stones	19th Nervous Breakdown	19-756	LE
Rolling Stones	19th Nervous Breakdown	14-403	PT
Rolling Stones	Angie	19-750	LE
Rolling Stones	Angie	14-393	PT
Rolling Stones	As Tears Go By	19-751	LE
Rolling Stones	Beast Of Burden	18-20	LE
Rolling Stones	Beast Of Burden	14-397	PT
Rolling Stones	Bitch **	18-23	LE
Rolling Stones	Brown Sugar	19-759	LE
Rolling Stones	Brown Sugar	14-391	PT
Rolling Stones	Carol	12-152	DK
Rolling Stones	Doo Doo Doo Heartbreaker	20-201	SC
Rolling Stones	Emotional Rescue	18-24	LE
Rolling Stones	Fool To Cry	18-29	LE
Rolling Stones	Get Off Of My Cloud	19-850	LE
Rolling Stones	Get Off Of My Cloud	14-400	PT
Rolling Stones	Gimme Shelter	18-15	LE
Rolling Stones	Harlem Shuffle	16-868	DK
Rolling Stones	Harlem Shuffle	14-394	PT
Rolling Stones	Honky Tonk Woman	19-849	LE
Rolling Stones	Honky Tonk Woman	14-398	PT
Rolling Stones	It's All Over Now	18-18	LE
Rolling Stones	It's Only Rock & Roll	18-25	LE
Rolling Stones	It's Only Rock & Roll	14-395	PT
Rolling Stones	Jumpin' Jack Flash	19-758	LE
Rolling Stones	Jumpin' Jack Flash	14-396	PT
Rolling Stones	Last Time	19-755	LE
Rolling Stones	Let It Bleed	18-16	LE
Rolling Stones	Let's Spend The Night Together	19-752	LE
Rolling Stones	Let's Spend The Night Together	17-182	SC
Rolling Stones	Little Queenie	12-130	DK
Rolling Stones	Little Red Rooster	12-339	DK
Rolling Stones	Miss You	14-399	PT
Rolling Stones	Mixed Emotions	20-206	SC
Rolling Stones	Mother's Little Helper	19-754	LE
Rolling Stones	Mother's Little Helper	14-402	PT
Rolling Stones	Not Fade Away	11-276	DK
Rolling Stones	Not Fade Away	14-401	PT
Rolling Stones	Paint It Black	19-753	LE
Rolling Stones	Play With Fire	18-17	LE
Rolling Stones	Rock & A Hard Place	20-194	SC
Rolling Stones	Ruby Tuesday	18-19	LE
Rolling Stones	Satisfaction	19-126	KC
Rolling Stones	Satisfaction	19-746	LE
Rolling Stones	Satisfaction	14-390	PT
Rolling Stones	She's So Cold	20-199	SC
Rolling Stones	She's So Cold	47-871	SC
Rolling Stones	Some Girls	49-775	SC
Rolling Stones	Star Star	20-204	SC
Rolling Stones	Start Me Up	18-22	LE
Rolling Stones	Street Fighting Man	18-21	LE
Rolling Stones	Street Fighting Man	14-404	PT
Rolling Stones	Sympathy For The Devil	19-748	LE
Rolling Stones	Tell Me You're Coming Back	18-26	LE
Rolling Stones	Time Is On My Side	11-397	DK
Rolling Stones	Time Is On My Side	19-749	LE
Rolling Stones	Time Is On My Side	14-392	PT
Rolling Stones	Tumbling Dice	18-28	LE
Rolling Stones	Under My Thumb	18-27	LE
Rolling Stones	Under My Thumb	21-243	SC
Rolling Stones	Undercover Of The Night	21-628	SC
Rolling Stones	Wild Horses	19-757	LE
Rolling Stones	You Can't Always Get What U Want	19-125	KC
Rolling Stones	You Can't Always Get What U Want	19-747	LE

ARTIST	SONG TITLE	#	TYPE
Rolling Stones	You Got Me Rocking	20-202	SC
Romantics	Our Day Will Come	4-37	SC
Romantics	Talking In Your Sleep	14-570	AH
Romantics	Talking In Your Sleep	21-744	MH
Romantics	What I Like About You	9-352	AH
Romantics	What I Like About You	2-45	SC
Ronettes	Be My Baby	35-57	CB
Ronettes	I Saw Mommy Kissing Santa Claus	47-589	ZM
Ronettes	Xmas - I Saw Mommy Kissing Santa Claus	47-589	ZM
Ronnettes	Walkin' In The Rain	11-639	DK
Ronny & Daytonas	GTO	3-551	SC
Ronstadt & Ingram	Duet - Somewhere Out There	11-805	DK
Ronstadt & Ingram	Duet - Somewhere Out There	6-335	MM
Ronstadt & Ingram	Duet - Somewhere Out There	13-185	P
Ronstadt & Ingram	Duet - Somewhere Out There	9-205	SO
Ronstadt & Ingram	Somewhere Out There	11-805	DK
Ronstadt & Ingram	Somewhere Out There	6-335	MM
Ronstadt & Ingram	Somewhere Out There	13-185	P
Ronstadt & Ingram	Somewhere Out There	9-205	SO
Ronstadt & Neville	All My Life	11-821	DK
Ronstadt & Neville	All My Life	6-236	MM
Ronstadt & Neville	All My Life	12-890	P
Ronstadt & Neville	Don't Know Much	6-337	MM
Ronstadt & Neville	Duet - All My Life	11-821	DK
Ronstadt & Neville	Duet - All My Life	6-236	MM
Ronstadt & Neville	Duet - All My Life	12-890	P
Ronstadt & Neville	Duet - Don't Know Much	6-337	MM
Ronstadt, Linda	Am I Blue	49-208	MM
Ronstadt, Linda	Blue Bayou	16-767	DK
Ronstadt, Linda	Blue Bayou	9-3	MH
Ronstadt, Linda	Blue Bayou	12-736	P
Ronstadt, Linda	Blue Bayou	10-4	SC
Ronstadt, Linda	Blue Train the	14-875	SC
Ronstadt, Linda	Can't We Be Friends	9-832	SAV
Ronstadt, Linda	Different Drum	12-323	DK
Ronstadt, Linda	Different Drum	13-304	P
Ronstadt, Linda	Different Drum	9-696	SAV
Ronstadt, Linda	Faithless Love	9-487	SAV
Ronstadt, Linda	Heartbeats Accelerating	16-361	CB
Ronstadt, Linda	Heat Wave	22-924	SC
Ronstadt, Linda	High Sierra	6-855	MM
Ronstadt, Linda	How Do I Make You	10-8	SC
Ronstadt, Linda	Hurt So Bad	11-182	DK
Ronstadt, Linda	I've Got A Crush On You	34-8	CB
Ronstadt, Linda	I've Got A Crush On You	12-565	P
Ronstadt, Linda	It's So Easy	8-801	CB
Ronstadt, Linda	It's So Easy	11-161	DK
Ronstadt, Linda	It's So Easy	10-3	SC
Ronstadt, Linda	Just One Look	10-5	SC
Ronstadt, Linda	Long Long Time	10-2	SC
Ronstadt, Linda	Love Is A Rose	29-631	CB
Ronstadt, Linda	Mean To Me	15-530	MM

ARTIST	SONG TITLE	#	TYPE
Ronstadt, Linda	Ooh Baby Baby	10-366	KC
Ronstadt, Linda	Poor Poor Pitiful Me	9-634	SAV
Ronstadt, Linda	Round Midnight	10-705	JVC
Ronstadt, Linda	Silver Threads And Golden Needles	29-622	CB
Ronstadt, Linda	Someone To Lay Down Beside Me	20-101	SC
Ronstadt, Linda	Someone To Watch Over Me	7-186	MM
Ronstadt, Linda	That'll Be The Day	34-36	CB
Ronstadt, Linda	That'll Be The Day	10-7	SC
Ronstadt, Linda	Walk On	2-825	SC
Ronstadt, Linda	What'll I Do	15-582	MM
Ronstadt, Linda	When Will I Be Loved	16-766	DK
Ronstadt, Linda	When Will I Be Loved	9-7	MH
Ronstadt, Linda	When Will I Be Loved	12-639	P
Ronstadt, Linda	When Will I Be Loved	10-1	SC
Ronstadt, Linda	You're No Good	35-123	CB
Ronstadt, Linda	You're No Good	10-6	SC
Rooftop Singers	Walk Right In	21-16	CB
Rooftop Singers	Walk Right In	12-141	DK
Rooftop Singers	Walk Right In	7-352	MM
Roommates	Glory Of Love	13-263	P
Rose Royce	Car Wash	11-405	DK
Rose Royce	Car Wash	3-559	SC
Rose, Amy	I Just Want You To Know	40-24	PHN
Rose, Maggie	Girl In Your Truck Song	47-714	BKD
Rose, Maggie	Looking Back Now	43-185	ASK
Rose, Rusty	Love You Save the	17-373	DK
Rosie & Originals	Angel Baby	6-144	MM
Rosie & Originals	Angel Baby	5-523	SC
Ross & Gaye	You Are Everything - duet	49-69	ZVS
Ross & Richie	Duet - Endless Love	15-354	LE
Ross & Richie	Duet - Endless Love	13-203	P
Ross & Temptations	Duet - I'm Gonna Make You Love Me	17-100	DK
Ross & Temptations	I'm Gonna Make You Love Me	17-100	DK
Ross, Diana	Ain't No Mountain High Enough	15-359	LE
Ross, Diana	Baby Love	15-363	LE
Ross, Diana	Best Years Of My Life	15-360	LE
Ross, Diana	Boss the	15-366	LE
Ross, Diana	Come See About Me	48-548	DK
Ross, Diana	Do You Know Where You're Goin' To	11-266	DK
Ross, Diana	Do you Know Where You're Goin' To	4-53	SC
Ross, Diana	Happening the	48-545	DK
Ross, Diana	Home	15-368	LE
Ross, Diana	I Hear A Symphony	48-547	DK
Ross, Diana	I'm Coming Out	9-763	SAV
Ross, Diana	I'm Still Waiting	15-365	LE
Ross, Diana	It's My Time	15-362	LE
Ross, Diana	It's My Turn	6-567	MM
Ross, Diana	Last Time I Saw Him	18-260	DK

ARTIST	SONG TITLE	#	TYPE
Ross, Diana	Last Time I Saw Him	15-364	LE
Ross, Diana	Love Child	35-82	CB
Ross, Diana	Love Child	15-367	LE
Ross, Diana	Love Child	4-520	SC
Ross, Diana	Love Hangover	33-297	CB
Ross, Diana	Love Hangover	11-773	DK
Ross, Diana	Love Is Here & Now You're Gone	48-546	DK
Ross, Diana	Mirror Mirror	15-358	LE
Ross, Diana	Missing You	15-361	LE
Ross, Diana	My Old Piano	48-779	P
Ross, Diana	Reach Out & Touch Somebody	11-808	DK
Ross, Diana	Someday We'll Be Together	15-353	LE
Ross, Diana	Stop In The Name Of Love	15-357	LE
Ross, Diana	Theme From Mahogany	14-891	DK
Ross, Diana	Touch Me In The Morning	16-741	DK
Ross, Diana	Touch Me In The Morning	15-356	LE
Ross, Diana	Touch Me In The Morning	9-657	SAV
Ross, Diana	Touch Me In The Morning	4-752	SC
Ross, Diana	Up The Ladder To The Roof	48-549	DK
Ross, Diana	Upside Down	16-730	DK
Ross, Diana	Upside Down	9-658	SAV
Ross, Diana	When You Tell Me That You Love Me	24-263	SC
Ross, Diana	Why Do Fools Fall In Love	15-355	LE
Rossdale, Gavin	Love Remains The Same	36-525	CB
Roth, Asher feat Cee-Lo	Be By Myself	36-299	PHM
Roth, David Lee	Goin' Crazy	47-467	CB
Roth, David Lee	Just A Gigolo	6-351	MM
Roth, David Lee	Just A Gigolo	12-805	P
Roth, David Lee	Just A Gigolo	2-142	SC
Roth, David Lee	Just Like Paradise	34-91	CB
Roth, David Lee	Yankee Rose	47-466	SC
Rothberg, Patti	Inside	24-117	SC
Rowland, K & Eve	Like This	30-561	CB
Rowland, Kelly	Can't Nobody	34-173	CB
Rowland, Kelly	Can't Nobody	19-348	STP
Rowland, Kelly	Can't Nobody	32-166	THM
Rowland, Kelly	Like This	30-561	CB
Rowland, Kelly	Stole	35-267	CB
Rowland, Kelly	Stole	32-15	THM
Roxette	Crash Boom Bang	29-133	ST
Roxette	Dangerous	18-247	DK
Roxette	Duet - Dangerous	18-247	DK
Roxette	Fading Like A Flower	18-495	SAV
Roxette	It Must Have Been Love	28-419	DK
Roxette	It Must Have Been Love	12-811	P
Roxette	It Must Have Been Love	9-693	SAV

ARTIST	SONG TITLE	#	TYPE
Roxette	Joyride	18-496	SAV
Roxette	Listen To Your Heart	18-232	DK
Roxette	Look the	11-513	DK
Roxette	Wish I Could Fly	14-27	THM
Roxy Music	Jealous Guy	13-317	P
Roy, Lesley	Unbeautiful	36-252	PHM
Royal Crown Revue	Beyond The Sea	15-212	AMS
Royal Crown Revue	Hey Pachuco	13-691	SGB
Royal Crown Revue	Walkin' Blues	15-211	AMS
Royal Crown Revue	Zip Gun Bop	13-694	SGB
Royal Guardsmen	Snoopy VS The Red Baron	15-140	SC
Royal Guardsmen	Snoopy Vs. The Red Baron	6-520	MM
Royal Guardsmen	Snoopy's Christmas	45-742	SC
Royal Guardsmen	Xmas - Snoopy's Christmas	45-742	SC
Royal Teens	Duet - Short Shorts	29-830	SC
Royal Teens	Short Shorts	29-830	SC
Royal, Billy Joe	Boardwalk Angel	47-371	VH
Royal, Billy Joe	Cherry Hill Park	6-782	MM
Royal, Billy Joe	Down In The Boondocks	6-791	MM
Royal, Billy Joe	Down In The Boondocks	5-97	SC
Royal, Billy Joe	I'm Okay And Getting Better	24-128	SC
Royal, Billy Joe	If The Jukebox Took Teardrops	47-373	SRK
Royal, Billy Joe	Love Has No Right	29-650	SC
Royal, Billy Joe	Out Of Sight And On My Mind	47-370	SC
Royal, Billy Joe	Searchin' For Some Kind of Clue	47-372	SC
Royal, Billy Joe	Tell It Like It Is	33-92	CB
Royal, Billy Joe	Tell It Like It Is	4-657	SC
Roys	I Only Have Good Days	36-219	PHM
Roys	Still Standing	39-76	PHN
Rubio, Paulina	Don't Say Goodbye	17-593	PHM
Ruby & Romantics	Hey There Lonely Boy	7-38	MM
Ruby & Romantics	Our Day Will Come	35-50	CB
Ruby & Romantics	Our Day Will Come	11-599	DK
Ruby & Romantics	Our Day Will Come	19-617	MH
Rucker, Darius	Alright	36-48	PT
Rucker, Darius	Candy Cane Christmas	45-769	CK
Rucker, Darius	Don't Think I Don't Think About It	47-374	CB
Rucker, Darius	Homegrown Honey	47-375	SSC
Rucker, Darius	It Won't Be Like This for Long	36-240	PHM
Rucker, Darius	Miss You	43-164	ASK
Rucker, Darius	Radio	41-49	ASK
Rucker, Darius	Radio	44-334	SSC
Rucker, Darius	Southern Style	49-783	SSC
Rucker, Darius	True Believers	40-44	PHN
Rucker, Darius	Wagon Wheel	40-43	ASK
Rucker, Darius	Xmas - Candy Cane Christmas	45-769	CK
Rudolph, Kevin feat Lil Wayne	Let It Rock	36-28	PT

ARTIST	SONG TITLE	#	TYPE
Ruffin, Jimmy	What Becomes of the Broken Hearted	35-84	CB
Ruffin, Jimmy	What Becomes Of The Broken Hearted	12-157	DK
Rufus	Along Comes Mary	4-512	SC
Rufus	Tell Me Something Good	4-52	SC
Rufus&Chaka Kahn	Hollywood	17-469	SC
Rufus&Chaka Kahn	Sweet Thing	5-108	SC
Ruiz, Rey	Latino - Desde Que No Estas	17-759	SC
Ruiz, Rey	Latino - Muevelo	17-790	SC
Run DMC	Walk This Way	13-282	P
Run DMC	You Be Illin'	14-444	SC
Rundgren, Todd	Bang The Drum All Day	2-553	SC
Rundgren, Todd	Hello It's Me	11-341	DK
Rush	Fly By Night	5-883	SC
Rush	Tom Sawyer	4-567	SC
Rush, Merilee	Angel Of The Morning	49-449	MM
Rushen, Patrice	Forget Me Nots	18-371	AH
Rushlow	I Can't Be Your Friend	19-64	ST
Rushlow	I Can't Be Your Friend	32-372	THM
Rushlow	Sweet Summer Rain	20-389	ST
Rushlow Harris	That's So You	30-253	CB
Rushlow, Tim	Crazy Life	15-610	ST
Rushlow, Tim	She Misses Him	34-343	CB
Rushlow, Tim	She Misses Him	22-467	ST
Rushlow, Tim	When You Love Me	9-396	CB
Russel, Brenda	Piano In The Dark	11-533	DK
Russell, Johnny	Rednecks White Sock & Blue Ribbon	5-623	SC
Russell, Leon	I'll Sail My Ship Alone	45-686	VH
Russell, Leon	Lady Blue	2-786	SC
Russell, Leon	Roll In My Sweet Baby's Arms	4-631	SC
Russell, Leon	Six Pack To Go	2-407	SC
Russell, Leon	Tight Rope	47-473	SC
Rutan, Deric	When You Come Around	19-368	ST
Ryan & Daniels	Duet - Wrong Side Of Sober	49-920	KVD
Ryan & Daniels	Wrong Side Of Sober - duet	49-920	KVD
Ryan, Derek	Irish - Irish Heart	48-722	KV
Ryan, Derek	Shut Up And Dance	45-25	KVD
Rydell, Bobbie	Wild One	13-73	P
Rydell, Bobby	Forget Him	47-475	SC
Rydell, Bobby	Sway	47-476	SF
Rydell, Bobby	Swinging School	47-474	PS
Rydell, Bobby	We Got Love	47-477	SRI
Ryder & Detroit Whe	Devil With a Blue Dress On	11-445	DK
Rzeznik, J	I'm Still Here (Jim's Theme)	32-27	THM
S.O.A.P.	This Is How We Party	16-225	PHM
S.O.A.P.	This Is How We Party	10-138	SC
S.O.S. Band	Just The Way You Like It	12-382	DK
S.O.S. Band	Take Your Time	18-373	AH

ARTIST	SONG TITLE	#	TYPE
Sade	By Your Side	20-618	CB
Sade	By Your Side	30-779	SF
Sade	Hang On To Your Love	10-503	DA
Sade	No Ordinary Love	6-415	MM
Sade	No Ordinary Love	14-867	PS
Sade	Paradise	14-869	PS
Sade	Smooth Operator	17-111	DK
Sade	Smooth Operator	13-182	P
Sade	Smooth Operator	14-866	PS
Sade	Sweetest Taboo	14-868	PS
Sade	Sweetest Taboo the	29-632	SC
Sadler, Ssgt Barry	Ballad Of The Green Beret	20-71	SC
Safaris	Image Of A Girl	25-167	MM
Sager, Carole Bayer	You're Moving Out Today	30-794	SF
Saliva	Always	18-831	THM
Saliva	Rest In Pieces	25-663	MM
Salt 'N Pepa	Ain't Nothin' But A She Thing	49-321	CB
Salt 'N Pepa	Duet - Shoop	16-573	SC
Salt 'N Pepa	Let's Talk About Sex **	2-191	SC
Salt 'N Pepa	Push It **	2-720	SC
Salt 'N Pepa	Shake Your Thang (It's Your Thing)	49-320	CB
Salt 'N Pepa	Shoop	16-573	SC
Salt 'N Pepa	Whatta Man	2-109	SC
Salt-N-Pepa	Expression	37-68	SC
Sam & Dave	Don't Make It So Hard On Me	9-755	SAV
Sam & Dave	Hold On I'm A Comin'	26-201	DK
Sam & Dave	Hold On I'm Coming	35-81	CB
Sam & Dave	Hold On I'm Coming	12-726	P
Sam & Dave	Hold On I'm Coming	3-261	SC
Sam & Dave	I Thank You	7-258	MM
Sam & Dave	I Thank You	12-727	P
Sam & Dave	Soul Man	12-92	DK
Sam & Dave	Soul Man	12-711	P
Sam & Dave	When Something Is Wrong	12-27	DK
Sam The Sham & Pharoahs	Little Red Riding Hood	13-117	P
Sam The Sham & Pharoahs	Little Red Riding Hood	14-345	SC
Sam The Sham & Pharoahs	Wooly Bully	16-836	DK
Sam The Sham & Pharoahs	Wooly Bully	13-64	P
Sam The Sham & Pharoahs	Wooly Bully	10-533	SF
Sam The Sham & Pharoahs	Wooly Bully	6-136	MM
Sampson, Daz	Teenage Life	30-695	SF
Sandford/Townsend	Smoke From A Distant Fire	21-505	SC
Sandler, Adam	Adam's Chanuka Song **	16-642	MM
Sandler, Adam	Ode To My Car **	13-728	SGB
Sandler, Adam	What The Hell Happened	5-555	SC

ARTIST	SONG TITLE	#	TYPE
	To Me **		
Sandler, Adam	What The Hell Happened To Me **	13-727	SGB
Sandpipers	Come Saturday Morning	11-348	DK
Sandpipers	Latino - Guatanamera	11-503	DK
Sang, Samantha	Emotion	11-326	DK
Santana	Anywhere You Want To Go	49-883	SF
Santana	Black Magic Woman	17-119	DK
Santana	Black Magic Woman (Radio Version)	5-878	SC
Santana	Everybody's Everything	21-514	SC
Santana	Evil Ways	11-831	DK
Santana	Maria Maria	14-182	CB
Santana	Open Invitation	9-377	AH
Santana	They All Went To Mexico	44-68	KV
Santana	Winning	29-264	SC
Santana & Band	Why Don't You & I	32-321	THM
Santana & Branch	Duet - Game Of Love the	18-580	NS
Santana & Branch	Game Of Love	25-392	MM
Santana & Branch	Game Of Love the	18-580	NS
Santana & Dido	Feels Like Fire	32-134	THM
Santana & Everlast	Put Your Lights On	9-338	PS
Santana & Everlast	Put Your Lights On	10-218	SC
Santana & Everlast	Put Your Lights On	19-824	SGB
Santana & Kroeger	Why Don't You & I	25-657	MM
Santana & Musiq	Nothing At All	20-631	NS
Santana & Musiq	Nothing At All	18-777	PHM
Santana & Thomas	Smooth	30-207	PHM
Santana & Thomas	Smooth	8-499	PHT
Santana feat Alex Band	Why Don't You & I	35-285	CB
Santana feat Chad Kroeger	Into The Night	36-450	CB
Santana feat M. Branch	Game Of Love	35-242	CB
Santana/Los Lonely	I Don't Wanna Lose Your Love	29-279	PHM
Santiago, Lina	Just Because I Love You	24-167	SC
Sanz, Alejandro	Latino - Cuando Nadie Me Ve	18-2	SC
Sanz, Victor	Destination Unknown	14-145	CB
Sarstedt, Peter	Where Do You Go To My Lovely?	10-633	SF
Savage Garden	Animal Song	7-846	PHM
Savage Garden	Animal Song	13-714	SGB
Savage Garden	Crash And Burn	14-178	CB
Savage Garden	I Knew I Loved You	5-791	SC
Savage Garden	To The Moon And Back	21-545	PHM
Savage Garden	Truly Madly Deeply	7-705	PHM
Savage Garden	Truly Madly Deeply	10-119	SC
Saving Abel	18 Days	36-384	SC
Saving Abel	Addicted	36-528	CB
Saving Jane	Girl Next Door (Radio Version)	30-273	SC
Sawyer Brown	800 Pound Jesus	23-373	SC
Sawyer Brown	Another Side	8-404	CB

ARTIST	SONG TITLE	#	TYPE
Sawyer Brown	Another Side	22-771	ST
Sawyer Brown	Another Side	46-244	CB
Sawyer Brown	Betty's Bein' Bad	29-695	SC
Sawyer Brown	Boys And Me the	17-164	JVC
Sawyer Brown	Café On The Corner	5-31	SC
Sawyer Brown	Can You Hear Me Now	17-576	ST
Sawyer Brown	Circles	16-104	ST
Sawyer Brown	Dirt Road the	2-353	SC
Sawyer Brown	Drive Me Wild	7-831	CHT
Sawyer Brown	Drive Me Wild	22-720	ST
Sawyer Brown	I Don't Believe In Goodbye	2-670	SC
Sawyer Brown	I Will Leave The Light On	4-197	SC
Sawyer Brown	I'll Be Around	19-373	ST
Sawyer Brown	I'm In Love With Her	16-196	THM
Sawyer Brown	Lookin' For Love	22-592	ST
Sawyer Brown	Lookin' For Love	16-271	TT
Sawyer Brown	Perfect World	14-76	CB
Sawyer Brown	Round Here	7-180	MM
Sawyer Brown	Round Here	3-662	SC
Sawyer Brown	She's Getting There	24-159	SC
Sawyer Brown	Six Days On The Road	7-611	CHM
Sawyer Brown	Some Girls Do	33-109	CB
Sawyer Brown	Some Girls Do	12-417	P
Sawyer Brown	Step That Step	20-15	SC
Sawyer Brown	Thank GOD For You	34-306	CB
Sawyer Brown	Thank God For You	2-515	SC
Sawyer Brown	They Don't Understand	23-481	CB
Sawyer Brown	They Don't Understand	29-615	ST
Sawyer Brown	This Missin' You Heart Of Mine	19-442	SC
Sawyer Brown	This Night Won't Last Forever	7-671	CHM
Sawyer Brown	This Thing Called Wantin' & Havin'	7-21	MM
Sawyer Brown	This Time	17-257	NA
Sawyer Brown	This Time	2-540	SC
Sawyer Brown	Treat Her Right	7-231	MM
Sawyer Brown	Treat Her Right	22-889	ST
Sawyer Brown	Trouble On The Line	2-340	SC
Sawyer Brown	Used To Blue	5-762	SC
Sawyer Brown	Walk the	12-56	DK
Sayer, Leo	Long Tall Glasses (I Can Dance)	47-479	SC
Sayer, Leo	Moonlighting	47-482	ZM
Sayer, Leo	More Than I Can Say	13-31	P
Sayer, Leo	More Than I Can Say	11-50	PX
Sayer, Leo	More Than I Can Say	21-799	SC
Sayer, Leo	One Man Band	47-481	SF
Sayer, Leo	Show Must Go On the	47-480	SF
Sayer, Leo	Thunder In My Heart	30-739	SF
Sayer, Leo	When I Need You	35-150	CB
Sayer, Leo	When I Need You	29-642	SC
Sayer, Leo	When I Need You	10-536	SF
Sayer, Leo	You Make Me Feel Like Dancing	33-304	CB
Sayer, Leo	You Make Me Feel Like	29-298	SC

ARTIST	SONG TITLE	#	TYPE
	Dancing		
Scaggs, Boz	Breakdown Dead Ahead	46-318	SC
Scaggs, Boz	Georgia	46-319	SC
Scaggs, Boz	Harbor Lights	15-749	AMS
Scaggs, Boz	Lowdown	7-97	MM
Scaggs, Boz	Some Change	24-27	SC
Scaggs, Boz	What Do You Want The Girl To Do	46-320	SC
Scandal	Goodbye To You	5-314	SC
Scandal	Warrior the	4-531	SC
Scarlet Pumpernel	Show - You Are My Home	18-810	PS
Schneider, Fred	Halloween - I'm Gonna Haunt You	16-283	TT
Schneider, Fred	Halloween - Monster in my pants	16-285	TT
Schneider, Fred	I'm Gonna Haunt You	16-283	TT
Schneider, John	At The Sound Of The Tone	5-774	SC
Schneider, John	Country Girls	5-415	SC
Schneider, John	I've Been Around Enough To Know	14-316	SC
Schneider, John	What's A Memory Like You Doing…	20-291	SC
Schneider, John	What's a Memory Like You...	33-90	CB
Schneider, John	You're The Last Thing I Needed…	5-675	SC
Scissor Sisters	Comfortably Numb	29-221	ZM
Scissor Sisters	Filthy/Gorgeous **	29-226	ZM
Scissor Sisters	Laura	29-222	ZM
Scissor Sisters	Mary	29-223	ZM
Scissor Sisters	Music Is The Victim **	29-224	ZM
Scissor Sisters	Take Your Mama	23-561	MM
Scissor Sisters	Take Your Mama	29-225	ZM
Scorpions	Always Somewhere	49-99	KVD
Scorpions	Believe In Love	49-101	KVD
Scorpions	Big City Nights	49-97	SC
Scorpions	Dust In The Wind	49-102	CDG
Scorpions	No One Like You	49-96	SC
Scorpions	Rock You Like A Hurricane	17-335	DK
Scorpions	Rock You Like A Hurricane	23-62	MH
Scorpions	Send Me An Angel	49-98	KVD
Scorpions	Still Lovin' You	5-494	SC
Scorpions	Still Lovin' You	49-95	SC
Scorpions	Winds Of Change	7-493	MM
Scorpions	Winds Of Change	8-611	TT
Scorpions	You And I	49-100	KVD
Scorpions	Zoo the	21-756	SC
Scott & O'Connor	Duet - I Will Fall - Nashville	45-477	KVD
Scott & O'Connor	I Will Fall - Nashville - duet	45-477	KVD
Scott & O'Connor	Show - I Will Fall - Nashville - duet	45-477	KVD
Scott, Dylan	Makin' This Boy Go Crazy	41-77	PHN

ARTIST	SONG TITLE	#	TYPE
Scott, Jack	Oh Little One	45-345	BSP
Scott, Jill	Getting In The Way	20-620	CB
Scott, Jill	Getting' In The Way	25-693	MM
Scott, Jill	He Loves Me	25-691	MM
Scott, Jill	Long Walk a	33-387	CB
Scott, Jill	Long Walk a	25-683	MM
Scott, Linda	I've Told Every Little…	3-464	SC
Scott, Ray	Gone Either Way	29-371	CB
Scott, Ray	My Kind Of Music	23-475	CB
Screaming Trees	All I Know	24-116	SC
Script	Broken Arrow	39-122	PHM
Script	Kaleidoscope	39-124	PHM
Seal	Every Time I'm With You	48-395	DCK
Seal	Fly Like An Eagle	4-612	SC
Seal	Kiss From A Rose	11-66	JTG
Seal	Kiss From A Rose	3-432	SC
Seal	Prayer For The Dying	6-636	MM
Seal	Waiting For You	32-429	THM
Seals & Croft	Diamond Girl	12-350	DK
Seals & Croft	Diamond Girl	17-560	PR
Seals & Croft	Diamond Girl	3-473	SC
Seals & Croft	Get Closer	12-351	DK
Seals & Croft	Get Closer	20-362	SC
Seals & Croft	Hummingbird	47-484	DCK
Seals & Croft	I'll Play For You	47-483	SC
Seals & Croft	Summer Breeze	29-634	SC
Seals & Croft	We May Never Pass This Way Again	3-456	SC
Seals & Croft	Windflowers	47-485	KKS
Seals & Osmond	Duet - Meet Me In Montana	8-119	CB
Seals & Osmond	Duet - Meet Me In Montana	2-309	SC
Seals & Osmond	Meet Me In Montana	8-119	CB
Seals & Osmond	Meet Me In Montana	2-309	SC
Seals, Brady	Another You Another Me	4-452	SC
Seals, Brady	Been There Drunk That	47-581	PHN
Seals, Brady	Best Is Yet To Come the	8-984	CB
Seals, Brady	Country As A Boy Can Be	45-829	VH
Seals, Brady	I Fell	5-297	SC
Seals, Brady	Natural Born Lovers	48-102	SC
Seals, Brady	Still Standing Tall	48-98	MM
Seals, Brady	Whole Lotta Hurt	8-856	CB
Seals, Dan	Addicted	14-424	SC
Seals, Dan	All Fired Up	4-117	SC
Seals, Dan	Big Wheels In The Moonlight	48-103	CB
Seals, Dan	Bop	38-43	CB
Seals, Dan	Bop	6-756	MM
Seals, Dan	Bop	8-692	SAV
Seals, Dan	Everything That Glitters Is Not Gol	4-554	SC
Seals, Dan	Good Times	48-104	CB
Seals, Dan	Healing Kind the	4-18	SC
Seals, Dan	I Will Be There	6-88	SC
Seals, Dan	I'd Really Love To See	4-151	SC

ARTIST	SONG TITLE	#	TYPE
	You Tonight		
Seals, Dan	Love On Arrival	6-540	MM
Seals, Dan	My Baby's Got Good Timin'	5-560	SC
Seals, Dan	My Old Yellow Car	46-112	SC
Seals, Dan	One Friend	48-106	SC
Seals, Dan	Three Time Loser	48-107	SC
Seals, Dan	When Love Comes Around The Bend	48-105	SC
Seals, Dan	You Still Move Me	5-671	SC
Searchers	Love Potion # 9	11-421	DK
Searchers	Love Potion # 9	6-656	MM
Searchers	Love Potion # 9	12-661	P
Searchers	Needles & Pins	11-252	DK
Searchers	Needles & Pins	20-33	SC
Searchers	When You Walk In The Room	9-700	SAV
Sears, Dawn	Nothin' But Good	4-475	SC
Sears, Dawn	Runaway Train	6-582	MM
Sears, Dawn	Runaway Train	13-20	P
Sebastian, Joan	Latino - Secreto De Amor	17-754	SC
Secada, John	Free	36-179	PHM
Secada, Jon	Angel Of Harlem	6-409	MM
Secada, Jon	I'm Free	4-281	SC
Secada, Jon	Too Late Too Soon	10-687	HH
Secret Affair	Time For Action	30-785	SF
Secret Garden	Show - Hold On	10-373	KC
Sedaka, Neil	Alice In Wonderland	45-357	CB
Sedaka, Neil	Bad Blood	9-170	SO
Sedaka, Neil	Breaking Up Is Hard To Do	11-268	DK
Sedaka, Neil	Breaking Up Is Hard To Do	12-743	P
Sedaka, Neil	Breaking Up Is Hard To Do	9-168	SO
Sedaka, Neil	Breaking Up Is Hard To Do (Slow V)	5-480	SC
Sedaka, Neil	Calendar Girl	26-417	DK
Sedaka, Neil	Calendar Girl	14-346	SC
Sedaka, Neil	Calendar Girl	9-164	SO
Sedaka, Neil	Diary the	45-356	CB
Sedaka, Neil	Happy Birthday Sweet Sixteen	11-253	DK
Sedaka, Neil	Happy Birthday Sweet Sixteen	12-740	P
Sedaka, Neil	Happy Birthday Sweet Sixteen	9-165	SO
Sedaka, Neil	I'm A Song (Sing Me)	45-851	VH
Sedaka, Neil	Laughter In The Rain	11-196	DK
Sedaka, Neil	Laughter in The Rain	9-169	SO
Sedaka, Neil	Let's Go Steady Again	45-60	CB
Sedaka, Neil	Little Devil	11-453	DK
Sedaka, Neil	Next Door To An Angel	45-355	CB
Sedaka, Neil	Oh Carol	11-197	DK
Sedaka, Neil	Oh Carol	13-121	P
Sedaka, Neil	Oh Carol	9-166	SO
Sedaka, Neil	One Way Ticket To The Blues	9-167	SO

ARTIST	SONG TITLE	#	TYPE
Sedaka, Neil	Run Samson Run	45-358	CB
Sedaka, Neil	Sweet Little You	45-354	CB
Sedaka, Neil	You Mean Everything To Me	45-353	CB
Seeger, Pete	Don't Fence Me In	7-347	MM
Seekers	Carnival Is Over the	10-664	SF
Seekers	Georgy Girl	16-810	DK
Seekers	Georgy Girl	9-836	SAV
Seekers	I'll Never Find Another You	10-590	SF
Seekers	Island Of Dreams	49-63	ZVS
Seekers	Morningtown Ride	49-62	ZVS
Seekers	World Of Our Own	49-61	ZVS
Seely, Jeannie	Don't Touch Me	8-389	CB
Seether	Rise Above This	36-506	CB
Seger & McBride	Chances Are - duet	46-342	MM
Seger & McBride	Duet - Chances Are	46-342	MM
Seger, Bob	Against The Wind	10-173	UK
Seger, Bob	Beautiful Loser	20-73	SC
Seger, Bob	Betty Lou's Getting Out	10-179	UK
Seger, Bob	C'Est La Vie	5-305	SC
Seger, Bob	Come to Poppa	19-276	SGB
Seger, Bob	Famous Final Scene the	10-178	UK
Seger, Bob	Feel Like A Number	46-345	SC
Seger, Bob	Fire Down Below	46-340	AH
Seger, Bob	Fire Lake	10-176	UK
Seger, Bob	Good For Me	10-180	UK
Seger, Bob	Her Strut	43-210	SC
Seger, Bob	Hollywood Nights	15-175	MH
Seger, Bob	Holywood Nights	10-174	UK
Seger, Bob	Horizontal Bop the **	2-731	SC
Seger, Bob	Katmandu	13-651	SGB
Seger, Bob	Like A Rock	35-184	CB
Seger, Bob	Little Drummer Boy - xmas	46-343	SC
Seger, Bob	Lock And Load	46-341	MM
Seger, Bob	Mainstreet	20-319	MH
Seger, Bob	Mainstreet	3-451	SC
Seger, Bob	Mainstreet	10-171	UK
Seger, Bob	Night Moves	2-790	SC
Seger, Bob	Night Moves	10-170	UK
Seger, Bob	Old Time Rock & Roll	12-674	P
Seger, Bob	Old Time Rock & Roll	2-39	SC
Seger, Bob	Old Time Rock & Roll	10-526	SF
Seger, Bob	Ramblin' Gamblin' Man	46-338	SC
Seger, Bob	Real Love the	46-344	SC
Seger, Bob	Rock And Roll Never Forgets	46-339	AH
Seger, Bob	Roll Me Away	17-527	SC
Seger, Bob	Shakedown	24-71	SC
Seger, Bob	Shame On The Moon	11-540	DK
Seger, Bob	Shame On The Moon	3-477	SC
Seger, Bob	Sock It To Me Santa - xmas	46-288	CB
Seger, Bob	Still The Same	10-172	UK
Seger, Bob	Sunspot Baby	19-282	SGB
Seger, Bob	Till It Shines	10-177	UK

ARTIST	SONG TITLE	#	TYPE
Seger, Bob	Tryin' To Live My Life Without You	46-362	LG
Seger, Bob	Turn The Page	19-122	KC
Seger, Bob	Turn The Page	10-169	UK
Seger, Bob	Wait For Me	46-346	SC
Seger, Bob	We've Got Tonight	34-70	CB
Seger, Bob	We've Got Tonight	6-446	MM
Seger, Bob	Xmas - Little Drummer Boy	41-40	CB
Seger, Bob	Xmas - Little Drummer Boy	46-343	SC
Seger, Bob	Xmas - Sock It To Me Santa	46-288	CB
Seger, Bob	You'll Accomp'ny Me	10-175	UK
Sego's	Gospel - Hallelujah Square	16-20	SX
Selena	Captive Heart	23-569	MM
Selena	Captive Heart	21-451	PS
Selena	Dreaming Of You	19-582	MH
Selena	Dreaming Of You	21-452	PS
Selena	Dreaming Of You	15-471	THM
Selena	I Could Fall In Love	21-449	PS
Selena	I Will Survive/Funkytown Medley	23-570	MM
Selena	I'm Getting Used To You	23-571	MM
Selena	I'm Getting Used To You	21-450	PS
Selena	Last Dance/The Hustle/On The Radio	19-161	SGB
Selena	Latino - Armor Prohibido (Forbidden	21-444	PS
Selena	Latino - Como La Flor (Like a Flowe	21-448	PS
Selena	Latino - El Toro Relajo (Crazy Bull	21-447	PS
Selena	Latino - Tu Solo Tu (You Only You)	21-446	PS
Selena	Missing My Baby	23-568	MM
Selena&Barrio Boys	Latino - Donde Estes (Where Are...)	21-445	PS
Sellars, Shane	Matthew Mark Luke & Earnhardt	9-872	ST
Sellers, Jason	Can't Help Calling Your Name	9-391	CB
Sellers, Jason	Matter Of Time a	8-985	CB
Sellers, Jason	Matter Of Time a	10-209	SC
Sellers, Jason	Matter Of Time a	22-383	ST
Sembello, Michael	Maniac	28-355	DK
Semisonic	Closing Time	10-142	SC
Semisonic	Secret Smile	7-809	PHT
Semisonic	Singing In My Sleep	14-286	MM
Sensations	Let Me In	9-285	SC
Seritti Politti	Perfect Way	29-14	MH
Sev	Same Old Song	23-157	PHM
Seven	Drunk Chicks	36-373	SC
Sevendust	Enemy	19-760	PHM
Seville, David	Witch Doctor	33-238	CB
Seville, David	Witch Doctor	6-856	MM
Seville, David	Witch Doctor	16-298	TT

ARTIST	SONG TITLE	#	TYPE
Seville, David & Chipmunks	Chipmunk Song the	49-126	TU
Sha-Na-Na	Born To Hand Jive	14-585	SC
Sha-Na-Na	Those Magic Changes	10-11	SC
Shadows Of Knight	Gloria	27-560	DK
Shaffer, Charlie	Pearly Shells	6-829	MM
Shaffer, Lisa	Just One	30-541	CB
Shaggy	Angel	12-391	PHM
Shaggy	Angel	18-544	TT
Shaggy	Dance And Shout	15-442	PHM
Shaggy	In The Summertime	25-390	MM
Shaggy	Strength Of A Woman	32-93	THM
Shaggy	Strength Of A Woman the	25-399	MM
Shaggy & Rayvon	Angel	16-483	MH
Shaggy & Rayvon	Duet - Angel	16-483	MH
Shaggy & Ricardo	Duet - It Wasn't Me	16-471	MH
Shaggy & Ricardo	Duet - It Wasn't Me	16-117	PRT
Shaggy & Ricardo	It Wasn't Me	16-471	MH
Shaggy & Ricardo	It Wasn't Me	16-117	PRT
Shaggy & Ricardo	It Wasn't Me	18-561	TT
Shai	I Don't Wanna Be Alone	4-344	SC
Shakira	Objection	18-424	CB
Shakira	One the	20-468	CB
Shakira	Underneath Your Clothes	18-294	CB
Shakira	Underneath Your Clothes	25-209	MM
Shakira	Whenever Wherever	25-77	MM
Shakira w Jean Wyclef	Hips Don't Lie	30-727	SF
Shakira&Wyclef Jean	Duet - Hips Don't Lie	30-727	SF
Shakira&Wyclef Jean	Hips Don't Lie	30-727	SF
Shalamar	Make That Move	15-38	SS
Shalamar	Second Time Around the	25-274	MM
Shand, Remy	Take A Message	18-229	CB
Shand, Remy	Take A Message	25-222	MM
Shand, Remy	Way I Feel the	20-519	CB
Shangri-Las	Give Him A Great Big Kiss	6-655	MM
Shangri-Las	Leader Of The Pack	11-777	DK
Shangri-Las	Leader Of The Pack	3-366	MH
Shangri-Las	Leader Of The Pack	6-158	MM
Shangri-Las	Leader Of The Pack	9-282	SC
Shangri-Las	Remember Walking In The Rain	6-646	MM
Shangri-Las	Remember Walking In The Rain	9-708	SAV
Shanice	I Love Your Smile	13-605	P
Shanice	Saving Forever For You	17-389	DK
Shannon	Let The Music Play	3-443	SC
Shapeshifters	Incredible	30-697	SF
Shapiro, Helen	There's Always Something	10-611	SF
Shapiro, Helen	Walkin' Back To Happiness	10-556	SF

ARTIST	SONG TITLE	#	TYPE
Shapiro, Helen	You Don't Know	19-109	SAV
Sharp, Dee Dee	Mashed Potato Time	27-492	DK
Sharp, Dee Dee	Mashed Potato Time - DANCE #	22-393	SC
Sharp, Kevin	Beautiful People	15-864	ST
Sharp, Kevin	If She Only Knew	8-744	CB
Sharp, Kevin	If You Love Somebody	7-677	CHM
Sharp, Kevin	If You Love Somebody	4-832	SC
Sharp, Kevin	If You Love Somebody	22-614	ST
Sharp, Kevin	Love Is All That Really Matters	8-461	CB
Sharp, Kevin	Love Is All That Really Matters	22-792	ST
Sharp, Kevin	Nobody Knows	7-392	MM
Sharp, Kevin	Nobody Knows	4-589	SC
Sharp, Kevin	She's Sure Taking It Well	14-657	CB
Sharp, Kevin	She's Sure Taking It Well	22-400	CHM
Sharp, Kevin	There's Only You	8-149	CB
Sharp, Kevin	There's Only You	22-415	ST
Sharp, Maia	Red Dress	29-320	PHM
Shaver, Billy Joe	Hottest Thing In Town	45-839	VH
Shaw, Artie	Begin The Beguine	11-761	DK
Shaw, Artie	Begin The Beguine	10-710	JVC
Shaw, Sandie	Long Live Love	10-591	SF
Shaw, Victoria	Cry Wolf	6-580	MM
Shaw, Victoria	Forgiveness	6-805	MM
Shaw, Victoria	Forgiveness	2-834	SC
Shawanda, Crystal	My Roots Are Showing	36-264	PHM
Shawanda, Crystal	You Can Let Go	36-583	CB
Shawanda, Crystal	You Can Let Go	36-226	PHM
Shay, Sam	Take a Letter Maria	17-34	DK
She Moves	Breaking All The Rules	5-188	SC
SheDaisy	Come Home Soon	20-447	ST
SheDaisy	Don't Worry 'Bout A Thing	22-20	CB
SheDaisy	Get Over Yourself	25-184	MM
SheDaisy	Get Over Yourself	16-685	ST
SheDaisy	I Will....But	13-810	CHM
SheDaisy	Little Goodbyes	8-333	CB
SheDaisy	Lucky 4 You (Tonite I'm Just Me)	22-572	ST
SheDaisy	Mine All Mine	25-235	MM
SheDaisy	Mine All Mine	17-569	ST
SheDaisy	Passenger Seat the	20-171	ST
SheDaisy	Santa's Got A Brand New Bag - xmas	45-246	CB
SheDaisy	Still Holding Out For You	15-96	ST
SheDaisy	This Woman Needs	19-232	SC
SheDaisy	This Woman Needs	22-500	ST
SheDaisy	Xmas - Santa's Got A Brand New Bag	45-246	CB
Sheik, Duncan	Barely Breathing	15-476	SC
Sheik, Duncan	On A High	25-314	MM
Sheik, Duncan	White Limousine	29-282	PHM
Sheila E	Glamorous Life	24-429	SC

ARTIST	SONG TITLE	#	TYPE
Shelby, David	Kick A Little Dirt Around	41-61	PHN
Shelton & Adkins	Duet - Hillbilly Bone	38-84	CB
Shelton & Adkins	Hillbilly Bone - duet	38-84	CB
Shelton & Aguilera	Duet - Just A Fool	47-449	MRH
Shelton & Aguilera	Just A Fool - duet	47-449	MRH
Shelton & Monroe	Duet - Lonely Tonight	45-329	CKC
Shelton & Monroe	Duet - You Ain't Dolly & You Ain't...	49-522	BKD
Shelton & Monroe	Duet - You Ain't Dolly... (Inst)	49-523	BKD
Shelton & Monroe	Lonely Tonight - duet	45-329	CKC
Shelton & Monroe	You Ain't Dolly & You Ain't Porter	49-522	BKD
Shelton & Monroe	You Ain't Dolly & You... (Inst)	49-523	BKD
Shelton, Blake	Addicted	38-212	PHN
Shelton, Blake	All About Tonight	37-332	CB
Shelton, Blake	All Over Me	25-64	MM
Shelton, Blake	All Over Me	15-854	ST
Shelton, Blake	Asphalt Cowboy	47-447	KV
Shelton, Blake	Austin	33-140	CB
Shelton, Blake	Austin	15-100	ST
Shelton, Blake	Baby the	34-353	CB
Shelton, Blake	Baby the	25-416	MM
Shelton, Blake	Baby the	18-463	ST
Shelton, Blake	Baby the	32-40	THM
Shelton, Blake	Boys 'Round Here	43-254	ASK
Shelton, Blake	Boys 'Round Here	43-261	KCD
Shelton, Blake	Came Here To Forget	49-370	BKD
Shelton, Blake	Came Here To Forget	49-3	DCK
Shelton, Blake	Country On The Radio	47-444	ASK
Shelton, Blake	Doin' What She Likes	43-135	PHN
Shelton, Blake	Don't Make Me	30-166	CB
Shelton, Blake	Don't Make Me	45-333	ASK
Shelton, Blake	Dreamer the	39-2	CB
Shelton, Blake	Drink On It	38-278	AS
Shelton, Blake	Footloose	47-448	KV
Shelton, Blake	Georgia In A Jug	38-113	AT
Shelton, Blake	GOD Gave Me You	38-89	CB
Shelton, Blake	Gonna	45-40	BKD
Shelton, Blake	Good At Startin' Fires	36-277	PHM
Shelton, Blake	Goodbye Time	22-30	CB
Shelton, Blake	Heavy Liftin'	25-611	MM
Shelton, Blake	Heavy Liftin'	19-84	ST
Shelton, Blake	Home	36-416	CB
Shelton, Blake	Honey Bee	37-206	AS
Shelton, Blake	I Need My Girl	45-376	BKD
Shelton, Blake	I'll Just Hold On	45-331	AC
Shelton, Blake	Kiss My Country Ass	38-116	CB
Shelton, Blake	Lay Low	45-385	BKD
Shelton, Blake	Mine Would Be You	40-56	ASL
Shelton, Blake	More I Drink the	30-471	CB
Shelton, Blake	My Eyes	44-166	BKD
Shelton, Blake	Neon Light	45-332	ASK
Shelton, Blake	Nobody But Me	23-407	CB
Shelton, Blake	Nobody But Me	29-845	SC
Shelton, Blake	Ol' Red	33-179	CB

ARTIST	SONG TITLE	#	TYPE
Shelton, Blake	Ol' Red	25-239	MM
Shelton, Blake	Ol' Red	16-687	ST
Shelton, Blake	Over	39-38	ASK
Shelton, Blake	Playboys of the Southwestern World	25-649	MM
Shelton, Blake	Playboys of the Southwestern World	19-266	ST
Shelton, Blake	Playboys Of The Southwestern World	32-343	THM
Shelton, Blake	Problems At Home	47-764	SRK
Shelton, Blake	Ready To Roll	47-446	KV
Shelton, Blake	Sangria	45-948	KV
Shelton, Blake	She Wouldn't Be Gone	36-203	PHM
Shelton, Blake	Some Beach	23-392	CB
Shelton, Blake	Some Beach	30-10	SC
Shelton, Blake	Some Beach	20-492	ST
Shelton, Blake	Sunny In Seattle	47-445	FTX
Shelton, Blake	Sure Be Cool If You Did	42-32	ASK
Shelton, Blake	Ten Times Crazier	41-50	ASK
Shelton, Blake	When Somebody Knows You	20-327	ST
Shelton, Blake	When Somebody Knows You...	39-1	CB
Shelton, Blake	Who Are You When I'm Not Looking	37-234	CB
Shenandoah	All Over But The Shouting	7-198	MM
Shenandoah	All Over But The Shouting	4-203	SC
Shenandoah	Always Have Always Will	3-623	SC
Shenandoah	Church On Cumberland Road	14-692	CB
Shenandoah	Darned If I Don't Danged If I Do	1-494	CB
Shenandoah	Darned If I Don't Danged If I Do	2-746	SC
Shenandoah	Deeper Than That	4-401	SC
Shenandoah	Ghost In This House	1-484	CB
Shenandoah	Ghost In This House	2-625	SC
Shenandoah	Heaven Bound	1-495	CB
Shenandoah	Heaven Bound	7-28	MM
Shenandoah	I Got You	1-485	CB
Shenandoah	I Want To Be Loved Like That	1-491	CB
Shenandoah	I Want To Be Loved Like That	2-8	SC
Shenandoah	I'll Go Down Loving You	2-423	SC
Shenandoah	If Bubba Can Dance I Can Too	1-492	CB
Shenandoah	If Bubba Can Dance I Can Too	6-498	MM
Shenandoah	If Bubba Can Dance I Can Too	2-208	SC
Shenandoah	Janie Baker's Love Slave	1-490	CB
Shenandoah	Janie Baker's Love Slave	6-763	MM
Shenandoah	Leavin's Been A Long Time Comin'	1-489	CB

ARTIST	SONG TITLE	#	TYPE
Shenandoah	Leavin's Been A Long Time Comin'	6-123	MM
Shenandoah	Mama Knows	5-559	SC
Shenandoah	Moon Over Georgia the	1-486	CB
Shenandoah	Next To You Next To me	1-483	CB
Shenandoah	Rock My Baby	1-488	CB
Shenandoah	Two Dozen Roses	1-482	CB
Shenandoah	What Children Believe	14-106	CB
Shenandoah	When You Were Mine	1-487	CB
Shenandoah/Krauss	Duet - Somewhere in the Vicinity of	17-259	NA
Shenandoah/Krauss	Duet - Somewhere in the Vicinity of	2-822	SC
Shenandoah/Krauss	Somewhere In The Vicinity/Heart	17-259	NA
Shenandoah/Krauss	Somewhere In The Vicinity/Heart	2-822	SC
Shep & Limelights	Daddy's Home	35-47	CB
Shep & Limelights	Daddy's Home	3-296	MM
Shep & Limelights	Daddy's Home	3-581	SC
Shepard, Jeanne	Dear John Letter	8-771	CB
Shepard, Jeanne	Second Fiddle To An Old Guitar	15-89	CB
Shepard, Jeanne	Slippin' Away	8-786	CB
Shepard, Vonda	Baby Don't You Break My Heart Slow	8-225	PHT
Shepard, Vonda	Baby Don't You Break My Heart Slow	16-193	THM
Shepard, Vonda	Searchin' My Soul	16-223	PHM
Shepard, Vonda	Searchin' My Soul	5-271	SC
Shepard, Vonda	This Old Heart Of Mine	48-556	DK
Shepherd, Ashton	Sounds So Good	36-604	CB
Shepherd, Ashton	Takin' Off This Pain	36-417	CB
Shepherd, Kenny	Blue On Black	21-558	PHM
Sheppard & Hill	Can't We Try - duet	35-313	CB
Sheppard & Hill	Duet - Can't We Try	35-313	CB
Sheppard, T.G.	Born In A High Wind	16-366	CB
Sheppard, T.G.	Devil In The Bottle	20-661	SC
Sheppard, T.G.	Do You Wanna Go To Heaven	34-242	CB
Sheppard, T.G.	Do You Wanna Go To Heaven	4-651	SC
Sheppard, T.G.	Finally	3-249	CB
Sheppard, T.G.	Finally	13-473	P
Sheppard, T.G.	I Feel Like Loving You Again	3-248	CB
Sheppard, T.G.	I Loved 'Em Every One	13-385	P
Sheppard, T.G.	I'll Be Coming Back For You	20-18	SC
Sheppard, T.G.	Last Cheater's Waltz	3-247	CB
Sheppard, T.G.	Last Cheater's Waltz	13-500	P
Sheppard, T.G.	Last Cheater's Waltz	4-581	SC
Sheppard, T.G.	One Owner Heart	43-322	CB
Sheppard, T.G.	Only One You	5-558	SC
Sheppard, T.G.	Party Time	3-379	SC
Sheppard, T.G.	Slow Burn	33-85	CB
Sheppard, T.G.	Strong Heart	5-673	SC
Sheppard, T.G.	War Is Hell On The Home Front Too	4-481	SC

ARTIST	SONG TITLE	#	TYPE
Sheriff	When I'm With You	21-751	MH
Sherman, Allan	Crazy Downtown **	23-17	SC
Sherman, Allen	Hello Muddah Hello Faddah	6-513	MM
Sherman, Allen	Hello Muddah Hello Faddah	5-638	SC
Sherman, Allen	Xmas - Twelve Days Of Christmas	5-714	SC
Sherman, Bobby	Easy Come Easy Go	21-800	SC
Shiek, Duncan	She Runs Away	10-95	SC
Shields	You Cheated You Lied	25-546	MM
Shifty	Slide Along Side	20-545	PHM
Shinedown	Fly From The Inside	32-254	THM
Shinedown	I Dare You	30-284	SC
Shinedown	Save Me	29-256	SC
Shinedown	Secong Chance	36-22	PT
Shirelles	Baby It's You	15-404	MM
Shirelles	Dedicated To The One I Love	3-283	MM
Shirelles	Dedicated To The One I Love	4-14	SC
Shirelles	Foolish Little Girl	48-374	LE
Shirelles	I Met Him On A Sunday	27-499	DK
Shirelles	Mama Said	19-611	MH
Shirelles	My Boyfriend's Back	48-373	SGB
Shirelles	Sha La La	48-377	RB
Shirelles	Soldier Boy	17-316	SS
Shirelles	Tonight's The Night	48-375	MM
Shirelles	Welcome Home Baby	48-376	RB
Shirelles	Will You Love Me Tomorrow	11-129	DK
Shirelles	Will You Love Me Tomorrow	3-286	MM
Shirelles	Will You Love Me Tomorrow	12-714	P
Shirelles	Will You Love Me Tomorrow	4-9	SC
Shirley & Lee	Duet - Let The Good Times Roll	6-142	MM
Shirley & Lee	Duet - Let The Good Times Roll	4-241	SC
Shirley & Lee	Let The Good Times Roll	6-143	MM
Shirley & Lee	Let The Good Times Roll	4-241	SC
Shocking Blue	Venus	3-475	SC
Shontelle	T-Shirt	48-698	PHM
Shore, Dinah	Anniversary Song	27-410	DK
Shore, Dinah	Blue Canary	15-408	NK
Shore, Dinah	Blues In The Night	11-580	DK
Shore, Dinah	Blues In The Night	4-347	SC
Shore, Dinah	Blues In The Night	47-721	DKM
Shore, Dinah	Buttons And Bows	17-399	DK
Shore, Dinah	Buttons And Bows	21-17	SC
Shore, Dinah	Doin' What Comes Natur'ly	2-243	SC
Show Boat	Show - Old Man River	27-447	DK
Show Boat	Show - Why Do I Love You	17-803	PS

ARTIST	SONG TITLE	#	TYPE
Shrek	Show - I'm A Believer	18-669	PS
Shrek	Show - I'm On My Way	18-670	PS
Shupe&Rubberband	Dream Big	23-126	CB
Shyne & Ashanti	Duet - Jimmy Choo	30-807	PHM
Shyne & Ashanti	Jimmy Choo	30-807	PHM
Sia	Day Too Soon	37-151	SC
Side Show	Show - Who Will Love Me As I Am	18-807	PS
Sider, Lizzie	I Love You That Much	41-62	PHN
Silhouettes	Get A Job	15-479	MM
Silkk the Shocker	It Ain't My Fault **	28-28	DK
Silverchair	Ana's Song	8-507	PHT
Silverchair	Straight Lines	37-122	SC
Simmons, "Jumpin" Gene	Halloween - Haunted House	45-117	SC
Simmons, "Jumpin" Gene	Haunted House - Halloween	45-117	SC
Simon & Garfunkel	50 Ways To Leave Your Lover	23-636	BS
Simon & Garfunkel	59th Street Bridge Song	23-634	BS
Simon & Garfunkel	All I Know	15-397	DM
Simon & Garfunkel	America	49-763	LG
Simon & Garfunkel	Boxer the	5-310	SC
Simon & Garfunkel	Bridge Over Troubled Water	23-635	BS
Simon & Garfunkel	Bridge Over Troubled Water	10-367	KC
Simon & Garfunkel	Bridge Over Troubled Water	21-242	SC
Simon & Garfunkel	Bye Bye Love	49-767	LG
Simon & Garfunkel	Cecelia	5-304	SC
Simon & Garfunkel	Duncan	15-469	DM
Simon & Garfunkel	El Condor Pasa	23-641	BS
Simon & Garfunkel	Feelin' Groovy	15-474	DM
Simon & Garfunkel	Hazy Shade Of Winter	49-761	LG
Simon & Garfunkel	Homeward Bound	23-642	BS
Simon & Garfunkel	Homeward Bound	15-494	DM
Simon & Garfunkel	I Am A Rock	15-499	DM
Simon & Garfunkel	Kodachrome	23-633	BS
Simon & Garfunkel	Leaves That Are Green	49-765	LG
Simon & Garfunkel	Loves Me Like A Rock	49-762	LG
Simon & Garfunkel	Me & Julio Down By The Schoolyard	23-637	BS
Simon & Garfunkel	Me & Julio Down By The Schoolyard	15-529	DM
Simon & Garfunkel	Mother And Child Reunion	15-534	DM
Simon & Garfunkel	Mrs. Robinson	23-643	BS
Simon & Garfunkel	Mrs. Robinson	5-302	SC
Simon & Garfunkel	My Little Town	15-536	DM
Simon & Garfunkel	Scarborough Fair	4-714	SC
Simon & Garfunkel	Slip Slidin' Away	23-638	BS
Simon & Garfunkel	Slip Slidin' Away	15-560	DM
Simon & Garfunkel	Sound Of Silence	17-174	SC
Simon & Garfunkel	Sound Of Silence	23-639	BS
Simon & Garfunkel	Take Me To The Mardi Gras	49-764	LG
Simon & Garfunkel	We've Got A Groovy Thing Going	49-766	LG

ARTIST	SONG TITLE	#	TYPE
Simon & Garfunkel	You Can Call Me Al	23-640	BS
Simon & Garfunkel	You Can Call Me Al	15-590	DM
Simon, Carly	Anticipation	4-50	SC
Simon, Carly	As Time Goes By	18-67	MM
Simon, Carly	Better Not Tell Her	49-152	CB
Simon, Carly	Coming Around Again	4-388	SC
Simon, Carly	Devoted To You	49-157	LG
Simon, Carly	Haven't Got Time For The Pain	12-703	P
Simon, Carly	In The Wee Small Hours	6-447	MM
Simon, Carly	Jesse	49-153	CB
Simon, Carly	Legend In Your Own Time	49-151	CB
Simon, Carly	Let The River Run	49-155	CB
Simon, Carly	Like A River	49-159	SC
Simon, Carly	Mockingbird	49-149	CB
Simon, Carly	Moonlight Serenade	49-160	ST
Simon, Carly	Nobody Does It Better	33-299	CB
Simon, Carly	Nobody Does It Better	11-520	DK
Simon, Carly	Nobody Does It Better	12-881	P
Simon, Carly	Nobody Does It Better	9-57	SC
Simon, Carly	Right Thing To Do	49-150	CB
Simon, Carly	Stuff That Dreams Are Made Of	49-148	CB
Simon, Carly	That's The Way I've Always...	2-559	SC
Simon, Carly	Touched By The Sun	24-29	SC
Simon, Carly	Two Little Sisters	49-156	DCK
Simon, Carly	We're Not Makin' Love Anymore	49-158	MM
Simon, Carly	You Belong To Me	49-154	CB
Simon, Carly	You're So Vain	11-198	DK
Simon, Carly	You're So Vain	13-181	P
Simon, Carly	You're So Vain	10-537	SF
Simon, Joe	Get Down Get Down	17-105	DK
Simon, Paul	50 Ways To Leave Your Lover	2-144	SC
Simon, Paul	Father & Daughter	25-437	MM
Simon, Paul	Kodachrome	9-318	AG
Simon, Paul	Kodachrome	20-318	MH
Simon, Paul	Loves Me Like A Rock	3-615	SC
Simon, Paul	Still Crazy After All These Years	46-128	SC
Simone, N.	Wild Is The Wind	23-355	MM
Simple Minds	Alive And Kicking	9-692	SAV
Simple Minds	Alive And Kicking	5-479	SC
Simple Minds	Don't You Forget About Me	11-392	DK
Simple Minds	Don't You Forget About Me	16-58	SC
Simple Plan	How Can This Happen To Me	23-320	CB
Simple Plan	I'd Do Anything	35-300	CB
Simple Plan	Perfect	20-232	MM
Simple Plan	Shut Up	47-583	CB
Simple Plan	Welcome To My Life	22-346	CB
Simple Plan	Welcome To My Life	30-817	PHM
Simple Plan	When I'm Gone	36-474	CB

ARTIST	SONG TITLE	#	TYPE
Simply Re	Sunrise	32-392	THM
Simply Red	Holding Back The Years	11-120	DK
Simply Red	Holding Back The Years	12-826	P
Simply Red	If You Don't Know Me By Now	19-123	KC
Simply Red	If You Don't Know Me By Now	13-184	P
Simpson & Lachey	Duet - Where Are You	20-127	PHM
Simpson & Lachey	Duet - Where You Are	14-183	CB
Simpson & Lachey	Duet - Where Are You	20-127	PH
Simpson & Lachey	Where Are You	20-127	PHM
Simpson & Lachey	Where You Are	14-183	CB
Simpson, Ashlee	Boyfriend	30-143	PT
Simpson, Ashlee	La La	22-353	CB
Simpson, Ashlee	Pieces Of Me	23-567	MM
Simpson, Jenny	Ticket Out Of Kansas	8-216	CB
Simpson, Jessica	Angels	23-566	MM
Simpson, Jessica	Come On Over	36-605	CB
Simpson, Jessica	I Think I'm In Love	33-420	CB
Simpson, Jessica	I Think I'm In Love With You	14-482	SC
Simpson, Jessica	I Think I'm In Love With You	19-835	SGB
Simpson, Jessica	I Think I'm In Love With You	15-637	THM
Simpson, Jessica	I Wanna Love You Forever	8-523	PHT
Simpson, Jessica	I Wanna Love You Forever	17-538	SC
Simpson, Jessica	Irresistible	35-220	CB
Simpson, Jessica	Irresistible	18-524	TT
Simpson, Jessica	Little Bit a	33-384	CB
Simpson, Jessica	Remember That	36-242	PHM
Simpson, Jessica	Sweetest Sin	32-359	THM
Simpson, Jessica	Where You Are	15-330	PHM
Simpson, Jessica	With You	35-291	CB
Sin Bandera	Latino - Entra En Mi Vida	23-245	AI
Sinatra & Davis	Duet - Me And My Shadow	49-502	MM
Sinatra & Davis	Me And My Shadow (Live)	49-502	MM
Sinatra & Franklin	Duet - What Now My Love	15-580	MM
Sinatra & Franklin	What Now My Love	15-580	MM
Sinatra, Frank	Ain't She Sweet	34-441	CB
Sinatra, Frank	All Of Me	15-398	NK
Sinatra, Frank	All Of Me	21-212	SGB
Sinatra, Frank	All Or Nothin At All	9-234	PT
Sinatra, Frank	All The Way	11-306	DK
Sinatra, Frank	All The Way	10-715	JVC
Sinatra, Frank	All The Way	20-757	KB
Sinatra, Frank	All The Way	12-521	P
Sinatra, Frank	All The Way	16-416	PR
Sinatra, Frank	All The Way	21-226	SGB
Sinatra, Frank	Almost Like Being In Love	21-227	SGB
Sinatra, Frank	Amapola	45-582	OZP
Sinatra, Frank	Anything Goes	14-268	MM

ARTIST	SONG TITLE	#	TYPE
Sinatra, Frank	At Long Last Love	14-273	MM
Sinatra, Frank	Brazil	28-508	DK
Sinatra, Frank	Call Me Irresponsible	15-462	DK
Sinatra, Frank	Can I Steal A Little Love	10-721	JVC
Sinatra, Frank	Can I Steal A Little Love	49-484	MM
Sinatra, Frank	Chicago	34-11	CB
Sinatra, Frank	Chicago	11-567	DK
Sinatra, Frank	Chicago	18-70	MM
Sinatra, Frank	Chicago	9-236	PT
Sinatra, Frank	Chicago	21-229	SGB
Sinatra, Frank	Chicago (That Toddlin' Town)	28-503	DK
Sinatra, Frank	Come Dance With Me	49-505	MM
Sinatra, Frank	Come Fly With Me	9-249	PT
Sinatra, Frank	Come Fly With Me	21-211	SGB
Sinatra, Frank	Day By Day	28-504	DK
Sinatra, Frank	Didn't We	9-253	PT
Sinatra, Frank	Don't Get Around Much Anymore	9-241	PT
Sinatra, Frank	Flowers Mean Forgiveness	10-722	JVC
Sinatra, Frank	Fly Me To The Moon	21-215	SGB
Sinatra, Frank	For Once In My Life (80th Live)	49-500	MM
Sinatra, Frank	Forget Domani	49-487	MM
Sinatra, Frank	French Foreign Legion	49-495	MM
Sinatra, Frank	From This Moment On	14-265	MM
Sinatra, Frank	Get Happy	14-272	MM
Sinatra, Frank	Here's That Rainy Day	15-490	SGB
Sinatra, Frank	Hey Jealous Lover	49-503	MM
Sinatra, Frank	High Hopes	12-198	DK
Sinatra, Frank	High Hopes	10-716	JVC
Sinatra, Frank	High Hopes	12-490	P
Sinatra, Frank	High Hopes	9-238	PT
Sinatra, Frank	High Hopes	4-349	SC
Sinatra, Frank	House I Live In the (What is...)	49-489	MM
Sinatra, Frank	How About You	9-257	PT
Sinatra, Frank	How Deep Is The Ocean	14-277	MM
Sinatra, Frank	How Do You Keep The Music Playing	9-239	PT
Sinatra, Frank	How Insensitive	15-497	SGB
Sinatra, Frank	I Get A Kick Out Of You	17-381	DK
Sinatra, Frank	I Get A Kick Out Of You	14-270	MM
Sinatra, Frank	I Get A Kick Out Of You	12-560	P
Sinatra, Frank	I Get A Kick Out Of You	21-213	SGB
Sinatra, Frank	I Get Along Without You Very Well	49-506	MM
Sinatra, Frank	I Had The Craziest Dream	9-248	PT
Sinatra, Frank	I Love Paris	11-760	DK
Sinatra, Frank	I Only Have Eyes For You	49-718	KV
Sinatra, Frank	I Wish I Were In Love Again	14-275	MM
Sinatra, Frank	I Won't Dance	14-267	MM
Sinatra, Frank	I'll Be Seeing You	9-259	PT
Sinatra, Frank	I'll Never Smile Again	11-570	DK
Sinatra, Frank	I'll Never Smile Again	10-719	JVC
Sinatra, Frank	I'm Gonna Sit Right Down & Write...	14-276	MM
Sinatra, Frank	I've Got The World On A String	9-244	PT
Sinatra, Frank	I've Got You Under My Skin	16-731	DK
Sinatra, Frank	I've Got You Under My Skin	10-717	JVC
Sinatra, Frank	I've Got You Under My Skin	20-759	KB
Sinatra, Frank	I've Got You Under My Skin	9-261	PT
Sinatra, Frank	It Was A Very Good Year	11-569	DK
Sinatra, Frank	It Was A Very Good Year	9-260	PT
Sinatra, Frank	It's All Right With Me	9-237	PT
Sinatra, Frank	It's Nice To Go Traveling	49-496	MM
Sinatra, Frank	Just In Time	49-256	DFK
Sinatra, Frank	Just One Of Those Things	14-264	MM
Sinatra, Frank	L.A. Is My Lady	49-501	MM
Sinatra, Frank	Lady Is A Tramp the .	34-14	CB
Sinatra, Frank	Lady Is A Tramp the	28-495	DK
Sinatra, Frank	Lady is A Tramp the	20-766	KB
Sinatra, Frank	Lady Is A Tramp the	14-266	MM
Sinatra, Frank	Lady Is A Tramp the	9-250	PT
Sinatra, Frank	Lady Is A Tramp the	13-633	SGB
Sinatra, Frank	Learnin' The Blues	10-714	JVC
Sinatra, Frank	Learning The Blues	35-29	CB
Sinatra, Frank	Let It Snow	45-738	SFX
Sinatra, Frank	Let Me Try Again	12-493	P
Sinatra, Frank	Let's Fall In Love	9-262	PT
Sinatra, Frank	Love And Marriage	27-405	DK
Sinatra, Frank	Love And Marriage	2-864	SC
Sinatra, Frank	Love And Marriage	21-218	SGB
Sinatra, Frank	Love Is Here To Stay	14-274	MM
Sinatra, Frank	Luck Be A Lady	12-155	DK
Sinatra, Frank	Luck Be A Lady	21-210	SGB
Sinatra, Frank	Makin' Whoopee	9-245	PT
Sinatra, Frank	Making Whoopee	34-4	CB
Sinatra, Frank	Memories Of You	45-597	OZP
Sinatra, Frank	More	13-655	SGB
Sinatra, Frank	My Funny Valentine	49-483	MM
Sinatra, Frank	My Kind Of Town	9-233	PT
Sinatra, Frank	My Kind Of Town	21-209	SGB
Sinatra, Frank	My Kind Of Town, Chicago Is	20-768	KB
Sinatra, Frank	My Way	17-145	DK
Sinatra, Frank	My Way	7-190	MM
Sinatra, Frank	My Way	12-522	P
Sinatra, Frank	My Way	9-242	PT
Sinatra, Frank	My Way	2-202	SC
Sinatra, Frank	New York New York	11-104	DK
Sinatra, Frank	New York New York	20-761	KB
Sinatra, Frank	New York New York	6-355	MM
Sinatra, Frank	New York New York	12-504	P
Sinatra, Frank	New York New York	16-410	PR
Sinatra, Frank	New York New York	9-258	PT

ARTIST	SONG TITLE	#	TYPE
Sinatra, Frank	New York New York	2-194	SC
Sinatra, Frank	Nice 'N Easy	21-220	SGB
Sinatra, Frank	Nice Work If You Can Get It	14-271	MM
Sinatra, Frank	Night And Day	42-31	CB
Sinatra, Frank	Night And Day	10-720	JVC
Sinatra, Frank	Night And Day	45-7	KV
Sinatra, Frank	Night And Day (Faster Version)	28-500	DK
Sinatra, Frank	Oh Look At Me Now	15-540	SGB
Sinatra, Frank	On A Clear Day	12-552	P
Sinatra, Frank	One For My Baby	21-223	SGB
Sinatra, Frank	Please Be Kind	25-262	MM
Sinatra, Frank	Put Your Dreams Away	49-485	MM
Sinatra, Frank	Ring A Ding Ding	49-491	MM
Sinatra, Frank	S'Posin'	49-493	MM
Sinatra, Frank	Same Old Saturday Night	49-488	MM
Sinatra, Frank	Saturday Night Is The Lonliest Nigh	9-252	PT
Sinatra, Frank	Second Time Around	12-49	DK
Sinatra, Frank	Second Time Around	12-503	P
Sinatra, Frank	Show - Anything Goes	12-296	DK
Sinatra, Frank	So Rare	25-269	MM
Sinatra, Frank	Softly As I Leave You	49-486	MM
Sinatra, Frank	Someone To Watch Over Me	4-353	SC
Sinatra, Frank	Somethin' Stupid	27-565	DK
Sinatra, Frank	Something Stupid	11-466	DK
Sinatra, Frank	Something Stupid	21-225	SGB
Sinatra, Frank	Something Stupid	49-492	MM
Sinatra, Frank	South Of The Border	28-505	DK
Sinatra, Frank	South Of The Border	12-499	P
Sinatra, Frank	Stars Fell On Alabama	19-790	SGB
Sinatra, Frank	Stella By Starlight	28-498	DK
Sinatra, Frank	Strangers In The Night	11-568	DK
Sinatra, Frank	Strangers In The Night	10-723	JVC
Sinatra, Frank	Strangers In The Night	12-520	P
Sinatra, Frank	Strangers In The Night	9-251	PT
Sinatra, Frank	Summer Wind	34-15	CB
Sinatra, Frank	Summer Wind	20-763	KB
Sinatra, Frank	Summer Wind	12-558	P
Sinatra, Frank	Summer Wind	9-256	PT
Sinatra, Frank	Summer Wind	2-204	SC
Sinatra, Frank	Taking A Chance On Love	14-278	MM
Sinatra, Frank	Taking A Chance On Love	21-216	SGB
Sinatra, Frank	Talk To Me	10-718	JVC
Sinatra, Frank	Tangerine	9-243	PT
Sinatra, Frank	Tender Trap the	9-255	PT
Sinatra, Frank	Tender Trap the	21-214	SGB
Sinatra, Frank	Thanks For The Memories	15-567	MM
Sinatra, Frank	That Old Black Magic	21-217	SGB
Sinatra, Frank	That's Life	11-184	DK
Sinatra, Frank	That's Life	12-523	P
Sinatra, Frank	They All Laughed	49-499	MM

ARTIST	SONG TITLE	#	TYPE
Sinatra, Frank	They Can't Take That Away	9-240	PT
Sinatra, Frank	They Can't Take That Away	21-221	SGB
Sinatra, Frank	This Love Of Mine	49-490	MM
Sinatra, Frank	Too Marvelous For Words	9-254	PT
Sinatra, Frank	Volare	48-586	DK
Sinatra, Frank	Way You Look Tonight the	49-498	MM
Sinatra, Frank	When You're Smiling	21-12	CB
Sinatra, Frank	Where Or When (Live at Sands)	49-494	MM
Sinatra, Frank	Witchcraft	20-771	KB
Sinatra, Frank	Witchcraft	12-559	P
Sinatra, Frank	Wives And Lovers	21-228	SGB
Sinatra, Frank	Xmas - Let It Snow	45-738	SFX
Sinatra, Frank	You Brought A New Kind Of Love	9-235	PT
Sinatra, Frank	You Do Something To Me	9-805	SAV
Sinatra, Frank	You Go To My Head	49-497	MM
Sinatra, Frank	You Make Me Feel So Young	9-246	PT
Sinatra, Frank	You Make Me Feel So Young	21-222	SGB
Sinatra, Frank	You Will Be My Music	49-504	MM
Sinatra, Frank	You'd Be So Nice To Come Home To	17-158	DK
Sinatra, Frank	You'd Be So Nice To Come Home To	10-713	JVC
Sinatra, Frank	You'd Be So Nice To Come Home To	14-269	MM
Sinatra, Frank	Young At Heart	12-524	P
Sinatra, Frank	Young At Heart	9-232	PT
Sinatra, Frank	Your Nobody Till Somebody Loves You	48-580	DK
Sinatra, N & Hazelwood	Summer Wine	44-322	DFK
Sinatra, N. & Hazelwood	Duet - Some Velvet Morning	47-513	VH
Sinatra, N. & Hazelwood	Some Velvet Morning - duet	47-513	VH
Sinatra, Nancy	Bang Bang	49-756	LGK
Sinatra, Nancy	Sugar Town	12-719	P
Sinatra, Nancy	Sugar Town	6-49	SC
Sinatra, Nancy	These Boots Are Made For Walkin'	17-47	DK
Sinatra, Nancy	These Boots Are Made For Walkin'	10-730	JVC
Sinatra, Nancy	These Boots Are Made For Walkin'	13-96	P
Sinatra, Nancy	You Only Live Twice	9-62	SC
Sinatra, Nancy	You Only Live Twice	30-791	SF
Singletary, Daryle	Amen Kind Of Love	7-580	CHM
Singletary, Daryle	Amen Kind Of Love	7-377	MM
Singletary, Daryle	Amen Kind Of Love	4-508	SC
Singletary, Daryle	I Let Her Lie	7-26	MM
Singletary, Daryle	I Let Her Lie	3-655	SC
Singletary, Daryle	I'd Love To Lay You	18-454	ST

ARTIST	SONG TITLE	#	TYPE
	Down		
Singletary, Daryle	I've Thought Of Everything	10-273	CB
Singletary, Daryle	Jesus And Bartenders	30-458	CB
Singletary, Daryle	My Baby's Lovin'	8-765	CB
Singletary, Daryle	Note the	7-728	CHM
Singletary, Daryle	Note the	22-776	ST
Singletary, Daryle	Now And Again	29-353	CB
Singletary, Daryle	That's Where You're Wrong	8-475	CB
Singletary, Daryle	Too Much Fun	35-413	CB
Singletary, Daryle	Too Much Fun	7-167	MM
Singletary, Daryle	Too Much Fun	4-19	SC
Singletary, Daryle	Used To Be's the	10-77	SC
Singletary, Daryle	Workin' It Out	7-254	MM
Siouxsie&Banshees	Kiss Them For Me	6-44	SC
Sir Douglas Quint	Mendocino Ragazzina	13-109	P
Sir Mix-A-Lot	Baby Got Back	33-440	CB
Sir Mix-A-Lot	Baby Got Back **	12-1	DK
Sir Mix-A-Lot	Baby Got Back **	2-178	SC
Sisquo	Dance For Me	18-552	TT
Sisquo	Incomplete	30-646	THM
Sisquo	Incomplete	23-259	HS
Sisquo	Incomplete (Radio Version)	14-496	SC
Sisquo	Thong Song the	29-171	MH
Sisquo	Unleash The Dragon	19-822	SGB
Sister Hazel	All For You	33-364	CB
Sister Hazel	Change Your Mind	33-378	CB
Sister Hazel	Change Your Mind	15-640	THM
Sister Hazel	Happy	5-184	SC
Sister Sledge	We Are Family	26-371	DK
Sister Sledge	We Are Family	9-6	MH
Sister Sledge	We Are Family	13-5	P
Sister Sledge	We Are Family	9-218	PT
Sister Sledge	We Are Family	2-33	SC
Sisters Wade	Don't Let Me Down	8-900	CB
Sisters Wade	How Much Longer	10-214	SC
Sixpence None The	Breathe	34-139	CB
Sixpence None The	Breathe Your Name	25-429	MM
Sixpence None The	Breathe Your Name	18-587	NS
Sixpence None the	Breathe Your Name	32-25	THM
Sixpence None The	Don't Dream It's Over	25-538	MM
Sixpence None The	Don't Dream It's Over	32-171	THM
Sixpence None The	Kiss Me	7-807	PHT
Sixpence None The	Kiss Me	13-703	SGB
Sixpence None The	Kiss Me	35-216	CB
Sixpence None The	Safety Line	39-131	PHM
Sixpence None The	There She Goes	8-502	PHT
Sixwire	Look At Me Now	16-709	ST
Sixwire	Way Too Deep	25-418	MM
Sixwire	Way Too Deep	18-470	ST
Skaggs & White	Duet - Love Can't Ever Get Better	5-450	SC
Skaggs & White	Love Can't Ever Get Better	5-450	SC
Skaggs, Ricky	Back Where We Belong	4-227	SC

ARTIST	SONG TITLE	#	TYPE
Skaggs, Ricky	Cajun - Cajun Moon	49-388	SC
Skaggs, Ricky	Cajun Moon	20-22	SC
Skaggs, Ricky	Cajun Moon	49-388	SC
Skaggs, Ricky	Cat's In The Cradle	7-246	MM
Skaggs, Ricky	Country Boy	33-88	CB
Skaggs, Ricky	Country Boy	11-799	DK
Skaggs, Ricky	Country Boy	5-409	SC
Skaggs, Ricky	Crying My Heart Out Over You	49-632	CB
Skaggs, Ricky	Don't Cheat in Our Hometown	4-547	SC
Skaggs, Ricky	Get Rhythm	12-485	P
Skaggs, Ricky	Halfway Home Café	18-215	ST
Skaggs, Ricky	Heartbroke	8-202	CB
Skaggs, Ricky	Heartbroke	8-701	SAV
Skaggs, Ricky	Highway 40 Blues	8-702	SAV
Skaggs, Ricky	Honey Open That Door	33-82	CB
Skaggs, Ricky	Honey Open That Door	4-485	SC
Skaggs, Ricky	I Don't Care	34-252	CB
Skaggs, Ricky	I Wouldn't Change You If I Could	4-652	SC
Skaggs, Ricky	Same Ol' Love	12-439	P
Skaggs, Ricky	Solid Ground	4-28	SC
Skaggs, Ricky	When	24-162	SC
Skaggs, Ricky	You May See Me Walkin'	5-856	SC
Skid Row	18 And Life	23-59	MH
Skid Row	Wasted Time	23-101	SC
Skid Row	Youth Gone Wild	5-67	SC
Sky Kings	Picture Perfect	7-244	MM
Skylark	Wildflower	7-466	MM
Skylark	Wildflower	3-482	SC
Skylark	Wildflower	13-668	SGB
Skyliners	Since I Don't Have You	17-418	DK
Skyliners	Since I Don't Have You	6-261	MM
Skyliners	This I Swear	18-66	MM
Slade	Merry Christmas Everybody	45-770	SF
Slade	Xmas - Merry Christmas Everybody	45-770	SF
Slaughter	Fly To The Angels	24-689	SC
Slaughter	Up All Night	23-60	MH
Slaughter, Shannon & Heather	Duet - If I Were A Carpenter	41-92	PHN
Slaughter, Shannon & Heather	If I Were A Carpenter - duet	41-92	PHN
Sledge, Percy	When A Man Loves A Woman	17-40	DK
Sledge, Percy	When A Man Loves A Woman	12-712	P
Sledge, Percy	When A Man Loves A Woman	2-274	SC
Sleeper Agent	Get It Daddy	38-243	PHM
Sleepless In Seattl	Show - Stand By Your Man	6-894	MM
Sleepless In Seattle	Show - When I Fall In Love	48-787	MM
Sleepless In Seattle	When I Fall In Love - show	48-787	MM
Slocum, Jamie	Say Hello To Heaven	30-344	CB

ARTIST	SONG TITLE	#	TYPE
Sly & Family Stone	Dance To The Music	35-76	CB
Sly & Family Stone	Duet - Everyday People	17-116	DK
Sly & Family Stone	Duet - Everyday People	12-911	P
Sly & Family Stone	Everyday People	17-116	DK
Sly & Family Stone	Everyday People	12-911	P
Sly & Family Stone	Family Affair	33-272	CB
Sly & Family Stone	Family Affair	11-671	DK
Sly & Family Stone	Family Affair	9-756	SAV
Sly & Family Stone	Hot Fun In The Summertime	12-63	DK
Sly & Family Stone	Hot Fun In The Summertime	13-606	P
Sly & Family Stone	If You Want Me To Stay	10-672	HE
Sly & Family Stone	Thank You	27-344	DK
Sly & Family Stone	Thank You	14-360	MH
Sly & Family Stone	Thank You	7-40	MM
Sly & Family Stone	Thank You	5-458	SC
Small Faces	Itchycoo Park	13-322	P
Small Faces	Sha La La La Lee	10-578	SF
Small Town Pistols	I Only Smoke When I Drink	49-742	DCK
Small, Millie	My Boy Lollipop	11-511	DK
Small, Millie	My Boy Lollipop	14-338	SC
Smash Mouth	All Star	29-169	MH
Smash Mouth	All Star	7-873	PHM
Smash Mouth	Can't Get Enough Of You	7-772	PHT
Smash Mouth	Can't Get Enough Of You Baby	34-147	CB
Smash Mouth	Holiday In My Head	18-286	CB
Smash Mouth	Holiday In My Head	25-143	MM
Smash Mouth	I'm A Believer	18-399	MM
Smash Mouth	I'm A Believer	16-392	SGB
Smash Mouth	Pacific Coast Party	33-392	CB
Smash Mouth	Pacific Coast Party	25-40	MM
Smash Mouth	Pacific Coast Party	16-79	ST
Smash Mouth	Then The Morning Comes	35-256	CB
Smash Mouth	Then The Morning Comes	8-524	PHT
Smash Mouth	Then The Morning Comes	5-789	SC
Smash Mouth	Walkin' On The Sun	30-211	CB
Smash Mouth	Walkin' On The Sun	7-687	PHM
Smash Mouth	You Are My Number One	25-654	MM
Smashing Pumpkins	1979	34-356	CB
Smashing Pumpkins	1979	13-603	P
Smashing Pumpkins	1979	4-176	SC
Smashing Pumpkins	Bullet With Butterfly Wings	28-442	DK
Smashing Pumpkins	Bullett With Butterfly Wings	34-141	CB
Smashing Pumpkins	Landslide	29-130	ST
Smashing Pumpkins	Muzzle	24-364	SC
Smile Empty Soul	Bottom Of A Bottle	32-290	THM
Smilez & Southstar	Tell Me (What's Goin' On)	32-128	THM
Smith, Anthony	Half A Man	18-799	ST

ARTIST	SONG TITLE	#	TYPE
Smith, Anthony	Half A Man	32-153	THM
Smith, Anthony	If That Ain't Country	33-170	CB
Smith, Anthony	If That Ain't Country	16-710	ST
Smith, Anthony	John J. Blanchard	18-332	ST
Smith, Anthony	John J. Blanchard	32-9	THM
Smith, Cal	Country Bumpkin	15-834	CB
Smith, Cal	Country Bumpkin	4-303	SC
Smith, Cal	Lord Knows I'm Drinking the	33-29	CB
Smith, Canaan	Hole In A Bottle	49-673	KCD
Smith, Canaan	Love You Like That	48-743	KCD
Smith, Carl	Are You Teasing Me	22-109	CB
Smith, Carl	Back Up Buddy	22-115	CB
Smith, Carl	Deep Water	8-649	SAV
Smith, Carl	Don't Just Stand There	22-108	CB
Smith, Carl	Don't Just Stand There	6-8	SC
Smith, Carl	Go Boy Go	22-116	CB
Smith, Carl	Hey Joe	22-114	CB
Smith, Carl	Hey Joe	5-852	SC
Smith, Carl	If Teardrops Were Pennies	5-362	SC
Smith, Carl	Kisses Don't Lie	22-120	CB
Smith, Carl	Let Old Mother Nature Have Her Way	22-107	CB
Smith, Carl	Let Old Mother Nature Have Her Way	4-803	SC
Smith, Carl	Let's Live A Little	22-106	CB
Smith, Carl	Loose Talk	22-110	CB
Smith, Carl	Loose Talk	14-333	SC
Smith, Carl	Lord Knows I'm Drinkin' the	8-806	CB
Smith, Carl	Mr. Moon	22-111	CB
Smith, Carl	Orchids Mean Goodbye	22-112	CB
Smith, Carl	Take My Ring Off Your Finger	46-29	SSK
Smith, Carl	There She Goes	22-117	CB
Smith, Carl	Trademark	22-113	CB
Smith, Carl	When You Feel Like You're In Love	43-281	SC
Smith, Carl	Why Why	22-119	CB
Smith, Carl	You Are The One	22-118	CB
Smith, Carl	You Are The One	22-253	SC
Smith, Connie	Ain't Had No Lovin'	8-387	CB
Smith, Connie	Ain't Had No Lovin'	14-332	SC
Smith, Connie	Burning A Hole In My Mind	48-95	CB
Smith, Connie	Cincinnati Ohio	8-269	CB
Smith, Connie	He'll Have To Stay	49-298	KST
Smith, Connie	Hurtin's All Over the	15-80	CB
Smith, Connie	I Never Once Stopped Loving You	48-93	CB
Smith, Connie	I'll Come Running	5-842	SC
Smith, Connie	If I Talk To Him	6-13	SC
Smith, Connie	If It Ain't Love	8-285	CB
Smith, Connie	Just For What I Am	4-793	SC
Smith, Connie	Just One Time	8-843	CB
Smith, Connie	Nobody But A Fool Would Love You	48-97	CB

ARTIST	SONG TITLE	#	TYPE
Smith, Connie	Once A Day	15-542	CMC
Smith, Connie	Once A Day	20-288	SC
Smith, Connie	Ribbon Of Darkenss	8-391	CB
Smith, Connie	Ribbon Of Darkness	6-779	MM
Smith, Connie	Run Away Little Tears	48-96	CB
Smith, Connie	Then And Only Then	5-756	SC
Smith, Connie	You And Your Sweet Love	48-94	CB
Smith, Frankie	Double Dutch Bus	14-361	MH
Smith, Granger	Backroad Song	48-697	KRG
Smith, Granger	Backroad Song	47-488	DCK
Smith, Granger	Letters To London	47-486	PHN
Smith, Granger	Miles And Mud Tires	42-5	PHN
Smith, Granger	Red Dirt	47-487	PHN
Smith, Granger	We Do It In The Field	39-56	PHN
Smith, Kate	God Bless America	11-571	DK
Smith, Kate	My Old Kentucky Home	11-492	DK
Smith, Margo	It Only Hurts For A Little While	29-779	CB
Smith, Margo	You Take My Breath Away	8-272	CB
Smith, Michael M	Let It Rain	34-426	CB
Smith, Michael W	Gospel - Place In This World	35-317	CB
Smith, Michael W	Place In This World	35-317	CB
Smith, Michael W.	Gospel - Live The Life	20-152	KB
Smith, Michael W.	This Is Your Time	9-334	PS
Smith, Michael W.	This Is Your Time	14-488	SC
Smith, O.C. & Page	Little Green Apples	27-547	DK
Smith, O.C.R.	Little Green Apples	4-242	SC
Smith, O.C.R.	Son Of Hickory Holler's Tramp	10-632	SF
Smith, Rex	You Take My Breath Away	5-684	SC
Smith, S & Legend	Duet - Lay Me Down	48-441	KCD
Smith, S & Legend	Lay Me Down - duet	48-441	KCD
Smith, Sam	Drowning Shadows	45-395	DCK
Smith, Sam	I'm Not The Only One	44-317	SBI
Smith, Sam	Leave Your Lover	44-316	SBI
Smith, Sam	Like I Can	45-137	BHK
Smith, Sammi	Help Me Make It Through The Night	17-154	DK
Smith, Sammi	Help Me Make It Through The Night	9-594	SAV
Smith, Will	Black Suits Comin'	18-216	CB
Smith, Will	Black Suits Comin'	25-255	MM
Smith, Will	Black Suits Comin'	18-144	PHM
Smith, Will	Getting Jiggy Wit' It	13-686	SGB
Smith, Will	Getting' Jiggy Wit It	10-130	SC
Smith, Will	Just The Two Of Us	7-771	PHT
Smith, Will	Men In Black	10-107	SC
Smith, Will	Miami	7-794	PHT
Smith, Will	Wild Wild West	7-891	PHT
Smith, Will	Wild Wild West	13-781	SGB
Smithereens	Girl Like You a	9-842	SAV
Smithereens	Girl Like You a	5-610	SC
Smokin' Armadillos	Let Your Heart Lead Your Mind	4-121	SC

ARTIST	SONG TITLE	#	TYPE
Smokin' Armadillos	Miracle Man	4-888	SC
Smokin' Armadillos	Thump Factor	7-278	MM
Smyth & Henley	Duet - Sometimes Love Just Ain't...	6-229	MM
Smyth & Henley	Duet - Sometimes Love Just Ain't...	9-674	SAV
Smyth & Henley	Sometimes Love Just Ain't Enough	6-229	MM
Smyth & Henley	Sometimes Love Just Ain't Enough	9-674	SAV
Smyth, Patty	Beat Of A Heart	24-426	SC
Smyth, Patty	Because The Night	7-489	MM
Smyth, Patty	No Mistakes	6-178	MM
Smyth, Patty	No Mistakes	24-146	SC
Snake Oil Willie Band	I Don't Look Good Naked Anymore - F	45-325	CK
Snake Oil Willie Band	I Don't Look Good Naked Anymore - M	45-324	DFK
Snap	Rhythm Is A Dancer	6-410	MM
Sneaker Pimps	6 Underground	10-110	SC
Sniff 'N The Tears	Driver's Seat	5-679	SC
Snoop Dogg w Pharrell	Drop It Like It's Hot (Radio Vers)	37-94	SC
Snoop Dogg, Pharrell, Wilson	Beautiful	32-315	THM
Snoop Doggy Dogg	Gin & Juice	25-473	MM
Snoop Doggy Dogg	Gin & Juice	14-447	SC
Snow Patrol	Chasing Cars	30-261	CB
Snow Patrol	Chasing Cars	30-61	PHM
Snow Patrol	Chasing Cars	30-726	SF
Snow, Hank	Down The Trail Of Achin' Hearts	22-125	CB
Snow, Hank	Fool Such As I a	8-652	SAV
Snow, Hank	Gold Rush Is Over the	22-126	CB
Snow, Hank	Gold Rush Is Over the	5-700	SC
Snow, Hank	Golden Rocket the	22-123	CB
Snow, Hank	Golden Rocket the	5-576	SC
Snow, Hank	Hello Love	22-131	CB
Snow, Hank	Hello Love	5-561	SC
Snow, Hank	I Don't Hurt Anymore	22-128	CB
Snow, Hank	I Don't Hurt Anymore	4-806	SC
Snow, Hank	I Went To Your Wedding	22-132	CB
Snow, Hank	I'm Movin' On	8-791	CB
Snow, Hank	I'm Movin' On	12-407	P
Snow, Hank	I'm Movin' On	9-512	SAV
Snow, Hank	I've Been Everywhere	22-122	CB
Snow, Hank	I've Been Everywhere	8-653	SAV
Snow, Hank	I've Been Everywhere	5-366	SC
Snow, Hank	Lady's Man	22-127	CB
Snow, Hank	Lady's Man	5-850	SC
Snow, Hank	Last Ride the	22-135	CB
Snow, Hank	Let Me Go Lover	22-129	CB
Snow, Hank	Miller's Cave	22-247	SC
Snow, Hank	Ninety Miles An Hour	22-130	CB
Snow, Hank	Rhumba Boogie the	22-124	CB
Snow, Hank	Rhumba Boogie the	5-425	SC
Snow, Hank	Somewhere My Love	48-581	DK
Snow, Hank	Spanish Fire Ball	22-133	CB

ARTIST	SONG TITLE	#	TYPE
Snow, Hank	Tangled Mind	22-134	CB
Snow, Hank	Tangled Mind	37-302	SC
Snow, Phoebe	Poetry Man	2-778	SC
Sobule, Jill	I Kissed A Girl	3-500	SC
Social Distortion	I Was Wrong	24-546	SC
Socialburn	Down	23-154	PHM
Socialburn	Everyone	32-330	THM
Soft Cell	Tainted Love	11-655	DK
Soft Cell	Tainted Love	29-3	MH
Soggy Bottom Boys	I Am A Man Of Constant Sorrow	30-35	CB
Soggy Bottom Boys	I Am A Man Of Constant Sorrow	9-873	ST
Soho	Hippy Chick	30-771	SF
Soleii, Stella	Kiss Kiss	15-456	PHM
Something/People	Duet - My Love Is The Shhh	7-719	PHM
Something/People	My Love Is The Shhh	7-719	PHM
Something/People	With You	24-57	SC
Sommers, Joanie	Johnny Get Angry	20-62	SC
Sommers, Joanie	One Boy	19-111	SAV
Son By Four	Purest Of Pain (A Puro Dolor)	30-645	THM
Sondheim, Stephen	Being Alive	17-778	PS
Sondheim, Stephen	Broadway Baby	17-770	PS
Sondheim, Stephen	Children Will Listen	17-780	PS
Sondheim, Stephen	Everybody Says Don't	17-783	PS
Sondheim, Stephen	Not While I'm Around	17-781	PS
Sondheim, Stephen	Show - Anyone Can Whistle	17-777	PS
Sondheim, Stephen	Show - Comedy Tonight	17-775	PS
Sondheim, Stephen	Show - Could I Leave You	17-771	PS
Sondheim, Stephen	Show - Do I Hear A Waltz	17-773	PS
Sondheim, Stephen	Show - Everybodys' Out to Have/Maid	17-772	PS
Sondheim, Stephen	Show - I'm Still Here	17-774	PS
Sondheim, Stephen	Show - Ladies Who Lunch the	17-779	PS
Sondheim, Stephen	Show - Losing My Mind	17-776	PS
Sondheim, Stephen	Show - Loving You	17-785	PS
Sondheim, Stephen	Show - Putting It Together	17-782	PS
Sondheim, Stephen	Sooner Or Later	17-784	PS
Song And Dance	Show - Unexpected Song	18-812	PS
Sonique	I Put A Spell On You	18-520	TT
Sonique	It Feels So Good	20-623	CB
Sonique	It Feels So Good	18-525	TT
Sonique	Sky	18-531	TT
Sonny & Cher	All I Ever Need Is You	6-239	MM
Sonny & Cher	All I Ever Need Is You	14-65	RS
Sonny & Cher	All I Ever Need Is You	15-133	SGB
Sonny & Cher	Baby Don't Go	14-57	RS
Sonny & Cher	Beat Goes On	35-62	CB
Sonny & Cher	Beat Goes On the	11-543	DK
Sonny & Cher	Beat Goes On the	13-257	P

ARTIST	SONG TITLE	#	TYPE
Sonny & Cher	Beat Goes On the	14-55	RS
Sonny & Cher	Beat Goes On the	9-661	SAV
Sonny & Cher	Beat Goes On the	15-127	SGB
Sonny & Cher	Cowboy's Work Is Never Done	14-48	RS
Sonny & Cher	Duet - All I Ever Need Is You	6-239	MM
Sonny & Cher	Duet - All I Ever Need Is You	14-65	RS
Sonny & Cher	Duet - All I Ever Need Is You	15-133	SGB
Sonny & Cher	Duet - Baby Don't Go	14-57	RS
Sonny & Cher	Duet - Beat Goes On the	11-543	DK
Sonny & Cher	Duet - Beat Goes On the	13-257	P
Sonny & Cher	Duet - Beat Goes On the	14-55	RS
Sonny & Cher	Duet - Beat Goes On the	9-661	SAV
Sonny & Cher	Duet - Beat Goes On the	15-127	SGB
Sonny & Cher	Duet - Cowboy's Work Is Never Done	14-48	RS
Sonny & Cher	Duet - I Got You Babe	11-446	DK
Sonny & Cher	Duet - I Got You Babe	14-59	RS
Sonny & Cher	Duet - I Got You Babe	15-121	SGB
Sonny & Cher	Duet - Little Man	14-67	RS
Sonny & Cher	I Got You Babe	11-446	DK
Sonny & Cher	I Got You Babe	14-59	RS
Sonny & Cher	I Got You Babe	15-121	SGB
Sonny & Cher	Little Man	14-67	RS
Sons Of Pioneers	Cool Water	12-305	DK
Sons Of Pioneers	Cool Water	5-424	SC
Sons Of Pioneers	Ghost Riders In The Sky	8-434	CB
Sons Of Pioneers	Tumbling Tumbleweeds	17-348	DK
Sons Of Pioneers	Tumbling Tumbleweeds	35-341	CB
Sons Of Pioneers	Tunbling Tumbleweeds	5-369	SC
Sons Of The Desert	Albuquerque	8-978	CB
Sons Of The Desert	Change	13-825	CHM
Sons Of The Desert	Everybody's Gotta Grow Up	14-84	CB
Sons Of The Desert	Hand Of Fate	22-422	ST
Sons Of The Desert	Leaving October	8-405	CB
Sons Of The Desert	What About You	8-918	CB
Sons of the Desert	What About You	43-7	SC
Sons Of The Desert	What About You	22-749	ST
Sons Of The Desert	What I Did Right	14-845	ST
Sons Of The Desert	Whatever Comes First	10-73	SC
Sons Of The Pioneers	Teardrops In My Heart	45-708	VH
Soraya	Suddenly	24-49	SC
Sosoreny, Greg	Gently Breathe	41-84	PHN
Soul Asylum	Misery	3-497	SC
Soul Asylum	Runaway Train	35-206	CB
Soul Asylum	Runaway Train	28-440	DK
Soul Asylum	Runaway Train	6-366	MM
Soul Decision	Faded	35-225	CB
Soul Decision	Faded (Radio Version)	14-508	SC
Soul Decision w Thrust	Faded	30-640	THM
Soul Food	Show - Song For Mama	18-182	DK
Soul II Soul	Back To Life	12-383	DK

ARTIST	SONG TITLE	#	TYPE
Soul II Soul	Keep On Movin'	16-540	P
Soul Survivor	Expressway To Your Heart	28-109	DK
Soul Survivor	Expressway To Your Heart	9-835	SAV
Soul, David	Don't Give Up On Us Baby	2-557	SC
Soul, Jimmy	If You Wanna Be Happy	17-396	DK
Soul, Jimmy	If You Wanna Be Happy	10-739	JVC
Soul, Jimmy	If You Wanna Be Happy	12-643	P
Soul, Jimmy	If You Wanna Be Happy	2-69	SC
Soulja Boy Tell 'Em	Crank That (Soulja Boy)	37-110	SC
Sound Of Music	Edelweiss	10-45	SC
Sound Of Music	Show - Climb Every Mountain	10-48	SC
Sound Of Music	Show - Do-Re-Mi	11-796	DK
Sound Of Music	Show - Do-Re-Mi	10-44	SC
Sound Of Music	Show - Edelweiss	10-45	SC
Sound Of Music	Show - I Have Confidence	10-46	SC
Sound Of Music	Show - My Favorite Things	27-381	DK
Sound Of Music	Show - My Favorite Things	10-47	SC
Sound Of Music	Show - Sixteen Going on Seventeen	10-41	SC
Sound Of Music	Show - So Long Farewell	10-43	SC
Sound Of Music	Show - Sound Of Music the	27-379	DK
Sound Of Music	Show - Sound Of Music the	10-42	SC
Sound Of Music	Sixteen Going On Seventeen	10-41	SC
Soundgarden	Black Hole Sun	30-744	SF
Soundgarden	Burdening My Mind	24-112	SC
Source	You Got The Love	30-736	SF
South Pacific	My Girl Back Home	17-708	SC
South Pacific	Show - Cockeyed Optimist	17-710	SC
South Pacific	Show - Honey Bun	17-709	SC
South Pacific	Show - I'm Gonna Wash That Man…	7-372	MM
South Pacific	Show - I'm Gonna Wash That Man…	17-705	SC
South Pacific	Show - I'm In Love w/Wonderful Guy	17-712	SC
South Pacific	Show - My Girl Back Home	17-708	SC
South Pacific	Show - Some Enchanted Evening	27-400	DK
South Pacific	Show - Some Enchanted Evening	17-707	SC
South Pacific	Show - There Is Nothing Like a Dame	7-373	MM
South Pacific	Show - There Is Nothing Like a Dame	17-706	SC
South Pacific	Show - This Nearly Was Mine	18-196	PS
South Pacific	Show - This Nearly Was	17-711	SC

ARTIST	SONG TITLE	#	TYPE
	Mine		
South Pacific	Show - Younger Than Springtime	27-399	DK
South Pacific	Show - Younger Than Springtime	14-380	PS
South Park	Blame Canada	15-340	MM
South Park	Xmas - I'm A Lonely Jew	5-709	SC
South Sixty Five	Love Bug (Bite Me)	14-78	CB
South Sixty Five	No Easy Goodbye	8-932	CB
South Sixty Five	No Easy Goodbye	14-605	SC
South Sixty Five	Random Act Of Senseless Kindness	10-161	SC
South, Joe	Don't It Make You Wanna Go Home	7-163	MM
South, Joe	Games People Play	6-784	MM
South, Joe	Games People Play	3-262	SC
South, Joe	Games People Play the	33-263	CB
South, Joe	I Knew You When	16-648	JTG
South, Joe	Walk A Mile In My Shoes	10-753	JVC
Souther, J.D.	You're Only Lonely	21-802	SC
Southern Gospel	Gospel - Blessed Assurance	16-617	CB
Southern Gospel	Gospel - Blood Will Never Lose It's	16-612	CB
Southern Gospel	Gospel - Both Sides Of The Road	16-15	SX
Southern Gospel	Gospel - Farther Along	16-18	SX
Southern Gospel	Gospel - God On The Mountain	16-19	SX
Southern Gospel	Gospel - He Loves Me	16-604	CB
Southern Gospel	Gospel - I Can't Even Walk	16-21	SX
Southern Gospel	Gospel - I Saw The Light	16-605	CB
Southern Gospel	Gospel - I'll Fly Away	16-22	SX
Southern Gospel	Gospel - I'm Standing On The Solid.	16-23	SX
Southern Gospel	Gospel - In The Garden	16-606	CB
Southern Gospel	Gospel - John The Relevation	16-25	SX
Southern Gospel	Gospel - Just A Closer Walk W/Thee	16-607	CB
Southern Gospel	Gospel - Just A Little Talk w/Jesus	16-608	CB
Southern Gospel	Gospel - King Of Eternity	16-613	CB
Southern Gospel	Gospel - Old Time Way	16-609	CB
Southern Gospel	Gospel - One Day At A Time	16-610	CB
Southern Gospel	Gospel - Sailing Away	16-611	CB
Southern Gospel	Gospel - Softly And Tenderly	16-26	SX
Southern Gospel	Gospel - Standing On The Promises	16-28	SX
Southern Gospel	Gospel - Where Would I Be	16-615	CB
Sovine, Red	Teddy Bear	8-276	CB
Space Jam	I Believe I Can Fly	18-178	DK
Space Jam	Show - I Believe I Can Fly	18-178	DK
Spacehog	I Want To Live	15-306	THM

ARTIST	SONG TITLE	#	TYPE
Spandau Ballet	True	7-105	MM
Spaniels	Goodnight Sweetheart	12-673	P
Spaniels	Goodnight Sweetheart	2-75	SC
Spanky & Our Gang	Duet - Like To Get To Know You	14-450	SC
Spanky & Our Gang	Lazy Days	9-710	SAV
Spanky & Our Gang	Like To Get To Know You	14-450	SC
Sparks, Jordin	Battlefield	36-25	PT
Sparks, Jordin	One Step At A Time	36-471	CB
Sparks, Jordin	Tattoo	30-588	PHM
Sparks, Jordin	This Is My Now	30-563	CB
Sparks, Larry	Smokey Mountain Memories	36-352	CB
Sparls, Jordin feat Chris Brown	No Air	36-486	CB
Spartz, Doug	Colors And Numbers	2-669	SC
Spears, Billie Jo	57 Chevrolet	47-591	KV
Spears, Billie Jo	57 Chevrolet	47-590	MRE
Spears, Billie Jo	Blanket On The Ground	33-17	CB
Spears, Billie Jo	Blanket On The Ground	10-505	SF
Spears, Billie Jo	I'm Gonna Be A Country Girl Again	47-510	VH
Spears, Billie Jo	Lonely Hearts Club	45-720	VH
Spears, Billie Jo	Misty Blue	39-7	CB
Spears, Billie Jo	Sing Me An Old Fashioned Song	47-593	P
Spears, Billie Jo	Stay Away From The Apple Tree	49-377	CB
Spears, Billie Jo	Sugar And Spice	10-565	SF
Spears, Billie Jo	What I've Got In Mind	8-359	CB
Spears, Britney	Baby One More Time	13-557	LE
Spears, Britney	Baby One More Time	13-706	SGB
Spears, Britney	Born To Make You Happy	13-559	LE
Spears, Britney	Boys	34-152	CB
Spears, Britney	Boys	25-304	MM
Spears, Britney	Break The Ice	36-473	CB
Spears, Britney	Crazy (You Drive Me)	8-279	PHT
Spears, Britney	Don't Let Me Be The Last To Know	15-455	PHM
Spears, Britney	From The Bottom Of My Broken Heart	15-294	CB
Spears, Britney	From The Bottom Of My Broken Heart	13-560	LE
Spears, Britney	I'm A Slave 4 U	35-234	CB
Spears, Britney	I'm A Slave 4 U	25-28	MM
Spears, Britney	I'm A Slave For You	16-304	PHM
Spears, Britney	I'm Not A Girl Not Yet A Woman	20-615	CB
Spears, Britney	I'm Not A Girl Not Yet A Woman	25-148	MM
Spears, Britney	I'm Not A Girl Not Yet A Woman	16-93	SC
Spears, Britney	Lucky	14-3	PHM
Spears, Britney	Lucky	14-506	SC
Spears, Britney	One Kiss From You	15-811	CB
Spears, Britney	Oops I Did It Again	13-562	LE
Spears, Britney	Overprotected	25-207	MM

ARTIST	SONG TITLE	#	TYPE
Spears, Britney	Perfume	43-159	PHM
Spears, Britney	Piece Of Me	36-524	CB
Spears, Britney	Radar	36-303	PHM
Spears, Britney	Sometimes	13-561	LE
Spears, Britney	Sometimes	8-160	PHT
Spears, Britney	Sometimes	13-700	SGB
Spears, Britney	Stronger	33-435	CB
Spears, Britney	Stronger	15-427	PHM
Spears, Britney	Toxic	20-535	CB
Spears, Britney	Womanizer	36-522	CB
Spears, Britney	You Drive Me Crazy	13-558	LE
Spears, Britney	You Drive Me Crazy	10-200	SC
Spears, Jamie Lynn	How Could I Want More	44-276	PHN
Specials	Ghost Town - Halloween	45-115	ZM
Specials	Halloween - Ghost Town	45-115	ZM
Spencer Davis Grp	Gimme Some Lovin'	15-480	SC
Spencer Davis Grp	Keep On Running	10-577	SF
Spencer Davis Grp	Somebody Help Me	10-643	SF
Spencer, Kevin	God Bless America Again	48-668	VH
Spice Girls	2 Become 1	21-547	PHM
Spice Girls	Love Thing	28-185	SF
Spice Girls	Say You'll Be There	28-186	SF
Spice Girls	Spice Up Your Life	7-702	PHM
Spice Girls	Stop	10-141	SC
Spice Girls	Stop	21-594	SF
Spice Girls	Too Much	7-713	PHM
Spice Girls	Too Much	5-185	SC
Spice Girls	Wannabe	16-44	SC
Spice Girls	Who Do You Think You Are	9-99	PS
Spin Doctors	Little Miss Can't Be Wrong	17-387	DK
Spin Doctors	Two Princes	12-74	DK
Spin Doctors	Two Princes	5-375	MM
Spin Doctors	Two Princes	12-782	P
Spinal Tap	Big Bottom **	23-18	SC
Spinal Tap	Sex Farm	37-83	SC
Spinners	Could It Be I'm Falling In Love	28-113	DK
Spinners	Duet - They Just Can't Stop It	17-142	DK
Spinners	I'll Be Around	16-559	P
Spinners	I'll Be Around	5-613	SC
Spinners	Mighty Love	28-114	DK
Spinners	One Of A Kind Love Affair	16-560	P
Spinners	Rubberband Man	7-477	MM
Spinners	Rubberband Man	9-767	SAV
Spinners	Rubberband Man	4-295	SC
Spinners	They Just Can't Stop It	17-142	DK
Spinners	They Just Can't Stop It	9-667	SAV
Spiral Staircase	More Today Than Yesterday	9-362	MG
Spiral Staircase	More Today Than Yesterday	7-75	MM
Sponge	Wax Ecstatic	24-106	SC
Springfield, Dusty	Brand New Me a	11-404	DK

ARTIST	SONG TITLE	#	TYPE
Springfield, Dusty	I Close My Eyes And Count To Ten	10-636	SF
Springfield, Dusty	I Only Want To Be With You	5-77	SC
Springfield, Dusty	I Only Want To Be With You	10-651	SF
Springfield, Dusty	In Private	49-239	DFK
Springfield, Dusty	In The Middle Of Nowhere	10-658	SF
Springfield, Dusty	Maybe I Know	10-728	JVC
Springfield, Dusty	Sit Down I Think I Love You	9-726	SAV
Springfield, Dusty	Son Of A Preacher Man	21-196	DK
Springfield, Dusty	Son Of A Preacher Man	10-732	JVC
Springfield, Dusty	Son Of A Preacher Man	6-785	MM
Springfield, Dusty	Son Of A Preacher Man	17-312	NA
Springfield, Dusty	Spooky	48-585	DK
Springfield, Dusty	Wishin' And Hopin'	10-731	JVC
Springfield, Dusty	You Don't Have To Say You Love Me	19-615	MH
Springfield, Rick	Don't Talk To Strangers	24-75	SC
Springfield, Rick	Jesse's Girl	16-160	SC
Springfields	Island Of Dreams	29-824	SF
Springsteen, Bruce	Ain't Good Enough For You	49-103	CDG
Springsteen, Bruce	Backstreets	20-241	LE
Springsteen, Bruce	Badlands	17-611	LE
Springsteen, Bruce	Blinded By The Light	20-249	LE
Springsteen, Bruce	Born In The USA	17-615	LE
Springsteen, Bruce	Born In The USA	30-4	MM
Springsteen, Bruce	Born To Run	17-607	LE
Springsteen, Bruce	Born To Run	3-454	SC
Springsteen, Bruce	Brilliant Disguise	17-613	LE
Springsteen, Bruce	Cadillac Land	20-240	LE
Springsteen, Bruce	Cover Me	20-252	LE
Springsteen, Bruce	Dancing In The Dark	17-608	LE
Springsteen, Bruce	Dancing In The Dark	3-486	SC
Springsteen, Bruce	Darlington County	20-248	LE
Springsteen, Bruce	Fade Away	20-251	LE
Springsteen, Bruce	Fire	20-245	LE
Springsteen, Bruce	Glory Days	17-620	LE
Springsteen, Bruce	Human Touch	20-247	LE
Springsteen, Bruce	Hungry Heart	17-610	LE
Springsteen, Bruce	I'm Going Down	20-239	LE
Springsteen, Bruce	I'm On Fire	17-609	LE
Springsteen, Bruce	I'm On Fire	17-179	SC
Springsteen, Bruce	Jersey Girl	20-246	LE
Springsteen, Bruce	Lonesome Day	18-598	ST
Springsteen, Bruce	Lonesome Day	32-28	THM
Springsteen, Bruce	My Hometown	35-185	CB
Springsteen, Bruce	My Hometown	17-612	LE
Springsteen, Bruce	No Surrender	20-243	LE
Springsteen, Bruce	Pay Me My Money Down	36-178	PHM
Springsteen, Bruce	Pink Cadillac	17-430	KC
Springsteen, Bruce	Pink Cadillac	17-621	LE
Springsteen, Bruce	Rising the	25-305	MM
Springsteen, Bruce	River the	20-237	LE
Springsteen, Bruce	Rosalita Come Out	20-236	LE

ARTIST	SONG TITLE	#	TYPE
	Tonight		
Springsteen, Bruce	Rosa ita Come Out Tonight	21-513	SC
Springsteen, Bruce	Secret Garden	17-618	LE
Springsteen, Bruce	Secret Garden	14-878	SC
Springsteen, Bruce	Streets Of Philadelphia	17-617	LE
Springsteen, Bruce	Tenth Avenue Freezeout	17-616	LE
Springsteen, Bruce	Tenth Avenue Freezeout	13-671	SGB
Springsteen, Bruce	Thunder Road	17-619	LE
Springsteen, Bruce	Thunder Road	17-177	SC
Springsteen, Bruce	Tougher Than The Rest	17-614	LE
Springsteen, Bruce	Tunnel Of Love	20-238	LE
Springsteen, Bruce	Two Hearts	20-242	LE
Springsteen, Bruce	Waiting On A Sunny Day	25-540	MM
Springsteen, Bruce	War	20-250	LE
Springsteen, Bruce	Xmas - Merry Christmas Baby	41-39	CB
Springsteen, Bruce	Xmas - Merry Christmas Baby	22-839	ST
Springsteen, Bruce	Xmas - Santa Claus Is Comin' To...	34-433	CB
Springsteen, Bruce	Xmas - Santa Claus Is Coming/Town	7-7	MM
Springsteen, Bruce	You Can Look But You Better Not...	20-244	LE
Squeeze	Tempted	29-4	MH
Squeeze	Tempted	2-562	SC
Squier, Billy	Stroke the **	2-726	SC
Squire Parsons	Gospel - Beluah Land	16-603	CB
Squirrel Nut Zipper	Hell	10-92	SC
Squirrel Nut Zipper	Hell	13-689	SGB
Squirrel Nut Zipper	Put A Lid On It	13-695	SGB
SR-71	Right Now	15-788	THM
SR-71	Tomorrow	18-828	THM
St. James, Rebecca	Breathe	35-306	CB
St. James, Rebecca\	Gospel - God	20-149	KB
St. Louis Blues	Show - Come Rain Or Come Shine	12-295	DK
St. Louis, Louis	Rock & Roll Party Queen	10-10	SC
St. Peters, Crispian	Pied Piper	10-669	SF
Stabbing Westward	What Do I Have To Do	4-669	SC
Stacey, Phil	If You Didn't Love Me	36-403	CB
Stafford, Jim	Cow Patti	15-145	SC
Stafford, Jim	My Girl Bill **	23-25	SC
Stafford, Jim	Spiders & Snakes	8-450	CB
Stafford, Jim	Spiders & Snakes	11-347	DK
Stafford, Jim	Swamp Witch	47-521	VH
Stafford, Jim	Wildwood Weed	2-134	SC
Stafford, Jo	Oh London Bridge	16-792	DK
Stafford, Jo	On London Bridge	15-541	CMC
Stafford, Jo	You Belong To Me	11-576	DK
Stafford, Terry	Suspicion	11-530	DK
Stafford, Terry	Suspicion	7-69	MM
Stagga Lee	Roll Wit MVP	32-271	THM
Staind	Believe	36-537	CB
Staind	Epiphany	21-650	CB
Staind	Fade	16-316	TT

267

ARTIST	SONG TITLE	#	TYPE
Staind	For You	33-437	CB
Staind	For You	32-212	THM
Staind	How About You	23-274	THM
Staind	It's Been Awhile	35-250	CB
Staind	It's Been Awhile	18-395	MM
Staind	It's Been Awhile	16-384	SGB
Staind	Price To Pay	32-288	THM
Staind	Right Here	30-223	PHM
Staind	Right Here	30-223	PHM
Staind	Right Here	30-157	PT
Staind	So Far Away	20-229	MM
Staind	So Far Away	32-329	THM
Staley, Karen	Somebody's Child	8-245	CB
Stallone, Frank	Far From Over	27-395	DK
Stampeders	Sweet City Woman	9-367	MG
Stampeders	Sweet City Woman	5-381	SC
Stampley, Joe	All These Things	5-760	SC
Stampley, Joe	Do You Ever Fool Around	43-302	CB
Stampley, Joe	If You've Got 10 Minutes	43-301	CB
Stampley, Joe	Put Your Clothes Back On	43-299	CB
Stampley, Joe	Red Wine And Blue Memories	43-300	CB
Stampley, Joe	Roll On Big Mama	8-838	CB
Stampley, Joe	Roll On Big Mama	9-598	SAV
Stampley, Joe	Soul Song	5-537	SC
Stampley, Joe	Whiskey Chasin'	45-843	VH
Stampley, Tony	Waste Of Good Whiskey	17-577	ST
Standaed	Who Can I Turn To	47-825	DK
Standard	After You've Gone	27-427	DK
Standard	Ain't We Got Fun	35-23	CB
Standard	Alexander's Ragtime Band	27-463	DK
Standard	All Of Me	27-422	DK
Standard	Am I Blue	9-468	SAV
Standard	America The Beautiful	23-219	SM
Standard	America the Beautiful - Patriotic	34-436	CB
Standard	America The Beautiful/Battle Hymn o	20-164	BCI
Standard	Angel Eyes	13-634	SGB
Standard	Auld Lang Syne	14-308	MM
Standard	Autumn Leaves	15-403	SGB
Standard	Baby Face	11-758	DK
Standard	Beautiful Brown Eyes	17-398	DK
Standard	Beautiful Dreamer	11-493	DK
Standard	Because Of You	47-822	DK
Standard	Beer Barrel Polka	27-448	DK
Standard	Beer Barrel Polka	7-412	MM
Standard	Beyond The Sunset	12-70	DK
Standard	Bill Bailey Won't You Please Come..	27-458	DK
Standard	Blame It On My Youth	15-407	SGB
Standard	Blue Moon	35-32	CB
Standard	Bluebird Of Happiness	47-829	PS
Standard	Blues In The Night	47-818	DK
Standard	Buffalo Gals	27-415	DK

ARTIST	SONG TITLE	#	TYPE
Standard	Cab Driver (Quartet)	10-474	MG
Standard	Cab Driver (Solo)	10-464	MG
Standard	Call Me Irresponsible	47-821	DK
Standard	Carry Me Back To Old Virginny	47-826	JVC
Standard	Cheek To Cheek	47-832	SC
Standard	Chicken Dance the - DANCE #	22-390	SC
Standard	Child Is Born a	15-464	SGB
Standard	Clementine	11-479	DK
Standard	Clementine	23-222	SM
Standard	Come Rain Or Come Shine	9-833	SAV
Standard	Cotton Fields	11-473	DK
Standard	Crawdad Song, the	44-51	KV
Standard	Cry Me A River	9-795	SAV
Standard	Cry Me A River	19-788	SGB
Standard	Daddy's Little Girl	19-789	SGB
Standard	Danny Boy	17-346	DK
Standard	Day By Day	12-67	DK
Standard	Days Of Wine And Roses	13-627	SGB
Standard	Deep In The Heart Of Texas	27-464	DK
Standard	Dixie	26-500	DK
Standard	Dixie	2-65	SC
Standard	Dixie	23-227	SM
Standard	Dollar Wine Dance	49-464	MM
Standard	Don't Fence Me In	10-471	MG
Standard	Down By he Riverside	27-446	DK
Standard	Down In My Heart	46-292	CB
Standard	Everything Happens To Me	15-472	SGB
Standard	Five Foot Two Eyes Of Blue	35-18	CB
Standard	For He's A Jolly Good Fellow	34-437	CB
Standard	For Me And My Gal	23-223	SM
Standard	Frankie & Johnny	11-476	DK
Standard	Georgie Porgie	47-833	SDK
Standard	Give A Little Whistle	21-10	SC
Standard	Go Tell It On The Mountain	10-247	SC
Standard	God Bless America	20-160	BCI
Standard	God Bless America - Patriotic	33-209	CB
Standard	Good Morning Heartache	13-639	SGB
Standard	Goodnight My Love	10-460	MG
Standard	Goosey Goosey Gander	47-834	SDK
Standard	Gospel - Good Christain Friends Rej	15-481	SC
Standard	Gospel - Swing Low Sweet Chariot	11-481	DK
Standard	Gospel - Swing Low Sweet Chariot	21-621	SF
Standard	Gospel - Will The Circle Be Unbroke	11-478	DK
Standard	Grandfather's Clock	11-484	DK

ARTIST	SONG TITLE	#	TYPE
Standard	Greensleeves	11-474	DK
Standard	Happy Birthday (Short Vers)	35-45	CB
Standard	Happy Birthday To You	11-585	DK
Standard	Happy Birthday To You	12-607	P
Standard	Happy Days Are Here Again	35-21	CB
Standard	Happy Days Are Here Again	12-570	P
Standard	Heart & Soul	27-462	DK
Standard	High Hopes	35-24	CB
Standard	Home On The Range	11-494	DK
Standard	Home On The Range	23-221	SM
Standard	Honeysuckle Rose	12-32	DK
Standard	I Can't Get Started	11-834	DK
Standard	I Love To Tell The Story	47-830	SC
Standard	I Love You Truly	10-469	MG
Standard	I'm Forever Blowing Bubbles	47-819	DK
Standard	I'm Getting Sentimental Over You	15-502	DK
Standard	I'm Old Fashioned	13-630	SGB
Standard	I've Forever Blowing Bubbles	11-584	DK
Standard	I've Got A Lovely Bunch Of Coconuts	11-583	DK
Standard	I've Got You Under My Skin	35-28	CB
Standard	Irish - Goodnight Irene	21-504	SC
Standard	It Could Happen To You	15-512	SGB
Standard	It Don't Mean A Thing	12-548	P
Standard	Jeanie With The Light Brown Hair	11-491	DK
Standard	Jimmy Crack Corn	23-229	SM
Standard	Let Me Call You Sweetheart	35-22	CB
Standard	Let Me Call You Sweetheart	11-475	DK
Standard	Let Me Call You Sweetheart	12-535	P
Standard	Let Me Call You Sweetheart	23-224	SM
Standard	Like Someone In Love	13-640	SGB
Standard	Little Green Apples	10-466	MG
Standard	Long Long Ago	47-827	JVC
Standard	Love Is A Many Splendored Thing	35-30	CB
Standard	Lover Come Back To Me	17-363	DK
Standard	Lullaby Of Broadway	11-817	DK
Standard	Lullaby Of Broadway	9-808	SAV
Standard	Make Someone Happy	9-579	SAV
Standard	Making Memories	10-461	MG
Standard	Man On The Flying Trapeze	9-858	SAV
Standard	Maybe It's Because I'm A Londoner	17-397	DK
Standard	Misty	17-345	DK
Standard	Moonlight Bay	11-582	DK
Standard	Moonlight Serenade	10-459	MG
Standard	My Bonnie	12-608	P
Standard	My Grandfather's Clock	47-840	SFM
Standard	My Heart Cries For You	10-470	MG
Standard	My Little Grass Shack	9-825	SAV
Standard	My Old Dog Tray	47-836	SDK
Standard	My Romance	13-631	SGB
Standard	Nearness Of You the	15-537	DK
Standard	Nevertheless (I'm In Love With You)	47-516	VH
Standard	Oh Susanna	11-490	DK
Standard	Oh Susanna	23-225	SM
Standard	Ol' Man River	17-159	DK
Standard	Old Blue	47-837	SDK
Standard	Old Folks At Home - Swanee River	11-485	DK
Standard	On A Slow Boat To China	17-160	DK
Standard	On A Slow Boat To China	13-632	SGB
Standard	On The Sunny Side Of The Street	12-13	DK
Standard	On Top Of Old Smoky	27-461	DK
Standard	Patriotic - America the Beautiful	34-436	CB
Standard	Patriotic - God Bless America	33-209	CB
Standard	Patriotic - Star Spangled Banner	33-210	CB
Standard	Patriotic - You're a Grand Old Flag	34-440	CB
Standard	Pennies From Heaven	11-301	DK
Standard	Polka Dots & Moonbeams	15-551	SGB
Standard	Puttin' On The Ritz	10-472	MG
Standard	Red River Valley	11-487	DK
Standard	Rocky Top	13-416	P
Standard	Rocky Top	2-34	SC
Standard	Route 66	26-487	DK
Standard	San Francisco Bay Blues	12-180	DK
Standard	San Francisco Bay Blues	47-722	DKM
Standard	Santa Lucia	27-449	DK
Standard	Satin Doll	27-420	DK
Standard	Satin Doll	13-635	SGB
Standard	Scotch & Soda	13-638	SGB
Standard	She'll Be Comin' 'Round the Mtn	23-228	SM
Standard	Shenandoah	11-486	DK
Standard	Shortnin' Bread	47-838	SDK
Standard	Sidewalks Of New York the	27-444	DK
Standard	Sloop John B	27-368	DK
Standard	Someone To Watch Over Me	27-430	DK
Standard	Song Is You the	15-561	SGB
Standard	South Of The Border	11-298	DK
Standard	Spanish Eyes	10-465	MG
Standard	St. Louis Blues	12-14	DK

ARTIST	SONG TITLE	#	TYPE
Standard	Star Spangled Banner	12-106	DK
Standard	Star Spangled Banner	12-614	P
Standard	Star Spangled Banner - Patriotic	33-210	CB
Standard	Stardust	27-54	DK
Standard	Stella By Starlight	15-562	SGB
Standard	Streets Of Laredo	27-445	DK
Standard	Summertime	13-637	SGB
Standard	Swanee River (Old Folks At Home)	27-457	DK
Standard	Sweet Leilani	47-831	SC
Standard	Take Me Out To The Ballgame	12-609	P
Standard	Take Me Out To The Ballgame	23-220	SM
Standard	That Old Feeling	47-518	VH
Standard	There Will Never Be Another You	15-569	SGB
Standard	This Land Is Your Land	20-159	BCI
Standard	This Time The Dream's On Me	15-570	SGB
Standard	Thou Swell	15-571	SGB
Standard	Till Then	10-473	MG
Standard	Tom Dooley	18-171	DK
Standard	Toot Toot Tootsie Goodbye	35-26	CB
Standard	Turkey In The Straw	47-839	SDK
Standard	Very Thought Of You the	47-828	PS
Standard	Waltzing Matilda	47-835	SDK
Standard	Wave	15-577	SGB
Standard	Way You Look Tonight the	13-629	SGB
Standard	Wearin' Of The Green	12-142	DK
Standard	Wedding March the	49-465	MM
Standard	Wedding Song the	2-67	SC
Standard	What Kind Of Fool Am I	47-824	DK
Standard	When I Fall In Love	12-838	P
Standard	When The Saints Go Marching In	34-439	CB
Standard	Willow Weep For Me	12-50	DK
Standard	Won't You Come Home Bill Bailey	11-483	DK
Standard	Wreck Of The John B.	47-823	DK
Standard	Xmas - Carol Of The Bells	41-7	CB
Standard	Xmas - Christ Was Born on Xmas Day	41-3	CB
Standard	Xmas - Christmas Time Is Here	41-19	PR
Standard	Xmas - Christmas Waltz	41-18	PR
Standard	Xmas - Do You Hear What I Hear?	41-13	CB
Standard	Xmas - It Won't Seem Like Xmas w/o You	41-4	CB
Standard	Xmas - My Favorite Things	41-1	CB
Standard	Xmas - Nuttin' For Christmas	41-11	CB
Standard	Xmas - Twas the Night	41-6	CB

ARTIST	SONG TITLE	#	TYPE
	Before Xmas		
Standard	Xmas - Two-Step 'Round the Xmas Tree	41-16	PR
Standard	Xmas - We Need A Little Christmas	41-5	CB
Standard	Xmas - We Three Kings	41-12	CB
Standard	Yankee Doodle Dandy	23-230	SM
Standard	Yellow Rose Of Texas the	23-226	SM
Standard	Yes Sir That's My Baby	35-31	CB
Standard	You Are My Sunshine	26-413	DK
Standard	You Belong To Me	47-817	DK
Standard	You Don't Know What Love Is	13-641	SGB
Standard	You Go To My Head	19-784	SGB
Standard	You Made Me Love You	15-598	DK
Standard	You Stepped Out Of A Dream	15-591	SGB
Standard	You Took Advantage Of Me	15-592	SGB
Standard	You Turned The Tables On Me	15-593	SGB
Standard	You'd Be So Nice To Come Home To	47-820	DK
Standard	You're A Grand Old Flag - Patriotic	34-440	CB
Standard	Young And Foolish	15-597	SGB
Stanley Brothers	Pig In The Pen	8-260	CB
Stanley Brothers	Rank Stranger	38-28	CB
Stanley, Ralph	Little Cabin Home On The Hill	49-328	CB
Stanley, Ralph	Little Maggie	8-253	CB
Stansfield & Mic	Duet - These Are The Days of/ Life	18-235	DK
Stansfield & Mic	These Are The Days Of Our Lives	18-235	DK
Stansfield, Lisa	All Around The World	17-95	DK
Stansfield, Lisa	All Around The World	6-166	MM
Stansfield, Lisa	All Around The World	16-539	P
Staple Singers	Duet - Respect Yourself	27-259	DK
Staple Singers	Duet - Respect Yourself	12-920	P
Staple Singers	I'll Take You There	2-443	SC
Staple Singers	Let's Do It Again	11-373	DK
Staple Singers	Respect Yourself	27-259	DK
Staple Singers	Respect Yourself	12-920	P
Stapleton, Chris	Daddy Doesn't Pray Anymore	49-788	DCK
Stapleton, Chris	Devil Named Music the	49-650	KV
Stapleton, Chris	Fire Away	48-671	KVD
Stapleton, Chris	Fire Away	46-134	FMK
Stapleton, Chris	More Of You	49-652	KV
Stapleton, Chris	Nobody To Blame	47-395	BKD
Stapleton, Chris	Parachute	49-10	KV
Stapleton, Chris	Sometimes I Cry - live	49-651	KV
Stapleton, Chris	Tennessee Whiskey	45-439	KV
Stapleton, Chris	Traveller	45-438	BKD
Stapleton, Chris	What Are You Listening To	45-437	BKD
Stapleton, Chris	Whiskey And You	48-679	KVD

ARTIST	SONG TITLE	#	TYPE
Star Academy	Locomotion the	45-944	KV
Star Is Born a - Streisand	Show - Evergreen	49-568	PS
Starbuck	Moonlight Feels Right	7-100	MM
Starland Local	Duet - Afternoon Delight	11-394	DK
Starland Vocal Band	Afternoon Delight	11-394	DK
Starr, Edwin	25 Miles	25-277	MM
Starr, Kay	Rock & Roll Waltz the	5-15	SC
Starr, Kay	Rock & Roll Waltz the	10-598	SF
Starr, Kay	Side By Side	11-312	DK
Starr, Kay	Side By Side	15-845	MM
Starr, Kay	Side By Side	4-348	SC
Starr, Kay	Wheel Of Fortune	4-182	SC
Starr, Ringo	No No Song	2-752	SC
Starr, Ringo	Oh My My	49-779	SC
Starr, Ringo	Photograph	49-780	SC
Starr, Ringo	You're Sixteen	33-296	CB
Starr, Ringo	You're Sixteen	9-840	SAV
Starr, Ringo	You're Sixteen	11-145	DK
Starship	Count On Me	15-225	LE
Starship	Nothing's Gonna Stop Us	7-55	MM
Starship	Nothing's Gonna Stop Us Now	35-143	CB
Starship	We Built This City	20-305	CB
Starship	We Built This City	17-76	DK
Starship	We Built This City	7-60	MM
State Fair	Show - It Might As Well Be Spring	27-398	DK
Statesboro Revue	Fade My Shade Of Black the	41-68	PHN
Static X	Only the	19-857	PHM
Statler Brothers	Bed Of Roses	19-390	CB
Statler Brothers	Bed Of Roses	5-822	SC
Statler Brothers	Class Of ' 57	19-387	CB
Statler Brothers	Do You Know You Are My Sunshine	19-380	CB
Statler Brothers	Do You Know You Are My Sunshine	4-270	SC
Statler Brothers	Do You Remember These	19-379	CB
Statler Brothers	Do You Remember These	4-583	SC
Statler Brothers	Elizabeth	19-383	CB
Statler Brothers	Elizabeth	5-569	SC
Statler Brothers	Flowers On The Wall	19-378	CB
Statler Brothers	Flowers On The Wall	11-782	DK
Statler Brothers	Flowers On The Wall	12-468	P
Statler Brothers	Flowers On The Wall	9-442	SAV
Statler Brothers	Flowers On The Wall	5-93	SC
Statler Brothers	How To Be A Country Star	19-389	CB
Statler Brothers	I'll Go To My Grave Lovin' You	19-376	CB
Statler Brothers	I'll Go To My Grave Lovin' You	4-632	SC
Statler Brothers	Let's Get Started If We're Gonna	5-773	SC
Statler Brothers	More Than A Name On A	49-795	DFK

ARTIST	SONG TITLE	#	TYPE
	Wall		
Statler Brothers	Movies the	8-826	CB
Statler Brothers	My Only Love	19-384	CB
Statler Brothers	My Only Love	5-754	SC
Statler Brothers	Oh Baby Mine	19-382	CB
Statler Brothers	Thank God I've Got You	19-388	CB
Statler Brothers	Too Much On My Heart	19-385	CB
Statler Brothers	Too Much On My Heart	11-722	DK
Statler Brothers	Too Much On My Heart	5-527	SC
Statler Brothers	Who Am I To Say	19-381	CB
Statler Brothers	Who Am I To Say	14-261	SC
Statler Brothers	You Can't Have Your Kate & Edith To	19-386	CB
Statler Brothers	You'll Be Back	6-83	SC
Stealers Wheel	Stuck In The Middle With You	2-151	SC
Steam	Na Na Hey Hey Kiss Him Goodbye	33-446	CB
Steam	Na Na Hey Hey Kiss Him Goodbye	11-664	DK
Steam	Na Na Hey Hey Kiss Him Goodbye	7-54	MM
Steam	Na Na Hey Hey Kiss Him Goodbye	13-94	P
Steam	Na Na Hey Hey Kiss Him Goodbye	9-766	SAV
Steam	Na Na Hey Hey Kiss Him Goodbye	3-260	SC
Steel Pulse	Brown Eyed Girl	25-386	MM
Steeldrivers	If It Hadn't Been For Love	49-921	KVD
Steele, Jeffrey	Good To Go	17-587	ST
Steele, Jeffrey	I Can Give You Love Like That	17-487	CB
Steele, Jeffrey	Somethin' In The Water	25-5	MM
Steele, Jeffrey	Something In The Water	15-861	ST
Steele, Tommy	My Side Of The Street	39-70	PHN
Steelheart	I'll Never Let You Go (Angel Eyes)	24-690	SC
Steely Dan	Black Friday	15-382	RS
Steely Dan	Bodhisattva	15-396	RS
Steely Dan	Deacon Blues	13-16	P
Steely Dan	Deacon Blues	15-390	RS
Steely Dan	Dirty Work	15-394	RS
Steely Dan	Do It Again	11-500	DK
Steely Dan	Do It Again	15-169	MH
Steely Dan	Do It Again	15-384	RS
Steely Dan	Do It Again	20-52	SC
Steely Dan	Do It Again	10-540	SF
Steely Dan	Fez the	15-395	RS
Steely Dan	FM (No Static At All)	15-393	RS
Steely Dan	Hey 19	15-383	RS
Steely Dan	Josie	15-392	RS
Steely Dan	Kid Charlemagne	15-389	RS
Steely Dan	My Old School	15-388	RS
Steely Dan	Peg	15-391	RS
Steely Dan	Reelin' In The Years	12-818	P
Steely Dan	Reelin' In The Years	15-381	RS

ARTIST	SONG TITLE	#	TYPE
Steely Dan	Rikki Don't Lose That Number	17-337	DK
Steely Dan	Rikki Don't Lose That Number	15-386	RS
Steely Dan	Show Biz Kids	15-385	RS
Steely Dan	Time Out Of Mind	15-387	RS
Stefani & Eve	Duet - Rich Girl	22-357	CB
Stefani & Eve	Rich Girl	22-357	CB
Stefani, Gwen	4 In The Morning	30-565	CB
Stefani, Gwen	Cool	23-312	SC
Stefani, Gwen	Hollaback Girl **	30-130	PT
Stefani, Gwen	Wind It Up	30-266	CB
Stefani,Eve & Gwen	Let Me Blow Ya Mind	18-527	TT
Stegal, Rod	Lonestar Beer	47-489	OZP
Stegall, Keith	1969	4-132	SC
Steiner, Tommy S.	Tell Me Where It Hurts	25-298	MM
Steiner, Tommy S.	Tell Me Where It Hurts	17-586	ST
Steiner, Tommy S.	What If She's An Angel	25-124	MM
Steiner, Tommy S.	What If She's An Angel	16-103	ST
Steiner, Tommy S.	What If She's An Angel	33-190	CB
Steiner, Tommy S.	What We're Gonna Do About It	18-460	ST
Steppenwolf	Born To Be Wild	11-352	DK
Steppenwolf	Born To Be Wild	6-139	MM
Steppenwolf	Born To Be Wild	13-39	P
Steppenwolf	Born To Be Wild	2-44	SC
Steppenwolf	Magic Carpet Ride	11-502	DK
Steppenwolf	Magic Carpet Ride	13-227	P
Steppenwolf	Magic Carpet Ride	3-259	SC
Steppenwolf	Pusher the	2-757	SC
Steps	Summer Of Love	20-5	SGB
Steps	Tragedy	15-331	PHM
Steps	When I Said Goodbye	19-658	SGB
Stereo Fuse	Everything	18-611	PHM
Stereophonics	Have A Nice Day	25-79	MM
Steve Miller Band	Abracadabra	33-307	CB
Steve Miller Band	Fly Like An Eagle	35-129	CB
Steve Miller Band	Fly Like An Eagle	10-361	KC
Steve Miller Band	Fly Like An Eagle	3-530	SC
Steve Miller Band	Jet Airliner	16-595	MM
Steve Miller Band	Joker the	16-779	DK
Steve Miller Band	Joker the	5-313	SC
Steve Miller Band	Over My Head	4-874	SC
Steve Miller Band	Rock 'N Me	3-483	SC
Steve Miller Band	Swingtown	5-309	SC
Steve Miller Band	Take The Money And Run	4-90	SC
Stevens, Cat	Another Saturday Night	23-655	BS
Stevens, Cat	Another Saturday Night	13-583	NU
Stevens, Cat	Can't Keep It In	23-646	BS
Stevens, Cat	Can't Keep It In	13-574	NU
Stevens, Cat	Father & Son	13-580	NU
Stevens, Cat	Father And Son	23-652	BS
Stevens, Cat	Hard Headed Woman	23-647	BS
Stevens, Cat	Hard Headed Woman	13-575	NU
Stevens, Cat	Hurt the	23-656	BS
Stevens, Cat	Hurt the	13-584	NU

ARTIST	SONG TITLE	#	TYPE
Stevens, Cat	Longer Boats	46-161	SC
Stevens, Cat	Moonshadow	23-648	BS
Stevens, Cat	Moonshadow	13-576	NU
Stevens, Cat	Moonshadow	5-303	SC
Stevens, Cat	Morning Has Broken	23-654	BS
Stevens, Cat	Morning Has Broken	13-582	NU
Stevens, Cat	Morning Has Broken	2-777	SC
Stevens, Cat	Oh Very Young	23-645	BS
Stevens, Cat	Oh Very Young	13-573	NU
Stevens, Cat	Peace Train	23-650	BS
Stevens, Cat	Peace Train	13-578	NU
Stevens, Cat	Ready	23-651	BS
Stevens, Cat	Ready	13-579	NU
Stevens, Cat	Sitting	23-653	BS
Stevens, Cat	Sitting	13-581	NU
Stevens, Cat	Two Fine People	23-649	BS
Stevens, Cat	Two Fine People	13-577	NU
Stevens, Cat	Wild World	9-317	AG
Stevens, Cat	Wild World	23-644	BS
Stevens, Cat	Wild World	13-572	NU
Stevens, Cat	Wild World	15-801	SC
Stevens, Dodie	Pink Shoelaces	6-857	MM
Stevens, Dodie	Pink Shoelaces	5-231	SC
Stevens, Ray	Ahab The Arab	16-487	CB
Stevens, Ray	Ahab The Arab	15-347	MM
Stevens, Ray	Along Came Jones	16-496	CB
Stevens, Ray	Back In The Doghouse Again	16-498	CB
Stevens, Ray	Bad Little Boy - xmas	47-903	CB
Stevens, Ray	Ballad Of The Blue Cyclone (Rasslin	16-495	CB
Stevens, Ray	Deer Slayer	47-904	TU
Stevens, Ray	Duet - Guitarzan	15-346	MM
Stevens, Ray	Everything Is Beautiful	8-45	CB
Stevens, Ray	Everything Is Beautiful	22-926	SC
Stevens, Ray	Guitarzan	16-492	CB
Stevens, Ray	Guitarzan	15-346	MM
Stevens, Ray	Haircut Song the	16-491	CB
Stevens, Ray	Haircut Song the	15-139	SC
Stevens, Ray	I'm My Own Grandpa	15-343	MM
Stevens, Ray	It's Me Again Margaret	16-490	CB
Stevens, Ray	Jeremiah Peabody's Song	6-863	MM
Stevens, Ray	Mississippi Squirrel Revival	16-486	CB
Stevens, Ray	Mississippi Squirrel Revival	6-515	MM
Stevens, Ray	Mississippi Squirrel Revival	15-137	SC
Stevens, Ray	Misty	16-493	CB
Stevens, Ray	Misty	4-634	SC
Stevens, Ray	Motel Song the	16-499	CB
Stevens, Ray	Osama Yo Mama	16-338	ST
Stevens, Ray	Redneck Christmas	46-289	CB
Stevens, Ray	Shriner's Convention	16-494	CB
Stevens, Ray	Spanish Fireball	6-766	MM
Stevens, Ray	Streak the	16-489	CB
Stevens, Ray	Streak the	2-179	SC

ARTIST	SONG TITLE	#	TYPE
Stevens, Ray	Too Drunk To Fish	47-846	FMG
Stevens, Ray	Turn Your Radio On	16-497	CB
Stevens, Ray	Would Jesus Wear A Rolex	47-905	VH
Stevens, Ray	Xmas - Bad Little Boy	47-903	CB
Stevens, Ray	Xmas - Redneck Christmas	46-289	CB
Stevens, Ray	Xmas - Santa Claus Is Watching You	16-500	CB
Stevens, Ray	Xmas - Santa Claus is Watching You	5-707	SC
Stevenson, B.W.	My Maria	34-42	CB
Stevie B	Because I Love You (Postman Song)	28-117	DK
Steward, Rod	Tonight I'm Yours Don't Hurt Me	48-215	LE
Stewart & Sting	All For Love	18-481	NU
Stewart & Sting	Duet - All For Love	18-481	NU
Stewart, Al	Time Passages	21-508	SC
Stewart, Al	Year Of The Cat the	2-785	SC
Stewart, Billy	Summertime	11-224	DK
Stewart, Billy	Summertime	3-318	MH
Stewart, Billy	Summertime	7-71	MM
Stewart, Gary	Drinkin' Thing	14-313	SC
Stewart, Gary	Out Of Hand	20-287	SC
Stewart, Gary	Quits	14-423	SC
Stewart, Gary	She's Actin' Single	4-571	SC
Stewart, Gary	Whiskey Trip	29-691	SC
Stewart, Larry	Alright Already	2-332	SC
Stewart, Larry	Always A Woman	7-424	MM
Stewart, Larry	Always a Woman	4-621	SC
Stewart, Larry	Losing Your Love	2-644	SC
Stewart, Larry	Losing Your Love	22-860	ST
Stewart, Larry	Rockin' The Rock	2-744	SC
Stewart, Larry	Why Can't You	7-324	MM
Stewart, Larry	Why Can't You	4-411	SC
Stewart, Rod	Angel	14-850	LE
Stewart, Rod	Baby Jane	14-848	LE
Stewart, Rod	Do Ya Think I'm Sexy	35-139	CB
Stewart, Rod	Do Ya Think I'm Sexy	16-735	DK
Stewart, Rod	Do Ya Think I'm Sexy	25-597	MM
Stewart, Rod	Do Ya Think I'm Sexy	9-651	SAV
Stewart, Rod	Downtown Train	22-922	SC
Stewart, Rod	Duet - This Old Heart Of Mine	6-233	MM
Stewart, Rod	Every Beat Of My Heart	14-855	LE
Stewart, Rod	Faith Of The Heart	7-813	PHT
Stewart, Rod	First Cut Is The Deepest the	14-852	LE
Stewart, Rod	Forever Young	11-70	JTG
Stewart, Rod	Have I Told You Lately	14-859	LE
Stewart, Rod	Have I Told You Lately	10-17	SC
Stewart, Rod	Have I Told You Lately That I Love	25-599	MM
Stewart, Rod	Having A Party	14-858	LE
Stewart, Rod	Hot Legs	16-151	SC
Stewart, Rod	Human	16-254	TT
Stewart, Rod	I Don't Want To Talk	14-851	LE

ARTIST	SONG TITLE	#	TYPE
	About It		
Stewart, Rod	If I Had You	16-256	TT
Stewart, Rod	If Lovin' You Is Wrong I Don't	14-853	LE
Stewart, Rod	If We Fall In Love Tonight	24-631	SC
Stewart, Rod	Killing Of Georgie the	14-846	LE
Stewart, Rod	Leave Virginia Alone	3-439	SC
Stewart, Rod	Love Touch	48-541	DK
Stewart, Rod	Maggie May	15-177	MH
Stewart, Rod	Maggie May	25-598	MM
Stewart, Rod	Moonglow	25-594	MM
Stewart, Rod	My Heart Can't Tell You No	12-187	DK
Stewart, Rod	Oh No Not My Baby	14-849	LE
Stewart, Rod	People Get Ready	4-291	SC
Stewart, Rod	Reason To Believe	14-857	LE
Stewart, Rod	Reason To Believe	6-363	MM
Stewart, Rod	Reason To Believe	29-640	SC
Stewart, Rod	Rhythm Of My Heart	14-856	LE
Stewart, Rod	Some Guys Have All The Luck	11-285	DK
Stewart, Rod	Some Guys Have All The Luck	25-604	MM
Stewart, Rod	Superstar	16-219	MM
Stewart, Rod	That Old Feeling	25-596	MM
Stewart, Rod	These Foolish Things	25-592	MM
Stewart, Rod	They Can't Take That Away From Me	25-595	MM
Stewart, Rod	This Old Heart Of Mine	14-847	LE
Stewart, Rod	This Old Heart Of Mine	6-233	MM
Stewart, Rod	To Be With You	16-261	TT
Stewart, Rod	Tonight I'm Yours	14-860	LE
Stewart, Rod	Tonight I'm Yours (Don't Hurt Me)	24-68	SC
Stewart, Rod	Tonight's The Night	25-601	MM
Stewart, Rod	Tonight's The Night	2-859	SC
Stewart, Rod	Way You Look Tonight the	25-593	MM
Stewart, Rod	What Am I Gonna Do	14-854	LE
Stewart, Rod	You Go To My Head	25-591	MM
Stewart, Rod	You Wear It Well	25-603	MM
Stewart, Rod	You Wear It Well	3-526	SC
Stewart, Rod	You're In My Heart	25-600	MM
Stewart, Rod	You're In My Heart	9-652	SAV
Stewart, Rod	Young Turks	14-861	LE
Stewart, Rod	Young Turks	25-602	MM
Stewart, Wynne	It's Such A Pretty World Today	8-670	SAV
Stigers, Curtis	Never Saw A Miracle	7-474	MM
Stills, Stephen	Love The One You're With	33-278	CB
Stills, Stephen	Love The One You're With	10-356	KC
Stills, Stephen	Love The One You're With	2-784	SC
Sting	Desert Rose	15-635	THM
Sting	Desert Rose	18-553	TT
Sting	Desert Rose (Radio	14-481	SC

ARTIST	SONG TITLE	#	TYPE
	Version)		
Sting	Fields Of Gold	6-368	MM
Sting	If I Ever Lose My Faith In You	24-142	SC
Sting	If You Love Somebody Set 'Em Free	4-316	SC
Sting	My Funny Friend And Me	17-721	THM
Sting	Send Your Love	20-230	MM
Stone Sour	Bother	25-431	MM
Stone Sour	Inhale	32-220	THM
Stone Temple Pilots	All In The Suit That You Wear	23-270	THM
Stone Temple Pilots	Interstate Love Song	2-476	SC
Stone Temple Pilots	Interstate Love Song	13-750	SGB
Stone Temple Pilots	Lady Picture Show	24-633	SC
Stone Temple Pilots	Plush	13-749	SGB
Stone, Angie	I Wish I Didn't Miss You	25-224	MM
Stone, Angie	Mad Issues	25-692	MM
Stone, Angie	Wish I Didn't Miss You	18-222	CB
Stone, Angie	Wish I Didn't Miss You	33-449	CB
Stone, Doug	Addicted To A Dollar	20-603	CB
Stone, Doug	Addicted To A Dollar	6-501	MM
Stone, Doug	Born In The Dark	7-148	MM
Stone, Doug	Born in The Dark	3-572	SC
Stone, Doug	Christmas Card a	45-751	CB
Stone, Doug	Come In Out Of The Pain	20-597	CB
Stone, Doug	Faith In Me Faith In You	2-663	SC
Stone, Doug	Fourteen Minutes Old	20-592	CB
Stone, Doug	Fourteen Minutes Old	6-617	MM
Stone, Doug	Gone Out Of My Mind	8-492	CB
Stone, Doug	I Never Knew Love	20-602	CB
Stone, Doug	I Thought It Was You	20-595	CB
Stone, Doug	I Thought It Was You	3-643	SC
Stone, Doug	I'd Be Better Off In A Pine Box	20-591	CB
Stone, Doug	I'd Be Better Off In A Pine Box	9-453	SAV
Stone, Doug	In A Different Light	20-594	CB
Stone, Doug	Jukebox With A Country Song	20-596	CB
Stone, Doug	Jukebox With A Country Song	9-543	SAV
Stone, Doug	Little Houses	20-604	CB
Stone, Doug	Little Houses	17-267	NA
Stone, Doug	Little Houses	2-546	SC
Stone, Doug	Made For Loving You	20-600	CB
Stone, Doug	Made For Loving You	6-311	MM
Stone, Doug	Make Up In Love	19-208	CB
Stone, Doug	Make Up In Love	14-629	SC
Stone, Doug	Make Up In Love	22-490	ST
Stone, Doug	More Love	2-322	SC
Stone, Doug	Sometimes I Forget	3-537	SC
Stone, Doug	Sometimes I Forget	7-25	MM
Stone, Doug	Surprise	9-421	CB
Stone, Doug	These Lips Don't Know How To Say	12-160	DK

ARTIST	SONG TITLE	#	TYPE
Stone, Doug	These Lips Don't Know How To Say..	20-593	CB
Stone, Doug	These Lips Don't Know How To Say..	6-625	MM
Stone, Doug	Too Busy Being In Love	20-599	CB
Stone, Doug	Too Busy Being In Love	6-218	MM
Stone, Doug	Too Busy Being In Love	2-710	SC
Stone, Doug	Warning Labels	20-598	CB
Stone, Doug	Warning Labels	2-351	SC
Stone, Doug	Why Didn't I Think Of That	20-601	CB
Stone, Doug	Why Didn't I Think Of That	2-626	SC
Stone, Doug	Xmas - All I Want For Xmas Is You	18-757	CB
Stone, Doug	Xmas - Christmas Card a	45-751	CB
Stone, Doug	You Have The Right To Remain Silent	6-818	MM
Stone, Joss	Dirty Man	43-119	ZMP
Stone, Joss	Free Me	43-117	CB
Stone, Joss	High Road the	44-162	BKD
Stone, Joss	Right To Be Wrong	22-367	CB
Stone, Joss	Right To Be Wrong	43-118	ASK
Stone, Joss	Super Duper Love	43-120	ZPA
Stone, Joss	Tell Me 'Bout It	30-566	CB
Stone, Joss	You Had Me	21-162	PHM
Stone, Keys & Eve	Brotha (Part II)	25-686	MM
Stories	Brother Louie	11-382	DK
Stories	Brother Louie	2-441	SC
Storm, Gale	I Hear You Knockin'	17-72	DK
Strait & Jackson	Duet - Murder On Music Row	34-338	CB
Strait & Jackson	Murder On Music Row	19-258	CSZ
Strait & Jackson	Murder On Music Row - duet	34-338	CB
Strait, George	Ace In The Hole	28-78	DK
Strait, George	Ace In The Hole	20-399	MH
Strait, George	Adalida	1-247	CB
Strait, George	Adalida	2-697	SC
Strait, George	Adalida	22-877	ST
Strait, George	All My Ex's Live In Texas	1-257	CB
Strait, George	All My Ex's Live In Texas	13-378	P
Strait, George	All My Ex's Live In Texas	9-431	SAV
Strait, George	All My Ex's Live In Texas	3-373	SC
Strait, George	Always Never The Same	38-153	CB
Strait, George	Am I Blue	16-584	SC
Strait, George	Amarillo By Morning	1-241	CB
Strait, George	Amarillo By Morning	13-453	P
Strait, George	Baby Blue	34-278	CB
Strait, George	Baby Blue	2-510	SC
Strait, George	Baby's Gotten Good At Goodbye	8-167	CB
Strait, George	Baby's Gotten Good At Goodbye	4-553	SC

ARTIST	SONG TITLE	#	TYPE
Strait, George	Best Day Of My Life the	22-527	ST
Strait, George	Big One the	6-663	MM
Strait, George	Big One the	2-487	SC
Strait, George	Blue Clear Sky	7-227	MM
Strait, George	Blue Clear Sky	22-878	ST
Strait, George	Breath You Take the	38-140	CB
Strait, George	Carried Away	1-249	CB
Strait, George	Carried Away	7-275	MM
Strait, George	Carried Away	4-364	SC
Strait, George	Carried Away	22-893	ST
Strait, George	Carrying Your Love With Me	1-264	CB
Strait, George	Carrying Your Love With Me	7-638	CHM
Strait, George	Carrying Your Love With Me	10-97	SC
Strait, George	Carrying Your Love With Me	22-597	ST
Strait, George	Chair the	8-161	CB
Strait, George	Chair the	8-694	SAV
Strait, George	Check Yes Or No	1-248	CB
Strait, George	Check Yes Or No	7-136	MM
Strait, George	Chill Of An Early Fall	8-173	CB
Strait, George	Chill Of An Early Fall	3-649	SC
Strait, George	Chill Of An Early Fall a	9-542	SAV
Strait, George	Christmas Cookies	45-754	CB
Strait, George	Cold Beer Conversations	45-389	BKD
Strait, George	Cowboy Rides Away the	4-543	SC
Strait, George	Cowboys Like Us	25-703	MM
Strait, George	Cowboys Like Us	19-362	ST
Strait, George	Cowboys Like Us	32-377	THM
Strait, George	Desperately	19-762	ST
Strait, George	Does Ft. Worth Ever Cross Your Mind	1-242	CB
Strait, George	Does Ft. Worth Ever Cross Your Mind	9-518	SAV
Strait, George	Don't Make Me Come Over There...	14-130	CB
Strait, George	Don't Make Me Come Over There...	22-584	ST
Strait, George	Down And Out	5-318	SC
Strait, George	Down Louisiana Way	49-228	DFK
Strait, George	Drinkin' Champagne	2-411	SC
Strait, George	Drinking Champagne	1-244	CB
Strait, George	Drinking Champagne	8-601	TT
Strait, George	Drinking Man	39-35	ASK
Strait, George	Easy Come Easy Go	8-175	CB
Strait, George	Easy Come Easy Go	6-391	MM
Strait, George	Easy Come Easy Go	2-508	SC
Strait, George	Famous Last Words Of A Fool	8-166	CB
Strait, George	Fire I Can't Put Out a	8-171	CB
Strait, George	Fire I Can't Put Out a	24-77	SC
Strait, George	Fireman the	8-164	CB
Strait, George	Fireman the	4-484	SC
Strait, George	Fool Hearted Memory	8-162	CB
Strait, George	Fool Hearted Memory	4-819	SC

ARTIST	SONG TITLE	#	TYPE
Strait, George	Give It All We Got Tonight	44-154	BKD
Strait, George	Give It Away	30-15	CB
Strait, George	Go On	14-101	CB
Strait, George	Go On	13-857	CHM
Strait, George	Go On	19-209	CSZ
Strait, George	Gone As A Girl Can Get	1-259	CB
Strait, George	Gone As A Girl Can Get	49-276	CB
Strait, George	Heartland	1-250	CB
Strait, George	Heartland	20-400	MH
Strait, George	Heartland	6-125	MM
Strait, George	Heartland	2-803	SC
Strait, George	Here For A Good Time	38-86	AT
Strait, George	High Tone Woman	29-33	CB
Strait, George	Home Improvement	38-142	CB
Strait, George	Honk If You Honky-Tonk	38-143	CB
Strait, George	House Of Cash	49-420	CB
Strait, George	How 'Bout Them Cowgirls	30-544	CB
Strait, George	I Believe	40-59	ASK
Strait, George	I Believe	41-97	PHN
Strait, George	I Can Still Make Cheyenne	1-265	CB
Strait, George	I Can Still Make Cheyenne	4-464	SC
Strait, George	I Cross My Heart	1-245	CB
Strait, George	I Cross My Heart	6-110	MM
Strait, George	I Cross My Heart	12-434	P
Strait, George	I Cross My Heart	2-12	SC
Strait, George	I Got A Car	42-21	ASK
Strait, George	I Gotta Get To You	38-144	CB
Strait, George	I Hate Everything	30-797	PHM
Strait, George	I Hate Everything	20-485	ST
Strait, George	I Just Can't Go On Dying Like This	42-12	PHN
Strait, George	I Just Wanna Dance With You	7-740	CHM
Strait, George	I Just Want To Dance With You	1-251	CB
Strait, George	I Know She Still Loves Me	4-17	SC
Strait, George	I Look At You	38-145	CB
Strait, George	I Saw GOD Today	36-391	CB
Strait, George	I'd Like To Have That One Back	1-260	CB
Strait, George	I'd Like To Have That One Back	2-808	SC
Strait, George	I've Come To Expect It From You	8-163	CB
Strait, George	I've Come To Expect It From You	3-650	SC
Strait, George	If I Know Me	8-168	CB
Strait, George	If I Know Me	6-627	MM
Strait, George	If I Know Me	17-244	NA
Strait, George	If You Ain't Lovin'	5-317	SC
Strait, George	If You Ain't Lovin' You Ain't Livin'	34-281	CB
Strait, George	If You Can Do Anything Else	34-361	CB

ARTIST	SONG TITLE	#	TYPE
Strait, George	If You Can Do Anything Else	14-836	ST
Strait, George	If You're Thinkin' You Want A Stran	5-323	SC
Strait, George	It Ain't Cool to Be Crazy Over You	5-330	SC
Strait, George	It Just Comes Natural	30-163	CB
Strait, George	Just Look At Me	24-10	SC
Strait, George	King Of Broken Hearts the	24-121	SC
Strait, George	King Of The Mountain	1-266	CB
Strait, George	King Of The Mountain	7-579	CHM
Strait, George	King Of The Mountain	22-909	ST
Strait, George	Lead On	1-262	CB
Strait, George	Lead On	6-806	MM
Strait, George	Lead On	3-416	SC
Strait, George	Let It Go	46-12	BKD
Strait, George	Let's Fall To Pieces Together	2-363	SC
Strait, George	Living & Living Well	25-183	MM
Strait, George	Living And Living Well	33-194	CB
Strait, George	Living And Living Well	16-428	ST
Strait, George	Living For The Night	37-58	CB
Strait, George	Love Bug	8-174	CB
Strait, George	Love Bug	6-506	MM
Strait, George	Love Without End Amen	1-258	CB
Strait, George	Love Without End Amen	11-705	DK
Strait, George	Love Without End Amen	4-61	SC
Strait, George	Love's Gonna Make It Alright	38-215	PHN
Strait, George	Make Her Fall In Love With Me Song	45-684	VH
Strait, George	Man In Love With You the	1-246	CB
Strait, George	Man In Love With You the	6-605	MM
Strait, George	Man In Love With You the	17-216	NA
Strait, George	Man In Love With You the	2-449	SC
Strait, George	Marina Del Rey	2-367	SC
Strait, George	Meanwhile	8-353	CB
Strait, George	Meanwhile	7-825	CHT
Strait, George	Meanwhile	22-724	ST
Strait, George	Merry Christmas Wherever You Are	45-765	CB
Strait, George	Nerve the	1-252	CB
Strait, George	Night Is Young the	42-7	PHN
Strait, George	Nobody In His Right Mind	5-316	SC
Strait, George	Nobody In His Right Mind...	34-268	CB
Strait, George	Ocean Front Property	8-165	CB
Strait, George	Ocean Front Property	9-472	SAV
Strait, George	Ocean Front Property	2-18	SC
Strait, George	Old Time Christmas	45-764	CB
Strait, George	One Night At A Time	14-650	CB
Strait, George	One Night At A Time	7-605	CHM
Strait, George	One Of You	38-147	CB

ARTIST	SONG TITLE	#	TYPE
Strait, George	Out Of The Blue Clear Sky	1-263	CB
Strait, George	Overnight Male	2-812	SC
Strait, George	Overnight Success	1-253	CB
Strait, George	Overnight Success	5-133	SC
Strait, George	Overnight Success	8-597	TT
Strait, George	Piece Of Mind	38-148	CB
Strait, George	Right Or Wrong	9-170	CB
Strait, George	River of Love	38-149	CB
Strait, George	Road Less Traveled the	38-150	CB
Strait, George	Round About Way	8-231	CB
Strait, George	Round About Way	7-721	CHM
Strait, George	Run	25-47	MM
Strait, George	Run	16-3	ST
Strait, George	Seashores Of Old Mexico	29-197	CB
Strait, George	Seashores Of Old Mexico	29-843	SC
Strait, George	She Let Herself Go	23-464	CB
Strait, George	She'll Leave You With A Smile	25-349	MM
Strait, George	She'll Leave You With A Smile	18-324	ST
Strait, George	So Much Like My Dad	6-185	MM
Strait, George	Somewhere Down In Texas	38-154	SC
Strait, George	Stars On The Water	18-208	ST
Strait, George	Stay Out Of My Arms	4-119	SC
Strait, George	Take Me Back To Tulsa	38-151	CB
Strait, George	Take Me To Texas	47-400	BKD
Strait, George	Tell Me Something Bad About Tulsa	25-609	MM
Strait, George	Tell Me Something Bad About Tulsa	19-45	ST
Strait, George	Tell Me Something Bad About Tulsa	32-228	THM
Strait, George	Texas	23-292	CB
Strait, George	That's What Breakin' Hearts Do	41-100	PHN
Strait, George	Thoughts Of A Fool	4-144	SC
Strait, George	Today My World Slipped Away	1-254	CB
Strait, George	Today My World Slipped Away	22-626	ST
Strait, George	Troubadour	36-593	CB
Strait, George	True	1-269	CB
Strait, George	True	22-807	ST
Strait, George	Twang	49-524	BKD
Strait, George	Unwound	38-152	SC
Strait, George	We Really Shouldn't Be Doin' This	8-494	CB
Strait, George	Wha't Going On In Your World	1-243	CB
Strait, George	What Do You Say To That	5-729	SC
Strait, George	What Do You Say To That	22-429	ST
Strait, George	What's Going On In Your World	14-688	CB

ARTIST	SONG TITLE	#	TYPE
Strait, George	What's Going On In Your World	5-121	SC
Strait, George	When Did You Stop Loving Me	8-172	CB
Strait, George	When Did You Stop Loving Me	24-248	SC
Strait, George	Where The Sidewalk Ends	45-363	DFK
Strait, George	Without Me Around	4-479	SC
Strait, George	Wrapped	30-352	CB
Strait, George	Write This Down	19-197	CB
Strait, George	Write This Down	7-884	CHT
Strait, George	Write This Down	22-738	ST
Strait, George	Xmas - Christmas Cookies	45-754	CB
Strait, George	Xmas - Merry Christmas Wherever You Are	45-765	CB
Strait, George	Xmas - Merry Xmas Strait To You	18-760	CB
Strait, George	Xmas - Old Time Christmas	45-764	CB
Strait, George	Xmas - There's A New Kid In Town	15-655	THM
Strait, George	Xmas - What A Merry Christmas This	18-748	CB
Strait, George	Xmas - When It's Xmas Time in Texas	18-751	CB
Strait, George	You Can't Make A Heart Love Some-..	1-261	CB
Strait, George	You Can't Make A Heart Love Some-..	17-274	NA
Strait, George	You Can't Make A Heart Love Some-.d	22-851	ST
Strait, George	You Haven't Left Me Yet	8-496	CB
Strait, George	You Know Me Better Than That	8-169	CB
Strait, George	You Know Me Better Than That	12-441	P
Strait, George	You Know Me Better Than That	2-702	SC
Strait, George	You Look So Good In Love	1-256	CB
Strait, George	You Look So Good In Love	6-759	MM
Strait, George	You Look So Good In Love	4-648	SC
Strait, George	You'll Be There	22-337	CB
Strait, George	You'll Be There	23-385	SC
Strait, George	You're Something Special To Me	4-647	SC
Stranglers	Uptown	11-675	DK
Strawberry Alarm	Incense & Peppermints	11-344	DK
Stray Cats	I Won't Stand In Your Way	48-166	KV
Stray Cats	Lonely Summer Nights	48-167	SS
Stray Cats	Rev It Up And Go	48-168	SS
Stray Cats	Rock This Town	13-4	P
Stray Cats	Rock This Town	5-142	SC
Stray Cats	Rock This Town	13-698	SGB
Stray Cats	Runaway Boys	48-165	EK

ARTIST	SONG TITLE	#	TYPE
Stray Cats	Sexy & 17	3-446	SC
Stray Cats	Stray Cat Strut	35-168	CB
Stray Cats	Stray Cat Strut	2-32	SC
Stray Cats	Stray Cat Strut	13-697	SGB
Street, Mel	Lovin' On Back Streets	29-655	SC
Streets	Never Went To Church	30-718	SF
Streets	When You Wasn't Famous **	30-693	SF
Streisand & Adams	Duet - I Finally Found Someone	20-120	PHM
Streisand & Adams	I Finally Found Someone	20-120	PHM
Streisand & Buble	Duet - It Had To Be You	49-544	CK
Streisand & Buble	It Had To Be You - duet	49-544	CK
Streisand & Crawford	Duet - Music Of The Night	49-573	PS
Streisand & Crawford	Music Of The Night - duet	49-573	PS
Streisand & Dion	Duet - Tell Him	7-693	PHM
Streisand & Dion	Duet - Tell Him	10-118	SC
Streisand & Dion	Tell Him	7-693	PHM
Streisand & Dion	Tell Him	10-118	SC
Streisand & Gibb	Duet - Guilty	15-485	MM
Streisand & Gibb	Duet - What Kind Of Fool	15-579	MM
Streisand & Gibb	Duet - What Kind Of Fool	49-608	PS
Streisand & Gibb	Guilty	15-485	MM
Streisand & Gibb	What Kind Of Fool	15-579	MM
Streisand & Gibb	What Kind Of Fool - duet	49-608	PS
Streisand & Gill	Duet - If You Ever Leave Me	15-288	PS
Streisand & Gill	Duet - If You Ever Leave Me	10-217	SC
Streisand & Gill	If You Ever Leave Me	15-288	PS
Streisand & Gill	If You Ever Leave Me	10-217	SC
Streisand & Johnson	Duet - Till I Loved You	49-539	CB
Streisand & Johnson	Till I Loved You - duet	49-539	CB
Streisand & Manilow	Duet - I Won't Be the One To Let Go	49-622	ST
Streisand & Manilow	I Won't Be The One To Let Go	49-622	ST
Streisand & Mathis	Duet - I Have A Love	49-540	MM
Streisand & Mathis	I Have A Love - duet	49-540	MM
Streisand, Barbra	All I Ask Of You	49-562	PRS
Streisand, Barbra	All Is Fair In Love	49-546	PS
Streisand, Barbra	As Time Goes By	49-561	MM
Streisand, Barbra	Before The Parade Passes	49-547	PS
Streisand, Barbra	Being Alive	49-569	PS
Streisand, Barbra	But Beautiful	49-605	PS
Streisand, Barbra	Calling You	49-611	PS
Streisand, Barbra	Chidren Will Listen	49-554	KKS
Streisand, Barbra	Christmas Lullaby	49-588	PS
Streisand, Barbra	Christmas Memories	49-589	PS
Streisand, Barbra	Circle	49-614	PS
Streisand, Barbra	Comin' In And Out Of Your Life	49-543	MM
Streisand, Barbra	Crazy He Calls Me	49-383	PS

ARTIST	SONG TITLE	#	TYPE
Streisand, Barbra	Cry Me A River	49-469	MM
Streisand, Barbra	Cry Me A River	49-215	MM
Streisand, Barbra	Don't Rain On My Parade	26-372	DK
Streisand, Barbra	Emily	49-603	PS
Streisand, Barbra	Evergreen	12-879	P
Streisand, Barbra	Everybody Says Don't	49-559	PS
Streisand, Barbra	Everything	47-847	FMG
Streisand, Barbra	For All We Know	24-18	SC
Streisand, Barbra	Free Again	49-576	PS
Streisand, Barbra	Free Again	49-209	MM
Streisand, Barbra	Gentle Rain	49-593	PS
Streisand, Barbra	Goodbye For Now	49-612	PS
Streisand, Barbra	Grown-Up Christmas List	49-591	PS
Streisand, Barbra	Happy Days Are Here Again	15-841	MM
Streisand, Barbra	He Touched Me	49-558	LG
Streisand, Barbra	Hello Dolly	49-572	PS
Streisand, Barbra	Here's That Rainy Day	49-597	PS
Streisand, Barbra	Here's To Life	49-598	PS
Streisand, Barbra	Higher Ground	5-280	SC
Streisand, Barbra	Higher Ground	49-616	PS
Streisand, Barbra	How Do You Keep the Music Playing	49-604	PS
Streisand, Barbra	I Believe	49-618	PS
Streisand, Barbra	I'll Be Home For Christmas	49-590	PS
Streisand, Barbra	I'm A Fool To Want You	49-382	PS
Streisand, Barbra	I'm In The Mood For Love	49-601	PS
Streisand, Barbra	I'm In The Mood For Love	45-521	SS
Streisand, Barbra	I've Dreamed Of You	15-285	PS
Streisand, Barbra	I've Got A Crush On You	49-579	PS
Streisand, Barbra	I've Got A Crush On You	49-381	PS
Streisand, Barbra	I've Never Been In Love Before	49-548	PS
Streisand, Barbra	If As We Never Said Goodbye	49-553	KKS
Streisand, Barbra	If I Could	49-617	PS
Streisand, Barbra	If You Ever Leave Me	49-555	KKS
Streisand, Barbra	In The Wee Small Hours Of The AM	49-592	PS
Streisand, Barbra	Island the	15-289	PS
Streisand, Barbra	It Must Have Been The Mistletoe	48-514	KVD
Streisand, Barbra	Just One Lifetime	15-291	PS
Streisand, Barbra	Kiss Me In The Rain	29-268	SC
Streisand, Barbra	Ladies Who Lunch the	49-577	PS
Streisand, Barbra	Leading With Your Heart	49-615	PS
Streisand, Barbra	Life Story	49-624	SF
Streisand, Barbra	Lost Inside Of You	49-549	PS
Streisand, Barbra	Love Like Ours	15-286	PS
Streisand, Barbra	Love Theme from A Star Is Born	49-625	TOS
Streisand, Barbra	Lover (When You're Near Me)	49-385	PS
Streisand, Barbra	Lover Man	49-380	PS

ARTIST	SONG TITLE	#	TYPE
Streisand, Barbra	Luck Be A Lady	49-563	PS
Streisand, Barbra	Main Event Fight the	49-550	PS
Streisand, Barbra	Make Someone Happy	49-594	PS
Streisand, Barbra	Man I Love a	15-527	MM
Streisand, Barbra	Moon River	49-609	PS
Streisand, Barbra	More In Love With You	49-610	PS
Streisand, Barbra	Music That Makes Me Dance	15-287	PS
Streisand, Barbra	My Funny Valentine	49-580	PS
Streisand, Barbra	My Heart Belongs To Me	10-497	DA
Streisand, Barbra	My Man	49-564	PS
Streisand, Barbra	My Man	49-448	MM
Streisand, Barbra	New York State Of Mind	46-280	KV
Streisand, Barbra	No Matter What Happens	49-578	PS
Streisand, Barbra	Not While I'm Around	49-565	PS
Streisand, Barbra	On A Clear Day You Can See Forever	48-783	MM
Streisand, Barbra	Ordinary Miracles	49-570	PS
Streisand, Barbra	Papa Can You Hear Me	9-49	MM
Streisand, Barbra	People	16-804	DK
Streisand, Barbra	People	45-52	AHM
Streisand, Barbra	Piece Of Sky	48-424	IDM
Streisand, Barbra	Piece Of Sky a	49-575	PS
Streisand, Barbra	Places That Belong To You	49-621	SC
Streisand, Barbra	Queen Bee	45-796	SBI
Streisand, Barbra	Sam, You Made the Pants Too Long	49-560	LG
Streisand, Barbra	Second Hand Rose	18-60	MM
Streisand, Barbra	Second Hand Rose	49-538	MM
Streisand, Barbra	Second Time Around the	49-606	PS
Streisand, Barbra	Send In The Clowns	49-567	PS
Streisand, Barbra	Send In The Clowns	49-552	FH
Streisand, Barbra	Show - Evergreen	16-736	DK
Streisand, Barbra	Silent Night	49-545	PS
Streisand, Barbra	Smoke Gets In Your Eyes	49-596	PS
Streisand, Barbra	Some Enchanted Evening	49-574	PS
Streisand, Barbra	Someone To Watch Over Me	49-620	SC
Streisand, Barbra	Somewhere	33-322	CB
Streisand, Barbra	Song Bird	49-541	MM
Streisand, Barbra	Speak Low	15-292	PS
Streisand, Barbra	Spring Can Really Hang You Up...	49-599	PS
Streisand, Barbra	Stoney End	11-735	DK
Streisand, Barbra	Stranger In A Strange Land	49-623	ST
Streisand, Barbra	Summer Knows the	12-887	P
Streisand, Barbra	Superman	45-867	VH
Streisand, Barbra	Tomorrow	49-571	PS
Streisand, Barbra	Way He Makes Me Feel the	17-786	PS
Streisand, Barbra	Way We Were the	18-124	DK
Streisand, Barbra	Way We Were the	6-354	MM
Streisand, Barbra	Way We Were the	12-512	P

ARTIST	SONG TITLE	#	TYPE
Streisand, Barbra	We Must Be Loving Right	15-290	PS
Streisand, Barbra	We're Not Makin' Love Anymore	6-441	MM
Streisand, Barbra	We've Only Just Begun	9-879	DK
Streisand, Barbra	What Are You Doing The Rest Of ...	15-848	MM
Streisand, Barbra	What Are You Doing The Rest Of...	12-575	P
Streisand, Barbra	What Did I Have That I Don't Have..	15-847	MM
Streisand, Barbra	What Kind Of Fool	49-556	KKS
Streisand, Barbra	Where Do You Start	49-595	PS
Streisand, Barbra	Where You Lead	49-551	PS
Streisand, Barbra	Wild Is The Wind	49-602	PS
Streisand, Barbra	With One Look	49-557	KKS
Streisand, Barbra	Woman In Love	28-286	DK
Streisand, Barbra	Woman In Love	18-72	MM
Streisand, Barbra	Woman In Love	8-612	TT
Streisand, Barbra	Xmas - Christmas Lullaby	49-588	PS
Streisand, Barbra	Xmas - Christmas Memories	49-589	PS
Streisand, Barbra	Xmas - Grown-Up Christmas List	49-591	PS
Streisand, Barbra	Xmas - I'll Be Home For Xmas	49-590	PS
Streisand, Barbra	Xmas - It Must Have Been The Mistletoe	48-514	KVD
Streisand, Barbra	Xmas - Silent Night	49-545	PS
Streisand, Barbra	You Go To My Head	49-384	PS
Streisand, Barbra	You Must Believe In Spring	49-600	PS
Streisand, Barbra	You'll Never Walk Alone	49-619	PS
Streisand, Barbra	You're Gonna Hear From Me	49-607	PS
Streisand, Barbra	You're The Top	49-542	MM
Streisand&Diamond	Duet - You Don't Bring Me Flowers	7-547	AH
Streisand&Diamond	Duet - You Don't Bring Me Flowers	18-51	MM
Streisand&Diamond	Duet - You Don't Bring Me Flowers	9-206	SO
Streisand&Diamond	You Don't Bring Me Flowers	7-547	AH
Streisand&Diamond	You Don't Bring Me Flowers	18-51	MM
Streisand&Diamond	You Don't Bring Me Flowers	9-206	SO
Streisand&Summer	Duet - No More Tears	10-546	SF
Streisand&Summer	Duet - No More Tears (Enough Is..)	26-95	DK
Streisand&Summer	Duet - No More Tears/Enough is Enou	13-155	P
Streisand&Summer	No More Tears - Enough Is Enough	26-95	DK
Streisand&Summer	No More Tears - Enough Is Enough	13-155	P
Streisand&Summer	No More Tears - Enough Is Enough	10-546	SF

ARTIST	SONG TITLE	#	TYPE
Stricklin, Luke	American By God's Amazing Grace	23-469	CB
Strokes	12:51	19-761	PHM
Strunk, Judd	Daisy A Day	49-252	DFK
Stryper	Halloween - To Hell With The Devil	16-294	TT
Stryper	Honestly	23-111	SC
Stuart, Marty	Burn Me Down	3-640	SC
Stuart, Marty	Hillbilly Rock	17-219	NA
Stuart, Marty	If I Ain't Got You	16-576	SC
Stuart, Marty	If There Ain't There Oughta Be	34-414	CB
Stuart, Marty	If There Ain't There Oughta Be	19-375	ST
Stuart, Marty	Kiss Me I'm Gone	6-499	MM
Stuart, Marty	Kiss Me I'm Gone	2-400	SC
Stuart, Marty	Likes Of Me the	2-698	SC
Stuart, Marty	Now That's Country	5-414	SC
Stuart, Marty	Red Red Wine & Cheatin' Songs	8-966	CB
Stuart, Marty	Red Red Wine & Cheatin' Songs	10-190	SC
Stuart, Marty	Tempted	9-538	SAV
Stuart, Marty	Thanks To You	4-430	SC
Stuart, Marty	Too Much Month at the End of/Money	19-706	ST
Stuart, Marty	You Can't Stop Love	7-401	MM
Stuart, Marty	You Can't Stop Love	24-658	SC
Stuart, Michael	Latino - Casi Perfecta	17-793	SC
Stuckey, Nat	Plastic Saddle	47-730	SRK
Studdard, Ruben	Flying Without Wings	34-150	CB
Studdard, Ruben	Flying Without Wings	25-635	MM
Studdard, Ruben	Flying Without Wings	32-317	THM
Studdard, Ruben	Sorry 2004	20-538	CB
Studdard, Ruben	Sorry 2004	36-327	PS
Studdard, Ruben	Superstar	36-326	PS
Studdard, Ruben	Superstar	19-543	SC
Studdard, Ruben	What If	36-328	CB
Studdard, Ruben	What If	36-328	PS
Stylistics	Betch By Golly Wow	9-830	SAV
Stylistics	Break Up To Make Up	49-455	MM
Stylistics	I'm Strong In Love With You	20-366	SC
Stylistics	You Are Everything	9-760	SAV
Stylistics	You Are Everything	24-332	SC
Stylistics	You Make Me Feel Brand New	11-213	DK
Stylistics	You Make Me Feel Brand New	7-480	MM
Stylistics	You Make Me Feel Brand New	9-757	SAV
Styx	Babe	11-192	DK
Styx	Best Of Times	47-379	LE
Styx	Blue Collar Man (Long Nights)	5-592	SC
Styx	Boat On The River	47-378	KV
Styx	Come Sail Away	16-600	MM
Styx	Come Sail Away	17-516	SC
Styx	Crystal Ball	47-381	SC

ARTIST	SONG TITLE	#	TYPE
Styx	Don't Let It End	47-384	SC
Styx	Don't Let It End	47-380	LE
Styx	Fooling Yourself	47-385	SC
Styx	Grand Illusion the	47-382	SC
Styx	Lady	35-125	CB
Styx	Lady	24-64	SC
Styx	Light Up	2-751	SC
Styx	Lorelei	47-383	SC
Styx	Miss America	5-63	SC
Styx	Mr. Roboto	38-47	SC
Styx	Renegade	4-559	SC
Styx	Show Me The Way	47-377	CB
Styx	Snowblind	47-386	SC
Styx	Suite Madam Blue	47-376	AH
Styx	Too Much Time On My Hands	20-88	SC
Sublime	Santeria	30-215	PHM
Sublime	Wrong Way	7-689	PHM
Sugababes	About You Now (Radio Vers)	49-888	SC
Sugababes	Follow Me Home	30-715	SF
Sugar Ray	Answer The Phone	33-386	CB
Sugar Ray	Answer The Phone	25-32	MM
Sugar Ray	Bartender (It's So Easy)	19-592	CB
Sugar Ray	Chasin' You Around	19-670	CB
Sugar Ray	Evert Morning	16-199	PHT
Sugar Ray	Falls Apart	9-337	PS
Sugar Ray	Falls Apart	5-890	SC
Sugar Ray	Fly	30-221	PHM
Sugar Ray	Is She Really Going Out With Him	25-662	MM
Sugar Ray	Mr. Bartender (It's So Easy)	25-662	MM
Sugar Ray	Mr/ Bartender (It's So Easy)	32-283	THM
Sugar Ray	When It's Over	35-259	CB
Sugarhill Gang	Rapper's Delight	15-805	SC
Sugarland	All I Want To Do	36-591	CB
Sugarland	Already Gone	36-223	PHM
Sugarland	Baby Girl	35-449	CB
Sugarland	Baby Girl	30-232	RS
Sugarland	Baby Girl	20-491	ST
Sugarland	Down In Mississippi	30-236	RS
Sugarland	Down In Mississippi	29-370	CB
Sugarland	Everyday America	30-457	CB
Sugarland	Fly Away	30-237	RS
Sugarland	Hello	30-233	RS
Sugarland	Just Might (Make Me Believe)	23-474	CB
Sugarland	Just Might (Make Me Believe)	29-856	SC
Sugarland	Just Might Make Me Believe	30-235	RS
Sugarland	Settlin'	30-197	CB
Sugarland	Small Town Jerico	30-239	RS
Sugarland	Something More	23-115	CB
Sugarland	Something More	30-231	RS
Sugarland	Something More	23-382	SC

ARTIST	SONG TITLE	#	TYPE
Sugarland	Speed Of Life	30-238	RS
Sugarland	Stand Back Up	23-480	CB
Sugarland	Stand Back Up	30-241	RS
Sugarland	Stay	30-452	CB
Sugarland	Tennessee	30-234	RS
Sugarland	Time Time Time	30-240	RS
Sugarland	Want To	30-44	CB
Sugarland	Want To	30-96	PHM
Sugarland/Little Big Town/Owen,J	Life In A Northern Town	36-398	CB
Sugarloaf	Green Eyed Lady	19-133	KC
Sugarloaf	Green Eyed Lady	9-366	MG
Sugarloaf	Green Eyed Lady	2-783	SC
Sugarloaf&Corbetta	Don't Call Us We'll Call You	5-586	SC
Suggs	Cecelia	25-381	MM
Sum 41	Fat Lip	16-383	SGB
Sum 41	Hell Song the	32-216	THM
Sum 41	Still Waiting	23-160	PHM
Summer, Donna	Any Way At All	14-882	SC
Summer, Donna	Bad Girls	11-209	DK
Summer, Donna	Bad Girls	4-529	SC
Summer, Donna	Could It Be Magic	15-204	LE
Summer, Donna	Dim All The Lights	17-58	DK
Summer, Donna	Dim All The Lights	15-207	LE
Summer, Donna	Hot Stuff	35-154	CB
Summer, Donna	Hot Stuff	16-781	DK
Summer, Donna	Hot Stuff	2-506	SC
Summer, Donna	I Don't Want To Get Hurt	15-200	LE
Summer, Donna	I Feel Love	15-203	LE
Summer, Donna	I Will Go With You	15-198	LE
Summer, Donna	Last Dance	17-41	DK
Summer, Donna	Last Dance	9-219	PT
Summer, Donna	Love To Love You Baby	15-201	LE
Summer, Donna	Love To Love You Baby	24-337	SC
Summer, Donna	MacArthur Park	35-148	CB
Summer, Donna	MacArthur Park	11-715	DK
Summer, Donna	MacArthur Park	13-134	P
Summer, Donna	MacArthur Park	4-850	SC
Summer, Donna	On The Radio	15-206	LE
Summer, Donna	On The Radio	16-153	SC
Summer, Donna	She Works Hard For The Money	11-524	DK
Summer, Donna	Spring Affair	15-205	LE
Summer, Donna	This Time I Know It's For Real	15-199	LE
Summer, Donna	Try Me I Know We Can Make It	15-202	LE
Summer, Donna	Unconditional Love	17-59	DK
Summer&New Row	New Money	14-94	CB
Sunset Blvd - Streisand	Show - With One Look	49-566	PS
Sunset Boulevard	Show - Too Much Love To Care	19-591	SC
Sunset Boulevard	Show - With One Look	10-380	KC
Sunset Boulevard	Show - With One Look	17-802	PS
Sunset Boulevard	Too Much In Love To Care	19-591	SC

ARTIST	SONG TITLE	#	TYPE
Superdrag	Sucked Out	24-228	SC
Supernaw, Doug	Honky Tonkin' Fool	4-471	SC
Supernaw, Doug	Long Tall Texan	4-501	SC
Supernaw, Doug	Not Enough Hours In The Night	7-141	MM
Supernaw, Doug	Not Enough Hours In The Night	3-569	SC
Supernaw, Doug	Reno	6-528	MM
Supernaw, Doug	She Never Looks Back	7-200	MM
Supernaw, Doug	She Never Looks Back	4-228	SC
Supernaw, Doug	State Fair	2-321	SC
Supernaw, Doug	What In The World	4-201	SC
Supernaw, Doug	What'll You Do About Me	6-718	MM
Supernaw, Doug	What'll You Do About Me	17-277	NA
Supernaw, Doug	What'll You Do About Me	22-863	ST
Supernaw, Doug	You Still Got Me	4-97	SC
Supernaw/Beach Boys	Duet - Long Tall Texan	24-411	SC
Supernaw/Beach Boys	Long Tall Texan	7-385	MM
Supernaw/Beach Boys	Long Tall Texan	24-411	SC
Supertramp	Breakfast In America	5-587	SC
Supertramp	Breakfast In America	30-754	SF
Supertramp	Give A Little Bit	6-492	MM
Supertramp	Give A Little Bit	12-790	P
Supertramp	Give A Little Bit	29-269	SC
Supertramp	Take The Long Way Home	17-515	SC
Supremes	Baby Love	11-119	DK
Supremes	Baby Love	9-311	STR
Supremes	Back In My Arms Again	17-358	DK
Supremes	Come See About Me	14-889	DK
Supremes	Come See About Me	12-630	P
Supremes	Come See About Me	4-13	SC
Supremes	Happening the	14-885	DK
Supremes	I Hear A Symphony	14-888	DK
Supremes	I Hear a Symphony	4-43	SC
Supremes	Love Child	11-755	DK
Supremes	Love Child	5-10	SC
Supremes	Love Is Here And Now You're Gone	14-887	DK
Supremes	My World Is Empty Without You Babe	12-102	DK
Supremes	Someday We'll Be Together	14-886	DK
Supremes	Stop In The Name Of Love	29-842	SC
Supremes	Stop! In The Name Of Love	11-173	DK
Supremes	Stop! In The Name Of Love	12-631	P
Supremes	Stop! In The Name Of Love	9-23	PS
Supremes	Up The Ladder To The Roof	17-340	DK

ARTIST	SONG TITLE	#	TYPE
Supremes	Where Did Our Love Go	16-727	DK
Supremes	Where Did Our Love Go	19-616	MH
Supremes	Where Did Our Love Go	12-629	P
Supremes	Where Did Our Love Go	4-31	SC
Supremes	You Can't Hurry Love	16-794	DK
Supremes	You Can't Hurry Love	4-719	SC
Supremes	You Keep Me Hangin' On	11-178	DK
Supremes	You Keep Me Hanging On	35-89	CB
Supremes&Temptat	Duet - I'm Gonna Make You Love Me	9-765	SAV
Supremes&Temptation	I'm Gonna Make You Love Me	9-765	SAV
Surface	First Time the	2-270	SC
Surface	Shower Me With Your Love	34-100	CB
Surface	Shower Me With Your Love	9-683	SAV
Survivor	Eye Of The Tiger	20-365	SC
Survivor	I Can't Hold Back	24-688	SC
Survivor	Search Is Over the	16-155	SC
Sutherland, Christy	Freedom	22-74	CB
Swan, Billy	Bop To Be	47-539	VH
Swan, Billy	Everything's The Same	47-540	VH
Swan, Billy	I Can Help	17-415	DK
Swan, Billy	I Can Help	9-596	SAV
Swan, Billy	Lover Please	47-538	VH
Swayze, Patrick	She's Like The Wind	6-449	MM
Sweat & Cage	Duet - Nobody	20-128	PHM
Sweat & Cage	Duet - Nobody	24-372	SC
Sweat & Cage	Nobody	20-128	PHM
Sweat & Cage	Nobody	24-372	SC
Sweeney, Sunny	Drink Myself Single	45-271	DCK
Sweet	Ballroom Blitz	12-347	DK
Sweet	Blockbuster	48-761	P
Sweet	Halloween - Hell Raiser	45-116	SF
Sweet	Hell Raiser - Halloween	45-116	SF
Sweet	Little Willy	15-804	SC
Sweet	Wig Wam Bam	49-56	ZVS
Sweet Charity	Hey Big Spender	15-492	MM
Sweet Charity	Show - If My Friends Could See Me..	6-244	MM
Sweethearts/Rodeo	Chains Of Gold	19-425	SC
Sweethearts/Rodeo	Midnight Girl In A Sunset Town	6-778	MM
Sweethearts/Rodeo	Midnight Girl In A Sunset Town	5-241	SC
Sweetnam, S.	Billy S.	32-282	THM
Sweetwater Rain	StarShine	39-59	PHN
Swift, Taylor	All You Had To Do Was Stay	48-301	KV
Swift, Taylor	Bad Blood	48-298	KV
Swift, Taylor	Begin Again	44-326	SSC
Swift, Taylor	Best Day the	43-173	CB
Swift, Taylor	Blank Space	48-308	MRH
Swift, Taylor	Breathe	43-169	ASK
Swift, Taylor	Change	43-174	CB

ARTIST	SONG TITLE	#	TYPE
Swift, Taylor	Clean	48-300	KV
Swift, Taylor	Cold As You Say	36-83	BM
Swift, Taylor	Eyes Open	39-45	ASK
Swift, Taylor	Fearless	38-131	CB
Swift, Taylor	Fifteen	37-28	CB
Swift, Taylor	Forever And Always	43-172	ASK
Swift, Taylor	I Heart Question Mark	44-141	BKD
Swift, Taylor	I Knew You Were Trouble	42-33	ASK
Swift, Taylor	I Know Places	48-299	KV
Swift, Taylor	I'm Only Me When I'm With You	36-423	CB
Swift, Taylor	Invisible	36-91	BM
Swift, Taylor	Jump Then Fall	37-324	CB
Swift, Taylor	Love Story	36-5	PT
Swift, Taylor	Mary's Song (Oh My My My)	36-88	BM
Swift, Taylor	Mean	37-210	AS
Swift, Taylor	Mine	38-280	CB
Swift, Taylor	New Tomantics	48-306	KV
Swift, Taylor	Our Song	30-548	CB
Swift, Taylor	Ours	44-271	KV
Swift, Taylor	Out Of The Woods	48-428	MRH
Swift, Taylor	Outside the	36-84	BM
Swift, Taylor	Perfectly Good Heart	36-92	BM
Swift, Taylor	Picture To Burn	36-390	CB
Swift, Taylor	Place In This World a	36-82	BM
Swift, Taylor	Red	43-148	ASK
Swift, Taylor	Shake It Off	48-307	KV
Swift, Taylor	Should've Said No	36-596	CB
Swift, Taylor	Sparks Fly	38-206	AS
Swift, Taylor	Stay Beautiful	36-86	BM
Swift, Taylor	Story Of Us	37-357	CB
Swift, Taylor	Style	48-304	KV
Swift, Taylor	Sweeter Than Fiction	42-23	ASK
Swift, Taylor	Sweeter Than Fiction	44-310	SBI
Swift, Taylor	Teardrops On My Guitar	30-312	CB
Swift, Taylor	Tell Me Why	43-170	ASK
Swift, Taylor	This Love	48-305	KV
Swift, Taylor	Tied Together With a Smile	36-85	BM
Swift, Taylor	Tim McGraw	30-23	CB
Swift, Taylor	Today Was A Fairytale	36-53	PT
Swift, Taylor	Umbrella (So Ho Mix)	48-608	DK
Swift, Taylor	Untouchable	37-334	CB
Swift, Taylor	Way I Love You the	43-171	ASK
Swift, Taylor	We Are Never Ever Getting Back...	39-24	ASK
Swift, Taylor	White Christmas	45-791	KV
Swift, Taylor	White Horse	43-175	CB
Swift, Taylor	Wildest Dreams	48-309	MRH
Swift, Taylor	Wonderland	48-302	KV
Swift, Taylor	Xmas - White Christmas	45-791	KV
Swift, Taylor	You Are In Love	48-303	KV
Swift, Taylor	You Belong With Me	37-213	AS
Swift, Taylor	You Belong With Me	36-21	PT
Swift, Taylor	You're Not Sorry	36-382	SC

ARTIST	SONG TITLE	#	TYPE
Swindell, Cole	Ain't Worth The Whiskey	44-287	KCD
Swindell, Cole	Chillin' It	40-58	ASK
Swindell, Cole	Hope You Get Lonely	44-268	PHN
Swindell, Cole	Hope You Get Lonely Tonight	45-393	KCDC
Swindell, Cole	Let Me See Ya Girl	45-378	BKD
Swindell, Cole	Should've Ran After You	45-394	DCK
Swindell, Cole	Should've Ran After You (Inst)	49-760	BKD
Swindell, Cole	You Should Be Here	48-742	BKD
Swindell, Cole	You Should Be Here	46-97	DCK
Swindell, Cole	You Should Be Here (Inst)	49-416	BKD
Swing Out Sister	Break Out	20-83	SC
Swingin' Medallions	Double Shot Of My Baby's Love	13-268	P
Swinging Blue Jeans	Hippy Hippy Shake	5-179	SC
Switchfoot	Meant To Live	19-854	PHM
Swon Brothers	Danny's Song	44-212	DCK
Swon Brothers	Later On	44-200	BKD
SWV	Anything	12-250	DK
SWV	Can We	10-91	SC
SWV	Duet - You're Always On My Mind	12-249	DK
SWV	I'm So Into You	34-126	CB
SWV	I'm So Into You	6-418	MM
SWV	I'm So Into You	13-22	P
SWV	Let's Talk About Sex **	12-251	DK
SWV	Use Your Heart	24-169	SC
SWV	You're Always On My Mind	12-249	DK
Sylvers	Boogie Fever	27-577	DK
Sylvers	Boogie Fever	2-494	SC
Sylvers	Hot Line	11-383	DK
Sylvers	Hot Line	2-495	SC
Sylvester	You Make Me Feel Mighty Real	15-701	LE
Sylvia	Drifter	20-23	SC
Sylvia	Falling In Love	45-925	SC
Sylvia	Nobody	11-724	DK
Sylvia	Nobody	13-437	P
Sylvia	Pillow Talk	2-847	SC
Sylvia	Snapshot	5-776	SC
Sylvia	Tumbleweed	14-431	SC
Sylvia	Y Viva Espana	16-370	SF
Syms, Sylvia	I Could Have Danced All Night	12-556	P
Syndicate of Sound	Hey Little Girl	10-492	DA
Syndicate of Sound	Hey Little Girl	10-649	SF
System of a Down	Innervision	23-159	PHM
T-Pain & Akon	Bartender (Radio Vers)	37-109	SC
T. Rex	Bang A Gong (Get It On)	13-229	P
T.A.T.U.	All The Things She Said	25-541	MM
T.A.T.U.	All The Things She Said	18-608	PHM
T.A.T.U.	All The Things She Said	23-340	SC
T.A.T.U.	Not Gonna Get Us	32-244	THM
T.I.	Rubber Band Man **	23-251	THM
Taco	Puttin' On The Ritz	4-842	SC

ARTIST	SONG TITLE	#	TYPE
Taff, Russ	Bein' Happy	6-847	MM
Taff, Russ	Long Hard Road	20-655	SC
Taff, Russ	One And Only Love	2-699	SC
Tag Team	Whoomp! There It Is	12-133	DK
Tah, Geggy	Whoever You Are	24-370	SC
Take 6	Gospel - Soemthing Within Me	13-114	P
Take That	Back For Good	28-445	DK
Talent, Billy	Try Honesty	23-182	PHM
Talking Heads	And She Was	12-788	P
Talking Heads	Burning Down The House	11-623	DK
Talking Heads	Burning Down The House	12-787	P
Talking Heads	Burning Down The House	29-260	SC
Talking Heads	Life During Wartime	21-412	SC
Talking Heads	Take Me To The River	12-795	P
Talking Heads	Wild Wild Life	14-572	AH
Tamia	Officially Missing You	32-345	THM
Tamia	Questions	20-569	CB
Tamia	Stranger In My House	12-388	PHM
Tamia	There's A Stranger In My House	18-538	TT
Tams	What Kind Of Fool Do You Think I Am	6-787	MM
Tank	Please Don't Go	30-491	CB
Taproot	Poem	32-68	THM
Taste Of Honey	Boogie Oogie Oogie	17-130	DK
Taste Of Honey	Boogie Oogie Oogie	15-42	SS
Taste Of Honey	Sukiyaki	13-290	P
Tavares	Heaven Must Be Missing An Angel	24-338	SC
Tavares	It Only Takes A Minute	27-359	DK
Taylor & Simon	Duet - Mochingbird	46-120	SC
Taylor & Simon	Duet - Mockingbird	13-44	P
Taylor & Simon	Mochingbird - duet	46-120	SC
Taylor & Simon	Mockingbird	13-44	P
Taylor, Ben	I Will	14-880	SC
Taylor, Dean	There's A Ghost In My House	30-792	SF
Taylor, James	Carolina In My Mind	10-66	SC
Taylor, James	Copperline	45-544	SC
Taylor, James	Country Road	11-272	DK
Taylor, James	Don't Let Me Be Lonely Tonight	33-289	CB
Taylor, James	Don't Let Me Be Lonely Tonight	10-72	SC
Taylor, James	Everyday	45-535	OZP
Taylor, James	Fire & Rain	11-236	DK
Taylor, James	Fire & Rain	6-423	MM
Taylor, James	Fire & Rain	10-69	SC
Taylor, James	Handy Man	11-345	DK
Taylor, James	Handy Man	6-431	MM
Taylor, James	Her Town Too	45-537	RSZ
Taylor, James	How Sweet It is To Be Loved By You	9-882	DK
Taylor, James	How Sweet It Is To Be Loved By You	6-434	MM

ARTIST	SONG TITLE	#	TYPE
Taylor, James	How Sweet It Is To Be Loved By You	12-635	P
Taylor, James	Little More time With You	10-65	SC
Taylor, James	Long Ago And Far Away	45-540	CB
Taylor, James	Mexico	17-525	SC
Taylor, James	Never Die Young	45-543	SC
Taylor, James	Riding On A Railroad	45-536	OZP
Taylor, James	Shed A Little Light	45-539	CB
Taylor, James	Shower The People	10-71	SC
Taylor, James	Something In The Way She Moves	45-541	RSZ
Taylor, James	Steamroller (Live)	14-600	SC
Taylor, James	Steamroller Blues	11-278	DK
Taylor, James	Steamroller Blues	10-68	SC
Taylor, James	Sweet Baby James	2-560	SC
Taylor, James	That Lonesome Road	45-522	SC
Taylor, James	Traffic Jam (Live)	45-523	SC
Taylor, James	Up On The Roof	45-538	RSZ
Taylor, James	Walking Man	45-542	RSZ
Taylor, James	You Can Close Your Eyes	49-2	DCK
Taylor, James	You've Got A Friend	11-86	DK
Taylor, James	You've Got A Friend	10-67	SC
Taylor, James	Your Smiling Face	6-427	MM
Taylor, James	Your Smiling Face	10-70	SC
Taylor, Johnnie	Cheaper To Keep Her	24-344	SC
Taylor, Johnnie	Disco Lady	17-138	DK
Taylor, Johnnie	Who's Making Love	12-158	DK
Taylor, Johnnie	Who's Making Love	26-234	DK
Taylor, Johnnie	Who's Making Love	15-13	SC
Taylor, Koko	Wang Dang Doodle	15-310	SC
Taylor, R. Dean	There's A Ghost In My House	30-792	SF
Taylor, Rachel	Light A Fire	48-402	DCK
Tears For Fears	Break It Down Again	16-630	MM
Tears For Fears	Everybody Wants To Rule The World	20-292	CB
Tears For Fears	Everybody Wants To Rule The World	13-253	P
Tears For Fears	Everybody Wants To Rule The World	5-150	SC
Tears For Fears	Head Over Heels	29-10	MH
Tears For Fears	Shout	26-348	DK
Tebey	We Shook Hands (Man To Man)	25-448	MM
Tebey	We Shook Hands (Man to Man)	18-600	ST
Tebey	We Shook Hands (Man to Man)	32-158	THM
Technotronic	Pump Up The Jam	14-642	SC
Teddy Bears	To Know Him Is To Love Him	19-622	MH
Teddy Bears	To Know Him Is To Love Him	22-446	SC
Tedeschi, Susan	Black Velvet	17-457	AMS
Tedeschi, Susan	Evidence	29-216	PHM
Tedeschi, Susan	Give Me One Reason	17-458	AMS
Tedeschi, Susan	It Hurts So Bad	17-451	AMS

ARTIST	SONG TITLE	#	TYPE
Tedeschi, Susan	It Hurts So Bad	23-345	MM
Tedeschi, Susan	It Hurts So Bad	15-18	SC
Tedeschi, Susan	Move Over	17-454	AMS
Tedeschi, Susan	Piece Of My Heart	17-455	AMS
Tedeschi, Susan	Rock Me Right	17-453	AMS
Tedeschi, Susan	Rock Me Right	15-25	SC
Tedeschi, Susan	Runaway	17-456	AMS
Tedeschi, Susan	You Need To Be With Me	17-452	AMS
Tee Set	Ma Belle Amie	16-666	LC
Temperance Seven	You're Driving Me Crazy	10-654	SF
Temple, Shirley	On The Good Ship Lollipop	12-547	P
Temptations	Ain't Too Proud To Beg	16-839	DK
Temptations	Ain't Too Proud To Beg	4-691	SC
Temptations	All I Need	14-897	DK
Temptations	Ball Of Confusion	11-775	DK
Temptations	Beauty Is Only Skin Deep	12-84	DK
Temptations	Cloud Nine	12-83	DK
Temptations	Don't Look Back	49-859	DCK
Temptations	Get Ready	4-42	SC
Temptations	I Can't Get Next To You	17-128	DK
Temptations	I Know I'm Losing You	26-515	DK
Temptations	I Wish It Would Rain	14-896	DK
Temptations	Lady Soul	49-249	DFK
Temptations	My Girl	17-127	DK
Temptations	My Girl	12-625	P
Temptations	My Girl	9-659	SAV
Temptations	My Girl	2-89	SC
Temptations	Papa Was A Rollin' Stone	7-101	MM
Temptations	Papa Was A Rolling Stone	35-112	CB
Temptations	Papa Was A Rolling Stone	11-269	DK
Temptations	Psychedelic Shack	34-34	CB
Temptations	Psychedelic Shack	17-395	DK
Temptations	Runaway Child Running Wild	11-756	DK
Temptations	Since I Lost My Baby	14-894	DK
Temptations	Treat Her Like A Lady	15-699	LE
Temptations	War	11-380	DK
Temptations	Way You Do The Things You Do	11-175	DK
Tenacious D	F### Her Gently **	37-91	SC
Tenacious D	Tribute **	37-90	SC
Tennison, Chalee	Go Back	14-168	CB
Tennison, Chalee	Go Back	22-468	ST
Tennison, Chalee	Handful Of Water	5-727	SC
Tennison, Chalee	Lonesome Road	18-458	ST
Tennison, Chalee	Makin' Up With You	14-112	CB
Tennison, Chalee	Someone Else's Turn To Cry	8-477	CB
Tennison, Chalee	Someone Else's Turn To Cry	14-617	SC
Tennison, Chalee	What I Tell Myself	14-912	CB
Terry Baxter Orch.	You're Gonna Lose That	16-783	DK

ARTIST	SONG TITLE	#	TYPE
	Girl		
Tesh & Dalia	Mother I Miss You	14-280	MM
Tesh & Ingram	Show - Give Me Forever I Do	17-654	PR
Tesh, John	Give Me Forever I Do	10-18	SC
Tesla	What You Give	6-21	SC
Tex, Joe	Sweet Woman Like You	17-317	SS
Texas Lightning	Highway To Hell	49-922	KVD
Texas Tornados	Hey Baby Que Paso	44-78	KV
Texas Tornados	Little Bit Is Better Than Nada a	10-693	HH
Texas Tornados	Little Bit Is Better Than Nada a	44-79	KV
Texas Tornados	She Never Spoke Spanish To Me	49-750	KV
Thalia	Baby I'm In Love	19-655	CB
Thalia & Fat Joe	Duet - I Want You	25-719	MM
Thalia & Fat Joe	Duet - I Want You	32-349	THM
Thalia & Fat Joe	I Want You	25-719	MM
Thalia & Fat Joe	I Want You - Duet	32-349	THM
Thalia feat Fat Joe	I Want You	19-603	CB
The Wiz	Believe In Yourself	49-434	SDK
The Wiz	Brand New Day	49-433	SDK
The Wiz	Don't Nobody Bring Me No Bad News	49-438	SDK
The Wiz	Ease On Down The Road	49-435	SDK
The Wiz	He's The Wizard	49-436	SDK
The Wiz	Home	49-432	SDK
The Wiz	I'm A Mean Ol' Lion	49-437	SDK
The Wiz	Show - Believe In Yourself	49-434	SDK
The Wiz	Show - Brand New Day	49-433	SDK
The Wiz	Show - Don't Nobody Bring Me No Bad..	49-438	SDK
The Wiz	Show - Ease On Down The Road	49-435	SDK
The Wiz	Show - He's The Wizard	49-436	SDK
The Wiz	Show - Home	49-432	SDK
The Wiz	Show - I'm A Mean Ol' Lion	49-437	SDK
The Wiz	Show - Y'All Got It	49-439	SDK
The Wiz	Y'All Got It	49-439	SDK
Them	Baby Please Don't Go	10-640	SF
Them	Here Comes The Night	10-574	SF
Theory of/Deadman	Make Up Your Mind	23-168	PHM
They Might B Giants	Istanbul Not Constantinople	6-859	MM
They Might B Giants	Istanbul Not Constantinople	15-135	SC
They Might B Giants	Particle Man	5-641	SC
Thicke, Robin	Magic	36-520	CB
Thin Lizzie	Jailbreak	5-875	SC
Third Day	Come Together	34-420	CB
Third Day	You Are So Good To Me	34-422	CB
Third Eye Blind	10 Days Late	14-490	SC
Third Eye Blind	Blinded (When I See You)	25-630	MM
Third Eye Blind	Blinded (When I See	32-285	THM

ARTIST	SONG TITLE	#	TYPE
	You)		
Third Eye Blind	Deep Inside of You	33-421	CB
Third Eye Blind	Deep Inside Of You	14-498	SC
Third Eye Blind	How's It Going To Be	35-210	CB
Third Eye Blind	How's It Going To Be	7-707	PHM
Third Eye Blind	How's It Going To Be	5-187	SC
Third Eye Blind	Jumper	33-370	CB
Third Eye Blind	Jumper	13-681	SGB
Third Eye Blind	Never Let You Go	15-323	PHM
Third Eye Blind	Semi Charmed Life	30-213	PHM
Thom, Sandi	I Wish I Was A Punk Rocker	30-709	SF
Thomas & Springfield	As Long As We Got Each Other - duet	47-599	SAV
Thomas & Springfield	Duet - As Long As We Got Each Other	47-599	SAV
Thomas, B.J.	Another Somebody Done Somebody	13-430	P
Thomas, B.J.	Another Somebody Done Somebody	36-153	LE
Thomas, B.J.	Another Somebody Done Somebody..	11-669	DK
Thomas, B.J.	Another Somebody Done Somebody…	5-23	SC
Thomas, B.J.	Everybody Loves A Rain Song	9-570	SAV
Thomas, B.J.	Everybody Loves a Rain Song	38-44	GMG
Thomas, B.J.	Eyes Of A New York Woman	5-211	SC
Thomas, B.J.	Eyes Of A New York Woman the	36-155	LE
Thomas, B.J.	Hooked On A Feeling	11-255	DK
Thomas, B.J.	Hooked On A Feeling	13-174	P
Thomas, B.J.	Hooked On A Feeling	35-106	CB
Thomas, B.J.	Hooked On A Feeling	36-157	LE
Thomas, B.J.	I Just Can't Help Believing	36-152	LE
Thomas, B.J.	I'm So Lonesome I Could Cry	47-388	MM
Thomas, B.J.	Jingle Bells - xmas	46-96	CB
Thomas, B.J.	Let It Snow	45-737	CB
Thomas, B.J.	Mama	36-154	LE
Thomas, B.J.	Mighty Clouds Of Joy	21-518	SC
Thomas, B.J.	New Looks From An Old Lover	9-511	SAV
Thomas, B.J.	New Looks From An Old Lover	5-248	SC
Thomas, B.J.	New Looks From An Old Lover	47-387	SC
Thomas, B.J.	Raindrops Keep Fallin' On My Head	16-852	DK
Thomas, B.J.	Raindrops Keep Fallin' On My Head	12-686	P
Thomas, B.J.	Raindrops Keep Fallin' On My Head	36-151	LE
Thomas, B.J.	Rock & Roll Lullaby	21-807	SC
Thomas, B.J.	Rock And Roll Lullaby	36-156	LE
Thomas, B.J.	Two Car Garage	20-673	SC
Thomas, B.J.	Whatever Happened to	44-323	DFK

ARTIST	SONG TITLE	#	TYPE
	Old Fashioned Love		
Thomas, B.J.	Xmas - Jingle Bells	46-96	CB
Thomas, B.J.	Xmas - Let It Snow	45-737	CB
Thomas, Carl	I Wish (Radio Version)	14-504	SC
Thomas, Carl	Summer Rain	14-20	THM
Thomas, Carla	B-A-B-Y	7-70	MM
Thomas, Carla	B-A-B-Y	12-715	P
Thomas, Carla	Gee Whiz	35-38	CB
Thomas, Carla	Gee Whiz Look At His Eyes	12-902	P
Thomas, Keni	Gloryland	23-488	CB
Thomas, Rhett	It Goes Like This	43-14	ASK
Thomas, Rob	Ever The Same	47-609	CB
Thomas, Rob	Her Diamonds	36-296	PHM
Thomas, Rob	Little Wonders	47-613	THM
Thomas, Rob	Lonely No More	47-607	SC
Thomas, Rob	Someday	47-610	CB
Thomas, Rob	Streetcorner Symphony	47-608	SC
Thomas, Rob	This Is How A Heart Breaks	23-314	CB
Thomas, Rufus	Do The Dog	47-611	RB
Thomas, Rufus	Walking The Dog	17-134	DK
Thomas, Rufus	Willy Nilly	47-612	RB
Thomas&Springfield	As Long As We Got Each Other	9-828	SAV
Thomas&Springfield	Duet - As Long As We Got Each Other	9-828	SAV
Thompson Square	Are You Gonna Kiss Me Or Not	37-199	AS
Thompson Square	Duet - I Got You	37-228	CB
Thompson Square	Everything I Shouldn't Be Thinkin' About	47-35	BKD
Thompson Square	Glass	38-277	AS
Thompson Square	I Got You - duet	37-228	CB
Thompson Square	Let's Fight	47-389	PHN
Thompson Twins	Hold Me Now	2-846	SC
Thompson, Cyndi	I Always Liked That Best	33-160	CB
Thompson, Cyndi	I Always Liked That Best	25-50	MM
Thompson, Cyndi	I Always Liked That Best	16-2	ST
Thompson, Cyndi	I'm Gone	25-228	MM
Thompson, Cyndi	I'm Gone	15-856	ST
Thompson, Cyndi	If You Could Only See	18-452	ST
Thompson, Cyndi	What I Really Meant To Say	33-172	CB
Thompson, Cyndi	What I Really Meant To Say	15-105	ST
Thompson, Gina	Things That You Do the	24-52	SC
Thompson, Hank	Answer Me My Love	48-578	DK
Thompson, Hank	Blackboard Of My Heart	19-327	CB
Thompson, Hank	Honky Tonk Girl	19-330	CB
Thompson, Hank	Humpty Dumpty Heart	19-321	CB
Thompson, Hank	I've Come Awful Close	19-328	CB
Thompson, Hank	New Green Light the	19-323	CB
Thompson, Hank	Oklahoma Hills	45-727	VH
Thompson, Hank	Older The Violin, Sweeter the Music	19-333	CB
Thompson, Hank	On Tap In The Can Or In The Bottle	19-331	CB

ARTIST	SONG TITLE	#	TYPE
Thompson, Hank	Rub A Dub Dub	19-326	CB
Thompson, Hank	Rub A Dub Dub	5-370	SC
Thompson, Hank	Six Pack To Go	19-329	CB
Thompson, Hank	Smoky The Bar	19-332	CB
Thompson, Hank	Smoky The Bar	5-854	SC
Thompson, Hank	Squaws Along The Yukon	19-324	CB
Thompson, Hank	Waiting In The Lobby Of Your Heart	19-325	CB
Thompson, Hank	Wake Up Irene	19-322	CB
Thompson, Hank	Who Left The Door To Heaven Open	21-637	CB
Thompson, Hank	Wild Side Of Life the	19-320	CB
Thompson, Hank	Wild Side Of Life the	9-607	SAV
Thompson, Hank	Yesterday's Girl	45-726	VH
Thompson, Josh	Beer On The Table	36-316	PHM
Thompson, Josh	Cold Beer With Your Name On It	41-96	PHN
Thompson, Josh	Comin' Around	45-563	BKD
Thompson, Josh	Down For A Get Down	45-281	BKD
Thompson, Josh	Wanted Me Gone	45-564	BKD
Thompson, Josh	Way Out Here	45-562	CB
Thompson, Josh	Won't Be Lonely Long	38-107	CB
Thompson, Sue	How I Love Them Old Songs	49-393	VH
Thompson, Sue	Norman - (Lots of backup)	49-302	LRT
Thompson, Sue	Norman (Inst)	49-392	KV
Thompson, Sue	Sad Movies	5-82	SC
Thornton, Marsha	Bottle Of Wine And Patsy Cline	45-508	CB
Thorogood, George	Bad To The Bone	20-146	KB
Thorogood, George	Bad To The Bone	15-171	MH
Thorogood, George	Bad To The Bone	21-563	MM
Thorogood, George	I Drink Alone	43-9	CB
Thorogood, George	I Drink Alone	20-320	MH
Thorogood, George	If You Don't Start Drinkin' I'm...	5-743	SC
Thorogood, George	Move It On Over	20-80	SC
Thorogood, George	One Bourbon One Scotch One Beer	2-566	SC
Thorogood, George	Rock & Roll Christmas	45-763	CB
Thorogood, George	Who Do You Love	46-208	SC
Thorogood, George	Woman With The Blues	48-406	DFK
Thorogood, George	Xmas - Rock & Roll Christmas	45-763	CB
Thousand Horses	Smoke	45-27	BKD
Thousand Horses	Smoke (Inst)	49-665	BKD
Thrasher Shiver	Goin' Goin' Gone	4-426	SC
Three Days Grace	I Hate Everything About You	20-575	CB
Three Days Grace	I Hate Everything About You	35-287	CB
Three Days Grace	I Hate Everything About You	23-176	PHM
Three Days Grace	Riot	36-484	CB
Three Degrees	When Will I See You Again	35-117	CB
Three Degrees	When Will I See You Again	12-104	DK

ARTIST	SONG TITLE	#	TYPE
	Again		
Three Degrees	When Will I See You Again	24-345	SC
Three Dog Night	An Old Fashioned Love Song	11-636	DK
Three Dog Night	An Old Fashioned Love Song	13-302	P
Three Dog Night	Black & White	24-328	SC
Three Dog Night	Celebrate	35-91	CB
Three Dog Night	Celebrate	5-597	SC
Three Dog Night	Easy To Be Hard	34-28	CB
Three Dog Night	Joy To the World	11-686	DK
Three Dog Night	Just An Old Fashioned Love Song	34-54	CB
Three Dog Night	Liar	29-635	SC
Three Dog Night	Mama Told Me Not To Come	11-542	DK
Three Dog Night	Mama Told Me Not To Come	15-173	MH
Three Dog Night	Mama Told Me Not To Come	29-284	SC
Three Dog Night	Never Been To Spain	2-435	SC
Three Dog Night	One	33-268	CB
Three Dog Night	One	11-595	DK
Three Dog Night	One	13-301	P
Three Dog Night	Pieces Of April	4-329	SC
Three Dog Night	Shambala	4-49	SC
Three Hanks	Move It On Over	4-626	SC
Thrice	All That's Left	23-187	PHM
Thrills	Big Sur	21-606	SF
Thunder	Boys Like Girls	36-531	CB
TI	Whatever You Like	36-6	PT
Tiffany	Could've Been	12-4	DK
Tiffany	Could've Been	4-296	SC
Tiffany	I Saw Him Standing There	28-388	DK
Til Tuesday	Voices Carry	4-875	SC
Tillis & Bryce	Don't Let Go	9-593	SAV
Tillis & Bryce	Duet - Don't Let Go	9-593	SAV
Tillis & Bryce	Duet - Take My Hand	5-448	SC
Tillis & Bryce	Take My Hand	5-448	SC
Tillis, Mel	Charlie's Angel	48-101	FMK
Tillis, Mel	Coca Cola Cowboy	19-465	CB
Tillis, Mel	Coca Cola Cowboy	5-37	SC
Tillis, Mel	Good Woman Blues	19-458	CB
Tillis, Mel	Heart Healer	19-459	CB
Tillis, Mel	Heart Over Mind	19-452	CB
Tillis, Mel	I Ain't Never	19-451	CB
Tillis, Mel	I Ain't Never	4-642	SC
Tillis, Mel	I Believe In You	3-862	CB
Tillis, Mel	I Believe In You	5-753	SC
Tillis, Mel	I Got The Hoss	19-460	CB
Tillis, Mel	Looking For Tomorrow	45-844	VH
Tillis, Mel	Memory Maker	3-865	CB
Tillis, Mel	Midnight Me & The Blues	14-428	SC
Tillis, Mel	New Patches	19-464	CB
Tillis, Mel	Sawmill	19-453	CB

ARTIST	SONG TITLE	#	TYPE
Tillis, Mel	Sawmill	5-814	SC
Tillis, Mel	Send Me Down To Tucson	19-461	CB
Tillis, Mel	Southern Rains	19-463	CB
Tillis, Mel	Southern Rains	13-521	P
Tillis, Mel	Stomp Them Grapes	19-456	CB
Tillis, Mel	Who's Julie	45-730	VH
Tillis, Mel	Your Body Is An Outlaw	19-462	CB
Tillis, Pam	After A Kiss	14-697	CB
Tillis, Pam	After A Kiss	5-730	SC
Tillis, Pam	After A Kiss	22-508	ST
Tillis, Pam	All The Good Ones Are Gone	1-461	CB
Tillis, Pam	All The Good Ones Are Gone	7-621	CHM
Tillis, Pam	Betty's Got A Bass Boat	1-462	CB
Tillis, Pam	Betty's Got A Bass Boat	4-504	SC
Tillis, Pam	Blue Rose the	1-454	CB
Tillis, Pam	Cleopatra Queen Of Denial	1-457	CB
Tillis, Pam	Cleopatra Queen Of Denial	26-574	DK
Tillis, Pam	Cleopatra Queen of Denial	2-30	SC
Tillis, Pam	Deep Down	7-139	MM
Tillis, Pam	Deep Down	3-565	SC
Tillis, Pam	Do You Know Where Your Man Is	6-393	MM
Tillis, Pam	Don't Tell Me What To Do	1-451	CB
Tillis, Pam	Don't Tell Me What To Do	10-782	JVC
Tillis, Pam	Don't Tell Me What To Do	2-105	SC
Tillis, Pam	Every Time	8-191	CB
Tillis, Pam	How Gone Is Goodbye	17-166	JVC
Tillis, Pam	I Said A Prayer	22-798	ST
Tillis, Pam	I Said A Prayer For You	1-464	CB
Tillis, Pam	I Was Blown Away	2-661	SC
Tillis, Pam	I Was Blown Away	22-868	ST
Tillis, Pam	In Between Dances	1-459	CB
Tillis, Pam	In Between Dances	6-797	MM
Tillis, Pam	In Between Dances	2-831	SC
Tillis, Pam	It's Lonely Out There	22-901	ST
Tillis, Pam	Land Of The Living	1-465	CB
Tillis, Pam	Land Of The Living	22-632	ST
Tillis, Pam	Let That Pony Run	1-456	CB
Tillis, Pam	Let That Pony Run	19-299	MH
Tillis, Pam	Let That Pony Run	12-422	P
Tillis, Pam	Maybe It Was Memphis	1-453	CB
Tillis, Pam	Maybe It Was Memphis	11-806	DK
Tillis, Pam	Maybe It Was Memphis	6-188	MM
Tillis, Pam	Maybe It Was Memphis	13-399	P
Tillis, Pam	Maybe It Was Memphis	4-62	SC
Tillis, Pam	Mi Vida Loca	1-458	CB
Tillis, Pam	Mi Vida Loca	17-258	NA
Tillis, Pam	Mi Vida Loca	2-551	SC
Tillis, Pam	One Of Those Things	1-452	CB

ARTIST	SONG TITLE	#	TYPE
Tillis, Pam	Please	22-590	ST
Tillis, Pam	River And The Highway the	1-460	CB
Tillis, Pam	River And The Highway the	4-159	SC
Tillis, Pam	Shake The Sugar Tree	1-455	CB
Tillis, Pam	Shake The Sugar Tree	10-763	JVC
Tillis, Pam	Shake The Sugar Tree	12-423	P
Tillis, Pam	Shake The Sugar Tree	2-792	SC
Tillis, Pam	Spilled Perfume	2-211	SC
Tillis, Pam	Train Without A Whistle	47-795	SRK
Tillis, Pam	We've Tried Everything	6-507	MM
Tillis, Pam	When You Walk In The Room	26-573	DK
Tillis, Pam	When You Walk In The Room	6-606	MM
Tillis, Pam	When You Walk In The Room	17-225	NA
Tillis, Pam	When You Walk In The Room	2-454	SC
Tillotson, Johnny	It Keeps Right On A Hurtin'	7-259	MM
Tillotson, Johnny	Judy Judy Judy	49-285	CAK
Tillotson, Johnny	Little Sparrow	47-738	SRK
Tillotson, Johnny	Poetry In Motion	11-116	DK
Tillotson, Johnny	Poetry In Motion	4-3	SC
Tillotson, Johnny	Princess Princess	46-592	DCK
Tillotson, Johnny	Without You	20-32	SC
Tillotson, Johnny	You're The Reason	49-286	CAK
Timbaland & Hilson	Way I Are the - duet	37-152	SC
Timbaland & Keri Hilson	Duet - Way I Are the	37-152	SC
Timbaland feat One Republic	Apologize	36-453	CB
Timbaland feat One Republic	Apologize	30-589	PHM
Timberlake, Justin	Cry Me A River	25-423	MM
Timberlake, Justin	Cry Me A River	18-605	PHM
Timberlake, Justin	I'm Lovin' It	19-666	CB
Timberlake, Justin	Like I Love You	25-345	MM
Timberlake, Justin	Rock Your Body	20-513	CB
Timberlake, Justin	Rock Your Body	25-579	MM
Timberlake, Justin	Rock Your Body	19-336	STP
Timberlake, Justin	Rock Your Body	32-205	THM
Timberlake, Justin	Senorita	32-355	THM
Timberlake, Justin	Still On My Brain	19-656	CB
Timberlake, Justin	Still On My Brain	32-384	THM
Time	Jungle Love	16-61	SC
Ting Tings	Shut Up And Let Me Go	47-586	MRH
Tiny Tim	Tiptoe Through The Tulips With Me	9-839	SAV
Tiny Tim	Tiptoe Through The Tulips With Me	5-645	SC
Tippin & Tippin	Duet - Love Like There's No Tomorro	25-450	MM
Tippin & Tippin	Love Like There's No Tomorrow	25-450	MM
Tippin, Aaron	Always Was	15-611	ST
Tippin, Aaron	Call Of The Wild the	2-703	SC

ARTIST	SONG TITLE	#	TYPE
Tippin, Aaron	Come Friday	23-293	CB
Tippin, Aaron	Everything I Own	4-366	SC
Tippin, Aaron	Everything I Own	22-900	ST
Tippin, Aaron	For You I Will	22-693	ST
Tippin, Aaron	He Believed	30-202	CB
Tippin, Aaron	Her	22-437	ST
Tippin, Aaron	How's The Radio Know	7-389	MM
Tippin, Aaron	How's The Radio Know	4-594	SC
Tippin, Aaron	I Got It Honest	2-714	SC
Tippin, Aaron	I'll Take Love Over Money	25-229	MM
Tippin, Aaron	I'll Take Love Over Money	16-711	ST
Tippin, Aaron	I'm Leaving	8-375	CB
Tippin, Aaron	I'm Leaving	7-858	CHT
Tippin, Aaron	I'm Leaving	22-736	ST
Tippin, Aaron	If Her Lovin' Don't Kill Me	18-133	ST
Tippin, Aaron	If Her Loving Don't Kill Me	34-346	CB
Tippin, Aaron	Kiss This	14-69	CB
Tippin, Aaron	Kiss This	19-243	CSZ
Tippin, Aaron	Love Like There's No Tomorrow	18-792	ST
Tippin, Aaron	My Blue Angel	2-519	SC
Tippin, Aaron	Patriotic - Where the Stars & Stripes	33-158	CB
Tippin, Aaron	People Like Us	22-587	ST
Tippin, Aaron	People Like Us	15-217	THM
Tippin, Aaron	Ready To Rock	30-81	CB
Tippin, Aaron	She Feels Like A Brand New Love	2-664	SC
Tippin, Aaron	That's As Close As I'll Get	7-82	MM
Tippin, Aaron	That's As Close As I'll Get	3-539	SC
Tippin, Aaron	That's What Happens When I Hold U	7-428	MM
Tippin, Aaron	There Ain't Nothin' Wrong W/Radio	6-201	MM
Tippin, Aaron	There Ain't Nothin' Wrong W/Radio	2-24	SC
Tippin, Aaron	What This Country Needs	5-826	SC
Tippin, Aaron	What This Country Needs	22-519	ST
Tippin, Aaron	Where The Stars&Stripes&Eagle Flys	20-580	CB
Tippin, Aaron	Where The Stars&Stripes&Eagle Flys	25-46	MM
Tippin, Aaron	Where The Stars&Stripes&Eagle Flys	16-7	ST
Tippin, Aaron	Without Your Love	4-99	SC
Tippin, Aaron	Working Man's PHD	20-405	MH
Tippin, Aaron	Working Man's PHD	17-233	NA
Tippin, Aaron	You've Got To Stand For Something	20-576	CB

ARTIST	SONG TITLE	#	TYPE
Tippin, Aaron	You've Got To Stand For Something	8-599	TT
Titanic	Show - My Heart Will Go On	18-177	DK
TLC	Ain't 2 Proud 2 Beg	34-115	CB
TLC	Baby Baby Baby	33-342	CB
TLC	Baby Baby Baby	12-747	P
TLC	Come On Down	15-425	CB
TLC	Creep	16-624	MM
TLC	Damaged	25-580	MM
TLC	Damaged	19-345	STP
TLC	Damaged	32-233	THM
TLC	Dear Lie	15-423	CB
TLC	Diggin' On You	15-422	CB
TLC	Girl Talk	32-92	THM
TLC	Girl Talk **	25-468	MM
TLC	Hands Up	32-161	THM
TLC	No Scrubs	7-842	PHM
TLC	No Scrubs	28-222	SF
TLC	No Scrubs	13-704	SGB
TLC	Red Light Special	16-629	MM
TLC	Switch	15-424	CB
TLC	Unpretty	8-295	PHT
TLC	Waterfalls	14-904	SC
TLC	What About Your Friends	35-204	CB
Toad&Wet Sprocket	All I Want	13-240	P
Toad&Wet Sprocket	Good Intentions	15-482	THM
Tokens	Lion Sleeps Tonight the	12-129	DK
Tokens	Lion Sleeps Tonight the	3-327	MH
Tokens	Lion Sleeps Tonight the	6-657	MM
Tokens	Lion Sleeps Tonight the	13-58	P
Tokens	Tonight I Fell In Love	25-547	MM
Toliver, Tony	Bettin' Forever On You	24-152	SC
Toliver, Tony	He's On The Way Home	4-629	SC
Tomlinson, Trent	Drunker Than Me	29-22	CB
Tomlinson, Trent	Drunker Than Me	29-505	SC
Tomlinson, Trent	Drunker Than Me	23-462	ST
Tomlinson, Trent	Henry Cartrights Prayer & Produce	37-54	CB
Tomlinson, Trent	Just Might Have Her Radio On	30-364	CB
Tomlinson, Trent	One Wing In The Fire	30-26	CB
Tomlinson, Trent	One Wing In The Fire	30-103	PHM
Tone-Loc	Funky Cold Medina	33-438	CB
Tone-Loc	Funky Cold Medina	12-110	DK
Tone-Loc	Funky Cold Medina	16-542	P
Tone-Loc	Funky Cold Medina	2-183	SC
Tone-Loc	Wild Thing the	12-154	DK
Tonic	If You Could Only See	10-112	SC
Tonic	Open Up Your Eyes	5-284	SC
Tonic	You Wanted More	8-508	PHT
Tonight Da Buzz	Let Me Love You	21-727	TT
Tony Rich Project	Nobody Knows	4-168	SC
Tony! Toni! Tone!	Anniversary	2-232	SC
Tony! Toni! Tone!	Leavin'	15-757	NU
Tool	Schism	16-378	SGB

ARTIST	SONG TITLE	#	TYPE
Top Gun	Show - Take My Breath Away	6-873	MM
Top Gun	Show - Take My Breath Away	13-193	P
Top Loader	Breathe	16-312	TT
Torme, Mel	Again	4-184	SC
Torme, Mel	Blue Moon	9-737	SAV
Torme, Mel	Sweet Georgia Brown	9-802	SAV
Total	Do you Think About Us	4-615	SC
Total	Kissin' You	4-341	SC
Toto	Africa	7-91	MM
Toto	Africa	14-636	SC
Toto	I Won't Hold You Back	20-99	SC
Toto	Rosanna	16-523	P
Townsend, Ed	For Your Love	6-262	MM
Townsend, Ed	For Your Love	9-739	SAV
Townsend, Pete	Let My Love Open The Door	20-79	SC
Toy Dolls	Nellie The Elephant	16-374	SF
Toya	I Do	35-232	CB
Toys	Lover's Concerto a	11-563	DK
Tractors	Baby Likes To Rock It	30-107	CB
Tractors	Baby Likes To Rock It	17-255	NA
Tractors	Baby Likes To Rock It	2-450	SC
Tractors	Badly Bent	2-766	SC
Tractors	Can't Get Nowhere	17-480	CB
Tractors	I Wouldn't Tell You No Lies	8-948	CB
Tractors	I Wouldn't Tell You No Lies	14-627	SC
Tractors	Poor Boy Shuffle	45-859	VH
Tractors	Shortenin' Bread	8-399	CB
Tractors	Shortenin' Bread	10-157	SC
Tractors	Xmas - Santa Claus Boogie	3-392	SC
Traffic	Lowspark Of High Heeled Boys	13-654	SGB
Trailer Trash	Daddy's Drinking Up Our Xmas	46-286	CB
Trailor Choir	Off The Hillbilly Hook	36-201	PHM
Trailor Choir	Off The Hillbilly Hook	49-17	KV
Trailor Choir	Rockin' The Beer Gut	37-62	CB
Trailor Choir	Rockin' The Beer Gut	45-369	BKD
Trailor Choir	What Would You Say	37-44	CB
Trailor Choir	Xmas - Daddy's Drinking Up Our Xmas	46-286	CB
Train	50 Ways To Say Goodbye	48-266	KV
Train	Angel In Blue Jeans	48-267	KV
Train	Better Off Alive	48-263	KV
Train	Bruises	48-265	KV
Train	Cab	29-278	PHM
Train	Cadillac Cadillac	48-269	ZPC
Train	Calling All Angels	19-596	CB
Train	Calling All Angels	25-622	MM
Train	Calling All Angels	32-281	THM
Train	Drive By	48-261	FTX
Train	Drive By	46-191	BHK

ARTIST	SONG TITLE	#	TYPE
Train	Drops Of Jupiter	15-810	CB
Train	Drops Of Jupiter	16-477	MH
Train	Drops Of Jupiter	21-609	SF
Train	Drops Of Jupiter	16-388	SGB
Train	Drops Of Jupiter	15-303	THM
Train	Drops Of Jupiter	18-554	TT
Train	Following Rita	48-262	KV
Train	Free	48-270	SC
Train	Get To Me	37-315	THM
Train	Give Myself To You	48-268	THM
Train	Hey Soul Sister	37-316	PHM
Train	I Am	37-317	SC
Train	I Am	15-790	THM
Train	If It's Love	37-318	PHM
Train	Lincoln Avenue	48-264	KV
Train	Marry Me	37-261	PHM
Train	Meet Virginia	35-211	CB
Train	Meet Virginia	10-184	SC
Train	Ordinary	23-559	MM
Train	Respect	37-319	PHM
TRain	Save Me San Francisco	38-200	PHM
Train	Shake Up Christmas	45-774	KV
Train	She's On Fire	18-290	CB
Train	She's On Fire	25-200	MM
Train	She's On Fire	37-320	PHM
Train	Something More	25-41	MM
Train	Something More	37-321	SC
Train	When I Look To The Sky	19-662	CB
Train	When I Look To The Sky	37-322	SC
Train	Xmas - Shake Up Christmas	45-774	KV
Trainor & Legend	Duet - Like I'm Gonna Lose You	45-144	BH
Trainor & Legend	Like I'm Gonna Lose You - duet]	45-144	BH
Trainor, Meghan	03:00:00 AM	45-145	DCK
Trainor, Meghan	All About That Bass	45-1	ASK
Trainor, Meghan	Bang Them Sticks	45-146	KCD
Trainor, Meghan	Better When I'm Dancing	46-11	BKD
Trainor, Meghan	Close Your Eyes	45-55	BKD
Trainor, Meghan	Credit	45-150	KVD
Trainor, Meghan	Dear Future Husband	45-142	ASK
Trainor, Meghan	Good To Be Alive	48-449	KCD
Trainor, Meghan	I'll Be Home	48-513	KVD
Trainor, Meghan	Lips Are Moving	45-138	BKD
Trainor, Meghan	My Selfish Heart	45-151	KVD
Trainor, Meghan	NO	49-659	BKD
Trainor, Meghan	No Good For You	45-152	KVD
Trainor, Meghan	Title	45-149	KJ
Trainor, Meghan	What If I	45-644	KV
Trainor, Meghan	What If I Wanna Kiss You Tomorrow	45-147	KCD
Trammps	Disco Inferno	9-226	PT
Trammps	Disco Inferno	20-368	SC
Transmatic	Come	25-86	MM
Transplants	Diamonds And Guns	23-169	PHM

ARTIST	SONG TITLE	#	TYPE
Trapt	Headstrong	19-598	CB
Trapt	Still Frame	23-179	PHM
Travares	More Than A Woman	13-323	P
Traveling Wilburys	Handle With Care	30-764	SF
Travers, Pat	Boom Boom	3-614	SC
Travers, Pat	Snortin' Whiskey	40-32	KV
Travis	Why Does It Always Rain On Me	15-789	THM
Travis & Jones	Few Old Country Boys a	9-483	SAV
Travis, Merle	Divorce Me C.O.D.	19-623	CB
Travis, Merle	I Am A Pilgrim	45-692	CB
Travis, Merle	So Round So Firm So Fully Packed	19-633	CB
Travis, Randy	1982	1-391	CB
Travis, Randy	1982	8-699	SAV
Travis, Randy	America Will Always Stand	20-577	CB
Travis, Randy	Angels	23-124	CB
Travis, Randy	Angels	29-510	SC
Travis, Randy	Angels	29-609	ST
Travis, Randy	Are We In Trouble Now	7-334	MM
Travis, Randy	Are We in Trouble Now	4-392	SC
Travis, Randy	Before You Kill Us All	6-496	MM
Travis, Randy	Before You Kill Us All	2-209	SC
Travis, Randy	Better Class Of Losers	17-148	DK
Travis, Randy	Better Class Of Losers	6-204	MM
Travis, Randy	Box the	4-64	SC
Travis, Randy	Box the	22-855	ST
Travis, Randy	Card Carrying Fool	47-767	SRK
Travis, Randy	Cowboy Boogie	6-760	MM
Travis, Randy	Deeper Than The Holler	1-401	CB
Travis, Randy	Deeper Than The Holler	13-328	P
Travis, Randy	Diggin' Up Bones	1-393	CB
Travis, Randy	Diggin' Up Bones	11-437	DK
Travis, Randy	Diggin' Up Bones	8-700	SAV
Travis, Randy	Forever And Ever Amen	1-395	CB
Travis, Randy	Forever And Ever Amen	12-105	DK
Travis, Randy	Forever And Ever Amen	13-361	P
Travis, Randy	Forever Together	2-396	SC
Travis, Randy	Hard Rock Bottom Of My Heart	1-404	CB
Travis, Randy	Hard Rock Bottom Of My Heart	12-437	P
Travis, Randy	Hard Rock Bottom Of My Heart	26-549	DK
Travis, Randy	He Walked On Water	1-405	CB
Travis, Randy	He Walked On Water	20-397	MH
Travis, Randy	He Walked On Water	2-362	SC
Travis, Randy	Heroes And Friends	20-588	CB
Travis, Randy	Heroes And Friends	3-646	SC
Travis, Randy	Hole the	8-728	CB
Travis, Randy	Hole the	22-803	ST
Travis, Randy	Honky Tonk Moon	1-400	CB
Travis, Randy	I Told You So	1-399	CB
Travis, Randy	I Told You So	35-398	CB
Travis, Randy	I Told You So	11-424	DK
Travis, Randy	I Told You So	5-123	SC
Travis, Randy	I Won't Need You	1-396	CB

ARTIST	SONG TITLE	#	TYPE
Travis, Randy	I Won't Need You Anymore	9-520	SAV
Travis, Randy	I Won't Need You Anymore	5-661	SC
Travis, Randy	I'd Surrender All	2-419	SC
Travis, Randy	I'll Be Right Here Lovin' You	14-99	CB
Travis, Randy	Is It Still Over	14-684	CB
Travis, Randy	Is It Still Over	3-371	SC
Travis, Randy	It's Just A Matter Of Time	1-403	CB
Travis, Randy	Little Left Of Center	14-710	CB
Travis, Randy	Little Left Of Center a	22-554	ST
Travis, Randy	Look Heart No Hands	10-759	JVC
Travis, Randy	Man Ain't Made Of Stone a	5-735	SC
Travis, Randy	Man Ain't Made Of Stone a	22-510	ST
Travis, Randy	My Heart Cracked	47-791	SRK
Travis, Randy	No Place Like Home	1-394	CB
Travis, Randy	Old 8 X 10	1-397	CB
Travis, Randy	On The Other Hand	1-392	CB
Travis, Randy	On The Other Hand	17-408	DK
Travis, Randy	Out Of My Bones	22-785	ST
Travis, Randy	Out Of My Bones	49-378	CB
Travis, Randy	Patriotic - America Will Always Stand	34-383	CB
Travis, Randy	Point Of Light	9-533	SAV
Travis, Randy	Pray For The Fish	19-367	ST
Travis, Randy	Promises	20-651	SC
Travis, Randy	Spirit Of A Boy Wisdom Of A Man	22-674	ST
Travis, Randy	Stranger In My Mirror	8-929	CB
Travis, Randy	Stranger In My Mirror	7-888	CHT
Travis, Randy	Stranger In My Mirror	22-729	ST
Travis, Randy	This Is Me	6-666	MM
Travis, Randy	Three Wooden Crosses	34-378	CB
Travis, Randy	Three Wooden Crosses	25-525	MM
Travis, Randy	Three Wooden Crosses	18-594	ST
Travis, Randy	Three Wooden Crosses	32-223	THM
Travis, Randy	Too Gone Too Long	1-398	CB
Travis, Randy	Too Gone Too Long	9-498	SAV
Travis, Randy	Too Gone Too Long	3-380	SC
Travis, Randy	Whisper My Name	20-409	MH
Travis, Randy	Whisper My Name	6-598	MM
Travis, Randy	Whisper My Name	17-236	NA
Travis, Randy	Whisper My Name	2-323	SC
Travis, Randy	White Christmas Makes Me Blue	45-790	CB
Travis, Randy	Would I	4-507	SC
Travis, Randy	Xmas - Christmas Song the	30-394	SC
Travis, Randy	Xmas - How Do I Wrap My Heart Up	8-62	CB
Travis, Randy	Xmas - Jingle Bell Rock	22-845	ST
Travis, Randy	Xmas - Meet Me Under the Mistletoe	15-651	THM
Travis, Randy	Xmas - Oh What A Silent	15-659	THM

ARTIST	SONG TITLE	#	TYPE
	Night		
TRavis, Randy	Xmas - White Christmas Makes Me Blue	45-790	CB
Travis, Randy	Xmas - White Xmas Makes Me Blue	15-663	THM
Travolta & Newton-John	Duet - Grease Megamix (Rad Vers)	20-118	PHM
Travolta & Newton-John	Duet - Summer Nights	12-95	DK
Travolta & Newton-John	Duet - Summer Nights	13-142	P
Travolta & Newton-John	Duet - Summer Nights	9-277	SC
Travolta & Newton-John	Duet - Summer Nights	10-531	SF
Travolta & Newton-John	Duet - You're The One That I Want	11-172	DK
Travolta & Newton-John	Duet - You're The One That I Want	6-339	MM
Travolta & Newton-John	Duet - You're The One That I Want	9-280	SC
Travolta & Newton-John	Grease Megamix (Radio Version)	20-118	PHM
Travolta & Newton-John	Summer Nights	12-95	DK
Travolta & Newton-John	Summer Nights	13-142	P
Travolta & Newton-John	Summer Nights	9-277	SC
Travolta & Newton-John	Summer Nights	10-531	SF
Travolta & Newton-John	We Go Together	6-869	MM
Travolta & Newton-John	We To Together	10-12	SC
Travolta & Newton-John	You're The One That I Want	11-172	DK
Travolta & Newton-John	You're The One That I Want	6-339	MM
Travolta & Newton-John	You're The One That I Want	9-280	SC
Travolta, John	Greased Lightning	9-274	SC
Travolta, John	Sandy	10-13	SC
Tre	Take Your Time	10-688	HH
Tremeloes	Number One (Call Me)	10-638	SF
Tremeloes	Silence Is Golden	10-592	SF
Tresvant, Ralph	Sensitivity	28-404	DK
Trevino, Rick	Bobbie Ann Mason	3-415	SC
Trevino, Rick	Honky Tonk Crowd	16-593	MM
Trevino, Rick	I Only Get This Way With You	7-629	CHM
Trevino, Rick	I Only Get This Way With You	10-80	SC
Trevino, Rick	In My Dreams	19-374	ST
Trevino, Rick	Learning As You Go	7-331	MM
Trevino, Rick	Learning As You Go	4-369	SC
Trevino, Rick	Learning As You Go	22-904	ST
Trevino, Rick	Looking For The Light	2-655	SC
Trevino, Rick	Looking For The Light	22-873	ST
Trevino, Rick	Only Lonely Me	8-154	CB

ARTIST	SONG TITLE	#	TYPE
Trevino, Rick	Running Out Of Reasons To Run	4-593	SC
Trevino, Rick	Save This One For Me	7-85	MM
Trevino, Rick	See Rock City	8-128	CB
Trevino, Rick	See Rock City	22-638	ST
Trevino, Rick	Separate Ways	30-320	CB
Trevino, Rick	She Can't Say I Didn't Cry	6-611	MM
Trevino, Rick	She Can't Say I Didn't Cry	3-44	SC
Trick Pony	Ain't Wastin' Good Whiskey On You	23-468	CB
Trick Pony	Ain't Wastin' Good Whiskey On You	29-850	SC
Trick Pony	Boy Like You a	34-401	CB
Trick Pony	Boy Like You a	25-573	MM
Trick Pony	Boy Like You a	18-798	ST
Trick Pony	Boy Like You a	32-230	THM
Trick Pony	Bride the	30-803	PHM
Trick Pony	Bride the	20-472	ST
Trick Pony	It's A Heartache	22-317	CB
Trick Pony	Just What I Do	34-397	CB
Trick Pony	Just What I Do	25-128	MM
Trick Pony	Just What I Do	16-101	ST
Trick Pony	On A Mission	33-181	CB
Trick Pony	On A Mission	25-359	MM
Trick Pony	On A Mission	18-206	ST
Trick Pony	On A Night Like This	34-347	CB
Trick Pony	On A Night Like This	15-190	ST
Trick Pony	Pour Me	14-153	CB
Trick Pony	Pour Me	22-593	ST
Trick Pony	Pour Me	16-274	TT
Triggs, Trini	Horse To Mexico	8-933	CB
Triggs, Trini	Straight Tequila	8-179	CB
Triggs, Trini	Wreckin' Crew	14-733	CB
Triggs, Trini	Wreckin' Crew	6-65	SC
Tritt & Mellencamp	What Say You	20-510	ST
Tritt & Stuart	Duet - Whiskey Ain't Workin' Anymor	2-410	SC
Tritt & Stuart	Whiskey Ain't Workin' Anymore	12-442	P
Tritt & Stuart	Whiskey Ain't Workin' Anymore	2-410	SC
Tritt & White	Duet - Helping Me Get Over You	7-670	CHM
Tritt & White	Duet - Helping Me Get Over You	4-840	SC
Tritt & White	Helping Me Get Over You	7-670	CHM
Tritt & White	Helping Me Get Over You	4-840	SC
Tritt, Travis	Anymore	1-661	CB
Tritt, Travis	Best Of Intentions	14-92	CB
Tritt, Travis	Best Of Intentions	13-862	CHM
Tritt, Travis	Best Of Intentions	19-212	CSZ
Tritt, Travis	Best Of Intentions	22-567	ST
Tritt, Travis	Between An Old Memory & Me	22-854	ST
Tritt, Travis	Between An Old	2-537	SC

ARTIST	SONG TITLE	#	TYPE
	Memory & Me		
Tritt, Travis	Bible Belt	24-88	SC
Tritt, Travis	Can I Trust You With My Heart	1-662	CB
Tritt, Travis	Can I Trust You With My Heart	17-386	DK
Tritt, Travis	Can I Trust You With My Heart	6-222	MM
Tritt, Travis	Country Ain't Country	25-523	MM
Tritt, Travis	Country Ain't Country	18-788	ST
Tritt, Travis	Country Ain't Country	32-156	THM
Tritt, Travis	Country Club	1-663	CB
Tritt, Travis	Drift Off To Dream	1-664	CB
Tritt, Travis	Foolish Pride	6-592	MM
Tritt, Travis	Foolish Pride	2-217	SC
Tritt, Travis	Girl's Gone Wild	35-436	CB
Tritt, Travis	Girl's Gone Wild	20-341	ST
Tritt, Travis	Help Me Hold On	1-666	CB
Tritt, Travis	Help Me Hold On	11-717	DK
Tritt, Travis	Here's A Quarter Call Someone Who	1-667	CB
Tritt, Travis	Here's A Quarter Call Someone Who	26-288	DK
Tritt, Travis	Here's A Quarter Call Someone Who	6-184	MM
Tritt, Travis	Here's A Quarter Call Someone Who	13-380	P
Tritt, Travis	Here's A Quarter Call Someone Who	9-488	SAV
Tritt, Travis	I See Me	22-22	CB
Tritt, Travis	I'm Gonna Be Somebody	1-665	CB
Tritt, Travis	If I Lost You	8-177	CB
Tritt, Travis	It's A Great Day To Be Alive	22-585	ST
Tritt, Travis	Lonesome On'Ry Mean	19-270	ST
Tritt, Travis	Lord Have Mercy On The Workin Man	1-669	CB
Tritt, Travis	Lord Have Mercy On The Workin Man	10-755	JVC
Tritt, Travis	Lord Have Mercy On The Workin Man	2-1	SC
Tritt, Travis	Love Of A Woman	15-185	ST
Tritt, Travis	Modern Day Bonnie & Clyde	33-176	CB
Tritt, Travis	Modern Day Bonnie & Clyde	25-126	MM
Tritt, Travis	Modern Day Bonnie & Clyde	16-99	ST
Tritt, Travis	More Than You'll Ever Know	1-670	CB
Tritt, Travis	More Than You'll Ever Know	7-317	MM
Tritt, Travis	More Than You'll Ever Know	4-899	SC
Tritt, Travis	No More Looking Over My Shoulder	8-354	CB
Tritt, Travis	No More Looking Over My Shoulder	22-719	ST
Tritt, Travis	Nothing Short Of Dying	1-672	CB

ARTIST	SONG TITLE	#	TYPE
Tritt, Travis	Nothing Short Of Dying	17-369	DK
Tritt, Travis	Nothing Short Of Dying	6-197	MM
Tritt, Travis	Only You And You Alone	4-157	SC
Tritt, Travis	Put Some Drive In Your Country	1-673	CB
Tritt, Travis	Put Some Drive In Your Country	34-286	CB
Tritt, Travis	She's Going Home With Me	7-610	CHM
Tritt, Travis	Something Stronger Than Me	30-582	CB
Tritt, Travis	Start The Car	14-613	SC
Tritt, Travis	Still In Love With You	8-144	CB
Tritt, Travis	Still In Love With You	22-420	ST
Tritt, Travis	Strong Enough To Be Your Man	34-392	CB
Tritt, Travis	Strong Enough To Be Your Man	18-129	ST
Tritt, Travis	Tell Me I Was Dreaming	2-732	SC
Tritt, Travis	Ten Feet Tall & Bulletproof	1-674	CB
Tritt, Travis	Trouble	1-675	CB
Tritt, Travis	Trouble	6-538	MM
Tritt, Travis	Trouble	13-526	P
Tritt, Travis	Trouble	2-102	SC
Tritt, Travis	What Say You	22-63	CB
Tritt, Travis	What's In It For Me	6-668	MM
Tritt, Travis	Where Corn Don't Grow	7-584	CHM
Tritt, Travis	Where Corn Don't Grow	7-399	MM
Tritt, Travis	Where Corn Don't Grow	24-659	SC
Tritt, Travis	Whiskey Ain't Workin' Anymore	7-413	MM
Tritt, Travis	Xmas - Christmas In My Hometown	18-754	CB
Tritt, Travis	You Can't Count Me Out Yet	18-593	ST
Tritt, Travis	You Never Take Me Dancing	30-465	CB
Triumph	Lay It On The Line	6-17	SC
Triumph	Lay It On The Line	13-666	SGB
Triumph	Magic Power	23-106	SC
Troccoli, Kathy	You've Got A Way	6-177	MM
Troggs	Anyway That You Want Me	37-275	CMC
Troggs	Love Is All Around	46-312	SC
Troggs	Wild Thing	11-246	DK
Troggs	Wild Thing	13-164	P
Troggs	Wild Thing	16-297	TT
Troggs	With A Girl Like You	37-274	ZM
Troutman, Roger	I Want To Be Your Man	11-407	DK
Trower, Robin	Bridge Of Sighs	18-257	DK
Trower, Robin	Lady Love	13-652	SGB
Troy, Doris	Just One Look	35-70	CB
Troy, Doris	Just One Look	13-116	P
Troy, Doris	Just One Look	5-461	SC
Troy, Doris	Just One Look	10-568	SF
Troys	What Do You Do	32-249	THM
TRUST Company	Running From Me	32-105	THM

ARTIST	SONG TITLE	#	TYPE
Tubb & Foley	Duet - Tennesse Border #2	22-302	CB
Tubb & Foley	Tennessee Border #2	22-302	CB
Tubb, Ernest	Drivin' Nails In My Coffin	22-306	CB
Tubb, Ernest	Filipino Baby	8-443	CB
Tubb, Ernest	Half A Mind	45-710	VH
Tubb, Ernest	Have You Ever Been Lonely	8-393	CB
Tubb, Ernest	I Love You Because	8-388	CB
Tubb, Ernest	It's Been So Long Darlin'	22-293	CB
Tubb, Ernest	Let's Say Goodbye Like….Hello	22-303	CB
Tubb, Ernest	Letters Have No Arms	4-802	SC
Tubb, Ernest	Missing In Action	22-304	CB
Tubb, Ernest	Rainbow At Midnight	19-636	CB
Tubb, Ernest	Slipping Around	22-300	CB
Tubb, Ernest	Soldier's Last Letter	8-796	CB
Tubb, Ernest	Thanks A Lot	22-305	CB
Tubb, Ernest	Try Me One More Time	22-301	CB
Tubb, Ernest	Walking The Floor Over You	22-292	CB
Tubb, Ernest	Walking The Floor Over You	11-709	DK
Tubb, Ernest	Walking The Floor Over You	8-661	SAV
Tubb, Ernest	Waltz Across Texas	33-2	CB
Tubb, Ernest	Waltz Across Texas	4-864	SC
Tubes	Don't Touch Me There **	15-6	SC
Tubes	Duet - Don't Touch Me There **	15-6	SC
Tucker & Brown	Don't Go Out	2-346	SC
Tucker & Brown	Duet - Don't Go Out	2-346	SC
Tucker & Campbell	Dream Lover - duet	49-655	KV
Tucker & Campbell	Duet - Dream Lover	49-655	KV
Tucker & McClinton	Duet - Tell Me About It	8-112	CB
Tucker & McClinton	Duet - Tell Me About It	6-527	MM
Tucker & McClinton	Duet - Tell Me About It	2-338	SC
Tucker & McClinton	Tell Me About It	2-338	SC
Tucker & McClinton	Tell Me About It	8-112	CB
Tucker & McClinton	Tell Me About It	6-527	MM
Tucker, Davis, Overstreet	Duet - I Won't Take Less Than...	34-276	CB
Tucker, Davis, Overstreet	I Won't Take Less Than... - duet	34-276	CB
Tucker, Tanya	Already Gone	38-9	CB
Tucker, Tanya	Bed Of Roses	45-123	THM
Tucker, Tanya	Between The Two Of Them	1-613	CB
Tucker, Tanya	Between The Two Of Them	2-649	SC
Tucker, Tanya	Blood Red & Going Down	13-458	P
Tucker, Tanya	Call On Me	38-10	CB
Tucker, Tanya	Can I See You Tonight	5-56	SC
Tucker, Tanya	Can't Run From Yourself	38-11	CB
Tucker, Tanya	Come In Our Of The World	24-134	SC
Tucker, Tanya	Daddy And Home	45-124	THM

ARTIST	SONG TITLE	#	TYPE
Tucker, Tanya	Danger Ahead	38-12	CB
Tucker, Tanya	Delta Dawn	8-15	CB
Tucker, Tanya	Delta Dawn	7-112	MM
Tucker, Tanya	Delta Dawn	8-679	SAV
Tucker, Tanya	Don't Believe My Heart Can Stand…	19-429	SC
Tucker, Tanya	Down To My Last Teardrop	16-343	CB
Tucker, Tanya	Down to My Last Teardrop	13-384	P
Tucker, Tanya	Find Out What's Happening	1-614	CB
Tucker, Tanya	Find Out What's Happening	2-828	SC
Tucker, Tanya	Hangin' In	1-612	CB
Tucker, Tanya	Hangin' In	6-597	MM
Tucker, Tanya	Hangin' In	2-795	SC
Tucker, Tanya	Here's Some Love	1-606	CB
Tucker, Tanya	Here's Some Love	9-583	SAV
Tucker, Tanya	Here's Some Love	14-262	SC
Tucker, Tanya	Highway Robbery	1-608	CB
Tucker, Tanya	I Believe the South is Gonna Rise	38-13	CB
Tucker, Tanya	I'll Come Back As Another Woman	16-351	CB
Tucker, Tanya	I'll Come Back As Another Woman	9-445	SAV
Tucker, Tanya	I've Learned To Live	24-243	SC
Tucker, Tanya	If It Don't Come Easy	16-342	CB
Tucker, Tanya	If It Don't Come Easy	5-18	SC
Tucker, Tanya	If Your Heart Ain't Busy Tonight	1-609	CB
Tucker, Tanya	If Your Heart Ain't Busy Tonight	33-102	CB
Tucker, Tanya	If Your Heart Ain't Busy Tonight	6-187	MM
Tucker, Tanya	If Your Heart Ain't Busy Tonight	3-651	SC
Tucker, Tanya	It Hurts Like Love	4-598	SC
Tucker, Tanya	It Won't Be Me	16-352	CB
Tucker, Tanya	It's A Cowboy Lovin' Night	45-125	THM
Tucker, Tanya	It's A Little Too Late	16-345	CB
Tucker, Tanya	It's A Little Too Late	10-788	JVC
Tucker, Tanya	It's A Little Too Late	6-131	MM
Tucker, Tanya	It's A Little Too Late	12-478	P
Tucker, Tanya	It's Only Over For You	16-348	CB
Tucker, Tanya	It's Only Over For You	5-164	SC
Tucker, Tanya	Jamestown Ferry the	19-434	SC
Tucker, Tanya	Just Another Love	16-349	CB
Tucker, Tanya	Just Another Love	4-783	SC
Tucker, Tanya	Let The Good Times Roll	24-76	SC
Tucker, Tanya	Little Things	14-662	CB
Tucker, Tanya	Little Things	7-616	CHM
Tucker, Tanya	Lizzie And The Rainman	1-605	CB
Tucker, Tanya	Lizzie And The Rainman	5-55	SC
Tucker, Tanya	Love Me Like You Used To	16-340	CB

ARTIST	SONG TITLE	#	TYPE
Tucker, Tanya	Love Me Like You Used To	5-47	SC
Tucker, Tanya	Love's The Answer	14-254	SC
Tucker, Tanya	Man That Turned My Mama On	15-64	CB
Tucker, Tanya	Man That Turned My Mama On	13-338	P
Tucker, Tanya	Memory Like I'm Gonna Be	25-356	MM
Tucker, Tanya	Memory Like I'm Gonna Be	18-455	ST
Tucker, Tanya	My Arms Stay Open All Night	16-347	CB
Tucker, Tanya	My Arms Stay Open All Night	2-813	SC
Tucker, Tanya	Oh What It Did To Me	16-353	CB
Tucker, Tanya	Old Weakness (Comin' On Strong)	25-529	MM
Tucker, Tanya	Old Weakness (Comin' On Strong)	18-805	ST
Tucker, Tanya	Old Weakness (Coming On Strong)	32-194	THM
Tucker, Tanya	One Love At A Time	16-341	CB
Tucker, Tanya	One Love At A Time	5-58	SC
Tucker, Tanya	Pecos Promenade	38-15	CB
Tucker, Tanya	Ridin' Out The Heartache	16-578	SC
Tucker, Tanya	San Antonio Stroll	8-451	CB
Tucker, Tanya	San Antonio Stroll	6-770	MM
Tucker, Tanya	San Antonio Stroll - DANCE #	22-385	SC
Tucker, Tanya	Some Kind Of Trouble	16-344	CB
Tucker, Tanya	Some Kind Of Trouble	19-303	MH
Tucker, Tanya	Some Kind Of Trouble	6-111	MM
Tucker, Tanya	Soon	1-611	CB
Tucker, Tanya	Soon	6-378	MM
Tucker, Tanya	Strong Enough To Bend	16-339	CB
Tucker, Tanya	Strong Enough To Bend	11-719	DK
Tucker, Tanya	Texas When I Die	17-309	NA
Tucker, Tanya	Texas When I Die	9-478	SAV
Tucker, Tanya	Two Sparrows In A Hurricane	1-610	CB
Tucker, Tanya	Two Sparrows In A Hurricane	6-213	MM
Tucker, Tanya	Two Sparrows In A Hurricane	12-416	P
Tucker, Tanya	Walking Shoes	16-350	CB
Tucker, Tanya	Walking Shoes	26-579	DK
Tucker, Tanya	Walking Shoes	9-454	SAV
Tucker, Tanya	Walking Shoes	2-352	SC
Tucker, Tanya	We Don't Have To Do This	6-462	MM
Tucker, Tanya	What's Your Mama's Name	8-42	CB
Tucker, Tanya	What's Your Mama's Name	5-52	SC
Tucker, Tanya	Without You What Do I Do With Me	16-346	CB
Tucker, Tanya	Would You Lay With Me	1-603	CB
Tucker, Tanya	You Just Watch Me	6-505	MM

ARTIST	SONG TITLE	#	TYPE
Tucker, Tanya	You Just Watch Me	2-430	SC
Tuesdays	I'll Be Here	21-559	PHM
Tull, Jethro	Aqualung	26-336	DK
Tull, Jethro	Bungle In The Jungle	14-559	AH
Tull, Jethro	Bungle In The Jungle	12-329	DK
Tull, Jethro	Bungle In The Jungle	20-313	MH
Tull, Jethro	Bungle In The Jungle	17-513	SC
Tull, Jethro	Living In The Past	20-92	SC
Tull, Jethro	Locomotive Breath	12-328	DK
Tune Weavers	Happy Happy Birthday Baby	4-211	SC
Tune Weavers	Happy Happy Birthday Baby	30-777	SF
Tunstall, K.T.	Another Place To Fall	30-704	SF
Tunstall, K.T.	Black Horse And The Cherry Tree	29-276	PHM
Tunstall, K.T.	Hold On	30-593	PHM
Tunstall, K.T.	Hold On	37-112	SC
Tunstall, K.T.	Little Favours	49-885	SC
Tunstall, K.T.	Suddenly I See	30-267	CB
Turner & Stanley	Duet - Me And God	30-196	CB
Turner & Stanley	Me And God	30-196	CB
Turner & Yearwood	Another Try	36-432	CB
Turner, Ike & Tina	I Want To Take You Higher	15-505	CMC
Turner, Ike & Tina	Oh My My Can You Boogie	7-61	MM
Turner, Ike & Tina	Proud Mary	7-35	MM
Turner, Joe	Corrina Corrina	20-59	SC
Turner, Joe	Corrina Corrina	17-325	SS
Turner, Josh	All Over Me	38-129	CB
Turner, Josh	Another Try	48-609	DK
Turner, Josh	Everything Is Fine	36-227	PHM
Turner, Josh	Firecracker	30-533	CB
Turner, Josh	Haywire	44-296	BKD
Turner, Josh	I Had One One Time	49-229	DFK
Turner, Josh	I Wouldn't Be A Man	38-104	CB
Turner, Josh	Long Black Train	19-176	ST
Turner, Josh	Long Black Train	32-302	THM
Turner, Josh	One Woman Man	44-297	BKD
Turner, Josh	She'll Go On You	18-212	ST
Turner, Josh	Time Is Love	39-22	ASK
Turner, Josh	Time Is Love	44-148	BKD
Turner, Josh	What It Ain't	20-343	ST
Turner, Josh	Whatcha Reckon	49-105	CDG
Turner, Josh	Why Don't We Just Dance	36-34	PT
Turner, Josh	Why Don't We Just Dance	46-299	BKD
Turner, Josh	Would You Go With Me	29-601	CB
Turner, Josh	Your Man	23-418	CB
Turner, Josh	Your Man	29-846	SC
Turner, Sammy	Lavender Blue	7-305	MM
Turner, Tina	Addicted To Love	10-427	LE
Turner, Tina	Best the	10-431	LE
Turner, Tina	Better Be Good To Me	11-376	DK
Turner, Tina	Better Be Good To Me	10-426	LE
Turner, Tina	Golden Eye	10-425	LE

ARTIST	SONG TITLE	#	TYPE
Turner, Tina	Golden Eye	9-68	SC
Turner, Tina	I Don't Wanna Fight	27-310	DK
Turner, Tina	I Don't Wanna Fight	10-429	LE
Turner, Tina	I Don't Wanna Fight	6-363	MM
Turner, Tina	I Don't Wanna Fight	13-23	P
Turner, Tina	I Don't Wanna Lose You	10-424	LE
Turner, Tina	Let's Stay Together	10-423	LE
Turner, Tina	Missing You	4-688	SC
Turner, Tina	Nutbush City Limits	10-419	LE
Turner, Tina	Private Dancer	10-418	LE
Turner, Tina	Private Dancer	16-525	P
Turner, Tina	Proud Mary	10-428	LE
Turner, Tina	Proud Mary	47-406	SC
Turner, Tina	Proud Mary	47-405	CB
Turner, Tina	River Deep Mountain High	10-417	LE
Turner, Tina	Something Beautiful Remains	24-286	SC
Turner, Tina	Steamy Windows	9-685	SAV
Turner, Tina	Two People	10-422	LE
Turner, Tina	Typical Male	10-421	LE
Turner, Tina	Way Of The World	10-432	LE
Turner, Tina	We Don't Need Another Heartache	10-430	LE
Turner, Tina	What's Love Got To Do With It	10-420	LE
Turner, Tina	What's Love Got To Do With It	12-678	P
Turner, Tina	Whatever You Need	14-477	SC
Turner, Tina	When The Heartache is Over	5-892	SC
Turtles	Elenore	12-869	P
Turtles	Elenore	20-60	SC
Turtles	Happy Together	17-67	DK
Turtles	It Ain't Me Babe	7-64	MM
Turtles	She'd Rather Be With Me	3-457	SC
Turtles	She's My Girl	6-51	SC
Turtles	You Showed Me	5-175	SC
TV Themes	Addams Family TV Theme	2-162	SC
TV Themes	All In The Family	2-161	SC
TV Themes	American Bandstand	2-164	SC
TV Themes	Beverly Hillbillies	2-152	SC
TV Themes	Brady Bunch	2-155	SC
TV Themes	Brady Bunch the	27-404	DK
TV Themes	Casper The Friendly Ghost - Halloween	45-119	SC
TV Themes	Cheers	2-170	SC
TV Themes	Daniel Boone	2-165	SC
TV Themes	Duet - All In The Family	2-161	SC
TV Themes	Duet - Green Acres	2-156	SC
TV Themes	Duet - Three's Company	2-174	SC
TV Themes	F Troop	2-159	SC
TV Themes	Flintstones	2-164	SC
TV Themes	Gilligan's Island	27-401	DK
TV Themes	Gilligan's Island	2-160	SC
TV Themes	Greatest American Hero	2-176	SC

ARTIST	SONG TITLE	#	TYPE
TV Themes	Green Acres	2-156	SC
TV Themes	Halloween - Casper the Friendly Ghost	45-119	SC
TV Themes	Happy Days	2-172	SC
TV Themes	Jefferson's the	2-173	SC
TV Themes	Laverne & Shirley	2-163	SC
TV Themes	Laverne & Shirley Theme	27-402	DK
TV Themes	Love Boat the	2-171	SC
TV Themes	Meet The Flintstones	12-616	P
TV Themes	Monkees the	2-169	SC
TV Themes	Mr. Ed	2-157	SC
TV Themes	Partridge Family	2-153	SC
TV Themes	Petticoat Junction	2-154	SC
TV Themes	Rawhide	2-158	SC
TV Themes	Secret Agent Man	2-175	SC
TV Themes	Three's Company	2-174	SC
TV Themes	WKRP In Cincinatti	2-164	SC
Twain & Currington	Duet - Party For Two	22-61	CB
Twain & Currington	Party For Two	21-164	CB
Twain & Krauss	Coat Of Many Colors	20-270	SC
Twain & White	Duet - From This Moment On	8-2	CB
Twain & White	Duet - From This Moment On	7-745	CHM
Twain & White	Duet - From This Moment On	14-293	MM
Twain & White	From This Moment On	8-2	CB
Twain & White	From This Moment On	7-745	CHM
Twain & White	From This Moment On	14-293	MM
Twain, Shania	Ain't No Particular Way	45-530	CB
Twain, Shania	Any Man Of Mine	1-511	CB
Twain, Shania	Any Man Of Mine	7-436	MM
Twain, Shania	Any Man Of Mine	2-773	SC
Twain, Shania	C'Est La Vie	23-429	CB
Twain, Shania	Coat Of Many Colors	19-712	ST
Twain, Shania	Come On Over	8-6	CB
Twain, Shania	Come On Over	5-797	SC
Twain, Shania	Come On Over	22-499	ST
Twain, Shania	Dance With The One That Brought You	3-644	SC
Twain, Shania	Don't	22-18	CB
Twain, Shania	Don't	21-654	SC
Twain, Shania	Don't Be Stupid	8-140	CB
Twain, Shania	Don't Be Stupid (You Know I Love..)	22-410	ST
Twain, Shania	Forever And For Always	34-359	CB
Twain, Shania	Forever And For Always	25-613	MM
Twain, Shania	Forever And For Always	19-46	ST
Twain, Shania	Forever And For Always	32-232	THM
Twain, Shania	From This Moment On	15-625	PHM
Twain, Shania	God Bless The Child	1-518	CB
Twain, Shania	God Bless The Child	24-650	SC
Twain, Shania	Home Ain't Where His Heart Is..	4-893	SC
Twain, Shania	Home Ain't Where His Heart Is...	1-517	CB
Twain, Shania	Home Ain't Where His	7-441	MM

ARTIST	SONG TITLE	#	TYPE	ARTIST	SONG TITLE	#	TYPE
	Heart Is...				Face		
Twain, Shania	Honey I'm Home	8-3	CB	Twain, Shania	Shoes	23-465	CB
Twain, Shania	Honey I'm Home	22-824	ST	Twain, Shania	Thank You Baby (For Makin' Some...	23-432	CB
Twain, Shania	I Ain't Goin' Down	45-526	CB	Twain, Shania	That Don't Impress Me Much	8-860	CB
Twain, Shania	I Ain't No Quitter	23-116	CB	Twain, Shania	That Don't Impress Me Much	10-162	SC
Twain, Shania	I Ain't No Quitter	23-37	SC	Twain, Shania	That Don't Impress Me Much	22-695	ST
Twain, Shania	I'm Gonna Getcha Good	33-191	CB	Twain, Shania	That Good (Wanna Get To Know You	23-428	CB
Twain, Shania	I'm Gonna Getcha Good	25-408	MM	Twain, Shania	Up	34-363	CB
Twain, Shania	I'm Gonna Getcha Good	18-447	ST	Twain, Shania	Up	25-454	MM
Twain, Shania	I'm Gonna Getcha Good	32-38	THM	Twain, Shania	Up	18-590	ST
Twain, Shania	I'm Holdin' On To Love	14-85	CB	Twain, Shania	Up	32-112	THM
Twain, Shania	I'm Holdin' On To Love	13-858	CHM	Twain, Shania	Waiter! Bring Me Water!	23-433	CB
Twain, Shania	I'm Holdin' On To Love	22-557	ST	Twain, Shania	Wanna Get To know You That Good	45-531	CB
Twain, Shania	I'm Jealous	23-430	CB	Twain, Shania	What I Wanna Be	45-532	CB
Twain, Shania	I'm Not In The Mood (To Say No)	45-533	CB	Twain, Shania	What Made You Say That	19-289	MH
Twain, Shania	I'm Outta Here	7-444	MM	Twain, Shania	What Made You Say That	16-658	THM
Twain, Shania	I'm Outta Here	3-659	SC	Twain, Shania	When	1-525	CB
Twain, Shania	If It Don't Take Two	7-439	MM	Twain, Shania	When	22-550	ST
Twain, Shania	If You Wanna Touch Her, Ask	45-528	ASK	Twain, Shania	When You Kiss Me	20-446	ST
Twain, Shania	If You're Not In It For Love	1-513	CB	Twain, Shania	When You Kiss Me	32-83	THM
Twain, Shania	If You're Not In It For Love	7-444	MM	Twain, Shania	Whose Bed Have Your Boots Been	17-276	NA
Twain, Shania	If You're Not In It For Love	3-659	SC	Twain, Shania	Whose Bed Have Your Boots Been	16-657	THM
Twain, Shania	In My Car (I'll Be The Driver)	45-519	SC	Twain, Shania	Whose Bed Have Your Boots Been..	7-438	MM
Twain, Shania	Is There Life After Love	7-443	MM	Twain, Shania	Whose Bed Have Your Boots Been...	1-512	CB
Twain, Shania	Is There Life After Love	4-457	SC	Twain, Shania	Woman In Me the	1-514	CB
Twain, Shania	It Only Hurts When I'm Breathing	19-763	ST	Twain, Shania	Woman In Me the	7-450	MM
Twain, Shania	Juanita	45-529	CB	Twain, Shania	You Lay A Whole Lot Of Love On Me	16-659	THM
Twain, Shania	Ka-Ching!	23-431	CB	Twain, Shania	You Win My Love	1-515	CB
Twain, Shania	Leaving Is The Only Way Out	45-534	CB	Twain, Shania	You Win My Love	7-448	MM
Twain, Shania	Looking Through Your Eyes	45-527	BS	Twain, Shania	You're Still The One	35-416	CB
Twain, Shania	Love Gets Me Every Time	8-125	CB	Twain, Shania	You're Still The One	8-304	CB
Twain, Shania	Love Gets Me Every Time	22-639	ST	Twain, Shania	You're Still The One	7-712	PHM
Twain, Shania	Man I Feel Like A Woman	7-861	CHT	Twain, Shania	You're Still The One	22-765	ST
Twain, Shania	Man! I Feel Like A woman	8-5	CB	Twain, Shania	You've Got A Way	22-424	ST
Twain, Shania	Man! I Feel Like A Woman	8-519	PHT	Twain, Shania	You've Got A Way - Pop Mix	8-108	PHT
Twain, Shania	Nah!	22-14	CB	Tweet	Oops (Oh My) **	25-218	MM
Twain, Shania	No One Needs To Know	1-516	CB	Tweet	Smoking Cigarettes	32-19	THM
Twain, Shania	No One Needs To Know	7-271	MM	Twinkle	Terry	10-662	SF
Twain, Shania	No One Needs To Know	22-880	ST	Twisted Sister	We're Not Gonna Take It	23-61	MH
Twain, Shania	Raining On Our Love	7-446	MM	Twister Alley	Dance	6-752	MM
Twain, Shania	Rock This Country	5-408	SC	Twitty & Lynn	After The Fire Is Gone - duet	48-242	CB
Twain, Shania	Rock This Country	22-533	ST	Twitty & Lynn	Duet - After The Fire Is Gone	48-242	CB
Twain, Shania	She's Not Just A Pretty Face	20-269	SC	Twitty & Lynn	Duet - Feelings	48-243	CB
Twain, Shania	She's Not Just A Pretty	19-528	ST				

ARTIST	SONG TITLE	#	TYPE
Twitty & Lynn	Duet - I Can't Love You Enough	5-449	SC
Twitty & Lynn	Duet - Lead Me On	5-446	SC
Twitty & Lynn	Duet - Louisiana Woman Miss..Man	8-110	CB
Twitty & Lynn	Duet - My Elusive Dreams	48-247	THM
Twitty & Lynn	Feelings - duet	48-243	CB
Twitty & Lynn	I Can't Love You Enough	5-449	SC
Twitty & Lynn	Lead Me On	5-446	SC
Twitty & Lynn	Louisiana Woman Mississippi Man	8-110	CB
Twitty & Lynn	My Elusive Dreams - duet	48-247	THM
Twitty, Conway	After All The Good Is Gone	8-835	CB
Twitty, Conway	Ain't She Something Else	4-817	SC
Twitty, Conway	Baby's Gone	48-239	CB
Twitty, Conway	Between Blue Eyes And Jeans	4-549	SC
Twitty, Conway	Boogie Grass Band	20-660	SC
Twitty, Conway	Bridge That Just Won't Burn	6-76	SC
Twitty, Conway	Clown the	14-312	SC
Twitty, Conway	Crazy In Love	43-202	CB
Twitty, Conway	Desperado Love	2-632	SC
Twitty, Conway	Desperado Love	49-347	CB
Twitty, Conway	Don't Call Him A Cowboy	43-193	CB
Twitty, Conway	Don't Cry Joni	8-799	CB
Twitty, Conway	Don't It Make You Lonely	4-120	SC
Twitty, Conway	Don't Take It Away	8-824	CB
Twitty, Conway	Duet - Don't Cry Joni	8-799	CB
Twitty, Conway	Fallin' For You For Years	43-197	CB
Twitty, Conway	Fifteen Years Ago	4-575	SC
Twitty, Conway	Games That Daddies Play	43-198	CB
Twitty, Conway	Georgia Keeps Pullin On My Ring	43-195	CB
Twitty, Conway	Goodbye Time	5-868	SC
Twitty, Conway	Happy Birthday Darlin'	29-777	CB
Twitty, Conway	Happy Birthday Darling	4-767	SC
Twitty, Conway	Hello Darlin'	1-151	CB
Twitty, Conway	Hello Darlin'	26-373	DK
Twitty, Conway	Hello Darlin'	13-462	P
Twitty, Conway	How Much More Can She Stand	48-240	CB
Twitty, Conway	I Couldn't See You Leaving	43-199	CB
Twitty, Conway	I Don't Know A Thing About Love	2-364	SC
Twitty, Conway	I Don't Know A Thing About Love	1-163	CB
Twitty, Conway	I Love You More Today	5-100	SC
Twitty, Conway	I May Never Get To Heaven	4-779	SC
Twitty, Conway	I See The Want To In Your Eyes	43-201	CB
Twitty, Conway	I Want To Know You Before We Make Love	48-244	CB
Twitty, Conway	I Wish I Was Still In Your Dreams	48-241	CB
Twitty, Conway	I'd Love To Lay You Down	1-160	CB
Twitty, Conway	I'd Love To Lay You Down	4-658	SC
Twitty, Conway	I'm Not Through Loving You Yet	43-200	CB
Twitty, Conway	I'm The Only Thing	48-246	SC
Twitty, Conway	I've Already Loved You In My Mind	20-277	SC
Twitty, Conway	Image Of Me the	22-248	SC
Twitty, Conway	It's Only Make Believe	8-268	CB
Twitty, Conway	It's Only Make Believe	7-304	MM
Twitty, Conway	It's Only Make Believe	13-420	P
Twitty, Conway	Julia	43-194	CB
Twitty, Conway	Life's Little Ups and Downs	9-504	SAV
Twitty, Conway	Linda On My Mind	1-155	CB
Twitty, Conway	Linda On My Mind	3-598	SC
Twitty, Conway	Lonely Blue Boy	45-93	HCK
Twitty, Conway	Making Believe	8-665	SAV
Twitty, Conway	Next In Line	4-860	SC
Twitty, Conway	Next In Line	48-245	SC
Twitty, Conway	On Our Last Date	49-301	LOU
Twitty, Conway	Play Guitar Play	43-196	CB
Twitty, Conway	Red Neckin' Love Makin' Night	1-165	CB
Twitty, Conway	Red Neckin' Love Makin' Night	4-774	SC
Twitty, Conway	Rest Your Love On Me	5-864	SC
Twitty, Conway	Road That I Walk	49-125	SBI
Twitty, Conway	Rose the	48-238	CB
Twitty, Conway	She Needs Someone To Hold Her	14-427	SC
Twitty, Conway	She Needs Someone To Hold Her..	1-153	CB
Twitty, Conway	She's Got A Single Thing In Mind	11-780	DK
Twitty, Conway	Slow Hand	8-200	CB
Twitty, Conway	Slow Hand	9-436	SAV
Twitty, Conway	Slow Hand	4-266	SC
Twitty, Conway	Somebody's Needin' Somebody	4-494	SC
Twitty, Conway	That's My Job	4-769	SC
Twitty, Conway	There's A Honky Tonk Angel	29-617	CB
Twitty, Conway	This Time I've Hurt Her More Than..	8-363	CB
Twitty, Conway	This Time I've Hurt Her More Than..	13-513	P
Twitty, Conway	Tight Fittin' Jeans	8-41	CB
Twitty, Conway	Tight Fittin' Jeans	2-640	SC
Twitty, Conway	To See My Angel Cry	22-251	SC
Twitty, Conway	Touch The Hand	1-156	CB

ARTIST	SONG TITLE	#	TYPE
Twitty, Conway	Touch The Hand	13-518	P
Twitty, Conway	Who Did They Think He Was	48-248	THM
Twitty, Conway	You've Never Been This Far Before	15-72	CB
Twitty, Conway	You've Never Been This Far Before	4-780	SC
Twitty, Conway	Your Love Had Taken Me That High	48-237	CB
Two Tons O' Fun	It's Raining Men	12-22	DK
Tyler, Bonnie	Holding Out For A Hero	11-422	DK
Tyler, Bonnie	It's A Heartache	35-141	CB
Tyler, Bonnie	It's A Heartache	2-554	SC
Tyler, Bonnie	Lost In France	48-774	P
Tyler, Bonnie	Total Eclipse Of The Heart	14-571	AH
Tyler, Bonnie	Total Eclipse Of The Heart	18-231	DK
Tyler, Bonnie	Total Eclipse Of The Heart	9-16	MH
Tyler, Dean	Built For Blue Jeans	30-118	CB
Tyler, Kris	What A Woman Knows	10-127	SC
Tyler, Kris	What A Woman Knows	22-421	ST
Tyler, Ryan	Last Thing She Said the	30-799	PHM
Tyler, Ryan	Last Thing She Said the	20-477	ST
Tyler, Ryan	Run Run Run	19-371	ST
Tymes	So Much In Love	25-166	MM
Tyrell, Steve	Give Me The Simple Life	30-191	LE
Tyrell, Steve	Never The Less	30-190	LE
Tyrese	How You Gonna Act Like That	20-521	CB
Tyrese	How You Gonna Act Like That	32-272	THM
Tyrese	Lately	16-191	THM
Tyrese	Signs Of Love Makin'	32-420	THM
Tyrese	Sweet Lady	7-834	PHM
U2	All Because Of You	22-366	CB
U2	Angel Of Harlem	17-471	SC
U2	Bad	30-69	CB
U2	Bad	30-69	SC
U2	Beautiful Day	23-264	HS
U2	Beautiful Day	16-479	MH
U2	Beautiful Day	30-78	SC
U2	Beautiful Day	18-547	TT
U2	Desire	11-766	DK
U2	Desire	30-70	SC
U2	Desire	30-759	SF
U2	Electrical Storm	23-150	PHM
U2	Elevation	48-311	SC
U2	Even Better Than The Real Thing	30-66	SC
U2	Get On Your Boots	48-315	SF
U2	Ground Beneath Her Feet the	48-310	MM
U2	Hold Me Thrill Me Kiss Me Kill Me	30-73	SC
U2	I Still Haven't Found What I'm Look	17-147	DK
U2	I Still Haven't Found	13-274	P

ARTIST	SONG TITLE	#	TYPE
	What I'm Look		
U2	I Will Follow	30-68	SC
U2	In A Little While	48-312	SC
U2	Mysterious Ways	13-272	P
U2	Mysterious Ways	6-32	SC
U2	New Year's Day	30-75	SC
U2	One	13-276	P
U2	One	30-77	SC
U2	Original Of The Species	29-213	PHM
U2	Please	48-314	SFG
U2	Pride (In The Name of Love)	30-72	SC
U2	Pride In The Name Of Love	13-275	P
U2	Sometimes You Can't Make It On Your Own	48-313	ST
U2	Stuck In A Moment You Can't Get..	15-817	CB
U2	Sunday Bloody Sunday	16-71	SC
U2	Sweetest Thing	16-211	MM
U2	Sweetest Thing	7-818	PHM
U2	Vertigo	22-341	CB
U2	Walk On	30-76	SC
U2	Where The Streets Have No Name	30-74	SC
U2	With Or Without You	12-341	DK
U2	With Or Without You	13-273	P
U2	With Or Without You	30-79	SC
UB40	Blue Eyes Crying In The Rain	49-929	KVD
UB40	Here I Am Come And Take Me	12-20	DK
UB40	Higher Ground	25-387	MM
UB40	Red Red Wine	7-418	MM
Ugly Kid Joe	Cat's In The Cradle	23-100	SC
Ugly Kid Joe	Everything About You	13-747	SGB
Uncle Kracker	Drift Away	25-532	MM
Uncle Kracker	Drift Away	19-342	STP
Uncle Kracker	Follow Me	35-241	CB
Uncle Kracker	Follow Me	16-472	MH
Uncle Kracker	Follow Me	15-300	THM
Uncle Kracker	Follow Me	18-556	TT
Uncle Kracker	In A Little While	25-335	MM
Uncle Kracker	In A Little While	18-344	PHM
Uncle Kracker	Memphis Soul Song	20-234	MM
Uncle Kracker	Memphis Soul Song	32-432	THM
Uncle Kracker	Rescue	23-553	MM
Uncle Kracker w Gray	Drift Away	32-245	THM
Uncle Mac	All Things Bright And Beautiful	48-764	P
Underwood, Carrie	All American Girl	37-14	CB
Underwood, Carrie	Before He Cheats	29-202	CB
Underwood, Carrie	Before He Cheats	30-98	PHM
Underwood, Carrie	Before He Cheats	29-847	SC
Underwood, Carrie	Blown Away	39-34	ASK
Underwood, Carrie	Church Bells	49-11	KV
Underwood, Carrie	Clock Don't Stop	49-641	KV

ARTIST	SONG TITLE	#	TYPE
Underwood, Carrie	Cowboy Cassanova	36-50	PT
Underwood, Carrie	Crazy Dreams	37-6	CB
Underwood, Carrie	Dirty Laundry	49-719	KV
Underwood, Carrie	Do You Think About Me	39-29	KV
Underwood, Carrie	Don't Forget To Remember Me	30-119	AS
Underwood, Carrie	Don't Forget To Remember Me	29-364	CB
Underwood, Carrie	First Noel the	45-783	KV
Underwood, Carrie	Flat On The Floor	37-2	CB
Underwood, Carrie	Girl You Think I Am the	49-12	KV
Underwood, Carrie	Good Girl	44-206	MRH
Underwood, Carrie	Hark The Herald Angels Sing	45-784	KV
Underwood, Carrie	Heartbeat	45-463	BKD
Underwood, Carrie	Home Sweet Home	37-35	CB
Underwood, Carrie	Home Sweet Home	36-381	SC
Underwood, Carrie	I Just Can't Live A Lie	30-120	AS
Underwood, Carrie	I Told You So	37-5	CB
Underwood, Carrie	I'll Stand By You	30-473	CB
Underwood, Carrie	Inside Your Heaven	30-121	AS
Underwood, Carrie	Inside Your Heaven	23-282	CB
Underwood, Carrie	Inside Your Heaven	30-141	PT
Underwood, Carrie	Jesus Take The Wheel	30-122	AS
Underwood, Carrie	Jesus Take The Wheel	29-25	CB
Underwood, Carrie	Jesus Take The Wheel	23-450	ST
Underwood, Carrie	Just A Dream	37-8	CB
Underwood, Carrie	Last Name	37-9	CB
Underwood, Carrie	Lessons Learned	30-123	AS
Underwood, Carrie	Like I'll Never Love You Again	47-703	BKD
Underwood, Carrie	More Boys I Meet the	37-12	CB
Underwood, Carrie	Night Before (Life Goes On)	30-126	AS
Underwood, Carrie	O Holy Night	45-785	KV
Underwood, Carrie	See You Again	40-50	ASK
Underwood, Carrie	Smoke Break	45-348	BKD
Underwood, Carrie	So Small	30-545	CB
Underwood, Carrie	Some Hearts	30-124	AS
Underwood, Carrie	Some Hearts	29-61	CB
Underwood, Carrie	Some Hearts	29-504	SC
Underwood, Carrie	Starts With Goodbye	30-125	AS
Underwood, Carrie	Two Black Cadillacs	39-33	ASK
Underwood, Carrie	Undo It	36-45	PT
Underwood, Carrie	Wasted	30-127	AS
Underwood, Carrie	Wasted	30-245	CB
Underwood, Carrie	We're Young And Beautiful	30-128	AS
Underwood, Carrie	We're Young And Beautiful	37-13	CB
Underwood, Carrie	What Child Is This	45-786	KV
Underwood, Carrie	Wine After Whiskey	47-579	KV
Underwood, Carrie	Xmas - First Noel the	45-783	KV
Underwood, Carrie	Xmas - Hark The Herald Angels Sing	45-784	KV
Underwood, Carrie	Xmas - O Holy Night	45-785	KV
Underwood, Carrie	Xmas - What Child Is This	45-786	KV
Underwood. Carrie	Some Hearts	30-124	AS
Undisputed Truth	Smiling Faces Sometimes	24-339	SC
Unit 4 Plus 2	Concrete And Clay	10-615	SF
Unknown	Ullo John Got A New Motor	21-605	SF
UNV	Something's Goin' On	13-21	P
Unwritten Law	Rest Of My Life	23-166	PHM
Up Close&Personal	I Finally Found Someone	18-184	DK
Up Close&Personal	Show - I Finally Found Someone	18-184	DK
Urban & Dunn	Duet - Raise The Barn	42-27	CB
Urban & Dunn	Raise The Barn - duet	42-27	CB
Urban & Lambert	Duet - We Were Us	43-87	PHN
Urban & Lambert	We Were Us	43-87	PHN
Urban, Keith	Better Life	23-413	CB
Urban, Keith	Better Life	29-606	ST
Urban, Keith	Break On Me	48-738	KV
Urban, Keith	Break On Me	48-1	KCD
Urban, Keith	Break On Me - instrumental	48-746	BKD
Urban, Keith	But For The Grace Of God	14-124	CB
Urban, Keith	But For The Grace Of God	14-16	CHM
Urban, Keith	But For The Grace Of God	19-217	CSZ
Urban, Keith	Cop Car	43-168	PHN
Urban, Keith	Days Go By	20-444	ST
Urban, Keith	Die Of A Broken Heart	20-385	ST
Urban, Keith	Even The Stars Fell For You	42-22	ASK
Urban, Keith	Everybody	30-550	CB
Urban, Keith	For You	39-32	PHM
Urban, Keith	Hit The Ground Runnin'	46-155	KV
Urban, Keith	I Told You So	30-438	CB
Urban, Keith	I'm In	37-337	CB
Urban, Keith	It's A Love Thing	14-693	CB
Urban, Keith	It's A Love Thing	19-229	SC
Urban, Keith	It's A Love Thing	22-535	ST
Urban, Keith	Jeans On	29-367	CB
Urban, Keith	John Cougar, John Deere, John 3:16	45-24	BKD
Urban, Keith	Kiss A Girl	37-34	CB
Urban, Keith	Little Bit Of Everything	45-626	ASK
Urban, Keith	Live To Love Another Day	30-80	CB
Urban, Keith	Long Hot Summer	38-45	PHM
Urban, Keith	Making Memories Of Us	22-327	CB
Urban, Keith	Making Memories Of Us	23-378	SC
Urban, Keith	Marry For Money	46-154	CB
Urban, Keith	Once In A Lifetime	30-104	CB
Urban, Keith	Once In A Lifetime	30-95	PHM
Urban, Keith	Only You Can Love Me This Way	36-311	PHM
Urban, Keith	Put You In A Song	46-156	PHN
Urban, Keith	Raining On Sunday	34-373	CB
Urban, Keith	Raining On Sunday	25-445	MM

ARTIST	SONG TITLE	#	TYPE
Urban, Keith	Raining On Sunday	18-589	ST
Urban, Keith	Raining On Sunday	32-81	THM
Urban, Keith	Raise 'Em Up	45-62	SBI
Urban, Keith	Somebody Like You	33-180	CB
Urban, Keith	Somebody Like You	25-292	MM
Urban, Keith	Somebody Like You	18-127	ST
Urban, Keith	Somewhere in My Car	45-625	SSC
Urban, Keith	Stupid Boy	30-244	CB
Urban, Keith	Sweet Thing	36-257	PHM
Urban, Keith	Till Summer Comes Around	37-323	SF
Urban, Keith	Tonight I Wanna Cry	29-36	CB
Urban, Keith	Tu Compania	36-597	CB
Urban, Keith	Walk In The Country	46-153	CAP
Urban, Keith	Wasted Time	49-639	DCK
Urban, Keith	Where The Blacktop Ends	34-350	CB
Urban, Keith	Where The Blacktop Ends	9-862	ST
Urban, Keith	Who Wouldn't Wanna Be Me	25-639	MM
Urban, Keith	Who Wouldn't Wanna Be Me	32-340	THM
Urban, Keith	Who Wouldn't Wanna Be Me	19-171	ST
Urban, Keith	Without You	37-235	CB
Urban, Keith	You Gonna Fly	45-624	ASK
Urban, Keith	You Look Good In My Shirt	23-396	CB
Urban, Keith	You'll Think Of Me	19-699	ST
Urban, Keith	You're My Better Half	22-92	CB
Urban, Keith	You're My Better Half	21-664	SC
Urban, Keith	Your Everything	35-424	CB
Urban, Keith	Your Everything	13-824	CHM
Urban, Keith	Your Everything	6-68	SC
Uriah Heep	Stealin'	19-138	SGB
USA For Africa	We Are The World	20-297	CB
USA For Africa	We Are The World	19-124	KC
Used	Buried Myself Alive	32-179	THM
Usher	Can U Help Me	34-172	CB
Usher	Caught Up	22-342	CB
Usher	Love In This Club	48-594	DK
Usher	Moving Mountains	36-530	CB
Usher	Nice And Slow	16-229	PHM
Usher	Nice And Slow	5-194	SC
Usher	U Don't Have To Call	35-271	CB
Usher	U Don't Have To Call	25-212	MM
Usher	U Got It Bad	33-422	CB
Usher	U Got It Bad	25-82	MM
Usher	U Remind Me	15-814	CB
Usher	U Remind Me	23-588	PHM
Usher	U Remind Me	16-386	SGB
Usher	You Make Me Wanna	7-701	PHM
Usher	You Make Me Wanna	5-285	SC
Usher & Keys	Duet - MY Boo	30-805	PHM
Usher & Keys	My Boo - duet	30-805	PHM
Usher feat Young Jeezy	Love In The Club	36-482	CB

ARTIST	SONG TITLE	#	TYPE
Usher/Lil Jon/Ludac	Duet - Yeah	23-253	THM
Usher/Lil Jon/Ludac	Yeah	23-263	THM
Valasquez, Jaci	Gospel - You're My GOD	34-427	CB
Vale, Jerry	Al Di La - Spanish	49-211	MM
Vale, Jerry	Mama - Spanish	49-210	MM
Valens, Richie	Boney Maronie	45-433	SRK
Valens, Richie	Come On Let's Go	12-744	P
Valens, Richie	Donna	35-15	CB
Valens, Richie	Donna	12-742	P
Valens, Richie	Framed	45-677	DCK
Valens, Richie	La Bamba	11-171	DK
Valens, Richie	Oh Donna	35-15	CB
Valens, Richie	Tell Laura I Love Her	10-552	SF
Valens, Richie	We Belong Together	45-432	KV
Valentino w Timbaland	Anonymous	30-584	CB
Valentino, Bobby	Anonymous	30-564	CB
Vallee, Rudy	As Time Goes By	12-516	P
Vallejo, Al & Kendall Beard	Duet - Outta State, Outta Mind	42-10	PHN
Vallejo, Al & Kendall Beard	Outta State, Outta Mind - duet	42-10	PHN
Valli, Frankie	Can't Take My Eyes Off Of You	11-335	DK
Valli, Frankie	Can't Take My Eyes Off Of You	9-37	MM
Valli, Frankie	Grease	9-276	SC
Valli, Frankie	My Eyes Adored You	12-24	DK
Valli, Frankie	My Eyes Adored You	2-850	SC
Valli, Frankie	Our Day Will Come	49-472	MM
Valli, Frankie	Walk Like A Man	4-34	SC
Valli, June	I Understand	9-745	SAV
Van Dyke, Leroy	Auctioneer	8-720	CB
Van Dyke, Leroy	Auctioneer	5-364	SC
Van Dyke, Leroy	If A Woman Answers	5-429	SC
Van Dyke, Leroy	My World Is Caving In	45-887	VH
Van Dyke, Leroy	Walk On By	8-780	CB
Van Dyke, Leroy	Walk On By	12-474	P
Van Dyke, Leroy	Walk On By	4-310	SC
Van Halen	And The Cradle Will Rock	13-618	LE
Van Halen	Beautiful Girls	10-488	DA
Van Halen	Dancing In The Street	13-617	LE
Van Halen	Dreams	21-771	SC
Van Halen	Feel Your Love Tonight	13-642	SGB
Van Halen	Hot For Teacher	5-62	SC
Van Halen	Human Beings	4-333	SC
Van Halen	I Feel Your Love Tonight	19-136	SGB
Van Halen	Ice Cream Man	20-81	SC
Van Halen	Jamie's Cryin'	5-884	SC
Van Halen	Jump	13-615	LE
Van Halen	Jump	2-42	SC
Van Halen	Just A Gigolo	13-619	LE
Van Halen	Panama	13-620	LE
Van Halen	Panama	20-45	SC
Van Halen	Pretty Woman	13-616	LE
Van Halen	Right Now	5-740	SC
Van Halen	Runnin' With The Devil	4-563	SC

ARTIST	SONG TITLE	#	TYPE
Van Halen	Unchained	23-110	SC
Van Halen	When It's Love	13-614	LE
Van Halen	Why Can't This Be Love	9-379	AH
Van Halen	Why Can't This Be Love	13-613	LE
Van Halen	Why Can't This Be Love	13-755	SGB
Van Halen	You Really Got Me	13-751	SGB
Van Zant	Get What You Got Comin'	15-307	THM
Van Zant	Goes Down Easy	30-587	CB
Van Zant	Help Somebody	22-332	CB
Van Zant	Nobody Gonna Tell Me What To Do	23-472	CB
Van Zant	That Scares Me	30-448	CB
Van Zant	Things I Miss The Most	29-580	CB
VanBeethoven,Camper	Take The Skinheads Bowling **	23-22	SC
Vance & Valients	Xmas - All I Want For Xmas Is You	8-93	CB
Vance & Valients	Xmas - All I Want For Xmas Is You	5-711	SC
Vandross, Luther	Always And Forever	10-19	SC
Vandross, Luther	Anyone Who Had A Heart	48-286	KV
Vandross, Luther	Best Things In Life Are Free	48-291	LE
Vandross, Luther	Buy Me A Rose	46-200	SC
Vandross, Luther	Dance With My Father	20-376	HP
Vandross, Luther	Dance With My Father	25-659	MM
Vandross, Luther	Dance With My Father	19-539	SC
Vandross, Luther	Dance With My Father	32-388	THM
Vandross, Luther	Don't Want To Be A Fool	48-292	MM
Vandross, Luther	Every Year Every Christmas	45-772	KV
Vandross, Luther	Going In Circles	48-295	SC
Vandross, Luther	Here And Now	28-107	DK
Vandross, Luther	Here And Now	6-437	MM
Vandross, Luther	Here And Now	13-205	P
Vandross, Luther	Here And Now	2-276	SC
Vandross, Luther	House Is Not a Home a	14-574	SC
Vandross, Luther	I Can Make It Better	24-644	SC
Vandross, Luther	I Know	48-324	SC
Vandross, Luther	I Really Didn't Mean It	48-325	SFM
Vandross, Luther	If Only For One Night	48-323	SC
Vandross, Luther	Impossible Dream the	48-289	LE
Vandross, Luther	Little Miracles	48-296	SC
Vandross, Luther	Love Don't Love You Anymore	48-293	MM
Vandross, Luther	Love The One You're With	48-285	KV
Vandross, Luther	Never Let Me Go	18-482	NU
Vandross, Luther	Never Too Much	48-288	LE
Vandross, Luther	Power Of Love	16-404	PR
Vandross, Luther	Power Of Love (Love Power)	33-337	CB
Vandross, Luther	Since I Lost My Baby	48-290	LE
Vandross, Luther	Since You've Been Gone	48-297	SC
Vandross, Luther	So Amazing	48-287	KV
Vandross, Luther	Sometimes It's Only Love	24-264	SC

ARTIST	SONG TITLE	#	TYPE
Vandross, Luther	Stop To Love	12-78	DK
Vandross, Luther	Take You Out	48-294	MM
Vandross, Luther	Think About You	23-248	THM
Vandross, Luther	Xmas - Every Year Every Christmas	45-772	KV
Vandross, Luther	Your Secret Love	24-292	SC
Vanilla Ice	Ice Ice Baby	5-334	SC
Vanity Fare	Hitchin' A Ride	9-801	SAV
Vanity's	Nasty Girl **	5-546	SC
Vannelli, Gino	I Just Wanna Stop	17-561	PR
Vannelli, Gino	I Just Wanna Stop	4-59	SC
Vannett, Connie	Pussycat Song the **	30-669	RSX
Vannett, Connie	Pussycat Song the **	5-553	SC
VanRay	Inside Out	32-135	THM
VanShelton, Ricky	After The Lights Go Out	8-548	CB
VanShelton, Ricky	Backroads	8-557	CB
VanShelton, Ricky	Call Me Crazy	14-144	CB
VanShelton, Ricky	Crime Of Passion	20-658	SC
VanShelton, Ricky	Don't We All Have The Right	34-285	CB
VanShelton, Ricky	Don't We All Have The Right	8-558	CB
VanShelton, Ricky	Don't We All Have The Right	5-526	SC
VanShelton, Ricky	From A Jack To A King	33-98	CB
VanShelton, Ricky	From A Jack To A King	14-680	CB
VanShelton, Ricky	I Am A Simple Man	8-549	CB
VanShelton, Ricky	I Am A Simple Man	17-146	DK
VanShelton, Ricky	I Am A Simple Man	2-397	SC
VanShelton, Ricky	I Meant Every Word He Said	8-550	CB
VanShelton, Ricky	I Meant Every Word He Said	4-68	SC
VanShelton, Ricky	I'll Leave This World Loving You	8-560	CB
VanShelton, Ricky	I'll Leave This World Loving You	9-527	SAV
VanShelton, Ricky	I've Cried My Last Tear For You	8-561	CB
VanShelton, Ricky	I've Cried My Last Tear For You	11-718	DK
VanShelton, Ricky	Just As I Am	8-551	CB
VanShelton, Ricky	Just Say Goodbye	8-552	CB
VanShelton, Ricky	Keep It Between The Lines	8-553	CB
VanShelton, Ricky	Keep It Between The Lines	6-195	MM
VanShelton, Ricky	Life Turned Her That Way	4-659	SC
VanShelton, Ricky	Life's Little Ups And Downs	8-554	CB
VanShelton, Ricky	Living Proof	9-459	SAV
VanShelton, Ricky	Lola's Love	22-861	ST
VanShelton, Ricky	Somebody Lied	8-562	CB
VanShelton, Ricky	Somebody Lied	13-502	P
VanShelton, Ricky	Somebody Lied	8-703	SAV
VanShelton, Ricky	Statue Of A Fool	8-555	CB
VanShelton, Ricky	Statue Of A Fool	17-288	NA
VanShelton, Ricky	Statue Of A Fool	2-621	SC

ARTIST	SONG TITLE	#	TYPE
VanShelton, Ricky	Wherever She Is	2-489	SC
VanShelton, Ricky	Wild Man	8-556	CB
VanShelton, Ricky	Wild Man	2-713	SC
VanShelton, Ricky	Xmas - C-H-R-I-S-T-M-A-S	8-60	CB
VanShelton, Ricky	Xmas - Please Come Home For Xmas	18-750	CB
Vanwarmer, Randy	Just When I Needed You Most	35-156	CB
Vanwarmer, Randy	Just When I Needed You Most	2-552	SC
Vapors	Turning Japanese	21-399	SC
Various	Irish - When Irish Eyes Are Smiling	48-583	DK
Various	When Irish Eyes Are Smiling	48-583	DK
Various Artists	Ain't Nobody Here But Us Chickens	47-757	SRK
Vassar, Phil	American Child	25-231	MM
Vassar, Phil	American Child	17-568	ST
Vassar, Phil	An American Child - Patriotic	34-381	CB
Vassar, Phil	Carlene	8-895	CB
Vassar, Phil	Carlene	5-837	SC
Vassar, Phil	Carlene	22-538	ST
Vassar, Phil	Good Ole Days	23-289	CB
Vassar, Phil	Good Ole Days	29-607	ST
Vassar, Phil	I Would	36-607	CB
Vassar, Phil	I Would	36-209	PHM
Vassar, Phil	I'll Take That As A Yes (Hot Tub)	23-8	CB
Vassar, Phil	In A Real Love	21-660	SC
Vassar, Phil	In A Real Love	20-340	ST
Vassar, Phil	Just Another Day In Paradise	14-70	CB
Vassar, Phil	Just Another Day In Paradise	19-214	CSZ
Vassar, Phil	Last Day Of My Life	29-191	CB
Vassar, Phil	Last Day Of My Life	29-848	SC
Vassar, Phil	Love Is A Beautiful Thing	36-404	CB
Vassar, Phil	Patriotic - An American Child	34-381	CB
Vassar, Phil	Rose Bouquet	22-591	ST
Vassar, Phil	Six Pack Summer	15-187	ST
Vassar, Phil	That's When I Love You	17-604	CB
Vassar, Phil	That's When I Love You	25-65	MM
Vassar, Phil	That's When I Love You	16-6	ST
Vassar, Phil	This Is God	25-518	MM
Vassar, Phil	This Is God	18-785	ST
Vassar, Phil	This Is God	32-121	THM
Vassar, Phil	This Is My Life	30-461	CB
Vassar, Phil	Ultimate Love	19-174	ST
Vassar, Phil	Woman In My Life the	30-53	CB
Vaughn, Sarah	All The Things You Are	12-533	P
Vaughn, Sarah	Lullaby Of Birdland	10-709	JVC
Vaughn, Sarah	Make Yourself Comfortable	5-84	SC
Vaughn, Sarah	Moonlight In Vermont	2-249	SC

ARTIST	SONG TITLE	#	TYPE
Vaughn, Sarah	Whatever Lola Wants	23-347	MM
Vaughn, Sarah	Whatever Lola Wants	3-503	SC
Vaughn, Stevie Ray	Cold Shot	7-212	MM
Vaughn, Stevie Ray	Cold Shot	13-765	SGB
Vaughn, Stevie Ray	Couldn't Stand The Weather	46-310	SC
Vaughn, Stevie Ray	Crossfire	20-138	KB
Vaughn, Stevie Ray	Crossfire	7-214	MM
Vaughn, Stevie Ray	Give Me Back My Wig	46-31	SSK
Vaughn, Stevie Ray	House Is Rockin'	7-213	MM
Vaughn, Stevie Ray	Look At Little Sister	13-764	SGB
Vaughn, Stevie Ray	Pride And Joy	7-211	MM
Vaughn, Stevie Ray	Pride And Joy	15-317	SC
Vaughn, Stevie Ray	Sky Is Crying the	20-132	KB
Vaughn, Stevie Ray	Sky Is Crying the	15-17	SC
Vaughn, Stevie Ray	Texas Flood	15-26	SC
Vaughn, Stevie Ray	Willie The Wimp	45-361	KV
Vaughn, Stevie Ray & Jimmie	Tick-Tock	48-509	KVD
Vaughn, Tyrone	Downtime	38-248	PHN
Vedder, Eddie	Hard Sun	37-121	SC
Vedder, Eddie	You've Got To Hide Your Love Away	25-140	MM
Vee, Bobby	Christmas Wish	45-788	TB
Vee, Bobby	Come Back When You Grow Up	5-232	SC
Vee, Bobby	Devil Or Angel	13-104	P
Vee, Bobby	Forever Kind Of Love	47-844	DCK
Vee, Bobby	How Many Tears	49-64	ZVS
Vee, Bobby	More Than I Can Say	49-65	ZVS
Vee, Bobby	Night Has A Thousand Eyes the	5-166	SC
Vee, Bobby	Night Has A Thousand Eyes the	10-618	SF
Vee, Bobby	Please Don't Ask About Barbara	49-66	ZVS
Vee, Bobby	Rubber Ball	49-67	ZVS
Vee, Bobby	Run To Him	4-253	SC
Vee, Bobby	Sharing You	49-68	ZVS
Vee, Bobby	Take Good Care Of My Baby	11-361	DK
Vee, Bobby	Take Good Care Of My Baby	7-267	MM
Vee, Bobby	Take Good Care Of My Baby	13-258	P
Vee, Bobby	Take Good Care Of My Baby	9-713	SAV
Vee, Bobby	Xmas - Christmas Wish	45-788	TB
Vega, Ray	Remember When	7-404	MM
Vega, Suzanne	Luka	9-324	AG
Vega, Suzanne	Luka	9-13	MH
Velasquez, Jaci	On My Knees	35-316	CB
Vella, Billy	At This Moment	9-829	SAV
Velvet Revolver	Fall To Pieces	22-354	CB
Vendetta Red	Shatterday	32-332	THM
Venga Boys	We Like To Party	7-838	PHM
Venga Boys	We Like To Party	13-785	SGB
Vera & Beaters	At This Moment	35-194	CB

ARTIST	SONG TITLE	#	TYPE
Vera & Beaters	At This Moment	11-653	DK
Vera & Beaters	At This Moment	20-317	MH
Vera & Beaters	At This Moment	12-833	P
Verne, Larry	Mr. Custer	5-633	SC
Veronicas	Untouched	36-251	PHM
Vertical Horizon	Everything You Want	16-234	PHM
Vertical Horizon	Everything You Want (Radio Vers)	5-893	SC
Vertical Horizon	I'm Still Here	20-228	MM
Vertical Horizon	I'm Still Here (Jim's Theme)	32-27	THM
Vertical Horizon	You're A God	15-645	THM
Vertical Horizon	You're A God (Radio Version)	14-500	SC
Verve	Sonnet	8-514	PHT
Verve Pipe	Photograph	24-111	SC
Via, Angela	Picture Perfect (Radio Version)	14-473	SC
Victor Victoria	Show - Le Jazz Hot	10-372	KC
Vidal, Daniele	Les Champs Ulysees	15-521	CMC
Videos	Trickle Trickle	20-67	SC
Village People	In The Navy	45-618	CBE
Village People	Macho Man	35-142	CB
Village People	Macho Man	9-217	PT
Village People	YMCA	18-363	AH
Village People	YMCA	9-216	PT
Vincent, Gene	Be Bop A Lula	11-399	DK
Vincent, Gene	Be Bop A Lula	7-256	MM
Vincent, Gene	Blue Jean Bop	49-232	DFK
Vincent, Gene	Race With The Devil	49-233	DFK
Vincent, Rhonda	I've Forgotten You	23-144	CB
Vincent, Rhonda	If Heartaches Had Wings	19-707	ST
Vincent, Rhonda	What More Do You Want From Me	4-240	SC
Vincent, Rhonda	You Can't Take It With You	19-682	ST
Vincent, Rhonda	You Can't Take It With You...	36-370	CB
Vines	Ms. Jackson	32-177	THM
Vines	Outtathaway	23-152	PHM
Vinton, Bobby	Beer Barrel Polka	21-20	CB
Vinton, Bobby	Blue On Blue	11-368	DK
Vinton, Bobby	Blue On Blue	4-35	SC
Vinton, Bobby	Blue Velvet	33-240	CB
Vinton, Bobby	Blue Velvet	9-892	DK
Vinton, Bobby	Blue Velvet	13-101	P
Vinton, Bobby	Coming Home Soldier	46-33	SSK
Vinton, Bobby	Halfway To Paradise	49-88	SAV
Vinton, Bobby	I Love How You Love Me	49-87	LE
Vinton, Bobby	Just As Much As Ever	45-337	BSP
Vinton, Bobby	Mr. Lonely	5-177	SC
Vinton, Bobby	My Heart Belongs To Only You	7-261	MM
Vinton, Bobby	My Melody Of Love	7-43	MM
Vinton, Bobby	Please Love Me Forever	7-264	MM
Vinton, Bobby	Roses Are Red My Love	11-778	DK
Vinton, Bobby	Sealed With A Kiss	49-89	FH
Vinton, Bobby	Take Good Care Of My	35-46	CB

ARTIST	SONG TITLE	#	TYPE
	Baby		
Vinton, Bobby	There I've Said It Again	4-720	SC
Violent Femmes	Add It Up **	5-544	SC
Vitamin C	Graduation (Friends Forever)	14-185	CB
Vitamin C	Graduation (Friends Forever)	19-825	SGB
Vitamin C	Itch the	35-238	CB
Vitamin C	Me Myself & I	16-187	PHM
Vitamin C	Smile	10-202	SC
Vixen	Cryin'	19-558	SC
Vixen	Edge Of A Broken Heart	24-435	SC
Voegele, Kate	99 Times	36-298	PHM
Vogues	Five O'Clock World	3-25	SC
Vogues	Turn Around Look At Me	11-560	DK
Vogues	You're The One	5-512	SC
Voices of Theory	Say It	15-631	PHM
VonRay	Inside Out	32-135	THM
Wagoner & Parton	Duet - Last Thing On My Mind	9-613	SAV
Wagoner & Parton	Duet - Please Don't Stop Loving Me	5-442	SC
Wagoner & Parton	Last Thing On My Mind	9-613	SAV
Wagoner & Parton	Please Don't Stop Loving Me	5-442	SC
Wagoner, Porter	Big Wind	19-310	CB
Wagoner, Porter	Carroll County Accident	19-309	CB
Wagoner, Porter	Cold Hard Facts Of Life	19-307	CB
Wagoner, Porter	Cold Hard Facts Of Life	5-699	SC
Wagoner, Porter	Company's Comin'	19-318	CB
Wagoner, Porter	Eat Drink & Be Merry	19-311	CB
Wagoner, Porter	Eat Drink & Be Merry	5-38	SC
Wagoner, Porter	Green Green Grass Of Home	19-319	CB
Wagoner, Porter	I'll Go Down Swinging	19-316	CB
Wagoner, Porter	I've Enjoyed As Much Of This As I..	19-313	CB
Wagoner, Porter	Misery Loves Company	19-306	CB
Wagoner, Porter	Misery Loves Company	5-217	SC
Wagoner, Porter	Satisfied Mind	19-308	CB
Wagoner, Porter	Satisfied Mind	8-668	SAV
Wagoner, Porter	Skid Row Joe	19-317	CB
Wagoner, Porter	Sorrow On The Rocks	19-315	CB
Wagoner, Porter	Tryin' To Forget The Blues	19-312	CB
Wagoner, Porter	Xmas - We Wish You A Merry Xmas	8-76	CB
Wagoner, Porter	Y'All Come	19-305	CB
Wagoner, Porter	Your Old Love Letters	19-314	CB
Wainwright, Loudin	Dead Skunk	2-789	SC
Wainwright, Rufus	Hallelujah	44-306	SC
Waite, John	Change	37-67	SC
Waite, Tom	Piano Has Been Drinking the	7-407	MM
Waiting To Exhale	Show - Let It Flow	18-821	PS
Waitresses	Christmas Wrapping	45-743	SC
Waitresses	I Know What Boys Like	15-14	SC
Waitresses	Xmas - Christmas	14-304	MM

ARTIST	SONG TITLE	#	TYPE
	Wrapping		
Waitresses	Xmas - Christmas Wrapping	45-743	SC
Wakely, Jimmy	I Love You So Much It Hurts	19-844	CB
Wakely, Jimmy	One Has My Name, Other My Heart	19-839	CB
Wakely, Jimmy	One Has My Name, Other My Heart	5-218	SC
Walk The Moon	Different Colors	48-414	BKD
Walk The Moon	Shut Up And Dance	47-585	MRH
Walker & All Stars	Shotgun	3-22	SC
Walker Brothers	Sun Ain't Gonna Shine Anymore	3-127	SC
Walker, Billy	Charlie's Shoes	5-223	SC
Walker, Charlie	Don't Squeeze My Sharmon	46-39	SSK
Walker, Charlie	Foggy River	45-833	VH
Walker, Charlie	Pick Me Up On Your Way Down	8-776	CB
Walker, Charlie	Pick Me Up On Your Way Down	14-329	SC
Walker, Charlie	Who Will Buy The Wine	5-426	SC
Walker, Clay	Bury The Shovel	1-99	CB
Walker, Clay	Bury The Shovel	4-463	SC
Walker, Clay	Chain Of Love the	8-897	CB
Walker, Clay	Chain Of Love the	13-827	CHM
Walker, Clay	Chain Of Love the	5-839	SC
Walker, Clay	Dreaming With My Eyes Wide Open	17-239	NA
Walker, Clay	Dreaming With My Eyes Wide Open	1-93	CB
Walker, Clay	Dreaming With My Eyes Wide Open	12-186	DK
Walker, Clay	Dreaming With My Eyes Wide Open	6-600	MM
Walker, Clay	Dreaming With My Eyes Wide Open	2-325	SC
Walker, Clay	Fall	30-449	CB
Walker, Clay	Few Questions a	34-409	CB
Walker, Clay	Few Questions a	25-615	MM
Walker, Clay	Few Questions a	19-62	ST
Walker, Clay	Few Questions a	32-301	THM
Walker, Clay	Fore She Was Mama	30-174	CB
Walker, Clay	Hypnotize The Moon	1-98	CB
Walker, Clay	Hypnotize The Moon	4-92	SC
Walker, Clay	I Can't Sleep	19-703	ST
Walker, Clay	I Don't Know How Love Starts	24-241	SC
Walker, Clay	I Won't Have The Heart	4-235	SC
Walker, Clay	If I Could Make A Living	1-94	CB
Walker, Clay	If I Could Make A Living	2-485	SC
Walker, Clay	If You Ever Feel Like Lovin' Me Aga	15-605	ST
Walker, Clay	Jesus Was A Country Boy	20-448	ST
Walker, Clay	Live Laugh Love	5-726	SC
Walker, Clay	Live Laugh Love	22-502	ST
Walker, Clay	Live Until I Die	1-91	CB

ARTIST	SONG TITLE	#	TYPE
Walker, Clay	My Heart Will Never Know	1-97	CB
Walker, Clay	My Heart Will Never Know	6-800	MM
Walker, Clay	My Heart Will Never Know	2-763	SC
Walker, Clay	Once In A Lifetime Love	14-96	CB
Walker, Clay	One Two I Love You	1-101	CB
Walker, Clay	One Two I Love You	10-86	SC
Walker, Clay	Only On Days That End In "Y"	22-895	ST
Walker, Clay	Only On Days That End In Y	7-248	MM
Walker, Clay	Only On Days That End In Y	4-361	SC
Walker, Clay	Ordinary People	1-104	CB
Walker, Clay	Ordinary People	22-800	ST
Walker, Clay	Rumor Has It	14-661	CB
Walker, Clay	Rumor Has It	7-591	CHM
Walker, Clay	Rumor Has It	7-422	MM
Walker, Clay	Say No More	30-32	CB
Walker, Clay	Say No More	9-865	ST
Walker, Clay	She Likes It In The Morning	36-428	CB
Walker, Clay	She's Always Right	8-928	CB
Walker, Clay	She's Always Right	7-887	CHT
Walker, Clay	She's Always Right	22-728	ST
Walker, Clay	Then What	8-226	CB
Walker, Clay	Then What	7-720	CHM
Walker, Clay	Then What	22-757	ST
Walker, Clay	This Woman And This Man	1-96	CB
Walker, Clay	This Woman And This Man	17-284	NA
Walker, Clay	This Woman And This Man	22-865	ST
Walker, Clay	Watch This	1-102	CB
Walker, Clay	Watch This	22-617	ST
Walker, Clay	What's It To You	2-804	SC
Walker, Clay	Where Do I Fit In The Picture	1-92	CB
Walker, Clay	Where Do I Fit In The Picture	2-820	SC
Walker, Clay	Who Needs You Baby	1-95	CB
Walker, Clay	Who Needs You Baby	7-77	MM
Walker, Clay	Who Needs You Baby	3-538	SC
Walker, Clay	You're Beginning To Get To Me	8-156	CB
Walker, Jerry Jeff	Pissin' In The Wind **	30-664	RSX
Walker, Jerry Jeff	Up Against The Wall	15-15	SC
Walker, Junior	What Does It Take To Win Your Love	17-376	DK
Walker, Mike	Stones In The Road	17-606	CB
Walker, Mike	Who's Your Daddy	17-486	CB
Walker, T-Bone	Stormy Monday	15-321	SC
Walker, Tamara	Circle Of Love	34-413	CB
Walker, Tamara	Didn't We Love	14-128	CB
Wall Of Voodoo	Mexican Radio	21-400	SC
Wallace, Jerry	If You Leave Me Tonight	14-323	SC

ARTIST	SONG TITLE	#	TYPE
Wallace, Jerry	In The Misty Moonlight	16-368	CB
Wallace, Jerry	Primrose Lane	29-620	CB
Wallace, Jerry	Primrose Lane	20-61	SC
Wallflowers	6th Avenue Heartache	24-120	SC
Wallflowers	Heroes	16-231	PHM
Wallflowers	Three Marlenas	7-694	PHM
Wallis, Ruth	You've Gotta Have Boobs **	30-670	RSX
Walsh & Earle	Honey Don't	24-350	SC
Walsh, Joe	All Night Long	17-512	SC
Walsh, Joe	Funk #49	15-710	LE
Walsh, Joe	Ordinary Average Guy	15-709	LE
Walsh, Joe	Rocky Mountain Way	12-695	P
Walsh, Joe	Walk Away	15-711	LE
Walters, Jamie	Hold On	3-438	SC
Walters, Jamie	Why	3-490	SC
Waltz Favorites	Blue Skirt Waltz	29-810	SSR
Waltz Favorites	Waltz - Blue Skirt Waltz	29-810	SSR
Wang Chung	Dance Hall Days	29-638	SC
Wang Chung	Everybody Have Fun Tonight	26-272	DK
Wang Chung	Everybody Have Fun Tonight	15-799	SC
War	Cisco Kid the	12-171	DK
War	Cisco Kid the	4-57	SC
War	Low Rider	4-86	SC
War	Why Can't We Be Friends	12-166	DK
War	Why Can't We Be Friends	15-800	SC
Ward & Dominos	60 Minute Man	2-82	SC
Ward & Dominos	Stardust	12-528	P
Ward, Anita	Ring My Bell	2-492	SC
Ward, Chris	Fall Reaching	24-160	SC
Ward, Damon	Keys In The Mailbox the	37-226	DW
Ward, Mike	Neon Wishing Well	10-85	SC
Ward, Shayne	No Promises	30-705	SF
Warden, Monte	Someday	8-940	CB
Wariner & Brooks	Duet - Katie Wants A Fast One	14-93	CB
Wariner & Brooks	Duet - Katie Wants A Fast One	19-220	CSZ
Wariner & Brooks	Katie Wants A Fast One	14-93	CB
Wariner & Brooks	Katie Wants A Fast One	19-220	CSZ
Wariner & Brooks	Katie Wants A Fast One	22-559	ST
Wariner & Larson	Duet - That's How You Know When...	5-443	SC
Wariner & Larson	That's How You Know When...	5-443	SC
Wariner w/Brooks	Burnin' The Roadhouse Down	22-826	ST
Wariner, Steve	All Roads Lead To You	14-257	SC
Wariner, Steve	Burnin' The Roadhouse Down	8-738	CB
Wariner, Steve	Can I Come Over Tonight	8-931	CB
Wariner, Steve	Crash Course In The Blues	3-50	SC
Wariner, Steve	Divorce Me C.O.D.	5-220	SC
Wariner, Steve	Domino Theory the	1-497	CB
Wariner, Steve	Drive	1-505	CB
Wariner, Steve	Drivin' And Cryin'	1-503	CB
Wariner, Steve	Drivin' And Cryin'	3-45	SC
Wariner, Steve	Every Little Whisper	8-221	CB
Wariner, Steve	Every Little Whisper	22-690	ST
Wariner, Steve	Faith In You	13-834	CHM
Wariner, Steve	Faith In You	19-257	CSZ
Wariner, Steve	Heart Trouble	5-326	SC
Wariner, Steve	Holes In The Floor Of Heaven	8-473	CB
Wariner, Steve	I Got Dreams	14-259	SC
Wariner, Steve	I'm Already Taken	19-200	CB
Wariner, Steve	I'm Already Taken	22-425	ST
Wariner, Steve	If I Didn't Love You	6-387	MM
Wariner, Steve	In A Heartbeat	8-395	CB
Wariner, Steve	It Won't Be Over You	1-504	CB
Wariner, Steve	It Won't Be Over You	6-577	MM
Wariner, Steve	Kansas City Lights	8-689	SAV
Wariner, Steve	Leave Him Out Of This	1-500	CB
Wariner, Steve	Life's Highway	13-536	P
Wariner, Steve	Life's Highway	5-20	SC
Wariner, Steve	Like A River To The Sea	1-506	CB
Wariner, Steve	Lynda	29-75	CB
Wariner, Steve	Lynda	5-319	SC
Wariner, Steve	Precious Thing	1-498	CB
Wariner, Steve	Road Trippin'	8-739	CB
Wariner, Steve	Small Town Girl	5-321	SC
Wariner, Steve	Snow Fall On The Sand	18-790	ST
Wariner, Steve	Some Fools Never Learn	4-824	SC
Wariner, Steve	There For Awhile	1-499	CB
Wariner, Steve	Tips Of My Fingers	1-501	CB
Wariner, Steve	Tips Of My Fingers	17-254	NA
Wariner, Steve	Two Teardrops	8-923	CB
Wariner, Steve	Two Teardrops	7-866	CHT
Wariner, Steve	Weekend the	5-320	SC
Wariner, Steve	What I Didn't Do	4-656	SC
Wariner, Steve	When I Could Come Home To You	2-507	SC
Wariner, Steve	Where Did I Go Wrong	1-496	CB
Wariner, Steve	Where Did I Go Wrong	5-328	SC
Wariner, Steve	Woman Loves a	1-502	CB
Wariner, Steve	You Can Dream Of Me	20-17	SC
Warnes, Jennifer	I Know A Heartache When I See One	33-308	CB
Warnes, Jennifer	Right Time Of The Night	4-377	SC
Warrant	Cherry Pie	5-485	SC
Warrant	Cherry Pie **	23-51	MH
Warrant	Down Boys	6-28	SC
Warrant	Heaven	24-207	SC
Warrant	I Saw Red	24-686	SC
Warrant	Uncle Tom's Cabin	5-69	SC
Warren Brothers	Better Man	8-352	CB
Warren Brothers	Change	23-489	CB
Warren Brothers	Guilty	22-694	ST
Warren Brothers	Hey Mr. President	19-51	ST
Warren Brothers	Hey Mr. President	32-231	THM

ARTIST	SONG TITLE	#	TYPE
Warren Brothers	It Ain't Me	29-350	CB
Warren Brothers	Move On	14-132	CB
Warren Brothers	Move On	22-463	ST
Warren Brothers	Sell A Lot Of Beer	20-511	ST
Warren Brothers	Sell A Lot Of Beer	47-504	SC
Warren Brothers	That's The Beat Of A Heart	9-393	CB
Warren Brothers	That's The Beat Of A Heart	13-862	CHM
Warren Brothers	That's The Beat Of A Heart	19-251	CSZ
Warren Brothers	Where Does It Hurt	15-192	ST
Warren, Darren	Cowboy Up & Party Down	38-102	PHM
Warrens & Evans	Duet - That's The Beat Of A Heart	13-862	CHM
Warrens & Evans	Duet - That's The Beat Of A Heart	19-251	CSZ
Warwick & Friends	Duet - That's What Friends Are For	9-876	DK
Warwick & Friends	That's What Friends Are For	9-876	DK
Warwick & Friends	That's What Friends Are For	17-421	KC
Warwick & Friends	That's What Friends Are For	6-343	MM
Warwick, Dionne	Alfie	11-314	DK
Warwick, Dionne	Alfie	13-163	P
Warwick, Dionne	All The Love In The World	48-763	P
Warwick, Dionne	Anyone Who Had A Heart	13-324	P
Warwick, Dionne	Anyone Who Had A Heart	4-249	SC
Warwick, Dionne	Do You Know The Way To San Jose	11-216	DK
Warwick, Dionne	Do You Know The Way To San Jose	3-360	MH
Warwick, Dionne	Do You Know The Way To San Jose	4-698	SC
Warwick, Dionne	Don't Make Me Over	20-58	SC
Warwick, Dionne	Heartbreaker	12-373	DK
Warwick, Dionne	I Say A Little Prayer	16-831	DK
Warwick, Dionne	I Say A Little Prayer	5-464	SC
Warwick, Dionne	I'll Never Fall In Love Again	16-802	DK
Warwick, Dionne	I'll Never Fall In Love Again	30-750	SF
Warwick, Dionne	Message To Michael	5-6	SC
Warwick, Dionne	Then Came You	26-394	DK
Warwick, Dionne	Valley Of The Dolls	5-233	SC
Warwick, Dionne	Walk On By	11-793	DK
Warwick, Dionne	Walk On By	14-341	SC
Warwick, Dionne	Wishing And Hoping	34-135	CB
Was (Not Was)	Walk The Dinosaur	34-101	CB
Washington, Dinah	This Bitter Earth	23-354	MM
Washington, Dinah	Trust In Me	23-353	MM
Washington, Dinah	What A Difference A Day Makes	19-614	MH
Washington, Dinah	What A Difference A Day	5-451	SC

ARTIST	SONG TITLE	#	TYPE
	Makes		
Washington, Grover	Just The Two Of Us	35-162	CB
Washington, Grover	Just The Two Of Us	12-886	P
Washington, Grover	Just The Two Of Us	2-275	SC
Waters, Ethyl	Show - Am I Blue	12-286	DK
Watkins, Sara	You And Me	41-73	PHN
Watley, Jodi	Don't You Want Me	11-767	DK
Watley, Jodi	Don't You Want Me	20-55	SC
Watley, Jodi	Looking For A New Love	11-787	DK
Watley, Jodi	Looking For A New Love	33-326	CB
Watley, Jodi	Real Love	11-532	DK
Watley, Jodi	Real Love	16-519	P
Watley, Jodi	Some Kind Of Lover	11-316	DK
Watley, Jodi	You Love Keeps Working	15-763	NU
Watson, Aaron	That Look	49-406	BKD
Watson, Aaron	That Look (Inst)	49-407	BKD
Watson, Gene	Drinkin' My Way Back Home	14-675	CB
Watson, Gene	Farewell Party	8-830	CB
Watson, Gene	Farewell Party	14-314	SC
Watson, Gene	Forever Again	14-676	CB
Watson, Gene	Fourteen Carat Mind	14-664	CB
Watson, Gene	Fourteen Carat Mind	2-633	SC
Watson, Gene	Gospel - the City	43-100	CB
Watson, Gene	Got No Reason Now For Going Home	14-677	CB
Watson, Gene	Got No Reason Now For Going Home	5-780	SC
Watson, Gene	Love In The Hot Afternoon	14-667	CB
Watson, Gene	Love In The Hot Afternoon	7-154	MM
Watson, Gene	Nothing Sure Looked Good On You	14-671	CB
Watson, Gene	Nothing Sure Looked Good On You	19-435	SC
Watson, Gene	Old Man And His Horn the	29-703	SC
Watson, Gene	Old Porch Swing	4-140	SC
Watson, Gene	Paper Rosie	14-666	CB
Watson, Gene	Paper Rosie	5-619	SC
Watson, Gene	Pick The Wildwood Flower	14-670	CB
Watson, Gene	Pick The Wildwood Flower	5-812	SC
Watson, Gene	Should I Come Home	14-663	CB
Watson, Gene	Sometimes I Get Lucky & Forget	14-674	CB
Watson, Gene	Speak Softly (You're Talking To My.	14-672	CB
Watson, Gene	That Evil Child	45-869	VH
Watson, Gene	Where Love Begins	14-668	CB
Watson, Gene	Where Love Begins	29-697	SC
Watson, Gene	You Could Know As Much About...	14-669	CB
Watson, Gene	You Gave Me A Mountain	24-353	SC
Watson, Gene	You're Just Another	47-492	CB

ARTIST	SONG TITLE	#	TYPE
	Beer Drinking Song		
Watson, Gene	You're Out Doing What I'm Doing Without	14-673	CB
Watson, Johnny "Guitar"	Ain't That A Bitch	36-137	SGB
Wayne, Jimmy	I Love You This Much	25-708	MM
Wayne, Jimmy	I Love You This Much	19-262	ST
Wayne, Jimmy	I Love You This Much	32-417	THM
Wayne, Jimmy	I Will	36-245	PHM
Wayne, Jimmy	Paper Angels	22-96	CB
Wayne, Jimmy	Paper Angels	23-32	SC
Wayne, Jimmy	Paper Angels	19-769	ST
Wayne, Jimmy	Stay Gone	34-368	CB
Wayne, Jimmy	Stay Gone	25-521	MM
Wayne, Jimmy	Stay Gone	18-804	ST
Wayne, Jimmy	Stay Gone	32-187	THM
Wayne, Jimmy	That's All I'll Ever Need	30-168	CB
Wayne, Jimmy	You Are	30-804	PHM
Wayne, Jimmy	You Are	20-329	ST
Wayne, Thomas	Tragedy	20-31	SC
We Five	You Were On My Mind	16-881	DK
We the Kings	Secret Valentine	36-268	PHM
Weather Girls	It's Raining Men	20-373	SC
Weaver, Patty	Xmas - Joy To The World	33-207	CB
Weavers	Goodnight Irene	8-419	CB
Weber, Joan	Let Me Go Lover	33-241	CB
Weezer	Beverly Hills	23-318	CB
Weezer	Hashpipe	16-380	SGB
Weezer	Island In The Sun	25-37	MM
Weezer	Pork And Beans	36-470	CB
Weezer	Say It Isn't So	5-737	SC
Weezer	Troublemaker	36-521	CB
Welch, Larry	Since I Fell For You	6-256	MM
Welk, Lawrence	Alley Cat the - DANCE #	22-389	SC
Weller, Freddie	Games People Play	8-634	SAV
Wells & Foley	As Long As I Live - duet	48-201	CB
Wells & Foley	Duet - As Long As I Love	48-201	CB
Wells & Foley	Duet - Make Believe (Till We Can...)	48-203	CB
Wells & Foley	Duet - One By One	6-4	SC
Wells & Foley	Duet - One By One	48-200	CB
Wells & Foley	Duet - You And Me	48-202	CB
Wells & Foley	Make Believe (Till We Can...) - duet	48-203	CB
Wells & Foley	One By One	6-4	SC
Wells & Foley	One By One - duet	48-200	CB
Wells & Foley	You And Me - duet	48-202	CB
Wells, Junior	Messin' With The Kid	15-29	SC
Wells, Kitty	Amigo's Guitar	20-644	SC
Wells, Kitty	Heartbreak USA	8-778	CB
Wells, Kitty	Heartbreak USA	4-748	SC
Wells, Kitty	I Can't Stop Loving You	34-194	CB
Wells, Kitty	I Can't Stop Loving You	47-390	CB
Wells, Kitty	I'll Always Be Your Fraulein	48-204	SSK
Wells, Kitty	It Wasn't God Who Made	7-119	MM

ARTIST	SONG TITLE	#	TYPE
	Honky Tonk		
Wells, Kitty	It Wasn't God Who Made HonkyTonk	26-490	DK
Wells, Kitty	Jealousy	47-393	CB
Wells, Kitty	Left To Right	47-394	CB
Wells, Kitty	Making Believe	13-348	P
Wells, Kitty	Making Believe	14-326	SC
Wells, Kitty	Mommy For A Day	4-737	SC
Wells, Kitty	Password	4-739	SC
Wells, Kitty	Paying For That Back Street Affair	48-205	SSK
Wells, Kitty	Searching For Someone Like You	5-571	SC
Wells, Kitty	There's Poison In Your Heart	47-391	CB
Wells, Kitty	This White Circle On My Finger	47-392	CB
Wells, Kitty	Will Your Lawyer Talk To My Lawyer	4-742	SC
Wells, Kitty	You Don't Hear	4-738	SC
Wells, Mary	Don't Mess With Bill	49-452	MM
Wells, Mary	My Guy	9-880	DK
Wells, Mary	My Guy	10-727	JVC
Wells, Mary	My Guy	3-268	MM
Wells, Mary	One Who Really Loves You	6-559	MM
Wells, Mary	One Who Really Loves You the	49-479	MM
Wells, Mary	Two Lovers	6-565	MM
Wells, Mary	You Beat Me To The Punch	12-66	DK
West & Foxx	Gold Digger **	30-138	PT
West & Rogers	Duet - Every Time Two Fools Collide	8-117	CB
West & Rogers	Duet - Every Time Two Fools Collide	2-298	SC
West Side Story	Show - Gee Officer Krupke	7-369	MM
West Side Story	Show - I Feel Pretty	6-251	MM
West Side Story	Show - I Feel Pretty	5-647	SC
West Side Story	Show - Maria	12-31	DK
West Side Story	Show - Maria	5-657	SC
West Side Story	Show - Something's Coming	6-877	MM
West Side Story	Show - Tonight	27-377	DK
West Side Story	Show - Tonight	6-254	MM
West Side Story	Show - Tonight	19-587	SC
West Side Story	Tonight	19-587	SC
West, Dottie	Are You Happy Baby	29-785	CB
West, Dottie	Are You Happy Baby	14-322	SC
West, Dottie	Before The Ring On Your Finger Turn	5-841	SC
West, Dottie	Come See Me And Come Lonely	15-231	CB
West, Dottie	Come See Me And Come Lonely	47-815	SRK
West, Dottie	Country Sunshine	8-795	CB
West, Dottie	Country Sunshine	13-494	P
West, Dottie	Country Sunshine	5-418	SC

ARTIST	SONG TITLE	#	TYPE	ARTIST	SONG TITLE	#	TYPE
West, Dottie	Every Word I Write	15-229	CB	Wheatus	Teenage Dirtbag	15-447	PHM
West, Dottie	Here Comes My Baby	33-22	CB	Whiskey Falls	Falling Into You	36-566	CB
West, Dottie	Here Comes My Baby	8-383	CB	Whiskey Falls	Last Train Running	30-476	CB
West, Dottie	Last Time I Saw Him	15-519	CB	Whispers	And The Beat Goes On	15-39	SS
West, Dottie	Lesson In Leavin'	8-840	CB	White Lion	Wait	5-64	SC
West, Dottie	Reaching Out To Hold You	15-232	CB	White Lion	When The Children Cry	23-56	MH
West, Dottie	Sometimes When We Touch	49-774	SC	White Lion	When The Children Cry	24-684	SC
West, Dottie	Tonight You Belong To Me	15-230	CB	White Plains	My Baby Loves Lovin'	20-48	SC
West, Dottie	Tonight You Belong To Me	47-816	SRK	White Stripes	Hardest Button To Button	23-185	PHM
West, Dottie	When It's Just You & Me	15-228	CB	White Stripes	Seven Nation Army	19-604	CB
West, Dottie	Would You Hold It Against Me	6-1	SC	White Stripes	Seven Nation Army	19-545	SC
West, Dottie	You're Not Easy To Forget	15-227	CB	White Stripes	Seven Nation Army	32-218	THM
West, Emily	Rocks In Your Shoes	36-578	CB	White Stripes	You Don't Know What Love Is	49-908	SC
West, Kanye	Gold Digger **	30-138	PT	White Town	Your Woman	10-685	HH
West, Kanye	Heartless	36-267	PHM	White Town	Your Woman	10-94	SC
West, Kanye	Love Lockdown	49-906	SC	White, Barry	Can't Get Enough Of Your Love	35-118	CB
West, Kanye & Foxx	Gold Digger (Radio Vers)	37-95	SC	White, Barry	Can't Get Enough Of Your Love	6-566	MM
West, Keith	Excerpt From A Teenage Opera	10-647	SF	White, Barry	Can't Get Enough Of Your Love	16-553	P
West, Shelly	Jose Quervo	7-414	MM	White, Barry	Can't Get Enough Of Your Love	4-758	SC
West, Shelly	Jose Quervo	2-26	SC	White, Barry	Come On	46-196	SC
Western Flyer	Cherokee Highway	2-734	SC	White, Barry	I'm Gonna Love You Just A Little...	9-764	SAV
Western Flyer	Friday Night Stampede	7-23	MM	White, Barry	Let The Music Play	48-772	P
Western Flyer	His Memory	4-21	SC	White, Barry	Never Gonna Give You Up	10-678	HE
Western Flyer	What Will You Do With M-E	4-892	SC	White, Barry	Never Never Gonna Give You Up	6-560	MM
Westlife	Swear It Again	16-233	PHM	White, Barry	You See The Trouble With Me	15-696	LE
Westlife	World Of Our Own	18-343	PHM	White, Barry	You're The First The Last My Everyt	17-99	DK
Weston & Gaye	Duet - It Takes Two	26-524	DK	White, Bryan	Bad Day To Let You Go	8-467	CB
Weston & Gaye	It Takes Two	26-524	DK	White, Bryan	Between Now And Forever	7-234	MM
Wet Wet Wet	Love is All Around	12-181	DK	White, Bryan	Eugene You Genius	6-669	MM
Wet Willie	Keep On Smilin'	18-156	CB	White, Bryan	God Gave Me You	5-827	SC
Wet Willie	Keep On Smilin'	7-462	MM	White, Bryan	How Long	14-127	CB
Wet Willie	Keep On Smilin'	2-534	SC	White, Bryan	How Long	22-464	ST
Wham!	Careless Whisper	16-721	DK	White, Bryan	I'm Not Supposed To Love You Anymor	4-233	SC
Wham!	Careless Whisper	13-206	P	White, Bryan	Look At Me Now	24-126	SC
Wham!	Careless Whisper	24-66	SC	White, Bryan	Love Is The Right Place	7-679	CHM
Wham!	Everything She Wants	20-298	CB	White, Bryan	Love Is The Right Place	22-615	ST
Wham!	Everything She Wants	28-337	DK	White, Bryan	One Small Miracle	8-148	CB
Wham!	Everything She Wants	16-522	P	White, Bryan	One Small Miracle	22-753	ST
Wham!	Everything She Wants	4-847	SC	White, Bryan	Rebecca Lynn	3-625	SC
Wham!	Freedom	11-648	DK	White, Bryan	Sittin' On Go	14-656	CB
Wham!	Freedom	21-607	SF	White, Bryan	Sittin' On Go	7-609	CHM
Wham!	Wake Me Up Before You Go Go	35-176	CB	White, Bryan	So Much For Pretending	4-420	SC
Wham!	Wake Me Up Before You Go-Go	16-777	DK	White, Bryan	Someone Else's Star	6-845	MM
Wham!	Wake Me Up Before You Go-Go	12-760	P	White, Bryan	Someone Else's Star	2-775	SC
Wham!	Wake Me Up Before You Go-Go	10-532	SF	White, Bryan	That's Another Song	7-378	MM
Wham!	Xmas - Last Christmas	11-725	DK	White, Bryan	That's Another Song	4-596	SC

ARTIST	SONG TITLE	#	TYPE
White, Bryan	Tree Of Hearts	8-746	CB
White, Bryan	Tree Of Hearts	22-833	ST
White, Bryan	You're Still Beautiful To Me	22-432	ST
White, Clarence	Bury Me Beneath The Willow	45-685	VH
White, Karyn	Superwoman	19-359	DK
White, Lari	Don't Fence Me In	16-645	MM
White, Lari	John Wayne Walking Away	14-611	SC
White, Lari	Lay Around And Love On You	8-880	CB
White, Lari	Lead Me Not	2-794	SC
White, Lari	Now I Know	8-881	CB
White, Lari	Now I Know	6-664	MM
White, Lari	Now I Know	2-420	SC
White, Lari	Ready Willing And Able	4-22	SC
White, Lari	Stepping Stone	8-495	CB
White, Lari	Stepping Stone	22-806	ST
White, Lari	Take Me	22-677	ST
White, Lari	Test the	4-230	SC
White, Lari	That's How You Know	8-882	CB
White, Lari	That's How You Know When You're..	6-712	MM
White, Lari	That's How You Know When You're...	17-281	NA
White, Lari	That's My Baby	19-300	MH
White, Lari	That's My Baby	16-592	MM
White, Lari	What A Woman Wants	10-787	JVC
White, Lari	Wild At Heart	7-284	MM
White, Lari	Wishes	4-469	SC
Whites	Hangin' Around	8-705	SAV
Whites	Keep On The Sunny Side	33-224	CB
Whitesnake	Here I Go Again	13-37	P
Whitesnake	In The Still Of The Night	5-61	SC
Whitesnake	Is This Love	13-36	P
Whitesnake	Slow An' Easy	6-18	SC
Whitesnake	Steal Away	48-568	DK
Whiting & Wakely	Duet - Slippin' Around	19-640	CB
Whiting & Wakely	Duet - Slippin' Around	6-3	SC
Whiting & Wakely	Slippin' Around	19-640	CB
Whiting & Wakely	Slippin' Around	6-3	SC
Whitley & Morgan	Duet - Till A Tear Becomes A Rose	8-118	CB
Whitley & Morgan	Duet - Till a Tear Becomes a Rose	2-302	SC
Whitley & Morgan	Till A Tear Becomes A Rose	8-118	CB
Whitley & Morgan	Till A Tear Becomes A Rose	2-302	SC
Whitley, Keith	Birmingham Turnaround the	49-401	KVD
Whitley, Keith	Dance With Me Molly	47-742	SRK
Whitley, Keith	Don't Close Your Eyes	11-738	DK
Whitley, Keith	Going Gone	11-739	DK
Whitley, Keith	Hard Livin'	14-422	SC
Whitley, Keith	Heartbreak Highway	49-497	CB
Whitley, Keith	Homecoming ' 63	8-697	SAV

ARTIST	SONG TITLE	#	TYPE
Whitley, Keith	Homecoming ' 63	19-446	SC
Whitley, Keith	I Never Go Around Mirrors	47-766	SRK
Whitley, Keith	I Wonder Do You Think Of Me	4-654	SC
Whitley, Keith	I Wonder Do You Think Of Me	8-595	TT
Whitley, Keith	I Wonder where You Are Tonight	49-402	KVD
Whitley, Keith	I'm No Stranger To The Rain	9-510	SAV
Whitley, Keith	I'm No Stranger To The Rain	16-583	SC
Whitley, Keith	I'm Over You	34-296	CB
Whitley, Keith	I'm Over You	4-545	SC
Whitley, Keith	It Ain't Nothin'	14-682	CB
Whitley, Keith	It Ain't Nothin'	6-621	MM
Whitley, Keith	It Ain't Nothing	34-298	CB
Whitley, Keith	Miami My Amy	5-557	SC
Whitley, Keith	Same Old Side Road	49-400	CB
Whitley, Keith	Somebody's Doing Me Right	33-111	CB
Whitley, Keith	Talk To Me Texas	49-396	CB
Whitley, Keith	Tell Lorrie I Love Her	49-395	JER
Whitley, Keith	Ten Feet Away	49-398	CB
Whitley, Keith	Till A Tear Becomes A Rose	6-616	MM
Whitley, Keith	When You Say Nothing At All	35-395	CB
Whitley, Keith	When You Say Nothing At All	2-99	SC
Whitley, Keith	Would These Arms Be In Your Way	49-399	CB
Whitley, Keith	Xmas - There's A New Kid In Town	18-753	CB
Whitman, Slim	Indian Love Call	5-581	SC
Whittaker, Roger	Blue Eyes Crying In The Rain	13-586	PL
Whittaker, Roger	But She Loves Me	13-593	PL
Whittaker, Roger	Durham Town	13-587	PL
Whittaker, Roger	Have I Told You Lately	13-591	PL
Whittaker, Roger	I Love You Because	13-589	PL
Whittaker, Roger	I'd Fall In Love Tonight	13-592	PL
Whittaker, Roger	Keep On Chasing Rainbows	13-594	PL
Whittaker, Roger	Last Farewell the	13-585	PL
Whittaker, Roger	New World In The Morning	13-590	PL
Whittaker, Roger	There Goes My Everything	13-588	PL
Who	Anyway Anyhow Anywhere	28-142	DK
Who	Anyway Anyhow Anywhere	19-735	LE
Who	Baba O'Reilly	10-481	DA
Who	Behind Blue Eyes	19-736	LE
Who	Happy Jack	28-143	DK
Who	Happy Jack	19-731	LE
Who	I Can See For Miles	28-144	DK
Who	I Can See For Miles	19-729	LE

ARTIST	SONG TITLE	#	TYPE
Who	I Can See For Miles	3-129	SC
Who	I Can't Explain	19-742	LE
Who	I'm A Boy	28-149	DK
Who	I'm A Boy	19-741	LE
Who	I'm Free	19-738	LE
Who	Join Together	19-733	LE
Who	Kids Are Alright the	19-745	LE
Who	Magic Bus	28-145	DK
Who	Magic Bus	19-734	LE
Who	My Generation	28-146	DK
Who	My Generation	7-53	MM
Who	My Generation	3-857	SC
Who	Pictures Of Lily	28-147	DK
Who	Pictures Of Lily	19-737	LE
Who	Pinball Wizard	19-730	LE
Who	Squeeze Box	35-122	CB
Who	Squeeze Box	19-744	LE
Who	Squeeze Box	2-721	SC
Who	Substitute	28-148	DK
Who	Substitute	19-743	LE
Who	Summertime Blues	13-222	P
Who	Who Are You	19-740	LE
Who	Who Are You	5-596	SC
Who	Won't Get Fooled Again	19-732	LE
Who	You Better You Bet	19-739	LE
Who	You Better You Bet	5-877	SC
Who	Behind Blue Eyes	37-69	SC
Whodini	Freaks Come Out At Night	17-530	SC
Whodini	Halloween - Haunted House Of Rock	45-139	GGZ
Whodini	Haunted House Of Rock - Halloween	45-139	GGZ
Wicks, Chuck	All I Ever Wanted	36-413	CB
Wicks, Chuck	Hold That Thought	48-453	CB
Wicks, Chuck	I Don't Do Lonely Well	48-451	KCD
Wicks, Chuck	Man Of The House	48-455	CB
Wicks, Chuck	Old School	48-454	CB
Wicks, Chuck	Saturday Afternoon	48-456	KCD
Wicks, Chuck	Stealing Cinderella	30-580	CB
Wiggins, J & A	Has Anybody Seen Amy	17-240	NA
Wiggins, J & A	Has Anybody Seen Amy	2-484	SC
Wiggins, J & A	Memory Making Night	2-696	SC
Wiggins, J & A	She's In the Bedroom Crying	2-573	SC
Wiggins, J & A	Somewhere In Love	10-83	SC
Wiggles	Away In A Manger - xmas	45-241	WIG
Wiggles	Go Santa Go - xmas	45-239	WIG
Wiggles	Here Come The Reindeer - xmas	45-238	WIG
Wiggles	Rockin' Santa - xmas	45-237	WIG
Wiggles	Unto Us This Holy Night - xmas	45-240	WIG
Wiggles	Xmas - Away In A Manger	45-241	WIG
Wiggles	Xmas - Go Santa Go	45-239	WIG
Wiggles	Xmas - Here Come The	45-238	WIG

ARTIST	SONG TITLE	#	TYPE
	Reindeer		
Wiggles	Xmas - Rockin' Santa	45-237	WIG
Wiggles	Xmas - Unto Us This Holy Night	45-240	WIG
Wilburn Brothers	Roll Muddy River	33-14	CB
Wild Cherry	Play That Funky Music	26-295	DK
Wild Cherry	Play That Funky Music	10-528	SF
Wild Horses	I Will Survive	16-39	ST
Wild Orchid	At Night I Pray	24-543	SC
Wilde, Kim	Kids In America	24-422	SC
Wilde, Kim	You Keep Me Hangin' On	6-491	MM
Wilder, Matthew	Break My Stride	4-58	SC
Wilkinson, Amanda	Gone From Love Too Long	22-3	CB
Wilkinson, Amanda	Gone From Love Too Long	19-695	ST
Wilkinson, Amanda	No More Me And You	23-132	CB
Wilkinsons	26 Cents	8-745	CB
Wilkinsons	26 Cents	22-810	ST
Wilkinsons	Boy Oh Boy	8-956	CB
Wilkinsons	Boy Oh Boy	22-676	ST
Wilkinsons	Fly (The Angel Song)	8-242	CB
Wilkinsons	Fly (The Angel Song)	22-687	ST
Wilkinsons	Jimmy's Got A Girlfriend	22-480	ST
Wilkinsons	Shame On Me	14-711	CB
Williams & Harris	Duet - If I Needed You	45-231	CB
Williams & Harris	If I Needed You - duet	45-231	CB
Williams & Jennings	Conversation the - duet	45-186	KV
Williams & Jennings	Duet - Conversation the	45-186	KV
Williams & Kid Rock	Duet - The "F" Word	45-133	SC
Williams & Kid Rock	The "F" Word - duet	45-133	SC
Williams Andy	Aloha Oe	15-399	NK
Williams, Andy	Born Free	13-553	LE
Williams, Andy	Can't Get Used To Losing You	12-29	DK
Williams, Andy	Can't Get Used To Losing You	2-199	SC
Williams, Andy	Can't Take My Eyes Off You	49-42	ZVS
Williams, Andy	Days Of Wine And Roses	27-393	DK
Williams, Andy	Days Of Wine And Roses	13-555	LE
Williams, Andy	Days Of Wine And Roses	12-553	P
Williams, Andy	Days Of Wine And Roses	33-214	CB
Williams, Andy	Dear Heart	33-216	CB
Williams, Andy	Exodus Song	46-283	UBS
Williams, Andy	Hawaii - Aloha Oe	15-399	NK
Williams, Andy	Lonely Street	46-119	SC
Williams, Andy	Love Is Blue	45-605	OZP
Williams, Andy	Love Me With All Your Heart	49-212	MM
Williams, Andy	Love Story	13-556	LE
Williams, Andy	Moon River	11-307	DK
Williams, Andy	Moon River	13-550	LE
Williams, Andy	Moon River	12-514	P

ARTIST	SONG TITLE	#	TYPE
Williams, Andy	Moon River	2-203	SC
Williams, Andy	More	13-552	LE
Williams, Andy	Music To Watch Girls Go By	49-43	ZVS
Williams, Andy	On The Street Where You Love	49-44	ZVS
Williams, Andy	Red Roses For A Blue Lady	16-845	DK
Williams, Andy	Red Roses For A Blue Lady	13-551	LE
Williams, Andy	Somewhere My Love	11-305	DK
Williams, Andy	Somewhere My Love	13-549	LE
Williams, Andy	Theme From Exodus	13-554	LE
Williams, Andy	Three Coins In A Fountain	34-7	CB
Williams, Andy	Where Do I Begin	11-308	DK
Williams, Andy	Xmas - Happy Holiday	18-745	CB
Williams, Andy	Xmas - Happy Holiday	14-302	MM
Williams, Andy	Xmas - Happy Holidays/Holiday Season	41-14	CB
Williams, Andy	Xmas - Home For The Holidays	18-746	CB
Williams, Andy	Xmas - It's The Most Wonderful Time	14-305	MM
Williams, Andy	Xmas - Silver Bells	14-300	MM
Williams, BeBe	Oh Happy Day	48-553	DK
Williams, Billy	I'm Gonna Sit Right Down & Write...	5-518	SC
Williams, Christoph	All I See	18-393	SAV
Williams, Deniece	It's Gonna Take A Miracle	13-195	P
Williams, Deniece	It's Gonna Take A Miracle	5-384	SC
Williams, Deniece	Let'e Hear It For The Boy	27-295	DK
Williams, Deniece	Let's Hear It For The Boy	7-52	MM
Williams, Deniece	Let's Hear It For The Boy	16-546	P
Williams, Don	Ain't It Amazing	45-221	DFK
Williams, Don	Amanda	35-364	CB
Williams, Don	Amanda	8-627	SAV
Williams, Don	And So It Goes	39-88	PHN
Williams, Don	And So It Goes	45-215	PHN
Williams, Don	Back In My Younger Days	45-223	CB
Williams, Don	Come A Little Closer	45-220	DCK
Williams, Don	Come Early Morning	5-201	SC
Williams, Don	Falling Again	45-217	SC
Williams, Don	Good Ol' Boys Like Me	5-198	SC
Williams, Don	Heartbeat In the Darkness	5-197	SC
Williams, Don	I Believe In You	13-407	P
Williams, Don	I Believe In You	9-848	SAV
Williams, Don	I Recall A Gypsy Woman	10-519	SF
Williams, Don	I Sing For Joy	48-672	DCK
Williams, Don	I Wouldn't Want To Live If You...	8-836	CB
Williams, Don	I Wouldn't Want To Live...	4-773	SC
Williams, Don	I'm Just A Country Boy	4-775	SC
Williams, Don	I've Got A Winner In You	45-225	CB
Williams, Don	If Hollywood Don't Need You	4-548	SC
Williams, Don	Infinity	39-97	PHN
Williams, Don	It Must Be Love	29-626	CB
Williams, Don	It Must Be Love	5-208	SC
Williams, Don	It's Who You Love	4-474	SC
Williams, Don	Lay Down Beside Me	44-56	CB
Williams, Don	Lay Down Beside Me	45-228	CB
Williams, Don	Listen To The Radio	45-230	CB
Williams, Don	Lord Have Mercy On A Country Boy	17-353	DK
Williams, Don	Lord I Hope This Day Is Good	33-74	CB
Williams, Don	Lord I Hope This Day Is Good	3-600	SC
Williams, Don	Love Is On A Roll	4-491	SC
Williams, Don	Love Me Over Again	4-776	SC
Williams, Don	Love Me Tonight	4-578	SC
Williams, Don	Miracles	45-229	CB
Williams, Don	My Rifle My Pony And Me	45-216	SC
Williams, Don	Nobody But You	45-218	SC
Williams, Don	One Good Well	20-21	SC
Williams, Don	Please Don't Let Me Love You	45-222	CB
Williams, Don	Rake And Ramblin' Man	45-227	CB
Williams, Don	Say It Again	4-770	SC
Williams, Don	Shadow Land	10-75	SC
Williams, Don	She Never Knew Me	29-702	SC
Williams, Don	She's In Love With A Rodeo Man	47-761	SRK
Williams, Don	Some Broken Hearts Never Mend	34-227	CB
Williams, Don	Some Broken Hearts Never Mend	13-465	P
Williams, Don	Some Broken Hearts Never Mend	5-128	SC
Williams, Don	Stay Young	9-437	SAV
Williams, Don	Stay Young	5-556	SC
Williams, Don	Story Of My Life	45-219	SFM
Williams, Don	That's The Thing About Love	4-766	SC
Williams, Don	Then It's Love	5-866	SC
Williams, Don	Ties That Bind	45-226	CB
Williams, Don	Till The Rivers All Run Dry	5-202	SC
Williams, Don	Too Late To Turn Back Now	48-552	DK
Williams, Don	True Love	22-288	CB
Williams, Don	Tulsa Time	17-289	NA
Williams, Don	Turn Out the Light & Love Me...	34-216	CB
Williams, Don	Turn Out The Lights & Love Me...	8-364	CB
Williams, Don	Walkin' A Broken Heart	5-622	SC

311

ARTIST	SONG TITLE	#	TYPE
Williams, Don	We Should Be Together	45-224	CB
Williams, Don	You're My Best Friend	8-628	SAV
Williams, Hank III	I Don't Know	14-841	ST
Williams, Hank Jr.	All Jokes Aside	14-735	CB
Williams, Hank Jr.	All My Rowdy Friends/Comin...	16-682	C2C
Williams, Hank Jr.	All My Rowdy Friends/Comin...	13-467	P
Williams, Hank Jr.	All My Rowdy Friends/Settled..	2-122	SC
Williams, Hank Jr.	America Will Survive - patriotic	34-365	CB
Williams, Hank Jr.	American Way the	16-683	C2C
Williams, Hank Jr.	Attitude Adjustment	16-681	C2C
Williams, Hank Jr.	Born To Boogie	6-754	MM
Williams, Hank Jr.	Born To Boogie	13-405	P
Williams, Hank Jr.	Both Sides Of Goodbye	4-149	SC
Williams, Hank Jr.	Cajun - Cajun Baby	49-387	SC
Williams, Hank Jr.	Cajun Baby	49-387	SC
Williams, Hank Jr.	Country Boy Can Survive a	13-382	P
Williams, Hank Jr.	Country State Of Mind	8-206	CB
Williams, Hank Jr.	Country State Of Mind	5-411	SC
Williams, Hank Jr.	Dinosaur	45-694	TBR
Williams, Hank Jr.	Dirty Mind	16-676	C2C
Williams, Hank Jr.	Dixie On My Mind	16-672	C2C
Williams, Hank Jr.	Don Juan D' Bubba	4-429	SC
Williams, Hank Jr.	Don't Ask Me No Questions	45-207	CZC
Williams, Hank Jr.	Eleven Roses	4-814	SC
Williams, Hank Jr.	Eyes of Waylon	16-674	C2C
Williams, Hank Jr.	Family Tradition	7-109	MM
Williams, Hank Jr.	Family Tradition	13-333	P
Williams, Hank Jr.	Family Tradition	2-123	SC
Williams, Hank Jr.	Finders Are Keepers	19-422	SC
Williams, Hank Jr.	Gonna Go Huntin' Tonight	16-680	C2C
Williams, Hank Jr.	Hank	16-677	C2C
Williams, Hank Jr.	Hog Wild	2-690	SC
Williams, Hank Jr.	Honky Tonkin'	9-455	SAV
Williams, Hank Jr.	Honky Tonkin'	2-414	SC
Williams, Hank Jr.	Hotel Whiskey	16-362	CB
Williams, Hank Jr.	I Ain't Goin' Peacefully	45-696	VH
Williams, Hank Jr.	I'd Love To Knock the Hell Out Of You	47-594	CB
Williams, Hank Jr.	I'm One Of You	19-536	ST
Williams, Hank Jr.	I'm One Of You	32-413	THM
Williams, Hank Jr.	I'm Tired	16-675	C2C
Williams, Hank Jr.	If Heaven Ain't A Lot Like Dixie	33-71	CB
Williams, Hank Jr.	If You Don't Like Hank Williams	16-678	C2C
Williams, Hank Jr.	It's All Over But The Crying	49-299	KWC
Williams, Hank Jr.	It's All Over But The Crying	45-695	KWC
Williams, Hank Jr.	Just Call Me Hank	48-748	BKD
Williams, Hank Jr.	Kaw-Liga	16-671	C2C
Williams, Hank Jr.	Keep The Change	38-211	PHN
Williams, Hank Jr.	Last Pork Chop	45-697	VH
Williams, Hank Jr.	Man Of Steel	16-679	C2C
Williams, Hank Jr.	Mind Your Own Business	9-494	SAV
Williams, Hank Jr.	Naked Woman And Beer	9-402	CB
Williams, Hank Jr.	Old Habits	37-297	CB
Williams, Hank Jr.	Outland Women	49-18	KV
Williams, Hank Jr.	Patriotic - America Will Survive	34-365	CB
Williams, Hank Jr.	Rainin' In My Heart	37-298	CB
Williams, Hank Jr.	Texas Women	37-305	CB
Williams, Hank Jr.	There's A Tear In My Beer	7-420	MM
Williams, Hank Jr.	This Ain't Dallas	14-432	SC
Williams, Hank Jr.	Tuesday's Gone	16-673	C2C
Williams, Hank Jr.	Whiskey Bent & Hell Bound	16-669	C2C
Williams, Hank Jr.	Whiskey Bent & Hell Bound	5-151	SC
Williams, Hank Jr.	Why Can't We All Just Get A Longneck	45-520	SC
Williams, Hank Jr.	Why Can't We All Just Get/Longneck	20-258	PHM
Williams, Hank Jr.	Why Can't We All Just Get/Longneck	20-176	ST
Williams, Hank Jr.	Woman I Never had	16-670	C2C
Williams, Hank Jr.	Women I've Never Had	37-299	SC
Williams, Hank Jr/S	There's A Tear In My Beer	9-449	SAV
Williams, Hank Sr.	Alone And Forsaken	45-704	CB
Williams, Hank Sr.	Angel Of Death the	37-198	CB
Williams, Hank Sr.	Baby We're Really In Love	14-229	CB
Williams, Hank Sr.	Calling You	37-197	CB
Williams, Hank Sr.	Cold Cold Heart	11-187	DK
Williams, Hank Sr.	Cold Cold Heart	13-436	P
Williams, Hank Sr.	Cold Cold Heart	8-635	SAV
Williams, Hank Sr.	Cold Cold Heart	5-101	SC
Williams, Hank Sr.	Crazy Heart	14-227	CB
Williams, Hank Sr.	Dear Brother	37-188	CB
Williams, Hank Sr.	Dear John	14-225	CB
Williams, Hank Sr.	Dear John	34-187	CB
Williams, Hank Sr.	First Year Blues	45-698	CB
Williams, Hank Sr.	Gospel - Angel Of Death the	37-198	CB
Williams, Hank Sr.	Gospel - Calling You	37-197	CB
Williams, Hank Sr.	Gospel - Dear Brother	37-188	CB
Williams, Hank Sr.	Gospel - House Of Gold	37-191	CB
Williams, Hank Sr.	Gospel - How Can You Refuse HIM Now	37-189	CB
Williams, Hank Sr.	Gospel - I Dreamed About Mama...	37-186	CB
Williams, Hank Sr.	Gospel - I Saw The Light	37-185	CB
Williams, Hank Sr.	Gospel - I'll Have A New Body	37-196	CB
Williams, Hank Sr.	Gospel - Jesus Remembered Me	37-190	CB
Williams, Hank Sr.	Gospel - Prodigal Son the	37-193	CB

ARTIST	SONG TITLE	#	TYPE
Williams, Hank Sr.	Gospel - Ready To Go Home	37-184	CB
Williams, Hank Sr.	Gospel - Sing Sing Sing	37-293	CB
Williams, Hank Sr.	Gospel - Thank GOD	37-192	CB
Williams, Hank Sr.	Gospel - Thy Burdens Are Greater...	37-194	CB
Williams, Hank Sr.	Gospel - Tramp On The Street the	37-195	CB
Williams, Hank Sr.	Half As Much	14-219	CB
Williams, Hank Sr.	Half As Much	8-636	SAV
Williams, Hank Sr.	Hey Good Lookin'	16-752	DK
Williams, Hank Sr.	Hey Good Lookin'	7-156	MM
Williams, Hank Sr.	Hey Good Lookin'	13-434	P
Williams, Hank Sr.	Hey Good Lookin'	8-637	SAV
Williams, Hank Sr.	Honky Tonk Blues	14-220	CB
Williams, Hank Sr.	Honky Tonk Blues	9-489	SAV
Williams, Hank Sr.	Honky Tonkin'	22-307	CB
Williams, Hank Sr.	Howlin' At The Moon	14-226	CB
Williams, Hank Sr.	I Can't Help It If I'm Still In...	16-754	DK
Williams, Hank Sr.	I Can't Help It If I'm Still In...	8-638	SAV
Williams, Hank Sr.	I Can't Help It If I'm Still In...	5-98	SC
Williams, Hank Sr.	I Dreamed About Mama Last Night	37-186	CB
Williams, Hank Sr.	I Saw The Light	37-185	CB
Williams, Hank Sr.	I'll Never Get Out Of This World Al	14-228	CB
Williams, Hank Sr.	I'll Never Get Out Of This World Al	6-15	SC
Williams, Hank Sr.	I'm A Long Gone Daddy	14-230	CB
Williams, Hank Sr.	I'm So Lonesome I Could Cry	18-123	DK
Williams, Hank Sr.	I'm So Lonesome I Could Cry	13-351	P
Williams, Hank Sr.	I'm So Lonesome I Could Cry	8-639	SAV
Williams, Hank Sr.	Jambalaya	17-31	DK
Williams, Hank Sr.	Jambalaya	12-745	P
Williams, Hank Sr.	Jambalaya	9-486	SAV
Williams, Hank Sr.	Kaw-Liga	11-801	DK
Williams, Hank Sr.	Kaw-Liga	13-435	P
Williams, Hank Sr.	Lonesome Whistle	14-232	CB
Williams, Hank Sr.	Long Gone Lonesome Blues	22-308	CB
Williams, Hank Sr.	Lost Highway	45-700	CB
Williams, Hank Sr.	Lovesick Blues	19-845	CB
Williams, Hank Sr.	Lovesick Blues	13-367	P
Williams, Hank Sr.	Lovesick Blues	9-622	SAV
Williams, Hank Sr.	Lovesick Blues	5-215	SC
Williams, Hank Sr.	Mansion On The Hill	8-640	SAV
Williams, Hank Sr.	Message To My Mother	45-705	CB
Williams, Hank Sr.	Mind Your Own Business	14-224	CB
Williams, Hank Sr.	Moanin' The Blues	22-309	CB
Williams, Hank Sr.	Move It On Over	8-641	SAV
Williams, Hank Sr.	My Bucket's Got A Hole In It	22-310	CB
Williams, Hank Sr.	Nobody's Lonesome For Me	14-233	CB
Williams, Hank Sr.	Please Make Up Your Mind	37-187	CB
Williams, Hank Sr.	Ready To Go Home	45-703	CB
Williams, Hank Sr.	Rockin' Chair Money	45-699	CB
Williams, Hank Sr.	Settin' The Woods On Fire	14-221	CB
Williams, Hank Sr.	Settin' The Woods On Fire	19-399	SC
Williams, Hank Sr.	Sing Sing Sing (I'm Gonna	37-293	CB
Williams, Hank Sr.	Someday You'll Call My Name	45-701	CB
Williams, Hank Sr.	Take These Chains From My Heart	34-190	CB
Williams, Hank Sr.	Take These Chains From My Heart	8-642	SAV
Williams, Hank Sr.	Tramp On The Street the	45-707	CB
Williams, Hank Sr.	Wealth Won't Save Your Soul	45-706	CB
Williams, Hank Sr.	Weary Blues From Waitin'	45-702	CB
Williams, Hank Sr.	Wedding Bells	14-222	CB
Williams, Hank Sr.	Wedding Bells	17-307	NA
Williams, Hank Sr.	Wedding Bells	5-373	SC
Williams, Hank Sr.	Why Don't You Love Me	4-869	SC
Williams, Hank Sr.	You Win Again	14-223	CB
Williams, Hank Sr.	You Win Again	8-643	SAV
Williams, Hank Sr.	You're Gonna Change Or I'm Gonna Le	14-231	CB
Williams, Hank Sr.	Your Cheatin' Heart	16-809	DK
Williams, Hank Sr.	Your Cheatin' Heart	13-345	P
Williams, Larry	Bony Moronie	6-686	MM
Williams, Larry	Bony Moronie	11-53	PX
Williams, Larry	Bony Moronie	4-244	SC
Williams, Larry	Short Fat Fannie **	5-519	SC
Williams, Lucinda	Righteously	32-381	THM
Williams, Lucinda	Righteously	25-629	MM
Williams, Maurice	Stay	34-1	CB
Williams, Maurice	Stay	17-106	DK
Williams, Maurice	Stay	6-654	MM
Williams, Pharrell	Come Get It Bae	49-74	ZPC
Williams, Pharrell	Happy	43-177	SF
Williams, Pharrell	Marilyn Monroe	49-73	ZPC
Williams, Robbie	Angels	8-517	PHT
Williams, Robbie	Feel	25-533	MM
Williams, Robbie	Millennium	11-75	JTG
Williams, Robbie	Millennium	7-892	PHT
Williams, Robbie	Millennium	10-185	SC
Williams, Tex	Smoke Smoke Smoke That Cigarette	19-632	CB
Williams, Tex	Smoke Smoke Smoke That Cigarette	19-405	SC
Williams, Trent	Beer Man	20-346	ST
Williams, Vanessa	Just For Tonight	6-96	MM
Williams, Vanessa	Oh How The Years Go By	9-98	PS
Williams, Vanessa	Oh How The Years Go	5-181	SC

ARTIST	SONG TITLE	#	TYPE
	By		
Williams, Vanessa	Save The Best For Last	26-279	DK
Williams, Vanessa	Save The Best For Last	19-575	MH
Williams, Vanessa	Save The Best For Last	36-364	SC
Williams, Vanessa	Sweetest Days the	9-270	SC
Williams, Vanessa	Sweetest Days the	29-124	ST
Williams, Vanessa	Work To Do	18-384	SAV
Williams, Vanessa	Xmas - What Child Is This	22-837	ST
Williams, w/Wilson.	That's How They Do It In Dixie	29-363	CB
Williams&McKnight	Duet - Love Is	6-332	MM
Williams&McKnight	Duet - Love Is	12-746	P
Williams&McKnight	Love Is	6-332	MM
Williams&McKnight	Love Is	12-746	P
Williamson, Sonny	Bring It On Home To Me	14-596	SC
Willie, Boxcar	Joy To The World - xmas	45-257	CB
Willie, Boxcar	Xmas - Joy To The World	45-257	CB
Willis, Bruce	Here Comes Trouble Again	49-726	HGK
Willis, Bruce	Respect Yourself	49-730	KVD
Willis, Chris	Love Is Gone	49-911	SC
Willis, Chuck	Betty And Dupree	49-734	SRK
Willis, Chuck	It's Too Late	17-324	SS
Willis, Chuck	See See Rider	49-733	P
Willis, Chuck	What Am I Living For	49-728	CB
Willis, Kelly	Don't Come the Cowboy With Me	49-735	TU
Willis, Kelly	Getting To Me	49-729	DCK
Willis, Kelly	Heaven's Just A Sin Away	6-531	MM
Willis, Kelly	If I Left You	18-473	ST
Willis, Kelly	Not Forgotten You	49-727	CB
Willis, Matt	Don't Let It Go To Waste	49-732	MRE
Willis, Matt	Up All Night	49-731	KVD
Willmon, Trent	Dixie Rose Deluxe's Honky Tonk...	23-402	CB
Willmon, Trent	On Again Tonight	29-204	CB
Willmon, Trent	So Am I	30-115	CB
Wills & O'Neal	Duet - I'm Gonna Do Anything	15-863	ST
Wills & O'Neal	Duet - I'm Not Gonna Do Anything...	25-124	MM
Wills & O'Neal	I'm Gonna Do Anything	15-863	ST
Wills & O'Neal	I'm Not Gonna Do Anything	15-863	ST
Wills, Bob	Across The Alley From The Alamo	45-693	OZP
Wills, Bob	Big Ball In Cowtown a	20-702	CB
Wills, Bob	Bubbles In My Beer	20-691	CB
Wills, Bob	Bubbles In My Beer	47-496	CB
Wills, Bob	Faded Love	20-699	CB
Wills, Bob	Faded Love	17-366	DK
Wills, Bob	Faded Love	8-647	SAV
Wills, Bob	Heart To Heart Talk	20-694	CB
Wills, Bob	I Ain't Got Nobody	20-698	CB
Wills, Bob	Ida Red Like To Boogie	20-697	CB

ARTIST	SONG TITLE	#	TYPE
Wills, Bob	Ida Red Like To Boogie	45-351	CBE
Wills, Bob	Maiden's Prayer	20-692	CB
Wills, Bob	Milk Cow Blues	20-693	CB
Wills, Bob	New San Antonio Rose	5-704	SC
Wills, Bob	New Spanish Two Step	19-625	CB
Wills, Bob	Roly Poly	9-460	SAV
Wills, Bob	San Antonio Rose	20-690	CB
Wills, Bob	San Antonio Rose	17-384	DK
Wills, Bob	San Antonio Rose	13-356	P
Wills, Bob	St. Louis Blues	20-700	CB
Wills, Bob	Stay A Little Longer	20-703	CB
Wills, Bob	Stay A Little Longer	6-6	SC
Wills, Bob	Sugar Moon	19-634	CB
Wills, Bob	Take Me Back To Tulsa	20-696	CB
Wills, Bob	Time Changes Everything	20-695	CB
Wills, Bob	Time Changes Everything	8-646	SAV
Wills, Bob	Wabash Blues	20-704	CB
Wills, Mark	19 Somethin'	34-379	CB
Wills, Mark	Almost Doesn't Count	9-405	CB
Wills, Mark	Almost Doesn't Count	13-830	CHM
Wills, Mark	Almost Doesn't Count	19-253	CSZ
Wills, Mark	And The Crowd Goes Wild	35-429	CB
Wills, Mark	And The Crowd Goes Wild	25-697	MM
Wills, Mark	And The Crowd Goes Wild	19-365	ST
Wills, Mark	And The Crowd Goes Wild	32-376	THM
Wills, Mark	Back At One	5-829	SC
Wills, Mark	Back At One	22-515	ST
Wills, Mark	Days Of Thunder	30-467	CB
Wills, Mark	Don't Laugh At me	8-748	CB
Wills, Mark	Don't Laugh At Me	22-816	ST
Wills, Mark	Everything There Is To Know	10-266	SC
Wills, Mark	Hank	29-594	CB
Wills, Mark	High Low And In Between	7-383	MM
Wills, Mark	High Low And In Between	24-655	SC
Wills, Mark	I Do (Cherish You)	8-410	CB
Wills, Mark	I Do (Cherish You)	22-787	ST
Wills, Mark	I Want To Know	14-135	CB
Wills, Mark	Jacob's Ladder	4-371	SC
Wills, Mark	Life Ain't Always Beautiful	29-708	ST
Wills, Mark	Loving Every Minute	15-95	ST
Wills, Mark	Nineteen Somethin'	25-409	MM
Wills, Mark	Nineteen Somethin'	18-449	ST
Wills, Mark	Nineteen Somethin'	32-6	THM
Wills, Mark	Places I've Never Been	7-637	CHM
Wills, Mark	Places I've Never Been	22-606	ST
Wills, Mark	She's In Love	19-206	CB
Wills, Mark	She's In Love	10-195	SC
Wills, Mark	Take It All Out On Me	30-318	CB

ARTIST	SONG TITLE	#	TYPE
Wills, Mark	That's A Woman	22-6	CB
Wills, Mark	That's A Woman	20-262	SC
Wills, Mark	That's A Woman	19-848	ST
Wills, Mark	When You Think Of Me	34-404	CB
Wills, Mark	When You Think Of Me	25-528	MM
Wills, Mark	When You Think Of Me	18-794	ST
Wills, Mark	When You Think Of Me	32-190	THM
Wills, Mark	Wish You Were Here	8-374	CB
Wills, Mark	Wish You Were Here	7-829	CHT
Wills, Mark	Wish You Were Here	22-717	ST
Wilmon, Trent	Beer Man	47-494	CB
Wilmon, Trent	Cold Beer And A Fishing Pole	47-495	CB
Wilmon, Trent	Dixie Rose's Deluxe Honky Tonk..	20-494	ST
Wilshire	Special	32-322	THM
Wilson & Haggard	Duet - Politically Uncorrect	29-199	CB
Wilson Phillips	Daniel	24-259	SC
Wilson Phillips	Hold On	11-694	DK
Wilson Phillips	Hold On	12-748	P
Wilson Phillips	I'll Never Get Over You Getting…	12-73	DK
Wilson Phillips	Release Me	28-411	DK
Wilson Phillips	Release Me	13-248	P
Wilson Phillips	Xmas - Silent Night	22-838	ST
Wilson Phillips	You Won't See Me Cry	6-370	MM
Wilson Pickett	Funky Broadway	11-792	DK
Wilson Pickett	Funky Broadway	17-330	SS
Wilson Pickett	I'm In Love	10-368	SS
Wilson Pickett	In The Midnight Hour	35-71	CB
Wilson Pickett	In The Midnight Hour	26-446	DK
Wilson Pickett	In The Midnight Hour	13-93	P
Wilson Pickett	In The Midnight Hour	2-83	SC
Wilson Pickett	Land Of 1000 Dances	35-92	CB
Wilson Pickett	Mustang Sally	26-273	DK
Wilson Pickett	Mustang Sally	6-483	MM
Wilson, Al	Show And Tell	35-120	CB
Wilson, Al	Show And Tell	11-673	DK
Wilson, Al	Show And Tell	7-479	MM
Wilson, Gretchen	All Jacked Up	23-408	CB
Wilson, Gretchen	All Jacked Up	36-376	SC
Wilson, Gretchen	California Girls	30-82	CB
Wilson, Gretchen	Come To Bed	30-170	CB
Wilson, Gretchen	Crazy	41-72	PHN
Wilson, Gretchen	Don't Do Me No Good	36-608	CB
Wilson, Gretchen	Earrings Song the	37-41	CB
Wilson, Gretchen	Full Time Job	29-508	SC
Wilson, Gretchen	Grandma	41-76	PHN
Wilson, Gretchen	Here For The Party	35-446	CB
Wilson, Gretchen	Here For The Party	20-443	ST
Wilson, Gretchen	Homewrecker	22-311	CB
Wilson, Gretchen	I Don't Feel Like Loving You Today	29-23	CB
Wilson, Gretchen	I Don't Feel Like Loving You Today	23-452	ST
Wilson, Gretchen	I Got Your Country Right Here	37-340	CB

ARTIST	SONG TITLE	#	TYPE
Wilson, Gretchen	If I Could Do It All Again	37-60	CB
Wilson, Gretchen	Midnight Oil	30-164	CB
Wilson, Gretchen	One Bud Wiser	29-372	CB
Wilson, Gretchen	One Of The Boys	30-444	CB
Wilson, Gretchen	Redneck Woman	35-438	CB
Wilson, Gretchen	Redneck Woman	20-254	PHM
Wilson, Gretchen	Redneck Woman	20-324	ST
Wilson, Gretchen	Skoal Ring	29-511	SC
Wilson, Gretchen	When I Think About Cheating	22-84	CB
Wilson, Gretchen	When It Rains	23-138	CB
Wilson, Gretchen	Work Hard Play Harder	37-225	CB
Wilson, Gretchen	You Don't Have To Go Home	30-564	CB
Wilson, J. Frank	Last Kiss	2-57	SC
Wilson, Jackie	Higher And Higher	12-753	P
Wilson, Jackie	Lonely Teardrops	2-87	SC
Wilson, Jackie	Reet Petite	11-45	PX
Wilson, Jackie	That's Why	7-300	MM
Wilson, Kevin Bloody	Kev's Courtin' Song **	37-81	SC
Wilson, Meri	Peter The Meter Reader **	15-2	SC
Wilson, Meri	Telephone Man **	2-182	SC
Wilson, Nancy	Best Is Yet To Come the	23-348	MM
Wilson, Nancy	I Wish You Love	15-506	MM
Wilson, Nancy	Xmas - What Are You Doing NYE	14-307	MM
Winans & P Diddy	I Don't Wanna Know	20-570	CB
Winans & P. Diddy	Duet - I Don't Wanna Know	20-570	CB
Winbush, Angela	Treat U Rite	15-761	NU
Winehouse, Amy	Back To Black	37-142	SC
Winehouse, Amy	He Can Only Hold Her	49-58	ZVS
Winehouse, Amy	Just Friends	49-60	ZVS
Winehouse, Amy	Love Is A Losing Game	49-59	ZVS
Winehouse, Amy	Me And Mr. Jones	49-57	ZVS
Winehouse, Amy	Rehab	48-596	DK
Winehouse, Amy	Tears Dry On Their Own	30-590	PHM
Winehouse, Amy	You Know I'm No Good	36-476	CB
Winger	Miles Away	24-687	SC
Winger	Seventeen	6-20	SC
Wings	Listen To What The Man Said	35-130	CB
Wings	Listen To What The Man Said	4-76	SC
Winter, Johnny	Drinkin' Blues	49-677	SC
Winter, Johnny	Ganster Of Love	49-678	VH
Winter, Johnny	Mojo Boogie	14-597	SC
Winter, Johnny	Mojo Boogie	49-676	DJ
Winter, Johnny	Rock And Roll Hoochie Koo	49-373	CB
Winwood, Steve	Back In The High Life Again	33-318	CB
Winwood, Steve	Back In The High Life Again	29-267	SC
Winwood, Steve	Higher Love	4-378	SC
Winwood, Steve	Holding On	34-99	CB

ARTIST	SONG TITLE	#	TYPE
Winwood, Steve	While You See A Chance	7-483	MM
Wiseman, Mac	Footprints In The Snow	8-258	CB
Wiseman, Mac	Jimmie Brown the Newsboy	36-355	CB
Withers, Bill	Ain't No Sunshine	33-273	CB
Withers, Bill	Ain't No Sunshine	17-137	DK
Withers, Bill	Ain't No Sunshine	13-143	P
Withers, Bill	Lean On Me	16-854	DK
Withers, Bill	Lean On Me	13-107	P
Withers, Bill	Use Me	16-159	SC
Witherspoon,Jimmy	Ain't Nobody's Business	15-314	SC
Witter, Jim	All My Life	8-925	CB
Wizard Of Oz	Ding Dong The Witch Is Dead - Show	33-219	CB
Wizard Of Oz	Show - Ding Dong the Witch Is Dead	33-219	CB
Wizard Of Oz	Show - Ding Dong the Witch is Dead	9-815	SAV
Wizard Of Oz	Show - If I Only Had A Brain	9-813	SAV
Wizard Of Oz	Show - Merry Old Land Of Oz the	9-816	SAV
Wizard Of Oz	Show - Over The Rainbow	9-812	SAV
Wizard Of Oz	Show - We're Off to See the Wizard	33-221	CB
Wizard Of Oz	Show - We're Off To See the Wizard	9-814	SAV
Wizard Of Oz	We're Off To See The Wizard - Show	33-221	CB
Womack, Lee Ann	Ashes By Now	14-121	CB
Womack, Lee Ann	Ashes By Now	22-571	ST
Womack, Lee Ann	Ashes By Now	14-31	THM
Womack, Lee Ann	Blame It On Me	48-484	CKC
Womack, Lee Ann	Buckaroo	34-326	CB
Womack, Lee Ann	Buckaroo	7-748	CHM
Womack, Lee Ann	Chances Are	49-408	BKD
Womack, Lee Ann	Chances Are (Inst)	49-409	BKD
Womack, Lee Ann	Does My Ring Burn Your Finger	25-66	MM
Womack, Lee Ann	Does My Ring Burn Your Finger	16-32	ST
Womack, Lee Ann	Don't Tell Me	22-517	ST
Womack, Lee Ann	Finding My Way Back Home	30-106	CB
Womack, Lee Ann	Fool the	35-412	CB
Womack, Lee Ann	Fool the	7-659	CHM
Womack, Lee Ann	Forever Everyday	25-412	MM
Womack, Lee Ann	Forever Everyday	18-451	ST
Womack, Lee Ann	Forever Everyday	32-43	THM
Womack, Lee Ann	He Oughta Know That By Now	23-119	CB
Womack, Lee Ann	He Oughta Know That By Now	23-390	SC
Womack, Lee Ann	He'll Be Back	48-482	CKC
Womack, Lee Ann	I Hope You Dance	13-821	CHM
Womack, Lee Ann	I Know Why The River Runs	48-480	CKC

ARTIST	SONG TITLE	#	TYPE
Womack, Lee Ann	I May Hate Myself In The Morning	22-94	CB
Womack, Lee Ann	I'll Think Of A Reason Later	8-879	CB
Womack, Lee Ann	I'll Think Of A Reason Later	22-711	ST
Womack, Lee Ann	King Of Broken Hearts	36-260	PHM
Womack, Lee Ann	Last Call	36-600	CB
Womack, Lee Ann	Last Call	36-206	PHM
Womack, Lee Ann	Little Past Little Rock a	8-761	CB
Womack, Lee Ann	Lord I Hope This Day Is Good	48-481	CKC
Womack, Lee Ann	Man With 18 Wheels a	48-479	CKC
Womack, Lee Ann	Never Again Again	7-619	CHM
Womack, Lee Ann	Never Again Again	10-79	SC
Womack, Lee Ann	Now You See Me Now You Don't	10-197	SC
Womack, Lee Ann	Now You See Me Now You Don't	22-427	ST
Womack, Lee Ann	Solitary Thinkin'	37-43	CB
Womack, Lee Ann	Some Things I Know	8-962	CB
Womack, Lee Ann	Something Worth Leaving	17-565	ST
Womack, Lee Ann	Something Worth Leaving Behind	25-289	MM
Womack, Lee Ann	Stronger Than I Am	48-483	CKC
Womack, Lee Ann	There's More Where That Came From	29-499	SC
Womack, Lee Ann	Twenty Years & Two Husbands Ago	29-40	CB
Womack, Lee Ann	Why They Call It Falling	33-185	CB
Womack, Lee Ann	Why They Call It Falling	9-863	ST
Womack, Lee Ann	Wrong Girl	35-425	CB
Womack, Lee Ann	Wrong Girl the	20-169	ST
Womack, Lee Ann	Xmas - What Are You Doing NYE	30-401	SC
Womack, Lee Ann	You've Got To Talk To Me	22-413	ST
Wonder, Stevie	Boogie On Reggae Woman	11-825	DK
Wonder, Stevie	Don't You Worry 'Bout A Thing	17-338	DK
Wonder, Stevie	Fingertips Pt. 2	10-734	JVC
Wonder, Stevie	For Once In My Life	11-732	DK
Wonder, Stevie	For Once In My Life	4-692	SC
Wonder, Stevie	Higher Ground	24-336	SC
Wonder, Stevie	I Just Called To Say I Love You	35-173	CB
Wonder, Stevie	I Just Called To Say I Love You	11-644	DK
Wonder, Stevie	I Was Made To Love Her	15-714	LE
Wonder, Stevie	I Wish	15-716	LE
Wonder, Stevie	If You Really Love Me	34-38	CB
Wonder, Stevie	Isn't She Lovely	35-165	CB
Wonder, Stevie	Isn't She Lovely	27-258	DK
Wonder, Stevie	Livin' For The City	27-267	DK
Wonder, Stevie	Livin' For The City	10-676	HE
Wonder, Stevie	Master Blaster (Jammin')	46-164	SC

ARTIST	SONG TITLE	#	TYPE
Wonder, Stevie	My Cherie Amour	11-811	DK
Wonder, Stevie	My Cherie Amour	9-46	MM
Wonder, Stevie	Part Time Lover	20-304	CB
Wonder, Stevie	Part Time Lover	11-749	DK
Wonder, Stevie	Place In The Sun the	15-715	LE
Wonder, Stevie	Ribbon In The Sky	10-363	KC
Wonder, Stevie	Shoo Be Doo Be Doo Da Da	15-717	LE
Wonder, Stevie	Signed Sealed Delivered	34-31	CB
Wonder, Stevie	Signed Sealed Delivered I'm Yours	11-776	DK
Wonder, Stevie	Sir Duke	15-559	CMC
Wonder, Stevie	Sir Duke	27-262	DK
Wonder, Stevie	Superstition	12-26	DK
Wonder, Stevie	Superstition	25-282	MM
Wonder, Stevie	Uptight Everything Is Alright	17-377	DK
Wonder, Stevie	Uptight Everything Is Alright	13-138	P
Wonder, Stevie	Yester Me Yester You Yesterday	49-476	MM
Wonder, Stevie	You Are The Sunshine Of My Life	27-256	DK
Wonder, Stevie	You Are The Sunshine Of My Life	14-367	MH
Wonder, W.	No Letting Go	32-213	THM
Wonders	That Thing You Do	24-542	SC
Wood & Beymer	Duet - Tonight	11-795	DK
Wood & Beymer	Tonight	11-795	DK
Wood, Brenton	Gimme Little Sign	27-285	DK
Wood, Brenton	Gimme Little Sign	5-460	SC
Wood, David	Ride The Wild West	38-214	PHN
Wood, Jeff	Use Mine	10-76	SC
Wood, Jeff	You Just Get One	7-426	MM
Woodward, Lucy	Dumb Girls	32-139	THM
Woodward, Lucy	Dumb Girls	20-526	CB
Wooley, Sheb	Halloween - Purple People Eater	16-288	TT
Wooley, Sheb	Purple People Eater	4-2	SC
Wooley, Sheb	Purple People Eater	16-288	TT
Worley, Darryl	Awful Beautiful Day	20-490	ST
Worley, Darryl	Awful Beautiful Life	23-11	CB
Worley, Darryl	Awful Beautiful Life	21-656	SC
Worley, Darryl	Family Tree	25-411	MM
Worley, Darryl	Family Tree	18-448	ST
Worley, Darryl	Family Tree	32-39	THM
Worley, Darryl	Family Tree	32-39	THM
Worley, Darryl	Good Day To Run a	14-143	CB
Worley, Darryl	Good Day To Run a	14-13	CHM
Worley, Darryl	Good Day To Run a	19-223	CSZ
Worley, Darryl	Good Day To Run a	22-582	ST
Worley, Darryl	Have You Forgotten	25-561	MM
Worley, Darryl	Have You Forgotten	19-3	ST
Worley, Darryl	Have You Forgotten	32-186	THM
Worley, Darryl	Have You Forgotten - Patriotic	34-407	CB
Worley, Darryl	I Just Came Back (From a War)	30-172	CB

ARTIST	SONG TITLE	#	TYPE
Worley, Darryl	I Love Her She Hates Me	23-415	CB
Worley, Darryl	I Miss My Friend	33-171	CB
Worley, Darryl	I Miss My Friend	25-187	MM
Worley, Darryl	I Miss My Friend	16-688	ST
Worley, Darryl	I Will Hold My Ground	22-10	CB
Worley, Darryl	I Will Hold My Ground	19-692	ST
Worley, Darryl	If Something Should Happen	22-28	CB
Worley, Darryl	Living In The Here And Now	30-356	CB
Worley, Darryl	Nothin' But A Love Thang	29-602	CB
Worley, Darryl	Patriotic - Have You Forgotten	34-407	CB
Worley, Darryl	Second Wind	15-213	NSC
Worley, Darryl	Second Wind	15-99	ST
Worley, Darryl	Sideways	25-53	MM
Worley, Darryl	Sideways	16-11	ST
Worley, Darryl	Tennessee River Run	25-645	MM
Worley, Darryl	Tennessee River Run	19-264	ST
Worley, Darryl	Tennessee River Run	32-374	THM
Worley, Darryl	Tequila On Ice	36-228	PHM
Worley, Darryl	When You Need My Love	9-394	CB
Worley, Darryl	When You Need My Love	13-852	CHM
Worley, Darryl	When You Need My Love	19-248	CSZ
Worley, Darryl	When You Need My Love	22-551	ST
Worsham, Charles	Could It Be	41-95	PHN
Worsham, Charlie	Rubberband	42-4	PHN
Wreckers	Good Kind the	30-316	CB
Wreckers	Leave The Pieces	29-587	CB
Wreckers	My Oh My	30-112	CB
Wreckers	Tennessee	30-361	CB
Wreckx-N-Effect	Rump Shaker	14-437	SC
Wright, Betty	Clean Up Woman	24-343	SC
Wright, Chely	Back Of The Bottom Drawer	20-259	PHM
Wright, Chely	Back Of The Bottom Drawer	20-332	ST
Wright, Chely	Bumper Of My SUV the	22-102	CB
Wright, Chely	He's A Good Ol' Boy	6-672	MM
Wright, Chely	He's A Good Ol' Boy	17-213	NA
Wright, Chely	He's A Good Ol' Boy	3-48	SC
Wright, Chely	I Already Do	8-472	CB
Wright, Chely	It Was	5-799	SC
Wright, Chely	It Was	22-505	ST
Wright, Chely	Jezebel	25-75	MM
Wright, Chely	Jezebel	16-36	ST
Wright, Chely	Just Another Heartache	8-153	CB
Wright, Chely	Just Another Heartache	22-763	ST
Wright, Chely	Listenin' To The Radio	4-24	SC
Wright, Chely	Love That We Lost the	4-156	SC
Wright, Chely	Never Love You Enough	29-355	CB
Wright, Chely	Never Love You Enough	15-188	ST
Wright, Chely	River the	23-492	CB

ARTIST	SONG TITLE	#	TYPE
Wright, Chely	River the	29-614	ST
Wright, Chely	Sea Of Cowboy Hats	4-107	SC
Wright, Chely	Sea Of Cowboy Hats	22-875	ST
Wright, Chely	She Went Out For Cigarettes	14-719	CB
Wright, Chely	She Went Out For Cigarettes	22-547	ST
Wright, Chely	Shut Up And Drive	7-669	CHM
Wright, Chely	Shut Up And Drive	4-835	SC
Wright, Chely	Shut Up And Drive	22-621	ST
Wright, Chely	Single White Female	8-953	CB
Wright, Chely	Single White Female	7-869	CHT
Wright, Chely	Single White Female	14-604	SC
Wright, Chely	Till I Was Loved By You	2-550	SC
Wright, Gary	Back On The Chain Gang	4-526	SC
Wright, Gary	Don't Try To Own Me	24-17	SC
Wright, Gary	Dream Weaver	35-134	CB
Wright, Gary	Dream Weaver	13-11	P
Wright, Gary	Love is Alive	4-56	SC
Wright, Michelle	Answer Is Yes the	4-622	SC
Wright, Michelle	He Would Be Sixteen	6-214	MM
Wright, Michelle	Nobody's Girl	7-342	MM
Wright, Michelle	Nobody's Girl	4-408	SC
Wright, Michelle	One Good Man	6-612	MM
Wright, Michelle	One Good Man	3-541	SC
Wright, Michelle	One Time Around	6-119	MM
Wright, Michelle	Take It Like A Man	35-399	CB
Wright, Michelle	Take it Like A Man	6-535	MM
Wright, Michelle	Take It Like A Man	12-480	P
Wright, Michelle	Take It Like A Man	2-103	SC
Wrights	Down This Road	22-27	CB
Wurzels	Combine Harvester (Brand New..)	44-63	STTW
Wyatt & Avant	Duet - Nothing In This World	20-616	CB
Wyatt & Avant	Nothing In This World	20-616	CB
Wycliff	Bubblegoose **	13-724	SGB
Wynette & Houston	Duet - My Elusive Dreams	7-118	MM
Wynette & Houston	Duet - My Elusive Dreams	4-306	SC
Wynette & Houston	My Elusive Dreams	7-118	MM
Wynette & Houston	My Elusive Dreams	4-306	SC
Wynette & Jones	Ceremony the	9-591	SAV
Wynette & Jones	Duet - Ceremony the	9-591	SAV
Wynette & Jones	Duet - Golden Ring	8-114	CB
Wynette & Jones	Duet - Take Me	49-358	CB
Wynette & Jones	Golden Ring	8-114	CB
Wynette & Jones	Golden Ring	5-441	SC
Wynette & Jones	Take Me - duet	49-358	CB
Wynette & Parton	Silver Threads & Golden Needles	6-476	MM
Wynette, Tammy	Almost Persuaded	49-354	CB
Wynette, Tammy	Another Lonely Song	9-589	SAV
Wynette, Tammy	Another Lonely Song	49-359	CB
Wynette, Tammy	Apartment # 9	8-381	CB
Wynette, Tammy	Bedtime Story	49-356	CB

ARTIST	SONG TITLE	#	TYPE
Wynette, Tammy	Cowboys Don't Shoot Straight	49-357	CB
Wynette, Tammy	DIVORCE	15-824	CB
Wynette, Tammy	DIVORCE	16-737	DK
Wynette, Tammy	DIVORCE	10-746	JVC
Wynette, Tammy	DIVORCE	13-417	P
Wynette, Tammy	DIVORCE	8-675	SAV
Wynette, Tammy	DIVORCE	3-377	SC
Wynette, Tammy	Enough Of A Woman	45-668	DCK
Wynette, Tammy	Good Lovin'	13-534	P
Wynette, Tammy	Good Lovin'	9-602	SAV
Wynette, Tammy	He Loves Her All The Way	6-767	MM
Wynette, Tammy	I Believe	49-362	CB
Wynette, Tammy	I Don't Wanna Play House	33-3	CB
Wynette, Tammy	I Don't Wanna Play House	4-265	SC
Wynette, Tammy	I Still Believe In Fairytales	49-363	CB
Wynette, Tammy	I'll See Him Through	4-745	SC
Wynette, Tammy	I'm Not A Candle In The Wind	49-355	CB
Wynette, Tammy	Kids Say The Darndest Things	15-70	CB
Wynette, Tammy	Kids Say The Darndest Things	9-592	SAV
Wynette, Tammy	Let's Get Together One Last Time	49-364	CB
Wynette, Tammy	Lighter Shade Of Blue a	45-721	VH
Wynette, Tammy	My Man	4-749	SC
Wynette, Tammy	One Of A Kind	29-625	CB
Wynette, Tammy	Run Woman Run	6-86	SC
Wynette, Tammy	Singing My Song	4-747	SC
Wynette, Tammy	Slow Burning Fire	47-783	SRK
Wynette, Tammy	Stand By Your Man	11-427	DK
Wynette, Tammy	Stand By Your Man	13-343	P
Wynette, Tammy	Stand By Your Man	9-614	SAV
Wynette, Tammy	Take Me To Your World	4-744	SC
Wynette, Tammy	This Time I Almost Made It	49-366	CB
Wynette, Tammy	Till I Can Make It On My Own	8-371	CB
Wynette, Tammy	Till I Get It Right	35-367	CB
Wynette, Tammy	Till I Get It Right	4-746	SC
Wynette, Tammy	Too Far Gone	49-361	CB
Wynette, Tammy	Ways To Love A Man the	9-618	SAV
Wynette, Tammy	Ways To Love A Man the	20-639	SC
Wynette, Tammy	We Sure Can Love Each Other	49-365	CB
Wynette, Tammy	Womanhood	49-360	CB
Wynette, Tammy	You And Me	12-408	P
Wynette, Tammy	Your Good Girl's Gonna Go Bad	8-278	CB
Wynette, Tammy	Your Good Girl's Gonna Go Bad	17-13	DK
Wynette, Tammy	Your Good Girl's Gonna	14-324	SC

ARTIST	SONG TITLE	#	TYPE
	Go Bad		
Wynette, Tammy	Divorce Sale the	45-670	DCK
Wynonna	Heaven Help Me	32-416	THM
Wynonna	Tell Me Why	34-308	CB
Wynonna	To Be Loved By You	35-408	CB
Wynonna	What The World Needs	34-403	CB
Wynonna	What The World Needs	32-263	THM
X-Ecutioners	It's Goin' Down	18-230	CB
Xscape	Arms Of The One Who Loves You	10-144	SC
Xscape	Love On Your Mind	15-758	NU
Xscape	Understanding	17-407	DK
Y & T	Mean Streak	23-109	SC
Y & T	Summertime Girls	6-24	SC
Yamin, Elliott	Wait For You	49-901	SC
Yankee Doodle Dandy	Give My Regards To Broadway	49-442	MM
Yankee Doodle Dandy	Show - Give My Regards To Broadway	49-442	MM
Yankee Grey	All Things Considered	19-201	CB
Yankee Grey	All Things Considered	10-215	SC
Yankee Grey	All Things Considered	22-495	ST
Yankee Grey	Another Nine Minutes	22-475	ST
Yankee Grey	This Time Around	14-90	CB
Yankee Grey	This Time Around	22-560	ST
Yankovic, Weird Al	Achy Breaky Heart (Parody)	15-349	MM
Yankovic, Weird Al	Addicted To Spuds	49-837	SC
Yankovic, Weird Al	Alimony	49-846	SGB
Yankovic, Weird Al	Amish Paradise **	23-20	SC
Yankovic, Weird Al	Another One Rides The Bus	49-845	SGB
Yankovic, Weird Al	E-BAY	37-82	SC
Yankovic, Weird Al	Eat It	6-512	MM
Yankovic, Weird Al	Eat It	12-597	P
Yankovic, Weird Al	Fat	49-843	SGB
Yankovic, Weird Al	Grapefruit Diet	49-848	SGB
Yankovic, Weird Al	I Lost On Jeopardy	49-842	SC
Yankovic, Weird Al	I Love Rocky Road	49-838	SC
Yankovic, Weird Al	I Think I'm A Clone Now	15-342	MM
Yankovic, Weird Al	I Want A New Duck	49-849	SGB
Yankovic, Weird Al	Like A Surgeon	6-525	MM
Yankovic, Weird Al	My Bologna	49-844	SGB
Yankovic, Weird Al	Phony Calls	49-850	SGB
Yankovic, Weird Al	Polka Your Eyes Out	49-749	KV
Yankovic, Weird Al	Ricky	49-839	SC
Yankovic, Weird Al	Saga Begins the	49-841	SC
Yankovic, Weird Al	She Drives Like Crazy	49-847	SGB
Yankovic, Weird Al	Smells Like Nirvana	15-344	MM
Yankovic, Weird Al	Spam	49-840	SC
Yankovic, Weird Al	Truck Drivin' Song	44-82	KV
Yankovic, Weird Al	Xmas - Christmas At Ground Zero	5-715	SC
Yankovic, Weird Al	Yoda	15-351	MM
Yankovic, Weird Al	You Don't Love Me Anymore	49-836	SC
Yankovik, Weird Al	Truck Driving Song	46-281	KV
Yarbrough, Glenn	Baby The Rain Must Fall	7-74	MM

ARTIST	SONG TITLE	#	TYPE
Yardbirds	For Your Love	11-258	DK
Yardbirds	For Your Love	13-226	P
Yardbirds	Heart Full Of Soul	20-66	SC
Yardbirds	I'm A Man	14-461	SC
Yardbirds	Shapes Of Things	6-56	SC
Yates, Billy	Daddy Had A Cadillac, & Mama Got A C...	48-712	CB
Yates, Billy	Flowers	7-641	CHM
Yates, Billy	Flowers	22-607	ST
Yates, Billy	Shadows	48-713	CB
Yates, Billy	What Do You Want From Me	14-795	ST
Yearwood & Brooks	Duet - Love Will Always Win	49-345	CB
Yearwood & Brooks	Love Will Always Win - duet	49-345	CB
Yearwood & Diffie	Duet - Walkaway Joe	8-121	CB
Yearwood & Diffie	Walkaway Joe	8-121	CB
Yearwood, Trisha	Believe Me Baby I Lied	1-639	CB
Yearwood, Trisha	Believe Me Baby I Lied	7-335	MM
Yearwood, Trisha	Believe Me Baby I Lied	4-406	SC
Yearwood, Trisha	Better Your Heart Than Mine	6-473	MM
Yearwood, Trisha	Better Your Heart Than Mine	2-708	SC
Yearwood, Trisha	Come Back When It Ain't Rainin'	48-337	SC
Yearwood, Trisha	Down On My Knees	6-381	MM
Yearwood, Trisha	Everybody Knows	1-640	CB
Yearwood, Trisha	Everybody Knows	16-661	CHM
Yearwood, Trisha	Everybody Knows	24-649	SC
Yearwood, Trisha	For Reasons I've Forgotten	48-342	THM
Yearwood, Trisha	Georgia Rain	23-127	CB
Yearwood, Trisha	Hearts In Armor	48-339	SC
Yearwood, Trisha	How Do I Live	1-641	CB
Yearwood, Trisha	How Do I Live	7-635	CHM
Yearwood, Trisha	I Can't Understand	24-122	SC
Yearwood, Trisha	I Don't Paint Myself Into Corners	18-130	ST
Yearwood, Trisha	I Need You	22-401	CHM
Yearwood, Trisha	I Wanna Go Too Far	6-849	MM
Yearwood, Trisha	I Wanna Go Too Far	3-417	SC
Yearwood, Trisha	I Would Have Loved You Anyway	9-861	ST
Yearwood, Trisha	I'll Still Love You More	14-619	SC
Yearwood, Trisha	I'll Still Love You More	22-739	ST
Yearwood, Trisha	I'm Still Alive	48-340	SC
Yearwood, Trisha	If I Ain't Got You	48-334	MM
Yearwood, Trisha	Inside Out	25-57	MM
Yearwood, Trisha	Inside Out	16-33	ST
Yearwood, Trisha	Like We Never Had A Broken Heart	1-632	CB
Yearwood, Trisha	Nothin' Bout Memphis	36-283	PHM
Yearwood, Trisha	O Mexico	24-87	SC
Yearwood, Trisha	Oh Lonesome You	6-135	MM
Yearwood, Trisha	On A Bus To St. Cloud	3-628	SC
Yearwood, Trisha	Perfect Love	8-233	CB

ARTIST	SONG TITLE	#	TYPE
Yearwood, Trisha	Powerful Thing	8-866	CB
Yearwood, Trisha	Powerful Thing	10-164	SC
Yearwood, Trisha	Powerful Thing	22-698	ST
Yearwood, Trisha	Real Live Woman	34-336	CB
Yearwood, Trisha	Real Live Woman	23-365	SC
Yearwood, Trisha	Real Live Woman	22-472	ST
Yearwood, Trisha	Restless Kind the	48-333	C2C
Yearwood, Trisha	She's In Love With The Boy	1-631	CB
Yearwood, Trisha	She's In Love With The Boy	13-524	P
Yearwood, Trisha	She's In Love With The Boy	9-637	SAV
Yearwood, Trisha	Something So Right	48-331	CB
Yearwood, Trisha	Song Remembers When the	1-636	CB
Yearwood, Trisha	Song Remembers When the	2-349	SC
Yearwood, Trisha	Sweetest Gift	48-341	SC
Yearwood, Trisha	That's What I Like About You	1-633	CB
Yearwood, Trisha	That's What I Like About You	6-186	MM
Yearwood, Trisha	That's What I Like About You	13-337	P
Yearwood, Trisha	That's What I Like About You	2-327	SC
Yearwood, Trisha	There Goes My Baby	1-643	CB
Yearwood, Trisha	There Goes My Baby	7-761	CHM
Yearwood, Trisha	They Call It Fallin' For A Reason	36-611	CB
Yearwood, Trisha	They Call It Fallin' For A Reason	36-210	PHM
Yearwood, Trisha	Thinkin' About You	1-637	CB
Yearwood, Trisha	Thinkin' About You	6-709	MM
Yearwood, Trisha	Thinkin' About You	17-285	NA
Yearwood, Trisha	Thinkin' About You	22-866	ST
Yearwood, Trisha	This Is Me You're Talking To	36-411	CB
Yearwood, Trisha	Those Words He Said	48-335	SC
Yearwood, Trisha	Too Bad You're No Good	48-336	SC
Yearwood, Trisha	Try Me Again	48-338	SC
Yearwood, Trisha	Trying To Love You	29-27	CB
Yearwood, Trisha	Trying To Love You	23-455	ST
Yearwood, Trisha	Walkaway Joe	10-758	JVC
Yearwood, Trisha	Walkaway Joe	6-211	MM
Yearwood, Trisha	Walkaway Joe	12-477	P
Yearwood, Trisha	Walkaway Joe	9-676	SAV
Yearwood, Trisha	Where Are You Now	14-71	CB
Yearwood, Trisha	Where Are You Now	13-847	CHM
Yearwood, Trisha	Where Your Road Leads	8-185	CB
Yearwood, Trisha	Woman Before Me the	1-634	CB
Yearwood, Trisha	Woman Before Me the	19-290	MH
Yearwood, Trisha	Woman Before Me the	6-200	MM
Yearwood, Trisha	Woman Walk The Line	24-253	SC
Yearwood, Trisha	Wrong Side Of Memphis	1-635	CB
Yearwood, Trisha	Wrong Side Of Memphis	12-445	P
Yearwood, Trisha	Wrong Side Of Memphis	2-800	SC

ARTIST	SONG TITLE	#	TYPE
Yearwood, Trisha	Xmas - It Wasn't His Child	18-749	CB
Yearwood, Trisha	Xmas - It Wasn't His Child	7-6	MM
Yearwood, Trisha	Xmas - It Wasn't His Child	15-656	THM
Yearwood, Trisha	Xmas - Santa Claus is Back in Town	18-728	CB
Yearwood, Trisha	Xmas - Sweetest Gift the	30-398	SC
Yearwood, Trisha	Xmas - Take A Walk Thru Bethlehem	15-664	THM
Yearwood, Trisha	Xmas - There's A New Kid In Town	22-844	ST
Yearwood, Trisha	XXX's And OOO's	1-638	CB
Yearwood, Trisha	XXX's And OOO's	12-183	DK
Yearwood, Trisha	XXX's And OOO's	6-588	MM
Yearwood, Trisha	XXX's And OOO's	17-211	NA
Yearwood, Trisha	XXX's And OOO's	12-481	P
Yearwood, Trisha	XXX's And OOO's	2-452	SC
Yearwood, Trisha	You Can Sleep While I Drive	6-801	MM
Yearwood, Trisha	You Can Sleep While I Drive	2-693	SC
Yearwood, Trisha	You Done Me Wrong	6-210	MM
Yearwood, Trisha	You Say You Will	6-312	MM
Yearwood, Trisha	You Say You Will	2-817	SC
Yearwood, Trisha	You're Where I Belong	9-403	CB
Yearwood, Trisha	You're Where I Belong	22-528	ST
Yes	Long Distance Runaround	20-100	SC
Yes	Owner Of A Lonely Heart	11-698	DK
Yoakam & Crow	Baby Don't Go - duet	49-692	DFK
Yoakam & Crow	Duet - Baby Don't Go	49-692	DFK
Yoakam & Loveless	Duet - Send A Message To My Heart	49-689	CB
Yoakam & Loveless	Send A Message To My Heart	49-689	CB
Yoakam & Owens	Duet - I Was There	49-687	CB
Yoakam & Owens	Duet - Streets Of Bakersfield	49-686	CB
Yoakam & Owens	I Was There - duet	49-687	CB
Yoakam & Owens	Streets Of Bakersfield - duet	49-686	CB
Yoakam, Dwight	Ain't That Lonely Yet	12-465	P
Yoakam, Dwight	Ain't That Lonely Yet	2-336	SC
Yoakam, Dwight	Always Late (With Your Kisses)	49-685	CB
Yoakam, Dwight	Back Of Your Hand the	49-681	SC
Yoakam, Dwight	Blue Moon Of Kentucky	49-700	KV
Yoakam, Dwight	Carmelita	45-854	VH
Yoakam, Dwight	Claudette	4-836	SC
Yoakam, Dwight	Close Up The Honky Tonks	49-697	KV
Yoakam, Dwight	Crazy Little Thing Called Love	8-969	CB
Yoakam, Dwight	Crazy Little Thing Called Love	7-879	CHT
Yoakam, Dwight	Crazy Little Thing Called Love	14-626	SC

ARTIST	SONG TITLE	#	TYPE
Yoakam, Dwight	Dim Lights Thick Smoke And...	49-698	KV
Yoakam, Dwight	Fast As You	2-345	SC
Yoakam, Dwight	Gone	4-163	SC
Yoakam, Dwight	Guitars Cadillacs	6-536	MM
Yoakam, Dwight	Guitars Cadillacs	13-452	P
Yoakam, Dwight	Heart Of Stone	4-898	SC
Yoakam, Dwight	Heartaches By The Number	49-699	KV
Yoakam, Dwight	Honky Tonk Man	20-652	SC
Yoakam, Dwight	I Got You	49-684	SC
Yoakam, Dwight	I Sang Dixie	33-91	CB
Yoakam, Dwight	I Want You To Want Me	15-334	CB
Yoakam, Dwight	I Want You To Want Me	15-193	ST
Yoakam, Dwight	Intentional Heartache	49-701	ST
Yoakam, Dwight	It Only Hurts When I Cry	12-440	P
Yoakam, Dwight	King Of Fools	49-691	CK
Yoakam, Dwight	Little Ways	6-87	SC
Yoakam, Dwight	Long White Cadillac	49-682	SC
Yoakam, Dwight	My Heart Skips A Beat	49-695	DCK
Yoakam, Dwight	Near You	49-630	DCK
Yoakam, Dwight	Nothing	7-143	MM
Yoakam, Dwight	Nothing	3-571	SC
Yoakam, Dwight	Nothing's Changed Here	49-683	SC
Yoakam, Dwight	Only You	49-696	SRK
Yoakam, Dwight	Please Baby Please	14-421	SC
Yoakam, Dwight	Pocket Of A Clown	6-608	MM
Yoakam, Dwight	Pocket Of A Clown	2-313	SC
Yoakam, Dwight	Ring Of Fire	49-703	SRK
Yoakam, Dwight	She Wore Red Dresses	49-702	SRK
Yoakam, Dwight	Sitting Pretty	17-590	ST
Yoakam, Dwight	Sitting Pretty	49-688	CB
Yoakam, Dwight	Smoke Along The Track	49-693	DFK
Yoakam, Dwight	Sorry You Asked	7-245	MM
Yoakam, Dwight	Sorry You Asked?	22-890	ST
Yoakam, Dwight	Stop The World	49-694	DCK
Yoakam, Dwight	Streets Of Bakersfield	49-679	STT
Yoakam, Dwight	Suspicious Minds	49-680	SC
Yoakam, Dwight	Takes A Lot To Rock You	49-690	CB
Yoakam, Dwight	These Arms	16-662	CHT
Yoakam, Dwight	Things Change	22-804	ST
Yoakam, Dwight	Thinking About Leaving	14-698	CB
Yoakam, Dwight	Thousand Miles From Nowhere	9-623	SAV
Yoakam, Dwight	Thousand Miles From Nowhere	2-371	SC
Yoakam, Dwight	Try Not To Look So Pretty	3-36	SC
Yoakam, Dwight	Turn It On Turn It Up Turn Me Loose	34-294	CB
Yoakam, Dwight	Turn It On Turn It Up Turn Me Loose	4-143	SC
Yoakam, Dwight	What Do You Know About Love	14-149	CB
Yoakam, Dwight	What Do You Know About Love	10-261	SC
Yoakam, Dwight	What Do You Know	22-575	ST

ARTIST	SONG TITLE	#	TYPE
	About Love		
Yoakam, Dwight	Xmas - Here Comes Santa Claus	30-393	SC
Yoakam, Dwight	Xmas - Santa Claus Is Back In Town	15-653	THM
Yoakam, Dwight	Xmas - Santa Claus Is Coming/Town	7-10	MM
Yoakam, Dwight	You're The One	26-540	DK
Yoakam, Dwight	You're The One	20-665	SC
Young & Pope	Duet - Think Of You	48-2	BKD
Young & Pope	Think Of You - duet	48-2	BKD
Young & Singleton	Duet - Keeping Up With the Joneses	20-740	CB
Young & Singleton	Duet - Keeping Up With The Joneses	46-57	CB
Young & Singleton	Keeping Up With The Joneses	20-740	CB
Young & Singleton	Keeping Up With The Joneses - duet	46-57	SSK
Young Divas	This Time I Know It's For Real	47-675	SFK
Young MC	Bust A Move	34-136	CB
Young MC	Bust A Move	11-496	DK
Young MC	Bust A Move	16-531	P
Young Rascals	Girl Like You a	3-461	SC
Young Rascals	Good Lovin'	35-58	CB
Young Rascals	Good Lovin'	11-690	DK
Young Rascals	Groovin'	35-63	CB
Young Rascals	Groovin'	11-93	DK
Young Rascals	Groovin'	13-115	P
Young Rascals	How Can I Be Sure	3-462	SC
Young, Chris	A.M.	47-934	BKD
Young, Chris	Aw Naw	40-55	ASK
Young, Chris	Drinkin' Me Lonely	30-24	CB
Young, Chris	Gettin' You Home (Black Dress)	37-32	CB
Young, Chris	I Can Take It From There	47-933	BKD
Young, Chris	I'm Coming Over	45-26	BKD
Young, Chris	Lonely Eyes	49-782	SSC
Young, Chris	Lonely Eyes	45-377	ASK
Young, Chris	Man I Want To Be the	36-40	PT
Young, Chris	Neon	38-217	PHN
Young, Chris	Shoebox the	48-736	KV
Young, Chris	Text Me Texas	45-54	VH
Young, Chris	Tomorrow	37-207	AS
Young, Chris	Voices	47-932	CB
Young, Chris	Who I Am With You	43-259	ASK
Young, Chris	You're Gonna Love Me	30-362	CB
Young, Faron	All Right	20-732	CB
Young, Faron	Alone With You	8-797	CB
Young, Faron	Alone With You	3-594	SC
Young, Faron	Country Girl	20-735	CB
Young, Faron	Face To The Wall	20-738	CB
Young, Faron	Goin' Steady	20-729	CB
Young, Faron	Goin' Steady	9-847	SAV
Young, Faron	Goin' Steady	5-664	SC
Young, Faron	Hello Walls	20-736	CB
Young, Faron	Hello Walls	17-298	NA

ARTIST	SONG TITLE	#	TYPE
Young, Faron	Hello Walls	13-492	P
Young, Faron	Hello Walls	8-632	SAV
Young, Faron	I Just Came In To Get My Baby Out Of..	46-53	SSK
young, Faron	If I Ever Fall In Love (With a Honky...)	47-737	SRK
Young, Faron	If You Ain't Lovin'	7-164	MM
Young, Faron	If You Ain't Lovin' You Ain't Livin	20-730	CB
Young, Faron	It's Four In The Morning	4-314	SC
Young, Faron	It's Four In The Morning	20-728	CB
Young, Faron	Leavin' And Sayin' Goodbye	46-54	SSK
Young, Faron	Live Fast Love Hard Die Young	20-731	CB
Young, Faron	Riverboat	20-737	CB
Young, Faron	Sweet Dreams	20-734	CB
Young, Faron	This Little Girl Of Mine	5-816	SC
Young, Faron	Wine Me Up	20-741	CB
Young, Faron	You're Still Mine	20-733	CB
Young, Faron	Your Old Used To Be	20-739	CB
Young, Faron	Your Time's Comin'	46-58	VH
Young, Faron	Step Aside	45-729	VH
Young, Kathy	Thousand Stars a	30-760	SF
Young, Kathy	Thousand Stars In The Sky	7-306	MM
Young, Neil	After The Gold Rush	37-72	SC
Young, Neil	Cinnamon Girl	5-879	SC
Young, Neil	Heart Of Gold	17-68	DK
Young, Neil	Heart Of Gold	15-168	MH
Young, Neil	Heart Of Gold	5-138	SC
Young, Neil	Needle & Damage Damage Damage	15-752	AMS
Young, Neil	Rockin' In The Free World	46-337	SC
Young, Neil	Southern Man	10-502	DA
Young, Paul	Every Time You Go Away	20-300	CB
Young, Paul	Every Time You Go Away	13-35	P
Young, Paul	Every Time You Go Away	16-814	DK
Young, Paul	Every Time You Go Away	4-322	SC
Young, Paul	Love Is In The Air	9-48	MM
Young, Paul	Oh Girl	11-98	DK
Young, Paul	Oh Girl	9-672	SAV
Youngbloods	Get Together	34-49	CB
Youngbloods	Get Together	11-828	DK
Youngbloodz & Lil Jon	Damn! - duet	32-422	THM
Youngbloodz & Lil Jon	Duet - Damn!	32-422	THM
Zac Brown Band	All Alright	44-161	BKD
Zac Brown Band	Beautiful Drug	49-418	BKD
Zac Brown Band	Beautiful Drug (Instrumental)	47-705	BKD
Zac Brown Band	Big Fat Bitch **	43-473	KV
Zac Brown Band	Castaway	46-69	KV

ARTIST	SONG TITLE	#	TYPE
Zac Brown Band	Chicken Fried	36-615	CB
Zac Brown Band	Chicken Fried	36-199	PHM
Zac Brown Band	Cold Hearted	46-62	FTX
Zac Brown Band	Colder Weather	37-201	AS
Zac Brown Band	Devil Went Down To Georgia	48-642	KV
Zac Brown Band	Different Kind Of Fine	43-472	CB
Zac Brown Band	Dress Blues	46-76	BKD
Zac Brown Band	Fox On The Run	43-469	KV
Zac Brown Band	Free	37-335	CB
Zac Brown Band	Goodbye In Her Eyes	43-155	ASK
Zac Brown Band	Goodbye In Her Eyes	43-462	SBI
Zac Brown Band	Highway 20 Ride	38-126	CB
Zac Brown Band	I Play The Road	43-467	KV
Zac Brown Band	I Play The Road	38-260	PHN
Zac Brown Band	Island Song	43-471	KV
Zac Brown Band	It's Not OK	46-64	KV
Zac Brown Band	Jolene	43-466	KV
Zac Brown Band	Jump Right In	43-470	KV
Zac Brown Band	Keep Me In Mind	38-170	FTX
Zac Brown Band	Knee Deep	43-463	FTX
Zac Brown Band	Knee Deep	43-474	QH
Zac Brown Band	Lance's Song	46-74	BKD
Zac Brown Band	Last But Not Least	46-71	KV
Zac Brown Band	Let It Go	47-762	SRK
Zac Brown Band	Let It Go	46-66	KV
Zac Brown Band	Loving You Easy	45-51	BKD
Zac Brown Band	Make This Day	49-725	KV
Zac Brown Band	Make This Day	46-73	DFK
Zac Brown Band	Martin	46-65	KV
Zac Brown Band	Mary	43-464	FTX
Zac Brown Band	Mary	49-242	DFK
Zac Brown Band	Natural Disaster	46-70	KV
Zac Brown Band	No Hurry	38-279	BKD
Zac Brown Band	No Hurry	45-797	SBI
Zac Brown Band	Overnight	49-13	KV
Zac Brown Band	Overnight	46-72	KV
Zac Brown Band	Quiet Your Mind	46-67	KV
Zac Brown Band	Settle Me Down	46-68	KV
Zac Brown Band	Sic 'Em On A Chicken	43-465	KV
Zac Brown Band	Sweet Annie	43-89	HM
Zac Brown Band	Toes	36-315	PHM
Zac Brown Band	Toes (Female Version)	49-287	CK
Zac Brown Band	Tomorrow Never Comes	46-77	BKD
Zac Brown Band	Whatever It Is	37-33	CB
Zac Brown Band	Where The Boat Leaves From	46-63	FTX
Zac Brown Band	Whiskey's Gone	43-468	KV
Zac Brown Band	Wind the	44-151	BKD
Zac Brown Band & Alan Jackson	As She's Walking Away - duet	37-344	CB
Zac Brown Band & Alan Jackson	Duet - As She's Walking Away	37-344	CB
Zac Brown Band & Bareillas	Duet - Mango Tree	48-510	KVD
Zac Brown Band & Bareillas	Mango Tree - duet	48-510	KVD
Zac Brown Band &	Duet - Knee Deep	37-216	CB

ARTIST	SONG TITLE	#	TYPE	ARTIST	SONG TITLE	#	TYPE
Buffett							
Zac Brown Band & Buffett	Knee Deep - duet	37-216	CB				
Zac Brown Band & Cornell	Heavy Is The Head	46-78	KV				
Zac Brown Band & Jackson	As She's Walking Away - duet	46-79	CB				
Zac Brown Band & Jackson	Duet - As She's Walking Away	46-79	CB				
Zager & Evans	In The Year 2525	11-832	DK				
Zappa, Frank	Dinah Moe Humm **	2-729	SC				
Zappa, Frank	Dirty Love	10-484	DA				
Zayn	It's You	49-931	MRH				
Zedd feat Hayley Williams	Stay The Night	43-158	PHM				
Zero, Remy	Save Me	30-655	THM				
Zevon, Warren	Halloween - Werewolves Of London	16-296	TT				
Zevon, Warren	Werewolves Of London	17-466	SC				
Zevon, Warren	Werewolves Of London	16-296	TT				
Zombie, Rob	Halloween - Living Dead Girl	45-323	SC				
Zombie, Rob	Living Dead Girl - Halloween	45-323	SC				
Zombies	She's Not There	17-42	DK				
Zombies	She's Not There	13-71	P				
Zombies	She's Not There	5-456	SC				
Zombies	She's Not There	10-656	SF				
Zombies	Tell Her No	11-555	DK				
Zombies	Tell Her No	14-460	SC				
Zombies	Time Of The Season	11-554	DK				
Zombies	Time Of The Season	12-651	P				
Zutons	Valerie	30-723	SF				
Zutons	Why Won't You Give Me Your Love	30-751	SF				
Zwan	Honestly	23-163	PHM				
ZZ Top	Beer Drinkers & Hell Raisers	13-766	SGB				
ZZ Top	Blue Jean Blues	13-768	SGB				
ZZ Top	Cheap Sunglasses	16-150	SC				
ZZ Top	Gimme All Your Lovin'	13-208	P				
ZZ Top	I'm Bad I'm Nationwide	13-763	SGB				
ZZ Top	La Grange	20-54	SC				
ZZ Top	Legs	12-170	DK				
ZZ Top	Legs	4-297	SC				
ZZ Top	Mexican Blackbird	13-643	SGB				
ZZ Top	Sharp Dressed Man	12-814	P				
ZZ Top	Tush	33-303	CB				
ZZ Top	Tush	2-728	SC				
ZZ Top	What's Up With That	24-362	SC